LAND LAW

Sweet & Maxwell's Textbook Series

4th Edition

John Stevens
Senior Lecturer in Law, University of Birmingham

Robert Pearce
Vice Chancellor, The University of Wales Lampeter

and

Nicola Jackson
University of East Anglia

LONDON
SWEET & MAXWELL
2008

First published 1997
Third edition 2005
Fourth edition 2008

Published in 2008 by
Sweet & Maxwell Limited of
100 Avenue Road, London NW3 3PF
(*http://www.sweetandmaxwell.thomson.com*)

Typeset by LBJ Typesetting Ltd of Kingsclere, Newbury
Printed in Great Britain by TJ International of Padstow, Cornwall

No natural forests were destroyed to make this product:
only farmed timber was used and replanted.

A CIP catalogue record for this book is available from the
British Library

ISBN 978 0 421 96070 1

PREFACE

When we produced the first edition of *Stevens & Pearce* in 1999, our aim was to write a text-book that was sensitive to the needs of students who find Land Law a difficult and demanding subject whilst not lacking anything in academic rigour. We have sought to maintain this objective through three editions. However our personal circumstances have now changed such that it is impossible for us to continue this task alone into the future. We are therefore delighted to be able to pass this edition largely into the capable hands of Nicola Jackson. It would be hard to imagine anyone more ideally suited to this task. Nicola is an outstanding legal scholar, who has a glittering publication record in the Property Law field. She manages to combine her scholarly talent with enthusiasm for teaching undergraduates Land Law, inspiring them with her love of the subject and assisting them with clarity of explanation. The future development of this textbook could not be in better hands. We are very grateful to Nicola for undertaking the revision of the majority of chapters, with the exception of Chapters 1-5 and 9-10, which we have revised for this edition.

John Stevens and Robert Pearce

I am delighted to have undertaken much of the revision for this edition. My aim has been to work with the existing structure of the book and to incorporate developments as unobtrusively as possible.

By far the most developments have been brought about in the courts, rather than through legislation, although there has been some legislative activity in specific areas. For example, after a long and tortuous journey it has finally become compulsory for house sellers to have a "Home Information Pack". In relation to mortgages, the Consumer Credit Act 2006 gives the courts the power to intervene where there is an unfair credit relationship. This is designed to replace the previous power to reopen an extortionate credit bargain. Under the Civil Partnerships Act 2004 same-sex couples who have registered a civil partnership now have similar rights as married couples, e.g. pension rights, and the court now has discretion to adjust their property rights. Since the last edition the Law Commission has been active in reviewing aspects of land law. It has recently considered the property rights of cohabitees, and has proposed a scheme for the distribution of property rights on break-up of the cohabitation.[1] The law relating to easements and freehold covenants is currently being reviewed by the Law Commission and it published its consultation paper just in time to be included in this edition.[2]

There has been considerable case law development in land law since the last edition and I can only give some of the more important illustrations here. There has been much activity in the area of adverse possession. *Roberts v Swangrove Estates* elaborated both on acts that could constitute factual possession and on the question of what intention is required[3]; The Court of Appeal has been much occupied with the question of when possession can be construed as adverse to the interests of the owner, considering the nature of conduct required, *Allen v Matthews*[4] and *Ofulue v Bossert*,[5] and expanding on the issue of implied licences, *Colin Dawson Windows Ltd v King's Lynn and West Norfolk BC*,[6] *Barrett v Tower Hamlets LBC*,[7] *Batsford Estates (1983) Co Ltd v Taylor*.[8] The long awaited House of Lords decision in *Stack v Dowden*[9] was perhaps not all one could have hoped for in terms of a thorough review of the law in the area of when an interest in land can be acquired informally through a constructive trust. However, it clarifies the law in relation to how shares in property are quantified once it has been decided that some interest exists. The case raises a number of questions in relation to the framework of co-ownership, joint tenancies and tenancies in common, as seen in *Adekunle v Ritchie*.[10] I have been able to incorporate some useful case law on the interpretation of the *Royal Bank of Scotland v Etridge* criteria for establishing whether a mortgage may be set aside for undue influence, for example, *Abbey National Bank Plc v Stringer*[11] and *Goodchild v Bradbury*.[12] There have been developments surrounding the concept of unconscionability and proprietary estoppel, particularly in the context of the acquisition of property for development.[13] Last but not least the courts have recently considered whether some of the rules of land law are compatible with the Human Rights Act 1998: in adverse possession, *Beaulane Properties Ltd. v Palmer*[14] and the decision of the Grand Chamber of the European Court of Human Rights in *J.A. Pye (Oxford) Ltd v United Kingdom*.[15] A number of cases have recently showed concern as to whether the test for postponing sale of the family home on insolvency in order to satisfy the bankrupt's creditors

---

[1] Law Commission, "Cohabitation: The Financial Consequences of Relationship Breakdown" Consultation Paper No. 179 (2006); Law Commission, "Cohabitation: The Financial Consequences of Relationship Breakdown" (Law Com No. 307 (2007)).

[2] "Easements, Covenants and Profits /ga Prendre" Law Com No. 186 (2008).

[3] [2007] EWHC 513, the case was affirmed on appeal: *Roberts v Swangrove Estates Ltd* [2008] EWCA Civ 98.

[4] [2007] EWCA Civ 216; [2007] 2 P. & C.R. 21.

[5] [2008] EWCA Civ 7.

[6] [2005] 2 P & CR 19.

[7] [2005] EWCA Civ 923.

[8] [2006] 2 P. & C.R. 5.

[9] [2007] 2 AC 432.

[10] [2007] 2 P & CR DG20.

[11] [2006] EWCA Civ 338.

[12] [2006] EWCA Civ 1868.

[13] *Yeoman's Row Management Ltd v Cobbe* [2006] 1 W.L.R. 2964.

[14] [2006] Ch. 79.

[15] *The Times,* October 1, 2007.

might not be too harsh, particularly in the light of the right to enjoyment of property and the right to private and family life afforded by the HRA.[16]

Finally, I would like to express my thanks to Sweet & Maxwell. Publishing editor Constance Sutherland has been extremely helpful and patient. I was at Lancaster University when I completed this work and would like to thank my friends and colleagues in the School of Law. In particular, David Milman and Mike Doupe have shown such kindness and encouragement and have discussed with me many of the new developments in land law. I would of course like to thank John Stevens and Robert Pearce for their support and encouragement and can only hope that I have done justice to their faith in me in asking me to undertake this work. On a more personal note, thank you to my husband Colin and my one-in-a-million friend Gill Fraser. I have attempted to state the law up to the end of April 2008.

Nicola Jackson
University of East Anglia

---

[16] *Barca v Mears* [2005] 1 P. & C.R. DG 7; *Nicholls v Lan* [2007] 1 F.L.R. 744; *Donoghue v Ingram* [2006] EWHC 282.

TABLE OF CONTENTS

Part II: The Ownership of Land

Part III Subsidiary Interests in Land

TABLE OF CASES

1

TABLE OF STATUTES

Part I

INTRODUCTORY

Chapter 1

ORIENTATION

WHAT IS PROPERTY?

1. Property Concerns the Ownership of Things

At a basic level everyone is familiar with the idea of property, since they have some experience of owning things. For example if Damon is given a car by his parents for his 18th birthday, he becomes its owner, and it can be said to belong to him. As a consequence of his ownership he is able to do whatever he wants with it. He can make use of it himself and enjoy the privileges of his ownership. He can lend the car to a friend, or perhaps offer it for hire. He can sell it and thus realise its value in money. He can destroy it, if he so chooses. All of these options are made possible by the fact that he owns the car. Integral to his ownership of the car is the fact that his rights in relation to it are exclusive, that other people have no rights in it. For example, if Murray takes the car without permission and sells it to Frank, it is clear that Frank should not become the owner of the car. Murray had no right to the car himself and cannot pass to Frank a better right than he himself possessed. Even though the car may now be in the possession of Frank, this does not mean that he owns it. It still belongs to Damon and he can insist that it be returned to him.

1–001

2. A Wide Variety of "Things"

If property is concerned with the ownership of things, it should be obvious that there is a wide variety of things which can be owned. For example, a person may own money, clothes, shares in a company, a ticket to a pop concert, a house or flat. These are all different "things" which may be owned. An important distinction is drawn between tangible and intangible property. Tangible property consists of things which are physical in nature, for example a car. Intangible property consists of things which are not physical in nature but which are regarded as property because they are capable of being owned. For example, shares in a company may be owned

1–002

and traded, but they are not physical things. Although the share certificates are in some sense "physical", they are only evidence of the existence of the property right to which they relate, namely the notional share of the ownership of the company and its assets. Other examples of intangible property are intellectual property rights such as copyrights and patents. Some of these rights exist only because there is legislation conferring exclusivity, as is the case for instance with copyrights and patents. Other rights have their origin in the common law.

3. Proprietary Rights

(a) *The Nature of Proprietary Rights*

1–003   A proprietary right is a right which exists in relation to a thing, whether tangible or intangible. The most important proprietary right is that of ownership, but this is by no means the only right which may exist in relation to a thing. For example, a house which is owned by one person may be leased to a tenant and mortgaged to a building society. In such a case the owner, the tenant and the building society all enjoy proprietary rights in the house. An important distinction is drawn between rights which are proprietary in nature, and rights which are purely personal. A personal right is an entitlement which a person enjoys against another specific individual, and its central characteristic is that it can only be enforced against that specific person. It is often referred to by Latin terminology as a right *in personam*. In contrast, a proprietary right is a right existing "in" the item of property, or thing, to which it relates. The right is enforceable against the thing, irrespective of who possesses or owns it at the time that the right is sought to be enforced. Such rights are described in Latin as rights *in rem*, which means "in the thing itself". The central characteristic of a proprietary right is that it is capable of enduring through changes in ownership of the property to which it relates, so that it will be enforceable against the new owner.

(b) *An Illustration of Personal Rights*

1–004   Imagine that Andy goes up to read law at the University of Barsetshire. He is in need of accommodation and answers an advert in a local newspaper placed by Beryl, an elderly lady, who provides students with bed and breakfast accommodation for £75 per week. If Beryl and Andy agree that he can stay in her house for his first year, his right to live there will be founded upon a contractual agreement between himself and Beryl and will be purely personal in nature. He will not be a trespasser on her land, because she has granted him permission to be there, but he in no sense owns the land, nor does he enjoy any proprietary right in it. His right is technically termed a licence. Unless Beryl has agreed not to terminate his licence before the end of the year, she will be entitled to withdraw her permission for him to live in her house at any time. If she does tell him to leave, he may well be entitled to a remedy against her for breach of contract, for which he would be entitled to recover damages to compensate him for any loss he suffered as a result of the breach, but he is not entitled to continue living in the house, and if he attempts to do so he will be committing a trespass. He cannot transfer his right to anyone else: for example, he cannot decide that after the first week he is going to return

4

home and allow Charlotte to take over his licence and insist that she lives in the house. More importantly, if Beryl decides to sell the house to David, Andy will not be entitled to assert his contractual right to live in the room against David. David will be entitled to take the house free from any rights of Andy, since Andy's rights do not exist in the house as such but only against Beryl personally. Similarly, if Beryl were to mortgage the house to Barset Bank and it subsequently turned out that she was unable to keep up the repayments so that Barset Bank can enforce its mortgage by taking possession of the house in order to sell it, Andy would not be able to assert his right to occupy against the Bank to prevent the repossession.

(c) *An Illustration of Proprietary Rights*

If, however, rather than taking Andy as a lodger into her house, Beryl owned a self-contained **1–005** single-bedroom flat and agreed to grant Andy a lease for a year at a rent of £300 a month, Andy's interest would no longer be purely personal, for his lease would constitute a proprietary interest in the flat. Unless Andy committed a breach of the terms of his lease entitling Beryl to forfeit his interest, she would not be able simply to decide that she no longer wanted him to live there. He would be entitled to remain for as long as the term he had been granted. Unless the lease specifically prevented him from so doing, he would be able to transfer his right to occupy to someone else, such as Charlotte, who would then be entitled to occupy the flat in his stead. If Beryl were to sell the flat to David, or to mortgage it to the bank, Andy's interest would be enforceable against both David and the bank, because they would have acquired the flat subject to his pre-existing right to occupy it.

CENTRAL CONCERNS OF THE LAW OF PROPERTY

1. Function of the Law of Property

The law of property comprises the range of legal rules and principles which regulate propri- **1–006** etary rights in things. It is an analytically coherent body of law as, for example, is criminal law which concerns itself with how the law determines if conduct is criminal in the eyes of the state, or the law of contract which comprises the legal rules regulating obligations voluntarily entered into by consensual agreement. Although there is an inevitable overlap with other subject areas a number of prime concerns may be identified which property law addresses.

2. Ownership

The question of ownership is one of the central concerns of the law of property. Who is the owner **1–007** of a particular thing, whether tangible or intangible? For example, if a wallet is found in the street containing a large quantity of money, who is the owner? Does it belong to the finder, the state, or to the person who lost it? Central to issues of ownership are questions as to how the ownership of property can be acquired and transferred. For example, if Damon agrees to sell his car to Frank, at what point does Damon cease to be the owner of his car and Frank become the new owner? By what mechanism is the ownership transferred from Damon to Frank? Alternatively, if Beryl agrees to grant Andy a lease of her flat, at what point does he become entitled to a lease and the concomitant right to occupy it? If Charlotte owns shares in Marks & Spencer and merely gives the share certificates to David for his birthday, does this transfer the ownership of them to her? If Edward owns an estate in Cornwall, but for the last five years a group of travellers led by Francesca has been living there, have they acquired the ownership by virtue of their possession for that period? In many cases the transfer of property might require special formalities or procedures to be observed, and the transfer will be ineffective if they have not been followed.

3. Creation of Subsidiary Interests

1–008   A second major issue is whether there are any lesser, or subsidiary, rights existing in a thing which is owned by someone else. Imagine, for example, that Frank purchases a car but then pledges it to Murray as security for a loan: what sort of right, if any, does Murray have in the car? Such subsidiary rights and interests are common in relation to land. As has been seen, a house or flat may be owned by one person, leased to another, and mortgaged to a bank. How and when are such subsidiary interests as leases and mortgages created over the land? What do they entitle the holder of the subsidiary right to do in relation to the thing they affect?

4. Priorities Between Competing Interests

1–009   A third major issue addressed by the law of property is that of determining which of several competing proprietary rights in the same thing should enjoy priority over the others. For example, if Beryl owns a flat and on Monday grants a lease for a year to Andy and then on Wednesday grants a lease for a year to Charlotte, which of these two proprietary rights will have priority over the other, since it is impossible for both to be enjoyed simultaneously? Similarly, if Beryl granted a lease for a year to David last month and this month sold her house to Charlotte, who did not know of the existence of David's interest, will David's right enjoy priority over Charlotte's, or will Charlotte's ownership enjoy priority so that she can effectively evict David? Will it make any difference if Charlotte was merely given the house by Beryl rather than purchasing it?

LAND LAW

1. The Distinction Between Real and Personal Property

1–010   In English law a fundamental distinction was historically drawn between what was termed "real property" and "personal property". At its simplest, real property consists of what today would be called "land", and personal property is all property which is not land. Historically there were significant distinctions between the regimes applicable to each, especially regarding the law of succession. Despite more recent attempts to eliminate unnecessary distinctions between the two types of property, the difference between land and personal property is still important, especially as legislation has introduced a statutory framework governing many of the important property issues which are exclusive to land. The following chapter will consider what is meant by "land" in the technical sense.

2. The Social and Cultural Context of Land Law

Land law comprises the body of law which regulates proprietary issues concerning things classified as "land". The content of such law is obviously of tremendous social significance, since the ownership and exploitation of land is of fundamental importance to society and its functioning. No one can live without reference to land, whether as their home, place of work or for recreation. The nature of land ownership has changed dramatically over the centuries. Initially, land was owned by a small number of people for whom it was a source of power and income, and the majority of the population had no real rights at all. As a consequence of industrialisation and the agricultural revolution, land became less significant as a source of revenue, and other forms of investment emerged. There has been a gradual increase in the number of people buying land of their own, so that today a majority of people own the land which provides their home. For many people their home is their greatest asset in terms of value, and it has usually been acquired by the use of a mortgage. Given the social background, a number of central principles underlying English land law and have influenced its development and structures. There is nothing necessarily objectively correct about these principles but they are a reflection of the cultural background within which English land law has evolved. **1–011**

(a) *The Individual Ownership of Land*

Unlike other cultures, which may emphasise tribal, family, or state ownership of land, English land law primarily regards land as an individual asset. This is closely related to the concepts of freedom and self-determination so that the owner is entitled to use his land as he chooses, or indeed to fail to use it, no matter how little benefit this may bring to others or how much more effectively the land could be used. He can transfer it to whoever he wants, and on death he can leave it by will to whoever he wants. Closely allied to this is the fact that English law also protects an owner's land from any interference by others. He is entitled to exclude whoever he wants. It is a truism that an "Englishman's home is his castle", no matter how small the particular castle may be! **1–012**

(b) *Facilitation of the Use of Land*

At the same time as emphasising individual ownership as a cardinal principle, English land law aims to facilitate the efficient use of land by enabling the owner to create subsidiary **1–013** interests that will benefit himself and others. If he does not wish to inhabit land himself, he may wish to grant a lease to someone else, entitling them to the benefit of occupation and entitling him to the benefit of rent. Similarly, if a neighbouring landowner wishes, for example, to start industrial production on his land which will necessitate a means of access that he does not otherwise possess, he may be able to obtain a right of way in return for the payment of an appropriate price. Thus the variety of subsidiary interests which may be created in land and which are enjoyed by someone other than the owner are a means by which efficient use may be made of what is inevitably a scarce resource.

(c) *Free Marketability of Land*

1–014   A further objective is to ensure that land remains a readily tradable market commodity. English land law has sought to reduce the difficulties inherent in the buying and selling of land, in particular by seeking to ensure that a prospective purchaser can be confident that the vendor is entitled to sell the land in question, and by providing that the purchaser is not taken unawares by the existence of subsidiary interests which affect the value or utility of the land to him. In more recent years many developments in land law have been affected by the need to ensure that mortgage lenders are able to lend without risk that their security will be subsequently compromised by undiscovered third party interests in the land. Without the willingness of lenders to provide purchase money on the security of land, the housing market would grind to a virtual standstill, since there are relatively few buyers who are able to raise the purchase price from their own resources alone.

(d) *Fair Protection of Third Party Interests*

1–015   A further objective is to ensure that subsidiary interests in land enjoy fair protection when the land is transferred, so that they are not easily defeated by a mere transfer of the land to a new owner. However, this is balanced against the desire to ensure that a transferee, and especially a purchaser of the land, is not unfairly burdened by subsidiary interests in the land of which he was unaware, and perhaps could not have been aware, at the time when he acquired the land.

ARRANGEMENT OF THIS BOOK

1–016   It is not the object of this book to provide a detailed and comprehensive guide to every issue that may arise in relation to land and its use and ownership. It is intended to provide a guide to the most important concepts and mechanisms in English land law. The book is divided into three parts. Part I introduces the most important concepts and structures of English land law. It will examine the historic foundations of land law, before turning to explain the contemporary framework of land registration. Part II, "The Ownership of Land", will examine the various types of ownership of land which can be enjoyed and how they may be acquired and transferred. Freehold, leasehold, commonhold and equitable ownership will be considered in detail. Part III, "Subsidiary Interests in Land", will examine the most important of the various subsidiary interest in land, including easements, restrictive covenants, mortgages, estate contracts, estoppel equities and licences and it will be considered how such interests can be acquired and what rights they confer upon the holder.

Chapter 2

WHAT IS LAND?

LAND AS THE PHYSICAL GROUND

Most people would naturally define "land" in terms of the physical ground. There is a scene **2–001**
in Woody Allen's film *Love and Death* where it is announced that the central character's
Uncle Boris owns a small piece of land. The said uncle is then shown holding a piece of turf
in his hands with the rest of the family rejoicing around it. Somewhat later in the film it is
announced that Uncle Boris has gone into hotel development, and he is shown holding the
same piece of turf but with a minute Monopoly-style hotel placed in the middle. Many people conceive of their "land" in a similar way. Although this is not wrong in itself, it is inadequate from a legal point of view, because "land" enjoys a wider technical meaning.

THE LEGAL CONCEPT OF LAND

1. A Statutory Definition

"Land" is given a wider meaning by s.205(i)(ix) of the Law of Property Act 1925, which **2–002**
provides that:

> " 'Land' includes land of any tenure, and mines and minerals, whether or not held apart
> from the surface, buildings or parts of buildings (whether the division is horizontal, verti-
> cal or made in any other way) and other corporeal hereditaments; also a manor, an advow-
> son, and a rent and other incorporeal hereditaments; and an easement, right, privilege, or
> benefit in, over or derived from land."

It is obvious that there is a circularity in this definition. Land is defined by reference to itself.
The definition goes further, however, by including some things that the layman would not

11

otherwise consider to be land. So, for instance, the rights of a lord of the manor are included as land, and to modern eyes, more strangely, also an advowson. This is the right to nominate the incumbent minister of a church. The logic of this right being treated as land is that it was not uncommon for manor houses to have a church alongside the house and within its grounds. It therefore made sense for the right to nominate the minister of that church to be treated for legal purposes in the same way as the manor house and grounds.

Although we have yet to consider some of the unfamiliar terms in this definition, it is clear that land is not regarded as the mere ground, but is a category describing a whole range of rights associated with the ground. The section distinguishes between two very important categories of rights which comprise land, namely corporeal and incorporeal hereditaments.

2.   Corporeal Hereditaments

2–003   Hereditaments are rights which, until the reform of succession laws by the significant legislative changes of 1925, passed on the death of the current owner under the laws of inheritance. Under these rules, the property concerned was inherited by the eldest male descendant in direct line of blood (the "heir"), rather than being shared between the whole of the nearest class of relatives. Despite the fact that it is now some 80 years since the laws of inheritance disappeared, the concept of an hereditament has been preserved in this definition. We will, in the study of land law, come across other instances where relics of old law linger on in the use of terminology which no longer has any modern practical consequence.

Corporeal hereditaments were those physical items of property which passed on death before 1926 according to the old laws of inheritance. Most obviously, this includes the physical features of land comprising the surface itself and everything attached to the land such as permanent buildings and any plants or trees growing[1] on the land. It also includes mines and minerals (which are capable of being owned separately from the surface: the Channel Tunnel, where it passes through English territorial limits, is owned separately from the surface, and constitutes a corporeal hereditament).

3.   Incorporeal Hereditaments

2–004   In contrast to corporeal hereditaments, incorporeal hereditaments are rights which under the old law of inheritance would have passed to the heir but which had no direct physical identity. So the right to take a short cut across someone's land in order to reach your own, the right to take water from a spring on another person's land and the (now outmoded) right to take wood from someone else's land to repair your house or farming tools, would all be considered to be incorporeal hereditaments. They are proprietary rights in land which are themselves classified as "land". They are therefore regulated by the rules appropriate to land rather than personal property. Most of these rights recognised as incorporeal hereditaments benefit

---

[1] See *Stukeley v Butler* (1615) Hob. 168.

neighbouring land, but there are some examples, such as the right to fish in a river, which are capable of being enjoyed independently of the ownership of any neighbouring land.

4. Special Cases

There are some special situations in which property is treated as land under the statutory definition. We have come across manors and advowsons already. Manors were ancient land holdings, dating from the Middle Ages and before. A "lord" owned a tract of land, part of which he enjoyed for his personal use, and part of which was used by others ("tenants") in a subservient relationship to him. He held courts in which disputes between tenants were resolved, and he retained rights over the land used by his tenants, frequently including the rights to any minerals. Despite the fact that most of the rights of lords of the manor have now disappeared or been abolished (for instance, manor courts can no longer be held), there are still residual rights belonging to lords of manors. Those rights are governed by the rules relating to land set out in the 1925 legislation and in subsequent legislation.

2–005

Leasehold interests were in a special position before 1925. Although treated as land for many purposes, for historical reasons they were not corporeal hereditaments. In consequence, on the death of a tenant, different rules of inheritance applied from those applying to freehold land. By stating that "land includes land of any tenure", the Law of Property Act 1925 makes it clear that leases are included in the definition.

RIGHTS ABOVE AND BELOW THE SURFACE

1. The Traditional Maxim

It is clear that ownership of the surface of land carries with it rights to what is below the surface and to control of the airspace above. Historically, it was said that *cuius est solum, eius est usque ad coelum et ad inferos* ("whoever owns the sod owns everything up to the heavens and down to the depths of the earth"). Although this may well have proved practical when there was virtually no possibility of the exploitation of the airspace above land, the principle has had to be substantially modified in the light of the evolution of flight to strike a sensible balance between the rights of the surface owner and the right to overflight of land.

2–006

2. Rights Below the Surface of Land

(a) *Rights to Mineral Deposits*

The owner of land is prima facie entitled to the ownership of any mineral deposits found beneath the surface. However, even this right is qualified in the national interest. At common

2–007

law any unmined gold and silver belongs to the Crown as a prerogative right.[2] By statute, deposits of oil, coal and natural gas also belong to the Crown.[3] Crown or statutory authority is therefore required to remove these natural resources.

(b) *Right to Spaces Below the Surface*

2–008   Space below the surface, whether natural or man-made, is land and is capable of ownership and protection from intrusion by trespassers. In *The Metropolitan Railway Co v Fowler*[4] it was held that ownership of a tunnel was to be regarded as ownership of an interest in land, so as to attract the equivalent of rates. In *Grigsby v Melville*[5] the Court of Appeal held that the owner of a house also owned a cellar underneath it, even though he could not gain access to it from his own land, and that he was entitled to an injunction to prevent his neighbour, who did have a means of access, from using it for storage without permission.[6] Title to the Channel Tunnel is registered separately from the registration of the owners of the surface below which the tunnel passes.

(c) *Rights to Items Found in the Land*

2–009   The owner of land is also entitled to the ownership of any lost items of property found in the land, unless they are treasure trove, in which case ownership will vest in the Crown.[7] Thus, in *Elwes v Brigg Gas Company*,[8] when a tenant of land unearthed a pre- historic boat it was held to belong to the landowner. Similarly in *Waverley B C v Fletcher*[9] the Court of Appeal held that a brooch unearthed by a metal detecting enthusiast in a public park belonged to the Council which owned the land.

3.   Rights to the Airspace Above the Land

2–010   The owner of the physical surface also owns the airspace above the land, and is entitled to assert his rights in relation to it and to restrain others from trespassing into it. In *Kelsen v Imperial Tobacco*[10] an owner of the surface of land was granted an injunction to restrain a

---

[2] *Case of Mines* (1567) 1 Plowd. 310; *Attorney-General v Morgan* [1891] 1 Ch. 432.
[3] Petroleum (Production) Act 1934 s.1; Coal Industry Act 1994 s.9.
[4] [1892] 1 Q.B. 165.
[5] [1974] 1 W.L.R. 80.
[6] See also *Edwards v Lee's Administrator* (1936) 96 S.W.2d 1028.
[7] At common law an item was only treasure trove if it contained a substantial quantity of gold or silver and it had been hidden rather than lost. The scope of treasure trove has been widened by the Treasure Act 1996, the provisions of which are too technical for detailed discussion here. See also *Attorney-General v Trustees of the British Museum* [1903] 2 Ch. 598; *Attorney-General of the Duchy of Lancaster v GE Overton (Farms) Ltd* [1982] Ch. 277.
[8] (1886) 33 Ch.D. 562.
[9] [1995] 4 A11 E.R. 756; [1996] Conv. 216 (Stevens).
[10] [1957] 2 Q.B. 334.

trespass by the neighbouring landowner who had erected a sign which projected into the airspace above his land by some four inches. In such cases an injunction is available even though the infringement causes no damage to the land affected, because trespass is actionable per se. In *Anchor Brewhouse Developments Ltd v Berkley House Ltd*[11] a developer allowed the jib of a tower crane to swing over the plaintiff's property. Scott J. granted an injunction to restrain the trespass.[12] Similarly in *Laiqat v Majid*[13] Silber J. held that an extractor fan which projected over the claimant's land by some 750 millimetres and at a height of 4.5 metres constituted a trespass, even though the county court judge first hearing the case had come to a different conclusion because whilst "it is something which is not particularly attractive, [it] certainly cannot be said to be at a height which would interfere with any normal activity within the garden". However, because no objection had been made to the fan for many years before the current dispute arose, Silber J. remitted to the county court the question of whether damages might be a more appropriate remedy than an injunction. However, although there need not be any interference with normal activities, the caselaw makes it clear that the owner of the surface does not enjoy rights over the superjacent airspace to an unlimited height. In *Bernstein v Skyviews and General Ltd*[14] a landowner claimed that there had been a trespass when a light aircraft had overflown his land to take an aerial photograph at a height of several hundred feet. The landowner relied on the maxim *cuius est solum, eius est usque ad coelum et ad inferos* (a Latin phrase meaning that whoever owns the surface also owns up to the heavens and down to the depths) to justify a remedy, but Griffiths J. held that no actionable trespass had occurred. He concluded that, in the light of the scientific developments enabling use of airspace, the maxim was incapable of balancing the rights of landowners against the rights of the public. He held that the rights of a landowner to the airspace above his land should be restricted "to such a height as is reasonably necessary for the ordinary use and enjoyment of his land and the structure upon it" and that "above that height he has no greater rights in the airspace than any other member of the public". Thus the extent to which a landowner enjoys rights to the airspace above his land is dependent upon the nature and use to which he has put his land. Statute has also intervened, so that overflight by aircraft is not actionable if they were flying at a height reasonable in the circumstances.[15]

4. Possible Division of Land into Horizontal Strata

The fact that "land" extends to rights enjoyed to the space above and below the physical surface opens the possibility of the horizontal division of land into strata capable of ownership by different persons. This is most clearly seen in the case of flats, where the owners of an upper floor flat do not own the surface itself. The possibility of such horizontal division of **2–011**

[11] [1987] E.G.L.R. 172.
[12] Compare *Woolerton and Wilson v Costain* [1970] 1 W.L.R. 411 where an injunction was suspended by Stamp J. in a similar case, but this decision was doubted in *Charrington v Simons Ltd* [1971] 1 W.L.R. 598 and *John Trenberth Ltd v National Westminster Bank* (1979) 39 P. & C.R. 104.
[13] [2005] EWHC 1305, QB.
[14] [1978] Q.B. 479.
[15] Civil Aviation Act 1982 s.76(1).

15

land is expressly recognised in the definition of land in s.205(l)(ix) of the Law of Property Act 1925.

5. Protection from Illegitimate Entry and Interference

(a) *Protection from Unauthorised Entry*

2–012 Since the ownership of land carries rights to the space both above and beneath the surface, an owner, or a person enjoying exclusive possession as a tenant under a lease, enjoys protection from illegitimate entry. Any unauthorised physical intrusion onto his land, whether on the surface, under the surface, or into the airspace at a height within that necessary for the reasonable use and enjoyment of the land, will constitute a trespass. Such a trespass is actionable per se without the need for the landowner to demonstrate that he has suffered any loss. The court will usually grant an injunction to remove any continuing trespass and damages for any loss which has been caused. In some circumstances the court may be prepared to grant damages in lieu of an injunction. The vigour with which a landowner's rights will be defended is well illustrated *by John Trenberth Ltd v National Westminster Bank Ltd*.[16] The defendant bank owned a building fronting a highway which they were under a statutory duty to maintain in a safe condition. It needed to be repaired but the repairs could only be completed by the erection of scaffolding on the plaintiff's neighbouring land. After some months of inconclusive negotiations in which the defendants sought permission to erect the scaffolding, they went ahead without having obtained consent. Walton J. held that an injunction was appropriate because there had been a flagrant invasion of the plaintiff's land, despite the fact that the refusal of permission was irrational. He commented that the protection of the rights of a landowner was so comprehensive that the defendants might have to demolish and rebuild their building if permission could not be obtained. Although the general principle of the protection of private property still stands, the position of persons such as the defendants has been ameliorated by the intervention of statute. The Access to Neighbouring Land Act 1992 allows a person requiring access to neighbouring land for carrying out specified works to apply to the court for an access order entitling him to enter the land for that purpose.

(b) *Protection from Unauthorised Interference with Use*

2–013 A landowner is also entitled to protection from illegitimate interference with his use and enjoyment of his land occasioned by the activities of another landowner on his own land, for example, by the emission of noise, smell or smoke. A person's activities will be actionable in tort as a nuisance if they cause physical damage or amount to an unreasonable interference with the use of the land. For example, in *St Helens Smelting Co v Tipping*[17] it was held that a nuisance

[16] (1979) 39 P. & C.R. 104.
[17] (1965) 11 E.R. 1483.

16

had been committed when noxious gases and vapours from the defendant's smelting works damaged trees and hedges on the plaintiff's land. Clearly what constitutes an unreasonable interference will depend upon the circumstances of the land affected, and especially its location. As Thesiger L.J. said in *Sturges v Bridgman*[18] "what would be a nuisance in Belgrave Square would not necessarily be so in Bermondsey", a district known at that time for its air-polluting tanneries. Not every possible use of land is subject to protection from interference. In *Hunter v Canary Wharf Ltd*[19] the House of Lords held that interference with potential television reception by the building of a tower block was not actionable as a nuisance,[20] in just the same way that the erection of a building which obscures a view is riot a nuisance.[21] Where an actual nuisance has occurred, the landowner may be entitled to an injunction or damages.

OWNERSHIP OF THINGS ATTACHED TO LAND

1.   The General Principle

A second Latin maxim provides: *quicquid plantatur solo, solo cedit* ("whatever is attached to the soil becomes part of it"). This provides the rationale for the principle that items of personal property, known as chattels, become land if they are attached to it so as to become part of it. Chattels which have become attached so as to form part of the land are known as fixtures. Whether an item has become a fixture will be especially important in two contexts. First, where land is transferred, a conveyance of the land will transfer with it all the fixtures which are not expressly excluded.[22] Even more importantly, from the very moment that an owner of land has entered into a contract to sell, he is no longer entitled to remove fixtures since they henceforth belong to the purchaser.[23] Secondly, where land is subject to a lease, any chattels which the tenant attaches to the land so as to become fixtures will belong to the landlord, and prima facie the tenant will not be entitled to remove them when the lease comes to an end. However, as will be seen, the law has developed to allow a tenant to remove specific categories of fixture he has added to the land. Fixtures are also treated as forming part of land when it has been mortgaged.

2-014

2.   When does a Chattel Become a Fixture?

The criteria for determining whether a chattel has become a fixture are easily stated, but are much more difficult to apply. In *Elitestone Ltd v Morris* Lord Lloyd reviewed the authorities and stated that whether a chattel had becomes a fixture:

2-015

---

[18] (1879) 11 Ch.D. 852 at 865.
[19] [1997] 2 All E.R. 426.
[20] See also *Bridlington Relay Ltd v Yorkshire Electricity Board* [1965] Ch. 436.
[21] See *Attorney-General v Doughty* (1752) 2 Ves. Sen. 453; *Fishmongers' Co v East India Co* (1752) 1 Dick. 164.
[22] Law of Property Act 1925 s.62.
[23] The contract operates to transfer the equitable ownership of the land to the purchaser immediately.

"depends on the circumstances of each case, but mainly on two factors, the degree of annexation and the object of annexation."[24]

The "degree of annexation" concerns the extent to which the chattel has become attached to the land. The more firmly it is attached, the more likely it is to have become a fixture. However the fact of attachment is not determinative of whether a chattel has become a fixture. The court must also consider the "object of annexation", in other words it must take into account the reason why the chattel was attached to the land. The combination of these two factors means that in some circumstances a chattel which has been firmly attached to the land might remain a chattel, or that a chattel which is not attached to the land at all might become a fixture. The operation of these tests will be examined in the context of the three most common situations in which it will need to be determined whether a chattel has become a fixture.

(a) *Chattels Attached to the Land*

2–016   Prima facie, a chattel will become a fixture when it is physically attached, or annexed, to the land. In *Holland v Hodgson*[25] the owner of a mill installed looms which were attached to the stone floor by means of nails driven through holes in their feet. Blackburn J. held that, even though they were easily removable, the looms had become fixtures and therefore passed with the land when it was repossessed under a mortgage which had not been repaid. He stated the general principle:

> "an article which is affixed to the land even slightly is to be considered as part of the land, unless the circumstances are such as to shew that it was intended to all along to continue a chattel, the onus lying on those who contend that it is a chattel."

This suggests that the mere fact that an item has been attached to the land will tend towards the conclusion that it has become a fixture, but with the qualification that such attachment is not always in itself to make the item a fixture. As Blackburn J. indicated earlier in his judgment, there are two relevant factors to be take into account, namely "the degree of annexation and the object of the annexation". In practice this has meant that chattels which are attached to the land merely to enable them to be better enjoyed as chattels will not be regarded as fixtures and will retain their status as personal property. In *Leigh v Taylor*[26] the tenant for life of a mansion house had hung valuable tapestries in a drawing room. Although they were affixed to the land the House of Lords held that they remained chattels because they were never intended to form part of the structure of the house and were only attached to enable them to be better enjoyed as ornamental decoration. This can be contrasted with *D'Eyncourt v Gregory*,[27] where tapestries were held to be fixtures because they were just as integral to the

---

[24] [1997] 2 All E.R. 513 at 518.
[25] (1872) L.R. 7 C.P. 328.
[26] [1902] A.C. 157.
[27] (1866) Law Rep. 3 Eq. 382.

decoration of the room where they were attached as wallpaper or frescos. In *Leigh v Taylor* Lord Halsbury suggested that the difference between these two cases was not one of law but due to the fact that fashions had changed so that attitudes to styles of ornamentation were different. Although not stated, it may also be relevant that in *Leigh v Taylor* the owner of the tapestries did not have a right to the land extending beyond his own death, and the Court may therefore have been slow to infer that he was intending to gift the tapestries to the future owner of the land.

In *Berkley v Poulett*[28] the Court of Appeal indicated that the "purpose of annexation" test was pre-eminent over the fact of physical attachment, but Scarman L.J. noted that there was a close relationship between the two:

> "If the purpose of the annexation be for the better enjoyment of the object itself, it may remain a chattel, notwithstanding a high degree of physical annexation. Clearly, however, it remains significant to discover the extent of physical disturbance of the building or the land involved in the removal of the object. If an object cannot be removed without serious damage to, or destruction of, some part of the realty, the case for its having become a fixture is a strong one."

The vendor of land had removed a number of pictures affixed by screws into the panelling of a dining room after contracting to sell, and the purchaser claimed that these had been fixtures. The court held that although they were attached to the wall, they had retained their character as mere chattels because they had been fixed so that they could be better enjoyed as pictures. Thus they were not part of an overall design for the room which would be lost if they were removed. They could easily be replaced by other pictures.

The operation of the two tests can also been seen in the contrast between two cases involving cinema chairs. In *Lyon & Co v London City and Midland Bank*,[29] chairs were hired and fastened to the floor of a cinema with screws. It was held that they remained chattels despite their annexation to the land, because they had only been installed for a temporary duration of 12 weeks, and they were easily removable without causing damage to the premises. In *Vaudeville Electric Cinema Ltd v Muriset*[30] it was held that cinema chairs attached to the floor had become fixtures and therefore passed to a person who enjoyed a mortgage over the land. The central difference seems to have been that in the latter case the chairs were part of the permanent equipment of the building and the annexation was not merely for a temporary use. The relationship between the "degree of annexation" and "purpose of annexation" in determining whether a chattel had become a fixture can also be seen in the more recent case of *Chelsea Yacht and Boat Co Ltd v Pope*.[31] The case concerned a houseboat which was moored at a boatyard on the River Thames. The boat was attached to a pontoon by mooring lines, to an anchor in the river bed at the foot of an embankment wall and to rings in the wall. The boat was also connected to services provided by the boatyard owners. The occupier of the boat claimed that he enjoyed a tenancy of the houseboat, but the boatyard owners claimed that the

2–017

[28] (1976) 241 E.G. 911.
[29] [1903] 2 K.B. 135.
[30] [1923] 2 Ch. 74.
[31] [2001] 2 All E.R. 409.

boat was a chattel, and that therefore it could not be subject to a lease. The Court of Appeal held that the houseboat had remained a chattel. Even though it was secured by ropes and the services to the river bank, the degree of annexation was insufficient to make the houseboat part of the land. All the attachments could be undone simply, and the houseboat could easily be moved without injury to itself or the land. More importantly, the Court held that it was not necessary for the houseboat to be attached to the land so as to provide a permanent home. The attachment was rather intended to prevent it being carried away by the tide or the weather. The purpose of the annexation was not, therefore, to make the houseboat part of the land.

In *Elitestone Ltd v Morris*[32] the House of Lords stressed that the "purpose of annexation" test did not mean that the subjective intentions of the owners of the land or chattels attached were determinative of their status. Lord Lloyd stated:

> "the intention of the parties is only relevant to the extent that it can be derived from the degree and object of the annexation. The subjective intention of the parties cannot affect the question whether the chattel has, in law, become part of the freehold, any more than the subjective intention of the parties can prevent what they have called a licence from taking effect as a tenancy, if that is what the law is."[33]

2–018 This principle had been applied by the House of Lords in *Melluish (Inspector of Taxes) v BMI (No.3) Ltd*,[34] which concerned the question whether various items, including central heating installed in council flats, lifts in council car parks, cremators in a council crematorium and a filtration plant in a council swimming pool, had become fixtures, making them the property of the council, or remained chattels so that they were owned by companies which had leased them to the councils. Lord Browne-Wilkinson explained that it was irrelevant that the lease demonstrated a common intention of the parties that the chattels should continue to belong to the companies fixing them to the land. Such a contractual agreement may regulate the right to sever the chattels from the land between the parties, but it cannot prevent the chattel, once fixed, becoming part of the land in law, and as such owned by the owner of the land so long as it remains fixed.

(b) *Chattels Resting on Land*

2–019 The corollary to the presumption that a chattel attached to the land becomes a fixture is that a chattel which is not attached to the land retains its status as such. As Blackburn J. stated in *Holland v Hodgson*:

> "articles not otherwise attached to the land than by their own weight are not to be considered as part of the land, unless the circumstances are such as to shew that they were intended to be part of the land, the onus of shewing that they were so intended lying on those who assert that they have ceased to be chattels."[35]

---

[32] [1997] 2 All E.R. 513.
[33] [1997] 2 All E.R. 513 at 519.
[34] [1995] 4 All E.R. 453.
[35] (1872) L.R. 7 C.P. 328. Compare the quotation from *Holland v Hodgson*, para.2–016, above.

It can be seen that Blackburn J. therefore treats the degree of annexation as shifting the burden of proof: articles attached to land are presumed fixtures unless a contrary intention is shown; by contrast articles merely resting on land are presumed to be chattels unless the contrary is shown. The general rule was applied in *Jordan v May*,[36] where the issue was whether an electric motor and batteries were fixtures. It was held that as the motor was sunk in concrete it was attached to the land and a fixture, but the batteries remained chattels because they were resting by their own weight. However, the purpose for which chattels are allowed to remain on the land by their own weight is again the pre-eminent test, so that the mere fact that there is no attachment does not prevent a chattel becoming a fixture. In *Hamp v Bygrave*[37] the vendors of land removed a number of items from their garden, including a stone statue and other stone ornaments, after entering into a contract with the purchasers. It was held that these items were fixtures despite the fact that they merely rested by their own weight, because they formed "part and parcel of the garden" and had been installed primarily to improve the land. Similarly it had been held in *D'Eyncourt v Gregory*[38] that ornamental statues of lions in the garden and house were fixtures because they were a integral part of the overall architectural design of the land. By contrast, in *Berkley v Poulett*[39] the vendor of land removed a half-ton statute of a Greek athlete from the garden which the purchaser claimed had been a fixture. The Court of Appeal held that it had remained a chattel, since it was not part of an architectural design to improve the land, as evidenced by the fact that a different ornament had previously stood in the same place.

(c) *Buildings*

In *Billing v Pill* Lord Goddard C.J. stated: **2–020**

> "What is a fixture? First, the commonest fixture is a house. A house is built into the land, so the house, in law, is regarded as part of the land; the house and the land are one thing."[40]

Although a house attached to the land by its foundations will clearly be a fixture, greater problems have arisen in connection with buildings merely resting on the land by their own weight. In a number of early cases wooden buildings resting on land were held to have remained chattels.[41] In *Webb v Frank Bevis Ltd*[42] a large shed attached to a concrete floor by iron straps was held to have become part of the land, although as a trade fixture the tenant was entitled to sever it at the end of his tenancy. In *Elitestone Ltd v Morris*[43] the House of Lords was required to determine whether a bungalow which rested on concrete foundation blocks by its own

---

[36] [1947] K.B. 427.
[37] (1982) 266 E.G. 720.
[38] (1866) Law Rep. 3 Eq. 382.
[39] (1976) 241 E.G. 911.
[40] [1954] 1 Q.B. 70 at 75.
[41] *Elwes v Maw* (1802) 3 East 38; *R. v Otley (Inhabitants)* (1830) 1 B. & Ad. 161; *Wansbrough v Maton* (1836) 4 Ad. & E. 884; *Wiltshear v Cottrell* (1853) 1 E. & B. 674.
[42] [1940] 1 All E.R. 247.
[43] [1997] 2 All E.R. 513.

weight was a fixture or a chattel. It was held that although it rested by its own weight, it had become part of the land. The central factor in determining whether it had become part of the land was whether it was capable of being removed without demolition. Lord Lloyd referred to the two tests outlined by Blackburn J. in *Holland v Hodgson*[44] and concluded:

> "These tests are less useful when one is considering the house itself. In the case of the house the answer is as much a matter of common sense as precise analysis. A house which is constructed in such a way so as to be removable, whether as a unit or in sections, may well remain a chattel, even though it is connected temporarily to mains services such as water and electricity. But a house which is constructed in such a way that it cannot be removed at all, save by destruction, cannot have been intended to remain as a chattel. It must have been intended to form part of the realty."[45]

2–021 He therefore held that the bungalow had become part of the land because it could not be taken down and re-erected elsewhere without demolition. However, buildings such as Portacabins, mobile homes and similarly relocatable prefabricated buildings are capable of retaining their status as chattels.

3. Rights to Remove Fixtures

(a) *Severance of Fixtures by the Owner of Land*

2–022 If a chattel has become a fixture it is perfectly possible for it to be severed from the land so as to regain its status as a chattel. The owner of land can clearly sever any fixtures whenever he wishes.

(b) *Severance of Fixtures by the Vendor of Land*

2–023 It has already been noted that the effect of a contract to sell land is to pass the ownership of the land to the purchaser immediately.[46] From that time the vendor is only entitled to remove such fixtures as the contract entitles him to sever from the land. As has been noted, a number of the cases discussed above involved claims by purchasers of land that fixtures had been wrongly removed.[47] To reduce the scope for disputes, it is now common practice for the vendor and purchaser to draw up a schedule prior to exchange of contracts of what will and will not be included in the sale.

---

[44] (1872) L.R. 7 C.P. 328.
[45] [1997] 2 All E.R. 513 at 519.
[46] As will be seen, the ownership which passes in this situation is the equitable ownership of the land and the vendor retains the legal ownership.
[47] For example, see *Berkley v Poulett* (1976) 241 E.G. 911 and *Hamp v Bygrave* (1983) 266 E.G. 720, [1931] 2 Ch. 183.

(c)   Severance of Fixtures by a Tenant of Land on the Termination of his Lease

Where a tenant has attached chattels to the land he is leasing such that they have become fix-   **2–024**
tures, they thenceforth belong to the landlord who owns the land. However, the common law
and statute have intervened so that the tenant is entitled to remove some categories of fixtures
which he adds to the land, to prevent the landlord unjustifiably gaining the benefit of them.
Such fixtures can only be severed from the land if they can be removed without causing
severe structural damage, and the severing tenant is required to make good any damage
caused by their removal.

(i)   Tenant's Right to Remove Ornamental and Domestic Fixtures

A tenant is entitled to remove fixtures which he added to the land purely for decoration or   **2–025**
ornament. For example, in *Spyer v Phillipson*[48] a tenant who had installed antique paneling
in the room of a house to give it a Jacobean appearance was held entitled to remove it,
because it was only attached by screws and was readily removable.

(ii)   Tenant's Right to Remove Trade Fixtures

It has long been recognised that a tenant is entitled to remove fixtures installed during the   **2–026**
term of his lease for the purpose of carrying on his business.[49] For example, in *Smith v City
Petroleum*[50] it was held that a tenant could remove petrol pumps from the land because they
were trade fixtures and could be easily removed since they were only bolted to the land.
However it was held that the petrol tanks could not be removed because they had become an
integral part of the land and could not easily be detached. In *Young v Dalgety Plc*[51] a tenant
had installed light fittings and a carpet which had become fixtures by virtue of their attachment to the land, but the Court of Appeal held that they were trade fixtures and removable
because they were attached to render the premises convenient for the tenant's business use.
In *Mancetter Developments Ltd v Garmanson Ltd*[52] it was held that tenants were entitled to
remove an extractor fan from a wall of premises used for their chemical business.

(iii)   Agricultural Tenant's Right to Remove Fixtures

Historically, fixtures installed by a tenant of agricultural land could not be removed because   **2–027**
they were not categorised as "trade fixtures".[53] However, statute has intervened so that an

---

[48] [1931] 2 Ch. 183.
[49] *Poole's Case* (1703) 1 Salk. 368.
[50] [1940] 1 All E.R. 260.
[51] [1987] 1 E.G.L.R. 116.
[52] [1986] Q.B. 1212.
[53] See *Elwes v Maw* (1802) 3 East 38.

agricultural tenant is entitled to remove fixtures added during the term, either before the termination of the tenancy or within two months thereof.[54]

(iv) Duty of Tenant Removing Fixtures to Make Good any Damage to the Land

2–028　A tenant who legitimately severs any fixtures from the land is under a duty to make good the damage that may be caused by such removal. This principle was recognised by the Court of Appeal in *Mancetter Developments Ltd v Garmanson Ltd* where the tenants who had removed the extractor fan had failed to fill in the holes left in the wall. Dillon L.J. stated:

> "The analysis of the liability at common law is, in my judgment, that the liability to make good the damage is a condition of the tenant's right to remove tenant's fixtures: therefore removal of the fixtures without making good the damage, being in excess of the tenant's right of removal, is waste, actionable in tort, just as much as removal by the tenant of a landlord's fixture which the tenant has no right to remove is waste."[55]

The tenant who fails to make good damage to the land occasioned by the legitimate removal of fixtures will therefore be liable to compensate the owner for the loss suffered. However, Dillon L.J. also noted that such things as holes left by the removal of screws or nails are *de minimis* and unlikely to be actionable. In *Re de Falbe*[56] it was held that a tenant was not obliged to redecorate a wall after the removal of a fixture.

4. Ownership of Chattels Found on Land

2–029　It has already been noted that items of personal property found buried in land will belong to the landowner if they are not treasure trove. The position in relation to such items found on the surface of land is different, and they do not automatically belong to the landowner. If a chattel is found on the surface of land and its original owner cannot be found, and it is not treasure trove, the central question is whether it belongs to the finder or to the occupier of the land, whether the occupier be the owner or a tenant. The relevant principles were considered by the Court of Appeal in *Parker v British Airways Board*,[57] where a passenger had found a gold bracelet in the executive lounge at Heathrow airport. Donaldson L.J. held that unless the finder was a trespasser, in which case the occupier of the land where the chattel was found would always have a better entitlement to it than the finder, the occupier of the land would only have a better right to the item than the finder if he had manifested a sufficient intention to exercise control over the land and anything which might be found on it. He considered that a bank would certainly exercise sufficient control over a bank vault to gain a better

---

[54] Agricultural Holdings Act 1986 s.10.
[55] [1986] Q.B. 1212 at 1219. "Waste" is a technical term meaning unauthorised damage to property made by someone such as a tenant with only a limited right to the land.
[56] [1901] 1 Ch. 523.
[57] [1982] Q.B. 1004.

entitlement to a chattel found there than the finder, and that the owner of a public park clearly would not have exercised such control. However, there remains a wide area between these extremes where it is unclear whether sufficient control is exercised, for example, if a chattel is found on a petrol station forecourt, the public part of a supermarket,[58] or a private front garden. Although British Airways exercised a degree of control over the airport lounge, admitting only those with appropriate business class tickets and seeking to exercise a right to refuse entry where necessary, it was held that their control was not sufficient to give a right to the found property superior to the finder who was not a trespasser. It therefore seems that only in cases where an occupier of land exercises a very high degree of control over it will the occupier gain a better entitlement to lost chattels than a finder who is legitimately present on the land. In *Waverley BC v Fletcher*[59] it was held that the Council, which owned a public park, had a better claim than the finder, who had dug up a valuable brooch after finding it with a metal detector. Not only was the object concerned beneath the surface,[60] but the finder was trespassing by digging in the park. In all cases there is an obligation on the finder or occupier to take reasonable steps to return the found item to its true owner.

Although it may seem certain and clear-cut, the distinction which the courts have drawn between articles on the surface and those below leaves unanswered the issue of articles which have only temporarily been buried. For instance, how would the principles apply to a ring which has fallen off someone's finger on a sand dune and is found the following day by a child building a sandcastle? Would it make any difference if a rain storm washed away the covering of sand? The bipolar test set out in the twin cases of *Fletcher* and *Waverley* fails to deal with ambiguous situations such as these.

---

[58] See *Bridges v Hawkesworth* (1851) 21 L.J. Q.B. 75.
[59] [1995] 4 All E.R. 756.
[60] See above para.2–009.

Chapter 3

HISTORIC FOUNDATIONS OF LAND LAW

TENURES AND ESTATES

1. The Feudal System

Modern land law has developed by a process of evolution over a period of nearly one **3–001** thousand years. The shape of the present law is far removed from that of the medieval period, but some of the fundamental concepts which make up the framework of English land law, and in particular concepts of the ownership of land, are derived from that time. It is commonly assumed today that land is "owned" by those who hold title to it. Historically this was not the case. English law was founded upon the premise that all land was owned by the King.[1] His subjects were merely permitted to make use of it, holding it on the basis of some form of tenancy, either from the King directly, or indirectly through a chain of others deriving their holding ultimately from the King himself. Those who held their land directly from the King were known as *tenants in capite* or tenants in chief. Such tenants were then able to grant what were in effect sub-tenancies of the land that they themselves held, and their sub-tenants were known as *tenants in demesne*. By means of such sub-grants a feudal ladder was constructed of persons who held their land as tenants of their immediate overlord, who would in turn hold the land as tenant of their lord, until the ladder culminated in the tenants *in capite* who held directly from the King. The intermediate lords between the King and the person actually enjoying the tenure of the land were know as mesne lords. Crucial to an understanding of this feudal structure of land holding were the twin doctrines of tenures and estates.

---

[1] See Pollock and Maitland, *History of English Law* (2nd edn), Vol.I, p.237.

2. The Doctrine of Tenure

(a) *Meaning of Tenure*

3–002 Since no one within the feudal system owned land except the King, those who enjoyed its use did so only as tenants. The terms under which such persons enjoyed the right to a tenancy of the land were known as tenure. Tenure is therefore best understood as the terms under which a person held land, either as a tenant *in capite* of the King or as a tenant in demesne of their immediate overlord. Generally tenure required the tenant to perform services for the King or his overlord. There was a wide variety of tenures, classified according to the nature of the services that had to be performed.

(b) *Free and Unfree Tenures*

3–003 In the system of tenure two types of tenants should be distinguished. Some tenants enjoyed tenure of land in their own right, and therefore enjoyed a place on the feudal ladder that stretched from the relatively minor and insignificant lords, through the nobility, to the King himself. Such persons enjoyed what is known as free tenure. However in most parts of England and Wales the ordinary common people (villeins) enjoyed no such place on the feudal ladder. They only occupied their land on behalf of their lords, rather than in their own right, and it was the lord who was regarded by law as having possession, technically the *seisin*, of the land. This was known as unfree tenure or villeinage. In more recent times unfree tenure was known as "copyhold tenure". The villein owed duties to the lord in return for being allowed the use of the land, and the lord often retained a range of rights over the land such as the right to hunt. Over time the rights of the occupiers of copyhold land became more secure, but until copyhold tenure was abolished, special forms of transfer applied.

(c) *Types of Free Tenure*

3–004 The terms under which land was held by those enjoying free tenure varied, though they were intended to ensure that the country's military, spiritual and agricultural needs were met. The majority of those whose held their tenure directly from the King as tenants *in capite* did so on the basis of knights' service, a tenure in chivalry, which required them to provide the King with a specified number of armed horsemen for a number of days each year. This was the means by which the army was raised. Other forms of tenure included "frankalmoign" and "divine service", where the land was held in return for the performance of religious functions, and "tenure in socage", where the tenant was required to perform agricultural services (normally by supplying agricultural produce) for his lord. From an early stage those enjoying tenure of land on the basis of knights' service were required to pay the King a sum of money, known as scutage, rather than provide actual horsemen. What started as a feudal system in which tenants provided services in kind therefore developed into what would now be described as a system of taxation linked to the use of land.

28

(d) *Transfer of Tenure: Subinfeudation and the Statute of Quia Emptores*

Under a fully developed feudal system of land holding, one issue which arose was how a   **3–005**
tenant could transfer his interest in land to another person. One means was by the grant of
new sub-tenancies and tenure. This had the advantage to the transferor that he would continue
to receive services or an income from the person to whom the land was transferred, although
remaining liable to provide services to his own lord. The consequence of this form of
transfer was to add further rungs of mesne lords to the feudal ladder. This process of transfer
through the creation of new tenancies was known as subinfeudation, and was common until
prohibited by the Statute *Quia Emptores* of 1290, which had the effect that only the King was
entitled to grant new tenures. From that time tenure to land was transferred by the substitution of a new tenant for the old in the place that he had enjoyed on the feudal ladder. In time
the conversion of most feudal obligations into obligations to pay money combined with the
effect of inflation meant that most mesne lordships were unenforced and in due course
became untraceable.

(e) *Modern Relevance of Tenure*

Although of historical importance it is almost impossible to find any practical significance for   **3–006**
the doctrine of tenure in modern land law. The Tenures Abolition Act 1660 converted most
free tenures into tenure in socage, so that the only remaining tenures were socage and copyhold. Copyhold tenure was finally abolished by the Law of Property Act 1925 and converted
into freehold tenure in socage. The consequence was that following the Law of Property
Act 1925 all land was held by its owners as tenants of the Crown in socage, but that apart
from some exceptional cases where ceremonial services were still attached to that tenure, all
vestiges of that tenure had disappeared. Such aspects of tenure as remain are in most cases
indistinguishable from the rights of the Crown relating to personal property. For instance, it
is said that be virtue of the doctrine of tenure, the Crown is entitled by escheat to any land for
which no other owner can be identified. However, substantially the same concept applies to
personal property where under the doctrine of *bona vacantia* (property without an owner) the
right to any property which would otherwise be ownerless vests in the Crown. The point has
probably now been reached where it is possible to declare that the doctrine of tenure has
ceased to have any practical effect. The time is now ripe to follow the example set in Scotland
by the Abolition of Feudal Tenure etc. (Scotland) Act 2000 (which came into effect on
November 28, 2004) and to abolish feudal tenure. That task would be much simpler for
England and Wales than it was for Scotland since feudal tenure retained more significance in
modern Scottish law than it does in the law of England and Wales.[2] Even there the law was
described as in urgent need of reform since the feudal system prior to abolition "now serves
no useful function. It has become an anachronism which needlessly complicates the law".[3]

---

[2] For further information about the abolition of feudal tenure in Scotland, see *Report on Abolition of the Feudal
System* Scottish Law Commission (SCOT LAW COM No.168) (1999).
[3] *Report on Abolition of the Feudal System* Scottish Law Commission (SCOT LAW COM No.168) (1999) para.1.15.

3. The Doctrine of Estates

(a) *The Meaning of an Estate in Land*

3–007 Since ultimate ownership of land remained with the King it was clear that tenants did not own the land itself. Instead what the tenant was regarded as enjoying was a right to possession, or seisin of the land. The common law would protect the tenant's right to seisin of the land against everyone except a person who had a better right to the land. Instead of speaking of ownership of the land the person who enjoyed the right to seisin enjoyed an estate in the land. The estate is best understood as the grant of a right of seisin, or proprietorial rights, over the land for a period of time. Whereas the doctrine of tenures refers to the terms under which a tenant enjoys his right to the land, the doctrine of estates relates to the period of time during which his rights to the land will endure. Rather than owning the land itself, the doctrine of estates means that a person enjoys a notional period of time in the land, during which period he is entitled to enjoy tenure of it. By means of the doctrine of estates, English land law conceptually distinguishes between the ownership of the land itself and the enjoyment of rights to use and enjoy land to the exclusion of all others. As was stated in *Walsingham's Case*[4]:

> "the land itself is one thing, and the estate in the land is another thing, for an estate in the land is a time in the land, or land for a time, and there are diversities of estates, which are no more than diversities of time . . ."

As is noted in this comment, English law recognised a number of different types of estate in land, and the key distinguishing feature between them is the period of time for which the grant of the land may be enjoyed. The relationship between the doctrines of tenures and estates was thus that tenure represented the terms under which a person enjoyed rights to the land, and the estate was the period of time for which such rights were to endure.

(b) *Freehold Estates in Land*

3–008 There were three main types of freehold estate, each of which differed in the length of time for which the grant of the land would last.

(i) Fee Simple Estate

3–009 The first and most important of the estates was the fee simple. This is a perpetual grant of proprietorship of land, meaning that the grant can never come to an end. A person who enjoys a fee simple in the land is technically a tenant of the Crown, but since the interest can never end

---

[4] (1573) 2 Plowd. 547 at 555.

it is tantamount to absolute ownership of the land for all practical purposes. In *Walsingham's Case*[5] an estate in fee simple was described as "a time in the land without end". The estate in fee simple may be transferred to others and on death will pass as part of the owner's estate, either by will or according to the rules of intestacy.

(ii)   Fee-tail Estate

The fee tail, or entailed estate, was a grant of land which can only pass to the lineal descen-   **3–010**
dants of the original grantee. Therefore if the family to which the land was granted dies out, it will revert back to the Crown. In *Walsingham's Case* the fee tail was described as "time in the land . . . for as long as [the grantee] has issues of his body". The precise terms of the fee tail could vary, so that in some cases the land was granted only so long as the original grantee had male lineal descendants, or in some rare cases female lineal descendants. Obviously the fee tail is not as durable an interest in land as the fee simple. It was, however, possible to convert the fee tail into a fee simple by means of "barring the entail". This may be done by the tenant in possession by will[6] or through an inter vivos declaration by deed that he is henceforth holding the land as a tenant in fee simple. The Trusts of Land and Appointment of Trustees Act 1996 amended the law so that it is impossible to create an entailed estate. A grant of such an interest in land will instead take effect as an absolute interest under a trust of the land.[7]

(iii)   Life Estate

A life estate is a grant of the land for the lifetime of the grantee only, and it automatically   **3–011**
comes to an end on his death. The life interest is transferable, but the estate will still come to an end on the death of the original grantee and not on the death of the transferee. In the modern law a life estate can only take effect behind a trust of the land.[8]

(c)   *Flexibility of Land Ownership through Estates*

The concept of the estate has enabled English law to develop a complex and flexible means   **3–012**
of land ownership since a person does not own the land itself but an abstract estate in the land. It is possible for a lesser estate to be carved out of a greater estate. For example, a person holding an estate in fee simple of the land can grant a life interest out of his estate to another. The holder of the life interest will then be entitled to enjoy immediate possession and use of the land for the period of his life, at which point the holder of the fee simple will be entitled to enjoy his full unencumbered rights over the land again. Thus a number of people may enjoy different rights in the same piece of land at the same time, and different people may be

---

[5] (1573) 2 Plowd. 547
[6] Law of Property Act 1925 s.176.
[7] Sch.1 para.5(1).
[8] See below, Ch.14.

regarded as "owners" of the same piece of land at the same time because the nature of their "ownership" varies. As between themselves the rights of such simultaneous "owners" will depend upon who has the better right to immediate possession of the land, and their relationship inter se will be regulated by the incidents of their various rights of ownership.

(d) Leasehold Estates in Land

3–013   As well as the freehold estates in land English law also recognised leasehold estates, which are created by leases. Historically leasehold estates were not regarded as real property but as personal proprietary interests where the freehold owner of land had granted a tenant a right to occupy the land for a period of time, usually in return for the payment of rent. The leasehold estate therefore enables a separation between the ownership of the land and its use, since the landlord remains the full owner whilst the tenant under the lease is entitled to a more limited range of rights including the exclusive use of the land. In the modern law leases, which take a very wide range of forms and lengths, provide an important means of enjoying interests in land, and very long leases are almost equivalent to actual ownership.

COMMON LAW AND EQUITY[9]

1. Introduction

3–014   Another important factor which underpins much of the language used to describe rights and interests in land is the distinction between the common law and equity. Due to historical factors English law developed two completely separate jurisprudential systems, each of which recognised its own body of rights and interests, enforced and protected by its own courts. One body of law was the common law, which was administered by the common law courts, and the other was equity, which was administered by the Courts of Chancery.

2. The Common Law

3–015   Prior to the Norman Conquest in 1066 there was no single legal system operating in England. Instead there were a variety of decision-making bodies, some local and some national, applying a system of customary law which varied by geographical location. The common law was the system of justice which emerged after the Norman Conquest, when it was established that justice flowed from the King, and was administered by the Royal Courts. It was "common" in the sense that it applied to the whole Kingdom, thus eliminating the previous regional variation. By 1234

---

[9] See Holdsworth, *A History of English Law* (7th edn, 1956), Vol.1, Ch.V; J.H. Baker, *An Introduction to English Legal History* (2nd edn, 1979), Ch.6; Pearce and Stevens, *The Law of Trusts and Equitable Obligations* (4th edn, 2002), Ch.1.

the origins of the two common law courts, the Court of Common Pleas and the King's Bench, had emerged. The common law courts naturally applied the common law and protected the interests in land which were recognised by the common law. However, the common law system was subject to a number of important defects. First, in order to start an action it was necessary to obtain a writ. As a consequence of the Provisions of Oxford in 1258 it was no longer possible for the courts to create new writs, and therefore actions had to be brought within the narrow range of writs that were available. The common law also had a limited range of remedies.

3.   The Development of Equity

(a)   *Motivations for the Development of Equity*

Equity was a parallel system of law which developed initially to remedy the defects of the common law system. The equity jurisdiction had its origins in appeals by aggrieved parties directly to the King, and the delegation of this appellate role to the King's Council and ultimately to the Chancellor acting in his own right. The Court of Chancery developed as a court of "conscience" where justice would be done between the parties. Actions were started by means of a simple subpoena which avoided the need for a writ. Although the Court of Chancery initially operated as a court of conscience, over a period of time equity began to develop its own body of rights, rules and principles which it would enforce. Its relationship with the common law was a matter of ongoing conflict, which was finally settled in 1616 when James I ordered that the Chancery courts were entitled to grant "common injunctions" which had the effect of restraining a person from pursuing an action at common law or from enforcing a judgment which had been given by the common law courts. This had the practical effect of enabling the Chancery courts to establish primacy over the common law and thus to achieve the supremacy of equity. **3–016**

(b)   *Equity Prior to the Judicature Acts*

By the middle of the nineteenth century equity was an established body of law recognising and protecting its own rights and interests in property, including interests in land. There were in effect two separate court systems operating side by side: the common law courts where a plaintiff could obtain remedies to enforce his common law rights, and the Chancery courts where a plaintiff could enforce his rights in equity. It was not possible to obtain equitable relief in a common law court, nor common law remedies in the Court of Chancery. In order to overcome the administrative difficulties of having two parallel systems of law administered by different courts the structure of the English legal system was radically reshaped by the Judicature Acts of 1873 and 1875. **3–017**

(c)   *Effect of the Judicature Acts*

The central effect of the Judicature Acts was to create a single Supreme Court from the common law and Chancery courts. This Supreme Court comprises the High Court and the Court of **3–018**

Appeal, and although the court is organised into divisions, such as the Queen's Bench and Chancery Division, these are divisions of administrative convenience rather than of jurisdiction. The judges of the Supreme Court were given both common law and equitable jurisdiction.[10] The amalgamation of the courts thus meant that it was no longer necessary to start separate actions in separate courts to obtain both common law and equitable relief. The Act also incorporated the supremacy of equity in s.25 of the Judicature Act 1873, which provided that in matters where there was a conflict between the rules of equity and the rules of the common law the rules of equity were to prevail.[11] It has long been a question of debate whether the Judicature Acts brought about a fusion of the common law and equity into a single body of law, or whether there was merely a fusion of administration, so that they remained essentially separate systems administered by the same court. Although the traditional view has been that there was merely a fusion of administration, well expressed by Ashburner's famous fluvial metaphor that "the two streams of jurisprudence, though they run in the same channel, run side by side and do not mingle their waters", more recent cases take the view that there has been a substantive fusion to produce a single body of law.[12] This does not mean that the distinction between legal and equitable rights and interests in land is unimportant, and it may still be essential to distinguish between them since their character may determine whether such rights are binding upon a particular person claiming interests in the land to which they relate.

TRUSTS

1. The Nature of a Trust

3–019   One of the most important creations of equity is the trust. This is best defined as a means by which property may be held by one person for the benefit of another. For example, if a famous pop star wants to purchase a house in a village without it being known that he is the owner, he may wish someone else to appear to be the owner. He may ask his friend to purchase the house with money that he provides. Here the friend will appear from the legal documents to be the owner of the house, but the reality behind that "front" is that the pop star is the true owner. The friend cannot treat the house as if it were his own property but must instead treat it as the property of the star. As the paper owner, he will have the power to deal with the property, but he not must do so in his own interests but on behalf of the star. The essence of a trust is that there is a separation of the ownership of property into two distinct types, namely the legal ownership and the equitable ownership. The equitable ownership is sometimes called the beneficial ownership. The legal ownership is the ownership which would have been recognised by the common law, and the legal owners are the trustees of the property. This means that they have all the powers over the property that are the proper incidents of legal

---

[10] Judicature Act 1973 s.24. See now Supreme Court Act 1981 s.49(1).
[11] See *Walsh v Lonsdale* (1882) 21 Ch.D. 9; *United Scientific Holding v Burnley BC* [1978] A.C. 904.
[12] See *United Scientific Holding v Burnley BC* [1978] A.C. 904; *Aquaculture Corp v New Zealand Green Mussel Co Ltd* [1990] 3 N.Z.L.R. 299; *Canson Enterprises Ltd v Broughton & Co* (1993) 85 D.L.R. (4th) 129; *Tinsley v Milligan* [1993] 3 All E.R. 65.

ownership, including the power to transfer title to the property. However, although they hold these powers by virtue of their legal ownership, they are not entitled to use them for their own advantage, since the persons who are the "real" owners of the trust property are the beneficiaries. The trustees must always act in the interests of the beneficiaries, and if they fail to do so the beneficiaries will be entitled to remedies against them for breach of trust. The beneficiaries are regarded as the owners of the property held on trust for them and, under the rule in *Saunders v Vautier*,[13] are entitled to demand that the trustees transfer the legal title to them, provided that they are unanimous in their demand and are all of age and legally competent. Trusts may be created of all types of property, personal property, intellectual property and land, and they provide a vital means of facilitating flexible arrangements for the ownership and management of property. The nature of a trust is well illustrated by the facts of *Tinsley v Milligan*.[14] A house was purchased by a lesbian couple who both contributed equally to the purchase price. The house was purchased in the name of Tinsley alone, so that she was the sole legal owner, with the object of ensuring that Milligan would appear to be a lodger in the house, to enable her to continue claiming housing benefit. However, the consequence of her contribution to the purchase price was to give rise to a special type of trust called a resulting trust. Thus although Tinsley was the sole legal owner, she held the house as trustee on trust for herself and Milligan in equal shares. Milligan therefore enjoyed a beneficial interest in a half share of the property, which she was able to assert against Tinsley when their relationship broke up.

2. The Importance of Trusts to the Ownership of Land

Although trusts may be created over any type of property, they form a vital aspect of modern land law. For reasons which will be explained more fully in Chapters 11 and 12, every situation where there is co-ownership of land will take place behind a trust of land, as will life interests and other successive interests.[15] Only where land is owned by a single absolute owner for his own sole benefit will the land be free from the existence of a trust.

3–020

3. Historical Origins of the Trust

(a) *The Development of the "Use"*

The modern concept of the trust began with the development of the "use" in the medieval period to avoid some of the difficulties associated with the feudal system of landholding. It was common for land to be conveyed to X "to the use of Y" so that X was not to enjoy the property for his own benefit but was to apply it for the benefit of Y. X was known as the *feoffee* and Y as the *cestui que use*. The legal ownership of the land was vested in the feoffee. One

3–021

---

[13] (1841) 4 Beav. 115.
[14] [1993] 3 All E.R. 65.
[15] See below, Ch.14.

advantage of the use included the ability to give property to religious orders that were prevented from owning property, such as the order of St Francis. More importantly, they enabled a landowner to avoid the strict rules of inheritance by enabling them to direct the feoffees by will as to how the property should be held on their death, and to avoid the payment of feudal dues payable on inheritance by ensuring that the land was perpetually held by a group of feoffees, so that there was no succession to the legal title. The death of the *cestui que use* did not require the payment of such dues. A use was also a means of avoiding forfeiture of land to the Crown if the tenant committed high treason. Uses were not recognised and enforced by the common law, but they were enforced by the Chancellor, who would act against feoffees who did not observe the rights and interests of the cestui que use. The development of the use therefore marked the beginning of the distinction between legal and equitable ownership.

(b) *Statute of Uses 1535*

3–022 The development of the use was so successful that by 1500 the majority of land was held in use, with consequent detrimental effects on the revenue of the Crown through the avoidance of the feudal dues. To reverse this reduction in revenue the King attempted to abolish the use by the Statute of Uses 1535, which had the effect of executing the use by statutorily vesting legal ownership in the *cestui que use*, thus bringing the use to an end. However, the statute did not abolish all uses, and those where the feoffees had active duties to perform (for example, the collection and distribution of profits and the management of an estate) were excluded. The effects of the statute could also be avoided by means of a "use upon a use", where property was conveyed "to X to the use of Y, to the use of Z". The Statute of Uses only executed the first use, and equity was prepared to accept that Y was holding the land to the use of Z. Recognition of the second use had originally been rejected by both the common law[16] and equity, but by the later part of the sixteenth century the "use upon the use" was recognised in equity in order to give effect to the transferor's intentions.[17] This second use was referred to as a "trust", which is the origin of the modern terminology.[18] A simple conveyance of land "upon trust" was effective to create a trust of the land without any mention of the first use, under which the trustee received the legal title to the land and the beneficiary enjoyed the equitable ownership.

4. Legal and Equitable Ownership Compared

3–023 By means of the trust English law has developed a system of dual ownership of property, including land. It is important to recognise that the beneficiary of a trust of land is, in a real sense, an owner of it. There has been some debate as to whether the interest of a beneficiary is to be regarded as a proprietary interest *in rem* or a personal interest *in personam*. Those who

---

[16] *Jane Tyrrel's Case* (1557) 2 Dyer 155a.
[17] See, for example, *Sambach v Dalston* (1635) Toth 188.
[18] Although the term trust had also been used for a single use prior to the development of the "use upon a use".

have argued that the beneficial interest is a right in personam have done so on the grounds that, as with all equitable rights, it was enforced *in personam*[19] by the Chancery Court ordering the trustee to observe the trust. It was also liable to be defeated by the interest of a person who purchased the legal title from the trustees, *bona fides* (in good faith), without notice of the existence of the trust, at which point the beneficiary would be restricted to his remedies against the trustee for breach of trust. This was a consequence of the operation of the doctrine of notice which will be considered more fully below. The better view seems to be that the rights of the beneficiary of a trust, including a trust of land, should be regarded as proprietary rights, although of a special character. As Lord Browne-Wilkinson observed in *Tinsley v Milligan*[20]:

> "Although for historical reasons legal estates and equitable estates have differing incidents, the person owning either type of estate has a right of property, a right *in rem* and not merely a right *in personam*."

The reality of the proprietary status of the equitable interest is evidenced by the fact that the beneficiary can deal with it in much the same way as he could deal with other property. It is an asset which he can transfer to others, provided that the appropriate formalities required by the Law of Property Act 1925 s.53(1)(c).[21] He can dispose of it by will, or in the event of his intestacy it will devolve to his heirs. He can use his interest as security for a loan, and he may incur tax upon its value. The equitable interest behind a trust is capable of enduring through changes in the legal ownership of the property. However, the beneficiary clearly cannot transfer a title better than that which he himself enjoys, so that he is not able to transfer the full legal title to the land. Equitable ownership behind a trust is also, as has been noted above, less durable than legal ownership, since it is liable to be defeated by the rights of a person who acquires the legal title *bona fides* without notice of its existence.

5. The Creation of Trusts of Land

There are three main ways that a trust of land may come into being. These will be examined in detail in Chapter 6, but here an outline is provided.

3–024

(a) *Express Trusts*

As the name suggests, express trusts are those which are created by the deliberate act of the legal owner of the land. He may either declare himself to be a trustee in favour of the beneficiary, at which point he will retain the legal title himself but only in the capacity as trustee for the beneficiary, or alternatively he may transfer the land to a person who has agreed to take it

3–025

---

[19] It is one of the maxims of Equity that "equity acts in personam".
[20] [1993] 3 All E.R. 65 at 86.
[21] The disposition of the subsisting equitable interest must be made in writing, signed by the person disposing of it.

as trustee. According to the Law of Property Act 1925 s.53(1)(b) an *inter vivos* declaration of trust of land must be evidenced by writing, signed by the person creating the trust or his agent.

(b) *Resulting Trusts*

3–026 Resulting trusts are trusts which arise automatically in certain circumstances. The most important situation is where one person has contributed to the price of land purchased in the name of another. This was the case in *Tinsley v Milligan*,[22] noted above. By the Law of Property Act 1925 s.53(2) there are no formal requirements for the creation of resulting trusts. Under a resulting trust of land the equitable ownership of land will be held in the same proportions as the contributions that have been made to the purchase price.

(c) *Constructive Trusts*

3–027 Constructive trusts are trusts which arise as a result of the conduct of the parties. The principles were expounded by the House of Lords in *Lloyds Bank v Rosset*,[23] namely that where the legal ownership of land is held in the name of one person, but there was a common intention[24] that someone else was to enjoy a share of the ownership a constructive trust will arise if the person claiming a share had acted to his detriment on the basis of the common intention. Again by virtue of the Law of Property Act 1925 s.53(2) there is no necessity for writing. The parties' respective shares of the equitable ownership will be determined in accordance with their common intention.

LEGAL AND EQUITABLE RIGHTS AND INTERESTS IN LAND

1. Subsidiary Rights and Interests in Land

3–028 Although ownership, whether legal or equitable under a trust, is the most important right that a person may enjoy in land there are many other lesser interests or rights in land which a person may enjoy. For example, a person may have a right of way to cross another's land, which right is known as an easement. A person may have borrowed money on the security of his land by means of a mortgage, or he may have granted a tenant a lease of his land. Many of these subsidiary rights or interests in land may exist with either legal or equitable status. Lord Browne-Wilkinson's statement in *Tinsley v Milligan*[25] that English law "has one single law of property made up of legal and equitable interests" is an appropriate description.

[22] [1993] 3 All E.R. 65.
[23] [1991] 1 A.C. 107.
[24] The common intention may be express or implied from the facts of the parties dealing with each other.
[25] [1993] 3 All E.R. 65 at 86.

2. The Origin of Equitable Interests in Land

Common law rights and interests in land were those which were historically recognised and enforced by the common law courts prior to the Judicature Acts. Equitable rights and interests were those which were recognised and enforced by the Chancery courts. One of the main circumstances in which an equitable right arose is where there was a contract to create a legal right but the necessary formalities had not been observed, generally because no deed had been executed. However equity, following the maxim that "equity treats as done that which ought to be done", was willing to treat a specifically enforceable contract to create an interest in land as effective to create an equitable interest on equivalent terms to those agreed in the contract. The operation of this principle can be illustrated from the facts of *Walsh v Lonsdale*.[26] The defendant had entered into a contract to grant the plaintiff a lease of his land under the terms of which the rent was to be payable yearly in advance. No legal lease was ever granted by the defendant by deed. However, since there was a valid and enforceable contract, it was held that there was an equitable lease on the terms contained in the contract, namely requiring the rent to be paid in advance. This principle that equitable rights are generated on the basis of contract where the requisite common law formalities have not been observed is also applicable to easements and mortgages.

3-029

3. The Modern Distinction between Legal and Equitable Estates and Interests in Land

Today the question whether estates and interests in land are legal or equitable in character is not determined by their historical origins, but is fixed by means of the statutory definition in s.1 of the Law of Property Act 1925. This section outlines the categories of estates and interests which are capable of assuming legal character, and by a process of elimination all other estates and interests are deemed equitable. A fuller consideration of this section and its effects is given below, but it is to be noted that although an interest may be capable of enjoying legal status, whether it is in fact legal will often depend on whether the appropriate formalities have been followed for its creation.

3-030

Rules Governing Priority Between Legal and Equitable Rights

1. The Problem of Priority and Interests in Land

One of the central issues with which land law has to grapple is the problem of determining priorities between competing interests in land. This difficulty arises in particular where a person

3-031

---

[26] (1882) 21 Ch.D. 9.

purchases land and there are third parties who enjoyed interests in it prior to the purchase. Is the purchaser to be bound by such pre-existing third party interests? For example, imagine a situation where Mark is the legal owner of a house. He may have granted Norma a three-year lease of the house so that she could live there while she studies at a local university. Owen may enjoy a right of way across the drive of the house so that he can have access to his own garage. Penelope, who owns land at the back of the house, may enjoy the benefit of a restrictive covenant entered by Mark agreeing that he will not use his land for business purposes. Mark may have declared himself a trustee of a half share of the house in favour of his girlfriend Roberta. In this situation Norma, Owen, Penelope and Roberta all have proprietary interests in the house owned by Mark. No doubt their interests are valid and enforceable against him but what happens if he decides to sell the house to Stephanie? Is she still bound to observe their interests when the house is transferred into her name? This will depend upon whether their interests have priority over the interest in the house she has acquired. If they do, then their rights will bind her. If not, she will take the land free from them. The same question would arise if, for example, instead of selling the house to Stephanie, Mark merely transferred it to her as a gift, or alternatively if he decided to grant his bank a mortgage over the house to secure a loan.

2. The Basic Principle of Priority by Date of Creation

3–032   Perhaps the simplest way to determine priority between competing rights and interests in land would be to apply a rule that pre-existing rights gain priority over subsequently created rights, so that priority is determined by the order of their creation. However such a simple approach fails to take account of the fact that some rights and interests in land are inherently more important than others, and that some rights are legal and others equitable in nature. Thus a more nuanced means of determining priorities evolved, which differentiated between rights according to their character. Whilst priority between competing legal interests, or competing equitable interests, would be determined by the order of their creation, so that an earlier right would gain priority over a later right, the doctrine of notice developed as a means by which legal interests could gain priority over pre-existing equitable interests, thus subverting any precedence based on the order of creation.

3. Rules of Priority Governing Legal Rights

3–033   Legal rights were historically indefeasible, so that at common law a legal right would never lose priority to a subsequently created legal or equitable right. Priorities thus followed strictly the order in which the legal rights had been created. This indefeasibility was expressed in the maxim "legal rights bind the world". To return to the example cited above, if Mark owned the fee simple of a house and had granted Norma a legal lease for three years and then sold the house to Stephanie, Stephanie would be bound by Norma's lease because it was a legal interest and gained priority over Stephanie's subsequently acquired ownership of the house. Legal interests were not, therefore, defeated by changes in the ownership of the land or by the acquisition of other interests. If Mark had granted a legal mortgage to his bank, the bank would acquire its security subject to Norma's prior legal lease and would not gain priority over it. Whether the person acquiring the subsequent interest in the house knew about the subsisting legal interest was irrelevant. He would be bound by it even if he had no idea that it existed.

4. Rules of Priority Governing Equitable Rights

(a) *The Doctrine of Notice*

As has been noted above in the context of the difference between legal ownership and equitable ownership under a trust, equitable interests were not so durable as legal interests and did not bind the world automatically. As between themselves, priority to equitable interests was governed by the order of their creation, so that pre-existing equitable interests took priority over those which were created subsequently. However, in relation to legal interests it was not necessarily the case that a pre-existing equitable interest would have priority over a subsequently created legal interest. In a sense legal interests had the ability to operate as "trump" cards which could in some cases defeat pre-existing equitable interests. However, it was not inevitable that they would do so. The principle, known as the doctrine of notice, was that equitable interests took priority to all subsequently created interests except those of a person who purchased a legal estate in the land, bona fide (in good faith), for valuable consideration and without notice of the existence of the equitable interest. The element of notice is the most significant, and means that if a purchaser knew, or should have known, of the existence of the equitable interest he cannot acquire his legal estate free from it. He knew or should have known what he was getting. Returning to the example above, if Norma enjoyed only an equitable lease then Stephanie would take free from it only if she was a bona fide purchaser of a legal estate without notice.

A person would only acquire land free from pre-existing equitable interests if they satisfied the three constituent elements of the doctrine of notice.

3–034

(i) Bona Fides

Bona fides is a Latin expression meaning "good faith". There is a general requirement that a person claiming to take advantage of the doctrine of notice must have acted in good faith, and it adds little in substance to the requirements. A person engaging in a corrupt transaction would almost certainly be aware of the rights which he was trying to defeat.

3–035

(ii) Purchaser of a Legal Estate for Value

A person will only obtain the protection of the doctrine of notice if they purchased a legal estate in return for valuable consideration. The modern definition of a legal estate will be considered below. "Value" means consideration which is recognised by equity and includes marriage consideration (for instance where a gift of land is made as a wedding present), but

3–036

not nominal consideration. The donee of a gift of land will not therefore obtain the protection of the doctrine of notice, nor will a person who inherits the land on the death of the owner. In *Midland Bank Trust Co v Green*[27] the House of Lords held that the requirement that consideration must be valuable did not mean that it had to be adequate, so that a payment of £500 to purchase a legal estate in farmland which was worth hundreds of times more was still treated as "valuable consideration".

(iii)   Without Notice

3–037   The most important element of the doctrine of notice is that the purchaser of the legal estate must have no notice (sometimes referred to as "knowledge") of the existence of the equitable right. The foundation of this principle is that if the purchaser knows of the equitable interest their conscience is affected and they should not have gone ahead with the purchase if they had not wanted to be bound by the interest. However, if they did not know that it existed their conscience was not affected and there is no reason why they should be bound by it.

(b)   *Types of Notice*

3–038   English law identified three distinct types of notice, actual, constructive and imputed notice, which are now codified in s.199(1) of the Law of Property Act 1925. As a result of an extended understanding of notice a purchaser of a legal estate will acquire it subject to pre-existing equitable interests not only where he was personally aware of the existence of those interests, but where he should have been aware of their existence.

(i)   Actual Notice

3–039   A person has actual notice of an interest in land when he is consciously aware of its existence. As Cairns L.C. stated in *Lloyd v Banks* actual notice exists where the mind of a person:

> ". . . has in some way been brought to the intelligent apprehension of the nature of [an interest] which has come upon the property, so that a reasonable man, or an ordinary man of business, would act upon the information and would regulate his conduct by it."[28]

It is clear that justice demands that a person who has actual notice of an equitable interest affecting land should take the land subject to it. As Lord Cranworth said in *Ware v Lord Egmont*:

> "Where a person has actual notice of any matter of fact, there can be no danger of doing injustice if he is held to be bound by all the consequences of that which he knows to exist."[29]

---

[27] [1981] A.C. 517.
[28] (1868) 3 Ch. App. 488 at 490–491.
[29] (1854) 4 De G.M. & G. 460 at 473.

(ii) Constructive Notice

Prospective purchasers of land are expected to take all reasonable steps to inquire whether there are any equitable interests adversely affecting the land, and they cannot take advantage of their failure to take such steps. Equity therefore deemed them to have notice of the existence of such interests affecting the land as they would have discovered if they had made all reasonable inquiries. This principle is placed on a statutory footing in the Law of Property Act 1925, s.199(1)(ii)(a) which provides that a purchaser is to be affected by notice of any instrument, matter or fact if:

3–040

> "it is within his own knowledge, or would have come to his knowledge if such inquiries and inspections had been made as ought reasonably to have been made by him".

A prospective purchaser of a legal estate in land was firstly expected to make an inspection of the vendor's title documents. If he failed to do so he would be held to have notice of such interests as would have been revealed by an inspection.[30] Secondly he was expected to make a physical inspection of the land, and would have constructive notice of any equitable rights which would have been evident from such an inspection of the land. Sometimes this principle was taken to extreme lengths: for example, in *Hervey v Smith*[31] it was held that a purchaser had notice of his neighbour's equitable easement to make use of two flues in his house because the Court held that he should have noticed that he had 14 chimney pots but only 12 flues.

A prospective purchaser was expected to make inquiries of any persons who were discovered to be in occupation of the land by an inspection. If they failed to do so they would have constructive notice of the occupier's interests in the land. For example, if an occupier was a beneficiary of a trust of the land, the purchaser would have constructive notice of that equitable interest. This principle was adopted by the Court of Appeal in *Hunt v Luck*, where Vaughan Williams L.J. stated:

> ". . . if a purchaser or a mortgagee has notice that the vendor or mortgagor is not in possession of the property, he must make inquiries of the person in possession . . . and find out from him what his rights are, and if he does not choose to do that, then whatever title he acquires as purchaser or mortgagee will be subject to the title or right of the tenant in possession."[32]

---

[30] If the purchaser failed to make any inquiry for the title deeds at all, but allowed them to remain in the hands of a third person, such as an equitable mortgagee, he would be taken to have constructive notice of the equitable interests of the possessors of the deeds: *Walker v Linom* [1907] 2 Ch. 104. If he inquires after them, but the vendor fails to produce them, the purchaser will have notice of any equitable interests which they would have revealed unless there was gross negligence on the part of the person asserting an equitable right: *Oliver v Hinton* [1899] 2 Ch. 264; *Hewitt v Loosemore* (1851) 9 Hare 449. Although a prospective purchaser is entitled to insist on proof of title for at least 15 years by statute, if the parties choose they can agree to a lesser period in their contract. If a lesser period is stipulated the purchaser will have constructive notice of any equitable interests which would have been disclosed if he had insisted on proof of title for the whole period: *Re Cox and Neve's Contract* [1891] 2 Ch. 109; *Re Nisbet and Pott's Contract* [1906] 1 Ch. 386.

[31] (1856) 22 Beav. 299.

[32] [1902] 1 Ch. 428, at 433.

3–041 At the time of this decision the rights most likely to be involved were those of tenants. In the case of *Hunt v Luck* itself, since the freehold owner was not in occupation it was likely that the occupier was a tenant holding under a lease. If the purchaser did not make enquiries to verify this, he would be bound by the interests of the possessor. Ignorance would be no defence since the purchaser had only himself to blame for not asking the relevant questions. If the purchaser's enquiries could or should have revealed that the possessor was paying rent to a third party the purchaser would also be bound by the interests of that third party.

In the modern law the principle remains but has been given broader application. A purchaser is expected to make reasonable inquiries of all persons who are occupying the land, whether that occupation is exclusive or contemporaneous with the occupation of the owner. In *Caunce v Caunce*[33] Stamp J. held that a mortgagee did not have constructive notice of the trust interest of a wife who shared occupation of her matrimonial home with her husband, who was the sole legal owner and had granted the mortgage, because her occupation was "wholly consistent with the title offered". However, such sentiments were rejected by the House of Lords in *Williams & Glyn's Bank Ltd v Boland*[34] and today it cannot be presumed that a person in actual occupation of the land has no rights enforceable against the land after sale.

Failure to make any inspection of the land at all will clearly cause a purchaser to be deemed to have constructive notice of the existence of the rights of all the persons whose existence he would have discovered by making such an inspection.[35] In addition, a purchaser who makes some inspection will still be affixed with constructive notice if that inspection was inadequate. In *Kingsnorth Finance v Tizard*[36] a matrimonial home was co-owned in equity by a husband and wife, but he was the sole legal owner. Following the breakdown of their marriage the wife slept elsewhere, but returned every day to care for their twin children, which led the judge to conclude that she was in continued occupation. The husband subsequently mortgaged the property and disappeared with the money he had raised. The mortgagees accepted the mortgage after their agent had inspected the property on Sunday shortly after lunchtime, a time arranged by the husband to ensure that his wife and children would not be present on the property. When the agent visited the house the husband told him that his wife had left many months ago and that they were separated and she was living with someone else nearby. The agent inspected the property and looked round inside and out, discovering evidence of occupation by the two children but finding no evidence of female occupation other than by the teenage daughter. Judge Finlay Q.C. held that, in the circumstances, the inspection which had been made was inadequate because it had been conducted at a time arranged by the husband to ensure that his wife would not be present. He stated:

> "... if the purchaser or mortgagee carries out such inspections 'as ought reasonably to be made' and does not find the claimant in occupation or find evidence of that occupation, then I am not persuaded that the purchaser or mortgagee is in such circumstances ... fixed with notice of the claimant's rights. One of the circumstances, however, is that such inspection is made 'as ought reasonably to be made'. Here [the agent] carried out his inspection on a

[33] [1969] 1 W.L.R. 286.
[34] [1981] A.C. 487.
[35] See *Lloyds Bank v Carrick* [1996] 4 All E.R. 630.
[36] [1986] 1 W.L.R. 783.

Sunday afternoon at a time arranged with Mr Tizard. If the only purpose of such an inspection were to ascertain the physical state of the property, the time at which the inspection is made and whether or not that time is one agreed in advance with the vendor or the mortgagor appears to me to be immaterial. Where, however, the object of the inspection (or one of the objects) is to ascertain who is in occupation, I cannot see that an inspection at a time pre-arranged with the vendor will necessarily attain that object. Such a pre-arranged inspection may achieve no more than an inquiry of the vendor or mortgagor and his answer to it."[37]

At first sight the decision may seem somewhat harsh, since it begs the question how purchasers or mortgagees could protect themselves against vendors or mortgagors who deliberately conceal the occupation of some other person. There must clearly be limits to what an inspection can demand. For example, the judge agreed that it was not reasonable for the agent to open cupboards and drawers to look for signs of occupation. The central inadequacy therefore seems to have been the unusual timing of the inspection and that this should have alerted the agent to the possibility of concealment. However it was not merely the inadequacy of the inspection which led to a finding of constructive notice. In the course of the inspection the agent had been made aware by Mr Tizard that he was married, albeit separated, whereas on the application form for the loan he had declared himself single. Therefore when it became apparent that he was in fact married, and that a spouse was in existence, the mortgagees should have been put on notice that further inquiries were appropriate to ascertain whether the wife enjoyed any interests in the land. No reasonable mortgagee would have accepted a mortgage over what had been a matrimonial home knowing of the existence of a spouse but having failed to ensure that she had no interests in the land. The decision is more easily supported on the grounds that the inspection was inadequate because it failed to investigate further into circumstances which it had revealed. **3–042**

(iii) Imputed Notice

By a process of extension a purchaser will be treated as enjoying notice of any equitable interests affecting the land of which an agent acting on his behalf had notice. This will be so whether the agent's notice was actual or constructive. This principle is again evident in *Kingsnorth Finance v Tizard* since it was the agent instructed to act by the mortgagees who had constructive notice of the interests of Mrs Tizard. Notice was therefore imputed to the mortgagees. As a result their mortgage did not have priority over Mrs Tizard's share of the equitable ownership of the house. Imputed notice was also placed on a statutory basis in the Law of Property Act 1925 s.199(1)(ii)(b). **3–043**

(c) *Failure to Disclose an Interest*

Although the burden of making enquiries falls to the prospective purchaser of land, in some circumstances a person with an equitable interest is under an obligation to disclose its **3–044**

---

[37] [1986] 1 W.L.R. 783 at 794–795.

existence, so that he will not enjoy priority if he fails to do so. In *Midland Bank Ltd v Farmpride Hatcheries Ltd*[38] a man occupied a farm under a contractual licence granted by the company which owned the land, which he in turn co-owned and controlled with his wife. The company granted the bank a mortgage of the land, and he negotiated the details of the loan acting as the agent of the company. Although the bank was aware that he and his family occupied the land at no point did he disclose the existence of the licence to them, and it was not revealed by their negotiations. He subsequently claimed that the bank had taken the mortgage subject to his contractual licence on the grounds that they had constructive notice of its existence. The Court of Appeal held that he could not assert the priority of his interest over the mortgage because he was estopped by his failure to disclose it. Shaw L.J. explained:

> "In my judgment Mr Willey set up a smoke-screen designed to hide even the possible existence of some interest in himself which could derogate from the interest of the company ostensibly conferred by the mortgage. To change the metaphor, he deliberately put [the bank] off the scent and the bank accepted the mortgage as a consequence. They would not have done so but for Mr Willey's subtle but positive indication that he had communicated all that had to be told which could be relevant to the bank's consideration of the company's application. This being so, I am of the opinion that Mr Willey is estopped from setting up any facts which would go to show that he held an interest which overrides or stands in priority of the company's application."[39]

(d) *Effects of the Doctrine of Notice on Equitable Interests*

3–045 Where an equitable interest is defeated by application of the doctrine of notice the interest is completely destroyed and is not resurrected even if the land is subsequently purchased by someone who had actual notice of its existence.[40] To return to the example outlined above, if Norma enjoyed an equitable lease over Mark's house and Stephanie was a bona fide purchaser for value without notice of a legal estate in the house then the consequence would be that Stephanie would take the house free from Norma's equitable interest. That equitable interest would therefore be destroyed and if Stephanie subsequently sold the house to Timothy it would not revive to bind him even though he had actual knowledge that Norma's had enjoyed an equitable lease.

THE PROPERTY LEGISLATION OF 1925

1. Objectives of the Legislation

3–046 In 1925 English land law was subjected to a comprehensive programme of statutory reform. Four major pieces of legislation were enacted: the Law of Property Act 1925; the Land Registration

---

[38] (1980) 260 E.G. 493.
[39] (1980) 260 E.G. 497.
[40] See, for example, *Wilkes v Spooner* [1911] 2 K.B. 473.

Act 1925; the Settled Land Act 1925; and the Trustee Act 1925. These reforms were intended to simplify the ownership of land, reshaping the system so that unnecessary complications and difficulties were removed, and establishing a central, state-maintained, Land Registry, which would govern the ownership and transfer of land and replace the doctrine of notice as a means of determining issues of priority. The legislative framework introduced in 1925 establishes the basic framework of modern English land law, although as will be seen in Chapter 5, the system of land registration has itself been modernised, and the Land Registration Act 1925 has been repealed and replaced by the Land Registration Act 2002. The prime objective of the reforms introduced in 1925 was to reduce the difficulties encountered in the transfer of land through the existence of a multiplicity of legal estates and the doctrine of notice, thus making conveyancing a simpler and safer process. In order to achieve this end the legislation introduced a number of key reforms.

2. Reducing the Number of Legal Estates and Interests in Land

Prior to the reforms introduced in 1925 there was a bewildering array of different estates and interests in land, which could enjoy either legal or equitable character. One essential aspect of the reform was to simplify this complex mosaic of estates and interests. Section 1 of the Law of Property Act 1925 therefore reduced the number of legal estates that could exist in land to two, and the number of legal interests to five. Section 1(3) provides that all other estates, interests and charges in land "take effect merely as equitable interests".   **3–047**

(a) *The Two Legal Estates*

Section 1(1) of the Law of Property Act 1925 provides that there are only two legal estates in land, namely the fee simple absolute in possession (better known as the freehold) and the term of years absolute (better known as the leasehold).   **3–048**

(i) Fee Simple Absolute in Possession

In s.1(1)(a) the first of the two legal estates is "an estate in fee simple absolute in possession". This is a freehold estate and, as has been noted above, is an estate which has perpetual duration. The limitation that the estate must be "absolute" is intended to differentiate it from conditional and determinable fee simples, and the requirement that it must be in possession is intended to distinguish reversionary or remainder interests. These distinctions will be considered in detail in Chapter 8.   **3–049**

(ii) Term of Years Absolute

Section 1(1)(b) states that the second of the legal estates is the term of years absolute. This is a lease, and therefore it constitutes the legal leasehold estate in land. The nature of leasehold interests will be considered in detail in Chapter 6.   **3–050**

(b) *The Five Legal Interests*

3–051 Section 1(2) then specifies the five interests and charges which are capable of enjoying legal status.

(i)   Easements

3–052 By s.1(2)(a) an easement which is granted for a period equivalent to the duration of either of the two legal estates is capable of being a legal easement. This means, for example, that a right of way will only be capable of legal status if it is granted perpetually or for a specified and fixed period of time. A grant of an easement for life would not qualify for legal status. Whether an easement is in fact legal will also be dependent upon the manner of its creation. Easements are examined in detail in Chapter 9.

(ii)   Rentcharges

3–053 A rentcharge is an entitlement to be paid a periodic sum by the owner of a piece of land, which is neither the rent payable under a lease nor payments due under a mortgage. In common with easements they are only capable of attaining legal status if created for a period equivalent to either of the two legal estates. Rentcharges are of limited significance since the Rentcharges Act 1977 prohibits the creation of new rentcharges and those existing as of the date of the act will ultimately be extinguished.

(iii) Charges by Way of Legal Mortgage

3–054 Where a mortgage, which is a security interest over land, is created in the appropriate form as a charge by way of legal mortgage, it is capable of existing as a legal interest. Mortgages are considered in detail in Chapter 11.

(iv)   Miscellaneous Charges

3–055 Section 1(2)(d) provides that similar charges to those by way of legal mortgage which are "not created by an instrument" are also capable of legal status. This category contained predominantly statutory charges and is now of limited significance.

(v)   Rights of Entry

3–056 Rights of entry are the means by which a lease is forfeited if the tenant is in breach of its terms. An estate may also be forfeited if the terms of a rentcharge to which it is subject have been broken. The legal quality of a right of entry is dependent upon the legal quality of the lease or rentcharge to which it relates.

3. Reducing the Maximum Number of Legal Owners of Land

The legal title to land can only be transferred by the legal owners.[41] In order to simplify transfers of land, the Trustee Act 1925 s.34(2) limited the maximum number of co-owners of the legal title to four. This is therefore the maximum number of trustees of land. This limit on the number of trustees does not affect the number of equitable co-owners who can share in the beneficial interest in the property by means of the trust. It means only that if there are more than four co-owners, not all of them can be trustees holding the legal estate. The reason for imposing this limit is to make a transfer of the land less complicated since a potential transferee has only to deal with a limited number of legal owners.

3–057

4. Purchasers of Land should not have to Concern Themselves with Beneficial Interests

(a) *The Centrality of Overreaching*

As should be evident from the reforms noted above, one of the objects of the 1925 legislation was to ensure that the legal ownership of land was kept as simple as possible. This was achieved by reducing the number of legal estates, and imposing a maximum number of legal co-owners of the legal title. The inevitable consequence of these reforms was that all complexities in the ownership of land would have to take place behind a trust of the legal title. However the legislation sought to ensure that a potential purchaser of the legal title to land would not need to be concerned with the complexities in the beneficial ownership which lay behind the legal title, and to provide a way in which he would only need to deal with the legal owners. This objective was achieved through the mechanism of overreaching, which is a statutory means by which any equitable trust interests in the land are converted into trust interests of the same character enforceable over the purchase money that a transferee of the land paid to the legal owners. Where overreaching operates a purchaser acquires the land free from any existing trust interests affecting it, even if he had notice of their existence.

3–058

The fact that a purchaser of land may overreach any pre-existing beneficial interests is a key underpinning element of the system of land registration introduced in 1925, since it means the beneficial interests behind a trust need not appear on the face of the register of title. The desire to ensure that such beneficial interests do not have to appear on the registered is termed the curtain principle, in the sense that the register draws a curtain between the legal and beneficial ownership of the land. It ensures that the register is kept relatively simple and

---

[41] The transfer will normally require a deed which is a formal document which makes it clear on its face that it is a deed and which is signed by the person making it in the presence of a witness who also signs: Law of Property (Miscellaneous Provisions) Act 1989 s.1.

that the complexities of the enjoyment of ownership in equity take place "off register" behind the legal ownership. Although the concept of overreaching is an essential prerequisite to the operation of the system of land registration, it is not exclusive to it, and the 1925 legislation provides for the operation of overreaching irrespective of whether the title is registered or unregistered.

(b) *How Overreaching Works*

3–059   The essence of overreaching is that, if certain statutory criteria are satisfied when a legal estate in land subject to a trust is sold or mortgaged, any equitable ownership is removed from the land and transferred to the proceeds of sale paid to the trustees. As a consequence the beneficiaries no longer retain any equitable ownership in the land but their rights are preserved and transferred exclusively to the proceeds of sale, which the trustees who have received them continue to hold on trust for them. The purchaser of the land who has complied with the statutory criteria therefore acquires his interest in the land entirely free from the equitable ownership of the beneficiaries. Overreaching thus effects a substitution of the subject matter of the trust, so that whereas prior to overreaching the beneficiaries enjoyed the equitable ownership of land, after overreaching they enjoy only the equitable ownership of money. Lord Oliver explained the rationale of overreaching in *City of London Building Society v Flegg*:

> "The whole philosophy of the [Law of Property Act 1925] . . . was that a purchaser of a legal estate (which by s.205(1)(xxi) includes a mortgagee) should not be concerned with the beneficial interests of the [co-owners] which were shifted to the proceeds of sale."[42]

He stated that overreaching was critical to achieving the legislative policy of "keeping the interests of beneficiaries behind the curtain and confining the investigation of title to the devolution of the legal estate".[43] These sentiments were approved by the Court of Appeal in *State Bank of India v Sood* where Peter Gibson L.J. summarised that:

> "A principal objective of the 1925 property legislation was to simplify conveyancing and the proof of title to land. To this end equitable interests were to be kept off the title to the legal estate and could be overreached on a conveyance to a purchaser who took free from them."[44]

It had been assumed that overreaching would only occur where a transaction affecting the legal title of land held on trust resulted in the payment of capital moneys into which the beneficial interests could be transferred. However in *State Bank of India v Sood* the Court of Appeal held that overreaching could occur even where a transaction did not produce a money substitute for the beneficiaries' equitable ownership of land. The court regarded overreaching as a means by which a purchaser of a legal estate in land or a mortgagee could gain priority over equitable interests irrespective of whether they were preserved in other property or not.

[42] [1988] A.C. 54 at 77.
[43] [1988] A.C. 54 at 77.
[44] [1997] 1 All E.R. 169 at 172–173.

Peter Gibson L.J. defined overreaching as "the process whereby existing interests are subordinated to a later interest or estate created pursuant to a trust or power".[45]

(c) An Example of Overreaching in Practice

In *City of London Building Society v Flegg*[46] the House of Lords considered the effects of the   **3–060**
statutory overreaching provisions. The case concerned a house which had been purchased in the names of Mr and Mrs Maxwell-Brown, who were the registered proprietors, but the purchase money had been partly provided by Mr and Mrs Flegg, who were Mrs Maxwell-Brown's parents, with the intention that they would be able to share occupation of the property. Mr and Mrs Flegg had in fact lived in the house since the date of the purchase. The effect of their contribution was that they enjoyed a share of the equitable ownership by way of a resulting trust, and that Mr and Mrs Maxwell-Brown held the legal title as trustees for them. Unfortunately Mr and Mrs Maxwell-Brown suffered severe financial difficulties, and granted the plaintiff a charge by way of legal mortgage over the house. The Fleggs were unaware of this transaction and did not consent to it. The plaintiff advanced £37,500 to the Maxwell-Browns which they used to discharge their debts. Inevitably they defaulted on their mortgage repayments, and the mortgagee sought possession of the house. The main issue was whether the mortgagee took its legal mortgage subject to the Fleggs' pre-existing equitable ownership. The House of Lords held that since the statutory criteria for overreaching had been satisfied the Fleggs' equitable ownership had been transferred from the house to the money which had been advanced to Mr and Mrs Maxwell-Brown, and that they therefore had no interests in the land capable of taking priority to the mortgage. Lord Oliver explained the effect of overreaching on their rights in the land:

> "If, then, one asks what were the subsisting rights of [Mr and Mrs Flegg] . . . the answer must, in my judgment, be that they were rights which, *vis-à-vis*[47] the [mortgagee], were *eo instanti*[48] with the creation of the charge, overreached and therefore subsisted only in relation to the equity of redemption."[49]

As a consequence the mortgagee could force a sale of their home to recover the amount of the loan and, since the trustees had dissipated the proceeds of sale, the preservation of their beneficial interests in the proceeds of sale was merely theoretical and they would only recover their initial contribution to the purchase price of the house if there was sufficient capital remaining after sale and the discharge of the mortgage. Their only other remedies would lie against the trustees for breach of trust. Although this result may seem unfair, in reality they were the victims of the trustees' dishonesty, and the case demonstrates that overreaching operates primarily as a mechanism to protect the interests of purchasers, not to safeguard the entitlements of

---

[45] [1997] 1 All E.R. 169 at 172, citing with approval [1990] C.L.J. 277 (Harpum).
[46] [1988] A.C. 54.
[47] i.e. in relation to.
[48] Latin for "at the same moment".
[49] The equity of redemption is the residual interest in the property subject to the mortgage, and includes, for instance the right to live in the property provided that the mortgage repayments are made, and the right to recover the property free from the mortgage once the loan has been discharged. See Ch.17.

beneficiaries. When one innocent party must inevitably lose out, the system favours the third party who has taken an interest in the land as any other result would act as a disincentive to those contemplating acquiring interests in land, especially mortgagees, thus affecting the stability of the housing market and the wider economy.

(d) *Statutory Criteria for Overreaching*

(i) An Interest Susceptible to Overreaching

3–061   Only specified interests in land are capable of being overreached. Section 2(1) of the Law of Property Act 1925 makes a general assertion that: "A conveyance to a purchaser of a legal estate in land shall overreach any equitable interest or power affecting that estate, whether or not he has notice thereof . . .". The breadth of this subsection, which suggests a general overreaching of equitable interests in land, is curtailed by s.2(3) which provides that certain categories of equitable interest cannot be overreached. This subsection excludes all the most important equitable rights in land from the consequences of overreaching, including equitable mortgages; equitable easements; equitable restrictive covenants; equitable estoppel interests and estate contracts. There are thus two categories of rights in land: those that can be overreached, and those that cannot. The rights that cannot be overreached are typically commercial rights whose very existence depends upon them being enforceable against the land itself. The rights that can be overreached are typically "family" rights that can only be given effect to by means of a trust. The net impact is that overreaching operates principally against equitable ownership of land arising behind a trust.

(ii) A Transaction which has Overreaching Effect

3–062   In order for a beneficial interest behind a trust to be overreached a transaction must occur which is capable of having an overreaching effect. Section 2(1) of the Law of Property Act 1925 provides that a conveyance of a legal estate in the land will have a potentially overreaching effect in four situations. The most significant of these in practice is where the conveyance is made by trustees of land,[50] but a conveyance under the powers conferred by the Settled Land Act 1925, by a mortgagee or personal representative in the exercise of his paramount powers, or under an order of the court will also have overreaching effect. By s.205(1)(ii) "conveyance" is given an extended meaning and includes "a mortgage, charge, lease, assent, vesting declaration, vesting instrument, disclaimer, release and every other assurance of property or of an interest therein by any instrument, except a will".

(iii) Purchase of a Legal Estate

3–063   By s.2(1) of the Law of Property Act 1925, overreaching will only operate in favour of a person who is a "purchaser of a legal estate of land". This means overreaching will only occur

---

[50] Law of Property Act 1925 s.2(1)(i).

where a person purchases either the freehold of land or a legal lease. By statutory extension in s.205(1)(xxi) of the Law of Property Act 1925, "purchaser of a legal estate" includes "a chargee by way of legal mortgage" so that a mortgagee will also enjoy the benefits of over-reaching, as in *City of London Building Society v Flegg*.[51] Since the overreaching provisions are found in Part I of the Law of Property Act 1925 s.205(xxi) defines a purchaser as "a person who acquires an interest in or charge on property for money or money's worth". There is therefore no requirement that a person seeking to take advantage of the overreaching mechanism must have acted in good faith,[52] nor must they have provided adequate consideration in return for the legal estate they acquired.[53] In *State Bank of India v Sood*[54] the Court of Appeal expressly stated that the payment of a mere nominal consideration in money would have over-reaching effect.

(iv) Appropriate Application of Capital Moneys Arising from the Transaction

The central limitation to the operation of overreaching is that the purchaser of the legal estate **3–064** must pay any capital moneys arising under the conveyance in the appropriate manner required by the statute. These requirements are intended to provide the persons whose interests are overreached with some measure of protection against fraud, but they are only relevant where a conveyance gives rise to capital moneys.[55]

Where land is held upon a trust of land, s.2(1)(ii) of the Law of Property Act 1925 provides that the beneficiaries' interests will only be overreached if "the requirements of section 27 of this Act respecting the payment of capital money arising on such a conveyance are complied with". Section 27 provides that:

> "(1) A purchaser of a legal estate from trustees of land shall not be concerned with the trusts affecting the land, the net income of the land or the proceeds of sale of the land whether or not those trusts are declared by the same instrument as that by which the trust of land is created.
>
> (2) Notwithstanding anything to the contrary in the instrument (if any) creating a trust of land or in any trust affecting the net proceeds of sale of the land if it is sold, the proceeds of sale or other capital money shall not be paid to or applied by the direction of fewer than two persons as trustees, except where the trustee is a trust corporation, but this subsection does not affect the right of a sole personal representative as such to give valid receipts for, or direct the application of, proceeds of sale or other capital money, nor, except where capital money arises on the transaction, render it necessary to have more than one trustee."

A strict reading of s.27 would seem to suggest that a transaction cannot be effective at all if the proceeds of sale are paid to less than two trustees for sale, or to a trust corporation.

[51] [1988] A.C. 54.
[52] Contrast *Peffer v Rigg* [1977] 1 W.L.R. 285 in the context of minor interest under the Land Registration Act 1925.
[53] Compare *Midland Bank Trust Co v Green* [1981] A.C. 513 in the context of the registration of land charges in unregistered land.
[54] [1997] 1 All E.R. 169.
[55] *State Bank of India v Sood* [1997] 1 All E.R. 169.

However, transactions have not been held void even where the capital moneys arising on a conveyance were paid to a sole trustee (as, for example, in *Williams & Glyn's Bank Ltd v Boland*[56] and *Abbey National v Cann*[57]). The failure to pay the capital moneys arising under the conveyance to two or more trustees, or to a trust corporation, does nevertheless deprive the conveyance of overreaching effect. In such cases the equitable ownership of the beneficiaries is not automatically deprived of priority over the legal estate of the purchaser or mortgagee. Instead, questions of priority will be determined, if the land is registered, by whether the equitable interest was a properly protected minor interest or an overriding interest.

Where a conveyance of land is made by a mortgagee or personal representative, s.2(1)(iii) of the Law of Property Act 1925 provides that overreaching will take effect if any capital moneys arising are paid to the mortgagee or the personal representative. A conveyance of land under an order of the court has overreaching effect under s.2(1)(iv) of the Law of Property Act 1925 provided that any capital moneys arising are either paid into court or in accordance with the order of the court.

(v)   No Capital Moneys Need Arise from the Transaction

3–065   In *State Bank of India v Sood*[58] the Court of Appeal held that it was not a necessary requirement of overreaching that the conveyance with claimed overreaching effect must have resulted in the payment of capital moneys which were appropriately applied. Rather, appropriate payment of capital moneys is only required where the conveyance gives rise to them. The case concerned the claim of four family members that their trust interests in their home had not been overreached when the two registered proprietors, who were holding the house on trust for sale, had granted a legal charge over the property to a bank in 1989 in order to secure the present and future liabilities of a company. The bank claimed that this charge was a conveyance which had overreached their interests. The defendants argued that their interests had not been overreached because, unlike *City of London Building Society v Flegg* where the money raised by way of mortgage had been paid over to Mr and Mrs Maxwell-Brown, no capital moneys had arisen contemporaneously with the grant of the legal charge. Since the facts were not in dispute Peter Gibson L.J. stated the legal question which was at issue:

> "The crucial issue is the construction of the final condition of section 2(1)(ii) of the Law of Property Act 1925 relating to the statutory requirements respecting the payment of capital money. There is no dispute that if capital money does arise under a conveyance by trustees for sale to a purchaser it must be paid or applied as section 27(2) of that Act dictates. But for overreaching to occur, does capital money have to arise on and contemporaneously with the conveyance?"[59]

3–066   The court held that, as a matter of construction, s.2(1)(ii) did not require the payment of capital moneys since the identical requirement was imposed in s.2(1)(i) in relation to settled land.

[56] [1981] A.C. 487.
[57] [1991] 1 A.C. 56.
[58] [1997] 1 All E.R. 169.
[59] [1997] 1 All E.R. 169 at 177.

Since capital moneys would not arise in consequence of every conveyance made under the powers conferred by the Settled Land Act 1925 the statutory requirement could only apply to those conveyances which did give rise to such capital money. The presence of the phrase "any capital money" in s.2(1)(iii) and (iv) was not taken to indicate that the payment of capital moneys was itself a requirement under s.2(1)(ii). Peter Gibson L.J. pointed out that there were several types of conveyance of land which would not give rise to a contemporaneous payment of capital moneys other than a charge to secure existing or future indebtedness, including an exchange of land and the grant of a lease without a premium and questioned why the legislature had intended to exclude such conveyances from having an overreaching effect.[60] Pill L.J. pointed out that since it was accepted that even a nominal payment of capital at the time of a conveyance would have overreaching effect this would have the effect of rendering largely illusory any protection of the beneficiaries. He therefore considered that the legislation did not require any payment on conveyance:

> "Had Parliament intended to protect those interests by requiring the contemporaneous payment of capital money if overreaching is to occur, I would have expected express and stringent provision."[61]

The court also considered and dismissed the policy arguments against permitting overreaching where no capital moneys were paid over. Peter Gibson L.J. stated:

> "A more substantial argument of policy advanced on behalf of [the defendants] is that if overreaching occurs where no capital money arises, the beneficiaries' interests may be reduced by the conveyance leaving nothing to which the interests can attach by way of replacement save the equity of redemption, and that may be or become valueless. I see considerable force in this point, but I am not persuaded that it suffices to defeat what I see to be the policy of the legislation, to allow valid dispositions to overreach equitable interests. In my judgment, on its true construction section 2(1)(ii) only requires compliance with the statutory requirements respecting payment of capital money if capital money arises. Accordingly, I would hold that capital money did not have to arise under the conveyance."[62]

The conclusion reached demonstrates the power of overreaching as a mechanism for defeating pre-existing equitable interests and the supremacy given to conveyancing considerations. As Peter Gibson L.J. pointed out, commercial lenders have consistently acted as though such charges confer priority by overreaching and to have allowed the defendants to succeed would have undermined a system which had proved an important means of small businessmen obtaining finance for their ventures:

> "I accept that a novel and important point of law is raised by this appeal. Lending institutions regularly take security from businessmen in the form of a legal charge on property (which very frequently means that the matrimonial home is charged) to secure existing and

---

[60] [1997] 1 All E.R. 169 at 178.
[61] [1997] 1 All E.R. 169 at 182.
[62] [1997] 1 All E.R. 169 at 178.

future indebtedness, and very commonly that property will be registered land held by two registered proprietors on trust for sale with no restriction registered in respect of their power to transfer or mortgage that property. It was not suggested that it had ever been the practice of mortgagees to make enquiries of occupiers of the property as to any claimed rights. Yet if the [defendants] are right, that is what the mortgagees must do if they are not to take subject to the beneficial interests of the occupiers."[63]

(vi)   Overreaching Operates Irrespective of Notice

3–067   Section 2(1) of the Law of Property Act 1925 states that overreaching occurs in favour of a purchaser of a legal estate in land "whether or not he has notice thereof". It is therefore entirely irrelevant whether a purchaser of land knew that it was held on trust, and the beneficiaries' equitable ownership will be overreached provided that the statutory requirements are met. This again emphasises how overreaching is a mechanical process operating to secure conveyancing efficiency rather than as a genuine means of preserving the rights of the beneficiaries against unjust misappropriation.

(vii)   Reform of Overreaching

3–068   The way in which overreaching can defeat the claims of individuals like the parents in *City of London Building Society v Flegg*[64] has been the subject of criticism. The Fleggs could, of course, have protected themselves by registering their interest, and it was likely to have been a deliberate choice on their part not to do so. In some cases, however, protection through the registration of an interest will be less likely, for instance where a beneficial interest has arisen through a constructive trust. The suggestion of the Law Commission[65] that the rights of occupiers should always be protected against the loss of their interest unless they consent has not been adopted, nor has an alternative suggestion that trustees of land should only be able to grant a mortgage with overreaching effect if it is used to finance the purchase or improvement of the land.[66]

5.   Introduction of a Universal System of Land Registration

(a)   *Registration of Title to Land*

3–069   The ultimate object of the 1925 legislation was to introduce a universal system of land registration, whereby ownership of land would be constituted by being registered as the owner on a central land register. This would greatly simplify the conveyancing process, since anyone needing to establish the identity of the legal owners of the land would be able to do so merely

---

[63] [1997] 1 All E.R. 169 at 176.
[64] [1988] A.C. 54.
[65] Law Com. No.188, *Transfer of Land: Overreaching: Beneficiaries in Occupation* (1989).
[66] Harpum [1990] C.L.J. 275 at 332.

by looking at the register. Such a scheme of registration was introduced by the Land Registration Act 1925. The legislation envisaged that, by means of a gradual process occurring over a period of time, the ownership of all legal estates in land, i.e. freehold ownership and leasehold ownership, would become registered. A piecemeal process of registration was set in motion by designating specific geographical areas to be areas of compulsory registration, with the consequence that the land would have to be registered when next transferred. In 1925 the legislators anticipated that full registration would take some 30 years. In the event it has taken nearly twice as long since it was not until the Registration of Title Order 1989[67] that the whole of England and Wales was finally designated an area of compulsory registration. The Land Registration Act 1925 has now been repealed and replaced by the Land Registration Act 2002. This new legislation provides the framework for contemporary land law, and it is examined in detail in Chapter 5.

(b) *Protecting Third Party Interests in Registered Land*

The creation of a system of land registration was not merely intended to facilitate simpler conveyancing, but also to provide a mechanism by which third party subsidiary rights and interests in land could be protected. The essence of the system of registration is that third party rights can be protected on the Land Register against the title of the land to which they relate. In theory a person who is contemplating a purchase of the land will be able to find out if there are any adverse interests affecting it by simply looking at the register, a process known as a search. A purchaser would only be bound by those interests which were properly protected by means of an entry on the register, irrespective of whether he knew of them or not. As was recognised by the House of Lords in *Midland Bank Trust Co v Green*,[68] this system firmly places the burden of protecting interests in land on those who hold them. It is their responsibility to ensure that they are properly protected by registration and they take the risk that they will lose priority to a subsequent purchaser if they have failed to register. However, this general rule is subject to the exception that certain interests in land, which are known as overriding interests and are defined by statute,[69] are binding on a person who purchases the land even though they do not appear on the register. The presence of such overriding interests has proved one of the most important and controversial aspects of the scheme of land registration. In the registered land system there is no continuing place for the doctrine of notice.

3–070

[67] SI 1989/1347.
[68] [1981] A.C. 513.
[69] See Land Registration Act 2002 Sch.3.

Chapter 4

UNREGISTERED LAND

REGISTERED TITLE AND UNREGISTERED TITLE

In the last chapter we saw how it had been the intention of the land law reforms of 1925 to move rapidly towards a system in which ownership of land was proved by means of a national publicly administered system of registration. This system was to replace the previous system of proof of land ownership which had been in place for several hundred years. It was also intended to replace the equitable doctrine of notice dealing with priorities between legal and equitable rights in the land. It was obviously not possible for the new system to be introduced overnight. To ameliorate the transitional problems of an interim period the original legislation made provision for a special regime for land that had not yet been registered. Such land is known as unregistered land, and although many of the reforms already outlined applied to such land (for example the limitation of the maximum number of legal owners and the principles of overreaching), the old rules relating to proof of ownership continued to apply and there was no general scheme of registration for the protection of third party interests.

4–001

    The gradual extension of the obligation to register title to land, and the enactment of the Land Registration Act 2002, have significantly reduced the importance of the rules governing unregistered land. The only cases in which these rules are now relevant are in the very limited number of situations where transactions affecting unregistered land can take place without an obligation to register the land, and to determine the priority of rights at the time when the land is first registered. Although the Land Registration Act 2002, which is considered extensively in the next chapter, sets out a code for determining the priority of interests following registration, the old rules determine which rights should be recorded on the register when the land is first registered.

PROOF OF TITLE

1. Title to Land

4–002 Ownership consists of a bundle of rights to something: principally the right to use it, to alter or destroy it, to prevent others from interfering with those rights, and the right to transmit to others this bundle of rights. For all land there will be an owner. But who is that owner? A person is said to have title to land when they have the rights of the owner. Since it is only the owner who can grant rights over land, a person buying land or taking a mortgage over it will want to be sure that the person selling or giving the mortgage has the right or title to do so.

2. Establishing Title to Unregistered Land

4–003 In the registered land system the identity of the owner of a legal estate in land is relatively easy to establish, since the owner will be registered as the proprietor of the estate in question. The person whose name appears on the register as proprietor is the person with title to that registered estate. Where title is not registered any potential purchaser must satisfy himself that the vendor does enjoy good title to the legal estate claimed. This is usually achieved by allowing the potential purchaser to examine the vendor's title deeds. These consist of the collection of conveyances or other deeds and documents by which the estate in issue has been created or disposed of in the past, which together provide a historical record demonstrating how the vendor has come to enjoy good title to the land.

(a) *A Good Root of Title*[1]

4–004 Where land is unregistered a prospective purchaser or mortgagee will want the vendor or mortgagor to establish that he enjoys a "good root of title". This may be evidenced by a document which clearly identifies the land in question and establishes the existence of the estate which can then be traced into the hands of the present vendor. Although there is no statutory or judicial definition of a "good root of title" it was described in *Williams on Vendor and Purchaser as*:

> ". . . an instrument or disposition dealing with or proving on the face of it, without the aid of extrinsic evidence, the ownership of the whole legal and equitable estate in the property sold, containing a description by which the property can be identified and showing nothing to cast any doubt on the title of the disposing parties."[2]

---

[1] For further information see *Barnsley's Conveyancing Law and Practice* (4th edn, 1996), pp.265–331.
[2] (4th edn), p.124.

(b) *Establishing a Good Root of Title to a Freehold Estate*

In the case of a freehold estate the best root of title is a past conveyance which was executed **4–005** when the freehold estate was sold. Such a conveyance on sale indicates that the title was investigated and accepted at the date that the conveyance was made. By the Law of Property Act 1925 s.44(1) the purchaser of land may require that the vendor demonstrate 15 years' good title.[3] This means that he must be able to point to a conveyance on sale dating back at least 15 years. Obviously if there was such a conveyance to himself more than 15 years previously, this will be sufficient to demonstrate good title and no further investigation need be made.[4] However, if the land had been conveyed to him 10 years ago, by a vendor who derived his own title from a conveyance made in 1930, the earlier conveyance would form the good root of title.

A good title can also be acquired by adverse possession of 12 years. However, a vendor may be extremely wary about transacting with such an adverse possessor, since there will be some risk that the claim cannot be substantiated and that rights in existence before the commencement of the adverse possession will remain enforceable. For this reason the purchaser may insist upon proof of the earlier title which has been displaced by adverse possession.

(c) *Establishing a Good Root of Title to a Legal Leasehold Estate*

If a purchaser is seeking an assignment of a leasehold estate he will obviously wish to satisfy him **4–006** self that the vendor or mortgagor is entitled to the estate claimed. To do this the tenant must produce an abstract or copy of the lease from which his estate derives and proof of dealings with the leasehold estate dating back at least 15 years, thus establishing that he is currently the tenant. For example, if a 99-year lease was granted in 1920 a vendor must both produce the lease itself and demonstrate that he has good title to the tenancy thereby created. If the tenancy was assigned to him more than 15 years ago, this will be sufficient. However, if it was assigned to him 10 years ago, by a tenant who had previously taken an assignment in 1960, he must produce the earlier assignment in order to establish a good root of title. By the Law of Property Act 1925 s.44(2) the vendor of a leasehold estate is not required to prove the validity of the freehold title of his landlord.

PRIORITIES IN UNREGISTERED LAND

1. A Limited Scheme of Registration for some Interests in Unregistered Land

Although land is termed "unregistered" because there is no registration of title of legal estates, **4–007** a limited system of registration was introduced for certain specified subsidiary interests in land.

---

[3] Reduced from 30 years by Law of Property Act 1969 s.23.
[4] The parties may contractually agree on a shorter period of time.

These interests were termed "land charges" and the Land Charges Act 1925, replaced by the Land Charges Act 1972, introduced a land charges register. This register is a names-based register, so that land charges are protected by an entry against the name of the estate owner of the land to which they relate. This reflects the interim and short-term nature of the land charges register. The system was neither intended nor designed to remain in operation for over 80 years. Inevitably this has led to difficulties which will only be overcome when all land is registered.

(a) *Interests Which are Land Charges*

4–008   Section 2 of the Land Charges Act 1972 provides that certain interests in unregistered land are land charges. There are six basic categories of land charge, termed "classes", although within some classes there is a further subdivision. The majority of land charges are uncontroversial. However, there has been much debate as to the precise scope of some rights which are accorded the status of land charges.

(i)   Class A Land Charges

4–009   Class A land charges comprise rights to receive a sum of money from the owner of land, for example an annuity, arising only by an application under an Act of Parliament to recover money spent on the land under the provisions of such an Act. An example of such a land charge is a landlord's right to compensation under the Agricultural Holdings Act 1986.[5]

(ii)   Class B Land Charges

4–010   Class B land charges comprise rights identical to those in Class A which are not dependent for their creation on the application of any person, but which arise automatically by operation of statute, excluding local land charges. An example of such a land charge is the charge over land recovered in a legally aided action arising to recoup the client's unpaid legal aid contributions.[6]

(iii) Class C(i) Land Charges

4–011   Class C(i) land charges comprise the "puisne mortgage", which is defined as a "legal mortgage which is not protected by the deposit of documents relating to the legal estate affected". Such mortgages will generally be second mortgages, since the mortgagee of a first mortgage will usually insist on holding the title documents, to prevent the mortgagor dealing with the legal estate. The puisne mortgage is unusual in that it is a legal interest ranking as a land

---

[5] ss.85 and 86.
[6] Legal Aid Act 1988 s.16(6).

charge. This anomaly is explicable by the importance of affording adequate protection to the mortgagee, since it is obvious that the title documents (of which there is only one set since the documents are the original documents used to transfer ownership[7]) cannot be deposited with two or more separate lenders.

(iv)   Class C(ii) Land Charges

Class C(ii) land charges comprise the "limited owner's charge", which is defined as "an equitable charge acquired by a tenant for life or statutory owner under the Inheritance Tax Act 1984 or under any other statute by reason of the discharge by him of any capital transfer tax or other liabilities and to which special priority is given by statute". This would include, for example, a charge in favour of a tenant for life under a strict settlement who pays inheritance tax on the estate from which his life interest is derived.   **4–012**

(v)   Class C(iii) Land Charges

Class C(iii) land charges consist of the "general equitable charge". This is a catch-all category which will include all equitable charges over land except those excluded by the Land Charges Act 1972 s.2(4)(iii), which provides that: **4–013**

"A general equitable charge is any equitable charge which—

(a)   is not secured by a deposit of documents relating to the legal estate affected; and
(b)   does not arise or affect an interest arising under a trust of land or a settlement; and
(c)   is not a charge given by way of indemnity against rents equitably apportioned or charged exclusively on land in exoneration of other land and against the breach or non-observance of covenants or conditions; and
(d)   is not included in any other class of land charge."

This category of land charge will include an equitable mortgage of a legal estate not secured by title deeds, and an unpaid vendor's lien.

(vi)   Class C(iv) Land Charges

Class C(iv) land charges comprise "estate contracts", and are probably the single most significant category of land charge. They are defined by s.2(4)(iv):   **4–014**

---

[7] The exception to the documents being originals is where land has been subdivided, in which case certified copies of documents will be used in relation to that part of the root of title predating the subdivision. The title deeds will, however, consist of the original documents for the period when the plot of land concerned has been in separate ownership, and that must include at least the most recent conveyance.

> "An estate contract is a contract by an estate owner or by a person entitled at the date of the contract to have a legal estate conveyed to him to convey or create a legal estate, including a contract conferring either expressly or by statutory implication a valid option to purchase, a right of pre-emption or any other like right."

Estate contracts will therefore include contracts for the sale of the freehold of land and contracts to grant a lease.[8] They also include the grant of an option to acquire such a legal estate[9] and a right of pre-emption.

(vii)   Class D(i) Land Charges

4–015   Class D(i) land charges comprise the "Inland Revenue Charge", which is a charge acquired over land by the Board of Inland Revenue under the Inheritance Act 1984.

(viii)   Class D(ii) Land Charges

4–016   Class D(ii) land charges comprise restrictive covenants. However not every restrictive covenant in unregistered land is a land charge. By the Land Charges Act 1972 s.2(5)(ii) only those restrictive covenants "entered into on or after 1st January 1926" are within Class D(ii). Issues of priority relating to restrictive covenants created before that date will fall to be determined by the doctrine of notice.

(ix)   Class D(iii) Land Charges

4–017   Class D(iii) land charges comprise "equitable easements", which are defined by s.2(5)(iii) as:

> ". . . an easement right or privilege over or affecting land created or arising on or after 1st January 1926, and being merely an equitable easement."

Although this definition seems relatively straightforward, comprising easements coming into existence after the specified date which are not legal in status, its precise scope has been the subject of some controversy. In *ER Ives Investment Ltd v High*[10] Lord Denning M.R. adopted a restrictive interpretation that Class D(iii) only included easements which would have enjoyed legal status if they had been granted prior to 1926:

> "It appears, then, that an 'equitable easement' is a proprietary interest in land such as would before 1926 have been recognised as capable of being conveyed or created at law, but which since 1926 only takes effect as an equitable interest."

---

[8] *Phillips v Mobil Oil Co Ltd* [1989] 1 W.L.R. 888.
[9] *Midland Bank Trust Co v Green* [1981] A.C. 513 (option to purchase freehold); *Taylor Fashions Ltd v Liverpool Victoria Trustees Co Ltd* [1982] Q.B. 133 (option to renew lease).
[10] [1967] 2 Q.B. 379.

Although Lord Denning's view has not been expressly disapproved,[11] it should be rejected as highly artificial and inconsistent with the plain meaning of the statute. All easements which are purely equitable in character created after 1926 should rank as land charges, irrespective of what their status would have been prior to that date.

(x) Class E Land Charges

Class E land charges comprise annuities affecting land which were created prior to January 1, 1926 but which had not been registered in a pre-existing register of annuities which was closed when the Land Charges Act 1925 was brought into force. Clearly this is a very narrow category. **4–018**

(xi) Class F Land Charges

Class F land charges comprise the rights of occupation of a matrimonial home enjoyed by a spouse under Part IV of the Family Law Act 1996. **4–019**

(b) *Registration of Land Charges*

Land charges can be protected by registration on the land charges register. Section 3(1) of the Land Charges Act 1972 provides that "a land charge shall be registered in the name of the estate owner whose estate is intended to be affected". The register which is maintained is therefore based on the "names" of the persons who owned the land at the date when the land charge was registered, and not on entries referenced to the land itself. **4–020**

(i) The Appropriate Name in Which a Land Charge should be Registered

One potential difficulty with a names based register is that many people use a number of different versions of their name. They may be known by a nickname, or use an informal version of their name for personal relationships but the full formal version for important transactions. In *Standard Property Investment Plc v British Plastics Federation*[12] Walton J. held that the appropriate name for the purposes of registration was the name of the owner of the estate affected as found in the conveyance by which the estate had been conveyed to him or her. This would serve as a "fixed point of reference". **4–021**

(ii) Effect of Registration of a Land Charge in the Appropriate Name

The correct registration of a land charge is deemed by statute to give everyone in the world actual knowledge of its existence. Section 198(1) of the Law of Property Act 1925 provides that: **4–022**

---

[11] See *Poster v Slough Estates Ltd* [1968] 1 W.L.R. 1515 at 1520–1521, per Cross J.
[12] (1985) 53 P. & C.R. 25.

"The registration of any instrument or matter in any register kept under the Land Charges Act 1972 or any local land charges register, shall be deemed to constitute actual notice of such instrument or matter, and of the fact of such registration, to all persons, and for all purposes connected with the land affected, as from the date of registration or other prescribed date and so long as the registration continues in force."

In consequence any person acquiring a legal interest in the land will take subject to the registered land charge.

This provision was initially the cause of problems because a search of the land charges register would often only reveal adverse interests after contracts for the sale of the land had been exchanged, and the purchaser was already obliged to go through with the purchase. Since the purchaser was deemed by s.198(1) to have had actual notice of the existence of the land charge at the date of the contract, a subsequent revelation of its existence did not entitle him to refuse to complete the purchase.[13] This difficulty was remedied by the Law of Property Act 1969 s.24(1), which provided that:

"Where under a contract for the sale or other disposition of any estate or interest in the land the title to which is not registered . . . any question arises whether the purchaser had knowledge, at the time of entering into the contract, of a registered land charge, that question shall be determined by reference to his actual knowledge and without regard to the provisions of section 198 . . ."

This provision has the effect that a purchaser will be entitled to refuse to complete a contract if a registered land charge comes to light by search after it was entered, provided that the purchaser did not have actual knowledge of its existence at the time that he entered the contract.

(iii)   Effect of Registration of a Land Charge in an Incorrect Name

4–023   Due to ignorance or mistake the owner of a land charge may register it against an incorrect version of the name of the estate owner. This occurred in *Diligent Finance v Alleyne*.[14] In this case the legal title to a house was owned by a husband, whose name on the conveyance was Erskine Owen Alleyne. His wife registered a Class F land charge against the name Erskine Alleyne. He subsequently granted a mortgage to a finance company, which requisitioned an official search against the correct name. It was held that the incorrect registration did not affix the finance company with actual notice, so that it took priority over the wife's interest. However in some circumstances even an incorrect registration may prove effective. In *Oak Co-operative Building Society v Blackburn*[15] the legal owner of a house was Francis David Blackburn. He entered into an estate contract to sell the property to the defendant, who registered a Class C(iv) land charge against the name *Frank* David Blackburn, since this was how he was known locally. He subsequently mortgaged the property and, before agreeing to

---

[13] *Re Forsey and Hollebone's Contract* [1927] 2 Ch. 379.
[14] (1971) 23 P. & C.R. 346.
[15] [1968] Ch. 730.

make the loan, the building society requisitioned an official search of the land charges register. Due to an error the search was requisitioned in the name of Francis *Davis* Blackburn. The Court of Appeal held that the use of an incorrect name in the initial registration was not ineffective because the search had also been requisitioned in the wrong name. Russell L.J. stated the principle:

". . . if there be a registration in what may be fairly described as a version of the full names of the vendor, albeit not a version which is bound to be discovered on a search in the correct full names, we would not hold it a nullity against someone who does not search at all, or who (as here) searches in the wrong name."

The circumstances of this case were unusual, and the exception set out in the judgment is likely to have relatively limited scope.

(c) *Discovering the Existence of Registered Land Charges*

(i) Searches of the Land Charges Register

When a person is considering the acquisition of an interest in unregistered land he has the opportunity to search the land charges register in order to discover whether any interests have been protected by registration. Such a search may either be undertaken personally, or alternatively an official search may be requisitioned, in which case the person searching will submit the appropriate names to the registry which will carry out the search and then issue a certificate indicating any land charges which have been registered against them. In *Oak Co-operative Building Society v Blackburn*[16] Russell L.J. expressed the clear preference of the law in favour of an official search, and regarded a personal search as "foolish".[17]

4–024

(ii) Effect of an Official Search Certificate

When an official search is requisitioned the resulting official search certificate is of vital importance. The Land Charges Act 1972, s.10(4) provides that:

4–025

"In favour of a purchaser or an intending purchaser, as against persons interested under or in respect of matters or documents entries of which are required or allowed as aforesaid, the certificate, according to its tenor, shall be conclusive, affirmatively or negatively, as the case may be."

This means that if a mistake is made by the Land Registry, so that a land charge which had been registered was not included in the official search certificate, the purchaser is entitled to rely on the certificate and, if the other relevant statutory criteria are satisfied, will acquire the

[16] [1968] Ch. 730.
[17] [1968] Ch. 730 at 744.

land free from the otherwise properly protected land interest. In such cases the holder of the land charge would have a remedy against the Land Registry for negligence, thus enabling him to recover compensation for any loss that he suffered as a result.[18]

(iii)   The Problem of Inaccessible Registrations

4–026   A major difficulty with the names-based register of land charges is that a prospective purchaser may need to know the names of all the estate owners after 1925 in order to be certain that there are no adverse land charges affecting the land. For example, if the freehold owner of land granted a 99-year option to purchase in 1927, which was registered as a Class C(iv) land charge, a prospective purchaser in 2009 would only be able to ascertain its existence if he knew the name of the owner against whom it had been registered. However, a prospective purchaser only enjoys the statutory right to examine the title deeds establishing a good root of title dating back at least 15 years. Since he does not have the right of access to earlier documents and conveyances he may find that it is impossible to discover the names of previous estate owners in order to requisition a search against them. Thus if the land subject to the option had been sold by the subsequent estate owners in 1947, 1967, 1987 and 1997, a prospective purchaser in 2009 would have the right to examine the conveyance of 1987 to establish title but not to examine any earlier documents. Although this might reveal the name of the transferee of the estate under the 1967 conveyance, it would not reveal the name of the person who had been the estate owner in 1927 when the estate contract had been registered. The problem is compounded because effective registration is deemed to constitute actual notice of the registered land charge. Therefore, a prospective purchaser could go ahead and acquire the land in 2009 without being able to discover the existence of the registered charge because the essential information concerning the name of the estate owner was unavailable to him, yet find that he was still bound by the option because he was deemed to have actual notice of it. In order to prevent any unfairness which might arise from these difficulties the Law of Property Act 1969 introduced a right to statutory compensation for anyone who suffers loss as a result of the existence of a land charge registered against the name of an estate owner who was in no way connected with the present transaction. Such compensation is not available to a person who had actual notice of the existence of the land charge.[19]

(d)   *Unregistered Land Charges Rendered Void if Statutory Criteria Satisfied*

4–027

Failure to register a land charge will have the effect that the interest is rendered void if the appropriate statutory criteria are fulfilled. A person who satisfies these criteria will thus acquire the land free from the unprotected interest. The exact criteria vary, depending upon the type of land charge.

---

[18] *Ministry of Housing and Local Government v Sharp* [1970] 2 Q.B. 223.
[19] Land Charges Act 1972 s.25(1)(b).

(i) Unregistered Land Charges of Classes C(iv) and D

Section 4(6) of the Land Charges Act 1972 provides that:

4–028

> "An estate contract and a land charge of Class D created or entered into on or after 1st January 1926 shall be void as against a purchaser for money or money's worth . . . of a legal estate in the land charged with it, unless the land charge is registered in the appropriate register before the completion of the purchase."

Thus a person will only take free from an unprotected land charge of these classes if he has purchased a legal estate in the land (i.e. a freehold or leasehold estate)[20] or obtained a charge by way of legal mortgage[21] for money or money's worth. A person acquiring title by gift, through succession, in return for marriage consideration or for nominal non-monetary consideration will not be entitled to protection and will take his interest subject even to unprotected land charges.

An unregistered estate contract or Class D land charge is, however, at risk where a purchaser gives money consideration. In *Midland Bank Trust Co Ltd v Green*[22] the House of Lords held that there was no need for the consideration to be adequate, so that an unprotected land charge would be rendered void on the purchase of a legal estate even though the consideration provided was merely nominal. On the facts, an unprotected option was rendered void when the owner's wife purchased the farm to which the option related for £500, even though the farm was worth some £40,000 at the date of the transaction. It is also clear from the decision of the House of Lords in *Midland Bank Trust Co Ltd v Green*[23] that it is irrelevant that a person had actual notice of the existence of an unprotected land charge, if he satisfies these statutory criteria. It will still be rendered void against him irrespective of his knowledge. In the Court of Appeal, Lord Denning M.R. had construed s.4(6) so as to introduce an additional requirement of "good faith" by referring to the definition of a purchaser in the Law of Property Act 1925 s.205(xxi) and concluded that where a mother had purchased a farm with full knowledge that her son had been granted an option over it, she could not claim the benefit of the statute to render the unprotected estate contract void. However, the House of Lords rejected Lord Denning's interpretation and Lord Wilberforce held that it was entirely inappropriate to read a requirement of good faith into s.4(6) by reference to contemporaneous Acts, and that the omission of such a requirement had been deliberate. It was therefore held that the wife acquired the freehold of the farm free from the estate contract of her son, even though she knew full well of its existence at the time of the transaction.

Whilst the estate contract is not enforceable against the purchaser, it remains contractually enforceable against the person who granted it. The normal remedy in such a case will be damages, but in an exceptional case, specific performance might still be available. In *Coles v Samuel Smith Old Brewery*[24] the defendant brewery company had conveyed the freehold of a

---

[20] The statutory protection will not therefore apply to a person who acquires an equitable interest in the land: *McCarthy and Stone Ltd v Hodge* [1971] 1 W.L.R. 1547.
[21] Law of Property Act 1925 s.87(1).
[22] [1981] A.C. 513.
[23] [1981] A.C. 513.
[24] [2007] EWCA Civ 1461.

property which it owned to an associated company which it controlled. The purpose of this sale was to defeat an unregistered estate contract enjoyed by the claimants. The Court of Appeal held that specific performance could be ordered against the brewery company because it was in a position to compel its associated company to comply with that order.

(ii) Unregistered Land Charges of the Other Classes

4–029 With some slight variations the remaining land charges will be rendered void when unprotected if slightly lesser statutory conditions are met. The formula used is that they are void "as against a purchaser of the land charged with it, or of any interest in such land, unless the land charge is registered in the appropriate register before the completion of the purchase".[25] In comparison with s.4(6), such unprotected land charges will be rendered void even against a person who does not acquire a legal estate in the land, for example the mortgagee of an equitable mortgage. The requirement as to consideration is also different. Rather than requiring "money or money's worth", statutory protection is given to any purchaser, a term which is defined in s.17 to mean:

> "any person (including a mortgagee or lessee) who, for valuable consideration, takes any interest in land or in a charge on land . . ."

This will include marriage consideration and nominal consideration, but again an unprotected land charge will not be rendered void as against a person who acquires an interest in the land by way of a gift or through succession.

(e) *Exceptional Cases in which Void Land Charges Remain Binding*

4–030 Although an unregistered land charge would ordinarily be rendered void by statute against a purchaser who meets the relevant criteria of s.4 of the Land Charges Act 1972, in exceptional circumstances it may still be found to be binding.

(i) Statutorily Void Land Charge Binding Because of the Purchaser's Fraud

4–031 The courts will not permit an unregistered land charge to be defeated by a fraudulent transaction. However it is clear that a transaction will not be regarded as fraudulent simply because a purchaser of the land knew of the existence of an unprotected minor interest and now claims to have taken free from it. In *Midland Bank Trust Co Ltd v Green*[26] the House of Lords held that it was not fraud for a person to take advantage of his legal rights.[27] Lord Wilberforce held that equitable

---

[25] See s.4(2) (Class A charges created after December 31, 1888); s.4(3) (Class A land charges created before January 1, 1889); s.46(4) (Classes B and C(i), (ii) and (iii)); s.46(8) (Class F).

[26] [1981] A.C. 513.

[27] Citing Lord Cozens-Hardy M.R. in *Re Monolithic Building Co* [1915] 2 Ch. 643. The same reasoning was applied in *Coles v Samuel Smith Old Brewery* [2007] EWCA Civ 1461.

doctrines such as notice and fraud should not be read into modern Acts of Parliament, and that clear enactments as to registration and priority should be interpreted according to their tenor.[28] In the view of the House of Lords, therefore, the mere fact that a person knew of a failure to register a land charge appropriately does not mean that it would be fraudulent to exploit that opportunity and acquire the land free from it, even if this is the sole object of the transaction. Whilst this might result in some seemingly harsh outcomes, it is consistent with the policy of the 1925 legislation which shifted the emphasis from the obligation of the prospective purchaser to make adequate inquiries to protect himself to the obligation of the holder of subsidiary interests to take the necessary steps to ensure that they were protected. As Lord Wilberforce noted:

> "The case is plain: the Act is clear and definite. Intended as it was to provide a simple and understandable system for the protection of title to land, it should not be read down or glossed; to do so would destroy the usefulness of the Act. Any temptation to remould the Act to meet the facts of the present case, on the supposition that it is a hard one and that justice requires it, is, for me at least, removed by the consideration that the Act itself provides a simple and effective protection for persons in [the son's] position, viz. by registration."[29]

However this does not mean that a transaction which is deliberately designed to defeat an unprotected land charge will never be regarded as fraudulent. A sham transaction is likely to be disregarded. For example it is unlikely that a land charge would be rendered void if the purchaser was in effect the same person as the present owner subject to the unprotected interest, either because the purchaser was a nominee of the owner and held the land acquired on bare trust for him, or was a company which was a mere shell for the owner.[30] Similarly if the purchaser of the land stood as a fiduciary of the holder of the unprotected land charge it is unlikely that he could acquire the land free from it.[31]

(ii) Purchaser has Expressly Agreed to Take the Land Subject to an Incumbrance

In *Lyus v Prowsa Developments*,[32] a case involving registered land, it was held that a purchaser was bound by an unprotected interest, which would otherwise have been rendered void against him by statute, because he had expressly agreed to take subject to it. The express agreement affects the conscience of the purchaser, generating a constructive trust which arises outside the statute, causing the unprotected interest binds the purchaser in equity. There is no reason to doubt that the same principle would operate in relation to the limit scheme of registration of land charges in unregistered land. Such a trust will only arise where the purchaser

4–032

---

[28] [1981] A.C. 513 at 531.

[29] In the event it should be noted that although the son's family failed to establish that the mother's estate was bound by the unprotected option they were able to recover damages from the son's solicitors for their negligence in not advising him to protect his option as soon as it had been granted.

[30] See *Jones v Lipman* [1962] 1 W.L.R. 832. The test may be hard to apply: see *Coles v Samuel Smith Old Brewery* [2007] EWCA Civ 1461.

[31] See *Du Boulay v Raggett* (1989) 58 P. & C.R. 138.

[32] [1952] 1 W.L.R. 1044.

had agreed to take the land subject to the specific interest, so that a mere general agreement to take subject to third party interests affecting the land would not be sufficient. The vendor of the land must also have detrimentally relied upon such an express undertaking, usually evidenced by accepting a reduced price for the land so as to reflect the diminished value to the purchaser because he has promised to observe the specified third party interest.[33]

(iii)   Statutorily Void Land Charge Binding by Estoppel

4–033   Even if a land charge would be rendered statutorily void by operation of the Land Charges Act 1972 it is possible that it might be binding on a purchaser who is estopped from denying its existence. Although this principle is closely related to the concept of the independent constructive trust it seems that a lower threshold would be required to establish the estoppel since there is no need to demonstrate an agreement to take the land subject to the interest. This possibility was raised in *ER Ives Investment Ltd v High*,[34] and accepted by Oliver J. in *Taylor Fashions Ltd v Liverpool Victoria Friendly Society*.[35]

2.   Residual Operation of the Doctrine of Notice

4–034   Although the Land Charges Act introduced a limited system of registration for specific interests, priority between all other types of interest continued to be determined by the operation of the traditional doctrine of notice. Thus a purchaser of a legal estate in the land would take priority over any pre-existing equitable interests which were not registrable as land charges, provided that he did not have actual, constructive, or imputed notice of their existence. By far the most significant category of such interests were beneficial interests arising behind a trust of the legal title. If the legal title were owned by at least two co-owners, the principles of overreaching would operate. Thus the doctrine of notice would only operate in practice in relation to trust interests where a sole legal owner held the land on trust. This was the case in *Kingsnorth Finance Co Ltd v Tizard*,[36] which was discussed above and which is a paradigm example of the continuing operation of the doctrine of notice in relation to unregistered land.

THE CONTEMPORARY SIGNIFICANCE OF UNREGISTERED LAND

4–035   Although of historic interest, unregistered land is of rapidly diminishing significance. There is now a requirement that title to land anywhere in England and Wales must be registered whenever it is sold, mortgaged or inherited. In consequence fewer and fewer properties will be unregistered. Over a number of years all land in private hands will become registered, since

---

[33] See *Ashburn Anstalt v Arnold* [1989] Ch. 1.
[34] [1967] 2 Q.B. 379.
[35] [1979] EWHC Ch 1; [1981] 1 All ER 897; [1981] 2 WLR 576; [1982] QB 133.
[36] [1986] 1 W.L.R. 783.

registration must take place at the latest when the current owner or owners die. In time the application of the new regime of compulsory land registration will mean that the only land which will not be registered is land which is owned by corporations such as the Crown, companies, or universities and colleges, provided that they do not seek voluntary registration or mortgage the land. Once land is registered, the unregistered land rules cease to have any application, whether this relates to proof of title or to priorities. In most cases, therefore, the only relevance of the unregistered land rules concerns the issue of proof of title and priorities at the time the land is dealt with in such a way as to enter the registered land system.

Chapter 5

REGISTERED LAND: THE FRAMEWORK OF CONTEMPORARY LAND LAW

INTRODUCTION

In the last two chapters the historic foundations of English land law were examined. In this chapter we turn to consider the framework of contemporary land law. The Land Registration Act 1925 sought to introduce a comprehensive system of registration of title to land which would determine the ownership of land and resolve issues of priorities between competing interests in land. Such a system of registration was intended to improve the efficiency of conveyancing, by making it easier to conduct transactions affecting the land. The framework of registration introduced in 1925 has since been reformed, and the Land Registration Act 1925 has been repealed and replaced by the Land Registration Act 2002. This chapter provides an overview of the system as a whole, and an understanding of the topics which it covers is critical to understanding modern land law. The next two chapters will examine alterations to the Register and priorities in registered land.

5–001

THE SYSTEM OF LAND REGISTRATION

1.   The Introduction of a System of Registration of Title to Land

In Chapter 3 it was seen that there are only two legal estates in land, the fee simple absolute in possession, and the term of years absolute, otherwise known as freehold and leasehold ownership. These two legal estates are the most important interests in land, and the system of land registration is based upon the registration of freehold and long leasehold estates on a centrally maintained land register. Although we have already dealt with some of the background

5–002

to the system of land registration, a recapitulation will help to explain the background and objectives of the system.

(a) *Title to Land Prior to the Introduction of Registration*

5–003 Registration of title is a relatively modern concept. Although all English land titles are historically derived from grants from the Crown,[1] no contemporaneous central record was kept of these grants, nor was there a general requirement in the UK for subsequent transfers of the land to be recorded. Indeed, it was originally the case that land transfers were made in the same sort of way as transfers of most goods still are today, with a physical handing over of possession coupled with an intention to transfer ownership. In the early period of English land law, there would therefore in most cases have been no written record of title to land, let alone one supervised by a public authority. Over the centuries the practice developed of transfers of land being made or recorded in writing, until finally the Law of Property Act 1925[2] made it compulsory for all transfers of legal estates in land to be made by deed. It also became common practice for the vendor of land to be required to prove his or her title to the land. In the absence of any central record of land ownership or central record of land transfers, the only way in which this could be done was through a chain of title deeds. The vendor (with rare exceptions, such as where title had been acquired through adverse possession[3]) would have become owner through a transfer by deed from a person who in turn would have become owner through a similar transfer, and so on. The vendor's proof of ownership would therefore consist of the deed conveying the land to him, the deed conveying the land to his predecessor in title, and all the other deeds conveying the land to previous owners. This chain of title deeds would have to go back to what was considered to be a "good root of title" of sufficient antiquity. The good root of title had to be a deed transferring the whole legal estate in a transaction in which the person acquiring the land could have been expected to conduct a full investigation of the adequacy of the documents. A transfer on sale would satisfy this test, but a transfer by way of gift would not. The chain also had to extend back over a substantial period, which has become progressively shorter over the years, and is now (in the absence of any special contractual provision) 15 years.[4] The logic of this period is that if a landowner and his predecessors have been in possession of the land for this length of time, it is relatively unlikely that any adverse claim will exist against the land. The possibility of adverse claims is not, however, completely eliminated. It is, for instance, possible that Albert, the then owner of Wellington House, granted a lease to Edward for 99 years in 1919. When that lease expires in 2018, Albert or his successors in title will be able to recover possession of the land. What may have happened in the interim is that Frank acquired title by 12 years' adverse possession expiring in 1957 (possibly being unaware of the lease to Edward), and the land was then sold on a number of times until it was purchased by Peter

---

[1] See Ch.3.
[2] s.52.
[3] See Ch.8.
[4] Law of Property Act 1969 s.23. The Law of Property Act 1925 s.44 had previously reduced the statutory root of title from 40 years to 30.

in 1996. Despite the fact that none of the deeds examined by Peter disclose the fact that Albert has superior rights, or that Peter's title derives from Frank's adverse possession (which could only have extinguished Edward's leasehold interest), Peter could find himself being evicted by Albert in 2018.[5]

The fact that some adverse claims may not appear from the examination of title deeds is not the only inconvenience. Where land is subdivided (as for instance where a field is developed as a housing estate), several properties will trace title to the same root, which will therefore need to be proved by certified copies and not by the original deeds. Some of the copies may not have been reproduced well; over the years some of the deeds may have become damaged or lost; and key documents might be suppressed by a dishonest vendor. Most inconveniently of all, on every sale the whole history has to be re-examined for the requisite period. For instance, if Victoria had bought Osborne House in 1965 and lived there until 1995, when she sold to Gladstone, who then sold in 1998 to Palmerston, who sold to Asquith in 2001, then it would be necessary for Asquith, Palmerston and Gladstone all to examine the title back to 1965 in order to cover the statutory period of 15 years' investigation of title, despite the degree of repetition which this involves. In *Williams & Glynn's Bank Ltd v Boland*[6] Lord Scarman commented that this system involved the "wearisome and intricate task of examining title". **5–004**

(b) *Schemes of Registration of Deeds*

Whilst English law originally had no system for recording title or land transactions for historical reasons, registration systems were established from the outset in some other jurisdictions. For instance, in Ontario, significant areas of land were distributed by way of Crown grants based on carefully surveyed tracts. Legislation required any subsequent dealings with the land to be recorded by means of copies of the relevant deeds being deposited in a central registry. Similar systems operated in Ireland, in Yorkshire and in Middlesex, although these were based on records of summaries only of the relevant deeds. These systems of registration of deeds had the advantage of providing a central repository for all such deeds, reducing the possibility that deeds might be suppressed, and also providing a safeguard against their loss or damage. However, the systems generally offered no guarantee as to the validity of the documents, did not obviate the need to conduct a full investigation of title each time land is sold, and did not capture non-documentary land transactions. **5–005**

(c) *The Advantages of Registration of Title*

A more comprehensive system of registration is one in which the register does more than record transactions in land. Instead it provides a definitive record of ownership. It is this system which has been adopted as the model for England and Wales. A register, maintained **5–006**

---

[5] See *St Marylebone Property Co Ltd v Fairweather* [1963] A.C. 510.
[6] [1981] A.C. 487.

by the Land Registry, records details of the land including information about its physical extent; who is currently the owner of it; any rights which exist for its benefit; any mortgages to which it is subject; and any other incumbrances or burdens to which it is subject. Instead of a purchaser verifying that the vendor has the right to sell by checking through a chain of title deeds, all that is needed is for a simple check to be made with the Land Registry. For instance, if the title to Osborne House were registered, then Asquith would not need, when he acquired it in 2001, to check the transfers from Victoria to Gladstone and from Gladstone to Palmerston. He would merely need to check that Palmerston was registered as proprietor. The examination of the register should also disclose whether there was a mortgage on Osborne House, whether the land was crossed by any rights of way, and whether any leases had been granted. In the most comprehensive of systems of land registration, everything which Asquith might want to know should be disclosed by the register, and he would not be bound by any rights affecting the property which were not recorded. As will be seen, the system of land registration adopted in England and Wales is not as comprehensive as this.

(d) *The Introduction of Registration in England*

5–007   Although the property legislation of 1925 began the process of the introduction of a universal scheme of registration of land in England and Wales, a system of registration was first introduced by the Land Registry Act 1862,[7] the preamble to which stated that the object was to "facilitate the proof of title". The Land Transfer Act 1897 provided for compulsory registration of title in designated areas. The process of introducing registration of title was accelerated by the Land Registration Act 1925. Lord Oliver noted in *City of London Building Society v Flegg* that this Act:

> ". . . was introduced as part and parcel of the overall property legislation enacted in that year and it introduced for the first time . . . a power in central government to designate areas in which registered conveyancing would be compulsory".[8]

As it was obviously impossible for all land to be registered immediately, land was to be registered either voluntarily by its owners or compulsorily on sale in designated geographical areas, with the object that eventually all land would be registered. For land remaining unregistered, a partial scheme of registration for some important interests was introduced by the Land Charges Act 1925. It was initially anticipated that universal registration would be accomplished within 30 years of the Land Registration Act 1925, but this goal proved impossible to attain. The final stage of the transition to such universal coverage was set in place by the Registration of Title Order 1989, under which the entire country was designated an area of compulsory registration. The Land Registration Act 1997 widened the circumstances in which title to remaining unregistered land must be registered, reflecting a desire to speed the completion of the process. A further expansion of the number of situations in which

---

[7] See (1972) 36 Conv. 390 (H.W. Wilkinson).
[8] [1988] A.C. 54 at 84.

registration is compulsory was made by the Land Registration Act 2002 which has replaced the Land Registration Act 1925 as the governing statute.

(e) The System of Land Registration is not Intended to be Identical in Effect to Unregistered Land

It has sometimes been thought that the legislation introducing the system of registration of title was merely intended to place the existing principles relating to unregistered land on a statutory footing, so that there would be no substantive difference in the circumstances in which a purchaser would take title free from subsidiary interests in the land. If this analysis is correct then obviously much help could be derived in interpreting the various statutory provisions by examining the pre-existing law. However, the House of Lords has made clear that there should be no presumption that the legislation intended to leave the substantive law unchanged. In *Midland Bank Trust Co v Green* Lord Wilberforce stated in relation to a question of interpretation of the Land Charges Act 1925:

> "My lords, I do not think it is safe to seek the answer to this question by means of a general assertion that the property legislation of 1922–25 was not intended to alter the law, or not intended to alter it in a particular field, such as that relating to purchasers of a legal estate. All the Acts of 1925, and their precursors, were drafted with the utmost care, and their wording, certainly where this is apparently clear, has to be accorded firm respect."[9]

The differences between the land registration system and unregistered land are even more pronounced following the changes made by the Land Registration Act 2002. The system of land registration must therefore be taken on its own terms as an integral whole transforming the law rather than codifying it.[10]

2. Key Features of the System of Land Registration

(a) The "Mirror", "Curtain" and "Compensation" Principles

The English system of land registration is sometimes said to be founded upon three key principles. The first is the mirror principle. This means that the register of land ownership is intended to be an accurate reflection of the range of rights with which a purchaser is likely to be concerned. The second is the curtain principle. This means that rights with which a purchaser is not concerned are not disclosed on the register, but are hidden behind the curtain of registration. Finally, the compensation or indemnity principle means that where loss is caused through

5–008

5–009

---

[9] [1981] A.C. 513 at 529.
[10] See also *Lloyds Bank Plc v Carrick* [1996] 4 All E.R. 630; Law Com. No.158, *Land Registration for the Twenty-First Century* (1998) para.1.6.

an inaccuracy in the register, compensation will be paid to anyone who has suffered loss through reliance upon it.

(b) *Register Maintained by the State*

5–010   The Land Register of ownership of land titles is maintained by the state under the control of the Chief Land Registrar. The register is maintained centrally and by 19 district land registries. The system is self-funding through the imposition of fees for searches and registrations. The register is open to general public inspection.[11] An index (which includes an index map) makes it possible to discover whether any parcel of land is registered.[12]

(c) *The Terminology of Land Registration*

5–011   The word "register" is used in a variety of ways in the Land Registration Acts. In some instances it is used to refer to the whole of the register maintained by the Land Registry; in other instances it refers to the record for each individual title; and in other instances again it refers to three separate parts of the record kept for each individual title. Using the language of electronic storage, the word "register" is used to describe the directory of all registered titles, the folder for each individual registered title, and the files contained within each folder (see below). This overlapping use of the word "register" can be confusing, and it is regrettable that the Land Registration Acts did not adopt a clearer terminology.

The structure of the Land Register

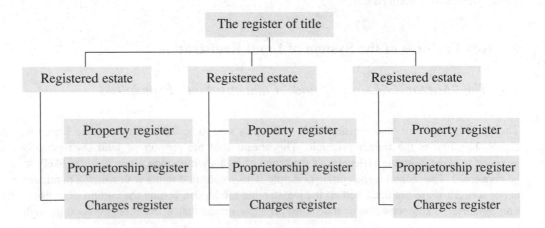

---

[11] Land Registration Act 2002 s.66. The Register could originally only be inspected with the authority of the registered proprietor, but public access first became available in 1990: Land Registration Act 1925 s.112(1) (as substituted by Land Registration Act 1988, s.1(1)).
[12] Land Registration Act 2002 s.68.

There can be a similar difficulty in relation to the descriptions of rights in registered land. Only certain rights are capable of being registered independently with their own folder. These, once registered, are called registered estates. Other rights are registered by means of entries against the registered estate or registered estates to which they relate. A legal mortgage, for instance, can exist only as a registered charge, recorded by registration against the registered estate to which it relates. There is also the full range of other rights, such as easements, covenants, options and contracts, which exist only as subordinate rights against the land of another. In the Land Registration Act 1925 rights of this kind, which could be entered on the register, but only against some other registered title or registered estate, were described as minor interests. That terminology is not used in the Land Registration Act 2002, but since no other description for these rights has been introduced in its place, it is convenient to continue to use the phrase. There are two further categories of rights in registered land. Some minor interests, such as the rights of beneficiaries under a trust of land, can never be recorded on the register. For convenience these can be called unregistrable minor interests, although this is again not a phrase used in the Land Registration Acts. Finally, there are certain rights which are automatically enforceable against a person acquiring registered land even when they are not recorded on the register. These are usually described as overriding interests.[13] To confuse things still further, it is possible for the same right to be capable of being a registered estate, for it to be capable of being recorded against another registered title, and for it to be protected as an overriding interest. In other words, the categories of rights in registered land are not mutually exclusive.

(d) *Registered Estates*

The Land Registration Act 1925 recognised just two kinds of registered estate, the freehold and the long lease. The Land Registration Act 2002[14] extends the categories of right which can be registered as independent registered estates to comprise freehold estates,[15] leasehold estates with more than seven years unexpired,[16] leases for discontinuous periods,[17] leases taking effect in possession more than three months from the date of their grant,[18] certain leases to which the Housing Act 1985 applies,[19] and rentcharges, franchises and profits à prendre in gross. **5–012**

(e) *Compulsory First Registration*

The register of title maintained by the Land Registry does not provide a comprehensive list of all land ownership in England and Wales. Instead, land registration was introduced progressively **5–013**

---

[13] The phrase "overriding interest" is used in the Land Registration Rules 2003 although it is not used in the Land Registration Act 2002.
[14] s.3.
[15] Land Registration Act 2002 s.3(1)(a) and s.4(2)(a).
[16] Land Registration Act 2002 s.3(1)(a) and (3); s.4(2)(b). Under the Land Registration Act 1925, the lease had to have 21 years unexpired to be registrable as a registered estate.
[17] Land Registration Act 2002 s.3(4). Such a lease can be used to create a timeshare arrangement under which the tenant has the right to use a property for, say, the first week in August each year.
[18] Land Registration Act 2002 s.4(1)(d) and s.6(3)(a). The consequence of this is that a legal lease, even for a period as short as one week, will have to be registered if it is to commence more than three months from the date of its grant.
[19] Land Registration Act 2002 s.4(1)(b), (e) and (f).

through a process of voluntary and compulsory registration, the latter operating when certain dealings with land took place. It is currently possible for the owner of a freehold estate, a long lease (i.e. one with more than seven years unexpired), of a rentcharge, franchise or profit à prendre to apply for voluntary registration.[20] In addition, following certain dealings in land, it is compulsory for the person acquiring a freehold estate, a leasehold estate with at least seven years unexpired, and certain other legal interests to apply for registration.[21] Because of progressive extensions to the scope of compulsory registration, and because of the rate at which most property is transferred, it has been estimated that 90 per cent of all land transactions involve title to land which has already been registered. Since the scope of compulsory registration now includes dispositions by will or on intestacy, all registrable estates in land owned by individuals will become registered within a generation. The Lord Chancellor can add to the events upon which compulsory registration applies,[22] but since registration only becomes compulsory when some specified event occurs, land held by corporations (including universities or Oxford or Cambridge colleges) or the Crown may remain outside the land registration system for a considerable time. A point may be reached where in order to tidy loose ends it is appropriate to require the owners of land to register their title even though there is no transaction.

(f)   Subsequent Dealings with Registered Land

5–014   Once land falls within the system of land registration, all subsequent dealings with the land operate within that system, and there is no scope for the operation of the rules relating to unregistered land. Any transfers of registered land require registration for their completion.[23] The effect of registration is to vest the legal title in the person registered as owner, even if the transaction on which the registration was based was imperfect.[24] The register thus becomes a mirror of title to the land.

(g)   The Format of the Register

5–015   Although each independently registered estate, whether freehold or leasehold, has a single entry at the Land Registry, which is given an individual title number, each entry is divided into three sections detailing different aspects of the land to which it relates.[25]

(i)   Property Register

5–016   The property register is the first section of the entry for any registered estate. It identifies the land in relation to which the estate exists, by means of a verbal description and reference to

---

[20] Land Registration Act 2002 s.3.
[21] Land Registration Act 2002 s.4.
[22] Land Registration Act 2002 s.5.
[23] Land Registration Act 2002 s.27.
[24] Land Registration Act 2002 s.58.
[25] Land Registration Rules 2003 (SI 2003/1417) r.4(2).

a map, and states whether the estate is freehold or leasehold. The property register may also contain details of benefits attached to the land, such as easements and restrictive covenants enjoyed over other land of which the registered estate is the dominant tenement.[26] Where the estate is leasehold the property register will also contain brief details of the lease.[27] The description of the boundaries is normally "general" only and does not, unless the contrary is made clear, establish the exact line of any boundary.[28]

(ii) Proprietorship Register

The second section of the register entry is the proprietorship register, which contains the name and address of the present registered proprietor and states the quality of title with which the estate has been registered.[29] The proprietorship register also contains details of any restrictions which have the effect of restricting or limiting the rights of the registered proprietor to dispose of the land.[30] A restriction might provide, for instance, that no registration is to take place without the consent of a named individual. **5–017**

(iii) Charges Register

The third section of the register is the charges register, which contains details of third party rights which burden the land. For example the charges register may contain details of mortgages and other financial charges which are secured on the land, restrictive covenants limiting its use and easements which third parties enjoy over it.[31]

(h) *Other Registrable Dispositions*

Although only a limited range of legal estates are capable of being registered as separate titles at the land registry some subsidiary interests in land are only capable of being created at law by registration. These are rights which arise as a result of a registrable disposition. The list of dispositions required to be registered is set out in Land Registration Act 2002 s.27. In particular, a charge by way of legal mortgage and express legal easements will only be created when the chargee or the proprietor of the easement is registered as such on the title to which it relates. This is another **5–018**

---

[26] Land Registration Rules 2003 (SI 2003/1417) r.5. The dominant tenement is the property which benefits from a right such as a right of way or other easement. The property over which the right is exercised is known as the servient tenement.

[27] Land Registration Rules 2003 (SI 2003/1417) r.6.

[28] Land Registration Act 2002 s.60.

[29] Land Registration Rules 2003 (SI 2003/1417) r.8.

[30] The Land Registration Act 2002 recognises the restriction as the only category of limit to the exercise by an estate owner of his or her powers. Under the Land Registration Act 1925 the limitation was described as a restriction if agreed to by the registered proprietor (Land Registration Act 1925 s.58). If imposed by the registrar or by court order, it was known as an inhibition (Land Registration Act 1925 s.57). It was also possible for there to be a caution requiring the person named to be informed in writing before any dealing was registered (Land Registration Act 1925 s.55).

[31] Land Registration Rules 2003 (SI 2003/1417) r.9.

way in which the register is intended to reflect accurately the state of title and subsidiary rights. In the absence of such registration the mortgage or easement granted will be equitable only and will rank alongside other subsidiary interests as an unregistered "minor interest".

(i)   *Minor Interests*

5–019   The Land Registration Act 2002 does not restrict the range of rights affecting land that can be created by the registered proprietor.[32] In addition to registrable dispositions, which can have full effect only if they are registered, it is possible for rights not listed in s.27 to be created in the same way for registered land as they can for unregistered land. The collective description for these rights is minor interests.[33] Most of these rights are equitable rights, rather than legal rights, although this is a distinction of much less importance in relation to registered land than it is for unregistered land. Many of these rights are capable of being recorded on the register of the land to which they relate, although some are not. The advantage of recording a minor interest on the register is that it guarantees that the right will have priority over any rights subsequently created. For example, if Kevin is the registered owner of a farm, which he agrees to sell to Ian, this gives Ian an equitable right arising from the specifically enforceable contract. If Ian protects the contract by means of an entry on the register, then the contract will be enforceable against the land, even if Kevin subsequently sells the farm to Leonard. The entry on the register will mean that Leonard is aware of the contract at the time of his purchase, another application of the mirror principle. If Ian fails to record his contract by an entry on the register, then his contract will not be enforceable against Leonard, because of the special statutory priority rules which govern registrable dispositions.

(j)   *Overriding Interests*

5–020   Overriding interests represent the greatest breach in the mirror principle. The essential characteristic of overriding interests is that they bind a purchaser of the land even where they have not been protected on the register of the estate they affect. In a sense they are rather like "trump cards" of the registered land system, taking automatic priority to any rights which are subsequently acquired by a person in the land. The list of overriding interests is set out in two schedules to the Land Registration Act, one list applying to first registration, and the other to subsequent registration. The most prominent category of overriding interest concerns the rights of a person who is in occupation of the land at the time that another right comes into existence and is registered. Suppose, for example that, although Ian had not recorded the existence of his contract to buy Kevin's farm, he was managing the farm on Kevin's behalf at the time of the sale to Leonard. Even though not recorded on the register, Ian's contract would be enforceable against Leonard.

---

[32] Land Registration Act 2002 s.23.
[33] See Land Registration Act 1925 s.3(xv). This description is no longer used in the Land Registration Act 2002, but remains a convenient phrase which is used in the Land Registration Rules 2003.

It can be seen that overriding interests are a significant gap in the comprehensiveness of the land registration system, since they mean that a purchaser of land may find that it is subject to third party interests which were not revealed on the register. A prospective purchaser cannot therefore rely on the register alone to satisfy himself whether there might be any adverse interests affecting the land.

(k) *Eliminating the Complexity of Equitable Ownership from the Register*

Although the register is based on the registration of legal ownership it has also been seen how a person can enjoy the equitable ownership of land through a trust. Such trust interests can be more easily created and transferred than their legal equivalents, and historically their existence was not generally evident from the title deeds of land. This is particularly true of resulting or constructive trusts. It would have been possible to require all such beneficial interests to appear on the register of the legal estate to which they relate, but this would have led to extreme complexity. Instead, the legislation of 1925 introduced a means by which, as far as possible, equitable ownership need not appear on the register, and indeed cannot be recorded on the register.[34] Overreaching provides a mechanism whereby a purchaser of land can be sure that he will acquire it free from any existing beneficial interests by paying the purchase price to at least two legal owners, who would be the trustees holding the land subject to the trust. If this condition is met the trust interests no longer affect the land and the purchaser will take his title unencumbered by them. The interests of the beneficiaries are not destroyed by overreaching, but transferred to the purchase moneys in the hands of the trustees. The operation of overreaching means that beneficial interests under a trust are concealed behind the curtain of registration. Overreaching has proved so effective as a means of keeping equitable ownership off the register that the majority of problems associated with trust interests in registered land have occurred where it has not taken place because a person has acquired the legal ownership from a sole proprietor.

5–021

(l) *Facilitating Electronic Conveyancing*

The Land Registration Act 2002 contains provisions which will enable the introduction of electronic conveyancing. Under current arrangements, land transactions are completed in a traditional manner. For instance, where land is sold, the sale is completed by the execution of a deed of transfer which is then submitted by the purchaser to the Land Registry for registration. When the electronic conveyancing provisions of the Land Registration Act 2002 come into operation, this will change. By s.91, a deed disposing of a registered estate or charge can be made electronically. By s.92,[35] the Land Registry can establish a secure electronic network which will provide conveyancers with direct access to the register of titles. Finally, by s.93, rules may be made requiring contracts and deeds dealing with registered estates and rights

5–022

---

[34] Rights which may not be recorded on the register are enumerated in Land Registration Act 2002 s.33.
[35] And Sch.5.

recorded on the register to be made electronically and recorded simultaneously on the register. The effect of this will be to eliminate the time gap that currently exists between the execution of a deed or of a contract and its registration. Moreover, when the rules are brought into operation, no contract or deed will be effective unless it is simultaneously registered. In consequence, the register will become a more accurate mirror the state of ownership and of rights affecting registered land.

(m) *Accuracy of the Register Guaranteed*

5–023   Subject to powers given to the Court and to the Land Registrar to rectify or amend the register,[36] the register is conclusive as to title.[37] Where there is a doubt about the quality of the title, the Land Registrar can reflect this in the type of registration, thereby qualifying or limiting the extent of the guarantee of title.[38] The register is not, however, conclusive as to the validity of matters other than title to a registered estate.[39] If Martin claimed to have an easement over Nicola's land, and registered a notice recording this, although the notice would confer priority for the easement over any subsequently created rights in the land, it does not have the effect of guaranteeing the validity of Martin's claimed easement should it be subject to any defect, either in its inherent character, or in the way in which it was created.

The Land Registration Act 2002 contains complex provisions under which compensation is payable to persons who have suffered loss as a result of a mistake in the register, or in consequence of the correction of a mistake in the register.[40] The Act therefore reflects the compensation or indemnity principle.

REGISTRATION OF TITLE TO LAND

1.   Interests Which may or must be Registered

5–024   It has been noted that the scheme of the 1925 property legislation was to create just two legal estates in land, the fee simple absolute in possession, and the term of years absolute. All other rights in land were to be subordinate or derivative. The Land Registration Act 1925 contemplated that only these two estates could be registered. The Land Registration Act 1925 s.2(1) stated:

> "After the commencement of this Act, estates capable of subsisting as legal estates shall be the only interests in respect of which a proprietor can be registered . . ."

[36] Land Registration Act 2002 s.65 and Sch.4.
[37] Land Registration Act 2002 s.11 (first registration of a freehold title), s.12 (first registration of a leasehold title), s.58 (effect of registration in general).
[38] Land Registration Act 2002 ss.9, 10.
[39] Land Registration Act 2002 s.32.
[40] Land Registration Act 2002 s.103 and Sch.8.

It was not practicable for all leasehold estates to be registered and it was only leasehold estates with more than 21 years unexpired that were capable of registration as registered estates.

The categories of registrable estates have been expanded by the Land Registration Act 2002. As has already been described, the categories of leasehold interests which can now be registered (and in some cases must be registered) include leases with seven years unexpired, discontinuous leases (such as timeshare leases), leases taking effect in possession more than three months from the date of their grant, and certain leases to which the Housing Act 1985 applies. The Act also makes rentcharges, franchises, manors[41] and profits à prendre in gross registrable as registered estates.[42] A rentcharge is a right to receive a rent payable by the owner of freehold land (rent payable by the tenant of leasehold land is known as rent service). A franchise is a right granted by the Crown in years gone by to enjoy rights which at common law were reserved to the Crown. Franchises can include, for instance, the right to hold a fair or a market (and to collect the rents from the stallholders) or to salvage wrecks in various parts of territorial waters. Manors fall within the definition of land contained in the Law of Property Act 1925[43]; although they may include a tract of land in its usual sense, their main commercial value lies in the title (lordship of the manor) which accompanies them, and the fact that they occasionally confer benefits such as franchises or mineral rights upon the owner. The main forms of profit à prendre in gross are the rights to fish in a river and the right to hunt over land, both of which are capable of being owned independently of the right to possess the land (or water) itself.

2. First Registration of Title to Unregistered Land

(a) *When Must Title be Registered for the First Time?*

Where title to land is currently unregistered, the occurrence of certain events renders it com-   **5–025**
pulsory to apply for registration. This will be the case when a freehold estate or a lease with more than seven years unexpired is sold, transferred by way of gift,[44] or mortgaged by way of first legal mortgage,[45] or where one of the leasehold estates described in the previous paragraph is granted out of a freehold or leasehold estate.[46] In each of these cases it is necessary

---

[41] Although not explicitly listed in s.3 as a registrable estate, manors are referred to in s.88 and are also registrable as freehold estates in land.

[42] To be pedantically accurate, independently registered rentcharges and profits à prendre should be described as independently registrable *interests* (rather than *estates*), since the Law of Property Act 1925 recognised only two legal estates, the fee simple absolute in possession and the term of years absolute, all other legal rights being described as legal interests: Law of Property Act 1925 s.1. See also Land Registration Act 2002 Sch.2 para.6. Franchises and manors fall within the definition of "land" contained in the Law of Property Act 1925 s.205 and so would be capable of independent registration as a registrable estate if held for a freehold or appropriate leasehold estate, even if express provision had not been made in the Land Registration Act 2002.

[43] Law of Property Act 1925 s.205(1)(ix).

[44] Land Registration Act 2002 s.4(1)(a). This includes where there is a succession on death completed by way of an assent by the personal representatives of the deceased: s.4(1)(a)(ii).

[45] Land Registration Act 2002 s.4(1)(g).

[46] Land Registration Act 2002 s.4(1)(c).

for the person to whom the transfer or grant has been made to apply for the interest to be registered.[47] In the special situation where the interest granted is a mortgage, then it is the owner of the estate out of which the mortgage is granted who must apply for the estate to be registered.[48] In addition to the circumstances where registration is compulsory, it is also possible for an estate owner to apply for voluntary registration.[49] There are currently no requirements for the compulsory registration of rentcharges, franchises or profits à prendre, but voluntary registration of these rights is possible.[50] In addition, there is an incentive to register franchises or manors. If they are not registered within a period of 10 years from the commencement of the Land Registration Act 2002, they will cease to be enforceable against land following first registration or following a registrable disposition of land which has already been registered, unless their existence has been noted against the registered estate affected.[51]

Where registration is compulsory, a failure to apply for registration within two months[52] means that the transaction will fail to transfer, grant or create a legal estate.[53] Subject to a discretion given to the Land Registrar to extend the time limit,[54] it will be necessary to repeat the transaction to make good the deficiency.[55] The grantee will, however, enjoy an equitable interest in the land pending registration,[56] although this may be vulnerable to subsequent dealings with the land by the grantor.

(b) *Grades of Title Awarded on First Registration of Ownership*

5–026   When land is registered for the first time the Land Registrar is required to investigate the title of the person seeking to be registered as owner. The registrar will then register the land with a class of title appropriate to the degree to which the owner has been able to satisfy him of their entitlement. In the case of freehold ownership the registrar may grant absolute, possessory or qualified title. In the case of leasehold ownership the additional grade of "good leasehold title" may be awarded. Absolute title is the appropriate where the registrar "is of the opinion that the person's title is such as a willing buyer could properly be advised by a competent professional adviser to accept"[57] and where, if the land concerned is leasehold, the registrar approves the lessor's title to grant the lease.[58] Where the registrar is satisfied about the quality of a leasehold interest, but has not approved the lessor's title to grant the lease, then registration will be with

---

[47] Land Registration Act 2002 s.6(1) and (3).
[48] Land Registration Act 2002 s.6(1) and (2).
[49] See Cooke [2002] Conv. 11.
[50] Land Registration Act 2002 s.3.
[51] Land Registration Act 2002 s.117. The record on the register would be by way of a caution against first registration, or by way of a notice where the estate affected had already been registered.
[52] Land Registration Act 2002 s.6(4).
[53] Land Registration Act 2002 s.7.
[54] Land Registration Act 2002 s.6(5).
[55] Land Registration Act 2002 s.8. The additional costs so incurred fall upon the person who should have applied for registration.
[56] By way of being the beneficiary of a bare trust from the transferor in the case of a transfer of a freehold or leasehold estate, and by way of a contract for valuable consideration in the case of a purported grant of a new leasehold interest or of a mortgage: s.7(2).
[57] Land Registration Act 2002 s.9(2).
[58] Land Registration Act 2002 s.10(2).

good leasehold title. Qualified title and possessory title are appropriate where the registrar has reservations which are significant enough to give cause to believe that the title might be disturbed. The registrar will register with qualified title where the reservations relate to a specific matter such as the absence of a sufficiently long root of title, or to the fact that a key document cannot be furnished, and no copy is available. The qualification concerned will be expressed as part of the grant. Where the reservations are more general, for instance because there is no satisfactory proof of title at all, but the person seeking registration is in actual occupation of the land,[59] then possessory title may be used. Possessory title is not used automatically where the person seeking first registration relies on title by adverse possession, for there are cases where such a title will be accepted by a competent professional adviser, for instance where the claim to adverse possession is supported by appropriate statutory declarations or other evidence.

(c) *Upgrading Title*

The registrar has power to upgrade title if he is satisfied in relation to the matters which gave rise to the initial registration with qualified, possessory or good leasehold title.[60] Registration with possessory title will normally be upgraded to title absolute or good leasehold title, as appropriate, after the registered proprietor has been in possession for twelve years.[61]   **5–027**

(d) *The Effect of First Registration*

First registration has the effect of vesting legal title in the person registered as proprietor, even if there may have been some defect in the title presented to the registrar.[62] The registration is subject to the reservations relating to the nature of the title, if the registration is not with title absolute, and is also subject to: **5–028**

   (i) any adverse rights recorded on the register for the property;

   (ii) overriding interests; and

   (iii) any rights acquired by adverse possession of which the registered proprietor has notice.

Where the registered proprietor is not wholly entitled to the estate for his own benefit, then "as between himself and the persons beneficially entitled to the estate, the estate is vested in him [the registered proprietor] subject to such of their interests as he has notice of".[63] Suppose that Peter buys Rossiter House in his own name, but his wife Meryl contributes to the purchase. That is likely to give Meryl a share in the beneficial ownership by way of resulting or constructive trust. Peter will not be able to claim that the trust is not binding on him because of the effect of

---

[59] Or in receipt of the rents and profits: Land Registration Act 2002 s.9(5) and 10(5).
[60] Land Registration Act 2002 s.62.
[61] Land Registration Act 2002 s.62(4) and (5).
[62] Land Registration Act 2002 s.11 (freeholds); s.12 (leaseholds).
[63] Land Registration Act 2002 s.11(5). See also s.12(5).

the first registration of the property. If the first registration relates to leasehold property, then the registration is also subject to the express and implied covenants which relate to the lease.[64]

(e)   *Overriding Interests Applying on First Registration*

5–029   First registration is subject to the overriding interests set out in Sch.1 of the Land Registration Act 2002. These are similar to, but are not identical to, the overriding interests which apply in relation to subsequent registered dispositions. Nor are they identical to the list of overriding interests contained in the previous legislation, the Land Registration Act 1925.[65]

As has already been explained, overriding interests are enforceable against registered land even though they have not been recorded in the register, and even though the registered proprietor may be unaware of them. The rights which are treated as overriding interests on first registration are, by and large, legal rights which would have been binding on the owner of unregistered land, even though the owner may have been unaware of their existence. They include legal easements and profits à prendre,[66] customary and public rights,[67] legal leases which are not themselves registrable estates,[68] certain rights to mines and minerals,[69] and for a transitional period of 10 years, franchises, manorial rights, Crown rents, common law obligations to repair or contribute to the cost of repairing embankments, sea or river walls, and payments in lieu of tithes.[70] Local land charges, which are recorded in a separate register, are also overriding interests.[71] In addition, the interests of persons in actual occupation are overriding interests.[72] This important category of overriding interest is not confined to legal rights, and can therefore include equitable interests such as the right of a person to an interest by way of resulting or constructive trust, under an equitable lease, or under a specifically enforceable contract relating to the land. The mere fact that a person is in occupation does not in itself create any new rights,[73] and the categorisation of a right as overriding gives it no special status other than priority over certain subsequent transactions.[74] The Act defines the category thus:

> "An interest belonging to a person in actual occupation, so far as relating to land of which he is in actual occupation, except for an interest under the Settled Land Act 1925."

This category of overriding interest is of considerable importance, and will be discussed in detail in the context of subsequent registered dispositions. It should be noted, however, that

---

[64] Land Registration Act 2002 s.12(4).

[65] Land Registration Act 1925 s.70.

[66] Land Registration Act 2002 Sch.1 para.3.

[67] Land Registration Act 2002 Sch.1 paras 4 and 5.

[68] Land Registration Act 2002 Sch.1 para.1.

[69] Land Registration Act 2002 Sch.1 paras 7 to 9.

[70] Land Registration Act 2002 Sch.1 paras 10 to 14. See s.117 which deprives these rights of the status of overriding interests as from 10 years from the coming into operation of this part of the Act.

[71] Land Registration Act 1925 Sch.1 para.6.

[72] Land Registration Act 1925 Sch.1 para.2.

[73] The occupier must have a legal or an equitable interest rather than simply a personal right: *Williams & Glyn's Bank Ltd v Boland* [1981] AC 487. This may include a right arising by virtue of proprietary estoppel: *Sommer v Sweet* [2005] EWCA Civ 227 at 25.

[74] *Fairclough v Salmon* [2006] EWCA Civ 320 at 22.

the definition of this category of overriding interest is not in the same terms as that for sub-sequent registered dispositions. In particular, it is irrelevant whether the actual occupation is or is not reasonably discoverable from an inspection of the property.

(f) *The Dual Operation of Unregistered and Registered Land Rules*

Although the Land Registration Act 2002 does not make this explicit, first registration will often combine the operation of both the unregistered land rules and of the rules relating to first registration of registered land. Where registration is voluntary registration by an existing estate owner, the rules relating to first registration of registered land will operate on their own. Where, however, registration follows an event as a consequence of which registration has become compulsory, then there will be a sequential application of the rules relating to unregistered land and those relating to first registration. In some cases this will have little consequence, but there will be others where the consequences are more significant.

5–030

Consider first the situation where land is registered following a voluntary disposition, such as succession on death. In such a case, under the unregistered land rules, the new owner takes subject to all rights which affected the estate in the hands of the previous owner. The effect of first registration, however, may be to render unenforceable certain rights affecting the land. Suppose that Oliver was the owner of Bleak House, title to which is not registered, and he contracted to sell the property to Petula. Petula does not register the contract under the Land Charges Act,[75] and before the contract is completed, Oliver dies, leaving Bleak House to his daughter Rebecca. Although under the unregistered land rules Petula can enforce the contract against Rebecca, the effect of the first registration of Rebecca as owner would be to render Petula's contract unenforceable against Bleak House, unless Petula had an overriding interest by virtue of actual occupation. The same would be true if Petula's claim was based on a resulting trust arising from a contribution to the purchase price of Bleak House. Such a beneficial interest is enforceable against a successor in title to unregistered land, but ceases to be enforceable following first registration unless it is an overriding interest by virtue of actual occupation or is a beneficial interest of which the newly registered proprietor had notice.[76]

Where first registration follows a disposition of unregistered land for valuable consideration, then one must first apply the unregistered land rules (including the equitable doctrine of notice), and then the rules relating to first registration. Again, the rules will not necessarily produce the same results. Imagine that Hugh is the owner of River Cottage, title to which has not yet been registered. Jamie has an equitable easement to cross the garden, and this is evident from the fact that there is a gate in the garden wall at River Cottage which gives access to Jamie's neighbouring cottage. If Hugh sells River Cottage to Rick, then Rick acquires the property subject to Jamie's equitable interest. The physical evidence means that Rick would acquire River Cottage with notice of the equitable easement.[77] The easement would, however, probably cease to be enforceable by Jamie following Rick's first registration. Equitable easements are not overriding interests which are automatically protected on first registration. Nor is it likely that Jamie would

---

[75] See Ch.4 for the provisions relating to registration of charges against unregistered land.
[76] Land Registration Act 2002 s.11(5) or s.12(5).
[77] The situation is similar to *Hervey v Smith* (1856) 22 Beav. 299.

be considered to be in actual occupation of his right of way, even if he were using it regularly, since actual occupation is not a concept that is likely to apply to easements. Nor would Jamie be protected on the basis that he had a beneficial interest of which Rick had notice, for the entitlement to an equitable easement is unlikely to be considered to be a beneficial interest. There could equally be situations relating to registration following sale where the unregistered land rules result in the destruction of a right affecting the property, which will not then be revived because it falls within the list of overriding interests automatically protected on first registration.[78]

(g) Subsequent Dealings with the Registered Legal Ownership

5–031 Once the freehold or leasehold ownership of land is registered, all subsequent dealings with the legal title to the land must take place through the application of the rules set out in the Land Registration Act 2002.

(h) Cautions Against First Registration

5–032 A person with an interest in unregistered land can register a caution against first registration.[79] The effect of this is that the cautioner must be notified by the registrar of any proposal to register the estate concerned, and given an opportunity to object within a fixed period.[80] Lodging a caution is not a substitute for registering a registrable legal estate since a caution against first registration procured by a person entitled to a fee simple absolute in possession or a term of years absolute expires automatically two years after the Land Registration Act 2002 comes into force.[81]

3. Land Which is Already Registered

(a) Multiple Registered Estates in Relation to the Same Physical Land

5–033 Because it is the estate in land which is registered, rather than the physical land itself, it is possible for there to be more than one independently registered estate in relation to the same physical tract of land. For instance, where a leasehold estate is registered, it will often be the case that the freehold out of which the lease was created will also be registered. Each of these registered titles or registered estates will contain a cross-reference to the other.

Although the circumstances are likely to be relatively rare, it is also possible for land, once registered, to fall out of the system of registered land. Since leasehold estates are of finite duration, it would be possible for the owner of an unregistered freehold, such as an Oxford

---

[78] For instance an estate contract in favour of a person in actual occupation, but which is void for lack of registration under the Land Charges Acts.
[79] Land Registration Act 2002 s.15.
[80] Land Registration Act 2002 s.16. This period is normally 15 working days: Land Registration Rules 2003 r.53.
[81] Land Registration Act 2002 Sch.12 para.14.

college, to grant a lease for, say, 12 years. Being for more than seven years' duration, the lease would be registrable, but the freehold would not be registrable. Once the lease terminates by expiry, there would cease to be any registered interest in relation to the tract of land. Any new lease, if for more than seven years, would of course be registrable.

(b) *Dealings with Registered Interests*

Where an estate in land has been registered, it is dealings with that registered estate which fall **5–034** to be governed by the registered land rules, not any dealings with the tract of land. Thus where a leasehold estate has been registered, but the freehold has not been registered, dealings with the lease are governed by the Land Registration Act 2002. Dealings with the freehold, such as the grant of short leases taking effect in possession, fall outside the ambit of the registered land system, unless the dealing is such as to attract compulsory registration.

Since in the majority of cases it is the freehold estate which is first registered, and all other interests in land subsequently created must derive from that freehold estate, in practice once the land (i.e. the freehold) has been registered, all subsequent dealings will be governed by the registered land system.

4. The Land Certificate

The registered proprietor of land is provided with a copy of the entry for his title on the register.[82] **5–035** This copy is known as a land certificate, and although in practice it may be treated as such, it should not be regarded as the equivalent of title deeds. The land certificate is only evidence of title, which is in fact constituted by the entry on the land register. It used to be the case that the land certificate had to be provided to the Land Registry when a charge was submitted for registration or when the land register entry was amended, for example where a restriction or notice was applied for.[83] In keeping with the principles of electronic record keeping, this is no longer a requirement.

DISPOSITIONS OF REGISTERED LAND

1. The Owner's Powers of Disposition

The Land Registration Act 2002 does not curtail the powers of the owner of registered land. **5–036** Indeed it expressly provides in s.23 that the registered proprietor, or a person entitled to be registered as proprietor,[84] has:

---

[82] Land Registration Act 2002 Sch.10 para.4. The previous statutory provision was Land Registration Act 1925 s.63.
[83] Land Registration Act 1925 s.65 and s.64(1). This matter is now to be determined by rules to be made under the Land Registration Act 2002: see Sch.10 para.4(c), but the Land Registration Rules 2003 do not require the land certificate to be submitted when a charge is registered or when an application is made for an agreed notice to be registered.
[84] Land Registration Act 2002 s.24.

"power to make a disposition of any kind permitted by the general law in relation to an interest of that description . . ."

The only exception to the generality of that power is that although the registered proprietor can "charge the estate at law with the payment of money", he cannot do this by way of a mortgage by demise or by sub-demise, but only by way of a charge by way of legal mortgage[85] which must then be registered as a registered charge.

2. Requirement of Registration

5–037   Although the 2002 Act does not restrict the powers of an owner, it does impose an obligation to register certain dispositions or dealings with the registered land. The dealings required to be registered are called registrable dispositions. A failure to register has a number of consequences. First, the registration of a registrable disposition gives it priority over certain earlier rights. A failure to register means that this right to priority will be lost. Second, registration confers priority for the registrable disposition over all subsequent rights. Again, a failure to register will mean that this automatic protection is lost. Thirdly, a failure to register means that the disposition "does not operate at law".[86] In other words, it creates only equitable rights. Where the transaction is for valuable consideration, these rights will arise by virtue of a specifically enforceable contract, provided that any necessary formalities have been observed.[87] Where the transaction is voluntary, the disposition may nevertheless be considered effective in equity where the grantor has completed all that is required on his part for an effective transfer,[88] or where the grantor is estopped from denying that the transfer has become effective.[89] Finally, the failure to complete a transfer by registration means that the previous registered proprietor continues to appear on the register as proprietor. As such, he continues to be able to exercise owner's powers, and may therefore create rights which, although subsequent in time to the registrable disposition, may themselves be registrable dispositions and so take priority over it. This is known as the "registration gap".

3. What Dispositions are Registrable?

5–038   The list of registrable dispositions is contained in s.27 of the Act. Not surprisingly, transfers of the registered estate must be completed by registration.[90] Expressly created easements

---

[85] Land Registration Act 2002 s.23(1). See Ch.17 for the means by which it is possible to create mortgages. It should be noted that the prohibition in s.23 on the way in which legal mortgages or charges of registered land can be created does not affect the creation of equitable mortgages or charges.

[86] Land Registration Act 2002 s.27(1).

[87] Since all registrable dispositions are legal interests, they can be created only by deed: see Law of Property Act 1925 s.52. Since the formality requirements for a deed include all of the requirements for a contract (except for the need to incorporate all the agreed terms), it will be rare that a deed does not automatically satisfy the requirements for an enforceable contract, even where there is no separate written contract: see Law of Property (Miscellaneous Provisions) Act 1989.

[88] See *Mascall v Mascall* (1985) 50 P. & C.R. 119; *Brown & Root Technology Ltd v Sun Alliance and London Assurance Co Ltd* [2001] Ch.33; Dowling (1999) 50 N.I.L.Q. 90.

[89] See Pearce and Stevens, *The Law of Trusts and Equitable Obligations* (4th edn) pp.177–178.

[90] Land Registration Act 2002 s.27(2)(a).

must also be registered,[91] as must expressly created rentcharges.[92] So must charges by way of legal mortgage.[93] In addition, newly granted leases must be completed by registration if they are[94]:

    (i) for more than seven years; or

    (ii) they take effect in possession more than three months from the date of their grant; or

    (iii) they are for discontinuous periods; or

    (iv) they fall within certain provisions of the Housing Act 1985; or

    (v) they are leases of a franchise or manor.[95]

The registration will take effect by means of the appropriate entry in the register of the registered estate concerned, and in cases where this is applicable (for instance in the case of the grant of leases), the creation of a new registered estate or title.[96]

4. Dispositions other than Registrable Dispositions

There is a wide range of rights which the registered proprietor can create but which do not **5–039** fall within the category of registrable dispositions. This includes, for instance, express trusts of the land, contracts for the sale or disposition of an interest in the land, equitable grants of easements, equitable mortgages, contractual licences, and restrictive covenants. It is, in addition, possible for rights to arise without an express grant or contract. Thus easements can be acquired through prescription, and rights to possession through adverse possession. Finally, rights may arise informally through resulting or constructive trusts or through the operation of the doctrine of proprietary estoppel. The registered land system, since it does not restrict the powers of a registered proprietor, must be capable of accommodating all of these rights, and any new rights that may be created.

    The way in which the system accommodates these rights is, first by recognising the existence of an unfettered variety of rights. Second, it provides a method for recording the existence of rights on the register. Finally, it provides what is intended to be a comprehensive set of rules for determining the priority of rights where two or more rights come into conflict. The Land Registration Act 2002 achieves this through the overlapping application of rules governing three categories of right: minor interests, overriding interests, and overreachable interests. It should be noted, however, that the registered land system should be seen as a whole, and it is not possible fully to understand the operation of the system in relation to any of these categories of right without understanding how the rules apply to other categories.

[91] Land Registration Act 2002 s.27(2)(d).
[92] Land Registration Act 2002 s.27(2)(e).
[93] Land Registration Act 2002 s.27(2)(f).
[94] Land Registration Act 2002 s.27(2)(b).
[95] Land Registration Act 2002 s.27(2)(c).
[96] Land Registration Act 2002 Sch.2.

PROTECTING MINOR INTERESTS

5–040   As was noted above, one consequence of the introduction of a system of registration of title is that third party interests affecting the land can be recorded on the register of title of the land to which they relate. A prospective purchaser should thus be able to discover whether there are any such interests affecting the land merely by looking at the register. Under the Land Registration Act 1925 third party interests affecting land which could not be registered as independent tiles were termed minor interests, and the owners of such interests were able to protect them on the register by entering a caution, notice, inhibition or restriction. The Land Registration Act 2002 has reformed the means by which such interests may be protected on the register, and it is now only possible to protect such interests by entering a notice or a restriction. In very general terms a restriction will be the appropriate means of protecting a beneficial interest arising under a trust, whilst most other forms of interest will be protected by means of a notice.

1.   Protecting an Interest by Entering a Notice

(a)   *What is a Notice?*

5–041   A notice is defined by s.31(1) of the Land Registration Act 2002 as "an entry in the register in respect of the burden of an interest affecting a registered estate or charge." Since interests created by a registrable disposition will have to be completed by registration, the entry of a notice will only be appropriate for the protection of interests which are not created by means of a registrable disposition. A notice will therefore be appropriate for the protection of equitable interests, such as equitable leases, easements or restrictive covenants, or of an estate contract affecting the land, for example an option to purchase or a right of pre-emption arising from a contract. Section 33 expressly stipulates that certain interests cannot be protected by the entry of a notice in the register. The most important of these excluded rights are a beneficial interest arising under a trust of land and a lease for a term of less than three years.[97]

(b)   *Procedure for Entering a Notice*

5–042   Any person who claims to be entitled to the benefit of an interest affecting the registered land may apply to the registrar for the entry of a notice in the register in respect of the interest.[98] A notice may take the form either of an agreed notice or a unilateral notice. An agreed notice may only be entered if the applicant is the registered proprietor, the registered proprietor consents

---

[97] s.33 also excludes a settlement under the Settled Land Act 1925, a restrictive covenant made between a lessor and lessee of land, an interest capable of being registered under the Commons Registration Act 1965, and an interest in any coal or coal mine.
[98] Land Registration Act 2002 s.34(1).

to the entry of the notice, or the registrar is satisfied of the validity of the applicants claim to the interest in question.[99] A unilateral notice may be entered without the consent of the registered proprietor, but the registrar must give notice of the entry to the registered proprietor,[100] and the unilateral notice entered in the register must indicate that it is unilateral and identify the beneficiary of the notice.[101] The fact that a notice is identified as unilateral in nature will indicate that the validity of the beneficiary's interest has not been established and accepted. The registered proprietor of land is entitled to apply to the registrar for the cancellation of a unilateral notice, but the registrar must first give the beneficiary of the notice an opportunity to oppose its cancellation.[102]

(c) The Effect of Entering a Notice

Where an interest is protected on the register by the entry of a notice, it will enjoy priority over any subsequently created interests in the land. In particular a person who subsequently acquires an interest in the land by means of a registered disposition will acquire his interest subject to the interest which is protected by the notice.   **5–043**

2. Protecting an Interest by Entering a Restriction

(a) What is a Restriction?

A restriction is defined by s.40(1) as "an entry in the register regulating the circumstances in which a disposition of a registered estate or charge may be subject of an entry in the register". The entry of a restriction prevents the proprietor of the land making a disposition which would require registration. The restriction may prohibit such transactions either indefinitely,[103] for a specified period of time,[104] or until the occurrence of a specified event,[105] for example the giving of notice, the obtaining of consent or the making of an order by the court or registrar.[106]   **5–044**

Restrictions are particularly important for protecting beneficial interests in land arising under a trust since, as was noted above, such interests cannot be protected by means of a notice. Where land is held on trust a restriction may be entered by the registrar which prevents the proprietor making a registered disposition, for example transferring on sale or granting a mortgage, unless overreaching takes place. In other words the restriction will have the effect of ensuring that any capital moneys arising from the transaction are paid to two trustees of the legal title.

---

[99] Land Registration Act 2002 s.34(3). Land Registration Rules 2003 r.81.
[100] Land Registration Act 2002 s.35(1). Land Registration Rules 2003 r.89.
[101] Land Registration Act 2002 s.35 (2)(a).
[102] Land Registration Act 2002 s.36.
[103] Land Registration Act 2002 s.40(2)(b)(i).
[104] Land Registration Act 2002 s.40(2)(b)(ii).
[105] Land Registration Act 2002 s.40(2)(b)(iii).
[106] Land Registration Act 2002 s.40(3). Land Registration Rules 2003 Sch.4 sets out the standard forms of restriction.

(b) *Procedure for Entering a Restriction*

5–045 Section 42(1) provides that the registrar may only enter a restriction on the register if it appears to him that it is necessary or desirable to do so for the purpose of:

(a) preventing invalidity or unlawfulness in relation to dispositions of a registered estate or charge;

(b) securing that interests which are capable of being overreached on a disposition of a registered estate or charge are overreached; or

(c) protecting a right or claim in relation to a registered estate or charge.

A restriction cannot, however, be used as a means of protecting the priority of an interest which could have been protected by the entry of a notice.[107] A restriction can only be entered on the application of the registered proprietor,[108] with the consent of the registered proprietor,[109] of by a person who has "a sufficient interest in making the entry".[110] Where an application for the entry of a restriction is made without the consent of the registered proprietor, the registrar must give the registered proprietor notice of the application and of the right to object to it.[111]

---

[107] Land Registration Act 2002 s.42(2).
[108] Land Registration Act 2002 s.43(1)(a).
[109] Land Registration Act 2002 s.43(1)(b).
[110] Land Registration Act 2002 s.43(1)(c).
[111] Land Registration Act 2002 s.45(1).

Chapter 6

ALTERATIONS TO THE REGISTER: RECTIFICATION AND INDEMNITY

1. Potential Alteration of the Register

At the heart of the system of land registration is the idea that the land is owned by the person(s) who are registered as the proprietor(s) and that this title is good against all the world, so that a person seeking to acquire ownership or an interest in the land can be confident that he or she is transacting with the person(s) entitled to make dispositions of the land. It has already been noted that registration with absolute title is sufficient to constitute the person so registered proprietor, with ownership that is good against the entire world,[1] even if his title prior to registration was defective. It is possible for the wrong person to be registered as proprietor, either as the consequence of deliberate fraud, or as a consequence of mistake. In such a situation, given the effect of registration, the interests of the true owner are defeated by the registration. It is also possible for matters other than proprietorship to be incorrectly recorded, either by the inclusion of erroneous matters, or by the omission of matters which should appear on the register. The Land Registration Act 2002 contains provision for the register to be corrected in such eventualities. Such correction is technically called alteration, apart from the special situation in which an alteration involves the correction of a mistake and prejudicially affects the title of a registered proprietor. In that latter situation alone, an alteration is called rectification.[2]

6–001

---

[1] Land Registration Act 2002 ss.11, 12 and 58.
[2] Land Registration Act 2002 Sch.4 para.1. Prior to the 2002 Act, the term rectification was used for all alterations of the register. The reason for changing the terminology is not clear, but reflects the special restrictions on alterations which affect the title of a proprietor in possession.

2. Potential Indemnity

6–002 Inaccuracies in the register can potentially cause loss. In a limited range of circumstances an indemnity, or compensation, is payable by the Land Registry. These circumstances include where loss is caused by a rectification (but not by an alteration) of the register and where loss is caused by a mistake which would require rectification for its correction.

3. Jurisdiction to Alter the Register

(a) *Circumstances in which Alteration is Possible*

6–003 Schedule 4 to the Land Registration Act 2002 provides that the register may be altered by order of the court or at the discretion of the registrar[3]:

> "for the purpose of
>
>   (a) correcting a mistake;
>   (b) bringing the register up to date; or
>   (c) giving effect to any estate, right or interest excepted from the effect of registration."

In addition, the registrar has authority to remove a superfluous entry.[4]

   Where the amendment of the register amounts to a rectification, in other words an amendment which corrects a mistake and which prejudicially affects the title of a registered proprietor, then it is possible for the amendment to have prospective effect by changing the priority of any interest affecting the registered estate.[5]

(b) *Bringing the Register Up To Date*

6–004 Entries on the register may no longer accurately reflect the legal position. For instance, a lease noted on the register may have been terminated by forfeiture proceedings, or it may be determined in court proceedings that an option to purchase registered land noted on the register is unenforceable. Similarly, new rights may have arisen which are enforceable for the benefit of or against the land, but which are not recorded on the register. This might include an easement which has been acquired through prescription. Altering the register in order accurately to reflect these matters is an administrative alteration bringing the register up to date, but having no effect upon the legal position.

---

[3] Land Registration Act 2002 Sch.4 paras 2(1) and 5(1); Land Registration Rules 2003 r.126
[4] Land Registration Act 2002 Sch.4, para.5(1)(d); *Stein v Stein* [2004] EWHC 3212, removal of a superfluous restriction.
[5] Land Registration Act 2002 Sch.4 para.8.

(c) Giving Effect to any Estate, Right or Interest Excepted from the Effect of Registration

It is possible that when land was first registered, the title deeds contained reference to a document which the person applying for registration was for some reason unable to supply. In such a situation, if the registrar considered the matter sufficiently important to create a significant reservation about title, registration may have been granted with qualified title, reserving any matters that might be disclosed by the missing document. If evidence of the missing document later came to light, disclosing that the land was subject to defined restrictive covenants, the register could be altered to reflect these matters which had been excepted from the effect of registration. Again, this is an administrative matter which does not affect legal rights.

6–005

(d) Alteration for the Purpose of Correcting Mistakes

The correction of a mistake is much more likely to have an impact upon legal rights, although this will not necessarily be the case. It is possible for an administrative error to have occurred, either on the part of a solicitor prior to the submission of documents for registration, or on the part of the Land Registry, as a result of which a minor interest has been noted against the wrong registered estate. The statutory provision allows alteration to delete the entry against the wrong estate and to add it to the correct estate. If at the time when the alteration is made no further transaction has taken place affecting either registered estate, no loss will have been caused by the mistake or by its alteration. A failure to record a minor interest against the correct estate could, however, have adverse consequences since it would deprive the minor interest of protected priority. Suppose that Derek, the registered proprietor of 57 London Road, granted an option to sell the house to Eric, who applied to the Land Registry to register a notice of the option. If, as a result of an error at the Land Registry, the option was not recorded against the title of 57 London Road, the option would not be enforceable against Francis if he later purchased the house from Derek and became registered as proprietor. In such a case, however, an indemnity would be payable to Eric if the register was not altered to give effect to his rights.[6]

6–006

(e) Meaning of "Mistake"

The Land Registration Act 2002 provides no guidance as to what constitutes a mistake affecting the register. The Law Commission has suggested that there might be cases where there is no mistake in the register even if it fails accurately to mirror the position relating to title prior to registration. For instance, if a person had acquired title to land by adverse possession, but

6–007

---

[6] An indemnity is payable by the Land Registry for mistakes the correction of which would require a rectification of the register (i.e. an alteration prejudicially affecting the title of a registered proprietor such as Francis). Oddly, it seems that there is no provision in the Act for indemnity if the registered disposition creates only a lease which is not capable of independent registration, for in such a case the alteration of the register would not prejudicially affect a registered proprietor.

was not at the date of first registration in actual occupation of it, under the rules relating to first registration, the rights of the adverse possessor are binding on a registered proprietor only if the registered proprietor had notice of them. According to the Law Commission, the adverse possessor would not be able to seek alteration of the register because "there is . . . no mistake in the register that requires rectification".[7] The logic is that the rights of the adverse possessor have been affected, not by the failure to record them in the register, but by the operation of the rules contained in Land Registration Act 2002. If this logic is followed, it is hard to see how there could ever be a situation in which it could be said that the wrong person has been registered as proprietor of the legal estate because of the curative effect of s.58 of the Act under which even if the wrong person is registered as proprietor, the legal estate is deemed to have vested in him. In order to give the provisions of the Act a sensible effect in relation to the correction of mistakes, a common sense interpretation of that phrase will be required. As will be seen, because indemnity is in most cases only available in situations in which mistakes have occurred, it is desirable for the concept of mistake to be interpreted broadly rather than narrowly.

Cases decided prior to the Land Registration Act 2002 considered different provisions and must therefore be treated with caution. Nevertheless, *Norwich and Peterborough Building Society v Steed*[8] provides an illustration which is worth considering. Derek Steed was the registered proprietor of a house in London, which had been purchased with the aid of a loan from a local authority which was protected in the charges register. Derek's mother, sister and her husband also lived at the house. Derek emigrated to California and granted his mother a power of attorney in relation to the house. A transfer was then executed, purportedly by Mrs Steed, transferring the title into the names of Derek's sister and her husband, who purchased the property with the help of a building society mortgage which was protected as a registered legal charge. The mortgage payments fell into arrears and the building society sought repossession. When Derek returned he joined the proceedings for possession and claimed that he was entitled to rectification of the register as against his sister and her husband and the building society, contending that his mother's signature on the transfer was a forgery. Eventually the forgery allegation was dropped and Derek instead claimed that his mother had not known what she was signing and that the transfer was void on grounds of *non est factum*. Knox J. held that the transfer was not void but voidable because of the fraud that had been perpetrated, and he ordered that the register be rectified to restore Derek as the registered proprietor, but he did not order rectification against the building society by removal of their charge. The Court of Appeal held that the *non est factum* plea should fail for lack of evidence and that the exercise of the power of attorney was not *ultra vires*. There was no doubt that the transfer was induced by the sister's fraud and the question was whether this entitled Derek to rectification against the building society. The most relevant provision was s.82(1)(h) of the Land Registration Act 1925. This provided that amendment to the register was possible "in any other case where, by reason of any error or omission in the register, or by reason of any entry made under a mistake, it may be deemed just to rectify the register." Scott L.J. rejected the

---

[7] Law Com. No.271, para.3.47. If this analysis is correct, the Land Registration Act 2002 reverses *Chowood Ltd v Lyall* [1930] 2 Ch. 156 where the Court of Appeal ordered rectification where the plaintiffs had been registered as the first proprietors of land they had purchased and the defendant, who was the neighbouring landowner, had previously become entitled by adverse possession of two narrow strips of woodland.

[8] [1993] Ch. 116.

view that there was a general power to rectify the register and instead held that there had to be some "error or omission" in the register or some "entry made under a mistake" in order for an amendment to the register to be possible. Since the building society's charge was not registered against the property by virtue of an error or mistake of any kind there was no ground for rectification under para.(h).

(f) *Mistakes by the Registrar*

There can be little doubt that mistakes made within the Land Registry can be corrected by means of alterations to the register. Although decided under previous legislation, the result in *Freer v Unwins*[9] would almost certainly be the same. The plaintiffs were the freeholders of a tobacconist shop and the defendant was the lessee of a separate shop in the same parade. The plaintiffs' shop enjoyed the benefit of a restrictive covenant affecting the shop leased by the defendant, preventing its use for the sale of tobacco. The burden of this covenant was protected against the freeholders of the defendant's shop under the Land Charges Act 1925. When title to the shops was registered, the title of the shop occupied by the defendants did not show the burden of the restrictive covenant. The Land Registrar subsequently rectified the register so that the burden of the restrictive covenant appeared against the freehold to the defendant's land.[10] It is worth noting, however, that the court held that, since the covenant did not appear on the register on the date when the lease was granted, the lessees did not take the lease subject to the restrictive covenant. The effect of this decision was that the covenant was binding upon the freehold of the shop but not on the lessees for the duration of the lease. **6–008**

(g) *Registration Procured by Fraud*

It is not entirely clear whether registration procured by fraud can be corrected by means of alteration of the register. The previous statutory provisions contained an express rule relating to registration obtained by fraud. For instance in *Re Leighton's Conveyance*[11] the plaintiff claimed rectification of the register when her daughter had obtained a transfer of the registered title into her name by fraudulently misrepresenting the nature of documents that she asked her to sign. The daughter subsequently mortgaged the property and the mortgagee's interests were effected as registered charges. Luxmore J., applying the provision relating to registration obtained by fraud, ordered rectification of the register so that the plaintiff was inserted as the owner of the land with absolute title, but there was no interference with the registered charges which remained enforceable against the property. By contrast, in *Nouri v Marvi*[12] the owner had gone abroad leaving another in occupation. That person fraudulently caused themselves to be registered as proprietor and then transferred the property to an innocent third party. Rich J. held that **6–009**

---

[9] [1976] Ch. 288; [1976] C.L.J. 215 (Hayton); (1976) 30 Conv. 304 (Crane); (1976) 92 L.Q.R. 338.

[10] It should be noted that this rectification was probably inconsistent with s.82(3) of the Land Registration Act 1925, which protected the rights of a proprietor in possession, but the freeholder did not appeal against it.

[11] [1936] 1 All E.R. 1033.

[12] [2005] EWHC 2996.

it would be unjust to order rectification against the third party as the claimant had not monitored the position of the title and thus prevented the involvement of third parties.

It cannot be predicted with certainty whether the same result would apply under the legislation currently in force. In one sense, a registration obtained by fraud constitutes a mistake. Had the registrar been aware of the fraud, the disposition so secured would never have been registered. If the registration of the daughter in *Re Leighton's Conveyance* were a mistake, then it would surely also follow that the registration of the charges was a mistake, for although the creation of the charges would fall within the owner's powers exercisable by the registered proprietor, that person should never have been registered as proprietor. This is not, however, the only possible view. The registrar could be said to be acting entirely properly in acting upon a disposition which on its face appears to be in order, both in registering the daughter and subsequently in registering the charges.[13] It would be regrettable if this latter view were adopted, for the consequence, although maintaining the sanctity of the register, would be to allow the process of registration to be used as an instrument of fraud.

(h) *Rectification Affecting the Title of a Registered Proprietor*

6–010   There are limits upon amendments of the register which correct mistakes and which prejudicially affect the title of a registered proprietor in possession.

(i) Title of Registered Proprietor is not Prejudicially Affected

6–011   Not every amendment of the register which affects the title of a registered proprietor causes a prejudice. The amendment may merely give effect to rights which are already binding upon the registered proprietor. The case of *Hodgson v Marks*[14] provides an example. In this case Mr Evans, a lodger, persuaded Mrs Hodgson to transfer her house into his name on the basis that she would remain the beneficial owner. He then, in breach of trust, sold the house to Mr and Mrs Marks. Mrs Hodgson remained living in the house throughout. If the Land Registration Act 2002 were to apply to these facts, then Mrs Hodgson would be entitled to be reregistered as proprietor, even though it would entail deleting the names of Mr and Mrs Marks as registered proprietors. The actual occupation of Mrs Evans would mean that her rights would be binding on them as an overriding interest.

(ii) Registered Proprietor in Possession

6–012   Where an amendment of the register is for the purpose of correcting a mistake and which will cause a prejudice to a registered proprietor who is in possession, the Land Registration Act 2002 provides that rectification is possible only if the registered proprietor consents, or has

---

[13] A view which is arguably supported by *Norwich and Peterborough Building Society v Steed* [1993] Ch. 116.
[14] [1971] Ch. 892.

"by fraud or lack of proper care caused or substantially contributed to the mistake" for which rectification is sought, or "it would for any other reason be unjust for the alteration not to be made".[15] A failure by the registered proprietor to investigate his title properly before applying for registration could deprive him of protection. In *Re 139 Deptford High Street*[16] Wynn-Parry J. held that a person who had been registered as the first proprietor of land including a small plot belonging to the British Transport Commission was not entitled to the protection against rectification because he had contributed to the error by putting forward an application for registration containing the error, despite the fact that his mistake was completely innocent. However, this decision was made under an earlier provision and the current provisions require a lack of proper care by the registered proprietor.

Cases decided under previous legislation may provide some guidance as to when it would be unjust not to make an alteration. In *Chowood v Lyall*[17] Luxmore J. held that it would be unjust not to rectify where otherwise a person who was entitled to land by adverse possession would be deprived of his ownership. However, in *Epps v Esso Petroleum*[18] Templeman J. held that it would not have been unjust to refuse rectification against the registered proprietor. The defendants had purchased land and were registered as first proprietors of it and a strip of frontage previously conveyed to the predecessors in title of the plaintiffs. When the land was conveyed to the plaintiffs they were registered as proprietors of the same strip of frontage, so that there was a double registration. Templeman J. held that since the plaintiffs' vendor had taken the land subject to a covenant to build a wall marking the boundary, which they had failed to fulfil, it would not be unjust to refuse rectification of the defendants' title, thus depriving them of ownership of the strip of land. He noted that there was "nothing on the register or on the ground on or before the date when the defendants became the registered proprietors of the disputed strip which put [them] on inquiry" and that the plaintiffs should have been aware of a potential dispute concerning the boundary from their vendor's documents of title. In *London Borough of Hounslow v Hare*[19] Knox J. similarly held that a refusal to rectify would not be unjust. The defendant was granted a 125-year lease of a flat which was protected on the title of the freehold to which it related and was also independently registered as a title at the Land Registry. The lease should not have been granted, since the land was owned by a charity and the consent of the Commissioners had not been obtained as required by s.29(1) of the Charities Act 1960. Knox J. took into account the fact that the plaintiff was entirely innocent and noted the effect that registration would have upon the nature of her interests[20]:

> "What I primarily . . . have to look at is whether it is considered that it would be unjust not to rectify the register against Miss Hare and I cannot reach that conclusion. She has been in possession of this property for a very long time . . . it seems to me that when one is dealing with a person's home the change from the near equivalent of a freehold that a 125 year lease gives to somebody of that age nearing forty to that of a tenant, assured or not, is one

[15] Land Registration Act 2002 Sch.4 paras 3 and 6.
[16] [1951] Ch. 884.
[17] [1930] 2 Ch. 156.
[18] [1973] 2 All E.R. 465.
[19] (1992) 24 H.L.R. 9; [1993] Conv. 224.
[20] (1992) 24 H.L.R. 9 at 27.

of very considerable significance. That feature does, in my judgment, far outweigh any financial considerations that there may be the other way."[21]

A case considering whether it would be unjust to rectify the register against a proprietor in possession under the 2002 Act is *Sainsbury's Supermarkets Ltd v Olympia Homes Ltd*.[22] Sainsbury's had an option over neighbouring land to acquire part of it for a roundabout for public access to their new outlet. The land was sold to Olympia but the sale was such as to pass only an equitable interest.[23] Sainsbury's had not registered their option but as it had been created before Olympia's equitable interest it took priority in principle. However, Olympia was mistakenly registered as proprietors of the legal estate. Sainsbury's claimed rectification of the register, because otherwise their option would be defeated. Although Olympia was in possession of the land, it was held that it would be unjust not to rectify the register:

> "The whole basis on which Olympia acquired the . . . site was that land would be taken from it for the purposes of the roundabout. Were the register not to be rectified then it would have acquired a windfall which would be potentially very significant indeed."[24]

(iii)   Registered Proprietor not in Possession

6–013   Even if an amendment to the register amounts to a rectification prejudicially affecting the title of a registered proprietor, if the proprietor is not in possession of the property, the court or the registrar must follow the normal rule that the alteration should be made to correct a mistake "unless there are exceptional circumstances which justify not making the alteration".[25] In *Derbyshire C C v Fallon*[26] Chrstopher Nugee Q.C. found that the circumstances were sufficiently exceptional to justify refusing the alteration of a boundary line that had been wrongly drawn. The respondent proprietors had built on the land with no objection by the appellants and had made attempts to resolve the boundary dispute.

(iv)   Reform of Alterations and Rectification

6–014   The provisions in the Land Registration Act 2002 relating to alteration reflect the recommendations of the Law Commission. The consultation document, *Land Registration for the Twenty-First Century*, suggested that, whilst the then current law "works without undue difficulty in practice", there were defects in drafting which should be corrected in the interests of attaining

---

[21] In *Pinto v Lim* [2005] EWHC 630, a case under the 1925 Act, the court refused rectification against a proprietor in possession following a forged transfer into the sole name of one of two co-owners, who then transferred to a purchaser. Influential factors were the length of time the purchaser had been in possession, the absence in the purchaser of awareness of any wrongdoing at the material time, and the comparatively small size of the claimant's interest.
[22] [2005] EWHC 1235; [2006] 1 P. & C.R. 17; Dixon [2005] Conv. 447–459.
[23] It was sold by a chargee of the equitable estate.
[24] Per Mann J., para.95, Olympia were registered as subject to Sainsbury's option; Dixon [2005] Conv. 447–459; Also *James Hay Pension Trustees Ltd v Cooper Estates Ltd* [2005] EWHC 36.
[25] Land Registration Act 2002 Sch.4 paras 3(3) and 6(3); Land Registration Rules 2003 r.126.
[26] [2007] EWHC 1326.

greater certainty. It is regrettable that the form of the legislation which has resulted continues to contain defects in drafting which leave the scope of alteration and rectification unclear.

4. Circumstances Where an Indemnity is Payable

(a) *Indemnity not always Payable*

The circumstances where an indemnity is payable are set out in Sch.8 of the Land Registration Act 2002. It should be noted that an indemnity or compensation is not payable in every situation where the Land Registry has made an error or the register is inaccurate. The principal situations in which an indemnity is payable are set out below. In addition there are certain other situations where an indemnity is payable, for instance where documents lodged at the registry have been lost or destroyed.[27] **6–015**

(b) *Rectification of the Register*

The first situation where an indemnity is payable is where a person suffers loss by reason of a rectification of the register.[28] It will be recalled that rectification is the correction of a mistake which prejudicially affects the title of a registered proprietor.[29] If the register is merely altered, for instance to give effect to an overriding interest, then no indemnity is payable. There are two reasons. The first is that an alteration is not rectification. The other is that the alteration has caused no loss. The registered proprietor would in any event have been subject to the overriding interest. It also follows that because no indemnity is payable for alterations to the register other than rectifications, no indemnity would be payable if, for instance, the registration of an easement is deleted. **6–016**

(c) *Failure to Rectify the Register*

An indemnity is also payable for "a mistake whose correction would involve rectification of the register".[30] Thus, for instance, if owing to a Land Registry error, a registered charge had not been registered, and the registered proprietor had sold the property to an innocent purchaser who moved into possession, it is unlikely that the register would be rectified to disclose the charge. The register could only be rectified in a case such as this either with the consent of the registered proprietor or if there is some other substantial reason which would make it unjust not to rectify the register. In consequence of the mistake, the chargee has suffered loss, and the correction of the mistake to avoid this loss would have involved rectification. This loss would be subject to indemnity. **6–017**

---

[27] For the list of situations where an indemnity is payable see Land Registration Act 2002 Sch.8 para.1.
[28] Land Registration Act 2002 Sch.8 para.1(1)(a).
[29] See also Land Registration Act 2002 Sch.8 para.11(2).
[30] Land Registration Act 2002 Sch.8 para.1(1)(b).

(d) *Mistakes in Searches etc.*

6–018 An indemnity is payable for losses arising from mistakes (whether of commission or omission[31]) in an official search, an official copy, in copy documents retained by the registrar and referred to in the register.[32]

(e) *Forgeries*

6–019 An indemnity is payable to a person who suffers loss by reason of the rectification of the register to correct a registration obtained as a result of a forgery where that person is the proprietor of a registered estate or charge claiming in good faith under the forged disposition.[33] Suppose that Drake is the registered proprietor of Meadow Cottage. Whilst he is overseas on a two-year expatriate assignment he rents the house to Gosling. Gosling forges Drake's signature on a transfer of Meadow Cottage to himself. He then mortgages the property to Mallard Bank Plc. Mallard Bank Plc would be entitled to an indemnity if, on Drake's return from his overseas posting, the register is rectified to restore Drake to the register. It should be noted that this provision for indemnity would not apply if instead of granting a mortgage, Gosling had granted a short lease to Coote. Coote might be able to assert a claim to indemnity by reason of having suffered loss by reason of the rectification of the register, but the special provision for forgeries applies only to the proprietor of a registered estate or charge. This limitation appears to have no logical foundation.

(f) *Claimant's Fraud or Lack of Proper Care*

6–020 A claimant is not entitled to any indemnity if he has caused or contributed to a loss by his own fraud. Where he has caused or contributed to a loss through a lack of proper care, then this will debar or reduce the indemnity as the case may be.[34] The same restriction applies to anyone whose predecessor in title caused or contributed to a loss through fraud or lack of care, unless the claimant derived title under a disposition for valuable consideration which has been registered or protected by an entry on the register.

(g) *Calculation of Indemnity*

6–021 The amount of an indemnity is normally the amount which the claimant has lost, but where that loss comprises the loss of an estate or interest, the amount is limited to the value of the

---

[31] Land Registration Act 2002 Sch.8, para.11(1).
[32] Land Registration Act 2002 Sch.8 paras 1(1)(c) to (e).
[33] Land Registration Act 2002 Sch.8 para.1(2)(b).
[34] Land Registration Act 2002 Sch.8 para.5.

estate or interest at the time of the rectification, or at the time of any mistake which has not been rectified.[35] This rule applies even though there may be no practical means by which the owner of the estate or interest concerned could have discovered that the mistake had taken place, and even though land values in the meantime may have increased by substantially more than the rate of interest payable.[36]

---

[35] Land Registration Act 2002 Sch.8 para.6.
[36] Interest can be paid on an indemnity payment, excluding periods where the claimant has not diligently pursued a claim: Land Registration Rules 2003 r.195.

Chapter 7

PRIORITY BETWEEN INTERESTS IN REGISTERED LAND

1. Introduction to Priorities

One major objective of the introduction of a system of land registration was to replace the doc- **7–001**
trine of notice as the mechanism determining issues of priority between competing interests in
land. Whilst this doctrine was founded on principles of justice and fairness, the concept of constructive notice was difficult to apply in practice. Under the doctrine of notice those acquiring an
interest in land bore the burden of establishing to their satisfaction that the land was not subject
to any pre-existing interests which would affect them by making reasonable inspections of the
land, in much the same way that the purchaser of a second-hand car bears the burden of ensuring that it is free from defects. In contrast the basic premise of land registration is that people who
are seeking to acquire an interest in the land should only have to examine the register in order to
establish whether the land is subject to any adverse interests. Under a system of land registration,
those who enjoy interests in land are required to take action to protect them by ensuring that they
are entered appropriately on the register. If they fail to do so a person who subsequently acquires
an interest in the land will take free from the unprotected interest. In practice this basic premise
has not been applied absolutely. This is a recognition that the owners of some rights and interests
in land cannot fairly be expected to take action to protect them by registration, for example where
they may not even realise that they have a right. The determination of priorities between competing interests in registered land will vary depending upon the nature of the interests concerned.

2. Overreaching of Beneficial Interests Behind a Trust

Not all issues of priority between interests affecting registered land are determined by the pro- **7–002**
visions of the Land Registration Act 2002. As was noted above, beneficial interests arising
where there is a trust of registered land are capable of being overreached in accordance with the

provisions of the Law of Property Act 1925. These provisions were discussed in detail in Chapter 3, and it should be remembered that they have the effect that beneficial interests affecting the land will be overreached if there is a conveyance, which includes the grant of a legal mortgage, by at least two trustees, to whom any capital moneys arising from the transaction are paid. Where overreaching takes place, the beneficial interests are eliminated from the land altogether with the consequence that they are incapable of gaining priority over any other interests. Issues of priority regarding the interests of the beneficiaries of a trust of registered land will therefore only arise where overreaching has not occurred, which will be the case where the land was owned by a sole registered proprietor, as was the case in *Willams & Glyn's Bank v Boland*[1] and *Abbey National v Cann*.[2]

3. The Basic Rule for Determining Priorities Between Interests in Registered Land

7–003   The starting point of the Land Registration Act 2002 is that priority between interests in registered land should be determined by the order of their creation, so that an earlier interest prima facie gains priority over a later interest. This general rule is stated in s.28, which provides that "the priority of an interest affecting a registered estate or charge is not affected by a disposition of the estate or charge",[3] and further that it makes no difference to the operation of this basic rule "whether the interest or disposition is registered".[4] However this basic rule is subject to significant qualifications in ss.29 and 30, which have the effect that in some circumstances an interest arising under a disposition will gain priority over previously created interests affecting the estate or charge.

4. Priority Accorded to Registered Dispositions Over Unprotected Interests

7–004   The general rule established in s.28 that priority between interests is determined by the order of their creation is reversed by s.29 in favour of registered dispositions. Section 29 of the Land Registration Act provides:

> "If a registrable disposition of a registered estate is made for valuable consideration, completion of the disposition by registration has the effect of postponing to the interest under the disposition any interest affecting the estate immediately before the disposition whose priority is not protected at the time of registration."

A registered disposition falling within s.29 will therefore take priority over earlier rights unless those earlier rights have protected priority. Section 29(2) identifies four circumstances in which an interest will enjoy protected priority:

---

[1] [1981] A.C. 487.
[2] [1991] 1 A.C. 56; Jackson, "Overreaching in Registered Land Law" (2006) 69 M.L.R. 214.
[3] Land Registration Act 2002 s.28(1).
[4] Land Registration Act 2002 s.28(2).

"(2) For the purposes of subsection (1), the priority of an interest is protected—

(a) in any case, if the interest—
   (i) is a registered charge or the subject of a notice in the register
   (ii) falls within any of the paragraphs of Schedule 3, or
   (iii) appears from the register to be excepted from the effect of registration, and
(b) in the case of a disposition of a leasehold estate, if the burden of the interest is incident to the estate."

The most important categories of interests which enjoy protected priority are those which have been protected by an entry on the register (s.2(a)(i)) and overriding interests (s.2(a)(ii)), which are defined in Sch.3 to the Act. These will be examined in detail below.

(a) *Requirements for Registered Dispositions to Take Priority Over Earlier Interests*

Section 29 specifies four requirements which must be satisfied before a registered disposition can gain priority over earlier interests which do not enjoy protected priority.   **7–005**

(i) The Disposition Must be of a Registered Estate

Section 29 only operates in relation to land which has already been registered. It has no application to unregistered land, even where the disposition is one for which registration is compulsory.   **7–006**

(ii) The Disposition Must be Made for Valuable Consideration

The section does not alter priorities where a disposition is not for valuable consideration. It does not apply, for instance, to succession on death, or to transfers by way of gift. Valuable consideration does not include marriage consideration, nor does it include a nominal consideration in money.[5] It is not clear what marks the difference between nominal consideration and valuable consideration. In *Peffer v Rigg*[6] it was held by Goulding J. that the sum of £1 constituted only nominal consideration for the purposes of a similar provision in the Land Registration Act 1925. However, in *Midland Bank Trust Co v Green*,[7] the House of Lords considered that the sum of £500 represented more than nominal consideration for the sale of a farm worth £40,000 on the open market. Lord Wilberforce stressed that "nominal consideration" was not synonymous with "inadequate" or even "grossly inadequate" consideration.[8] It is impossible to say whether the payment of £250, or £100, or £50, or £10, or £5 would have been regarded as nominal.   **7–007**

---

[5] Land Registration Act 2002 s.132(1).
[6] [1977] 1 W.L.R. 285.
[7] [1981] A.C. 513.
[8] [1981] A.C. 513 at 532.

(iii) The Disposition Must be a Registrable Disposition

7–008 The statutory variation to the ordinary priority rule applies only to those dealings which constitute registrable dispositions as set out in s.27. The section would not, therefore apply to an equitable mortgage created by means of a specifically enforceable contract. There are special provisions for legal leases, described below.

It was suggested in *Malory Enterprises Ltd v Cheshire Homes (UK) Ltd*[9] that a forged transfer would not qualify as a disposition, even where it was made in favour of an innocent third party. If this decision is correct, a distinction must be drawn between a case where Andrew forges a transfer of 77 High Street from Bernard directly to Patrick, when s.29 would not operate (since a forged transfer is not a disposition, even if for valuable consideration); by contrast if Andrew first forged a transfer of 77 High Street from Bernard to himself, and then sold to Patrick, s.29 would operate, since a sale by a registered proprietor (even where he had procured his registration illegally) would constitute a disposition for valuable consideration. This distinction is both surprising and hard to defend.

(iv) The Disposition Must be Completed by Registration

7–009 It is only once registration has taken place that s.29 operates. At present, of course, that requires that the transaction be first completed in the prescribed statutory form[10] and that it subsequently be submitted for registration. When electronic conveyancing is introduced, the two processes will be simultaneous.

(b) *The Special Position of Leases*

7–010 By s.29(4) the grant of a leasehold estate which does not constitute a registered disposition, for instance because it is for seven years or less, is treated as if it were a registered disposition and had actually been registered. Where it is granted for valuable consideration, it therefore benefits from the priority advantages of s.29 without the need for registration. Although the section does not state this explicitly, the use of the word "estate" implies that the lease must be a legal lease.[11] That means that to fall within the scope of s.29 it must have been granted by deed, or must take effect in possession for three years or less at a full market rent.[12]

(c) *The Irrelevance of Notice of Unprotected Interests*

7–011 As will be seen below, a person to whom a registered disposition is made will take subject to the interests of any occupier of the land concerned if he had actual knowledge of the

---

[9] [2002] EWCA Civ 151. The case was decided upon the basis that the registered proprietor had remained in occupation, and so had an overriding interest.
[10] Land Registration Act 2002 s.25.
[11] See Law of Property Act 1925 s.1(1) and (3).
[12] Law of Property Act 1925 s.54.

existence of the interest, since Sch.3 para.2(1)(c) of the Land Registration Act 2002 grants such an interest overriding status. However, outside of this limited context the doctrine of notice is irrelevant to the operation of s.29 of the Act. An interest affecting the estate will lose priority to a registered disposition if it was not protected at the time of registration even where the person to whom the registered disposition was made had actual knowledge of the existence of the unprotected interest. Whilst the Land Registration Act 1925 had seemingly also rendered the concept of notice irrelevant in relation to unprotected minor interests, in *Peffer v Rigg*[13] Goulding J. proposed an interpretation of the legislation which would have entailed its reintroduction. A house was purchased with money provided by Mr Peffer and Mr Rigg in the sole name of Mr Peffer, who was the registered proprietor, in order to provide a home for their mother-in-law. Mr Rigg therefore enjoyed a half share of the equitable ownership by way of a resulting trust. His beneficial interest was clearly a minor interest, but he took no steps to protect it on the register. Following a marital breakdown Mr Peffer transferred the title to his wife for £1. She was fully aware of the existence of Mr Rigg's trust interest at the time that the transaction took place. Under s.20(1) of the Land Registration Act 2002, which was the equivalent of s.29 of the Land Registration Act 2002, a transferee or grantee of a legal estate for valuable consideration would acquire the land free from any unprotected minor interests which were not otherwise overriding. In this case Mr Rigg had an unprotected minor interest which was not overriding under s.70(1)(g) because he was not in actual occupation of the land. Graham J. held that the term "transferee" in s.20(1) should be read to mean "purchaser", since this term was used in the parallel provision s.59(6), and that since a purchaser was defined as a "purchaser in good faith for valuable consideration", s.20 should also be subject to a requirement of good faith on the part of the transferee providing valuable consideration. He further concluded that a "transferee" could not be regarded as having acted in good faith where he purchased land knowing of the existence of an unprotected interest, thus reintroducing the concept of actual notice to issues of priority regarding unprotected minor interests. However this analysis was highly dubious and, in any event, merely obiter because he had also found that Mrs Peffer had in fact failed to provide valuable consideration and did not therefore gain the protection of s.20(1) at all. Despite appearing to achieve justice, there was no legitimate reason for equating the position of a "transferee or grantee" in s.20(1) with that of a "purchaser" in s.59(6). More importantly, even if a requirement of good faith were to be incorporated into s.20(1), there was no reason why it should be equated with the presence of "notice". Section 59(6) itself incorporated "good faith", because the term "purchaser" was used, but it also stated that notice was irrelevant, thus clearly refuting the suggestion that the absence of actual notice is synonymous with "good faith". Finally the decision was inconsistent with the underlying philosophy of registration, namely to render the doctrine of notice redundant, which was accepted by higher courts.[14] The new provisions of s.29 of the Land Registration Act 2002 do not employ language which could be interpreted in such a creative way, and it was the intention of the draftsmen to ensure that the concept of actual notice could not be reintroduced so as to protect the priority of an unprotected minor interest which was not otherwise overriding.[15]

---

[13] [1977] 1 W.L.R. 285.
[14] *Midland Bank Trust Co v Green* [1981] A.C. 513; *Williams & Glyn's Bank Ltd v Boland* [1981] A.C. 487.
[15] See Law Com. No.254, *Land Registration for the Twenty-First Century*, paras 3.44–3.50.

5. Protected Priority Accorded to Interests Entered on the Register

7–012   Section 29(2)(a)(i) grants statutory priority to any interests which have been protected on the register either as a registered charge or by means of the entry of a notice. Such interests cannot, therefore, lose their lose priority to a later interest.

6. Priority Accorded to Overriding Interests

(a) *What are Overriding Interests?*

7–013   Section 29(2)(a)(ii) grants statutory priority to any interest which "falls within any of the paragraphs of Sch.3". Schedule 3 specifies 14 categories of "unregistered interests which override registered dispositions". These interests are extremely important, because they gain priority over later interests even though they are not protected by any entry on the register. As such they are a significant exception to the "mirror" principle of land registration, and they have the effect that a potential purchaser of land cannot simply look at the register alone to satisfy himself of all possible adverse interests.[16]

(b) *Overriding Interests Under the Land Registration Act 1925*

7–014   Overriding interests were introduced by the Land Registration Act 1925, which provided that a purchaser of a legal estate would take the land subject to any overriding interests affecting it.[17] Although these categories no longer apply, they illustrate how the concept of overriding interests has developed and they are relevant in considering the leading cases under the Land Registration Act 1925, many of which are relevant in understanding the current legislation. Section 70(1) of the 1925 Act defined the interests which enjoyed overriding status:

> "All registered land shall, unless under the provisions of this Act the contrary is expressed on the register, be deemed to be subject to such of the following overriding interests as may be for the time being subsisting in reference thereto, and such interests shall not be treated as incumbrances within the meaning of this Act, that is to say—
>
> (a) rights of common, drainage rights, customary rights (until extinguished), public rights, profits a prendre, rights of sheepwalk, rights of way, watercourses, rights of water, and other easements not being equitable easements required to be protected by notice on the register;

---

[16] There is a duty imposed on a person seeking to register a disposition to "provide information to the registrar about any of the interests that fall within Schedule 3" of which he has actual knowledge and which affect the title. There are certain exceptions, e.g. a lease of less than one year, a trust interest. The registrar may then register the interest by way of notice: Land Registration Rules 2003 r.57.

[17] s.20(1)(b) Land Registration Act 1925.

(b) liability to repair highways by reason of tenure, quit-rents, Crown rents, heriots, and other rents and charges (until extinguished) having their origin in tenure;

(c) liability to repair the chancel of any church;

(d) liability in respect of embankments, and sea and river walls;

(e) . . . payments in lieu of tithe, and charges annuities payable for the redemption of tithe rentcharges;

(f) subject to the provisions of this Act, rights acquired or in course of being acquired under the Limitation Acts;

(g) the rights of every person in actual occupation of the land or in receipt of the rent and profits thereof, save where enquiry is made of such person and the rights are not disclosed;

(h) in the case of a possessory, qualified, or good leasehold title, all estates, rights, interests, and powers excepted from the effect of registration;

(i) rights under local land charges unless and until protected on the register in the proscribed manner;

(j) rights of fishing and sporting, seignorial and manorial rights of all descriptions (until extinguished), and franchises;

(k) leases granted for a term not exceeding twenty-one years;

(l) in respect of land registered before the commencement of this Act, rights to mines and minerals, and rights of entry, search, and user, and other rights and reservations incidental to or required for the purpose of giving full effect to the enjoyment of rights to mines and minerals or of property in mines and minerals, being rights which, where the title was first registered before the first date of January, eighteen hundred and ninety-eight, were created before that date, and where the title was first registered after the thirty-first day of December eighteen hundred and ninety-seven, were created before the date of first registration."

Although it may not be immediately apparent, this section provided for two different types of overriding interests.

(i) Specific Interests Enjoying Overriding Status

It is plain from s.70(1) of the Land Registration Act 1925 that the majority of paragraphs pro-   **7–015**
vided that specific interests were to enjoy overriding status by virtue simply of being interests of that description. For example, para.(k) accorded short leases overriding status. Similarly many of the other paragraphs stipulated that certain rights which burden the land were overriding interests. For example, in older villages it is relatively common for the most important properties to be subject to an obligation to repair the main part of the local parish church, an obligation which in the event of severe damage could be extremely onerous.[18] These rights are generally either of great civic importance, such as the obligation to upkeep sea walls, or those which it cannot be expected that the holder will protect, such as rights in the process of being acquired by adverse possession.

---

[18] In reality such obligations are generally fulfilled by means of an insurance policy taken out by all the landowners in the area who are so affected.

(ii) Other Interests Capable of Enjoying Overriding Status if the Relevant Statutory Criteria were Satisfied

7–016 As well as providing that certain specific interests were to have overriding status, s.70(1) also had the effect of conferring overriding status on the rights enjoyed by people who were in actual occupation of the land, or receiving rent and profits from it. Thus rights which would otherwise lose priority because they had not been protected on the register were elevated to overriding status if the statutory criteria of s.70(1)(g) were satisfied. This elevation of general rights affecting the land to overriding interests if coupled with actual occupation of the receipt of rents and profits was a very significant derogation from the mirror principle of registration. The impact of s.70(1)(g) was seen especially clearly in the context of trust interests in registered land, where the beneficiary would often be in actual occupation of the land. The decision of the House of Lords in *Williams & Glyn's Bank Ltd v Boland*[19] is the leading case, and the facts provide a very good illustration of the operation of overriding interests. Mr Boland was the sole registered proprietor of his matrimonial home, and he held it on trust for himself and his wife, who was entitled to a share of the equitable ownership by way of a resulting trust. He subsequently granted a mortgage of the house to a bank, which entered its charge on the register. Mr Boland was unable to keep up the necessary mortgage payments and the bank sought to repossess and sell the property. Mrs Boland argued that her equitable interest under a trust for sale was binding on the bank so that it was not entitled to possession. The House of Lords held that even though Mrs Boland's interest was a minor interest which had not been protected on the register of title, and that the bank was otherwise entitled to statutory priority under s.20(1) of the Land Registration Act 1925, she was a person who was in "actual occupation" of the land and her interest was therefore binding under s.70(1)(g).

(c) *Overriding Interests Under the Land Registration Act 2002*

7–017 The Land Registration Act 2002 retains the concept of overriding interests as interests which enjoy priority over later interests even though they have not been protected on the register. However the new legislation has reduced the number of specific interests which are accorded overriding status, and also reduced the scope of the protection conferred on the rights of the occupiers of land. Schedule 3 to the Act sets out the rights which constitute overriding interests. Because of their significance, these are set out in full:

> **"Unregistered interests which override registered dispositions**
> **Leasehold estates in land**
> 1. A leasehold estate in land granted for a term not exceeding seven years from the date of the grant, except for—
>   (a) a lease the grant of which falls within s.4(1)(d), (e) or (f);
>   (b) a lease the grant of which constitutes a registrable disposition.
>
> **Interests of persons in actual occupation**
> 2. An interest belonging at the time of the disposition to a person in actual occupation, so far as relating to land of which he is in actual occupation, except for—

---

[19] [1981] A.C. 487.

(a) an interest under a settlement under the Settled Land Act 1925;

(b) an interest of a person of whom inquiry was made before the disposition and who failed to disclose the right when he could reasonably have been expected to do so;

(c) an interest—

   (i) which belongs to a person whose occupation would not have been obvious on a reasonably careful inspection of the land at the time of the disposition, and

   (ii) of which the person to whom the disposition is made does not have actual knowledge at that time;

(d) a leasehold estate in land granted to take effect in possession after the end of the period of three months beginning with the date of the grant and which has not taken effect in possession at the time of the disposition.

Easements and profits à prendre

3. (1) A legal easement or profit à prendre, except for an easement or profit à prendre which is not registered under the Commons Registration Act 1964, which at the time of the disposition—

(a) is not within the actual knowledge of the person to whom the disposition is made, and

(b) would not have been obvious on a reasonably careful inspection of the land over which the easement or profit is exercisable.

(2) The exception in sub-paragraph (1) does not apply if he person entitled to the easement or profit proves that it has been exercised in the period of one year ending with the day of the disposition.

Customary and public rights

4. A customary right

5. A public right.

Local land charges

6. A local land charge

Mines and Minerals

7. An interest in any coal or coal mine, the rights attached to any such interest and the rights of any person under s.38, 49 or 51 of the Coal Industry Act 1994.

8. In the case of land to which title was registered before 1898, rights to mines and minerals (and incidental rights) created before 1898.

9. In the case of land to which title was registered between 1898 and 1925 inclusive, rights to mines and minerals (and incidental rights) created before the date of registration of the title.

Miscellaneous

10. A franchise.[20]

11. A manorial right.

---

[20] Interests 10–15 will no longer override registered dispositions after October 13, 2013: Harpum and Bignell, *Registered Land—Law and Practice under the Land Registration Act 2002* (2004), Jordans, pp.148–149, 467.

12. A right to a rent which was reserved to the Crown on the granting of any freehold estate (whether or not he right is still vested in the Crown).
13. A non-statutory right in respect of an embankment or sea or river wall.
14. A right to payment in lieu of a tithe.
15. A Right in respect of the repair of a church chancel.[21]

The overriding status of specific interests, such as leases for a term not exceeding seven years or easements and profits à prendre, will be examined in detail in the relevant sections of the book dealing with the interest in question. Here we will concentrate on the overriding status conferred on the rights of actual occupiers of the land.

(d) *Interests Capable of Enjoying Overriding Status Under Paragraph 2*

7–018 Paragraph 2 of Sch.3 replaces s.70(1)(g) of the Land Registration Act 1925 and confers overriding status on the interests of those who are in actual occupation of land. It is noteworthy that para.2 does not accord overriding status to the interests of those who are merely "in receipt of rent and profits" from the land. The case law interpreting and applying s.70(1)(g) remains relevant, as it helps to identify the interests which will be capable of enjoying overriding status and also to define what will constitute actual occupation.

(i) Only Interests in Land can Enjoy Overriding Status

7–019 Paragraph 2 of Sch.3 confers overriding status on an "interest" belonging to a person in actual occupation of the land. This language is slightly more precise than that of s.70(1)(g), which spoke of the "rights" of a person in actual occupation. It had already been held that s.70(1)(g) only operated in favour of proprietary rights in the land, so that the personal rights of an actual occupier were not given overriding status. In *Provincial Bank Ltd v Ainsworth*,[22] for example, the House of Lords held that the right of a wife to remain living in her matrimonial home even when she was not entitled to any share of the ownership was incapable of constituting an overriding interest. Lord Wilberforce rejected the argument that all "rights", irrespective of whether they were purely personal in character, were converted into binding overriding interests by the statute:

> "To ascertain what 'rights' come within this provision, one must look outside the Land Registration Act to see what rights affect purchasers under the general law. To suppose that the subsection makes any right, of howsoever a personal character, which a person in occupation may have, an overriding interest by which a purchaser is bound, would involve

---

[21] This paragraph was inserted by SI 2003/2431. It will cease to be overriding after October 13, 2013: Harpum and Bignell, *Registered Land—Law and Practice under the Land Registration Act 2002* (2004), Jordans, pp.148, 467. The Land Registration Bill 2001 included it but before the Bill had passed through Parliament the Court of Appeal decided that these interests contravened the European Convention on Human Rights: *Aston Cantlow and Wilmcote with Billesley Parochial Church Council v Wallbank and Another* [2002] Ch.51. Accordingly, the interest was removed from the Bill. It was reinstated when the House of Lords overturned this decision: *Aston Cantlow and Wilmcote with Billesley Parochial Church Council v Wallbank and Another* [2004] 1 A.C. 546: Harpum and Bignell, p.54: [2003] Conv. 351.
[22] [1965] A.C. 1175.

two consequences: first that the Act, in this respect, brings about a substantive change in real property law by making personal rights bind purchasers; second, that there is a difference as to the nature of the rights by which a purchaser may be bound between registered and unregistered land, for purely personal rights including the wife's right to stay in the house cannot affect purchasers of unregistered land even with notice. One may have to accept that there is a difference between unregistered land and registered land as regards what kind of notice binds a purchaser. But there is no warrant in the terms of this paragraph or elsewhere in the Act for supposing that the nature of the rights which are to bind a purchaser is to be different, excluding personal rights in one case, including them in another."[23]

It followed that all proprietary rights in land were capable of gaining overriding status under s.70(1)(g), including, for example, an estate contract such as an option to purchase land,[24] an equitable lease and most importantly a beneficial interest arising under a trust of the land.[25] In contrast personal rights, such as a bare or contractual licence, would be incapable of gaining overriding status. This can be seen in *Strand Securities v Caswell*[26] where Eric Caswell was the tenant of a flat. He was not living there himself, but allowed his step-daughter to reside rent-free. Since the step-daughter was a bare licensee of the flat, she had no right which was capable of constituting an overriding interest under s.70(1)(g), despite the fact that she was in actual occupation.[27]

(ii) Trust Interests which have been Overreached cannot form the Subject Matter of an Overriding Interest

The case law relating to the operation of s.70(1)(g) also considered the interrelationship between overreaching and overriding interests. As has been noted above, beneficial interests arising under a trust of land will be overreached where there is a conveyance executed by at least two trustees. Since overreaching eliminates the beneficial interest from the land it follows that a beneficial interest which has been overreached cannot form the subject matter of an overriding interest. This was so held by the House of Lords in *City of London Building Society v Flegg*.[28] It will be recalled that in this case Mr and Mrs Maxwell-Browne were the registered proprietors of a house which they held on trust for themselves and Mr and Mrs Flegg as co-owners in equity. They subsequently mortgaged the house without Mr and Mrs Flegg's knowledge. Mr and Mrs Flegg claimed that as they had been in actual occupation of the house throughout, their equitable interest was binding on the mortgagee as an overriding interest under s.70(1)(g). Lord Oliver explained how the overreaching mechanisms deprived Mr and Mrs Flegg of any rights in the land capable of falling within the ambit of s.70(1)(g):

7–020

> "I cannot, for my part, accept that, once what I may call the parent interest, by which alone the occupation can be justified, has been overreached and thus subordinated to a legal

[23] [1965] A.C. 1175 at 1261.
[24] *Webb v Pollmount* [1966] Ch. 584; see also *Bridges v Mees* [1957] Ch. 475.
[25] *Hodgson v Marks* [1971] Ch. 892; *Williams & Glyn's Bank Ltd v Boland* [1981] A.C. 487.
[26] [1965] Ch. 958.
[27] As will be seen later, there was also an issue as to whether Mr Caswell had an overriding interest.
[28] [1988] A.C. 54.

estate properly created by the trustees under their statutory powers, it can, in relation to the proprietor of the legal estate so created, be any longer said to be a right 'for the time being subsisting.' Section 70(1)(g) protects only the rights in reference to the land of the occupier whatever they are at the material time—in the instant case the right to enjoy in specie the rent and profits of the land held in trust for him. Once the beneficiary's rights have been shifted from the land to capital moneys in the hands of the trustees, there is no longer an interest in the land to which the occupation can be referred or which it can protect. If the trustees sell in accordance with the statutory provisions and so overreach the beneficial interests in reference to the land, nothing remains to which a right of occupation can attach and the same result must, in my judgment, follow vis-a-vis a chargee by way of legal mortgage so long as the transaction is carried out in the manner proscribed by the Law of Property Act 1925, overreaching the beneficial interests by subordinating them to the estate of the chargee which is no longer 'affected' by them . . . In the instant case, therefore, I would, for my part, hold that the charge created in favour of the [building society] overreaches the beneficial interests of the Mr and Mrs Flegg and that there is nothing in s.70(1)(g) of the Land Registration Act 1925 or in Boland's case which has the effect of preserving against the [building society] any rights of Mr and Mrs Flegg . . ."[29]

7–021 In consequence, the equitable ownership of a beneficiary behind a trust of land will only be capable of overriding status if it has not been overreached. A beneficial interest under a trust of land is therefore only likely to obtain overriding status where the land was owned by a sole registered proprietor, as was the case in *Williams & Glyn's Bank Ltd v Boland*.[30]

(iii) The Owner of the Interest Must have been in Actual Occupation of the Land at the Date of the Disposition

7–022 An interest which is capable of obtaining overriding status under para.2 of Sch.3 will only do so if its owner meets the specified criteria of actual occupation. The interest will become overriding if either of two criteria are met. First, the interest will be overriding if the person claiming that interest was in actual occupation of the land at the date of the disposition and the occupation would have been obvious from a reasonably careful inspection of the land. Second the interest will be overriding if the person claiming the interest was in occupation but that occupation would not have been obvious from a reasonably careful inspection of the land, provided that the person to whom the disposition was made had actual knowledge of the existence of the interest. Thus an overriding interest will require one of the following equations to be satisfied:

Either
INTEREST + OBVIOUS ACTUAL OCCUPATION = OVERRIDING STATUS

Or
INTEREST + NON-OBVIOUS ACTUAL OCCUPATION + ACTUAL
KNOWLEDGE = OVERRIDING STATUS

[29] [1988] A.C. 54 at 90–91.
[30] [1981] A.C. 487.

However, an interest does not become overriding merely because the person to whom a disposition is made has actual knowledge of its existence. As has already been indicated, an interest will only be protected as an overriding interest if it is proprietary in character.

(e) *What is Meant by Actual Occupation?*

Paragraph 2 of Sch.3 provides that a proprietary interest will only become an overriding interest **7–023** if the person to whom it belongs is "in actual occupation" of the land to which it relates. In the absence of any statutory definition the meaning can only be construed from the authorities which considered the meaning of actual occupation for the purposes of s.70(1)(g). Although para.2 introduces an additional requirement that the occupation must have been obvious from a reasonably careful inspection of the land, an interest may still be overriding even though the occupation would not have been obvious, provided that the person to whom a disposition was made had actual knowledge of the interest. It is therefore necessary to understand the general meaning of actual occupation before turning to consider whether such occupation would have been obvious.

(i) Occupation is a Straightforward Question of Fact

Under s.70(1)(g) of the Land Registration Act 1925 the requirement of "actual occupation" was **7–024** consistently interpreted as a simple matter of fact,[31] namely whether the person claiming entitlement to an overriding interest was physically present on the land to which that interest relates. It was not to be regarded as a term of legal art, with a peculiarly limited meaning, nor as requiring that the person factually occupying land enjoyed a legal entitlement to do so. In *Williams & Glyn's Bank Ltd v Boland* Lord Wilberforce considered the meaning of "actual occupation" and concluded:

> "The words are ordinary words of plain English, and should, in my opinion, be interpreted as such ... Given occupation, i.e. presence on the land, I do not think that the word 'actual' was intended to introduce any additional qualification, certainly not to suggest that possession must be 'adverse': it merely emphasises that what is required is physical presence, not some entitlement in law."[32]

In many cases it will be clear that a person is in actual occupation of land, especially residential property, since as Nicholls L.J. observed in *Lloyds Bank v Rosset*, residential premises are occupied by "those who live in them".[33] Most cases which concerned straightforward situations of a person living in property only considered the meaning of "actual occupation" because some limited interpretation was being advocated. For example, in *Hodgson v Marks*[34] Mrs Hodgson transferred the legal title of her house into the name of her lodger, Evans, who sold the property

---

[31] In *Williams & Glyn's Bank v Boland* [1979] Ch. 312 at 322 Lord Denning M.R. stated that actual occupation "is a matter of fact, not a matter of law".
[32] [1981] A.C. 487 at 504–505.
[33] [1989] Ch. 350 at 376–377.
[34] [1971] Ch. 892.

to Marks. She had continued to live there, and when Marks came to view the property he saw her coming up a path to the house but did not ascertain who she was. The first instance judge held that she was not in "actual occupation" for the purposes of s.70(1)(g) because the word "actual" limited protection to those persons whose occupation was by an act recognisable to any person seeking to acquire an interest in the land. However, the Court of Appeal rejected this analysis and concluded that Mrs Hodgson had clearly been in actual occupation of the property at all material times as she was "de facto living in the house as her house",[35] and it was irrelevant that the purchaser had assumed her to be Evans' wife. In *Williams & Glyn's Bank Ltd v Boland*[36] Mrs Boland was living in the matrimonial home she shared with her husband and in which she enjoyed a share of the equitable ownership. The bank, which had granted him a mortgage, argued that she was not to be regarded as enjoying "actual occupation" within s.70(1)(g) on three grounds: first, because the vendor (mortgagor) was in occupation; secondly, because her occupation as a wife was merely a shadow of her husband's occupation; and, thirdly, because her occupation was not inconsistent with the title of the vendor. Lord Wilberforce rejected these proposed qualifications. He held that the occupation of a vendor does not exclude the possible occupation of others, approving comments to that effect in *Caunce v Caunce*[37] and *Hodgson v Marks*.[38] He rejected as obsolete the argument raised in *Bird v Syme-Thomson*[39] that the unity of a husband and wife meant that a wife's occupation was merely a shadow of her husband's. He held that there was no requirement that the occupation must be inconsistent with the title of the vendor, and concluded:

> "The only solution which is consistent with the Act and with common sense is to read the paragraph for what it says. Occupation, existing as a fact, may protect rights if the person in occupation has rights."

Whilst the concept of shadow occupation may be redundant between spouses, it has more recently been reasserted in respect of minor children by the Court of Appeal in *Hypo-Mortgage Services Ltd v Robinson*, where Nourse L.J. held that it was "axiomatic that minor children of the legal owner are not in actual occupation within s.70(1)(g)" because they are a "shadow of occupation of their parent.[40] He considered that this conclusion was further supported by the fact that it would be impossible to make inquiries of such children in the manner anticipated by the provision.

Although in many cases the question of actual occupation will be straightforward because the claimant of an overriding interest clearly lives in the property to which it relates, difficulties have arisen in relation to how far the concept of occupation can be carried. As was observed by Lord Oliver in *Abbey National Building Society v Cann* the issue of whether a person was in actual occupation may essentially be a matter of fact, but:

> "There is the serious question of what, in law, can amount to 'actual occupation' for the purposes of s.70(1)(g). In Williams & Glyn's Bank Ltd v Boland Lord Wilberforce observed

[35] [1971] Ch. 892 at 932.
[36] [1981] A.C. 487.
[37] [1969] 1 W.L.R. 286.
[38] [1971] Ch. 892.
[39] [1991] 1 W.L.R. 440.
[40] [1997] 2 F.L.R. 71 at 72.

that these words should be interpreted for what they are, that is to say, ordinary words of plain English. But even plain English may contain a variety of shades of meaning."[41]

(ii) Actual Occupation Requires a Sufficient Physical Presence on the Land

In the absence of sufficient physical presence on the land it will be impossible to establish **7–025** actual occupation. In *Epps v Esso Petroleum*[42] the plaintiffs claimed that they enjoyed actual occupation of a strip of land where they had parked their car on an unidentified part for an undefined time. Templeman J. held that they had failed to establish that they were entitled to an overriding interest:

"But even if Mr Jones regularly parked his car on the disputed strip I do not consider that this constituted actual occupation of the disputed strip in the circumstances of the present case. I reach this conclusion for the following reasons; first, the parking of a car on a strip 11 feet wide by 80 feet long does not actually occupy the whole, or a substantial, or any defined part of that disputed strip for the whole or any defined time. Secondly, the parking of a car on an unidentified piece of land, apparently comprised in garage premises, is not an assertion of actual occupation of anything."[43]

(iii) Residence is not Required to Establish Actual Occupation

Although it is clear that slight physical presence will not amount to actual occupation, residence **7–026** is not a necessary criterion. The level of presence necessary will depend on the nature of the land over which an overriding interest is claimed. In *Lloyds Bank v Rosset*[44] the issue was whether a wife could claim an overriding interest against the bank, which had granted a mortgage when her husband purchased a derelict farmhouse. Prior to the completion of the sale the vendors had allowed the Rossets to begin renovation work of the property. The builders that they employed were on the premises daily, and one of the men slept there most nights. The wife spent almost every day at the house, arriving at 10am and leaving just after 4pm, urging the builders on and decorating rooms, and also spent two nights sleeping there. The majority of the Court of Appeal held that in these circumstances she was in actual occupation of the house even though she was not resident as such. Nicholls L.J. explained and applied the principles:

". . . I accept that in ordinary speech one normally does equate occupation in relation to a house with living there. If a person is intending to move into a house but has not yet done so, he would not normally be regarded as having gone into occupation. That is the normal position, with a house which is fit for living in. But that does not provide the answer in the present case, where the house was semi-derelict . . . If, day after day, workmen are actively building a house on a plot of land, or actively and substantially renovating a semi-derelict

[41] [1991] 1 A.C. 56 at 93.
[42] [1973] 1 W.L.R. 1071.
[43] [1973] 1 W.L.R. 1071 at 1079–1080. It appears from these remarks that the question of what constitutes actual occupation cannot entirely be divorced from the issue of whether the occupation is reasonably apparent.
[44] [1989] Ch. 350.

house, it would be contrary to the principle underlying paragraph (g) if a would be purchaser or mortgagee were entitled to treat that site as currently devoid of an occupant for
the purpose of the paragraph . . . In my view, the test of residence propounded by the bank
is too narrow. As the judge observed, what constitutes occupation will depend upon the
nature and state of the property in question. I can see no reason, in principle or in practice,
why a semi-derelict house such as Vincent farmhouse should not be capable of actual occupation whilst the works proceed and before anyone has started to live in the building."[45]

The House of Lords[46] subsequently held that the wife was not entitled to any overriding interest, on the grounds that she was unable to establish that she enjoyed any share of the equitable ownership of the land by way of a constructive trust.[47] Sadly this meant that there was
no need for the House of Lords to determine if she had been in actual occupation and Lord
Bridge refused to go into a question that he saw as of only academic interest.

(iv)   Occupation by the Physical Presence of a Representative

7–027   It seems clear that a person may be regarded as being in actual occupation of land even when
she is not physically present if someone is "living there" on her behalf in a representative
capacity. This was recognised by Lord Oliver in Abbey National Building Society v Cann,
who stated that actual occupation does not necessarily involve the personal presence of the
claimant, so that a caretaker or representative of a company could occupy on behalf of his
employer. Similarly in Lloyds Bank v Rosset[48] the Court of Appeal considered that builders
employed to renovate a property were capable of occupying on behalf of their employers. In
Strand Securities v Caswell[49] the Court of Appeal held that representative occupation was
possible by an agent or employee. Although the court considered that a contractual relationship was not essential for finding representative occupation, and Harman L.J. suggested that
a house occupied by a wife could also be regarded as being occupied by her husband since
she occupied as his representative,[50] it held that the tenant did not enjoy actual occupation of
the flat in which he had allowed his step-daughter to occupy as a licensee. Lord Denning M.R.
explained his reluctance at the inevitability of this conclusion:

> "I would like to hold that the [father] was sharing the occupation of the flat with the
> [step-daughter]. But I cannot bring myself to this conclusion. The truth is that he allowed
> her to be in actual occupation, and that is all there is to it. She was a licensee rent free
> and I fear that it does not give him protection. It seems to me to be a very rare case—a
> case which the legislature did not think of for it is quite clear that if the [daughter] had
> paid a token sum as rent, or for use and occupation, to the [father], he would be 'in
> receipt of rents and profits' and his rights would be protected under s.70(1)(g). Again if
> the [father] put his servant or caretaker into the flat, rent free, he would be protected

[45] [1989] Ch. 350 at 376–377.
[46] [1991] 1 A.C. 107.
[47] See above Ch. 11.
[48] [1989] Ch. 350.
[49] [1965] Ch. 958.
[50] [1965] Ch. 984.

because his agent would have actual occupation on his behalf. It is odd that the [father] is not protected simply because he let his stepdaughter in rent free. Odd as it is, I fear the words of the statute do not cover this case . . ."[51]

It should, of course be noted that the new provisions relating to actual occupation do not put the receipt of rent and profits on the same footing as under the Land Registration Act 1925.

(v) Actual Occupation Preserved through Temporary Absence by Symbolic Occupation

Although in *Abbey National Building Society v Cann* Lord Oliver stressed that actual occupation must "involve some degree of permanence and continuity",[52] it is clear that persons who can be properly described as "living there" may not in fact enjoy continuous physical occupation of land. For example, if an MP owns a flat in London which he shares with his mistress, he may be living there during the week, but living back with his family in his constituency during the week-end. The same is true of persons who own second homes. Alternatively a co-owner of a property may be called away for a period of time on a business trip, or take a holiday for a week or so. Does their actual occupation cease during this time that they are "away"? Although with relatively short absences the answer must certainly be no, the problems posed are greater if a person is absent for a longer period of time. For example, a co-owner may decide to spend a month inter-railing in Europe, six months sailing round the world, or be seconded by their business to Saudi Arabia for six weeks. During such an absence there may be ample opportunity for the legal owner of the land to arrange things so that there are few obvious physical signs of their occupation to a potential purchaser or mortgagee. The question arises whether, in the event of a disposition during their absence, the co-owner's interests will be binding on the mortgagee or transferee as overriding interests. As was seen above, a person who is not physically present on the land can preserve actual occupation through the occupation of a representative. It similarly seems that a person can preserve actual occupation through temporary absences by the continued presence of their personal belongings on the land. Such "symbolic" occupation was a factor in finding that a wife's share of the equitable ownership of her matrimonial home was protected as an overriding interest in *Chhokar v Chhokar*.[53] Mr Chhokar was the sole legal owner of a house, which he held on trust for himself and his wife. Intending to leave his wife, he sold the house to his friend Mr Parmar, deliberately arranging that completion of the sale should occur while his wife was in hospital giving birth to their child. Ewbank J. explained the circumstances of the transaction:

> "On 19 February, the date of completion, the husband made special arrangements to have the net proceeds of sale in cash in his hands. He paid his debts and then he set off for India. That was the last the wife saw of him for some two years. The wife and baby were discharged from hospital on 22 February. They went home. They found the locks had been changed . . . on 1 March 1979 Mr Parmar registered the conveyance to him at the Land Registry. The wife at that date was not in the house because he had put her out, but some

7–028

---

[51] [1965] Ch. 984 at 981.
[52] [1991] 1 A.C. 56 at 93.
[53] [1984] F.L.R. 313. See also *Hoggett v Hoggett* (1980) 39 P. & C.R. 121.

of her furniture was there. I have to consider whether she was in actual occupation on the day of the registration of the conveyance. I have no difficulty in deciding that she was in actual occupation. Her interest, accordingly, in the house is an overriding interest . . ."[54]

Such symbolic occupation was also recognised in *Kling v Keston Properties*,[55] where Vinelott J. held that the plaintiff had enjoyed actual occupation of a garage, partly because his wife's car had been trapped in it by the defendant parking her car across the entrance.

(vi)   Is Symbolic Occupation Alone enough to Constitute Actual Occupation?

7–029   Although *Chhokar v Chhokar* suggests that symbolic occupation by furniture and personal belongings may prove sufficient to preserve a pre-existing actual occupation established by physical presence, it is less certain whether it can alone establish actual occupation. This issue arose in *Abbey National Building Society v Cann*[56] where it was argued that following the purchase of a house a mother enjoying an equitable interest in the purchase moneys was entitled to an overriding interest binding a mortgage company which had taken a security over the property, on the grounds that at the moment of completion of the purchase she had been in actual occupation. Since she had been abroad on holiday at the time that completion occurred, her claim of actual occupation was founded on the fact that some 35 minutes before completion took place the vendors had allowed her son to begin to unload her furniture into the house and permitted carpet fitters to begin laying her carpets. The House of Lords held that these acts were wholly insufficient to constitute actual occupation. Lord Oliver commented that much more was required than a mere fleeting presence:

> "A prospective tenant or purchaser who is allowed, as a matter of indulgence, to go into property in order to plan decorations or measure for furnishings would not, in ordinary parlance, be said to be occupying it, even though he might be there for hours at a time. Of course, in the instant case, there was, no doubt, on the part of the persons involved in moving Mrs Cann's belongings, an intention that they should remain there and would render the premises suitable for her ultimate use as a residential occupier. Like the trial judge, however, I am unable to accept that acts of this preparatory character, carried out by courtesy of the vendor prior to completion can constitute 'actual occupation' for the purposes of s.70(1)(g)."[57]

This does not, however, mean that actual occupation can never be established by purely symbolic occupancy. For example if the case had concerned a three-year lease of the house granted by Mr Cann to a third party on the day before his mother returned from holiday, it is likely that Mrs Cann would have been able to claim an overriding interest against the lessor. The presence of her furniture and belongings would have been permanent and not merely fleeting, and not dependent on the indulgence of the vendor.

[54] [1984] F.L.R. 313 at 317.
[55] (1985) 49 P. & C.R. 212.
[56] [1991] 1 A.C. 56.
[57] [1991] 1 A.C. 56 at 94.

(vii)   Occupation of Part of the Land

In *Wallcite Ltd v Ferrishurst Ltd*[58] the Court of Appeal held that it was not necessary for an occu-   **7–030**
pier to be in actual occupation of the whole of the land in order to enjoy an overriding interest
under s.70(1)(g) of the Land Registration Act. Thus a plaintiff who was only in occupation of a
part of the land to which an interest related was able to gain priority for the interest over the whole
of the land. This decision has now been reversed by para.2 of Sch.3, which makes clear that the
interest of the occupier is only protected in relation to the land which is actually occupied.

(f)   *The Date at which Actual Occupation must be Established*

One particular problem associated with overriding interests has been the relevant date at   **7–031**
which the criteria must be established. This issue causes difficulty because of the so-called
"registration gap" which occurs between the completion of a sale of land and the date at which
the purchaser is registered as the new proprietor. As will be explained in the next chapter, completion is the moment at which the purchase money is paid, the legal documents
effecting transfer is signed, and the keys handed over. However the transfer of the legal title
is only effected by subsequent registration. If the relevant date for the establishment of "actual
occupation" is the date of the registration of the transfer, rather than the date of completion,
then it is possible that rights arising during the registration gap might become binding on the
purchaser, who would have no possibility of protecting himself against them. This issue arose
in relation to the operation of s.70(1)(g) of the Land Registration Act 1925. In *Abbey National
Building Society v Cann*[59] George Cann purchased a house in circumstances in which part of
the purchase moneys were provided by his mother, so that she was entitled to a share of the
equitable ownership. Completion occurred on August 13, but George granted a mortgage to
the building society and kept part of the intended purchase money for himself. The charge was
also executed on August 13, but it was not until September 13 that the charge was registered
and George was registered as proprietor. By that date Mrs Cann was in actual occupation of
the property, and one argument on her behalf was that she was entitled to an overriding interest taking priority over the charge of the building society. Although she had not been in actual
occupation at the date of completion, she had entered into actual occupation during the "registration gap". Did this have the effect that the interest gained priority as an overriding interest? The House of Lords held that it did not. Lord Oliver explained that, in order to prevent a
"conveyancing absurdity" s.70(1)(g) should be interpreted so as to require that the claimant
of an overriding interest must have been in actual occupation of the land at the date at which
the transaction was completed. Any other interpretation would mean that a potential purchaser
was unable to protect himself by making inquiries of any occupiers.

However Sch.3 para.2 appears to alter the relevant date for determining whether the owner
of an interest was in actual occupation. The relevant time is "the time of the disposition." This
may have been intended to confirm the decision in *Abbey National Building Society v Cann*.
However, since s.27(1) provides that a disposition "does not operate at law until the relevant

---

[58] [1999] 1 All E.R. 977.
[59] [1991] 1 A.C. 56. See also *Barclays Bank Plc v Zaroovabli* [1997] 2 All E.R. 19.

registration requirements are met" this means that on a strict interpretation the relevant date is the date of registration. The Land Registration Act 2002 clearly intends that the introduction of electronic conveyancing will eliminate the problem of the registration gap, since completion and registration will then be simultaneous. However until this facility is operational the new legislation reintroduces the potential for overriding interests to arise during the period of the registration gap unless the courts choose to adopt the interpretation that the date of the disposition is the date of completion in the case of a sale, or the date on which the transaction is intended to have effect rather than the later date on which the disposition is registered.

(g)   Was the Occupation Obvious?

7–032   As has been noted above, an interest no longer gains overriding status merely because its owner is in actual occupation of the land. Paragraph 2(c)(i) provides that an interest will not be overriding if the occupation of the owner "would not have been obvious on a reasonably careful inspection of the land." This limitation was intended to limit the scope of overriding interests, and in particular to ensure that purchasers of the land would not find themselves bound by interests which would not have been readily discoverable by an inspection of the land.[60] Whilst the requirement of apparancy is not intended to re-introduce the concept of constructive notice into registered land it is hard not to avoid the conclusion that this is the practical effect of Sch.3 para.2(c)(i), and authorities such as that in *Kingsnorth Finance v Tizard*[61] will be especially relevant in determining the meaning of a "reasonably careful inspection" and what such an inspection would have revealed. The limitation will make no difference to clearly straightforward cases such as *Williams & Glyn's Bank Ltd v Boland*[62] or *Hodgson v Marks*,[63] where the owner of the interest was obviously in occupation of the land. However the requirement may cause uncertainty where the owner of the interest was only periodically present on the land, or was temporarily absent from the land, or most especially where the owner of the land took steps to conceal the fact of occupation of a person who was temporarily absent from the land. It seems likely that a similar result would be reached on the facts of cases such as *Lloyds Bank v Rosset*[64] and *Chhokar v Chhokar*,[65] since the presence of the wife in both cases would have been obvious from a reasonably careful inspection of the land. In the case of *Lloyds Bank v Rosset* it would have revealed the presence of the wife on the building site, and in *Chhokar v Chhokar* it would have revealed the presence of the wife through the presence of her furniture and personal possessions. However, if the husband in *Chhokar v Chhokar* had ensured that all evidences of his wife's existence were removed from the property, or were hidden in a way that would not have been revealed by a "reasonably careful inspection", then her interest would not have been protected unless the purchaser had actual knowledge.

---

[60] See Law Com. No.254, *Land Registration for the Twenty-First Century*, paras 5.71–5.75.
[61] [1986] 1 W.L.R. 783.
[62] [1981] A.C. 487.
[63] [1971] Ch. 892.
[64] [1989] Ch. 350.
[65] [1984] F.L.R. 313. See also *Hoggett v Hoggett* (1980) 39 P. & C.R. 121.

(h) *Loss of Overriding Status if the Occupier Failed to Disclose his Rights*

Although the existence of overriding interests appears to undermine the "mirror" principle of **7–033**
land registration, potential purchasers of land have the ability to protect themselves against the
interests of occupiers which might become overriding against them. Schedule 3 para.2(b) provides that "an interest of a person of whom inquiry was made before the disposition and who
failed to disclose the right when he could reasonably have been expected to do so" will not
gain overriding status. Thus a purchaser of land can gain protection against potentially adverse
overriding interests by inspecting the land and asking all those persons in actual occupation
whether they have any interests in the land. If such occupiers reveal their interests then the purchaser must beware. If they do not reveal their interests then they will not become overriding
and the purchaser can safely take free of them. Schedule 3 para.2(b) continues the caveat to
s.70(1)(g) of the Land Registration Act 1925 that the rights of an actual occupier would be
overriding "save where enquiry is made of such person and the rights are not disclosed".
However, the new provision has added the important caveat that the rights of the occupier will
only be prevented from attaining overriding status if he could reasonably have been expected
to disclose the right in question. Depending upon how it is interpreted, this added requirement
of reasonableness has the potential to greatly increase the protection of the rights of occupiers,
and to diminish the ability of purchasers to protect themselves against adverse interests.

(i)   The Inquiry Must be Made by the Prospective Purchaser or his Agent

The nature of inquiries which will be effective to protect a purchaser from an overriding inter-   **7–034**
est were considered in reference to s.70(1)(g) of the Land Registration Act 1925 in *London
& Cheshire Insurance Co Ltd v Laplagrene Property Co. Ltd*.[66] Brightman J. stated:

> "the inquiry which paragraph (g) envisages is readily and sensibly confined to inquiry by or
> on behalf of the intending transferee or grantee for the purposes of the intended disposition."

This suggests that the inquiries can be made either by the prospective purchaser himself, or
by an agent acting on his behalf, provided that the inquiries are made in the course of the
transaction. To this extent any inquiries made by any person, however disinterested in or
unconnected with the property, will not suffice.

(ii)   The Inquiry Must be Addressed to the Person Entitled to the Right or
her Agent

An inquiry will only be effective to protect a purchaser if it was made of the person entitled   **7–035**
to the right claimed to enjoy overriding status. For example, in *Hodgson v Marks*[67] Russell
L.J. held that a purchaser would not be protected when he had failed to make any inquiry of

---

[66] [1971] Ch. 499 at 505.
[67] [1971] Ch. 892.

Mrs Hodgson as to her rights in the property he was acquiring, and that he would not be entitled to rely on the "untrue ipse dixit[68] of the vendor" that she had no rights, nor on his assumption that she was the vendor's wife. In *Winkworth v Edward Baron Developments Ltd*[69] the Court of Appeal considered that an inquiry made of an agent, for example a solicitor, acting for the party entitled to a right in the land would be effective to protect a potential purchaser from an overriding interest if the agent failed to disclose its existence. However in the circumstances, where a husband mortgaged the matrimonial home of which his wife was an equitable co-owner, the court held that there had been no effective inquiry made of the wife since the solicitor acting for her and her husband was not asked to answer an inquiry on her behalf but merely to pass a letter to them, which he passed to the husband who did not pass it on to his wife but answered the inquiries falsely.

(iii)   The Inquiry Must be Made as to the Existence of Rights in the Land

7–036   An inquiry will only be effective to protect the potential purchaser if it is directed to the question whether the person of whom it is made enjoys rights in the land. If an inquiry is made as to whether the person enjoys certain specific rights in the land this will be inadequate to protect against the overriding status of other rights in relation to which no inquiry was addressed. In *Winkworth v Edward Baron Developments Ltd*[70] a mortgage company had asked a husband and wife to acknowledge that they occupied their house as licensees and not by virtue of any tenancy or lease. Nourse L.J. held that this amounted to no more than "an inquiry as to the capacity in which the husband and wife occupied the property"[71] and did not prevent the wife's beneficial interest acquiring overriding status. The court indicated that an inquiry did not need to be specific in order to be effective, and Nourse L.J. implied that an inquiry "as to their rights in the land generally" would have been sufficient to protect the mortgagee from any rights that they then failed to disclose.

(iv)   It Must be Reasonable to Expect the Occupier to Disclose his Right

7–037   The added requirement of reasonableness by Sch.3 para.2(b) introduces an element of uncertainty, especially since many of the rights which are protected as overriding interests arise informally, and the owner may not be aware of their existence, or even of the very possibility of their existence. This is perhaps especially the case with resulting or constructive trusts of land. A woman who has moved in to live with a man and then contributed to the mortgage repayments may be entirely unaware that she perhaps thereby gained an interest in the land by way of a resulting or constructive trust. Would it be reasonable to expect such an ignorant occupier to disclose the existence of her right to a potential purchaser?

[68] The phrase ipse dixit translates as "he says it himself". In colloquial English we would probably refer to the vendor's "say so".
[69] (1986) 52 P. & C.R. 67.
[70] (1986) 52 P. & C.R. 67.
[71] (1986) 52 P. & C.R. 67 at 77.

(i) *Actual Knowledge of the Interest of an Occupier whose Occupation would not have been Obvious on a Reasonably Careful Inspection of the Land*

As was noted above, an interest of a person in actual occupation of the land will still enjoy over-riding status, even though the occupation would not have been obvious from a reasonably careful inspection of the land, if the person to whom the disposition is made had actual knowledge of the interest at the time. Schedule 3 para.2(1)(c) thus reintroduces the concept of notice to registered land, albeit in very limited and unlikely circumstances. *Chhokar v Chhokar*[72] perhaps provides an example of the kind of circumstances in which Sch.3 para.2(1)(c) would come into play. In that case the purchaser of the house knew that Mrs Chhokar had an interest in the matrimonial home. Thus even if her continued occupation during the time that she was in hospital were not to be regarded as "obvious" on a reasonably careful inspection of the land, her rights would still be overriding. Whilst the introduction of actual notice in this context may seem just, it might also be difficult to apply in practice. In many cases the interests of occupiers arise informally, for example by way of a constructive or resulting trust. Whilst a purchaser may have actual knowledge of the existence of an occupier he may not be aware that such an occupier has any specific interest in the land. Schedule 3, para.2(1)(c) seems to require actual knowledge of the interest itself, not merely actual knowledge of the fact that a person was in occupation.

7–038

7. Circumstances in which an Unprotected Interest may Gain Priority Over a Registered Disposition even though it is not Overriding

As has been seen, the provisions of the Land Registration Act 2002 have the effect that a person who acquires a registered estate for valuable consideration will take his estate free from any unprotected earlier interests unless they are overriding, in which case they will enjoy protected priority. However cases decided under the preceding regime of the Land Registration Act 1925 have held that in some limited circumstances an unprotected interest which is not an overriding interest may still be binding on the purchaser of a legal estate because of the operation of equitable doctrines operating outside of the legislation. There is no reason to suspect that the Land Registration Act 2002 has negated the operation of these equitable doctrines, so it remains possible that a purchaser of a registered estate may be prevented from taking advantage of the statutory priority accorded by s.29.[73]

7–039

(a) *An Unprotected Interest may be Binding by Means of an Independent Constructive Trust*[74]

Although an interest which has not been protected on the register will not usually be binding upon a person entitled to statutory priority unless it is also an overriding interest, it seems to have

7–040

---

[72] [1984] F.L.R. 313. See also *Hoggett v Hoggett* (1980) 39 P. & C.R. 121.
[73] See Cooke and O'Connor, "Purchaser Liability to Third Parties in the English Land Registration System: A Comparative Perspective" (2004) 120 L.Q.R. 640.
[74] [1983] C.L.J. 54 (Harpum); [1983] Conv. 64 (Jackson); (1983) 46 M.L.R. 96; (1984) 47 M.L.R. 476 (Bennett).

been recognised that in very limited circumstances a constructive trust of such an unprotected interest can arise wholly outside of the registered land system, such that it is binding upon a transferee or grantee acquiring title to the land. The possibility of such a trust was raised by Graham J. in *Peffer v Rigg*[75] where he suggested that Mrs Peffer might be bound by Mr Rigg's equitable trust interest even if his analysis of the requirement of good faith under s.20(1) of the Land Registration Act 1925 was incorrect. He stated:

> "On the evidence in this case I have found that [Mrs Peffer] knew quite well that [Mr Peffer] held the property on trust for himself and [Mr Rigg] in equal shares. [Mrs Peffer] knew this was so and that the property was trust property when the transfer was made to her, and therefore she took the property on a constructive trust in accordance with general equitable principles . . . This is a new trust imposed by equity and is distinct from the trust which bound [Mr Peffer]. Even if, therefore, I am wrong as to the proper construction of ss.20 and 59, when read together, and even if s.20 strikes off the shackles of the express trust which bound [Mr Peffer], this cannot invalidate the new trust imposed on [Mrs Peffer]."[76]

This somewhat novel approach, that an express trust defeated by the appropriate rules of priority is replaced by a distinct constructive trust, seems inconsistent with the traditional rule that acquisition of the legal title by a bona fide purchaser for value without notice has the effect of permanently extinguishing pre-existing equitable interests.[77] It has, however, been approved and applied in subsequent cases. In *Lyus v Prowsa Developments*[78] Mr and Mrs Lyus had entered into a contract with a building company for the purchase of a plot of land on which they were intending to build a house. They therefore enjoyed a minor interest, namely an estate contract, against the building company which was the registered proprietor of the land. The company had previously mortgaged the land to a bank, which enjoyed a registered charge over it. The building company went into liquidation before construction had started, and the land was sold by the mortgagee bank to a further building company. Although Mr and Mrs Lyus had protected their interest by means of a caution, the bank would have been able to sell the land free from their estate contract because of their prior registered charge, thus leaving them with only a personal right to prove for damages for breach of contract in the company's liquidation. However, the contract under which the bank sold the land to the second building company contained a clause that it was sold "subject to" Mr and Mrs Lyus' estate contract. Dillon J. held that, in these circumstances, the building company had acquired the land subject to the Lyus' estate contract by way of a constructive trust, and it was not entitled to rely on the provisions of the Land Registration Act 1925 granting it statutory priority.[79] He stated his reasoning as follows:

> "It seems to me that the fraud on the part of the defendants in the present case lies not just in relying on the legal rights conferred by an Act of Parliament, but in the [purchaser] reneging on a positive stipulation in favour of [Mr and Mrs Lyus] in the bargain under which [they] acquired the land. That seems to me to make all the difference. It has

[75] [1977] 1 W.L.R. 285.
[76] [1977] 1 W.L.R. 265 at 294.
[77] *Wilkes v Spooner* [1911] 2 K.B. 473.
[78] [1982] 1 W.L.R. 1044.
[79] See ss.20 and 34.

long since been held, for instance in *Rochefoucauld v Boustead*,[80] that the provisions of the Statute of Frauds 1677 cannot be used as an instrument of fraud, now incorporated in certain sections of the Law of Property Act 1925, and that it is fraud for a person to whom the land is agreed to be conveyed as trustee for another to deny the trust and relying on the terms of the statute to claim the land for himself . . . it seems to me that the same considerations are applicable in relation to the Land Registration Act 1925."[81]

The potential for a constructive trust arising independently so as to bind the purchaser of land with an interest from which they would otherwise have taken free was also recognised by the Court of Appeal in *Ashburn Anstalt v Arnold*[82] in the context of contractual licences. Fox L.J. stated that the rationale for the imposition of such a trust was that "the conscience of the estate owner is affected"[83] and warned that such trusts should not be easily established:

"In matters relating to title to land, certainty is of prime importance. We do not think it desirable that constructive trusts of land should be imposed in reliance on inferences from slender materials."[84]

Although the possibility of an independent constructive trust of an unprotected minor interest has been accepted, it is likely that it will only be established if stringent criteria are satisfied.

(i) An Independent Constructive Trust will not Arise Merely Because the Transferee had Actual Notice of the Existence of an Unprotected Interest

It seems clear that the mere fact that a transferee of land had actual notice of the existence of an unprotected minor interest will not give rise to a constructive trust. It was implicit in *Lyus v Prowsa Developments*[85] that the building company would not have been affected by Mr and Mrs Lyus' estate contract if they had merely purchased the land from the bank knowing of its existence. In such circumstances they would have been entitled to rely on the statutory priority afforded by the Land Registration Act 1925 to take their title free from it.

7–041

(ii) An Independent Constructive Trust will not Arise Merely because the Transferee had Agreed to Take the Land Subject to Interests Affecting it in General

Crucial to the emergence of an independent constructive trust in *Lyus v Prowsa Developments* was the fact that the building company had expressly agreed to take title to the land "subject to" the estate contract. Contracts of sale often contain a term that the purchaser agrees to take

7–042

[80] [1897] 1 Ch. 196.
[81] [1982] 1 W.L.R. 1044 at 1054–1055.
[82] [1989] Ch. 1.
[83] [1989] Ch. 1 at 25.
[84] [1989] Ch. 1 at 26.
[85] [1982] 1 W.L.R. 1044.

subject to all rights affecting the land. It seems that such general agreements are not sufficient to give rise to a constructive trust. The trust arises only because the conscience of the purchaser is affected, and this will only be so if there was an agreement to take subject to the specific interest concerned.

(iii) An Independent Constructive Trust will not Arise Unless there was Detrimental Reliance by the Transferor in Consequence of the Transferee's Agreement to Take Title Subject to a Specific Interest

7–043   In *Ashburn Anstalt v Arnold*[86] the Court of Appeal emphasised that the mere fact that a transferee of the title of land had agreed to take it subject to a specific interest from which he would otherwise take free was not alone sufficient to give rise to a constructive trust, since it was not inevitable that the conscience of the transferee would have been affected. There may be other reasons for the inclusion of such stipulations, for example the duty of the vendor to disclose all possible incumbrances known to him. As Fox L.J. stated[87]:

> "The mere fact that land is expressly to be conveyed 'subject' to a contract does not necessarily imply that the grantee is to be under an obligation, not otherwise existing, to give effect to the provisions of the contract. The fact that the conveyance is expressed to be subject to the contract may often . . . be at least as consistent with an intention merely to protect the grantor against claims by the grantee as an intention to impose an obligation on the grantee. The words 'subject to' will, of course, impose notice. But notice is not enough to impose on somebody an obligation to give effect to a contract into which he did not enter. Thus, mere notice of a restrictive covenant is not enough to impose upon the estate owner an obligation to give effect to it: *London County Council v Allen*.[88]"

The Court of Appeal held that a constructive trust would only arise where there was some detrimental reliance by the transferor selling the land, and a corresponding advantage to the transferee, as a consequence of his agreeing to take the land subject to the interest. Where such detriment and advantage are present the conscience of the transferee is affected so that he cannot be allowed to take the advantage flowing from his agreement only to renege on it subsequently and assert that by statute the land is not encumbered by the interest he agreed to take "subject to". The most obvious form of such advantage is a reduction in the price paid for the land in recognition that he had agreed to abide by the interest. In *Ashburn Anstalt v Arnold*, Fox L.J. stressed that there had been no finding of fact that the purchaser had "paid a lower price in consequence of the finding that the sale was subject" to a contractual licence, and therefore there was no constructive trust. Another example of such advantage would be if the vendor had sold the land to the purchaser ahead of a rival bidder, albeit at the same price, on the grounds that he had agreed to take subject to an interest.

---

[86] [1989] Ch. 1.
[87] [1989] Ch. 1 at 26.
[88] [1914] 3 K.B. 642.

(b) *An Unprotected Interest may be Binding Because of Fraud*

(i) Deliberate Schemes to Defeat Unprotected Interests

The question arises whether there are any other circumstances in which the conduct of a transferee or grantee is fraudulent so as to disentitle him from the protection of statutory priority.
Several older authorities suggest that a deliberate scheme to defeat the interests of a third party
in the land will be regarded as fraud. For example, in *Waimiha Sawmill Co Ltd v Waione Timber
Co Ltd*[89] Lord Buckmaster stated: "If the designed object of a transfer be to cheat a man of a
known existing right, that is fraudulent." In *Jones v Lipman*,[90] Benny Lipman agreed to sell a
house to Mr and Mrs Jones for £5,250. He subsequently refused to perform his contract and, to
avoid specific performance, transferred title to the house into the name of a company, Alamed
Ltd, who were registered as proprietors. Mr Lipman and his solicitor's clerk were the sole share-
holders of the company. Russell J. held that in these circumstances the company should be
bound by the contract to sell and he ordered specific performance. He emphasised that:

7–044

> "The defendant company is the creature of the first defendant, a device and a sham, a
> mask which he holds before his face in an attempt to avoid recognition by the eye of
> equity. The cases cited illustrate that an equitable remedy is rightly to be granted directly
> against the creature in such circumstances."[91]

However it is questionable whether a general principle that a scheme deliberately to defeat the
unprotected interests of a third party is fraudulent can survive the decision of the House of Lords
in *Midland Bank Trust Co v Green*. In the Court of Appeal Lord Denning M.R. had held that
the transaction in question was fraudulent because it was "executed deliberately to deprive"[92]
a person enjoying an unprotected option to purchase land of his right. This was rejected by the
House of Lords, where Lord Wilberforce stated that it was not fraud for a person to rely on legal
rights to which they are entitled by statute, even though the circumstances suggested a transaction arranged with the prime object of defeating the unprotected estate contract. *Jones v
Lipman*[93] can be distinguished because the rationale for finding fraud vitiating the availability
of statutory priority was the absence in reality of a genuine transfer of the land. Since the company could be regarded as an extension of Mr Lipman he had, in substance, transferred the legal
title to himself. In *Midland Bank Trust Co v Green* there was a genuine transfer of the legal title
to the land from husband to wife and it was impossible to prove that the sole motivation was to
achieve the defeat of their son's interests. As Lord Wilberforce commented:

> "Any advantage to oneself seems necessarily to involve a disadvantage for another: to
> make the validity of the purchase depend upon which aspect of the transaction was

---

[89] [1926] 101 at 106.
[90] [1962] 1 W.L.R. 832.
[91] [1989] Ch. 1 at 836–837.
[92] [1980] Ch. 590 at 625.
[93] [1962] 1 W.L.R. 832.

prevalent in the purchaser's mind seems to create distinctions equally difficult to analyse in law as to establish in fact; avarice and malice may be distinct sins, but in human conduct they are liable to be intertwined. The problem becomes even more acute if one supposes a mixture of motives. Suppose—and this may not be far from the truth—that the purchaser's motives were in part to take the farm from Geoffrey, and in part to distribute it between Geoffrey and his brothers and sisters, but not at all to obtain any benefit for herself, is this acting in 'good faith' or not? Should, family feeling be denied a protection afforded to simple greed?"[94]

It may be that if it had been established that the wife had been acting solely at the direction of her husband, so that she was in effect his nominee and held the legal title she acquired on a bare trust for him, that this would have constituted sufficient fraud to negate the operation of statutory priority. It is therefore possible to accept a general principle that where it can be shown that a transaction was a sham, in that the transferee of the legal title was in reality the transferor, either by the device of a company or a bare trust, there is a fraud which vitiates the operation of s.29 of the Land Registration Act 2002.

(ii)   A Person who Acquires Land in a Fiduciary Capacity is not Entitled to Rely on Statutory Priority

7–045   It also seems that a person who acquires the title to land will not be entitled to statutory priority so as to defeat the unprotected interests of a third party to whom that person also owed a fiduciary duty. *Du Boulay v Raggett*[95] concerned a plot of land which had been purchased at an auction by Mr Raggett, which he had subsequently transferred to his wife. Prior to the auction Mr and Mrs Raggett had agreed with the plaintiffs that they would bid for the land for themselves and also on the plaintiffs' behalf, so that the plaintiffs would not have to bid independently, and that they would then convey parts of the plot to the plaintiffs. After the land was purchased Mr Raggett refused to convey the agreed parts to the plaintiffs, alleging that he had only said that he would consider leasing them the areas in which they were interested. Mr Raggett then conveyed the plot to his wife, who claimed that she had taken her title free from the agreement to convey as it had not been protected as a minor interest and she was entitled to statutory priority under the Land Registration Act 1925 s.20(1). However, Robert Wright Q.C. held that as a consequence of their dealings Mr and Mrs Raggett stood in a fiduciary relationship to the plaintiffs in respect of the purchase at auction, and that Mrs Raggett was not entitled to acquire the land free from their interests. He considered the argument from *Midland Bank Trust Co v Green* that Mrs Raggett was entitled to rely on her statutory rights:

"I recognise the force of that argument but I do not think that it avails Mrs Raggett for the reason that she acquired the title already impressed with a trust . . . The question, therefore, is whether Mrs Raggett, in the light of the facts . . . had imposed upon herself

---

[94] [1981] A.C. 513 at 530.
[95] (1989) 58 P. & C.R. 138.

a fiduciary duty to hold any title she might obtain upon trust for herself and Mr Raggett and the plaintiffs. I think the answer is yes."[96]

Although this principle is clearly similar to the imposition of an independent constructive trust, the fraud arises because the transferee enjoys a particular status in relation to the third party who enjoys an unprotected interest in the land, not because they have entered a specific agreement with the transferor that they will take the land subject to it.

[96] (1989) 58 P. & C.R. 154

Part II

THE OWNERSHIP OF LAND

Chapter 8

FREEHOLD OWNERSHIP OF LAND

The most important interest in land which can be held by a person is the freehold. As has been **8–001**
seen, this is the interest which is tantamount to the actual ownership of the land. Although
such ownership prima facie carries with it the right of the freeholder to do whatever he wants
with his land, in reality his freedom is circumscribed by state intervention. The ownership of
certain valuable minerals in a freeholder's land is, for example, vested in the Crown. More
significantly, a freeholder's ability to develop and build on his land, and the use to which he
may put it, are regulated by planning controls.

The freehold interest is the most fundamental interest in land since all other lesser rights
and interests in the land are derived from it. Indeed, the life estate and the fee tail used to be
called "particular estates" because they constituted part only of the totality of rights in land
making up full ownership. Similarly, where a lease of land has been granted the leasehold
interest is simply carved out from the landlord's freehold interest. Again, where there is a trust
of land, the equitable interest is enjoyed by the beneficiaries of the trust but the freehold is
generally held by the trustees. It follows that the freehold interest in every piece of land will
be held by someone, although that person's rights will be qualified to the extent that third parties enjoy interests in that land which detract from his right to enjoy the freehold for himself.

A relatively recent development in land tenure has been the creation by statute of commonhold ownership. This is a specialised form of freehold ownership in which the owners of residential property can own the freehold of their individual units whilst enjoying shared ownership
of common areas such as car parking spaces or staircases or of amenities such as swimming
pools. Commonhold ownership is considered at the end of this chapter.

THE FREEHOLD AS A LEGAL ESTATE IN LAND

As a consequence of the Law of Property Act 1925 the freehold ownership in land is capable **8–002**
of existing as a legal estate. Section 1(1)(a) provides that "an estate in fee simple absolute in

143

possession" is "capable of subsisting or of being conveyed or created at law". The purpose of this definition is to differentiate freehold estates which are capable of attaining legal status from those which are not. If a fee simple estate fails to satisfy all three requirements in the definition it cannot take effect as a legal estate but only as an equitable interest behind a trust.

1. "Fee Simple"

8–003   As was noted in Chapter 3, the fee simple is one of the estates in land which was recognised in English law. The essence of the fee simple is that it is a perpetual grant of the land which cannot be brought to an end, in contrast to the estate in fee tail and the life interest.

2. "Absolute"[1]

(a) *Meaning of the Requirement*

8–004   The requirement in s.1(1)(a) that a freehold interest in land must be absolute in order to enjoy legal status is intended to exclude all grants of a fee simple estate where there is some possibility that the grant may fail in the future. This will generally be the case if the owner of a fee simple has transferred it to another person subject to a condition, so that in the event of the condition occurring the estate would revert back to him. In this way he has not fully divested himself of all his interest in the land, since there is a possibility that it will revert to him if the condition occurs, and the recipient cannot be said to enjoy an unqualified perpetual entitlement to the land. The requirement that the fee simple be absolute would be expected to exclude conditional and determinable fee simples alike from the class of legal estates. However, it should be noted that legislation intervenes to accord legal status to many conditional fee simples.

(b) *Conditional Fee Simple*

(i) Definition

8–005   A conditional fee simple will arise whenever a fee simple is transferred subject to the provision that it will fail on the happening of a condition subsequent.[2] For example, the freehold owner of land may transfer it to his mistress "on condition that she does not marry"; to his son "unless he becomes a Roman Catholic"; or to to his daughter "provided that she does not become a doctor".

---

[1] See Cheshire and Burn, *Modern Law of Real Property* (14th edn), Ch.15.
[2] In the case of a condition precedent the interest will not take effect until the condition is satisfied. If the condition is invalid for public policy reasons, then it follows that the interest will fall with the invalid condition. If the condition is impossible to fulfil, then similarly the interest will never take effect.

(ii)   Effect of the Occurrence of the Condition Subsequent

At common law if the condition occurs the land is not automatically transferred or revested   **8–006**
in the grantor, thus leaving the grantee with no interest. Instead, the occurrence of the condition gives the grantor the right to terminate the interest by "re-entering" the land.[3] Conditions
operate differently when they apply to a beneficial interest under a trust: they are then essentially directions to the trustees defining the nature of the beneficiary's interest. No entry on
the part of the trustees is therefore required to terminate the rights of the beneficiary.

(iii)   Void Conditions

Although the owner of land is generally free to restrict a grant with whatever conditions he   **8–007**
chooses, the law has always intervened to strike out conditions which are considered to be
contrary to public policy. The reason for this is that the imposition of a condition is a powerful means of exercising control over the behaviour of the grantee, since he will not wish to
lose his interest in the land. The law has always regarded as void conditions which impose a
complete restriction on the ability of the grantee to sell or transfer the land to others.[4]
Technically such conditions are said to restrict the ability to alienate the land. In *Re Brown*,[5]
a father left his freehold interest in land by will to his four sons subject to the condition that
they were only to alienate their shares to each other. Harman J. held that as they were a small
and diminishing class this amounted to a general restriction on alienation and was therefore
void. In contrast, in *Re Macleay*,[6] a condition not to alienate land other than within "the
family" was upheld, since this constituted a large group of people which would be increasing
in size. Conditions which are in complete restraint of marriage are regarded as contrary to
public policy.[7] However, conditions which restrain the freedom to remarry have been upheld,[8]
as have conditions which restrict the right of the grantee to marry a particular individual[9] or
persons from a specified group. For example, in *Jenner v Turner*[10] a condition imposed by a
sister on her brother that he should not marry a "domestic servant" was upheld by Bacon V.C.
Similarly a condition that the grantee not marry a "Papist" was upheld in *Duggan v Kelly*,[11]
as was a condition not to marry a "Scotchman" in *Perrin v Lyon*.[12] Conditions which encourage the separation or divorce of a husband and wife,[13] which seek to separate a parent from

---

[3] See *Challis's Real Property* (3rd edn, 1911), pp.219, 261.
[4] See *Muschamp v Bluett* (1617) J. Bridge 132; *Hood v Oglander* (1865) 34 Beav 513; *Re Rosher* (1884) 26 Ch.D.
801; *Corbett v Corbett* (1888) 14 P.D. 7; *Re Dugdale* (1888) 38 Ch.D. 176; *Re Cockerill* [1929] 2 Ch. 131.
[5] [1954] Ch. 39.
[6] (1875) L.R. 20 Eq. 186.
[7] *Long v Dennis* (1767) 4 Burr 2052; *Low v Peers* (1770) Wilm. 364.
[8] *Jordan v Holkham* (1753) Amb. 209. Contrast the Irish case of *Duddy v Gresham* (1878) 2 L.R.Ir. 422 where a condition in the testator's will that his wife should not remarry but enter a convent of her choice was held void.
[9] *Re Bathe* [1925] Ch. 377; *Re Hanlon* [1933] Ch. 254.
[10] (1880) 16 Ch.D. 188.
[11] (1848) 10 Ir. Eq. R. 295.
[12] (1807) 9 Est. 170.
[13] *Wren v Bradley* (1848) 2 de G. & Sm. 49; *Re Moore* (1888) 39 Ch.D. 116; *Re Caborne* [1943] Ch. 224;
Re Johnson's Will Trusts [1967] Ch. 387.

child,[14] or which interfere with the exercise of parental duties[15] have also been held to be void. However conditions which restrict the religion of the grantee have never been held to be contrary to public policy, and such a restriction was upheld by the House of Lords in *Blathwayt v Baron Cawley*.[16] Conditions will also be regarded as void if they are uncertain, since as Lord Cranworth stated in *Clavering v Ellison* the court must be able to "see from the beginning, precisely and distinctly, upon the happening of what event it was that [the gift] was to determine".[17] In *Clayton v Ramsden*[18] it was held that a condition forfeiting an interest in the event of marriage to a person "not of Jewish parentage" was void on the grounds of uncertainty.

(iv)   Consequence of a Void Condition Subsequent

8–008   Where a conditional fee simple is granted, but the condition is held to be void, the grantee takes his interest in the land free from the condition.[19] He therefore receives a fee simple absolute. This result will also follow if the condition cannot possibly occur.[20]

(v)   Status of a Conditional Fee Simple

8–009   Although s.1(1)(a) of the Law of Property Act 1925 would seem to indicate that a conditional fee simple cannot rank as a legal estate in land, s.7 has the effect that most conditional fee simples will enjoy legal status. This section, which was introduced by the Law of Property (Amendment) Act 1926,[21] has the effect that:

> "a fee simple subject to a legal or equitable right of entry or re-entry is for the purposes of this Act a fee simple absolute."

As has already been noted, the interest under a conditional fee simple does not automatically terminate if the condition occurs but must be forfeited by means of the exercise of a power of re-entry. Therefore the majority of conditional fee simples will fall within the ambit of s.7 unless they have been created expressly by means of a trust.

---

[14] *Re Morgan* (1910) 26 T.L.R. 398; *Re Sandbrook* [1912] 2 Ch. 471; *Re Boulter* [1922] 1 Ch. 75; *Re Piper* [1946] 2 All E.R. 503.

[15] See *Re Borwick* [1933] Ch. 657, where a condition that a child would forfeit her interest if she became a Roman Catholic was held void as it interfered with a parent's duty to provide his children with religious instruction.

[16] [1976] A.C. 397.

[17] (1859) 7 H.L. Cas. 7070 at 725.

[18] [1943] A.C. 320.

[19] *Re Croxon* [1904] 1 Ch. 252.

[20] *Re Turton* [1926] Ch. 96.

[21] The section was introduced because in some parts of the country the purchaser of land did not pay the seller the full price of the land but instead granted a perpetual annual land charge over it. In the event of the failure to repay the seller could re-enter the land and reacquire the fee simple. The section was intended to prevent the inconvenience of the fee simple not enjoying the status of a legal estate in such arrangements.

(c) *Determinable Fee Simple*

(i) Definition

The distinction between a fee simple which is subject to a condition subsequent and a fee simple **8–010** which is determinable is extremely fine, and was described in *Re King's Trusts* as "little short of disgraceful to our jurisprudence"[22] and in *Re Sharp's Settlement* as "extremely artificial".[23] The essence of the distinction seems to be that in the case of a determinable fee simple the grant of the land is never contemplated as being absolute, but only as lasting until the determining event occurs. The grant is only absolute in practice if the determining event never occurs. In the case of a conditional gift the grant is of a prima facie absolute interest in the land which will be cut short if the condition occurs. The difference between the two often comes down to a matter of the language that has been used to phrase the gift.[24] If the grant is said to be "until", "so long as", "whilst" or "during" the general conclusion is that it is determinable. In contrast, if phrases such as "on condition that", "provided that", and "if" are used the grant will be conditional in form. Therefore a grant of a fee simple to Peter "until he becomes a fighter pilot" will be determinable, but a grant "unless he becomes a fighter pilot" will be conditional. The problems occasioned by the artificiality of this distinction are compounded by the fact that the distinction is not trivial, but rather has important consequences for the nature of the interest which is enjoyed by the grantee.

(ii) Effect of the Occurrence of the Determining Event

If the event which is stipulated as the determining event of a determinable fee simple occurs, **8–011** the consequence is that the grant is automatically brought to an end and the fee simple revests in the grantee.[25] Unlike a conditional fee simple there was no need at common law for the grantee to take the initiative to forfeit the interest by exercising of a right of re-entry. Where the interest is created by way of trust, the beneficiary's interest similarly ceases automatically when the event occurs.

(iii) Effect if the Determining Event is Held Void

As was noted above, certain conditions are liable to be held void for reasons of public policy. If **8–012** a determining event is held void the grant itself fails and the interest reverts back to the grantee. For example in *Re Moore*,[26] a trust to pay a weekly sum to a woman "whilst . . . living apart from her husband" was held to be void because the determining event was itself void. This is exactly the opposite result to the outcome where a condition subsequent is held void and the grant becomes absolute.

---

[22] (1892) 29 L.R.Ir 410 at 410, per Porter M.R.
[23] [1973] Ch. 331 at 340, per Pennycuick V.C.
[24] See Challis, *Law of Real Property* (3rd edn), p.283.
[25] *Re Evan's Contract* (1920) 2 Ch. 469.
[26] (1888) 39 Ch.D. 116.

(iv)   Effect if the Determining Event Becomes Impossible

8–013   If the determining event becomes impossible, so that it will never happen, the interest automatically becomes absolute.[27]

(v)   Status of a Determinable Fee Simple

8–014   Unless a determinable fee simple is accompanied by a right of re-entry, it will fall outside the scope of the Law of Property Act 1925, s.7 and cannot enjoy the status of a legal estate. It can only take effect as an equitable interest behind a trust.

3.   "In Possession"

8–015   The meaning of the limitation that the fee simple must be "in possession" is not that the fee simple owner must necessarily be enjoying the actual use and possession of the land. For example, a freehold owner who has let his land does not enjoy the factual possession since the tenant has the right to "exclusive possession" of the land for the duration of the lease.[28] The requirement therefore refers to the fact that the holder of the fee simple is entitled to immediate enjoyment of his full rights as owner of the land, differentiating it from circumstances where he will only come to enjoy his full rights in the future. As Viscount Dilhorne stated in *Pearson v IRC* an estate in possession gives "a present right of present enjoyment".[29]

(a)   *Fee Simple Estates in Remainder*

8–016   A person will not be entitled to a fee simple absolute in possession if he holds a mere remainder interest in the land. This means that for the present someone else enjoys immediate rights over the land and that the fee simple owner will only become entitled to his full rights when those immediate rights are exhausted. For example, if James transferred the fee simple in his land to Karen, subject to a life interest for Leon, Karen's interest would be an interest in remainder since she would not be entitled to immediate enjoyment of her rights over the land but only on the death of Leon. It is not that the person with a remainder interest has no present rights in the land, the remainder interest is itself a present interest, but that his rights over the land will only come into full effect in the future. For historical reasons a fee simple estate out of which a lease has been granted is not considered to be an estate in remainder. It is only where the fee simple is subject to a particular estate, namely subject to a life estate or a fee tail, that it will be considered to be in remainder.[30]

---

[27] *Re Leach* [1912] 2 Ch. 422.

[28] See Law of Property Act 1925 s.205(1)(xix) where "possession" includes the "receipt of rents or profits or the right to receive the same."

[29] [1981] A.C. 753 at 772.

[30] Similarly, a fee simple cannot exist in remainder or in reversion upon another fee simple. Therefore, where the owner of a fee simple creates a fee simple defeasible by condition subsequent, he is considered only to retain the right of entry; where he creates a determinable fee simple, he is considered to retain a possibility of reverter.

(b) *Fee Simple Estates in Reversion*

An estate in reversion is similar to a remainder interest in that the owner's rights will simi- **8–017** larly not be fully enjoyed until the future. Reversionary interests arise where the original fee simple owner of land has failed to divest himself fully of his interests in the land, leaving a residue of rights which will result in the possession of the land reverting to him (or to his successors should he die before this occurs). For example, if instead of transferring the fee simple to Karen, James had simply granted Leon a life interest over his land, James would himself retain the reversionary interest, since on the death of Leon he would again be entitled to exercise his immediate rights as the fee simple owner. The difference between a remainder and a reversion is that the remainder arises where a fee simple owner creates a particular estate and simultaneously conveys what remains of the fee simple to someone else; by contrast a reversion exists where the fee simple owner creates a particular estate but retains the fee simple so that possession will revert to him or his successors on the ending of the particular estate.

DETERMINING WHO OWNS THE FREEHOLD

1. Introduction to Freehold Title

Having examined the theoretical nature of the freehold interest in the form of a fee simple **8–018** absolute in possession, the question arises as to who actually enjoys the freehold ownership, or title, to a particular piece of land. What constitutes good title will depend upon whether the land is registered or unregistered, and is subject to the qualification that a person who has adversely possessed the land may have gained a title which displaces that of the paper owner.

2. Freehold Title in Unregistered Land

Where land is unregistered, ownership of the freehold is not constituted by the possession of **8–019** any particular document or piece of paper. Title is constituted by being able to demonstrate an entitlement to the ownership of the land which is superior to the claims of any others. The most important means by which a person can establish such a title is by showing that he has derived his interest from a good root of title. This is done by showing that the land was transferred to him by a person who himself enjoyed a good title and was entitled to transfer it. Such a transfer is described as a conveyance, and by s.52(1) of the Law of Property Act 1925 it must be made by deed. What are known as the "title deeds" of unregistered land are simply a collection of the conveyances of the land which demonstrate how the title to the land has been derived. It is only necessary for a person claiming the land to demonstrate a good root of title stretching back 15 years, since if he has possessed the land for that period he will have gained a title good against anyone else by means of adverse possession.

3. Freehold Title in Registered Land

8–020 One of the most significant reforms introduced by the Land Registration Act 1925, which has now been replaced by the Land Registration Act 2002, was the establishment of a comprehensive system of land registration. Where title to land has been registered it is no longer necessary to demonstrate a good root of title on every occasion. Instead legal ownership of land is definitively constituted by being registered as the "registered proprietor" of the land on the centrally maintained Land Register. The registration of freehold ownership is the foundational building block of the system of land registration. The circumstances in which it is necessary for the freehold ownership of land to be registered, and the consequences of registration or of a failure to register, were examined in detail in Chapter 5 and will not be repeated here.

ACQUISITION OF THE FREEHOLD TITLE TO LAND BY TRANSFER FROM THE EXISTING FREEHOLD OWNER

1. General Principles

8–021 The most important means by which a person can obtain the freehold ownership of land is by way of a valid transfer of title from the present freehold owner. The transfer may either be by gift, or more usually as a result of a contract between the parties for the sale and transfer of the land. The principles governing transfers of freehold ownership differ depending upon whether the land in question is registered or unregistered. The process by which the ownership is transferred is known as conveyancing.

(a) *Transferring Freehold Ownership in Unregistered Land*

8–022 Where land is unregistered the freehold may be transferred by means of a conveyance from the transferor to the transferee. By s.52(1) of the Law of Property Act 1925, a conveyance of land is "void for the purpose of conveying or creating a legal estate unless made by deed".[31] In every case the transfer will now have to be completed by registration.[32]

(b) *Transferring Freehold Ownership in Registered Land*

8–023 Where land is registered, a transfer of the freehold estate is a disposition which is required to be completed by registration.[33] It follows that the freehold estate will only pass from the current

---

[31] Law of Property (Miscellaneous Provisions) Act 1989 s.1.
[32] Land Registration Act 2002 s.4(1).
[33] Land Registration Act 2002 s.27(2)(a).

registered proprietor to the intended transferee of the estate by the entry of the transferee as the new registered proprietor of the land at the Land Registry. To accomplish this process the transferor of the freehold estate must complete a land transfer form, authorising the Land Registrar to alter the register entry. Once completed by the transferor this form is passed to the transferee, who completes it by entering his own details. The form is then forwarded to the Land Registry and the register is amended.[34]

2. The Conveyancing Process

By far the most common circumstance in which the freehold ownership of land will be transferred is where the land is sold. In the case of unregistered land this will give rise to the need to register the title. Ultimately in the case of both registered and unregistered land a sale will only effect a transfer of the legal freehold ownership through registration of the transferee as the registered proprietor. Although the means by which freehold ownership is transferred is by registration of the transferee, the process of conveyancing is complex because of the inter-relationship between the contract entered into by the parties and their proprietary entitlements to the land. This section will outline the key stages of the conveyancing process, and the effects that they have on the rights and entitlements of the parties.[35]   **8–024**

(a) Distinguishing Contract, Completion and Registration

Where land is transferred by sale there are a number of important stages to the conveyancing process. Three separate elements of such a transaction must be distinguished. First, there is the contract between the purchaser and the vendor, which constitutes a binding agreement to sell and transfer the land in return for the payment of an agreed price. However the mere entering of a binding contract does not itself transfer the legal ownership of the land from the vendor to the purchaser. A second stage to the transaction is required when the contract is carried into effect, the purchase price is paid, and possession of the land is transferred to the purchaser. This stage is termed completion, and is accompanied by the execution of a conveyance of the land by the transferor to the transferee using an appropriate land transfer form.[36] However even the execution of a conveyance and land transfer form is not effective to transfer the legal freehold estate in the land to the purchaser. This will only happen when the transferor is registered as the new proprietor of the estate, and thus a third stage of registration is required. There is inevitably a time gap between the completion of the sale, when the purchaser will usually move into the property, and the point at which the purchaser becomes the legal owner of the property.   **8–025**

---

[34] See *Mascall v Mascall* (1984) 50 P. & C.R. 119.

[35] For a full discussion of the conveyancing process see: Thompson, *Barnsley's Conveyancing Law and Practice* (4th edn, 1996).

[36] The land transfer form is the form of transfer prescribed for the transfer of registered land. For unregistered land the conveyance must contain all the relevant information but need not use any prescribed form.

(b) *Reaching Agreement "Subject to Contract"*

8–026   A vendor seeking to sell land will obviously seek a buyer, probably through the services of an estate agent, and advertise the land as available for purchase stipulating an expected price. Potential buyers offer a price they are willing to pay. When an offer is made it is for the vendor to decide whether to accept or reject it. Although in conventional bargains the contract comes into existence and is binding on the parties at the moment that an offer is accepted, in land sales the offer is usually accepted by the vendor "subject to contract". This operates as a provisional acceptance of the offer, signifying that the vendor is willing to sell at that price, but without creating a binding agreement. Both parties remain free not to go ahead with the transaction and they will have no remedies if the other decides to withdraw from the transaction. This "sale" may fall through for a number of common reasons, for example if the vendor accepts and subsequently receives a higher offer from someone else, a practice known as gazumping. Alternatively, if the price of property is falling the purchaser may wish to pull out of the sale if he feels the offer is too high. During the period between acceptance subject to contract and exchange of contracts the purchaser will have opportunity to make inquiries concerning the land. The basic rule remains caveat emptor so the burden falls on the purchaser to satisfy himself of what he is getting. The buyer's solicitor will therefore conduct a number of searches, for example of the Land Register, to ascertain that the seller genuinely owns the property and has the right to sell it, and to discover if there are any adverse interests affecting it, such as easements or restrictive covenants. The buyer's solicitor will also search the local land charges register maintained by the relevant local authority which contains other information relevant to the land such as planning permissions and similar matters. The buyer might also conduct an environmental search to ensure that there are no problems with the land, and most buyers will also undertake some kind of structural survey of the property. If the purchase is being financed with the help of a mortgage the lender will usually also conduct a survey to confirm that the land is of sufficient value to provide security for the proposed mortgage advance. The complexity of these pre-contract inquiries and searches, and the possibility that they might need to be repeated multiple times if potential sales fall through before a contract is entered into, has prompted legislative intervention in the property transfer market.[37] The Housing Act 2004 provides that sellers must produce a "Home Information Pack" before their property is put on the market,[38] which must include, inter alia, an energy performance certificate,[39] a home condition report (which is voluntary), evidence of title, and standard searches.[40] For newly built houses marketed for sale the Home Information Pack must contain a "Sustainability Certificate" incorporating

---

[37] There has been criticism that this is not beneficial to the consumer: Riddall [2001] Conv. 206, 206; Kenny [2003] Conv. 263.

[38] s.156. The provisions relating to Home Information Packs were brought fully into force on March 13, 2008, in relation to all remaining residential properties: Housing Act 2004 (Commencement No.11) (England and Wales) Order (SI 2008/898).

[39] "Containing advice on how to cut carbon emissions and fuel bills": *http://www.homeinformationpacks.gov.uk*. This part of the provision appears to be part of the implementation of the European Buildings Directive (Directive 2002/91) which "required Member States by January 4, 2006 to provide energy performance certificates on the sale and renting of buildings": [2006] Conv. 497, 497.

[40] Housing Act 2004 s.163; Home Information Pack (No.2) Regulations 2007 (SI 2007/1667) Pt 3 reg.8; See also *http://www.homeinformationpacks.gov.uk*; K. Fenn (2006) 10(1) L. & T.R. 15.

information about, e.g. how materials are used, aspects of design and construction, ensure "the health, safety, welfare and convenience of persons in or about the property".[41] The provision of the Home Information Pack is intended to reduce dramatically the time between the acceptance of an offer and exchange of contracts. However it shifts costs which are currently borne by prospective purchasers to intending vendors. It is also likely to have less impact on dealing with delays in house sales than intended since many of these delays relate to difficulties in obtaining a mortgage for reasons unrelated to the matters contained in the HIP, and to the need for most purchasers (other than those making their first purchase) to coordinate the purchase with the sale of an existing property, and so on through occasionally lengthy chains of related transactions.[42] There are other problems with the HIP, including the willingness of purchasers to rely upon surveys conducted on behalf of the seller, and the possibility that a survey will become out of date if a property remains on the market for any length of time.[43]

(c) *Exchange of Contract*

Exchange is the moment at which a fully binding contract comes into force between the parties. **8–027** Neither party can then withdraw from the sale without committing a breach of contract. If one party does breach the contract the other will be able to seek a remedy from the courts. It is possible for the contract to be made using only a single document signed by both parties. It is more usual, however, for the contract to be made using two identical documents, one of which is signed by the purchaser, with the other being signed by the seller. These documents are exchanged when it is intended that the contract should come into effect.

(i) *Formalities Required for the Creation of Contracts for the Sale of Land*

A contract for the sale of land will be void unless the requisite formalities have been satisfied. **8–028** For contracts entered after September 27, 1989 the formal requirements are stipulated in the Law of Property (Miscellaneous Provisions) Act 1989. Section 2(1) provides that:

> "A contract for the sale or other disposition of an interest in land can only be made in writing and only by incorporating all the terms which the parties have expressly agreed in one document or, where contracts are exchanged, in each."

Where a prior valid contract has granted a person an option to purchase land Hoffman J. held in *Spiro v Glencrown*[44] that there was no need for a notice exercising the option to comply

---

[41] Home Information Pack (Amendment) Regulations 2008 (SI 2008/572) reg.2.

[42] See also Kenny [2004] Conv. 81.

[43] HIPS (previously known as "the Seller's Pack" and "Sellers' Information Pack") are discussed in *The Conveyancer and Property Lawyer* going back to their conception. The conclusion appears to be that their purpose is oblique, ill-conceived and unlikely to solve many of the problems they have set out to rectify: Kenny [1999] Conv. 78; [2003] Conv. 263; [2004] Conv. 81; [2005] Conv. 185; [2005] Conv. 277; [2006] Conv. 497; [2006] Conv. 319; Riddall [2001] Conv. 206]; also K. Fenn (2006) 10(1) L. & T.R. 15.

[44] [1991] Ch. 537.

with s.2. This follows from the fact that an option is exercised by the grantee and it is unrealistic to expect the grantor to sign such a notice. Contracts made prior to September 27, 1997 merely needed to be evidenced in writing by the Law of Property Act 1925 s.40. If there was no writing the contract was unenforceable unless there had been some act of part performance by the parties, such as entering into possession of the land, in which case it would be enforceable in equity. The fact that a contract which does not comply with the formalities requirements of the Law of Property (Miscellaneous Provisions) Act 1989 is rendered void has abolished the doctrine of part performance, which is therefore no longer applicable.

(ii) The Mechanism of Exchange

8–029 Exchange consists of the vendor signing and passing a copy of the contract to the purchaser, and the purchaser signing and passing a copy of the contract to the vendor. This may be effected by post, in which case the contractual postal rule[45] will apply, by telephone,[46] or in person. Customarily a deposit is paid by the purchaser when the contracts are exchanged.

(iii) Specific Performance is Normally Available

8–030 Since the property involved is land, which is unique, the equitable remedy of specific performance will generally be available once a contract has been concluded so that the other party can compel the party in breach to perform the contract. As Lord Diplock said in *Sudbrook Trading Estate Ltd v Eggleton*, damages alone would "constitute a wholly inadequate and unjust remedy for the breach" and therefore "the normal remedy is by way of specific performance".[47] However, because specific performance is an equitable remedy and therefore discretionary, it may be unavailable if the party seeking it has acted unconscionably, the award would prejudice the interests of third parties, or it would cause a hardship amounting to an injustice. For example, in *Patel v Ali*[48] Mr and Mrs Ali had entered a contract to sell their house to Mr and Mrs Patel. Mr Ali was then adjudicated bankrupt and spent a year in prison. Mrs Ali was diagnosed as suffering from cancer and had a leg amputated just before the birth of her second child and then subsequently had a third child. Goulding J. refused an order for specific performance on the ground of undue hardship, but emphasised that:

> "only in extraordinary and persuasive circumstances can hardship supply an excuse for resisting performance of a contract for the sale of [land]".

[45] *Adams v Lindsell* (1818) 1 B. & Ald. 681; *Household Fire and Carriage Accident Insurance Co Ltd v Grant* (1879) 4 Ex.D. 216; *Henthorn v Fraser* [1892] 2 Ch. 27. See also *Entores v Miles Far East Corp* [1955] 2 Q.B. 327; *Brinkibon Ltd v Stahag* [1983] A.C. 34.
[46] *Midland Bank Trust Co v Green* [1981] A.C. 513.
[47] [1983] 1 A.C. 444 at 478.
[48] [1984] Ch. 283.

(iv) The Contract for Sale Gives Rise to a Constructive Trust

Although entering a binding contract does not itself effect the transfer of the legal title of the land to the purchaser, the equitable ownership passes by means of a constructive trust as soon as the contract is entered because the contract is specifically enforceable and "equity treats as done that which ought to be done". As Lord Jessel M.R. said in *Lysaght v Edwards*: **8–031**

> "the moment you have a valid contract for sale the vendor becomes in equity a trustee for the purchaser of the estate sold".[49]

One consequence of this is that from the moment of contract the purchaser is required to insure the land since risk passes to him when he obtains the equitable ownership of the land. Similarly from the moment of contract the vendor is no longer entitled to sever fixtures from the land as they belong to the purchaser in equity.

(v) The Contract for Sale Constitutes an Interest in Land

Since a contract for sale of land involves the transfer of property, the contract itself is regarded as a type of interest in land, which is known as an estate contract. Since it falls outside of the scope of s.1(2) of the Law of Property Act 1925, the estate contract is merely an equitable interest in the land.[50] If the land is wrongly conveyed to someone other than the purchaser by the vendor it is possible that such a transferee will be bound by the purchaser's estate contract. This will be a question of priorities. In the case of registered land it will depend upon whether the estate contract was properly protected on the register, or whether the purchaser was in actual occupation of the land he had contracted to buy, in which case his estate contract may be an overriding interest. In the case of unregistered land an estate contract is a land charge and whether it binds the third party transferee will depend on whether it was properly protected on the land charges register.[51] **8–032**

(d) *Completion*

Completion is the final stage of the transfer where the legal title is transferred from the vendor to the purchaser. The mere fact that the new freehold owner has taken possession of the land in pursuance of the contract is not itself effective to transfer title. In the case of unregistered land the conveyance is executed after the purchaser has paid over the purchase moneys and the appropriate title deeds are then handed over. In the case of registered land the vendor hands over the form of transfer which must be completed and sent to the Land Registry. Completion is the usual time at which the purchaser is entitled to enter into the land being transferred, so that in the case of a transfer of domestic accommodation it usually equates with the date of moving. **8–033**

---

[49] [1876] 2 Ch.D. 499.
[50] Law of Property Act 1925 s.1(3).
[51] *Midland Bank Trust Co v Green* [1981] A.C. 513.

(e) *Registration*

8–034 As has been noted above, the legal title is not technically transferred by conveyance but by registration of the transferee as the new proprietor of the land, or by first registration if the land was previously unregistered. Inevitably this process takes time and it means that the purchaser will not be registered as owner at the time that completion takes place. The gap between the date of completion and the date at which the purchaser is registered as the new owner is referred to as the "registration gap".

(f) *Electronic Conveyancing*

8–035 The Law Commission Consultative document, *Land Registration for the Twenty-First Century*,[52] anticipates a future move towards a system of electronic conveyancing. This will replace the current procedures for completion and registration of the transfer of a registered estate in land, and will enable completion and registration to take place simultaneously. This will mean that there will no longer be any "registration gap" between the current paper exercise of completion and the registration of the transferee as the proprietor of the freehold of the land. The Land Registration Act 2002 makes provision for the introduction of a new system of electronic conveyancing in Pt 8 and Sch.5. These provisions have not yet been fully brought into force.[53] E-conveyancing services are to be introduced incrementally, avoiding a "big bang" approach to change.[54] The Land Registry already has a number of online services, for example, "Land Registry Direct" which provides access to information, including title registers to "the great majority of properties in England and Wales".[55] Title information is now available to members of the public for download for a small fee from "Land Register Online".[56] There is also a system enabling the electronic discharge of mortgages.[57]

3. Priority of Interests where Freehold Land is Transferred

8–036 Where the title to freehold land is transferred the question arises as to whether the transferee acquires the title subject to the pre-existing rights and interests of third parties. The means by which such priorities issues are resolved were examined in detail in Chapter 7 (and in Chapter 4 for unregistered land), and only a brief summary will be provided here. The relevant principles will differ depending upon whether the land was registered or unregistered.

---

[52] Law Com. No.254 (1998), para.11.2.
[53] See Harpum and Bignell, *Registered Land: The New Law* (2002), Jordans, Ch.7.
[54] *http://www1.landregistry.gov.uk/e-conveyancing/projects.*
[55] *http://www1.landreg.gov.uk/direct/.*
[56] *http://www.landregisteronline.gov.uk/.*
[57] *http://www1.landregistry.gov.uk/e-conveyancing/ends/;* [2003] Conv. 263.

(a) Determining Priorities where the Land was Registered

Where the title to freehold land was already registered, issues of priority are determined by a combination of the statutory rules regarding overreaching and the provisions of the Land Registration Act 2002 as to the effect of registered dispositions of land. Where the transfer has overreaching effect the transferor will acquire the land free from any pre-existing trust interests. Overreaching will only occur where the land was conveyed by at least two trustees, to whom any capital moneys arising from the transfer were paid. Since a transfer of freehold title is a registered disposition of the land, s.29 of the Land Registration Act 2002 has the effect that a transferor of the freehold title for valuable consideration gains priority over all pre-existing interests except those which have "protected priority", which are:

8–037

(i) any registered charges or interests protected by a notice in the register;

(ii) the overriding interests set out in Sch.3;

(iii) any interest which appears from the register to be excepted from the effect of registration.

(b) Determining Priorities where the Land was Unregistered

Where the freehold title to unregistered land is transferred, the transfer will have to be completed by registration. Issues of priority are therefore determined by a combination of the statutory rules regarding overreaching and the effect of first registration of title. Where the transfer has over-reaching effect the transferor will acquire title free from any pre-existing trust interests affecting the land. Any existing legal interests will bind the purchaser, as will any equitable interests which have not been overreached, other than those equitable interests in respect of which the purchaser can claim to be a bona fide purchaser for value without notice. All such rights which are binding on the purchaser and of which the Land Registrar is aware will be recorded on the register. Following first registration, under the provisions of the Land Registration Act 2002 the first registered proprietor will acquire the land subject only to the following interests:

8–038

(i) any adverse rights recorded on the register for the property;

(ii) the overriding interests set out in Sch.1[58];

(iii) any rights acquired by adverse possession of which the registered proprietor has notice.

[58] The rights which are treated as overriding interests on first registration are, by and large, legal rights which would have been binding on the owner of unregistered land, even though the owner may have been unaware of their existence. They include legal easements and profits à prendre, customary and public rights, legal leases which are not themselves registrable estates, certain rights to mines and minerals, and for a transitional period of 10 years, franchises, manorial rights, Crown rents, common law obligations to repair or contribute to the cost of repairing embankments, sea or river walls, payments in lieu of tithes and chancel repair liability. Local land charges, which are recorded in a separate register, are also overriding interests.

ACQUISITION OF THE FREEHOLD TITLE TO LAND BY ADVERSE POSSESSION

8–039   In the previous section it has been seen how the usual means of acquiring the freehold ownership of land is by effective transfer from the present freeholder. However it is also possible for a person to gain title to the land by taking possession of it for a sufficient period of time. By this means a squatter may, in effect, "steal" land from its true owner, who will be incapable of recovering it. Such a person is said to have acquired title to the land by adverse possession.

Although it might initially appear to be against public policy to allow persons to "steal" land merely by taking possession of it, as this might encourage squatting, the law regards an owner of land as being under a duty to protect his own interests. If his land is occupied by squatters, he is expected not to stand by and do nothing to have them removed, but to seek his rightful remedies to evict them because they are trespassers. If he does not take advantage of the remedies that are available to him, the law supposes that he does not particularly value the land that is adversely possessed, or at least not sufficiently to take action to protect his rights. This rationale was articulated in *RB Policies at Lloyd's v Butler*,[59] where it was said that landowners should not "go to sleep on their claims" and cannot expect the assistance of the courts in recovering their land if they do so. The inherent limitations in the operation of the principles of adverse possession mean that only in extreme cases will squatters qualify to oust the rights of landowners.

The exact means by which a squatter can obtain title to land by adverse possession will vary, depending upon whether the land in question is registered or unregistered. In the case of unregistered land, the title of a freehold owner is extinguished where a squatter is in adverse possession for a period of 12 years. In the case of registered land a rather more complex procedure is necessary, because legal ownership is constituted by registration as the proprietor of the estate in question. Under the regime of the Land Registration Act 1925 a squatter would be entitled to be registered as proprietor of the land after it had been adversely possessed for 12 years or more,[60] and in the interim period before such registration the proprietor would hold the land on trust for him.[61] Under the new regime introduced by the Land Registration Act 2002 a squatter does not automatically acquire the right to be registered as proprietor of the land by virtue of a period of adverse possession. Rather he will only be entitled to be registered as proprietor if specific statutory criteria are met, which have the effect of greatly limiting the circumstances in which title to registered land will be acquired by adverse possession. The consequence is that there are now two distinct regimes for adverse possession, one applying to unregistered land, and the other to registered land. There are, however, a number of common features.

1. The Essential Elements of Adverse Possession

8–040   There are two main requirements that a squatter must satisfy before he is able to claim adverse possession of land. First, he must show that he was in factual possession of the

---

[59] [1950] 1 K.B. 76.
[60] Land Registration Act 1925 s.75(2).
[61] Land Registration Act 1925 s.75(1).

land. Second, he must show that he possessed the land with the necessary intention to possess.[62]

(a) *Factual Possession of the Land*

A person will only be able to claim adverse possession if he has taken physical possession of the land. Under the provisions of the Limitation Act 1980 a person claiming an interest by way of adverse possession will only be entitled to claim that his possession was adverse from the date that the true owner was dispossessed or discontinucd his possession.[63] In *Treloar v Nute* Sir John Pennycuick stated that:

    8–041

> "the person claiming by possession must show either (1) discontinuance by the paper owner followed by possession or (2) dispossession (or as it is sometimes called 'ouster') of the paper owner".[64]

(i) What Constitutes Factual Possession of Land

The question whether a person has taken factual possession of the land is complex, since what will be sufficient to constitute such possession will depend upon the nature of the land concerned.[65] What seems to be required is that the possessor must have taken exclusive physical control of the land. However what will be sufficient to constitute control will itself vary with the nature of the land.[66] As Slade J. stated in *Powell v McFarlane*:

    8–042

> "Factual possession signifies an appropriate degree of physical control. It must be a single and [exclusive] possession, though there can be a single possession exercised by or on behalf of several persons jointly. Thus an owner of land and a person intruding on that land without his consent cannot both be in possession of the land at the same time. The question what acts constitute a sufficient degree of exclusive physical control must depend on the circumstances, in particular the nature of the land and the manner in which land of that nature is commonly used or enjoyed . . . Everything must depend on the particular circumstances, but broadly, I think what must be shown as constituting factual possession is that the alleged possessor has been dealing with the land in question as an occupying owner might have been expected to deal with it and that no-one else has done so."[67]

---

[62] These requirements were recognised by the Court of Appeal in *Powell v McFarlane* (1977) 38 P. & C.R. 452 and approved by the House of Lords in *Pye (JA) (Oxford) Ltd v Graham* [2003] 1 A.C. 419.
[63] Limitation Act 1980 s.15(6) Sch.1 para.1.
[64] [1976] 1 W.L.R. 1295.
[65] *Lord Advocate v Lord Lovat* (1880) 5 App. Cas. 273 at 288, per Lord O'Hagan.
[66] In *Palfrey v Wilson The Times* May 3, 2007; [2007] Conv. 191, the claimant had done everything required to maintain a wall, repairing it, adding a damp-proof course, etc. These were sufficient acts of possession of the wall.
[67] (1970) 38 P. & C.R. 452 at 471, as approved by the House of Lords in *Pye (JA) (Oxford) Ltd v Graham* [2002] UKHL 30; [2002] 3 All E.R 865.

It is clear that physically fencing the land will generally be sufficient to establish factual possession.[68] In *Seddon v Smith*[69] Cockburn C.J. said that "enclosure is the strongest possible evidence of adverse possession".[70] Therefore there was no doubt that land had been factually possessed in *Buckinghamshire CC v Moran*,[71] where the claimant had completely enclosed an area belonging to the council with fences and hedges and incorporated it as part of his garden by adding a new gate and lock. In *Barrett v Tower Hamlets LBC*[72] the tenants of a public house used and occupied adjacent land and repaired and maintained a fence which secured it from access by third parties, whilst believing the land to be comprised in their tenancy. Neuberger L.J. held that this established a "strong" case.[73] It did not matter that they themselves had not erected the fence.[74] Neither was it important that the fence did not cover the whole area, the material issue being whether they had dealt with the land as an occupying owner. The enclosure of the land is not a necessary requirement for factual possession, and in some cases has been held to be insufficient,[75] for example where a fence was erected for only 24 hours,[76] or for the purpose of preventing a senile family member from straying.[77] In many cases it has been held that factual possession has been established even without fencing or otherwise enclosing the land. In *Treloar v Nute*[78] grazing cows and storing timber on land was held to amount to factual possession. In *Red House Farms (Thorndon) Ltd v Catchpole*,[79] shooting over marshy ground was also held to be sufficient. In *Leigh v Jack*[80] Bramwell L.J. suggested that building on land or cultivating it could constitute factual possession. In *Roberts v Swangrove Estates Ltd*[81] it was held that in appropriate circumstances fishing could constitute an act of possession.[82] In this case a claim to foreshore succeeded by an accumulation of acts of possession and control, e.g. the grant of shooting and fishing licences, collecting payment under those licences, and substantial dredging of the river bed.[83] However, the performance of purely trivial acts will not generally constitute factual possession of the land. In *Tecbild v Chamberlain*[84] it was held that children who had played on land and tethered and exercised their ponies there had not done sufficient to establish factual possession.[85] In *Pye (JA) (Oxford) Ltd v Graham*[86] the House of Lords held that the requirement of factual

---

[68] See for example: *Williams v Usherwood* (1983) P. & C.R. 235.

[69] (1877) 36 L.T. 168.

[70] Approved by the House of Lords in *Pye (JA) (Oxford) Ltd v Graham* [2003] 1 A.C. 419; In *Mulcahy v Curramore Ltd* [1974] 2 N.S.W.L.R. 464 fencing was described as "useful evidence of occupation to the exclusion of others."

[71] [1990] Ch. 623.

[72] [2005] EWCA Civ 923.

[73] [2005] EWCA Civ 923, para.38.

[74] An analogy was drawn with *Pye v Graham*.

[75] See: *Basildon DC v Manning* (1975) 237 E.G. 879; *Boosey v Davis* (1987) 55 P. & C.R. 83.

[76] *Marsden v Miller* (1992) 64 P. & C.R. 239.

[77] *Fruin v Fruin* (unreported, 1983, CA).

[78] [1976] 1 W.L.R. 1295.

[79] (1977) 244 E.G. 295.

[80] (1870) 5 Ex.D. 264.

[81] [2007] EWHC 513, the case was affirmed on appeal: *Roberts v Swangrove Estates Ltd* [2008] EWCA Civ 98.

[82] [2007] EWHC 513 para.46. Permanent acts such as "fixtures into the soil of the foreshore are more likely to be regarded as acts of possession of the soil itself" than more superficial acts: Para.46.

[83] This was only one of the claims for adverse possession dealt with in this case.

[84] (1969) 20 P. & C.R. 633.

[85] See also *Bills v Fernandez-Gonzales* (1981) 132 N.L.J. 60; *Boosey v Davis* (1987) 55 P. & C.R. 83; *Wilson v Marton's Executors* [1993] 24 E.G. 119.

[86] [2003] 1 A.C. 419.

possession was readily satisfied where the defendants had farmed land belonging to the claimants, including grazing between 80 and 140 cattle, liming and re-seeding the land, trimming the hedges every year and maintaining the boundary fencing and ditches. The owners were physically excluded from the land by the hedges and the lack of any key to the road gate providing access.

(ii) Possession Must be Exclusive

The claimant must have been in possession to the exclusion of the paper owner and all others.[87] In *Leigh v Jack*[88] the person claiming adverse possession had used land for the storage of materials. The owner had also made occasional use of the land. The claim to adverse possession failed because, as the case was subsequently interpreted in *Buckinghamshire CC v Moran*,[89] the claimant never had possession to the exclusion of the owner. In *British Waterways Board v Toor*[90] a claim to an alleyway failed, inter alia, because the squatter had not excluded others from parking there. In contrast, in *Barrett v Tower Hamlets LBC*[91] the exercise of the paper owner's responsibility to support the adjacent building by erecting props on the area, was not a sufficient reassertion of possession against the squatters.

8–043

(iii) Possession Must be Adverse to the Interests of the Owner

This means that the claimant must be exercising factual possession of the land as a trespasser, rather than as someone who is entitled because he has the permission of the owner to occupy the land. Therefore a tenant[92] of the freeholder or a person to whom he has granted a licence,[93] whether consensual or unilateral,[94] cannot maintain that his possession was adverse. However, his possession may become adverse if it continues beyond the time when his lease or licence[95] has come to an end. As Slade L.J. stated in *Buckinghamshire CC v Moran*:

8–044

> "Possession is never 'adverse' . . . if it is enjoyed by lawful title. If, therefore, a person occupies or uses land by licence of the owner with the paper title and his licence has not been duly determined, he cannot be treated as having been in 'adverse possession' as against the owner of the paper title."[96]

---

[87] i.e. unauthorised others. In *Roberts v Swangrove Estates Ltd* [2007] EWHC 513, para.45, Lindsay J. held that "the required exclusivity of possession is not negated by the exercise of the legal rights of others such as public rights of way or of fishing or navigation or private rights such as easements". Affirmed on appeal: [2008] EWCA Civ 98.
[88] (1870) 5 Ex.D. 264 (as interpreted in *Buckinghamshire CC v Moran* [1990] Ch. 623).
[89] [1990] Ch. 623.
[90] [2006] EWHC 1256.
[91] [2005] EWCA Civ 923.
[92] *Colchester BC v Smith* [1991] Ch. 448.
[93] *BP Properties v Buckler* [1987] 2 E.G.L.R. 168.
[94] See *Markfield Investments Ltd v Evans* [2001] 2 All E.R. 238.
[95] *Colchester BC v Smith* [1991] Ch. 448.
[96] [1990] Ch. 623 at 626.

In *Allen v Matthews*[97] the Court of Appeal held that a person who had been given limited permission to use a yard for storage had successfully established that his possession was adverse because his use substantially exceeded the permission in both degree and nature. In *Ofulue v Bossert*[98] it was held that a person who believed he was a tenant could be in adverse possession as the owner did not accept that he was a tenant. All that was necessary is that the owner had not given consent to the possession.

In one case prior to the Limitation Act 1980 a licence was implied where the owner of land left it unoccupied because he had no present use for it but intended to make some use in the future. The case was *Wallis's Cayton Bay Holiday Camp Ltd v Shell Mex and BP Ltd*,[99] where a farmer sold land to a petroleum company which intended to use it for the construction of a filling station in the future, once a new road had been built. The road was not built, and the farmer used the land in a variety of ways, including extending his caravan park. Action was taken by the petroleum company only after the farmer had been using the land he had sold for more than 12 years. Lord Denning M.R. held that there was an implied licence so that the farmer had not defeated the petroleum company's title to the land. If the case had established a general principle, the implication of such licences would have made it extremely difficult to establish adverse possession of unoccupied land.[100] In *Buckinghamshire CC v Moran*[101] Nourse L.J. described the implied licence theory introduced by Lord Denning as "an original heresy of his own", and the law was reformed by the Limitation Act 1980, which provides that a licence will not be implied "merely by virtue of the fact that [the claimant's] occupation is not inconsistent with the [owner's] present or future enjoyment of the land".[102]

Nevertheless, this provision expressly does not prevent the court from finding that there is an implied licence "where such a finding is justified on the actual facts of the case".[103] In *Colin Dawson Windows Ltd v King's Lynn and West Norfolk BC*[104] a licence was implied because the paper owner, during negotiations with the claimant squatters for sale of the land, asked the claimants to leave if the sale did not proceed, which demonstrated implied permission to be on the land during negotiations. Rix L.J. outlined the test for implied licences[105]:

> "But in order to establish permission in the circumstances of any case, two matters must be established. First there must have been some overt act by the landowner or some demonstrable circumstances from which the inference can be drawn that permission was in fact given. Secondly, a reasonable person would have appreciated that the user was with the permission of the landowner."

In *Barrett v Tower Hamlets LBC*[106] Neuberger L.J. said that "[t]he court will readily infer the grant of a licence during negotiations for the purchase or letting of land, where the negotiating

---

[97] [2007] EWCA Civ 216; [2007] 2 P. & C.R. 21.
[98] [2008] EWCA Civ 7.
[99] [1975] Q.B. 94.
[100] See also *Gray v Wykeham Martin & Goode* (unreported, January 17, 1977).
[101] [1990] Ch. 623.
[102] Limitation Act 1980 s.15(6) Sch.1 para.8(4).
[103] See (1980) 96 L.Q.R. 333 (P. Jackson); [1986] Conv. 434 (G. McCormack).
[104] (2005) 2 P. & C.R. 19.
[105] Para.34 quoting *Bath & North Somerset DC v Nicholson* (February 22, 2002, unreported), per Mr Kim Lewison Q.C. quoting *Lambeth v Rumbelow* (unreported) January 25, 2001 per Etherton J.
[106] [2005] EWCA Civ 923.

purchaser or tenant is in occupation".[107] However, in this case there could be no implied licence because the negotiations did not involve the claimant possessors.[108] In *Batsford Estates (1983) Co Ltd v Taylor* the Court of Appeal recognised that "the test is a general one" and not solely applicable to circumstances where there are negotiations.[109]

A claim to adverse possession will be defeated if the squatter acknowledges the paper owner's superior title. What constitutes such an acknowledgement will be a question of fact, but it must be made by the person in possession.[110]

(iv) Possession Must be Open

The adverse possession of the land must be open and unconcealed.[111] This requirement means that the period of adverse possession cannot start running against a true owner where he would not have been able to observe that the land was being possessed. Section 32 of the Limitation Act 1980 provides that any actions of the possessor which were fraudulent or deliberately concealed from the owner do not cause the limitation period to run until the owner discovered, or should reasonably have discovered, the fraud or concealment.[112]

8–045

(b) *Intention to Possess the Land*

(i) Meaning of the Requirement

The mere fact that a person enjoys factual possession of the land adverse to the owner is not itself sufficient to entitle him to defeat the owner's title. He must demonstrate that he possessed the land with the requisite intention. This elusive requirement has also been known as the animus possidendi. Historically it was thought that the necessary intention was an intention to own the land.[113] However in the recent case of *Pye (JA) (Oxford) Ltd v Graham*[114] the House of Lords categorically held that there was no need for a squatter to demonstrate an intention to own the land in order to gain title by means of adverse possession. All that is required is the demonstration of an "intention to possess" the land. Lord Browne-Wilkinson explained:

8–046

> "Once it is accepted that in the Limitation Acts, the word 'possession' has its ordinary meaning (being the same as in the law of trespass or conversion) it is clear that, at any given moment, the only relevant question is whether the person in factual possession also

---

[107] [2005] EWCA Civ 923, paras 66–68, referring to *Colin Dawson*.
[108] [2005] EWCA Civ 923, paras 66–68. To conclude otherwise would be "legal fairyland", the paper owners being unaware of the occupation: [2005] EWCA Civ 923, paras 66–68.
[109] (2006) 2 P. & C.R. 5, para.23, per Sir Martin Nourse.
[110] *Allen v Matthews* [2007] 2 P. & C.R. 21; *Barrett v Tower Hamlets LBC* [2005] EWCA Civ 923.
[111] *Pye (JA) (Oxford) v Graham* [2003] 1 A.C. 419 at 446d–e, *Roberts v Swangrove Estates Ltd* [2007] EWHC 513, per Lindsay J.
[112] *Beaulane Properties Ltd v Palmer* [2006] Ch. 79.
[113] *Littledale v Liverpool College* [1900] 1 Ch. 19; *George Wimpey & Co Ltd v Sohn* [1967] Ch. 47 at 510, per Russell L.J.
[114] [2003] 1 A.C. 419.

has an intention to possess: if a stranger enters onto land occupied by a squatter, the entry is a trespass against the possession of the squatter whether or not the squatter has any long-term intention to acquire a title."[115]

He further opined that confusion had been caused by the definition of this element as an "intention to possess," and that it might have been clearer to have required an intention to exercise physical control and custody of the land "on one's own behalf and for one's own benefit".[116]

A dubious decision suggests that if the squatter believes that he enjoys possession by virtue of a lawful title, e.g. a licence to occupy, then he does not have the necessary intention to possess: *Clowes Developments (UK) Ltd v Walters*.[117] In *British Waterways Board v Toor*[118] a potential adverse possessor's claim to title to an alleyway was defeated, inter alia, because his (mistaken) belief that he had rights of access was insufficient to constitute an intention to possess the land. An unusual point arose in *Roberts v Swangrove Estates Ltd*,[119] where the Crown claimed adverse possession of riparian land. Roberts argued that the Crown's policy of not contesting claims to riparian land meant that it could not establish the required intention. Lindsay J. dismissed this argument:

"an intention on a squatter's part exclusively to possess at least unless and until he is dispossessed by another or until the paper owner shows to him both a good title and a real will to repossess suffices."[120]

(ii) Intention to Possess Demonstrated by an Intention to Exclude the World at Large, Including the Paper Owner

8–047 The requisite intention to possess will be demonstrated by an intention on the part of the squatter to exclude the world at large, including the paper owner, so far as is reasonably possible.[121] This will most easily be established where the squatter has enclosed the land so as to prevent the paper owner exercising access. In *Buckinghamshire CC v Moran*, for example, the Court of Appeal took the view that the fact of physical enclosure of land "itself prima facie indicates the requisite animus possidendi". Slade L.J. cited the judgment of Lord Halsbury L.C. in *Marshall v Taylor*, who stated in relation to the piece of land in question:

"The true nature of this particular strip of land is that it is enclosed. It cannot be denied that the person who now says he owns it could not get to it in any ordinary way. I do not deny that he could have crept through the hedge, or, if it had been a brick wall that he

---

[115] [2003] 1 A.C. 419 at [42].
[116] [2003] 1 A.C. 419 at [40].
[117] [2006] 1 P. & C.R. 1. Compare *Ofulue v Bossert* [2008] EWCA Civ 7. The Court of Appeal held that a person who believed they were a tenant could be in adverse possession.
[118] [2006] EWHC 1256.
[119] [2007] EWHC 513.
[120] Upheld on appeal: [2008] EWCA Civ 98.
[121] *Pye (JA) (Oxford) Ltd v Graham* [2003] 1 A.C. 419 at [46]; [2002] 3 All E.R. 865.

could have climbed over the wall; but that was not the ordinary and usual mode of access."[122] There is thus a very close relationship between the requirement of an intention to possess and the fact of possession. It will be more difficult to establish the requisite intention to possess where the claimant has taken factual possession of the land other than by enclosure. In *Powell v Macfarlane*[123] a claim of adverse possession was made where a boy had started grazing his cow on the land in question at the age of 14. Slade J. held that this did not itself demonstrate the necessary intention to exclude the true owner from the land. He considered that compelling evidence of an intention to possess would be necessary where the claimant's use of the land did not itself indicate such an intention.

(iii) Intention to Possess Where the True Owner has a Future use for the Land

Prior to the decision of the House of Lords in *Pye (JA) (Oxford) Ltd v Graham*[124] some **8–048** authorities suggested that a squatter could not have the necessary intention to possess the land if he was aware that the owner intended to put the land to some use in the future. In *Leigh v Jack*[125] the claimant had stored scrap metal on land which he knew was intended to be used in the future by the owners for the construction of a street. It was held that he had not dispossessed the true owner and Cockburn C.J. stated that his knowledge of the future intended use meant that he did not intend to act as a trespasser. In *Buckingham CC v Moran*[126] the Court of Appeal rejected any contention that *Leigh v Jack* meant that there could never be sufficient intention to possess where the possessor was aware of a future intended use of the land, and in *Pye (JA) (Oxford) Ltd v Graham* Lord Browne-Wilkinson considered that "the suggestion that the sufficiency of the possession can depend upon the intention not of the squatter but of the true owner is heretical and wrong".[127] He went on to explain that a squatter's knowledge of an intended future purpose would only prevent the establishment of an intention to possess in very rare circumstances:

"The highest it can be put is that, if the squatter is aware of a special purpose for which the paper owner uses or intends to use the land and the use made by the squatter does not conflict with that use, that may provide some support for a finding as a question of fact that the squatter had no intention to possess the land in the ordinary sense but only an intention to occupy it until needed by the paper owner. For myself I think that there will be few occasions in which such inference could properly be drawn in cases where the true owner has been physically excluded from the land. But it remains a possible, if improbable, inference in some cases."[128]

---

[122] [1895] 1 Ch. 641 at 645.
[123] (1977) 38 P. & C.R. 452 at 476.
[124] [2003] 1 A.C. 419.
[125] (1876) 5 Ex.D 264.
[126] [1990] Ch. 623.
[127] [2003] 1 A.C. 419 at [45].
[128] [2003] 1 A.C. 419 at [45].

(iv) Intention to Possess Where the Squatter would have been Willing to Pay the Owner to Occupy the Land if Asked

8–049   The central issue in *Pye (JA) (Oxford) Ltd v Graham*[129] was whether the requisite intention to possess could be established where the defendant would have been willing to pay the owner to occupy the land if the owner had asked for payment. The defendant had first entered into occupation of the land in question, which consisted of four fields, under a written agreement permitting him to graze cattle thereon. On the expiry of this agreement the owners refused to grant a request for a further grazing agreement because they anticipated seeking planning permission for the development of the land. The defendants remained in occupation, and the owners failed to reply to their subsequent letters requesting to cut hay and asking for a further grazing agreement. Lord Browne-Wilkinson explained that a squatter's willingness to pay for his occupation of the land did not prevent the establishment of an "intention to possess":

> "Once it is accepted that the necessary intent is an intent to possess not to own, and an intention to exclude the paper owner only so far as is reasonably possible, there is no inconsistency between a squatter being willing to pay the paper owner if asked and his being in the meantime in possession. An admission of title by the squatter is not inconsistent with the squatter being in possession in the meantime."[130]

He also pointed out that the defendant had not remained in occupation in just the same way as he had under the grazing agreement. He had done things on the land which he would have had no right to do under that agreement, had acted in a way which he knew was contrary to the wishes of the true owner, and had treated the land as if it were his own by treating as part of his own farm and maintaining it on the same basis as the rest of the farm. Together these actions showed that his willingness to pay for the use of the disputed land if asked was not inconsistent with an intention to possess it in the meantime.

2. Adverse Possession of Unregistered Land

(a) *Squatter Acquires Good Title After 12 Years' Adverse Possession*

8–050   Where title to land is unregistered, a squatter will acquire good title simply by adversely possessing it for the requisite period of time. Where the land has been adversely possessed for 12 years or more the Limitation Act 1980 prevents the owner of the land taking action to assert his rights against the adverse possessor. Section 15(1) provides that:

> "No action shall be brought by any person to recover any land after the expiration of twelve years from the date on which the right of action accrued to him or, if it first accrued to some person through whom he claims, to that person."

---

[129] [2003] 1 A.C. 419.
[130] At [46].

The effect of this section is to extinguish the rights of the owner in favour of the adverse possessor, who will be able to claim a new title of his own.[131] The adverse possessor will not be able to prove his title through title deeds, but will have to rely on the fact of his adverse possession for 12 years or more. Such an adverse possessor will take his freehold interest in the land subject to all other third party interests which affect the land.

A squatter will only be entitled to defeat the title of the paper owner if he can demonstrate that he enjoyed a continuous period of adverse possession for 12 years. If at any point the true owner regained possession and broke the continuity of the period of adverse possession, then the claimant will be unable to defeat his title. The Limitation Act 1980 expressly anticipates that the 12-year period may comprise the accumulation of several persons' adverse possession, provided there is no break in the chain of possession. For example, if Peter began to possess land in 1990 and Quentin joined him in 2000 and then Peter left the land in 2001, Quentin will be able to claim adverse possession. There was a continuous period of possession exceeding 12 years even though Quentin had not himself possessed the land for 12 years. However the 12-year period of adverse possession must be continuous, so that if Peter began to possess the land in 1992, abandoned his possession in 2001, and Quentin took possession in 2002, Quentin would not be able to assert a right to adverse possession.[132]

The mere fact that the landowner served a writ to start proceedings to recover land will not stop time running against him for the purposes of adverse possession. In *Markfield Investments Ltd v Evans*[133] adverse possession began running against the owners of a house which had been adversely possessed in 1979 at the latest. In 1990 the owners issued a writ to recover possession of the land, but the writ was dismissed in 1999 for want of prosecution. The Court of Appeal held that the mere fact that the writ had been issued in 1990 did not stop time running against the occupiers, and is of no more significance than a demand for possession. It therefore followed that the occupiers were entitled to the land by adverse possession.

(b) *Squatters' Rights are Protected if the Land is Sold and Registered*

Difficulties may arise if a squatter has been in adverse possession of the land for more than 12 years, but after this time the paper owner sells the land to a third party who is registered as proprietor. The rights of such a squatter are, however, protected as overriding interests on first registration, and will therefore be binding on the new registered proprietor, who will take the land subject to them. During the three years after the coming into force of the Land Registration Act 2002 the rights of the squatter constitute overriding interests irrespective of whether he was in actual occupation of the land or not, and irrespective of whether the registered proprietor knew of their existence or not.[134] This means, for example, that a squatter who adversely possessed the land for a continuous period of 12 years or more, but who is now no longer in possession of the land, will be able to assert good title against the registered

8–051

---

[131] *St Marylebone Property Co Ltd v Fairweather* [1963] A.C. 510.

[132] See Limitation Act s.15(6) and Sch.1 para.8(2); *Trustees Executors and Agency Co Ltd v Short* (1888) 13 App. Cas. 793; *Wills v Earl Howe* [1893] 2 Ch. 545; *Samuel Johnson and Sons Ltd v Brock* [1907] 2 Ch. 533; *Mulcahy v Curramore Pty Ltd* [1974] 2 N.S.W.L.R. 464.

[133] [2001] 2 All E.R. 238.

[134] Land Registration Act 2002 Sch.12 para.7.

proprietor. However three years after the coming into force of the 2002 Act the rights of the squatter are only overriding if he was in actual occupation at the date of registration, or if the new proprietor has notice of his interest.[135] It seems that notice for this purpose must include constructive notice and is not limited to actual notice.

3. Adverse Possession of Registered Land

8–052 As was noted above, under the regime of the Land Registration Act 1925 a squatter who had adversely possessed registered land for a period of at least 12 years was entitled by s.75(2), to be registered as proprietor. Prior to registration as proprietor, s.75(1) deemed that the current proprietor held his freehold estate on trust for the squatter. Thus, although the squatter did not automatically become entitled to the legal title to the land after adversely possessing for the requisite period, he did become automatically entitled to the equitable ownership of the land. His equitable interest was protected as an "overriding interest" under s.70(1)(f), which meant that it would bind any transferee of the land.

The Land Registration Act 2002 has introduced an entirely new approach to the acquisition of title by adverse possession in registered land. Section 96 provides for the disapplication of s.15 of the Limitation Act 1980 in respect of registered land.[136] This means that the title of a registered proprietor is not automatically extinguished, whether in law of in equity, by the mere fact of adverse possession for the requisite period of time. Instead a squatter will only be entitled to be registered as proprietor in place of the current proprietor if stringent statutory criteria are satisfied. These criteria are found in Sch.6 to the Act, which establishes a procedure by which a squatter may apply to be registered as proprietor of the land. In essence a person who has adversely possessed land will only be entitled to be registered as proprietor with the consent of the current owner, whether given actively or passively, or if the present owner fails to take action to recover the land after he has been informed that the adverse possessor wishes to be registered as proprietor.

(a) *A Squatter can Apply for Registration as Proprietor After 10 Years' Adverse Possession*

8–053 Schedule 6, para.1(1) provides that:

> "A person may apply to the registrar to be registered as the proprietor of a registered estate if he has been in adverse possession of the estate for the period of ten years on the date of the application."

Whilst this provision clearly reduces the duration of the adverse possession required before a squatter can obtain title to the land, it does not in itself entitle the squatter to be registered as the proprietor merely because he has been in possession for 10 years.

---

[135] Land Registration Act 2002 s.11(4)(c).

[136] With the exception that the limitation period may run against a registered chargee of the land.

(b) *The Registrar must give Notice of a Squatter's Application to Interested Parties*

If a squatter applies to be registered as the proprietor of the freehold estate of the land, **8–054**
the registrar must give notice of the application to the persons who would be affected by
such registration. Where the application relates to the freehold estate, Sch.2(1) provides
that the registrar will have to give notice, amongst others, to the proprietor of the estate[137]
and the proprietor of any registered charge on the estate.[138] The purpose of requiring such
a notice is to enable the interested parties to object to the registration of the squatter as
proprietor. The address to which such a notice is to be sent is the address of the registered
proprietor. If the only land which the registered proprietor owns is the land which is
being adversely possessed, then the chances are that this will have been the address provided for the registered proprietor. In consequence any notice to the registered proprietor
is likely to be intercepted by the squatter and will never reach the registered proprietor
himself.

(c) *The Recipient of a Notice may Require the Registrar to Deal with the Application under the Provisions of Para.5 of Sch.6*

A person who receives notice of a squatter's application to be registered as proprietor has the **8–055**
option of requiring the application to be dealt with by the registrar under the provisions of
para.5 of Sch.6. Paragraph 5 limits the circumstances in which an applicant is entitled to be
registered as proprietor.

(d) *An Applicant will be Registered as Proprietor if the Recipients of the Notice do not Require the Registrar to Deal with the Application under the Provisions of Para.5*

A squatter who has applied to be registered as proprietor of the freehold estate will be **8–056**
entitled to be registered as the new proprietor if the recipients of the notice of his application
fail to exercise their right to require the registrar to deal with the application under para.5
within a period of 65 days after the date of issue of the notice.[139] By failing to respond to
the notice, which must specify the consequences of a failure to require the registrar to deal
with the application under para.5,[140] the interested parties are taken to have consented to the
registration of the squatter as the new registered proprietor, thereby surrendering their own
rights to the land.

---

[137] Land Registration Act 2002 Sch.6 para.2(1)(a).
[138] Land Registration Act 2002 Sch.6 para.2(1)(b).
[139] Land Registration Act 2002 Sch.6 para.4; Land Registration Rules r.189.
[140] Land Registration Act 2002 Sch.6 para.2(2).

(e) *An Applicant will be Entitled to be Registered as Proprietor if any of the Conditions of Para.5 are Met*

8–057   If the recipients of a notice of an application by a squatter to be registered as proprietor require the registrar to deal with it under para.5, the applicant will only be entitled to be registered as the new proprietor if one of three specified conditions is met.[141]

(i) The Registered Proprietor is Estopped from Seeking to Dispossess the Applicant

8–058   Paragraph 5(2) provides that the applicant will be entitled to be registered as proprietor if it would be "unconscionable because of an equity by estoppel for the registered proprietor to seek to dispossess the applicant"[142] and "the circumstances are such that the applicant ought to be registered as the proprietor".[143] This will be the case where the registered proprietor has in some way assured the squatter that he is entitled to the estate in question, or that he will not seek to dispossess him so as to deprive him of the estate, and the squatter has relied on the assurance and acted to his detriment on the basis of it. The requirements of estoppel are discussed in detail in Chapter 19.

(ii) The Applicant is for Some Other Reason Entitled to be Registered as the Proprietor of the Estate

8–059   Paragraph 5(3) provides that the applicant is entitled to be registered as proprietor if he "is for some other reason entitled to be registered as the proprietor of the estate". This would cover the situation where the applicant had contracted to purchase the land, paid the price and moved into possession, but where the title had never been effectively transferred to him.[144]

(iii) The Application Concerned a Boundary Dispute and the Applicant had Reasonably Believed that the Land Belonged to Him

8–060   The third, and most significant, condition is found in para.5(4), which in effect provides that a squatter is entitled to be registered as proprietor if the application arises as a result of a boundary dispute, and he reasonably believed that the land he possessed belonged to him. This condition will only be met if:

> (a) the land to which the application relates is adjacent to land belonging to the applicant;

---

[141] Land Registration Act 2002 Sch.6 para.5(1).
[142] Land Registration Act 2002 Sch.6 para.5(2)(a).
[143] Land Registration Act 2002 Sch.6 para.5(2)(b).
[144] *Bridges v Mees* [1957] Ch. 475; (2001) Law Com. No.271, *Land Registration for the Twenty-First Century—A Conveyancing Revolution*, para.698.

(b) the exact line of the boundary between the two has not been determined under rules under s.60;

(c) for at least 10 years of the period of adverse possession ending on the date of the application, the applicant (or any predecessor in title) reasonably believed that the land to which the application relates belonged to him;

(d) the estate to which the application relates was registered more than one year prior to the date of the application; and

(f) An applicant will be entitled to be registered as proprietor if he reapplies for registration two years after a previous application has been rejected.

As has been seen, a squatter will only be entitled to be registered as proprietor after 10 years' adverse possession if other interested parties, including the current registered proprietor, consent to his application, or if his application satisfies any of the three conditions set out in para.5(3). However, the mere fact that a squatter's initial application is rejected is not necessarily the end of the story. Having been made aware of the squatter's claim by the receipt of a notice of his application, the current registered proprietor, who has objected to his registration, is expected to take action to recover possession of his land. If he fails to take action to assert his rights for a period of two years the squatter will be entitled to be registered as the proprietor of the land. Paragraph 6(1) provides that a squatter whose initial application has been rejected "may make a further application to be registered as the proprietor of the estate if he is in adverse possession of the estate from the date of the application until the last day of the period of two years beginning with the date of its rejection". Paragraph 7 provides that where such a further application is made the squatter "is entitled to be entered in the register as the new proprietor of the estate". **8–061**

The net effect of these provisions is that a squatter will gain the right to be registered as the proprietor of the land after he has adversely possessed the land for at least 12 years, but that this right will not automatically accrue to him. He will only acquire the right to be so registered where the current proprietor was made aware of his claims by way of an application after at least ten years possession, but who failed to take the necessary action to evict him from the property. In practise this will greatly reduce the likelihood of a squatter gaining ownership of the land by adverse possession, since most proprietors will seek to protect their interest when they are informed of the claim of the squatter.

4. Adverse Possession of Freehold Land Subject to a Lease

(a) *No Adverse Possession of the Freehold Title while the Lease is in Force*

Where land is subject to a lease the tenant enjoys possession of the land whilst the landlord retains the freehold title. Any adverse possession is only therefore adverse to the interests of the tenant and not of the freeholder whilst the lease remains in force. The landlord cannot himself seek possession until the lease is determined, since he is not entitled to possession until that point. However, where a tenant is no longer able to assert his rights against an **8–062** adverse possessor because the land has been possessed for the 12-year period, it was held in *St Marylebone Property Co Ltd v Fairweather*[145] that in the case of unregistered land, he may voluntarily surrender his lease to the landlord, which has the effect of bringing the lease to an end thus enabling the landlord to recover possession from the adverse possessor because the adverse possession does not defeat the rights of the landlord as the freehold owner. This conclusion has been questioned because where an adverse possessor has defeated the interest of the tenant the tenant has no lease which can be surrendered to the landlord. His rights have passed to the possessor. In the case of registered land, the effect of adverse possession under the Land Registration Act 1925 was that the paper owner held the land on trust for the squatter. The squatter held an overriding interest. The surrender of a lease could therefore give no better right to the landlord to evict the squatter than the tenant had.[146] The position under the Land Registration Act 2002 is different and the position will depend upon whether the squatter has been registered as proprietor of the leasehold interest.

(b) *Adverse Possession against the Landlord's Freehold Title Once the Lease has Come to an End*

8–063 The adverse possessor will only defeat the freehold title of the landlord if he remains in adverse possession for the requisite period after the expiry of the lease, since the limitation period runs against the freeholder from this date.[147] If he completes the necessary period he will be entitled to invoke the procedure for registration by virtue of adverse possession.

5. Priority of Interests where Title to Freehold Land is Acquired by Adverse Possession

8–064 A squatter who acquires title to land by adverse possession will not usually gain priority over any pre-existing rights and interests in the land. Overreaching will clearly not operate in favour of an adverse possessor since the land is not conveyed by at least two trustees. In the case of unregistered land an adverse possessor is neither entitled to claim statutory priority over unprotected land charges, or of the traditional doctrine of notice, because he has not provided valuable consideration. In registered land, Sch.6 para.9(2) specifically provides that the registration of an adverse possessor as the proprietor of an estate in the land "does not affect the priority of any interests affecting the estate". This general rule is subject to a limited exception. Paragraphs 9(3) and 9(4) have the effect that an adverse possessor who is registered as the new proprietor of the land will take free from any registered charge affecting the estate, except where he was entitled to be registered as proprietor under the three conditions specified in para.5.

---

[145] [1963] A.C. 510.
[146] See *Spectrum Investment Co Ltd v Holmes* [1981] 1 W.L.R. 221 and *Central London Estates v Kato Ltd* [1998] 4 All E.R. 948.
[147] Limitation Act 1980 Sch.1 para.4.

172

6. Adverse Possession and the Human Rights Act 1998

In *Beaulane Properties Ltd v Palmer*[148] Nicholas Strauss Q.C. held that the effect of the 1980 **8–065**
Act and the Land Registration Act 1925 was to deprive the owner of his possessions contrary
to art.1 of the first protocol. The effect of the doctrine in the present case was disproportionate and did not promote the aims of the relevant legislation, here (at this time) the Land
Registration Act 1925. The status quo was restored by the judgment of the Grand Chamber
of the European Court of Human Rights in *Pye (JA) (Oxford) Ltd v United Kingdom*.[149] The
applicants argued that they had been deprived of their ownership "as a result of the operation
of the 1925 and 1980 Acts".[150] "The applicant companies contended that their loss was so
great, and the windfall to the Grahams so significant, that the fair balance required by article
1 . . . was upset".[151] The European Court of Human Rights held that the Land Registration
Act 1925 and the Limitation Act 1980 constituted a deprivation of title, and "upset the
fair balance between the demands of the public interest on the one hand and the applicants'
right to the peaceful enjoyment of their possessions on the other".[152] In *Pye (JA) (Oxford)
Ltd v United Kingdom*[153] the Grand Chamber overturned this ruling and held that the law on
adverse possession did not contravene art.1.[154]

> "Such [legislation] fell within the state's margin of appreciation, unless [it] gave rise to
> results which were so anomalous as to render the legislation unacceptable. The acquisi-
> tion of unassailable rights by the adverse possessor had to go hand-in-hand with a
> corresponding loss of property rights for the former owner . . . The possibility of unde-
> serving tenants being able to make windfall profits did not affect the overall assessment
> of the proportionality of the legislation"[155]

ACQUISITION OF THE FREEHOLD TITLE TO LAND BY PROPRIETARY ESTOPPEL

A further means by which a person may acquire the freehold title of land is if the court orders **8–066**
that it should be transferred to him as a remedy where he has established an entitlement by
way of proprietary estoppel. The general doctrine of proprietary estoppel is examined in detail

---

[148] [2006] Ch. 79; J.Howell, "The Human Rights Act 1998: Land, Private Citizens, and the Common Law" (2007)
123 L.Q.R. 618; [2005] Conv. 345.
[149] *The Times* October 1, 2007.
[150] Summarised in *The Times* October 1, 2007: *Pye (JA) (Oxford) Ltd v United Kingdom* (2006) 43 E.H.R.R. 3, *The
Times* November 23, 2005. The UK government valued the land at £2.5m in July 2002.
[151] *The Times* October 1, 2007.
[152] Summarised in *The Times* October 1, 2007; *JA. Pye (Oxford) Ltd v United Kingdom* (2006) 43 E.H.R.R. 3.
See generally J. Howell, "The Human Rights Act 1998: Land, Private Citizens, and the Common Law" (2007) 123
L.Q.R. 618.
[153] *The Times* October 1, 2007.
[154] *The Times* October 1, 2007.
[155] *The Times* October 1, 2007, referring to *James v UK* (1986) 8 E.H.R.R. 123. In any case, they might have brought
an action to recover possession.

in Chapter 19 below. The essence of the doctrine is that if the owner of land has made an assurance to someone else that he is or will become entitled to some interest in the land, he will be estopped from denying that person any interest if he has subsequently acted to his detriment in reliance upon the assurance. A person who fulfils the requirements of an assurance, reliance and detriment will enjoy an estoppel "equity" which the court will "satisfy" by the award of an appropriate remedy. In circumstances where the nature of the assurance is that the person will receive the ownership of the land the court may satisfy the equity by ordering the owner to transfer the freehold title to the claimant.[156] For example, in *Pascoe v Turner*[157] the plaintiff and defendant lived together in a house owned by the plaintiff. He had told her that the house was hers, and in reliance on this representation she spent money redecorating and improving the property, and purchased furniture and furnishings. When their relationship ended the plaintiff purported to determine any licence the defendant might have to occupy the property and sought possession. The Court of Appeal held that the defendant had established an entitlement to an estoppel equity since she had clearly acted to her detriment in reliance upon the plaintiff's assurances, and that the appropriate remedy for the satisfaction of that equity was to order the plaintiff to fulfil the defendant's expectations by transferring the freehold ownership to her.

COMMONHOLD: A FORM OF FREEHOLD OWNERSHIP[158]

1. Introduction to Commonhold

(a) *What is Commonhold?*

8–067 Commonhold is a new form of landholding which was introduced into English law by the Commonhold and Leasehold Reform Act 2002. It is not a new type of estate in land, to sit alongside freehold and leasehold estates, but is a specialised form of freehold ownership,[159] hence the fact that it will be addressed in this chapter. Commonhold provides a means of facilitating the freehold ownership of land where there are a number of separate residential units which share the use of some common areas and facilities, for example where a large house has been divided into a number of separate flats which share a common entrance and stairway, a block of residential flats, an estate intended to provide retirement homes for the elderly together with appropriate facilities and services, or a residential development providing facilities such as a swimming pool or sports club for the use of residents. Commonhold will enable the owners of each unit within the commonhold property to own the freehold of their individual unit, and to own the freehold of the common areas together. In some ways commonhold is a hybrid of elements of freehold and leasehold ownership. Other jurisdictions

---

[156] See: *Dillwyn v Llewelyn* (1862) 4 De G.F. & J. 517.
[157] [1979] 1 W.L.R. 431.
[158] For detailed analysis of commonhold see Clarke, *Commonhold—The New Law*, Jordans (2002).
[159] See [2003] 67 Conv. 358 (Riddall).

have already introduced forms of landholding similar to commonhold, for example condominium title in New Zealand and strata title in Australia. The precise nature of commonhold is, however, unique to English law.

(b) *The Need for Commonhold*

Commonhold ownership was introduced to overcome the deficiencies of freehold or leasehold ownership to facilitate the kinds of development which have just been described.

8–068

(i) The Deficiencies of Freehold Ownership

The central difficulty with freehold ownership is that it is currently impossible under English law to impose positive obligations on a freehold owner which will be capable of binding successors in title to the land.[160] The effect of this long-established rule can be illustrated by the case of *Rhone v Stephens*.[161] The case involved a semi-detached property, each part of which shared a common roof. The original freehold owners had entered a covenant that they would maintain the common roof. However the House of Lords held that this covenant was not enforceable against their successors in title, because it was a positive obligation and was therefore incapable of running with the land. This limitation, which will be considered in detail in Chapter 16, means that freehold ownership is unsuitable as a form of landholding where it is necessary to require the freeholders to repair and maintain their property, or to contribute towards the cost of the maintenance of common areas. In relation to flats, for example, there is no theoretical difficulty with the grant of a freehold title to a flat, even if it is not attached directly to the land. However there are very substantial difficulties with conventional freehold ownership in arranging for the use of common facilities such as roads and drains, and for amenities such as a shared swimming pool or concierge service. Such facilities and amenities clearly require contributions to operating costs. It would be possible to require each purchaser in a new development containing such facilities to undertake to contribute to the maintenance costs, but an undertaking of this kind would constitute a positive covenant—one to contribute financially—and such covenants are not normally binding on a purchaser following sale. The devices which have been used to circumvent this difficulty are imperfect. Even arrangements for the combined maintenance or upkeep of essential services such as the roof or the support provided by lower floor flats for upper floor flats are difficult to create using conventional freeholds.

8–069

(ii) The Deficiencies of Leasehold Ownership

Given the deficiencies of freehold ownership, prior to the introduction of commonhold such developments could only be facilitated on a leasehold basis. The owners of each individual unit within the development would enjoy a lease from a landlord, who would retain the

8–070

---

[160] *Austerberry v Oldham Corp* (1885) 29 Ch.D. 750.
[161] [1994] 2 A.C. 310.

ownership of the common areas and be responsible for their maintenance and for the provision of services. The tenants would be required to pay some kind of service charge to the landlord to cover the cost of the upkeep of the common parts or in return for the services provided, and their rights and obligations would be defined by the terms of their lease. Whilst many developments have successfully taken place on a leasehold basis, it was recognised that there were inadequacies with such an arrangement. Firstly most property owners instinctively prefer to own a freehold rather than a leasehold estate in land. A lease is intrinsically a "wasting asset", even though it can be granted for a very long period of time. Secondly there are often tensions between landlords and tenants in respect of the maintenance of the common parts of leasehold land, and especially over the amount of the service charge. Tenants often wish to be able to manage the repair and maintenance of the common areas themselves.

(c) *The Introduction of Commonhold*

8–071   In the light of these deficiencies a working party of the Law Commission proposed the introduction of commonhold in 1987,[162] and in 1990 the Lord Chancellor's department issued a Consultation Paper proposing draft legislation to implement it.[163] This paper explained the main advantages of commonhold ownership:

> "The adoption of the commonhold scheme would lead to savings in the time and complexity of conveyancing by reducing to an absolute minimum the need for conveyancers to consider the rules applicable to essentially similar arrangements, and by ensuring that departures from the standard rules were quickly identifiable. Most importantly, it would institutionalise arrangements for the democratic management by and for the benefit of the freehold unit owners within a commonhold, through a 'commonhold association' (a corporate body controlled exclusively by them)".[164]

As was noted above, commonhold has now been introduced by the Commonhold and Leasehold Reform Act 2002.

2. The Essential Features of Commonhold Ownership[165]

8–072   There are three essential elements to the commonhold ownership of land.

(a) *Freehold Ownership by the Unit-holders of their Units*

8–073   Commonhold ownership is a type of freehold ownership. The owners of the individual units within the commonhold therefore own the freehold of their respective units. As such they are

---

[162] Cm.179, *Commonhold: Freehold Flats and Freehold Ownership of Other Interdependent Buildings* (1987).
[163] Cm.1345, *Commonhold—A Consultation Paper* (1990); see [1991] Conv. 70 and 170.
[164] Cm.1345 (1990) at para.1.2.
[165] S. Wong [2006] Conv. 14. There does not appear to be much practical demand for the tenure: [2005] Conv. 185.

free to transfer their unit without restriction[166] or to mortgage their unit.[167] The right to lease their unit may, however, be made subject to prescribed conditions.[168] A commonhold unit may be jointly owned,[169] and made the subject of a trust.

(b) *Freehold Ownership of the Common Parts by a Commonhold Association*

Whilst the unit-holders are the freehold owners of their individual units, the ownership of the common areas is vested in a commonhold association. Section 34(1) of the Commonhold and Leasehold Reform Act 2002 states that a commonhold association is a "private company limited by guarantee".[170] Every unit holder of the commonhold land is entitled to be registered as a member of the commonhold association.[171] Where a unit is jointly owned, only one of the joint proprietors is entitled to become a member of the commonhold association.[172] The members of the commonhold association thus control the company by the exercise of their votes,[173] including the appointment of officers and directors. Section 35(1) of the Commonhold and Leasehold Reform Act 2002 specifies the duties of the directors of the commonhold association:

8–074

> "The directors of a commonhold association shall exercise their powers so as to permit or facilitate so far as is possible—
>
> (a) the exercise by each unit-holder of his rights, and
> (b) the enjoyment by each unit holder of the freehold estate in his unit."

The directors are also required to enforce the obligations of the unit-holders.[174]

(c) *A Commonhold Community Statement*

Alongside the existence of a commonhold association, there must be a commonhold community statement. In effect this statement creates a "local law" of rights and obligations regarding the commonhold land. By s.31(1) of the Commonhold and Leasehold Reform Act 2002 the commonhold community statement makes provision for:

8–075

---

[166] The Commonhold and Leasehold Reform Act 2002 s.15(2) prevents the commonhold community statement from preventing or restricting the transfer of a commonhold unit.

[167] Commonhold and Leasehold Reform Act 2002 s.20(2).

[168] Commonhold and Leasehold Reform Act 2002 s.17.

[169] Commonhold and Leasehold Reform Act 2002 s.13. See Ch.12 below where the nature of co-ownership is discussed.

[170] See Companies Act 1985 s.1(2)(b). S.34(1)(b) of the Commonhold and Leasehold Reform Act 2002 provides that the sum of £1 is to be specified as the amount of the members guarantee.

[171] Commonhold and Leasehold Reform Act 2002 Sch.3 para.7.

[172] Commonhold and Leasehold Reform Act 2002 Sch.3 para.8.

[173] See Commonhold and Leasehold Reform Act 2002 s.36 for the conduct of voting by the members of the commonhold association.

[174] Commonhold and Leasehold Reform Act 2002 ss.35 and 37.

(a) the rights and duties of the commonhold association, and

(b) the rights and duties of the unit-holders.

The commonhold community statement must be made in the prescribed form,[175] and must make provisions regulating the use of the common parts, requiring the commonhold association to insure the common parts, and requiring the commonhold association to repair and maintain the common parts.[176] In relation to the use of common parts, the commonhold community statement may make provisions restricting the used of a specified part of the common parts, either as to the classes of person who may use it, or the kind of use to which it may be put.[177]

The duties which the commonhold community statement may impose on the commonhold association, or the unit-holders, include the following[178]: to pay money; to undertake works; to grant access; to give notice; to refrain from entering into transactions of a specified kind in relation to a commonhold unit; to refrain from using the whole or part of a commonhold unit for a specified purpose or for anything other than a specified purpose; to refrain from undertaking works (including alterations) of a specified kind; to refrain from causing nuisance or annoyance; to refrain from specified behaviour; to indemnity the commonhold association or a unit-holder in respect of costs arising from the breach of a statutory requirement. As will be seen in the subsequent chapter, many of these duties are of a kind imposed in leases to control the conduct of the tenant. In a commonhold context they limit the freedom of the freehold owners to deal with their units as they wish.

3. The Creation of a Commonhold

(a) *The Requirements of Commonhold*

8–076 Section 1(1) of the Commonhold and Leasehold Reform Act 2002 specifies the circumstances in which land will become commonhold:

> "Land is commonhold land if—
>
> (a) the freehold estate in the land is registered as a freehold estate in commonhold land,
> (b) the land is specified in the memorandum of association of a commonhold association as the land in relation to which the association is to exercise functions, and
> (c) a commonhold community statement makes provision for rights and duties of the commonhold association and unit-holders (whether or not this statement has come into force)."

---

[175] Commonhold and Leasehold Reform Act 2002 s.31(2).
[176] Commonhold and Leasehold Reform Act 2002 s.26.
[177] Commonhold and Leasehold Reform Act 2002 s.25(2).
[178] Commonhold and Leasehold Reform Act 2002 s.31(5).

Thus a commonhold may only be created where the three essential elements are present. The land will be registered as a "freehold estate in commonhold land" when the registered freeholder applies for it to be so registered.[179] Where the land is subject to a lease or a mortgage the application cannot be made without the consent of the landlord or mortgagee.[180] The registrar is required to ensure that the prescribed details of the commonhold association, the prescribed details of the registered freeholder of each commonhold unit, a copy of the commonhold community statement and a copy of the memorandum of and articles of association of the commonhold association are kept in his custody and referred to in the register.[181] A commonhold can be registered by a developer before there are any unit holders,[182] or where there are already unit holders.[183] This latter possibility allows for the conversion of a leasehold into a commonhold, although such conversion cannot occur without the consent of the landlord and the registered leaseholders. Where a commonhold is registered with unit-holders the application for registration as a commonhold must be accompanied by a list of the commonhold units, giving prescribed details of the proposed initial unit holders.[184]

(b) *Land which cannot be Commonhold*

It follows from the provisions of s.1(1) that unregistered land and leasehold land are incapable of being commonhold land. The Commonhold and Leasehold Reform Act 2002 also exclude certain type of registered freehold land from being commonhold. Under Sch.2 para.1 a "flying freehold" of land cannot be commonhold unless "all the land between the ground and the raised land" is part of the commonhold. Agricultural land and certain types of contingent freehold estates are also incapable of being commonhold.[185]   **8–077**

4. The Liability of Unit-holders

(a) *The Rights and Duties of Unit-holders Pass with the Land*

One of the key features of commonhold ownership is that the rights and duties imposed by the commonhold community statement are capable of passing so as to bind successors in title to the individual units. Section 16(1) of the Commonhold and Leasehold Reform Act 2002 provides that: **8–078**

---

[179] Commonhold and Leasehold Reform Act 2002 s.2.
[180] Commonhold and Leasehold Reform Act 2002 s.3.
[181] Commonhold and Leasehold Reform Act 2002 s.5(1).
[182] Commonhold and Leasehold Reform Act 2002 s.7.
[183] Commonhold and Leasehold Reform Act 2002 s.9.
[184] Commonhold and Leasehold Reform Act 2002 s.9(2).
[185] Commonhold and Leasehold Reform Act 2002 Sch.2 paras 2 and 3.

"A right or duty conferred or imposed—

    (a) by a commonhold community statement, or

    (b) in accordance with s.20,

shall affect a new unit-holder in the same way as it affected the former unit-holder."

This statutory provision had the effect of overcoming the problem identified above, namely that the burden of a positive covenant affecting freehold land is incapable of binding successors in title. It follows that, if the land in *Rhone v Stephens*[186] had been commonhold, with the roof regarded as a common part, the obligation to contribute towards the maintenance and repair would have been capable of being enforced against a successor in title. However although the duties imposed by the commonhold community statement can be enforced against the unit-holders, the commonhold association does not have the right to forfeit the interest of the unit-holders for breach of duty. As will be seen in the next chapter, tenants face the ultimate sanction of forfeiture of their estate in the land if they breach the terms of their lease.

(b) *Unit-holders are only Liable for their own Breaches of Duty*

8–079   A unit holder is only liable for any breach of duty that occurs during the time that he is the owner of a unit. Section 16(2) provides that "a former unit-holder shall not incur a liability or acquire a right". It follows that a unit holder cannot be held liable for any breaches of duty committed by his successors in title after he has transferred his unit, or for breaches of duty committed by former owners.

5. The Termination of a Commonhold

A commonhold may be terminated in one of two ways. It may be voluntarily wound up by the members, or it may be wound up by order of the court.

(a) *Voluntary Winding-up*

8–080   A commonhold association may be wound up voluntarily by its members. Where this happens the freehold interest in the commonhold units is transferred by registration to the commonhold association.[187] The commonhold may only be wound up in this way if the commonhold association is solvent, and at least 80 per cent of the member of the association vote in favour of a resolution that it be wound-up.[188] The members must also pass a

---

[186] [1994] 2 A.C. 310.
[187] Commonhold and Leasehold Reform Act 2002 s.49(3).
[188] Commonhold and Leasehold Reform Act 2002 s.43(1)(c).

termination-statement resolution,[189] specifying the association's proposals for the transfer of the commonhold land following its registration as the freehold proprietor of the commonhold unit, and how the assets of the association will be distributed.[190] Where the winding-up resolution is passed by 100 per cent of the members of the association the liquidator of the association can make a termination application direct to the registrar.[191] However if then resolution did not attract unanimous support the court must approve the terms of the termination statement before a termination application is made.[192] This will ensure that the rights of the minority members of the commonhold association are protected.

(b) *Winding-up by the Court*

An insolvent commonhold association may also be wound up by the court where a creditor presents a petition for bankruptcy under s.124 of the Insolvency Act 1986.[193] In such cases the court may grant a succession order allowing a successor commonhold association to be registered as the proprietor of the freehold estate in the common parts.[194] A succession order should be granted unless the court thinks that "the circumstances of the insolvent commonhold association make a succession order inappropriate".[195] If no succession order is made, the liquidator must inform the registrar, who is then required to make "such arrangements as appear to him to be appropriate for ensuring that the freehold estate in the land in respect of which the commonhold association exercises functions ceases to be registered as a freehold estate in commonhold land as soon as is reasonably practicable".[196]

8–081

---

[189] Commonhold and Leasehold Reform Act 2002 s.43(1)(b).
[190] Commonhold and Leasehold Reform Act 2002 s.47.
[191] Commonhold and Leasehold Reform Act 2002 s.44.
[192] Commonhold and Leasehold Reform Act 2002 s.45.
[193] Commonhold and Leasehold Reform Act 2002 s.50(1).
[194] Commonhold and Leasehold Reform Act 2002 s.51.
[195] Commonhold and Leasehold Reform Act 2002 s.51(4).
[196] Commonhold and Leasehold Reform Act 2002 s.54(4)(a).

Chapter 9

LEASEHOLD OWNERSHIP

INTRODUCTION TO LEASES AND LEASEHOLD OWNERSHIP

1. The Nature of Leases

In the previous chapter it has been seen that the closest concept to the absolute ownership of **9–001** land in English law is offered by the legal freehold. However it is not always the case that the freehold owner of land wishes to use and occupy it himself. Leasehold ownership provides a mechanism by which a freeholder can grant another person the right to occupy and use his land. Such a right is usually granted in return for the payment of rent. The freeholder is thus able to exploit his land economically by selling the right of occupation and use to someone else. The person who grants a lease becomes a landlord, and the person who enjoys the lease-hold interest in the land is the tenant. The landlord does not lose all entitlement to the land. He retains his ownership subject to the rights of the tenant. His interest is known as the freehold reversion. When the lease comes to an end, either through the passage of time or if it is terminated for some reason, the full unencumbered freehold title to the property will return to him. It is also possible for a new leasehold interest to be carved out of an existing leasehold. For example, if David enjoys a 99-year lease of a house he may, subject to any lim-itations in his own lease, grant a 12 months' tenancy to Elizabeth. Such a lease is described as a "sub-lease", whereas the lease between David and the freehold owner is the "head lease".

The concept of leasehold title has proved extremely flexible as a means of facilitating a separation between the ownership and use of land. Leases may be granted for any period of time, and it is not uncommon for a lease to be granted for 999 years or more. On the other hand leases can also be granted for very short periods of time, so many students rent houses during their university studies for periods of six months or a year. Leasehold interests are sig-nificant in commercial contexts, for example the majority of shops in modern developments are granted a lease of their premises, but also residentially, whether in the private sector or public council housing.

(a) *Leases Confer a Right to the "Exclusive Possession" of Land*

9–002   A lease is not the only means by which an owner can enable another person to use and occupy his land. A person who enters onto land owned by another without permission is a trespasser. However an owner may grant a person permission to enter, use or even occupy his land. Such permission is known as a licence. Problems of differentiation between leases and licences arise because they can appear to have the identical effect in practice of permitting a third person to occupy and use land. However there is a crucial legal distinction between a lease and a licence. A lease confers on a tenant the right to "exclusive possession", whereas a licence does not confer such a right on the licensee. The right to exclusive possession means the right to exclude all persons from the land, including the landlord who has granted the lease. A tenant is therefore entitled to refuse the landlord entry to the land. If the landlord attempts to enter without permission he will stand as a trespasser vis-à-vis the tenant, who will be entitled to seek appropriate relief. In contrast a licensee enjoys a mere permission to be present on the licensor's land and usually has no right to exclude the licensor. If the licensor enters the land without the licensee's permission he will not, in most cases, commit a trespass and there are no remedies available to the licensee.[1] The conferral, or not, of exclusive possession is the main determinant whether a grant of a right to occupy land is to be characterised as a lease or a licence.

(b) *Leases Usually Create an Estate in the Land*

9–003   Traditionally a further distinction between leases and licenses was thought to be the fact that a lease created a proprietary interest in the land, whereas a licence conferred a purely personal right on the licensee to occupy the land. The key difference between personal and proprietary rights is that a personal right is only binding as against the person who granted it, whereas a proprietary right is capable of enduring through changes in the ownership of the land to which it relates. A licence is therefore incapable of enduring through changes of ownership of the land, so that if the owner/licensor transfers or sells the property to a third person, that third person will not be bound by the licence previously granted by the owner. Despite a number of attempts by Lord Denning to elevate contractual licences to a proprietary status, the purely personal character of licences was categorically affirmed by the Court of Appeal in *Ashburn Anstalt v Arnold*.[2] In some exceptional circumstances a licence may be binding on a transferee of the land by means of a constructive trust, but this is as result of the conduct of the transferee rather than as a consequence of the inherent nature of the licence itself.[3]

Whilst it is clear that a licence can only exist as a personal right, it is no longer clear that a lease must, of necessity, give rise to a proprietary estate in the land. Somewhat surprisingly,

---

[1] In some cases a licence can confer a contractual right to exclusive possession and in these situations the licensee can maintain an action for breach of contract against the licensor and possibly also for trespass. Even without exclusive possession the licensee may have contractual rights to prevent interference by the licensor with his or her enjoyment of the land in accordance with the terms of the contract.
[2] [1989] Ch. 1.
[3] See below Ch.20.

in *Bruton v London and Quadrant Housing Trust*[4] the House of Lords came to the conclusion that an agreement conferring exclusive possession on an occupier was to be regarded as a lease, and the resulting entitlement of the occupier as a tenancy, even though the grantor did not itself enjoy any proprietary interest in the land. The resulting "lease" would therefore create a tenancy which was not a proprietary interest in the land and did not confer an estate on the tenant. The case concerned a charitable trust (LQHT) which provided short term accommodation for homeless people. The accommodation was provided in a block of flats, which was owned by Lambeth LBC. The council had granted LQHT a contractual licence in 1986 to use the flats to provide accommodation for the homeless. The House of Lords held that a contractually binding occupancy agreement between the charitable trust and the plaintiff was a lease, even though LQHT did not have any proprietary interest in the land itself. Lord Hoffman suggested that a contractual right of occupancy may constitute a lease even where it does not confer a proprietary estate in the land:

> "A lease may, and usually does, create a proprietary interest called a leasehold estate or, technically, a 'term of years absolute'. This will depend upon whether the landlord had a interest out of which he could grant it. Nemo dat quod non habet. But it is the fact that the agreement is a lease which creates the proprietary interest. It is putting the cart before the horse to say that whether the agreement is a lease depends upon whether it creates a proprietary interest".[5]

Whilst this conclusion enabled the House of Lords to find that LQHT was subject to a contractual obligation to keep the premises in repair, an obligation which is implied into tenancies but not licences,[6] the judgment has been criticised[7] since it appears to have eroded the sharp conceptual distinction between leases and licences. There are two alternative arguments. The first is that LQHT could not have conferred a tenancy upon the plaintiff because it did not enjoy an estate in the land from which such an interest could have been derived. The right conferred upon the plaintiff should properly have been regarded as a contractual licence. The converse view is that even a person with a deficient title (or even with no title) can grant an estate in land, although that estate is vulnerable to being defeated by anyone who has a better title than the grantor. A person who does not own land can therefore grant a lease of it, and that lease will become complete if the grantor subsequently acquires title.[8] This argument relies upon the concept of relative title, a feature of unregistered land ownership. However, since only registration can constitute title, and the Land Registry would not register conflicting titles, the concept of relative title plays no part in registered land. The argument that a licensee cannot grant a lease therefore has greater strength.

The unconventional nature of the "tenancy" created in *Bruton v London and Quadrant Housing Trust*[9] was confirmed by the more recent decision of the House of Lords in *Lambeth LBC v Kay*,[10] which arose from the aftermath of the *Bruton* decision. In 1995 the council had

---

[4] [1999] 3 All E.R. 481.
[5] [1999] 3 All E.R. 481 at 487.
[6] Under Landlord and Tenant Act 1985 s.11.
[7] [2000] C.L.J. 25 (M. Dixon).
[8] This is a process known as "feeding the estoppel". A circumstance in which a person with no title might grant a lease is where a person negotiating for the purchase of land grants leases in anticipation of the acquisition.
[9] [1999] 3 All E.R. 481.
[10] [2006] UKHL 10; [2006] 4 All E.R. 128.

granted LQHT a 10-year lease in place of the initial licence agreement under which the Bruton "tenancy" had been created. Immediately following the decision in *Bruton v London and Quadrant Housing Trust* the council gave notice to terminate the 10-year lease to LQHT, and notified the occupiers that they would soon become trespassers and would have to leave their respective residences, on the grounds that the "tenancies" carved out of the licence agreement with LQHT were not binding on them. The residents argued that the common law rule established by *Mellor v Watkins*,[11] namely where A has granted a tenancy to B and B has granted a sub-tenancy to C, a surrender by B to A of B's tenancy does not determine C's sub-tenancy but has the effect that A become's C's landlord, applied to the grant of the 10-year lease to the charity in 1995, because the grant involved, by necessary implication, a surrender by the charity of the licence it had been granted. If this were correct, the "tenancies" of the residents deriving form the licence would became tenancies directly held by the council in the *scintilla temporis* between the surrender of the licence and the grant of the lease. This argument was rejected by the House of Lords, on the grounds that the *Mellor v Watkins* principle could have no relevance to a case where a tenancy had been granted by someone without an estate in the land in question. Lord Scott explained:

> "The *Bruton* tenancies are all of the same character. LQHT was, when it granted the *Bruton* tenancies, merely a licensee of Lambeth. The tenancies were not granted by Lambeth and were not carved by LQHT out of any estate that Lambeth had granted to LQHT. They were not derivative estates. LQHT, prior to the grant of the 1995 lease, had no estate in the land. It merely had a contractual licence. In these circumstances the *Mellor v Watkins* point that the intermediate landlord cannot by a consensual surrender give away an interest that belongs to a sub-tenant has no substance. True it is that LQHT could not by surrender of its licence give away or prejudice the rights of the *Bruton* tenants against itself, LQHT. But these rights never were enforceable against Lambeth. Once the LQHT licence had been terminated the appellants were trespassers as against Lambeth."[12]

Lord Scott referred to the entitlement of the residents as "non estate" tenants, and said that the consensual termination of the licence granted by Lambeth Council to LQHT could not turn them into "estate tenants" of the council.[13] There is thus a highly unsatisfactory distinction to be drawn between leases which create an "estate tenancy" that confers a genuine interest in land on the tenant, and leases which create a "non-estate tenancy" which confers only a personal right against the landlord on the tenant. In practice the vast majority of leases are likely to create a true "estate tenancy," as the landlord is likely to have proprietary interest in the land, and it would therefore have been better if the House of Lords had never introduced the concept of a "non estate" tenancy but had recongised the interest in *Bruton* for what it was, a contractual licence.

Where a true "estate tenancy" is created by a lease the tenant enjoys a proprietary interest in the land which may be transferred from one person to another. A landlord's "freehold reversion"

---

[11] (1874) L.R. 9 Q.B. 400.
[12] [2006] UKHL 10 at [143].
[13] [2006] UKHL 10 at [145].

and a tenant's leasehold interest are transferable to third parties by assignment, subject to any provisions in the lease.

(c) *Leases may be Legal Estates*

Leasehold interests are also capable of enjoying the status of legal estates in land. By s.1(1)(b) of the Law of Property Act 1925 a "term of years absolute" is capable of existing as a legal estate in land. The definitions section of the Act makes clear that a "term of years" includes a lease for a period of less than a year,[14] so that leases of any duration are capable of creating a legal estate in the land. However, as will be seen below, whether a lease in fact creates a legal estate or merely an equitable interest will depend upon whether it was created in the appropriate formal manner.

9–004

(d) *The Terms of Leases*

Leasehold interests arise in a wide range of circumstances. Although in all cases a relationship is established between the landlord and the tenant, it is obvious that the terms of the relationship will differ widely depending upon the circumstances. The terms of lease which define the respective rights and obligations of the landlord and tenant are described as the covenants of the lease. A simple covenant ordinarily entered into by the tenant is the obligation to pay rent to the landlord. A landlord may promise to keep the leased premises in good repair. Some covenants are implied into every lease by statute or the common law. A number of the most common and important covenants will be examined below, although a full analysis is outside of the scope of this book and is more properly the subject of specialist textbooks on landlord and tenant law.

9–005

2. State Regulation of Leases

When an owner of land agrees to grant a lease to a tenant he effectively enters into a contractual bargain. However there is generally a disparity between the relative bargaining strengths of the parties, so that the landlord is in a stronger position and is able to dictate the terms of the lease. The tenant is usually more vulnerable since he needs to find somewhere to live. If the law merely allowed unrestrained freedom of contract to operate, tenants would be open to unmitigated exploitation by landlords imposing extremely harsh terms upon them. In particular they would be able to charge unacceptably high rents during a housing shortage, securing compliance by the threat of termination of the lease and eviction. Given the potential vulnerability of the tenant to exploitation the state has intervened to regulate the relationship of landlord and tenant. This state control has had a marked impact on the development of the law relating to

9–006

---

[14] Law of Property Act 1925 s.205(10)(xxvii).

leases, as will be seen below. A detailed analysis is again beyond the scope of this book and only a brief outline of the most important legislation will be given here by way of introduction.[15]

(a) *"Protected Tenancies" under the Rent Acts*

9–007   After the First World War tenants were protected against poor quality housing. The Rent Acts were enacted after the Second World War to provide tenants with security of tenure and rent control, so that they could not be easily removed or charged excessive rents. Leases granted before January 15, 1989 are still capable of enjoying status as a "protected" or "statutory" tenancy under the Rent Act 1977. A tenancy is a "protected tenancy" during the contractually agreed term and a "statutory tenancy" arises when the agreed term has come to an end.[16] The landlord cannot terminate the tenancy without a court order and this will only be given in limited circumstances, such as the non-payment of rent or neglect causing the condition of the premises to deteriorate.[17] In a Rent Act tenancy the rent is also controlled so that the tenant is only obliged to pay a "fair rent", which overrides any rent agreed by the parties and is often lower than the market rent for the property. Under the provisions of the Rent Acts the surviving spouse of the original tenant may succeed to the tenancy.[18] In *Ghaidan v Godin-Mendoza*[19] the House of Lords held that the relevant provision could be read so as to extend this right to same-sex partners, so as to elimate its discriminatory effect and ensure a meaning compliant with arts 8 and 14 of the European Convention on Human Rights, without contradicting any cardinal principle of the Act.

(b) *"Assured Tenancies" under the Housing Act 1988*

9–008   During the 1980s government policy considered that the Rent Acts provided too much protection to tenants, with the consequence that they operated as a disincentive to private landlords letting property and were stultifying the private rented sector. The Housing Act 1988 therefore introduced the "assured tenancy", which offered a reduced level of protection with the objective of encouraging landowners to grant leases without the fear of being stuck with a tenant paying uneconomic rent who could not be removed. Tenancies created after January 15, 1989 may take the form of an "assured tenancy". A tenant under an assured tenancy enjoys similar protection from eviction but there is no provision for payment of a fair rent. There is no control of initial rents except where a landlord serves notice to increase the rent under an assured periodic tenancy, in which case a rent assessment committee can determine the rent that the landlord might reasonably be expected to have obtained on the open market.[20]

---

[15] For further information see: Bright and Gilbert, *Landlord and Tenant Law: The Nature of Tenancies* (1995); Davey, *Landlord and Tenant Law* (1999).
[16] Rent Act 1977 s.2.
[17] See: Rent Act 1977 Sch.15.
[18] Rent Act 1977 Sch.1 para.2.
[19] [2004] UKHL 30; [2004] 2 A.C. 557.
[20] Housing Act 1988 s.14(1).

(c) *"Assured Shorthold Tenancies" under the Housing Act 1988*

The Housing Act 1988 also introduced the "assured shorthold tenancy", which is a lease for a **9–009** specified period of not less than six months. The chief difference between the assured shorthold tenancy and the assured tenancy is that an assured shorthold does not offer security of tenure, so that at the end of the fixed term a new shorthold tenancy arises which can be terminated by the landlord giving two months' notice. The tenant is entitled to refer the initial rent of a shorthold tenancy to a rent assessment committee, but the committee is only entitled to make a determination if the rent is "significantly" higher than the landlord might reasonably be expected to obtain having regard to the rents payable under assured tenancies of similar houses in the locality.[21] Assured shorthold tenancies therefore provide relatively little protection for tenants in terms of rent control or security of tenure and have proved popular with landlords as a means of facilitating short-term letting. The majority of students renting private housing during their courses will do so on the basis of such an assured shorthold tenancy.

(d) *A Strong Presumption on Favour of an "Assured Shorthold Tenancy"*

The most recent legislation introduces a strong presumption that all leases will take the form of **9–010** an assured shorthold tenancy. Any tenancy created after February 28, 1997 will be an assured shorthold tenancy unless the tenancy expressly provided that it was not to be an assured shorthold tenancy, or the landlord gave the tenant notice that it was not to be an assured shorthold tenancy. There is thus no requirement of a fixed term,[22] but where an assured shorthold tenancy is not granted for a fixed period the landlord is not entitled to recover possession until at least six months has elapsed from the grant of the tenancy.[23]

DISTINGUISHING BETWEEN LEASES AND LICENCES

One of the most difficult issues of the post-war period has been to differentiate satisfactorily **9–011** between leases and licences. Two factors have generated difficulty. First, some leases and licences often appear very similar in their effect "on the ground", in that they enable a person to occupy land exclusively in practice. Thus it may be impossible to tell whether a particular exclusive occupier has been granted a lease or a licence from the mere fact of his exclusive occupation. The fact of his exclusive occupation may be explicable either by way of a lease or a licence. In the case of a licence his exclusive occupation arises simply because the owner does not choose to avail himself of his legal right to enter into the property. If the owner chose to do so the occupier would have no right to exclude him, but there is no opportunity for this to be demonstrated. In the case of a lease the occupation is exclusive precisely because the

---

[21] s.20.
[22] s.19A, as introduced by Housing Act 1996 s.96.
[23] s.21(5), as amended by Housing Act 1996 s.99.

occupier is entitled to exclude the owner. Second, at the time that the Rent Acts were in force, landowners sought to avoid creating protected tenancies by granting licences, which would not attract statutory protection. It therefore became common for landowners to grant rights of occupancy which were in practical effect identical to leases but which were stated by the parties to be mere licences. In the light of these difficulties the courts have had to determine how to approach the problem of differentiating between leases and licences. Two rival approaches have been adopted at different times. The objective approach determines whether a grant confers a lease or a licence by identifying the reality of the entitlement conferred rather than to the form of the grant. Under this approach the court looks to the substance of the occupancy enjoyed rather than the form of the agreement granting it, so that the conferral of exclusive possession in practice will give rise to a lease even if the grant is termed a licence by the parties. The subjective approach determines whether a grant confers a lease or a licence by looking to the intentions of the parties as expressed in their agreement rather than to the nature of the occupancy conferred in practice. Thus an agreement couched in the form of a licence will give rise to a licence even though in substance a right to exclusive occupation has been conferred which has all the characteristics of a lease.

1.   Historic Adoption of an Objective Approach

9–012   Initially the courts adopted an objective approach and, as a matter of policy, refused to allow property owners to avoid Rent Act provisions by framing their agreements as licences. For example in *Facchini v Bryson*[24] it was held that a tenancy had been created even where the agreement between the parties was stated to be a licence and it contained a provision that "nothing in this agreement shall be construed to create a tenancy". The policy was stated by Denning L.J.:

> "The occupation has all the features of a tenancy, and the parties cannot by the mere words of their contract turn it into something else. Their relationship is determined by the law and not by the label which they choose to put on it . . . It is most important that we should adhere to this principle, or else we might find all landlords granting licences and not tenancies, and we should make a hole in the rent acts through which could be driven—I will not say in these days a coach and four—but an articulated vehicle."[25]

2.   Rejection of the Objective Approach in Favour of a Subjective Approach

9–013   In a series of cases during the 1970s the courts changed approach and came to give primacy to the parties' intentions rather than to the objective nature of what had been created. This change reflected a feeling that, far from providing fair and necessary protection for tenants, the Rent

---

[24] [1952] 1 T.L.R. 1386.
[25] [1952] 1 T.L.R. 1386 at 1389–1390.

Acts had increasingly become a burden to landlords, which was acting as a disincentive to private owners renting their property, thus stultifying the private rental market. In marked contrast to his comments on the policy of preventing avoidance of the Rent Acts in *Facchini v Bryson*,[26] in *Shell-Mex and BP Ltd v Manchester Garages Ltd* Lord Denning M.R. recognised that giving primacy to the parties' intentions would enable landlords to avoid the protection offered by the Rent Acts:

> "I realise that this means that the parties can, by agreeing on a licence, get out of the Act; but so be it; it may be no bad thing."[27]

This new subjective approach was exemplified by the decision of the Court of Appeal in *Somma v Hazelhurst*.[28] An unmarried couple entered into an agreement with the owner of a house for the use of a double bed-sitting room. The agreement stated that it was a licence, the two partners were required to sign separate agreements and an agreed licence fee was paid separately by each of them to the owner. It was a term of the agreement that the licensees share the room with "such other licensees or invitees whom the licensor shall from time to time permit to use the room". Although it was patently clear that in practice the couple enjoyed exclusive occupancy of the room, the casting of the agreement as a licence was intended to avoid Rent Act control of the rent payable.

This decision clearly exposes the essence of the subjective approach to differentiating between leases and licences. The prime factor to be taken into consideration is the expressed intentions of the parties, not the substantive and objective reality of what they created.[29] Cumming-Bruce L.J. took the view that the agreement was clearly in the form of a licence and that the terms of the agreement were consistent with there being a licence and not a lease. Although some of the provisions of the agreement, especially in relation to sharing the room with other occupants, may prove unattractive there was no reason to undo the bargain that the parties had knowingly entered. He stated:

> "We can see no reason why an ordinary landlord . . . should not be able to grant a licence to occupy an ordinary house. If that is what both he and the licensee intend and if they can frame any written agreement in such a way as to demonstrate that it is not really an agreement for a lease masquerading as a licence, we can see no reason in law or justice why they should be prevented from achieving that object. Nor can we see why their common intentions should be categorised as bogus or unreal or as sham merely on the ground that the court disapproves of the bargain."[30]

However although this approach may be said to uphold the complete freedom of contract of the parties, the characterisation of the interest as a licence was surely somewhat disingenuous. The room occupied by the couple was a mere 22 feet by 18 feet, and the suggestion that the owner had the right to impose other occupiers on them is ridiculous. Similarly the licence

---

[26] [1952] 1 T.L.R. 1386.
[27] [1971] 1 All E.R. 841 at 845.
[28] [1978] 1 W.L.R. 1014.
[29] See also: *Aldrington Garages Ltd v Fielder* (1978) 37 P.& C.R. 461; *Sturlson and Co v Weniz* (1984) 17 H.L.R. 140.
[30] [1978] 1 W.L.R. 1014 at 1025.

agreement contained terms that, if either of the couple left, the owner was entitled to impose another occupier on the remaining licensee. As was pointed out this could mean that if one of the couple left the owner could introduce another person of a different sex to occupy the same room. Although the court concluded that these provisions were not a sham, in reality the landlord never had any intention of introducing additional or replacement occupiers. The whole purpose of the provisions was to ensure that the agreement appeared to have the character of a licence rather than a lease.

3. Reassertion of the Objective Approach

9–014   The primacy of the subjective approach, which paid closer attention to the parties' expressed intention than the reality of their arrangement, was finally ended by the decision of the House of Lords in *Street v Mountford*.[31] Mr Street granted Mrs Mountford a licence to occupy furnished rooms in a house. The agreement was stated to be a licence and a "licence fee" of £37 per week was payable. Mrs Mountford then claimed that the agreement created a Rent Act protected tenancy. The House of Lords, whose judgment was delivered by Lord Templeman, concluded that in reality a tenancy had been created. Central to this conclusion was the adoption of an objective approach to determining what the parties' agreement had created. He explained that the key elements of a tenancy were "exclusive possession at a rent for a term". If these factors were present, then a tenancy had been created and not a mere licence, irrespective of what the parties had chosen to call the right of occupancy:

> "In my opinion in order to ascertain the nature and quality of the occupancy . . . the court must decide whether upon its true construction the agreement confers on the occupier exclusive possession. If exclusive possession at a rent for a term does not constitute a tenancy then the distinction between a contractual tenancy and a contractual licence of land becomes wholly unidentifiable."[32]

The description given by the parties to their agreement is not, therefore, determinative of its legal character:

> "[T]he consequences in law of the agreement, once concluded, can only be determined by consideration of the effect of the agreement. If the agreement satisfied all the requirements of a tenancy, then the agreement produced a tenancy and the parties cannot alter the effect of the agreement by insisting that they only created a licence."[33]

Lord Templeman expressed the objective nature of the test in the memorable aphorism that "the manufacture of a five-pronged implement for manual digging results in a fork even if the manufacturer, unfamiliar with the English language, insists that he intended to make and has

---

[31] [1985] A.C. 809.
[32] [1985] A.C. 809 at 825.
[33] [1985] A.C. 809.

made a spade".[34] The objective approach had also been adopted by the High Court of Australia in *Radaich v Smith*[35] where Windeyer J., whose sentiments were approved by Lord Templeman,[36] held that it was inherently contradictory to say that a man who had been granted a right of exclusive possession of land was not a tenant but a mere licensee. In the later case of *Antoniades v Villiers*[37] Lord Templeman re-emphasised this objective approach:

> "an express statement of intention is not decisive and . . . the court must pay attention to the facts and surrounding circumstances and to what people do as well as to what people say".

The objective approach is not confined to residential leases but also applies to leases of commercial property. In *Rochester Poster Services Ltd v Dartford BC*[38] the plaintiffs had made an agreement for the use of a poster site at the perimeter of business premises under an agreement described as a licence. Despite this nomenclature it was held that the agreement in fact conferred exclusive possession of the site and therefore their interest was in the nature of a tenancy.

4. Assessing the Objective Approach

(a) *Advantages of the Objective Approach*

The objective approach adopted by the House of Lords in *Street v Mountford* prevents the use of false agreements to avoid the provisions of the Rent Acts. The Rent Acts were put in place for the very purpose of protecting vulnerable tenants with little bargaining power against the might of landlords, and to allow such protection to be avoided by the simple device of licence agreements was unacceptable. Such cases as *Somma v Hazelhurst* would clearly be caught by the objective approach. Lord Templeman disapproved of the decision, holding that the "court should be astute to detect and frustrate sham devices and artificial transactions whose only object is to disguise the grant of a tenancy and to evade the Rent Acts".[39]   **9–015**

(b) *Difficulties in Applying the Objective Approach*

However, despite the advantages of preventing easy avoidance of the Rent Acts, the objective approach in *Street v Mountford* does not provide a comprehensive and easy solution to the problem of determining whether an agreement creates a lease or a licence. Although attention is now focused on the factual nature of the parties' occupancy rather than on their agreement, the fundamental characteristic of leases, namely "exclusive possession" is essentially a legal   **9–016**

---

[34] [1985] A.C. 809.
[35] (1959) 101 C.L.R. 209.
[36] [1985] A.C. 809 at 827.
[37] [1990] 1 A.C. 417.
[38] (1991) 63 P. & C.R. 88.
[39] [1985] A.C. 809 at 825.

rather than a factual concept. It is perfectly possible for a person to enjoy exclusive occupation of premises without enjoying a legal entitlement to exclusive possession. For example, if an owner of a house goes abroad for a year and allows a friend to live in his house for that time in order to keep it secure, and to allow the friend to continue a search for her own accommodation, the friend may in fact enjoy the exclusive use of the house for the time the owner is away, but this does not mean that she enjoys the right to exclude the owner from the house. If the owner were to return to the house for the Christmas holiday without the friend's permission he would not be a trespasser. The mere fact of exclusive occupation will not always mean that there is also a right to exclusive possession in law, and therefore a tenancy. However, the existence of factual exclusive occupation is the essential starting point to the determination whether there is exclusive possession. Where a person enjoys exclusive occupation he may also be entitled to exclusive possession, but where he does not have exclusive occupation he cannot be entitled to exclusive possession and his interest must constitute a licence. The difficulties were identified by Lord Donaldson M.R. in *Aslan v Murphy*:

> "The occupier has in the end of the day to be a tenant or a lodger. He cannot be both. But there is a spectrum of exclusivity ranging from the occupier of a detached property under a full repairing lease, who is without doubt a tenant, to the overnight occupier of a hotel bedroom who, however upmarket the hotel, is without doubt a lodger. The dividing line—the sorting of the forks from the spades—will not necessarily or even usually depend upon a single factor, but upon a combination of factors."[40]

(c) *Extreme Application of the Objective Approach*

9–017 The objective approach to the differentiation of leases and licences adopted in *Street v Mountford* was recently reaffirmed by the House of Lords in *Bruton v London and Quadrant Housing Trust*.[41] However it is submitted that the House of Lords applied it in an extreme manner by holding that an agreement which purported to confer exclusive possession upon the occupier of a flat had conferred a tenancy even though the charitable trust which had granted the right did not have any proprietary interest in the flat. Whilst satisfaction of the criteria identified in *Street v Montford* is pre-requisite to the establishment of a tenancy, these criteria are not exhaustive. It is suggested that the case was wrongly decided and that a genuine tenancy can only be created where the grantor of a right of occupancy was capable of conferring a tenancy on the occupier.

THE ESSENTIAL REQUIREMENTS OF A LEASE

9–018 In the leading case of *Street v Mountford*[42] Lord Templeman propounded a definition of a lease which included three essential criteria. He stated that:

---

[40] [1990] 1 W.L.R. 766 at 770.
[41] [1999] 3 All E.R. 481.
[42] [1985] A.C. 809.

"to constitute a tenancy the occupier must be granted exclusive possession for a fixed or periodic term certain in consideration of a premium or periodic payments".[43]

The three elements are therefore (i) the grant of exclusive possession; (ii) for a time period which is certain; and (iii) the payment of rent. As these are examined it will be seen that the crucial criterion is usually the presence or absence of exclusive possession.

1. Exclusive Possession

The identification of exclusive possession is complex in practice because it is a legal entitlement rather than a factual state. As such it cannot be observed directly. In contrast exclusive occupation is a factual matter, which can be identified by observation of the nature of the occupancy in question. In determining whether a particular grant is a lease or a licence there is a close connection between the identification of exclusive occupation and exclusive possession. Since exclusive possession confers the right to exclude all other persons from occupation of the land, including the owner, it follows that a person cannot be entitled to exclusive possession unless he in fact enjoys exclusive occupation. Thus a grant of a right of occupation will only be capable of being a lease if the grantee in fact enjoys the exclusive occupancy of the land. If the grantee does not enjoy exclusive occupancy then the grant can only be a licence. If the grant does confer exclusive occupation in fact, then this will raise a presumption that it also confers the right to exclusive possession. This presumption will be rebutted if the circumstances are such as to suggest that the parties did not intend to confer a right of exclusive possession.

9–019

(a) *Exclusive Occupation*

Exclusive occupation is a purely factual state. It arises where a person, or number of persons, enjoy the sole and exclusive use of premises. For example, in *Somma v Hazelhurst*[44] it could be said that the couple in question in fact enjoyed exclusive occupation of their double room. Similarly in *Street v Mountford*[45] Mr and Mrs Mountford enjoyed exclusive occupation of their two rooms. In other cases it is clear that there is no exclusive occupation, for example if an elderly lady in a university town allows a student to live in one of her spare rooms as a lodger. In such circumstances the lodger cannot be said to exclusively occupy the house. The requirement of exclusive occupation is just as applicable to business premises as to residential property. In *Shell-Mex and BP Ltd v Manchester Garages Ltd*[46] the plaintiffs owned a petrol-filling station and granted the defendants the right to occupy for a year under an agreement called a licence. The defendants claimed that they were tenants. The agreement restricted the defendants to selling the plaintiff's brand of petrol and allowed the plaintiffs to enter the premises whenever they wanted to alter the layout, decoration or equipment of the

9–020

---

[43] [1985] A.C. 809 at 818.
[44] [1978] 1 W.L.R. 1014.
[45] [1985] A.C. 809.
[46] [1971] 1 All E.R. 841.

premises. Given these circumstances the Court of Appeal held that the plaintiffs did not enjoy exclusive occupation and that therefore the agreement did not confer a tenancy.

A number of common circumstances and problem areas can be identified in respect of the requirement of exclusive occupation.

(i)   Lodgers

9–021   It is clear that lodgers, that is, people who share the occupation of premises with the owner, cannot enjoy the status of tenants. They are mere licensees of the premises in which they lodge. As Lord Templeman stated in *Street v Mountford*:

> "In the case of residential accommodation there is no difficulty in deciding whether the grant confers exclusive possession. An occupier of residential accommodation at a rent for a term is either a lodger or a tenant. The occupier is a lodger if the landlord provides attendance or services which require the landlord or his servants to exercise unrestricted access to and use of the premises. A lodger is entitled to live in the premises but cannot call the place his own."[47]

The central characteristic of lodgers is their inability to refuse access to the premises they occupy to the owner or his servants acting on his behalf. For example, in the case of a student living with an elderly lady, the student does not enjoy the right to exclude her from the premises. Even though he may not wish it, she remains entitled to enter his room whenever she chooses.

(ii)   Shared Occupation of Premises

9–022   The mere fact that a number of people occupy the same premises does not necessarily mean that there is no exclusive occupancy, since they may jointly occupy the premises. For example if a group of students join together to rent a house they do not individually enjoy exclusive occupation. However they may be said to be the joint exclusive occupiers of the house. Particular difficulties have arisen in determining whether shared occupation of premises is a genuine joint tenancy, or the grant of separate licences to the individual occupiers. In *AG Securities v Vaughan*[48] an owner of a four-bedroomed flat entered into separate agreements with the four occupiers, each expressed to be licences. The agreements contained provisions requiring the individual licensees to share the flat with all the other occupiers granted licences by the owner. The flat was kept fully occupied over a period of time and whenever one occupier left another would be granted a licence by the owner. The occupiers had the sole use of a bedroom and shared use of the lounge, kitchen and bathroom. The House of Lords held that in these circumstances the occupiers were licensees and not joint tenants. Lord Templeman explained the crucial factors leading to this conclusion:

[47] [1985] A.C. 809 at 818.
[48] [1990] 1 A.C. 417.

"In the present case, if the four [occupiers] had been jointly entitled to exclusive occupation of the flat then, on the death of one of [them] the remaining three would be entitled to joint and exclusive occupation. But, in fact, on the death of one [occupier] the remaining three would not be entitled to joint and exclusive occupation of the flat. They could not exclude a fourth person nominated by the [owner]."[49]

In contrast in *Antoniades v Villiers*,[50] which was decided at the same time, the House of Lords found there was a joint tenancy rather than individual licences. A couple occupied a flat and enjoyed exclusive occupation. However the owner had required them to enter separate agreements with himself described as licences and required them to separately undertake to pay half the rent. The licences also contained a clause reserving the owner the right to go into occupation of the flat with the couple or to nominate others to occupy it with them. The House of Lords took the view that this provision in the agreements was a pretence and that there had never been any real intention on the part of the owner to enter occupation himself or to impose any other occupiers on the couple. The couple were therefore held to be tenants in joint possession.[51] In *The Mortgage Corp v Ubah*[52] it was held that there was no tenancy where the occupier of premises shared the kitchen with the owner, since there was no exclusive possession.

(iii)   Owner's Retention of Keys

The mere fact that an owner retains keys to premises does not prevent exclusive occupation. **9–023** In *Aslan v Murphy*[53] the owner of premises had entered into a "licence" agreement which included a term that he, as the licensor, would retain the keys and enjoy an absolute right of entry at all times. The Court of Appeal rejected the argument that the retention of the keys inevitably prevented the agreement conferring a tenancy. The principles were stated by Lord Donaldson M.R.:

"What matters is what underlies the provision as to keys. Why does the owner want a key, want to prevent keys being issued to the friends of the occupier or want to prevent a lock being changed? A landlord may well need a key in order that he may be able to enter quickly in the event of emergency: fire, burst pipes or whatever. He may need a key to enable him or those authorised by him to read meters or do repairs which are his responsibility. None of these underlying reasons would of themselves indicate that the true bargain between the parties was such that the occupier was in law a lodger."[54]

In contrast, if the keys were retained to enable the owner to provide services such as cleaning or bed-making, retention would indicate that a tenancy had not been conferred.

---

[49] [1990] 1 A.C. 417 at 460.
[50] [1990] 1 A.C. 417.
[51] See also *Hadjiloucas v Crean* [1988] 1 W.L.R. 1006, where sharing occupiers were found to be tenants; *Stribling v Wickham* [1989] 2 E.G.L.R. 35, where there was held to be a licence.
[52] (1997) 73 P. & C.R. 500.
[53] [1990] 1 W.L.R. 767.
[54] [1990] 1 W.L.R. 767 at 773.

(iv) Provision of Attendance

9–024   One of the most common factors preventing a finding of exclusive occupation is where the owner of the occupied property has agreed to provide regular services on behalf of the occupier. Such services are described as attendance This comprises only those services which are personal to the occupier's use of the premises he is occupying, and not services in regard to the common areas.[55] For example, the owner may agree to provide an occupier with daily cleaning of his room. Such services would constitute attendance whereas an agreement to clean the common staircase of a house divided into separate flats would not. An example of a case where occupants were found to be mere lodgers because of the provision of attendance is *Marcou v De Silvesa*.[56] A number of persons occupied flats in a house on the basis of agreements with the owner described as a licences. These agreements included provisions that the licensor would retain keys to the flats and enjoy the absolute right of entry at all times; that the licensor could require the licensees to vacate their flat at any time and move to another flat of comparable size in the house; and that the licensor would provide attendance for the licensees, including acting as housekeeper, cleaning the flats, collecting rubbish and cleaning windows. In the light of these provisions the Court of Appeal held that the occupiers did not enjoy exclusive occupation and were therefore mere lodgers and not tenants.

In general a person who occupies furnished rooms will be characterised as a lodger rather than a tenant. In *Marchant v Charters*[57] a man occupied what had been described as an "attractive bachelor service apartment", which comprised a bed-sitting room. The owner provided regular services, including daily cleaning and weekly provision of clean linen. In these circumstances the Court of Appeal held that the occupier was a mere licensee. In relation to the provision of attendance it was held irrelevant that on some occasions he had refused the services. For similar reasons students who occupy rooms in a university halls of residence will not be regarded as tenants, since the university requires access for cleaning and the provision of other services.

(v) Long-term Hotel Residents

9–025   It seems clear that a person who is a long-term hotel resident does not enjoy a tenancy of the room occupied. In *Appah v Parncliffe Investments Ltd*[58] a woman occupying a room at the "Emperor's Gate Hotel" was held to be a licensee and not a tenant. The provision of cleaning, bed-making and linen by the owners all necessitated entry, which was inconsistent with exclusive occupation.[59] The large numbers of persons now housed in bed and breakfast accommodation rather than council housing are mere licensees.

---

[55] See *Pasler v Grinling* [1948] A.C. 291; *Marchant v Charters* [1977] 1 W.L.R. 1181.
[56] (1986) 52 P. & C.R. 204.
[57] [1977] 1 W.L.R. 1181.
[58] [1964] 1 W.L.R. 1064.
[59] See also *Luganda v Service Hotels Ltd* [1969] 2 Ch. 209; *Mayflower Cambridge Ltd v Secretary of State* (1975) 30 P. & C.R. 28.

(vi)   Residents of Homes for the Elderly

It is also clear that a resident of a home for the elderly will not enjoy a tenancy. In *Abbeyfield*   **9–026**
(Harpenden) Society v Woods[60] a man of 85 occupied a room at a home for old people in
return for a weekly payment. A letter he received stated that he was entitled to "sole occupation" of his room, and that the society would provide service, meals, heating, lighting and a
resident housekeeper. When the man was asked to leave he refused, claiming that he enjoyed
exclusive possession and was entitled to Rent Act protection from eviction. The Court of
Appeal held that, given the provision of services and the entirely personal nature of the
arrangement between the man and the society, he was a mere licensee.

(vii)   Hostel Accommodation

Occupation of hostel accommodation is also unlikely to give rise to the exclusive occupation   **9–027**
which is a necessary pre-requisite of a tenancy. In *R. v South Middlesex Rent Tribunal Ex p.
Beswick*[61] a lady who lived in a room at a YWCA hostel was held to be a licensee and not a
tenant. In *Westminster City Council v Clarke*[62] the House of Lords considered the case of a man
who was housed in a hostel containing 31 single rooms for homeless men. Their agreements
entitled the Council to change the accommodation without notice and to require occupants to
share. Occupiers were required to be in their room by 11 pm and not to entertain visitors after
that time. The House of Lords held that in these circumstances the grant of exclusive possession would have been inconsistent with the purposes for which they provided the accommodation, and that the occupants were licensees and not tenants.

However the provision of short term accommodation for homeless people may sometimes
confer exclusive occupation, which is the necessary pre-requisite of exclusive possession and
a tenancy. In *Bruton v London and Quadrant Housing Trust*[63] the House of Lords held that a
man who occupied a flat under an agreement granted by a charitable housing trust which provided short-term accommodation for the homeless and others in need of housing was a tenant, even though the agreement was called a licence. The agreement contained a term that the
occupier would "permit the Trust or its Agents, Surveyors, or Consultants to enter the property for the purpose of inspecting the state of repair, and cleanliness of the property or for any
purpose connected at all reasonable hours of the day". Lord Hoffman explained that the terms
of this agreement did not detract from a grant of exclusive possession:

> "In this case, it seems to me that the agreement, construed against the relevant background,
> plainly gave Mr Bruton a right to exclusive possession. There is nothing to suggest that he
> was to share possession with the trust, the council or anyone else. The trust did not retain
> such control over the premises as was inconsistent with Mr Bruton having exclusive pos-
> session, as was the case in *Westminster City Council v Clarke*. The only rights which it
> reserved were for itself and the council to enter at certain times and for limited purposes.

[60] [1968] 1 W.L.R. 374.
[61] *The Times*, March 26, 1976.
[62] [1992] 2 A.C. 288.
[63] [1999] 3 All E.R. 481.

As Lord Templeman said in *Street v Mountford* such an express reservation 'only serves to emphasise the fact that the grantee is entitled to exclusive possession and is a tenant'."[64]

Whilst it is questionable whether the House of Lords was correct to hold that Mr Bruton enjoyed a tenancy in circumstances where the trust itself had no proprietary interest in the land, it is clear that an occupier of short term low-cost accommodation may sometimes enjoy exclusive possession and therefore a tenancy. It will be a matter for interpretation in each case whether a particular agreement confers exclusive possession or not.

(viii) Sham or Pretence Provisions

9–028 The mere presence of provisions in an agreement which seem to suggest that exclusive occupation is not enjoyed will not be conclusive if they can be shown to be a sham.[65] In other words, if the agreement contains terms which the owner had inserted merely to ensure that it appeared to confer a licence rather than a tenancy, the court will look to the reality of the parties' actions and give no regard to purported terms. As Lord Templeman stated in *Street v Mountford*,[66] commenting on the decision of the Court of Appeal in *Somma v Hazelhurst*[67]: "the court should, in my opinion, be astute to detect and frustrate sham devices and artificial transactions whose only object is to disguise the grant of a tenancy and to evade the Rent Acts". In *Marcou v De Silvaesa*[68] it was argued that the agreements between the occupiers and the owner were sham provisions. In particular it was provided that the occupiers were not entitled to use the premises between 10.30 am and 12.00 noon each day and that the licensor was entitled to remove and substitute furniture in the flats. It was held that, although these terms might be sham provisions, this did not mean that the agreement as a whole was a sham because the other terms of the agreements did envisage the performance of attendance and services which detracted from exclusive occupation. In contrast, in the very similar case of *Aslan v Murphy*,[69] the Court of Appeal held that an agreement did contain sham provisions which were to be ignored and held that a tenancy had been conferred. The occupier had entered into a licence agreement for a small basement room which included provisions that the licensee had no right to use the room between 10.30am and 12.00 noon and that the licensor would retain the keys to the room. Lord Donaldson M.R. took the view that "both provisions were wholly unrealistic and were clearly pretences", since no services had been provided.

(b) *Exclusive Possession*

9–029 Although a tenancy cannot arise in the absence of exclusive occupation, the presence of exclusive occupation does not conclusively indicate the presence of exclusive possession. Once factual exclusive occupation has been found it is necessary to consider whether the circumstances

---

[64] [1999] 3 All E.R. 481 at 486.
[65] In *Antoniades v Villiers* [1990] 1 A.C. 417 Lord Templeman preferred to use the term "pretence".
[66] [1985] A.C. 809 at 825.
[67] [1978] 1 W.L.R. 1014.
[68] (1986) 52 P. & C.R. 204.
[69] [1990] 1 W.L.R. 766.

of the occupancy, or of the relationship between the owner and occupier, negative any intention to confer exclusive possession. As Lord Templeman stated in *Street v Mountford*:

> "Sometimes it may be difficult to discover whether, on the true construction of an agreement, exclusive possession is conferred. Sometimes it may appear from the surrounding circumstances that there was no intention to create legal relationships. Sometimes it may appear from the surrounding circumstances that the right to exclusive possession is referable to a legal relationship other than a tenancy. Legal relationships to which the grant of exclusive possession might be referable and which would or might negative the grant of an estate or interest in the land include occupancy under a contract for the sale of the land, occupancy pursuant to a contract of employment or occupancy referable to the holding of an office."[70]

It is clear from these comments that there are a number of well-recognised circumstances where the enjoyment of exclusive occupation will not be taken to indicate the grant of a tenancy. However, where the only circumstances are that residential accommodation is offered and accepted with exclusive occupation for a term, at a rent, a tenancy will definitely result. This method of establishing factual exclusive occupation before examining whether any other factors indicate that a tenancy was not intended echoes the approach advocated by Denning L.J. in *Facchini v Bryson*:

> "In all the cases where an occupier has been held to be a licensee there has been something in the circumstances, such as a family arrangement, an act of friendship or generosity or such like to negative any intention to create a tenancy. In such circumstances it would be unjust to saddle the owner with a tenancy, with all the momentous consequences that that entails nowadays, when there was no intention to create a tenancy at all."[71]

(i) Service Occupancy

An occupier who enjoys exclusive occupation of premises as a consequence of his employment will not enjoy a tenancy if his occupancy is characterised as "service occupancy". The general principles were stated by Lord Templeman in *Street v Mountford*: **9–030**

> "A service occupier is a servant who occupies his master's premises in order to perform his duties as a servant. In those circumstances the possession and occupation of the servant is treated as the possession and occupation of the master and the relationship of landlord and tenant is not created."[72]

Where a person is required to occupy premises by his employer his occupation is likely to be characterised as a licence rather than a tenancy. In *Smith v Seghill Overseers*[73] Mellor J.

[70] [1985] A.C. 809 at 826.
[71] [1952] 1 T.L.R. 1386 at 1389.
[72] [1985] A.C. 809 at 818. See *Mayhew v Suttle* (1854) 4 El. & Bl. 347.
[73] (1875) L.R. 10 Q.B. 422 at 428.

suggested that the relevant test was whether the servant is required to occupy premises in order to better perform his duties as a servant. For example, a school housemaster who occupies a school house within the school grounds is unlikely to enjoy a tenancy and will be a mere licensee of the school because his occupancy is to enable him to act more effectively as a housemaster. Other common examples of service occupancies include farm workers, police officers and members of the armed forces. It does not have to be strictly necessary for the employee to occupy the premises provided he is required to do so with a view to the more efficient performance of his duties. Thus in *Fox v Dalby*[74] a sergeant required to occupy a particular house by his commanding officer was held not to be a tenant. In *Glasgow Corp v Johnstone*[75] the question arose as to whether a non-conformist clergyman, who occupied a house which was part of the church building, was a tenant or whether the church itself occupied the building.[76] The minister's duties included attending the services, counting the collection and acting as caretaker of the church. The House of Lords held that although it was not strictly necessary for him to reside in the house, since he could still have performed his duties if he had lived a short distance away though with some loss of efficiency, he was not a tenant because he was required to live there and this was of material assistance to the carrying out of his duties.[77] However, if the occupancy was in no sense required by the nature of his employment it is unlikely to constitute a service occupancy. In *Murray Bull & Co Ltd v Murray*[78] the defendant was appointed managing director of the plaintiff chemical research company and was granted a lease of a flat in the company's premises which enjoyed independent access to the street but also had direct access to the company's offices and laboratory. McNair J. held that in these circumstances his occupancy was not a service occupancy because the defendant was never required by the terms of his employment to live in the flat and he did so only because it was convenient for both parties. Similarly in *Facchini v Bryson*[79] an ice-cream manufacturer allowed his assistant to enter into occupation of a house in return for the payment a weekly sum. Although the agreement between the parties expressly stated that a tenancy was not intended, the Court of Appeal held that there was nothing in the circumstances of the occupation to negate the finding of a tenancy. The assistant's occupation was neither required by his employer nor necessary to enable him to perform his job more effectively. In *Crane v Morris*[80] the Court of Appeal seemed to suggest that a requirement to live in the occupied premises was not necessary to constitute a service occupancy. Lord Denning M.R. held that a service occupancy could arise even where the occupier was only permitted to live in the premises for the convenience of his work.[81] However, in the more recent case of *Norris v Checksfield*[82] the Court of Appeal seemed to reaffirm the need for a requirement to occupy. Woolf L.J. stated:

[74] (1874) L.R. 10 C.P. 285.
[75] [1965] A.C. 609.
[76] If the church could be said to occupy the building it would enjoy exemption from rates as a charity.
[77] See also *Reed v Cattermole* [1937] 1 K.B. 613.
[78] [1953] 1 Q.B. 211.
[79] [1952] 1 T.L.R. 1386.
[80] [1965] 3 All E.R. 77.
[81] See *Torbett v Faulkner* [1952] 2 T.L.R. 660.
[82] [1991] 1 W.L.R. 1241.

"an employee can be a licensee, although his occupation of the premises is not necessary for the purposes of the employment, if he is genuinely required to occupy the premises for the better performance of his duties. In my judgment this . . . accurately reflects the law."[83]

A mechanic was allowed to occupy a bungalow close to the depot where he worked on condition that he would apply for a PSV licence to be able to drive his employer's coaches. Prior to taking up occupation he failed to inform his employer that he was disqualified from driving. The Court of Appeal held that although his presence in the bungalow was not strictly required in relation to his employment as a mechanic, the occupancy had been granted with the expectation that he would qualify as a coach driver, which would require his presence in the premises to enable him to assist with emergencies more effectively. That expectation provided "a sufficient factual nexus between the commencement of the occupation of the premises and the employment which would benefit from that occupation".[84] He was therefore a service occupier and a mere licensee.

(ii) Family Relationships

Where occupation is allowed on the basis of family ties it may be found that there was no inten- **9–031** tion to create a legal relationship, and that therefore no tenancy was created. For example, in *Cobb v Lane*[85] a sister owned a house in which she allowed her brother to live for more than 13 years without paying rent. The Court of Appeal affirmed the decision of the judge at first instance that there had been no intention to grant a lease and that the brother was in occupation as a mere licensee. However the mere existence of a family relationship does not necessarily preclude a finding that the creation of a legal relationship was intended. In *Nunn v Dalrymple*[86] a man entered into an agreement with his parents-in-law that he would renovate a lodge on an estate that they owned. On completing the renovation he gave up his tenancy of a council house and moved into the lodge, paying rent. The Court of Appeal held that since he enjoyed exclusive occupation of the lodge he was entitled to a tenancy, and that in the circumstances the presence of a family relationship did not negate that conclusion. A significant factor seems to have been that he did not need to move house and he had given up his secure tenancy.

(iii) Friendship

Just as occupation on the basis of family relationships may negate the finding of a tenancy, **9–032** occupation granted on the basis of friendship may have the same effect. In *Booker v Palmer*[87] the owner of a cottage allowed evacuees who had been bombed out of their home to occupy it at the request of a friend. The Court of Appeal held that in these circumstances there was no intention to create legal relations. In *Heslop v Burns*[88] Edward Timms purchased a cottage for

---

[83] [1991] 1 W.L.R. 1241 at 1244. he approved the judgements of the House of Lords in *Glasgow Corp v Johnstone* [1965] A.C. 609.
[84] [1991] 1 W.L.R. 1241 at 1245.
[85] [1952] 1 T.L.R. 1037.
[86] (1990) 59 P. & C.R. 231.
[87] [1942] 2 All E.R. 674.
[88] [1974] 3 All E.R. 406.

Mr and Mrs Burns to occupy in 1951 after developing a romantic attraction to Mrs Burns and becoming concerned over their poor living conditions when they were expecting a child. He subsequently became the god-father of the child and paid for her education. They remained in accommodation provided by him until after his death in 1970. At no point did they pay any rent. They claimed that their occupancy was in the nature of a tenancy.[89] The Court of Appeal held that there was a mere licence because there was no intention to create legal relations at all. As Stamp L.J. observed, "The home was not to be the [Burns'] castle but the house in which he allowed them to live".[90] In *Rhodes v Dalby*[91] Goff J. held that no tenancy was created where a farmer allowed a teacher to live in a bungalow on his farm for two years on the basis of what was described as a "gentleman's agreement".

(iv) Charity and Generosity

9–033   Closely related to the preceding category, if an occupancy is granted on the basis of charitable or other motives of kindness or generosity, this may indicate that no tenancy was intended. For example, in *Marcroft Wagons Ltd v Smith*,[92] a daughter lived with her mother who was the statutory tenant of a house. On the mother's death the daughter asked the landlord to transfer the tenancy to herself, but the landlord refused. He did, however, allow her to remain in occupation for a short period in return for the payment of a rent to give her time to look for alternative accommodation. The Court of Appeal held that she was not entitled to a tenancy but was a mere licensee. Lord Evershed M.R. took the view that it would be wrong to give landlords a disincentive to act out of "ordinary human instincts of kindliness and courtesy" because of the fear that they would be stuck with tenants they could no longer remove if they allowed persons to remain in occupation for short periods in such circumstances.

In the more recent case of *Gray v Taylor*[93] the Court of Appeal held that a person who occupied an almshouse, which was administered by the trustees of a charity for the provision of accommodation for poor persons of good character who were not less than 60 years of age, was a licensee and not a tenant. Although the defendant claimed that she enjoyed exclusive possession in return for the payment of a weekly sum, Vinelott J. held that she only occupied the almshouse as a beneficiary of the charitable trust. He held that finding a tenancy would have imposed a burden on the charitable trustees which might have made it impossible for them to ensure that the occupation of the almshouse was restricted to persons who satisfied the criteria specified in the trust deed. For example, an almsperson who inherited a substantial legacy or won the national lottery would no longer be a poor person and a proper object of the charity, and would thus be required to cease occupation. Since the defendant was not a tenant the charity was entitled to give her notice to quit her flat on the grounds of her vexatious behaviour, which had disturbed the quiet enjoyment of the almshouse.

---

[89] A tenancy at will.
[90] [1974] 3 All E.R. 406 at 411.
[91] [1971] 2 All E.R. 1144.
[92] [1951] 2 K.B. 497.
[93] [1998] 4 All E.R. 17.

(v) Occupation of Premises Prior to Completion of Sale

Traditionally a person allowed into occupation of premises which he had agreed to purchase prior to completion was regarded as a tenant at will.[94] However in *Street v Mountford*[95] Lord Templeman suggested that in such cases there was no intention to create a tenancy.[96] This approach has not been universally applied. In *Javad v Mohammed Aqil*[97] the defendant was allowed into occupation of business premises owned by the plaintiff in anticipation of their being able ultimately to agree the terms of a lease. The Court of Appeal held that the defendant was a tenant at will. This case may not be determinative since there was no express contract between the parties and the issue before the court was not whether there was a tenancy or a licence but a tenancy at will or a periodic tenancy. In *Essex Plan Ltd v Broadminster*[98] the plaintiffs occupied premises of the defendant under a licence agreement which granted them an option to call for a long lease. After the licence had expired they remained in occupation. Hoffman J. held that irrespective of whether the agreement had granted the plaintiffs exclusive possession it had not created a tenancy:

9–034

> "contracts for the sale of land commonly provide for the purchaser to be allowed into occupation as a licensee pending completion on terms that he is to pay all outgoings together with interest on the purchase money and is to keep the premises in good repair. The purchaser's possession is ancillary and referable to his interest in the land created by his contractual right to a conveyance and Lord Templeman acknowledges that such a relationship, although exhibiting the ordinary badges of a tenancy, does not create one."

2. A Period which is Certain

The second requirement for a valid lease identified by Lord Templeman in *Street v Mountford*[99] was a "term". The effect of this requirement is that a lease must confer a right to exclusive possession of land for a limited period of time, which is identified with sufficient certainty. A grant will fail to create a lease if there is any uncertainty as to the date of commencement or as to the duration of the intended tenancy. This is a long-established requirement. As Lush L.J. observed in *Marshall v Berridge*:

9–035

> "There must be a certain beginning and a certain ending, otherwise it is not a perfect lease, and a contract for a lease must . . . contain those elements."[100]

---

[94] *Doe d. Tomes v Chamberlaine* (1839) 5 M. & W. 14.
[95] [1985] A.C. 809.
[96] See also *Errington v Errington* [1952] 1 K.B. 290; *Hyde v Pearce* [1982] 1 W.L.R. 560.
[97] [1991] 1 W.L.R. 1007.
[98] [1988] 56 P. & C.R. 353.
[99] [1985] A.C. 809.
[100] (1881) 19 Ch.D. 233 at 245.

(a) *Certainty of Commencement of the Tenancy*

(i) Agreement for a Lease with no Certain Start Date

9–036 Where an agreement contains no clear and certain date for the tenancy to commence it will not create a valid lease. In *Harvey v Pratt*,[101] for example, the parties made a written agreement for the lease of a garage which included the length of the term and details of the rent but did not give a date for commencement of the tenancy. The intended tenant had never entered into occupation. The Court of Appeal held that, in the absence of a commencement date, there was no valid contract for the lease.

(ii) Agreement for a Lease with an Uncertain Start Date

9–037 An agreement for the creation of a lease commencing on the occurrence of an uncertain event will not be invalid, and will be enforceable on the occurrence of the specified event. In *Brilliant v Michaels*[102] Evershed J. held that a contract for a lease of a flat entered in 1943, and which was to take effect when the flat became vacant, was enforceable because the tenant had actually taken possession on the flat becoming vacant. He stated the principle:

> "a contract for a lease is enforceable notwithstanding that the commencement of the term may be expressed by reference to the happening of a contingency which is at the time uncertain provided that, at the time that the contract is sought to be enforced, the event has occurred and the contingency has happened."[103]

Similarly, in *Swift v Macbean*[104] an agreement for a lease made in August 1939, to run from the outbreak of any hostilities between Britain and another power, was held valid because the war had broken out and the tenants had taken possession.

(iii) Reversionary Leases

9–038 Where an agreement is entered for the creation of a lease from a specified future date the lease is described as reversionary. For example, in *Mann, Crossman & Paulin Ltd v Registrar of the Land Registry*[105] a deed was executed by the lessor of a pub in 1917, which granted a lease to run for 30 years from 1946. This was held to create a vested proprietary interest in favour of the tenant, which could be registered. However the position was reformed by the Law of Property Act 1925 which renders void the creation of leases which will take effect more than 21 years after the date of the instrument creating them.[106] Contracts to create such void reversionary leases are themselves void.

---

[101] [1965] 1 W.L.R. 1025.
[102] [1945] 1 All E.R. 121.
[103] [1945] 1 All E.R. 121 at 128.
[104] [1942] 1 K.B. 375.
[105] [1918] 1 Ch. 202.
[106] Law of Property Act 1925 s.149(3).

(c) *Certainty as to the Maximum Duration of a Lease*

(i) A Traditional Common Law Requirement

It has long been established at common law[107] that a lease is invalid unless it has a fixed max-   **9–039**
imum duration, meaning that there is a clear point in time at which the tenancy will come to
an end. This requirement is intended to prevent the possibility that a lease might last forever,
since this would be incompatible with the fee simple estate out of which the leasehold interest is carved. In most cases leases have a clearly defined length, as for example a lease for 99
years. However difficulties have arisen when the duration of a tenancy is defined in relation
to the happening of an event, rather than by a specified period. In *Lace v Chantler*[108] a tenant
of a house granted a sub-lease to the defendant during the Second World War which was
expressed to be "for the duration of the war". The Court of Appeal held that this did not create a good leasehold interest for a fixed term because the term was uncertain.[109] Lord Greene
M.R. stated:

> "A term created by a leasehold tenancy agreement must be expressed either with cer-
> tainty and specifically or by reference to something which can, at the time when the lease
> takes effect, be looked to as a certain ascertainment of what the term is meant to be. In
> the present case, when this tenancy agreement took effect, the term was completely
> uncertain. It was impossible to say how long the tenancy would last."

The court felt unable to follow the example of Rowlatt J. in *Great Northern Railway Co v
Arnold*,[110] who had construed a similar agreement during the First World War as a lease for 999
years determinable on the cessation of the war. Although the Court of Appeal did not feel such
a construction was permissible, the fact that the lease could have been drafted in such a way
demonstrates the ease with which the purported difficulty of an uncertain term can be avoided.
The decision in *Lace v Chantler* had the effect of rendering many wartime leases invalid, and
led to the passage of remedial legislation in the form of the War-Time Leases Act 1944.

(ii) An Attempted Reinterpretation of the Requirement

Although the requirement of a fixed maximum duration was well established, in *Ashburn*   **9–040**
Anstalt v Arnold[111] the Court of Appeal proposed a radical reinterpretation. The occupier of
a shop, which was part of a complex that was being redeveloped by its owners, was permitted to remain in occupation rent-free until given a quarter's notice. The Court of Appeal

---

[107] See *Say v Smith* (1563) Plowd. 269.
[108] [1944] K.B. 368.
[109] The Court held, however, that because there was a clear intention to create a lease (the tenant had been given a rent
book in which the payments of rent were recorded) and had been paying rent weekly, this created a weekly tenancy.
[110] (1916) 33 T.L.R. 114.
[111] [1989] Ch. 1.

held that this agreement was a lease rather than a licence, but was then faced with the problem that it did not appear to satisfy the requirement of certainty because the agreement did not specify a fixed maximum duration, so that the occupancy could have continued for ever. However the Court of Appeal distinguished *Lace v Chantler*, holding that the real principle was not that a lease must have a fixed maximum duration, but that a lease must be brought to an end by the occurrence of a sufficiently certain event. On this analysis the real problem in *Lace v Chantler* was not the theoretical possibility that the war might last forever, but that it would not be possible to tell with sufficient certainty when the war ended. As Fox L.J. explained:

> "In *Lace v Chantler* the duration of the war could not be predicted and there was no provision for either party to bring the tenancy to an end before the war ended, and that event itself might be very hard to pinpoint."

In contrast, in *Ashburn Anstalt v Arnold* the event which would bring the tenancy to an end, namely the giving of a quarter's notice, was sufficiently certain. Fox L.J. therefore explained this new approach to the requirement of certainty:

> "The result . . . is that the arrangement could be brought to an end by both parties in circumstances which are free from uncertainty in the sense that there would be no doubt whether the determining event had occurred. The vice of uncertainty in relation to the duration of the term is that the parties do not know where they stand."[112]

(iii)   A Reassertion of the Traditional Requirement

9–041   Despite the attempt of the Court of Appeal to introduce a more liberal interpretation of the requirement in *Ashburn Anstalt v Arnold*, in *Prudential Assurance Co Ltd v London Residuary Body*[113] the House of Lords firmly reasserted the traditional approach and overruled the innovative interpretation of *Lace v Chantler*. The case concerned an agreement made in 1930 between the London County Council and the owner of a strip of land fronting a highway. The owner sold the land to the Council, and in return leased it back at a rent of £30 per annum. The agreement stated that the tenancy should "continue until the . . . land is required by the Council" for the purpose of widening the highway. The plaintiffs and defendants were the successors in title to the original council and owner. The central question was whether the agreement had created a lease. Lord Templeman held that *Ashburn Anstalt v Arnold* had been wrongly decided because it hade made it "unnecessary for a lease to be of a certain duration".[114] He explained that the reasoning of the Court of Appeal, which had led it to hold that it was only necessary for the event which would bring the lease to an end to be certain, was fallacious:

---

[112] [1989] Ch. 1 at 12.
[113] [1992] 2 A.C. 386.
[114] [1992] 2 A.C. 386 at 395.

"A lease can be made for five years subject to the tenant's right to determine if the war ends before the expiry of five years. A lease can be made from year to year subject to a fetter on the right of the landlord to determine the lease before the expiry of five years unless the war ends. Both leases are valid because they create a determinable certain term of five years. A lease might purport to be made for the duration of the war subject to the tenant's right to determine before the end of the war. A lease might be made from year to year subject to a fetter on the right of the landlord to determine the lease before the war ends. Both leases would be invalid because each purported to create an uncertain term. A term must either be certain or uncertain. It cannot be partly certain because the tenant can determine it at any time and partly uncertain because the landlord cannot determine it for an uncertain period. If the landlord does not grant and the tenant does not take a certain term the grant does not create a lease."[115]

The reassertion of the traditional requirement, although orthodox and in accord with the doctrine of precedent, was a matter of some regret to the House of Lords. The consequence was that the original lease was ineffective to create a tenancy on its terms. However, the fact that rent had been paid and accepted by the owners of the land was sufficient to generate an implied yearly periodic tenancy of the land. The nature of periodic tenancies is explained more fully below, but the consequence of this for the parties in *Prudential Assurance Co Ltd v London Residuary Body*[116] was that the owners of the land had the right to terminate the Prudential's tenancy by giving six months' notice. Lord Browne-Wilkinson pointed out that this led to a result wholly contrary to what the parties had intended when they contracted in 1930. The agreement was intended to ensure that the owners of the premises enjoyed a permanent road frontage for their premises, and that the only circumstances in which this could be lost was if the Council decided to widen the road, thus bringing the road closer to the premises. Instead the owners of the premises were left with unguaranteed frontage, and the Council with the freehold to a strip of land that they could not in practice use for any other purpose. In the light of this Lord Browne-Wilkinson questioned the appropriateness of the present rule, but felt that the security of existing property interests militated against a judicial change:

"This bizarre outcome results from the application of an ancient and technical rule of law which requires the maximum duration of a term of years to be ascertainable from the outset. No one has produced any satisfactory rationale for the genesis of that rule. No one has been able to point to any useful purpose that it serves at the present day. If, by overruling the existing authorities, this House were able to change the law for the future only I would have urged your Lordships to do so. But for this house to depart from a rule relating to land law which has been established for many centuries might upset long established titles. I must therefore confine myself to expressing the hope that the Law Commission might look at the subject to see whether there is in fact any good reason now for maintaining a rule which operates to defeat contractually agreed arrangements between the parties."

[115] [1992] 2 A.C. 395.
[116] [1992] 2 A.C. 386.

(iv) Drafting Leases which Comply with the Requirement

9–042 Although in both *Lace v Chantler*[117] and *Prudential Assurance Co Ltd v London Residuary Body*[118] the respective agreements were held ineffective to create valid leases according to their express terms, the difficulties could have been avoided by relatively simple drafting devices. There is no difficulty in providing that a lease is to be determinable by one, or both, of the parties upon the happening of a particular event, and therefore to draft such leases with reference to a fixed maximum term coupled with a right to determine would satisfy the requirements. A lease for 99 years subject to the tenant's or landlord's right to determine "if the war ends" would have created a valid lease in *Lace v Chantler*. Similarly, a lease for 999 years subject to the landlord's right to determine "if the land should be required for a road widening scheme" would have created a valid lease in *Prudential Assurance Co Ltd v London Residuary Body*.

(v) Statutory Solutions to Common Cases of Uncertain Terms

9–043 In a number of cases where parties might accidentally create a lease for an uncertain term statute has intervened to ensure that a valid lease is created. By s.149(6) of the Law of Property Act 1925, a lease granted for the period of a person's life will take effect as a lease for 90 years determinable on the death of that person.[119] Under the same section a lease granted to a person until marriage also takes effect as a 90-year lease determinable on marriage. A lease which is perpetually renewable, and therefore potentially capable of permanent endurance, takes effect as a lease for 2,000 years determinable only by the lessee.[120]

(vi) A Single Continuous Term?

9–044 Provided that the overall term is certain, it seems that a single continuous term is not a necessity for a valid lease. In *Cottage Holiday Associates Ltd v Customs and Excise Commissioners*[121] the question arose whether leases of time-share cottages were leases for a period exceeding 21 years. The leases granted the right to occupy a cottage for one week a year for 80 years. Woolf J. held that the effect of these agreements was to create leases of discontinuous periods less than 21 years in duration, since a distinction was to be drawn between the duration of the lease creating the interest and the duration of the interest itself.[122]

---

[117] [1944] K.B. 368.
[118] [1992] 2 A.C. 386.
[119] Provides that the lease was granted "at a rent, or in consideration of a fine".
[120] Law of Property Act 1925 s.145 Sch.15 para.1. See *Re Greenwood's Agreement* [1950] 1 All E.R. 436; *Re Hopkins Lease* [1972] 1 All E.R. 248.
[121] [1983] Q.B. 735.
[122] See also *Smallwood v Sheppards* [1895] 2 Q.B. 627. Such leases are now required to be registered under the Land Registration Act 2002 s.27(2).

(vii) The Requirement of a Fixed Maximum Duration and Periodic Tenancies

The requirement that the term of a lease must be of a fixed certain duration is especially difficult to apply in the context of periodic tenancies. The conceptual relationship between this requirement and periodic tenancies will be considered below, when the nature and operation of periodic tenancies is examined.

9–045

3. Payment of Rent

(a) *Meaning of Rent*

One of the main functions of leases is to enable landowners to profit from land which they do not intend to use themselves. Rent is the consideration which is paid by the tenant to the landlord in return for the tenancy. Rent only includes payments made in return for the use of the land,[123] and would not therefore include any money which the tenant was required by the lease to expend on repair to the property. Rent will usually take the form of a money payment, but could also comprise benefits in kind, such as the performance of services for the landlord, or the provision of some token such as a peppercorn (hence the expression "a peppercorn rent" for a low rent).

9–046

(b) *Is Rent a Necessity?*

In *Street v Mountford*[124] Lord Templeman seemed to suggest that the payment of rent was an essential criterion for the existence of a lease, since his repeated refrain through the judgment was that a tenancy consists of "exclusive possession, for a term, at a rent". However, in *Ashburn Anstalt v Arnold*[125] the Court of Appeal held that a tenancy could arise where exclusive possession was granted for a term even though no rent was payable. Fox L.J. concluded that Lord Templeman had not intended to suggest that rent was essential:

9–047

> "We are unable to read Lord Templeman's speech . . . as laying down a principle of 'no rent, no lease'."[126]

There were two main reasons why the Court of Appeal was able to reach this conclusion. First, to hold that a rent was essential would be inconsistent with s.205(1)(xxvii) of the Law of Property Act 1925, which defines a "term of years absolute" as a "term of years (taking effect either in possession or in reversion whether or not at a rent)". Secondly, it would be

---

[123] *Bostock v Bryant* (1990) 61 P. & C.R. 23.
[124] [1985] A.C. 809.
[125] [1989] Ch. 1.
[126] [1989] Ch. 1 at 9.

inconsistent with the judgment of Windeyer J. in the Australian case of *Radaich v Smith*,[127] which Lord Templeman had expressly approved, and which made no reference to a rent. Although many of the elements of the Court of Appeal's decision in *Ashburn Anstalt v Arnold*[128] have been overruled in subsequent cases, this rejection of the requirement of a rent as an integral feature of a tenancy has been followed and remains good law.[129]

(c) *Absence of a Rent may Indicate that no Tenancy was Intended*

9–048 Although rent is not a necessary requirement of a lease, it may prove an important relevant factor in determining if there was an intention on the part of the parties to grant a tenancy of land. In *Colchester Council v Smith*[130] a man had occupied agricultural land under an agreement with the Council in 1967 allowing him to remain in occupation for the rest of that year without charge and at his own risk. Ferris J. held that this agreement was a licence and not a tenancy, even though he in fact enjoyed exclusive use of the land. The absence of rent was highly relevant to this conclusion:

> "Although in this case the council did, in my judgment, grant exclusive possession to Mr Tillson it did not do so at a rent and only in a limited sense can it be said to have done so for a term. In my view the rejection of Mr Tillson's implied offer to pay a reasonable rent, the expression of the transaction in terms of non-objection to continued occupation as distinct from the grant, the insistence that Mr Tillson must occupy at his own risk and must give up possession at short notice if the land were required for other purposes, all point towards this being an exceptional transaction, not intended to give rise to legal obligations on either side."[131]

GRANTING FIXED TERM LEASES

1. Basic Principles

(a) *A Lease is a Conveyance*

9–049 A tenancy of land is created is by the grant of a lease. A lease is technically a conveyance,[132] which transfers the intended leasehold estate in the land to the tenant and leaving the owner

---

[127] (1959) 101 C.L.R. 209.
[128] [1989] Ch. 1.
[129] *Birrell v Carey* (1989) 58 P. & C.R. 184; *Prudential Assurance Co Ltd v London Residuary Body* (1992) 63 P. & C.R. 386, CA; *Canadian Imperial Bank of Commerce v Bello* (1992) 64 P. & C.R. 48; *Skipton Building Society v Clayton* (1993) P. & C.R. 223.
[130] [1991] Ch. 448.
[131] [1991] Ch. 485.
[132] Law of Property Act 1925 s.205(1)(ii) states that a "Conveyance" includes a lease.

holding the freehold reversion. In general a conveyance requires the execution of a deed,[133] but in the case of leases this is subject to an exception where the lease is for a period not exceeding three years. The precise requirements for the creation of a valid lease are determined by the duration of the tenancy, so that more formalities must be observed for the creation of longer leases. Very short leases (i.e. for up to three years) can be created orally without the need for further formalities, medium-term leases (i.e. those over three years and up to seven years) have to be granted by deed, and longer-term leases (i.e. those for more than seven years) have to be granted by deed and the grant completed by registration. If the appropriate formalities are observed the grant of the lease will create a legal estate in the land.

(b) Contracts to Grant Leases

In many circumstances a lease will be granted by a landowner in fulfilment of a contractual **9–050** promise to grant a lease. A valid contract to grant a lease is specifically enforceable in equity. The operation of the maxim "equity treats as done that which ought to be done" has the effect that equity treats a contract to grant a lease as effective to create a lease which is equitable in character. Such an equitable lease might arise where there is a valid contract to grant a lease but the landowner has made no attempt to grant a lease, or where the owner has purported to grant a lease but has failed to comply with the requisite formalities for the creation of a legal lease. The operation of equitable leases will be examined in detail below.

(c) Formal Requirements for Deeds and Contracts

The legal or equitable character of a lease will generally depend on whether the parties have **9–051** observed the appropriate formalities. For transactions occurring after September 26, 1989 the formality requirements are found in the Law of Property (Miscellaneous Provisions) Act 1989.[134] An instrument will only be valid as a deed if it makes clear on its face that it is intended to be a deed, and it is signed by the person creating it in the presence of a witness who attests the signature.[135] A contract will only be valid if made in writing and incorporating all the terms which the parties have expressly agreed. The document incorporating the terms must be signed by or on behalf of each party to the contract.[136]

(d) Registration

In some cases a legal lease will only be created if the grant is completed by registration. **9–052** Under the Land Registration Act 1925 only leases for more than 21 years were required to be

---

[133] Law of Property Act 1925 s.52.
[134] See above, para.8–028.
[135] Law of Property (Miscellaneous Provisions) Act 1989 s.1. Alternatively, it may be signed at the direction of the person creating the instrument in the presence of two witnesses who attest the signature.
[136] Law of Property (Miscellaneous Provisions) Act 1989 s.2.

registered. The Land Registration Act 2002 has greatly extended the circumstances in which the grant of a lease will have to be completed by registration. Section 27(2)(b) specifies five circumstances where the grant of a term of years absolute is a "disposition required to be completed by registration":

   (i) for a term of more than seven years from the date of the grant;

   (ii) to take effect in possession after the end of the period of three months beginning with the date of the grant;

   (iii) under which the right to possession is discontinuous;

   (iv) in pursuance of Part 5 of the Housing Act 1985 (c.68) (the right to buy); or

   (v) in circumstances where s.171A of that Act applies (disposal by landlord which leads to a person no longer being a secure tenant).

Failure to comply with the requirement of registration has the effect that the disposition "does not operate at law until the registration requirements are met",[137] although it may take effect in equity.

2. Legal Leases for a Fixed Term

(a) *Leases for a Term not Exceeding Three Years*

9–053 Although a lease is a conveyance, and would ordinarily have to be granted be deed, s.54(2) of the Law of Property Act 1925 introduces an exception in the case of short leases. It provides that a lease for a term "not exceeding three years" can be created orally without the need for further formalities, provided that it takes effect "in possession . . . at the best rent which can be reasonably obtained without taking a fine". An oral grant of a lease for a period of less than three years will thus create a legal term of years absolute provided that it is at a full rent (sometimes called a rack rent) and takes effect immediately.[138]

Section 54(2) will only apply if a lease is for a definite period of less than three years. In *Kushner v Law Society*[139] it was therefore held that it did not apply to a lease for 14 years which might have been terminated by the tenant within a three-year period. Section 54(2) has no application to the grant of a lease, whether orally or in writing but not by deed, which does not entitle the tenant to immediate possession of the land. In *Long v Tower Hamlets LBC*[140] the Council wrote to the plaintiffs confirming that they would grant a quarterly tenancy of a shop at a rent of £55. The letter was written on September 4 and stated that the tenancy would commence on September 29. James Munby Q.C. held that the letter had not given rise to a legal lease. It was wholly outside of the scope of s.54(2) because it purported to grant a reversionary lease, which could only have been granted by deed.

---

[137] Land Registration Act 2002 s.27(1).
[138] Law of Property Act 1925 s.1(1)(b).
[139] [1952] 1 K.B. 264.
[140] [1996] 2 All E.R. 683.

(b) *Leases for a Term Exceeding Three Years but not More than Seven Years*

Section 54(2) has no application to a lease for a period exceeding three years. Section 52 **9–054** therefore applies. This section provides:

> "All conveyances of land or of any interest therein are void for the purpose of conveying or creating a legal estate unless made by deed."

A legal lease for more than three years can, therefore, only be created by deed. There is no need, however, for the grant of a lease for a term exceeding three years but not more than seven years to be completed by registration, unless it falls within any of the other circumstances identified in s.27(2)(b) of the Land Registration Act 2002. A lease for more than three years which is granted by deed will thus create a legal term of years absolute.

(c) *Leases for a Term of More than Seven Years*

Section 27(2)(b)(i) of the Land Registration Act 2002 provides that a lease for a period of **9–055** more than seven years is a registrable disposition. As such a lease for more than seven years will have to be granted by deed and completed by registration. If these formal requirements are not satisfied the lease will only be able to take effect in equity.

3. Equitable Leases

(a) *The Concept of an Equitable Lease*

Where the parties have failed to comply with the appropriate formalities for the creation of a **9–056** legal lease it is still possible that an equitable lease may have been created. An equitable lease is created where there is a specifically enforceable contract between the parties for the grant of a legal lease, which contract has not been performed. The rationale underlying the concept of an equitable lease is the maxim that equity "treats as done that which ought to be done". Where a landowner contracts to grant a lease but fails to do so, an intended tenant could seek the aid of equity to force the landlord to grant the promised lease, equity treats the contract as generating the intended estate in the land.[141] The lease is equitable rather than legal in character, but is held on the same terms or covenants as were promised in the contract.[142] The principle was recognised in *Parker v Taswell*[143] but the classic case where an equitable lease was

---

[141] This doctrine operates in relation to contracts to create other interests in land besides leases, for example in *Mason v Clarke* [1955] A.C. 778 an agreement to grant a profit \ga prendre was held to create a equitable profit despite the absence of a deed.
[142] *Rochester Poster Services Ltd v Dartford BC* (1991) 63 P. & C.R. 88.
[143] (1858) 2 De. G. & J. 559.

held to have been created is *Walsh v Lonsdale*.[144] The theory was well summarised by Stamp L.J. in *Warmington v Miller*:

> "The equitable interests which the intended lessee has under an agreement for a lease do not exist in vacuo, but arise because the intended lessee has an equitable right to specific performance of the agreement. In such a situation that which is agreed to be and ought to be done is treated as having been done and carrying with it in equity the attendant rights."[145]

In *Walsh v Lonsdale*[146] the defendant agreed in 1879 to grant the plaintiff a lease of a cotton mill for seven years, at a rent of 30 shillings a year for each loom run. The rent was stipulated to be payable in advance. No deed was ever executed and the plaintiff entered into possession of the mill and ran 560 looms. The plaintiff paid his rent in arrears. In 1882 the defendant claimed that the plaintiff was obliged to pay rent in advance in accordance with the terms of the agreement and exercised the remedy of distress to recover the alleged arrears. The plaintiff claimed that distress had been unlawful exercised, arguing that he occupied the mill under an implied periodic tenancy because the agreed lease had not been granted. Under such an implied periodic tenancy the rent would have been payable in arrears and not in advance. The Court of Appeal, however, held that the plaintiff enjoyed an equitable lease of the mill on the same terms as the contract, i.e. at the agreed rent which was payable in advance. The exercise of the remedy of distress was therefore legitimate and the plaintiff's claim for damages for illegal distress was rejected. Lord Jessel M.R. stated the principles under which an equitable lease was found to exist:

> "There is an agreement for a lease under which possession has been given . . . [The tenant] holds, therefore, under the same terms in equity as if a lease had been granted, it being a case in which both parties admit that relief is capable of being given by specific performance. That being so, he cannot complain of the exercise by the landlord of the same rights as the landlord would have had if a lease had been granted."[147]

A more recent example of an equitable lease is *Rochester Poster Services Ltd v Dartford BC*.[148] In 1980 Forrest Amusements granted Rochester Poster Services the right to erect poster panels on the perimeter of their premises in return for a rent of £2,800 per annum. The agreement was for 12 years initially. The landlords failed to execute a deed granting the agreed lease to the tenants. However it was held that the contract operated to create an equitable lease. The plaintiffs were therefore entitled to receive compensation from the Council when they compulsorily purchased the land because they were in lawful possession under an equitable lease.

[144] (1882) 21 Ch.D. 9.
[145] [1973] Q.B. 877 at 887.
[146] (1882) 21 Ch.D. 9.
[147] (1882) 21 Ch.D. 9 at 14–15.
[148] (1991) 63 P. & C.R. 88.

216

(b) *Essential Conditions for the Existence of an Equitable Lease*

(i) A Valid Contract for a Lease

An equitable lease will only arise where there was a valid contract for the grant of a lease. As has been noted above, after September 26, 1989 such a contract must be made in writing which incorporates all the terms the parties have expressly agreed and is signed by or on behalf of them. In the case of contracts entered before the Law of Property (Miscellaneous Provisions) Act 1989 came into effect such contracts had merely to be evidenced in writing.[149] However the doctrine of part performance was also operative, so that a tenant who entered into possession on the basis of a purely oral agreement would enjoy an equitable lease even though there was no written evidence of the contract.[150] After September 26, 1989 a contract which does not comply with the new requirements will be ineffective to give rise to an equitable lease even if there was part performance. The scope of operation of *Walsh v Lonsdale*[151] and the equitable lease is therefore much reduced.

9–057

(ii) Availability of Specific Performance

Even where there is a valid contract for the creation of a lease, an equitable lease will only come into existence if specific performance of that contract is available. Specific performance is an equitable remedy and is not therefore available as of right. A number of factors may prevent the award of an order for specific performance, in which case the contract will not give rise to an equitable lease. Specific performance is not available in favour of a volunteer. It is also unavailable if the party seeking it is in breach of the covenants agreed in the contract. In *Coatsworth v Johnson*,[152] for example, a tenant had entered into possession of agricultural land under an agreement for a lease for 21 years. The contract contained a number of covenants, including an obligation to cultivate the land in a good and husband-like manner. As the tenant was in breach of this covenant, the Court of Appeal held that specific performance would have been unavailable to him, and that there was therefore no equitable lease. The court will also refuse to grant specific performance of a person's contract if this would necessitate him breaching a contract with a third person. In *Warmington v Miller*[153] a tenant's lease contained an express term prohibiting him from granting a sub-lease. In breach of this term the defendant granted the plaintiff an oral sub-lease of the premises, following which the plaintiff took possession. The Court of Appeal held that in these circumstances the plaintiff did not enjoy an equitable lease because specific performance of the contract would not have been available.[154]

9–058

---

[149] Law of Property Act 1925, s.40.
[150] See, for example, *Mason v Clarke* [1955] A.C. 778; [1974] 2 All E.R. 977.
[151] (1882) 21 Ch.D. 9.
[152] (1886) 55 L.J.Q.B. 220; [1886–1890] All E.R. 547.
[153] [1973] Q.B. 877.
[154] Following *Willmott v Barber* (1880) 15 Ch.D. 96.

(iii)   Electronic Conveyancing and Equitable Leases

9–059   When the provisions of the Land Registration Act 2002 concerning electronic conveyancing are brought into force some contracts for the grant of a lease will no longer automatically give rise to an equitable lease. This follows from s.93(2) of the Act, which provides that:

> "A disposition to which this section applies, or a contract to make such a disposition, only has effect if it is made my means of a document in electronic form and if, when the document purports to take effect—
>
> (a) it is electronically communicated to the registrar, and
> (b) the relevant registration requirement are met."

Section 93(2) applies to a disposition which "would trigger the requirement of registration",[155] which therefore includes the grant of a lease for more than seven years.[156] Since a contract to grant a lease for more than seven years will be ineffective as a contract unless made electronically (when this provision comes into effect), it will not trigger the operation of the equitable maxim that "equity treats as done that which ought to be done", and will not give rise to an equitable lease. Contracts for the grant of a lease of more than three years[157] but less than seven years will continue to give rise to an equitable lease.

(c)   *Primacy of an Equitable Lease*

9–060   Where there is a contract for a lease, and the tenant has taken possession of the land and paid a periodic rent to the landlord, the tenant's interest could be analysed in two ways. First, as has been seen, he would be entitled to an equitable lease on the same terms as were agreed in the contract. Secondly, the common law would regard the payment of periodic rent as giving rise to an implied periodic tenancy, which would generate a legal interest in the land. Given that both these conclusions can be construed from the same facts, the question arises as to how the tenant's interest should be characterised. This was the central issue in *Walsh v Lonsdale*.[158] As has been seen, the landlord claimed that the exercise of distress was justified under the terms of the contract for a lease requiring rent to be paid in advance. The tenant claimed that his interest was in the form of a periodic tenancy, under which the rent would be payable in arrears, thus rendering the distress illegal. The Court of Appeal held that following the Judicature Acts, which provide that in cases of conflict equity is to prevail over the common law, the tenant enjoyed an equitable lease and not a legal periodic tenancy. As Lord Jessel M.R. stated:

---

[155] Land Registration Act 2002 s.91(2).
[156] s.27(2)(b).
[157] No formalities are required for the grant of a lease not exceeding three years: Law of Property Act 1925 s.54(2).
[158] (1882) 21 Ch.D. 9.

"There is agreement for a lease under which possession has been given. Now since the Judicature Act the possession is held under the agreement. There are not two estates as there were formerly, one estate at common law by reason of the payment of the rent from year to year, and an estate in equity under the agreement. There is only one Court and the equity rules prevail in it. The tenant holds under an agreement for a lease."[159]

4. Leases Granted by the Court as a Remedy to Satisfy an Equity Raised by way of Proprietary Estoppel

Although leases are generally created only by the express acts of the parties, a leasehold interest may be awarded to a person by the court as one of the range of potential remedies to satisfy an equity raised by way of proprietary estoppel. Such tenancies were awarded by the court in *Siew Soon Wah v Yong Tong Hong*[160] and *Andrews v Colonial Mutual Life Assurance Society Ltd*.[161] The principles of proprietary estoppel are examined in detail in Chapter 19.

9–061

PERIODIC TENANCIES

A fixed term lease is simply the grant of a tenancy for a specified period of time. The tenant will enjoy his interest until the lease comes to an end naturally through the passage of time, unless the terms permit an earlier termination or either of the parties is entitled to terminate the lease because of the other's breach of covenant. A periodic tenancy has no fixed maximum duration at its inception. The essential nature of a periodic tenancy was identified by Nicholls L.J. in *Javad v Mohammed Aqil*:

9–062

"A periodic tenancy . . . is one which continues from period to period indefinitely, until determined by proper notice. For example, from year to year, quarter to quarter, month to month, or week to week."[162]

1. Express Periodic Tenancies

The landlord and tenant may expressly agree to create a periodic tenancy rather than a fixed term lease. They are free to stipulate whatever term they choose. The landlord may, for example, create a tenancy from "week to week", "month to month" or "year to year". Provided that the period does not exceed three years there is no need to observe any formalities, and the tenancy will be legal in nature.[163]

9–063

---

[159] (1882) 21 Ch.D. 9 at 14.
[160] [1973] A.C. 836.
[161] [1982] 2 N.Z.L.R. 556.
[162] [1991] 1 W.L.R. 1007 at 1009.
[163] Law of Property Act 1925 at s.54(2)

2. Implied Periodic Tenancies

(a) *When will a Periodic Tenancy be Implied?*

(i) Tenancy Implied from the fact of Exclusive Possession and Payment of Periodic Rent

9–064 A periodic tenancy will be implied whenever a person is permitted to enjoy the exclusive possession of land in return for the payment of a periodic rent. The general principles were stated by Nicholls L.J. in *Javad v Mohammed Aqil*:

> "A tenancy, or lease is an interest in land . . . [it] springs from a consensual arrangement between two parties . . . As with other consensually-based arrangements, parties frequently proceed with an arrangement whereby one person takes possession of another's land for payment without having agreed or directed their minds to one or more fundamental aspects of their transaction. In such cases the law, where appropriate, has to step in and fill the gaps in a way which is sensible and reasonable. The law will imply, from what was agreed and all the surrounding circumstances, the terms the parties are to be taken to have intended to apply. Thus if one party permits another to go into possession of his land on the payment of a rent of so much per week or month, failing more the inference sensibly and reasonably to be drawn is that the parties intended that there should be a weekly or monthly tenancy."[164]

In practice a periodic tenancy will often be implied where a person has entered into exclusive possession of premises and paid rent to the owner on the basis of a lease which was subsequently found to be invalid. For example, in *Prudential Assurance Co Ltd v London Residuary Body*[165] it was held that a lease was invalid because it did not specify a maximum duration. However the House of Lords found that the tenants enjoyed an implied periodic tenancy because they had taken possession and paid a yearly rent.[166] An implied periodic tenancy may also commonly arise where a tenant initially occupied premises under a fixed term lease which has expired. If he is allowed to remain in possession paying rent to the landlord after the lease has expired he will enjoy a periodic tenancy.

As has been noted above, if the facts of occupation would support either the finding of an equitable lease, on the basis of a specifically enforceable contract for a lease, or an implied periodic tenancy, the equitable lease will take primacy and govern the relationship between the landlord and tenant.[167]

---

[164] [1991] 1 W.L.R. 1007 at 1012.
[165] [1992] 2 A.C. 386.
[166] A similar conclusion was reached in *Lace v Chantler* [1944] K.B. 368.
[167] *Walsh v Lonsdale* (1882) 21 Ch.D. 9.

(ii) No Implied Periodic Tenancy if there are Factors which Indicate that there was No Intention to Create a Tenancy

The mere fact that a person has entered into the occupation of premises and paid rent does not incontrovertibly generate an implied periodic tenancy. As has already been seen in the context of fixed term leases, the circumstances of the occupancy may indicate that no tenancy was intended. As Russell L.J. observed in *Lewis v MTC (Cars) Ltd*: **9–065**

> "It is quite plain that if you find one person in occupation paying sums by way of rent quarterly or half yearly to another person, ordinarily speaking it is a right conclusion that there is a relationship between them of contractual landlord and tenant; but, of course, the circumstances may show that there is no justification for such an inference."[168]

In *Javad v Mohammed Aqil*[169] the owner of business premises allowed the defendant into occupation on the payment of £2,500, said to represent three months' rent, in anticipation of the parties being able to agree the terms of a lease. Two further payments of quarterly rent were made. When negotiations eventually broke down the defendant claimed that he was a tenant under an implied periodic tenancy. The Court of Appeal upheld a finding that in these circumstances no periodic tenancy was intended but merely a tenancy at will.[170] The defendant was entitled to nothing more than a permissive occupation while negotiations proceeded.

(b) Identifying the Term of an Implied Periodic Tenancy

Where a periodic tenancy is implied, the length of the term is not expressly agreed between the parties. It is therefore necessary to determine the length of the period of the tenancy from the facts. Older cases seem to suggest that whenever rent is payable in reference to a year, or a proportion of a year, then a yearly tenancy is created. More recent cases, for example *Javad v Mohammed Aqil*,[171] confirm that the correct principle is that the length of the term is determined by the period with reference to which the rent is calculated.[172] For example, if the rent is £100 per month then there will be an implied monthly periodic tenancy. If the rent is £1,200 per year then the tenancy will be yearly. It does not matter how the rent is actually paid, so if the £100 per month were collected in weekly instalments by the landlord this would not create a weekly tenancy. In *Ladies Hosiery and Underwear Ltd v Parker*[173] Maugham J. held that a payment of £2 per week gave rise to a weekly and not a yearly tenancy. **9–066**

---

[168] [1975] 1 W.L.R. 457 at 462.
[169] [1991] 1 W.L.R. 1007. See also *Sopwith v Stutchbury* (1983) 17 H.L.R. 50.
[170] See also *Cardiothoracic Institute v Shrewdcrest Ltd* [1986] 1 W.L.R. 368.
[171] [1991] 1 W.L.R. 1007.
[172] *Martin v Smith* (1874) L.R. 9 Ex. 50; *Adams v Cairns* (1901) 85 L.T. 10.
[173] [1930] 1 Ch. 304.

(c) *Problems Relating to the Duration of a Periodic Tenancy*

(i) A Fixed Maximum Duration?

9–067 In *Prudential Assurance Co Ltd v London Residuary Body*[174] the House of Lords reasserted the requirement that a lease must have a fixed maximum duration. However, this requirement is not easily applied to periodic tenancies, since by their very nature the period is continually renewed unless and until appropriate notice is given to bring the tenancy to an end. It is therefore uncertain at the beginning of the tenancy how long it will last in total, since it is uncertain when, or if, notice will be given. This problem was addressed by the Court of Appeal in *Re Midland Railway Co's Agreement*, where Russell L.J. stated:

> "If you have an ordinary case of a periodic tenancy (for example, a yearly tenancy) it is plain that in one sense at least it is uncertain at the outset what will be the maximum duration of the term created, which term grows year by year as a single term springing from the original grant. It cannot be predicated that in no circumstances will it exceed, for example, 50 years; there is no previously ascertained maximum duration for the term; its duration will depend upon the time that will elapse before either party gives notice of determination. The simple statement of the law that the maximum duration of a term must be certainly known in advance of its taking effect cannot therefore have direct reference to periodic tenancies."[175]

Although this approach has the merit of simplicity, more recent cases have tended to attempt to accommodate periodic tenancies with the requirement of a certain term rather than declare that they are an exception. The approach of Russell L.J. was expressly rejected by Lord Templeman in *Prudential Assurance Co Ltd v London Residuary Body*[176] where he stated:

> "I consider that the principle in *Lace v Chantler* reaffirming 500 years of judicial acceptance of the requirement that a term must be certain applies to all leases and tenancy agreements. A tenancy from year to year is saved from being uncertain because each party has power by notice to determine at the end of the year. The term continues until determined as if both parties made a new agreement at the end of each year for a new term for the ensuing year."

The justification for the validity of periodic tenancies seems therefore to be that each period is itself certain. There remains some difficulty in attempting to reconcile the certainty of the individual periods with the fact that the entire period of occupation under a periodic tenancy is viewed by English law as a single period. In *Hammersmith LBC v Monk*[177] Lord Bridge

---

[174] [1992] 2 A.C. 386.
[175] [1971] Ch. 725 at 732.
[176] [1992] 2 A.C. 386.
[177] [1992] 1 A.C. 478.

seemed to take the view that although retrospectively the period possessed is viewed as a single term, the continuation of the tenancy at the end of each term depends upon the will of the parties such that prospectively it should continue no further than they have impliedly agreed, namely one term. Therefore each period is in itself certain, but once commenced is agglomerated into the single continuous period comprised of any earlier periods. As he explained "the law regards a tenancy from year to year which has continued for a number of years, considered retrospectively, as a single term".[178] Despite the complexity of this distinction in comparison to the practical realism of Russell L.J. the effect is the same, namely that a periodic tenancy does not fall foul of the requirement that a lease must have a certain maximum duration.

(ii)   Limiting the Right to Determine

A further associated problem is whether a periodic tenancy can be created where the landlord **9–068** has agreed not to determine the tenancy except in specified circumstances. In *Re Midland Railway Co's Agreement*[179] the Court of Appeal upheld as valid a periodic tenancy which contained a clause that the landlords could not terminate the tenancy until they required the land for their purposes. This approach was extended by the decision of the Court of Appeal in *Ashburn Anstalt v Arnold*,[180] but both authorities were overruled by the House of Lords in *Prudential Assurance Co Ltd v London Residuary Body*.[181] Lord Templeman considered that they there were inconsistent with the rule that a lease must be for a fixed maximum duration. He concluded that: "A grant for an uncertain term which takes the form of a yearly tenancy which cannot be determined by the landlord does not create a lease".[182] A periodic tenancy of the land in question from year to year which could not be determined by the landlord except when it was needed for road-widening would therefore be invalid.

(d)   *Termination of a Periodic Tenancy*

A periodic tenancy, whether express or implied, will continue until proper notice is given to **9–069** terminate. The notice period will normally be specified in any express agreement. Failing express agreement, the notice period will be implied. With the exception of tenancies from year to year, notice of one period must be given to terminate. For example, a monthly tenancy can only be determined by a month's notice. However in the case of yearly tenancies six months' notice is sufficient. The precise mechanics of notice to determine will be examined below in the context of the determination of leasehold interests.

---

[178] [1992] 1 A.C. 478 at 490.
[179] [1971] Ch. 725.
[180] [1989] Ch. 1.
[181] [1992] 2 A.C. 386.
[182] [1992] 2 A.C. 386 at 395.

TENANCIES AT WILL

9–070 The central characteristic of a tenancy at will was identified by Nicholls L.J. in *Javad v Mohammed Aqil*:

> "a tenancy at will exists where the tenancy is on terms that either party may determine it at any time".[183]

Thus although the tenant enjoys exclusive occupation[184] of the land he enjoys no security. He does not have an estate in the land which he can transfer to others. To this extent his relationship with his landlord is personal rather than proprietary, and more akin to a licence. Unlike a licensee, however, he is able to maintain an action in trespass against strangers.[185] A tenancy at will may be created expressly or impliedly. Common situations where such a tenancy may arise are when a purchaser of property goes into possession before completion, or a tenant takes possession of premises in anticipation of negotiations for a lease, as was the case in *Javad v Mohammed Aqil*.[186] In the absence of an agreement that the occupation be rent-free, the tenant must pay the landlord compensation for his period of occupation. However the mere fact that rent is paid does not automatically raise a presumption of a periodic tenancy.[187] The crucial factor is the intention of the parties, which must be determined form all the circumstances.

A tenancy at will may be determined by either the tenant or the landlord, but no notice to quit is required. A mere demand for possession is sufficient.[188] The death of either party automatically determines the tenancy. Since a tenancy at will can end without any notice, the tenant must be given a reasonable period of grace following termination in order to vacate the premises promptly.

ACQUIRING A TENANCY BY ASSIGNMENT OR ADVERSE POSSESSION

9–071 Where land is subject to a valid lease, the tenant owns a proprietary interest, an estate in the land. This interest is capable of being transferred to a third party by way of assignment, and may be particularly valuable where the rent payable is below current market levels. A tenancy of either residential or commercial property is a marketable commodity, and the person to whom the lease is assigned will enjoy the same interest as was enjoyed by the original tenant. The same principles apply whether a lease is for a fixed term or is a periodic tenancy, although in practice fixed term leases are the more likely to be assigned. A leasehold estate in land may also be acquired by way of adverse possession.

---

[183] [1991] 1 W.L.R. 1007 at 1009.
[184] *Goldsack v Shore* [1950] 1 K.B. 708.
[185] *Heslop v Burns* [1974] 1 W.L.R. 1241.
[186] See also *Ramnarace v Lutchman* [2001] 1 W.L.R. 1651.
[187] *London Baggage Co (Charing Cross) Ltd v Railtrack Plc* [2000] E.G.C.S. 57. See also *Walji v Mount Cookland Ltd* [2002] 1 P. & C.R. 13.
[188] *Doe d. Price v Price* (1832) 9 Bing 356.

1. Assignment of the Tenant's Leasehold Estate

(a) *Tenant's Right to Assign*

In the absence of any express provision to a contrary effect in the lease, a tenant enjoys an absolute right to assign his tenancy.[189] When the tenancy is validly assigned the assignee stands in the shoes of the assignor as tenant under the lease and the assignor retains no interest in the land.[190]

9–072

(b) *Covenants against Assignment*

A tenant's absolute right to assign his tenancy interest may be qualified by the presence of an express covenant in the lease restricting his right to assign. Such restrictions may take the form of an absolute or qualified covenant against assignment, and are most commonly found in short term leases. Under an absolute covenant the tenant has no right to assign at all. Under a qualified covenant he cannot assign without the consent of the landlord. In *International Drilling Fluids Ltd v Louisville Investments (Uxbridge) Ltd*,[191] Balcombe L.J. stated that the purpose of such covenants was "to protect the lessor from having his premises used or occupied in an undesirable way, or by an undesirable tenant or his assignee".

9–073

In the case of qualified covenants, s.19(1) of the Landlord and Tenant Act 1927 provides that a landlord shall not withhold his consent from an assignment "unreasonably". Section 1 of the The Landlord and Tenant Act 1988 enacts a procedure for ensuring that a tenant's written request for consent is dealt with rapidly. It imposes a duty on the landlord:

> "(a) to give consent, except in a case where it is reasonable not to give consent,
> (b) to serve on the tenant written notice of his decision whether or not to give consent specifying in addition:
>
> (i) if the consent is given subject to condition, the conditions,
> (ii) if the consent is withheld, the reasons for withholding it."

He must fulfil his duty within a reasonable time of receipt of the request. The refusal of consent may be reasonable for example because of the proposed use of the premises by the assignee,[192] the unsatisfactory nature of the assignee's references[193] or of his financial position.[194] It is unclear whether the court should take into account the effects on the tenant if

---

[189] *Keeves v Dean* [1924] 1 K.B. 685; *Leith Properties v Byrne* [1983] Q.B. 433.
[190] *Milmo v Carreras* [1946] K.B. 306.
[191] [1986] Ch. 513.
[192] *Bates v Donaldson* [1896] 2 Q.B. 241.
[193] *Rossi v Hestdrive* [1985] E.G.L.R. 50.
[194] *British Bakeries (Midlands) Ltd v Michael Testler & Co Ltd* [1986] 1 E.G.L.R. 64.

consent is refused.[195] In each case it is a question of fact whether consent has been unreasonably withheld.[196] The landlord's duty not to withhold consent unreasonably was examined by the House of Lords in *Ashworth Frazer Ltd v Gloucester City Council*.[197] The case concerned a proposed assignment of a lease which might lead to a breach of a covenant in the lease prohibiting certain specified uses of the land. The House of Lords held that the court should not determine whether the grounds on which a landlord might reasonably or unreasonably withhold consent to a proposed assignment by strict rules. The concept of reasonableness was rather to be given a broad and common sense meaning so as to prevent the law "becoming unduly rigid".[198] However a landlord is not permitted to withhold consent on grounds wholly extraneous to the relationship of landlord and tenant with regard to the subject of the lease, and it would be unusual to find it unreasonable for the landlord to refuse consent to a proposed assignment which might lead to a breach of a covenant of the lease. The "indubitably correct" principles adopted by the House of Lords in that case were repeated by Peter Gibson L.J. in *Channel Hotels and Properties (UK) Ltd v Fahad Al Tamimi, First Penthouse Ltd*:

> "(i) a landlord is not entitled to refuse consent to an assignment on grounds which have nothing whatever to do with the relationship of landlord and tenant in regard to the subject matter of the lease;
> (ii) it is not necessary for the landlord to prove that the conclusions which led him to refuse to consent were justified, if they were conclusions which might be reached by a reasonable man in the circumstances;
> (iii) in each case it is a question of fact, depending on all the circumstances, whether the landlord's consent to an assignment has been unreasonably withheld."[199]

The withholding of consent on racial grounds is also unlawful.[200] Section 22 of the Landlord and Tenant (Covenants) Act 1995 allows landlords of commercial premises to include a specific clause in a lease stipulating circumstances in which they are entitled to withhold consent. Any subsequent withholding of consent in such circumstances is automatically reasonable. This provision only applies to leases commencing after 1995.

An assignment in breach of covenant does not prevent the transfer of an estate in the land. However the landlord may be entitled to forfeit the lease or seek damages from the ex-tenant in breach.[201]

---

[195] For cases which suggest that the consequences for the tenant are relevant see: *Sheppard v Hong Kong and Shanghai Banking Corp* (1872) 20 W.R. 459; *Houlder Brothers & Co Ltd v Gibbs* [1925] Ch. 575; *Leeward Securities Ltd v Lilyheath Properties Ltd* (1983) 271 E.G. 279. For cases which suggest that the landlord's interests are also relevant see: *Viscount Tredegar v Harwood* [1929] A.C. 72; *West Layton Ltd v Ford* [1979] Q.B. 593; *Bromley Park Gardens Estate Ltd v Moss* [1982] 1 W.L.R. 1019.

[196] *Bickell v Duke of Westminster* [1977] Q.B. 517; *West Layton Ltd v Ford* [1979] Q.B. 593.

[197] [2001] 1 W.L.R. 2180.

[198] [2001] 1 W.L.R. 2180 at [67] per Lord Rodger.

[199] [2004] EWCA Civ 1072 at [48].

[200] Race Relations Act 1976 s.24.

[201] See *Peabody Fund v Higgins* [1983] 3 All E.R. 122.

(c) Formalities

(i) Formalities for an Assignment

Where a lease has created a legal estate in land, any subsequent transfer thereof is a con-   **9–074**
veyance and must be effected by deed.[202] This is true even where the original lease had been
granted orally because it was for a period not exceeding three years. An assignment of an equitable interest in land must be effected by writing.[203] An oral assignment is of no effect at all.

(ii) Completion by Registration

The assignment of a tenancy may need to be completed by registration in order to take effect.   **9–075**
Where the title to the land is unregistered, the assignment of a leasehold estate which has
more than seven years will require the title to be registered.[204] Where a lease is itself a registered estate, then a transfer of the estate is a registrable disposition and will not take effect at
law until the registration requirements are met.[205]

2. Acquisition of a Leasehold Estate by Adverse Possession

In Chapter 8 it was seen that a freehold estate in land could be acquired by way of adverse   **9–076**
possession. The same principles apply to a leasehold estate, so that a squatter can acquire the
ownership of a tenancy by way of adverse possession. Where land is subject to a tenancy a
squatter's adverse possession will not run against the freehold estate until the lease has
expired.[206] In order to obtain a tenancy by adverse possession the squatter must satisfy the
twin requirements of factual possession and the intention to possess. These requirements were
examined in detail above. The precise way in which a squatter will acquire a tenancy by
adverse possession will depend upon the nature of the land in question.

(a) *Adverse Possession of a Leasehold Estate in Unregistered Land*

If the title to the land concerned is unregistered, then the rights of the current tenant will be   **9–077**
extinguished by 12 years' adverse possession. The squatter will then become the owner of the
erstwhile tenant's leasehold estate.

   There is some authority that a dispossessed tenant of unregistered land may be able to
surrender the lease to the landlord, thus bringing it to an immediate end and entitling the
landlord to repossess the property. If this is correct, the squatter remains in an insecure posi-

---

[202] Law of Property Act 1925 s.52(1). See *Crago v Julian* [1992] 1 W.L.R. 372.
[203] Law of Property Act 1925 s.53(1)(a).
[204] Land Registration Act 2002 ss.4(1)(a) and 4(2)(b).
[205] Land Registration Act 2002 s.27.
[206] Limitation Act 1980 Sch.1 para.4.

tion even despite having adversely possessed for the requisite period of time. The possibility of surrender by the original tenant was accepted in *St Marylebone Property Co Ltd v Fairweather*.[207] The ongoing entitlement of a dispossessed tenant to surrender his lease to the landlord has been strongly criticised by academics[208] and has not been followed by the Irish Supreme Court.[209] It is difficult to see how it can be correct that such a tenant can surrender his interest, since it has been extinguished by the adverse possession. The possibility that a dispossessed tenant of unregistered land might be able to surrender his tenancy was was left open by the Privy Council in *Chung Ping Kwan v Lam Island Development Co Ltd*,[210] but it has no application where the estate is registered.

Where a leasehold estate of unregistered land is acquired by adverse possession it appears that the leasehold covenants will not be directly enforceable between the landlord and the squatter. The adverse possessor is not an assignee of the tenant, and therefore does not enjoy "privity of estate" with the landlord.[211] However, if the squatter breaches the covenant the landlord may forfeit the lease against the dispossessed tenant, which will have the effect of bringing the lease to an end, and along with it any entitlement of the adverse possessor to continue in possession. In such circumstances the adverse possessor has no right to apply for relief against forfeiture of the lease.[212]

(b) *Adverse Possession of a Leasehold Estate in Registered Land*

(i) Adverse Possession of a Leasehold Estate in Registered Land where the Lease was Created for 21 Years or Less Prior to the Coming into Force of the Land Registration Act 2002

9–078   Where title to the land is registered, but the tenancy being adversely possessed was created by a lease for 21 years or less which was granted prior to the coming into force of the Land Registration Act 2002, the rights of the tenant will be extinguished by 12 years' adverse possession, just as in the case of unregistered land. The reason for this is that the lease for 21 years or less took effect as an overriding interest when created,[213] and did not therefore have to be registered. The new statutory framework regarding adverse possession of registered estates is thus inapplicable to such an interest.

(ii) Adverse Possession of a Leasehold Estate in Registered Land

9–079   In all other cases involving a tenancy which is a registered estate, a squatter will only be entitled to be registered as the new proprietor of the estate in accordance with the provisions of

---

[207] [1963] A.C. 510.
[208] H.W.R. Wade, "Landlord, Tenant Squatter" (1962) 78 L.Q.R. 541.
[209] *Perry v Woodfarm Homes Ltd* [1975] I.R. 104.
[210] [1997] A.C. 38.
[211] As there is no "assignment", the Landlord and Tenant (Covenants) Act 1995 is also inapplicable.
[212] *Tickner v Buzzacott* [1965] Ch. 426.
[213] Under the Land Registration Act 1925 s.70(1)(k).

Sch.6 to the Land Registration Act 2002. With limited exceptions, such a squatter will only be entitled to be registered as proprietor with the consent of the current proprietor, or if the current proprietor fails to take action to recover the land after being notified of the fact that it is being adversely possessed. The provisions of Sch.6 have already been examined in detail in Chapter 8, and will not be repeated here.

CREATING A SUB-LEASE

Where a tenant assigns his interest he transfers it to another person who takes over his place as tenant of the land. However instead of assigning his interest a tenant may grant a sub-lease, thus carving a tenancy out of his own leasehold estate. In such a situation he will stand as a tenant in relation to his original landlord, but will stand as landlord in relation to his sub-tenant, who will in turn stand as tenant in relation to him but enjoy no direct relationship with the landlord of the headlease.   **9–080**

Although a tenant is prima facie entitled to grant a sub-lease, the lease may contain a covenant against sub-letting which is either absolute or qualified. The statutory provisions regulating the right of a landlord to refuse consent to an assignment also govern his right to refuse consent to a sub-lease.

Where a sub-lease is granted the tenant must observe the same formalities as if it were an ordinary headlease.

ENFORCING LEASES FOLLOWING TRANSFER OF THE FREEHOLD REVERSION

Just as a tenant is able to assign his tenancy, so a landlord is able to transfer his freehold rever-   **9–081**
sion to a third party. In order to transfer the freehold reversion the landlord must comply with all the relevant requirements for a transfer of a freehold estate in the land. Where the freehold reversion is transferred the question will arise as to whether the transferee acquires his estate subject to the pre-existing lease, or whether he gains priority over it. The relevant principles vary depending upon whether the land was registered or unregistered.

1.   Priority of Leases of Registered Land

Where the freehold title to land is registered, and the freehold reversion is transferred, issues   **9–082**
of priority will be determined by the rules governing the effect of registered dispositions.[214]
These were examined in detail in Chapters 5 and 7, and only a brief summary of their effect

---

[214] Land Registration Act 2002 s.29.

on leases will be given here. A legal lease for a term exceeding seven years will have had to have been completed by registration, and will therefore bind the transferee of the freehold reversion. Subject to limited exceptions,[215] a legal lease for a term not exceeding seven years will be binging as an overriding interest.[216] An equitable lease will similarly be binding as an overriding interest if the tenant is in actual occupation of the land, which occupation would have been obvious on a reasonably careful inspection of the land, or if the transferee had actual knowledge of the existence of the equitable lease.[217]

2. Priority of Leases of Unregistered Land

9–083   A transfer of the freehold reversion of unregistered land will trigger compulsory registration. Issues of priority will therefore be determined by the rules concerning the effect of first registration.[218] These rules ensure that the registered proprietor will take the land subject to any legal lease. A legal lease for more than 21 years will take priority on first registration of the freehold title because it will have had to be registered already.[219] A legal lease for less than 21 years, which was granted before the coming in to force of the Land Registration Act 2002, will be binding as an overriding interest.[220] A legal lease for less than seven years granted after the Act has come in to force will, with certain exceptions,[221] also bind a registered proprietor on first registration as an overriding interest.[222] An equitable lease will gain priority and bind the registered proprietor as an overriding interest if the tenant was in actual occupation of the land.[223]

TERMINATION OF LEASES

1. Consequences of Termination

9–084   When a lease is terminated the leasehold interest of the tenant comes to an end, he no longer has any estate in the land, and the freehold owner will be entitled to immediate possession of the land. If the ex-tenant remains in occupation without permission his possession of the land will be adverse to the freehold owner. The freehold owner must use the appropriate legal procedure to remove such a squatting ex-tenant.[224]

---

[215] Land Registration Act 2002 Sch.3 para.1.
[216] Land Registration Act 2002 s.29(2)(a)(ii) and Sch.3 para.1.
[217] Land Registration Act 2002 s.29(2)(a)(ii) and Sch.3 para.2.
[218] Land Registration Act 2002 s.11.
[219] Land Registration Act 2002 s.1(4)(a).
[220] Land Registration Act 2002 s.11(4)(b) and Sch.12 para.12.
[221] Land Registration Act 2002 Sch.1 para.1.
[222] Land Registration Act 2002 s.11(4)(b) and Sch.1 para.1.
[223] Land Registration Act 2002 Sch.1 para.2.
[224] Protection from Eviction Act 1977 s.3(1).

2. Termination by Expiry

In the case of a fixed term lease, the lease will automatically terminate at the end of the spec- **9–085**
ified term without the need for the landlord to serve notice on the tenant. It should be noted
that many residential leases are converted on expiry by statute into periodic tenancies[225] and
business tenants generally have the right to request a new lease.[226]

3. Termination by Notice

(a) *Termination of Fixed Leases by Notice*

A fixed term lease is only determinable by notice if such a possibility is expressly provided **9–086**
for in the terms of the lease. For example, a lease for life, which by statute becomes a lease
for 90 years determinable on the death of the original lessee, is determinable by "one month's
notice in writing" from the lessor.[227] Long-term leases may include a "break clause" allowing the parties to terminate it before the expiry of the full term by appropriate notice.[228] Where
the lease is held by joint tenants, then such a break clause requires all the joint tenants to join
in giving notice, otherwise it will be ineffective.[229] The exercise of such a "break clause" was
examined by the House of Lords in *Mannai Investment Co Ltd v Eagle Star Life Assurance
Co Ltd*.[230] The case concerned a lease for 10 years commencing on January 13, 1992. The
lease contained a clause entitling the tenant to determine the lease by serving not less than six
months' notice in writing to expire on the third anniversary of the commencement date. The
tenant purported to give notice to determine the lease on January 12, 1995, whereas the third
anniversary of the commencement date was in fact January 13, 1995. The question was
whether the tenant had given effective notice to determine the lease. A majority of the House
of Lords held that the tenants had given valid notice. Lord Hoffman explained that notice to
terminate a tenancy should be effective if the notice was "quite clear to a reasonable tenant
reading it"[231] such that he could not be misled by it.[232] In reaching this conclusion the majority overturned a strict rule of construction which had been applied to the interpretation of
notices for 200 years, and which had been approved by the Court of Appeal in *Hankey v
Clavering*.[233]

---

[225] See Rent Act 1977; Housing Acts 1985 and 1988.
[226] Landlord and Tenant Act 1954.
[227] Law of Property Act 1925 s.149(6).
[228] *Industrial Properties (Barton Hill) Ltd v Associated Electrical Industries Ltd* [1977] Q.B. 580.
[229] *Hounslow LBC v Pilling* [1993] 1 W.L.R. 1242. See also *Hammersmith and Fulham LBC v Monk* [1992] 1 A.C. 478.
[230] [1997] 3 All E.R. 352.
[231] [1997] 3 All E.R. 352 at 381.
[232] Citing the test adopted by Goulding J. in *Carradine Properties Ltd v Aslam* [1976] 1 All E.R. 573.
[233] [1942] 2 K.B. 326.

(b) *Termination of Periodic Tenancies*

9–087   As has been noted above the very essence of a periodic tenancy is that the period continues until it is determined by proper notice given by either the landlord or the tenant.[234] It has also been seen that the House of Lords held in *Prudential Assurance Co v London Residuary Body*[235] that no limits can be imposed as to when the parties are entitled to determine a periodic tenancy.[236] Such limitations would mean that the tenancy contravened the rule that a lease must be for a fixed maximum duration.

(i)   Length of Notice which Must be Given

9–088   In the absence of express contrary provisions[237] the common law position is that the tenancy can only be determined by giving notice of the duration of one whole period, with the exception of a yearly periodic tenancy which can be determined by six months' notice.[238] Therefore, a weekly periodic tenancy can be determined by a week's notice, a monthly tenancy by a month's and a quarterly tenancy by a quarter's notice. However, in the case of dwelling-houses, statute intervenes to require a period of at least four weeks' notice to quit.[239]

(ii)   Time at which Notice Should be Given

9–089   The mere giving of a sufficient length of notice will not alone bring a periodic tenancy to an end. The notice must be given at the appropriate time since the tenancy can only end at the end of a relevant period. Notice of the relevant period must be given in such a way that the notice period itself expires at the end of a completed period of the tenancy.[240] This is known as the "corresponding date" rule. In practice it means that a notice for the shortest permitted period must be served on the tenant either on the anniversary of the period, or the day preceding that anniversary. For example, in the case of a monthly tenancy which commenced on the first of the month (and therefore expires on the last day of the month), one month's notice will only be effective to terminate the tenancy if it is given on first of that month or the last day of the preceding month. If the notice is not given at the appropriate time it will not terminate the tenancy and the tenancy will continue into the following period. Thus, using the same example of a monthly tenancy beginning on the first day of the month, if the landlord served notice on the tenant on the 20th of a month this could only be effective to terminate the tenancy on the last day of the following month since otherwise

---

[234] *Javad v Mohammed Aqil* [1991] 1 W.L.R. 1007; *Prudential Assurance Co v London Residuary Body* [1992] 2 A.C. 386.

[235] [1992] 2 A.C. 386.

[236] Overruling *Re Midland Railway Co's Agreement* [1971] Ch. 725; *Ashburn Anstalt v Arnold* [1989] Ch. 1.

[237] *Re Threlfall* (1880) 16 Ch.D. 274; *Queen's Club Gardens Estates Ltd v Bignell* [1924] 1 KB 117; *Lemon v Lardeur* [1946] K.B. 613. See *Land Settlement Association Ltd v Carr* [1944] K.B. 657 where a periodic tenancy for 364 days was expressly stated to be determinable by three calendar months' notice.

[238] *Prudential Assurance Co v London Residuary Body* [1992] 2 A.C. 386.

[239] Protection from Eviction Act 1977 s.5(1)(b).

[240] *Lemon v Lardeur* [1946] K.B. 613; *Queen's Club Garden Estates Ltd v Bignell* [1924] 1 K.B. 117; *Bathavon RDC v Carlile* [1958] 1 Q.B. 461.

the notice period would not have corresponded with the end of a period of the lease.[241] The tenancy could not (without agreement on the part of the tenant) be brought to an end on the 20th or the 21st of the month. In the case of yearly periodic tenancies, notice must be given at least given six months before the end of the particular period. In the case of a yearly tenancy beginning on a quarter day,[242] notice of at least two quarters must be given. In the case of a yearly tenancy beginning on any other day, notice of at least 182 days is required.[243]

(iii) Effectiveness of Notice to Terminate by Joint Tenants

Problems have arisen in the context of periodic tenancies where the freehold or the lease are held by two or more persons as joint tenants. The issue in such circumstances is whether notice given by one of the joint owners, without the concurrence of the others, is effective to terminate the tenancy. This question was considered at length by the House of Lords in *Hammersmith and Fulham LBC v Monk*[244] where, on grounds of principle, it was held that notice served by any joint tenant was effective to terminate the tenancy, irrespective of the intentions of the others that it should continue. Mr and Mrs Monk enjoyed a joint tenancy of a council flat determinable on four weeks' notice. They fell out and Mrs Monk left the flat. The Council agreed to rehouse her if she terminated the tenancy by appropriate notice and she duly gave notice without Mr Monk's knowledge. The House of Lords held that this was effective to determine the periodic tenancy on the basis that the tenancy could only continue with the consent of all parties. As Lord Bridge explained:

9–090

> "in any ordinary agreement for an initial term which is to continue for successive terms unless determined by notice, the obvious inference is that the agreement is intended to continue beyond the initial term only if and so long as all parties to the agreement are willing that it should do so . . . Thus the application of ordinary contractual principles leads me to expect that a periodic tenancy granted to two or more joint tenants must be terminable at common law by an appropriate notice to quit given by any one of them whether or not the others are prepared to concur."

This principle only applies because a continuing intention is assumed until notice is served, and the serving of notice is a negative dealing with the tenancy. As Lord Bridge stated:

> "The action of giving notice to determine a periodic tenancy is in form positive; but . . . the substance of the matter is that it is by his omission to give notice of termination that each party signifies the necessary positive assent to the extension of the term for a further period."[245]

That notice given by one joint tenant is effective to terminate a periodic tenancy has been confirmed by the House of Lords in *London Borough of Harrow v Qazi*.[246] A council flat had

---

[241] *Lemon v Lardeur* [1946] K.B. 613.
[242] Lady Day (March 25); Midsummer Day (June 24); Michaelmas (September 29); Christmas (December 25).
[243] *Sidebottom v Holland* [1895] 1 Q.B. 378.
[244] [1992] 1 A.C. 478; [1992] C.L.J. 218 (Tee); [1992] Conv. 279; (1992) 109 L.Q.R. 375 (Dewar).
[245] [1992] 1 A.C. 478 at 490–491.
[246] [2003] UKHL 43 at 40 (Lord Hope) and 113 (Lord Scott of Foscote).

been let to Mr and Mrs Qazi. After Mrs Qazi moved out, she served a notice to quit on the council. Lord Hope of Craighead said:

> "the joint tenancy has been brought to an end by the service of a tenant's notice to quit. The position in domestic law is that in these circumstances, as a result of the joint tenant's action and in terms of the lease, the whole of the joint tenancy is terminated. So neither joint tenant has any longer any right to remain in the premises."[247]

In contrast all positive dealings with a joint tenancy require the concurrence of all joint tenants. Such positive dealings include the exercise of an option to renew, the exercise of a break clause in the lease, making a disclaimer or applying for relief from forfeiture. Therefore, in *Hounslow LBC v Pilling*[248] it was held that a purported exercise of a break clause in a lease by a single joint tenant giving notice was ineffective to terminate the lease.

(c) *Termination of Tenancies at Will*

9–091   As has been noted, a tenancy at will may be determined by either party at any time. It is also brought to an end automatically if either party performs acts inconsistent with the continuation of the tenancy. Unless the tenant has been given sufficient notice to allow him to vacate the premises, he will not, however be treated as a trespasser immediately and will be given a sufficient period of grace to allow him to leave with his belongings. The period of grace is only that which is required to leave, and does not extend to remaining whilst the tenant secures alternative accommodation.

4.   Termination by Surrender

(a)   *Meaning of Surrender*

9–092   Since a tenancy is an interest in land carved out of the landlord's freehold ownership,[249] the return of the tenancy to the landlord will have the consequence of bringing the leasehold interest to an end, leaving the landlord with the unencumbered freehold. This process of returning the tenancy to the landlord is known as surrender.

(b)   *Express Surrender of a Tenancy*

9–093   A tenancy may be surrendered expressly to the landlord. Such a surrender is a conveyance of an interest in land and under s.52(1) of the Law of Property Act 1925 it must be effected by a deed.

---

[247] [2003] UKHL 43 at 74.
[248] [1993] 1 W.L.R. 1242; [1994] C.L.J. 227 (Tee).
[249] Or in the case of a sub-tenancy out of the superior landlord leasehold estate.

(c) Surrender by Operation of Law

In some circumstances a tenant will be taken to have impliedly surrendered his interest to the landlord, which takes effect as a surrender by operation of law and is exempt from any formalities requirement by s.52(1)(c) of the Law of Property Act 1925. Most commonly the tenant will be taken to have surrendered his interest if he gives up possession of the land subject to the tenancy. The principle stated in *Hill and Redman's Law of Landlord and Tenant* was accepted by the Court of Appeal in *Hoggett v Hoggett*,[250] namely "delivery of possession by the tenant to the landlord and his acceptance of possession effect a surrender by operation of law". However, it was held that in the circumstances there had been no effective surrender. Mr Hoggett enjoyed a weekly periodic tenancy of a house which he occupied with his wife and son. After arguments and violence the wife left home. Her husband brought a Miss Willis to share the house with him. He then purported to surrender the tenancy to the landlord and asked him to accept Miss Willis as a tenant, which he did, providing her with a rent book. Two days later he left the house. The Court of Appeal held that this purported surrender was a sham. There had been no delivery of possession to the landlord as the intention had been for Mr Hoggett to continue to occupy. He had left his furniture in the premises, along with his dog and motor car, and had never returned his rent book to the landlord. In contrast the most common circumstances which would give rise to an implied surrender would be if the tenant left possession of the land and returned the key to the landlord.[251] A tenant's acceptance of a new status from the landlord inconsistent with the continuation of a tenancy will also effect an implied surrender, as in *Foster v Robinson*[252] where a tenant accepted a licence for life of the premises.

9–094

(d) Effect of Surrender on a Subtenant

Where a tenancy is subject to a sub-tenancy, the principle established in *Mellor v Watkins*[253] has the effect that the surrender of the head lease by the head tenant to the landlord does not determine the sub-tenancy. Instead the surrender has the effect that the subtenant holds his tenancy directly from the landlord. However this principle will not apply if the termination of the lease is provided for in the terms of the lease itself.[254]

9–095

5. Termination by Merger

If the tenant acquires the landlord's freehold reversion this will have the immediate effect of bringing the lease to an end, as will the acquisition of both the interests of the landlord and tenant by a third party.

9–096

---

[250] (1980) 39 P. & C.R. 121.
[251] *ES Schwab & Co Ltd v McCarthy* (1976) 31 P. & C.R. 196.
[252] [1951] 1 K.B. 149.
[253] (1874) LR 9 QB 400
[254] *Pennell v Payne* [1995] Q.B. 192.

6. Termination by Disclaimer

9–097   As has been noted above, every lease contains an implied covenant that the tenant will not disclaim the landlord's title to the land he leases. Breach of this covenant entitles the landlord to forfeit the lease.[255] Section 315 of the Insolvency Act 1986 permits a trustee in bankruptcy to disclaim the tenant's lease if it is "unsaleable or not readily saleable, or is such that it may give rise to a liability to pay money or perform any other onerous act".

7. Termination by Forfeiture

9–098   As will be seen in the next chapter, where the tenant is in breach of other covenants of the lease the landlord may be entitled to forfeit it, which has the effect of bringing the tenant's interest to an end.

8. Termination by Repudiation

9–099   In a contract, if one party breaches a fundamental condition the other party is entitled to treat the breach as a repudiation of the contract and to sue for damages. Historically English law has held that the doctrine of repudiation does not apply to leases,[256] on the grounds that they are not to be assimilated with other contracts. However in *Hussein v Mehlman*[257] Stephen Sedley Q.C. held that the concept of repudiatory breach should be applied to leases, pointing to various decisions where the courts had tended to assimilate contract and leases, especially by the extension of the concept of frustration to leases.[258] He held that a tenant who had failed to keep the demised premises in repair, so that they were uninhabitable, and who had made it clear that he would not effect the repairs, had committed a repudiatory breach. He also indicated that the extension of the doctrine of repudiation to leases may have implications for cases where a tenant was in arrears of rent:

> "if the obligation to pay rent is as fundamental as the obligation to keep the house habitable, it will follow that a default in rent payments is a repudiatory act on the tenant's part. That this may follow is not, however, a reason for going back on what appears to me to be the inexorable effect of binding authority. It will, however, have effect subject only to all the statutory provisions which now hedge the right to recover possession, but also, I would think, to the provisions contained in the contract of letting itself in relation to forfeiture."

---

[255] *Wisbech St Mary Parish Council v Lilley* [1956] 1 W.L.R. 121; *Warner v Sampson* [1959] 1 Q.B. 297; *W.G. Clark (Properties) Ltd v Dupre Properties Ltd* [1992] Ch. 297.

[256] *Total Oil Great Britain Ltd v Thompson Garages (Biggin Hill) Ltd* [1972] 1 Q.B. 318.

[257] [1992] 2 E.G.L.R. 87; [1993] C.L.J. 212; [1993] Conv. 71.

[258] See *National Carriers Ltd v Panalpina (Northern) Ltd* [1981] A.C. 675. See also *United Scientific Holdings Ltd v Burnley BC* [1978] A.C. 904.

9. Termination by Frustration

Traditionally the doctrine of frustration applied only to suspend or discharge individual terms of a lease affected by supervening impossibility of performance.[259] However, in *National Carriers Ltd v Panalpina (Northern) Ltd*[260] the House of Lords held by a bare majority that frustration could discharge a lease as a whole. This does not mean that frustration of leases will be widespread. The defendants were the tenants of a warehouse leased from the plaintiffs under a 10-year fixed term lease. After five years the closure of the access road by a local authority would prevent them using the warehouse for 20 months. The House of Lords held that this interruption, which would last only a relatively short period of the duration of the tenancy and leave a further three years remaining after access was restored, did not "approach the gravity of a frustration event".[261]

10. Human Rights Aspects of Termination

Where the landlord is a public authority, the right to terminate a lease may be subject to art.8 of the European Convention on Human Rights, which has been incorporated into domestic law,

"1. Everyone has the right to respect for his private and family life, his home and his correspondence.

2. There shall be no interference by a public authority with the exercise of this right except such as in accordance with the law and is necessary in a democratic society in the interests of national security, public safety or the economic well-being of the country, for the prevention of disorder or crime, for the protection of health or morals, or for the protection of the rights and freedoms of others."

These provisions fell for interpretation and application by the House of Lords in *Harrow LBC v Qazi*.[262] Mr Qazi had been the joint tenant of a council house with his wife. His wife moved out and served notice to quit which had the effect of terminating the periodic tenancy of the house. Mr Qazi remarried and applied for a new tenancy, but this was declined, and the council's decision on this point was not challenged. The council sought possession from Mr Qazi on the basis that he had no right to remain in the house. Mr Qazi invoked art.8. The House of Lords was unanimous in holding that the house was his home. It did not matter that he no longer had any right to be there. The house was where he lived, and this was unchanged by the termination of the tenancy: "A person may make his home where he has no right to be; and a person may choose not to make his home where he has a right to live".[263] This much was agreed by all of the Law Lords.[264] However, they differed on whether there had been an

---

[259] *Cricklewood Property and Investment Trust Ltd v Leighton's Investment Trust Ltd* [1945] A.C. 221.
[260] [1981] A.C. 675.
[261] [1981] A.C. 675 at 697, per Lord Wilberforce.
[262] [2003] UKHL 43.
[263] [2003] UKHL 43 at 97 (Lord Millett).
[264] See [2003] UKHL 43 at 29 (Lord Steyn).

interference with the "right to a home". As Lord Hope said, "Article 8(1), as the Strasbourg Court has repeatedly said, does not guarantee a right to a home. What it guarantees to the individual is respect for his home, which is an entirely different concept".[265] A minority of the House of Lords considered that where possession proceedings were being taken by a public authority, then there would, in principle, be a situation where art.8 was "engaged", and the court invited to order possession would therefore need to consider whether the grant of possession was justified and proportionate. The majority, however, was of the opinion that there was no need for such a balancing. Lord Scott was most forthright on this point. In his view, "Article 8 cannot be raised to defeat contractual and proprietary rights to possession".[266] That view, although expressed in other words, was shared by Lords Hope[267] and Millett.[268] This did not deprive art.8 of any meaning. The article "does not concern itself with the person's right to the peaceful enjoyment of his home as a possession or as a property right".[269] "The emphasis is on the person's home as a place where he is entitled to be free from arbitrary interference by the public authorities"[270] such as conducting a search without a warrant. The House of Lords accordingly held that the council was entitled to an automatic order for possession since the lease had come to an end. If the council had itself been seeking to terminate the tenancy, then it would, of course, have had to comply with the statutory provisions and demonstrate that the relevant criteria for terminating the tenancy had been satisfied. The application of art.8 was further considered by the House of Lords in *Leeds City Council v Price*,[271] where a group of travelers who had parked their caravans on a recreation ground owned by a local authority claimed that their human rights were violated in contravention of art.8(1). Their argument that a local authority had to plead or prove in every case that domestic law complies with art.8 was rejected. Instead the House of Lords stated that courts should proceed on the assumption that domestic law strikes a fair balance and is compatible with art.8. It therefore follows that if the court, following its usual procedures, is satisfied that the domestic law requirements for making a possession order have been met, it should make a possession order unless the occupier shows that, highly exceptionally, he has a seriously arguable case on one of two ground: either (a) that the law which requires the court to make a possession order despite the occupier's personal circumstances is Convention-incompatible; or (b) that, having regard to the occupier's personal circumstances, the local authority's exercise of its power to seek a possession order is an unlawful act within the meaning of s.6.[272] It should be stressed that the Convention rights are have no application to a landlord or owner which is not a public authority.

---

[265] [2003] UKHL 43 at 69. See also Lord Bingham (one of the minority) at 6: "Article 8 does not in terms give a right to be provided with a home and does not guarantee the right to have one's housing problem solved by the authorities".
[266] [2003] UKHL 43 at 149.
[267] [2003] UKHL 43 at 84.
[268] [2003] UKHL 43 at 103.
[269] [2003] UKHL 43 at 50 (Lord Hope). Art.1 of the First Protocol was concerned with the protection of property rights.
[270] [2003] UKHL 43 at 50.
[271] [2006] UKHLC 10.
[272] [2006] UKHL 10 at [29] per Lord Bingham.

Chapter 10

LEASEHOLD COVENANTS

Having examined the essential nature of leasehold interests in land it is the purpose of this chapter to examine the substantive content of leases. The terms of a lease, determining the rights and obligations of the parties, are known as the covenants of the lease. The leasehold covenants are normally expressly agreed between the parties, but many of the most important covenants are implied by law or imposed by statute. The precise covenants in any lease will vary depending upon the terms of the parties' agreement, and it is the purpose of this section to consider only the most common and most significant of such covenants.

10–001

1. Covenants of the Landlord

(a) *Covenant to Provide Quiet Enjoyment*

Every lease contains an implied covenant that the landlord will provide the tenant with quiet enjoyment of the premises let.

10–002

(i) The Meaning of the Covenant

The covenant to provide quiet enjoyment can relate to noise, but is actually an obligation on the part of the landlord to provide the tenant with what has been contracted for, namely the use of the premises let. It provides the tenant with redress if the landlord interferes with the tenant's possession or legitimate enjoyment of the land. The nature of the obligation imposed by the covenant on the landlord was explained by Lord Alverstone C.J. in *Budd-Scott v Daniell*:

10–003

> "When one person agrees to give possession of his house for a time to another that ought to carry with it an agreement that he, the landlord, and those claiming through him, will not dispossess the tenant during that time. Therefore, a covenant or contract was to be

implied that the landlord and those claiming under him would not disturb the possession of the tenant."[1]

In *McCall v Abelesz*[2] Lord Denning M.R. identified the obligation as extending to "any conduct of the landlord or his agents which interferes with the tenant's freedom of action in exercising his rights as tenant". In *Kenny v Preen*[3] Pearson L.J. pointed out that the covenant meant that the tenant was entitled to have the full benefit of his tenancy and not merely to derive some pleasure from it.

In the recent decision of the House of Lords in *Southwark LBC v Mills* Lord Millett defined the obligations of the covenant as follows:

> "the covenant for quiet enjoyment is broken if the landlord or someone claiming under him does anything that substantially interferes with the tenant's title to or possession of the demised premises or with his ordinary and lawful enjoyment of the demised premises."[4]

(ii)   Breach of the Covenant by Acts of the Landlord

10–004   It is clear that acts of the landlord, or his agents, which interfere with the tenant's possession will amount to a breach of the covenant to provide quiet enjoyment. In *Lavender v Betts*[5] a landlord breached his covenant to provide quiet enjoyment when he removed the doors and windows of the rented premises. In *Perera v Vandiyar*[6] the disconnection of the gas and electricity supplies was held to constitute a breach, as was the removal of the central heating in *Mallay and Lunt v Alexander*.[7] In *Owen v Gadd*[8] a landlord was held to be in breach where he erected scaffolding outside a shop occupied by the tenant, preventing customers' access to the window. Although some earlier cases suggested that a breach would only be committed if the landlord physically interfered with the land,[9] it is now clear that such physical interference is not essential. In *Kenny v Preen*[10] a landlord let two rooms of a flat to an elderly widow. After serving a notice to quit he intimidated her in a variety of ways, including writing letters threatening to evict her from the rooms and put her property in the street, repeatedly knocking at the door and shouting threats. Pearson L.J. held that this was a breach of the covenant despite the absence of physical interference since it amounted to an "invasion of her rights as tenant to remain in possession undisturbed".[11] In *McCall v Abelesz*[12] Lord Denning M.R. held that the covenant is not confined to direct physical interference but extends to "any acts calculated to interfere with the peace or comfort of the tenant or his family".[13]

---

[1] [1902] 2 K.B. 351.
[2] [1976] Q.B. 585 at 594.
[3] [1963] 1 Q.B. 499.
[4] [1999] 4 All E.R. 448.
[5] [1942] 2 All E.R. 72.
[6] [1953] 1 W.L.R. 672.
[7] [1982] C.L.Y. 1747.
[8] [1956] 2 Q.B. 99.
[9] See *Browne v Fletcher* [1991] 1 Ch. 219; *Owen v Gadd* [1956] 2 Q.B. 99.
[10] [1963] 1 Q.B. 499.
[11] He also held that there was sufficient physical interference with the land if that was a necessary criterion.
[12] [1976] Q.B. 585.
[13] See also *McMillan v Singh* (1985) 17 H.L.R. 120.

Any remaining doubt as to the current position was eliminated by *Southwark LBC v Mills*.[14] The House of Lords held that the scope of the covenant to provide quiet enjoyment should not be restricted to acts which were a "direct and physical" interference with the tenant's use and enjoyment of the land. Earlier cases suggesting that the making of noise,[15] emanation of fumes, or interference with privacy or amenity did not constitute breaches of the covenant were doubted. Lord Hoffman therefore concluded that "regular excessive noise"[16] was capable of being a substantial interference with the ordinary enjoyment of premises, and hence a breach of covenant.

(iii)   The Landlord's Liability for the Acts of Others

A landlord will also be liable to his tenant for any breaches of the covenant to provide quiet **10–005** enjoyment arising through the acts of his agents or other persons claiming their title from him. For example, if a house has been converted into a number of self-contained flats, the landlord will be liable if the tenant of one flat disturbs the quiet enjoyment of another tenant. In *Sanderson v Berwick-upon-Tweed Corp*[17] a landlord was therefore held liable for breach of covenant where the tenant of one of his farms caused damage, by his use of drains, to a neighbouring farm which was occupied by another of his tenants. However, a landlord will only be liable for the lawful acts of those claiming title from him. Landlords are not liable for interference caused by a person claiming a superior title[18] or claiming under a predecessor in title to the landlord.[19]

(iv)   No Liability for Interference Caused by Circumstances Arising before the Grant of the Tenancy

The covenant to provide quiet enjoyment only operates prospectively. This means that a tenant **10–006** cannot complain of circumstances which interfere with his enjoyment of the premises if those circumstances were operative when he acquired the tenancy. A tenant is required to take the premises in the physical condition in which he finds them. Interference with the enjoyment of possession caused by the inherent structural state of the property cannot constitute a breach of the covenant. For example, in *Anderson v Oppenheimer*[20] a pipe in an office building burst, such that water from a cistern in the roof flooded the premises of the tenant of the ground floor. The Court of Appeal held that the escape of water was not a breach of the covenant to provide quiet enjoyment, even though it was a consequence of the maintenance of the cistern and water supply by the landlord. There had been no act or omission by the landlord after the lease had been granted. The water system had been present when the lease was granted, and the tenant had to take the building as he found it. Similarly in *Spoor v Green*[21] houses were damaged by

---

[14] [1999] 4 All E.R. 449.
[15] *Phelps v City of London Corp* [1916] 2 Ch. 255.
[16] [1999] 4 All E.R. 449 at 455.
[17] (1884) 13 Q.B.D. 547.
[18] *Jones v Lavington* [1903] 1 K.B. 253.
[19] *Celsteel Ltd v Alton House Holdings Ltd (No.2)* [1987] 1 W.L.R. 291.
[20] (1880) 5 Q.B.D. 602.
[21] (1874) L.R. 9 Exch. 99.

subsidence caused by underground mining. It was held that the landlord was not in breach of the covenant to provide quiet enjoyment because the mining had taken place prior to the grant of the tenancy. Moreover a tenant is also required to take the premises subject to any uses of the parts retained by the landlord of which he should have been aware when the tenancy was granted. In *Lylleton Times Co Ltd v Warners Ltd*[22] the plaintiffs owned a hotel next to premises in which the defendants operated a printing press. They entered into an agreement under which the defendants rebuilt their premises and granted the plaintiffs a lease of the upper floors for use as additional bedrooms. It was held that the noise and vibrations of the defendants' press did not constitute a breach of the covenant to provide quiet enjoyment because the plaintiffs had known that the defendants intended to use the premises for printing. The more recent case of *Southwark LBC v Mills*[23] concerned an alleged breach of the covenant to provide quiet enjoyment where the possession of tenants was disturbed by noise from the everyday activities of tenants in neighbouring flats. The prime cause of this interference was the inadequate sound-proofing of the building. The House of Lords held that the landlords had not committed a breach of covenant because the undesirable feature of the building, namely its propensity to admit the sounds of the everyday activity of the occupants of neighbouring flats, was a consequence of the inadequate sound insulation, a problem which had existed prior to the commencement of the tenancy. Lord Hoffman explained that, in these circumstances, the plaintiff had no grounds for complaint:

"It is sufficient that the tenants must reasonably have contemplated that there would be other tenants in neighbouring flats. If they cannot complain of the presence of other tenants as such, then their complaint is solely as to the lack of soundproofing. And that is an inherent structural defect for which the landlord assumed no responsibility. The council granted and the tenant took a tenancy of that flat."[24]

(v) Remedies for Breach of the Covenant to Provide quiet Enjoyment

10–007   A number of remedies are available to a tenant where a landlord is in breach of his covenant to provide quiet enjoyment. He may seek an injunction to restrain the landlord from threatened or continuing breaches, as for example in *Kenny v Preen*.[25] Where a breach has been committed the tenant may also seek damages to compensate him for the disturbance he has experienced. In *Branchett v Beaney*[26] the Court of Appeal held that damages should not be awarded to compensate a tenant for mental distress or injured feelings arising from the breach because the covenant is not a contract to provide "pleasure, relaxation, peace of mind or freedom from molestation"[27] but merely to "enjoy" the use of the land. However, it is clear that if the defendant's breach of covenant involves a trespass to the land the tenant will be able to maintain an action in tort, for which the court can award compensation for mental distress and

---

[22] [1907] A.C. 476.
[23] [1999] 4 All E.R. 449.
[24] [1999] 4 All E.R. 449 at 457.
[25] [1963] 1 Q.B. 499.
[26] [1992] 3 All E.R. 910.
[27] See *Watts v Morrow* [1991] 1 W.L.R. 1421.

injured feelings, especially when awarded as aggravated or exemplary damages.[28] In *Branchett v Beaney* the Court of Appeal upheld an award of £3,250[29] exemplary damages for a trespass which was also a breach of the covenant to provide quiet enjoyment.

(vi) Breach of Covenant may also be a Criminal Offence

Action by a landlord which constitutes a breach of the covenant to provide quiet enjoyment may also amount to the offence of harassment, which is defined by s.1(3) of the Protection from Eviction Act 1977:   **10–008**

> "If any person with intent to cause the residential occupier of any premises—
>
> (a) to give up the occupation of the premises or any part thereof; or
> (b) to refrain from exercising any right or pursuing any remedy in respect of the premises or part thereof;
>
> does acts likely to interfere with the peace or comfort of the residential occupier or members of his household, or persistently withdraws or withholds services reasonably required for the occupation of the premises as a residence, he shall be guilty of an offence."

(b) *Covenant not to Derogate from the Grant*

Every lease contains an implied covenant that the landlord will not derogate from the grant that he has made to the tenant.   **10–009**

(i) Meaning of the Covenant

The obligation of a landlord not to derogate from his grant is closely related to the covenant to provide quiet enjoyment. The covenant prevents a landlord from acting in a manner which, given the purpose for which the tenancy was granted, would reduce the usability of the land by the tenant. Difficulties will usually arise where a landlord has let part of his land, but retained the rest, and uses the retained part in such a way as to affect the tenant's use of his land. Parker J. explained the purpose of the covenant in *Browne v Flower*:   **10–010**

> ". . . if the grant or demise be made for a particular purpose, the grantor or lessor comes under an obligation not to use the land retained by him in such a way as to render the land granted or demised unfit or materially less fit for the particular purpose for which the grant or demise was made".[30]

---

[28] *Cassell & Co Ltd v Broome* [1972] A.C. 1027; *Drane v Evangelou* [1978] 1 W.L.R. 455; *Guppy's (Bridport) Ltd v Brookling* (1983) 14 H.L.R. 1.
[29] [1992] 3 All E.R. 910.
[30] [1911] 1 Ch. 219 at 226.

The rationale for this limitation on the landlord's freedom of use of his own retained land is simply a "rule of common honesty"[31] that "a grantor having given a thing with one hand is not to take away the means of enjoying it with the other".[32]

(ii) Breach of the Covenant

10–011 In *Aldin v Latimer Clark Muirhead & Co*[33] a landlord was held to be in breach of this covenant where he had let premises to a tenant who was a timber merchant and then subsequently built on land he had retained in a way which would interfere with the access of air to the tenant's sheds, which were used for drying his timber. In *Grosvenor Hotel Co v Hamilton*[34] a landlord was in breach where he caused vibrations to the leased land by his use of powerful engines to pump water on the adjacent land he had retained. In *Browne v Flower*[35] the Court of Appeal held that there was no breach where an iron staircase was erected on the outside of a block of flats, because it did not render other flats materially unfit for the purposes of residential flats. It seems that there will be no breach of covenant where a landlord lets neighbouring premises to others who will be in competition with the original tenant. In *Port v Griffith*,[36] for example, there was no derogation from grant where a landlord had let a shop to the plaintiff with an express covenant that it was to be used for "the sale of wool and general trimmings" and then let an adjoining shop for the business of a tailor and the sale of dressmaking trimmings. In *Romulus Trading Co Ltd v Comet Properties Ltd*[37] Garland J. held that there was no breach of the covenant where a landlord had let one unit in his buildings to the plaintiffs who intended to use it for their banking business and as a safe deposit centre, and then leased another unit in the same building to a rival bank which also intended to use it to provide the public with safe deposit facilities. If a tenant wishes to ensure that his landlord does not let neighbouring or close premises to business rivals it seems that he will have to insist on an express covenant to that effect in the lease.

(iii) Landlord's Knowledge of the Purpose of the Tenancy

10–012 A landlord will only be liable for breach of covenant if he was aware of the purpose for which the tenant intended to use the leased land. In *Harmer v Jumbil (Nigeria) Tin Areas Ltd*[38] Younger L.J. stated that in all cases the obligation must "be such as, in view of the surrounding circumstances, was within the reasonable contemplation of the parties at the time when the transaction was entered into, and was at that time within the grantor's power to fulfil". The landlord had granted the tenant a lease of a disused mine for use as an explosives'

---

[31] *Harmer v Jumbil (Nigeria) Tin Areas Ltd* [1921] 1 Ch. 200 at 225, per Younger L.J.
[32] *Birmingham, Dudley and District Banking Co v Ross* (1888) 38 Ch.D. 295 at 313, per Bowen L.J.
[33] [1894] 2 Ch. 437.
[34] [1894] 2 Q.B. 836.
[35] [1911] 1 Ch. 219.
[36] [1938] 1 All E.R. 295.
[37] [1996] 468 E.G. 157.
[38] [1921] 1 Ch. 200.

magazine. He subsequently granted a lease of adjoining land to other tenants, which permitted the working of minerals and opening of mine shafts. The presence of mine working in such close proximity to the magazine would have the effect of invalidating his first tenant's operating licence. He was therefore held to have breached his covenant not to derogate from the grant. In *Johnston & Sons Ltd v Holland*[39] it was held that a landlord's duty not to derogate from grant did not extend to cover the use of land he had acquired after the lease had been granted, so that the erection of a large hoarding concealing an advertisement which the tenant displayed on the flank wall of the premises he rented was no breach because his landlord had not owned that land at the date of the lease.

(iv)   Remedies for Breach of Covenant

A tenant may seek an injunction to restrain any breach[40] and damages to compensate for any loss suffered as a consequence of the breach. In *Grosvenor Hotel Company v Hamilton*[41] such damages were held to include the cost of the plaintiff moving his business to alternative premises.   **10–013**

(c)   *Covenants to Repair*

The allocation of obligations to repair and maintain the property between landlord and tenant will largely be determined by the express covenants of the lease. The express provisions of the lease may themselves lead to the implication of additional repairing obligations as a matter of interpretation. In *Barrett v Lounova*,[42] for example, a lease contained an express term that the tenant was to repair the interior but there were no express terms concerning the exterior, which had fallen into serious disrepair. The Court of Appeal construed the lease so as to imply a covenant of the landlord to repair the exterior of the premises in order to give "business efficacy" to the agreement. Kerr L.J. held that these circumstances called for the implication of a covenant: **10–014**

> "It is obvious . . . that sooner or later the covenant imposed by the tenant in respect of the inside can no longer be complied with unless the outside has been kept in repair . . . In my view it is therefore necessary, as a matter of business efficacy to make this agreement workable, that an obligation to keep the outside in repair must be imposed on someone."

He held that the only solution which made business sense was to imply that the landlord was under an obligation to repair the exterior.

A number of obligations on landlords to repair and maintain the property are implied by the common law or statute. The precise nature of the covenants implied will depend upon the nature of the tenancy in question.

---

[39] [1988] 1 E.G.L.R. 264.
[40] As was granted in *Harmer v Jumbil (Nigeria) Tin Areas Ltd* [1921] 1 Ch. 200.
[41] [1894] 2 Q.B. 836.
[42] [1990] 1 Q.B. 348.

(i) Covenant that Furnished Premises are fit for Human Habitation at the Start of the Tenancy

10–015 In *Smith v Marrable*[43] it was held that a landlord impliedly undertakes that furnished premises[44] are fit for human habitation. This obligation was held to be breached where the premises were infested with bugs. In the event of breach the tenant is entitled to quit the premises immediately without notice. The obligation only applies to the condition of the premises at the commencement of the tenancy, and in *Sarson v Roberts*[45] the Court of Appeal held that there was no implied covenant that premises continue to be habitable throughout the term.

(ii) Covenant to Keep Common Areas in Good Repair

10–016 In *Liverpool City Council v Irwin*[46] the House of Lords held that the council landlord of a block of flats was under an obligation to maintain the staircases and common areas of access in reasonable repair and usability. The tenants occupied under a document described as "conditions of tenancy" which contained no provisions relating to the landlord's obligations. Lord Wilberforce held that the appropriate test for the implication of an obligation to repair was that of necessity:

> "Such an obligation should be read into the contract as the nature of the contract itself implicitly requires, no more, no less: a test in other words, of necessity. The relationship accepted by the corporation is that of landlord and tenant: the tenant accepts obligations accordingly, in relation inter alia to the stairs, the lifts and the chutes. All these are not just facilities, or conveniences provided at discretion: they are essentials of the tenancy without which life in the dwellings, as a tenant, is not possible. To leave the landlord free of contractual obligation as regards these matters, and subject only to administrative or political pressure, is, in my opinion, inconsistent totally with the nature of this relationship. The subject matter of the lease (high rise blocks) and the relationship created by the tenancy demand, of their nature, some contractual obligation on the landlord."[47]

The House of Lords held that an absolute obligation was inappropriate and therefore implied a covenant to maintain reasonable repair and usability, including taking reasonable care to keep the lifts working and staircases lit. A repairing obligation of necessity was also implied in *King v Northamptonshire DC*[48] where a tenant of a house was wheelchair bound and needed to use the rear access to the property by means of a path in poor repair. The Court of Appeal held that there was an implied obligation to maintain the rear access.[49]

---

[43] (1843) 11 M. & W. 5.
[44] Unfurnished premises are excluded from the scope of the implied covenant: *Hart v Windsor* (1843) 12 M. & W. 68; *Lane v Cox* [1897] 1 Q.B. 415.
[45] [1895] 2 Q.B. 395.
[46] [1977] A.C. 239.
[47] [1977] A.C. 239 at 254.
[48] (1992) 24 H.L.R. 284.
[49] Compare *Duke of Westminster v Guild* [1985] Q.B. 688.

(iii) Covenant to Keep a House Fit for Human Habitation if it is Let at a Low Rent

The Landlord and Tenant Act 1985 s.8 implies into every lease of a house at a low rent a condition that it is fit for human habitation at the commencement of the tenancy and an undertaking that the landlord will keep it fit during the tenancy. These obligations are only implied if the rent does not exceed £80 in London or £52 elsewhere,[50] and if the house is not let for a term of more than three years upon terms that the tenant puts the premises into a condition reasonably fit for human habitation.[51] The protection afforded by s.8 is therefore relatively narrow.

10–017

(iv) Covenant to Keep a Dwelling House in Repair if the Lease is for a Term of less than Seven Years

A more significant repairing obligation is implied by s.11 of the Landlord and Tenant Act 1985. This section applies to leases of dwelling-houses granted after October 24, 1964 for a term of less than seven years.[52] Section 11(1) implies the following obligations into such a lease:

10–018

"(a) to keep in repair the structure and exterior of the dwelling-house (including drains, gutters and external pipes),

(b) to keep in repair and proper working order the installations in the dwelling-house for the supply of water, gas and electricity and for sanitation (including basins, sinks, baths and sanitary conveniences, but not other fixture fittings and appliances for making use of the supply of water, gas or electricity), and

(c) to keep in repair and proper working order the installations in the dwelling-house for space heating and water heating."

Any express covenant by the tenant to repair the property in these respects is of no effect.[53] One common question which has arisen is whether particular parts of a dwelling-house are to be regarded as part of the "structure and exterior". In *Re Irwin's Estate*[54] it was held that window frames and sashes were within the scope of the covenant,[55] but that a garage and yard separate from the dwelling-house were not. In *Hussein v Mehlman*[56] wall plaster was held to be part of the structure. It has also been held that the covenant relates only to physical defects in the premises. In *Quick v Taff-Ely BC*[57] windows caused severe condensation. However, it was held that there was no breach of the covenant since they were not in a state of disrepair but merely inadequate for their task and no physical damage had been caused by the condensation. In contrast in *Stent v Monmouth DC*[58] it was held that there was a breach of covenant

---

[50] Landlord and Tenant Act 1985 s.1(4).
[51] Landlord and Tenant Act 1985 s.1(5).
[52] Landlord and Tenant Act 1985 s.13.
[53] Landlord and Tenant Act 1985 s.4.
[54] (1990) 24 H.L.R. 1.
[55] See also *Boswell v Crucible Steel of America* [1925] 1 K.B. 119.
[56] [1992] 32 E.G. 59.
[57] [1986] Q.B. 809.
[58] (1987) 19 H.L.R. 269.

when water had come into a house under the front door which had been physically damaged by the water.

(v)   Remedies for Breach of Covenant

10–019   Where a landlord is in breach of his repairing obligations, whether express, implied or statutory, a number of remedies are available to the tenant. The tenant will be entitled to damages for breach of covenant assessed as the difference between the value of the premises to the tenant in their condition of disrepair and what their value would have been if the covenants had been fulfilled.[59] The tenant may also be able to obtain an order for specific performance.[60] If the tenant undertakes the repairs himself he enjoys a common law right to recoup the reasonable costs from future rent, provided that he gave the landlord notice of the need to repair.[61] If the landlord sues for non-payment of rent, and the tenant cross-claims for damages for breach of a repairing covenant, including any consequential damage, the tenant has an equitable right to set his claim off against the landlord's.[62] Where a landlord is in serious breach of his repairing obligations a tenant may be able to ask the court to appoint an administrator to collect the rents and service charges due from tenants, and to use them to carry out the repairs.[63] This might be especially appropriate in the case where the landlord of a block of flats is failing to fulfil his obligations.[64] Indirect enforcement of repairing obligations may also be sought through the local housing authority, which possesses statutory powers to deal with problems where property is unfit for human habitation or in need of repair.[65]

(vi)   Other Potential Liability of a Landlord for Property in a State of Disrepair

10–020   A landlord may be subject to a number of other common law and statutory liabilities if the property is not kept in repair. Following the long-established authority of *Cavalier v Pope*,[66] a landlord is not liable in tort for negligence for premises which are defective at the commencement of a tenancy, except if he was also the builder.[67] A landlord may be liable for damage caused as a result of his failure to repair under the Defective Premises Act 1972. By s.4(1) a landlord who is under an obligation to maintain or repair premises owes a duty of care to all persons who might reasonably be expected to be affected by defects to "see that they are

---

[59] See *Calabar Properties Ltd v Sticher* [1984] 1 W.L.R. 287; *Wallace v Manchester City Council* (1998) 30 H.L.R. 1111.
[60] *Jeune v Queens Cross Properties Ltd* [1974] Ch. 97; *Francis v Cowcliffe* (1977) 33 P. & C.R. 368; *Rainbow Estates v Tokenhold* [1998] 2 All E.R. 860.
[61] See *Lee-Parker v Izzer* [1971] 1 W.L.R. 1688.
[62] *British Anzani (Felixstowe) Ltd v International Marine Management (UK) Ltd* [1979] 2 All E.R. 1063.
[63] *Hart v Emelkirk Ltd* [1983] 1 W.L.R. 1289.
[64] See also Landlord and Tenant Act 1987 ss.21–24B, which entitles the tenant of a property divided into two or more flats to apply to a leasehold valuation tribunal if the landlord is in breach of his repairing obligations for the appointment of a manager, who may be empowered to manage the property.
[65] For example by serving a repair notice under the Housing Act 1985 s.189.
[66] [1906] A.C. 428; *McInerny v London Borough of Lambeth* (1988) 21 H.L.R. 188.
[67] *Rimmer v Liverpool City Council* [1985] Q.B. 1.

reasonably safe from personal injury or from damage to their property caused by a relevant defect". By s.4(4) the landlord will attract liability even if the tenancy contains no repairing obligations provided that the tenancy "expressly or impliedly gives the landlord the right to enter the premises to carry out any description of maintenance or repair of the premises".

2.   Covenants of the Tenant

(a)   *Covenant not to Disclaim the Landlord's Title*

There is an implied covenant in every lease that the tenant will not do anything which might prejudice the title of the landlord.[68] The essence of this obligation is that the tenant must not do anything which evinces an intention to no longer be bound by the relationship of landlord and tenant. The tenant will be in breach of this covenant only where a disclaimer is "clear and unambiguous". This was so held by Thomas Morison Q.C. in *WG Clarke (Properties) Ltd v Dupre Properties Ltd*[69] by analogy with the doctrine of repudiation of contract. A tenant sued his landlord for damages where he had extended the premises let into a courtyard to which the landlord claimed title by adverse possession. As part of his pleadings the tenant alleged that the courtyard was owned by a third party, and the landlord claimed that this was a breach of covenant entitling him to forfeit the lease. It was held that denying the title to the court-yard was only a partial disclaimer and that this did not constitute a sufficiently clear and unambiguous repudiation of the relationship of landlord and tenant of the whole premises let.

10–021

(b)   *Covenant not to Commit Waste*

Waste means any physical alteration of the land which is the result either of action or inaction on the part of the tenant. For example, in *Mancetter Ltd v Garmanson Ltd*[70] it was held that a tenant who removed an extractor fan which he had installed, leaving a hole in the wall, was liable for waste. Waste may take two forms. Waste caused by the actions of the tenant is described as voluntary waste. Waste which is caused by inaction, in other words the failure to make good damage caused by external or natural factors, is described as permissive waste.

10–022

   Liability for waste is related to the liability, if any, which a tenant has for repairs. In the absence of express agreement to the contrary, all tenants are liable for voluntarily waste, but liability for permissive waste will vary depending upon the nature of the tenancy. A tenant under a fixed term lease will incur liability for permissive waste unless expressly agreed oth-erwise.[71] A tenant under a yearly periodic tenancy is only liable for permissive waste which

---

[68] *WG Clarke (Properties) Ltd v Dupre Properties Ltd* [1992] Ch. 297 at 303, approving *Hill and Redman's Law of Landlord and Tenant* (18th edn, 1991), Vol.1.
[69] [1992] Ch. 297.
[70] [1986] Q.B. 1212.
[71] *Yellowly v Gower* (1855) 11 Ex.D. 274.

occurs because he fails to keep the premises wind and watertight.[72] In *Haskell v Marlow*[73] it was held that a tenant under a yearly tenancy was not liable for the effect of "reasonable wear and tear" on the property. Tenants under other periodic tenancies are not subject to these minimal requirements and are only liable for voluntary waste.[74]

(c) Covenant to Use the Property in a "Tenantlike Manner"

10–023 A covenant is implied into every lease that the tenant will use the property in a "tenantlike manner".[75] This covenant imposes a minimal duty on the tenant to take care of the property. Denning L.J. attempted to give some shape to this duty in *Warren v Keen*:

> "But what does to use the premises in a tenantlike 'manner' mean? It can, I think, best be shown by some illustrations. The tenant must take proper care of the place. He must, if he is going away for the winter, turn off the water and empty the boiler. He must clean the chimneys, when necessary, and also the windows. He must mend the electric light when it fuses. He must unstop the sink when it is blocked by his waste. In short, he must do the little jobs about the place which a reasonable tenant would do."[76]

(d) Covenant to Repair

10–024 There are no implied covenants, either at common law or by statute, which require a tenant to repair the property. A tenant will only be subject to such repairing obligations as are included in the express covenants of the lease. The parties are free to incorporate whatever express repairing provisions they agree, with the exception that the obligations imposed on landlords by s.11 of the Landlord and Tenant Act 1985 cannot be excluded. Tenants' obligations to repair are more likely to be imposed in longer term leases. If the express covenant excludes liability for damage caused by "fair wear and tear", this only includes normal and reasonable use.[77]

(e) Covenant to Pay Rent

10–025 Since rent is not a necessary requirement of a lease there is no general implied covenant to pay it. However in the majority of cases the payment of rent will be the subject of an express

---

[72] *Autworth v Johnson* (1832) 5 C. & P. 239; *Leach v Thomas* (1835) 7 C. & P. 327; *Weld v Porter* [1916] 2 K.B. 45.
[73] [1928] 2 K.B. 45.
[74] See *Warren v Keen* [1954] 1 Q.B. 15.
[75] *Horsefall v Mather Holt* (1815) N.P. 7; *Marsden v Edward Heyes Ltd* [1927] 2 K.B. 1; *Warren v Keen* [1954] 1 Q.B. 15.
[76] [1954] 1 Q.B. 15 at 20.
[77] *Haskell v Marlow* [1928] 2 K.B. 45.

covenant, which will stipulate the amount of rent payable and whether it is to be paid in arrears or in advance. In the case of longer leases this will often include a provision for periodic rent review. Similarly the lease may contain an express covenant requiring the tenant to pay the landlord a service charge in respect of the property.

The rent payable under a tenancy may be subject to statutory limits. Where the tenancy is a protected tenancy under the Rent Acts the landlord will only be entitled to charge a "fair rent". A fair rent is determined by excluding the effect of market forces, so that it will be substantially lower than the market rent for the property.[78] As was noted above, the majority of tenancies of residential property today will be assured shorthold tenancies. In the case of such tenancies the tenant will only be entitled to relief if the rent payable was "significantly higher" than the local market rent for similar properties.[79]

(f) *Covenant to Pay a Service Charge*

A lease may also contain a covenant requiring the tenant to pay a service charge to the landlord in return for the performance of his obligations, such as the maintenance of common areas. In the case of long leases the service charge is often considerably higher than the rent payable. Tenants enjoy statutory protection against excessive service charges, for example a landlord may only recover for costs which were "reasonably incurred"[80] and must obtain estimates and notify tenants where he intended to do work exceeding a certain ceiling. A tenant is also entitled to require his landlord to supply a written summary of the costs incurred comprising the service charge.

10–026

(g) *Covenant not to Assign or Sub-let the Property*

Since a lease creates an estate in the land, and not a purely personal entitlement for the tenant, a tenant is prima facie entitled to transfer his interest in the land to a third party, who will become tenant in his place. The process by which such a transfer of the tenancy is effected is called assignment. A lease may contain an express covenant against assignment by the tenant. The effect of such a covenant is not to prevent assignment, since this is one of the essential characteristics of a lease. Instead, if the lease is assigned in breach of covenant, the tenant is exposed to liability for that breach, which may include forfeiture of the lease. A tenant may also be able to sub-let the property, carving a lesser leasehold interest out of his own estate. Again the lease may contain provisions preventing or restricting the ability of the tenant to sub-let.

10–027

---

[78] Rent Act 1977 s.70(2).
[79] Housing Act 1988 s.22(3).
[80] Landlord and Tenant Act 1985 s.19(1).

3. Landlord's Remedies where a Tenant is in Breach of Covenant

10–028   When a tenant commits a breach of covenant, whether express or implied, five potential remedies may be available to the landlord. First the landlord may be entitled to forfeit the lease. Forfeiture entitles the landlord to terminate the tenancy before the expiry of the agreed term. It is the most powerful of the remedies available to him, and its availability and exercise is therefore carefully circumscribed by the law. Secondly, the landlord may be entitled to exercise distress. Distress is a self-help remedy available to the landlord where the tenant has failed to pay his rent. It entitles the landlord to seize goods on the premises let and sell them to recover the arrears of rent. Thirdly, the landlord will be able to sue to recover damages for breach of covenant to compensate him for any loss he has suffered by reason of the tenant's breach. Fourthly, he will be able to bring an action for arrears of rent to recovery up to six years of unpaid rent. Finally, he may be able to obtain specific performance if the tenant is in breach of his obligations to keep the premises in good repair.

(a)   *Forfeiture of the Lease*

(i)   When is Forfeiture Available?

10–029   Not every breach of a covenant entitles a landlord to forfeit the lease and the ordinary remedy is simply one of damages. However forfeiture will be available in three circumstances. First, a landlord enjoys an implied right to forfeit if the tenant disclaims his title.[81] Secondly, a landlord will enjoy a right to forfeit if an obligation of the lease is formulated as a condition.[82] Thirdly, a landlord will be entitled to forfeit for breach of covenant if the lease contains an express forfeiture clause. In most professionally drawn leases the obligations of the lease are drafted as conditions and the lease will contain a general forfeiture clause. Even where a tenant commits a breach of covenant which would entitle the landlord to forfeit the lease, forfeiture is not automatic. The breach merely renders the lease voidable by the landlord.

One very significant limitation to the availability of forfeiture is that a landlord will not be entitled to forfeit the lease if he has expressly or impliedly waived the tenant's breach of covenant. The general principles of waiver were explained by Parker J. in *Matthews v Smallwood*:

> "Waiver of a right of re-entry can only occur where the lessor, with knowledge of the facts upon which his right to re-entry arises, does some unequivocal act recognising the continued existence of the lease. It is not enough that he should do the act which recognizes, or appears to recognize, the continued existence of the lease, unless, at the time when the act is done, he has knowledge of the facts under which, or from which, his right of entry arose."[83]

[81] *Clarke v Dupre Ltd* [1992] Ch. 297.
[82] *Doe d Lockwood v Clarke* (1807) 8 East 185.
[83] [1910] 1 Ch. 777 at 786.

252

These principles were adopted by the House of Lords in *Kammins Ballrooms Co v Zenith Investments*.[84] Waiver will most commonly occur if the landlord continues to accept rent from the tenant,[85] which indicates an intention to continue the lease despite the breach. As Buckley L.J. stated in *Central Estates (Belgravia) Ltd v Woolgar (No.2)*[86]:

> "If [the landlord] chooses to do something such as demanding or receiving rent which can only be done consistently with the existence of a certain state of affairs, viz, the continuance of the lease or tenancy in operation, he cannot thereafter be heard to say that that state of affairs did not then exist."

There is no need for the landlord to intend to waive the breach.[87]

In *Matthews v Smallwood* Parker J. indicated that since the issue whether an act constitutes a waiver is a matter of law, the landlord is not entitled to treat the tenancy as continuing and receive rent without prejudice to his right to re-enter. This position has been reiterated by later cases.[88] A mere demand for rent will also be sufficient.[89] If rent is in arrears a landlord cannot accept money and avoid waiver by stipulating that the money is not accepted as rent.[90] In the case of acts other than the continued receipt of rent Slade L.J. stated in *Expert Clothing Ltd v Hillgate House*[91] that the court is "free to look at all the circumstances of the case" to determine whether an act was so unequivocal as to amount to an election. Examples of conduct which may amount to an election include an agreement by the landlord to grant a new tenancy on the normal determination of the existing lease,[92] and an offer by the landlord to vary a lease or to purchase the tenant's interest.[93] A landlord who exercises his remedy of distress for failure to pay rent will also be unable to seek forfeiture. Although in *Expert Clothing Ltd v Hillgate House* it was recognised that the proffering of a mere negotiating document may amount to a waiver, the Court of Appeal held that on the facts the sending of a draft deed of variation did not, since it was not unequivocal in the light of the surrounding circumstances, including the service of a s.146 notice[94] seeking possession 14 days beforehand manifesting a clear intention to forfeit.

A landlord will only be taken to have waived a breach if he had knowledge that it had taken place. This does not require actual knowledge, constructive knowledge will suffice. The landlord will also be affixed with the knowledge of his agent or employee.[95] In *Matthews v Smallwood*[96] it was held that there was no waiver when a landlord continued to accept rent after a tenant had committed a breach of his covenant not to sub-let the premises by granting

---

[84] [1971] A.C. 850.

[85] *Segal Securities Ltd v Thoseby* [1963] 1 Q.B. 887.

[86] [1972] 1 W.L.R. 1048 at 1054.

[87] *Cornillie v Saha* (1996) 28 H.L.R. 561.

[88] *Segal Securities Ltd v Thoseby* [1963] 1 Q.B. 887; *Central Estates (Belgravia) Ltd v Woolgar (No.2)* [1972] 1 W.L.R. 1048; *Expert Clothing Services & Sales Ltd v Hillgate House Ltd* [1986] Ch. 340.

[89] *David Blackstone Ltd v Burnetts (West End) Ltd* [1973] 1 W.L.R. 1487.

[90] *Croft v Lumley* (1856) 6 H.L. Cas. 672; *Davenport v The Queen* (1877) 3 Ch. App. Cas. 115.

[91] [1986] Ch. 340 at 360.

[92] *Ward v Day* (1863) 5 B. & S. 359.

[93] *Bader Properties Ltd v Linley Property Investments Ltd* (1967) 19 P. & C.R. 620.

[94] This is part of the procedure for the exercise of forfeiture.

[95] *Metropolitan Properties Co Ltd v Cordery* (1979) 39 P. & C.R. 10.

[96] [1910] 1 Ch. 777.

a mortgage because the landlord did not have any knowledge that the mortgage had been granted. In *Chrisdell Ltd v Johnson*[97] the Court of Appeal held that a landlord's mere suspicion of a breach was insufficient to generate a waiver where he had received representations from the tenant that there had been no breach but was insufficiently confident that they were untrue to take proceedings for re-entry. In *Van Haarlam v Kasner*[98] widespread media coverage of a tenant's illegal and immoral conduct was held sufficient knowledge.[99] The principles of waiver were applied in *Cornillie v Saha*.[100] In February 1993 Mr Cornillie purchased the freehold reversion of a block of flats, flat 18 of which was leased to Mr and Mrs Saha on terms which included a covenant against sub-letting. In October 1993 Mr Cornillie served a s.146 notice. The county court judge held that this did not amount to a waiver because Mr Cornillie did not at that stage know the identity of all the occupiers of flat 18 and whether they enjoyed tenancies or mere licences, although he did know that one of them had a tenancy. However the Court of Appeal reversed this decision and held that Mr Cornillie had waived his right to forfeit. His wife had known from early February that flat 18 had been divided into six rooms and these had been sub-let in breach of covenant. Aldous L.J. concluded that it was irrelevant that he did not know the identity of all the occupiers and that the "near certainty" that they all occupied on the same terms was sufficient to inform him of the fact of the breach.

A waiver will only be effective in relation to the breach to which it relates as provided in s.148(1) of the Law of Property Act 1925. A waiver cannot therefore protect a tenant against future similar breaches.[101] It will thus be important to determine whether the tenant's breach of covenant constituted a "once-and-for-all breach" or whether the obligation is a continuing one which is broken each day that the tenant is in breach. This issue was considered by the House of Lords in *Channel Hotels and Properties Ltd v Fahad Al Tamimi, First Penthosue Ltd*,[102] which concerned an alleged breach of a covenant by a tenant to carry out and complete the development of a roof space as expeditiously as possible so that they should have been completed by a specified time. Failure to complete the works by this specified time was held to be a "once-for–all-breach," so that a waiver by the landlord occurring after the specified time for the completion of the work had passed operated to prevent forfeiture for this breach. In contrast, in the case of a continuing breach, for example of a covenant to repair the property throughout the lease, the landlord can withdraw the waiver and seek forfeiture.[103] If in such a case the landlord has already served the requisite s.146 notice he does not need to serve another.[104] The effect of waiver is only to prevent the landlord seeking to forfeit the lease. He will still be entitled to claim damages from the tenant.[105]

Even where a landlord is prevented from seeking forfeiture for breach of covenant because he has waived the breach, another tenant of the landlord will be able to enforce the covenant directly against the tenant in breach if the covenant is restrictive and the properties are

---

[97] (1897) 54 P. & C.R. 257.
[98] (1992) 64 P. & C.R. 214.
[99] But contrast *Official Custodian for Charities v Parway Estates Developments Ltd* [1985] Ch. 151.
[100] (1996) 28 H.L.R. 561.
[101] *Bilson v Residential Apartments* [1992] 1 A.C. 494.
[102] [2004] EWCA Civ 1072.
[103] *Greenwich LBC v Discreet Selling Estates Ltd* (1990) 61 P. & C.R. 405.
[104] *Penton v Barnett* [1898] 1 Q.B. 276; *Farimani v Gates* (1894) 271 E.G. 887.
[105] *Stephens v Junior Army and Navy Stores Ltd* [1914] 2 Ch. 516; *Greenwich LBC v Discreet Selling Estates Ltd* (1990) 61 P. & C.R. 405.

subject to a "letting scheme,"[106] which is the leasehold equivalent of a building scheme affecting freehold land, or if the lease to the tenant in breach falls within the ambit of the Contracts (Rights of Third Parties) Act 1999.

(ii) How is Forfeiture Exercised?

Where forfeiture is available the landlord forfeits the lease by means of exercising his right of re-entry, which simply means that he retakes possession of the land. Re-entry may involve physical entry of the premises, but service of possession proceedings is equivalent.[107] Forfeiture is effective from the moment of re-entry and the tenant is thereafter a trespasser.[108]   **10–030**

A landlord of residential property is only permitted to exercise forfeiture by means of court proceedings, so he cannot simply retake physical possession of the land. Section 2 of the Protection from Eviction Act 1977 provides that:

> "Where any premises are let as a dwelling on a lease which is subject to a right of re-entry or forfeiture it shall not be lawful to enforce that right otherwise than by proceedings in the court while any person is lawfully residing in the premises or part of them."

A landlord who re-enters other than by such proceedings thus commits a criminal offence.[109] As has already been noted in the context of the landlord's covenant to provide quiet enjoyment above, s.1(3) also establishes the offence of harassment. Section 27 of the Housing Act 1988 provides that a tenant will be entitled to recover damages[110] from a landlord who unlawfully deprives him of his occupation, whether by wrongful eviction or harassment.

The provisions of the Protection from Eviction Act do not apply to non-residential property, and there is therefore nothing to prevent a landlord exercising forfeiture by means of peaceable physical re-entry. However, under s.6(1) of the Criminal Law Act 1977 it is an offence to use or threaten violence without lawful authority for the purposes of securing entry into any premises where, to the knowledge of the entrant, there is someone present who is opposed to entry. This means that most cases of peaceful re-entry of business premises will have to take place outside of working hours. In *Billson v Residential Apartments Ltd*[111] the landlord of unoccupied residential premises re-entered at 6am and changed the locks. However, the House of Lords expressed a dislike of even peaceable re-entry and expressed a preference for the issue of a writ and a reduction of any incentives for landlords pursuing what Lord Templeman described as "the dubious and dangerous method of determining the lease by re-entering the premises".[112] Even where re-entry is available, the landlord will have to comply with the statutory requirement to serve notice on the tenant as required by s.146(1) of the Law of Property Act 1925, considered below.

---

[106] See *Williams v Kiley* [2002] EWCA Civ 1645.
[107] *Billson v Residential Apartments Ltd* [1992] 1 A.C. 494.
[108] *Canas Property Co Ltd v KL Television Services Ltd* [1970] 2 Q.B. 433.
[109] Protection from Eviction Act 1977 s.1(2).
[110] See *Tagro v Cafane* [1991] 1 W.L.R. 378.
[111] [1992] 1 A.C. 494.
[112] [1992] 1 A.C. 494 at 525.

(iii) Forfeiture for Non-payment of Rent or Service Charge

10–031 A landlord seeking to forfeit for non-payment of rent must first make a formal demand for rent from the tenant. However, no such formal demand is required if the lease expressly exempts the landlord from such a requirement, or if the tenant is more than six months in arrears and there are insufficient goods on the premises to satisfy the arrears by means of a distress.[113] If possession is sought through proceedings in the High Court and the tenant is more than six months in arrears[114] the proceedings will be stayed if the tenant[115] pays the arrears and landlord's costs before the date of judgment.[116] If possession is sought in the county court the proceedings will be stayed if the tenant pays the arrears and landlord's costs not later than five days before the date of the trial.[117]

Even where a landlord is entitled to forfeit a lease because of the tenant's breach of covenant to pay rent the tenant may be able to obtain relief against forfeiture. Where a landlord has been granted possession by the High Court, and the tenant is more than six months in arrears,[118] s.210 of the Common Law Procedure Act 1852 allows the tenant to claim relief if he pays the rent due and landlord's costs within six months of the execution of the judgment. Where possession has been ordered by the county court the tenant may prevent the execution of the order by paying the arrears and costs within a period specified by the court.[119] If the landlord has recovered possession the tenant may apply for relief within six months and the court has the discretion to grant such order as it thinks fit. The tenant may also apply to the county court for relief within six months of a peaceful re-entry.[120] Outside these statutory provisions there is a general equitable jurisdiction to grant relief where the tenant has paid all the arrears and costs.[121]

Even greater protection is provided where a tenant is in breach of a covenant to pay a service charge. In such circumstances the landlord is not permitted to forfeit the lease unless a leasehold valuation tribunal, court or arbitration tribunal has determined that the amount claimed is payable by the tenant, or the tenant has admitted that it is payable.[122]

(iv) Forfeiture for Breach of other Covenants

10–032 The procedure for forfeiture for other covenants is governed by s.146 the Law of Property Act 1925,which provides:

---

[113] Common Law Procedure Act 1852 s.210. Goods are regarded as unavailable for distress if the premises are locked.

[114] *Standard Pattern Co v Ivey* [1962] Ch. 432.

[115] Payment by a third party will not entitled the tenant to a stay of proceedings: *Matthews v Dobbins* [1963] 1 W.L.R. 227.

[116] Common Law Procedure Act 1855 s.212.

[117] County Courts Act 1984 s.138(2).

[118] *Billson v Residential Apartments Ltd* [1992] 1 A.C. 494.

[119] The period must not be less than four weeks.

[120] County Courts Act 1984 s.139(2).

[121] *Howard v Fanshawe* [1895] 2 Ch. 581; *Lovelock v Margo* [1963] 2 Q.B. 786.

[122] Housing Act 1996 s.80.

"A right of re-entry or forfeiture under any proviso or stipulation in a lease for a breach of any covenant or condition in the lease shall not be enforceable, by action or otherwise, unless and until the lessor serves on the lessee a notice—

(a) specifying the particular breach complained of; and
(b) if the breach is capable of remedy, requiring the lessee to remedy the breach; and
(c) in any case, requiring the lessee to make compensation in money for the breach;

and the lessee fails, within a reasonable time thereafter, to remedy the breach, if it is capable of remedy, and to make reasonable compensation in money, to the satisfaction of the lessor, for the breach."

The notice required by s.146(1) must be served on the "lessee", which is given the extended meaning of "an original or derivative under-lessee, and the persons deriving title under a lessee; also a grantee under any such grant as aforesaid and the persons deriving title from him".[123] Where the lease has been assigned service of a notice on the original tenant will be insufficient.[124] The notice will be ineffective if it fails to specify the specific breach of covenant for which forfeiture is sought. Thus in *Akici v Butlin Ltd*[125] Neuberger L.J. held that the exercise of a rich of re-entry by a landlord against a tenant who had committed a breach of a covenant by sharing possession of the premises with a pizza delivery company had been invalid because the s.146 notice issued preceding the forfeiture had specified that the tenant was in breach of a covenant not to part with possession. The element of the notice offering the tenant the chance to remedy breaches of covenant or provide adequate financial compensation were said by Slade L.J. in *Expert Clothing Service & Sales Ltd v Highgate House Ltd*[126] to give tenants "one last chance" to comply with their obligations. The tenant is entitled to a reasonable time to comply with the notice. What is reasonable will depend upon the nature and remediability of the breach.[127] The need to offer a "reasonable period" to remedy any breach is only required if the breach is remediable. In general positive covenants, requiring the tenant to do something such as repair or maintain the premises, are capable of remedy.[128] In regard to negative covenants *Scala House and District Property Co Ltd v Forbes*[129] suggested that breaches can never be remedied since the breach cannot be undone,[130] for example a breach of a covenant not to assign, sub-let or alter the premises. As Bingham L.J. remarked in *Bass Ltd v Morton Ltd*,[131] the traditional view was that:

---

[123] Law of Property Act 1925 s.146(5)(b).
[124] *Fuller v Judy Properties Ltd* (1991) 64 P. & C.R. 176.
[125] [2005] EWCA Civ 1296.
[126] [1986] Ch. 340.
[127] In *Billson v Residential Aparments Ltd* [1992] 1 A.C. 494 a 14-day period was held sufficient where the tenants had no intention of remedying the breach. In *Horsey Estates v Steiger* [1899] 2 Q.B. 79 two days was insufficient where there was an irremediable breach.
[128] See *Expert Clothing Service and Sales Ltd v Hillgate House Ltd* [1986] Ch. 340 where it was held that a covenant to reconstruct premises was capable of remedy by performance and compensation.
[129] [1974] Q.B. 575.
[130] See also *Rugby School (Governors) v Tannahill* [1934] 1 K.B. 695.
[131] [1988] Ch. 493.

"A covenant to do something can be substantially performed even if late. A covenant not to do something, once broken, is broken for ever. As Lady Macbeth, referring to her breach of the sixth (negative) commandment observed: 'what's done is done'."

However, more recent decisions suggest a more flexible approach which differentiates between breaches of negative covenants which are "once for all" and cannot be undone, and breaches of a continuing nature which can be stopped and any harm the landlord has suffered effectively remedied.[132] In *Expert Clothing Service & Sales Ltd v Hillgate House Ltd*[133] Slade L.J. indicated that the ultimate question for the court was whether compliance with a s.146 notice, coupled with the payment of any appropriate monetary compensation, would "have effectively remedied the harm which the lessors had suffered or were likely to suffer from the breach". In *Bass Ltd v Morton Ltd*[134] Bingham L.J. indicated that a breach was only irremediable if the landlord could show "continuing damage" to himself once the breach had ceased and appropriate compensation been paid. Applying these tests a breach of a covenant not to use a premises for immoral purposes, as in *Rugby School (Governors) v Tannahill*,[135] would be irremediable,[136] since the harm caused to the landlord's reputation could not be undone. As O'Connor L.J. commented in *Expert Clothing Service & Sales v Hillgate House Ltd*[137]:

"To stop what is forbidden by a negative covenant may or may not remedy the breach even if accompanied by compensation in money. Thus to remove the window boxes and pay for the repair of any damage done will remedy the breach, but to stop using the house as a brothel will not, because the taint lingers on and will not dissipate within a reasonable time."

As a matter of principle a breach of a negative covenant against sub-letting is incapable of remedy, because it is impossible to uncreate an underlease. For the same reason an unlawful assignment very probably also constitutes an irremediabl;e breach. However in *Akici v Butlin Ltd*[138] Neuberger L.J. held that a breach of a covenant against parting with possession or sharing possession is not irremediable, provided that the breach falls short of creating or transferring a legal interest.

10–033   Thus use of premises for illegal purposes will generally constitute an irremediable breach, as for example in *Van Haarlam v Kasner*[139] where a tenant had used a flat for spying in breach of the Official Secrets Act 1911.

A tenant who has breached a covenant other than a covenant to pay rent may also be entitled to relief against forfeiture. Section 146(2) of the Law of Property Act 1925 gives the court a wide-ranging general jurisdiction to grant a tenant relief from forfeiture for breach of a covenant other than that to pay rent:

---

[132] *Savva v Hussein* (1997) 73 P & CR 150; *Akici v Butlin Ltd* [2005] EWCA Civ 1296.
[133] [1986] Ch. 340 at 358.
[134] [1988] Ch. 493 at 541.
[135] [1934] 1 K.B. 695.
[136] See also *Dunraven Securities Ltd v Holloway* (1982) 264 E.G. 709, where there was an irremediable breach of covenant when premises were used as a sex shop in Soho.
[137] [1986] Ch. 340 at 362.
[138] [2005] EWCA Civ 1296.
[139] (1992) 64 P. & C.R. 214.

"Where a lessor is proceeding, by action or otherwise, to enforce such a right of re-entry or forfeiture, the lessee may, in the lessor's action, if any, or in any action brought by himself, apply to the court for relief; and the court may grant or refuse relief, as the court, having regard to the proceedings and conduct of the parties . . . and to all the other circumstances, thinks fit; and in case of relief may grant it on such terms, if any, as to costs, expenses, damages, compensation, penalty or otherwise, including the granting of an injunction to restrain any like breach in the future, as the court, in the circumstances of each case, thinks fit."

In the case of forfeiture by court proceedings the tenant's right to apply for relief is only lost when the landlord has entered into possession of the premises. However, in the case of peaceable re-entry the House of Lords held in *Billson v Residential Apartments*[140] that the tenant can apply for relief even after the landlord has taken possession. Generally the courts will not grant relief for an irremediable breach where a third party's rights have intervened, for example by a re-letting of the premises after re-entry,[141] or where the breach involves immoral or illegal conduct.[142] Relief will usually be granted in the case of trivial breaches. Unlike the general equitable jurisdiction to grant relief, the jurisdiction under s.146(2) includes potential relief where the tenant committed a wilful breach of covenant.[143] It remains unclear whether in the light of s.146 the general equitable jurisdiction has survived and is available for breaches other than the non-payment of rent.[144]

(v) Additional Protection against Forfeiture for Breach of a Covenant to Pay a Service Charge

In many long leases the tenant is required to pay a service charge as well as a rent. The Housing Act 1996 has introduced provisions to protect tenants from forfeiture for non-payment of service charges because of the tendency of some landlords to exploit the levying of service charges as a way of terminating leases. The problem is particularly acute where the tenant contests the amount of the service charge levied. Section 81 of the Housing Act 1996 provides that a landlord cannot exercise a right of re-entry or forfeiture for non-payment of a service charge unless the amount of the service charge is agreed or admitted by the tenant, or has been the subject of determination by a court or tribunal. This does not prevent the landlord from serving a s.146 notice on a tenant for non-payment, but s.82 of the Housing Act 1996 provides that such a notice must inform the tenant of his rights under s.81.

10–034

---

[140] [1992] 1 A.C. 494.
[141] *Fuller v Judy Properties Ltd* (1991) 64 P. & C.R. 176.
[142] *Hoffman v Fineberg* [1949] Ch. 245; *Borthwick-Norton v Romney Warwick Estates Ltd* [1950] 1 All E.R. 798; *GMS Syndicate Ltd v Gary Elliott Ltd* [1982] Ch. 1.
[143] *Billson v Residential Apartments Ltd* [1992] 1 A.C. 494; *WG Clarke (Properties) Ltd v Dupre Properties Ltd* [1992] Ch. 297.
[144] *Official Custodian of Charities v Parway Estates Developments Ltd* [1985] Ch. 151; *Billson v Residential Apartments Ltd* [1992] 1 A.C. 494; [1991] C.L.J. 401 (Bridge); [1991] Conv. 380 (Goudling); [1992] Conv. 32 (Smith).

(vi) Additional Protection against Forfeiture for Breach of a Covenant to Repair

10–035 Where a tenant is in breach of his covenant to repair he can claim the additional protection afforded by the Leasehold Property Repairs Act 1938. This act applies to leases for a period of more than seven years with a term of at least three years to run. In the event of a breach the landlord must serve a s.146 notice on the tenant informing him that he has a 28-day period in which to serve a counter-notice on him claiming the protection of the Act. When such a counter-notice has been served the landlord requires leave of the court before enforcing the covenant. In *Associated British Ports v CH Bailey Plc*[145] Lord Templeman explained that this leave will generally be granted if "the immediate remedying of a breach of the repairing covenant is required in order to save the landlord from substantial loss of damage which the landlord would otherwise sustain".[146]

(vii) The Effect of Forfeiture on Third Parties

10–036 The forfeiture of a lease will have detrimental consequences for third parties, such as sub-tenants and mortgagees, who derive their interest from the terminated tenancy. Such third parties are thus entitled to seek relief from the effects of forfeiture to protect their interests. Since the forfeiture of a lease automatically extinguishes[147] any sub-tenancies, s.146(4) of the Law of Property Act 1925 allows sub-tenants to apply independently for relief from forfeiture of the head-lease. The court is granted jurisdiction to:

> "make an order vesting, for the whole term of the lease or any less term, the property comprised in the lease or any part thereof in any person entitled as under-lessee to any estate or interest in such property upon such conditions as to execution of any deed or other document, payment of rent, costs, expenses, damages, compensation, giving security, or otherwise, as the court in the circumstances of each case may think fit, but in no case shall such under-lessee be entitled to require a lease to be granted to him for any longer term than he had under his original sub-lease."

This entitles the court to grant the sub-tenant a direct lease from the landlord when the original tenant's head lease is forfeited. The right to seek relief against forfeiture under s.146(4) of the Law of Property Act 1925 also extends to a mortgagee of a leasehold interest.[148] The statutory jurisdiction is not available if the landlord has obtained possession by proceedings[149] although in *Abbey National Building Society v Maybeech Ltd*[150] Nicholls J. held that the equitable jurisdiction was still available in such circumstances.

---

[145] [1990] 1 All E.R. 929.

[146] See also *Sedac Investments v Tanner* [1982] 3 All E.R. 646; *Hamilton v Martell Securities* [1984] 1 All E.R. 665.

[147] *Great Western Railway Co v Smith* (1876) 2 Ch.D. 235; *GMS Syndicate Ltd v Gary Elliott Ltd* [1982] Ch. 1.

[148] Since the mortgage may take effect by way of a long lease, thus creating a sub-tenancy, or in the case of a charge by way of legal mortgage the mortgagee has a sub-term by virtue of Law of Property Act 1925 s.87(1). See: *Grand Junction Co Ltd v Bates* [1954] 2 Q.B. 160.

[149] *Rogers v Rice* [1892] 2 Ch. 170; *Abbey National Building Society v Maybeech Ltd* [1985] Ch. 190.

[150] [1985] Ch. 190.

(b) *Distress*

Distress is an ancient common law remedy available to a landlord where his tenant is in **10–037** arrears of rent. It allows the landlord to seize and sell goods found on the leased premises to recover the rent arrears. A landlord does not require the sanction of the court in order to distrain, so distress is therefore a form of self-help remedy. However a number of statutory and common law restrictions restrict the availability and exercise of distress.

Distress is only available to a landlord as a remedy for a tenant's failure to pay rent and not for breach of other covenants. It is only available where the rent is in arrears, namely the day after it is due.[151] As a result of the Limitation Act 1980 the remedy will be unavailable for rent more than six years in arrears.[152] If distress is exercised where rent is not due the distress will be unlawful, as was argued to be the case in *Walsh v Lonsdale*.[153] In some instances distress cannot be exercised by the landlord without the leave of the court. The most important situation in which leave is required is where the tenant is a Rent Act tenant.

Distress may be exercised by the landlord personally, or by a certified bailiff. Distress cannot be exercised between sunset and sunrise[154] and access cannot be gained forcibly to the premises.[155] The landlord cannot break down an outer door[156] or enter via a closed window.[157] He may, however, enter by means of an unlocked door[158] or open window.[159] Once he has gained entry he is entitled to break down internal doors and partitions.[160] At common law the landlord is entitled to seize any goods physically present on the land. However, this general right is subject to the exception that some goods and categories of goods are regarded as privileged and are not available for distress. Some goods enjoy absolute privilege and are exempt from seizure. These include perishable goods,[161] things in actual use by the tenant at the time he seeks to distrain,[162] clothes and bedding of the tenant and his family to a value of £100,[163] tools of the tenant's trade to the value of £150 and money which is not in a closed purse or bag.[164] Other goods enjoy a qualified privilege and may not be seized unless without them there would be insufficient goods to recover the rent arrears. This category includes the tools and implements of a man's trade,[165] animals which are used to plough the land[166] and animals on the land which belong to a third party which the tenant is feeding commercially.[167] Goods belonging to third

---

[151] *Duppa v Mayo* (1669) 1 Wms Saund 275; *Re Aspinall* [1961] 1 Ch. 526.
[152] Limitation Act 1980 s.19. In the case of agricultural land only one years rent may be recovered; Agricultural Holdings Act 1986 s.16.
[153] (1882) 21 Ch.D. 9.
[154] *Aldenburgh v Peaple* (1834) C. & P. 212; *Tutton v Drake* (1860) 29 L.J. Ex. 271.
[155] *Khazanchi v Faircharm Investments Ltd* [1988] 2 All E.R. 901.
[156] *Semayne's Case* (1605) 5 Co. Rep. 91a; *American Concentrated Must Corp v Hendry* (1893) 62 L.J.Q.B. 388; *Cassidy v Foley* [1904] 2 I.R. 427.
[157] *Nash v Lucas* (1867) L.R. 2 Q.B. 590.
[158] *Ryan v Shilock* (1851) 15 Q.B.D. 312.
[159] *Crabtree v Robinson* (1855) 15 Q.B.D. 312; *Long v Clarke* [1894] 1 Q.B. 308.
[160] *Browning v Dann* (1735) Buller's NP (7th ed.) 81c.
[161] *Morely v Pincombe* (1848) 2 Exch. 101.
[162] *Pitt v Shew* (1821) 4 B. & Ald. 206.
[163] Law of Distress Amendment Act 1888 s.4; Protection from Execution (Prescribed Value) Order (SI 1980/26).
[164] *East India Co v Skinner* (1695) 1 Botts P.L. 259.
[165] *Nargett v Nias* (1859) 1 E. & E. 439.
[166] *Simpson v Hartropp* (1744) Willes 512.
[167] Agricultural Holdings Acts 1986 s.18.

parties which are on the land may also enjoy an absolute privilege. The goods of undertenants and lodgers are privileged under the Law of Distress Amendment Act 1908.

Once distress has been levied the landlord must give the tenant notice, informing him of the reason for the distress, the proposed date of sale of the goods and of where goods have been removed to.[168] The goods may be sold at least five days after the tenant has been given such notice. The landlord must obtain the best price possible and he cannot purchase the goods himself.

The Law Commission has examined distress a number of times.[169] Its abolition was recommended by the Payne Committee in 1969[170] and by the Law Commission in 1991[171] on the grounds that it is "riddled with inconsistencies, uncertainties, anomalies and archaisms". However, it was recognised that abolition was only practical if a more rapid court procedure was introduced for the recovery of arrears of rent. In *Fuller v Happy Shopper Markets Ltd*[172] Lightman J. emphasised that in exercising distress the landlord must take the greatest care that there are no claims on the part of the tenant which may be available by way of equitable set off to be offset against and satisfy the demand of rent. He suggested that in the ordinary case the landlord would be well advised to give notice of his intention and invite the tenant to agree what is owing to him and to inform him whether there are any cross claims and, if so, to identify them. He also warned of the potential human rights implications of exercising distress:

> "The ancient (and perhaps anachronistic) self help remedy of distress involves a serious interference with the right of the tenant under Article 8 of the European Convention on Human Rights to respect for privacy and home under Article 1 of the First Protocol to the peaceful enjoyment of his possessions. The human rights implications of levying distress must be in the forefront of the mind of the landlord before he takes this step and he must fully satisfy himself that taking this action is in accordance with the law."[173]

(c) *Damages for Breach of Covenant*

10–038   A landlord will be entitled to recover damages wherever the tenant is in breach of his covenants, except the covenant to pay rent. He is entitled to recover the contractual measure of damages for the loss that he has suffered. The object is to restore the landlord to the position he would have been in if the breach had not been committed.

The provisions of the Leasehold Property Repairs Act 1938, which have been discussed above, apply to the recovery of damages for breach[174] of repairing covenants as well as to forfeiture.[175] Section 1 of the Landlord and Tenant Act 1927 provides that any award of damages cannot exceed the diminution in value of the landlord's reversionary interest caused by the breach.

---

[168] Distress for Rent Act 1689 s.1; Distress for Rent Act 1737 s.9.
[169] Law Com. No.5, Interim Report on Distress for Rent (1966); Law Commission Working Paper No.97, Landlord and Tenant: Distress for Rent (1986).
[170] Report of the Committee on the Enforcement of Judgement Debts (Cmnd. 3909, 1969).
[171] Law Com. No.194, *Landlord and Tenant: Distress for Rent* (1991).
[172] [2001] 1 W.L. 171945; [2001] 1 W.L.R. 1681
[173] [2001] 1 W.L.R. 1681 at [27].
[174] Leasehold Property Repairs Act 1938 s.1.
[175] [1986] Conv. 85 (Smith).

(d) *Action for Arrears of Rent*

By s.19 of the Limitation Act 1980 a landlord cannot bring an action to recover rent "after the   **10–039**
expiration of six years from the date on which the arrears became due".

(e) *Specific Performance of Repairing Obligations*

Historically it was generally accepted that repairing covenants could not be specifically   **10–040**
enforced, irrespective of whether the obligation to repair fell on the landlord or the tenant.[176]
However, as was explained above, it is now clear that a tenant may obtain specific performance of a landlord's obligations to repair premises.[177] In *Rainbow Estates Ltd v Tokenhold
Ltd*[178] Lawrence Collins Q.C. held that there was no reason in principle why a landlord should
not be able to obtain an order for specific performance against a tenant who was in breach of
his repairing covenants. He stressed that it was important to ensure that the tenants were not
subject to injustice or oppression, and especially that unscrupulous landlords are prevented
from purchasing the reversion of a lease with the intention of misusing a schedule of
dilapidations to pressure the tenant. He concluded:

> "It follows that not only is there a need for great caution in granting the remedy against
> a tenant, but also that it will be a rare case in which the remedy of specific performance
> will be the appropriate one: in the case of commercial leases, the landlord will normally
> have the right to enter and do the repairs at the expense of the tenant; in residential
> leases, the landlord will normally have the right to forfeit in appropriate cases."[179]

ENFORCING COVENANTS IN LEASES AFTER ASSIGNMENT

It has been seen how the grant of a lease creates an estate in land, and that the precise terms   **10–041**
of a lease, comprising the covenants of the landlord and the tenant, create contractual obligations between the parties. It has also been seen that a tenancy and a freehold reversion may
be transferred to successors in title to the original landlord and tenant. However the differences between proprietary and contractual rights creates problems in respect of the enforceability of the leasehold covenants where the tenancy, freehold reversion, or both, have been
transferred. Historically the doctrine of privity of contract ensured that contractual obligations
were only enforceable between the parties to the contract. Although the benefit of a contract
is capable of being transferred to a third party, and the reforms introduced by the Contracts
(Rights of Third Parties) Act 1999 have enabled third parties to enforce contracts created for

---

[176] *Hill v Barclay* (1810) 16 Ves 402.
[177] *Jeune v Queens Cross Properties Ltd* [1974] Ch. 97.
[178] [1998] 2 All E.R. 860.
[179] [1992] 2 All E.R. 860 at 869.

their benefit, there is still no means by which the burden of a contract can be enforced against anyone other than the original contracting party. The law has therefore had to develop alternative mechanisms to ensure that the provisions of a lease are binding between successors in title to an original landlord and tenant. The relevant principles are an amalgam of contractual rules and property principles, supplemented by statutory provisions in the Law of Property Act 1925. An entirely new statutory regime was introduced to govern the enforceability of covenants in leases granted after January 1, 1996 by the Landlord and Tenant (Covenants) Act 1995.

1. Privity of Estate

10–042   The central concept developed by the common law to ensure the ongoing enforceability of leasehold covenants between successors in title to the original landlord and tenant was that of "privity of estate". This concept was recognised as long ago as *Spencer's Case*[180] and its essence was identified by Nourse L.J. in *City of London Corp v Fell*:

> "The contractual obligations which touch and concern the land having become imprinted on the estate, the tenancy is capable of existence as a species of property independently of the contract."[181]

The contractual obligations which form part of the lease between the original landlord and tenant are thus considered as attached to the leasehold estate which exists between them, and not as mere personal obligations arising under their contract. When the estate is transferred to others, whether by assignment of the tenancy or the freehold reversion, the covenants are enforceable between the transferees who stand in the same positions in relation to the estate as the original landlord and tenant. The operation of privity of estate was further explained by Lord Templeman when *City of London Corp v Fell* came before the House of Lords. He stated that the solution to the problem of enforceability of covenants between assignees of the original parties to a lease was:

> "to annex to the term and the reversion the benefit and burden of covenants which touch and concern the land. The covenants having been annexed, every legal owner of the term granted by the lease and every legal owner of the reversion from time to time holds his estate with the benefit of and subject to the covenants which touch and concern the land."[182]

The enforceability of leasehold covenants is therefore a combination of the principles of privity of contract and privity of estate. Between the original landlord and tenant all covenants are enforceable by virtue of their contractual relationship. Between successors in title to the original landlord and tenant, covenants which "touch and concern" the land are enforceable on

---

[180] (1583) 5 Co Rep. 16a.
[181] [1993] Q.B. 589 at 604.
[182] [1994] 1 A.C. 459

the basis of privity of estate. The interaction between these two principles was summarised by Nourse L.J. in *City of London Corp v Fell*:

> "A lease of land, because it originates in contract, gives rise to obligations enforceable between the original landlord and the original tenant in contract. But because it also gives the tenant an estate in the land, assignable, like the reversion, to others, the obligations so far as they touch and concern the land, assume a wider influence, becoming, as it were, imprinted on the term of the reversion as the case may be, enforceable between the owners thereof for the time being as conditions of the enjoyment of their respective estates. Thus landlord and tenant stand together in one or other of two distinct legal relationships. In the first it is said that there is privity of contract between them, in the second privity of estate."[183]

2. Covenants which "Touch and Concern" Land

As is evident from the judicial descriptions of privity of estate, it is clear that not all covenants of the original landlord and tenant are enforceable between their successors in title. Only those covenants which can be said to "touch and concern" the land are enforceable on the basis of privity of estate. The object of this requirement is to differentiate those contractual terms which are genuinely imprinted on the estate from those which are purely personal and should not be binding on the land.   **10–043**

It has proved difficult to provide a simple comprehensive test to determine whether a covenant is to be regarded as touching and concerning the land. In *Hua Chiao Commercial Bank v Chiaphua Industries* Lord Oliver adopted the formulations of *Cheshire and Burn's Modern Law of Real Property*[184]:

> "If the covenant has direct reference to the land, if it lays down something which is to be done or is not to be done upon the land, or, and perhaps this is the clearest way of describing the test, if it affects the landlord in his normal capacity as landlord or the tenant in his normal capacity as tenant, it may be said to touch and concern the land . . . If a simple test is desired for ascertaining into which category a covenant falls, it is suggested that the proper inquiry should be whether the covenant affects either the landlord qua landlord or the tenant qua tenant. A covenant may very well have reference to the land, but, unless it is reasonably incidental to the relation of landlord and tenant, it cannot be said to touch and concern the land so as to be capable of running therewith or with the reversion."[185]

In the subsequent case of *P & A Swift Investments v Combined English Stores Group* he went on to offer a number of practical considerations which would identify whether a covenant was to be found to touch and concern land:

---

[183] [1993] Q.B. 589 at 603–604.
[184] (13th edn, 1982), pp.430–431.
[185] [1987] A.C. 99 at 107. See also *Congleton Corp v Pattison* (1808) 10 East 130; *Horsey Estate Ltd v Steiger* [1899] 2 Q.B. 79.

"Formulations of definitive tests are always dangerous, but it seems to me that, without claiming to expound an exhaustive guide, the following provides a satisfactory working test for whether, in any given case, a covenant touches and concerns the land: (1) the covenant benefits only the reversioner for the time being, and if separated from the reversion ceases to be of benefit to the covenantee; (2) the covenant affects the nature, quality, mode of user or value of the land of the reversioner; (3) the covenant is not expressed to be personal (that is to say neither being given only to a specific reversioner nor in respect of the obligations only of a specific tenant); (4) the fact that a covenant is to pay a sum of money will not prevent it from touching and concerning the land so long as the three forgoing conditions are satisfied and the covenant is connected with something to be done on, to or in relation to the land."[186]

10–044   Many leasehold covenants will obviously "touch and concern" the land since they are clearly referable to the relationship between the landlord and tenant. Covenants of the tenant which clearly touch and concern the land include: covenants to pay rent[187]; to keep the demised premises in repair[188]; to insure against fire[189]; not to use the premises other than as a dwelling-house[190]; not to assign the tenancy without consent.[191] Similarly a landlord's covenants to provide quiet enjoyment, to supply water,[192] to repair, and not to build on adjoining land[193] touch and concern the land. An option granted by the landlord to the tenant to purchase the freehold of the premises has been held not to touch and concern,[194] but an option to renew the lease does touch and concern the land.[195] Covenants that involve purely personal matters between the landlord and tenant will not touch and concern the land. In *Thomas v Hayward*[196] a covenant by the landlord of a pub not to open another within half a mile was held to be personal because it did not affect the landlord's behaviour on the land he had let. However, a covenant by the tenant of a pub not to do anything that would cause a suspension of a licence was held to touch and concern the land.[197] A covenant not to employ a named person on business premises was held to touch and concern the land[198] whereas a covenant not to employ a particular class of people on the property was not.[199] A covenant to provide personal services for the landlord would not touch and concern the land. In *Gower v Postmaster-General*[200] a covenant by a tenant to pay the rates due on land owned by the landlord other than that which he had rented was held not to touch and concern the land. In *P & A Swift Investments v Combined English Stores Group*[201] the

---

[186] [1989] A.C. 632 at 642.
[187] *Parker v Webb* (1693) 2 Salk. 5.
[188] *Matures v Westwood* (1598) Cro. Eliz. 599.
[189] *Vernon v Smith* (1821) 5 B. & Ald. 1.
[190] *Wilkinson v Rogers* (1864) 2 De G.J. & Sm. 62.
[191] *Williams v Earle* (1868) L.R. 3 Q.B. 739.
[192] *Jourdain v Wilson* (1821) 4 B. & Ald. 266.
[193] *Ricketts v Enfield Church Wardens* [1909] 1 Ch. 544.
[194] *Woodall v Clifton* [1905] 2 Ch. 257; *Griffiths v Pelton* [1958] Ch. 205.
[195] *Phillips v Mobil Oil Co Ltd* [1989] 1 W.L.R. 888.
[196] (1869) L.R. 4 Exch. 311.
[197] *Fleetwood v Hull* (1889) 23 Q.B.D. 35.
[198] *Re Hunters Lease* [1942] Ch. 124.
[199] *Mayor of Congleton v Pattison* (1808) 10 East 130.
[200] (1887) 57 L.T. 527.
[201] [1989] A.C. 632.

question arose whether a covenant to act as a surety of tenant's obligations touched and concerned the land. When the original landlord had granted an underlease of premises to a company the defendants acted as surety and guaranteed that the undertenant would pay the rent and observe all the covenants. The original landlord assigned the freehold reversion to the plaintiffs and the undertenants became insolvent and defaulted on the rent. The House of Lords held that the plaintiffs, as successors in title to the original landlords, could recover the £4,250 arrears of rent from the defendants because the surety agreement was a covenant which touched and concerned the land and was therefore enforceable by them.[202] Lord Oliver explained that since the tenant's covenant, which was guaranteed by the surety, touched and concerned the land the covenant of the surety must also touch and concern:

> "if [the primary obligation] of the tenant touches and concerns the land that of the surety must, as it seems to me, equally do so."[203]

In *Hua Chiao Commercial Bank v Chiaphua Industries*[204] the Privy Council held that a landlord's obligation to repay a tenant's deposit paid at the beginning of a lease was purely personal and did not touch and concern the land. The original landlord and tenant entered an agreement for a five-year lease. One term of their agreement was that the tenant should provide two months' rent as a security deposit, returnable at the end of the term. The landlord assigned his interest to the defendant bank as part of a mortgage arrangement. At the end of the term the plaintiff tenant sought to recover the deposit from the bank since the original landlord was insolvent. Lord Oliver explained the conclusion of the Privy Council that the obligation to repay the deposit was purely personal between the contracting parties:

> "It certainly does not per se affect the nature quality or value of the land either during or at the end of the term. It does not per se affect the mode of using or enjoying that which is demised. . . . Whilst it is true that the deposit is paid to the original payee because it is security for the performance of contractual obligations assumed throughout the term by the payer and because the payee is the party with whom the contract is entered into, it is, in their Lordship's view, more realistic to regard the obligation as one entered into with the landlord qua payee rather than qua landlord . . . The nature of the obligation is simply that of an obligation to repay money which has been received and it is neither necessary nor logical, simply because the conditions of repayment relate to the performance of covenants in a lease, that the transfer of the reversion should create in the transferee an additional and co-extensive obligation to pay money which he has never received and in which he never had any interest or that the assignment of the term should vest in the assignee the right to receive a sum which he has never paid."[205]

The decisions in these two cases are extremely difficult to reconcile, because in *P & A Swift Investments v Combined English Stores Group*[206] the surety covenant was held to touch and

---

[202] See also *Coronation Street Industrial Properties Ltd v Ignall Industries plc* [1989] 1 W.L.R. 304.
[203] [1989] A.C. 632 at 642.
[204] [1987] A.C. 99.
[205] [1987] A.C. 99 at 112–113.
[206] [1989] A.C. 632.

concern because it was linked to the performance of other covenants which did touch and concern, yet the obligation to repay a deposit in *Hua Chiao Commercial Bank v Chiaphua Industries*[207] was held not to touch and concern even though its return was linked to the performance of covenants which did touch and concern. The central distinction seems to be that a right to repay money is purely personal against the recipient, whereas a guarantee of the performance of a third party's obligations is enforceable by whoever performance is owed to.[208]

3. The Enforceability of Covenants in Legal Leases Granted Prior to January 1, 1996

10–045 The practical operation of the relevant rules of privity of contract and privity of estate can now be examined as they relate to legal leases granted prior to January 1, 1996.

(a) *The Enforcement of Covenants between the Original Landlord and the Original Tenant*

10–046

Since the original landlord and tenant are parties to the contract formed by the lease, all the covenants are enforceable between them on the simple basis of their contract, whether they touch and concern the land or not.

(b) *The Enforcement of Covenants between the Original Tenant and a Successor in Title to the Original Landlord*

10–047

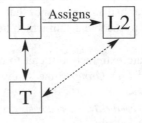

---

[207] [1987] A.C. 99.
[208] See also *Kumar v Dunning* [1989] Q.B. 193.

(i) Enforceability of the Landlord's Covenants by the Tenant against the Current Landlord

Although there is privity of estate between a tenant and an assignee of the freeholds reversion, the enforcement of the landlord's covenants has been placed on a statutory basis by s.142(1) of the Law of Property Act 1925. This has the effect that the burden of the covenants entered into by the original landlord pass with the assignment of the reversion, so that they are enforceable against him by the tenant. However, the statute only transfers the burden of covenants that are "with reference to the subject matter of the lease". This has been held to mean that the tenant may only enforce those leasehold covenants which "touch and concern the land" against the new landlord.[209] The new landlord will only be liable for breaches that occurred after the freehold reversion had been assigned to him. The tenant can therefore only seek a remedy for previous breaches against the landlord who had committed them.

10–048

(ii) Enforceability of the Tenant's Covenants by the Current Landlord

Section 141 (1) of the Law of Property Act 1925 has the effect that the assignee of the freehold reversion enjoys the benefit of every covenant of the tenant which has "reference to the subject matter" of the lease. This again means that the new landlord can enforce covenants which "touch and concern" the land against the tenant. It has been held that the effect of the assignment transfers to the assignee the exclusive right to seek remedies for breaches of covenant which occurred before the assignment took place.[210] Thus the current landlord will be the only person who is able to seek any remedy against the tenant, or indeed previous tenants, for breach of covenant. This means, for example, that if the tenant incurred arrears of rent before the freehold reversion was transferred, only the current landlord will be able to recover the arrears of rent from the tenant.

10–049

(iii) Continuing Contractual Liability of the Original Landlord to the Original Tenant

Where an original landlord has assigned his freehold reversion he remains liable to the original tenant in contract for any breaches of covenant, even those committed by the assignee, on the grounds of his continuing contractual liability under their contract.[211] The landlord will generally obtain an indemnity for any liability from the assignee, which will enable him to recover any compensation he may have to pay to the tenant for breaches committed, but this will prove ineffective if the assignee is insolvent.

10–050

---

[209] *Hua Chiao Commercial Bank v Chiaphua Industries* [1987] A.C. 99.
[210] *Re King* [1963] Ch. 459; *London & County (A & D) Ltd v Wilfred Sportsman Ltd* [1971] Ch. 764; *Arlesford Trading Co Ltd v Servansingh* [1971] 1 W.L.R. 1080.
[211] *Stuart v Joy* [1904] 1 K.B. 362.

(iv) Continuing Contractual Liability of the Original Tenant to the Original Landlord where the Freehold Reversion has been Assigned

10–051   Since s.141(1) of the Law of Property Act 1925 transfers the exclusive right to seek remedies for breach of covenants which touch and concern the land to the assignee of the landlord there is no continuing contractual liability between the original landlord and tenant. The tenant is only ever liable to the current landlord.

(c) *Enforceability between the Original Landlord and an Assignee of the Original Tenant*

10–052

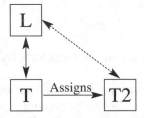

(i) Enforceability of the Tenant's Covenants by the Original Landlord against the Current Tenant

10–053   Since the original landlord and the assignee of the original tenant stand in privity of estate the covenants of the lease which "touch and concern" the land are enforceable between them. The assignee of the tenancy is only liable for breaches committed during the period of his tenancy, and he is liable neither for the breaches of his predecessors as tenant,[212] nor for the breaches of subsequent tenants after he has himself assigned the tenancy.[213] He remains liable to the current landlord for breaches committed during the period when he was the tenant even after he has assigned the lease such that he no longer stands in a tenant relationship.[214]

(ii) Enforceability of the Landlord's Covenants by the Current Tenant

10–054   Since there is privity of estate between the landlord and a successor in title to the original tenant, an assignee of the original tenant may enforce the covenants of the lease which touch and

---

[212] *Grescott v Green* (1700) 1 Salk. 199; *Granada Theatres Ltd v Freehold Investments (Leytonstone) Ltd* [1959] Ch. 592.
[213] *Onslow v Corrie* (1817) 2 Madd 330; *Paul v Nurse* (1828) 8 B. & C. 486.
[214] *J Lyons & Co Ltd v Knowles* [1943] K.B. 366; *Estates Gazette Ltd v Benjamin Restaurants Ltd* [1995] 1 All E.R. 129.

concern the land. In *Celsteel Ltd v Alton House Holdings Ltd (No.2)* it was suggested, both at first instance[215] and in Court of Appeal[216] that s.142(1) of the Law of Property Act 1925 has the effect that the original landlord remains liable to an assignee of the tenancy even where he has assigned his reversionary interest.

(iii) Continuing Contractual Liability of the Original Tenant to the Current Landlord

An original tenant who has assigned his tenancy remains liable to the original landlord in contract for any breaches of covenant, even those committed by his successors in title, on the grounds of his continuing contractual liability as a party to the lease. This means, for example, that the landlord will be able to recover any arrears of rent from an original tenant if his successors in title have failed to pay. In *Allied London Investments Ltd v Hambro Life Assurance Plc*[217] the plaintiff let premises to the defendant in 1972, and the defendant assigned his lease in 1973. In 1982 the assignee defaulted on the rent and it was held that the defendant was liable to the plaintiff for the arrears. An original tenant will even be liable for an assignee's failure to pay an increased rent agreed under the terms of the lease. In *Centrovincial Estates Ltd v Bulk Storage Ltd*[218] the original tenant had taken a lease for 21 years in 1965 at a rent of £17,000 per annum. The lease contained a provision to review the rent after 14 years and a new rent to be fixed by agreement between the parties. The tenant assigned his lease in 1978 and in 1979 the assignee agreed an increase in rent to £40,000 per annum with the landlord. The assignee subsequently defaulted on the payment of this rent and Harman J. held that the original tenant was liable to the landlord in contract for the arrears at the increased rent.[219] Similarly, in *Selous Street Properties Ltd v Oronel Fabrics Ltd*[220] the original tenant was held liable to pay a rent which had been increased because of improvements made by the assignee. An original tenant will also be liable to the landlord for any breach of a repairing covenant by an assignee, as was held in *Thames Manufacturing Co Ltd v Perrotts (Nichol & Peyton) Ltd*.[221] This contractual liability continues for the entire duration of the lease,[222] even if the lease is extended by the exercise of an option within it.[223] Obviously the continuation of contractual liability can impose a heavy burden on an original tenant, and breaches of covenant of a lease which was assigned many years before may come back to haunt him. The landlord can release an assigning tenant from such continuing liability but has little incentive to do so since this will reduce his own protection. The existence of continuing liability also acts as an incentive to ensure

10–055

[215] [1986] 1 W.L.R. 666.
[216] [1987] 1 W.L.R. 291.
[217] (1985) 50 P. & C.R. 207.
[218] (1983) 46 P. & C.R. 393.
[219] See also *Selous Street Properties Ltd v Oronel Fabrics Ltd* (1984) 270 E.G. 643; *Gus Property Management Ltd v Texas Homecare Ltd* [1993] 27 E.G. 130.
[220] (1984) 270 E.G. 643.
[221] (1985) 50 P. & C.R. 1.
[222] *Warnford Investments Ltd v Duckworth* [1979] Ch. 127.
[223] *Baker v Merckel* [1960] 1 Q.B. 657. In *City of London Corp v Fell* [1994] 1 All E.R. 458 the House of Lords held that a tenant's contractual liability did not continue after a statutory extension of a business tenancy.

that a tenant only assigns to a person who is likely to be able to perform the covenants of the lease. A tenant may obtain some protection for himself by obtaining an indemnity from his assignee and he has a right to restitution from the assignee if he is held liable for the assignee's breach.[224] In the event of a series of assignments there may well be a chain of indemnities. Such indemnities are implied by statute.[225] However, they provide the tenant with no protection if the assignee is insolvent, which may be the very reason he has breached his covenants. In *RPH Ltd v Mirror Group Newspapers and Mirror Group Holdings*[226] the plaintiffs were the original tenants of a lease which had been granted in 1970. The lease had been assigned three times to companies forming part of Robert Maxwell's business empire. First it was assigned to Mirror Group Holdings Ltd, which at the date of the action was insolvent, then to Mirror Group Newspapers, which remained solvent, and finally to Maxwell Communications Corp, which had defaulted on the rent. It was held that the plaintiffs were liable to pay the £1.5 million arrears of rent to the landlord even though they had assigned the lease more than 20 years previously. Their indemnity against Mirror Group Holdings was worthless because the company was insolvent, and although Mirror Group Holdings had an indemnity against Mirror Group Newspapers, which was solvent, the plaintiffs were not entitled to compel them to enforce it because the two indemnities were distinct. The plaintiff therefore had to bear the loss without the possibility of recourse against any of the assignees. Such far-reaching consequences of the continuing contractual liability between the original tenant and landlord were one of the major factors behind the reforms introduced by the Landlord and Tenant (Covenants) Act 1995, which has drastically curtailed the scope of such continuing liability in leases created after January 1, 1996.[227] However for leases outside of the scope of the statute the traditional rules continue to apply.

(d) Enforceability between Successors in Title to the Original Landlord and the Original Tenant

10–056

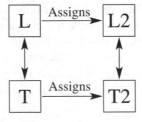

Where the interests of both the original landlord and original tenant have been assigned the covenants of the lease which "touch and concern" the land are enforceable between the current

---

[224] On the grounds of "legal compulsion". See *Moule v Garrett* (1872) L.R. 7 Exch. 101; *Selous Properties Ltd v Oronel Fabric Ltd* (1984) 270 E.G. 643; *Becton Dickinson Ltd v Zwebner* [1989] Q.B. 208.
[225] Law of Property Act 1925 s.77(1)(c); Land Registration Act 1925 s.24(1)(b).
[226] (1993) 65 P. & C.R. 252.
[227] See *Hindcastle Ltd v Barbara Attenborough Associate Ltd* [1996] 1 All E.R. 737.

landlord and tenant because they enjoy privity of estate. An assignee of the reversion of the tenancy is only liable for the breaches that he committed during the period of time that he stood in the position of landlord, and not for past or future breaches.

(e) *Enforceability between a Successor in Title to the Original Landlord and the Original Tenant where the Tenancy has also been Assigned*

10–057

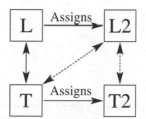

As has been noted above, it is clear that there is privity of estate between the successors in title to the original landlord and tenant, so that the landlord and tenant covenants which touch and concern the land will be enforceable between them. However, such a remedy may be of little practical value to the current landlord if the current tenant is insolvent. In such circumstances he may be able to enforce the covenants against the original tenant on the basis of his continuing liability under his contract with the original landlord.

The continuing contracted liability of the original tenant is not brought to an end when the original landlord assigns the freehold reversion. Rather, the assignee of the freehold reversion is entitled to the benefit of all the original tenant's covenants which touch and concern the land by virtue of s.141 of the Law of Property Act 1925. The assignee of the landlord may therefore enforce the covenants to that extent against the original tenant, even though the breach has been committed by an assignee of the tenancy. These principles were applied by the Court of Appeal in *Arlesford Trading Co Ltd v Servansingh*.[228] The defendant was the original tenant of a lease created in 1966. In 1969 he assigned the lease to his brother-in-law and a month later the landlord assigned the freehold to the plaintiffs. It was held that the plaintiffs could enforce the covenant to pay rent against the defendant who remained liable under his contract with the original landlord. The principle was stated by Russell L.J.:

> "an original lessee remains at all times liable under the lessee's covenants throughout the lease, and that assignment of the reversion does not automatically release him from that liability."[229]

---

[228] [1971] 1 W.L.R. 1080.
[229] [1971] 1 W.L.R. 1080 at 1082. See also *London and County (A & D) Ltd v William Sportsman Ltd* [1970] 3 W.L.R. 418.

(f) *The Enforcement of Covenants between the Landlord and a Sub-tenant*

10–058

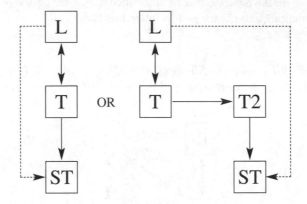

Where a tenant[230] has created a sub-tenancy there is no privity of estate between the landlord of the head-lease[231] and the sub-tenant. The tenant will be liable to his landlord for any breaches of covenant, and the sub-tenant will be liable to the tenant who granted him his sub-lease, but the landlord will be unable to obtain direct relief against the sub-tenant. However the fact that the landlord may be able to able to forfeit the head-lease if there is a breach of the tenants covenants, which will have the effect of destroying the sub-lease as well, provides an indirect means of enforcing the tenant covenants against a sub-tenant. Restrictive covenants of the lease may also be enforceable against the sub-tenant by the landlord by means of an injunction, as the burden of the covenant can pass to him under the equitable doctrine of *Tulk v Moxhay*.[232]

4. The Enforceability of Covenants in Equitable Leases Granted Prior to January 1, 1996

10–059 Where a lease is equitable rather than legal, or where there has been a merely equitable assignment of a legal lease, many of the same principles continue to operate. Thus the liability between the original parties is governed by their privity of contract, which will remain throughout the duration of the lease,[233] and the enforcement of the leasehold covenants between the original tenant and a successor in title to the original landlord assignee will be governed by ss.141 and 142 of the Law of Property Act 1925, which have been held to be equally applicable to equitable leases.[234] However there is some doubt as to whether the doctrine of privity of estate applies to equitable leases. Since the concept of privity of estate developed in *Spencer's Case*[235] was a creature of the common law, it has been questioned

---

[230] Whether the original tenant or an assignee of the tenancy.
[231] Whether the original landlord or an assignee of the reversion.
[232] (1848) 2 Ph. 774.
[233] *John Betts & Sons Ltd v Price* (1924) 40 T.L.R. 589.
[234] *Rickett v Green* [1910] 1 K.B. 253; *Weg Motors Ltd v Hales* [1962] Ch. 49.
[235] (1583) 5 Co Rep. 16a.

whether it should have any application to equitable leases. In *Purchase v Litchfield Brewery*[236] a tenant of a house under an equitable lease assigned his tenancy. The court held that there was no privity of estate and that therefore the assignees were not liable to the landlord for the rent. However the absence of privity of estate only prevents a landlord seeking to recover monetary remedies against an assignee. He will still be entitled to an injunction to restrain the assignee from breach of restrictive covenants in the lease, the burden of which passes in equity,[237] or to forfeit the lease by means of re-entry for breach.[238] Despite the authority of *Purchase v Litchfield Brewery*[239] it has been argued that the failure to extend privity of estate to equitable leases is anomalous. In *Boyer v Warbey*[240] Denning L.J. suggested that following the Judicature Acts the fusion of law and equity meant that there was no reason why the burden of leasehold covenants should not run with land in equity as well as in common law.[241] This conclusion is highly contentious since it is unlikely that the Judicature Acts effected such a fusion. An alternative possibility is that a new contract is implied between the landlord and the assignee when the assignee goes into possession and pays rent. If this is the case the covenants would be enforceable because of a new privity of contract between the landlord and the assignee. The possibility of such a conclusion seems to have been left open in *Purchase v Litchfield Brewery* where the judges stressed that the assignee had neither paid rent nor taken possession. These difficulties have been eliminated in relation to leases created after January 1, 1996 because the statutory regime introduced by the Landlord and Tenant (Covenants) Act 1995 is equally applicable to legal and equitable leases.

5. Enforceability of Covenants in Leases Granted after January 1, 1996

The traditional rules governing the enforceability of leasehold covenants were thoroughly examined by the Law Commission, which published a Report in 1988.[242] The Commission identified two central principles which it felt should underlie the law relating to the enforceability of leasehold covenants:

10–060

> "First a landlord or tenant of property should not continue to enjoy rights nor be under any obligation arising from a lease once he has parted with all interest in the property.
>
> Secondly, all terms of the lease should be regarded as a single bargain for letting the property. When the interest of one of the parties changes hands the successor should fully take his predecessor's place as landlord or tenant, without distinguishing between different categories of covenant."[243]

---

[236] [1915] 1 K.B. 184.

[237] *Tulk v Moxhay* (1848) 2 Ph. 774.

[238] In the case of unregistered land the assignee of the equitable lease will be bound by the restrictive covenant or right of re-entry as he is not a bona fide purchaser of a legal estate and therefore protected by the doctrine of notice. In the case of registered land a restrictive covenant or right of re-entry will constitute an overriding interest under s.70(1)(g) as the landlord is a person in receipt of the rent and profits of the land.

[239] [1915] 1 K.B. 184.

[240] [1953] 1 Q.B. 234.

[241] See also: [1978] C.L.J. 98 (Smith).

[242] Law Com. Report No.174, *Landlord and Tenant: Privity of Contract and Estate* (1988).

[243] Law Com. Report No.174, para.4.1.

The implementation of these cardinal principles would radically alter two foundations of the existing law. First, it would put an end to the continuing contractual liability of the original tenant to the original landlord or his assignees after the lease had been assigned. Secondly, it would mean the abolition of the limitation to enforceability on the basis of privity of estate to covenants which "touch and concern" the land. The Law Commission proposed that such reforms should be enacted to apply to both existing and new leases. However this recommendation was not followed, and a more limited reform was introduced by means of a private member's Bill in the Landlord and Tenant (Covenants) Act 1995. This Act radically reforms the rules of privity of estate and of continuing contractual liability, but it does not apply to all leases. In consequence the traditional rules and the statutory framework continue to operate side-by-side, thus complicating this field.

6. When does the Landlord and Tenant (Covenants) Act 1995 Apply?

10–061   By s.1(1) the provisions of the Act only apply to "new tenancies". A new tenancy is defined by s.1(3) as a tenancy "granted on or after the date on which this Act comes into force". Since the Act came into force on January 1, 1996 it will, subject to a number of exceptions, apply to all tenancies created since that date.[244] Where the terms of a lease are varied by the parties, and the law regards the variation as a deemed surrender and re-grant of the tenancy, there is in effect a fresh tenancy. This fresh tenancy falls within the scope of the Act.[245] Following *Friends Provident Life Office v British Railways Board*[246] such a surrender and re-grant is only likely to be deemed where the variation involves an increase in the property comprising the lease or the term extended. The provisions of the Landlord and Tenant (Covenants) Act 1995 are equally applicable to legal and equitable leases, since by s.28(1) a "tenancy" is defined to include "an agreement for a tenancy".

7. Statutory Transmission of the Benefit and Burden of Covenants

10–062   Section 3 of the Landlord and Tenant (Covenants) Act 1995 introduces a statutory framework governing the transmission and enforceability of the benefit and burden of leasehold covenants between successors in title to the original landlord and tenant of a lease. This places the traditional rules of privity of estate on a statutory footing. The limited statutory provisions in ss.141 and 142 of the Law of Property Act 1925 are superseded. Covenants are categorised as either "landlord covenants", which are covenants "falling to be complied with by the landlord of the premises demised by the tenancy", or "tenant covenants" which are covenants "falling to be complied with by the tenant of premises demised by the tenancy".[247]

---

[244] The Act does not apply to tenancies created after January 1, 1996 in pursuance of a prior agreement or court order (s.1(3)) or in pursuance of an option which had been granted before that date (s.1(6)).
[245] Landlord and Tenant (Covenants) Act 1995 s.1(5).
[246] [1995] 48 E.G. 106.
[247] Landlord and Tenant (Covenants) Act 1995 s.28(1).

(a) *The Annexation of Leasehold Covenants to the Demised Premises*

Section 3(1) provides that: **10–063**

"The benefit and burden of all landlord and tenant covenants of a tenancy—

(a) shall be annexed and incident to the whole, and to each and every part, of the premises demised by the tenancy and of the reversion in them, and

(b) shall in accordance with this section pass on an assignment of the whole or any part of those premises or of the reversion in them."

The most significant difference between the statutory scheme for the transmissibility of the benefit and burden of leasehold covenants to the assignees of the lease or the freehold reversion and the traditional rules of privity of estate is that the benefit and burden of covenants which do not touch and concern the land are also transmitted. The "touching and concerning" requirement is therefore completely eliminated. However covenants that were truly intended to be personal between a landlord and tenant will not be binding between successors in title. By s.3(6)(a) the rules of transmissibility do not apply to make a covenant enforceable "in the case of a covenant which (in whatever terms) is expressed to be personal to any person" against any other person. This means that such personal covenants must be expressly identified and such a characterisation will be not implied from the mere nature of the obligation a covenant imposes. The operation of this provision was considered by the Court of Appeal in *Chesterfield Properties Ltd v BHP Great Britain Petroleum Ltd*.[248] In this case a covenant by the original landlord of an office block agreeing to remedy any building work defects was expressly stated to be a personal obligation of the landlord in the terms of the lease. Jonathan Parker L.J. explained that such a personal covenant could not constitute a "landlord covenant" within the meaning of the Act since it does not fall to be performed by "the person who may from time to time be entitled to the reversion on the tenancy", which is the definition of a landlord in s.28(1). Whilst it is clearly correct that a personal covenant cannot bind a successor in title to the original landlord, the idea that a personal covenant cannot be a "landlord covenant" for the purpose of the Act renders s.3(6) superfluous to achieving this outcome.

(b) *Transmission of Covenants on Assignment by the Tenant*

Section 3(2) has the effect that, where a tenant assigns his tenancy, the assignee becomes   **10–064**
bound by the tenant covenants and becomes entitled to the benefit of the landlord covenants of the tenancy. The only exceptions are that the assignee will not be burdened by any covenants which did not burden the assignor immediately before the assignment,[249] nor by any covenants which affect any of the premises which are not assigned to him.[250] Similarly he does not enjoy the benefit of any covenants of the landlord which relate to premises not assigned to him.[251]

---

[248] [2001] EWCA Civ 1797.
[249] Landlord and Tenant (Covenants) Act 1995 s.3(2)(a)(i).
[250] Landlord and Tenant (Covenants) Act 1995 s.3(2)(a)(ii).
[251] Landlord and Tenant (Covenants) Act 1995 s.3(2)(b).

(c) *Transmission of Covenants on Assignment by the Landlord*

10–065   The same principles are mirrored where the freehold reversion is transferred. A successor in title to the landlord is bound by the landlord covenants and becomes entitled to the benefit of the tenant covenants. The assignee of the freehold reversion is similarly not bound by covenants which did not bind the assignor immediately before the assignment[252] and those which relate to part of the premises that have not been assigned to him.[253] Nor does he enjoy the benefit of covenants which do not relate to the land which has been assigned to him.[254] It should be noted that the assignment of a freehold reversion no longer has the automatic effect of transferring all of the assignor's rights of action against a tenant to the assignee.[255] By s.23 of the Act an assignee does not become entitled to any rights under the covenant arising prior to the time of the assignment, unless such rights are also expressly assigned. Thus if a landlord assigns his reversionary interests, and the tenant is in arrears of rent, in the absence of an express assignment the assignor remains the only person entitled to recover the arrears from the tenant. As the Court of Appeal noted in *Edlington Properties Ltd v Fenner & Co Ltd*,[256] s.3 has thus effected a change in the law. Unlike s.141 of the Law of Property Act 1925, the effect of the 1995 Act is to make the benefit and burden of covenants pass with the estate for the future but to leave past rights and obligations with the assignor.

8.   The Liability of Tenants after Assignment under Leases made after 1995

(a) *Automatic Release from the Tenant Covenants on Assignment*

10–066   As has been noted above, in the case of leases outside of the scope of the Landlord and Tenant (Covenants) Act 1995 the contractual liability of the original tenant to the landlord and his assignees continues even when he has assigned his tenancy. This continuing liability has now been removed for leases made after 1995 by s.5 of the Act. This section provides that where the tenant assigns the whole of the premises demised to him he is "released from the tenant covenants of the tenancy"[257] and "ceases to be entitled to the benefit of the landlord covenants of the tenancy".[258] An assignment of only part of the demised premises has the same effect to the extent that the tenant and landlord covenants "fall to be complied with in relation to [the assigned] part of the demised premises".[259] In *London Diocesan Fund v Avonridge Property Company Ltd*[260] the House of Lords held that the automatic release of the tenant from the ten-

---

[252] Landlord and Tenant (Covenants) Act 1995 s.3(3)(a)(i).
[253] Landlord and Tenant (Covenants) Act 1995 s.3(3)(a)(ii).
[254] Landlord and Tenant (Covenants) Act 1995 s.3(3)(b).
[255] In the case of tenancies created before January 1, 1996, the Law of Property Act 1925, s.141 had the effect of transferring all rights of action to the assignee save where provision was made to the contrary.
[256] [2006] EWCA Civ 403; [2006] 3 All E.R. 1200.
[257] s.5(2)(a).
[258] Landlord and Tenant (Covenants) Act 1995 s.5(2)(b).
[259] Landlord and Tenant (Covenants) Act 1995 s.5(3).
[260] [2005] UKHL 70.

ant covenant effected by s.5 cannot be excluded by express provision in the lease, for example by a clause providing that the original tenant's contractual liability should continue for the whole of the term. Such a provision would contravene the comprehensive anti-avoidance provision of s.25, because it would "exclude, modify or otherwise frustrate the operation of any provision" of the Act, and would be rendered void.

Since the tenant is automatically released from his covenants on assignment of the tenancy there will be no inherent liability for defaults committed by his assignees. The original tenant in such a case as *RPH Ltd v Mirror Group Newspapers and Mirror Group Holdings*[261] would no longer be liable for rent to the landlord where an assignee had defaulted. Similarly an original tenant would not be liable for an assignee's breaches of repairing covenants, as was the case in *Thames Manufacturing Co Ltd v Perrotts (Nichol & Peyton) Ltd*.[262] However, s.24(1) has the effect that the tenant remains liable to his landlord for any "liability of his arising from a breach of the covenant occurring before the release".

(b)   *Effect of Release of the Tenant on a Third Party Guarantor*

Where a third party has provided a guarantee of the tenant's performance of his covenants under the lease the release of the tenant from his covenants has the effect of releasing the guarantor to exactly the same extent.[263] Thus the guarantor will not be liable for breaches committed by the assignee, but will retain liability for any breaches committed by the tenant during his tenancy.   **10–067**

(c)   *Tenant's Continuing Rights against a Landlord in Breach after Release*

Although release from the tenant's covenants on assignment carries with it the corresponding cessation of entitlement of the tenant to the benefit of the landlord covenants, s.24(4) makes clear that "this does not affect any rights of his arising from a breach of the covenant occurring before he ceases to be so entitled". This means that he can maintain an action against the landlord for any breaches of covenant committed while he was the tenant. In *Edlington Properties Ltd v Fenner & Co Ltd*[264] the Court of Appeal held that the liability of a previous landlord to pay damages in respect of an accrued breach of covenant which occurred while he was the landlord does not run with the freehold reversion because it is a mere claim for money and not proprietary.[265] It was therefore held that a tenant was unable to set-off a claim for damages arising from a breach of covenant by a previous landlord who had performed defective building work against a demand for rent by the current landlord.   **10–068**

---

[261] (1993) 65 P. & C.R. 252.
[262] (1985) 50 P. & C.R. 1.
[263] Landlord and Tenant (Covenants) Act 1995 s.24(2).
[264] [2005] EWCA Civ 403; [2006] 3 All E.R. 1200.
[265] *Reeves v Pope* [1914] 2 K.B. 284; *Mortgage Corp Ltd v Ubah* (1996) 73 P. & C.R. 500; *Muscat v Smith* [2003] EWCA Civ 962.

(d) *Tenant may be Required to Grant an Authorised Guarantee Agreement*

10–069 Although the statutory cancellation of a tenant's liability on assignment of his lease prevents the unacceptable consequences of continuing contractual liability, it necessarily has a corresponding effect of reducing the protection afforded to the landlord. The possibility of continuing liability acts as a powerful incentive to a tenant to ensure that any assignment is only made to a tenant who is likely to be capable of meeting the obligations under the lease. For example, a tenant might think twice before assigning his interest to a company in danger of insolvency. In order to provide the landlord with some continuing protection and to provide tenants with a continuing incentive to make careful assignment decisions the Landlord and Tenant (Covenants) Act 1995 introduces a statutory system of guarantees, whereby a tenant who assigns his lease can be required by the landlord to execute a guarantee that the assignee will perform his obligations. In the event of default the landlord will have recourse against the assigning tenant not on the basis of any continuing contractual liability, but under the specific guarantee.

(i) Circumstances where an Authorised Guarantee Agreement can be Required

10–070 A valid authorised guarantee agreement can only be created in the circumstances outlined in s.16(3), namely if:

> "(a) by virtue of a covenant against assignment (whether absolute or qualified) the assignment cannot be effected without the consent of the landlord under the tenancy or some other person;
> (b) any such consent is given subject to a condition (lawfully imposed) that the tenant is to enter into an agreement guaranteeing the performance of the covenant by the assignee; and
> (c) the agreement is entered into by the tenant in pursuance of that condition."

An authorised guarantee agreement can never, therefore, be required where a lease does not contain a covenant against assignment. Since the landlord cannot unreasonably withhold consent for an assignment,[266] this means that the landlord's imposition of an authorised guarantee agreement as a condition of his consent must also be reasonable. In the case of a commercial lease[267] where the execution of an authorised guarantee agreement is expressly stated to be a condition of the grant of consent to assign, the Landlord and Tenant (Covenants) Act 1995 has amended s19 of the Landlord and Tenant Act 1927 so that the requirement of such a guarantee as a condition of consent cannot be regarded as unreasonable.[268]

---

[266] Landlord and Tenant Act 1927 s.19.
[267] i.e. non-residential leases: Landlord and Tenant Act 1927 s.19(1C).
[268] Landlord and Tenant Act 1927 s.19(1A).0

(ii) Enforceability of an Authorised Guarantee Agreement against the Direct Assignee Only

It is clear that an authorised guarantee agreement can only validly extend to a guarantee of **10–071** the obligations of the immediate assignee of the lease from the tenant executing it, and not to those of subsequent assignees. Section 16(4) provides:

"An agreement is not an authorised guarantee agreement to the extent that it purports—

(a) to impose on the tenant any requirement to guarantee in any way the performance of the relevant covenant by any person other than the assignee; or

(b) to impose on the tenant any liability . . . in relation to any time after the assignee is released from that covenant by virtue of this Act."

In other words, as soon as the assignee is no longer directly bound to the landlord by the tenant covenants in the lease, the former tenant who assigned his interest to him is no longer liable under the guarantee if the covenants are broken. Even where an authorised guarantee agreement is in place, s.17(2) provides that the former tenant will only be liable to pay any charge under that agreement if the landlord serves a notice on him within six months of the date that the charge became due informing him that the charge is now due and that he intends to recover form him the amount specified in the notice. The operation of this provision was recently considered by the in *Scottish & Newcastle v Raguz*.[269] This case concerned the liability of a former tenant under an authorised guarantee agreement to pay rent which was subject to a rent review process. The key question was whether the notice required under s.17(2) would have to be served within six months of the date that the rent became due, or six months of the date when the new rent had been determined by the review process, which might be some years later. The Court of Appeal held that the former tenant would only be liable to pay the rent if the notice was served by the landlord within six months of the date that the rent fell due, even though the review process had not been completed. The notice issued would then specify that the sum to be recovered was nil, but would note the possibility of the rent being determined to a greater sum. Lloyd L.J. noted that this procedure would be a burden to landlords, and could seem pointless and inconvenient to original tenants, but concluded that this was the only possible interpretation of the legislative language chosen for the provision.[270]

(iii) Authorised Guarantee Agreement does not Extend to Variations of the Lease Occurring after the Assignment

As was noted above, one of the harsh consequences of the continuing contractual liability of **10–072** a tenant was that he would be liable for breach of covenants even when they had been varied long after he had assigned his interest. In the case of covenants for rent this could mean that

---

[269] [2007] EWCA Civ 150; [2007] 2 All E.R. 871.
[270] ibid at [35].

he would be liable to pay an increased rent rather than the rent specified in the original lease, as happened in *Centrovincial Estates Ltd v Bulk Storage Ltd*.[271] The Landlord and Tenant (Covenants) Act 1995 introduces some limitations to the scope of a guarantor's liability under an authorised guarantee agreement where the terms of the lease are varied subsequently to the assignment. The general principle is that the former tenant is not liable for any amount "referable to any relevant variation of the tenant covenants".[272] Covenants are "relevant covenants" under, s.18(4) if:

(a) the landlord has, at the time of the variation, an absolute right to refuse to allow it; or

(b) the landlord would have had such a right if the variation had been sought by the former tenant immediately before the assignment by him but, between the time of the assignment and the time of the variation, the tenant covenants of the tenancy have been so varied as to deprive the landlord of such a right.

This complex provision has the following effect. First, the former tenant will be subject to increased liability where this is a consequence of the covenants of the lease itself, since such an increase will not constitute a "relevant variation". Most significantly this means that a former tenant will continue to be liable for rent increased under a rent review term in the lease after assignment. Secondly, the tenant will be freed from liability under his agreement where a variation amounts to an express or implied surrender or re-grant of the lease. This will include a variation by way of an increase in the term of the lease or of the extent of the demised property. Thirdly, he will not be liable under his agreement for any increased liability arising as a result of variations of the terms of the lease.

9. The Landlord's Liability after the Freehold Reversion is Assigned for Leases made after 1995

(a) *No Automatic Release from the Landlord Covenants*

10–073   Unlike the tenant, who is automatically released from his covenants on assignment by s.5, a landlord who assigns his freehold reversion is only freed from liability if he is actively released from his landlord covenants. Under s.8 the tenant alone is entitled to grant such a release. The effect of release is set out in s.6(2) of the Act, which provides that:

"If the landlord assigns the reversion in the whole of the premises of which he is the landlord—

(a) he may apply to be released from the landlord covenants of the tenancy in accordance with s.8; and

(b) if he is so released from all of those covenants, he ceases to be entitled to the benefit of the tenant covenants of the tenancy as from the assignment."

---

[271] (1983) 46 P. & C.R. 393.
[272] Landlord and Tenants (Covenants) Act 1995 s.18(2).

Section 6(3) provides for similar consequences where the landlord has assigned "part only of the premises of which he is the landlord" in which case he may be released from his landlord covenants and lose the benefit of the tenant's covenants "to the extent that they fall to be complied with" in relation to the part of the premises assigned. By s.8(3) any release from the landlord covenants is to be regarded as occurring at the date of assignment, even when the actual release was granted at a later date.

However the statutory provisions regarding the release of the landlord from the landlord covenant on the assignment of the freehold reversion may be supplemented by the inclusion of more generous provisions in the lease. In *London Diocesan Fund v Avonridge Property Company Ltd*[273] the House of Lords held that a landlord was entitled to curtail his liability under the landlord covenants from the outset of the lease, and that this would not contravene the anti-avoidance provisions of s.25 because it had never been the intention of the legislation to "close any other exit route already open to the parties".[274] In this case a landlord had granted a sublease containing a covenant for quiet enjoyment and for payment of the rent reserved by the head lease, but had specifically stated that it was not to be liable "after the Landlord has disposed of its interest in the property". The landlords subsequently assigned the head lease to a "man of straw" who disappeared leaving unpaid the rent due under the head lease. The House of Lords held that the original landlord's exclusion of liability was not rendered void by s.25, and that the tenants could not enforce the covenant against it.

(b) *Procedure for Obtaining Release from the Landlord Covenants*

(i) Application for a Release

Where a landlord seeks to be released from his landlord covenants on assignment of the freehold reversion by serving notice of the assignment on the tenant, s.8(1) provides that:

10–074

". . . an application for the release of a covenant to any extent is made by serving on the tenant, either before or within the period of four weeks beginning with the date of the assignment in question, a notice informing him of—

(a) the proposed assignment or (as the case may be) the fact that the assignment has taken place, and
(b) the request for the covenant to be released."

(ii) Release granted by Tenant's Counter-notice

By s.8(2)(c) the landlord will be released from his covenants if the tenant serves a notice in writing on him consenting to the release, to the extent mentioned in the notice.

10–075

---

[273] [2005] UKHL 70.
[274] [2005] UKHL 70 per Lord Nicholls.

(iii) Release Because of the Tenant's Failure to Respond to the Landlord's Notice

10–076   By s.8(2)(a) a landlord will be released from his covenants if he has requested release and the tenant does not "within the period of four weeks beginning with the day on which the notice is served, serve on the landlord . . . a notice in writing objecting to the release".

(iv) Tenant's Objection to Release

10–077   The landlord will not be released from his covenants if the tenant serves a counter-notice on him objecting to the release.

(v) Landlord's Application to the Court for a Declaration that Release is Reasonable

10–078   If the tenant serves a counter-notice on the landlord objecting to release the landlord is entitled under s.8(2)(b) to make an application to the county court,[275] and if appropriate the court may make a declaration that "it is reasonable for the covenant to be so released". The effect of such a declaration will be to release the landlord from his covenants.

(vi) Extension of Provisions Regulating Release from Landlord Covenants to "Former Landlords"

10–079   The provisions which govern the release of a landlord's covenants are also applicable in favour of a "former landlord" who had previously assigned his reversion but who "remains bound by a landlord covenant of the tenancy".[276] He will remain bound because, for whatever reason, he was not released from his landlord covenants when the tenancy was previously assigned. He is entitled to apply to the current tenant for release whenever the current landlord assigns the reversion. Whether he is released from his covenants is determined by the same provisions in s.8 as govern the release of the current assigning landlord.

(c) *Effect of Release on the Liability of a Landlord*

10–080   Where a landlord has been released from his covenants he will attract no liability for the acts of his assignee. However, by s.24(1) release will not affect his liability to the tenant for breaches of covenant committed beforehand. A landlord will not be released from his personal obligations to the tenant merely because he has been released from the "landlord

---

[275] Which has exclusive jurisdiction: Landlord and Tenant (Covenants) Act 1995 s.8(4)(c).
[276] Landlord and Tenant (Covenants) Act 1995 s.7(1).

covenants". In *Chesterfield Properties Ltd v BHP Great Britain Petroleum Ltd*[277] the Court of Appeal held that a landlord had not been released from the obligation to make good any building works defect which was expressly stated to be personal to him in the original lease. Even thought the freehold reversion had been assigned, and the landlord had been released from the "landlord covenants" because the tenant had not responded to the landlord's request to be released, he remained subject to the personal obligation.

(d) *Landlord's Continuing Rights against a Tenant in Breach after Release*

Although the release of a landlord from his landlord covenants has the effect that he ceases   **10–081**
from that moment to be entitled to the benefit of the tenant's covenants, s.24(4) makes clear that this "does not affect any rights of his arising from a breach of covenant occurring before he ceases to be so entitled". In other words the tenant will remain liable to him for breaches of covenant committed while he was the landlord.

---

[277] [2001] EWCA Civ 1797.

Chapter 11

EQUITABLE OWNERSHIP OF LAND

EQUITABLE OWNERSHIP IN ENGLISH LAND LAW

1. The Importance of Trusts in English Land Law

The preceding chapters have examined the two legal estates in land, namely the freehold and leasehold estates. These estates constitute the basis of legal ownership of land. However, in Chapter 3 it was explained how the Courts of Chancery developed the concept of the trust, whereby the owner of a legal estate in land holds it for the benefit of others, who are known as the beneficiaries. The beneficiaries of a trust are the equitable owners of the land. It follows that, where land is held on trust there is, in effect, a kind of "double ownership". The trustees are the legal owners, and they hold the land on trust for the beneficiaries, who are the equitable owners. Whilst the system of land registration was devised so as to keep the legal ownership of land as simple as possible, the complexities of land ownership take place behind the legal title through the mechanism of a trust. In order to gain a full understanding as to the ownership of land in English law it is therefore just as important to consider the equitable ownership as it is to identify the legal ownership.

11–001

2. Trusts and Shared Ownership of Land

The centrality of equitable ownership is evident from the fact that, under English law, all forms of shared ownership, whether concurrent ownership or successive ownership, must take place by way of a trust. For example, where a husband and wife wish to share the ownership of their matrimonial home this arrangement will have to be facilitated by means of a trust. Usually a husband and wife will be registered as joint proprietors of the legal title to their matrimonial

11–002

home, and will hold the property on trust for themselves jointly[1] or in equal shares. They will therefore be trustees of the legal title for themselves, and they will each have an equal entitlement to the beneficial ownership. There is, however, no necessity for people who are sharing the ownership of land to do so in equal shares. If, for example, a wealthy woman marries a relatively impoverished man, and they contribute unequally to the purchase of their matrimonial home, she may wish to ensure that she has a greater share of the ownership so as to reflect her greater contribution. They may thus be registered as joint proprietors of the legal title, but agree to share the equitable ownership in unequal proportions, for example the wife may insist on being entitled to three-quarters of the beneficial interest. In both these examples the same people own the legal title and the beneficial interest behind the trust, so that they are trustees for themselves. However this need not be the case. In *City of London Building Society v Flegg*,[2] for example, Mr and Mrs Maxwell-Browne were the joint proprietors of the legal title of a property which they held on trust for themselves and Mr and Mrs Flegg, who were Mrs Maxwell-Browne's parents.

Successive ownership must also take place behind a trust of the legal title. A life interest is an equitable interest in land which must take place behind a trust of the legal title. In fact the only situation in which a trust of land will not arise in English law is where there is a sole legal owner, who is solely entitled to it. In such circumstances the sole owner will be the registered proprietor of the land, and there will be no trust at all.

3. The Creation of Trusts of Land

11–003   Trusts of land may be created either expressly or by implication. Where the trust is created expressly the legal owner, or owners, of land declare that they are holding it on trust for specified beneficiaries, and stipulate the way in which the equitable ownership is to be shared. A couple who are living together and are about to purchase their first home may expressly declare that they will hold it on trust for themselves in equal shares. Alternatively, if a man moves in with a woman who is already the sole owner of a house, she may decide to declare that she is holding it on trust for them in equal shares. In this event she will remain the sole legal owner, but will hold the property on trust for herself and her partner in equal shares. Her partner will become entitled to a half-share of the beneficial interest in the land. However trusts of land may also arise by implication, so that the legal owner or owners hold it on trust even though they have not expressly declared that they are so doing. English law recognises two types of trust which arise informally in this way, resulting and constructive trusts. A resulting trust may be implied where a person has contributed to the purchase price of land. In the absence of a contrary intention, there is a presumption that the contributor will obtain a share of the equitable ownership proportionate to the contribution he or she had made to the purchase price. If, for example, a couple decide to buy a house together, and they each provide a half of the purchase price, but only one of them is registered as the proprietor, a

---

[1] The effect of joint ownership in equity is that when the first of the couple dies, the other becomes absolutely entitled to the property irrespective of the need to be given ownership of the matrimonial home under the laws of succession.

[2] [1988] A.C. 54.

resulting trust will be implied and the legal owner will hold the property on trust for them both in equal shares.[3] In contrast a constructive trust may arise where there was a common intention between the parties that the ownership of the land was to be shared, but the legal owner has not carried this intention into effect. Provided that the other party has acted to his or her detriment on the basis of the common intention, a constructive trust will be imposed to fulfil it. If, for example, a man and woman decide to move in together, and the man purchases a house in his sole name for them to live in, but tells the woman repeatedly that it is to be her house as much as his, and she acted to her detriment by making small contributions to the monthly mortgage payments, then this will give rise to a constructive trust and the man will hold the house on trust for himself and the woman in equal shares. The key difference between a resulting and a constructive trust is that the extent of the equitable interest obtained by way of a resulting trust is strictly limited to the value of the contribution to the purchase price, whereas the extent of the interest obtained by way of a constructive trust is determined by the nature of the common intention.

4. The Social Significance of Trusts of Land

It has been seen that trusts have a crucial role to play in determining the ownership of land, and in particular of enabling the ownership of land to be shared. The fact that resulting and constructive trusts can arise informally has been of great social importance, and the principles have evolved to take account of changes in society in regard to land ownership. **11–004**

In the early part of the twentieth century only a relatively small proportion of the population owned their own homes. The majority were tenants, either of private landlords or of the state in local authority housing. Most people cohabiting were married rather than "living in sin", and matrimonial homes were usually owned in the sole name of the husband. Wives were less likely to work, and therefore they often made little direct financial contribution to the purchase of the property. Divorce was rare, and it was often unnecessary for a wife to assert any proprietary entitlement to her matrimonial home, as it would never be in dispute between the parties. However, the traditional model of home ownership was increasingly rendered obsolete by post-war social changes. A rising divorce rate, women increasingly taking paid employment, and a lack of any statutory jurisdiction on the part of the courts to grant an unmarried partner a share of the family home on divorce, increasingly made it necessary for partners to assert an entitlement to a share of the equitable ownership of their home. The principles of resulting and constructive trusts enabled them to do so, either by demonstrating that they had contributed to the purchase price of the property, or by showing that there was a common intention that they were to share the ownership. Following the introduction of a statutory jurisdiction enabling the court to apportion the property of the parties on divorce, it became less necessary for wives to seek a resulting or constructive trust to protect their interests against their husbands. However the principles of resulting and constructive trusts proved capable of addressing other difficulties. Where a husband was the sole legal owner of a matrimonial home he would have the ability to mortgage the property without the permission, or even knowledge, of his wife. In such circumstances

---

[3] Unless there is evidence which rebuts the presumption that they intended to take equal shares.

the wife might claim entitlement of a share of the equitable ownership by way of a resulting or constructive trust so as to gain priority over the interests of the mortgage lender in the event that the mortgage could not be repaid. The principles of resulting and constructive trusts also took on greater significance as a consequence of the growing trend for couples to live together rather than to marry. Cohabitants are less likely to formalise the ownership of their home, and in the event of a breakdown of the relationship the court does not possess any jurisdiction to apportion their property between them, so that their entitlements must be determined by ordinary property principles. If, for example, a man moves in with a woman who already owns a house, and he helps make contribution to the mortgage repayments, or pays for a significant extension which increases the value of the property, he might obtain a share of the equitable interest by way of a resulting or constructive trust. Sometimes cohabiting couples fail to take steps to formalise their property rights because they mistakenly believe that they acquire such rights as a "common-law" husband or wife, whereas in fact no such relationship exists in English law. The nature of land ownership today is even more diverse and complex. Some 70 per cent of homes are now owned by one or more of their occupiers.[4] Whilst cohabitation continues to be a problem area where cohabitees fail to formalise their property rights, other types of shared ownership also cause difficulties. Increasingly a family home may be occupied by several generations simultaneously, for example as children continue to live with their parents, or elderly relatives come to live with their children. Elderly people or siblings may choose to live together, whether for comfort or companionship, or simply because it is too expensive to live in property alone. Resulting or constructive trusts may arise in such circumstances, for example where a child living at home makes contributions towards the payment of the mortgage, or where a child returns home to care for elderly parents, giving up a job or other opportunities on the basis of an expectation of gaining some share of the ownership of their house.

The principles of resulting and constructive trusts have therefore evolved, and are evolving, to meet changing social needs. As will be seen, they have often been criticised on the grounds that they have not been sufficiently progressive or responsive to the needs of society. The Law Commission has published a series of reports conducting an extensive review of the current law, proposing a number of modifications and clarifications,[5] and proposing a scheme of discretionary relief and property adjustment for cohabitants on breakdown of their relationship.[6] The proposed scheme would only apply to couples and not to co-habitation in any wider context such as that discussed at the end of the previous paragraph.

5.   The Nature of a Trust of Land

11–005   It has been seen how trusts are central to the ownership of land. Where land is held on trust, issues arise as to the respective rights and roles of the trustees and beneficiaries. The nature of the relationship between the trustees and beneficiaries will be examined in detail in the next chapter, whereas this chapter will largely explain how trusts of land are created.

---

[4] Law Commission, *Sharing Homes A Discussion Paper* (Law Com. No.278), 2002, para.1.7.

[5] Law Commission, *Sharing Homes: A Discussion Paper* (Law Com. No.278 (2002)).

[6] Law Commission, *Cohabitation: The Financial Consequences of Relationship Breakdown* Consultation Paper No.179 (2006); Law Commission, *Cohabitation: The Financial Consequences of Relationship Breakdown* (Law Com. No.307 (2007)).

(a) A Statutory Regime

Although personal property is equally capable of being held on trust, trusts of land are especially **11–006** significant and are subject to special statutory regimes. Under the Law of Property Act 1925 all forms of shared concurrent ownership of land took effect under a special form of trust known as a "trust for sale." Successive interests in land where there is some form of life estate, or other estates which cannot take effect at law as a consequence of s.1(1) of the Law of Property Act 1925, such as the determinable fee simple, took effect either under an express trust for sale or under the provisions of the Settled Land Act 1925 as a "strict settlement" of the land. However, following sustained criticism of this dual system over many years, and especially of the inappropriateness of the trust for sale as a vehicle for land holding, a single unitary statutory "trust of land" was introduced by the Trusts of Land and Appointment of Trustees Act 1996. This Act regulates the relationship between the trustees and beneficiaries where land is held on trust, defining their powers, duties and rights.

(b) Function of the Trustees of Land

The trustees of a trust generally enjoy the full legal ownership of the estate in the land to **11–007** which the trust relates.[7] Either a freehold or leasehold estate may be subject to a trust. By virtue of this ownership a trustee possesses the same powers of management and disposition over the property as would be held by an absolute owner unencumbered by the trust. This is confirmed by s.6(1) of the Trusts of Land and Appointment of Trustees Act 1996 which provides that:

> "For the purposes of exercising their functions as trustees, the trustees of land have in relation to the land subject to the trust all the powers of an absolute owner."

The trust does not ordinarily affect the trustee's capacity to deal with the land. As Lord Browne Wilkinson pointed out in *Hammersmith LBC v Monk*:

> "The fact that a trustee acts in breach of trust does not mean that he has no capacity to do the act he wrongly did."[8]

However, the terms of the trust impose obligations upon the trustee as to how he should deal with the property, and often more importantly how he should refrain from dealing with it. For example, it is clear that a trustee should not sell the land to a friend at a substantial undervalue in order to defeat the interests of the beneficiaries. If the trustees breach their obligations, and deal with the property in a manner inconsistent with the terms of the trust, the beneficiaries will be entitled to remedies against them for breach of trust.

---

[7] An equitable trust interest may itself form the subject matter of a trust, which is known as a sub-trust.
[8] [1992] 1 A.C. 478 at 493.

(c)   *Nature of the Beneficiaries' Interest Under a Trust*

(i)   A Proprietary Right in the Land

11–008   Where an estate in land is held on trust the beneficiaries enjoy rights to the trust property which are best considered as a form of ownership. It is clear from *Saunders v Vautier*[9] that the beneficiaries of a trust can demand that the trustees transfer the full legal title to them if they unanimously ask for it to be transferred.[10] The interests of the beneficiaries behind the trust can be dealt with in many of the ways that are indicative of a proprietary right. For example, the beneficiary can transfer his equitable interest to another person, whether by sale or as a gift, provided that he observes the necessary formalities for the transfer.[11] When he dies his beneficial interest can be validly disposed of by will, or pass under the rules of intestate succession. Most significantly his beneficial interests in the land are capable of enduring a change of ownership of the legal title. This capacity to endure changes of ownership was identified as the defining characteristic of property rights by Lord Wilberforce in *National Provincial Bank Ltd v Ainsworth*.[12] An example of the enduring character of beneficial interests can be seen in *Williams & Glyn's Bank v Boland*,[13] where a husband held a house on trust for himself and his wife. The husband alone was registered as the owner. The husband mortgaged the house without his wife's knowledge or consent. The House of Lords held that the wife's rights to equitable ownership were enforceable against the bank. The bank took subject to the wife's rights because she was living in the house, which meant that her beneficial interest in the land was an overriding interest under the provisions of the Land Registration Act 1925.

However the equitable ownership of the beneficiaries of a trust of land is not as durable as the legal ownership. Under the traditional doctrine of notice a bona fide purchaser of a legal estate for value without notice would take the land free from any pre-existing trust interests, which would thus be destroyed. This qualification has been the cause of much debate as to whether a trust interest is to be regarded as a genuine property right in rem. Maitland argued that equity had never regarded the beneficiary of a trust as the "owner" since the trust merely entitled him to enforce a personal obligation against the trustee to carry out the terms of the trust. He explained that:

> "[the trustee] is the owner, the full owner, of the thing, while the [beneficiary] has no rights in the thing . . ."[14]

However the whole character of beneficial interests behind trusts, and the ability of the beneficiaries to transfer them, is suggestive of a genuine property right, albeit one qualified to some extent by the doctrine of notice (and now the statutory rules concerning registered land).

---

[9] (1841) 4 Beav. 115.
[10] In order to do this they must all be of age and legally competent.
[11] Law of Property Act 1925 s.53(1)(c).
[12] [1965] A.C. 1175.
[13] [1981] A.C. 487.
[14] Maitland, *Equity*, p.17.

Even Maitland himself eventually came to the conclusion that more than a mere personal obligation was involved:

> ". . . I believe that for the ordinary thought of Englishmen 'equitable ownership' is just ownership pure and simple, though it is subject to a peculiar, technical and not very intelligible rule in favour of bona fide purchasers[15] . . . so many people are bound to respect these rights that practically they are almost as valuable as if they were dominium."[16]

It should be noted that not even legal ownership is absolute in its nature, so that third parties may defeat the interests of the legal owner. As has been seen, a person may effectively defeat the interests of the owner of an estate of land, whether freehold or leasehold, by means of adverse possession. Similarly, in the case of money the legal owner loses his ownership the moment that it becomes mixed with other money so that it is no longer identifiable.[17] These examples illustrate that if the defining characteristic of a property right is that it is absolutely indefatigable then there is no such thing as a proprietary right in English law. The better approach is that taken by Lord Browne-Wilkinson in *Tinsley v Milligan* who assimilated the proprietary character of legal and beneficial ownership:

> "Although for historical reasons legal estates and equitable estates have differing incidents, the person owning either type of estate has a right in property, a right in rem not merely a right in personam."[18]

(ii)   A Right to Occupy the Land

One question which has arisen in respect of trusts of land is whether the beneficiaries enjoy a right to occupy the land by virtue of their beneficial interest. Such a right of occupation would be indicative of a proprietary interest in the land itself. Historically this question was complicated by the uncertain impact of the doctrine of conversion. Since the majority of land held on trust was held under a "trust for sale", the key characteristic of which was the duty of the trustees to sell the land, an application of the doctrine of conversion would have the effect of treating the beneficiaries' interests as only arising in any potential proceeds of sale of the land and not in the land itself.[19] However, given the reality that most trusts of land have the practical object of enabling the beneficiaries to live in the property, the courts moved away from the full implications of the doctrine of conversion and regarded the beneficiaries as enjoying rights in the land itself and not merely the proceeds of sale. In *Williams & Glyn's Bank Ltd v Boland* Lord Wilberforce considered that:

11–009

> ". . . to describe the interests of spouses in a house jointly bought to be lived in as a matrimonial home as merely an interest in the proceeds of sale . . . is just a little unreal".[20]

---

[15] In other words, purchasers of a legal estate protected from earlier equitable interests by the doctrine of notice.
[16] *Collected Papers*, Vol. III, p.349.
[17] See *Taylor v Plumer* (1815) 3 M. & S. 562; *Agip (Africa) Ltd v Jackson* [1990] Ch. 265.
[18] [1993] 3 All E.R. 65 at 86.
[19] *Irani Finance Ltd v Singh* [1971] Ch. 59.
[20] [1981] A.C. 487 at 507.

In *City of London Building Society v Flegg*[21] the House of Lords held that the beneficiary of a trust for sale had the right to occupy the land. This more recent approach has now been placed on a statutory basis by the Trusts of Land and Appointment of Trustees Act 1996. Section 3 abolishes the doctrine of conversion completely and s.12(1) provides that, subject to limited exceptions:

> "a beneficiary who is beneficially entitled to an interest in possession in land subject to a trust of land is entitled by reason of his interest to occupy the land at any time."

EXPRESS TRUSTS OF LAND[22]

1. The Effect of an Express Declaration of Trust

11–010
An express trust of land is created by the deliberate intention of the legal owner, or owners, who declare a trust in favour of specified beneficiaries. The declaration of trust will both state the identity of the beneficiaries, and stipulate the proportions in which they are to share the beneficial ownership. An express trust will most commonly be declared when joint owners purchase land together, and the declaration will determine how the ownership of the land is to be shared. Where an express declaration has been made the beneficial interests in the land are determined by the terms of the declaration and there is no room for the operation of the principles of resulting or constructive trusts. In *Goodman v Gallant*,[23] for example, Mr Goodman and Mrs Gallant, who were living together, purchased a house together by acquiring the half share of Mrs Gallant's former husband. The transaction was completed by a transfer of the legal estate to Mr Goodman and Mrs Gallant with an express declaration that they held the property "on trust for themselves as joint tenants". When the relationship between Mr Goodman and Mrs Gallant broke down, Mrs Gallant argued that because she already had a half share, the effect of acquiring her ex-husband's share was to give her three quarters of the beneficial ownership. The Court of Appeal held that the express declaration of trust meant that they held the land on trust for themselves jointly, and that (unless Mrs Gallant could show that the declaration had been obtained through fraud or mistake) the extent of their contribution to the purchase price was therefore irrelevant.

The courts have expressed a strong preference for encouraging people who are purchasing property together to think about how they want the ownership to be shared, and to execute a declaration of trust accordingly. This will prevent subsequent uncertainty as to the equitable ownership of the land. In *Carlton v Goodman* Ward L.J. said:

> "I ask in despair how often this court has to remind conveyancers that they would save their clients a great deal of later difficulty if only they would sit the purchasers down,

---

[21] [1988] A.C. 54.
[22] See Pearce and Stevens, *The Law of Trusts and Equitable Obligations*, (4th edn., 2006), Ch. 6.
[23] [1986] Fam. 106.

explain the difference between a joint tenancy and a tenancy in common, ascertain what they want and then expressly declare in the conveyance of transfer how the beneficial interest is to be held because that will be conclusive and save all argument. When are conveyancers going to do this as a matter of invariable standard practice? This court has urged that time after time. Perhaps conveyancers do not read the law reports. I will try one more time: ALWAYS TRY TO AGREE ON AND THEN RECORD HOW THE BENEFICIAL INTEREST IS TO BE HELD. It is not very difficult to do."[24]

The Law Commission also concluded that it was desirable to encourage people to make express declarations of their beneficial entitlement in land whenever possible in its discussion paper *Sharing Homes*.[25] The Land Registry has introduced a requirement that those who purchase land as joint proprietors should stipulate their beneficial entitlements, and this may have the effect of reducing the scope for disputes in the future.[26]

2. Requirements of an Express Inter Vivos Declaration of a Trust of Land

(a) *An Intention to Create a Trust*

A trust of land will be expressly declared whenever the legal owner makes clear that he **11–011** intends to hold the land for the benefit of someone else. There is no need for the owner to use technical language to declare the trust.[27] As Scarman L.J. stated in *Paul v Constance*[28]:

> "there must be clear evidence from what is said or done of an intention to create a trust."

In practice the vast majority of express declarations of trust will be executed by legal practitioners on behalf of their clients and they will therefore clearly state an intention to create a trust.

(b) *Formalities*

There are no formalities required for a declaration of a trust of land. An oral declaration of trust **11–012** will be perfectly valid.[29] However the Law of Property Act 1925 renders a declaration of a trust of land unenforceable unless it is evidenced in writing. Section 53(1)(b) provides that:

---

[24] [2002] EWCA 545 at [44].
[25] Law Com. No.278, (2002), *Sharing Homes*: A Discussion Paper, para.2.52.
[26] *Stack v Dowden* [2007] 2 A.C. 432, per Baroness Hale at para.52.
[27] *Richards v Delbridge* (1874) L.R. 18 Eq. 11; *Re Kayford* [1975] 1 W.L.R. 279.
[28] [1977] 1 W.L.R. 527.
[29] *Gardener v Rowe* (1828) 5 Russ. 258; *Gissing v Gissing* [1969] 2 Ch. 85; *Cowcher v Cowcher* [1972] 1 W.L.R. 425; *Midland Bank Plc v Dobson* [1986] 1 F.L.R. 171.

"a declaration of a trust respecting any land or any interest therein must be manifested and proved by some writing signed by some person who is able to declare such trust or by his will."

The courts will therefore only enforce a declaration of trust if it is evidenced by some written documentation, containing all the material terms of the trust,[30] which is signed by the legal owner. This writing need not be contemporaneous with the declaration of the trust.[31] These requirements date back to the Statute of Frauds of 1677 and are intended to protect the legal owner of land against false claims that he had declared a trust.

(c) Transfer of the Legal Title to the Trustee

11–013 If the legal owner of land declares that he will henceforth hold the land on trust for specified beneficiaries no further action is necessary to bring the trust into existence. However the legal owner may intend to create an express trust by transferring the land to a third party, and declaring that the third party is to hold the land on trust for specified beneficiaries. In such circumstances the mere fact of a declaration will not create a trust. The trust will only come into existence when the land is transferred to the third party who is intended to hold it as trustee. This process is described as the constitution of the trust. The legal owner who wishes to create the trust must effectively transfer the legal title to the trustee. The transfer of the land will have to be completed by registration of the trustee as proprietor on the land register. However the creation of the trust is treated as effective from the moment that the transferee has done everything in his power to transfer the legal title to the transferor. This principle was established in *Re Rose*[32] in the context of a transfer of shares, but was applied to registered land in *Mascall v Mascall*.[33] A father wanted to transfer registered land to his son and completed the Land Registry transfer form. He then handed the form to his son, who needed to send it to the Land Registry to complete the transfer by registration. The Court of Appeal held that since the father had done all that he was required to do when he had handed the completed form to the son the transfer of the land was to be treated as effective from that moment and the father could not change his mind. Although the case involved a transfer of absolute title the principle would be equally applicable to a transfer on trust. If the son had been intended to take the land on trust the beneficiaries would have been entitled to equitable interests in the land from the moment that the father handed the completed form to his son.

(d) Enforcement of an Express Trust of Land even where the Necessary Formalities have not been Observed

11–014 Although s.53(1)(b) of the Law of Property Act 1925 appears to render an express declaration of trust unenforceable in the absence of appropriate writing, equity is unwilling to allow

[30] *Smith v Matthews* (1861) 3 De G.F. & J. 139; *Rochefoucauld v Boustead* [1897] 1 Ch. 196.
[31] *Forster v Hale* (1798) 3 Ves. 696; *Rochefoucauld v Boustead* [1897] 1 Ch. 196.
[32] [1952] Ch. 499.
[33] (1984) 50 P. & C.R. 119.

the statute to be used as an instrument of fraud. In some circumstances equity is willing to enforce a trust despite the absence of writing. This principle was developed in *Rochefaucauld v Boustead*.[34] Land in Ceylon was transferred to the defendant with the intention that it was to be held on trust for the Comtesse de la Rochefaucauld. The defendant subsequently mortgaged the land and the Comtesse sought a declaration that the defendant had acquired the land as a trustee. He claimed that the trust was unenforceable because of the absence of writing.[35] The Court of Appeal held that the existence of the trust could be proved by oral evidence, since to allow the defendant to rely on the lack of writing would be to permit him to commit a fraud against the Comtesse. The principle was explained by Lindley L.J.:

> "...the Statute of Frauds does not prevent the proof of a fraud; and it is a fraud on the part of a person to whom land is conveyed as a trustee, and who knows it was so conveyed, to deny the trust and claim the land himself. Consequently, notwithstanding the statute, it is competent for a person claiming land conveyed to another to prove by parol evidence that it was so conveyed upon trust for the claimant, and that the grantee, knowing the facts, is denying the trust and relying upon the form and conveyance and the statute, in order to keep the land himself."[36]

The application of what has become known as the rule in *Rochefaucauld v Boustead* has the clear merit of preventing injustice between the parties, but it also runs counter to the wording of the statute and has the danger of rendering the requirement of writing virtually irrelevant. In more recent cases such as *Bannister v Bannister*[37] an attempt has been made to explain the principle as resting on the doctrine of constructive trusts, so that in the absence of writing the court imposes a constructive trust on the land in the hands of the transferee who knew that he was intended to take it only as a trustee. This analysis has the advantage that it does not offend against the statute because s.53(2) of the Law of Property Act 1925 states that s.53(1)(b) has no application to the creation of constructive trusts. However, a mere shift of semantics should not hide the reality, which is that the court is in effect upholding and enforcing a trust obligation where the statutory requirement has not been met. The Court of Appeal in *Rochefaucauld v Boustead*[38] clearly thought that it was enforcing an express trust despite the absence of writing.

3. Express Trusts Void for Reasons of Perpetuity

(a) *Future Interests and the Problem of Perpetuity*

Following the legislation of 1925, and especially s.1(1) of the Law of Property Act 1925, which provides that only the fee simple absolute in possession and term of years absolute are

11–015

---

[34] [1897] 1 Ch. 196.
[35] Under what was then Statute of Frauds s.7.
[36] [1897] 1 Ch. 196 at 206.
[37] [1948] 2 All E.R. 133. See also *Neale v Willis* (1968) 19 P. & C.R. 836; *Re Densham* [1975] 1 W.L.R. 1519.
[38] [1897] 1 Ch. 196.

capable of existing as legal estates, all successive and future interests created after 1925 must take effect behind a trust. Future interests in land are interests which do not vest in an owner at the moment that they are granted, but are dependent upon some future contingency. For example, if a testator leaves land to "my first grandchild to be called to the Bar" this does not create a gift which is vested in anyone at the date of the testator's death. Similarly, if the owner of land were to transfer it to "my son for life, remainder to my first grandchild to be called to the Bar" the grant would not vest in its entirety at the date of the transfer. Either gift would only become vested when the contingency occurred, namely that a grandchild was called to the Bar.[39]

Where a gift is contingent it will only be valid if it does not offend the rule against perpetuities. This long-established rule (now modified by statute) operates to render a grant of a future contingent interest void if it is possible that it will not vest within the recognised perpetuity period. The rule is designed to prevent uncertainty as to the ownership of land, and also to prevent an owner of land predetermining its ownership beyond his death for an unacceptably long time. For example, if the owner of land were permitted to leave it to his son for life, remainder to his eldest grandson for life, remainder to his eldest great-grandson for life, remainder to his great-great grandson for life, this would have the effect of dictating the ownership of the land for four generations. Until statutory changes were made, it also potentially prevented the land from being sold.[40] Although this might facilitate an intention to keep the land within the family, it is not economically efficient that the land cannot be sold to a person who would derive a greater utility from it. The grant is likely to infringe the rule against perpetuities.[41] An exhaustive treatment of the rule is outside of the scope of this book and a more detailed consideration can be found elsewhere.[42] At common law the perpetuity period is defined as the period of a "life or lives in being at the date of the grant plus a further period of 21 years". A central question arises as to which life is to act as the "measuring life" of a contingent gift. The measuring life must be in existence at the date that the grant is made, either on the death of the testator if it is made by will, or at the time that an inter vivos grant is made. The grant may itself specify a "measuring life", and it is not necessary that the measuring life has any interest in the gift at all. It has been common to utilise a "royal lives clause" which nominates the life of the longest surviving lineal descendant of the monarch who is alive at the date of the grant. For example in *Re Villar*[43] a testator's gift to "such of my descendants as are living 20 years after the death of the last survivor of the lineal descendants of Queen Victoria living at my death" was valid as it did not offend the perpetuity period. However, it must be possible to ascertain without difficulty the date of death of the nominated life.[44] Often the relevant life will be that of the grantee or other persons expressly or impliedly mentioned in the grant and alive at the date that it takes effect. For example, if a testator

---

[39] Obviously the gift would not be contingent if there were a grandchild who had been called to the Bar, since it would be vested in that grandchild.

[40] Because it is only possible for successive interests in land to exist by means of a trust, with the trustees having the power to sell the land and to overreach the interests of the beneficiaries, the problem of inalienability no longer exists.

[41] It is difficult to envisage circumstances where the rule would apply to resulting or constructive trusts.

[42] See Cheshire and Burn, *Modern Law of Real Property*, (15th edn., 1994), pp.275–333; Gray, *Elements of Land Law* (2nd edn., 1993), pp.645–672; Riddall, *Introduction to Land Law* (5th edn., 1993).

[43] [1929] 1 Ch. 243.

[44] *Re Moore* [1901] 1 Ch. 936; *Re Warren's Will Trusts* (1961) 105 Sol. Jo. 511.

leaves land to "my first grandchild to be called to the Bar" the testator's own children and grandchildren living at the date of his death will be "lives in being" for the purposes of the rule against perpetuities, but not any grandchildren born subsequent to his death.

(b) *Application of the Common Law Rule Against Perpetuities*

At common law a grant of a contingent interest would be void ab intio if there was any **11–016** possibility at all that the gift could vest outside of the perpetuity period. It was irrelevant that the events that would have to happen to lead to such a result were wholly unlikely or improbable. For example, if a testator left land by will to "Albert for life, remainder to the first of Albert's sons to be called to the Bar", and at the date of the death of the testator Albert was alive and had no children, his life would be the only measuring life of the gift. Since it would be possible that Albert might yet have a child who could be called to the Bar more than 21 years after his (i.e. Albert's) death, the grant of the remainder interest would be void on grounds of perpetuity. If instead the grant was made to "Albert for life, remainder to the first of his sons to reach the age of eighteen" the contingent grant of the remainder interest would be valid. It is impossible that Albert could have a son who would not reach the relevant age within the perpetuity period, i.e. within 21 years of his own death. The extent to which the common law rule renders grants void despite ludicrously improbable events is well illustrated by *Ward v Van Der Leoff*[45] where a testator left property to his wife for life, terminable if she remarried anyone but a British subject, remainder to all or any of the children or child of his brothers and sisters who should be living at the death or remarriage of his wife who attained the age of 21. The House of Lords held that this gift was void for perpetuity since it was possible that a future born child of his brothers or sisters might attain the age of 21 outside of the perpetuity period. This was because his parents, or a surviving parent, might have another child after his death, which could itself have a child attaining the age of 21 more than 21 years after the death of everyone else named in his will who was living at his death, i.e. his brothers and sisters and their children. Such an eventuality would require both an immense family tragedy, and a miracle of Biblical proportions since his parents were 66 years old at the date of the will and his father had died since his death. However, Viscount Cave held that evidence of the inability of his mother to have further children was inadmissible.[46] In *Re Gaite's Will Trusts*[47] Roxburgh J. only avoided the absurdity of finding that a 65-year-old widow could become a grandmother within five years by having a newborn child who subsequently married and itself gave birth by holding that such a grandchild would be illegitimate.[48]

Where property is left to be divided proportionately between the members of a class it would be logical to assume that the grant would fail if there was any possibility that there might be members of the class arising outside of the perpetuity period. For example, if a testator left property to "Albert for life, remainder to all his children who attain the age of 25" it would be possible for a child to attain that age beyond the perpetuity period. However the

---

[45] [1924] A.C. 653.
[46] See also *Jee v Audley* (1787) 1 Cox. Eq. Cas. 324.
[47] [1949] 1 All E.R. 459.
[48] Since a five-year-old is too young to marry: Age of Marriage Act 1929 s.1(1).

rule in *Andrews v Partington*[49] provides that a class is treated as closed if one member is already qualified when the gift takes effect, and the class will only be open thereafter to the potential qualifiers in existence at that date. If Albert has a child who is over the specified age at the date of the testator's death the class is closed and only Albert's children also alive at that date can qualify. Any subsequently born child is not treated as a member of the class. Thus there would be no possibility of the interest vesting outside of the perpetuity period.

In cases where a grant would be void for perpetuity because a beneficiary is required to attain an age greater than 21, thus meaning that vesting could potentially occur outside the perpetuity period, s.163 of the Law of Property Act 1925 provides that the age of 21 shall be substituted. This provision only applies to instruments executed after 1925 and before July 14, 1964.

(c) *Application of the Perpetuity Rules to Gifts Taking Effect After July 16, 1964*

11–017   The application of the rule against perpetuities to gifts taking effect after July 16, 1964 has been substantially modified by the Perpetuities and Accumulations Act 1964, which has rendered the common law rule obsolete. The most important effect of the Act is to introduce a "wait and see" approach, so that a gift is not rendered void merely because there is a theoretical possibility that it might vest outside of the perpetuity period. Instead s.3(1) allows the gift to remain valid until it is established that vesting must occur outside of the perpetuity period. The relevant perpetuity period during which the court will "wait and see" if the gift vests can either be specified in the instrument as a period of up to 80 years,[50] or will comprise one of the statutory lives in being identified in s.3(5), plus 21 years. These lives include the life of the person making the disposition, the persons in whose favour the disposition was made, and in certain circumstances the parents and grandparents of the designated beneficiaries. Where a contingent grant is made to a class and at the end of the "wait and see" period there are potential members of the class, either alive or unborn, who would render the grant void, s.4(4) operates so that they are "deemed for all purposes of the disposition to be excluded from the class". This operates in a similar way to the class closing rule at common law. Section 4(1) provides that where a grant would be void because it requires an age of attainment exceeding 21 years, then the age specified will be substituted by the age, not less than 21, which would have prevented the grant being void. The Act also eliminates the problem of improbable possibilities inherent in the common law rule by enacting presumptions that a woman can only have a child between the ages of 12 and 55 and a man at 14 or above.[51]

(d) *Future of the Rule Against Perpetuities*

11–018   A number of significant criticisms have been raised in relation to the rule against perpetuities as it presently operates, including its complexity, uncertainty, inconsistency, interference with

---

[49] 1791) 3 Bro. C.C. 401.
[50] Perpetuities and Accumulations Act 1964 s.1(1).
[51] Perpetuities and Accumulations Act 1964 s.2(1).

commercial transactions, harshness, lack of adaptability and expense. It has been recently examined by the Law Commission, which recommends significant legislative reform.[52] Following consultation[53] the Law Commission rejects the suggestion that the rule against perpetuities should be abolished on the grounds that it is necessary to place "some restriction on the freedom of one generation to control the devolution of property at the expense of the generations that follow".[54] Instead the Law Commission proposes that the current rule be simplified by reducing its scope and by redefining the perpetuity period. It is of the opinion that the rule against perpetuities should only apply to successive estates and interests in property held on trust. This will encompass estates and interests under trusts which are determinable or subject to a condition precedent, and estates and interests held on trust subject to a condition subsequent.[55] The rule would no longer apply to interests such as easements granted or reserved to take effect at a future date, restrictive covenants which are to take effect at a future date, and options or rights of pre-emption.[56] The rule would similarly have no application to pension schemes.[57] The Commission further recommends that the perpetuity period should be a fixed period of 125 years,[58] which it is suggested would strike "the appropriate balance between the respective freedoms of the present generation and those to come to dispose of property as they wish, but does so with a far greater degree of simplicity than does the present law".[59] Whilst the introduction of this new perpetuity period would be prospective only, the Commission recommends that trustees of a trust created prior to any legislation should be able to elect by deed that the trust be subject to the new statutory perpetuity period if the trust contains an express perpetuity period of lives in being plus 21 years and the trustees believe that it is difficult or impracticable to ascertain the existence or whereabouts of the measuring lives, as would be the case, for example, if the trust contained a "Royal lives" clause.[60] It remains to be seen whether these proposals for simplification will be enacted.

RESULTING TRUSTS OF LAND[61]

Resulting trusts are trusts which arise in the absence of any expressed intention of the parties. In essence they are found where a person has received the legal title to property in circumstances where he cannot be regarded as having received the full equitable ownership. They derive from the general principle stated by Megarry J. in *Re Sick and Funeral Society of St John's Sunday School, Golcar*[62] that "any property a man does not effectually dispose of remains his own." For the sake of convenience two categories of resulting trust have been

11–019

---

[52] Law Com. No.251, *The Rule Against Perpetuities and Excessive Accumulations* (1998).
[53] Law Commission Consultation Paper No.133.
[54] Law Com. No.251, *The Rules Against Perpetuities and Excessive Accumulations* (1998).
[55] Law Com. No.251 para.7.31.
[56] Law Com. No.251 para.7.35.
[57] Law Com. No.251 para.7.36.
[58] Law Com. No.251 para.8.13.
[59] Law Com. No.251 para.8.9.
[60] Law Com. No.251 para.8.9.
[61] See Pearce and Stevens, *The Law of Trusts and Equitable Obligations*, (4th edn., 2006), pp.234–267.
[62] [1973] Ch. 51 at 59.

identified: automatic and presumed resulting trusts.[63] However, it should be noted that the legitimacy of this classification was called into question by the decision of the House of Lords in *Westdeutsche Landesbank Girocentrale v Islington LBC*,[64] where Lord Browne-Wilkinson emphasised that both categories were dependent upon the intentions of the original owner of the property. An automatic resulting trust will generally arise where the settlor of property has transferred it to the intended trustee but the trust has either failed for some reason[65] or the settlor has failed to identify the beneficiaries of the trust.[66] In such cases the holder of the legal title cannot retain the property for himself absolutely, so he is compelled to hold it on a resulting trust for the settlor. In this way the settlor retains his ownership of the property in equity, even though he has transferred the legal title. The most likely scenario in which such an automatic resulting trust of land would arise is if the settlor transferred the land to a person clearly as trustee but without specifying who was to be beneficially entitled. In such a case the trustee would hold the land on resulting trust for the settlor.

Of far greater significance to the equitable ownership of land are the principles of the presumed resulting trusts based upon voluntary transfer or contribution to the purchase price of an acquisition. These arise where an owner of property transfers it into the name of someone else, or where a person contributes to the acquisition price of property purchased in someone else's name. In both cases it is presumed that the person who has provided the essential material input to the transaction, whether the property or the money, cannot have intended to lose all interest in his wealth without making plain that it was his intention to do so. In the absence of a contrary intention he will be taken to have retained his interest by way of a resulting trust in either the property transferred or purchased. The basis of the operation of resulting trusts is therefore a rebuttable presumption that the owner of property does not intend to make a gift. However, in some circumstances, because of the nature of the relationship between the transferee or purchaser and the recipient of the property, there is a counter-presumption that a gift was intended. This counter-presumption is known as the presumption of advancement. Where the presumption of advancement applies there will only be a resulting trust if the presumption is rebutted, thus re-establishing that no gift was intended.[67]

1. Resulting Trusts where there is a Voluntary Conveyance of Land

11–020 Where property is transferred to a third party who does not provide any consideration for the transfer, there is a presumption of a resulting trust unless the relationship between the parties gives rise to the counter presumption of advancement. Unless this presumption of resulting trust is rebutted, the transferee will hold the transferred property on trust for the transferor. Although this presumption against a gift clearly applies in the case of a transfer of personal

---

[63] *Re Vandervell's Trusts (No.2)* [1974] Ch. 269.

[64] [1996] 2 All E.R. 961.

[65] For examples see *Re Ames Settlement* [1946] Ch. 217; *Re Chocrane* [1955] Ch. 309; *Re Astor's Settlement Trusts* [1952] Ch. 534.

[66] As in *Vandervell v IRC* [1967] 2 A.C. 291.

[67] Lord Neuberger was critical of the presumption of advancement in his dissenting opinion in *Stack v Dowden* [2007] 2 A.C. 432, para.112.

property[68] there is some controversy as to whether it applies in the case of a voluntary transfer of land. There is some uncertainty as to the impact of s.60(3) of the Law of Property Act 1925, which provides that:

> "In a voluntary conveyance a resulting trust for the grantor shall not be implied merely by reason that the property is not expressed to be conveyed for the use or benefit of the grantee."

Prior to the enactment of this section a voluntary conveyance of land would not be effective to transfer the land unless it contained an express declaration that the land was granted "unto and to the use of" the grantee. It is unclear whether the section has merely simplified conveyancing by making such a declaration unnecessary, or whether it has abrogated the presumption of resulting trust in relation to a voluntary conveyance of land altogether. In *Hodgson v Marks*[69] the Court of Appeal held that a resulting trust arose where an elderly lady had voluntarily transferred the legal title of her house to her lodger on the basis of an oral understanding that he would look after her affairs, and it was not suggested that s.60(3) would prevent the presumption of such a trust. However in *Tinsley v Milligan*[70] Lord Browne-Wilkinson opined that s.60(3) had arguably altered the law regarding the presumption of resulting trusts of land. In *Lohia v Lohia*[71] Nicholas Strauss Q.C. took the view that, on a "plain reading", s.60(3) had abolished the presumption of resulting trust in respect of a voluntary conveyance of land, so that a presumption would only arise if there were some other factor than the absence of consideration for the transfer, for example if the parties to the transaction were strangers. He therefore held that there was no presumption of resulting trust where a son had voluntarily transferred his share in the family home to his father. However it is submitted that the more traditional approach should be preferred. It is questionable whether there is any meaningful distinction between land and personal property so as to justify the operation of different presumptions. The effect of treating the presumption as abolished is to require to transferor to produce evidence that a gift of the beneficial interest was not intended.

2. Resulting Trusts where a Person has Contributed to the Purchase Price of Land

(a) *The Presumption that a Contribution to the Purchase Price Generates an Interest by way of a Resulting Trust*

As with the presumption against gifts, the presumption that a contribution to the purchase price of property will generate an interest in the equitable ownership in favour of the contributor by   **11–021**

---

[68] *Re Vindogradoff* [1935] W.N. 68; *Thavorn v Bank of Credit and Commerce International SA* [1985] 1 Lloyd's Rep 259.
[69] [1971] Ch. 892.
[70] [1993] 3 All E.R. 65.
[71] [2001] W.L.R. 101.

way of a resulting trust arises in relation to all types of property.[72] The general principle was identified by Eyre C.B. in *Dyer v Dyer*:

> "the trust of a legal estate . . . whether taken in the names of the purchasers and others jointly, or in the names of others without that of the purchaser; whether in one name or several; whether jointly or successive, results to the man who advances the purchase-money."[73]

It is clear that a contribution to the purchase price of land will gain the contributor a share of the equitable ownership by way of a resulting trust. As Lord Reid stated in *Pettitt v Pettitt*:

> "in the absence of evidence to the contrary effect a contributor to the purchase-price will acquire a beneficial interest in the property."[74]

This was reiterated by Lord Pearson in *Gissing v Gissing*,[75] where the issue was whether a wife was entitled to a share of the matrimonial home which had been purchased in the sole name of her husband:

> "If [she] did make contributions of a substantial amount towards the purchase of the house, there would be a resulting trust in her favour. That would be the presumption as to the intention of the parties at the time or times when she made and he accepted the contributions. The presumption is a rebuttable presumption: it can be rebutted by evidence showing some other intention."

(b)   *What will Constitute a Contribution to the Purchase Price?*

11–022   Only a direct contribution to the purchase price of property will give rise to a presumption of a resulting trust. Most straightforward is a direct contribution to the purchase price of land. For example in *Tinsley v Milligan*[76] a lesbian couple purchased a house which they intended to run as a lodging house. It was purchased in the name of Tinsley, who was registered as the sole legal owner. The purchase price of £29,000 was raised by way of a mortgage of £24,000 with the remainder raised from the sale of their jointly owned car. Since half of this money could be considered to be Milligan's, she had contributed half of the purchase price, and it was held that she was entitled to a half share of the property by way of a resulting trust. Although such a direct contribution to the purchase price will certainly give rise to a resulting trust other less direct contributions have also been held sufficient provided that they are sufficiently referable to the purchase price. Where land is purchased by means of a mortgage, it is possible to treat the money raised by mortgage as the equivalent of a cash contribution

---

[72] See *Fowkes v Pascoe* (1875) 10 Ch. App. 343 for an example of the presumption arising in the context of personal property.
[73] (1788) 2 Cox. Eq. Cas. 92 at 93.
[74] [1970] A.C. 777 at 794; see also Lord Neuberger's opinion in *Stack v Dowden* [2007] 2 A.C. 432.
[75] [1971] A.C. 886. Family home cases are now move commonly dealt with as constructive trusts *Stack v Dowden* [2007] 2 A.C. 432.
[76] [1993] 3 All E.R. 65.

by the person who is legally obliged to make the mortgage payments. This was at one time believed to be the technically correct conclusion. However more recent cases have taken the view that a person who has contributed to the mortgage repayments may be regarded as having contributed to the purchase price and will acquire an interest by way of a resulting trust. This possibility was examined by Bagnall J. in *Cowcher v Cowcher*,[77] where he considered the consequences of a conveyance of a house to A for £24,000 where A had provided £8,000 of his own money and the remainder was provided by way of a mortgage taken out in the name of B:

> ". . . suppose that at the time A says that as between himself and B he, A, will be responsible for half the mortgage repayments . . . Though as between A and B and the vendor A has provided £8,000 and B £16,000, as between A and B themselves A has provided £8,000 and made himself liable for the repayment of half the £16,000 mortgage namely a further £8,000, a total of £16,000; the resulting trust will therefore be as to two-thirds for A and one-third for B."

He concluded that a wife who had made some mortgage repayments was entitled to a share of the house by way of a resulting trust. In *Tinsley v Milligan*[78] it has already been noted that the majority of the purchase price was raised by way of a mortgage. This was repaid with money from a bank account in the sole name of Milligan. However, since it contained the proceeds of their business and was treated by them as their joint property this did not make any difference to the finding that they had contributed equally to the purchase price of the house. In *Curley v Parkes*,[79] Peter Gibson L.J. held that "[s]ubsequent payments of the mortgage instalments are not part of the purchase price already paid to the vendor, but are sums paid for discharging the mortgagor's obligations under the mortgage". In Lord Neuberger's dissenting judgment in *Stack v Dowden*,[80] he considered that "repayments of mortgage capital may be seen as retrospective contributions towards the cost of acquisition, or as payments which increase the value of the equity of redemption".[81] He thought this solution was attractive "perhaps particularly where a home is bought almost exclusively by means of a mortgage".[82]

Similarly, where one party has enabled another to purchase land at an undervalue or reduced price because he qualifies for some discount, then the amount of the discount will be regarded as a contribution to the purchase price. In *Marsh v Von Sternberg*[83] Bush J. held that a discount gained on the purchase of a long lease because one of the parties was a sitting tenant was to be assessed as a contribution to the purchase price for the purposes of determining their respective interests under a resulting trust. In *Springette v Defoe*[84] the Court of Appeal held that a discount of 41 per cent of the market value of a council flat, obtained because the

---

[77] [1972] 1 W.L.R. 425.
[78] [1993] 3 All E.R. 65.
[79] [2004] EWCA Civ 1515; [2005] 1 P. & C.R. DG15.
[80] [2007] 2 A.C. 432, para.117.
[81] [2007] 2 A.C. 432, para.117.
[82] [2007] 2 A.C. 432, para.120. However, the point had not been fully argued and the result would have been the same in that case, however the mortgage had been treated.
[83] [1986] 1 F.L.R. 526.
[84] [1992] 2 F.L.R. 388.

plaintiff had been a tenant for more than 11 years, was a contribution to the purchase price.[85] A gift from a third party may also be regarded as a contribution if it is applied towards the purchase of property. In *Midland Bank v Cooke*[86] a house was purchased in the sole name of a husband in 1971 for £8,500. The purchase price consisted of a mortgage of £6,450, with the balance provided by the husband's savings and a wedding gift of £1,100 given by his parents. The Court of Appeal held that since the gift was to regarded as made to them jointly, the wife had contributed half of the amount of the gift, namely £550, to the purchase price and to that extent was entitled to a share of the equitable ownership by way of a resulting trust. In contrast to these cases money contributions which cannot be related to the purchase price of the land will not be sufficient to give rise to a resulting trust. In *Burns v Burns*[87] Mr and Mrs Burns began living together as man and wife in 1961. In 1963 a house was purchased in the sole name of Mr Burns, who financed the purchase by way of a mortgage. Mrs Burns later worked and used part of her earnings to pay the rates, telephone bills and to buy various items of furniture for the house. When they separated in 1980 she claimed that she was entitled to a share of the house by reason of these contributions. The Court of Appeal held that because she had not made any direct contribution to the purchase price she was not entitled to any interest in the house by of a resulting trust. It should, however, be noted that the fact that contributions are ineffective to generate a resulting trust does not mean that it is inevitable that the contributor gains no equitable interest in the land, since they may give rise to a constructive trust which operates by applying different principles. Indeed, family home cases are now usually considered on the basis of constructive trust principles.

(c) *Quantification of the Extent of the Equitable Interest Under a Resulting Trust*

11–023 Where a person is entitled to a share of the equitable ownership of property by way of a resulting trust the quantification of his or her share is a matter of pure arithmetic. The court possesses no discretion and the share will be the equivalent of the exact proportion of the purchase price that was contributed. Thus in *Tinsley v Milligan*[88] Milligan was held entitled to a half share in the house because she had contributed exactly a half of the deposit that had been paid and half of the mortgage repayments. In *Midland Bank v Cooke*[89] the Court of Appeal held that Mrs Cooke would have been entitled to a 6.74 per cent share of the equitable ownership of the house by way of a resulting trust because this was the exact correspondence between her contribution of £550 and the purchase price of the property. In the event it was held that she was entitled to a half share of the house by way of a constructive trust. Despite the absence of any direct evidence, the Court of Appeal found that there was an implied intention that the parties would share ownership equally. In the case of a resulting trust the court is merely giving effect to the implication of any contribution that has been made, and the contributor will only be entitled to an equitable interest equivalent to that

---

[85] See also *Oxley v Hiscock* [2004] EWCA Civ 546; [2004] 3 W.L.R. 715.
[86] [1995] 4 All E.R. 562.
[87] [1984] Ch. 317.
[88] [1993] 3 All E.R. 65.
[89] [1995] 4 All E.R. 562.

contribution, no more and no less. In some contexts it may be difficult for the court to assess the extent of a contribution with exact precision, especially where the contribution was made by way of assistance with mortgage repayments. In such cases the court is prepared to adopt a practical approach, as was recognised by Lord Reid in *Gissing v Gissing*:

> "... where [the contributor] does not make direct payments towards the purchase it is less easy to evaluate her share. If her payments are direct she gets a share proportionate to what she has paid. Otherwise there must be a more rough and ready evaluation. I agree that this does not mean that she would as a rule get a half share ... There will be many others where a fair estimate might be a tenth or a quarter or something even more than a half."[90]

(d) Reliance on a Presumption of Resulting Trust where the Underlying Transaction was Effected to Pursue an Illegal Purpose

One question, which has been the subject of recent judicial consideration, is whether a person can rely on a presumption of resulting trust to claim an equitable interest in property which was acquired in pursuance of an illegal purpose. It is a maxim of equity that "he who comes to equity must come with clean hands", meaning that equity will not step in to assist a person whose conduct is illegal. In *Tinsley v Milligan*[91] there was no doubt that under the principles of presumed resulting trusts Milligan would be prima facie entitled to a half share of the house that had been purchased, but the House of Lords had to determine whether she should be entitled to assert her entitlement where the house had been conveyed into the sole name of Tinsley to enable her to continue to claim housing benefit, thus defrauding the Department of Social Security. Two members of the House of Lords held that the maxim should be applied strictly, so that Milligan could not maintain a claim to a half share of the house against Tinsley. However, the majority took the view that she should be entitled to assert her equitable proprietary interest provided that she did not have to rely on her illegal conduct to do so. Since the presumption of an automatic resulting trust arises from the mere fact of contribution it can be established without the need to demonstrate the purpose of the transaction. Milligan was not therefore prevented from claiming her half interest in the house. The principle was explained by Lord Browne-Wilkinson:

11–024

> "the time has come to decide clearly that the rule is the same whether a plaintiff founds himself on legal or equitable title: he is entitled to recover if he is not forced to plead or rely on the illegality, even if it emerges that the title on which he relied was acquired in the course of carrying through an illegal transaction."[92]

The approach adopted in *Tinsley v Milligan* was also applied by the Court of Appeal in *Lawson v Coombes*,[93] which concerned a house that had been purchased by a man and his

---

[90] [1971] A.C. 886 at 987. Note the principles of quantification that now apply in the context of family home cases: see para. 11–049 below.
[91] [1993] 3 All E.R. 65.
[92] [1993] 3 All E.R. 65 at 91.
[93] [1999] 2 W.L.R. 720.

mistress, in her sole name, with the illegal purpose of frustrating any claim to the house by his wife under the Matrimonial Causes Act 1973. It was held that the man was able to assert an interest by way of a resulting trust because he did not need to rely on the underlying illegal purpose of the transaction to establish his entitlement. A presumed resulting trust was generated by the mere fact of his contribution to the purchase price.

As will be seen, the problems are more complex in cases were the presumption of advancement applies and a plaintiff seeks to rebut the presumption on grounds which reveal an illegal purpose.

3. Rebuttal of the Presumption of a Resulting Trust

11–025   The presumption of resulting trust operating in favour of a contributor to the purchase price of property is capable of rebuttal by evidence that a gift was intended. As Lord Diplock observed in *Pettitt v Pettitt*,[94] the presumptions are "no more than a consensus of judicial opinion disclosed by reported cases as to the most likely inference of fact to be drawn in the absence of any evidence to the contrary". Where the presumption of a resulting trust is rebutted the person who enjoys the legal title of the property will be absolutely entitled to it, and the contributor will enjoy no interests in it by way of a trust.

(a)   *Evidence to Rebut the Presumption*

11–026   Any evidence that the transferor or contributor to the purchase price of the property was not intending to retain ownership for himself will be effective to rebut the presumption of a resulting trust. Evidence that a gift was intended will clearly rebut the presumption. This can be seen in the context of personal property in *Fowkes v Pascoe*[95] and *Re Young*,[96] and the principles are the same in relation to land. Evidence that a contribution was made by way of a loan will also rebut a presumption of resulting trust since a lender enjoys only a contractual entitlement to the repayment of the money lent and not an interest in the property acquired with it. For example in *Re Sharpe (A Bankrupt)*[97] Mr and Mrs Sharpe lived in a maisonette with their 82-year-old aunt, Mrs Johnson. The property had been purchased in the name of Mr Sharpe for £17,000, of which Mrs Johnson had provided £12,000 and the remainder was raised by way of a mortgage. Subsequently the Sharpes became bankrupt and Mrs Johnson claimed to be entitled to an interest in the property under a resulting trust. However, Browne-Wilkinson J. held that the money had been advanced by her by way of a loan, which she had intended that Mr Sharpe would repay, and this rebutted the presumption of a resulting trust.

[94] [1970] A.C. 777 at 823.
[95] (1875) 10 Ch. App. 343.
[96] (1889) 28 Ch.D. 705.
[97] [1980] 1 W.L.R. 219.

(b) Degree of Evidence Required to Rebut the Presumption of a Resulting Trust

The weight of evidence required to rebut a presumption of a resulting trust will vary with the nature of the circumstances in which property was transferred or a contribution made. In *Fowkes v Pascoe*[98] the Court of Appeal suggested that if a man invested in shares in the name of himself and his solicitor there would be a very strong inference that a trust was intended, because people do not usually make gifts to their professional advisers. In contrast the presumption of a resulting trust arising between a wife and her husband, which is somewhat anomalous because there is no presumption of advancement despite the nature of the relationship, is extremely weak and can be rebutted by slender evidence that a gift was intended. As Lord Upjohn remarked in *Pettitt v Pettitt*: **11–027**

> "If a wife puts property in her husband's name it may be that in the absence of all other evidence he is a trustee for her, but in practice there will in almost every case be some explanation (however slight) of this (today) rather unusual course. If a wife puts property into their joint names I would myself think that a joint tenancy was intended for I can see no other reason for it."[99]

4. The Counter-Presumption of Advancement

(a) The Presumption of Advancement

As has been seen, in cases where there is a voluntary transfer of property, or a contribution to the purchase price, there is a presumption of a resulting trust in favour of the transferor or the contributor. However in limited circumstances there is a counter-presumption that a gift was intended. This presumption is known as the presumption of advancement, and where such a presumption applies the transferor or contributor is presumed to have made a gift, and not to have intended to retain any interest in the property. As with the presumption of a resulting trust this presumption of advancement can be rebutted by evidence that no gift was intended. A presumption of advancement will only arise between parties who are in a relationship which was historically regarded as giving rise to a duty of one party to provide for the other's support. For this reason the contexts in which the presumption arises are reflective of Victorian concepts of family responsibility, and today there are anomalies which are purely anachronistic. In *Lowson v Coombes* Robert Walker L.J. commented that the presumption of advancement: **11–028**

> "has been cogently criticised both as out of date in modern social and economic conditions . . . and as being uncertain in its scope."[100]

---

[98] (1875) 10 Ch. App. 343.
[99] [1970] A.C. 777 at 815. See also *Knightly v Knightly* (1981) 11 Fam. Law 122.
[100] [1999] 2 W.L.R. 720 at 729; see also Lord Neuberger's criticism in *Stack v Dowden* [2007] 2 A.C. 432, para.112.

There is a clear presumption of advancement between a father and child[101] and between a child and a person standing in loco parentis to that child.[102] For example, in *Warren v Gurney*[103] it was held that a presumption of advancement applied where a father had purchased a house in the name of his daughter prior to her wedding. Similarly in *Webb v Webb*[104] there was a presumption of advancement where a father purchased an apartment in Antibes in the name of his son. In contrast there is no presumption of advancement between a mother and child[105] or in the context of other family relationships,[106] and therefore in such cases a presumption of resulting trust will continue to apply, although the nature of the relationship may mean that it is relatively easy to rebut. A presumption of advancement will also apply between a husband and wife, reflecting a traditional understanding that a husband would provide for his wife's material needs.[107] In *Pettitt v Pettitt*[108] the House of Lords affirmed the continuing application of the presumption between a husband and wife, although it was recognised that it had lost its force due to the increasing economic independence of wives. By analogy the presumption also applies between a man and his fiancé,[109] though not between a man and his mistress.[110] There is no presumption of advancement between a wife and her husband[111] or between co-habiting couples.[112] The gender bias currently enshrined in the presumption of advancement may contravene art.5 of the European Convention on Human Rights in its assertion of the equality of spousal rights.[113]

(b) *Rebutting the Presumption of Advancement*

11–029 When a presumption of advancement arises it may be rebutted by evidence demonstrating that no gift was intended by the transferor or contributor. For example, in *Warren v Gurney*[114] a father purchased a house for his daughter but retained the title deeds until his death. The

---

[101] *Re Roberts* [1946] Ch. 1; *B v B* (1975) 65 D.L.R. (3d) 460; For a modern application of the presumption of advancement in relation to company shares transferred between father and child, see *Antoni v Antoni* [2007] UKPC 10 Privy Council.

[102] *Hepworth v Hepworth* (1870) L.R. 11 Eq. 10; *Bennet v Bennet* (1879) 10 Ch.D. 474; *Re Orme* (1883) 50 L.T. 51; *Shephard v Cartwright* [1955] A.C. 431; *Re Paradise Motor Co Ltd* [1968] 1 W.L.R. 1125.

[103] [1944] 2 All E.R. 472.

[104] [1992] 1 All E.R. 17.

[105] *Re de Visme* (1863) 2 de G.J. & Sm. 17; *Bennet v Bennet* (1879) 10 Ch.D. 474.

[106] *Noack v Noack* [1959] V.R. 137 (sister); *Gorog v Kiss* (1977) 78 D.L.R. (3d) 690 (sister); *Knight v Biss* [1954] N.Z.L.R. 55 (son-in-law); *Dury v Cury* (1675) 75 S.S. 205 (nephew); *Russell v Scott* (1936) 55 C.L.R. 440 (nephew).

[107] *Re Eykyn's Trusts* (1877) 6 Ch.D. 115; *Silver v Silver* [1958] 1 All E.R. 523; *Heavey v Heavey* [1971] 111 I.L.T.R. 1; *M v M* [1980] 114 I.L.T.R. 46; *Doohan v Nelson* [1973] 2 N.S.W.L.R. 320; *Napier v Public Trustee (Western Australia)* (1980) 32 A.L.R. 153.

[108] [1970] A.C. 777.

[109] *Moate v Moate* [1948] 2 All E.R. 486; *Tinker v Tinker* [1970] P 136; *Mossop v Mossop* [1988] 2 All E.R. 202.

[110] *Diwell v Farnes* [1959] 1 W.L.R. 624; *Lowson v Coombes* [1999] 2 W.L.R. 720.

[111] *Re Curtis* (1885) 52 L.T. 244; *Mercier v Mercier* [1903] 2 Ch. 98; *Pearson v Pearson*, *The Times*, November 30, 1965; *Pettitt v Pettitt* [1970] A.C. 777; *Heseltine v Heseltine* [1971] 1 W.L.R. 342; *Northern Bank v Henry* [1981] I.R. 1; *Allied Irish Banks Ltd v McWilliams* [1982] N.I. 156.

[112] *Rider v Kidder* (1805) 10 Ves. 360; *Soar v Foster* (1858) 4 K. & J. 152; *Allen v Snyder* [1977] 2 N.S.W.L.R. 685; *Calverly v Green* (1984) 56 A.L.R. 483.

[113] Law Commission, *Sharing Homes: A Discussion Paper* (Law Com. No.278, 2002), para.2.60.

[114] [1944] 2 All E.R. 472.

Court of Appeal held that this rebutted the presumption of advancement because the father would have been expected to hand the deeds over to her if he had intended a gift. In *McGrath v Wallace*[115] a house was acquired by a father and son, in the sole name of the son, for their joint occupancy. The purchase price had been raised partly by the sale of the father's previous house and partly by means of a mortgage. The Court of Appeal held that the presumption of advancement was rebutted by evidence, including a declaration of trust which had never been signed, demonstrating that they intended to share the beneficial ownership in the proportions represented by the proceeds of sale and the mortgage. The mere fact that any rents and profits derived from land are returned to the contributor is not necessarily conclusive to rebut the presumption of advancement. In *Stamp Duties Comrs v Byrnes*[116] a father purchased property in Australia in the names of his sons, and they paid over to him the rents they received from the properties and he paid the cost of rates and repairs. The Privy Council held that the presumption of advancement was not rebutted because it was natural for the sons to feel some delicacy about taking the profits from the land during their father's lifetime.

(c) *Admissibility of Evidence to Rebut a Presumption of Advancement*

Since it would be very easy for a person who has made a gift of property to change his mind, and seek to have it set aside on the grounds that no advancement was intended, the Court has introduced a rule that a person may only rely on evidence of his acts and declarations which were contemporaneous with the transaction to rebut the presumption. Evidence of subsequent acts and declarations will only be admissible against a party and not in his favour.[117] **11–030**

(d) *Rebuttal of a Presumption of Advancement by Evidence of an Illegal Purpose*

It is a basic rule that the court will not allow a person to rely on evidence of his own illegal conduct to rebut a presumption of advancement. As was noted above, in *Tinsley v Milligan*[118] it was held that a party claiming a share of the beneficial ownership of land by way of a presumption of resulting trust does not need to rely on his illegal conduct in order to establish his interest, because the presumption arises from the mere fact of his contribution irrespective of his reasons for making it. However, where the presumption of advancement arises, a person seeking to claim an interest in land by way of a resulting trust may be required to rely on his illegality in order to rebut that counter-presumption and establish his interest. For example in *Gascoigne v Gascoigne*[119] a husband took a lease of land in the name of his wife in order to defeat his creditors. The Court of Appeal held that he could not rely on this to **11–031**

---

[115] *The Times*, April 13, 1995.
[116] [1911] A.C. 386.
[117] *Shepherd v Cartwright* [1955] A.C. 431.
[118] [1993] 3 All E.R. 65.
[119] [1918] 1 K.B. 223.

demonstrate that no gift was intended. The same principle was applied in *Tinker v Tinker*,[120] where a husband purchased a house in the name of his wife to prevent it being seized by creditors if his business failed.[121] Lord Denning M.R. held that he could not rebut the presumption of advancement:

"... he cannot say that the house is his own and, at one and the same time, say that it is his wife's. As against the wife, he wants to say that it belongs to him. As against his creditors, that it belongs to her. That simply will not do. Either it was conveyed to her for her own use absolutely; or it was conveyed to her as a trustee for her husband. It must be one or the other. The presumption is that it was conveyed to her for her own use; and he does not rebut that presumption by saying that he only did it to defeat his creditors ..."[122]

However, in *Tribe v Tribe*[123] the Court of Appeal held that a person could rebut a presumption of advancement, even though the property had been transferred in pursuance of an illegal purpose, if the purpose had not yet been carried into effect. A father owned 459 of 500 shares in a private company. He transferred them into the name of his son because of fears that he would become liable for the cost of repairs to two premises occupied by the company. In the event the father was never required to meet the cost of the repairs, and he demanded that his son return the shares to him. The son refused and the father sought a declaration that he had been holding them on resulting trust for him. The Court of Appeal held that the presumption of advancement applicable between a father and son could be rebutted by evidence of the purpose of the transaction, because the illegal objective of enabling the father to avoid his creditors had never been carried into effect. The principle was explained by Nourse L.J.:

"Certainly the transaction was carried into effect by the execution and registration of the transfer. But ... that is immaterial. It is the purpose which has to be carried into effect and that would only have happened if and when a creditor or creditors of the [father] had been deceived by the transaction. ... Nor is it any objection to the [father's] right to recover the shares that he did not demand their return until after the danger had passed and it was no longer necessary to conceal the transfer from his creditors. All that matters is that no deception was practised on them."[124]

5. The Practical Importance of Resulting Trusts

11–032   It has been seen that the presumption of a resulting trust is an important means by which a contributor to the purchase price of property can gain a share of the equitable ownership. However those seeking such an interest have often only contributed a very small percentage

---

[120] [1970] P. 136.
[121] See also *Re Emery's Investment Trusts* [1959] Ch. 410; [1962] 1 All E.R. 494.
[122] [1970] P. 136 at 141.
[123] [1995] 4 All E.R. 236.
[124] [1995] 4 All E.R. 236 at 248.

of the purchase price. This is not always the case, as in *Tinsley v Milligan*[125] where the parties had contributed equally to the purchase price. But a more usual scenario is that seen in *Midland Bank v Cooke*[126] where the wife had contributed only a very small proportion of the purchase price. Whether this matters to the claimant will depend upon the purpose for which he or she is seeking an equitable interest in the land. If she is merely seeking to demonstrate that she has some interest in the land, which will be binding upon some third party other than the legal owner who is claiming that she has no interest in the land, then the exact proportion of her equitable entitlement will be irrelevant as between her and the third party. For example, if a person is seeking to assert that she has an equitable interest in the land which is binding on a mortgage company which has lent money to the legal owner, it may only be necessary for her to show that she has some beneficial interest and the precise quantification of that interest is less important. This was the issue in *Williams & Glyn's Bank v Boland*[127] where a matrimonial home was owned in the sole name of a husband but the wife had contributed a substantial sum of her own money to the purchase price. The husband later mortgaged the house to the bank and the issue was whether the bank took its mortgage subject to any equitable interest of the wife. There was no question that the wife enjoyed an interest by way of a resulting trust arising from her contribution, but the precise extent of her interest was largely irrelevant to the issue in point, which was whether her actual occupation of the land converted her equitable interest into an overriding interest under the Land Registration Act 1925 s.70(1)(g) which would bind the mortgage company. Similarly in *Abbey National Building Society v Cann*[128] it was clear that the claimant enjoyed an interest in the equitable ownership of a house because of her contribution to the purchase price by way of a reduction to which she was entitled as a sitting tenant under a protected tenancy, but the extent of her interest was irrelevant to the question of whether it was binding on a subsequent mortgage lender. However if a person is claiming an entitlement against the legal owner of the land, it is much more likely that she will want to establish that she enjoys a substantial interest in it. If she has only contributed a small proportion of the purchase price this will not be possible by means of a resulting trust, but where it can be established that there was a common intention between the claimant and the legal owner that the claimant was to enjoy an interest in the land then she may be entitled to a constructive trust to give effect to that common intention, even where the practical effect is that she is thereby entitled to a much greater percentage of the equitable ownership of the land than would have been justified by her contribution alone. This is evident from the facts of *Midland Bank v Cooke*[129] where a wife contributed 6.74 per cent of the purchase price of her matrimonial home, which was registered in the sole name of her husband who had also contributed to the purchase price and made the mortgage contributions throughout. The Court of Appeal held that it was possible to infer a common intention that the husband and wife were to share the ownership of the house equally and therefore her interest was not limited to the strict proportion resulting from her cash contribution to the purchase price. Rather she was entitled to a half interest in the equitable ownership by way of a

---

[125] [1993] 3 All E.R. 65.
[126] [1995] 4 All E.R. 562.
[127] [1981] A.C. 487.
[128] [1991] 1 A.C. 56.
[129] [1995] 4 All E.R. 562.

constructive trust. This means that in practice where there is a relatively small financial contribution the person seeking a share of the equitable ownership of the property will prefer to demonstrate entitlement by way of a constructive trust.

6. Nature of the Co-ownership Arising Under a Resulting Trust

11–033   Where a person is entitled to a proportion of the equitable ownership of land by way of a resulting trust this will inevitably give rise to some species of co-ownership in equity. English law recognises two forms of co-ownership of the equitable interest of land, namely a joint tenancy and a tenancy in common. These concepts will be examined in more detail in the following chapter, but at this stage it is sufficient to know that where parties are joint tenants they are not treated as enjoying distinct and separate shares in the land which they can deal with individually. Most importantly the principle of survivorship operates between joint tenants so that when one joint tenant dies his interest in the land passes automatically to the other joint tenants and he cannot leave his notional share in the land to anyone else by means of a will.[130] Where a person is entitled to a share of the equitable ownership as a tenant in common he is regarded as holding that share distinctly from the interests of the other co-owners and the principle of survivorship does not apply to it. Where parties have contributed to the purchase price of land unequally, so that their entitlements are also unequal, they will be taken to hold their respective shares as tenants in common.[131] However where their contributions are identical there appears to be no reason why they should not be joint tenants.

7. Reform of Resulting Trusts

11–034   Although a well-established aspect of the law of trusts, and enjoying particular prominence in relation to land, the doctrine of resulting trusts has been criticised on the grounds that it contains many anomalies and anachronisms, especially in relation to the presumptions of advancement. The area was reviewed by the Law Commission in 1988.[132] The possibility of a generalised concept of community of property between husband and wife was rejected on the grounds that it would prevent the independent ownership and management of property during marriage. However, a revision of the presumptions operating was proposed so that they would correspond more closely to their likely intentions:

> "(i) Where money is spent to buy property, or property or money is transferred by one spouse to the other, for their joint use or benefit the property acquired or money transferred should be jointly owned.

---

[130] Nor will it pass to his heirs under the rules of intestacy if he dies without making a will.
[131] Note below the principles of quantification of a beneficial interest that apply in the context of purchase of a family home: see para.11–050.
[132] Law Com. No.175, *Family Law: Matrimonial Property* (1988).

(ii) Where money or property is transferred by one spouse to the other for any other purpose, it should be owned by that other.

In both cases, the general rule should give way to a contrary intention on the part of the paying or transferring spouse, provided that the contrary intention is known to that other spouse."[133]

This proposal has the effect of eliminating the anomaly that the presumption of advancement applies only between a husband and his wife and not between a wife and her husband.[134]

CONSTRUCTIVE TRUSTS OF LAND[135]

It has been seen how a contribution to the purchase price of land may give rise to a resulting trust of an equivalent share of the equitable ownership. In contrast constructive trusts arise where there was a common intention that the ownership of land was to be shared, but the intention has not been given effect by an express declaration of trust. The legal owner of the land will be required to hold it on constructive trust to fulfil the common intention if the claimant has acted to his or her detriment in reliance on the common intention. Constructive trusts are considerably more important in practice than resulting trusts because they enable a person to obtain a share of the equitable ownership of land far in excess of any financial contribution they have made to the purchase price, or in some circumstances even where there have made no such contribution at all.

    11–035

The underlying principles of constructive trusts were stated by Millett L.J. in *Paragon Finance Plc v DB Thakerar & Co*:

> "A constructive trust arises by operation of law whenever the circumstances are such that it would be unconscionable for the owner of property (usually but not necessarily the legal estate) to assert his own beneficial interest in the property and deny the beneficial interest of another."[136]

Whilst it is easy to state the underlying rationale in such general terms it will be seen that it is much more difficult in practice to identify the circumstances in which it will be "unconscionable" for a legal owner of land to deny that someone else enjoys a beneficial interest therein.

---

[133] Law Com. No.175, para.4.1.

[134] See *Stack v Dowden* [2007] 2 A.C. 432 for the effect of a conveyance of a house into joint names. The majority of the House of Lords decided (Lord Neuberger dissenting on the law) that there would be a presumption of joint beneficial ownership, rebuttable by evidence of circumstances indicating a contrary intention. This would have the incidental effect of superseding any presumption of advancement in cases of conveyance into both names.

[135] See Pearce and Stevens, *The Law of Trusts and Equitable Obligations*, (4th edn, 2006), pp.282–318.

[136] [1999] 1 All E.R. 400 at 408–409.

1. The Development of Constructive Trusts in England

(a) *The Seminal Authority*

11–036   The seminal authority on the development of the principles of constructive trusts of land was the decision of the House of Lords in *Gissing v Gissing*.[137] The principles established by this case have proved to be extremely robust and still underpin the concept of constructive trusts more than a quarter of a century later. The facts reveal the changing emphasis from the traditional paradigm of home ownership to the more modern realities of property ownership in families. The parties were husband and wife who had married in 1935 when they were in their early twenties. They were both in work, the wife as secretary for a firm of printers. The house that was the subject of the proceedings was purchased in 1951 for £2,695 and conveyed into the sole name of the husband. Of this, the husband was lent £500 by the managing director of the printing firm, £2,150 was raised by way of a mortgage, and he provided the balance of £45 from his own money. The wife then spent £220 of her money laying a lawn and providing furniture for the house. The wife continued to work and used her earnings to purchase clothes for herself and her child as well as adding to the housekeeping allowance provided by her husband. He paid all the instalments on the loan and the mortgage as well as the other outgoings of the home. In 1960, after 25 years of marriage, he left to live with a younger woman. She remained in the matrimonial home and was granted a divorce in 1966. She sought a declaration that she was beneficially entitled to the house. The House of Lords held that in these circumstances the husband was absolutely entitled to the house and that the wife had no interest in it by way of a trust. The central reason for this denial of any entitlement was that there was no conduct from which it could be inferred that the parties had a common intention that the wife was to be entitled to a share of the house. The general principles upon which such a trust would be inferred were stated by Lord Diplock:

> "A resulting, implied or constructive trust . . . is created by a transaction between the trustee and the [beneficiary] in connection with the acquisition by the trustee of a legal estate in the land, whenever the trustee has so conducted himself that it would be inequitable to allow him to deny to the [beneficiary] a beneficial interest in the land acquired. And he will be held so to have conducted himself if by his words or conduct he has induced the [beneficiary] to act to his own detriment in the reasonable belief that by so acting he was acquiring a beneficial interest in the land."[138]

This analysis of the circumstances under which a constructive trust may be established requires two central ingredients. First, that the legal owner of the land had in some way induced the claimant to believe that she would be entitled to a share of the ownership. This inducement could take either the form of an express agreement, or of an inference from the parties' conduct that an interest in the property was intended. Secondly, the person claiming

---

[137] [1971] A.C. 881.
[138] [1971] A.C. 881 at 905.

316

an interest must have acted to her detriment in some way by contributing to the purchase price of the land. Where these two factors were present the court would not allow the legal owner to enjoy the absolute ownership of the land free from the contributor's interests. As Lord Diplock explained:

"I take it to be clear that if the court is satisfied that it was the common intention of both spouses that the contributing wife should have a share in the beneficial interest and that her contributions were made upon this understanding, the court in the exercise of its equitable jurisdiction would not permit the husband in whom the legal estate was vested and who had accepted the benefit of the contributions to take the whole beneficial interest merely because at the time the wife made her contributions there had been no express agreement as to how her share in it was to be quantified."[139]

In the event Mrs Gissing was held not to have any interest because her contributions were not of such a type as would entitle the court to infer that there was a common intention that she was to be entitled to a share of the ownership of the house. As Lord Diplock explained: **11–037**

"On what is the wife's claim based? In 1951 when the house was purchased she spent about £190 on buying furniture and a cooker and refrigerator for it. She also paid £30 for improving the lawn. As furniture and household durables are depreciating assets whereas houses have turned out to be appreciating assets it may be that she would have been wise to have devoted her savings to acquiring an interest in the freehold; but this may not have been so apparent in 1951 as it has now become. The court is not entitled to infer a common intention to this effect from the mere fact that she provided chattels for joint use in the new matrimonial home; and there is nothing else in the conduct of the parties at the time of the purchase or thereafter which supports such an inference. There is no suggestion that the wife's efforts or her earnings made it possible for the husband to raise the initial loan or the mortgage or that her relieving her husband from the expense of buying clothing for herself and for their son was undertaken in order to enable him the better to meet the mortgage instalments or to repay the loan. The picture presented by the evidence is one of husband and wife retaining their separate proprietary interests in the property whether real or personal purchased with their separate savings and is inconsistent with any common intention at the time of the purchase of the matrimonial home that the wife, who neither then nor thereafter contributed anything to its purchase price or assumed any liability for it, should nevertheless be entitled to a beneficial interest in it."[140]

This passage shows the close relationship between constructive trusts and resulting trusts. Since there was no direct evidence of the parties' intentions, the court had to infer an intention from the circumstances. The only inference it was prepared to draw was that each party had a proprietary interest in the property he or she had paid for. The conclusion was therefore the same as with a resulting trust.

[139] [1971] A.C. 881 at 908.
[140] [1971] A.C. 881 at 911.

The essence of the constructive trust as adopted in *Gissing v Gissing* is that the court merely fulfils the intention of the parties. As Glass J.A. explained in the Australian case *Allen v Snyder*:

"... when it is called a constructive trust, it should not be forgotten that the courts are giving effect to an arrangement based upon the actual intentions of the parties, not a rearrangement in accordance with considerations of justice, independent of their intentions and founded upon their respective behaviour in relation to the matrimonial home."[141] However, in reality the circumstances in which such a trust arise are those where the parties have given little or no thought to their intentions, as issues such as the ownership of property have been assumed or misunderstood, or indeed one party has misrepresented his intentions to the other and taken advantage of the other's trusting nature or naivet\ae. In such cases the emphasis on the "actual intentions" of the parties is, to say the least, artificial, and the development of the doctrine of constructive trusts has been characterised by an ongoing tension between the desire to ensure that just results are achieved and the continued stress on the need to enforce the real intentions of the parties.

(b) A "New Model" Constructive Trust?

11–038   The principles expounded in *Gissing v Gissing* were extremely traditional and represented a strict property based approach which was more concerned with the nature of the parties' contributions to the property rather than to the nature of their relationship. Under this approach, contributions to family life which could not be related to ownership of a house, such as child-rearing or the performance of the usual domestic tasks that partners ordinarily have to do around the home, would not be sufficient to gain an interest in the property. Some judges preferred a less rigorous and limiting approach to the determination of constructive trust interests, and Lord Denning in particular was responsible for attempting to introduce a radically different approach by giving the court a wide discretion to determine on the facts of any given case whether a person should be entitled to an interest by way of a constructive trust. On his approach the chief criterion was that of "justice" and not the type of contribution which had been made.

Lord Denning advocated the adoption of what he described as a "new model" constructive trust which would give the court a wide discretion to award claimants' interests in property by way of constructive trusts so that the constructive trust would become a discretionary equitable remedy, as it is in the United States. Ironically he claimed authority for this development from the judgment of the House of Lords in *Gissing v Gissing*. However his use of citations was somewhat selective and he was prone to quote only those sentiments of the judges which indicated the inequitability of allowing the legal owner to enjoy an unencumbered legal title and not those where they attempted to lay down criteria for judging whether in the circumstances it would be inequitable. In *Hussey v Palmer* he explained the principles under which such a trust could be imposed:

---

[141] [1977] 2 N.S.W.L.R. 685 at 693.

318

". . . it is a trust imposed whenever justice and good conscience require it. It is a liberal process, founded on large principles of equity, to be applied in cases where the defendant cannot conscientiously keep the property for himself alone, but ought to allow another to have the property or a share in it. The trust may arise at the outset when the property is acquired, or later on, as the circumstances may require. It is an equitable remedy by which a court can enable an aggrieved party to obtain restitution."[142]

A classic example of a case where Lord Denning found that justice demanded the imposition of a constructive trust was *Eves v Eves*.[143] Janet Eves, who was 19, moved in with Stuart Eves and changed her name by deed poll. They intended to marry after his divorce and moved into a house which was purchased in his name alone. He told Janet that the house could not be put in their joint names because she was not yet 21, which was untrue, but that he intended to put it in their joint names in the future. She contributed no money to the purchase price, but did a great deal of work to improve the condition of the house, which had been very dirty and dilapidated. This included decorating and breaking up concrete in the front garden. Lord Denning considered that "she did much more than many wives would do". After a couple of years Stuart met another woman and decided to sell the house. The Court of Appeal held that in these circumstances Janet was entitled to a share of the equitable ownership by way of a constructive trust. Lord Denning M.R. explained the basis upon which such a trust would be imposed:

"It seems to me that this conduct by Mr Eves amounted to a recognition by him that, in all fairness, she was entitled to a share in the house equivalent in some way to a declaration of trust; not for a particular share, but for such share as was fair in view of all she had done and was doing. By so doing he gained her confidence. She trusted him. She did not make any financial contribution but she contributed in many other ways. She did much work in the house and garden. She looked after him and cared for the children. It is clear that her contribution was such that if she had been a wife she would have had a good claim to have a share in it on a divorce . . . In view of his conduct, it would, I think, be most inequitable for him to deny her any share in the house. The law will impute or impose a constructive trust by which he was to hold it on trust for them both."[144]

Having concluded that it was appropriate to impose a constructive trust, the extent of Janet's interest remained to be determined. Although the assurances of Stuart that he would ultimately place the house in their joint names suggested an equal sharing, Lord Denning took the view that the court should determine the appropriate share as an exercise of discretion. He therefore stated;   **11–039**

"But what should be the shares? I think one half would be too much. I suggest it should be one quarter of the equity."[145]

[142] [1975] 1 W.L.R. 1338.
[143] [1975] 1 W.L.R. 1338.
[144] [1975] 1 W.L.R. 1338.
[145] [1975] 1 W.L.R. 1338.

The decision in *Eves v Eves* illustrates the central aspects of the "new model" constructive trust and how it differs from the approach adopted by the House of Lords in *Gissing v Gissing*. First, it places greater emphasis on the totality of the parties' conduct and relationship and not merely on activities that can be related to the purchase price of the land. Secondly, the question of whether a constructive trust should be imposed, and the extent of the interest obtained thereby, is a matter for the court's discretion. Both of these elements introduce a degree of uncertainty into the process of determining whether a trust has arisen, and for this reason the "new model" constructive trust proved unacceptable to property lawyers.

(c) *Rejection of the "New Model" Constructive Trust*

Although some applications of Lord Denning's "new model" constructive trust may be regarded as achieving practical justice between the parties, and the outcomes have been regarded as correct by later cases, the concept of the "new model" constructive trust was categorically rejected on the grounds of its uncertainty and inconsistency with the earlier House of Lords' authorities. In *Grant v Edwards*[146] Nourse L.J. said that the basis of Lord Denning's decision in *Eves v Eves* had been "at variance with the principles stated in *Gissing v Gissing*". However, the major factor influencing this rejection was the concern of conveyancers that rights in property must be certain in relation to their existence, creation and extent. If this is not the case then there is a great danger that persons will be uncertain of their rights and entitlements, and in particular that third parties acquiring rights in land will not be able to be certain that their interests will not be prejudicially affected by the later imposition of a constructive trust because the court feels this to be just. Placing such a discretion in the hands of the court would lead inevitably to inconsistency of result and an impossibility of predicting whether a property right would be granted or not. It was thought that in principle property rights should not be determined by the individual moral feelings of a judge, which will inherently be subjective and unpredictable, but on more clearly defined criteria. These fears were well articulated by Bagnall J. in *Cowcher v Cowcher*[147] who considered the advantages of applying the more legalistic approach to constructive trusts adopted by the House of Lords in *Pettitt v Pettitt*[148] and *Gissing v Gissing*:

> "In any individual case the application of these propositions may produce a result which appears unfair. So be it; in my view, that is not an injustice. I am convinced that in determining rights, particularly property rights, the only justice that can be attained by mortals, who are fallible and are not omniscient, is justice according to law; the justice flows from the application of sure and settled principles to proved or admitted facts. So in the field of equity the length of the chancellor's foot has been measured or is capable of measurement. This does not mean that equity is past the age of child bearing: simply that

---

[146] [1986] Ch. 638 at 647.
[147] [1972] 1 W.L.R. 425 at 430.
[148] [1970] A.C. 777.

320

its progeny must be legitimate—by precedent out of principle. It is well that this should be so; otherwise no lawyer could safely advise on his client's title and every quarrel would lead to a law suit."[149]

This concept of justice was also echoed by Dillon L.J. in *Springette v Defoe*[150] who insisted that:

"the court does not as yet sit under a palm tree, to exercise a general discretion to do what the man in the street, on a general overview of the case, might regard as fair."

The "new model" constructive trust was also rejected by commonwealth jurisdictions, for example Australia in *Allen v Snyder*[151] and *Muschinski v Dodds*[152] In New Zealand, Mahon J. described the "new model" constructive trust in *Carly v Farrelly*[153] as a "supposed rule of equity which is not only vague in its outline but which must disqualify itself from acceptance as a valid principle of jurisprudence by its total uncertainty of application and result".

(d) *The Current Law*

Having rejected the "new model" constructive trust, the House of Lords restated the principles under which a constructive trust of land will arise in the leading case *Lloyds Bank v Rosset*.[154] The House of Lords effectively reaffirmed the approach adopted in *Gissing v Gissing*, namely that a constructive trust arises to give effect to the parties' intentions that they should share the ownership of the land. Since such shared ownership cannot be given effect at law in relation to the legal title, a constructive trust arises in equity and the legal owner is required to hold the land on trusts. The court is merely requiring the parties to give effect to their own intentions that there should be a sharing of the ownership of the land. The central question therefore becomes one of identifying when the parties can be said to have intended that they should share the ownership of the land. This essential requirement is termed the need to establish a "common intention" between the parties. Although the parties may sometimes have given a clear indication of their intentions in relation to the ownership of the property, which will not have been appropriately acted upon by means of an express declaration of trust by the legal owner, often there is no evidence that the parties have ever made an express agreement as to the ownership. However in some circumstances an intention to share the land can be inferred from the conduct of the parties, and the main issue in *Lloyds Bank v Rosset*[155] was as to the type of conduct from which such an inference can be drawn. The House of Lords held that only a financial contribution would be sufficient. *Lloyds Bank v Rosset*[156] therefore diminishes the significance of the nature of the parties' relationship as a factor determining

11–040

---

[149] [1971] A.C. 886.
[150] [1992] 2 F.L.R. 388 at 393.
[151] [1977] 2 N.S.W.L.R. 685.
[152] (1985) 160 N.Z.L.R. 356.
[153] [1975] 1 N.Z.L.R. 356.
[154] [1991] 1 A.C. 107.
[155] [1991] 1 A.C. 107.
[156] [1991] 1 A.C. 107.

whether there was a constructive trust, and also of non-financial contributions to family life. The central deficiency of the decision is that the House of Lords has seemingly reduced the importance of such contributions at a time when society seems to be increasingly concerned to value such non-financial contributions, which are more usually made by women, so as to eliminate discrimination in the context of the ownership of shared property.

Despite the seemingly universal rejection of the "new model" constructive trust, in *Oxley v Hiscock*[157] the Court of Appeal held that, where the parties had not reached a common intention as to the extent of their respective beneficial interests in the property, the court should hold that each is entitled to such share "as the court considers to be fair having regard to the whole course of dealings between them in relation to the property".[158] This seems suspiciously similar in practice to the "new model" constructive trust, although the element of discretion only applies to the determination of the respective beneficial interests of the parties, and not to the question whether there should be a constructive trust. In *Stack v Dowden*[159] the House of Lords confirmed the basic approach that the court, in order to quantify the size of a party's interest under a constructive trust, should have regard to the whole course of dealings of the parties, but that the relevant criteria was not what was "fair" but to find what was intended by the parties.[160]

(e) *Modern Significance of the Constructive Trust*

11–041   Despite the rejection of the "new model" constructive trust and the re-assertion of strict criteria in *Lloyds Bank v Rosset*, it is somewhat ironic that the need for a mechanism whereby the court can apportion the ownership of land justly between a husband and wife has been provided by statute. Under the Matrimonial Causes Act 1973 the court has the power to make orders adjusting the property rights of the parties on divorce. This effectively amounts to a discretion similar to that envisaged by Lord Denning under his "new model" constructive trust. The court now has a similar jurisdiction under the Civil Partnerships Act 2004 in relation to same-sex couples who have registered their partnership.[161] However, it may still be necessary for a husband, wife or civil partners to invoke the principles of constructive trusts if, rather than seeking to stake a claim to a share of the value of property owned at law by the other party to the marriage or partnership on divorce, he or she is seeking to claim an equitable interest in land which will take priority over the interests of a third party, frequently a mortgage company. For example, in *Lloyds Bank v Rosset* a wife was seeking to claim an interest in the matrimonial home, to which she had made no financial contribution, by way of a constructive trust so that she would have an interest binding on the bank to whom her husband had granted a mortgage. If she had been able to establish this interest she may have been able to prevent the bank from repossessing the house when the husband was no longer

---

[157] [2004] EWCA Civ 546.

[158] [2004] EWCA Civ 546 at [69], per Chadwick L.J.

[159] [2007] 2 A.C. 432.

[160] This was the criteria applied in *Midland Bank v Cooke* [1995] 4 All E.R. 562, but denounced in *Oxley v Hiscock* for being unrealistic. Couples do not usually formulate intentions about their respective shares.

[161] Pearce and Stevens, *The Law of Trusts and Equitable Obligations*, (4th edn, 2006), p.283.

able to pay the mortgage instalments. Similarly in *Midland Bank v Cooke*[162] Mrs Cooke was attempting to assert a share of the equitable ownership of her matrimonial home which would bind the bank which had been granted a mortgage to secure the husband's business overdraft. Whilst constructive trusts may still be relevant between married couples the most significant context in which they will determine proprietary rights is in cases of cohabitation, whether heterosexual or homosexual. In such cases the parties may never have agreed upon the ownership of any house they occupy and it is all too easy for a more legally aware partner to ensure that he or she remains the legal owner as an insurance that it will continue to belong to him or her if the relationship breaks down. The social context in which a constructive trust tends to be sought was recognised by the Court of Appeal in *Midland Bank v Cooke*, where Waite L.J. commented:

> "Equity has traditionally been a system which matches established principle to the demands of social change. The mass diffusion of home ownership has been one of the most striking social changes of our time. The present case is typical of hundreds, perhaps thousands, of others. When people, especially young people, agree to share their lives in joint homes they do so on a basis of mutual trust and in the expectation that their relationship will endure. Despite the efforts that have been made by many responsible bodies to counsel prospective cohabitants as to the risks of taking shared interests in property without legal advice, it is unrealistic to expect that advice to be followed on a universal scale. For a couple embarking on a serious relationship, discussion of the terms to apply at parting is almost a contradiction of the shared hope which brought them together. There will inevitably be numerous couples, married or unmarried, who have no discussion about ownership and who, perhaps advisedly, make no agreement about it."[163]

In such cases the other party will only be able to seek a share of the ownership by way of a resulting or constructive trust, and if his or her financial contribution is relatively small as a proportion of the purchase price then the only realistic prospect of securing a substantial benefit is by way of a constructive trust imposed on the basis of a common intention that they were to share the ownership of the land. Since the court has no discretion to apportion property between cohabitees when their relationship breaks down, the principles of constructive trusts will often be the only way that a party who was not the legal owner can maintain a claim. This was exactly the situation in which Janet Eves found herself and her position would be no different today. It remains to be seen whether the principles enunciated in *Lloyds Bank v Rosset* would continue to ensure her a share of the ownership of the house she had cohabited.

(f) *The Relationship Between Constructive Trusts and Proprietary Estoppel*

Although English law has adopted a restrictive concept of the constructive trust it must be noted that a constructive trust is not the only means by which a person can obtain an interest **11–042**

---

[162] [1995] 4 All E.R. 562.
[163] [1995] 4 All E.R. 575.

in land informally. The closely related doctrine of proprietary estoppel also enables a person to obtain an interest in land. There are three key differences between the operation of the two concepts. First, whereas constructive trusts are awarded because of a supposed common intention between the parties, an interest by way of proprietary estoppel will arise wherever a person has acted to his detriment in reliance upon a representation he received that he would enjoy an interest in the land. Secondly, whereas under a constructive trust the court has no remedial discretion but merely recognises that the claimant is entitled to a share of the equitable ownership of the land, in the case of proprietary estoppel once a party has demonstrated that he is entitled to some remedy because the requirements have been met, the precise remedy awarded is a matter for the court to determine in its discretion taking into account all the circumstances. In some cases the court has felt that it is appropriate to award the claimant the full fee simple ownership of the land concerned. In other cases a lesser interest, such as a right to occupy, has been granted. The court has also awarded merely monetary compensation. Thirdly, whereas a constructive trust arises at the moment when the common intention is acted upon, which means that it may bind third parties acquiring interests in the land after that time but before the court has recognised the entitlement, any interest by way of proprietary estoppel may only arise after it has been awarded by the court.

A number of recent cases, including *Lloyds Bank v Rosset*, have emphasised that there is a great deal of similarity between the principles of constructive trusts and proprietary estoppel, and that in many instances it may be possible for a plaintiff to make out a claim on either ground. In *Yaxley v Gotts* Robert Walker L.J. went so far as to suggest that:

> "in the area of a joint enterprise for the acquisition of land (which may be, but is not necessarily, the matrimonial home) the two concepts coincided."[164]

If this is indeed the case, then it is likely that the courts will develop a common set of principles which diminish or eliminate the differences between the doctrines as described above.[165] The approach taken by the Court of Appeal in *Midland Bank v Cooke*[166] could be seen as indication that the courts are likely to adopt a more flexible approach to finding a common intention than has been the case in the past. This has the potential to reduce some of the inadequacies of constructive trusts, but at the cost of reducing the predictability of the outcome of a dispute. However, Lord Walker has recently reconsidered his position in *Stack v Dowden*[167]:

> "I have to say that I am now rather less enthusiastic about the notion that proprietary estoppel and 'common interest' constructive trusts can or should be completely assimilated. Proprietary estoppel typically consists of asserting an equitable claim against the conscience of the 'true' owner. The claim is a 'mere equity'. It is to be satisfied by the minimum award necessary to do justice . . . which may sometimes lead to no more than

---

[164] [2000] 1 All E.R. 711. See also *Banner Homes Plc v Luff Developments Ltd* [2000] 2 W.L.R. 772.
[165] In the two recent cases of *Driver v Yorke* [2003] 2 P. & C.R. D10 and *Oxley v Hiscock* [2004] EWCA Civ. 546 the court drew from the principles of proprietary estoppel to determine whether a constructive trust had arisen.
[166] [1995] 4 All E.R. 562.
[167] [2007] 2 A.C. 432.

a monetary award. A 'common intention' constructive trust, by contrast, is identifying the true beneficial owner or owners, and the size of their beneficial interests."

Proprietary estoppel is considered in detail in Chapter 19.

2. Establishing a Constructive Trust: *Lloyds Bank v Rosset*

Mr and Mrs Rosset had married in 1972. In 1982 Mr Rosset became entitled to a substantial sum of money under a trust fund established by his grandmother in Switzerland. They decided to purchase and renovate a house, which was in a semi-derelict condition. The house was purchased for £57,000 and title was registered in the sole name of Mr Rosset. The purchase was made in his sole name at the insistence of the trustees advancing the money to him. The cost of the renovation work was also solely provided by Mr Rosset. Mrs Rosset helped with the renovation by decorating the bedrooms of the property and preparing other rooms for decoration. She also supervised and encouraged the builders who were employed to work on the house. Unknown to Mrs Rosset, Mr Rosset in fact mortgaged the house to the bank to secure his overdraft up to £15,000. After marital difficulties Mr Rosset left his wife and children in occupation of the house. He failed to keep up repayments on his loan and the bank demanded possession and sale of the house to enforce its security. Mrs Rosset claimed that she was entitled to a share of the ownership of the house by way of a constructive trust which was binding on the bank as an overriding interest under the Land Registration Act 1925, s.70(1)(g). The House of Lords was therefore asked to determine whether Mrs Rosset enjoyed a share of the equitable ownership of the house. It concluded that no trust had arisen.

11–043

The central reason why the House of Lords held that Mrs Rosset was not entitled to a constructive trust was that she was unable to demonstrate that there had been a common intention between herself and her husband that she was to enjoy a share of the ownership of the house. Lord Bridge, delivering the judgment of the House, drew a sharp distinction between two circumstances in which a common intention could be established, namely where there was evidence of an express intention which had been articulated between the parties that they were to share the ownership, and where there was no evidence of an express intention but an intention to share could nevertheless be inferred from their conduct. He criticised the judge at first instance, who had reached the conclusion that there was such an intention, on the grounds of his failure to keep these two categories distinct:

> "I cannot help thinking that the judge in the instant case would not have fallen into error if he had kept clearly in mind the distinction between the effect of evidence on the one hand which was capable of establishing an express agreement or an express representation that Mrs Rosset was to have an interest in the property and evidence on the other hand of conduct alone as a basis for an inference of the necessary common intention."[168]

---

[168] [1991] 1 A.C. 107 at 134.

The approach to constructive trusts adopted by the House of Lords therefore means that essentially different criteria apply depending upon whether a case involves an express or implied common intention.

(a) *Constructive Trusts Founded on an Express Common Intention*

(i) Establishing an Express Common Intention

11–044 The first category of circumstance in which a constructive trust may arise is where there was an express common intention between the parties that they were to share the ownership of the land. The establishment of such an express intention is a matter of evidence of what the parties said to each other at the time that the property was purchased and thereafter. Such an intention cannot be inferred from the nature of the parties' expectations arising from their relationship,[169] or from their conduct alone. In *Lloyds Bank v Rosset* Lord Bridge stated what a party must demonstrate in order to establish an express common intention:

> "The first and fundamental question which must always be resolved is whether . . . there has at any time prior to the acquisition, or exceptionally at any later date, been any agreement, arrangement or understanding reached between them that the property is to be shared beneficially. The finding of an agreement or arrangement to share in this sense can only, I think, be based on evidence of express discussions between the partners, however imperfectly remembered and however imprecise their terms may have been."[170]

On the evidence that was presented he concluded that no such common intention could be established. Lord Bridge explained that in the light of the known circumstances of the purchase a particularly heavy evidential burden would have to have been satisfied by Mrs Rosset that she was intended to be a joint owner of the house:

> "Spouses living in amity do not normally think it necessary to formulate or define their respective interests in property in any precise way. The expectation of parties to every happy marriage is that they will share the practical benefits of occupying the matrimonial home whoever owns it. But this is something quite distinct from sharing the beneficial interest in the property asset which the matrimonial home represents . . . Since Mr Rosset was providing the whole purchase price of the property and the whole cost of its renovation, Mrs Rosset would, I think, in any event have encountered formidable difficulty in establishing her claim to joint beneficial ownership. The claim as pleaded and as presented in evidence was, by necessary implication to an equal share in the equity. But to sustain this it was necessary to show that it was Mr Rosset's intention to make

---

[169] Thus, in *James v Thomas* [2007] EWCA Civ 1212, promises made that "this will benefit us both" during the course of improvements to a property related to improvements in the couple's quality of life and not to an interest in the house: para.33. Similarly, a representation that "you will be well provided for" was "a representation as to what the position would be after Mr Thomas' death": para.35.

[170] [1991] 1 A.C. 107 at 132.

an immediate gift to his wife of half the value of a property acquired for £57,000 and improved at a further cost of some £15,000. What made it doubly difficult for Mrs Rosset to establish her case was the circumstance, which was never in dispute, that Mr Rosset's uncle, who was trustee of his Swiss inheritance, would not release the funds for the purchase of the property except on terms that it was to be acquired in Mr Rosset's sole name. If Mr and Mrs Rosset had ever thought about it, they must have realised that the creation of a trust giving Mrs Rosset a half share, or indeed any other substantial share, in the beneficial ownership, of the property would have been nothing less than a subterfuge to circumvent the stipulation which the Swiss trustee insisted on as a condition of releasing the funds to enable the property to be acquired. In these circumstances, it would have required very cogent evidence to establish that it was the Rossets' common intention to defeat the evident purpose of the Swiss trustee's restriction by acquiring the property in Mr Rosset's name alone but to treat it nevertheless as beneficially owned by both spouses."[171]

Lord Bridge therefore emphasised that to establish that the parties had "entered into an agreement, made an arrangement, reached an understanding or formed a common intention that the beneficial interest in the property would be jointly owned", expressions that he felt were synonymous, required very clear evidence.

Although the Rossets had failed to satisfy this evidential burden, he noted cases where he considered that the burden would have been satisfied. He suggested that *Eves v Eves*[172] and *Grant v Edwards*[173] were "outstanding examples"[174] of cases where there had been an express common intention. In *Eves v Eves* Stuart had told Janet, when they set up home together, that the only reason why the house had not been put in their joint names was that she was too young. In *Grant v Edwards* a man set up home with a woman and told her that he was purchasing the house they shared in his name alone because adding her name to the title would prejudice her divorce proceedings. However, although superficially these assurances could be taken as evidence of an ultimate intention that the land should be co-owned when the supposed impediment was overcome, it is somewhat artificial to represent these statements as reflecting a real intention on the part of the legal owner of the property. In both cases the explanation given to the co-habiting woman was merely an excuse by the man to ensure that he was protected as the owner of the property if the relationship failed. There was never any genuine intention that the women should enjoy a share of the beneficial ownership. In fact the real intention was that they would never enjoy such an interest. This points to the artificiality of the imposition of a constructive trust as a fulfilment of the expressed common intention of the parties. It seems rather that what is important is that the legal owner gave the other person the impression that he intended the ownership of the land to be shared, and that having created that impression he cannot claim the defence of his "real" intentions. In this sense the express intention is extremely close to the concept of an express representation in cases of proprietary estoppel where a landowner deliberately misleads a person as to his rights in the

---

[171] [1991] 1 A.C. 107 at 128.
[172] [1975] 1 W.L.R. 1338.
[173] [1986] Ch. 638.
[174] [1991] 1 A.C. 107 at 133.

land. This overlap between the two concepts seems to have been recognised by Lord Bridge since he failed to distinguish them rigorously and suggested that in both *Eves v Eves* and *Grant v Edwards* the court had "rightly held" that the female partner was entitled to "a constructive trust or proprietary estoppel." However, as has been noted there are important conceptual distinctions between the doctrines of constructive trusts and proprietary estoppel, including the form of the remedy that is available and the time at which any interest in the land is taken to arise. Although the same facts may support both a claim to a constructive trust and an estoppel equity, it is important the principles should not be muddled.

In subsequent cases it has been made clear that the principles established in *Lloyds Bank v Rosset* do not require the parties to have reached a common intention as to the respective shares to be taken by the beneficial owners. In *Drake v Whipp* Peter Gibson L.J. explained:

> "All that is required for the creation of a constructive trust is that there should be a common intention that the party who is not the legal owner should have a beneficial interest and that that party should act to his or her detriment in reliance thereon."[175]

(ii)   Detriment where there was an Express Common Intention

11–045   The mere fact of an express common intention is not alone sufficient to entitle a person to an interest by way of a constructive trust. An owner of property is perfectly entitled to make unenforceable promises about what he will do with it and then fail to carry them into effect. For example, if a man promises to make a gift and then fails to do so the intended donor cannot claim entitlement to the property. A constructive trust is only enforced because it would be unconscionable in the circumstances for the legal owner to retain the absolute ownership of the land, in effect failing to abide by the expressed or agreed intentions. This will only be the case if the party claiming the interest had acted to his or her detriment in some way on the basis of the common intention. This raises the question as to what conduct will constitute sufficient detriment to establish the entitlement to a constructive trust. It is clear from *Lloyds Bank v Rosset*[176] that the level of conduct which will constitute detriment is significantly lower from that which is required in order to infer that there was a common intention in the first place. As Lord Bridge commented in relation to *Eves v Eves* and *Grant v Edwards*:

> "The subsequent conduct of the female partners in each case, which the court rightly held sufficient to give rise to a constructive trust . . . fell far short of such conduct as would by itself have supported the claim in the absence of an express representation by the male partner that she was to have such an interest."

The standard of conduct required to establish detriment to give effect to an express common intention is relatively low. Lord Bridge stated:

---

[175] [1996] 1 F.L.R. 826 at 830; A novel point arose in *Ledger-Beadell v Peach* [2006] EWHC 2940; [2007] 2 F.L.R. 210, in which judge Nicholas Strauss Q.C. held that a constructive trust had arisen where money had been advanced towards acquisition of a house and that it was the intention of all parties that the contributor would become entitled to a share, not immediately, but in the event of circumstances that, as it happened, took place.
[176] [1991] 1 A.C. 107.

"Once a finding [of an express common intention] is made it will only be necessary for the partner asserting a claim to a beneficial interest against the partner entitled to the legal estate to show that he or she acted to his or her detriment or significantly altered his position in reliance on the agreement in order to give rise to a constructive trust . . ."[177]

The affirmation of *Eves v Eves* on this basis suggests that the conduct need not involve significant financial contributions to constitute detriment, but that non-financial activity such as Janet's decoration and building work are themselves sufficient. The position of detriment was more fully considered by the Court of Appeal in *Grant v Edwards*, which also received the House of Lords' approval. Linda Grant moved in with George Edwards in circumstances where there was an express common intention that she would be entitled to a share of the house. George paid the mortgage but Linda made financial contributions to the housekeeping expenses and to the bringing up of their children. Nourse L.J. took the view that this could be regarded as making an indirect financial contribution to the mortgage instalments, because it enabled George to pay them out of his wages. However Browne-Wilkinson V.C. took a more liberal and expansive view:

"Once it has been shown that there was a common intention that the claimant should have an interest in the house, any act done by her to her detriment relating to the joint lives of the parties is, in my judgment, sufficient detriment to qualify. The acts do not have to be referable to the house . . . In many cases of the present sort, it is impossible to say whether or not the claimant would have done the acts relied on as a detriment even if she thought she had no interest in the house. Setting up house together, having a baby, making payments to general housekeeping expenses (not strictly necessary to enable the mortgage to be paid) may all be referable to the mutual love and affection of the parties and not specifically referable to the claimant's belief that she has an interest in the home."

Given that Lord Bridge spoke in terms of a "substantial change of position" as sufficient detriment it seems that Browne-Wilkinson V.C.'s views should be preferred and that any conduct of the claimant should be taken into account when determining if there was detriment, not merely conduct referable to the property. However although all varieties of conduct will be taken into account in assessing detriment a threshold must be exceeded so that conduct which is only "de minimis" will not amount to a "substantial change of position". On this basis Lord Bridge considered that even if there had been an express common intention Mrs Rosset's contributions to the work of renovating the house would have been insufficient to support a claim to a constructive trust.

The element of detriment was considered more recently in *Banner Homes Group Plc v Luff Developments Ltd*[178] in the context of an acquisition of commercial property. The plaintiff and the defendant reached an agreement to acquire and develop a site together. The defendant subsequently reneged on this agreement and acquired the land alone. While the agreement was

[177] [1991] 1 A.C. 107 at 132.
[178] [2000] 2 W.L.R. 772.

unenforceable as a contract due to its lack of formality, the Court of Appeal held that the defendant held the land on constructive trust. There was an express common intention that the land would be jointly owned, and the plaintiff had acted to its detriment by failing to consider acquiring the site for its own commercial portfolio. As Chadwick L.J. observed, given that the defendant had wanted to keep the plaintiff out of the market, "it does not lie easily in Luff's mouth to say that Banner suffered no detriment".[179] In *Pritchard Englefield v Steinberg*,[180] a son had bought a flat from the family company at a reduced price, the undervalue being the result of the fictional basis that his mother was a sitting tenant.[181] He had thereby acquired a considerable asset which he used to raise money for his business. She had not intervened to prevent him either from purchasing the flat or from using it to raise finance because he had assured her that she could live there. He held the property on constructive trust to give effect to her life interest.

(iii)   Quantifying the Equitable Interest

11–046   In principle, where a constructive trust arises because there was an express common intention, the claimant should be entitled to a share of the equitable ownership equivalent to that which it was intended she should enjoy. In this respect the decision of the Court of Appeal in *Eves v Eves*,[182] a supposed paradigm of a constructive trust imposed because of an express common intention, is anomalous. All the indications were that the intention was that Janet should be named as a joint owner of the legal title, but it was held that she was only entitled to a quarter share of the equitable interest. Brightman L.J. expressed some doubts about this and seemed to prefer the view that she should be entitled to a half share. In *Grant v Edwards*[183] Browne-Wilkinson L.J. suggested that this anomaly could be explained by analogy with the law of proprietary estoppel. The case was in any event decided applying Lord Denning's concept of the "new model" constructive trust which was subsequently rejected as heretical.

(b)   *Constructive Trusts Founded on an Inferred Common Intention*

(i)   Inferring a Common Intention from the Parties' Conduct

11–047   The absence of an express common intention between the legal owner and the claimant does not inevitably mean that there can be no constructive trust. As has already been noted, the most difficult situations arise where the parties have given no direct consideration to their respective proprietary entitlements and have acted on the basis of assumptions and preconceptions derived from the nature of their relationship, which only become apparent when some difficulties arise between them. It also seems that there is no difficulty inferring a common intention from the parties' conduct even when there is evidence that the parties

---

[179] [2000] 2 W.L.R. 772 at 769.
[180] [2005] 1 P. & C.R. DG2.
[181] Ensuring that the flat could not be reached by creditors: [2005] 1 P. & C.R. DG2.
[182] [1975] 1 W.L.R. 1338.
[183] [1986] Ch. 638 at 657–658.

had had no intentions as to the ownership of the property. In *Midland Bank Plc v Cooke*[184] the evidence presented at trial by a husband and wife demonstrated that at the time that their matrimonial home was purchased in the husband's name there had been no discussions as to how the property should be owned beneficially. Counsel for the bank argued that since the parties had testified on oath that they had made no agreement then there was no scope for equity to make one for them. Waite L.J., giving the judgment of the court, dismissed this argument as counter to the very system of equity:

> "It would be anomalous . . . to create a range of home-buyers who were beyond the pale of equity's assistance in formulating a fair presumed basis for sharing of beneficial title, simply because they had been honest enough to admit that they never gave ownership a thought or reached any agreement about it."[185]

However the courts have always been reluctant to infer that land would be jointly owned merely because the parties were in a relationship, whether marriage or of a quasi-matrimonial nature. Ownership of property is such a significantly more important entitlement than mere occupation that something beyond the ordinary course of human relationships has been expected. In *Pettitt v Pettitt*[186] Lord Diplock stressed that a common intention of joint ownership is not to be inferred from the mere fact that the parties have done what spouses or partners would ordinarily do:

> "It is common enough nowadays for husbands and wives to decorate and to make improvements in the family home themselves, with no other intention than to indulge in what is now a popular hobby, and to make the home pleasanter for their common use and enjoyment. If the husband likes to occupy his leisure by laying a new lawn in the garden or building a fitted wardrobe in the bedroom while the wife does the shopping, cooks the family dinner or bathes the children, I, for my part, find it quite impossible to impute to them as reasonable husband and wife any common intention that these domestic activities or any of them are to have any effect upon the existing proprietary rights in the family home on which they are undertaken."

Although these sentiments may reflect a more traditional concept of the family, and of family roles, than is current today, the basic proposition remains valid that only exceptional conduct by a party will give rise to an inference of a common intention. In *Lloyds Bank v Rosset*[187] the House of Lords took the view that only substantial financial contributions to the purchase price of the property could be regarded as sufficient to raise an inference of a common intention. Lord Bridge explained:

> "In sharp contrast [to the case where there is an express common intention] is the very different one where there is no evidence to support a finding of an agreement or arrangement

---

[184] [1995] 4 All E.R. 562.
[185] [1995] 4 All E.R. 562 at 575.
[186] [1970] A.C. 777 at 826.
[187] [1991] 1 A.C. 107 at 132–133.

to share, however reasonable it might have been for the parties to reach such an arrangement if they had applied their minds to the question, and where the court must rely entirely on the conduct of the parties both as the basis from which to infer a common intention to share the property beneficially and as the conduct relied on to give rise to a constructive trust. In this situation direct contributions to the purchase price by the partner who is not the legal owner, whether initially or by payment of the mortgage instalments, will readily justify the inference necessary to the creation of a constructive trust. But, as I read the authorities, it is at least extremely doubtful whether anything less will do."

11–048 Lord Bridge's statement of principle was greeted with criticism, on the grounds that it was unduly restrictive in requiring a direct contribution to the purchase price of the property. A common intention would thus be able to be inferred where a person had made a financial contribution to the purchase of the property, had enabled the property to be purchased at a discounted price,[188] had contributed to the payment of the mortgage, or had increased the value of the property by undertaking or contributing to the cost of improvements. However in *Lloyds Bank v Rosset* itself the House of Lords held that Mrs Rosset's conduct in decorating the house and supervising the work of the renovating builders was incapable of founding such an inference. As Lord Bridge commented:

"on any view the monetary value of Mrs Rosset's work expressed as a contribution to a property acquired at a cost exceeding £70,000 must have been so trifling as to be almost de minimis."

However even a direct financial contribution to the purchase price of property will not give rise to a constructive trust if the contribution was made in circumstances which demonstrate that there was no intention on the part of the contributor to obtain an interest in the property. Thus a contribution to the purchase price of land by way of gift or loan will not give rise to a trust.[189] In *Driver v Yorke*[190] the two sons of the purchaser of a flat made occasional contributions to the mortgage instalments. Judge Bowsher Q.C. held that these payments did not have the necessary connection with the purchase to be treated as a contribution to the purchase price. In *Lightfoot v Lightfoot-Brown*[191] the Court of Appeal held that no common intention of beneficial ownership could be inferred from a husband's £41,000 capital mortgage payment because his estranged spouse was unaware of the payment and a common intention must be "manifested" by the other's conduct.[192]

A common intention will not be able to be inferred in the absence of a relevant contribution to the purchase price of the property. In *Driver v Yorke*,[193] for example, a son of the purchaser of a flat had acted as a guarantor of the mortgage. Judge Bowsher Q.C. held that this was not a relevant contribution to the purchase price because he had not shown any intention of being liable for the mortgage instalments. In contrast to direct financial contributions to the

---

[188] As was the case in *Oxley v Hiscock* [2004] EWCA Civ. 546.
[189] See *Re Sharpe (A Bankrupt)* [1980] 1 W.L.R. 219.
[190] [2003] 2 P. & C.R. 210.
[191] [2005] EWCA Civ 201.
[192] [2005] EWCA Civ 201, para.27, relying on *Gissing v Gissing* [1971] A.C. 886 at 906.
[193] [2003] 2 P. & C.R. 210.

purchase price of the property, non-financial contributions to a partnership, such as providing childcare and looking after the house, would certainly be incapable of giving rise to a constructive trust. Similarly contributions towards household expenses would at first sight appear incapable of giving rise to a constructive trust. However in some subsequent cases the courts have adopted a more liberal approach than that indicated by a strict reading of Lord Bridge's statement, holding that a common intention can be inferred where a claimant made payments which indirectly contributed to the purchase price of the property by enabling the legal owner to pay the mortgage. In *Le Foe v Le Foe*[194] Nicholas Mostyn Q.C. held that a couples' financial contributions should be viewed as a whole, so that a wife's financial contributions towards household expenses could be regarded as an indirect contribution to the purchase price of the property. He explained:

> "Although I am sure that H earned more than W . . . I have no doubt that the family economy depended for its function on W's earnings. It was an arbitrary allocation of responsibility that H paid the mortgage, service charge and outgoings, whereas W paid for day-to-day domestic expenditure. I have clearly concluded that W contributed indirectly to the mortgage repayments, the principal of which furnished part of the consideration of the initial purchase price."[195]

Although the wife in question had in fact contributed directly to the purchase price, by using an inheritance she received to discharge a mortgage on the property, the more liberal approach adopted towards indirect financial contributions is consistent with the earlier judgement of the House of Lords in *Gissing v Gissing*,[196] where Lord Diplock indicated that a wife would be able to acquire a beneficial interest if she had contributed to the household expenditure and the husband would not have been able to afford to pay the mortgage instalments unless she had done so. Perhaps the best way to resolve any apparent contradiction with the statement of Lord Bridge in *Lloyd's Bank v Rosset* is to interpret a financial contribution to household expenses as a direct contribution to the purchase price if the legal owner of the property would not otherwise have been able to pay the mortgage. Even this expanded liberal interpretation will not assist a person who makes a contribution to general household expenses but this did not enable the owner to make the mortgage payments. Such a person will only be able to establish a constructive trust if there was an express common intention to share the ownership of the property.

In *Stack v Dowden*,[197] Lord Walker, strictly obiter, was critical of *Lloyds Bank v Rosset*:

> "Whether or not Lord Bridge's observation [that he doubted whether anything less than direct contributions would do to infer a common intention] was justified in 1990, in my opinion the law has moved on, and your Lordships should move it a little more in the same direction"[198]

---

[194] [2001] 2 F.L.R. 970.
[195] ibid. at 973.
[196] [1971] A.C. 886 at 907–908.
[197] [2007] 2 A.C. 432.
[198] [2007] 2 A.C. 432, para.26.

It was unreal and did not reflect the reality that property was purchased as part of the parties' joint lives. Wider evidence should be used to ascertain the cohabitants' common intentions,[199] and the idea of what constitutes a contribution should be broader, e.g. manual labour, improvements to the house.[200] However, his Lordship relied on *Drake v Whipp* and *Oxley v Hiscock*, cases primarily on quantifying the size of a beneficial interest once that interest has been established. So it is unclear the extent to which it is possible to rely on these comments as indicating a widening of the criteria for establishing a beneficial interest in the first place.[201]

In any case, it is appears harder to establish a beneficial interest in the situation where a person goes to live with their partner in property that is already owned by that partner. Although the point was mentioned in both *Gissing v Gissing* and *Lloyds Bank v Rosset*, two recent post-acquisition cases illustrate the trend. In *James v Thomas*[202] the claimant moved in with the defendant into his family home that he had acquired from his siblings following the death of their mother. The couple were partners in his business, to which the claimant contributed significantly, and the profits of the business were used to pay the mortgage. The Court of Appeal held that her claim to a beneficial interest in the home failed. No common intention could be inferred. The parties relied on the business to meet all their outgoings so it was not surprising that she contributed. "[W]hat she was doing was wholly explicable on other grounds".[203]

> "[I]n the absence of an express post-acquisition agreement, a court will be slow to infer from conduct alone that parties intended to vary existing beneficial interests established at the time of acquisition".[204]

James v Thomas was applied in *Morris v Morris*,[205] where the Court of Appeal held that in cases such as this the courts should be slow to interpret conduct of spouses or cohabitants as meaning that a beneficial interest of some sort should be acquired. The respondent and his mother were joint owners of a farmhouse that was part of the family farm. The claimant married and moved in with the respondent and contributed free of charge to the family farming business. She also provided the money to purchase an enclosure and started her own riding school funded partly by a free loan made by the respondent and his mother. The conduct was not exceptional, as required in post-acquisition cases, partly because she had received benefits towards her own business.[206]

(ii) Distinguishing a Constructive Trust Founded on an Inferred Common Intention from a Resulting Trust

11–049 Given that the decision of the House of Lords in *Lloyds Bank v Rosset* has effectively eliminated the possibility of finding a constructive trust in the absence of an express common

---

[199] [2007] 2 A.C. 432, para.31; also Baroness Hale at paras 60–63, where there is some support for this conclusion.
[200] "[W]hile remaining sceptical of the value of alleged improvements that are really insignificant": [2007] 2 A.C. 432, paras 34, 36.
[201] Also, *Stack v Dowden* was a case on quantifying the size of shares, not on establishing an interest in the first place: [2007] 2 A.C. 432, para.63, per Baroness Hale.
[202] [2007] EWCA Civ 1212.
[203] [2007] EWCA Civ 1212, per Sir John Chadwick at para.27.
[204] [2007] EWCA Civ 1212, per Sir John Chadwick at para.24, referring to *Gissing v Gissing*; also *Lloyds Bank v Rosset*.
[205] [2008] EWCA Civ 257.
[206] [2008] EWCA Civ 257 (Westlaw summary).

intention if there was no direct financial contribution to the purchase of the property the question arises as to whether there is any substantive difference between a constructive trust where a common intention is inferred from a contribution to the purchase price and a resulting trust. Despite the superficial similarity of the two principles, both of which confer a beneficial interest in the land informally as a consequence of financial contribution, the two concepts are distinct. This is evident at the level of the quantification of the share of the equitable ownership obtained. Under a resulting trust the share is determined mathematically as the proportion of the purchase price contributed. In the case of a constructive trust it is the inferred common intention which is given effect, and the share arising under the constructive trust may be far in excess of the relative proportion of the price contributed. This was recognised by Lord Bridge, who commented:

> "It is significant to note that the shares to which the female partners in *Eves v Eves* and *Grant v Edwards* were held entitled were one quarter and one half respectively. In no sense could these shares have been regarded as proportionate to what the judge in the instant case described as the 'qualifying contribution' in terms of the indirect contributions to the acquisition or enhancement of the value of the properties made by the female partners."[207]

As has already been noted above this distinction is also evident in the case of *Midland Bank v Cooke*[208] where a contribution to the purchase price which would have entitled a wife to a mere 6.74 per cent share of the equitable ownership by way of a resulting trust was held to be sufficient to lead to an inference of a common intention constructive trust of a half share. The difficulty with *Midland Bank v Cooke* as a precedent is that there was very little evidence from which the court could infer an intention to share equally. In the recent case of *Stack v Dowden*, the House of Lords held that where a house was conveyed into the joint names of a couple, then there would be a presumption that they intended to share the beneficial interest equally, irrespective of the size of the parties' respective contributions to the purchase price. The majority of the House of Lords held that it would require more than an examination of direct contributions to rebut this presumption and show that the parties' intended their beneficial interests to be different from their legal interests.

(iii) Determining the Beneficial Interests of the Parties Under a Constructive Trust Arising from an Inferred Common Intention

Although *Lloyds Bank v Rosset* clearly established that a common intention to share the beneficial ownership of land can only be inferred from a relevant financial contribution to the purchase price, it failed to address conclusively the way in which the respective shares of the parties in the beneficial interest should be determined. This has left room for uncertainty, judicial interpretation and for the reintroduction of an element of judicial discretion. It appears that the requirement of a financial contribution operates as a trigger to establish the necessary common intention, but that once a common intention to share has been inferred the court can

11–050

---

[207] [1991] 1 A.C. 107 at 133.
[208] [1995] 4 All E.R. 562.

take account of other non-financial considerations to determine the respective shares of the parties in the beneficial ownership. There were conflicting Court of Appeal authorities as to whether the court undertakes the determination of the respective interests of the parties by identifying their assumed intentions from the available evidence, or by exercising a discretion to decide what would be "fair" in all the circumstances. This matter has now been resolved by the House of Lords.[209]

In *Midland Bank v Cooke*[210] the Court of Appeal determined the respective interests of the parties by identifying their assumed intentions from all the available evidence. As has already been noted, the circumstances of the case were that Mrs Cooke had contributed 6.74 per cent of the purchase price of the matrimonial home by her half-share of a wedding gift of £1,100 which Mr Cooke's parents had made to them jointly when they married. However, she claimed entitlement to a half share by way of a constructive trust arising from their common intention that they were to share the house equally. The evidence clearly failed to establish that there was an express common intention to share the ownership, but the Court of Appeal held that her small direct financial contribution to the purchase price was sufficient to infer the necessary common intention. However the Court of Appeal held that it was necessary to consider the whole course of dealing between the parties so as to be able to identify their assumed intentions in respect of the property. Waite L.J. explained:

> "The general principle to be derived from *Gissing v Gissing* and *Grant v Edwards* can in my judgment be summarised in this way. When the court is proceeding, in cases like the present where the partner without legal title has successfully asserted an equitable interest through direct contribution, to determine (in the absence of express evidence of intention) what proportions the parties must be assumed to have intended for their beneficial ownership, the duty of the judge is to undertake a survey of the whole course of dealing between the parties relevant to their ownership and occupation of the property and their sharing its burdens and advantages. That scrutiny will not confine itself to a limited range of acts of direct contribution of the sort that are needed to found a beneficial interest in the first place. It will take into consideration all conduct which throws light on the question what shares were intended. Only if that search proves inconclusive does the court fall back on the maxim that 'equality is equity'."[211]

Having examined all the evidence of the parties' relationship the Court of Appeal concluded that their intentions should be assumed to have been to share the property equally. Waite L.J. pointed especially to the fact that she had looked after their children and maintained the property, contributed to household bills from her own salary and consented to a second mortgage of the house to guarantee her husband's business debts. He concluded:

> "One could hardly have a clearer example of a couple who had agreed to share everything equally: the profits of his business while it prospered, and the risks of indebtedness

---

[209] *Stack v Dowden*, discussed below.
[210] [1995] 4 All E.R. 562.
[211] [1995] 4 All E.R. 562 at 574.

suffered through its failure; the upbringing of their children; the rewards of her own career as a teacher; and most relevantly, a home into which he put his savings and to which she was to give over the years the benefit of the maintenance and improvement contribution. When to all this there is added the fact (still an important one) that this was a couple who had chosen to introduce into their relationship the additional commitment which marriage involves, the conclusion becomes inescapable that their presumed intention was to share the beneficial interest in the property in equal shares."

This broader approach was followed in *Le Foe v Le Foe*[212] by Nicholas Mostyn Q.C. who held that the Court of Appeal in *Midland Bank v Cooke* had decided to adopt "the more holistic approach of looking at the parties' global dealings over the span of their ownership of the property" rather than "the straightjacket of the mathematical resulting trust approach." Applying this holistic approach he inferred that a husband and wife who had been married for over forty years had intended to share their matrimonial home. This meant that the wife was entitled to a half share of the house, which was worth £1 million, not a 10 per cent share which would have reflected the £100,000 she had contributed to the purchase price.

A similar approach was adopted by the Court of Appeal in *Oxley v Hiscock*.[213] A house was purchased in 1991 to provide a home for Mr Hiscock and Mrs Oxley, who were living together. The house was purchased solely in the name of Mr Hiscock, and the purchase price was provided partly by the proceeds of sale of a previous property owned by Mrs Oxley, partly by a direct financial contribution from Mr Hiscock's savings, and partly by way of a mortgage. The parties' relationship ended in 1999, and in 2001 the house was sold. As Mrs Oxley had made a direct contribution to the purchase price of the house, there was no doubt that she was entitled to an interest by way of a constructive trust because the necessary common intention could be inferred. The case therefore concerned the extent of her beneficial interest in the house. At first instance it was held that she was entitled to a half-share of the equitable ownership by way of a constructive trust. Mr Hiscock appealed against this decision, arguing that because they had not discussed the extent of their respective beneficial interests at the time of the purchase they should each receive a share proportionate to their financial contributions, in other words that their interests should be determined by a resulting trust. On this basis he claimed that Mrs Oxley was only entitled to a 22 per cent share of the equitable ownership. The Court of Appeal rejected this argument, holding that Mrs Oxley was entitled to an interest by way of a constructive trust and not just a resulting trust. The Court of Appeal was therefore forced to consider how the respective interests of the parties should be determined in the absence of any evidence of any discussion between them as to the amount of the share they were each to have. It considered a number of alternative approaches which had been adopted at various times, including that of Waite L.J. in *Midland Bank v Cooke*,[214] and found them to be wanting. Chadwick L.J. stated the principle by which he thought that the court should determine the appropriate beneficial interests of the parties where there is no evidence of what their intentions were:

11–051

---

[212] [2001] 2 F.L.R. 970.
[213] [2004] EWCA Civ 546.
[214] [1995] 2 F.L.R. 915.

"It must now be accepted (at least in this Court and below) the answer is that each is entitled to that share which the court considers fair having regard to the whole course of dealing between them in relation to the property. And, in that context, the "whole course of dealing between them in relation to the property" includes the arrangements which they make from time to time in order to meet the outgoings (for example, mortgage contributions, council tax and utilities, repairs, insurance and housekeeping) which have to be met if they are to live in the property as their home."[215]

Applying this principle the Court of Appeal concluded that Mrs Oxley should only be entitled to a 40 per cent share of the equitable ownership of the house. Chadwick L.J. explained why he reached this conclusion:

"In my view to declare that the parties were entitled in equal shares would be unfair to Mr Hiscock. It would give insufficient weight to the fact that his direct contribution to the purchase price . . . was substantially greater than that of Mrs Oxley."[216]

There is a divergence between the "assumed intention" approach adopted by the Court of Appeal in *Midland Bank v Cooke* and the seeming "judicial discretion" approach adopted in *Oxley v Hiscock*. The approach adopted in *Oxley v Hiscock* owes more to the principles of proprietary estoppel rather than to the principles of constructive trusts, and indeed Chadwick L.J. relied primarily on estoppel authorities to conclude that the court should determine what was "fair" between the parties.[217] It will be seen below that the House of Lords has decided that the assumed intention, approach to quantification is the correct one. It is somewhat ironic that the decision as to what was "fair" on the facts of *Oxley* appears to have been less liberal than that in *Midland Bank v Cooke*. Chadwick L.J. placed greatest significance on the financial contributions of the parties, and not on the nature of their relationship. The judge at first instance had found that they had intended to share the ownership of the house in equal shares because it was a classic case of the "pooling of resources". Surely the fact that the parties had lived together in the property, which had been purchased to provide them with a home, for nearly 10 years should have taken precedence over the fact that one party had provided slightly more of the initial capital for the acquisition of the property.

(iv) Stack v Dowden and Determining the Beneficial Interests of the Parties where the House is Registered in Joint Names

11–052   In *Stack v Dowden*,[218] the House of Lords had to consider the principles by which beneficial interests are to be quantified. Mr Stack and Ms Dowden were unmarried cohabitees with four children. At first the couple lived in a house in Ms Dowden's name and she paid all the bills and the mortgage payments. They sold the property and bought another which was conveyed into joint names. Ms Dowden paid 65 per cent of the purchase price out of her savings account,

---

[215] [2004] EWCA Civ 546 at [69].
[216] [2004] EWCA Civ 546 at [74].
[217] In particular he relied on *Yaxley v Gotts* [2000] Ch. 162. See [2004] EWCA Civ 546 at [70].
[218] [2007] 2 A.C. 432.

which included the proceeds from the first property, and Mr Stack paid towards the mortgage repayments. The parties' paid off the mortgage as quickly as they could, Ms Dowden providing 60 per cent of these repayments. The couple separated in 2002 and Mr Stack argued that he was entitled to a 50 per cent interest in the house. The question in this case was "the effect of a conveyance into joint names without express declaration of the beneficial interests".[219] Would the beneficial interest follow the legal title so that the parties would be entitled to equal beneficial interests?[220] At first instance he was awarded a half share. Ms Dowden successfully appealed, the Court of Appeal awarding her a 65 per cent share. Baroness Hale, who gave the leading judgment in the House of Lords,[221] adopted a common-sense solution, and one which is likely to accord with most lay people's expectations of ownership. It was also aimed at reducing the possibility of litigation on the point which could be fuelled by bad feeling on the break-up of an intimate relationship.

> "It should only be expected that joint transferees would have spelt out their beneficial interests when they intended them to be different from their legal interests. Otherwise, it should be assumed that equity follows the law and that the beneficial interests reflect the legal interests in the property."[222]
>
> "Just as the starting point where there is sole legal ownership is sole beneficial ownership, the starting point where there is joint legal ownership is joint beneficial ownership. The onus is upon the person seeking to show that the beneficial ownership is different from the legal ownership."[223]

The question then naturally arose as to how the presumption of joint beneficial ownership could be rebutted. In a family home context "the importance to be attached to who paid for what in a domestic context may be very different from its importance in other contexts or long ago". Thus, in order to determine whether a common intention constructive trust arises to rebut the presumption of equality, "[t]he search is to ascertain the parties' shared intentions, actual, inferred or imputed, with respect to the property in the light of their whole course of conduct in relation to it".[224] She confirmed that this approach to quantifying beneficial interests, the approach of Chadwick L.J. in *Oxley v Hiscock*, applied in family home cases irrespective of whether legal title was registered in sole or joint names. In cases of sole ownership "the claimant had first to surmount the hurdle of showing that she had any beneficial interest at

---

[219] per Baroness Hale at para.48.

[220] The fact that this question has arisen at all was due to a change in conveyancing practice: *Stack v Dowden* [2007] 2 AC 432, per Baroness Hale at paras 49–50. The system of registration of title was designed to eliminate the purchaser's need to investigate the equitable interest under a trust. There is no need for the title to contain details of the beneficial interests so until recently the Land Registry has never required a declaration of how the beneficial interests are to be held. In 1998 the Land Registry introduced a requirement for those who purchase land as joint proprietors to declare how they are to hold the beneficial interest: Baroness Hale at para.52; also Law Commission, *Cohabitation: The Financial Consequences of Relationship Breakdown* (Law Com. No.307 (2007)), para.2.18.

[221] The majority agreed. Only Lord Neuberger dissented, on the law but not on the result.

[222] [2007] 2 A.C. 432, para.54; Baroness Hale relied on an analogy with *Malayan Credit Ltd v Jack Chia-MPH Ltd* [1986] A.C. 549, in the context of determining whether co-owners held as joint tenants or tenants in common in equity (see the next chapter).

[223] Para.56; For pre-*Stack v Dowden* recognition of the presumption that in joint ownership cases beneficial interests would follow the legal interests, see the Court of Appeal in *Crossley v Crossley* [2005] EWCA Civ 1581.

[224] [2007] 2 A.C. 432, para.60.

all,[225] before showing exactly what that interest was".[226] In cases of joint ownership, "a conveyance into joint names is sufficient, at least in the vast majority of cases, to surmount the first hurdle".[227] Baroness Hale added two clarifications to the principle in *Oxley v Hiscock*. First, the relevant search is not for what is "fair" but what was intended by the parties.[228] To allow the court to award the beneficial interest it thinks fair involved too large an element of discretion.[229] Secondly, the "whole course of dealing" examined by the court must relate to the property and not to the relationship in general. The first instance judge had wrongly directed himself to look "at their relationship rather than the matters which were particularly relevant to their intentions about this property".[230] Cases in which the presumption of joint beneficial ownership is rebutted would be "very unusual".[231] The party attempting to establish that the beneficial ownership was intended to be different from the legal ownership had to show much more than unequal contributions.[232] Baroness Hale stated a number of factors that are relevant to determining the parties' intentions, but each case depended on its own facts. Factors include:

> "[A]ny advice or discussions at the time of the transfer which cast light upon their intentions then;
> The reasons why the home was acquired in their joint names. . . .
> The purpose for which the home was acquired;
> The nature of the parties' relationship;
> Whether they had children for whom they both had responsibility to provide a home;
> How the purchase was financed, both initially and subsequently;
> How the parties arranged their finances, whether separately or together or a bit of both;
> How they discharged the outgoings on the property and their other household expenses;
> When a couple are joint owners of the home and jointly liable for the mortgage, the inferences to be drawn from who pays for what may be very different from the inferences to be drawn when only one is owner of the home. The arithmetical calculation of how much was paid by each is also likely to be less important. It will be easier to draw the inference that they intended that each should contribute as much to the household as they reasonably could and that they would share the eventual benefit or burden equally;
> The parties' individual characters and personalities. . . In the cohabitation context, mercenary considerations may be more to the fore than they would be in marriage, but it should not be assumed that they always take pride of place over natural love and affection."[233]

It is possible for intentions to change, for example, if "one party has financed (or constructed himself) an extension or substantial improvement to the property, so that what they have now

---

[225] To be established on *Rosset* principles.
[226] [2007] 2 A.C. 432, para.61.
[227] [2007] 2 A.C. 432, para.63.
[228] Which resolves the conflict in the Court of Appeal described above.
[229] [2007] 2 A.C. 432, para.61.
[230] [2007] 2 A.C. 432, per Baroness Hale at para.86.
[231] [2007] 2 A.C. 432, para.69.
[232] [2007] 2 A.C. 432, para.68. Thus, the presumption of resulting trust does not apply in such cases: *The Financial Consequences of Relationship Breakdown* Law Com. No.307 (2007), para.2.9.
[233] [2007] 2 A.C. 432, per Baroness Hale, para.69, formatting and some capital, supplied. Although she did not intend this to be an exhaustive list: para.70, also Law Com No.307 (2007).

is significantly different from what they had then".[234] Furthermore, joint ownership will have an effect on the court's perceptions of what the parties' intended as "it will almost always have been a conscious decision to put the house into joint names".[235]

On the facts of the case itself, Baroness Hale concluded that this was an unusual case and that Ms Dowden had successfully rebutted the strong presumption of joint beneficial ownership. The couple kept their affairs "rigidly separate"[236] and Ms Dowden had contributed much more to the financial acquisition of the property than Mr Stack had done.[237] "This is not a case in which it can be said that the parties pooled their separate resources, even notionally, for the common good . . . they undertook separate responsibility for that part of the expenditure which each had agreed to pay".[238] Mr Stack had not agreed to pay for "consumables and child minding" so it was not "possible to deduce some sort of commitment that each would do what they could".[239]

Lord Neuberger, in his dissenting opinion,[240] sought to apply ordinary principles of equity and took as his starting point the presumption of resulting trust, i.e. where property was conveyed into joint names each co-owner would get beneficial shares proportionate to their contributions.[241] However, this could be displaced by a constructive trust if the courts could find an agreement supported by detrimental reliance at the time of acquisition.[242] What would be required is "a discussion, statement or action which, viewed in its context, namely the parties' relationship, implied an actual agreement or understanding to effect such an alteration".[243] By themselves, living together, having children, sharing regular outgoings, or even joint bank accounts, would prove little in relation to ownership of an asset of substantial value such as the parties' home.[244] His lordship though that significant improvements to a home might suffice,[245] as might capital sum repayments to the mortgage, depending on circumstantces.[246] Lord Neuberger thought that there should be no difference of approach in family home cases and that any change such as a presumption of equality where there had been unequal contributions is a matter for parliament. Anything else constitutes a redistribution of assets akin to discredited doctrines that attempted to treat spouses' property as communal.[247] However, it is hard to see that this would have been anything other than a retrograde step. The family home context is different from the context in which the equitable principles relied upon were developed. It

11–053

---

[234] [2007] 2 A.C. 432, para.70; see also Law Com. No.307 (2007).

[235] [2007] 2 A.C. 432, para.66; Although the parties may not always understand the legal implications of joint legal ownership, or a lender might insist that the house is in joint names, Baroness Hale did not consider these factors to be heavily determinative.

[236] [2007] 2 A.C. 432, para.92.

[237] [2007] 2 A.C. 432, para.89.

[238] [2007] 2 A.C. 432, paras 90–91.

[239] [2007] 2 A.C. 432, para.91.

[240] He dissented on the law but agreed with the result.

[241] [2007] 2 A.C. 432, paras 110–111. Here he cited *Springette v Defoe*. Where there was no evidence such as contributions and the property had been taken in joint names, Lord Neuberger considered there to be a presumption of equality [2007] 2 A.C. 432, para. 109.

[242] [2007] 2 A.C. 432, paras 123–124.

[243] [2007] 2 A.C. 432, para.146.

[244] [2007] 2 A.C. 432, paras 131–134.

[245] [2007] 2 A.C. 432, para.139.

[246] [2007] 2 A.C. 432, para.140, e.g. "where both parties earn and share the home making, but one of them repays the mortgage by a single capital sum".

[247] Such as the rejected "family assets" doctrine of Lord Denning: Gissing v *Gissing; Pettitt v Pettitt* or the increasingly outdated presumption of advancement, [2007] 2 A.C. 432, para.112.

seems probable that even though parties' may not appreciate the legal significance of putting the home in joint names, or may not have the choice whether to do so given a lender who insists on it, most would attach some significance to it in terms of rights and would probably be surprised to think that a joint registration would not necessarily mean that they held in equal shares.[248] Lord Neuberger thought that there would be an inconsistency in the law. In cases where a non owner is seeking to establish a beneficial interest, a direct contribution will give him an interest under resulting trust principles.[249] However, this is to ignore the fact that in sole ownership cases a direct financial contribution is only the threshold required to recognise a common intention under a constructive trust and that the size of the interest would be determined by principles the same as those articulated by Baroness Hale. That notwithstanding, both judgments beg the question of whether the placing and order of these presumptions and surveys of dealings actually makes any difference. And indeed, they both came to the same conclusion on the facts. Baroness Hale gave considerable weight to the parties' financial contributions as rebutting the strong presumption of equality, precisely because in surveying the parties conduct in relation to the property there was so little else to go on. Lord Neuberger found nothing in the parties conduct, brought about by unequal contributions to rebut the presumption of resulting trust brought about by unequal contributions. The majority judgment makes more common sense and would discourage litigation, given that only exceptional cases would be able to rebut the presumption of equality. It also provided much needed clarification on the *Oxley v Hiscock* principle. Lord Neuberger's opinion would probably lead to more parties "chancing their arm" in litigation to prove they had a larger beneficial interest because of their higher initial contribution. This is exactly the sort of thing that the law should discourage, especially in the context of the break-up of intimate relationships. The House of Lords in *Stack v Dowden* did not conduct a comprehensive review of the law in this area, which is disappointing given that it has so many inherent problems.[250] Thus, issues of uncertainty remain undecided, such as, where title is in one of the parties' names only, whether indirect contributions to the mortgage will suffice to infer a common intention, and what precisely is the significance of non-financial contributions in a joint ownership case.[251] Also, the case does not make clear what would happen where one cohabitee moves into a house owned solely by the other and it is later conveyed into joint names. Would the presumption of equality apply here also, or might these circumstances make it easier to rebut that presumption?[252]

Adekunle v Ritchie[253] applied the *Stack v Dowden* presumption of joint beneficial ownership where a mother and son lived together and the house had been conveyed into joint names. It was held that the presumption that joint beneficial ownership followed joint legal ownership did not only apply to couples in a sexual or platonic relationship. This case was held to be "very unusual" and that the presumption of equality had been rebutted. It was found that they intended the son to have a third of the beneficial interest of the property. The reason the property was put in joint names was that the mother could not afford to purchase it without the son's

---

[248] cf. Lord Neuberger, [2007] 2 A.C. 432, paras 113–116.

[249] [2007] 2 A.C. 432, para.114.

[250] Law Com. No.307 (2007), para.2.14.

[251] Law Com. No.307 (2007), para.2.13.

[252] Law Com. No.307 (2007), para.2.13, given the recent trend in the Court of Appeal that it is harder to establish an interest in such circumstances: *James v Thomas* [2007] EWCA Civ 1212; *Morris v Morris* [2008] EWCA Civ 257.

[253] [2007] 2 P. & C.R. DG 20 (Westlaw summary).

assistance; it was purchased in order to provide a home for the mother; mother and son kept their finances separate; and she had 9 other children, so she clearly would not wish her son to have all her estate.[254] He was intended to have some interest as he lived there and contributed to the mortgage, but his contribution was less than hers.[255]

3. Criticism of the Common Intention Constructive Trust

Although in *Lloyds Bank v Rosset*[256] the House of Lords has clearly stated that a constructive trust will only arise where there is either an express or inferred common intention that the equitable ownership of land was to be shared, the principles identified can be subjected to a number of serious criticisms.

11–054

(a) *The Identification of Common Intention is Artificial*[257]

The very essence of the approach adopted in *Gissing v Gissing*[258] and *Lloyds Bank v Rosset*, namely that a constructive trust derives from the parties' intentions, is highly artificial. This is true whether the intention is express or implied. In *Lloyds Bank v Rosset* Lord Bridge described the cases of *Eves v Eves*[259] and *Grant v Edwards*[260] as "outstanding" examples where there had been an express common intention. However in reality in these cases there was no common intention at all as to sharing the ownership of the property. In each case the male partner had no intention of placing the house in joint names, and provided a convenient excuse to his partner explaining why it would not be possible to do so. It may well be that they had misrepresented their intentions to their partners, giving them the impression that they intended to share the ownership of the house, but this can hardly be described as a "common" intention. A constructive trust was imposed not because the man wanted his partner to enjoy a share of the ownership, but because she had acted to her detriment in circumstances where she believed that this was his intention. The true rationale for the imposition of the trust was therefore more akin to the principles of proprietary estoppel, where the key element is not a common intention but a representation which was acted upon to the claimant's detriment. Where there is no express common intention the process of inferring an intention is even less authentic. The court is engaged in a process of creative assessment of the parties' desires and it is entirely false to suggest that the court is fulfilling what they would have

11–055

---

[254] The *Stack v Dowden* presumption of equal beneficial ownership carries with it the presumption of a joint tenancy, which, as will be seen in the next chapter, means that on the death of one of two co-owners, the other takes the whole estate by right of survivorship: para.11–033 above.
[255] Not surprisingly, in *Laskar v Laskar* [2008] 7 E.G. 142(CS), the Court of Appeal held that the *Stack v Dowden* presumption of joint beneficial ownership did not apply in the context of a business venture. The doctrine of resulting trusts applied to determine the parties' shares.
[256] [1991] 1 A.C. 107.
[257] See (1993) 109 L.Q.R. 263 (S. Gardener).
[258] [1971] A.C. 886.
[259] [1975] 1 W.L.R. 1383.
[260] [1986] Ch. 638.

wanted. This artificiality is evident from the conflicting statements of the Court of Appeal in *Midland Bank v Cooke*.[261] At different points in the judgment Waite L.J. describes the parties as having "never given ownership a thought" and yet he ultimately finds that "their presumed intention was to share the beneficial ownership in the property in equal shares". Unfortunately this artificiality was perpetuated by the House of Lords in *Stack v Dowden*. This emphasis on the "presumption" of their intention makes clear what is really happening. The court is involved in a process of inventing a "common intention" in order to justify a conclusion that a person is entitled to a share of the equitable ownership. Most difficulty has been caused as the courts have sought to determine the extent to which non-financial contributions may give rise to a constructive trust of land. Although this debate has occurred under the rubric of supposed "common intention" the court could have imposed the limitation that in the absence of any financial contribution a party cannot be entitled to a share of the equitable interest unless there was an express declaration of trust, as a matter of policy. This would have been a more honest approach, avoiding the inherent uncertainty of the "new model" constructive trust and also the mystique of the language of common intention.

(b) *A Financial Contribution is Essential to Founding a Claim to a Constructive Trust where there is no Express Common Intention*

11–056   The practical effect of the decision in *Lloyds Bank v Rosset*, not, unfortunately greatly clarified in *Stack v Dowden*, is that a person not on legal titles who has made no financial contribution at all to the purchase or upkeep of land will be unable to claim entitlement to a share of the equitable ownership, unless she can establish an express common intention on the evidence. For example, a woman who moves in with a man, who does not work but who looks after the house and garden, who does a substantial amount of renovation work with materials provided by her partner, and who bears and brings up their children over many years, will be unable to establish a constructive trust. Even though everything about their relationship may suggest an intention to share this will not be sufficient if they never articulated that intention and the hurdle of the financial contribution cannot be overcome. Even once the financial hurdle is overcome, the court is no longer free to examine all the details of the parties' relationship to determine the extent of the shares, but must confine itself to details connected with ownership of the house.[262] It might be thought that in a modern age where the relative contributions of parties to relationships are not judged by society in purely economic and monetary terms, that non-financial contribution should be placed on a par with financial contributions for the purpose of inferring a common intention from which a constructive trust can be derived.[263] However, before the approach of English law is too quickly dismissed, it should be noted that non-financial contributions may be sufficient to establish an entitlement by way of the complementary and parallel principles of proprietary estoppel.

---

[261] [1995] 4 All E.R. 562.
[262] *Stack v Dowden* [2007] 2 A.C. 432.
[263] In *Stack v Dowden* [2007] 2 A.C. 432, Baroness Hale and Lord Walker considered, obiter, that the requirement of a financial contribution to the acquisition of the house in order to infer a common intention, was possibly inappropriately strict and the court should be able to take account of non-financial contributions. However, the matter was not resolved. The case itself concerned the issue of quantum of an interest once a common intention had been established.

4. Commonwealth Approaches to Constructive Trusts of Land

Whilst English law has adopted a relatively restrictive approach to constructive trusts of land, similar difficulties of determining when an interest in the equitable ownership of land should arise informally have been faced by other Commonwealth jurisdictions. In the main they have adopted more flexible approaches, but they have had to grapple with the same problems: the relevance of the parties' intentions; the extent to which non-financial contributions should give rise to an interest in the land; and whether any equitable interests in the land arise by right or from an exercise of the court's discretion.

11–057

(a) *Canada*

The Canadian courts have moved furthest from the traditional intention based constructive trust and have developed the concept of the constructive trust as a means of effecting restitution by reversing an unjust enrichment. In order to establish a constructive trust a person is required to demonstrate that the legal owner of the land had been enriched in a way which meant that he or she had experienced a corresponding deprivation.[264] For example in *Sorochan v Sorochan*[265] it was held that there was an enrichment and deprivation where a man and woman lived together for 42 years jointly working a farm which was owned at law by the man. He was held to have enjoyed the benefit of her years of labour in the farm and home. Similarly in *Peter v Beblow*[266] a man was held to have been enriched when the woman he lived with had acted as a housekeeper, home-maker and step-mother. Once enrichment is established, the claimant will be entitled to a constructive trust in the absence of any "juristic reason for the enrichment". This means that there must be no reason why the claimant would have conferred the enrichment without a reasonable expectation of retaining the benefit of it. The Canadian approach is different to that adopted in England in three major respects. First, it adopts a more positive attitude towards non-financial contributions to family life, such as housekeeping and child-rearing, which can constitute an enrichment calling for restitution but would not support the finding an inferred common intention under the principles of *Lloyds Bank v Rosset*. Secondly, once it is established that there is an enrichment which calls for restitution, the appropriate remedy is a matter for the court's discretion. The court may award a constructive trust, as for example in Sorochan v Sorochan where it was felt that a third share of the farm was appropriate, or alternatively a lesser remedy such as monetary compensation. Thirdly, if a constructive trust interest is awarded it does not necessarily affect other third party rights in the land since it does arise until granted by the court.

However the Canadian approach is also open to criticism. Despite the greater willingness to take account of the reality of the relationship between the parties, it places the focus on relationships which are "tantamount to spousal".[267] This leaves the court susceptible to value

11–058

---

[264] See *Pettkus v Becker* (1980) 117 D.L.R. (3d) 257.
[265] (1986) 29 D.L.R. (4th) 1.
[266] (1993) 101 D.L.R. (4th) 621.
[267] Wong, "Constructive trusts over the family home: lessons to be learned from other Commonwealth jurisdictions" [1998] 18 L.S. 369.

judgments, and ironically it may mean that the common intention approach is more flexible because it is able to take into account a wider range of relationships. At a conceptual level the Canadian approach has been criticised on the grounds that it has appropriated the language of restitution to justify the grant of constructive trusts to reverse unjust enrichment, but in doing so has violated restitutionary theory.[268] In particular the Canadian approach fails to explain why restitution should be available in such cases, takes account of detriments incurred by the claimant which do not enrich the landowner, and fails to award remedies which are strictly limited to reversing any enrichment conferred. In effect the Canadian courts have utilised the language of restitution to confer upon themselves a statutory-style discretion to adjust the property rights of cohabitees when their relationships end.

(b) *Australia*

11–059 The Australian courts initially adopted the common intention constructive trust[269] but now justify the imposition of constructive trusts on the grounds of "unconscionability." The essence of a constructive trust imposed under this principle was explained by Deane J. in *Muschinski v Dodds*[270] as a:

> "remedial institution which equity imposes regardless of actual or presumed intention . . . to preclude the retention or assertion of beneficial ownership to property to the extent that such retention or assertion would be contrary to equitable principle."

The main advantage of this approach is that it abandons the need to find any intention, reducing the degree of artificiality in rationalising the imposition of a trust. For example in *Baumgartner v Baumgartner*[271] the majority of the High Court held that a trust should be imposed in favour of a woman who had lived with a man even where there was no common intention because the pooling of their financial resources meant that it would be unconscionable for him to claim that the house was his sole property. As the constructive trust is imposed by the court rather than arising from the parties' intentions it is open to the court to determine if it should take effect retrospectively or only from the date of the judgment.

Whilst the concept of "unconscionability" seems less artificial than the English insistence upon a "common intention" to share the property, the courts still have to decide whether the parties' conduct in any particular case was "unconscionable" so as to merit the imposition of a constructive trust. In practice this requires the court to assess what the parties would have intended in respect of the ownership of the property given the nature of their relationship. Although earlier cases suggested a broader approach towards non-financial contributions, subsequent cases have adopted a narrow view that a constructive trust will not be raised expect by contributions which are directly related to the acquisition of the property.[272] These restrictions

---

[268] Mee, *The Property Rights of Cohabitees* (1999), p.226.
[269] *Allen v Snyder* [1977] 2 N.S.W.L.R. 685; *Baumgartner v Baumgartner* (1987) 164 C.L.R. 137.
[270] (1985) 160 C.L.R. 583.
[271] (1987) 164 C.L.R. 137.
[272] *Bryson v Bryant* (1992) 29 N.S.W.L.R. 188; *Stowe and Devereaux Holdings Pty Ltd v Stowe* (1995) 19 Fam L.R. 409; *W v G* (1996) 20 Fam L.R. 49.

mean that the doctrine of "unconscionability" may have become just as narrow as the English "common intention" constructive trust.[273] However a number of Australian jurisdictions have adopted legislative solutions to the problems posed by co-habitation, by permitting the courts the discretion to adjust the property rights of those who are party to a domestic relationship.[274] Whilst such regimes remove the need for cohabiting partners to establish an interest by way of a constructive trust, it is difficult to provide a satisfactory definition of the relationships falling within the ambit of the courts discretion.

(c) New Zealand

The New Zealand courts also began by adopting the common intention approach[275] but have more recently justified the imposition of constructive trusts on the basis of the fulfilment of the parties' "reasonable expectations." In *Gillies v Keogh*[276] Cooke P. regarded supposed common intentions as fictitious, and held instead that the parties' reasonable expectations should be construed from their conduct. Relevant factors in determining a reasonable expectation might include the length of the parties' relationship and the value of their contributions, whether financial or non-financial. The court is therefore involved in the process of objectively deciding whether conduct like that of the parties should give rise to a reasonable expectation of a share of the ownership of the land. If the legal owner made clear that the other party would not obtain an interest in the land then the court will not find that his or her conduct was based on a reasonable expectation because it was done in the full knowledge that no ownership was intended to be gained thereby. For this reason the Court of Appeal held that a man who had moved in with a woman who had purchased a house in her sole name and had indicated throughout the relationship that she regarded it as hers, did not have a reasonable expectation that by contributing to household expenses and improvements he would gain a share of the ownership.

11–060

However the New Zealand approach has also been subject to criticism. Whilst it avoids the need to find a fictitious "common intention", the New Zealand courts have failed to provide a coherent basis for the determination of the parties' reasonable expectations, so that there is uncertainty as to how the court might determine objectively what the parties would reasonably have expected.[277] In one case a judge suggested that a claimant could make a claim to an interest in the family home on any of eight separate bases, namely contract, express or implied or resulting trusts, common intention, unconscionability, estoppel and unjust enrichment.[278] It has also been suggested that the New Zealand approach enshrines gender bias. It will be more difficult for women, who are often in a weaker economic position, to establish a reasonable expectation, because a claimant will need to demonstrate that the contributions

---

[273] See (1990) 106 L.Q.R. 25 (Bryant); Wong, "Constructive trusts over the family home: lessons to be learned from other Commonwealth jurisdictions" [1998] 18 L.S. 369.
[274] See: New South Wales Property (Relationships) Act 1984; Victoria Property Law (Amendment) Act 1987; Northern Territories De Facto Relationships Act 1991; ACT Domestic Relationships Act 1994.
[275] *Hayward v Giordani* [1983] N.Z.L.R. 140.
[276] [1991] 2 N.Z.L.R. 327.
[277] Mee, *The Property Rights of Cohabitees* (1999), p.292.
[278] *Lankow v Rose* [1995] 1 N.Z.L.R. 277.

made manifestly exceeded any benefits received.[279] As in Australia, a legislative solution to the problem of home sharing has been introduced in New Zealand. From February 1, 2002 de facto relationships have been treated on the same basis as married couples for the purposes of property division on separation or death.[280] The relationship must usually have lasted for three years, and unmarried couples have the right to opt out of the statutory regime.

(d) *Summary*

11–061 Although these four jurisdictions have reached such varied solutions to the problem of the creation of informal trust interests in land, it should be noted that they are all attempting to wrestle with the same difficulties. None have been attracted by the idea of a wide discretion of the court to impose a trust on the basis of simple justice and have sought to establish criteria by which a situation where a constructive trust is justified can be differentiated from one where it is not, whether by the demonstration of a "common intention", an "enrichment" or an "expectation". In the application of all these criteria the parties' thinking remains relevant, and it may simply be that the Commonwealth approaches have avoided the artificial language of a real or presumed "common intention" with terminology that acknowledges the reality that the court is objectively assessing whether any share of the ownership of the land should arise in the circumstances rather than disguising it as an attempt to identify whether the parties subjectively wanted such an interest to arise. For this reason, in *Gillies v Keogh*[281] Cooke P. suggested that it may make little difference in practice which analysis is adopted:

> "Normally it makes no practical difference in the results whether one talks of constructive trust, unjust enrichment, imputed common intention or estoppel. In deciding whether any of these are established it is necessary to take into account the same factors."

The main difference between the English and Commonwealth approaches is not so much as to the circumstances in which a constructive trust can arise, but as to the nature of the remedy. The English concept is of an institutional constructive trust, in that the equitable trust interest arises in favour of the beneficiaries as of right from the facts. In theory the claimant's beneficial entitlement arises at the very moment in time that there was a common intention, so that the court is merely recognising the existence of the interest not awarding it as a remedy. In consequence the beneficial interest may affect the rights of third parties acquired subsequent to the creation of the constructive trust but prior to the date of the court's judgment recognising its existence. In contrast the Commonwealth cases adopt a more remedial approach. The award of a share of the equitable ownership is only one of a range of potential remedies which may be awarded by the court and the court has the discretion to determine whether a beneficial interest, if awarded, should take precedence over other third party rights in the land. To this extent these approaches to the constructive trust are a synthesis of the

---

[279] Wong, "Constructive trusts over the family home: lessons to be learned from other Commonwealth jurisdictions" [1998] 18 L.S. 369, 388.
[280] Property (Relationships) Act 1976.
[281] Property (Relationships) Act 1976.

English principles of constructive trusts and proprietary estoppel. Although at present in English law these doctrines are theoretically distinct, there is some evidence of an awareness by the courts of substantial overlap both in theory and practice,[282] and it is conceivable that in future the whole of English law in this area will develop in a manner more consistent with the Commonwealth approaches. That said, there are statements from the House of Lords that the doctrines should be kept separate and distinct.[283]

5. Reform of Constructive Trusts in England

The deficiencies of the English "common intention" constructive trust have been noted above, and the alternative approaches adopted in other jurisdictions have been considered. In a recent series of reports, the Law Commission has conducted an extensive survey of the law in this area.[284] In its first paper, *Sharing Homes*, the Law Commission concluded that it was impossible to devise a "statutory scheme for the ascertainment and quantification of beneficial interests in the shared home which can operate fairly and evenly across the diversity of domestic circumstances which are now encountered".[285] Instead it considered that further consideration should be given to the adoption of a legislative solution to the problems arising in the context of co-habitation, such as granting the court the power to adjust rights of people who have been living together for a specified period.[286] For same-sex couples who register their partnership, the Civil Partnerships Act 2004 now gives the court discretion similar to the discretion to adjust property rights on divorce under the Matrimonial Causes Act 1973. In its later reports the Law Commission recommended the enactment of a scheme of financial relief and property redistribution on the break-up of a quasi-matrimonial cohabitation.[287] But it has proved difficult to identify any viable alternative to the current law for the determination of property rights in all the different ways in which homes could be shared, e.g. siblings, parents and elder children, carers, friends, etc.[288] In *Sharing Homes*, in the absence of a more radical proposal, the Law Commission confined itself to making recommendations for the modification by the courts of the "common intention" constructive trust. As Baroness Hale stated in *Stack v Dowden*, it may take time for parliament to enact legislation along the lines recommended by the Law Commission in its 2006/2007 reports. Thus, the current law may be with us for some time yet.[289] It is perhaps unfortunate therefore that the proposals made in *Sharing Homes* seem simply to buttress the way in which the courts have already developed and applied the principles stated in *Lloyds Bank v Rosset*. The recommendations are as follows:

11–062

---

[282] For example, Chadwick L.J. in *Oxley v Hiscock*.

[283] *Stack v Dowden*, per Lord Walker, considered above.

[284] *Sharing Homes: A Discussion Paper* Law Com. No.278 (2002); *Cohabitation: The Financial Consequences of Relationship Breakdown* Law Com. Consultation Paper No.179 (2006); *The Financial Consequences of Relationship Breakdown* Law Com. No.307 (2007).

[285] Law Com. No.278 (2002), para.1.31(1).

[286] Law Com. No.278 (2002), para.1.31 and pp.886–87.

[287] Discussed below. It would also apply on the death of a cohabitant.

[288] *Sharing Homes: A Discussion Paper* Law Com. No.278 (2002).

[289] Law Com. No.278 (2002), paras 47–48.

(a) The Continued Necessity to Demonstrate a Common Intention to Share Ownership

11–063 Although *Sharing Homes* recognised that, because people do not think about their homes in legalistic terms, it could be unrealistic to demand proof of an intention to share the beneficial interest in a home,[290] it concluded that the concept of "common intention" should not be replaced as the basic criteria for the establishment of a constructive trust:

> "While we realise that the application of 'common intention' causes real difficulties to the courts and that it can lead to a highly artificial exercise, it is difficult to present a convincing case for any more effective criteria on which an assessment of beneficial entitlement could be based. Intention is clearly important, as it would be wholly unsatisfactory if a person were to obtain a beneficial interest where it was made extremely clear that a particular contribution, by financial or other contribution, would not be met this way."[291]

(b) Inferring a Common Intention from Indirect Financial Contributions

11–064 Rather than abandoning the concept of "common intention" the Law Commission instead advocated a widening of the circumstances in which a common intention would be inferred to include indirect financial contributions to the acquisition of the property[292]:

> "In many cases, a couple will not engage in discussion, but agree to an ordering of the household finances such that one pays off the mortgage while the other pays the household bills. In those circumstances, where the payment of those bills has enabled the other party to pay the mortgage instalments, we believe that the payer of the bills should be given due credit. In our view, an indirect contribution to the mortgage of this kind should be sufficient to enable the courts to infer that the parties had a common intention that the beneficial entitlement to the home be shared."[293]

However it is questionable whether this proposal requires any change in the current law. It amounts to a liberalisation of the strict language of Lord Bridge in *Lloyds Bank v Rosset*, but as was noted above this approach was already adopted by the court in *Le Foe v Le Foe*.[294] It does nothing, however, to assist a person who contributed to the payment of household bills where this did not enable the legal owner to pay the mortgage instalments, or a person who provided no financial contribution at all, for example a cohabitee who remained at home and provided child care.

---

[290] Law Com. No.278 (2002), para.2.112.
[291] Law Com. No.278 (2002), para.4.24.
[292] The House of Lords in *Stack v Dowden* seemed to indicate strong support for this, although the matter was not in issue and therefore not considered in any great detail.
[293] Law Com. No.278 (2002), para.4.26.
[294] [2001] 2 F.L.R. 970.

(c) *Quantifying the Extent of the Beneficial Interest Arising Under the Constructive Trust*

Finally the Law Commission advocated the adoption of a broad approach to the quantification of the extent of the beneficial interest arising where it was possible to infer a common intention from direct or indirect financial contributions: **11–065**

> "We consider that there is a strong case for the courts to adopt a broad approach here as well. If the question really is one of the parties' 'common intention', we believe that there is much to be said for adopting what has been called a "holistic approach" to quantification, undertaking a survey of the whole course of dealing between the parties and taking account of all conduct which throws light on the question what shares were intended."[295]

Again it seems that this approach has already been adopted by the courts, since it was applied in *Midland Bank v Cooke*[296] and *Le Foe v Le Foe*.[297] Although *Oxley v Hiscock*[298] rejected the idea that the court should determine "what shares were intended" by the parties in favour of the exercise of a judicial discretion to award the parties the shares which it considers "fair", this approach has itself been rejected recently by the House of Lords in favour of the Law Commission's formulation of "what shares were intended".[299]

The Law Commission reconsidered the need for legislative provision for financial relief on the breakdown of a cohabitation.[300] The courts can only develop the law so far, in accordance with the facts before them, as happened in *Stack v Dowden*, and cannot realistically perform a whole review of the defects in the law.[301] The Law Commission thought that reform was desirable. There is a significant increase in cohabitation outside marriage,[302] public acceptance of cohabitation has also increased, and many couples still believe erroneously that they have the same rights as married couples: "the common law marriage myth".[303] Although *Sharing Homes* had encouraged parties to make express declarations of how the beneficial interests should be held, there are a number of reasons identified in the later report why this is unrealistic. Couples may not appreciate the precise effect of opting for joint beneficial interests; they may be unwilling to consider relationship breakdown or too embarrassed to   **11–066**

---

[295] Law Com. No.278 (2002), para.4.27.

[296] [1995] 4 All E.R. 562.

[297] [2001] 2 F.L.R. 970.

[298] [2004] ECWA Civ. 546.

[299] *Stack v Dowden* [2007] 2 A.C. 432.

[300] It first published a Consultation Paper in 2006 (*Cohabitation: The Financial Consequences of Relationship Breakdown* Law Com. Consultation Paper No.179 (2006) and after the process of consultation, published a final report with a recommended scheme (*The Financial Consequences of Relationship Breakdown* Law Com. No.307 (2007)).

[301] Law Com. No.307 (2007), para. 2.12.

[302] Law Com. No.307 (2007), paras 1.8–1.10.

[303] Pearce and Stevens, *The Law of Trusts and Equitable Obligations*, (4th edn, 2006), p.283; "Surveys continue to find widespread belief in the 'common law marriage myth' that the law treats cohabiting couples, perhaps after they have been living together for a certain period of time, as if they were married": Law Com. No.307 (2007), para.2.49 citing Park et al, *British Social Attitudes. The 24th Report.*

discuss ownership issues.[304] Thus, given that the current law is inadequate and affecting an increasing number of people, reform is necessary:

> "The general law . . . is not equipped to provide a comprehensive solution to problems arising on separation, responding to the economic consequences of the parties' contributions to their relationship. Moreover, since it is limited to addressing the beneficial ownership of individual assets, the general law of property and trusts offers very little remedial flexibility. It provides no scope for orders that take effect, for example, over parties' pension funds. It offers no assistance where parties do not own the home that they have shared and do not have capital assets. A coherent set of statutory remedies providing financial relief between cohabitants would provide a way of doing better justice between the parties on separation, while respecting the interests of affected third parties."[305]

The Law Commission proposed a scheme allowing judicial discretion to award financial relief and property adjustment on the break-up of a cohabitation relationship. The types of remedies to which cohabitants would have access would be similar to those arising under the Matrimonial Causes Act 1973 and would be capable of addressing hardship, e.g. financial payments, transfer of ownership of the house, payments to the primary carer of children. There had been concern on the part of consultees that introducing a scheme of financial relief on separation of a cohabiting couple would undermine the institution of marriage and its important role in society.[306] However, the Law Commission thought that a scheme designed to prevent hardship to one party on the breakdown of a cohabitation would be more focused and not incompatible with any wider social policy to promote and protect "strong marriages".[307] It was emphasised that the proposed scheme would differ in certain key respects from the judge's discretion to adjust property rights on divorce of a married couple under the Matrimonial Causes Act 1973. "We do not think that all cohabitants should be able to obtain financial relief in the event of separation". To be eligible for the scheme the couple must have "had a child together or . . . lived together for a specified number of years". The Law Commission considers "that a period of between two and five years would be appropriate".[308] The couple may also "opt out" thereby disapplying the scheme.[309] As to the basis for a remedy, "applicants would have to prove that they had made qualifying contributions to the parties' relationship which had given rise to certain enduring consequences at the point of separation".[310] Thus, unlike the jurisdiction under the Matrimonial Causes Act 1973, this scheme is contributions-based rather than needs-based.

---

[304] Law Com No.307 (2007), para.2.20. The Law Commission did observe that "The Land Registry forms on which the declarations of trust are made cannot be a substitute for legal advice. However, it has been suggested that, suitably amended, the form could be a useful means of providing co-purchasers with clear information about the different models of beneficial ownership available to them and the implications of each, or about the importance of co-purchasers obtaining separate advice": Law Com. No.307 (2007), para.2.23. The Land Registry now publish user-friendly guidance on joint property ownership—Public Guide No.18 Nov 2007.

[305] Law Com. No.307 (2007), para.2.16 (footnotes omitted).

[306] Law Com. No.307 (2007), paras 2.36–2.39. The Law Commission observes that "the argument that it would do so underestimates marriage by suggesting that legal considerations are uppermost in couples' minds when they decide whether to marry." Law Com. No.307 (2007), Summary, para.1.21.

[307] Law Com. No.307 (2007), para.2.44.

[308] Law Com. No.307 (2007), Summary, para.1.14.

[309] Law Com. No.307 (2007), Summary, para.1.13.

[310] Law Com. No.307 (2007), Summary, para.1.17.

"The applicant would have to show that the respondent retained a benefit, or that the applicant had a continuing economic disadvantage, as a result of contributions made to the relationship. The value of any award would depend on the extent of the retained benefit or continuing economic disadvantage. The court would have discretion to grant such financial relief as might be appropriate to deal with these matters, and in doing so would be required to give first consideration to the welfare of any dependent children."[311]

The scheme is targeted at the *Burns v Burns*-type situation, where a couple had lived together over a number of years, had children, and one party had given up work to look after the children. It is in such cases that the injustices of the existing equitable rules are felt most keenly. That party will have given up the chance to accrue pension rights and earn higher wages, which is a significant economic disadvantage that would continue throughout the relationship. It is this type of situation that would fall within the proposed scheme.[312] The claim would not be based on lost earnings per se but "would be based upon the continuing economic impact of having given up work to look after [the child] and the need to care for [the child] after the separation".[313] The claimant is required to minimise any loss as far as practicable.[314]

Even the legal recognition of such de facto relationships would not resolve every difficulty, because there are increasing numbers of people who live together for mutual support or caring who are not in any sense "a couple".[315] The ordinary law would continue to be used to determine the parties' interests where they were ineligible for relief or where one party was claiming the priority of their interest as against a third party such as a mortgage lender.[316]

ASSIGNMENT OF EQUITABLE OWNERSHIP

1. A Beneficiary's Right to Deal with his Equitable Ownership

Where a person is entitled to a beneficial interest under a trust, whether it has arisen under an express, resulting or constructive trust, the beneficiary has an interest in the land which he is able to deal with as he chooses. For example he may use it as security to raise a loan by way of a mortgage. Alternatively, he has the ability to transfer his entitlement to someone else by way of an assignment. For example, if Brian holds land on trust for Charlotte and David, David is able to transfer his equitable interest in the land subject to the trust to Elizabeth. This process has exactly the same effect as a transfer of a legal estate in the land, so that Elizabeth will take David's place and Brian will henceforth hold the land on trust for Charlotte and Elizabeth. Similarly, if Brian held land on trust for Charlotte for life, with remainder to David, Charlotte could transfer her equitable life interest to Elizabeth. In such a case Elizabeth would enjoy the rights of Charlotte in the land as her substitute, so that the interest would continue until the

11–067

---

[311] Law Com. No.307 (2007), Summary, para.1.19.
[312] Law Com. No.307 (2007), Summary, paras 1.27–1.34.
[313] Law Com. No.307 (2007), Summary, para.1.33.
[314] Law Com. No.307 (2007), Summary, para.1.33.
[315] *Sharing Homes* at para.1.31 (4).
[316] Law Com No.307 (2007), para.2.25.

death of Charlotte. Such an interest is known as an interest pur autre vie since it is coterminous with the life of someone other than the person who enjoys the interest. Alternatively, David could transfer his remainder interest to Elizabeth, so that on the death of Charlotte she became entitled to the unencumbered freehold interest in the land.

2. Formalities Necessary for Assignment

(a) *Assignment by Appropriately Signed Writing*

A beneficial interest under a trust can only be effectively transferred if the appropriate formalities for an assignment are observed. Section 53(1)(c) of the Law of Property Act 1925 provides that:

> "a disposition of an equitable interest or trust subsisting at the time of the disposition, must be in writing signed by the person disposing of the same, or by his agent thereunto lawfully authorised in writing or by will."

If the assignment is not made by appropriately signed writing the purported transfer will be void and of no effect. For example, if David merely states orally that he is transferring his equitable interest to Elizabeth this will have no effect and David will remain the beneficiary of the trust.

(b) *A Specifically Enforceable Contract to Assign?*

11–068 Where there is a trust of personal property and a beneficiary enters into a purely oral contract to assign his interest, it has been held that the interest passes from the assignor to the assignee by means of a constructive trust if the contract was specifically enforceable.[317] However such a result is impossible in relation to a trust of land because the contract to assign would have to comply with the formalities' requirements for contracts for the sale or disposition of an interest in land. Under s.2 of the Law of Property (Miscellaneous Provisions) Act 1925 such contracts must be "made in writing" which is signed "by or on behalf of each party to the contract". Inevitably such a contract would itself satisfy the requirement of s.53(1)(c) of the Law of Property Act 1925 for a valid assignment.

PRIORITY AND EQUITABLE OWNERSHIP

11–069 The issue of priorities between different interests in land were fully considered in Chapters 4 and 7 above, so only a brief summary of the relevant provisions will be provided here in as

---

[317] See *Oughtred v IRC* [1960] A.C. 206; *Re Holt's Settlement* [1969] 1 Ch. 100; *Neville v Wilson* [1996] 3 All E.R. 171.

far as they apply to beneficial interests arising behind a trust. Historically priority between beneficial interests and subsequent interests in land was determined by the doctrine of notice, so that the rights of the beneficiary would take priority over all subsequent interests except those of a bona fide purchaser of a legal estate for value without notice, who would acquire his estate free form the trust, thus defeating the interests of the beneficiaries in the land. However the property reforms of 1925, and the introduction of a compulsory requirement of registration on the sale of unregistered land, has rendered the doctrine of notice all but irrelevant as a means of determining priority in relation to trust interests. The "curtain" principle of land registration means that, as far as is possible, beneficial interests will be kept off the face of the register. Under the provision of the Land Registration Act 2002 a beneficial interest cannot be protected on the land register by way of a notice,[318] although a beneficiary may be able to have a restriction entered which will have the effect of ensuring that the interest is overreached when there is a disposition of a registered estate or charge.[319]

1. Overreaching of Beneficial Interests

(a) *The Effect of Overreaching on Beneficial Interests*

The operation of overreaching was considered in detail in Chapter 3. Beneficial interests in **11–070**
land, whether arising under an express, resulting or constructive trust, are capable of being overreached. Overreaching occurs where the legal title of land is conveyed by at least two trustees,[320] to whom any capital money arising from the transaction is paid.[321] It has the effect that any beneficial interests are removed from the land and transferred into the capital money arising from the transaction. If overreaching occurs the purchaser of the land gains priority over any pre-existing beneficial interests, and takes the land free from them. Overreaching operates irrespective of whether the transferor of the land had actual notice of the existence of the beneficial interests.[322] The paradigm example of the operation of overreaching is *City of London Building Society v Flegg*,[323] in which the House of Lords held that a beneficial interest could not enjoy protection as an overriding interest if it was overreached.

(b) *Criticism of Overreaching*[324]

Although the operation of overreaching manifestly achieves the objective of ensuring that **11–071**
those seeking to purchase a legal estate in land, or to take a legal charge over it, need only

---

[318] Land Registration Act 2002 s.33(a).
[319] Land Registration Act 2002 s.42(1)(b).
[320] Law of Property Act 1925 s.27. See N. Jackson "Overreaching in Registered Land Law" (2006) 69 M.L.R. 214.
[321] *State Bank of India v Sood* [1997] 1 All E.R. 169.
[322] s.2(1) Law of Property Act 1925.
[323] [1988] A.C. 54.
[324] See J. Stevens, "Is Justice a Priority in Priorities?", Ch.8 in Meisel and Cook, *Property and Protection*, Hart (2000).

concern themselves with the legal title, the question arises whether this conveyancing efficiency is achieved at a disproportionately high cost, namely the unjust defeat of some beneficial interests. Overreaching places the beneficiaries in an extremely vulnerable position at the hands of their trustees, and there is little that they can do to protect themselves if the trustees act in fraud of their interests. The courts have applied the overreaching mechanism in such a way that it will defeat even the interests of a beneficiary who is in physical occupation of the land, and whose presence should therefore have been obvious to the potential purchaser, and the Law of Property Act 1925 makes clear that overreaching operates irrespective of whether the purchaser has notice of the existence of the beneficial interests. The courts have systematically rejected interpretations of the legislation which would have preserved the interests of beneficiaries in possession. In *City of London Building Society v Flegg*[325] the House of Lords refused to find that occupying beneficiaries' rights could be preserved as overriding interests. In *State Bank of India v Sood*[326] the Court of Appeal held that overreaching operated even where there were no capital moneys arising on a conveyance. It seems that a purchaser will be protected by overreaching even if he was fully aware that the effect of the transaction by the legal owners would be to ensure the practical elimination of the beneficiaries' interests in the land, for example if a purchaser acquired a freehold of land from legal owners desperate for money so that he was able to negotiate a price at a substantial undervalue whilst being fully aware of the beneficiaries' interests. Criticism of the operation of overreaching was voiced by the Court of Appeal in *State Bank of India v Sood*[327] where despite clear statements that conveyancing policy demanded that the beneficial interests of the defendants be overreached, there was some reluctance to reach that conclusion. Peter Gibson L.J. summarised:

> "Much though I value the principle of overreaching as having aided the simplification of conveyancing, I cannot pretend that I regard the position in the present case as entirely satisfactory. The safeguard for beneficiaries under the existing legislation is largely limited to having two trustees or a trust corporation where capital money falls to be received. But that is no safeguard at all, as this case has shown, when no capital money is received on and contemporaneously with the conveyance. Further, even when it is received by two trustees as in Flegg, it might be thought that the beneficiaries in occupation are insufficiently protected."[328]

Whilst it might be thought that the beneficiaries of a trust of land could protect their interests by means of an entry on the register of title this is less than likely to be satisfactory. A beneficial interest cannot be protected by means of a notice[329] and a restriction will only have the effect of ensuring that an interest which is capable of being overreached on a disposition of a registered estate or charge is in fact overreached. More significantly many beneficiaries will be unable to act to protect their interests precisely because they are unaware that they are

---

[325] [1988] A.C. 54.
[326] [1997] 1 All E.R. 169.
[327] [1997] 1 All E.R. 169.
[328] [1997] All E.R. 169 at 180.
[329] Land Registration Act 2002 s.33(a).

entitled to a beneficial interest in the land. This is especially the case where their equitable ownership of the land has arisen by means of a resulting or constructive trust. For example, in *State Bank of India v Sood*[330] four of the defendants claimed entitlement by way of resulting trusts and three by constructive trusts. It is unlikely that such beneficiaries even contemplated the existence of these rights until they were faced with the prospect of repossession of their home and sought legal advice to avoid it, much less that they would have considered the need to protect them against the other family members who held the legal title.

(c) *Reform of Overreaching*

In the light of these criticisms of the overreaching mechanism a number of possible reforms have been suggested which would increase the protection afforded to the beneficiaries of a trust of land. However none of the proposed reforms have been implemented.

11–072

(i) Overreaching Only with the Consent of Beneficiaries in Occupation

In *City of London Building Society v Flegg*[331] the Court of Appeal (in a decision overturned on appeal) effectively reached the conclusion that in registered land the rights of a beneficiary in occupation could not be defeated by overreaching because they would be protected as overriding interests under s.70(1)(g) of the Land Registration Act 1925. In such circumstances priority would only be gained if the potential purchaser had made inquiries of the beneficiary in occupation, and he or she had denied the existence of any right or consented to the conveyance. Although this approach attracted much criticism[332] and was overruled by the House of Lords[333] the Law Commission recommended statutory reform to protect the position of a beneficiary in occupation of the land in its report *Transfer of Land: Overreaching: Beneficiaries in Occupation*.[334] Its principal recommendation was summarised in para.4.3:

11–073

> "A conveyance of a legal estate in property should not have the effect of overreaching the interest of anyone of full age and capacity who is entitled to a beneficial interest in the property and who has a right to occupy it and is in actual occupation of it at the date of the conveyance, unless that person consents."

Such consent could be either express or implied. This would mean that such persons as Mr and Mrs Flegg, or the defendants in *Sood*, would not lose priority to a subsequent legal mortgagee without their consent, and it would impose on a person seeking to acquire a legal

---

[330] [1997] 1 All E.R. 169.
[331] [1986] Ch. 605.
[332] See: [1986] C.L.J. 202; [1986] Conv. 131; (1986) 102 L.Q.R. 349; (1986) 49 M.L.R. 519; [1987] Conv. 379.
[333] [1988] A.C. 54. See: [1987] C.L.J. 392; (1987) 103 L.Q.R. 520; [1987] Conv. 451; (1988) 51 M.L.R. 565.
[334] Law Com. No.188 (1989).

estate in the land or taking a legal mortgage the added burden of ensuring that the consent of all those in occupation had been received. It should be noted that this would not necessarily involve a greater degree of burden on potential purchasers because they already have a vested interest in making inquiries of occupiers to protect themselves against interests other than beneficial interests which might form the subject matter of a overriding interest.[335] Indeed the Law Commission stated:

> "We would not expect our recommendations to necessitate enquiries and inspections going beyond what is done at present."[336]

It was proposed that beneficiaries in occupation could give consent by any means, that no formalities would be required, and that the court should have an unfettered discretion to dispense with the consent requirement. The proposals of the Law Commission have been subjected to criticism by Harpum[337] who makes three main objections. First, he considers that it draws an unfair distinction between the rights of beneficiaries who are in occupation of the land and of those who are not. Secondly, he argues that it would defeat the curtain principle underlying the property legislation of 1925 by forcing purchasers of legal estates to make more extensive inquiries of persons in occupation to determine whether they have beneficial rights, thus meaning that trusts would again become a matter of title and a concern for purchasers. Thirdly, he suggests that it would weaken the system of land registration by extending the breadth of the category of overriding interests to include rights which are overreachable. It has now become clear that the reforms advocated by the Law Commission will not be implemented.[338]

(ii)   Restricting the Legal Powers of the Trustee to Dispose of the Land

11–074   Harpum advocates an alternative reform of the perceived defects of overreaching by restricting the legal owners' powers of disposition over land held on trust. He suggests that overreaching should continue to occur wherever there was a sale or lease of the land, but that the powers of the trustees to mortgage the land should be limited so that they would be able to raise a first mortgage to fund the purchase of property and to raise money for improvement or repair, but that they should have no power to raise a second mortgage. If the trustees were then to transact outside their powers it would require them to obtain the consent of all those beneficially entitled to the property. He concludes by summarising the perceived benefits of his alternative scheme:

> "The proposed scheme would facilitate most ordinary conveyancing transactions of sale and leasing. Purchasers and building societies would not need to investigate the rights of persons in actual occupation nor obtain their consent if there were two or more legal

---

[335] Law Com. No.188 (1989), paras 4.24–4.26.
[336] Law Com. No.188 (1989), para.4.24.
[337] [1990] C.L.J. 277.
[338] [1998] 12 L.S.G. 4.

owners. It would protect the rights of all beneficiaries, whether in actual occupation or not, in the case of dispositions outside the trustees' powers. Transactions such as second mortgages, which are likely to be detrimental to beneficiaries would be voidable, unless all beneficiaries under the trust had consented. This would of course constitute an exception to the general principle that trusts are to be kept off the title, but it is an exception that exists under the 1925 legislation."[339]

However, this recommendation was not enacted in the Trusts of Land and Appointment of Trustees Act 1996 which grants the trustees of a trust of land "all the powers of an absolute owner".[340]

2. Priority of Beneficial Interests which have not been Overreached

Where a beneficial interest has not been overreached, for example because the land subject to a trust was owned by a sole legal owner so that no disposition had overreaching effect, issues of priority will be determined by the relevant rules under the provisions of the Land Registration Act 2002.   **11–075**

(a) *Priority of Beneficial Interests in Registered Land*

If title to the land is already registered, issues of priority arise where a registered disposition takes place, for example when the land is sold or transferred, or where a lease for more than seven years or a legal mortgage is granted. In such circumstances a beneficial interest will enjoy protected priority if it is an overriding interest as defined in Sch.3 to the Land Registration Act 2002.[341] Under para.2 of Sch.3 a beneficial interest will only be overriding if the beneficiary is in actual occupation of the land at the date of the disposition, and either the occupation would have been obvious from a reasonably careful inspection of the land or the person to whom the disposition was made had actual notice of it. The interest will cease to be overriding if the disponee had made enquiry of the beneficiary before the disposition took place, and the beneficiary had failed to disclose his beneficial interest when he could reasonably have been expected to do so.   **11–076**

(b) *Priority of Beneficial Interests on First Registration*

Where the land is unregistered, and a transaction occurs which makes registration compulsory, then issues of priority will be determined by the special rules applicable to first   **11–077**

---

[339] [1990] C.L.J. 277, 332.
[340] Land Registration Act 2002 s.6(1).
[341] Land Registration Act 2002 s.29(2)(a)(ii).

registration. Under these rules the registered proprietor will take his estate in the land subject to any overriding interests.[342] These interests are defined in Sch.1 to the Land Registration Act 2002. Paragraph 2 provides that "an interest belonging to a person in actual occupation" of the land is an overriding interest, so it follows that a beneficiary who is in actual occupation of the land when it is first registered will gain priority, and that the registered proprietor will take his estate subject to the trust interest of the beneficiary. However if the beneficiary was not in actual occupation the registered proprietor will gain priority.

[342] Land Registration Act 2002 s.11(4)(b) and s.12(4)(c).

Chapter 12

CO-OWNERSHIP OF LAND

INTRODUCTION TO CO-OWNERSHIP[1]

1. The Meaning of Co-ownership

Although there are many situations where a person is the sole owner of land and no other indi- **12–001** vidual shares ownership of it, a more complex form of ownership is often required. For example where a couple, whether married or living together, purchase a house in which to live it is unlikely that they intend that only one of them will be the owner of the house. Instead they intend to share the ownership so that they are both owners of it simultaneously. Such rights are described as concurrent since they exist at the same time. As was seen in the previous chapter, in English land law all forms of concurrent sharing of land ownership must take place behind a trust of the land. A trust is a relationship which involves a separation of the legal title to the land, which is held by the trustees, from the equitable, or beneficial, interest which is enjoyed by the beneficiaries. Although it is possible for the ownership of the legal title to be shared between a number of persons, so that there will be multiple trustees, the reality of co-ownership takes place in relation to the beneficial interest and the beneficiaries are the true owners of the land. The purpose of this chapter is to examine the means by which co-ownership may be effected, and in particular to examine the forms of co-ownership and the consequent relationship between the trustees of the legal title and the beneficiaries, and between the co-owning beneficiaries themselves.

[1] See Smith, *Plural Ownership* (2005).

2. Forms of Co-ownership

12–002 English law recognises two forms of co-ownership: a joint tenancy and a tenancy in common.[2] Although both of these forms of co-ownership facilitate sharing of the ownership of land they are essentially different in terms of the conception of the nature of the rights that are conferred on the co-owners.

(a) *Joint Tenancy*

(i) Nature of a Joint Tenancy

12–003 Where co-ownership exists in the form of a joint tenancy all the co-owners are regarded as being wholly entitled to the whole of the property that is co-owned. In respect to land this means that each of the joint tenants is regarded as simultaneously owning the whole of the land concerned and that they cannot be regarded as holding specific shares of the property. For example if Kate and Martin are joint tenants of a cottage it is not appropriate to regard them as each owning a half share of it. Irrespective of whether they have contributed equally to the purchase price or not, if they have expressly taken the land as joint tenants they are each as much entitled to the whole of the cottage as the other. If the question was to be asked "who owns the cottage?" the appropriate answer would be that Kate owns the whole of the cottage and that Martin also owns the whole of the cottage at one and the same time. Expressed negatively there is no part of the cottage that they do not each completely own. The essence of a joint tenancy was expressed by Lord Browne-Wilkinson in *Hammersmith LBC v Monk*:

> "In property law, a transfer of land to two or more persons jointly operates so as to make them, vis-à-vis the outside world, one single owner."[3]

(ii) The Four Unities

12–004 A joint tenancy will only exist if what are described as the four unities are present.[4] If any of the essential unities are absent the parties cannot properly be said to be wholly entitled to the whole of the land. Unity of possession means simply that the co-owners must be entitled to possess the whole of the co-owned land, and that no joint tenant is entitled to exclude the

---

[2] Two other forms of co-ownership which were recognised in English land law are now virtually irrelevant. Tenancies by entireties was effectively abolished by the Law of Property Act 1925 which converted all such existing tenancies into conventional joint tenancies. Coparcenary, a form of joint tenancy without the operation of the principle of survivorship, is almost extinct since it will only arise where land which is subject to a fee tail is inherited by female heirs.
[3] [1992] 1 A.C. 478 at 492.
[4] *AG Securities v Vaughan* [1990] 1 A.C. 417.

others from possession of any part thereof.[5] Returning to the example of Kate and Martin introduced above, there would be no unity of possession, and therefore no joint tenancy, if Kate was entitled to exclude Martin from the first floor of the cottage, and Martin was entitled to exclude Kate from the lounge. Although unity of possession may subsequently be qualified by the intervention of the court, often because of a breakdown of the relationship between the co-owners, it is an essential pre-requisite at the outset of co-ownership by joint tenants. Unity of interest requires that the joint tenants must have identical interests in the land. For example, if Kate was the freehold owner of the land and Martin was entitled to a 99-year lease they could not be joint tenants. Likewise if Martin was the freehold owner but Kate was only entitled to a life interest. Unity of title means that the joint tenants must derive their identical interests in the land by an identical means, through the same act or document, for example if they have derived title by the same act of adverse possession from a single conveyance. Unity of time requires that the interests of the joint tenants must have been acquired by them at the same time.

(iii) Survivorship

The most important practical difference between a joint tenancy and a tenancy in common is that the principle of survivorship operates between co-owners who are joint tenants. The essence of survivorship is that when one of the joint tenants dies his interest in the land automatically passes to the remaining joint tenants. This is a logical consequence of the fact that all the joint tenants are regarded as being wholly entitled to the whole of the land. In a sense, when one of the joint tenants dies the extent of the interest of the others in relation to the land remains unchanged. They are entitled to no more than they were entitled to before the death of the joint tenant, namely the whole of the land. The main impact of the principle of survivorship is that a joint tenant is incapable of disposing of his interest in the land by means of a will. Nor, if he dies intestate, will those entitled under the rules of intestacy succeed to his interest. For example if Kate was to die leaving a will stating that she wanted her sister Naomi to inherit her interest in the cottage co-owned with Martin as joint tenants, Naomi would gain no interest in the cottage on her death because survivorship would operate between Kate and Martin and he would be left as the sole owner of the cottage. One potential problem with the operation of survivorship has been anticipated by statute, namely how to determine the order of death where joint tenants have died in circumstances where it is impossible to tell which has died first. If Martin and Kate were to be killed instantly in a car crash, would the cottage pass under the will of Kate or Martin as the survivor? Section 184 of the Law of Property Act 1925 adopts the somewhat arbitrary solution that where "two or more persons have died in circumstances rendering it uncertain which of them survived the other or others", it shall be presumed that the elder died first and the younger survived them. Thus if Kate were six months younger than Martin, she would be deemed to have survived him and the cottage would pass under her will, or to her heirs at law if she died intestate.

12–005

---

[5] See *Wiseman v Simpson* [1988] 1 W.L.R. 35 at 42, per Ralph Gibson L.J.; *Meyer v Riddick* (1990) 60 P. & C.R. 50.

(iv) Severance

12–006 Where property is co-owned by means of a joint tenancy, a tenant can separate his interest from that of the other joint tenants by means of severance. Severance has the effect that his interest in the land is transformed from entitlement to the whole of the land to a notional share of the ownership. For example if Martin decided to sever the joint tenancy he enjoyed of the cottage with Kate, his interest would be transformed into a half share of the land as a tenant in common. Inevitably Kate's interest would also become a half share as a tenant in common because she is the only other joint tenant. However, if there are more than two joint tenants, only the person who severs his interest will become a tenant in common and the others will remain joint tenants. For example, if Martin and Kate had purchased the cottage along with his parents, Olive and Peter, as joint tenants, and Martin subsequently severed his interest, he would become a tenant in common of a quarter share of the cottage and Kate, Olive and Peter would continue as joint tenants of the remaining three-quarters. Once a joint tenant has severed his interest the principle of survivorship no longer operates in relation to his interest as a tenant in common, nor does he retain any right to benefit from the operation of the right of survivorship between the remaining joint tenants. Therefore if Olive and Peter were killed in a plane crash Kate would acquire their interests by way of survivorship and she would be entitled to three-quarters interest as a tenant in common and Martin would still only be entitled to the quarter share he previously severed.

(b) *Tenancy in Common*

(i) Entitled to Shares in the Land

12–007 A person who enjoys an interest in property as a tenant in common is not regarded as owning it in its entirety. Instead he is regarded as enjoying a notional share of the ownership which is owned by him and by him alone. As already stated, if Martin and Kate were tenants in common of the cottage they would be entitled to a half share each. It should be noted that there is no requirement that the shares of the tenants in common must be equal in proportion.

(ii) Shares are Undivided

12–008 Although tenants in common can be regarded as owning separate shares in the land this does not mean that the land can be divided physically between them in proportion to their shares. The shares exist only in relation to the metaphysically abstract ownership of the land and not in the physical land itself. For example, if Martin and Kate are tenants in common of half shares in the cottage they cannot divide the property in two, so that Kate can claim the lounge, bathroom and back bedroom exclusively and Martin the dining room, kitchen and front bedroom. It would not be possible for Kate to maintain an action of trespass against Martin if he were to attempt to make use of the bathroom! The undivided nature of the shares and inability to demarcate the land physically follows from the fact that unity of possession remains a necessary requirement of a tenancy in common, thus entitling the tenants in common to possession of every part of the land. This entitlement to universal possession applies irrespective of the size of the share owned. Thus a tenant in common with a tenth share of land is as much entitled to possession of the whole of the land as the tenant in common owning the remaining nine-tenths.

(iii)   No Survivorship

The principle of survivorship has no application between persons who are tenants in common. **12–009**
Their respective shares will not pass automatically to the other tenants on death and can instead be effectively disposed of by will or in the event of intestacy will pass to the persons thereon entitled.

CO-OWNERSHIP OF THE LEGAL TITLE OF LAND

1.   When Co-ownership of the Legal Title Arises

Co-ownership of the legal title of land will occur if a legal estate in land, whether freehold or **12–010**
leasehold, is acquired by more than one person. This will happen where the land is conveyed into the name of more than one person, or if it is acquired by more than one person as adverse possessors.

2.   Form of Co-ownership of the Legal Title to Land

Historically the legal title to land could be co-owned either in the form of a joint tenancy or **12–011**
a tenancy in common. The availability of multiple forms of co-ownership of the legal title, coupled with the possibility of an unlimited number of legal owners, caused potentially severe problems in conveyancing practice. If the legal title were held by tenants in common, on the death of each tenant in common that person would be replaced as part legal owner with that person's testate or intestate successors. The number of legal owners was thus capable of multiplying exponentially. Any dealing with the land required the concurrence of all the legal owners, and this could on occasions be an almost insurmountable task, especially where some of the legal owners had emigrated or were otherwise hard to locate. Even if the legal owners began as joint tenants, the possibility of their shares being converted into shares as tenants in common left the possibility open of an indefinite expansion in the number of legal owners. In order to eliminate such problems the property legislation of 1925 provides that the legal title of land can only ever be held by co-owners as joint tenants. Section 1(6) of the Law of Property Act 1925 provides that:

"A legal estate in land is not capable of subsisting or of being created in an undivided share in land . . ."[6]

3. Severance of a Joint Tenancy of the Legal Title?

12–012 It follows logically from this policy that, where there is a joint tenancy of the legal title of land the joint tenants cannot sever their legal interests to give rise to a tenancy in common. Such a possibility is expressly prevented by s.36(2) of the Law of Property Act 1925, which provides that:

"No severance of a joint tenancy of the legal estate, so as to create a tenancy in common of land, shall be permissible, whether by operation of law or otherwise . . ."

This does not, however, prevent a joint tenant of the legal title releasing his interest to the other joint tenants and dropping out of the legal ownership of the land. Nor does it affect equitable ownership as joint tenants or as tenants in common.

4. A Maximum Number of Co-owners of the Legal Title

12–013 As well as forbidding a tenancy in common of the legal title of land, the legislation of 1925 removed a further obstacle to efficient conveyancing by limiting the number of persons who may hold the legal ownership as joint tenants. Section 34(2) of the Trustee Act 1925 provides that where the legal title to land is conveyed to more than four persons as joint tenants "the four first named (who are able and willing to act) shall alone be the trustees".[7] Therefore if land was transferred to Albert, Brian, Charlotte, David, Erica and Fatima only Albert, Brian, Charlotte and David would take the legal title. Although Erica and Fatima could be appointed as replacement trustees if a vacancy were to occur, they will not automatically succeed to a position of trusteeship if such a vacancy does arise, for example by the death of one of the trustees. It is important to note that although there can only be a maximum of four joint tenants of the legal title there is no limit to the number of persons who can share entitlement to the equitable interest.

[6] See also Law of Property Act 1925 s.34(1).
[7] See also Law of Property Act 1925 s.34(2).

Joint tenancy or tenancy in common in equity

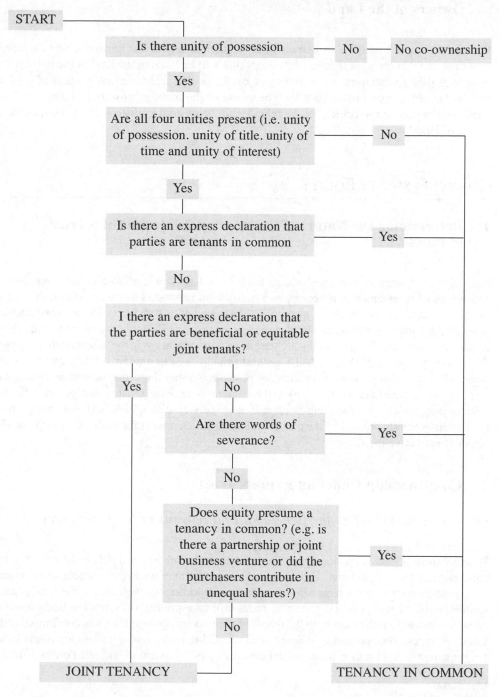

START

Is there unity of possession — No — No co-ownership

Yes

Are all four unities present (i.e. unity of possession. unity of title. unity of time and unity of interest) — No

Yes

Is there an express declaration that parties are tenants in common — Yes

No

I there an express declaration that the parties are beneficial or equitable joint tenants?

Yes   No

Are there words of severance? — Yes

No

Does equity presume a tenancy in common? (e.g. is there a partnership or joint business venture or did the purchasers contribute in unequal shares?) — Yes

No

JOINT TENANCY   TENANCY IN COMMON

5. Joint Tenants of the Legal Title as Trustees for the Beneficial Owners of the Land

12–014 Whenever there is a multiple ownership of the legal title to land it is inevitable that there will be a trust and that the joint tenants of the legal title will be holding the land as trustees for the benefit of the beneficiaries. As such they enjoy the powers conferred on trustees of land as well as the obligations arising thereby. The nature of the trustees' powers and duties will be considered below in the context of the relationship between the trustees and beneficiaries of a trust of land.[8]

CO-OWNERSHIP IN EQUITY

1. Determining the Nature of the Beneficial Interests of a Trust of Land

12–015 Irrespective of whether the legal title to land is held by a sole trustee or by a number of trustees as joint tenants it is necessary to identify who is entitled to the beneficial interest in the land so held. Three important questions have to be addressed. First, who are the beneficiaries of the trust? Secondly, do the beneficiaries enjoy their interests as joint tenants or as tenants in common? Thirdly, if they are tenants in common, what is the extent of their respective shares in the land? Although the general principles which address these questions are straightforward, complex arrangements are possible, so that there may at one and the same time be some beneficiaries who enjoy their interests as joint tenants and others who are tenants in common. As a starting point it is necessary to distinguish between trusts which have been expressly created by the parties and those which arise informally, whether as resulting or constructive trusts.

2. Co-ownership Under an Express Trust

(a) *Freedom to Define the Beneficial Entitlements of the Co-owners*

12–016 Where a trust of land is created expressly the express declaration will define the extent of the entitlement of the beneficiaries, both in regard to whether they are to be joint tenants or tenants in common, and if they are tenants in common the proportions of their shares. Such an express stipulation of the nature of the parties' interests will take priority over any implication which could be drawn from the facts as to the nature of their co-ownership. This was confirmed by the Court of Appeal in *Goodman v Gallant*,[9] where it held that an express declaration of the beneficial interest in land was exhaustive and conclusive of the position and left no room for the

---

[8] See Ch.13.
[9] [1986] 1 All E.R. 311.

doctrines of resulting or constructive trusts to be invoked. As has been noted in the previous chapter a declaration of a trust of land will only be enforceable if the necessary formalities have been observed, namely that the declaration is evidenced in writing.[10]

(b)   Declaration of a Trust of Land by the Legal Owner

The current legal owner may declare a trust of land through a declaration which is evidenced **12–017** in writing.[11] For example, if Kate is the sole legal owner of a cottage, and she decides that she wants Martin to enjoy a share of the ownership when he moves in with her, she can declare a trust of the cottage in their joint favour. If she declares that they are to enjoy the cottage jointly then the consequence will be that she will hold the legal title for them as joint tenants of the beneficial interest. Only if she makes clear in her declaration that they are to enjoy specific shares of the ownership will such a declaration be construed as giving rise to an express tenancy in common. If she were to declare that Martin was to enjoy a half share in the cottage this would give rise to a tenancy in common, with Kate holding the legal title on trust and each of them enjoying a half share of the equitable ownership thereof. If an express trust is declared of unequal shares in the land it is inevitable that the beneficiaries must hold their interests as tenants in common, since such an arrangement cannot be given effect by a joint tenancy. Thus if Kate declared that she held the cottage on trust for herself and Martin in shares of a third and two-thirds respectively this would create a tenancy in common.

(c)   Conveyance of the Land to Trustees

Alternatively a trust of the land may be created by a transfer of the legal title to a new owner or **12–018** owners, often on the sale of the land. For example if Martin and Kate were purchasing the cottage from Ian the conveyance may expressly state the terms under which the land is to be held. The conveyance may state that the land is transferred to Kate and Martin "on trust for themselves as joint tenants" or alternatively "on trust for themselves in equal shares". The first would create an express joint tenancy of the beneficial interest, the second a tenancy in common.

3.   Co-ownership where there is no Express Declaration of the Beneficial Entitlements

(a)   Lack of an Express Stipulation

Although parties creating a trust of land are free to define their respective beneficial entitle- **12–019** ments as they wish, they may have failed to do so. In such cases the law will have to presume

---

[10] Law of Property Act 1925 s.53(1)(b).
[11] Law of Property Act 1925 s.53(1)(b).

or imply the nature of their beneficial entitlements from their conduct. This will also clearly be necessary where a trust of land is created by means of a constructive or resulting trust.

(b) *Conveyance of the Land into the Names of More than one Person*

(i) A General Presumption that there is to be a Joint Tenancy

12–020 Where land is conveyed into the name of more than one person, and there is no express declaration of how the equitable ownership is to be shared, the general presumption is that the legal owners will hold the property on trust for themselves as joint tenants.[12] As has been noted above, if the land is conveyed into the name of more than four persons, only the first four named can take the legal title and the remainder will enjoy interests only as joint tenants of the beneficial interest.

(ii) Words of Severance

12–021 Even without any express declaration of trust, the words used in the documents may be compatible only with a tenancy in common. The essence of a joint tenancy is that there is no division into notional shares: the joint tenants all have indistinguishable interests in the land. If the transfer of the land uses any words which suggest that the owners are to have shares, then this is indicative of a tenancy in common. So phrases like "in equal shares", "share and share alike" or "equally" will show that a tenancy in common was intended. Words and phrases which show this intention to create notional shares on the part of the co-owners are known as words of severance.

(iii) Special Circumstances where the Presumption of a Joint Tenancy will be Displaced by a Tenancy in Common

12–022 Although a joint tenancy of the beneficial interest will generally be presumed where the legal title to land is conveyed to more than one owner, in some circumstances the law is prepared to displace that conclusion in favour of a tenancy in common because the nature of the relationship between the co-owners suggests that they did not intend the principle of survivorship to operate between themselves. This was recognised by the Privy Council in *Malayan Credit Ltd v Jack Chia-MPH Ltd*,[13] where Lord Brightman stated that the circumstances in which joint tenants at law would be presumed to hold their beneficial entitlements as tenants in common are not strictly circumscribed by the law and that equity may infer a tenancy in common wherever appropriate.[14] If the parties acquire land jointly as commercial partners they will not hold the legal title as joint tenants but as tenants in common in equal shares.[15] In *Malayan Credit Ltd v Jack Chia-MPH*

---

[12] Confirmed in *Stack v Dowden* [2007] 2 A.C. 432, per Baroness Hale at para.54, in a family home context.
[13] [1986] A.C. 549.
[14] [1986] A.C. 549 at 560.
[15] *Lake v Craddock* (1732) 3 P.Wms 158.

Ltd[16] the Privy Council held that a tenancy in common was to be inferred where a tenancy of business premises had been taken by a number of persons jointly at law to enable them to pursue their separate business purposes. Mortgagees who lend money on a joint legal mortgage are also inferred to hold their interests as tenants in common in equity[17] although they are joint tenants at law.[18] This again is because of the business character of the transaction. Another very significant circumstance where, in the absence of an express declaration, a tenancy in common will be preferred to a joint tenancy, is where the legal owners have contributed to the purchase price of the land in unequal proportions. A tenancy in common in equity is the only means of giving effect to the relative disparity of their contributions. This was a further reason for finding that there was a tenancy in common of the lease in *Malayan Credit Ltd v Jack Chia-MPH Ltd*.[19] The plaintiff and the defendant had agreed between themselves prior to the grant of the lease how they would apportion the space available, and roughly this meant the defendant occupying 62 per cent of the floor area and the plaintiff the remaining 38 per cent. They divided their liability for the rent and service charge in unequal shares in accordance with the area occupied. The Privy Council held that this feature of their relationship pointed unequivocally to a tenancy in common. A similar conclusion was reached in relation to residential property in *Walker v Hall*,[20] where a house had been purchased in the joint names of a man and his mistress. The Court of Appeal held that they held the property as on trust for themselves as tenants in common of a quarter and three-quarters of the beneficial interest, because the woman had contributed a quarter of the purchase price and the man the remainder.[21]

(iv) Conveyance of the Land into the Names of More than One Person as Tenants in Common

Slightly different difficulties arise if land is conveyed at law into the names of more than one person as tenants in common, since as has been noted above, the legal title cannot be held by co-owners other than in the form of a joint tenancy. The consequence is that the persons named in the conveyance, or if there are more than four the first four who are willing and able to act as trustees, will take the legal title as joint tenants and they will hold the land on trust for the persons named in the conveyance as tenants in common in equity.

12–023

(c) *Co-ownership through Resulting and Constructive Trusts of Land*

(i) Context of Informal Trusts

As has been seen in the previous chapter, there are many cases where a trust of land will be imposed on the legal owner or owners by means of a resulting or constructive trust. Most

12–024

---

[16] [1986] A.C. 549.
[17] *Re Jackson* (1887) 34 Ch.D. 732.
[18] Law of Property Act 1925 s.111.
[19] [1986] A.C. 549.
[20] [1984] 5 F.L.R. 126.
[21] This must now be considered in the light of *Stack v Dowden* [2007] 2 A.C. 432. The House of Lords held that where land was conveyed into joint names, more evidence than unequal contributions would be needed to rebut the strong presumption of equal beneficial ownership in family home cases.

commonly this has been so in cases of co-habitation of residential property where only one of the co-habitees is the legal owner of the land. If the other can establish that she is entitled to a share of the equitable ownership then the question will arise as to whether it is shared as joint tenants or tenants in common.

(ii) Co-ownership Under a Resulting Trust

12–025 A person will be entitled to a resulting trust interest in land if they have contributed directly to its purchase price. The extent of his or her interest is determined by means of an exact mathematical equivalence with the proportion of the contribution.[22] Only in circumstances where the contributions of the parties are exactly equal could a joint tenancy of the beneficial interest arise, and in cases where the contributions are unequal the parties must hold their respective interests as tenants in common.[23]

(iii) Co-ownership Under a Constructive Trust

12–026 A constructive trust arises not because of a person's financial contribution to the purchase price of property, but on the basis of a common intention with the legal owner that he or she was to be entitled to a share of the equitable ownership.[24] Only if the court finds that the common intention was that the parties were to share the property jointly will it be possible to find that there was a joint tenancy of the beneficial interest. However since the finding is usually that a party was entitled to a specific "share" of the ownership equity will generally prefer to find that the parties were tenants in common. For example in *Midland Bank v Cooke*[25] the Court of Appeal held where there was a common intention that a husband and wife were to share the ownership of a house the wife was entitled to an "equal share"[26] of the beneficial interest. Where a constructive trust gives rise to unequal shares of the beneficial interest, as in *Eves v Eves*[27] where a co-habiting girlfriend was held to be entitled to a third interest in the quasi-matrimonial home, the interest can only be given effect through a tenancy in common. In cases such as these, where the house is conveyed into joint names the position is that equity follows the law and presumes that the parties intended there to be equal beneficial ownership and for a joint tenancy to exist.[28]

---

[22] See *Huntingford v Hobbs* [1993] 1 F.L.R. 737; *Midland Bank plc v Cooke* [1995] 4 All E.R. 562.
[23] As in *Bull v Bull* [1955] 1 Q.B. 234.
[24] *Lloyds Bank v Rosset* [1991] 1 A.C. 107; *Stack v Dowden* [2007] 2 A.C. 432.
[25] [1995] 4 All E.R. 562.
[26] [1995] 4 All E.R. 562 at 576.
[27] [1975] 1 W.L.R. 1338.
[28] *Stack v Dowden* [2007] 2 A.C. 432. See Ch. 11.

SEVERANCE OF A JOINT TENANCY OF THE EQUITABLE OWNERSHIP OF LAND

1. The Consequences of Severance

It has been seen how co-ownership of the beneficial interest in land can be effected behind a trust either as a joint tenancy or a tenancy in common. Where there is a joint tenancy the co-owners are wholly entitled to the whole and the principle of survivorship operates between them. Severance is the process by which a joint tenant is enabled to separate his notional share of the ownership of the land from that of the other joint tenants, so that in relation to his share he ceases to be a joint tenant but becomes a tenant in common. As Dillon L.J. stated in *Harris v Goddard*:

12–027

> "Severance . . . is the process of separating off the share of a joint tenant, so that the concurrent ownership will continue but the right of survivorship will no longer apply. The parties will hold separate shares as tenants in common."[29]

As this statement indicates, one of the consequences of severance is that survivorship no longer operates in relation to the share of the tenant in common, and the tenant in common no longer enjoys the possibility of survivorship as regards the interests of the remaining joint tenants, if any. Where a joint tenancy is severed the party severing will be entitled to a share of the beneficial ownership directly proportionate to the number of joint tenants.[30] This will be the case even where the initial contributions of the joint tenants to the purchase price of the property were unequal.[31] For example, if there are two joint tenants and one severs they will become tenants in common of half shares. If one of six joint tenants were to sever his share he would become a tenant in common of a sixth share of the beneficial interest and the others would continue as joint tenants of the remaining five-sixths. These principles were stated by Russell L.J. in *Bedson v Bedson*:

> "On severance the beneficial joint tenancy becomes a beneficial tenancy in common in undivided shares and the right of survivorship no longer obtains. If there be two beneficial joint tenants, severance produces a beneficial tenancy in common in two equal shares. If there be three beneficial joint tenants and only one severs, he is entitled to a one-third undivided share and there is no longer survivorship between him and the other two, though the other two may remain inter se beneficial joint tenants of the other two-thirds."[32]

---

[29] [1983] 1 W.L.R. 203 at 210.
[30] See *Goodman v Gallant* [1986] 1 All E.R. 311.
[31] *Goodman v Gallant* [1986] 1 All E.R. 311. Such a situation would only arise if the beneficial interests of the contributors had been determined by an express declaration that they were to be joint tenants. In the absence of such a declaration they would be tenants in common of shares in proportion to their contributions under a resulting trust, unless it was in a family home situation where the *Stack v Dowden* presumption of equality arose. In *Singla (Brown's Trustee in Bankruptcy) v Brown* [2008] 2 W.L.R. 283, Thomas Ivory J. held that even though parties had intended one of them to have a minimal 1 per cent interest in a house, a transfer into both names "as joint tenants" and a subsequent severance, gave both equal shares in the property.
[32] [1965] 2 Q.B. 666.

Although the general rule is that a joint tenant severing his interest will be entitled to an equal share as a tenant in common, the parties may agree a different arrangement between themselves, so that an unequal share is severed.[33]

2. Means by which Severance may Occur

12–028 Five means are recognised by which the interest of a joint tenant may be severed. In many cases there may be an overlap between the different methods and one or more may be pleaded as alternative justifications for establishing that severance has taken place.

(a) *Statutory Severance*

12–029 Section 36(2) of the Law of Property Act 1925 provides for a statutory procedure by which a joint tenant may sever his interest merely by giving a written notice of his intention to sever to the other joint tenants.

(b) *Common Law Severance*

12–030 The statutory mechanism of severance was enacted as an addition to the three principal methods recognised by the common law. These were identified in *Williams v Hensman*[34] by Page-Wood V.C.:

> "A joint tenancy may be severed in three ways: in the first place, an act of any one of the persons interested operating upon his own share may create a severance as to that share . . . Secondly, a joint tenancy may be severed by mutual agreement. And, in the third place, there may be a severance by any course of dealing sufficient to intimate that the interests of all were mutually treated as consisting a tenancy in common."[35]

In *Bedson v Bedson*[36] Lord Denning M.R. suggested that it was a general rule that, where husband and wife are the beneficial joint tenants of land, and it is possessed by at least one of them, the joint tenancy cannot be severed.[37] Russell L.J. dissented and stated:

> "I am unable to accept the legal proposition of Lord Denning M.R. that when husband and wife are joint tenants of the legal estate in the matrimonial home and also beneficial joint tenants in respect of it, neither can, so long as one is in possession, sell his or her

---

[33] *Barton v Morris* [1985] 1 W.L.R. 1257.
[34] (1861) 1 J. & H. 546 at 557.
[35] (1861) 1 J. & H. 546 at 557.
[36] [1965] 2 Q.B. 666.
[37] [1965] 2 Q.B. 666 at 683.

beneficial interest therein or otherwise sever the beneficial joint tenancy. The proposition is, I think, without the slightest foundation in law or in equity."[38]

This rejection of the supposed limitation has been approved by all subsequent cases[39] and it seems that there is no inherent limitation on the right of joint tenants to sever their interests.

(c) *Forfeiture*

In rare cases where one joint tenant unlawfully kills another, severance may occur by operation of law so as to prevent the killer gaining the benefit of the principle of survivorship. **12–031**

3. Severance by Written Notice of a Joint Tenant

Section 36(2) of the Law of Property Act 1925 provides that: **12–032**

> "where a legal estate . . . is vested in joint tenants beneficially, and any tenant desires to sever the joint tenancy in equity, he shall give to the other joint tenants a notice in writing of such desire or do such other acts or things as would, in the case of a personal estate, have been effectual to sever the tenancy in equity . . ."

This section introduced a new[40] statutory mechanism for effecting severance whilst retaining the traditional common law means of severance which will be examined below. It has been argued that the wording of the section only permits severance by written notice where the legal and equitable ownership of land are held identically, i.e. by the same persons as joint tenants of both the legal and equitable title.[41] However, judicial pronouncements by the Court of Appeal in *Burgess v Rawnsley*[42] favour a wider interpretation that severance by written notice is available irrespective of whether or not the legal and equitable titles are identically held.

(a) *A Unilateral Intention to Sever will be Sufficient*

From the perspective of a joint tenant wishing to sever his share the main procedural advantage of severance by written notice is that he can act unilaterally without the need to obtain the consent, or even having to consult, his fellow joint tenants. **12–033**

---

[38] [1965] 2 Q.B. 666 at 690.
[39] *Re Draper's Conveyance* [1969] 1 Ch. 486; *Cowcher v Cowcher* [1972] 1 W.L.R. 425; *Harris v Goddard* [1983] 1 W.L.R. 203.
[40] Despite the view of Lord Denning M.R. in *Burgess v Rawnsley* [1975] Ch. 429 that the statute merely enacted the position at common law, the overwhelming judicial and academic opinion is that it introduced a new means of severance: *Re Draper's Conveyance* [1969] 1 Ch. 486; *Neilsen-Jones v Fedden* [1975] Ch. 222; [1975] C.L.J. 28 (Pritchard); [1976] C.L.J. 20 (Hayton). Although the statute clearly permits severance by written notice of a joint tenancy of land, it is unclear whether this method of severance is available in relation to a joint tenancy of personal property.
[41] [1976] C.L.J. 20 (Hayton).
[42] [1975] Ch. 429.

(b) *A Written Notice to Sever*

12–034   Severance under s.36(2) requires the giving of "written notice" to the other joint tenants. There is no specified form that such a notice must take. In *Re Draper's Conveyance*[43] Plowman J. held that the written notice did not need to be signed by the joint tenant as "there is no requirement in the subsection of a signature".

One question, which has caused some controversy, is whether the service of documents commencing legal proceedings claiming entitlement to a share of the ownership of land can constitute written notice for the purposes of s.36(2) and therefore effect a severance of a joint tenancy. The central obstacle to holding that such documents can constitute written notice is the concern that such proceedings need not be pursued once started. The issue arose in *Re Draper's Conveyance*,[44] where a husband and wife were the joint tenants of their matrimonial home under an express declaration of trust. They divorced in 1965, and in 1966 the wife started proceedings seeking an order[45] that the house be sold and the proceeds be divided according to their respective interests in it. The husband subsequently died intestate before the house had been sold. Plowman J. held that the joint tenancy had been severed by the issuing of the summons and accompanying affidavit of the wife because these documents constituted written notice that "clearly evinced an intention on the part of the wife that she wished the property to be sold and the proceeds distributed, a half to her and a half to the husband",[46] and this intention was inconsistent with the continuation of a joint tenancy. He therefore held that the joint tenancy had been severed before the death of the husband and that survivorship did not operate in favour of his ex-wife. In *Neilson-Jones v Fedden*[47] Walton J., relying on the earlier case *Re Wilks*,[48] doubted whether a mere summons and supporting affidavit could be taken to constitute written notice for the purpose of s.36(2) on the grounds that the mere issuing of proceedings is not irrevocable:

> "I am also troubled about the suggestion that the mere issue of the originating summons, coupled with the affidavit in support, could amount to a notice in writing . . . [I]t appears to me that s.36(2) contemplates an irrevocable notice, and that the issue of proceedings is the very reverse of an irrevocable act. If the proceedings are, indeed, to constitute a severance, it must, I think, follow as a consequence that they themselves become irrevocable, and this I find difficult to appreciate."[49]

However, his doubts were rejected by the Court of Appeal in *Harris v Goddard*[50] which held that *Re Draper's Conveyance*[51] had been correctly decided in so far as Plowman J. had held

---

[43] [1969] 1 Ch. 486.
[44] [1969] 1 Ch. 486.
[45] Under the Married Women's Property Act 1882 s.17.
[46] [1969] 1 Ch. 486 at 492.
[47] [1975] Ch. 222.
[48] [1891] 3 Ch. 59.
[49] [1975] Ch. 222 at 236.
[50] [1983] 1 W.L.R. 203.
[51] [1969] 1 Ch. 486.

that effective written notice had been given under s.36(2).[52] In *Burgess v Rawnsley*[53] Sir John Pennycuick had stated:

> "I do not see why the commencement of legal proceedings by writ or originating summons or the swearing of an affidavit in those proceedings, should not in appropriate circumstances constitute notice in writing within the meaning of s.36(2). The fact that the plaintiff is not obliged to prosecute the proceedings is I think irrelevant in regard to notice."

Indeed, in *Pudner v Pudner*[54] it was said that the execution of a will, which is inherently revocable, might be sufficient as a notice in writing if it contained words of severance and was communicated by the severing party to the other joint tenants in accordance with the terms of s.36.

(c) *Intention to Sever*

The mere fact that a written notice mentioning the possibility of severance has been given to the other joint tenants will not automatically effect severance. The crucial factor is the presence of an intention to sever. In *Gore and Snell v Carpenter*[55] a husband and wife were the beneficial joint tenants of two houses. They decided to divorce and the husband's solicitor was asked to draw up a separation agreement. The draft agreement included a clause severing the joint tenancy of the matrimonial home. The draft proposals were accepted in principle but no agreement was reached because some financial details remained to be settled. The husband was advised to serve a severance notice on his wife but refused to do so because he thought his wife might construe such action as hostile and detrimental to the negotiation of the divorce. He died a month after the divorce papers were served. In these circumstances Blackett-Ord J. held that the service of the draft separation agreement had not effected a severance of the joint tenancy because the necessary intention to sever was lacking:

12–035

> "It is, in my judgment, a question of intention . . . It is argued for the executors that the proposed separation agreement put forward . . . amounted to [a s.36(2)] notice. It will be recalled that the [proposed agreement] expressly refers to severance, but that was only part of the deed and the deed was never accepted. It was put forward . . . not in isolation but as part of a package of proposals, and was not intended in my judgment and therefore did not take effect as a notice under s.36(2)."[56]

The wife therefore enjoyed the entire beneficial interest in the houses by way of survivorship.

A notice will only be effective to sever if the intention is that it should effect an immediate severance, not that there should be a severance some time in the future. For this reason it

---

[52] Dillon L.J. stated that although *Re Wilks* [1891] 3 Ch. 59 may have been rightly decided in its time, it would be decided differently today because of s.36: [1983] 1 W.L.R. 1203 at 1210.
[53] [1975] Ch. 429 at 447.
[54] [2006] EWCA Civ 250 (obiter).
[55] [1990] 60 P. & C.R. 456. See also *McDowell v Hirshfield Lipson Rumney and Smith* [1992] 2 F.L.R. 126.
[56] [1990] 60 P. & C.R. 456 at 462.

was held that there was no severance in *Harris v Goddard*[57] although the facts are superficially similar to those in *Re Draper's Conveyance*.[58] A husband and wife were the joint tenants in equity under an express trust of their matrimonial home. In 1979 the wife left her husband and sought a divorce. Her petition for divorce sought that "such order may be made" in relation to the matrimonial home as "may be just", including transferring the property, settlement of the property or variation of the existing trust interests. Three days before the hearing of the petition was due the husband was injured in a car crash, and he died a month later. His executors claimed that the joint tenancy had been severed so that survivorship did not operate in favour of the wife. The Court of Appeal held that the divorce petition did not evince an intention to effect an immediate transformation in the nature of the parties' beneficial interests in the house, and that therefore the joint tenancy had not been severed. Slade L.J. explained why the petition was considered ineffective to sever:

> "I am unable to accept [the] submission that a notice in writing which shows no more than a desire to bring the existing interest to an end is a good notice. It must be a desire to sever which is intended to have the statutory consequence. Paragraph 3 of the prayer of the petition does no more than invite the Court to consider at some future time whether to exercise its jurisdiction under section 24 of the [Matrimonial Causes Act 1973] and if it does, to do so in one or more of three different ways. Orders under section 24(1)(a) and (b) could bring co-ownership to an end by ways other than by severance. It follows, in my judgment, that paragraph 3 of the prayer of the petition did not operate as a notice in writing to sever the joint tenancy in equity."[59]

Since there had been no severance of the joint tenancy the wife was entitled to the entire beneficial ownership as a consequence of the operation of survivorship on the death of her ex-husband.

(d) *Notice Given to the Other Joint Tenants*

12–036   Section 36(2) requires that the joint tenant intending to sever his interest must "give" the notice to the other joint tenants. Most cases examined have involved only two joint tenants. However where there are more than two the notice will only be effective if it is given to all of the others. Service to some, or even to the majority, will not be effective to sever.

(e) *Effective Service of Notice*

12–037   Section 196(3) of the Law of Property Act 1925 provides that a written notice to sever a joint tenancy will be "given" to the other joint tenant or tenants if it can be shown to have been left at their last known place of abode or business, irrespective of whether it was actually received

[57] [1983] 1 W.L.R. 1203.
[58] [1969] 1 Ch. 486.
[59] [1983] 1 W.L.R. 1203 at 1209.

or not. The notice may be left at such an address by the joint tenant personally, or by an agent acting on his behalf, for example by a postman where the notice has been sent by post. This was so held in the rather tragic case of *Kinch v Bullard*.[60] Mr and Mrs Johnson owned their matrimonial home as joint tenants in law and equity. Mrs Johnson petitioned for divorce and sent her husband a notice of severance by first class post in an envelope addressed to their home. The next day he suffered a heart attack and was taken to hospital. Whilst he was in hospital the postman delivered the letter. Mrs Johnson picked it up and destroyed it because she decided that she no longer wished to sever the tenancy. Mr Johnson subsequently died in hospital and Mrs Johnson died some five months later. The question at issue was whether notice to sever had been "given" so as to effect a severance. Neuberger J. held that severance had occurred, and stated:

> "Provided that it can be established that, irrespective of the identity of the person who delivered the notice to a particular address, it was delivered to that address, then the notice has been validly served at that address, provided that it is the addressee's last-known abode or place of business."[61]

It was therefore irrelevant that Mrs Johnson had changed her mind and had intercepted and destroyed the letter. The procedure had been set in train and the notice had been served. Neuberger J. was only willing to concede that the position would have been different if Mrs Johnson had informed her husband that she wished to revoke the notice before it was "given". Since severance had occurred suvivorship did not operate and Mr Johnson's half share of the house devolved according to the terms of his will.

Where the notice is given by registered post, it has been held to be effective even if not received. In *Re 88 Berkeley Road* [62] two single women, Miss Goodwin and Miss Eldridge, were the beneficial joint tenants of a house. A month before Miss Eldridge was married, Miss Goodwin sent a notice of severance by recorded delivery to the correct address. The notice had asked for acknowledgement of receipt of the notice, but no receipt was received. Since the ladies were living in the same house the post office records showed that the letter had been received and signed for by Miss Goodwin herself on behalf of Miss Eldridge who was away at the time. Miss Goodwin died soon after and her executors claimed that the joint tenancy had been severed. Plowman J. held that although the evidence supported Miss Eldridge's claim that she had never received the notice the posting alone was sufficient to constitute giving notice for the purposes of s.36(2). This was because s.196(4) of the Law of Property Act 1925 provides that a notice under the Act is deemed to have been served if "it is sent by post in a registered letter" and the letter is not returned to the post office undelivered. Plowman J. refused to distinguish "giving" notice under s.36(2) from "serving" notice under s.196(4) and held that Miss Goodwin had severed her interest and at the time of her death had been a tenant in common of a half share of the beneficial ownership.

---

[60] [1998] 4 All E.R. 650.
[61] [1998] 4 All E.R. 650 at 654.
[62] [1971] Ch. 648.

4. Severance by Unilateral Conduct of a Joint Tenant

12–038 The first of the three common law methods of severance identified in *Williams v Hensman*[63] is that a joint tenancy will be severed by "an act of any one of the persons interested operating upon his own share". This means of severance involves a degree of abstract inconsistency since the essence of a joint tenancy is that the joint tenants do not have individual shares in the land as such, hence it is somewhat inaccurate to speak about a tenant acting in relation to "his own share". In reality what is meant is that the joint tenant does some act which demonstrates that he is intending to treat his interest in the land as consisting of a specific share, which is therefore inconsistent with the continuation of a joint tenancy. As in the case of statutory severance by written notice this means of severance is capable of being exercised unilaterally by the joint tenant seeking to sever his share and does not require the consent or participation of the other joint tenants. A number of well-recognised categories of conduct by a joint tenant in relation to his interest in the land have been held to have the effect of severing his share.

(a) *Joint Tenant Transfers his Share in the Land to a Third Party*

12–039 One of the clearest unilateral acts a joint tenant can perform with severing effect is to transfer his interest in the land to a third party. Such a transfer is technically termed "alienation". In *Bedson v Bedson*[64] Russell L.J. stated generally that if a husband and wife were joint tenants "either husband or wife could . . . at any time by voluntary assignment or sale or mortgage of his or her beneficial interests have created a tenancy in common in undivided shares".[65] For example if there are two joint tenants of land and one sells his interests to a third party the joint tenancy will be severed and the remaining original tenant and the new co-owner will stand as tenants in common of half shares of the beneficial interest. If there are more than two joint tenants and one alienates his interests this will not have the effect of terminating the joint tenancy completely. The third party acquiring the interest of the alienating tenant will stand as a tenant in common of the relevant share in relation to the remaining co-owners, but as between themselves those co-owners will continue to hold their interests as joint tenants.[66] It is to be noted that where the joint tenant who alienates his interest is also a joint tenant of the legal title, the alienation takes effect only in equity and has no impact on the ownership of the legal title. He will remain a joint tenant[67] and trustee of the legal title even though he has no continuing beneficial interest in the land. In the absence of a specifically enforceable contract, severance will only occur if the transfer of the joint tenant's interest was completed and his share alienated. In the Australian case *Corin v Patton*[68] it was held that there was no severance where a joint tenant had executed a transfer of the land because

---

[63] (1861) 1 J. & H. 546.
[64] [1965] 2 Q.B. 666.
[65] [1965] 2 Q.B. 666 at 690.
[66] See *Bedson v Bedson* [1965] 2 Q.B. 666 at 689, referred to above at para.12–027.
[67] Or even the sole legal owner if there are no other trustees.
[68] (1990) 169 C.L.R. 540.

she had not done everything that was necessary for the transferee to be registered and the transfer was incomplete.[69]

(b) *Joint Tenant Transfers his Interest to One of his Fellow Joint Tenants*

A transfer of a joint tenant's share in the land to another joint tenant will inevitably have the effect of severing the share transferred. This follows from the fact that the transfer is intended to increase the extent of the interest of the acquiring joint tenant, and this cannot be given effect by means of a joint tenancy. For example if Philip, Quentin, Rowena and Stephanie are joint tenants of the beneficial interest in land and Philip sells his interest to Stephanie, the consequence will be that his share is severed so that Stephanie becomes a tenant in common of a quarter share and remains a joint tenant along with Quentin and Rowena of the remaining three-quarter share. Stephanie therefore has rights to the land in two different capacities.

12–040

(c) *Joint Tenant Mortgages his Interest in the Land*

In *Bedson v Bedson*[70] Russell L.J. stated that "a mortgage or charge of his interest by a beneficial joint tenant operates as a severance".[71] If a joint tenant mortgages his interest he will become entitled to an equal share of the beneficial interest as a tenant in common.[72] This provides one of the few means by which a joint tenant can sever his interest entirely secretly whilst retaining ownership. Virtually all other means of severance will be evident to the other joint tenants, or require mutual conduct or written notification of intention.

12–041

(d) *Joint Tenant Enters into a Contract to Transfer or Mortgage his Interest*

Even where the transaction has not yet been carried into effect severance will occur if a joint tenant enters into a specifically enforceable contract to alienate his share or to grant a mortgage.[73] This is a further application of the well-established maxim that equity treats as done that which ought to be done.

12–042

(e) *Joint Tenant Fraudulently Transfers or Mortgages the Entire Interest in the Land*

If a joint tenant purports to deal not merely with his own interest in the land but with the entire interest under the joint tenancy by transferring or mortgaging it, and thereby acts fraudulently

12–043

---

[69] Under the Australian Torrens system the certificate of land registration must be made available by the transferor for registration of the transferee. In *Corin v Patton* the certificate was held by the mortgagee of the land and the transferor never authorised the mortgagee to hand the certificate to the transferee.
[70] [1965] 2 Q.B. 666.
[71] [1965] 2 Q.B. 666 at 690.
[72] *First National Securities Ltd v Hegerty* [1985] Q.B. 850. See also: *Bedson v Bedson* [1965] 2 Q.B. 666 at 690.
[73] *Caldwell v Fellows* (1870) L.R. Eq. 410; *Re Hewett* [1894] 1 Ch. 362.

against the interests of the other joint tenants, this will have the effect of severing his share. In consequence his interest in the land will be bound by the fraudulent transaction but the interests of the other joint tenants will be left unaffected. For example, in *First National Securities Ltd v Hegerty*[74] a husband and wife were the beneficial joint tenants of a house which was intended to be their retirement home. The husband left and subsequently executed a legal mortgage of the property by forging his wife's signature on the application and charge. The Court of Appeal confirmed the holding of Bingham J. that "this disposition by the husband was a sufficient act of alienation to sever the beneficial joint tenancy and convert the husband and wife into tenants in common".[75] The reason is that the mortgage lender, which was not aware of the fraud, was entitled to have the transaction treated a being as fully effective as the husband had the power to make it. The husband had no power, acting alone, to mortgage the legal estate, but he did have power, even acting alone, to mortgage his own beneficial interest. Similarly in *Ahmed v Kendrick*[76] Mr and Mrs Ahmed were the beneficial joint tenants of a house, which Mr Ahmed sold and transferred to Kendrick by forging his wife's signature on the contract and transfer. The Court of Appeal again affirmed that the effect of this fraudulent transaction was to sever the joint tenancy. Mr and Mrs Ahmed became tenants in common of half shares in the house and Kendrick was only entitled to assert his entitlement against the half share of Mr Ahmed.[77]

(f) *Joint Tenant is Adjudicated Bankrupt*

12–044 When the court adjudicates a person bankrupt, all property owned by the bankrupt vests automatically in his trustee in bankruptcy.[78] Although this is not technically an act of the tenant it is a form of involuntary alienation of his interest which has the effect of severing any interest in land which he may enjoy as a joint tenant. The crucial moment is that of adjudication of bankruptcy by the court. In *Re Dennis*[79] a husband and wife were the beneficial joint tenants of two houses. In September 1982 the husband committed an act of bankruptcy[80] and in December a bankruptcy petition was presented. His wife died in February and he was adjudicated bankrupt in November 1983. Nicholls V.C. held that the effect of the relevant statute was not to vest the bankrupt's property retrospectively in the trustee but only when the adjudication order is made. Therefore at the date of the wife's death the joint tenancy had not been severed and survivorship operated so that at the date of adjudication the trustee in bankruptcy became entitled to the whole of both houses. The reverse of this situation arose in *Re Palmer*[81] where a husband, who was the joint tenant of a house with his wife, had died a debtor, which

---

[74] [1985] Q.B. 850.

[75] [1985] Q.B. 850 at 854.

[76] (1988) 56 P. & C.R. 120.

[77] As the wife had acquiesced in Kendrick discharging the mortgage over the property, the Court of Appeal also held that in determining the respective entitlements of Mrs Ahmed and Kendrick in the house, Kendrick should be given credit for the money paid to discharge the mortgage in priority to any interest she might have.

[78] Insolvency Act 1986 ss.283 and 306.

[79] [1993] Ch. 72.

[80] By failing to comply with a bankruptcy notice.

[81] [1994] Ch. 316.

led his executor to seek an insolvency administration order. The Court of Appeal held that such an administration order vested the property of the deceased in the trustee at the moment of his death, and that since at that moment there had been no severance the principle of survivorship operated and the wife was entitled to ownership of the house.

(g) *Charging Order Imposed on the Interest of a Joint Tenant*

The interest of a joint tenant will also be severed if a charge is imposed upon it by law. Such **12–045** charges may arise, for example, under the Charging Orders Act 1979. In *Bedson v Bedson*[82] Russell L.J. suggested that a charge imposed in favour of the Law Society to recover unpaid contributions to legal aid where the proceedings have recovered or preserved a beneficial interest for the claimant will effect severance.

(h) *Commencement of Proceedings by One Joint Tenant Against Others*

In *Re Draper's Conveyance*[83] which was considered above in the context of severance by writ- **12–046** ten notice, Plowman J. suggested that his conclusion that a wife had severed her joint tenancy of the matrimonial home could be supported on the grounds that her service of a summons, together with a supporting affidavit commencing litigation asserting her right to a half share of the beneficial interest, was itself an act by a joint tenant sufficient to sever her interest under the common law principles identified in *Williams v Hensman*[84] irrespective of whether the documents constituted written notice for the purposes of s.36(2) of the the Law of Property Act 1925. Subsequent cases have questioned whether the mere commencement of litigation is alone a sufficient act to effect severance. Walton J. expressed doubt in *Nielson-Jones v Fedden*.[85] citing the earlier case of *Re Wilks*[86] where Stirling J. had held that a beneficiary who was the joint tenant of a trust had not severed his interest merely by starting proceedings for payment of his share of the fund. The central criticism is that commencement of litigation is not a sufficiently irrevocable act because proceedings can be discontinued. However in *Harris v Goddard*[87] the Court of Appeal took the view that any danger of discontinuance is insufficient to invalidate the conclusion that the commencement of litigation amounts to unilateral conduct by a joint tenant which will sever his interest. Lawton L.J. commented:

> "I do not share the doubts about the correctness of [the] judgment on this point which Walton J. expressed in *Neilson-Jones v Fedden* relying on In *Re Wilks*. The fact that the wife in *Re Draper's Conveyance* could have withdrawn the summons is a factor which could have been taken into account in deciding whether what was done was effectual to

---

[82] [1965] 2 Q.B. 666.
[83] [1969] 1 Ch. 486.
[84] (1861) 1 J. & H. 546.
[85] [1975] Ch. 222.
[86] [1891] 3 Ch. 59.
[87] [1983] 1 W.L.R. 1206.

sever the joint tenancy in equity. The weight of that factor would have depended upon all the other circumstances and was in that case clearly negligible."[88]

The key question is therefore whether a clear intention to sever, declared unilaterally (for instance by initiating court proceedings) can operate as a severance.

(i) *Joint Tenant Declares his Intention to Sever?*

12–047   There has been some question whether a mere unilateral declaration by a joint tenant that he intends to sever his share is an act sufficient to effect severance under the first method identified in *Williams v Hensman*.[89] In *Hawkesley v May*[90] Havers J. stated that:

> "the first method indicated, namely an act of any one of the persons interested operating upon his own share, obviously includes a declaration of intention to sever by one party."

This was cited with approval by Plowman J. in *Re Draper's Conveyance*[91] but criticised by Walton J. in *Nielson-Jones v Fedden*.[92] as lacking any support in the authorities. However *Hawkesley v May*[93] was approved by Lord Denning M.R. in *Burgess v Rawnsley*[94] and in both that case and *Harris v Goddard*[95] the Court of Appeal rejected the criticisms Walton J. had levelled against *Re Draper's Conveyance*.[96] It is unclear whether these cases support the conclusion that a mere oral statement of intention is effective to sever (at least where it is communicated to the other joint tenants[97]), or whether they merely uphold the finding that severance had occurred in *Re Draper's Conveyance*,[98] a conclusion which could be justified perfectly adequately on the grounds that a written notice had been given. It seems as a matter of principle that a mere unilateral declaration of intention to sever, unaccompanied by any communication of that intention, should not be sufficient to sever a joint tenancy, otherwise it would be too easy for a declaration to be made but concealed and produced only if the party relying upon the severance would thereby be advantaged. The whole point about the statutory mechanism is that it relies upon communication. It could be argued that, even if a unilateral intention to sever is communicated, it would still not be adequate to effect a severance unless it complies with the statutory procedure. In the Australian High Court in *Corin v Patton*.[99] Mason C.J. and McHugh J. indicated that severance by unilateral intention was theoretically impossible because severance can only be brought about by the destruction of one of the four unities:

[88] [1983] 1 W.L.R. 1210.
[89] (1861) J. & H. 546.
[90] [1956] 1 Q.B. 304.
[91] [1969] 1 Ch. 486.
[92] [1975] Ch. 22
[93] [1956] 1 Q.B. 304.
[94] [1975] Ch. 429.
[95] [1983] 1 W.L.R. 203.
[96] [1969] 1 Ch. 486.
[97] In *Williams v Hensman* (1861) 1 J. & H. 546 at 557 Sir William Page Wood said that "it will not suffice to rely on an intention, with respect to the particular share, declared only behind the backs of the other persons interested".
[98] [1969] 1 Ch. 486.
[99] (1990) 169 C.L.R. 540.

"Unilateral action cannot destroy the unity of time, of possession or of interest unless the unity of title is also destroyed, and it can only destroy the unity of title if the title of the party acting unilaterally is transferred or otherwise dealt with or affected in a way which results in a change in the legal and equitable estates in the relevant property. A statement of intention, without more, does not affect the unity of title."[100]

They also pointed to two practical objections to finding that unilateral declaration would be sufficient to sever. First, uncertainty would follow, as "it would become more difficult to identify precisely the ownership of interests in land which had been the subject of statements said to amount to declarations of intention". Secondly, "there would then be no point in maintaining as a separate means of severance the making of mutual agreement between the joint tenants". The contrary argument is that a communicated intention to sever would go beyond severance by mutual agreement in cases where the communicated intention of one joint tenant is rejected by the others.

(j) *Joint Tenant Transfers his Share to Himself?*

Since a severance will occur if a joint tenant alienates his interest to a third party or to one of his fellow co-owners, the question has arisen as to whether a joint tenant can convert his interest into a joint tenancy by alienating his interest to himself. Following dicta of Lord Denning in *Rye v Rye*[101] it seems highly unlikely that such a transaction would effect severance. The joint tenant could, however, alienate his beneficial interest to third party trustees upon trust for himself, or upon trusts which include himself as a beneficiary, and in principle this should be effective to sever the joint tenancy.   **12–048**

(k) *Joint Tenant Disposes of his Interest by Will?*

The mere fact that a joint tenant has bequeathed his interest by will does not effect a severance inter vivos of the joint tenancy. Since survivorship operates immediately upon the death of a joint tenant, there is no interest in land which survives the death of the joint tenant and which is capable of passing under the joint tenant's will.[102]   **12–049**

5. Severance by Mutual Agreement of the Joint Tenants

Unlike the two means of severance which have been examined so far, severance under this second head of *Williams v Hensman*[103] cannot be exercised unilaterally by a joint tenant   **12–050**

---

[100] (1990) 169 C.L.R. 540 at 548.
[101] [1962] A.C. 496 at 514.
[102] *Moyse v Gyles* (1700) 2 Vern. 385.
[103] (1861) 1 J. & H. 546.

wishing to sever his share. Severance will only occur if all the joint tenants are agreed that it should.

(a) An Agreement does not Require an Enforceable Contract

12–051 For severance to occur by mutual agreement the joint tenants need not have entered into an enforceable contract inter se. The operation of this means of severance was explained by Sir John Pennycuick in *Burgess v Rawnsley*:

> "[counsel] contended that in order that rule 2 [severance by mutual agreement] should apply, the agreement must be specifically enforceable. I do not see any sufficient reason for importing this qualification. The significance of an agreement is not that it binds the parties; but that it serves as an indication of a common intention to sever, something which it was indisputably within their power to do. It will be observed that Page Wood V.-C. in his rule 2 makes no mention of specific enforceability."[104]

(b) An Agreement must have been Reached

12–052 The essential requirement for severance by mutual agreement is that the joint tenants actually reach an appropriate agreement in relation to the beneficial ownership of the land. Inconclusive negotiations and discussions may be sufficient to effect severance under the third head, namely mutual conduct, but there it is often a fine line which divides a finding of an agreement from a finding that negotiations were inconclusive.[105] The difficulties are well illustrated by *Burgess v Rawnsley*.[106] A house was purchased in the joint names of Mr Honick and Mrs Rawnsley, who had met at a religious rally in Trafalgar Square. He intended to marry her at the time that the purchase took place, but she had no intention of marrying him and intended that she would occupy a flat on the upper storey of the house and that he would occupy the lower storey. The conveyance expressly declared that they were to be joint tenants of the beneficial interest. Mr Honick paid for the property but Mrs Rawnsley gave him more than the entire purchase price in return for her interest. A year later Mr Honick sought to purchase Mrs Rawnsley's share in the property because it was clear that she would not marry him. He came to what he thought was an oral agreement with her to purchase her share for £750 and his solicitor wrote to her asking that she confirm her willingness to sell on those terms. The next day she went to the solicitors and said she was not willing to sell and that she wanted £1,000. A few days later Mr Honick told his solicitor to leave things as they were. Three years later he died. During the intervening time he had lived in the house alone, and paid all outgoings. His daughter, Mrs Burgess, claimed a half share in the house on the grounds that her father had severed his interest and that survivorship had not operated in favour of Mrs Rawnsley. The county court judge held as a fact that the parties had reached an agreement for the sale of Mrs Rawnsley's share for £750. Since the agreement was purely oral it

---

[104] [1975] Ch. 429.
[105] See for example *Barracks v Barracks* [2005] EWHC 3077; Westlaw document 2005 WL 3661975.
[106] [1975] Ch. 429.

would not have been enforceable.[107] The majority of the Court of Appeal held that severance had occurred because they were unwilling to upset the finding of fact that an agreement had been reached.[108] However, the judges expressed doubt whether this finding was truly justifiable on the evidence. Browne L.J. stated that he was "bound to say that the evidence about any such agreement seems to me to have been most unsatisfactory".[109] Lord Denning M.R. also concluded that severance had occurred on the basis of the agreement[110] but in his judgment was more concerned to demonstrate that severance could be supported even if there had been no agreement on the basis that the course of dealing of the parties "clearly evinced an intention by both parties that the property should henceforth be held in common and not jointly".[111] His comments in this respect will be examined below. What is clear from the decision of the Court of Appeal is that, if an agreement is established as a fact, it will have a severing effect. In the recent case of *Barracks v Barracks*,[112] Laddie J. considered that a negotiation for one co-owner to buy out the other would have amounted to a mutual agreement to sever, even when there appeared to be dispute between the parties as to timing and value of the property. Each negotiated on the basis that they were entitled to a half-share and this was sufficient agreement to sever.

(c) *The Agreement Need not be Express*

It is also clear from the judgments of the Court of Appeal in *Burgess v Rawnsley*[113] that an agreement need not have been concluded expressly but can be implied from the circumstances of the joint tenants' dealings. Browne L.J. stated that "an agreement to sever can be inferred from a course of dealing ... and there would in such a case ex hypothesi be no express agreement but only an inferred, tacit agreement".[114]   **12–053**

(d) *The Agreement must Relate to the Ownership of the Land*

There is no requirement that the agreement must specifically refer to severance. In *Burgess v Rawnsley*[115] Sir John Pennycuick indicated that "Rule 2 applies equally ... whether the agreement between the two joint tenants is expressly to sever or is to deal with the property in a manner which involves severance".[116] However the decision of Walton J. in *Nielsen-Jones v Fedden*[117] suggests that a mutual agreement will only sever a joint tenancy if   **12–054**

---

[107] Law of Property Act 1925 s.40.
[108] Sir John Pennycuick stated at 446 that "I do not think this court would be justified in holding that the judge's finding was so contrary to the weight of the evidence that it should be set aside."
[109] [1975] Ch. 429 at 442.
[110] [1975] Ch. 429 at 440.
[111] [1975] Ch. 429 at 442.
[112] [2005] EWHC 3077; Westlaw document 2005 WL 3661975, para.18.
[113] [1975] Ch. 429.
[114] [1975] Ch. 429 at 444, citing *Wilson v Bell* (1843) 5 Ir.Eq.R. and *Re Wilks* [1891] 3 Ch. 59.
[115] [1975] Ch. 429.
[116] [1975] Ch. 429 at 446.
[117] [1975] Ch. 222.

it relates to the actual ownership of the land and how it is held by the parties. The plaintiff and her ex-husband were the beneficial joint tenants of the matrimonial home. When the marriage broke down the house was too large for him to live in alone, and they reached an agreement, recorded in a written memorandum, that he should be entitled to sell the house at his discretion and use the proceeds to provide a new home where the children could come and visit. Before the house was sold he died. Walton J. held that the agreement they had reached did not sever their joint tenancy because it was concerned with the use of the land, or the proceeds of sale, and not the ownership:

> "can the memorandum be read as a severance of their joint beneficial interests: an agreement to the effect that each of them thereafter is to be solely entitled to his and her respective one half share in such proceeds? With the best will in the world I find myself wholly unable to give the memorandum such a construction. . . . It appears to me that the memorandum is dealing solely with the use by Mr Todd of the whole of the proceeds of sale, and that, qua ownership, use is wholly ambiguous: hence it cannot be implied from the fact the Mr Todd was to have the use of the whole of the money either that the title thereto was assigned to him or that he was entitled to have his own half absolutely, and Mrs Todd her own half share absolutely."[118]

(e) *The Agreement Need not have been Acted Upon*

12–055 Severance will occur if an agreement was reached and is not dependent upon the agreement having been carried into effect. This is clear from the facts of *Burgess v Rawnsley*[119] itself.

6. Severance by Mutual Conduct of the Joint Tenants

12–056 The essence of the third method of severance identified by Page Wood V.C. in *Williams v Hensman*[120] is that all the joint tenants have acted in such a way as to demonstrate that they intend to regard themselves as enjoying differentiated and specific shares in the land. It is said that it must be possible to infer from their conduct that they had a "common intention" to sever. Thus if joint tenants treat themselves as if they were tenants in common the law will regard the joint tenancy as having been severed, even though there was no express act of severance.

A unilateral act of a joint tenant will not be sufficient to effect severance under this head and will only be effective to sever if it falls within the first head examined above, namely if it is an act which operates on his own share. For this reason Page Wood V.C. stressed that a mere unilateral expression of intention to sever was not to be regarded as a "course of dealing" for the purposes of this third head of severance:

> "When severance depends on an inference of this kind without any express act of severance, it will not suffice to rely on an intention, with respect to the particular share, declared only

---

[118] [1975] Ch. 222 at 229.
[119] [1975] Ch. 222.
[120] (1861) 1 J. & H. 546.

behind the backs of the other persons interested. You must find in this class of cases a course of dealing by which the shares of all the parties to the contest have been affected."[121]

A number of categories of mutual conduct have come to be regarded as possessing potentially severing effect.

(a) Joint Tenants have Held Long-term Assumptions about their Ownership of the Land

Where joint tenants have held long-term assumptions about their ownership of the land which are inconsistent with the continuance of a joint tenancy this will be a sufficient course of conduct to effect a severance in fact. This was recognised by Blackett-Ord J. in Gore and *Snell v Carpenter*[122] where he stated:

> "A course of dealing is where over the years the parties have dealt with their interests in the property on the footing that they are interests in common and are not as joint."[123]

However having recognised that such a course of dealing could in principle effect severance he held none had in fact been established. A husband and wife were the joint tenants of two houses. In the course of separation negotiations it was suggested that one house should be transferred into the wife's name. Although she agreed to this in principle, there were further financial arrangements to be settled. No final agreement was ever reached and the wife continued to live in the house, which remained jointly owned, until the husband committed suicide some time later. Blackett-Ord J. held that this did not amount to a course of dealing sufficient to effect severance:

> "For severance to be effected by a course of dealings all the joint tenants must be concerned in such a course and in the present case there is no evidence that [the wife] was committing herself to accepting a tenancy in common prior to the property division which would have been made in the divorce proceedings."

Since there was no severance the entire ownership of the house vested in the wife by survivorship and did not form part of the husband's estate.

(b) Joint Tenants have Executed Mutual Wills

Although it has been seen that the unilateral act of a joint tenant purporting to dispose of his interest in land by will does not have the effect of severing his share inter vivos, the execution

12–057

12–058

---

[121] (1861) 1 J. & H. 546 at 557.
[122] (1990) 60 P. & C.R. 456.
[123] (1990) 60 P. & C.R. 456 at 462.

of mutual wills by all the joint tenants leaving their interests to agreed legatees will constitute a sufficient "course of dealing" to fall under the third head of *Williams v Hensman*. In *In the Estate of Heys*[124] a husband and wife were the joint tenants of a leasehold property. In 1907 they executed wills in identical terms leaving the property to each other if they predeceased, and to the defendants in the event that they died second. Sir Samuel Evans, President of the Court of Probate, held that the execution of these mutual wills severed their joint tenancy of the leasehold, so that from that time onwards they were holding as tenants in common. On the death of the husband his half share in the property passed to his wife under his will rather than by way of survivorship, and was bound by a trust in favour of the beneficiaries named in the mutual wills.[125]

(c) *Inconclusive Negotiations with Regard to the Ownership of the Land*

12–059
The most controversial issue to arise under this third head of severance is whether inconclusive negotiations between the joint tenants in regard to their ownership of the land are a sufficient course of conduct to effect severance. The possibility was raised by Lord Denning M.R. in *Burgess v Rawnsley*.[126] Whilst the majority of the Court of Appeal held that severance had occurred because Mrs Rawnsley had reached an oral agreement to sell her share of the co-owned house to Mr Honick, Lord Denning M.R. was prepared to find that "even if there was not any firm agreement" between the parties their negotiations amounted to a "course of dealing" which had evidenced a sufficient intention to sever. He stated a general principle that:

> "a 'course of dealing' need not amount to an agreement, expressed or implied, for severance. It is sufficient if there is a course of dealing in which one party makes clear to the other that he desires that their shares should no longer be held jointly but be held in common."[127]

The difficulty with this approach is that it seems to suggest that a mere unilateral statement of intention, provided that it is communicated to the other joint tenants, is sufficient to sever. It is clear that the other members of the Court of Appeal rejected the argument that a mere unilateral declaration of intention is sufficient, even if communicated,[128] but it is less clear whether the proposition that inconclusive negotiations would be a sufficient course of dealing was rejected. Browne L.J. doubted that the evidence would establish a sufficient course of dealing but refused to express a final opinion whether negotiation could ever be sufficient. Sir John Pennycuick seemed to anticipate that negotiations could have a severing effect, but not on the particular facts:

---

[124] [1914] P. 192.
[125] See also *Re Wilford's Estate* (1879) 11 Ch.D 267; *Gould v Kemp* 2 My. & K. 304.
[126] [1975] Ch. 429.
[127] [1975] Ch. 429 at 439.
[128] [1975] Ch. 429 at 444, per Browne L.J.; at 448, per Sir John Pennycuick.

"I do not doubt myself that where one tenant negotiates with another for some rearrangement of interest, it may be possible to infer from the particular facts a common intention to sever even though the negotiations break down. Whether such an inference can be drawn must I think depend upon the particular facts. In the present case the negotiations between Mr Honick and Mrs Rawnsley, if they can be properly described as negotiations at all, fall, it seems to me, far short of warranting an inference. One could not ascribe to joint tenants an intention to sever merely because one offers to buy out the other for £X and the other makes a counter offer of £Y."[129]

The evidence of later cases suggests that it is extremely difficult to establish a clear mutual intention to sever from inconclusive negotiations. In *McDowell v Hirschfield Lipson & Rumney and Smith*[130] it was submitted that inconclusive negotiations on the separation of a husband and wife and correspondence between their respective solicitors concerning the suggested sale of the matrimonial home were a sufficient course of dealing to effect severance. Eric Stockdale J. dismissed this submission finding that there was no course of dealing from which to justify a finding of a common intention to sever. He pointed out the crucial difficulty that in many such cases where negotiations have broken down severance is not at that stage inevitable for the parties.[131] Similarly, in *Gore and Snell v Carpenter*[132] Blackett-Ord J. held that a common intention to sever could not be inferred from abortive negotiations because at that stage the wife had not been prepared to commit herself to a tenancy in common.

(d) *Joint Tenants have Physically Divided their Possession of the Land*

It might be thought that physical division of the land could constitute a course of dealing **12–060** which manifests an intention to sever a joint tenancy. However it should be born in mind that unity of possession is a requirement of both joint tenancies and tenancies in common, and in *Greenfield v Greenfield*[133] Fox J. held that physical division of land was not automatically inconsistent with the continuance of a joint tenancy and was therefore insufficient as a course of dealing from which to infer an intention to sever. Two brothers were the joint tenants of a house which they had purchased as joint tenants in 1947 and converted into two separate maisonettes in 1962, in which they lived with their respective wives. When one brother died in 1975 his wife claimed to be entitled to ownership of their maisonette under his will. As there had been no severance it passed to the other brother by way of survivorship. Fox J. held that the long period of divided use did not indicate an intention on the part of the brothers to sever the joint tenancy:

"The onus of establishing severance must be on the plaintiff. It seems to me that on the facts [she] comes nowhere near discharging that onus. Neither side made clear any intention of ending the joint tenancy. The defendant had no intention of ending it

---

[129] [1975] Ch. 429 at 447.
[130] [1992] 2 F.L.R. 126.
[131] [1992] 2 F.L.R. 126 at 131.
[132] (1990) 60 P. & C.R. 456.
[133] (1976) 38 P. & C.R. 570.

and never thought that he or [his brother] had ended it. The defendant's understanding was that [his brother] was of exactly the same mind. Indeed their mutual intention in 1962 was to continue the joint tenancy. And so they agreed. The mere existence of the separate maisonettes and of their separate occupation is not inconsistent with the continuation of a joint tenancy. The two can perfectly well exist together. The matter must be considered in the light of the evidence of the actual intentions of the parties."[134]

(e) Joint Tenants Use their Land for a Business Partnership

12–061 In *Barton v Morris*[135] a man and woman purchased a farmhouse which they intended to run as a guest house. She provided the majority of the initial deposit, but the property was conveyed into their names as joint tenants in law and equity. The woman subsequently kept the accounts of their business, which differentiated between their respective capital contributions to the property. She was subsequently killed in a riding accident and the administratrix of her estate claimed that the joint tenancy had been severed by this course of dealing. The Court of Appeal held that the inclusion of the property in the account was not a course of dealing which reflected an intention that the joint tenancy should be severed, but rather an intention that the financial dealings of the parties should be accurately recorded, and for tax considerations. The property therefore passed absolutely to the man by survivorship.

7. Forfeiture

(a) Rationale of Forfeiture

12–062 Forfeiture occurs in order to prevent a person retaining property received as a consequence of unlawfully killing the owner. It has application where a person would receive property under the will of someone they unlawfully killed[136] or on intestacy.[137] It has potential application to situations where there is a joint tenancy, since if one joint tenant kills another he stands to gain thereby through the operation of survivorship. Rather than allow him to benefit, the law regards the unlawful killing as a severing event, thus preventing the operation of survivorship in the killer's favour. Given that the legal title to land can only be held as a joint tenancy, survivorship is allowed to operate in relation to the legal title if the killer is a trustee, but severance operates in relation to the equitable ownership so that the killer cannot derive any real benefit from his actions.

---

[134] (1976) 38 P. & C.R. 570 at 578.
[135] [1985] 2 All E.R. 1032
[136] See *Re Sigsworth* [1935] Ch. 89; *Re Callaway* [1956] Ch. 559; *Re Peacock* [1957] Ch. 310.
[137] *Re Crippen* [1911] P. 108.

(b) Scope of Forfeiture

Forfeiture will occur in the event of murder, but it remains unclear whether it will apply in all cases of manslaughter. Some cases suggest that it is inapplicable in cases of involuntary manslaughter[138] but the courts have generally shown reluctance to draw a distinction between voluntary and involuntary manslaughter.[139] In *Gray v Barr*[140] Geoffery Lane J. suggested at first instance that forfeiture would apply if a person was "guilty of deliberate, intentional and unlawful violence or threats of violence," a test approved by Vinelott J. in *Re K (deceased)*.[141] The forfeiture rule will apply even where there has been no criminal conviction if the unlawful killing can be established in the civil court where the burden of proof is the balance of probabilities.[142] In the more recent case of *Dunbar v Plant*[143] the Court of Appeal held that forfeiture might operate even where the surviving joint tenant had not used or threatened deliberate violence. Thus the interests of joint tenants were held to have been severed where one had aided and abetted the other to commit suicide, which is a criminal offence contrary s.2(1) of the Suicide Act 1961. Mummery L.J. explained why severance had occurred:

12–063

> "In my judgment . . . the presence of acts or threats of violence is not necessary for the application of the forfeiture rule. It is sufficient that a serious crime has been committed deliberately and intentionally. The references to acts or threats of violence in the cases are explicable by the facts of those cases. But in none of those cases were the courts legislating a principle couched in specific statutory language. The essence of the principle of public policy is that (a) no person shall take a benefit resulting from a crime committed by him or her resulting in the death of the victim and (b) the nature of the crime determines the application of the principle. On that view, the important point is that the crime that had fatal consequences was committed with a guilty mind (deliberately and intentionally). The particular means used to commit the crime (whether violent or non-violent) are not a necessary ingredient of the rule."[144]

(c) Jurisdiction to Grant Relief from Forfeiture

Although forfeiture prima facie operates in cases of unlawful killing, s.2(1) of the Forfeiture Act 1982 grants the court a jurisdiction to "make an order . . . modifying the effect of that rule" in cases other than murder. To exercise the jurisdiction the court must be satisfied that "having regard to the conduct of the offender and of the deceased and to such other circumstances as

12–064

---

[138] See *Tinline v White Cross Insurance Association Ltd* [1921] 3 K.B. 327; *James v British General Insurance Co Ltd* [1927] 2 K.B. 311.
[139] See *Re Giles* [1972] Ch. 544.
[140] [1971] 2 Q.B. 554.
[141] [1985] Ch. 85.
[142] *Gray v Barr* [1971] 2 Q.B. 554. See also *Re Sigsworth* [1935] Ch. 89 where forfeiture was applied when there was no criminal conviction because of the defendant's suicide.
[143] [1997] 4 All E.R. 289.
[144] [1997] 4 All E.R. 289 at 300.

appear to the court to be material, the justice of the case requires the effect of the rule to be modified in that case".[145] Relief from forfeiture was granted by Vinelott J. in *Re K (deceased)*[146] because the wife who had killed her husband had suffered grave violence at his hands. As a consequence of the court's order she was not prevented from taking his interest in their jointly owned matrimonial home by survivorship. Relief from forfeiture was also granted in *Dunbar v Plant*,[147] where the Court of Appeal stressed the tragic nature of the circumstances, in that the joint tenants had entered a suicide pact and one had survived, and that the jointly owned property had not been derived from the deceased tenant's family, who would have stood to gain if forfeiture had been permitted to take its course.

(d) *Effect of Forfeiture where there is a Joint Tenancy*

12–065 The exact effects of severance by operation of law through forfeiture will depend upon the nature of the joint tenancy in question.

(i) Operation of Forfeiture where there were only two Joint Tenants

12–066 Where land is held by two persons as joint tenants and one unlawfully kills the other the effect of the killing is to sever the joint tenancy. The consequence is that the killer will retain his half share of the land but will not receive the interest of his victim by survivorship. Instead, his victim's half share will pass under his will, or by the rules of intestacy. The operation of these principles are well illustrated in *Re K (deceased)*.[148] A husband and wife were the joint tenants at law and in equity of their matrimonial home. The wife subsequently shot the husband accidentally after threatening him with a loaded shotgun. Vinelott J. held that in these circumstances the forfeiture rule would prima facie apply so that although the wife held the entire legal title the joint tenancy had been severed in equity, there was a tenancy in common, and her husband's half share passed to whoever was entitled on his death.[149] In the event this result was only avoided because he felt able to grant relief from the effects of forfeiture.

(ii) Operation where there were more than two Joint Tenants and one has Killed Another

12–067 Where land is owned by more than two joint tenants and one is killed by another the operation of the forfeiture rule is less clear cut. For example, if Carolyn, Daniel, Ellen and Frank are the joint tenants in law and in equity of a house and Carolyn murders Daniel, the expected result would be that this would have the effect of severing Daniel's beneficial interest in the

---

[145] Forfeiture Act 1982 s.2(2).
[146] [1985] Ch. 85; affirmed [1986] Ch. 180.
[147] [1997] 4 All E.R. 289.
[148] [1997] 4 All E.R. 289.
[149] See also *Schobelt v Barbert* (1966) 60 D.L.R. (2d) 519; *Re Pechar* [1969] N.Z.L.R. 574.

land so that a quarter share would devolve to those entitled on his death, and that Carolyn, Ellen and Frank would continue as joint tenants of the remaining three-quarters. However this solution deprives the innocent joint tenants, namely Ellen and Frank, of benefiting from the death of Daniel by way of the principle of survivorship. To overcome such a problem an Australian court held[150] that the interests of the unlawfully killed joint tenant should be held on a constructive trust for the innocent joint tenants. If this approach were to be followed, Ellen and Frank would be joint tenants of a quarter share of the beneficial interest, representing Daniel's interest, and Ellen, Frank and Carolyn would be the joint tenants of the remaining three-quarters interest. There are no English cases which decide how such problems should be resolved and neither approach is ideal from the perspective of achieving justice between the surviving parties.

MUTUAL RIGHTS OF EQUITABLE CO-OWNERS OF LAND

1. Right to Occupation and Use of the Land

(a) *A Consequence of Unity of Possession*

It has already been noted that one essential element of both a joint tenancy and a tenancy in common is that the co-owners enjoy unity of possession of the co-owned land. This means that they are both entitled to occupy every part of the land and they cannot exclude each other from any part of it. This follows even if the parties are tenants in common, since their notional shares of the ownership of the land are not translated into a correspondingly proportionate right of occupation. The mutual right of occupation was recognised by the Court of Appeal in *Bull v Bull*[151] where a house was held by a man as trustee for himself and his mother as tenants in common. The Court of Appeal held that he was not entitled to evict her. Lord Denning M.R. explained:

12–068

> "when there are two equitable tenants in common, until the place is sold, each of them is entitled concurrently with the other to the possession of the land and to the use and enjoyment of it in a proper manner; and neither of them is entitled to turn the other out."[152]

Despite this general right it seems that in some circumstances the nature of the relationship of the original co-owners will prevent a successor in title who has acquired the share of one of them from exercising the right to occupation with the others. In *Chhokar v Chhokar*[153] Mr and Mrs Chhokar were the tenants in common in equity of their matrimonial home, the legal title to which was held by Mr Chhokar alone. After leaving his wife he sold the land to

---

[150] *Rasmanis v Jurewitsch* (1970) 70 S.R. (NSW) 407 (Court of Appeal of New South Wales).
[151] [1955] 1 Q.B. 234.
[152] [1955] 1 Q.B. 234 at 238.
[153] [1984] F.L.R. 313.

his friend Mr Parmar, who was fully aware of his wife's interest, and the sale was deliberately completed while Mrs Chhokar was in hospital. The effect of this transaction was that Parmar held the legal title to the house on trust for himself and Mrs Chhokar as equitable tenants in common of half shares because he had taken the land subject to Mrs Chhokar's interest which was binding on him as an overriding interest under the Land Registration Act 1925, s.70(1)(g). Subsequently Mr and Mrs Chhokar were reconciled and he moved back into the matrimonial home. The Court of Appeal assumed that in these circumstances Parmar had no right to occupation of the land, even though he was the owner of a half share by way of a tenancy in common, on the grounds that he stood in the shoes of Mr Chhokar as his successor in title, and that the right of occupation was dependent on the married status of the original co-owners. Cumming-Bruce L.J. explained:

> "[counsel for Parmar] submits that he has a right in law to occupy the property, but he goes on in the next breath to concede that it is a right that cannot be exercised because he succeeded to the rights of the husband in the matrimonial home. Mr Parmar is a married man himself and no court would allow him to try to occupy the matrimonial home in common with Mrs Chhokar (and for all I know Mrs Parmar might have something to say about it too, if he tried to do so). But for this purpose he stands in the shoes of [Mr Chhokar] . . ."[154]

This suggests that wherever the original co-owners entered into occupation of the land on the basis of an intimate relationship between themselves a successor in title will not be entitled to assert his right to occupy by virtue of his status as a co-owner alone.

It should also be noted that under s.12 of the Trusts of Land and Appointment of Trustees Act 1996 the beneficiaries of a trust of land have a statutory right to occupation of the land. This includes co-owners, who enjoy their rights behind a trust. Under s.13 the trustees have limited powers to exclude or restrict the occupation rights of the beneficiaries. The effect of these provisions are considered in detail below.

(b) One Co-owner cannot Trespass against Another

12–069   Since all the co-owners of land have rights to possession of the whole land, one co-owner cannot commit an act of trespass against another merely by exercising his or her own right to possession. For one co-owner to commit trespass, there must be something which amounts to an act excluding the other or other co-owners. In *Jacobs v Seward*[155] one tenant in common of land had cut hay in a field that was co-owned. The House of Lords held that a tenant in common could not maintain an action in trespass against a fellow tenant in common unless there had been an actual ouster of the allegedly trespassing tenant from the land. The argument that the placing of a lock on the gate to the field was a sufficient ouster was rejected, since the supposedly trespassing tenant had never been refused access to the field, and there was no

---

[154] [1984] F.L.R. 313.
[155] (1872) L.R. 5 H.L. 464.

evidence of anything passing between the parties to demonstrate that the lock had been placed with the intention of excluding the co-tenant. Lord Hatherley L.C. concluded that:

> "so far as trespass is concerned, it appears to me to be idle to talk of trespass as a consequence of a man making hay upon his own field—for it is his own—or a moiety of it at least, and no definite portion of it is mapped out as his moiety."[156]

(c)   *Payment of Rent between Co-owners*

Although all the co-owners are theoretically equally entitled to occupation of the land, it is inevitable that in some circumstances such shared occupation will be impossible. Such problems arise if the relationship of co-owners of residential property breaks down. In *Bull v Bull*[157] Lord Denning M.R. took the view that the solution to the inability of the co-owners to share the land was that it should be sold and the proceeds divided appropriately between the parties. However, as will be seen below, in many more recent cases where the relationship has disintegrated the courts have refused to order a sale of the land, with the effect that one co-owner remains in occupation of the land and the other is excluded. Where a co-owner does not enjoy the benefit of occupation of the land the question arises whether he is entitled to receive compensating payments of rent from the co-owners who continue to occupy. The traditional understanding is that since co-owners are equally entitled to occupy the land those that are not in occupation have no right to receive rent from those who are merely exercising their rights as co-owners. In *Henderson v Eason*, Parke B. stated:

12–070

> "There are obviously many cases in which a tenant in common may occupy and enjoy the land . . . and have all the benefit to be derived from it, and yet it would be most unjust to make him pay anything. For instance, if a dwelling house, or barn, or room, is solely occupied by one tenant in common without ousting the other . . . it would be most inequitable to hold that he thereby, by the simple act of occupation or use, without any agreement, should be liable to pay a rent or anything in the nature of compensation to his cotenants for that occupation or use to which to the full extent to which he enjoyed it he had a perfect right."[158]

(i)   No Right to Rent where a Co-owner Chooses not to Occupy

Where a co-owner voluntarily chooses not to exercise his right to occupy, he is not entitled to receive a rent from the co-owners in occupation. This was recognised in *Dennis v McDonald* where Purchas J. stated:

12–071

---

[156] (1872) L.R. 5 H.L. 464 at 473.
[157] [1955] 1 Q.B. 234.
[158] (1851) 17 Q.B. 701.

"Only in cases where the tenants in common not in occupation were in a position to enjoy their rights to occupy but chose not to do so voluntarily, and were not excluded by any relevant factor, would the tenant in common in occupation be entitled to do so free of liability to pay an occupation rent."[159]

(ii) Rent Payable where a Co-owner is Excluded by the Other or Others

12–072 It follows that were one co-owner is excluded from enjoyment of the co-owned land the co-owner(s) who continue to enjoy occupation will be required to pay a compensating rent to those deprived of their right. In *Dennis v McDonald*, Purchas J. examined the authorities[160] and summarised the approach of the Chancery courts:

"the Court of Chancery . . . would always be ready to enquire into the position as between co-owners being tenants in common, either at law or in equity, to see whether a tenant in common in occupation of the premises was doing so to the exclusion of one or more of the other tenants in common, for whatever purpose or by whatever means. If this was found to be the case, then if in order to do equity between the parties an occupation rent should be paid, this would be declared and the appropriate enquiry ordered."[161]

A man and woman had lived together as husband and wife for a number of years in a house which they owned as tenants in common in equity and occupied with their five children. The woman left the property as a result of the man's violence towards her. Purchas J. held that as she had been excluded from the family home she was entitled to receive a compensating payment from the man, who had remained in occupation. In contrast in *Jones v Jones*[162] a father purchased a house which was held on trust for himself and his son as tenants in common of three-quarters and a quarter share respectively. The purpose was to provide the son with somewhere to live. On the father's death his share passed to his wife, the son's step-mother, who wanted the house sold and who was not in occupation of it. Having refused to order a sale of the house Lord Denning M.R. held that in the absence of any ouster from the property, there was no obligation for the son to pay an occupational rent.[163] As will be seen later, the payment of a rent has often been imposed as a condition when the court has refused to order the sale of co-owned property so that one of the co-owners can remain living in it. For example, in *Harvey v Harvey*[164] a husband and wife were the equitable tenants in common of their matrimonial home in shares of a third and two-thirds respectively. The husband had left his wife and she remained in the house with three of their children. The Court of Appeal held that

---

[159] [1982] 3 F.L.R. 398 at 405.
[160] *M'Mahon v Burchell* (1846) 2 Ph. 127; *Henderson v Eason* (1851) 17 Q.B. 701; *Hill v Hickin* [1897] 2 Ch. 579; *Jones v Jones* [1977] 1 W.L.R. 438.
[161] [1982] 3 F.L.R. 398 at 404.
[162] [1977] 1 W.L.R. 438.
[163] Roskill L.J. held that there was no obligation to pay rent on the basis that the son's entitlement was by way of proprietary estoppel and that there was no jurisdiction for imposing rent as a condition of satisfying the estoppel equity.
[164] (1982) 3 F.L.R. 313.

any sale should be postponed[165] during the lifetime of the wife or until her remarriage, voluntary removal from the premises, or becoming dependent on another man. However it imposed the condition that after the mortgage was repaid, or the youngest child attained the age of 18, she was to pay an occupational rent for her continued occupancy. In *Bedson v Bedson*[166] the court awarded an occupational rent where one co-owner remained in occupation of the matrimonial home while divorce proceedings were pending. Where the co-owned property has been purchased by means of a mortgage the requirement that a co-owner who remains in occupation makes the mortgage repayments, thus freeing a co-owner who has been excluded, also amounts to the payment of a form of compensation for non-occupation.[167]

(iii)   Is an Occupational Rent Fair?

Given that the court is willing in some circumstances to require a co-owner in occupation to pay an occupational rent to those excluded, in *Chhokar v Chhokar*[168] the Court of Appeal suggested that the appropriate test to determine if rent should be required was whether it would be "fair" in the circumstances. As has been noted above, in the unusual circumstances of the case Mrs Chhokar and Mr Parmar were the tenants in common of Mrs Chhokar's matrimonial home. Ewbank J. held that as Mrs Chhokar had enjoyed the sole occupation of the property for three and a half years Mr Parmar should receive a rent of £8 per week. However the Court of Appeal rejected the contention that Mr Parmar was entitled to rent simply because he could not enjoy occupation, and deleted any requirement to pay from the judge's order. Cumming-Bruce L.J. stated that:

12–073

> "I have been unable to find anything in the authorities which should lead the court to hold that it would be fair, which I regard as the test, to require [Mrs Chhokar] to pay occupation rent to Parmar by way of payment for her occupation of the matrimonial home."[169]

Central to this conclusion seems to have been the fact that Mr Parmar in some sense stood in the shoes of the husband whose share he had purchased, and that the husband himself had not been excluded by the wife as she had taken him back and they were sharing occupation of the house.

(iv)   A Wider Jurisdiction to Award an Occupational Rent?

In *Re Pavlou (A Bankrupt)*[170] a husband and wife were the beneficial joint tenants of a house which they had purchased in 1973. In 1983 the husband left and the wife remained in sole occupation, paying the mortgage and making improvements to the property. Millet J. held that

12–074

---

[165] Even though it was held on trust for sale.
[166] [1965] 2 Q.B. 666.
[167] *Re Evers Trust* [1980] 1 W.L.R. 1327.
[168] [1984] F.L.R. 313.
[169] [1984] F.L.R. 313 at 332.
[170] [1993] 1 W.L.R. 1046.

on the evidence before him he could not determine whether an occupational rent should have been payable by the wife in respect of her sole occupation and set off against her mortgage interest payment when dividing the proceeds of sale. However he suggested a rather broader approach to the question of rent which did not necessarily require exclusion:

> "I take the law to be to the following effect. First, a court of equity will order an inquiry and payment of occupational rent, not only in the case where a co-owner in occupation has ousted the other, but in any other case in which it is necessary in order to do equity between the parties that an occupational rent should be paid. The fact that there has not been an ouster or forceful exclusion therefore is far from conclusive. Secondly, where it is a matrimonial home and the marriage has broken down, the party who leaves the property will, in most cases, be regarded as excluded from the family home, so that an occupation rent should be paid by the co-owner who remains. But that is not a rule of law; that is merely a statement of the prima facie conclusion to be drawn from the facts. The true position is that if a tenant in common leaves the property voluntarily, but would be welcome back and would be in a position to enjoy his or her right to occupy, it would normally not be fair or equitable on the remaining tenant in common to charge him or her with an occupation rent which he or she never expected to pay."[171]

He felt that there was insufficient evidence to determine whether the husband would have been welcomed back into occupation between 1983 when he left and 1986 when his wife petitioned for divorce, but that after the petition a rent was prima facie payable.

(v)   Assessment of the Occupational Rent

12–075   Where the court decides that the imposition of an occupational rent on a co-owner in sole occupation is appropriate the question arises as to how it should be assessed. In *Dennis v McDonald*[172] Purchas J. held that the man in sole occupation should pay his ex-partner a rent equivalent to half the fair rent which would have been assessed as payable by a rent officer for a letting of the whole premises unfurnished to a protected tenant for the period of the occupation, giving credit for any sums expended which improved the capital value of the property but not for the costs of ordinary repair and maintenance. The Court of Appeal rejected this approach on the grounds that it did not compensate the excluded co-owner for non-occupation but punished the occupier by regarding him as "illicitly enjoying and therefore accountable for the one half of what he would have had to pay for the property if he entered the property market as a willing tenant and found a willing landlord ready to let it to him." Sir John Arnold P. explained that he considered this inappropriate:

> "I am bound to say that in the circumstances of the case, that that is somewhat unrealistic. He occupies this property not because he has been able to negotiate in the market and obtain it but because he is a tenant in common. He occupies it in respect of, and by right

[171] [1993] 1 W.L.R. 1046 at 1050.
[172] [1982] F.L.R. 408.

of, his beneficial interest. He is not, therefore, subject to the vagaries of the market and starts off with a right of occupation. Something would have to be allowed in some way for that. Moreover, it is difficult to see what justification there is for charging a person in his position with such extra payment as a tenant would have to make by reason of the scarcity of relevant accommodation in the market."[173]

The Court of Appeal concluded that he should have to pay a "fair rent" as would be assessed under the Rent Act but eliminating the element for scarcity.[174] However it was stressed that the preferable solution was that the parties negotiate to determine an acceptable rent between themselves. Since the fundamental basis of rent assessment was compensation for non-occupation, rather than restitution of the benefit of sole-occupation to the co-owner remaining, the Court of Appeal further held that the man was not entitled to any set-off against rent because more of the parties' children were living with him than with her. Sir John Arnold P. explained why such considerations were irrelevant to the assessment of the rent:

"the nature of the payment, and the amount of the payment, should be regulated by reference to the circumstance that the payer is housed in the property of which he is a trustee to the exclusion of the payee, who is equally a beneficiary, and that the purpose to which the payer puts the property has nothing to do with the case."[175]

In *Harvey v Harvey*[176] the Court of Appeal held that an occupational rent should be determined at a "reasonable, market figure".

(vi)   Cost of Repairs Allowed against the Payment of Occupational Rent

In *Dennis v McDonald* the Court of Appeal also ordered an inquiry as to the costs or value of any improvements which the sole occupier had made to the land and that he should be entitled to set off half this amount against rent due.[177]   **12–076**

(vii)   Statutory Power of Trustees to Impose Rent

Under s.13 of the Trusts of Land and Appointment of Trustees Act 1996 the trustees of land are   **12–077**
entitled to impose conditions upon a co-owner who remains in occupation of co-owned land where the occupancy of other co-owners has been excluded or restricted by an exercise of their powers under s.12. The conditions which may be imposed specifically include requiring the beneficiary in occupation to "make payments by way of compensation to the beneficiary whose entitlement has been excluded or restricted".[178] This provision is discussed further below.

---

[173] [1982] F.L.R. 408 at 413.
[174] Assessment was ordered under s.70(1) and (2) of the Rent Act 1977 without regard to any other provisions of the Act.
[175] [1982] F.L.R. 408 at 412.
[176] [1982] 3 F.L.R. 141.
[177] See also *Re Pavlou* [1993] 1 W.L.R. 1046.
[178] Trusts of Land and Appointment of Trustees Act 1996 s.13(6)(a).

2. Right to Share in the Economic Exploitation of the Land

(a) *Profits Received from Someone who is not a Co-owner*

12–078 Land is an economically valuable commodity, which can be exploited so as to produce a profit for its owners. Obvious examples of such economic exploitation include leasing the land so as to produce an income in the form of rent, mining the land or farming the land. Where any profit is generated from a stranger's use or exploitation of the co-owned land the co-owners are entitled to a share proportionate to the extent of their interest. In *Henderson v Eason*[179] Parke B. held that a co-owner was obliged to account[180] for any profits he had received from third parties in excess of his legitimate entitlement:

> "where the tenant in common receives money or something else, where another person gives or pays it, which the cotenants are entitled to simply by reason of their being tenants in common, and in proportion to their interests as such, and of which one receives and keeps more than his just share according to that proportion."

These principles were applied in *Bernard v Josephs*[181] where a husband and wife were the tenants in common of half shares in their matrimonial home. After the breakdown of their marriage the wife left and the husband remained in occupation. He let part of the house to tenants. The Court of Appeal held that in assessing the price at which the husband should be allowed to purchase the wife's share she should be entitled to the credit of half the rent he had received.

(b) *Profits Generated by a Co-owner from his Own Use of the Land*

(i) No Duty to Account for Profit which is the Just Product of his Work

12–079 Where one co-owner has made a profit for himself by use of the land, for example by farming it or siting his production facility on it, he will not be accountable for the profit he made to the extent that it can be regarded as the legitimate product of his own investment, whether of labour or capital. As Parke B. stated in *Henderson v Eason*:

> "Again, there are many cases where profits are made, and are actually taken, by one co-tenant, and yet it is impossible to say that he has received more than comes to his just share. For instance, one tenant employs his capital and industry in cultivating the whole of a piece of land, the subject of the tenancy, in a mode in which the money and labour expended greatly exceed the value of the rent or compensation for the mere occupation

---

[179] (1851) 17 Q.B. 701.
[180] The co-owner liable to account is not, however, a fiduciary: *Kennedy v De Trafford* [1897] A.C. 180.
[181] [1982] Ch. 391.

of the land; in raising hops, for example, which is a very hazardous adventure. He takes the whole of the crops: and is he to be accountable for any of the profits in such a case, when it is clear that, if the speculation had been a losing one altogether, he could not have called for a moiety of the losses, as he would have been enabled to do had it been cultivated by the mutual agreement of the co-tenants? The risk of the cultivation, and the profits and loss, are his own; and with respect to all the produce of the land, the fructus industriales, which are raised by the capital and industry of the occupier, and would not exist without it. In taking all that produce he cannot be said to receive more than his just share and proportion to which he is entitled as a tenant in common. He receives in truth the return for his own labour and capital, to which his co-tenant had no right."[182]

(ii) Duty to Account where a Co-owner's Profits are not Merely the Product of his Own Work

In *Henderson v Eason* Parke B. anticipated that a co-tenant will not always be entitled to retain the entire profit generated by his use of the land as he cannot retain more than his just share and proportion. He will generally be liable to account if he has exploited the land itself, diminishing its capital value, for example by mineral extraction or quarrying. In *Job v Potton*[183] a mine was owned by a number of tenants in common, one of whom enjoyed a two-thirds share of the ownership. He extracted coal and one question was the extent to which he was required to account to his fellow tenants for the value of the coal extracted. Sir James Bacon V.C. presupposed that the tenant was entitled to extract the coal but that "he must not appropriate to himself more than his share". He held that he was liable to account to his fellow tenants for a third of the value of the coal that had been mined and brought to the surface, subject to a deduction of "the cost of the severance and the cost of bringing it to the pit's mouth". By means of this balance the co-tenants to whom he was obliged to account would not receive a windfall benefit of his work and investment, and he would not take more than his just share. In *Jacobs v Seward*[184] the House of Lords held that a tenant in common who had harvested hay from a co-owned field was not liable in tort to his fellow tenants. However it was assumed that if they had brought an action for account they would have been entitled to a share of the profits subject to allowance for the expense of making the hay.

12–080

3. Right to a Contribution Towards Repairs and Improvements

(a) *No Right to Contribution without Agreement, Request or Fulfilment of a Common Obligation*

Land, and especially buildings, will always require a degree of maintenance to prevent it falling into disrepair, which will inevitably diminish its value. If one co-owner pays for the

12–081

---

[182] (1851) 17 Q.B. 701.
[183] (1875) 20 L.R.Eq. 84.
[184] (1872) 5 L.R.App. Cas. 464.

cost of repairs or provides improvements to the land, is he entitled to proportionate contributions from his fellow tenants? In *Leigh v Dickson*[185] the Court of Appeal held that a tenant in common who pays for necessary repairs to the co-owned land is not entitled to a proportionate contribution to the cost from his co-owners unless there was an agreement that they would contribute. Brett M.R. explained why there was no right of contribution where one tenant in common had spent £80 on substantial repairs and improvement to the co-owned property:

> "The cost of the repairs was a voluntary payment by the defendant, partly for the benefit of himself and partly for the benefit of his co-owner; but the co-owner cannot reject the benefit of the repairs, and if she is held to be liable for a proportionate share of the cost, the defendant will get the advantage of the repairs without allowing his co-owner any liberty to decide whether she will refuse or adopt them . . . If the law were otherwise, a part-owner might be compelled to incur expense against his will: a house might be situated in a decaying borough, and it might be thought by one co-owner that it would be better not to repair it. The refusal of a tenant in common to bear any part of the cost of repair may be unreasonable; nevertheless, the law allows him to refuse and no action will lie against him."[186]

Consequently a co-owner will only be entitled to a contribution to the cost of repairs which he has incurred if there was an express or implied agreement that his co-tenants would contribute,[187] or an express or implied request[188] that the work be done. In *Leigh v Dickson* Cotton L.J. also suggested that there would be a right to contribution if a co-owner had funded repairs in fulfilment of an obligation to repair that he and his co-tenants jointly owed to a third party, since "when two persons are under a common obligation, one of them can recover from the other the amount expended in discharge or fulfilment of the common obligation". For example, if a lease containing a repairing covenant was held by two persons as tenants in common, and one of them paid for the costs of necessary repairs, he would be entitled to receive a contribution from his co-tenant proportionate to his interest.

(b) *An Equitable Lien to Recoup the benefit of Expenditure on Repairs or Improvements*

12–082   Although a co-owner will not be entitled to a contribution towards the costs of repairs or improvements it seems that he will be entitled to an equitable lien over the property which has been benefited by the repairs or improvements he funded, which must be satisfied from the proceeds of sale when the land is sold.[189] This possibility was recognised by Cotton L.J. in *Leigh v Dickson*:

---

[185] (1884) 15 Q.B.D. 60.
[186] (1884) 15 Q.B.D. 60 at 65–66.
[187] See *Bernard v Josephs* [1983] 4 F.L.R. 178; *Harwood v Harwood* [1991] 2 F.L.R. 274.
[188] *Leigh v Dickson* (1884) 15 Q.B.D. 60 at 67, per Cotton L.J.
[189] In *Bernard v Josephs* [1982] Ch. 391 the Court of Appeal held that only in exceptional circumstances would it be inferred that a co-owner's funding of repairs or improvements was intended to alter the extent of the beneficial interests in the property.

"Therefore, no remedy exists for money expended in repairs by one tenant in common, so long as the property is enjoyed in common; but in a suit for a partition it is usual to have an inquiry as to those expenses of which nothing could be recovered so long as the parties enjoyed their property in common; when it is desired to put an end to that state of things, it is then necessary to consider what has been expended in improvements or repairs; and whether the property is divided or sold by decree of the Court, one party cannot take the increase in value without making an allowance for what has been expended in order to obtain that increase in value; in fact, the execution of the repairs and improvements is adopted and sanctioned by accepting the increased value. There is, therefore, a mode by which money expended by one tenant in common for repairs can be recovered . . ."[190]

It is somewhat unclear from these comments whether the nature of the recovery by way of an equitable lien is of the costs of the repairs or improvements or of any increase in the value to the land flowing from such improvements. The cost of repairs may far exceed any increase in value, or work which one co-owner considers an improvement may be of such bad taste as to actually reduce the market value of the land. In *Gross v French*[191] where improvements to a house had been carried out at the expense of the legal owner, who was a bare trustee, the Court of Appeal held that he was entitled to an equitable lien over the land for the amount by which the value of the house had been enhanced by the work.[192] Walton J. had rejected the submission that the trustee should be entitled to a lien for the total expenditure he had incurred and not merely the enhancement value, and the Court of Appeal upheld this on the basis that his claim was analogous to that of a joint owner where the co-owned land is partitioned or sold. The entitlement of a co-owner to receive the value of improvements and repairs to land when it is sold is itself an equitable interest in the land, which is thus capable of binding successors in title.[193]

(c) *Equitable Lien Subject to Other Counterclaims*

Any equitable lien to which a co-owner may be entitled to recover enhancements to the value of the land flowing from repairs or improvements he funded will be subject to any counterclaims of his fellow co-owners. The lien will be subject to an occupational rent if he has enjoyed sole occupation of the land, and to an account of any profits he has made by the economic exploitation of it.[194]   **12–083**

---

[190] (1884) 15 Q.B.D. 60 at 67.
[191] (1975) 238 E.G. 39.
[192] See also *Re Cook's Mortgage* [1896] 1 Ch. 923.
[193] *Williams v Williams* (1899–1900) 81 L.T. (NS) 163.
[194] *Williams v Williams* (1899–1900) 81 L.T. (NS) 163.

Chapter 13

THE STATUTORY FRAMEWORK GOVERNING TRUSTS OF LAND

In the preceding chapter it has been seen that all forms of co-ownership must take effect **13–001** behind a trust of the land, irrespective of whether the co-owners are joint tenants or tenants in common of the beneficial interest. The consequence of this is that a significant proportion of land will be held on some type of trust, especially given that today the majority of homes are jointly owned rather than by the male partner alone. Trusts are therefore the major vehicle for residential land-owning in English land law. Given the significance of trusts to landholding, legislation has intervened to provide a framework for their operation, prescribing the nature of the trustee's rights and duties, rather than allowing them to be regulated by the general equitable principles governing the operation of trusts.

The property reforms of 1925 introduced a twin regime for trusts of land, which differentiated between successive and concurrent interests in the land. Successive interests would largely take place behind a special kind of trust, called a strict settlement, whilst concurrent co-ownership of land would take place behind a trust for sale. This regime was subject to extensive criticism, especially because of the perceived inappropriateness of a trust for sale as a vehicle for land ownership where the prime objective was usually to retain the land for occupation and use by the beneficiaries. In 1989 the Law Commission recommended reform,[1] and the Trusts of Land and Appointment of Trustees Act 1996 largely implemented its proposals. This act has introduced a single comprehensive regime regulating trusts of land, irrespective of whether the beneficial interests are successive or concurrent in nature. However, before turning to examine the new regime the main features of the historic trust for sale will be outlined, since many of the reforms introduced by the Trusts of Land and Appointment of Trustees Act 1996 can only be understood and evaluated in the light of the preceding law.

[1] Law Com. Report No.181, *Transfer of Land: Trusts of Land* (1989).

1. The Historic Trust for Sale

(a) *Trusts for Sale as the Universal Basis of Co-ownership*

13–002 Prior to the Trusts of Land and Appointment of Trustees Act 1996, all co-owned land was held on a trust for sale. The defining characteristic of the trust for sale, from which it derives it name, was that the trustees were placed under an overriding duty to sell the land.[2] This meant that their prime obligation was to arrange for the land to be sold, thereby converting the asset from an estate in land to a sum of money representing its value. This arrangement seems strange since the majority of trusts of land have as their prime object the retention of the land for occupation by the beneficiaries. Where a husband and wife are the joint legal and equitable owners of their matrimonial home their intention is generally to live in it and to keep hold of it. The trust for sale introduces an inherent inconsistency between their duties as trustees of the land, namely to sell it, and their intentions as beneficiaries to retain it for occupation. This tension inherent in the trust for sale was resolved by the fact that in most cases the trustees also enjoyed a power to postpone sale of the land.[3]

Under the 1925 regime a trust for sale could arise in one of two ways. First, a trust for sale could be created expressly by conveying the legal title to land to a trustee or trustees subject to an express duty to sell. Since the trust for sale was foundational to the 1925 legislation it became standard conveyancing practice to create express trusts for sale. However, the Law of Property Act 1925 also provided for a number of situations where a trust of land would be implied to take the form of a trust for sale. By s.36(1) a trust for sale would be implied in all situations where there was a joint tenancy of the legal ownership of the land, whether the beneficial interests behind the trust were in the form of a joint tenancy, a tenancy in common,[4] or even if there was no co-ownership but a single beneficiary.[5] In *Bull v Bull*[6] the Court of Appeal construed the statutory provisions so that a trust for sale would be implied even where there was no joint tenancy of the legal title of land, because there was a sole trustee, and a tenancy in common of the beneficial interest, despite the fact that such a situation was not apparently within the strict terms of s.36(1). A house was purchased by a mother and her son, with the son providing the majority of the purchase price, and the legal title was transferred into his name alone. The consequence of this arrangement was that he was a sole trustee holding the land on resulting trust for himself and his mother as tenants in common of shares of the beneficial interest proportional to their contributions. Denning L.J. concluded that this trust was an implied trust for sale, reasoning that since s.36(4) of the Settled Land Act 1925 stated that tenancies in common "shall only take effect behind a trust for sale", the legislation must have intended a trust for sale to be implied in such circumstances. The effect of this decision was to ensure that the regime of the trust for sale was given virtually universal coverage in cases of co-ownership of land behind

---

[2] Law of Property Act 1925 s.205(1)(xxix) defined a trust for sale as "an immediate binding trust for sale . . . with or without a power to postpone sale".

[3] By Law of Property Act 1925 s.25(1) a power to postpone sale was implied into every trust for sale "unless a contrary intention appears."

[4] As for example in *City of London Building Society v Flegg* [1988] A.C. 54.

[5] *Wilson v Wilson* [1969] 3 All E.R. 945.

[6] [1955] 1 Q.B. 234.

a trust. The only potential lacuna in the regime was a bare trust of the land, since the interpretative trickery of *Bull v Bull* would not work where there was no co-ownership of either the legal title or the beneficial interest. Therefore, although it would have been consistent with the general policy of the legislative framework to find that such a trust was a trust for sale, a bare trust where a sole trustee is holding the land on trust for a sole beneficiary would only have been subject to a duty to sell if expressly imposed.

(b) *The Powers and Duties of the Trustees of a Trust for Sale*

Under s.28 of Law of Property Act 1925 the trustees of a trust for sale were granted the same powers as conferred on both the tenant for life and on the trustees of a strict settlement governed by the Settled Land Act 1925. These were a limited range of rights including the right to sell,[7] to grant leases under defined conditions,[8] and to grant mortgages for a narrow range of purposes.[9] The trustees were, by s.26(3) of the Law of Property Act 1925, under a duty to consult the beneficiaries before exercising their powers. Their powers could also be made subject to the requirement of obtaining consent.[10] They had power to delegate a limited range of powers to the beneficiaries.[11] Most importantly the trustees possessed a power to postpone sale which, if validly exercised, would displace their duty to sell the land, thus enabling them to retain it. However, as trustees are required to act unanimously, the power to postpone sale could only be validly exercised if all the trustees were agreed that the land should be retained and not sold. As soon as one or more of the trustees refused to exercise the power to postpone the duty to sell would revive and could not be displaced. In such a situation the land would have to be sold. The operation of the trust for sale is well illustrated by *Re Mayo*[12] where land was held[13] by three trustees on an express trust for sale, one of whom wanted the land sold immediately whilst the others wished to retain it. Simmonds J. held that in the absence of a valid exercise of the power to postpone sale the trustees were under a duty to sell and he granted an order to enforce a sale by directing the trustees to take "all necessary steps for the sale of the property".[14] *Re Mayo* epitomises a strict approach to the enforcement of the duty to sell and it will be seen that in later cases the courts developed an entire jurisprudence of circumstances in which they would refuse to order a sale even though trustees were not unanimously exercising the power to postpone sale. Most of these cases involved land which had been acquired for purposes other than resale.

13–003

(c) *The Rights of the Beneficiaries of a Trust for Sale*

Where land was held by trustees on a trust for sale there was some question whether the beneficiaries were to be regarded as enjoying any interest in the land itself because of the potential

13–004

---

[7] Settled Land Act 1925 s.38.
[8] Settled Land Act 1925 s.41.
[9] Settled Land Act 1925 s.71.
[10] Law of Property Act 1925 s.26.
[11] Law of Property Act 1925 s.29.
[12] [1943] Ch. 302.
[13] The particular trust was a trust for sale arising by statute under the Settled Land Act 1925 s.36, but the principles are identical for all such trusts.
[14] [1943] Ch. 302 at 304.

application of the doctrine of conversion. Since the prime duty of the trustees in such a case was to sell the land, equity would anticipate the inevitability of such a sale because of the maxim that "equity treats as done that which ought to be done" with the result that the beneficiaries' interests existed only in relation to the purchase money which would be realised on sale.[15] Their interests were therefore in money and not in the land. However, with an increasing recognition that the central purpose of most trusts for sale was occupation of land by the beneficiaries the courts backed away from the logical consequences of a full-blown application of the doctrine of conversion. In *Williams & Glyn's Bank v Boland*[16] the House of Lords regarded it as unrealistic to regard a wife who was an equitable tenant in common of the matrimonial home she occupied with her husband as enjoying an interest only in the proceeds of sale of the land.[17] Her interest was held to be a right in land capable of forming the subject matter of an overriding interest under s.70(1)(g) of the Land Registration Act 1925.[18]

As the traditional doctrine of conversion suggested that the beneficiaries of a trust for sale enjoyed no actual rights in the land the concomitant effect of this would be that they had no right to occupy the land.[19] Their only right was to receive an appropriate share of the proceeds on sale. However the courts again backed away from the full logical implications of conversion and concluded that beneficiaries behind a trust for sale did enjoy rights of occupation. In *Bull v Bull*[20] Denning L.J. held that a mother, who was an equitable tenant in common of a house which her son held on trust for sale, was entitled to "possession of the land and to the use and enjoyment of it in a proper manner", on the grounds that these rights had been enjoyed by legal tenants in common.[21] This conclusion that an equitable tenant in common was entitled to occupation was expressly approved by the House of Lords in *Williams & Glyn's Bank Ltd v Boland*.[22] Most significantly, in *City of London Building Society v Flegg*[23] Lord Oliver stated that:

> "The beneficiary's possession or occupation is no more than a method of enjoying in specie the rent and profits pending sale in which he is entitled to share. It derives from and is . . . fathered by the interests under the trust for sale."[24]

His analysis reconciled both the essential nature of the trust for sale and the practical reality that the majority of such trusts had as their object the occupation of the land by the beneficiaries by making their right of occupation a present foretaste of their future entitlement to the proceeds of sale.

---

[15] See *Cooper v Critchley* [1955] Ch. 431; *Irani Finance Ltd v Singh* [1971] Ch. 59 at 80, per Cross L.J.; *Cedar Holdings Ltd v Green* [1981] Ch. 129.
[16] [1981] A.C. 487.
[17] See also the judgment of the Court of Appeal, which was approved: [1979] Ch. 312.
[18] See Chs 5 and 7.
[19] *Re Bagot's Settlement* [1894] 1 Ch. 177; *Re Earl of Stamford and Warrington* [1925] Ch. 162.
[20] [1955] 1 Q.B. 234.
[21] *Jacobs v Seward* (1872) L.R. 5 H.L. 464; *Re Warren* [1932] 1 Ch. 42. See also *Barclay v Barclay* [1970] 2 Q.B. 677.
[22] [1981] A.C. 487 at 510, per Lord Scarman.
[23] [1988] A.C. 54.
[24] [1988] A.C. 54 at 83.

(d)   *The Power of the Court to Resolve Disputes*

Under the regime of the trust for sale the court was given the power to resolve disputes **13–005** arising between or amongst the trustees and beneficiaries. Section 30 of the Law of Property Act 1925 provided:

> "If the trustees for sale refuse to sell or to exercise any of [their powers], or any requisite consent cannot be obtained, any person interested may apply to the court for a vesting or other order for giving effect to the proposed transaction or for an order directing the trustees for sale to give effect thereto, and the court may make such order as it thinks fit."

This section was interpreted by the courts as conferring a discretion which was sufficiently wide to entitle it to postpone a sale, even where the trustees did not unanimously agree to exercise their power to postpone, by refusing to order a trustee to sell. In this way the court could effectively order that the land be retained rather than sold. In *Re Buchanan-Wollaston's Conveyance*[25] Sir Wilfred Greene M.R. held that, when exercising the discretion under s.30, the court must:

> "look into all the circumstances and consider whether or not, at the particular moment and in the particular circumstances when the application is made to it, it is right and proper that such an order shall be made."[26]

In *Jones v Challenger*[27] Devlin L.J. adopted a generalised approach to the exercise of the jurisdiction which would consider the "prime object" of the trust that a sale need not be ordered "where the trust itself or the circumstances in which it was made show that there was a secondary or collateral object besides that of sale".[28] Given the willingness of the courts to refuse to order a sale in circumstances where there was a collateral object behind the trust there developed an entire jurisprudence, or catalogue, of such objects which would be sufficient to displace the duty to sell. Collateral objects might be found where the trustees had expressly agreed amongst themselves that the land was not to be sold unless they acted unanimously[29] or where the land had been purchased to provide a family home for the children of the trustees.[30] The cases relating to collateral objects are not rendered irrelevant by the new framework of the Trusts of Land and Appointment of Trustees Act 1996 and they are discussed more fully below in the context of the factors which must be considered by the court in exercising its new statutory discretion to make orders relating to the exercise of the trustees' functions.

---

[25] [1939] 1 Ch. 738.
[26] [1939] 1 Ch. 738 at 747.
[27] [1961] 1 Q.B. 176.
[28] [1961] 1 Q.B. 176 at 181.
[29] See *Re Buchanan-Wollaston's Conveyance* [1939] Ch. 217.
[30] See *Williams v Williams* [1976] Ch. 278.

2. Trusts of Land

(a) *Trusts of Land as the Universal Basis of Co-ownership*

13–006 As noted above, the Trusts of Land and Appointment of Trustees Act 1996 has now swept away the bifurcated approach adopted in 1925 in favour of the introduction of a unitary "trust of land," which will facilitate both co-ownership and successive ownership. It is no longer possible to create a strict settlement under the Settled Land Act 1925, although existing settlements will remain valid and remain governed by the old regime. All other trusts that include land amongst the trust property will take the form of a statutory "trust of land". This follows from s.1(a), which provides:

> " 'Trust of land' means . . . any trust of property which consists of or includes land."[31]

It is irrelevant how such a trust was created, since by s.1(2)(a) the statutory regime applies to "any description of trust (whether express, implied, resulting or constructive)." Logically, the "trustees of land" are defined as the "trustees of a trust of land".[32] Section 1(2)(a) also provides that a "trust of land" includes a "trust for sale and a bare trust", and s.1(2)(b) makes clear that all existing trusts for sale are brought within the new regime because a trust of land "includes a trust created, or arising, before the commencement of this Act".

The consequence of these provisions is that every trust consisting of interests in land (except for an existing strict settlement governed by the Settled Land Act 1925[33]) will be brought within the statutory framework of the Trusts of Land and Appointment of Trustees Act 1996. The Act defines the various powers and duties of the trustees who own the legal title, and the various rights and entitlements of the beneficiaries. It also provides a dispute resolution mechanism for situations where those relationships have broken down and there is no unanimity as to what should be done with the land. It is still possible for a trust of land to impose a duty to sell on the trustees, in which event they will continue to have an implied power to postpone sale, but such a duty will have to be imposed expressly when the trust is created.

(b) *Abolition of the Doctrine of Conversion*

13–007 As was noted above, one problem associated with the trust for sale was whether the presence of the duty to sell gave rise to the operation of the doctrine of conversion, thus depriving the beneficiaries of any right in the land itself and of the right to occupy the land. However as was seen the doctrine of conversion came to be increasingly marginalised and disregarded for the purpose of determining of the rights of the beneficiaries of a trust for sale. The Trusts of

---

[31] With the exception of land which is already settled land and land to which the University and Colleges Estates Act 1925 applies: s.1(3).

[32] Trusts of Land and Appointment of Trustees Act 1996, s.1(1)(b).

[33] See Ch.14.

Land and Appointment of Trustees Act 1996, has abolished it altogether, so that trust interests are to be treated as existing in the trust property, whether money or land. Section 3(1) provides:

> "Where land is held by trustees subject to a trust for sale, the land is not to be regarded as personal property; and where personal property is subject to a trust for sale in order that the trustees may acquire land, the personal property is not to be regarded as land."

Since the overall effect of the Act is that land will no longer be held with a duty to sell unless expressly imposed by the settlor in most cases the doctrine of conversion would have no application in any event. Section 3(1) makes clear that it has no application even in those rare instances where the trustees remain under an express duty to sell.

3. Powers and Duties of the Trustees of a "Trust of Land"

(a) *Trustees of Land Enjoy the Powers of an Absolute Owner in Relation to the Land*

Section 6(1) of the Trust of Land and Appointment of Trustees Act 1996 provides that: **13–008**

> "For the purposes of exercising their functions as trustees, the trustees of land have in relation to the land subject to the trust all the powers of an absolute owner."

This general principle means that the trustees are capable of dealing with the land in any way that an absolute owner is entitled to deal with his land. Clearly this general principle entitles the trustees to sell, mortgage or lease the land. This is a significant change from the previous position. Under the previous legislation the powers of trustees of land were restricted. The new policy relating to trusts, reflected in this change,[34] is to give trustees broad powers, but to impose upon the trustees a duty to exercise those powers in the interests of the beneficiaries. This general duty is inherent in all trust relationships but is confirmed by s.6(5) which provides that in exercising the powers conferred by the section "trustees shall have regard to the rights of the beneficiaries".

The following features of the trustees' powers may be noted:

(i) No duty to sell

Although s.6(1) clearly confers on a trustee of land the power to sell the land, it does not impose   **13–009**
a duty to sell. An absolute owner enjoys the discretion whether to sell or to retain his land.

---

[34] And in the wider powers now given to trustees to invest trust property.

(ii) Power to Purchase Land

13–010   Section 6(3) expressly provides that the trustees' powers to act as an absolute owner of land include the "power to purchase a legal estate in any land in England or Wales". This power may be exercised by way of investment, for the land to be occupied by any of the beneficiaries[35] or for any other reason.[36]

(iii) Express Qualification of the Trustees' General Powers

13–011   Although the trustees of a trust of land prima facie enjoy the same powers as an absolute owner, s.8 permits the settlor creating the trust to expressly restrict or qualify the trustees' powers. This allows the settlor, for example, to impose an express duty to sell, although in such a case there will be an implied power to postpone a sale.[37] This power to postpone sale cannot be excluded.[38] The settlor could, however, exclude the power of sale, thus obliging the trustees to retain the land.

(iv) Imposition of Requisite Consents

13–012   The trustees' right to deal with the property in the manner of an absolute owner can also be qualified by the express requirement of consents to the exercise of any power. This does not affect the intrinsic right of the trustees to act but s.8(2) provides that such powers "may not be exercised" without obtaining the appropriate consents.

(v) Trustees' Right to Terminate their Trusteeship by Conveyance of the Land to the Beneficiaries

13–013   The well-established rule in *Saunders v Vautier*[39] entitles the beneficiaries of a trust to demand that the trustees transfer the legal title to them if they are all agreed, of age and legally competent. This enables the beneficiaries to bring the trust to an end. Section 6(2) introduces a statutory equivalent in favour of the trustees, enabling them to bring their trusteeship to an end by forcing a transfer of the legal title to the beneficiaries if the beneficiaries could have exercised their right to terminate the trust. This right only arises if the beneficiaries of the trust of land are of full age and legally competent. If the trustees do convey the land to the beneficiaries the effect will be that they cease to have the onerous duties of trusteeship. If there is a sole beneficiary of the trust of land that person will become the absolute owner. If there are several co-owners of the beneficial interests those persons[40] will become the legal owners and therefore the beneficiaries will hold the land on a "trust of land" for themselves.

---

[35] Avoiding the implications of *Re Power* [1947] Ch. 547.
[36] Trusts of Land and Appointment of Trustees Act 1996 s.6(4).
[37] Trusts of Land and Appointment of Trustees Act 1996 s.4(1).
[38] Trusts of Land and Appointment of Trustees Act 1996 s.4(1).
[39] [1841] 4 Beav. 115.
[40] Note that there can still only be a maximum of four trustees of land.

(vi)   Trustees' Actions Subject to General Restrictions

Section 6(6) provides that the trustees' rights to deal with the land as absolute owners "shall not be exercised in contravention of, or of any order made in pursuance of, any other enactment or any rule of law or equity". The precise impact of this obscure subsection is unclear,[41] although a literal interpretation would suggest that any exercise of the trustees' powers which falls foul of it will be regarded as void and not simply as a breach of trust. The effective scope of s.6(6) is mitigated in respect of trusts of unregistered land as s.16(2) provides that a conveyance of such land in contravention of s.6(6) will not be invalidated unless the purchaser had actual notice of the contravention. Ferris and Battersby[42] have argued that s.6(6) had the effect of depriving dispositions of registered land in breach of trust of overreaching effect because they will be ultra vires and void. If this interpretation of the provisions were correct, then a disposition on sale of registered land would be invalid if the trustees did not sell at the best price reasonably obtainable, or if they used the proceeds to pay their own debts. If this were indeed the case, it would appear that there has been a dramatic legislative reversal of the decision of the House of Lords in *City of London Building Society v Flegg*,[43] something which seems most unlikely to have been intended given the conveyancing importance of the overreaching mechanism. However the problem has been resolved, at least as far as registered land is concerned, by the Land Registration Act 2002. Section 26(1) provides that:

> "a person's right to exercise owner's powers in relation to a registered estate or charge is to be taken to be free from any limitation affecting the validity of a disposition."

Ferris and Battersby admit that the effect of this provision is that "purchasers will continue to rely upon conveyances made by two trustees, or a trust corporation, to overreach the interests of beneficiaries of trusts of land".[44]

13–014

(b)   *Trustees' Right to Delegate their Powers in Relation to the Land*

Section 9(1) confers on trustees of land a general right to delegate any of their powers by power of attorney to "any beneficiary or beneficiaries of full age and beneficially entitled to an interest in possession in land subject to the trust". This includes the right to delegate the power of sale. The right to delegate cannot be excluded by the settlor. Section 9 only entitles the trustees to delegate their powers jointly as a body. The provision does not permit one

13–015

---

[41] One example of its use might be that if a family court made an order that sale of the former matrimonial home be postponed, to what extent will the court have jurisdiction under s.14 to make an order of sale at a later date? (Under s.14 the court can make any order it sees fit "relating to the exercise by the trustees of any of their functions": see below para.13–025). This could be an order relating to the trustees' powers under s.6(1), e.g. sale, but would it contravene the restriction in s.6(6)? The issue arose in *Avis v Turner* [2008] 2 W.L.R. 1, but Chadwick L.J. in the Court of Appeal dealt with the matter on the basis that this involved a trust for sale and did not concern a power conferred by s.6.

[42] "The Impact of the Trusts of Land and Appointment of Trustees Act 1996 on Purchasers of Registered Land" [1998] Conv. 169; "Overreaching and the Trusts of Land Act" [2001] Conv. 221; for counter-argument see "Overreaching and Unauthorised Dispositions of Registered Land" [2007] Conv. 120.

[43] [1988] A.C. 54.

[44] "The General Principles of Overreaching" (2003) 119 L.Q.R 94, at 125. See also Cooke [2002] Conv. 11.

trustee to delegate his power to the other trustees, nor to delegate his powers as trustees to the beneficiaries. Such an individual delegation is still possible under s.25 of the Trustee Act 1925. By s.9(8) the trustees enjoy protection from liability for the defaults of the beneficiaries to whom they have delegated their powers. They will only attract liability if they "did not exercise reasonable care in deciding to delegate the function to the beneficiary or beneficiaries".[45] Where trustees have jointly delegated their functions s.9(3) provides that the delegation can be revoked by "any one or more of them" at any time. A delegation is also revoked automatically if a new trustee is appointed[46] or when a person to whom a delegation was solely made ceases to be beneficially entitled under the trust.[47]

(c) *Trustees' Duty to Consult the Beneficiaries of the Trust*

13–016   Section 11(1) provides that:

> "The trustees of land shall in the exercise of any function relating to land subject to the trust—
>
> (a) so far as practicable, consult the beneficiaries of full age and beneficially entitled to an interest in possession in the land, and
> (b) so far as consistent with the general interest of the trust, give effect to the wishes of those beneficiaries, or (in case of dispute) of the majority (according to the value of their combined interests)."

This general requirement of consultation is subject to limited exceptions[48] and may be expressly excluded by the disposition creating the trust.[49] Where a trust of land was created prior to the commencement of the Act the trustees are under no duty to consult the beneficiaries unless the duty has been expressly incorporated into the trust by a deed executed by the settlor, or such of the persons who created the trust who are still alive and of full capacity.[50] Trustees do not need to consult when exercising their right under s.6(2) to convey the legal title to the beneficiaries of the trust.

The duty imposed by s.11 is not absolute. The trustees are not required to take unreasonable steps to attempt to consult beneficiaries, nor are they obliged to give effect to their wishes where consultations have taken place and the views of the beneficiaries are incompatible with the interest of the trust. Although the phrase "so far as is consistent with the general interest of the trust" seems vague, it has been taken from s.26(3) of the Law of Property Act 1925, and has not been the cause of litigation or dispute.

---

[45] Compare the problems associated with similar provisions in ss.23(1) and 30 of the Trustee Act 1925, as interpreted in *Re Vickery* [1931] Ch. 572.
[46] Trusts of Land and Appointment of Trustees Act 1996 s.9(3).
[47] Trusts of Land and Appointment of Trustees Act 1996 s.9(4)(a). Where a delegation was made to a number of beneficiaries jointly and one subsequently loses his entitlement under the trust the power is revoked in as far as it relates to him.
[48] Under s.11(2)(a) it does not apply to trusts created or arising under wills made before the commencement of the Act.
[49] Trusts of Land and Appointment of Trustees Act 1996 s.11(2)(a).
[50] Trusts of Land and Appointment of Trustees Act 1996 s.11(3).

(d) *Trustees' Power to Exclude Beneficiaries from Occupation of the Land*

As will be explained more fully below the co-owners of land, whether they are tenants in **13–017** common or joint tenants enjoy the right to occupy the land and cannot exclude each other from possession. This right is confirmed by s.12 of the Act. However, it is inevitable that on occasions the co-owners' relationship will deteriorate to such an extent that it is impossible for them to continue to share possession of the land. Section 13(1) grants the trustees the power to "exclude or restrict" the entitlement of any one or more beneficiaries of a trust of land who are concurrently entitled to occupation under s.12. They may not, however, exclude all the beneficiaries from occupation. The trustees must not exclude or restrict the occupation rights of any beneficiary unreasonably.[51] Although s.13(1) grants the trustees a wide power to exclude or restrict the occupation rights of the beneficiaries of the trust, the exercise of this power is effectively circumscribed by s.13(7) which provides that:

> "The powers conferred on the trustees by this section may not be exercised—
>
> (a) so as to prevent any person who is in occupation of land (whether or not by reason of entitlement under s.12) from continuing to occupy the land, or
>
> (b) in a manner likely to result in any such person ceasing to occupy the land, unless he consents or the court has given approval."

This means that a trustee can never force a beneficiary to cease occupation by exercise of this power and withdrawing his right to occupy without that beneficiary's consent or the approval of the court. Since the very situations in which it is likely to be necessary to force a co-owner to cease occupation, such as the breakdown of a relationship, are those where it is unlikely that the beneficiary will consent to such measures the practical effect of s.13(7) is that most cases of exclusion will have to be determined by the court. In most cases of co-ownership, the trustees are also the beneficiaries. Since the exercise of a power by trustees requires unanimity, the power is not exercisable unless the beneficiary-trustees are all in agreement.

Section 13 not only grants the trustees of land the power to exclude or restrict the occupation rights of beneficiaries but also specifies the factors which they must consider when contemplating the exercise of their power. These are listed in extremely general terms in s.13(4):

> "The matters to which trustees are to have regard in exercising the powers conferred by this section include—
>
> (a) the intentions of the person or persons (if any) who created the trust,
>
> (b) the purposes for which the land is held, and
>
> (c) the circumstances and wishes of each of the beneficiaries who is . . . entitled to occupy the land under section 12."

The central difficulty with this section is that concepts such as the "purposes for which the land is held" may not be immediately evident if not expressly stated in the instrument creating the trust.

---

[51] Trusts of Land and Appointment of Trustees Act 1996 s.13(2).

The trustees may impose reasonable conditions on any beneficiary "in relation to his occupation of land". Section 13(5) expressly permits the trustee to impose a condition on a beneficiary to "pay any outgoings or expenses in respect of the land". Section 13(6) permits the trustees to impose conditions where a beneficiary's rights of occupation have been excluded or restricted to receive compensation from those remaining in occupation. The court can review this power under s.14, with reference to the s.15 criteria.[52] For example, in the context where a matrimonial or quasi-matrimonial relationship has broken down and one party remains in occupation.[53]

4. Rights of the Beneficiaries of a Trust of Land

(a) *A Statutory Right to Occupy*

13–018 Section 12(1) of the Trusts of Land and Appointment of Trustees Act 1996 provides for a general right of occupation for the beneficiary of a trust of land:

> "A beneficiary who is beneficially entitled to an interest in possession in the land subject to a trust of land is entitled by reason of his interest to occupy the land at any time if at that time:
>
> (a) the purposes of the trust include making the land available for his occupation (or for occupations of beneficiaries of a class of which he is a member or of beneficiaries in general), or
> (b) the land is held by the trustees so as to be available."

The statutory right to occupy under s.12(1) only arises in favour of a beneficiary under a trust of land who is entitled to an interest "in possession". This means that only a person who enjoys a present and immediate right to possession of the land is entitled to occupy, and excludes a person whose interest is only in remainder or reversion. Most importantly it means that the person entitled to the remainder interest where a life interest has been granted has no right to occupation while the life tenant is alive. Where a trust of land facilitates co-ownership the co-owners are concurrently entitled to possession and therefore all enjoy rights of occupation under s.12.

Section 12(1)(a) has the effect that a beneficiary will only enjoy a statutory right of occupation if one of the purposes of the trust was to make the land available for his occupation. In the absence of express indications in a trust deed it is unclear how the purposes of a trust are to be defined. No doubt in many cases where there is co-ownership, whether on the basis of an express, constructive or resulting trust, it will be self evident that the purpose of the trust was to enable the co-owners to occupy the land. For example it was self-evidently the purpose of the trust in *City of London Building Society v Flegg*[54] that Mr and Mrs Maxwell-Browne were to

---

[52] See below for a discussion on the application of these sections, para.13–025.
[53] *Stack v Dowden* [2007] UKHL 17 [2007] 2 AC 432; *Murphy v Gooch* [2007] EWCA Civ 603; Westlaw document 2007 WL 1729776.
[54] [1988] A.C. 54.

share occupation of the house which had been purchased specifically to enable them to live with Mr and Mrs Flegg, their daughter and son-in-law. However, it seems likely that there would be no statutory right of occupation if the facts were similar to those of *Barclay v Barclay*.[55] In this case a man had died leaving his bungalow to be sold and divided in equal shares amongst his sons and daughters-in-law. One son continued to live in the bungalow and claimed that he was entitled to occupy as an equitable tenant in common. The Court of Appeal held that the bungalow should be sold and the proceeds divided. Lord Denning M.R. stated that this was because *Bull v Bull*[56] could be clearly distinguished:

> "In *Bull v Bull* the prime object was that the house should be occupied by them both. So they were tenants in common of the house itself. In the present case, the prime object of the testator was that the bungalow should be sold and the proceeds divided. So the beneficiaries were not tenants in common of the bungalow, but only of the proceeds after it was sold."

Although the analysis of the tenants rights would be different under the framework of the new trust of land, it seems unlikely that the "purpose" of the trust would be differently assessed under s.12(1)(a).

There is similarly no statutory right of occupation unless the land is held by the trustees so as to be "available" for occupation. This means that a beneficiary's rights of occupation will come to an end if the trustees decide to sell the land. The land must also be "suitable" for occupation. The exact scope of this restriction is unclear. It may be obvious that a mine held on trust is not suitable for the beneficiary's occupation, but it is less clear whether the statutory right of occupation would be excluded if the beneficiary were a drug-debauched heir to a stately home, or the co-owner of a farm incapable of running it. However in by far the majority of co-ownership cases there will be no difficulties of the suitability of residential property for occupation by the co-owners.

As has been noted above, under s.13 of the Act the trustees enjoy the power to exclude or restrict the right of occupation of some, but not all, of the beneficiaries. Most significantly the trustees cannot exercise their powers so that a person presently in occupation of the land will be prevented from continuing to occupy,[57] or made likely to cease occupation,[58] without the consent of that person unless the exercise of the power is approved by the court.

(b) *Right to be Consulted by the Trustees*

The corollary of the trustees' duty to consult with the beneficiaries of a trust of land over the exercise of their functions under s.11 of the Act is that the beneficiaries have a right to be consulted. As was noted above, this is not an absolute right and the trustees do not have to act according to their wishes if this is inconsistent with the general interest of the trust.

13–019

[55] [1970] 2 Q.B. 677.
[56] [1955] 1 Q.B. 234.
[57] Trusts of Land and Appointment of Trustees Act 1996 s.13(7)(a).
[58] Trusts of Land and Appointment of Trustees Act 1996 s.13(7)(b).

5. Resolving Disputes in Relation to the Co-owned Land

(a) *Context of Disputes*

13–020   Inevitably where a number of persons are simultaneously interested in land they will not always agree as to what should be done with it. A number of different scenarios of dispute may be noted:

(i) Disputes Among the Trustees

13–021   If land is held on trust by more than one trustee then it is possible that there will be disputes between the trustees as to how they should exercise their powers. Since the exercise of their powers requires the trustees to act unanimously this may result in a stalemate situation in which they cannot agree upon any course of action, for example some of the trustees may want to sell the land and others not.

(ii) Disputes between the Trustees and the Beneficiaries

13–022   Alternatively there may be a dispute between the trustee or trustees and the beneficiaries of the trust. For example, none of the trustees may want to sell the land but some of the co-owners want it sold. Obviously in the case of residential co-ownership some of the co-owners may also be the trustees of the land.

(iii) Disputes Among the Co-owners

13–023   Disputes may also arise amongst those who are the beneficial co-owners of the land.

(iv) Disputes between the Beneficiaries and their Creditors

13–024   Disputes may arise between the beneficiaries and their creditors as to whether the land should be sold so as to repay their debts. Such disputes are likely to arise if a beneficiary has become insolvent, or if their debts are secured on the co-owned land, whether by a charge or a mortgage.

(b) *Resolution of Disputes Arising in Relation to a Trust of Land*

13–025   Section 14 of the Trusts of Land and Appointment of Trustees Act 1996 grants the court a wide jurisdiction to make orders relating to the trust of land. Section 14(1) provides that: "Any person who is a trustee of land or has an interest in property subject to a trust of land may make an application to the court for an order under this section". Section 14(2) provides that:

"On an application for an order under this section the court may make any such order—

(a) relating to the exercise by the trustees of any of their functions (including an order relieving them of any obligation to obtain the consent of, or to consult, any person in connection with the exercise of any of their functions), or

(b) Declaring the nature or extent of a person's interests in property subject to the trust, as the court thinks fit."

Section 14 thus gives the court a wide scope of jurisdiction. This reflects the policy of the Law Commission report that the "courts should be able to intervene in any dispute relating to a trust of land".[59] Section 14(2)(a) is sufficiently wide to enable the court to authorise the trustees to carry out their functions in a manner which would otherwise constitute a breach of trust.[60] Section 14(2)(b) also expressly grants the court the power to determine the nature and extent of a claimant's interests in the land. However by far the most likely scenario which will call for the courts' intervention is the situation where co-owners cannot agree what should be done with the land and some wish it to be sold and others that it be retained. Despite the width of the jurisdiction granted, s.14(3) expressly stipulates that the court "may not under this section make any order as to the appointment or removal of trustees". The court enjoys the power to appoint and remove trustees under the general provisions of the Trustee Act 1925, as amended.

(c) *Factors which the Court must Consider*

Section 15(1) of the Trusts of Land and Appointment of Trustees Act 1996 places on a statutory footing a number of factors which the court should take into account when determining how to exercise its jurisdiction:

13–026

"The matters to which the court is to have regard in determining an application for an order under s.14 include—

(a) the intentions of the person or persons (if any) who created the trust,

(b) the purposes for which the property subject to the trust is held,

(c) the welfare of any minor who occupies or might reasonably be expected to occupy any land subject to the trust as his home, and

(d) the interests of any secured creditor of any beneficiary."

These factors are similar to those which had been considered relevant by the courts in exercising their jurisdiction in respect of trusts for sale arising under the earlier legislation, and therefore the relevant case law remains relevant as the best guide as to how the court would be likely to exercise its new powers.[61] Section 15(4) provides that the catalogue of factors

---

[59] Law Com. No.181, para.12.6.
[60] But the court cannot make an order under the section in relation to a power that trustees do not have. In *Hopper v Hopper* [2008] EWHC 228 it was noted that there was no power to require a compulsory purchase of the other co-owner's interest, because a trustee had no power of this kind under the 1996 Act; Westlaw document 2008 WL 371016.
[61] *TSB Bank v Marshall* [1998] 3 E.G.L.R. 100.

stipulated in s.15(1) does not apply to applications for an order made by a trustee in bankruptcy of a beneficiary. In such instances s.335A of the Insolvency Act applies.[62]

(i) The Intentions of the Persons Creating the Trust

13–027 Although s.15(1)(a) requires the court to have regard to the intentions of the persons creating the trust of land this will only be possible if their intentions are discernible. In some cases their intentions may have been stated in the instrument creating the trust, but where there is no such statement of intentions the courts may be able to infer an intention from the circumstances of the trust. There is clearly some overlap between an inference of intention and the assessment of the purpose of a trust.

(ii) The Purpose of the Trust

13–028 The cases suggest a number of means by which the purpose of the trust may be identified. The co-owners of land may reach an agreement external to the instrument creating the trust indicating the purpose for which the land is held. In *Re Buchanan-Wollaston's Conveyance*[63] a section of sea front land was conveyed to four people as joint tenants. They executed a deed stating that the land had been purchased so that it would not be used in a manner which would cause a depreciation in the value of their own adjacent properties. They also agreed not to deal with the land unless they were unanimous or approved by a majority vote. The Court of Appeal held that a sale should not be ordered against the terms of the co-owners' mutual covenant. Where land was purchased to provide a home for the co-owners the courts have found that this was the purpose of the trust. For example in *Jones v Challenger*[64] the Court of Appeal held that a house purchased as a matrimonial home was held on trust for the purpose of occupation by the spouses. However, the cases also suggest that the courts will have regard to whether the purposes of the trust are continuing or whether they have come to an end. In *Jones v Challenger* the husband and wife had divorced and the husband had moved out of the family home. The Court of Appeal therefore held that purpose was no longer "alive" but had been "dissolved"[65] and it therefore granted an order for sale. In *Rawlings v Rawlings*[66] it was held that the purpose of the trust had failed where a wife left her husband, even though there was no divorce. In the more recent case of *Bank of Ireland Home Mortgages Ltd v Bell*,[67] the Court of Appeal concluded similarly that, where a house had been purchased to provide a family home, the purpose "ceased to be operative"[68] when the husband left the family, so that this was an irrelevant consideration as regards the exercise of the discretion whether to order a sale of the property under s.14. In *Jones (A E) v Jones (F W)*[69] a father and son were the equitable joint

---

[62] Trusts of Land and Appointment of Trustees Act 1996 s.15(4).
[63] [1939] Ch. 738.
[64] [1961] 1 Q.B. 176.
[65] [1961] 1 Q.B. 176 at 419.
[66] [1964] P. 398.
[67] [2001] 2 All E.R. (Comm) 920; [2001] F.L.R. 805.
[68] per Peter Gibson L.J.
[69] [1977] 1 W.L.R. 438.

tenants of a house which had been purchased largely by the father for his son to live in. When the father died the son's step-mother, who had inherited his father's interest, sought to have the house sold. The Court of Appeal held that no order for sale would be granted since this would defeat the purposes of the trust, which were that the son was to be able to live in the house for life. In *Holman v Howes*,[70] an estranged husband and wife who were attempting to reconcile purchased a house, using the majority of the wife's savings, on the understanding that it would provide a home for her in case the reconciliation failed. The property was in the husband's name, but nothing turned on this, and he assured her that he would not attempt to evict her. The Court of Appeal refused to order sale. The purpose to provide a home for the wife still subsisted as the reconciliation had failed.

(iii)   The Welfare of Minors

Where land was purchased with the object of providing a home for the co-owners to share it has been seen that the courts tended to regard the purposes as at an end if their relationship ended. However, in *Rawlings v Rawlings*[71] Salmon L.J. suggested that the position might be different if the co-owners had children still in need of a home: **13–029**

> "If there were young children the position would be different. One of the purposes of the trust would no doubt have been to provide a home for them, and whilst that purpose still existed a sale would generally not be ordered. But when those children are grown up and the marriage is dead, the purposes of the trust have failed."[72]

This approach was adopted by the Court of Appeal in *Williams (JW) v Williams (MA)*,[73] where a house was owned jointly by a husband and wife who had four children. They divorced and the wife remained in the house with the children, the youngest of whom was 12. Lord Denning M.R. held that the primary purpose of the trust was to provide "a home in which the family is to be brought up",[74] and refused to order sale unless "it were shown that alternative accommodation could be provided at a cheaper rate, and some capital released". In *Dennis v McDonald*[75] the court refused to order sale where a house was owned by a husband and wife as tenants in common and the wife had left leaving the husband in occupation with three of their children. In some cases the courts have considered postponing an order for sale to protect the interests of children. In *Re Evers Trust*[76] a man and woman owned a house as joint tenants. When their relationship ended the man left and sought an order for sale. The first instance judge held that an order should be postponed until the couple's child was 16.[77] The Court of Appeal upheld his decision not to grant an immediate order for sale on the grounds that the underlying purpose of

---

[70] [2007] Fam Law 987.
[71] [1964] P. 398.
[72] [1964] P. 398 at 419.
[73] [1976] Ch. 278.
[74] [1976] Ch. 278 at 285.
[75] [1982] Fam. 398.
[76] [1980] 1 W.L.R. 1327.
[77] Compare *Bernard v Josephs* [1982] Ch. 391, where an order for sale was postponed for four months to enable the occupying partner to buy out the share of the other co-owner.

the trust was to provide a home for the couple and their children, but held that duration of the postponement was inappropriate because the parties' circumstances might change in the future. The courts are required to give consideration to the interests of children requiring a home under s.15. However, this does not mean that their needs will automatically prevail. The court will have to balance their interest against those of others interested in the land. Different weight may be given to the interests of minors where the dispute is between the co-owners inter se especially when a relationship has ended, and where there is a conflict between the interests of any minors and a creditor of the co-owners which is seeking to enforce its security. In *Bank of Ireland Home Mortgages Ltd v Bell*[78] the Court of Appeal held that only "very slight consideration" should have been given to the welfare of a son of the beneficiary who was not far short of 18 in deciding whether to grant an order for sale in favour of a mortgagee.

(iv)   The Interests of Secured Creditors of the Beneficiaries

13–030   Where a secured creditor, for example a mortgagee, has an interest in the co-owned property, the court must balance the interests of the secured creditor against those of the co-owners and any minors when making an order under s.14. Prior to the Trusts of Land and Appointment of Trustees Act 1996 the courts had held that, in exercising its discretion under s.30 of the Law of Property Act 1925, the interests of a secured creditor would always prevail over those of the beneficiaries and their children unless there were exceptional circumstances. In *Lloyds Bank Plc v Byrne & Byrne*,[79] for example, a husband, who was the joint tenant with his wife of their matrimonial home, had secured against the property a debt of £25,000 relating to a company of which he was a director. The bank obtained a charging order on the house when the debt was not repaid and subsequently sought an order for sale under s.30. The Court of Appeal ordered sale. Purchas L.J. held that no distinction was to be drawn between the position of a chargee of the land and a trustee in bankruptcy of one of the co-owners, and that therefore, in the absence of exceptional circumstances, the order for sale would be granted.[80] In *Abbey National Plc v Moss*[81] Hirst L.J. held that the same principle should apply where a mortgagee was seeking an order for sale, since a mortgagee was in "an almost identical position" to the bank in *Lloyds Bank Plc v Byrne & Byrne*.[82]

However in *Mortgage Corp v Shaire*[83] it was held that the pre-existing law had been changed by s.15 of the Trusts of Land and Appointment of Trustees Act 1996, so that it was no longer the case that the court should order sale in favour of a secured creditor unless there were exceptional circumstances. Neuberger J held that, as a result of s.15:

> "the court has greater flexibility than heretofore, as to how it exercises its jurisdiction on an application for an order for sale."[84]

---

[78] [2001] 2 All E.R. (Comm) 920; [2001] F.L.R. 805.
[79] [1991] 23 H.L.R. 472.
[80] This is the position where a trustee in bankruptcy seeks an order for sale of the property: see *Re Citro (A Bankrupt)* [1991] Ch. 142, which is discussed below.
[81] [1994] 26 H.L.R. 249.
[82] See also *Bank of Baroda v Dhillon* [1998] 1 F.L.R. 524.
[83] [2001] 4 All E.R. 364.
[84] [2001] 4 All E.R. 380.

It follows that the earlier cases considering the exercise of the court's discretion under s.30 of the Law of Property Act 1925 need to be "treated with caution", and that whilst they should not be disregarded altogether, they are unlikely to be of great, or decisive, assistance. The case concerned a house which had been purchased to provide a home for a Mr Fox and a Mrs Shaire, and Mrs Shaire's son from a previous marriage. Although the house was owned in their joint names, Mrs Shaire owned a 75 per cent share of the equitable ownership and Mr Fox 25 per cent. Unbeknown to Mrs Shaire, Mr Fox mortgaged the property by forging her signature on the relevant documents. Following the death of Mr Fox the mortgage company sought the sale of the house to enforce its security, which was clearly confined to his 25 per cent of the house. Having concluded that it was no longer necessary for Mrs Shaire to demonstrate "exceptional circumstances" in order for the court to refuse an order for sale, Neuberger J. considered the factors identified in s.15(1) of the Trusts of Land and Appointment of Trustees Act and, on balance, concluded that an order for sale should be refused. He explained his reasoning as follows:

"To my mind, for Mrs Shaire to have to leave her home of nearly a quarter of a century would be a real and significant hardship, but not an enormous one. She would have a substantial sum that could be put towards a smaller house . . . On the other hand I have no evidence as to what properties might be available for the sort of money she would be able to pay. For [the mortgagee] to be locked into a quarter of the equity of the property would be a significant disadvantage unless they had a proper return and a proper protection so far as insurance and repair is concerned.

It seems to me that if (a) [the mortgagee] can be protected by sorting out the equitable interest providing for a proper return and ensuring that the house is repaired and insured, and (b) Mrs Shaire can really pay a proper return, it would be right to refuse to make an order for possession and sale primarily because Mrs Shaire has a valid interest in remaining in the house and has a 75 per cent interest in it, and because [the mortgagee] is ultimately in the business of lending money on property in return for being paid interest."[85]

He therefore ordered that the mortgage be converted into a loan of 25 per cent of the value of the property,[86] and that Mrs Shaire should pay interest on the loan at 3 per cent above bank base rate. However, he was prepared to order sale if this solution would involve Mrs Shaire taking on a liability she could not meet.[87]

The greater flexibility of the court where considering a request for an order for sale by a secured creditor adopted in *Mortgage Corp v Shaire* was approved by the Court of Appeal in *Bank of Ireland Home Mortgages Ltd v Bell*.[88] However in this case the Court of Appeal ordered the sale of a property, and stressed that in exercising the discretion whether to order

---

[85] [2001] 4 All E.R. 380 at 383.
[86] Mrs Shaire would therefore become entitled to the entire beneficial interest in the property.
[87] See also *Swindale v Forder* [2007] EWCA Civ 29, where time was allowed against a chargee to permit the other co-owner to raise the funds to buy her out; Westlaw document 2007 WL 261185.
[88] [2001] 2 All E.R. (Comm.) 920; [2001] F.L.R. 805.

sale or not it should always be a "powerful consideration" whether a secured creditor was receiving proper recompense for being kept out of his money. A house had been purchased to provide a home for a husband and wife and their son. The husband, unbeknown to the wife, mortgaged the property. By the time that the mortgagee sought possession and sale of the property the beneficiaries' marriage had broken down, and their son was very nearly 18 years old. The Court of Appeal held that it was therefore an irrelevant consideration that the property had been purchased to provide a family home, and that the welfare of the minor should only merit very slight consideration. In contrast the Court of Appeal held that the creditor was not receiving proper recompense for being kept out of his money.[89] The debt to the mortgage company was some £300,000, which was increasing daily, and no payment of either capital or interest had been received for some eight years. Since the beneficiary only possessed a 10 per cent share of the beneficial ownership only a limited sum would be realised for her on the sale of the property, as the mortgagee would take the majority of the proceeds of sale. The Court of Appeal therefore ordered sale, holding that it would be "very unfair" to condemn the mortgagee to go on waiting for its money, with no prospect of recovering its debt from the owners, and with the debt increasing all the time and already exceeding what could be realised on sale. In contrast, in *Edwards v Lloyds TSB Bank Plc*,[90] a husband forged his wife's signature on a mortgage on jointly owned property. The bank applied for a sale in order to realise their security, which took effect against the interest of the husband. Even though no interest was being paid to the bank, immediate sale was not ordered because the consequences "would be unacceptably severe" on the wife and children. Sale was postponed for five years, until the youngest child reached majority, with the possibility of further postponement should the children be then in full-time education. Park J. distinguished *Bell* and the later, and very similar, case of *First National Bank Plc v Achampong*[91] for two reasons: first, unlike those cases, the debt was considerably less than the value of the husband's share of the house[92] and thus the creditor had prospect of payment in the future. Secondly, if sale were ordered it was doubtful whether the wife could purchase adequate alternative accommodation with what remained.[93]

(d) *Applications for an Order where a Beneficiary is Insolvent*

13–031   As was noted above, a different regime applies where an order is sought under s.14 by a trustee in bankruptcy. Section 15(4) provides that in such circumstances the application will be governed by the provisions of s.335A of the Insolvency Act 1985. The manner in which the court will exercise its discretion on such an application will vary depending upon the timing of the application.

---

[89] per Peter Gibson L.J.
[90] [2004] EWHC 1745; Westlaw document 2004 WL 1640344.
[91] [2003] EWCA 487; [2003] 2 P & CR DG 11.
[92] Para.32; She had acquired her husband's share in a divorce settlement and naturally stood in no better position in relation to the chargee than he had.
[93] Para.31. This latter point seems a somewhat dubious distinguishing feature from *Bell*.

(i) An Application made by a Trustee in Bankruptcy Less than a Year after the Bankrupt's Estate Vested in the Trustee

Where a beneficiary's trustee in bankruptcy applies to the court for an order for sale less than a year after the bankruptcy occurred, s.335A sets out the factors which the court must take into account:

13–032

> "On such an application the court shall make such order as it thinks just and reasonable having regard to—
>
> (a) the interests of the bankrupt's creditors;
> (b) where an application is made in respect of land which includes a dwelling house which is or has been the home of the bankrupt or the bankrupt's spouse or civil partner or former spouse or former civil partner—
>
>> (i) the conduct of the spouse, civil partner, former spouse or former civil partner so far as contributing to the bankruptcy;
>> (ii) the needs and financial resources of the spouse, civil partner, former spouse or former civil partner, and
>> (iii) the need of any children; and
>
> (c) all the circumstances of the case other than the needs of the bankrupt."

Prior to the enactment of this provision the court was required to prefer the interests of the creditor and order a sale unless there were "exceptional circumstances". Section 335A(2) clearly allows the courts to take into account a range of factors which would not necessarily have been regarded as exceptional. Some guidance as to the relevance of these factors may be gained from the decisions concerning the application of s.15(1), which was discussed above. In the light of the decision of the Court of Appeal in *Bank of Ireland Home Mortgages Ltd v Bell* [94] it seems that the interests of a creditor should still always be given "very powerful" consideration, and that they are not lightly to be set aside.

(ii) An Application made by a Trustee in Bankruptcy more than a Year after the Bankrupt's Estate Vested in the Trustee

Where a beneficiary's trustee in bankruptcy applies for an order for sale more than a year after the bankruptcy occurred, then the matter is governed by the much stricter provisions of s.335A(3) of the Insolvency Act 1986. This provides that:

13–033

> "Where such an application is made after the end of the period of one year beginning with the first vesting . . . of the bankrupt's estate in a trustee, the court shall assume, unless the circumstances of the case are exceptional, that the interests of the bankrupt's creditors outweigh all other considerations."

---

[94] [2001] 2 All E.R. (Comm.) 920; [2001] F.L.R. 805.

Prior to the enactment of s.335(A)(3) the courts had held that the rights of the creditor should prevail in all but the most exceptional circumstances, so the provision simply puts the existing law on a statutory footing. Guidance as to the meaning of "exceptional" circumstances can therefore be gained from the earlier authorities. The majority of the cases suggest that the court will take a strict approach, and that the court will not regard family disruption as an "exceptional" circumstance.[95] In *Re Citro (A Bankrupt)*[96] Nourse L.J. explained that the court should not treat disruption to family life as an exceptional circumstance:

> "Where a spouse who has a beneficial interest in the matrimonial home has become bankrupt under debts which cannot be paid without the realisation of that interest, the voice of the creditors will usually prevail over the voice of the other spouse and a sale of the property ordered within a short period. The voice of the other spouse will only prevail in exceptional circumstances ... What then are exceptional circumstances? As the cases show, it is not uncommon for a wife with young children to be faced with eviction in circumstances where the realisation of her beneficial interest will not produce enough to buy a comparable home in the same neighbourhood, or indeed elsewhere. And, if she has to move elsewhere, there may be problems over schooling and so forth. Such circumstances, while engendering a natural sympathy in all who hear of them, cannot be described as exceptional. They are the melancholy consequences of debt and improvidence with which every civilised society has been familiar."[97]

The only circumstances which seem likely to be regarded as "exceptional" by the court are an illness or disability[98] of a beneficiary, or of children living in the property, which would make it too disruptive for them to move from the property. Thus an order for sale has been refused where the spouse of a beneficiary has been suffering from paranoid schizophrenia[99] or renal failure and arthritis,[100] and where the bankrupt was suffering from terminal cancer with a life expectancy of six months.[101] An unusual case which stands apart from the majority of decisions is *Re Holliday (A Bankrupt)*.[102] This case suggested that in some circumstances the interests of children might be given priority over those of a creditor. A husband and wife were the co-owners of their matrimonial home. The husband left and his wife and three children continued to occupy the house. The husband subsequently became bankrupt in unusual circumstances. The petition for bankruptcy was made by the husband himself and not by any creditor, and the debts on which his bankruptcy was based were relatively small. It would not have been unreasonable to conclude that his bankruptcy was

---

[95] *Re Solomon (A Bankrupt)* [1967] Ch. 573; *Boydell v Gillespie* (1970) 216 E.G. 1505; *Re Turner (A Bankrupt)* [1974] 1 W.L.R. 1556; *Re Bailey (A Bankrupt)* [1977] 1 W.L.R. 278; *Re Lowrie (A Bankrupt)* [1981] 3 All E.R. 353; *Re Gorman (A Bankrupt)* [1990] 1 W.L.R. 616.

[96] [1991] Ch. 142.

[97] [1991] Ch. 142 at 157.

[98] See *Re Bailey* [1977] 1 W.L.R. 278, where Walton J. suggested that it might be an exceptional circumstance if a house were specially adapted to meet the needs of a disabled child.

[99] *Re Raval* [1998] 2 F.L.R. 718.

[100] *Claughton v Charalambous* [1999] 1 F.L.R. 740.

[101] *Re Bremner* [1999] 1 F.L.R. 912.

[102] [1981] Ch. 405.

engineered to enable the matrimonial home to be sold. The husband's trustee in bankruptcy sought an order for sale of the house. The Court of Appeal exercised its discretion by refusing to grant an order. Goff L.J. stated the principles under which the court should determine its proper response:

> "we have to decide having regard to all the circumstances, including the fact that there are young children, and that the debtor was made bankrupt on his own petition, whose voice, that of the trustee seeking to realise the debtor's share for the benefit of his creditors or that of the wife seeking to preserve a home for herself and her children, ought in equity to prevail."[103]

The court concluded that in all the circumstances the voice of the wife ought to prevail and that the sale of the house should be deferred for five years. But *Re Holliday* has been treated with caution and the courts are continuing to adopt the view that circumstances would have to be unusual,[104] rather than just ordinary, but severe, consequences of bankruptcy, to qualify as exceptional.[105] In *Barca v Mears*,[106] although the bankrupt's son had special educational needs, which were supported by his remaining living in the property for most of the week, these circumstances were not sufficiently "unusual" to be exceptional.

The courts have recently considered the extent to which this strict interpretation of the exceptional circumstances test is compatible with the rights enshrined in the Human Rights Act 1998.[107] In *Barca v Mears*[108] it was argued that the interpretation of "exceptional circumstances" was contrary to article 1 of the first protocol and article 8 of the European Convention on Human Rights i.e. the protection of property and the right to respect for private and family life. It was considered that these rights were "not absolute" and in most cases sale will be necessary for the protection of the rights of others, here creditors with a legitimate claim. Nevertheless, judge Nicholas Strauss QC questioned

> "whether the narrow approach as to what may be 'exceptional circumstances' . . . is consistent with the Convention. It requires the court to adopt an almost universal rule, which prefers the property rights of the bankrupt's creditors to the property and/or personal rights of third parties, members of his family, who owe the creditors nothing. . . . [I]t may be that, on a reconsideration of the sections in the light of the Convention, they are to be regarded as recognising that, in the general run of cases, the creditors' interests will outweigh all other interests, but leaving it open to a court to find that, on a proper consideration of the facts of a particular case, it is one of the exceptional cases in which this proposition is not true."[109]

---

[103] [1981] Ch. 405 at 420.
[104] e.g. illness, as considered above.
[105] Dixon [2005] Conv 161; Smith, "Plural Ownership" (2005); See also *Dean v Stout* [2006] 1 F.L.R. 725; *Donoghue v Ingram* [2006] EWHC 282; [2006] Fam. Law 733.
[106] [2005] 1 P. & C.R. DG7.
[107] Also Smith, *Plural Ownership* (2005).
[108] [2005] 1 P. & C.R. DG7.
[109] [2005] 1 P. & C.R. DG7; Smith, Plural Ownership (2005).

Thus, as Dixon observes, the claimant would not have to prove that the consequences were outside the usual consequences of bankruptcy, only that they were severe. This might trigger the jurisdiction to postpone sale, the judge properly weighing all the factors and not just assuming that sale should be ordered after one year.[110] In *Nicholls v Lan*,[111] it was held that where circumstances were exceptional, s.335A(3) required that all interests should be balanced against each other and the court should do what was just and reasonable, which may include making an order for sale. In the instant case the fairest order was to give the creditors access to the home, as the wife of the bankrupt had an interest in another property.[112] Judge Paul Morgan Q.C. held that s.335A was not inconsistent with arts 1 and 8. These rights were qualified. The judge had to conduct a balance of interests to include protection of the home and also the rights of creditors. In *Donoghue v Ingram*,[113] the judge observed that:

> "In [*Harrow LBC v Qazi* [2004] AC 983] the majority view of the House of Lords was that Article 8 could not be relied on to defeat proprietary or contractual rights to possession or confer a right to be provided with a home. . . . *Qazi* does not appear to have been cited to Mr Strauss QC in *Barca v Mears*."

However, almost as an aside the judge thought that neither s.14 of the Trusts of Land and Appointment of Trustees Act 1996 nor s.335A involved a "proprietary or contractual right to possession".[114]

---

[110] "[S]evere consequences of the usual type might now also fall within the definition, especially if little or no hardship would be caused to the creditors by further postponement": Dixon [2005] Conv. 161.
[111] [2007] 1 F.L.R. 744.
[112] [2007] Conv. 78.
[113] [2006] EWHC 282; [2006] Fam. Law 733; westlaw document 2006 WL 584538.
[114] at para 21, concluding that "I am inclined to accept . . . that Qazi does not establish that Article 8 is irrelevant in the present case": ibid.

Chapter 14

SUCCESSIVE OWNERSHIP AND LIMITED INTERESTS IN LAND

INTRODUCTION TO SUCCESSIVE AND LIMITED INTERESTS

1. Successive Interests Contrasted with Concurrent Interests

In Chapter 12 it has been seen how it is possible for two or more persons to enjoy simultaneous **14–001** rights of ownership in land by means of co-ownership, either as joint tenants or tenants in common. Such co-owners enjoy concurrent interests in the land, since they hold their respective entitlements at the same time. For this reason all the co-owners are entitled to occupy and enjoy the use of the land contemporaneously, and none can claim a right of occupation to the exclusion of the others. Successive interests, in contrast, divide the enjoyment and use of land over time, so that the rights of some persons are delayed until the rights of others have been exhausted. The classic example where there is a life interest in land. If Grant enjoys a life interest of Victoria Manor, and Phil the remainder interest, they share ownership by having simultaneous rights in the land, but their interests are not concurrent. Grant, as the life tenant, will be entitled to enjoy and use the land during his lifetime, either by living in the Manor or receiving any rents or profits which are generated from it. He will be entitled to transfer his life interest to someone else, but he cannot transfer or create any rights that will endure beyond his death. When Grant dies, Phil will become entitled to the full and unencumbered freehold ownership of the Manor. However during the lifetime of Grant he has no rights to use and enjoy the land. He has no right, for example, to live in the Manor, or to enjoy any share of the income it might generate, while Grant is alive. His interest is described as the freehold remainder,[1] since it consists of the rights which remain after the life interest. A freehold remainder confers no immediate right to possession. The remainder interest in land is also transferable, so that if Phil assigns it to Lorraine, on the death of Grant she will become entitled to the unencumbered freehold ownership of the Manor.

---

[1] His interest would be a freehold reversion if Phil had been the freehold owner who had created Grant's life estate.

2. The Regime for Successive Interests in Land

(a) *Trusts of Land*

14–002 In Chapters 12 and 13 it was seen that concurrent ownership must take place behind a trust. Successive interests are incapable of existing as legal estates[2] and must therefore also take effect in equity behind a trust of the legal title. The form of trust now used to give effect to equitable successive interests in land is the same as that now used for co-ownership, namely the "trust of land" regulated by the Trusts of Land and Appointment of Trustees Act 1996. This form of trust, much simplifying the previous law, applies to all successive interests in land created on or after January 1, 1997.

(b) *Successive Interests Created Before 1997*

14–003 The rules for successive interests in land created before the coming into operation of the Trusts of Land and Appointment of Trustees Act 1996 were complex. A successive interest could take effect behind an express trust for sale of the legal title. In the absence of an express trust for sale the creation of a successive interest would give rise to a strict settlement. The Settled Land Act 1925 introduced a special statutory regime for such settlements, which radically differed from conventional trusts. The Act contained complex rules that were designed for the great landed estates of the nineteenth century and before. These rules were far less appropriate for the simple situation of a person leaving the family home to his or her spouse for life, and then to their children on that spouse's death. Nevertheless, the elaborate rules of the Settled Land Act 1925 would still apply, creating what is called a "strict settlement", on occasions where the parties had no realisation that they were invoking the complex rules contained in the Settled Land Act 1925.

Following the introduction of the unitary trust of land by the Trusts of Land and Appointment of Trustees Act 1996 no new strict settlements may be created, but strict settlements created before 1997 continue to be governed by the Settled Land Act 1925. Settlements created before 1997 by means of an express trust for sale, however, have been converted into trusts of land to which the Trusts of Land and Appointment of Trustees Act 1996 applies.[3]

(c) *Forms of Successive Interest*

14–004 Life interests are the most common form of limited interest in land which can only take effect by means of a trust. Other limited interests include the entailed interest, a determinable interest in land, and a grant of land subject to a condition which leads to a gift over if the condition is broken. In addition, the grant of a freehold or leasehold in land to an infant gives rise to a trust (by way of a strict settlement before 1997, and by means of a trust of land if granted since then). This is because a person under the age of 18 is incapable of holding a legal estate.

[2] Law of Property Act 1925 s.1.
[3] Trusts of Land and Appointment of Trustees Act 1996 s.4.

SUCCESSIVE INTERESTS TAKING EFFECT BEHIND A TRUST OF LAND

In the previous chapter many of the key features of the trust of land have already been examined in the context of co-ownership. In this chapter some of the same details of the system will be repeated, although the emphasis will be upon how a trust of land may be utilised to give effect to successive or limited interests in land.   **14–005**

1. Creation of a Trust of Land

Section 1(1)(a) of the Trusts of Land and Appointment of Trustees Act 1996 provides that a trust of land means "any trust of property which consists of or includes land". A trust of land will arise irrespective of whether the trust was created expressly, or by an implied, constructive or resulting trust. A trust of land will arise irrespective of the type of equitable interest which arises behind it. All the interests which formerly gave rise to a settlement under Settled Land Act 1925 will now take effect behind a trust of land. Therefore any successive interests, determinable interests or trusts for the benefit of minors will give rise to a trust of land.   **14–006**

2. Position of the Trustees of a Trust of Land

(a) *Trustees have All the Powers of Management and Disposition Over the Land*

As a consequence of their position as holders of the legal title, the trustees of a trust of land enjoy all the powers of management and disposition over the land. Section 6(1) of the Trusts of Land and Appointment of Trustees Act 1996 provides that: **14–007**

> "[f]or the purpose of exercising their function as trustees, the trustees of land have in relation to the land subject to the trust all the powers of an absolute owner."

This means that they have the complete freedom to do what they choose with the land. By s.6(3) the trustees are given the power to purchase a legal estate in any land in England or Wales, and by s.6(5) they are required to "have regard to the rights of the beneficiaries" in exercising their powers.

(b) *Exercise of Trustees' Powers Subject to Consents*

Although the trustees of a trust of land are given the general power to deal with the land as if they were the absolute owner, their ability to exercise their powers may be made subject to the requirement that they gain the consent of persons nominated for that purpose in the instrument   **14–008** creating the trust. For example, in the case of a life interest the settlor may make the trustee's power of sale of the land subject to the consent of certain persons, perhaps of the life tenant or of other family members. Section 10 of the Trusts of Land and Appointment of Trustees Act 1996 has the effect that if the disposition creating the trust requires the consent of more than two persons to the exercise of any power by the trustees, a purchaser of the land is protected if the consent of "any two of them" is obtained. Although in such circumstances the purchaser would be protected, a trustee who has failed to obtain all the specified consents will have committed a breach of trust.

(c) *Requirement to Consult with the Beneficiaries Before Exercising Powers*

14–009 As well as the potential imposition of specific consents by the trust instrument, s.11 of the Trusts of Land and Appointment of Trustees Act 1996 places the trustees under a duty to consult with the beneficiaries of the trust when they exercise any of their functions. This is not an absolute duty, as s.11(1)(a) provides that they must:

> "so far as is practicable, consult the beneficiaries of full age and beneficially entitled to an interest in possession in the land".

Where there are successive interests in the land this means that there is only a need to consult with the present life tenant and not the remaindermen. For example, if trustees hold Victoria Manor on trust for Grant for life, remainder to Phil, and they intend to sell the land, they would be required to consult with Grant but not Phil, as he is not entitled to an interest in possession. Where the trustees are obliged to consult they are required "so far as is consistent with the general interest of the trust" to give effect to the beneficiaries' wishes, or the wishes of the majority.

(d) *Delegation of their Powers to the Beneficiaries of the Trust*

14–010 From the perspective of the creation of successive interests in land the most important aspect of the trust of land machinery is that the trustees are capable of delegating their powers to the beneficiaries of the trust. Section 9(1) provides that:

> "The trustees of land may, by power of attorney, delegate to any beneficiary or beneficiaries of full age and beneficially entitled to an interest in possession in land subject to the trust any of their functions as trustees which relate to the land."

The statutory power to delegate only applies to a delegation of the powers of the trustees as a body, and not to the individual powers of any of the trustees alone.

The beneficiary has no right to have the trustees' powers delegated to him and it is entirely within the trustees' discretion to decide whether to make a delegation. For example, if Victoria Manor is held on trust for Grant for life with remainder to Phil, Grant will only be entitled to exercise the powers of the trustees if they decide to delegate them to him. He cannot insist on such a delegation. Even where a delegation has been made the position of the beneficiary is somewhat insecure since s.9(3) provides that it can be revoked "by any one or more" of the trustees and it is automatically revoked if a new trustee is appointed.

Where the trustees have delegated their powers to the beneficiaries s.9(4) provides that the delegation will automatically be revoked if the beneficiary "ceases to be a person beneficially entitled to an interest in possession" in the land. For example, if Victoria Manor was held on trust for Grant for life, remainder to Phil for life, remainder to Lorraine, and the trustees had delegated their powers to Grant, the delegation would be automatically revoked if he were to surrender his interest to Phil as he would not longer enjoy any interest in possession of the land. A delegation will also be automatically revoked if one of the trustees who has granted it loses his mental capacity, because delegation cannot be made by an enduring power of attorney.[4] Section 9(7) makes clear that a delegation of the trustee's powers to the beneficiary cannot include the power to give a good receipt for any capital moneys arising as a result of a disposition of the land. This means that overreaching of the beneficial interests behind the trust cannot occur unless payment of any capital money arising is made to at least two trustees of land. If the trustees have delegated their functions to the beneficiaries s.9(8) protects them from potential liability arising by the beneficiaries' misuse. It provides that the trustees are liable for acts or defaults of the beneficiaries "if and only if the trustees did not exercise reasonable care in deciding to delegate the function to the beneficiary or beneficiaries".

(e) *Power to Convey the Land to the Beneficiaries if they are Absolutely Entitled*

If the beneficiaries of a trust of land are of age and capacity and absolutely entitled to the land the trustees enjoy the right to convey the legal title to them under s.6(2), thus relieving themselves of the responsibility of trusteeship. For example, if Victoria Manor is held by trustees for Grant for life, remainder to Phil, when Grant dies the trustees will be entitled to transfer the legal title to Phil even if he does not demand it. In such a case the beneficiary is under a duty to do "whatever is necessary" to secure that the land vests in him or her.[5]

14–011

3. Position of the Beneficiaries of the Trust of Land

(a) *Beneficiaries with an Interest in Possession Entitled to Occupy*

Section 12(1) of the Trusts of Land and Appointment of Trustees Act 1996 provides that:

14–012

> "A beneficiary who is beneficially entitled to an interest in possession in land subject to a trust of land is entitled by reason of his interest to occupy the land at any time if at that time—

---

[4] Trusts of Land and Appointment of Trustees Act 1996 s.9(6).
[5] Trusts of Land and Appointment of Trustees Act 1996 s.6(2)(a) and (b).

> (a) the purposes of the trust include making the land available for his occupation (or for the occupation of beneficiaries of a class of which he is a member or of the beneficiaries in general), or
>
> (b) the land is held by the trustees so as to be so available."

It has been seen that s.12 places the rights of concurrent owners of land to occupation on a statutory footing, a right which was somewhat unclear under the old trust for sale. It does the same for a beneficiary in a trust for successive interests. For example, if Victoria Manor is held on trust for Grant for life, remainder to Phil, Grant will enjoy the right to occupy under s.12 because he is entitled to an interest in possession.

Section 12(2) provides that a beneficiary with a right in possession does not enjoy a right to occupation if the land "is either unavailable or unsuitable for occupation by him". In some cases the operation of this limitation may be obvious. For example, if a factory site rather than Victoria Manor was held on trust for Grant for life it is unlikely that he would enjoy a right to occupy it residentially. However, it is unclear whether personal characteristics of the beneficiaries would prevent them enjoying a right to occupy. If Grant were an alcoholic, drug addict or member of a religious cult, would this render Victoria Manor "unsuitable for occupation by him"?

If there are two or more beneficiaries who are jointly entitled to occupy the land the trustees of the settlement may under s.13(1) "exclude or restrict the entitlement of any one or more (but not all) of them". This provision is not so relevant to situations of successive interests where there is more likely to be a sole person entitled to an interest in possession. However, if Victoria Manor were held by Grant and Mike jointly for life they would hold their interests concurrently and the trustees might be required to exercise their jurisdiction under s.13. The power to limit or exclude is rendered virtually nugatory by s.13(7) which prevents the trustees acting so as to cause a person to cease occupation unless he consents or an order of the court is obtained.

(b) *Powers of the Trustees may be Delegated to the Beneficiaries*

14–013 As has already been explained, the trustees possess the discretion to be able to delegate the exercise of some or all of their functions to the beneficiaries, but the beneficiaries do not have a right to have the functions delegated. Where any of the functions of the trustees have been delegated to the beneficiaries s.9(7) provides that they are "in relation to the exercise of the functions, in the same position as trustees (with the same duties and liabilities)". They are therefore fiduciaries and will attract liability for breach of trust if they do not exercise appropriate care in the exercise of such delegated functions.

4. The Role of the Court

(a) *A Wide Supervisory Jurisdiction*

14–014 Given the number of parties who may have interests in land which is held subject to successive interests under a trust of land, disputes will periodically occur. For example, if Victoria

Manor is held by trustees on trust for Grant for life, with remainder to Phil, Grant may want to see the house let to Lorraine, an up and coming pop star who is willing to pay an above market rent because of its location, in order to maximise his income, whereas Phil does not want the house let because he suspects that Grant is suffering from cancer and is likely to die soon and he wants to ensure that he can live in the house immediately. Alternatively, the trustees may be concerned about the costs of repairs to the houses that will soon be needed and would prefer that it be sold and a smaller more manageable property acquired, whereas Grant is wanting to start a business using the house as an up-market conference centre. To deal with any such difficulties concerning the trust the court is given a very wide jurisdiction to intervene under s.14 of the Trusts of Land and Appointment of Trustees Act 1996. Section 14(2) entitles the court to make orders:

(a) relating to the exercise by the trustees of any of their functions (including an order relieving them of any obligation to obtain the consent of, or to consult, any person in connection with the exercise of any of their functions), or

(b) declaring the nature or extent of a person's interest in property subject to the trust.

(b) *Persons who May Seek the Intervention of the Court*

Section 14(1) provides that: **14–015**

"Any person who is a trustee of land or has an interest in property subject to a trust of land may make an application to the court for an order under this section."

In the case of a trust of land facilitating successive interests all the relevant parties may seek the court's intervention, namely the trustees, the beneficiaries with interests in possession, any beneficiaries with subsequent limited interests, and those entitled to the remainder interest.

(c) *Factors Which the Court Must Consider in Exercising its Discretion*

When such an application is made, under s.14(2) the court has the discretion to make such   **14–016** order as it "thinks fit".[6] Section 15 outlines a number of factors which the court is required to take into account in determining an appropriate order. The relevance of these factors to disputes between co-owners of the land, where the most likely issue is whether the land should be sold, have been examined in the previous chapter. However, they may be relevant in a slightly different way to questions which concern land held subject to successive interests.

---

[6] Trusts of Land and Appointment of Trustees Act 1996 s.14(2).

(i) The Settlor's Intentions and the Purpose of the Trust

14–017 Section 15(1)(a) and (b) require the court to have regard to the "intentions of the person or persons (if any) who created the trust" and "the purposes for which the property subject to the trust is held". If, for example, a testator had established a trust of Victoria Manor for his son Grant for life with remainder to his grandson Phil, because he knew that Grant was a drug addict who only wanted to sell the house and he wanted to ensure that it remained in the family, this would be a factor, although not necessarily determinative, if there was a proposed sale of the house to which Phil objected and sought the intervention of the court.

(ii) Occupation Interests of Minors

14–018 Section 15(1)(c) requires the court to have regard to "the welfare of any minor who occupies or might reasonably be expected to occupy any land subject to the trust as his home". This might mean that the court would have to consider the interests of the children of a beneficiary in possession, even if they themselves were not entitled to any beneficial interests in the land. For example, if Victoria Manor was held on trust for Grant for life with remainder to Phil, the welfare of Grant's children who have been living in the house would be a relevant factor to consider if there was some dispute whether the house should be sold to enable the money to be more profitably invested.

(iii) Interests of Creditors

14–019 Under s.15(1)(c) the interests of any secured creditors of a beneficiary are to be taken into account.

(iv) Interests of Beneficiaries Entitled to Occupy

14–020 Where the trustees are seeking to exercise their powers under s.13 to exclude or restrict the right of beneficiaries with interests in possession and the intervention of the court is sought, s.15(2) provides that the court must have regard to the "circumstances and wishes of each of the beneficiaries of full age" who has a statutory right to occupy the land under s.12. If Victoria Manor is held on trust for Grant and Mike jointly for life, and Mike returns after a number of years in prison overseas for sexual abuse of children, the court would have to consider the circumstances and wishes of both Grant, who might have a family with small children living in the house, and Mike, who has nowhere else to live, in deciding whether the trustees should exclude his right to share occupation.

(v) Interests of Beneficiaries with Rights in Possession

14–021 The court is also required to have a general regard under s.15(3) to "the circumstances and wishes of any beneficiaries of full age and entitled to an interest in possession in the property subject to the trust or (in case of dispute) of the majority (according to the value of their combined interests)". In the case of successive interests this will mean the rights of the persons entitled to present enjoyment of the land, in other words the life tenants rather than the remainder beneficiaries. For example, if Grant, Phil and Lorraine are the joint life tenants of Victoria Manor, and Grant wishes the land to be sold and the money reinvested in a smaller property with the balance in a share portfolio, but Phil and Lorraine want the house retained, the court is required to have regard to the majority view.

(vi) Balance Between Competing Factors

Section 15 provides nothing more than a requirement that certain factors must be taken into account by the court and does not provide a definitive guide by which it can be predicted how disputes should be resolved. Often the various factors will point in the direction of different orders. For example, the intention and purpose of the trust may have been that specific land was retained for the family, whereas the interests of minors in occupation may point to the purchase of a more suitable property. In such cases it is simply a matter for the court to take into account all the competing factors before making whatever order it considers appropriate.

14–022

5. Third Parties Acquiring Interests in the Land Subject to a Trust of Land

(a) *Third Parties Acquiring the Interests of the Beneficiaries*

The beneficiaries under a trust of land are free to deal with their own equitable interests, For example, if Victoria Manor is held on trust for Grant for life he is perfectly able to assign his life interest to Lorraine. The powers of management would remain with the trustees so that unless Grant was also a trustee he would enjoy no continuing rights in the land. If the trustees had delegated any of their powers to him then the effect of his assignment of his interest would be to terminate the delegation automatically since by s.9(4) he would have ceased to be a person beneficially entitled to an interest in possession under the trust.

14–023

(b) *Third Parties Acquiring a Legal Estate in the Land*

(i) Dealing with Trustees who have not Delegated their Powers

Since the trustees retain the rights of management over the land they are entitled to transfer rights to third parties. For example, if trustees hold Victoria Manor on trust for Grant for life, remainder to Phil, they are entitled to transfer a freehold estate to Lorraine, or to grant her a legal lease. Any such grant or transfer would overreach the rights of Grant and Phil.

14–024

(ii) Dealing with Beneficiaries to whom the Trustees have Delegated their Powers

14–025 If the trustees have delegated their powers, or relevant powers, to a beneficiary or beneficiaries entitled to an interest in possession, then a third party can deal with such beneficiary. For example, if the trustees had delegated all their powers in relation to Victoria Manor to Grant, he would be able to transfer the freehold interest to Lorraine or to grant her a legal lease. This would again operate to overreach the rights of the beneficiaries provided that the capital money is properly applied. Under s.9(2), where the trustees have purported to delegate their powers to any person it will be presumed in favour of any third party who deals with them in good faith that the delegation was valid, unless the third party "has knowledge at the time of the transaction" that the trustees were not entitled to make the delegation.

(iii) Will a Third Party Acquire an Interest in the Land Free from the Existing Beneficial Interests?

14–026 By far the most significant question will be whether a third party who acquires a legal estate in the land, whether by dealing with the trustees or a delegate, takes his interest free from those of the beneficiaries. For example, if Lorraine purchases the freehold of Victoria Manor from the trustees, will she take the land free from Grant's life interest and Phil's remainder? Similarly, if the trustees had delegated their power of sale to Grant, would she take free from Phil's remainder interest? The central question will be whether the third party is entitled to the protection of overreaching. Provided the statutory requirements are satisfied, namely that the conveyance is made by the trustees of land[7] and the proceeds of sale are paid over to two trustees,[8] then the interests of the beneficiaries will be overreached and converted from interests in the land to interests in the purchase moneys in the hands of the trustees, and the purchaser will take the land free from the interests of the beneficiaries. If overreaching has not occurred then the equitable rights of the beneficiaries continue to be treated as enforceable against the land. The normal priority rules will determine the extent to which these rights will bind the purchaser. Since in many cases the beneficiary with the interest in possession is likely to be in occupation of the property, the beneficiary's rights will be enforceable as an overriding interest.

CONTINUING STRICT SETTLEMENTS

14–027 As has been seen, it is no longer possible to create a strict settlement of land. However those settlements which were created before 1997 continue to exist, and are governed by the regime of the Settled Land Act 1925.

---

[7] Law of Property Act 1925 s.2(1)(ii).
[8] Law of Property Act 1925 s.27.

1. The Creation of Strict Settlements

Before the enactment of the Trusts for Land and Appointment of Trustees Act 1996, a strict **14–028** settlement arose whenever land was "limited in trust for any persons by way of succession",[9] unless the land was subject to an express trust for sale.[10] Since the only estates in land which can exist as legal estates are the fee simple absolute in possession and the term of years absolute, all other interests in land conferring an entitlement to exclusive possession being equitable only, the effect of this provision was that all successive interests in land which were not created by means of a trust for sale could take effect only by way of a strict settlement. Thus the grant of an entailed interest,[11] or of an interest subject to defeasance by condition subsequent,[12] would all lead to the creation of a strict settlement. So, too, would the grant of a life interest, an interest subject to a condition precedent,[13] and the grant of land to a minor.[14] For instance, if Peggy had died before January 1, 1997, leaving Victoria Manor by will to her son Grant for life, and on Grant's death to her grandson Phil, the land would have been held on a strict settlement.

One of the central difficulties associated with the 1925 regime was that strict settlements would often arise accidentally. The breadth of circumstances which would constitute a settlement under s.1(1) of the Settled Land Act 1925, and the fact that a settlement arose whenever one of the interests in land specified in s.1(1)(i)–(v) was created, led to the inevitable result that a strict settlement may have arisen without the settlor ever having intended to subject his land in that way. This was especially likely where a testator had drawn up a home made will leaving his house to his spouse for life. A professionally drafted will, or declaration of trust, would generally have preferred an express trust for sale.

The Settled Land Act 1925 required the execution of two instruments in order to perfect a strict settlement. For the creation of a settlement inter vivos s.4(1) of the Settled Land Act, provided:

> "Every settlement of a legal estate in land inter vivos shall, save as in this Act otherwise provided, be effected by two deeds, namely a vesting deed and a trust instrument and if effected in any other way shall not operate to transfer or create a legal estate."

The trust instrument was the document in which the creator of the settlement specified the interests of the beneficiaries and appointed the trustees of the settlement.[15] The vesting deed was the means by which the legal title to the land was conveyed to the tenant for life.[16] Where the tenant for life was already the legal owner of the land the vesting deed was merely required to declare "that the land is vested in him for that estate".[17] Therefore, if Peggy was the freehold owner of Victoria Manor and wanted Grant to enjoy a life interest with remainder to Phil,

---

[9] Settled Land Act 1925 s.1(1)(i).
[10] Settled Land Act 1925 s.4(3).
[11] Settled Land Act 1925 s.1(1)(ii)(a).
[12] Settled Land Act 1925 s.1(1)(ii)(c).
[13] Settled Land Act 1925 s.1(1)(ii)(b).
[14] Settled Land Act 1925 s.1(1)(ii)(d).
[15] Settled Land Act 1925 s.4(3).
[16] Settled Land Act 1925 s.4(2).
[17] Settled Land Act 1925 s.4(2).

she would have had to execute both a trust instrument, and a vesting deed in favour of Grant. Section 5(1) of the Settled Land Act 1925 provided that a vesting deed should contain a number of statements:

(a) a description, either specific or general, of the settled land;

(b) a statement that the settled land is vested in the person or persons to whom it is conveyed or in whom it is declared to be vested upon the trusts from time to time affecting the settled land;

(c) the names of the persons who are the trustees of the settlement;

(d) any additional or larger powers conferred by the trust instrument relating to the settled land which by virtue of the Act operate and are exercisable as if conferred by the Act on a tenant for life;

(d) the name of any person for the time being entitled under the trust instrument to appoint new trustees of the settlement.

Failure to include all these details did not invalidate the vesting deed. Where a settlement was created by will rather than inter vivos the "two deed" requirement was maintained, but by s.6(a) of the Settled Land Act 1925 the will was regarded as a trust instrument for the purposes of the Act. Since the legal title to a testator's property vests in his personal representative on death, s.6(b) provided that:

"the personal representatives of the testator shall hold the settled land on trust, if and when required so to do, to convey it to the person who, under the will, or by virtue of this Act, is the tenant for life or statutory owner, and, if more than one, as joint tenants."

It is perfectly possible for a strict settlement of land to arise as a result of a declaration prior to January 1, 1997 even if there has been no execution of the necessary vesting deed prior to that date. For example, if Peggy declared a trust of Victoria Manor for Grant for life, remainder to Phil, on December 31, 1996 this would give rise to a strict settlement, as would a gift by will leaving Victoria Manor to Grant for life if the testator died on that date. However, although the instrument has created a strict settlement as yet the legal owner has not executed an appropriate vesting instrument in favour of the tenant for life or statutory owner. In such circumstances the Settled Land Act 1925 paralyses any dealings with the legal title of the land. Section 13 provides:

"Where a tenant for life or statutory owner has become entitled to have a principal vesting deed or a vesting assent executed in his favour, then until a vesting instrument is executed . . . any purported disposition thereof inter vivos by any person, other than a personal representative . . . shall not take effect except in favour of a purchaser of a legal estate [without notice of such tenant for life or statutory owner having become so entitled as aforesaid] but, save as aforesaid, shall operate only as a contract for valuable consideration to carry out the transaction after the requisite vesting instrument has been executed or made, and a purchaser of a legal estate shall not be concerned with such disposition unless the contract is registered as a land charge."

This section means that any third party who acquires a legal estate in the settled land from the legal owner before an appropriate vesting instrument has been executed will not obtain that interest in the land if they had notice of the existence of the settlement. Instead the purported disposition of the legal estate in their favour will be deemed to constitute an enforceable contract for the disposition of that interest, which they will be able to enforce after an appropriate vesting instrument has been executed. For example, if Peggy declared a settlement of Victoria Manor for Grant for life, remainder to Phil in November 1996, but has not yet executed a vesting instrument in favour of Grant as the tenant for life, and subsequently Grant purports to transfer the legal title to Lorraine, this will be ineffective to pass the legal title and will operate only as a contract to transfer when the legal estate is vested in him as tenant for life. Because the legal title remains vested in Peggy, it will be possible for her to effect a legal transfer, although this will be effective only if the purchaser had no notice of the existence of the settlement.

2. Key Features of the Strict Settlement

(a) *Location of the Legal Title*

One of the most important features of a strict settlement was that, unlike conventional trusts where the legal title is vested in the trustees, the legal title to the land was vested in the person presently entitled to possession. Such a person was termed the "tenant for life" of the settlement, and was defined by s.19(1) of the Settled Land Act 1925:   **14–029**

> "the person of full age who is for the time being beneficially entitled under a settlement to possession of settled land for his life is for the purposes of this Act the tenant for life of that land and the tenant for life under that settlement."

In the example which has been used above, if Grant enjoys a life interest in Victoria Manor created prior to January 1, 1997 he will be the tenant for life. To say that the tenant for life is the person presently entitled to possession of the land does not mean that they have to enjoy the physical occupation of it. It is a way of expressing that they are entitled to the immediate enjoyment of their rights and interests in the land, whether by actual possession or the receipt of any rents and profits that the land generates. Where two or more persons are entitled to possession of the land as joint tenants, for example if Phil and Kath were concurrently entitled to life interests of Victoria Manor "they together constitute the tenant for life".[18] If the settled land was registered, s.86(1) of the Land Registration Act 1925 provided that it was to be registered "in the name of the tenant for life". Where there was no person meeting the statutory definition of a tenant for life the Settled Land Act 1925 provided a list of persons who were to enjoy the powers of the tenant for life in relation to the land[19] and in the absence of any such persons the trustees of the settlement were to enjoy those powers,[20] as for example in the

---

[18] Settled Land Act 1925 s.19(2).
[19] Settled Land Act 1925 s.20(1)(i)–(x).
[20] Settled Land Act 1925 s.26.

case of a trust for the benefit of an infant.[21] Such persons were termed the "statutory owners." Therefore only as a last resort would the trustees of a strict settlement hold the legal title and the powers normally enjoyed by trustees of land.

(b) *Management of the Land by the Tenant for Life*

14–030 Under a strict settlement the tenant for life did not only hold the legal title of the land subject to the settlement, but he also enjoyed all the powers of management over it which are usually held and exercised by the trustees of a conventional trust. Most importantly he held the power to sell or exchange the land,[22] and to grant subsidiary interests such as leases or mortgages.[23] This meant that, where there was a life interest, there was no guarantee that the land would be retained for the remainder beneficiary. If Victoria Manor was held on a settlement for Grant for life, remainder to Phil, Grant as the tenant for life would have the right to sell the Manor to Lorraine so that she could become the absolute freehold owner. Grant would then have to apply the proceeds of the sale in accordance with the provisions of the Settled Land Act 1925.

(c) *Identity and Role of the Trustees of the Settlement*

14–031 It should already be evident that the trustees of a strict settlement enjoy a very different role to that of trustees of a conventional trust, or under a traditional trust for sale of land. Section 30(1)(i) of the Settled Land Act 1925 provided that the trustees of the settlement are any persons expressly granted the power of sale over the land[24] by the person creating the settlement, or whose consent is required before the exercise of such a power. If no one is granted a power of sale by the settlement, or required to consent to sale, s.30(1)(ii) provides that the trustees of the settlement will be those who are expressly declared to be the trustees in the instrument creating the settlement. If there is no-one within the statutory categories set out in s.30(1)(i)–(iv), the beneficiaries of the settlement are entitled to appoint trustees of the settlement by deed.[25] The trustees do not control or manage the land subject to the settlement and their chief role is rather to supervise the activities of the tenant for life so that the property subject to the settlement is conserved and not dissipated. The trustees are entitled to be informed if the tenant for life intends to exercise certain of his powers, including selling or mortgaging the land.[26] In the case of some transactions, for example the sale of the "principal mansion house" of a settlement, their consent is required.[27] Most importantly, where any

---

[21] Settled Land Act 1925 s.26.

[22] Settled Land Act 1925 s.38.

[23] Settled Land Act 1925 ss.41. and 71.

[24] Although on the face of the document establishing the settlement the trustees are granted this power, they would be unable to exercise it because the power of sale is enjoyed exclusively by the tenant for life.

[25] Settled Land Act 1925 s.30(1)(v).

[26] Settled Land Act 1925 s.101.

[27] Alternatively the tenant for life may obtain an order of the court.

transaction occurs which results in the realisation of the value of assets of the settlement in money, such "capital money" must be paid over to the trustees of the settlement and not to the tenant for life.[28] If such capital moneys are not paid to the trustees then the transaction is void. Overreaching of the beneficial interest behind a settlement can also only occur if the capital moneys are paid to at least two trustees of the settlement.[29]

3. Powers of the Tenant for Life Under a Strict Settlement

When a strict settlement has been validly created and the appropriate vesting deed executed the tenant for life is vested with the full legal ownership of the land. He does not, however, enjoy the unencumbered rights of an absolute owner to deal with the land as he wishes, and the scope of his powers are defined by the Settled Land Act 1925. **14–032**

(a) *Powers Granted to the Tenant for Life by the Settled Land Act*

(i) Power to Sell or Exchange the Land

By s.38 the tenant for life who has the legal title vested in him is entitled to sell, or exchange, the settled land, or any part of it, or any easement, right or privilege in the land, provided that the sale is made "for the best consideration in money that can reasonably be obtained".[30] **14–033**

(ii) Power to Grant Leases of the Land

By s.41 the tenant for life has the power to grant leases of the settled land for periods of up to 50 years, or longer in the cases of such leases as a mining or forestry lease. Again the lease must be for the "best rent that can reasonably be obtained".[31] **14–034**

(iii) Power to Grant Other Subsidiary Rights Over the Land

Section 38 also entitles the tenant for life to grant such subsidiary rights as easements, rights or privileges of any kind over the land. **14–035**

(iv) Power to Raise Money by Way of a Mortgage of the Land

Section 71 grants the tenant for life power to raise money by way of a mortgage of the settled land provided that the money is required for one of the narrow range of purposes specified. **14–036**

---

[28] Settled Land Act 1925 s.18.
[29] Law of Property Act 1925 s.2(3).
[30] Settled Land Act 1925 s.39(1).
[31] Settled Land Act 1925 s.42(1)(ii).

(b) Extension of the Statutory Powers Enjoyed by a Tenant for Life

14-037   Although the powers conferred on the tenant for life by the Settled Land Act 1925 cannot be excluded,[32] s.109 provides that the settlor who created the settlement can confer any additional powers on the tenant for life.

(c) Exercise of the Powers of the Tenant for Life

(i) Powers Held in a Fiduciary Capacity

14-038   The tenant for life enjoys his powers in relation to the settled land in a fiduciary capacity. This means that he cannot exercise them solely for his own benefit. Section 107(1) provides that:

> "A tenant for life or statutory owner shall, in exercising any power under this Act, have regard to the interests of all parties entitled under the settlement, and shall, in relation to the exercise thereof by him, be deemed to be in the position and to have the duties and liabilities of a trustee for those parties."

(ii) Powers Cannot be Assigned

14-039   Section 104(1) provides that the powers of the tenant for life are incapable of assignment and that if he does assign his interest he retains his powers and they are exercisable by him notwithstanding the assignment. Where the tenant for life has assigned his interests he may continue to exercise his powers without gaining the consent of the assignee.[33] Any contract that the tenant for life enters that he will not exercise some or all of his powers is void.[34]

(iii) Requirement to Inform the Trustees of the Settlement of Proposed Dealings with the Land

14-040   Where the tenant for life proposes to exercise certain of his powers he is first required to give notice of his intention to the trustees of the settlement. Section 101(1) of the Settled Land Act 1925 provides that he must give notice by registered letter to the trustees and to the solicitor for the trustees if he intends to "make a sale, exchange, lease, mortgage, or charge or to grant an option" in relation to the land. The notice must be given "not less than one month" before

---

[32] Settled Land Act 1925 s.106.
[33] Settled Land Act 1925 s.104(4).
[34] Settled Land Act 1925 s.104(2).

the proposed transaction is completed. By s.101(2) the notice need not be specific but may be "notice of a general intention" to make a transaction of the types covered by the section. By s.101(3) the tenant for life must make any information or particulars available to the trustees if they reasonably require it. The requirement of notice may be waived by the trustees, either in relation to a specific transaction or generally, and they may accept less than a month's notice.[35] Failure by the tenant for life to give appropriate notice does not affect the position of the third party with whom they transact concerning the land, provided that such a person was dealing in good faith, and the lack of notice does not invalidate the transaction.[36]

(iv) Exercise of Powers Requiring the Consent of the Trustees of the Settlement

In some cases the tenant must do more than simply give notice to the trustees of the settlement before exercising his powers and he must obtain their consent. Under s.58 the tenant for life must obtain the consent in writing of the trustees before compromising any claim relating to the settled land,[37] and before releasing, waiving or modifying any restrictive covenant or easement affecting other land for the benefit of the settled land.[38]   **14–041**

(v) Exercise of Powers Requiring Either the Consent of the Trustees or an Order of the Court

By s.65 the tenant for life cannot dispose of the principal mansion house[39] comprising the settled land, whether by sale or lease, without the consent of the trustees of the settlement or an order of the court. Similarly, under s.66 he cannot cut and sell timber on the land which is ripe for cutting without consent or a court order.[40]   **14–042**

(vi) Exercise of Powers Requiring an Order of the Court

Under s.57(2) the tenant for life cannot sell or lease an area of the land greater than that specified[41] for the purpose of providing housing or allotments for the working classes for less than the best price or rent that could be reasonably obtained, without an order of the court. By s.67(3) heirlooms included in the settlement cannot be sold by the tenant for life without an order for the court. Under s.46 the tenant for life may only make mining or building leases longer than the terms specified in s.41[42] where there is a court order.   **14–043**

---

[35] Settled Land Act 1925 s.101(4).
[36] Settled Land Act 1925 s.101(5).
[37] Settled Land Act 1925 s.58(1).
[38] Settled Land Act 1925 s.58(2).
[39] This is a house (other than a farmhouse) standing in grounds of more than 25 acres: Settled Land Act 1925 s.65(2).
[40] If he is impeachable for waste in respect of timber.
[41] Two acres in any one parish in urban districts, and 10 acres in rural districts.
[42] 999 years for building leases and 100 years for mining leases.

(vii) Trustees may Apply to the Court Concerning a Proposed Exercise of the Powers of the Tenant for Life

14–044 When the trustees receive notice of a proposed transaction by the tenant for life concerning the settled land they are entitled to apply to the court under s.93, which provides that:

> "If a question arises or a doubt is entertained—
>
> (a) respecting the exercise or intended exercise of any of the powers conferred by this Act . . . the tenant for life or statutory owner, or the trustees of the settlement, or any other person interested under the settlement, may apply to the court for its decision or directions thereon, or for the sanction of the court to any conditional contract, and the court may make such order or give such directions respecting the matter as the court thinks fit."

However, the trustees are not under any duty to seek the intervention of the court where a tenant for life proposes to exercise his powers and s.97(a) provides specifically that the trustees are not liable "for giving any consent, or for not making, bringing, taking or doing any such application, action, proceeding, or thing, as they might make, bring, take or do".

(viii) Capital Moneys Must be Paid to the Trustees of the Settlement

14–045 Where the tenant for life exercises his powers in relation to the land and any capital moneys arise, these are payable to the trustees of the settlement. This requirement is discussed below.

4. Rights and Powers of the Trustees of the Settlement

(a) *General Function in Relation to the Settlement*

14–046 Unlike the trustees of conventional trusts the trustees of a settlement are not invested with the legal title of the land, which is instead held by the tenant for life, or statutory owner as the case may be. The trustees do not therefore enjoy the day-to-day management and control of the property subject to the settlement and their role is rather one of overriding supervision. Their central role was characterised by Vaisey J. in *Re Boston's Will Trusts*[43] as ensuring that the trust property is conserved by the tenant for life. This is achieved by the requirements of the Settled Land Act concerning the payment of capital moneys realised by any transactions dealing with the settled property which are entered by the tenant for life. These have the effect that a third party will only gain the benefit of such a transaction if the capital moneys are paid to the trustees and such payment should prevent them being misappropriated or misapplied.

---

[43] [1956] Ch. 395 at 405.

The trustees also have to be informed of any dealing undertaken by the tenant for life and their written consent is required for some transactions.

(b) *Trustees Must be Informed of Intended Transactions by the Tenant for Life*

As has been noted above in the context of the powers of the tenant for life, by s.101 the **14–047** trustees must be informed if the tenant for life is intending to "make a sale, exchange, lease, mortgage or charge or to grant an option" of or over the settled property. The requirement of a month's written notice before the transaction, or contract for the transaction, is entered into enables the trustee to apply to the court under s.93 if they have any question or doubts about the proposed exercise of the power.

(c) *Trustees' Consent Must be Obtained to Exercise of Certain Powers*

As has been noted above, the provision of an excessive area of land by the tenant for life for **14–048** the provision of dwellings or allotments for the working classes, the sale of heirlooms and the grant of mining or building leases longer than the statutory maximum require the consent of the trustees of the settlement. Sale of the "principal mansion house" and the cutting of ripe timber require either the consent of the trustees or of an order of the court.

(d) *Trustees' Receipt of Capital Moneys*

(i) The Definition of Capital Moneys

Where property is held under a settlement the exercise of the powers of the tenant for life will **14–049** often result in the realisation of its value in money. It is important to distinguish whether such realised value is to be regarded as the capital or the income of the settlement, since this will determine the entitlements of the beneficiaries. The tenant for life, who enjoys a life interest, will be entitled to any income, whereas capital forms part of the remainder interest and should not be dissipated by the tenant for life. The Settled Land Act provides that the receipts from certain transactions are to be treated as capital money.[44] Most importantly the proceeds of sale of land or heirlooms[45] forming part of the settlement comprise capital money. Where the tenant for life leases the land and receives a fine (i.e. a lump sum rather than a periodical payment) in return it is deemed to be capital money,[46] as is the consideration paid for the grant of an option to purchase or take a lease.[47] Three-quarters of the rent of a mining

---

[44] The following examples are not exhaustive of what may constitute capital moneys for the purposes of the Settled Land Act 1925. See also ss.52, 54(4), 55(2), 56(4), 57(3), and 61(1).
[45] Settled Land Act 1925 s.67(2).
[46] Settled Land Act 1925 s.42(4).
[47] Settled Land Act 1925 s.51(5).

lease[48] and three-quarters of the money from the sale of timber[49] which is cut from the land are treated as capital money if the tenant for life is impeachable for waste. Money raised by way of a mortgage of the land[50] and received as compensation for a breach of covenant by a lessee or grantee of the tenant for life[51] is also capital money.

(ii) Requirement that Capital Moneys be Paid Over to the Trustees of the Settlement

14–050 When the tenant for life proposes to effect a transaction in exercise of his powers which will realise money which is capital money for the purpose of the Act, s.18(1) provides that:

> "Where land is the subject of a vesting instrument and the trustees of the settlement have not been discharged under this Act, then—
>
> (a) any *disposition by the tenant for life or statutory owner of the land*, other than a disposition authorised by this Act or any other statute, or made in pursuance of any additional or larger powers mentioned in the vesting instrument, *shall be void*, except for the purpose of conveying or creating such equitable interests as he has power, in right of his equitable interests and powers under the trust instrument, to convey or create; and
>
> (b) if any capital money is payable in respect of a transaction, a conveyance to a purchaser of the land shall only take effect under this Act if the capital money is paid to or by the direction of the trustees of the settlement or into court; and
>
> (c) notwithstanding anything to the contrary in the vesting instrument, or the trust instrument, *capital money shall not*, except where the trustee is a trust corporation, *be paid to or by the direction of fewer persons than two as trustees of the settlement*."

The comprehensive effect of this section is that unless the capital moneys are paid over to, or at the direction of, at least two trustees any dealings of the tenant for life in relation to the legal interest he holds in the land are void and ineffective to transfer any legal title to the person with whom he has transacted.[52] This operates as a safeguard to the interests of all the beneficiaries of the settlement from fraud by the tenant for life. On the other hand, where the statutory requirements are satisfied, then the transaction will operate both to convey the legal estate to the purchaser and to overreach the equitable interests of the beneficiaries.

---

[48] Settled Land Act 1925 s.47: note that only a quarter of the rent will constitute capital if the tenant is not impeachable for waste.
[49] Settled Land Act 1925 s.66(2).
[50] Settled Land Act 1925 s.71(1).
[51] Settled Land Act 1925 s.80(1).
[52] *Hughes v Hughes* [2005] 1 F.C.R. 679. The situation is different regarding registered land where, in the absence of a restriction on the register, a purchaser would take good title under the provisions that allow him to take free from all unregistered interests that are not overriding (Land Registration Act 2002 s.29), and this was accepted in this case.

(iii) Problems Where a Third Party is Unaware that He is Dealing with a Tenant for Life

If a third party acquires land which is settled and fails to pay over the capital moneys to the trustees of the settlement, but instead pays the tenant for life, there is some question as to whether the transaction is effective. Although s.18(1)(a) suggests that the failure to pay over to the trustees renders any disposition void s.110(1) provides that:

14–051

> "On a sale, exchange, lease, mortgage, charge or other disposition, a purchaser dealing in good faith with a tenant for life or statutory owner shall, as against all parties entitled under the settlement, be conclusively taken to have given the best price, consideration, or rent, as the case may require, that could reasonably be obtained by the tenant for life or statutory owner, and to have complied with all the requirements of this Act."

The question has arisen whether this section has the effect that a purchaser acting in good faith is deemed to have satisfied the requirement under s.18 that the purchase moneys must have been paid over to the trustees of the settlement. If so, a disposition to a purchaser who has acted in good faith without knowledge that he was dealing with a tenant for life will be effective and not rendered void by s.18. In *Weston v Henshaw*[53] Danckwerts J. held that s.110(1) only applied in favour of a purchaser who knew that he was dealing with a tenant for life and did not protect a third party who had acted under the misapprehension that he was transacting with an unencumbered legal owner. The case concerned unregistered settled land which was mortgaged by the tenant for life. The mortgagee had not paid the capital moneys arising to the trustees of the settlement as he was unaware that the land was subject to a settlement. The tenant for life had been able to pass himself off as the unencumbered legal owner using some earlier title deeds which had conveyed the land to him in fee simple before the settlement had been created. On his death the fraud was discovered and the beneficiary claimed that s.18(1)(a) rendered the mortgage void. Danckwerts J. rejected the argument that the innocent mortgagee was protected by s.110(1), stating: "I am satisfied . . . that that sub-section applies only to a person who is dealing with the tenant for life or statutory owner as such, whom he knows to be a limited owner, and with regard to whom he might be under a duty".[54] The mortgage was therefore void. He recognised that this result was in some measure unsatisfactory, since the case was "one of those unfortunate cases where an obvious fraud has been perpetrated by a person now deceased, with the result that one or other of two innocent persons must be deprived of what each of them naturally thought himself to be entitled to".[55] The right of the beneficiary was ultimately preferred to the right of the innocent third party. However, in *Re Morgan's Lease*[56] Ungoed-Thomas J. took a different approach to the scope of application of s.110(1). The case concerned the question whether the lessees of land subject to a settlement should be deemed to have paid the best rent that could reasonably be expected under s.110(1). He referred to the comments of Danckwerts J. and noted that the judgment did not

---

[53] [1950] Ch. 510.
[54] [1950] Ch. 510 at 519.
[55] [1950] Ch. 510 at 515.
[56] [1972] Ch. 1.

set out the reasoning which led to his conclusion as to the scope of s.110, nor had the earlier authority *Mogridge v Clapp*[57] been brought to the judge's attention. In that case the Court of Appeal had treated it "as self-evident that a person dealing with a life tenant without knowing that he was a life tenant would be entitled to rely on s.110 of the Settled Land Act 1925".[58] He therefore concluded that the section was available in favour of a person who was unaware that he was dealing with a life tenant:

> "There is, in the section, no express provision limiting its benefit to a purchaser who knows that the person with whom he is dealing is a tenant for life. On its face it reads as free of limitation and as applicable to a person without such knowledge as to a person who has it. There is a limitation, namely that the purchaser must act in good faith; but that limitation reads as applicable to a purchaser with such knowledge as to one without ... Thus my conclusion is that s.110 applies whether or not the purchaser knows that the other party to the transaction is a tenant for life."[59]

As a matter of statutory interpretation it seems that this view should be preferred, particularly when it is realised that the implication of the approach taken in *Weston v Henshaw*[60] is to create the only circumstance in which the bona fide purchaser of a legal estate in unregistered land takes subject to an equitable interest which falls outside of the limited system of registration of land charges.[61]

(e) *Trustees' Application of Capital Moneys which have been Received in Accordance with s.18*

14–052 The reason for requiring the trustees of the settlement to receive or direct the receipt of capital moneys consequential upon any dealings with the title to the land by the tenant for life is to ensure that they are then properly applied. Where the capital moneys have been raised for any special authorised object, for example improvements to the settled land, they must be used for that purpose.[62] Otherwise they are available for investment. Trustees, including trustees of settled land are now given wide powers of investment by the Trustee Act 2000. Prior to this, the trustees of settled land had only comparatively restricted powers of investment. Section 73 of the Settled Land Act 1925 provides that capital moneys "shall, when received, be invested or otherwise applied wholly in one, or partly in one, or partly in another or others" of the modes specified in detail in s.73(1)(i)–(xxi). This includes investments authorised under the Trustee Investment Act 1961[63] and importantly the purchase of freehold

---

[57] [1892] 3 Ch. 382.
[58] [1972] Ch. 1 at 9.
[59] [1972] Ch. 1 at 9.
[60] [1950] Ch. 510.
[61] See (1971) 87 L.Q.R. 338 (D.W. Elliott); (1973) 36 M.L.R. 28 (R.H. Maudsley); [1985] Conv. 377 (R. Warrington); (1991) 107 L.Q.R. 596 (J. Hill). *Hughes v Hughes* [2005] 1 F.C.R. 679, considered *Re Morgan's Lease* but concluded that the section did not apply in this case because of absence of good faith.
[62] Settled Land Act 1925 s.73(1).
[63] Settled Land Act 1925 s.73(1)(i) since the proceeds are "trust money".

land or a leasehold interest with 60 years of the term unexpired at the date of purchase.[64] In the absence of an express provision in the trust instrument capital money arising from the sale of settled land in England and Wales cannot be applied to the purchase of land other than in England and Wales.[65]

5. Termination of the Settlement

(a) *Duration of the Settlement*

Section 3 of the Settled Land Act 1925 provides:

14–053

"Land [which has been subject to a settlement which is a settlement for the purposes of this Act] shall be deemed for the purposes of this Act to remain and be settled land, and the settlement shall be deemed to be subsisting settlement for the purposes of this Act so long as—

(a) any limitation, charge or power of charging under the settlement subsists or is capable of being exercised; or

(b) the person who, if of full age, would be entitled as beneficial owner to have that land vested in him for a legal estate is an infant."

(b) *Disqualification of the Current Life Tenant*

Section 7(4) of the Settled Land Act 1925 makes provision for the eventuality that the current life tenant of a settlement ceases to have the statutory powers of a tenant for life "by reason of forfeiture, surrender or otherwise". In such a case "he shall be bound forthwith to convey the settled land to the person who under the trust instrument, or by virtue of [the Settled Land Act 1925] becomes the tenant for life" as his replacement. In the event that there is no replacement the settlement will be brought to an end, and he will be required to convey the legal title to the person entitled absolutely to the land. For example, if Victoria Manor is held on trust for Grant for life, remainder to Phil, and Grant surrenders his life interest to Phil, Grant will have to convey the legal title to him.

14–054

(c) *Effect of Death of the Tenant for Life*

When the tenant for life of the settlement dies the consequences will differ depending upon whether the settlement continues or whether the settlement comes to an end because the person entitled on his death is entitled absolutely and is not an infant.

14–055

---

[64] Settled Land Act 1925 s.73(1)(xi) and (xii). The Trustee Act 2000 confers wider powers to purchase land on trustees of land, but these wider powers do not apply to settled land: Trustee Act 2000 s.10.
[65] Settled Land Act 1925 s.73(2).

(i) Where the Settlement Continues

14–056   Section 7(1) of the Settled Land Act 1925 provides that:

> "If, on the death of a tenant for life or statutory owner . . . the land remains settled land, his personal representatives shall hold the settled land on trust, if and when required so to do, to convey it to the person who under the trust settlement or by virtue of the act becomes the tenant for life or statutory owner, and, if more than one, as joint tenants."

The "personal representatives" of the deceased life tenant who take the legal title to the land are not necessarily those who are his personal representatives in relation to the rest of his estate. By s.22(1) of the Administration of Estates Act 1925 the tenant for life may either appoint "special executors" in regard to the settled land expressly or alternatively, in the absence of an express appointment, the trustees of the settlement at the date of his death will become the special executors and hold the property on trust for the next tenant for life. By s.7(1) of the Settled Land Act 1925 the special executors must, when required, convey the legal title to the new tenant for life. It is clear from s.2(2)(a) of the Trusts of Land and Appointment of Trustees Act 1996 that a settlement created before January 1, 1997 will continue as a strict settlement where a life tenant dies and a new life tenant succeeds him.

(ii) Where the Settlement Ends

14–057   If the death of the life tenant has the effect that "any person of full age becomes absolutely entitled to the settled land . . . free from all limitations, powers and charges taking effect under the settlement" under s.7(5) of the Settled Land Act 1925 such a person may require the trustees of the settlement, or whoever the legal title to the land is vested in, "to convey the land to him". Thus if Victoria Manor is settled on trust for Grant for life, remainder to Phil in fee simple, on the death of Grant the legal title will pass to his special executors and Phil will be entitled to require them to transfer the legal title to him.

(d) *Termination During the Lifetime of the Tenant for Life*

(i) Termination if the Tenant for Life Becomes Absolutely Entitled to the Settled Land

14–058   If, during the course of the settlement, the tenant for life becomes absolutely entitled to the property subject to the settlement there is no need to convey the legal title to him since he will hold it already. For example, if Victoria Manor is held on trust for Grant for life, remainder to Phil, Grant will become absolutely entitled if he acquires Phil's remainder interest for himself. However by s.17(1) of the Settled Land Act 1925 the trustees of the settlement are "bound to execute, at the cost of the trust estate, a deed declaring that they are discharged from the trust so far as regards that land". Where such a deed of discharge contains no statement to the contrary a purchaser of a legal estate in the land is entitled to assume that the land has ceased to be settled land and that it is not subject to any trust for sale.[66]

(ii) Termination Because there is No Longer any Relevant Property Subject to the Settlement

Although settlements created before January 1, 1997 continue as strict settlements, s.2(4) of the Trust of Land and Appointment of Trustees Act 1996 provides that: **14–059**

> "Where at any time after the commencement of this Act there is in the case of any settlement which is a settlement for the purposes of the Settled Land Act 1925 no relevant property which is, or is deemed to be, subject to the settlement, the settlement permanently ceases at that time to be a settlement for the purposes of that Act."

"Relevant property" is defined to mean land and heirlooms.[67] This means that if all the land subject to a settlement is sold, and no heirlooms are held, then the purchase of new land with the capital moneys will give rise to a trust of land under the new regime and not to the revival of a settlement.

6. Overreaching of Beneficial Interests Under a Settlement

(a) *The Function of Overreaching*

Where land is held subject to a strict settlement the legal title is held by the tenant for life, and the beneficiaries of the settlement enjoy their interests in the equity. If a third party seeks to acquire the settled land they will wish to ensure that they can take the legal title free from the interests of any of the beneficiaries of the settlement. Overreaching provides a mechanism by which they can be sure that they will acquire the land unencumbered by any such third party trust rights by converting the trust interests of the beneficiaries in the land itself into identical interests in the purchase moneys which are paid over for the land. **14–060**

(b) *Essential Preconditions to the Overreaching of Equitable Interests in Settled Land*

(i) Compliance with Statutory Conditions

Overreaching will only occur if the conditions set out in s.2(1)(i) of the Law of Property Act 1925 are met. This section provides: **14–061**

---

[66] Settled Land Act 1925 s.17(3).
[67] Settled Land Act 1925 s.67(1).

"A conveyance to a purchaser of a legal estate in land shall overreach any equitable interest or power affecting that estate, whether or not he has notice thereof, if—

    (i) the conveyance is made under the powers conferred by the Settled Land Act 1925, or any additional powers conferred by a settlement, and the equitable interest or power is capable of being overreached thereby, and the statutory requirements respecting the payment of capital money arising under the settlement are complied with."

(ii) The Conveyance was Made Under an Exercise of the Settlement Powers

14–062 Overreaching can only occur if the conveyance of the relevant legal estate of the land subject to the settlement was made as a consequence of the exercise of the powers conferred by the settlement, either by the Act or through an express extension of those powers. If the conveyance was not a consequence of the exercise of such powers then overreaching cannot take place. For example, a conveyance by an erstwhile tenant for life in circumstances where the settlement has come to an end will not be capable of overreaching the equitable trust interests which exist behind what has become a bare trust of the legal title. For example, if Grant was the tenant for life of Victoria Manor and Phil was entitled to the remainder interests and Grant surrendered his life interest to Phil, the effect would be that the settlement was brought to an end. Until Grant conveyed the legal title to Phil he would hold it for him as a bare trustee. If Grant were to convey the legal title to Lorraine, this could not overreach Phil's equitable interest since the conveyance would not have been made in consequence of any exercise of the powers conferred by the settlement, which had ceased to exist.

(iii) The Equitable Interest is Capable of Being Overreached

14–063 Where land is not settled overreaching does not operate against all equitable interests in land but is largely reserved to trust interests, since the majority of other varieties of equitable interests are exempted from the effects of overreaching by s.2(3) of the Law of Property Act 1925.

However, s.2(3) only applies in the case of overreaching under a trust of land. In the case of settled land not only are the equitable interests of the beneficiaries of the settlement overreached,[68] but s.72(3) of the Settled Land Act 1925 provides that annuities affecting the settled land and a limited owner's charge or general equitable charge are capable of being overreached even if they have been properly protected as land charges.

(iv) Payment of the Capital Moneys to at Least Two Trustees of the Settlement

14–064 The most important requirement which must be satisfied before overreaching can take place is that the purchase moneys must be paid over according to the statutory requirements. It has

---

[68] Settled Land Act 1925 s.72(2).

already been seen that by s.18 of the Settled Land Act 1925 the capital moneys realised from a transaction must either be paid to or at the direction of at least two trustees of the settlement, or into court.[69] It has also been noted that failure to follow these requirements may have the effect not merely of preventing the overreaching of trust interests behind the settlement, but also of rendering the disposition of the legal estate void.

[69] Settled Land Act 1925 s.18(1)(b) and (c).

Part III

SUBSIDIARY INTERESTS IN LAND

Chapter 15

EASEMENTS AND PROFITS À PRENDRE

INTRODUCTION TO EASEMENTS

Whilst interests such as leases allow the owner of land to enable another person to enjoy the benefit of the possession and use of it in its entirety, an easement is a right which entitles a third party to exercise much more limited rights over land. One of the most common easement is a right of way. If, for example, Hamish and Isabelle own neighbouring terraced houses, and Hamish wants to build a garage at the end of his back garden, but it would be impossible for his car to gain access to it other than by using a track which runs across Isabelle's land, she could grant him an easement entitling him to enjoy the right of access and passage. An easement is not the only means by which such a right could have been facilitated. She could have granted Hamish a mere licence to use the track, which would give him a personal permission to use it. However an easement is not merely a personal right but is a right annexed to land, so that the benefit and burden are enjoyed by whoever owns the land to which it relates for the time being. If Isabelle were to grant Hamish a right of way it would not be his right alone, but a right annexed to the house he presently owns, so that if he was to sell the house to Jock, then Jock would also be entitled to exercise the right of way as the new owner. Similarly if Isabelle were to sell her house Hamish, or Jock would still be entitled to exercise it against the new owner, provided that any registration requirements were satisfied.

15–001

There are a number of means by which easements may be created. In the example of Hamish and Isabel it was assumed that the easement was expressly granted. However, in some circumstances an easement may be found to have been granted by implication from the parties' conduct. Easements may also be acquired by operation of statute and through long usage in a manner analogous to the principles of adverse possession. It has been seen from s.1(2)(a) of the Law of Property Act 1925 that an easement is an interest in land capable of enjoying legal status, provided that its duration is equivalent either to a fee simple estate or to a term of years absolute. Whether an easement which meets these criteria is in fact legal will depend on the manner in which it was created. Where land is subject to a valid easement and the title is transferred, the transferee will take the land subject to the easement unless he can establish that he enjoys priority over it. The rules of priority relating to the burden of easements are different depending on whether the land to which it relates is registered or unregistered, and in each case on whether the easement is legal or equitable.

ESSENTIAL CHARACTERISTICS OF EASEMENTS

1. No Complete Catalogue of Easements

15–002   It is impossible to draw up a complete catalogue of the rights which the law is prepared to recognise as easements, because new easements might come to be recognised with changing social circumstances and concepts of land usage. As Lord St Leonards observed in Dyce v Lady James Hay, with some prescience:

> "The category of servitudes and easements must alter and expand with the changes that take place in the circumstances of mankind."[1]

The law has been ready to recognise new easements which confer a positive benefit on the owner of the land holding the right, for example the right to use land as communal gardens,[2] for a washing line,[3] for aircraft movements[4] or for car parking.[5] However, there has been a much greater reluctance to recognise new negative rights, which entitle the holder to prevent the owner of the burdened land from doing something on it, as easements because they would unduly restrict a person's right to enjoy his own land. For example, in *Phipps v Pears*[6] the Court of Appeal held it would not recognise an easement of protection from the weather. The court accordingly held that a landowner was not liable to the damage resulting to his neighbour's house when he demolished his own, thus exposing its flank wall to the elements.

2. Easements Distinguished from Profits à Prendre

15–003   One important distinction which should be drawn is between easements and another category of analogous property rights termed profits à prendre. The key characteristic of a profit is that it entitles the owner to take some material benefit from land owned by another, by appropriating something from the land, or produced by the land, that belonged to the owner. For example, a right to take crops from land, to pasture cattle, or to take game would all constitute profits. In contrast an easement does not entitle the holder to take anything from the land at all, but merely to make use of it in some way. An easement may therefore be described as a privilege without a profit.[7] Profits à prendre are considered in greater detail

---

[1] (1852) 1 Macq. 305 at 312–313.
[2] *Re Ellenborough Park* [1956] Ch. 131.
[3] *Drewell v Towler* (1832) 3 B. & Ad. 735; *Mulvaney v Gough* [2002] EWCA Civ 1078; [2003] 4 All E.R. 83.
[4] *Dowty Boulton Paul Ltd v Wolverhampton Corporation (No.2)* [1976] Ch. 13.
[5] *London & Blenheim Estates Ltd v Ladbroke Retail Parks Ltd* [1992] 1 W.L.R. 1278.
[6] [1965] 1 Q.B. 76.
[7] See *Hewlins v Shippam* (1826) 5 B. & C. 221.

below. Somewhat anomalously the right to take water from the land of another is considered to be an easement and not a profit.

3. Easements Distinguished from Similar Rights

(a) *Natural Rights*

Every landowner automatically enjoys certain rights, similar to easements, as natural rights **15–004** incident to ownership and protected by means of the right to damages or an injunction for nuisance. These include the right to the natural flow of water through a defined channel such as a river[8] (although not the right to percolating water which is not in a defined channel[9]; the right to the natural drainage of surface water[10]; and the right to support for land in its natural state.[11] The right to support does not extend to the extra support which buildings require, although where a landowner has a right of action for damage caused to his land, he may recover compensation for the additional loss arising from any damage to buildings.[12] In *Holbeck Hall Hotel v Scarborough BC*[13] the claimants had lost their hotel when a large section of cliff fell away in a massive landslide in 1993. The defendants owned the land between the hotel and the sea, and were aware that the cliff was unstable as a result of maritime erosion. There had been previous slips, but nothing on the scale of the 1993 landslide, which had arisen because of geological conditions of which both parties were unaware. The Court of Appeal held that the defendants owed a duty of care to the claimants. Stuart-Smith L.J. said:

> "I conclude that the scope of Scarborough's duty was confined to an obligation to take care to avoid damage to the claimants' land which they ought to have foreseen without further geological investigation. It may also have been limited by other factors, . . . so that it is not necessarily incumbent on someone in Scarborough's position to carry out extensive and expensive remedial work to prevent the damage which they ought to have foreseen; the scope of the duty may be limited to warning claimants of such risk as they were aware of or ought to have foreseen and sharing such information as they had acquired relating to it."[14]

(b) *Public Customary Rights*

An activity which has been enjoyed as of right since 1189[15] will be considered to confer **15–005** legally enforceable rights upon those falling within the scope of the custom, even though it

---

[8] *Swindon Waterworks Co Ltd v Watts and Berks Canal Navigation Co* (1875) L.R. 7 H.L. 697.
[9] *Bradford Corp v Pickles* [1895] A.C. 587.
[10] *Palmer v Bowman* [2000] 1 All E.R. 22.
[11] *Redland Bricks Ltd v Morris* [1970] A.C. 652; *Lotus Ltd v British Soda Co Ltd* [1972] Ch. 123.
[12] *Lotus Ltd v British Soda Co Ltd* [1972] Ch. 123.
[13] [2000] 2 All E.R. 705.
[14] [2000] 2 All E.R. 705 at 725.
[15] See the section on prescription later in this chapter. 20 years' use as of right is sufficient to establish the right of the inhabitants of a locality to enjoy sports and pastimes under the Commons Registrations Act 1965: see *R. v Oxfordshire CC* [1999] 3 All E.R. 385.

may not satisfy the usual requirements for an easement. Thus in *New Windsor Corp v Mellor*[16] it was held that the inhabitants of Windsor had a legal right to use Bachelors' Acre, an open space within the town, for sports and pastimes despite their being no dominant tenement, a normal requirement for easements.[17] Other rights upheld on the same basis have included the right of fishermen to dry their nets on private land[18] and for the inhabitants of a parish to erect a maypole and dance around it.[19] Under the Commons Registration Act 1965, as amended by the Countryside and Rights of Way Act 2000, local common land that has been used over a long period for recreation or lawful pastimes may be registered as a "town or village green".[20] The Commons Act 2006 extends the law in relating to registration of common land and adds a more comprehensive administrative structure.[21]

(c) *Other Public Rights*

15–006   There are certain rights that may be enjoyed by any member of the public. For instance, there is a public right to navigate and fish in tidal waters, including over the foreshore (the area between high and low tide) when it is covered with water. Similarly, under the general law, any member of the public is entitled to use a public right of way.[22]

4.   The Positive Characteristics of Easements

(a) *Re Ellenborough Park*

15–007   The leading authority setting out the essential characteristics of easements is the decision of the Court of Appeal in *Re Ellenborough Park*.[23] The issue in this case was whether a right of the owners of freehold property to make use of neighbouring land as a park for leisure purposes was capable of existing as an easement. In answering this question in the affirmative, Evershed M.R. adopted a fourfold test to determine whether a right could be recognised as an easement:

> "(1) there must be a dominant and a servient tenement: (2) an easement must 'accommodate' the dominant tenement; (3) dominant and servient owners must be different persons, and (4) a right over land cannot amount to an easement, unless it is capable of forming the subject-matter of a grant."[24]

---

[16] [1975] Ch. 380.
[17] The case arose because of a campaign to stop the land being used to create a car park. The land, originally used for archery practice, is now used as a public park with some public lavatories being the most prominent feature.
[18] *Mercer v Denne* [1905] 2 Ch. 538.
[19] *Hall v Nottingham* (1875) 1 Ex. D. 1.
[20] See R. Meager [2006] Conv 265; *Oxfordshire CC v Oxford City Council* [2006] Ch. 43.
[21] Explanatory Notes.
[22] See [1993] Conv. 129 (M. Welstead).
[23] [1956] Ch. 131.
[24] [1956] Ch. 131 at 163, adopting the criteria formulated in *Cheshire's Modern Law of Real Property* (7th edn), pp.456 et seq.

Not all of these characteristics are equally significant and the technical language conceals what are often relatively straightforward propositions. As will be seen, the first three elements of this test can be conflated into a single principle, and the final element, which is of considerable importance, is so laconic as to be deficient as a guide to the recognition of new easements.

(b) *"A Dominant and a Servient Tenement"*

It has already been noted that an easement is a right annexed to particular land, which the owner thereof is entitled to exercise over other land. This requirement is expressed using the words "there must be a dominant and servient tenement". The dominant tenement is the piece of land which enjoys the benefit of the easement, and the servient tenement is the land burdened by it. In the example used at the start of this chapter, Hamish's house would be the dominant tenement since the right of way was a privilege attached to it, and Isabelle's the servient tenement. The requirement ensures that easements are rights which are only associated with the ownership of particular land.[25] The grant of a privilege over land by the owner to a person to be enjoyed independently of any land they own will be a mere licence and not an easement. For example, if Isabelle owned a country estate and granted Hamish, who lived in London, a right to come and walk there at weekends, this would not create an easement but confer a personal permission. In *Re Ellenborough Park*[26] this requirement was clearly met, because the freehold properties neighbouring the park were the dominant tenements and the park itself was the servient tenement. In *Alfred F Beckett Ltd v Lyons*[27] the Court of Appeal held an alleged right for all the inhabitants of the County Palatine of Durham to collect sea-washed coal from a stretch of foreshore was incapable of existing as an easement because there was no dominant tenement. Winn L.J. stated the principle that:

15–008

> ". . . no person can possess an easement otherwise than in respect of and in amplification of his enjoyment of some estate or interest in a piece of land."[28]

The dominant land may be identified in the document granting the easement, or it may be ascertained through extrinsic evidence.[29] Land that has not been identified at the time an easement is created cannot constitute the dominant tenement.[30] The owner of land cannot therefore acquire an existing easement to additional land which he may acquire in the future. There is no reason, however, why the dominant land cannot be treated as including other land enjoyed with it at the time of the grant of the easement.[31]

---

[25] See *Ackroyd v Smith* (1850) 10 C.B. 164; *Todrick v Western National Omnibus Co* [1934] Ch. 561; *Alfred F Beckett Ltd v Lyons* [1967] Ch. 449.

[26] [1956] Ch. 131.

[27] [1967] Ch. 449. Such rights could be public customary rights if enjoyed since 1189 (see above).

[28] [1967] Ch. 449 at 483.

[29] *Hamble PC v Haggard* [1972] 1 W.L.R. 122.

[30] *London and Blenheim Estates Ltd v Ladbroke Retail Parks Ltd* [1994] 1 W.L.R. 31.

[31] See *Britel v Nightfreight (GB) Ltd* [1998] 4 All E.R. 432 where it was held that the rights enjoyed by the dominant tenement could extend to other land enjoyed by way of lease, licence, or easement.

(c) A Right "Accommodating" the Dominant Tenement: An Easement Must Benefit the Land of the Dominant Owner

15–009 Behind the mystique of the language of rights "accommodating" the dominant tenement lies by far the most important limitation of the nature of the privileges over land which are capable of existing as easements. The essence of the requirement is that the right must in some way benefit the land itself, therefore increasing the utility of the dominant tenement, and not merely providing a personal advantage to the owner. In *Re Ellenborough Park*, Evershed M.R. adopted the following formulation of the meaning of the requirement as accurately representing the law:

> "A right enjoyed by one over the land of another does not possess the status of an easement unless it accommodates and serves the dominant tenement, and is reasonably necessary for the better enjoyment of that tenement, for if it has no necessary connexion therewith, although it confers an advantage upon the owner and renders his ownership of the land more valuable, it is not an easement at all, but a mere contractual right personal to and enforceable between the two contracting parties."[32]

Stated in this way, it can be seen that the requirement that an easement accommodate the dominant tenement is nothing more than an expansion of the requirement that there be a dominant tenement. Unless there is a link between the nature of the benefit conferred and some neighbouring land, the neighbouring land cannot constitute a dominant tenement. Expressed another way, it is inherent in the concept of a dominant tenement that it must be a property which in its own right benefits from the alleged easement.

Some early cases took a very narrow and restrictive approach to the application of the requirement that the right must accommodate the dominant tenement. For example, in *Ackroyd v Smith*[33] the owner of land granted the owners and occupiers of neighbouring land, and "all persons having occasion to resort thereto", a right to pass and repass along a road across his land for all purposes. Creswell J. held that this right was not capable of existing as an easement as it was a right unconnected with the dominant land. He stated:

> "It would be a novel incident annexed to land, that the owner and occupier should, for purposes unconnected with that land and merely because he is the owner and occupier, have a right of road over other land."[34]

The objection seems to have been that the scope of the right was so wide that it was not exclusively limited to use for the benefit of the land but could be utilised even when there was no benefit to the land as such but only personal benefit to the user. However, in *Todrick v Western National Omnibus Company Ltd*[35] Romer L.J. doubted whether as a matter of construction the grant should have been interpreted as a right of way for all purposes, whether or not connected with the land in question, and considered that the right should have been held to be an easement.[36] The Court of Appeal held that a right of way could serve more than one property.

---

[32] [1956] Ch. 131 at 170.
[33] (1850) 10 C.B. 164.
[34] (1850) 10 C.B. 164 at 188.
[35] [1934] Ch. 561.
[36] See also *Thorpe v Brumfitt* (1873) 8 Ch. App. 650.

It did not have to terminate at the dominant tenement. In *Re Ellenborough Park*, Lord Evershed M.R. considered that a right of way was not disqualified from enjoying status as an easement merely because it might be used by trespassers who had no connection with the dominant land at all, for example if they decided to take a short cut across the servient land.[37]

(i) Accommodation Requires more than Merely Enhancement of the Economic Value of Land

The mere fact that a privilege is annexed to the dominant land with the effect of thereby enhancing its value is not itself conclusive of the question whether the right "accommodates" the dominant land. This was stated by Evershed M.R. in *Re Ellenborough Park*:   **15–010**

> "It is clear that the right did, in some degree, enhance the value of the property, and this consideration cannot be dismissed as wholly irrelevant. It is, of course, a point to be noted; but . . . it is in no way decisive of the problem; it is not sufficient to show that the right increased the value of the property conveyed unless it is also shown that it was connected with the normal enjoyment of that property."[38]

(ii) Accommodation Requires a Sufficient Geographical Nexus Between the Dominant and Servient Land

A right will only be regarded as accommodating the dominant land to which it is annexed if that dominant land enjoys a sufficient geographical nexus with the servient land so that it can be said to benefit the land as such. In *Todrick v Western National Omnibus Co*[39] the Court of Appeal rejected a claimed principle that there must be contiguity between the dominant and servient tenements, but if they are separated by too much distance the right will be regarded as for the personal benefit of the owner of the dominant land and not for the land itself. For example, in *Bailey v Stephens*[40] Byles J. stated that it was impossible to have a right of way over land in Kent appurtenant to land in Northumberland.[41] In *Re Ellenborough Park*[42] one issue was whether the right to use the park could constitute an easement when some of the houses entitled were close, but not in fact fronting it. Evershed M.R. held that the fact that these houses were not adjacent to the servient land did not mean that the right did not accommodate them: **15–011**

> "We think that the extension of the right of enjoyment to these few houses does not negative the presence of the necessary 'nexus' between the subject-matter enjoyed and the premises to which the enjoyment is expressed to belong."[43]

---

[37] See also *Hamble PC v Haggard* [1972] 1 W.L.R. 122.
[38] [1956] Ch. 131 at 173.
[39] [1934] Ch. 561.
[40] (1863) 2 H. & C. 121.
[41] Comments which were approved by the Court of Appeal in *Todrick v Western National Omnibus Co Ltd* [1934] Ch. 190.
[42] [1956] Ch. 131 at 173.
[43] [1956] Ch. 131 at 175.

(iii)   Accommodation in the Context of Business Use of Land

15–012   Particular problems have arisen as to whether rights which enable the owner of the dominant tenement to carry out his business are capable of accommodating the dominant land and therefore existing as easements. In *Hill v Tupper*[44] the plaintiff had leased land adjoining a canal, and in the lease he was granted the exclusive right to put pleasure boats into the water and use the canal for that purpose. The defendant, landlord of an inn also adjacent to the canal, placed boats on it and the plaintiff claimed that this amounted to an interference with his right, which he alleged was an easement. The court held that his right was not an easement but a mere licence. Pollock C.B. stated that his right was "unconnected with the use and enjoyment of the land", and it has sometimes been thought that this indicates that rights which bring a commercial advantage to the owner of the dominant land cannot be regarded as accommodating it. However, this approach is clearly too narrow, and in *Re Ellenborough Park*[45] Lord Evershed M.R. considered that the true rational for the decision in *Hill v Tupper* was that the particular right claimed had no connection with the land:

> "It is clear that what the plaintiff was trying to do was to set up, under the guise of an easement, a monopoly which had no normal connexion with the ordinary use of his land, but which was merely an independent business enterprise. So far from the right claimed sub-serving or accommodating the land, the land was but a convenient incident to the exercise of the right."

Where a right does have sufficient connection with the use of the dominant land for business purposes, it will be regarded as accommodating the dominant land. For example, in *Moody v Steggles*[46] Fry J. held that the right of the owners of a pub to affix a sign-board to the wall of the neighbouring house was an easement.[47] He stated:

> "It is said that the easement in question relates, not to the tenement, but to the business of the occupant of the tenement, and that therefore I cannot tie the easement to the house. It appears to me that that argument is of too refined a nature to prevail, and for this reason, that the house can only be used by an occupant, and that the occupant only uses the house for the business which he pursues, and therefore in some manner (direct or indirect) an easement is more or less connected with the mode in which the occupant of the house uses it."[48]

Similarly in *Copeland v Greenhalf*[49] Upjohn J. held that he would have no difficulty in principle in finding that a right to deposit trade goods on neighbouring land was an easement

---

[44] (1863) 2 H. & C. 121.
[45] [1956] Ch. 131 at 173.
[46] (1879) 12 Ch.D. 261.
[47] The pub was located down an alleyway, and without a sign on the main street it would be unlikely that the pub would attract much passing trade.
[48] (1879) 12 Ch.D. 261 at 266. He cited *Wood v Hewett* 8 Q.B. 913; *Lancaster v Eve* (1859) 5 C.B. (N.S.) 717 and *Hoare v Metropolitan Board of Works* (1873–74) Law Rep. 9 Q.B. 296 as examples where an easement had been held to exist where it could only possibly be of benefit to the land because of the business of the particular occupant.
[49] [1952] Ch. 488.

capable of accommodating the dominant tenement, even though he held that the particular right claimed in the case was too extensive to constitute an easement. In *Wong v Beaumont Property Trust Ltd*[50] the Court of Appeal held that there was an easement entitling the tenants of premises used as a Chinese restaurant to erect a ventilation duct fixed to the wall of land owned by the landlord, which was only necessary because of the nature of the business pursued, and in *Woodhouse & Co Ltd v Kirkland Ltd*[51] Plowman J. held that a means of access utilised for a long period by a business and its customers and suppliers had become an easement, since it was for "their reasonable business purposes". However, although it is clear that rights are capable of existing as easements when they benefit commercial activities conducted on the dominant land, there will be no easement if the benefits are not confined to the business of the owner or occupier of the dominant land. In *Clapman v Edwards*[52] a tenant of a petrol station enjoyed the right in his lease to use the walls of the adjoining premises for advertising purposes. Bennett J. held that since the right was not limited to entitling the tenant to advertise his own business, it was not capable of existing as an easement:

> "If it were to enable the grantee, as I hold it does, to advertise anything he chooses upon the flank walls in question, there is no connection between the dominant tenement and the servient tenement in the flank walls in respect of such a user."

Even if the person holding the right to use the flank walls for advertising did not own the filling station, it would have been possible to make a profit from letting out the advertising space. There was therefore no necessary link between the right to advertise and the ownership or occupation of neighbouring land.

(iv) Accommodation and Recreational or Leisure Use of Land

As in the case of business rights, some older authorities suggest that rights to use land for **15–013** recreational or leisure purposes are not capable of existing as easements because they do not accommodate the dominant land. In *Mounsey v Ismay*[53] the court held that the claimed right of the freemen and citizens of Carlisle to hold an annual horse race on land belonging to the plaintiff was not capable of existing as an easement. Although this could be explained on the grounds that there was no dominant tenement, Martin B. held that the right did not confer a benefit in the character of an easement:

> ". . . we are of opinion that to bring the right within the term 'easement' . . . it must be a right of utility and benefit, and not one of mere recreation and amusement."[54]

In *International Tea Stores Company v Hobbs*[55] Farwell J. considered that the right of a tenant to use his landlord's park and gardens for his enjoyment was not capable of existing as an

---

[50] [1965] 1 Q.B. 173.
[51] [1970] 1 W.L.R. 1185.
[52] [1938] 2 All E.R. 507.
[53] (1865) 3 H. & C. 486.
[54] (1865) 3 H. & C. 486 at 498.
[55] [1903] 2 Ch. 165.

easement because it was a jus spatiandi and not a right of way leading to any particular place. He applied the same reasoning in *Attorney-General v Antrobus*[56] where it was held that access to Stonehenge was not a public right of way because such a jus spatiandi was not known to English law as a right capable of forming the subject matter of an easement by prescription or grant. Irish authorities also held that use of a walk "not . . . for the purpose of reaching any definite place, but as a place of recreation, to walk, to saunter, to lounge, to chat, to meet their friends" was not a public right of way, and by analogy would have been incapable of existing as an easement.[57] However, following *Re Ellenborough Park*[58] it is now clear that a right to make use of land even for recreational or leisure activities is capable of constituting an easement, provided that the use has sufficient connection with the dominant tenement to which it relates. The case concerned the question whether a right of the owners of houses fronting or extremely close to the allegedly servient land, which was to be maintained as an ornamental pleasure park, to make use of it for recreational purposes was an easement. Lord Evershed M.R. explained, with the help of an analogy, why the right in question accommodated the dominant tenement:

> "A much closer analogy, as it seems to us, is the case of a man selling the freehold of part of his house and granting to the purchaser . . . the right, appurtenant to such part, to use the garden in common with the vendor and his assigns. In such a case the test of connexion, or accommodation, would be amply satisfied; for just as the use of a garden undoubtedly enhances, and is connected with the use and enjoyment of the house to which it belongs, so also would the right granted, in the case supposed, be closely connected with the use and enjoyment of the part of the premises sold. Such, we think, is in substance the position in the present case. The park became a communal garden for the benefit and enjoyment of those whose houses adjoined it or were in its close proximity. Its flower beds, lawns and walks were calculated to afford all the amenities which it is the purpose of the garden of a house to provide; and, apart from the fact that these amenities extended to a number of holders, instead of being confined to one . . . we can see no difference in principle between Ellenborough park and a garden in the ordinary signification of that word. It is the collective garden of the neighbouring house, to whose use it was dedicated by the owners of the estate and as such amply satisfied, in our judgment, the requirement of connexion with the dominant tenements to which it is appurtenant."[59]

The court felt that the fact that the park could be used for such purposes as taking exercise and rest, or taking out small children, meant that the right to use it was of sufficient utility or benefit to the land and not for mere recreation or amusement.[60] In the recent case of *Mulvaney v Gough*[61] the Court of Appeal therefore held that the right of a cottage owner to use of a communal garden at the back of her cottages enjoyed an easement. However, as with rights bringing business advantage this does not mean that every recreational or leisure right will

[56] [1905] 2 Ch. 188.
[57] *Abercromby v Fermoy Town Commissioners* [1900] 1 I.R. 302.
[58] [1956] Ch. 131 at 173.
[59] [1956] Ch. 131 at 174–175.
[60] [1956] Ch. 131 at 179.
[61] [2002] EWCA Civ. 1078; [2003] 4 All E.R. 83.

necessarily accommodate the dominant tenement. In *Re Ellenborough Park* the Court of Appeal accepted that if the owner of particular land was to enjoy the right to visit a zoological garden free of charge, or to attend Lord's cricket ground without payment, these rights could not constitute easements because there would not be sufficient nexus between the enjoyment of the right and the use of the house. Evershed M.R. also indicated that a right to use land to play games may lack sufficient utility to accommodate the dominant tenement.[62]

(v) The Essence of the Requirement

Looking at the cases in the round, it can be seen that in many of them the essence of the requirement that an easement accommodate the dominant tenement appears to be that the rights concerned are only of value (or possibly are of greater value) if they are annexed to neighbouring land, than they would be if they were held separately and apart from the land. Rights such as the right to exploit boats on a canal, or to go to Lord's cricket ground, would have a commercial value as great if sold separately from land as if they would if sold with the land. They do not depend for their existence upon their being any dominant tenement. On the other hand, the right to use a driveway over a neighbour's property to drive a car into a garage would have neither meaning nor value if there were no garage at the end of the driveway into which to put the car. It is a right which can exist only because there is a dominant tenement.

15–014

(d) *"Dominant and Servient Owners Must be Different Persons"*

Again, this requirement is an expansion of the requirement that there be a dominant and a servient tenement. Without diversity of ownership there cannot be two tenements: a landowner owning two properties where one provides benefits to other can just as easily be considered to hold a single tenement in two parts. If Hamish owns a house with a garage at the rear, he does not need an easement to use the driveway which runs across his own land. He is able to use the driveway because it stands on his own land. It would make no difference if Hamish owned two adjoining terraced houses and used a driveway across one to reach a garage behind the other. Since an easement is a right exercised by virtue of the ownership of land over land belonging to another, it is impossible for an easement to exist if there is no diversity of ownership because the dominant and servient tenements are both owned by the same person.[63]

15–015

However, an easement may arise where there is diversity of ownership, for instance through the grant of a lease. If Hamish is the freehold owner of the houses but grants Isabelle a lease of one whilst retaining the other, she will enjoy exclusive possession of that land. If Hamish wishes to enjoy access across it he cannot do so by virtue of his freehold ownership alone. However, if when he grants the lease to Isabelle, Hamish provides in the lease that he is to have a right of way, this will be an easement during the period of the lease, since for that period there is diversity of ownership, as he is the owner of the dominant tenement but Isabel

---

[62] [1956] Ch. 131 at 179, commenting on the judgment of Martin B. in *Mounsey v Ismay* (1865) 3 H. & C. 486.
[63] *Bolton v Bolton* (1879) 11 Ch.D. 968; *Metropolitan Railway Co v Fowler* [1892] 1 Q.B. 165.

is the leasehold owner of the servient tenement. Similarly, a tenant would be able to enjoy an easement over land retained by her landlord.[64] A trustee is also able to enjoy an easement over other land of which he is the beneficial owner behind a trust.

Although rights exercised over land owned and possessed by the same person cannot be easements because there is no diversity of ownership between the dominant and servient tenement, they are not entirely irrelevant to the law relating to easements. They are regarded as quasi-easements, and as will be seen later, they may become full easements if the land is subdivided.

(e) *"Right Capable of Forming the Subject Matter of a Grant": It must have been Possible to Create Expressly by Deed*

15–016   Although an easement may in fact come into existence by a wide variety of means, the fourth requirement of *Re Ellenborough Park*[65] stipulates that a right will only exist as an easement if it could have been expressly granted by deed. This is often the most potent source of difficulty, and is an issue on which *Re Ellenborough Park* offers little guidance. It is in this respect that the *Re Ellenborough Park* test is deficient. The test identifies the requirement but offers no criteria which can be used to judge when the requirement is satisfied.

Two principal characteristics of the requirement can be identified. The first is that the right claimed must be sufficiently clear to be capable of description in a deed. The second is that the right claimed must be of a kind or type which the courts are prepared to admit to the category of easements. In addition, although this is not relevant to the essential character of easements, it is necessary to establish that there has in fact been a grant of the easement, expressly, by implication or by presumption, from the owner of the servient land to the owner of the dominant land.

(i) The Right Claimed must be Sufficiently Definite

15–017   A right will only be an easement if it allows those entitled to the benefit thereof to exercise rights of a sufficiently definite character. This requirement is intended to exclude rights which Evershed M.R. described in *Re Ellenborough Park*[66] as "too vague and wide". The court considered that a right to wander at will over all or every part of another person's land, which had been described by Farwell J. as a jus spatiandi in cases referred to above, would be too wide to constitute an easement and could only exist as a personal licence. However, it held that the right conferred to use the specific park in question was "both well defined and commonly understood".[67] The more general a right is claimed to be, the less likely that it will be held to constitute an easement. A right to light through a defined window may be an easement,[68] whereas a general right to light is not. A right to passage of air through a rock shaft was held to be an easement in *Bass v Gregory*,[69]

---

[64] *Borman v Griffiths* [1930] 1 Ch. 493.
[65] [1956] Ch. 131 at 173.
[66] [1956] Ch. 131 at 173.
[67] [1956] Ch. 131 at 176.
[68] *Easton v Isted* [1903] 1 Ch. 405; *Levet v Gas Light & Coke Co* [1919] 1 Ch. 24.
[69] (1890) 25 Q.B.D. 481.

as was a right to air through defined ventilation apertures in *Cable v Bryant*.[70] However, in *Chastey v Ackland*[71] the Court of Appeal held that an alleged right to ventilation by the general flow of air, which had been obstructed by the defendant's low building which thus prevented the smell from a public urinal being carried away, was not capable of existing as an easement. Nor are such general and intangible rights as a right to privacy,[72] or the right to a view,[73] easements.

(ii)   The Right must be of a Type Recognised as an Easement

Certain types of easement are so well established that there is no difficulty in recognising them. Rights of way are obvious examples, so too are wayleaves—rights to pass pipes or cables over or under another's land. However, it is said that the categories of easement are not closed.[74] So how is the decision made as to whether to recognise a new type of easement? One possibility is through reasoning by analogy, so that if there can be a right to supply water to a house by means of an underground pipe,[75] so also it is possible to have electricity supplied through a cable,[76] and presumably also to run telephone lines, computer cabling or cable television lines over a neighbour's property, although there is no case directly in point. This alone is not enough, since entirely new rights, such as the right to use a letterbox,[77] or the right to use an airfield[78] have sometimes been recognised. It is therefore necessary to identify some common characteristics of easements.

15–018

(iii)   The Right Claimed must not Amount to Possession of the Land

Since the very nature of an easement is that the owner of the dominant land enjoys limited rights of user over the servient land, any right the exercise of which would amount to the dominant owner enjoying possession of the servient land, either exclusively or jointly with the owner, will be regarded as granting an excessive entitlement. It is not that such rights cannot be granted, since a right to possession could be given by lease or licence, but they cannot be conferred as easements. For example, in *Mulvaney v Gough*[79] it was held that, whilst the right of a cottage owner to make use of a communal garden at the back of her cottage was capable of existing as an easement, she was not entitled to plant a flower bed in a specific location within the communal area, as this would amount to exclusive use.

A right will not be regarded as incapable of being an easement merely because the servient owner will not be able to use his land in the same way at the same time if the dominant owner

15–019

---

[70] [1908] 1 Ch. 259.
[71] [1895] 2 Ch. 389.
[72] *Browne v Flower* [1911] 1 Ch. 219.
[73] *William Aldred's Case* (1610) 9 Co Rep. 57b.
[74] *Dyce v Lady James Hay* (1852) 1 Macq. 305.
[75] *Goodhart v Hyatt* (1883) 25 Ch.D. 182.
[76] *Duffy v Lamb* (1997) 75 P. & C.R. 364.
[77] *Goldberg v Edwards* [1950] Ch. 247.
[78] *Dowty Boulton Paul Ltd v Wolverhampton Corporation (No.2)* [1976] Ch. 13.
[79] [2002] EWCA Civ. 1078; [2003] 4 All E.R. 83.

chooses to exercise it. In *Miller v Emcer Products*[80] a tenant was granted a right by his land-lord to use toilets on an upper floor of their building, which was occupied by third parties. The Court of Appeal rejected the argument that right could not exist as an easement because it involved an excessive user. Romer L.J. stated:

> "In my judgment the right had all the requisite characteristics of an easement . . . It is true that during the times when the dominant owner exercised the right, the owner of the servient tenement would be excluded, but this in greater or lesser degree is a common feature of many easements (for example, rights of way) and does not amount to an ouster of the servient owner's rights as [would be] incompatible with a legal easement."[81]

Most of the difficulties with this requirement have involved claims of rights of storage, or rights to park.

In relation to rights of storage, it is ultimately a matter of degree as to whether an alleged right to storage would constitute excessive use of the land. Some cases have concluded that the grant of a right of storage on the servient land was too extensive to be an easement. In *Copeland v Greenhalf*[82] the defendant claimed that he had acquired an easement by long usage to leave vehicles awaiting repair in the course of his business on a strip of adjoining land belonging to the plaintiff. Upjohn J. held that in the circumstances the right claimed was incapable of existing as an easement:

> "I think that the right claimed goes wholly outside any normal idea of an easement . . . This claim really amounts to a claim to a joint user[83] of the land by the defendant. Practically, the defendant is claiming the whole beneficial user of the strip of land on the south-east side of the track there; he can leave as many or as few lorries there as he likes for as long as he likes; he may enter on it by himself, his servants and agents to do repair work thereon. In my judgment, that is not a claim which can be established as an ease-ment. It is virtually a claim to possession of the servient tenement, if necessary to the exclusion of the owner; or, at any rate, to a joint user . . . It seems to me that to succeed, this claim must amount to a successful claim of possession by reason of long adverse possession."[84]

It should be noted, however, that Upjohn J. expressly limited his remarks to the creation of an easement by prescription, and did not apply them to the creation of such rights by express grant. In *Grigsby v Melville*[85] Brightman J. also held that a right of storage in a cellar under the servient land, which could only be accessed via the dominant land, was incapable of being an easement since it would amount to an exclusive right of user. In contrast, in *Wright v Macadam*[86] the Court of Appeal held that a right to store coal in a shed had been acquired by

---

[80] [1956] Ch. 304.
[81] [1956] Ch. 304 at 316.
[82] [1952] Ch. 488.
[83] "User" means simply use.
[84] [1952] Ch. 488 at 498.
[85] [1972] 1 W.L.R. 1355.
[86] [1949] 2 K.B. 744.

a tenant on the renewal of the lease.[87] In *London & Blenheim Ltd v Ladbroke Parks Ltd*[88] Judge Paul Baker Q.C. distinguished this case from *Copeland v Greenhalf* on the grounds that "a small coal shed in a large property is one thing. The exclusive use of a large part of the allegedly servient tenement is another".[89] As Alexander Hill-Smith observes:

> "The distinction between the two cases therefore on this analysis relates to the size of the property over which the easement is claimed. Many commentators have accepted as authoritative this reconciliation of the two authorities. If this reconciliation is correct, it means that the ouster principle does not apply where the area in question from which the owner has been ousted is small in comparison to the size of the servient tenement."[90]

In *Moncrieff v Jamieson*,[91] Lord Scott thought that Judge Paul Baker Q.C.'s reconciliation of the two cases "was addressing the wrong point":[92]

> "The servient land in relation to a servitude or easement is surely the land over which the servitude or easement is enjoyed, not the totality of the surrounding land of which the servient owner happens to be the owner."[93]

An analogous issue is whether a right to park is capable of existing as an easement.[94] In *Newman v Jones*[95] Megarry V.C. held that a right of the tenant of a flat to park a car in a defined area nearby was capable of existing as an easement, and a general right to park on defined land was held to be an easement in *Bilkus v London Borough of Redbridge*.[96] According to *London & Blenheim Ltd v Ladbroke Parks Ltd*,[97] it is a matter of degree whether the right claimed would amount to excessive use of the land:

> "If the right granted in relation to the area over which it is to be exercisable is such that it would leave the servient owner without any reasonable use of his land, whether for parking or anything else, it could not be an easement though it might be some larger or different grant."[98]

---

[87] Although the case is often cited to support the proposition that a right to store goods, even in a confined area, is capable of being an easement, the Court did not state that the right was in the nature of an easement. The right may therefore have been a right to joint or exclusive use arising in the special circumstances of an implied grant under Law of Property Act 1925 s.62. See also *Att-Gen of Southern Nigeria v John Holt (Liverpool) Ltd* [1915] A.C. 599.

[88] [1992] 1 W.L.R. 1278.

[89] A better distinction may be that where a right is expressly granted, it will be valid and enforceable whether it is an easement or a right to joint use. The right claimed in *Wright v Macadam* arose under s.62 of the Law of Property Act 1925 and was therefore to be treated as if it had been expressly granted.

[90] "Rights of Parking and the Ouster Principle After *Batchelor v Marlow*" [2007] Conv. 223 at 227 (footnote omitted); *Moncrieff v Jamieson* [2007] UKHL 42, para.55; [2007] 1 WLR 2620.

[91] [2007] UKHL 42; [2007] 1 WLR 2620, a House of Lords case on the Scottish law, which was acknowledged to be similar to English law on this point.

[92] [2007] UKHL 42, para.57.

[93] [2007] UKHL 42, para.57. Lord Scott relied on Hill-Smith's article. The alternative test proposed is discussed below from n. 102.

[94] Hill-Smith [2007] Conv. 223.

[95] March 22, 1982 (unreported).

[96] (1968) 207 E.G. 803.

[97] per Judge Paul Baker Q.C.

[98] [1992] 1 W.L.R. 1278.

According to this test a right granting a person the exclusive right to park their car in a particular space is therefore unlikely to be capable of being an easement.[99] In *Batchelor v Marlow*[100] the defendants, who ran a garage business, claimed to have acquired an easement by prescription to park and store six cars on land owned by the claimant between 8.30am and 6pm from Monday to Friday. The land in question was only large enough to accommodate six cars. At first instance it was held that the alleged entitlement to park was capable of existing as an easement because it was limited in time and did not therefore amount to an exclusion of the claimant. However the Court of Appeal held that the right was incapable of existing as an easement because it would deprive the owner of any reasonable use of his land. Tuckey L.J. explained as follows:

> "If one asks the simple question: 'Would the applicant have any reasonable use of the land for parking?' the answer, I think, must be 'No'. He has no use at all during the whole of the time that parking space is likely to be needed. But if one asks the question whether the applicant has any reasonable use of the land for any other purpose, the answer is even clearer. His right to use his land is curtailed altogether for intermittent periods throughout the week. Such a restriction would, I think, make his ownership of the land illusory."[101]

In *Moncrieff v Jamieson*,[102] Lord Scott (obiter) rejected the 'reasonable use' test:

> "[t]he claim in *Batchelor v Marlow* for an easement to park cars was a prescriptive claim based on over 20 years of that use of the strip of land. There is no difference between the characteristics of an easement that can be acquired by grant and the characteristics of an easement that can be acquired by prescription. If an easement can be created by grant it can be acquired by prescription and I can think of no reason why, if an area of land can accommodate nine cars, the owner of the land should not grant an easement to park nine cars on the land. The servient owner would remain the owner of the land and in possession and control of it. The dominant owner would have the right to station up to nine cars there and, of course, to have access to his nine cars. How could it be said that the law would recognise an easement allowing the dominant owner to park five cars or six or seven or eight but not nine? I would, for my part, reject the test that asks whether the servient owner is left with any reasonable use of his land, and substitute for it a test which asks whether the servient owner retains possession and, subject to the reasonable exercise of the right in question, control of the servient land."[103]

Thus, Lord Scott considered that an easement of car parking ought to be recognised even though this would limit the servient owner's use of that land, provided the servient owner retained sufficient control over the land. Lord Neuberger saw "considerable force" in Lord Scott's argument, and went on to observe that if that were the right test, *Batchelor v Marlow*

---

[99] The test was doubted by the House of Lords in *Moncrieff v Jamieson* [2007] UKHL 42; [2007] 1 WLR 2620.
[100] [2001] EWCA Civ. 1051; [2003] 4 All E.R. 78.
[101] [2003] 4 All E.R. 82.
[102] [2007] UKHL 42; [2007] 1 WLR 2620.
[103] [2007] UKHL 42, para.59. For these views, Lord Scott relied upon Alexander Hill-Smith's [2007] Conv. 223, see para 61.

was wrongly decided.[104] Given the limited argument on the point, the potential consequences, and the fact that it was unnecessary to pronounce on the point for the current appeal, Lord Neuberger went no further than this.

In *Montrose Court Holdings Ltd v Shamash*,[105] the Court of Appeal held that the owner of the servient tenement had the right to introduce a scheme of parking permits, which meant temporal and numeric restrictions on parking, in order to regulate the parking by residents to a development.[106]

(iv)   The Right must not Require the Servient Owner to Take Positive Action

Any right which requires the owner of the servient tenement to take positive action, and particularly to spend money, goes beyond what is characteristic of an easement. In *Regis Property Co Ltd v Redman*[107] the Court of Appeal therefore held that the obligation of a landlord to supply the premises of his tenant with constant hot water and central heating was not capable of existing as an easement as it involved the performance of services, which was essentially a matter of personal contract as distinct from a proprietary right. In *Duke of Westminster v Guild*[108] a tenant enjoyed an easement in the form of a right of drainage via a drain running through the landlord's land which had become blocked. The Court of Appeal held that, although such an easement carried with it the right of the tenant to enter the landlord's property to repair the drain, the landlord was not, as the owner of the servient tenement, under any obligation to execute any repairs necessary to ensure the enjoyment of the easement by the dominant land. The general rule also applies to easements of support, as was explained by Lord Greene M.R. in *Bond v Nottingham Corp*:

15–020

> "The owner of the servient land is under no obligation to repair that part of his building which provides support for his neighbour. He can let it fall into decay. If it does so, and support is removed, the owner of the dominant land has no cause for complaint. On the other hand, the owner of the dominant land is not bound to sit by and watch the gradual deterioration of the support constituted by his neighbour's building. He is entitled to enter and take the necessary steps to ensure that the support continues by effecting repairs, and so forth, to the part of the building which gives the support. But what the owner of the servient land is not entitled to do, is by an act of his own, to remove the support without providing an equivalent."[109]

Despite this general rule several limited exceptions have been recognised. A right to have the servient land fenced, or a fence or wall kept in repair, has been held to be an easement,

15–021

[104] [2007] UKHL 42, para.143. In its 2008 Consultation Paper "Easements, Covenants and Profits à Prendre Law Com No. 186 (2008), the Law Commission considered both the 'reasonable use' test in *London & Blenhein* and the test in Moncrieff v Jamieson, to be inappropriate. Instead, the Law Commission propared an alternative from "first principles": para 3.49. This will be discussed below at 15–097.
[105] [2006] EWCA Civ 251; Westlaw document 2006 WL 755478; [2006] Conv. 497.
[106] [2006] Conv. 497 (although the servient owner's right to do this had been expressly reserved, the only issue being the propriety of the regulations: [2006] EWCA Civ 251; [2006] Conv. 497).
[107] [1956] 2 Q.B. 613.
[108] [1985] Q.B. 688.
[109] [1940] Ch. 429 at 438–439.

and by its very nature imposes an obligation on the servient landowner to take positive action.[110] It also seems that an easement may carry with it positive obligations binding the servient landowner if this is inevitably required in the circumstances. *Liverpool City Council v Irwin*[111] concerned the liabilities of a council which was the landlord of a tower block, the flats of which were rented to tenants but the common parts of which were retained by the Council. The tenants enjoyed easements to use the stairs, the lifts and the rubbish chutes. The House of Lords held that in the particular circumstances these easements also imposed an obligation on the landlords to maintain the common parts of the building in a reasonable manner. Lord Wilberforce explained:

> "I accept, of course, the argument that a mere grant of an easement does not carry with it any obligation on the part of the servient owner to maintain the subject matter. The dominant owner must spend the necessary money, for example in repairing a driveway leading to his house. And the same principles may apply where a landlord lets an upper floor with access by a staircase; responsibility for maintenance may well rest on the tenant. But there is a difference between that case and the case where there is an essential means of access, retained in the landlord's occupation, to units in a building of multi-occupation, for unless the obligation to maintain is, in a defined manner, placed upon the tenants, individually or collectively, the nature of the contract, and the circumstances, require that it be placed on the landlord."[112]

There are suggestions in *Holbeck Hall Hotel Ltd v Scarborough BC* that there might be circumstances under which the servient owner might be required to take positive steps to maintain a right of support enjoyed by the dominant owner.[113]

CREATION OF EASEMENTS

15–022   There are a number of ways in which an easement may be created. An easement will only be legal in character if it is granted for a period equivalent to either a fee simple absolute or a term of years and the appropriate formalities are observed.[114] If these requirement are not met the easement will be equitable in nature.

1. Express Grant

15–023   A grant of an easement will occur when either there has been a prior diversity of ownership of the dominant and servient tenements and the owner of the dominant tenement grants an

---

[110] *Crow v Wood* [1971] 1 Q.B. 77. See also *Jones v Price* [1965] 2 Q.B. 618; *Egerton v Harding* [1975] Q.B. 62.
[111] [1977] A.C. 239.
[112] [1977] A.C. 239 at 256.
[113] [2000] 2 All E.R. 705.
[114] Law of Property Act 1925 s.1(2)(a).

easement to the owner of the servient tenement, or where the land has been previously owned in its entirety by the owner of the now servient tenement and when he transfers the dominant tenement he grants the transferee an easement over the land he retains. For example, if Hamish owns two neighbouring houses and sells one to Isabel, he can in the conveyance grant her a right of way across his garden. An express grant will only create a legal easement if it is made by a deed complying with the requirements of s.1 of the Law of Property (Miscellaneous Provisions) Act 1989. This requirement will be met if the grant is incorporated in a conveyance transferring title to the dominant land. If an easement is expressly granted but not by deed the purported grant will only create a licence.[115] However if there is a valid contract to grant the easement this will give rise to an equitable easement. Section 27(2)(d) of the Land Registration Act 2002 provides that the express grant of a legal easement over registered land is a disposition required to be completed by registration, irrespective of the duration of the grant. The grant of the easement is completed by the entry of a notice of the interest in the register of the title of the servient tenement to which it relates, and if the dominant tenement is a registered estate then the proprietor of the registered estate must be entered in the register as the proprietor of the easement.[116] Failure to comply with these requires will have the effect that the grant does not operate at law.[117]

2. Implied Grant

Where the owner of land conveys part of it to another person he is under a duty to give full effect to the intention of the parties in making the grant. He is therefore under a duty not to derogate from his grant of the land. The law is therefore willing to imply that the transferor granted easements to the transferee which are necessary for the proper use of the transferred land; which the parties had a common intention should be granted; or which were exercised by the transferor over his land before he transferred it and are necessary to the reasonable enjoyment of the land granted. Because the grant of such easements is implied into the deed they take effect as legal easements. Implied grants of easements do not need to be completed by registration, as s.27(2) of the Land Registration Act 2002 only renders the "express grant" of an easement a "disposition required to be completed by registration."   **15–024**

(a) *Easements Implied by Necessity*

A grant of land[118] impliedly includes[119] a grant of any easements which were necessary for the use of the land by the grantee. The most common situation in which such an easement will   **15–025**

---

[115] *Wood v Leadbitter* (1845) 13 M. & W. 838.
[116] Land Registration Act 2002 Sch.2 para.7.
[117] Land Registration Act 2002 s.27(1).
[118] An easement of necessity will only arise where there is a grant of land: *Proctor v Hodgson* (1855) 10 Ex. 824; *Wilkes v Greenway* (1890) 6 T.L.R. 449; *Nickerson v Barroughclough* [1981] Ch. 426.
[119] Despite some arguments that the rationale for the creation of easements of necessity was public policy, in *Nickerson v Barroughclough* [1981] Ch. 426 the Court of Appeal rejected these and reaffirmed that the easement is implied from the circumstances into the grant of land.

be implied into a grant is where there would be no means of access to the land granted unless there was a right of way over the land of the grantor. In such cases the land granted will become a dominant tenement and an easement will be implied over the land retained by the grantor. The requirement of necessity is construed strictly, so that an easement will not be implied against the grantor merely because this would provide a more convenient access to the land granted. As Stirling J. stated in *Union Lighterage Company v London Graving Dock Company*:

> "In my opinion, an easement of necessity ... means an easement without which the property retained cannot be used at all, and not merely necessary to the reasonable enjoyment of the property."[120]

15–026 Therefore if the land granted already enjoys a right of access, so that it is not "landlocked", no easement will be implied over the grantor's land no matter how inconvenient the existing access is.[121] However an easement of necessity will be implied even if the grantee enjoys access to the land if that access is either unlawful,[122] or not enjoyed "as of right". For example, in *Barry v Hasseldine*,[123] the grantee purchased land that was completely surrounded by the land of the grantor, or land owned by strangers over which he had no right of way. He in fact exercised access over a disused airfield with the permission of its owner. Danckwerts J. held that as he enjoyed no legal right of access to the land granted an easement of necessity should be implied over the grantor's land. Where such an easement of necessity is implied the route is determined by the grantor who retains the servient land.[124] As the easement of necessity is implied into the grant of the land at the date that the grant is made it does not terminate if an alternative means of access becomes available in the future. However, the extent of the easement is determined by what would be necessary for the use of the dominant land at the date of the grant, and its scope is not increased merely because of a change of use in the future.[125] Although easements of necessity have generally concerned rights of way, other rights have been held to be implied by necessity. In *Wong v Beaumont Property Trust Ltd*[126] the Court of Appeal held that the tenant of three cellars which he used as a Chinese restaurant was entitled to an easement of necessity to erect a ventilation duct on the outside of the landlord's building. However, it is questionable whether this case should genuinely be regarded as an example of an easement of necessity as a ventilation shaft was not required for any use of the land but only as a consequence of the particular use to which it was put. The creation of such an easement would have been better explained by finding a common intention of the landlord and the tenant.

---

[120] [1902] 2 Ch. 557 at 573; Also *Adealon International Corp Proprietary Ltd v Merton LBC* [2007] 1 W.L.R. 1898.
[121] *Titchmarsh v Royston Water Co Ltd* (1899) 81 L.T. 673; *MRA Engineering Ltd v Trimster Co Ltd* (1987) 56 P. & C.R. 1; *Manjang v Drammeh* (1990) 61 P. & C.R. 194. In *Sweet v Sommer* [2004] 4 All E.R. p. 288 an easement of necessity was implied where access would have required the demolition of a building; The decision was confirmed by the Court of Appeal: [2005] 2 All E.R. 64; 2005 WL 513419; the Court relying more on the alternative ground of estoppel: [2005] Conv. 545.
[122] *Hansford v Jago* [1921] 1 Ch. 322.
[123] [1952] Ch. 832.
[124] *Brown v Alabaster* (1887) 37 Ch. 490.
[125] *Corporation of London v Riggs* (1880) 12 Ch.D. 798.
[126] [1965] 1 Q.B. 173.

There is no rule of law that land cannot be acquired unless it has a means of access, and the circumstances may make it clear that no easement of necessity should be implied, for instance because the plaintiff expects to gain access through the purchase of another property or through negotiations with another adjoining landowner.[127]

(b) Easements Implied by the Common Intention of the Grantor and Grantee of the Land

Even where an easement is not strictly necessary for the use of the land it may be implied into the grant if it can be shown that the grantor and grantee of the land had a common intention that the right should be granted. In *Pwllbach Colliery Co Ltd v Woodman*[128] Lord Parker identified two circumstances in which such an easement will be implied. First, an implication arises "because the right in question is necessary for the enjoyment of some other right expressly granted". For example, if the grantor has expressly granted the grantee a right to draw water from a spring on his land this necessarily involves the right of going to the spring for that purpose. Secondly, and more importantly, he stated that easements could be implied from the circumstances in which a grant of land was made:

15–027

> "The law will readily imply the grant . . . of such easements as may be necessary to give effect to the common intention of the parties to a grant of real property, with reference to the manner or purposes for which the land was granted."

He further held that such a common intention will only be found if "the parties should intend that the subject of the grant . . . should be used in some definite and particular manner". These principles were applied by the Court of Appeal in *Stafford v Lee*[129] where a deed of gift of woodland mentioned the fact that it fronted a private road which was the only practicable means of access. Some years later the owners of the land wanted to build a house and claimed that they were entitled to a right of way over the road by foot or vehicles for all purposes associated with a residential dwelling. The owners of the servient land claimed that the right of way was limited to use for all purposes necessary for the reasonable enjoyment of the land as woodland. The court held that since the original deed granting the land was accompanied by a plan which indicated that the parties intended it to be used for the construction of a dwelling, the parties had a common intention to use the land for that definite and particular purpose and that an appropriate right of way had been impliedly granted. In *Davies v Bramwell*[130] the Court of Appeal implied an easement to give effect to the common intention of the parties that the land was to be used as a garage. This meant that large vehicles, for safety, had to be driven across the servient land. It has already been noted that the recognition of an easement in *Wong v Beaumont Property Trust Ltd*[131] would be better explained on the grounds of a common intention of the landlord and tenant that the land be used as a restaurant.

---

[127] *Nickerson v Barroughclough* [1981] Ch. 426.
[128] [1915] A.C. 634 at 646–647.
[129] (1993) 65 P. & C.R. 172.
[130] [2007] EWCA Civ 821; [2008] 1 P & CR DG2; 2007 WL 2479550 (Westlaw).
[131] [1965] 1 Q.B. 173.

(c) Easements Implied into the Grant from Quasi-Easements Previously Enjoyed by the Grantor

15–028   As was explained earlier, where the owner of land grants part of it and retains the rest, or divides his land by simultaneous transfers, any rights which he exercised over his land in the character of easements prior to the division are termed quasi-easements. The rule in *Wheeldon v Burrows*[132] has the effect that such rights may be implied into the grant of the land so that the grantee enjoys the same rights in relation to his land as were previously exercised by the owner himself. The rule was stated by Thesiger L.J.:

> "On the grant by the owner of a tenement of part of that tenement as it is then used and enjoyed, there will pass to the grantee all those continuous and apparent easements (by which, of course, I mean quasi-easements), or, in other words, all those easements which are necessary for the reasonable enjoyment of the property granted and which have been and are at the time of the grant used by the owner of the entirety for the benefit of the part granted."

It is clear from this statement that not every quasi-easement exercised by the owner over his land will be implied into the grant. First, they must have been exercised by him "continuously and apparently", which means that they must have left some permanent mark on the land. In *Borman v Griffiths*[133] it was therefore held that the grant of an easement was implied over a plainly visible road. However, in *Ward v Kirkland*[134] Ungoed-Thomas J. held that a right to go onto the grantor's land for the purpose of repairing a wall was not implied where the previous use was not "continuous and apparent" because there was no feature on the allegedly servient land which would have been obvious on inspection as indicating the exercise of the quasi-easement. He explained the meaning of the requirement:

> "The words 'continuous and apparent' seem to be directed to there being on the servient tenement a feature which would be seen on inspection and which is neither transitory nor intermittent; for example, drains, paths, as contrasted with the bowsprits of ships overhanging a piece of land."[135]

The principle seems to be one of "what you see is what you get". In other words, if the physical appearance of the land would lead the purchaser reasonably to conclude that the sale includes an easement, the onus shifts to the seller expressly to exclude that easement.

The second component of the rule is that, the quasi-easement must have been necessary for the reasonable enjoyment of the land. This does not require strict necessity, so that access exercised by the grantor as a quasi-easement may be implied into the grant even though it is merely more convenient than other means of access to the land.[136] In *Wheeler v JJ Saunders*

---

[132] (1879) 12 Ch.D. 31.
[133] [1930] 1 Ch. 493.
[134] [1967] Ch. 194.
[135] [1967] Ch. 194 at 225.
[136] *Borman v Griffiths* [1930] 1 Ch. 493; *Castagliola v English* (1969) 210 E.G. 1425.

Ltd[137] the majority of the Court of Appeal held that a means of access was not reasonably necessary for the enjoyment of the land and that there was therefore no implied easement. The plaintiffs had purchased a farmhouse which had previously been in common ownership with the adjacent land owned by the defendants. There were two possible means of access to the farmhouse, one of which involved crossing part of the defendants' land. Staughton and May L.JJ. held that this second means of access was not necessary for the reasonable enjoyment of the farmhouse because the other entrance would do just as well. The rule in *Wheeldon v Burrows* will not operate to confer an easement if it is excluded by the contrary agreement of the parties,[138] nor where the terms of the conveyance make clear that it was not intended to be exercised. For example, in *Wheeler v .J.J Saunders Ltd* the conveyance of the farmhouse contained a clause that the plaintiffs were to erect a fence along the southern boundary of their land, where they claimed they were entitled to a right of way through the operation of the rule in *Wheeldon v Burrows*. Peter Gibson L.J. held that the fencing obligation defeated the implication of the right of way because it did not anticipate the incorporation of a gate which would have enabled access to be maintained. The other members of the Court of Appeal did not express any concluded opinion on that issue having already found that no easement could be implied into the grant. The rule in *Wheeldon v Burrows* has been supplemented by the operation of s.62 of the Law of Property Act 1925, which is examined below and operates even in favour of rights in the nature of easements which were not exercised continuously and apparently.[139] However the rule is wider in two important respects. First, it operates even where there was no conveyance of a legal estate of land but merely a contract to convey.[140] Secondly, it operates where there was no prior diversity of occupation between the dominant and servient tenements, a condition which is an essential pre-requisite to the operation of s.62.

It remains unclear whether the two elements within the rule are cumulative or alternative. Does a purchaser have to show both that an easement is continuous and apparent and that it is reasonably necessary to the enjoyment of the land, or is it enough if one element only is present? Logic would suggest that the rule should apply if only one element is satisfied. This is because if the rule is based on the legitimate expectation arising on the purchaser's part that he will be able to enjoy the property he is purchasing on the basis of what appears to be sold, then that legitimate expectation can arise for either of the reasons set out in the rule. To require both elements to be satisfied sets up an illogical and unreasonable test. Surely if the purchaser of a house inspects it and sees that it has running water and functioning sanitary equipment, he is entitled to expect to be able to use the water and sewage pipes serving the property, even if they pass under land being retained by the vendor. The use of these pipes would be reasonably necessary for the enjoyment of the property. To require that the route of the pipes should also be evident from an inspection of the property would add an irrelevant consideration so far as the creation of a reasonable expectation is concerned.

---

[137] [1995] 2 All E.R. 697.

[138] *Borman v Griffiths* [1930] 1 Ch. 493; *Squarey v Harris-Smith* (1981) 42 P. & C.R. 118.

[139] For this reason the right to repair the wall in *Ward v Kirkland* [1967] Ch. 194 was held to have become an easement by operation of s.62 even though it had not been exercised continuously and apparently.

[140] *Borman v Griffiths* [1930] 1 Ch. 493; *Horn v Hiscock* (1972) 223 E.G. 1437.

3. Express Reservation

15–029   Reservation occurs where, rather than retaining the servient land on division of his property, the transferor retains the dominant tenement and wishes to be able to exercise rights in the character of easements over the servient land which he previously also owned. Rather than requiring the transferee to grant him the intended easements he can reserve such rights to himself in the conveyance, and the transferee will take the land as a servient tenement subject to those easements. For example, if Hamish owns two neighbouring houses and wishes to sell one to Isabelle, but he also wants to ensure that he is entitled to continue to use a path that runs across the garden of that house, he can reserve to himself a right of way to use the path when he transfers ownership of the house to her. An easement will only be reserved if the transferor of the servient tenement includes appropriate words of reservation in the conveyance or transfer. No special form of words are required as long as it is clear that the transferor intends to enjoy an easement over the land transferred. For example, a conveyance "subject to a right of way" has been held to create an easement by reservation.[141]

Historically the reservation of an easement was considered as operating by way of a re-grant by the transferee of the servient tenement, so that the reservation was only effective if the transferee also executed the conveyance. This requirement was removed by s.65 of the Law of Property Act 1925 so that a reservation is effective where only the transferor executes the conveyance of the land subject to it. Somewhat anomalously, however, the courts[142] have continued to regard the reservation as operating by a re-grant so that as a rule of construction an express reservation will be construed against the transferee of the servient tenement and in favour of the transferor retaining the dominant land.[143]

Section 27(2)(d) of the Land Registration Act 2002 provides that the express reservation of a legal easement is a disposition required to be completed by registration. Therefore just as in the case of an express grant, creation of an easement by express reservation must be completed by the entry of a notice of the interest in the register of the title of the servient tenement to which it relates.[144]

4. Implied Reservation

15–030   Although it has been seen that the law will imply the grant of easements into a deed on behalf of the grantee, there is a much greater reluctance to imply that a grantor has reserved easements to himself. This is because a grantor is expected to act in his own interests and deeds are construed in favour of the grantee.[145] The principle was stated by Thesiger L.J. in *Wheeldon v Burrows*:

---

[141] *Pitt v Buxton* (1969) 21 P. & C.R. 127; *Pallister v Clark* (1975) 30 P. & C.R. 84; *Wiles v Banks* (1983) 50 P. & C.R. 80.
[142] With the exception of *Cordell v Second Clanfield Properties Ltd* [1969] 2 Ch. 9.
[143] *Johnstone v Holdway* [1963] 1 Q.B. 601; *St. Edmundsbury and Ipswich Diocesan Board of Finance v Clark (No.2)* [1975] 1 W.L.R. 468.
[144] Land Registration Act 2002 Sch.2 para.7.
[145] *Neill v Duke of Devonshire* [1882] 8 App. Cas. 135.

"... if the grantor intends to reserve any right over the tenement granted, it is his duty to reserve it expressly in that grant."[146]

In that case the person claiming the easement had conveyed land adjacent to a workshop which had windows overlooking, and enjoying light from, the land sold. The purchaser of the land subsequently built so as to obstruct the windows. The Court of Appeal held that as the vendor had not expressly reserved a right to light in the conveyance it would not be implied and the owner of the allegedly servient land was entitled to build and obstruct the windows.[147] However, Thesiger L.J. recognised that there were some very limited exceptions to the general rule that the reservation of easements will not be implied into a grant.

(a) *Implied Reservation of Easements of Necessity*

Where the effect of a grant would be to landlock completely land retained by the grantee a reservation of a right of way may be implied into the grant.[148]   **15–031**

(b) *Implied Reservation by Common Intention*

An easement may also be found to have been impliedly reserved if it can be shown that the parties enjoyed a common intention that the grantee should be so entitled.[149] Since this is an exception to the general rule that a grantor must expressly reserve any right he wishes to retain over the land, a heavy evidential burden must be discharged before such a reservation will be implied. In *Re Webb's Lease*[150] Lord Evershed M.R. held that a grantor who claims such a reservation must be able "at least to prove affirmatively that such a reservation was clearly intended by him and his grantee at the time of the grant". The Court of Appeal held that a grantor had failed to discharge that burden when he claimed an implied reservation of an easement to maintain advertisements on the outside wall of the premises granted, and that the mere fact that the grantee was aware of the presence of the adverts at the date of the grant was insufficient to establish the necessary common intention.   **15–032**

5. Statutory Creation by s.62 Law of Property Act 1925

In essence s.62 of the Law of Property Act 1925 provides that, where land is conveyed, the conveyance automatically carries with it the rights and privileges which are annexed to the land, so that these do not need to be laboriously detailed in the conveyance. Section 62(1) and (2) provides: **15–033**

---

[146] (1879) 12 Ch.D. 31 at 49.
[147] See also *Ray v Hazeldine* [1904] 2 Ch. 17.
[148] See *MRA Engineering Ltd v Trimster Co Ltd* (1988) 56 P. & C.R. 1.
[149] See *Pwllbach Colliery Co Ltd v Woodman* [1915] A.C. 643 at 646–647, per Lord Parker.
[150] [1951] Ch. 808 at 820.

"(1) A conveyance of land shall be deemed to include and shall by virtue of this Act operate to convey, with the land, all buildings, erections, fixtures, commons, hedges, ditches, fences, ways, waters, watercourses, liberties, privileges, easements, rights and advantages whatsoever, appertaining or reputed to appertain to the land, or any part thereof, or, at the time of conveyance, demised, occupied, or enjoyed with, or reputed or know as part and parcel of or appurtenant to the land or any part thereof.

(2) A conveyance of land, having houses or other buildings thereon, shall be deemed to include and shall by virtue of this Act operate to convey, with the land, house or other buildings, all outhouses, erections, fixtures, cellars, areas, courts, courtyards, cisterns, sewers, gutters, drains, ways, passages, lights, watercourses, liberties, privileges, easements, rights and advantages whatsoever, appertaining or reputed to appertain to the land, houses, or other buildings conveyed, or any of them, or any part thereof, or, at the time of conveyance, demised, occupied, or enjoyed with, or reputed or know as part and parcel of or appurtenant to, the land, houses, or other buildings conveyed, or any part thereof."

Clearly this section has the effect that land which is conveyed carries with it the benefit of pre-existing easements,[151] but it has also been interpreted more widely so that rights enjoyed by the land conveyed over the land retained which were not formerly legal easements are converted into legal easements, and the conveyed land becomes a dominant tenement. Such easements are most likely to arise where a right in the nature of an easement was being exercised over the land retained by virtue of a mere licence. When the land is conveyed that right is converted into a full legal easement. For example, in *Wright v Macadam*[152] a tenant of a top floor flat was permitted to use a shed in the garden of the property to store coal. A new tenancy was granted making no mention of the shed. The landlord subsequently demanded payment of an additional rent for its use. The Court of Appeal held that the licence had been converted into a legal right by the grant of the new tenancy, which was a conveyance under s.62, and that the use of the shed as a matter of right meant that rent could not be charged. Jenkins L.J. accepted the principle that:

"a 'right' permissive at the date of the grant may become a legal right upon the grant by the force of the general words in [s.62 of the Law of Property Act 1925]."[153]

Similarly, in *International Tea Stores Company v Hobbs*[154] the tenant of a house had enjoyed a licence to cross the yard of the landlord's neighbouring property. When he purchased the freehold from the landlord, Farwell J. held that the licence was converted into a legal right of way enjoyed on the same terms as the licence, namely for the purposes of their business, between the appropriate hours and not by horse-drawn carts.[155] Section 62 would also have the effect of converting pre-existing equitable easements that were enjoyed by the land conveyed into legal easements.

---

[151] *Graham v Philcox* [1984] Q.B. 747.
[152] [1949] 2 K.B. 744.
[153] Citing *Lewis v Meredith* [1913] 1 Ch. 571, per Neville J. It was not necessary for the court to decide whether the right was an easement or a right to possession.
[154] [1903] 2 Ch. 165.
[155] See also: *Goldberg v Edwards* [1950] Ch. 247.

(a) Section 62 Only Operates where there is a Conveyance of the Land

Rights are only converted by s.62 into legal easements if there is a conveyance of the land. A **15–034** "conveyance" is given an extended meaning in s.205(1)(ii) of the Law of Property Act 1925 to include:

> "a mortgage, charge, lease, assent, vesting declaration, vesting instrument, disclaimer, release and every other assurance of property or of an interest therein, by any instrument, except a will."

There is no "conveyance" where an oral lease of land is granted,[156] an equitable lease is created or any other equitable interest is created by means of contract rather than by deed.[157]

(b) Section 62 only Operates in Favour of Rights being Exercised at the Date of the Conveyance

Only rights in use at the date of the conveyance will be converted into legal easements. As **15–035** Megarry V.C. stated in *Penn v Wilkins*:

> "Section 62 was apt for conveying existing rights, but it did not resurrect mere memories of past rights."[158]

(c) Section 62 only Operates where there was a Prior Diversity of Occupation

Although in *Long v Gowlett*[159] Sargant J. seemed to suggest that s.62 could operate even **15–036** though there was no prior diversity of occupation between the land conveyed and the servient tenement over which it would be enjoyed if it had been exercised continuously and apparently prior to the conveyance, the House of Lords held in *Sovmots Ltd v Secretary of State for the Environment*[160] that diversity of occupation was a necessary pre-requisite of the operation of s.62. As Lord Edmund-Davies succinctly stated:

> "But the section cannot operate unless there has been some diversity of ownership or occupation of the quasi-dominant and quasi-servient tenements prior to the conveyance."[161]

Lord Wilberforce explained that this was a necessary consequence of the theory by which s.62 operates:

---

[156] *Rye v Rye* [1962] 2 A.C. 496.
[157] *Borman v Griffiths* [1930] 1 Ch. 493.
[158] (1974) 236 E.G. 203.
[159] [1923] 2 Ch. 177.
[160] [1979] A.C. 144.
[161] [1979] A.C. 144 at 176.

"The reason is that when land is under one ownership one cannot speak in any intelligible sense of rights, or privileges, or easements being exercised over one part for the benefit of another. Whatever the owner does, he does as owner and, until a separation occurs, of ownership or at least of occupation, the condition for the existence of the rights, etc., does not exist."[162]

This requirement is most likely to be satisfied where the allegedly dominant land was subject to a tenancy, and the landlord has subsequently conveyed the freehold reversion or granted a new lease to the tenant, or where part of the land was occupied by a licensee who has been granted a tenancy or purchased the freehold.

(d) *Section 62 only Converts Rights into Easements if they have all the Characteristics Required of an Easement*

15–037   Section 62 will only operate to convert into legal easements such rights over the servient land as would have been capable of being expressly created as easements. If the right lacks any of the essential characteristics of an easement, as examined above, s.62 will not operate to cure the defect. As Lord Denning M.R. observed in *Phipps v Pears*:

". . . in order for s.62 to apply, the right or advantage must be one which is known to the law, in this sense, that it is capable of being granted at law so as to be binding on all successors in title."[163]

For this reason he held that whereas a right to use a coal shed or a right of way could be created as legal rights by operation of s.62, a right to protection from the weather, or a right to a fine view, could not, because they are not rights known to law. Similarly s.62 will not operate in favour of a right which the owner of the allegedly servient land would not have been entitled to grant expressly,[164] nor of rights which were intended by the parties to be merely temporary.[165]

(e) *Section 62 will not Operate if it is Expressly Excluded in the Conveyance of the Land*

15–038   A right will not be converted into an easement by operation of s.62 if the conveyance expressly excludes its operation. This follows from s.62(4) which provides:

"This section applies only if and as far as a contrary intention is not expressed in the conveyance, and has effect subject to the terms of the conveyance and to the provisions contained therein."

---

[162] [1979] A.C. 144 at 169. See also: *Bolton v Bolton* (1879) 11 Ch.D. 968; *Squarey v Harris-Smith* (1981) 42 P. & C.R. 118.
[163] [1965] 1 Q.B. 76 at 84.
[164] *Quicke v Chapman* [1903] 1 Ch. 659.
[165] *Birmingham and Dudley District Banking Co v Ross* (1888) 238 Ch.D. 295; *Green v Ashco Horticulturalist Ltd* [1966] 2 All E.R. 232.

(f) The Creation of an Easement by Operation of s.62 does not Need to be Completed by Registration

Section 27(7) of the Land Registration Act 2002 specifically exempts the creation of legal **15–039** easements by operation of s.62 of the Law of Property Act 1925 from the category of dispositions which are required to be completed by registration. Thus although s.62 technically operates as a form of express grant, it is treated in practice as a species of implied grant.

6. Acquisition of Easements by Prescription[166]

As was seen in Chapter 8, a squatter may obtain the legal ownership of land by means of **15–040** adverse possession for a requisite period of time. Prescription similarly enables a person to acquire a right as an easement by adverse usage over a sufficient period of time. The law of prescription is complex, and there are a number of different ways in which a prescriptive right may be obtained.

(a) General Requirements of Prescription

A right will only be obtained by way of prescription if it has been exercised in accordance **15–041** with the following principles for the requisite period of time.

(i) Use must have been Open

Long use, even of the requisite period, will be incapable of creating an easement unless it was **15–042** exercised openly and peacefully. In *Union Lighterage Co v London Graving Dock Co*[167] Romer L.J. stated that an easement was only acquired when:

> "the enjoyment has been open—that is to say, of such a character that an ordinary owner of the land, diligent in the protection of his interests, would have, or must be taken to have, a reasonable opportunity of becoming aware of that enjoyment."

For this reason the Court of Appeal held that no easement was acquired when a dock had been fixed to a wharf for more than 20 years by means of underground rods which were invisible to the owner of the servient land. Similarly, in *Liverpool Corp v H Coghill and Son Ltd*[168] no easement was acquired where the owner of the allegedly dominant land had discharged waste irregularly at night into a sewer for more than 20 years.[169]

---

[166] For a discussion of the underlying rationale, see F.R. Burns, "Prescriptive Easements in England and Legal 'Climate Change' " [2007] Conv. 133.
[167] [1902] 2 Ch. 557 at 571.
[168] [1918] 1 Ch. 307.
[169] For a consideration of the principle see *Williams v Sandy Lane (Chester) Ltd* [2007] P. & C.R. 27; [2007] Conv. 161.

(ii)   Use must have been Peaceable

15–043   No easement will be acquired by prescription if the user was forcible against the servient land, for example if the allegedly servient owner continually protested against the use.[170]

(iii)   Use must have been without Permission

15–044   Long use will only be effective to acquire an easement, other than a right to light, if it was exercised as of right[171] without the permission of the servient landlowner, since otherwise the user would derive from an express or implied licence.[172] In *Gardner v Hodgson's Kingston Brewery Co Ltd*[173] permission was implied where the user for 60 years of a right of way had made a periodic payment to the owner of the allegedly servient land. It does not matter that permission is unilateral: "the granting of an unsolicited consent is sufficient to prevent time running for the purpose of prescription".[174] Permission which has lapsed will not prevent the acquisition of an easement if the use continued for the appropriate period after the lapse. Use in excess of the permission will also acquire an easement because a radically different use means that the claimant is no longer entitled under the licence. In *Odey v Barber*[175] a change of use to transport calves in addition to sheep was not sufficiently different.[176] It should be noted that the effect of the Prescription Act is that easements other than rights of light may be acquired by 40 years use even if there was permission, unless that permission was granted in writing. The mere fact that the servient owner has tolerated the exercise of a use of which he was aware, and has taken no steps to prevent it, does not mean that the use was conducted with his permission so as to prevent the acquisition of an easement. As Dillon L.J. stated in *Mills v Silver*[177] "mere acquiescence in or toleration of the user by the servient owner cannot prevent the user[178] being as of right for the purposes of prescription". In the case of a right to light, 20 years' use without written agreement will be effective to acquire an easement by prescription even if the right was enjoyed with oral permission.[179] There is no need for the person claiming an easement through long use to believe they are entitled to it. As Lord Hoffmann said in *R. v Oxfordshire CC Ex p Sunningwell PC*,[180] "user which is apparently as of right cannot be discounted merely because, as will often be the case, many of the users over a long period were subjectively indifferent as to whether a right existed, or even had private knowledge that it did not".

---

[170] *Eaton v Swansea Waterworks Co* (1851) 17 Q.B. 267; *Dalton v Angus & Co* (1881) 6 App. Cas. 740.

[171] *Sturges v Bridgman* (1879) 11 Ch.D. 852; *Healey v Hawkins* [1968] 1 W.L.R. 1967.

[172] *Odey v Barber* [2008] 2 W.L.R. 618; [2006] EWHC 3109.

[173] [1903] A.C. 229.

[174] *Odey v Barber* [2008] 2 W.L.R. 618; [2006] EWHC 3109 at [70].

[175] [2008] 2 W.L.R. 618; [2006] EWHC 3109.

[176] [2008] 2 WLR 618, para 41–42.

[177] [1991] Ch. 271 at 279.

[178] "User" means use or usage.

[179] Prescription Act 1832 s.3. *Mallam v Rose* [1915] 2 Ch. 222; *Plasterers' Co v Parish Clerks Co* (1851) 6 Exch. 630.

[180] [1999] 3 All E.R. 385 at 396.

(iv) Use must have been Lawful

No easement by prescription can be acquired if no one could have unlawfully granted the easement claimed[181] or if the use claimed was prohibited by statute or constituted a criminal offence.[182]

15–045

(v) Use must have been Exercised by the Freehold Owner of Land

An easement can only be obtained by prescription in favour of a freehold owner of the dominant land against the freehold of the servient land. A tenant can never acquire an easement over neighbouring land owned by his landlord.[183] A tenant can gain an easement by prescription against neighbouring freehold land owned by a stranger who is not his landlord, but he acquires such a right for the benefit of the freehold of the land he leases and it endures beyond the termination of his tenancy.[184] Where user commences against a dominant tenement which is not subject to a tenancy, any easement which is acquired by prescription will bind the freehold title even if the land is subjected to a tenancy before the relevant period of user has been completed.[185] However, no easement can be acquired by prescription if the user commenced when the allegedly servient land was already subject to a tenancy.[186]

15–046

(b) *Legal Operation of Prescription*

If a right has been exercised in accordance with these principles it may give rise to an easement by prescription. However, whereas the doctrine of adverse possession is rooted in the concept that long use entitles the user to the right exercised, the acquisition of an easement by prescription operates on the basis of a fiction that the user was at some point in time granted the relevant right. There are now three ways in which prescription may operate, each of which requires different criteria to be satisfied.

15–047

(i) Right Presumed to have Existed "From Time Immemorial"

At common law an easement could be acquired by prescription if it was shown that it had been enjoyed from time immemorial, which is taken by the common law to mean AD 1189. Long usage is thus treated as giving rise to a presumption that the right claimed has been enjoyed from time immemorial.[187] However this presumption can be rebutted by the owner of the allegedly servient land demonstrating that this was not in fact the case, for example if

15–048

---

[181] *Neaverson v Peterborough RDC* [1902] 1 Ch. 557.
[182] *Cargill v Gotts* [1981] 1 W.L.R. 441; *Hanning v Top Deck Travel Group Ltd* (1993) 68 P. & C.R. 14.
[183] *Gayford v Moffatt* (1868) 4 Ch. App. 133; *Kilgour v Gaddes* [1904] 1 K.B. 457.
[184] *Wheaton v Maple & Co* [1893] 3 Ch. 48; *Pugh v Savage* [1970] 2 Q.B. 373.
[185] *Palk v Shinner* (1852) 18 Q.B. 568.
[186] *Daniel v North* (1809) 11 East 372; *Roberts v James* (1903) 89 L.T. 282 (life tenancy).
[187] *Bryant v Foot* (1867) L.R. 2 Q.B. 161.

the right could not have been enjoyed before that date[188] or because the land has been in common ownership at some point since 1189.

(ii)   Right Presumed to have been Granted by a "Lost Modern Grant"

15–049   Since the owner of the allegedly servient land will often be able to demonstrate that a claimed easement could not have existed since 1189 the courts introduced the doctrine of a "lost modern grant", under which evidence of 20 years' use generates a fiction that the right claimed was expressly granted after 1189 but that the grant has since been lost.[189] This fiction is irrebuttable, so that 20 years' use will give rise to a legal easement even if it can be shown that no grant was ever made,[190] although there will be no easement if it can be shown that such a grant could never have been made. An easement may be acquired by prescription under the doctrine of a lost modern grant even on the basis of a past period of 20 years' use which has since been interrupted or discontinued.[191]

(iii)   Prescription Operating by Statute

15–050   In addition to acquisition of easements by prescription on the basis of use since time immemorial and lost modern grant, the Prescription Act 1832 provides an alternative means of establishing entitlement to an easement by long use. In the case of rights other than the right to light, s.2 has the effect that use as of right for 20 uninterrupted[192] years immediately preceding an action disputing the existence of the right[193] cannot be defeated by mere evidence that use in fact began after time immemorial. However, 20 years' use will be ineffective to create such an easement if it can be shown that it was enjoyed by the agreement or consent of the owner of the servient land, even if merely oral.[194] Uninterrupted user for a 40-year period will render a right "absolute and indefeasible" even if it was enjoyed with the consent or agreement of the servient owner, unless that agreement or consent was given in writing.[195] By s.4 of the Act no physical obstruction of a right will be regarded as having interrupted use unless the claimant submitted or acquiesced in the obstruction for a year after he had notice of it and of the person responsible for it.[196] In relation to rights of light, s.3 provides that 20 years' uninterrupted use is "deemed absolute and indefeasible" unless it was enjoyed by written consent or agreement.

---

[188] *Hulbert v Dale* [1909] 2 Ch. 570.
[189] See *Dalton v Angus & Co* (1881) 6 App. Cas. 740.
[190] *Tehidy Minerals Ltd v Norman* [1971] 2 Q.B. 528.
[191] *Mills v Silver* [1991] Ch. 271; The doctrine of lost modern grant was considered in *Odey v Barber* [2008] 2 W.L.R. 618; [2006] EWHC 3109.
[192] See *Hyman v van den Bergh* [1907] 2 Ch. 516.
[193] *Reilly v Orange* [1955] 2 Q.B. 112.
[194] The 20-year prescription period under the 1832 Act appears to do little more than to re-state the doctrine of lost modern grant.
[195] See *Gardner v Hodgson's Kingston Brewery Co Ltd* [1903] A.C. 229.
[196] See *Davies v Du Paver* [1953] 1 Q.B. 184; *Dance v Triplow* (1991) 63 P. & C.R. 1.

(c) *Reform of Prescription*

As has been seen above, the acquisition of easements and profits by prescription is extremely   **15–051**
complex, with three separate means of prescription recognised by the common law and statute.
The role of prescription was examined by the Law Reform Committee in 1966, which recommended that it be abolished altogether for easements and profits.[197] In 1998 the Law Commission
recommended that the law be modified so as to accommodate the changes which will result from
the introduction of electronic conveyancing.[198] The Law Commission has recently recommended
a complete revision of the law of prescription, as part of its extensive review of the law of easements, covenants and profits à prendre.[199] This will be discussed below at paragraph 15 096
onwards.

7. Creation of Easements by Estoppel

Even where there is no grant, or contract for the grant, of an easement an owner of land will be   **15–052**
entitled to such a right if the owner of the servient tenement is estopped from denying that he
enjoys it. This is an application of the general doctrine of proprietary estoppel, examined in detail
in Chapter 19 below, which allows the court to grant a proprietary right as a remedy where an
"estoppel equity" has been raised. In order to establish an equity which requires satisfaction by
the court granting an easement the owner of the allegedly dominant land must show that there
was a representation or assurance by the owner of the servient land that he would be entitled to
exercise an easement, and that he has acted to his detriment on the basis of that assurance. For
example in *Ward v Kirkland*[200] the plaintiff owner of a cottage was granted permission by the
owners of neighbouring land to lay drains across her land, connected to a sceptic tank. The drains
were installed at the plaintiff's expense. The defendant subsequently claimed the right to terminate any licence enjoyed by the plaintiff to use the drains and demanded their removal. Ungoed-
Thomas J. held that since the defendant had granted permission for the drains to be installed for
an indefinite period and the plaintiff had incurred expenditure on the basis of that permission, an
easement to use the drains had arisen on the grounds of estoppel. In *Sweet v Sommer*[201] the Court
of Appeal held that an express grant, which as it turned out was invalid, gave rise to an easement
by proprietary estoppel as the owners of the purported servient tenement sat by and let the owners of the dominant tenement build on the land and exercise the right of way whilst all parties
assumed the right to exist. In *Crabb v Arun DC*[202] the plaintiff owned land which he intended
to sell in two plots. To achieve this it was necessary to establish a right of way onto a road
for one of the intended plots, and the defendants agreed in principle that there should be
such a right of way across the adjoining land owned by them. The defendants then fenced the

---

[197] 14th Report, Cmnd. 3100 (1966).
[198] Law Com. No.254, *Land Registration for the Twenty-First Century* (1998) paras 10.90–10.94.
[199] Consultation Paper "Easements, Covenants and Profits à Prendre's Law Com No 186 (2008).
[200] [1967] Ch. 194.
[201] [2005] EWCA Civ 227; Westlaw 2005 WL 513419, [2005] Conv. 545.
[202] [1976] Ch. 179. See also *ER Ives Investment Ltd v High* [1967] 2 Q.B. 379.

boundary of their land, leaving a gate at the agreed point of access. The plaintiff sold part of his land and retained the part which was intended to enjoy the right of way. The defendants subsequently removed the gate and fenced the gap, refusing to allow the plaintiff access. The Court of Appeal held that there was sufficient assurance to the plaintiff that he would be able to enjoy access, and that since he had acted to his detriment by selling part of his land without reserving a right of way over in his favour to raise an estoppel which was satisfied by the grant of an easement. Lord Denning M.R. explained:

> "The defendants actually put up the gates at point B at considerable expense. That certainly led the plaintiff to believe that he should have the right of access through point B without more ado . . . The defendants knew that the plaintiff intended to sell the two portions separately and that he would need an access point at point B as well as point A. Seeing that they knew of his intention—and they did nothing to disabuse him but rather confirmed it by erecting gates at point B—it was their conduct which led him to act as he did: and this raises an equity in his favour against them. In the circumstances it seems to me inequitable that the council should insist on their strict title as they did: and to take the high-handed action of pulling down the gates without a word of warning; and to demand of the plaintiff £30,000 as the price for the easement."[203]

Once an estoppel equity has been established, it is a matter for the court to award the appropriate remedy to "satisfy" it. In cases where the equity is established because of the denial of a right in the character of an easement the court will generally award the easement denied as the appropriate satisfaction. Although the estoppel right is described as an "equity" the court is perfectly capable of awarding a legal easement to the claimant.

8. Equitable Easements

15–053 Equitable easements may arise either where the nature of the right granted does not meet the requirements of a legal easement because it is not granted for a period equivalent to an estate in fee simple absolute in possession or a term of years absolute, or where the appropriate formalities have not been observed but there is a specifically enforceable contract for the grant of the easement.

(a) *Easements Granted by Deed which Fail to Meet the Requirements for Legal Status*

15–054 As has been noted, the mere fact that an easement has been granted or reserved by deed is not of itself conclusive of legal status. Section 1(2)(a) of the Law of Property Act 1925 provides for the circumstances in which an easement is capable of existing or being created at law:

---

[203] [1976] Ch. 179 at 189.

"An easement, right or privilege in or over land for an interest equivalent to an estate in fee simple absolute in possession or a term of years absolute."

This means that the easement must be granted either in perpetuity, or for a defined and specific period of time. Thus a right of way granted by Hamish to Isabel "for life" by deed would only be capable of creating an equitable easement. However, an equitable easement will only arise if the grant or reservation was made for valuable consideration.[204]

(b)   *A Contract to Create an Easement*

Since equity treats as done that which ought to be done, a specifically enforceable contract to grant an easement will give rise to an equitable right even though the requisite formalities for a legal easement have not been satisfied. This principle will clearly operate in relation to express grants and reservations, but also extends to situations where an easement is implied under the rule in *Wheeldon v Burrows*,[205] so that where an owner of land enters into a contract to convey part, any quasi-easements which he enjoyed continuously and apparently over the land will be implied into the contract.[206] Contracts entered into before September 27, 1989 are governed by the formalities provisions of the Law of Property Act 1925, s.40. Under these provisions a purely oral contract for the creation of an easement would be effective to generate an equitable easement if it was accompanied by part performance on the part of the person enjoying the benefit of the easement.[207] However contracts entered after September 27, 1989 contracts will only be effective to create an equitable easement if they fulfil the more stringent formalities requirements of s.2 of the Law of Property (Miscellaneous Provisions) Act 1989, which requires that they be made in writing, incorporating all the terms of the contract, signed by or on behalf of the parties. Thus a purely oral contract is incapable of creating an equitable easement, even if there is part performance, and will be construed as the grant of a mere licence over the property of the grantor.[208]

15–055

9.   Easements: "Reform and Rationalisation"

The Law Commission is currently undertaking "[a] project to examine easements, covenants and similar land law rights with a view to their reform and rationalisation". *http://www. lawcom.gov.uk/easements.htm.* In spring 2008 it published a Consultation Paper "praisionally proposing wide-ranging reform of the law governing easements, covenants and profits à prendre. The Commission's work in this area builds upon its joint work with the Land Registry which culminated in the Land Registration Act 2002" http://www.lawcom.gov.uk/ easements.htm. The Law Commissions proposals will be considered below at 15–096.

15–056

---

[204] *May v Belleville* [1905] 2 Ch. 605.
[205] (1879) 13 Ch.D. 31.
[206] *Borman v Griffith* [1930] 1 Ch. 493; *Horn v Hiscock* (1972) 223 E.G. 1437.
[207] *McManus v Cooke* (1887) 35 Ch.D. 681.
[208] *Wood v Leadbitter* (1845) 13 M. & W. 838.

SCOPE OF ENTITLEMENT CONFERRED BY AN EASEMENT

1. Scope of Entitlement to Rights of Way

15–057   The owner of the dominant tenement needs to know more than that he has an easement. He needs to know its extent. For instance, if David has a right of way over Goliath's field, does this permit him to cross only on foot, or may he travel with a wheelbarrow or in a car or lorry? Obviously in many cases the extent of the easement will be determined by the terms of the grant or reservation. Any use in excess of the entitlement will amount to a trespass. The means by which the scope of a right of way is determined will vary according to the way in which it was created.

(a) *Expressly Created Rights of Way*

15–058   Where a right of way has been expressly granted or reserved the scope of the easement will be determined by construction of the terms used in the deed creating it. The following principles are observed in regard to the interpretation of the scope of an expressly granted right of way:

(i)   The Grant should be Construed against the Grantor

15–059   In *Williams v James* Willes J. stated that the language of an express grant of an easement should be construed against the grantor:

> "In the case of a grant the language of the instrument can be referred to, and it is of course for the court to construe that language; and in the absence of any clear indication of the intention of the parties, the maxim that a grant must be construed most strongly against the grantor must apply."[209]

(ii) Consideration of the Physical Circumstances of the Land at the Date of the Grant

15–060   The precise scope of an expressly granted easement will also be construed in the light of the nature of the land over which it was granted.[210] Sir John Pennycuick stated in *St Edmundsbury and Ipswich Diocesan Board of Finance v Clarke*:

> "It is no doubt true that in order to construe an instrument one looks first at the instrument and no doubt one may form a preliminary impression upon such inspection. But it is not until one has considered the instrument and the surrounding circumstances in conjunction

---

[209] (1867) L.R. 2 C.P. 577, 581.
[210] See *Todrick v Western National Omnibus Co Ltd* [1934] Ch. 190; *Keefe v Amor* [1965] 1 K.B. 334.

that one concludes the process of construction. Of course one may have words so unambiguous that no surrounding circumstances could affect their construction."[211]

This principle was applied by the Court of Appeal in *White v Richards*,[212] where part of a plot of agricultural land was conveyed with an express reservation of a right of way over a designated track to "pass and repass on foot with or without motor vehicles . . . so far as . . . may be necessary for the use and enjoyment of the retained land". It was held that the scope of this easement should be construed in the light of the physical nature of the track over which it was enjoyed, so that since it was only eight feet ten inches wide and mainly dirt it could only be exercised by vehicles with a wheelbase of less than eight feet and width of less than nine, and with a laden weight of less than 10 tons. Use by 38-ton lorries, excavators and other heavy machinery was therefore excessive and damages for trespass were awarded. However, where a specific right has been expressly granted the courts will not allow the physical circumstances of the land to limit its scope. In *Keefe v Amor*[213] a right of way was granted over a strip of land 20 feet wide which at the time of the grant had an entrance some four feet six inches wide. The Court of Appeal held that there was no excessive user when the owner of the dominant land widened the entrance and a track over the land to seven feet six inches. Russell L.J. stated:

"... if the true conclusion is that the right granted embraces potentially the whole of the strip, the fact that the physical characteristics of the site (for example walls) make the exercise of the right at the time of the grant impossible over any but a limited route will not contradict or limit the scope of the grant . . . and . . . where the form of the grant shows perfectly clearly the quality of the right, and that it extends to every part of the whole area, topographical circumstances could not properly be regarded as restricting it."

(iii) Grant of a More Onerous Easement will Include a Grant of the Less Onerous Right

Where an easement has been expressly granted or reserved it will be held to include the right to exercise less onerous uses falling within its scope, since the grant of the greater is deemed to include the lesser.[214] Therefore in *White v Richards*[215] the grant of a right to "pass or repass on foot with or without motor vehicles" was also held to include the right to walk dogs and to lead a horse on foot, and to ride a pedal cycle on the grounds that it clearly included the greater right to ride a motor cycle which is a form of motor vehicle. Since a right to drive a motor vehicle includes the right to drive a horse-drawn carriage or cart,[216] it was also held to include the right to lead cows and other animals on foot, although not to drive them.

15–061

---

[211] [1975] 1 W.L.R. 468, affirming *Cannon v Villiers* (1878) 8 Ch.D. 415.
[212] (1994) 68 P. & C.R. 105.
[213] [1965] 1 Q.B. 334.
[214] *British Railways Board v Glass* [1965] Ch. 538.
[215] (1994) 68 P. & C.R. 105.
[216] *Ballard v Dyson* (1808) 1 Taunt. 279.

(iv) Subsequent Change of use of Dominant Land

15–062   The scope of an expressly granted or reserved easement is not automatically limited by the use to which the dominant tenement was put at the date that the easement was granted. In *White v Grand Hotel, Eastbourne Ltd*[217] a right of way benefiting the dominant land was expressly granted whilst it was a private dwelling-house. It was subsequently converted into a hotel, with the consequence that it was more heavily used since it led to a garage for the guests. The Court of Appeal held that as there was no limitation on the scope of the easement in the words of the grant it was a general right and not limited to purely domestic use. However, a change of use may mean that even an authorised easement is used excessively.[218] In *Rosling v Pinnegar*[219] a right of way benefiting a house was granted in 1923. In 1982 the house, which enjoyed the right of way along with the 25 residents of a hamlet, was restored and opened to the public, leading to an increased use. The Court of Appeal held that since the grant was "for all purposes" the use by visitors was not unauthorised, but that the quantity of visitors interfered unreasonably with the rights of those others entitled to use it, and was thus excessive.

(v) Enlargement of the Dominant Tenement

15–063   Where an easement has been expressly granted only for the benefit of specific land, the easement will not benefit additional land if the dominant tenement is subsequently enlarged. In *Peacock v Custins*[220] a right of way had been granted for the benefit of a 15-acre parcel of farmland (the red land) in a conveyance which stated that the right was to be "at all times and for all purposes in connection with the use and enjoyment of the property hereby conveyed". The owner of the red land subsequently purchased an adjacent 10-acre parcel of land (the blue land) and made use of the right of way for the purpose of farming the blue land. The Court of Appeal held that, even though the use of the right of way for the benefit of the blue land would not be excessive, the right of way did not extend for the benefit of the blue land. The task of the court was simply to declare the scope of the grant, "having regard to its purpose and the identity of the dominant tenement." The terms of the grant clearly restricted the use of the right of way to the red land. Schiemann L.J. stated the principles by which the Court would operate:

> "The authorities indicate that the burden on the owner of the servient tenement is not to be increased without his consent. But burden in this context does not refer to the number of journeys or the weight of the vehicles. Any use of the way is, in contemplation of law, a burden and one must ask whether the grantor agreed to the grantee making use of the way for that purpose."[221]

However an easement will be regarded as benefiting additional land where the dominant tenement has been enlarged, if the use for the benefit of the additional land can be regarded as

---

[217] [1913] 1 Ch. 113.
[218] See *Jelbert v Davis* [1968] 1 W.L.R. 589.
[219] [1987] 54 P. & C.R. 124.
[220] [2001] 2 All E.R. 827.
[221] [2001] 2 All E.R. 827 at 836.

"ancillary" to the use of the original dominant tenement. In *Peacock v Custins* the use of the right of way for the benefit of the blue land could not be regarded as purely ancillary to the use of the red land. However in *Massey v Boulden*[222] the Court of Appeal held that an easement which had been acquired initially for the benefit of a house continued to benefit the tenement when it was enlarged by the addition of two rooms from an adjoining property, because the use for the benefit of the two rooms could only sensibly be described as ancillary to its use for the original dominant tenement.

(b) *Implied Rights of Way*

Where a right of way has not been expressly granted or reserved, but is found to have been implied into a conveyance or transfer of land, the scope of the right is limited to the use which was contemplated at the date of the conveyance or transfer, which will often be determined by the actual use which was occurring at that date. In *Milner's Safe Company Ltd v Great Northern and City Railway Co*[223] Kekewich J. held that an implied right of way included business use because the owner conveying the land had been accustomed to using it to load and unload vans, but that it did not extend to allowing a railway company which now owned the land to use it as the main thoroughfare to and from their station. In *Corporation of London v Riggs*[224] Lord Jessel M.R. held that an impliedly reserved right of way to agricultural land must be limited to use for agricultural purposes, and that it did not extend to use which was necessary if the land was to be used for building purposes. Use beyond that exercised at the date of the conveyance will not be excessive if clearly contemplated by the parties. In *Stafford v Lee*[225] an easement of necessity benefiting woodland was held to include access to a house, since the conveyance indicated that it was anticipated that a residential dwelling would be constructed.

15–064

(c) *Right of Way Acquired by Prescription*

Where a right of way is acquired by prescription the scope of entitlement is limited to the user which acquired the easement. This follows from the fact that there is no other evidence than that of the user which obtained the right from which to determine its scope.[226] In consequence the scope of the entitlement acquired by prescription can only be determined by that user. As Mellish L.J. stated in *United Land Co v Great Eastern Railway Co*:

15–065

> "Where a right of way is claimed by user, then, no doubt, according to the authorities, the purpose for which the way may be used is limited by the user; for we must judge from the way in which it has been used what the purposes were for which the party claiming has gained the right."[227]

---

[222] [2002] EWCA Civ 1634; [2002] 2 All E.R. 87.
[223] [1907] 1 Ch. 208.
[224] (1880) 12 Ch.D. 798.
[225] (1965) P. & C.R. 172.
[226] See *Williams v James* (1867) L.R. 2 C.P. 577 at 581.
[227] (1875) 10 Ch. App 586 at 590.

A mere increase in the extent of use of a right acquired by prescription will not be excessive.[228] In *British Railways Board v Glass*[229] a right of way to a caravan park was acquired by prescription. The Court of Appeal held that an increase from six caravans to 30 was not excessive use. In *Woodhouse & Co Ltd v Kirkland Ltd*[230] Plowman J. held that there was no excessive user where a right of way used by a plumbers' merchant and their customers and suppliers was used to a greater extent when the owners of the servient land left a gate to the premises open for a longer period. However, user of a different kind, rather than mere increase in user, will be excessive. In *Williams v James*[231] it was held that a prescriptive right to carry agricultural produce to a farm did not extend to a right to carry those items necessary when the farm was converted into a factory.

2. Scope of Entitlement to Rights to Light

(a) *Restricted to Buildings*

15–066   Rights to light, which are almost exclusively obtained by prescription, are not capable of existing in the abstract, but rather only in relation to buildings and their "windows or apertures constructed for the purpose of admitting light".[232] For this reason in *Levet v Gas Light and Coke Co*[233] it was held that there could be no right to light through a door.

(b) *Restricted to Sufficient Light for Comfortable Enjoyment and Use*

15–067   Where a right to light has been acquired by prescription it does not entitle the owner of the dominant land to an absolute right to the amount of light he has been accustomed to enjoy. In *Colls v Home and Colonial Stores* Lord Lindley stated the rule that:

> ". . . generally speaking an owner of ancient lights is entitled to sufficient light according to the ordinary notions of mankind for the comfortable use and enjoyment of his house as a dwelling house, if it is a dwelling house, or for the beneficial use and occupation of the house if it is a warehouse, a shop, or other place of business."[234]

This principle was applied by Millet J. in *Carr-Saunders v Dick McNeil Associates*[235] where the light to the second floor of a building was reduced when the owners of the servient tenement added two storeys to their building. He held that the appropriate inquiry was not as to the extent

---

[228] See *Giles v County Building Constructors (Hertford) Ltd* (1971) 22 P. & C.R. 978; *Cargill v Gotts* [1981] 1 W.L.R. 441.
[229] [1965] Ch. 538.
[230] [1970] 1 W.L.R. 1185.
[231] (1867) L.R. 2 C.P. 577.
[232] *Levet v Gas Light and Coke Co* [1919] 1 Ch. 24 at 27, per Peterson J.
[233] [1919] 1 Ch. 24.
[234] [1904] A.C. 179. at 208, applying *City of London Brewery v Tennant* (1873–74) L.R. 9 Ch. 212.
[235] [1986] 1 W.L.R. 922.

of the reduction in light but as to the amount of light left, and whether this was reasonable not merely for the present use but also for other potential uses to which the dominant owner might reasonably be expected to put the premises in the future. He held that there had been actionable interference since it would mean that the space on the second floor could no longer be subdivided conveniently so that the subdivided areas would each receive an adequate amount of light.[236]

3. Interference with Exercise of Easements by the Owner of the Servient Land

Any wrongful interference by the servient owner with the exercise of an easement will be actionable by the dominant owner in nuisance. Interference per se is not actionable, but only such interference as substantially affects the use of the easement. The principles were set out by Scott J. in *Celsteel v Alton House Holdings Ltd*:

15–068

> "There emerge . . . two criteria relevant to the question whether a particular interference with a right of way is actionable. The interference will be actionable if it is substantial. And it will not be substantial if it does not interfere with the reasonable use of the right of way."[237]

Although the case concerned interference with a right of way the principles are more generally applicable. It has already been noted how in the case of rights to light, mere reduction in the quantity of light is not actionable, but only such a reduction as leaves too little light for the reasonable enjoyment of the premises. In *Keefe v Amor* Russell L.J. pointed out that what constitutes substantial interference will vary with the use to which the dominant tenement is put, so that an actionable interference will be caused by:

> "such obstacles as impede the user of the strip for such exercise of the right granted as from time to time is reasonably required by the dominant tenement."[238]

In assessing whether an interference is reasonable, the Court of Appeal indicated in *Saint v Jenner* that the entitlement of other users of the right of way must be considered. Stamp L.J. stated:

> ". . . it is to be observed that in deciding what is a substantial interference with the dominant owner's reasonable use of a right of way, all the circumstances must be considered, including the rights of other persons entitled to use the way."[239]

On this basis measures to reduce the speed of cars were not unreasonable when the right of way was also used by horses.

---

[236] In *Midtown Ltd v City of London Real Property Co Ltd* [2005] EWHC 33 it was held that there was interference with a right to light despite the reliance in office buildings on unnatural light; 2005 WL 62265 (Ch D) Westlaw document.
[237] [1985] 1 W.L.R. 204 at 217.
[238] [1965] 1 Q.B. 334.
[239] [1973] Ch. 275 at 279.

Most cases have concerned some kind of obstruction of rights of way. In *Clifford v Hoare*[240] the owner of the servient tenement erected a building which encroached two feet into a roadway 40 feet wide. It was held that this did not amount to an actionable interference with a right of way over the road because the encroachment was trivial and would not interfere with reasonable use and enjoyment of it. In *Petty v Parsons*[241] the Court of Appeal considered that the erection of a gate by the servient owner across the right of way would not be an actionable interference if the gate was kept open during business hours. In *Celsteel v Alton House Holdings Ltd*[242] Scott L.J. held that the narrowing of a driveway leading to garages would not be actionable if the only effect was that relatively easy manoeuvring would be required to drive in and out. In *Celsteel v Alton House Holdings Ltd* the occupiers of the servient land were proposing to build a car wash which would have the effect of reducing the width of a right of way over a driveway leading to garages from nine metres to four metres. Scott J. held that since this was hardly a trivial encroachment, and it was reasonable for the driveway to be used by large commercial vans and lorries, the interference would be substantial and therefore actionable. In *Saint v Jenner*[243] the owner of the servient tenement had surfaced a cart track over which the plaintiff enjoyed a right of way, and built speed-humps to reduce the speed of cars using the track, which was also used by horse-riders. The Court of Appeal held that this alone was not an actionable interference, but that large pot holes which had subsequently developed by the humps did constitute substantial interference. In *Mulvaney v Gough*[244] the same principles were applied outside of the context of a right of way. The case concerned an easement to use land behind a row of cottages as a communal garden. The owner of the dominant tenement sought to gravel part of the land so as to create a vehicular access. The Court of Appeal held that this would not necessarily constitute an interference with the easement to use the land as a whole as a communal garden, and that it would be matter for consideration on all the facts whether the proposal would substantially interfere with the claimant's rights.

Since wrongful interference constitutes the tort of nuisance the appropriate remedies are either an injunction to remove or prevent such interference, and damages to compensate for any loss that has occurred. The court has jurisdiction to award damages in lieu of an injunction. The case of *Shelfer v City of London Electric Lighting Co*[245] laid down a "good working rule" to determine whether the court should award damages instead:

> "(1) If the injury to the plaintiff's legal rights is small; (2) and is one which is capable of being estimated in money; (3) and is one which can be adequately compensated by a small money payment; (4) and the case is one in which it would be oppressive to the defendant to grant an injunction."[246]

In *Regan v Paul Properties Ltd*[247] the Court of Appeal applied the *Shelfer* criteria to interference with a right to light, where nearby land was developed and took light away from the

---

[240] (1874) L.R. C.P. 362.
[241] [1914] 2 Ch. 653.
[242] [1985] 1 W.L.R. 204 at 218.
[243] [1985] 1 W.L.R. 204 at 218.
[244] [2002] EWCA Civ 1078; [2003] 4 All E.R. 83.
[245] [1895] 1 Ch 287.
[246] [1895] 1 Ch. 287: Pearce and Stevens, "The Law of Trusts and Equitable Obligations" (4th edn, 2006), p.48.
[247] [2006] EWCA Civ 1391; [2007] Ch 135.

claimant's living room. Monetary compensation was not adequate in this case and the invasion of the right was significant. Thus, although an injunction would have serious consequences for a developer, who had completed a considerable amount of the construction, to grant an injunction requiring demolition of the construction was the proper course of action. Oppression was not the only criteria for the court to consider.[248]

EXTINGUISHMENT AND VARIATION OF EASEMENTS

1. Release

The owner of the dominant land is entitled to release the servient land from the burden of the easement which he is entitled to exercise over it. Once an easement has been released it cannot revive in his favour. Release is therefore similar to the surrender of a leasehold term. The dominant owner can grant a release either expressly or by implication from his conduct.

15–069

(a) *Express Release*

The dominant owner can only expressly release an easement at law by means of a deed.[249] However, even where no deed has been executed equity will refuse to allow an owner of the previously dominant land to assert his strict entitlement to an easement if he has released it informally and it would be inequitable to allow him to continue to use the easement, generally because he has acquiesced in some action taken by the servient owner in the belief that the easement had been released. For example in *Waterlow v Bacon*[250] the dominant owner of land entitled to a right to light entered into an agreement with the servient owner that he was to be allowed to increase the height of his wall if he built new and larger skylights in return. Having built the wall it considered that it would be inequitable for the dominant owner to complain of interference with his easement.

15–070

(b) *Implied Release*

If the dominant owner abandons his easement he will be taken to have impliedly released it so that it no longer burdens the servient land. The mere fact that the dominant owner has not used the easement is not conclusive of abandonment.[251] Buckley L.J. spelt out what was required in *Tehidy Minerals v Norman*:

15–071

---

[248] P. Chyneweth, [2007] Conv. 175.
[249] *Lovell v Smith* (1857) 3 C.B.N.S. 120.
[250] (1866) L.R. 2 Eq. 514.
[251] *Swan v Sinclair* [1924] 1 Ch. 254; *Williams v Sandy Lane (Chester) Ltd* [2007] P. & C.R. 27, Court of Appeal.

"Abandonment of an easement or of a profit can only, we think, be treated as having taken place where the person entitled to it has demonstrated a fixed intention never at any time thereafter to assert the right himself or to attempt to transmit it to anyone else."[252]

For this reason the Court of Appeal held that the fact that owners of land entitled to a prescriptive profit to graze on a down had allowed an association of commoners to control the management of the grazing was not an abandonment of their individual rights. Buckley L.J. stated that, although they had submitted to the control of the association for advantages of fencing and maintenance, it did not follow that "if at some time in the future the arrangement should come to an end, the commoners might not wish to reassert their common rights". In *Benn v Hardinge*[253] the Court of Appeal held that even a period of 175 years' non-user was ineffective to establish abandonment when it had not been used because an alternative had been available. In *Williams v Sandy Lane (Chester) Ltd*[254] the Court of Appeal held that a right of way had not been abandoned even where works had been carried out making continued use difficult. Use was not impossible. Further, the fencing that was obstructing the right of way was insubstantial and could be removed at little expense.

In contrast, an abandonment was held to have taken place in *Swan v Sinclair*[255] where a right of way at the back of houses had not been used for 38 years and the dominant owner had acquiesced in physical alterations in the land which would prevent its use as a right of way. Similarly, in *Moore v Rawson*[256] the owner of the dominant tenement was held to have abandoned his right to light when he demolished a building with windows and rebuilt a stables with no windows. The owner of the previously servient tenement then built a building which would have interfered with the light, but it was held that the dominant owner could not reassert his entitlement when three years later he made a window in the stable.

2. Unification of Title and Possession

15–072 The idea that an owner of one piece of land enjoys rights over land owned by someone else is the very essence of an easement. Therefore if ownership of the dominant and servient land is united in the same person any easements will cease to exist, since the owner will be entitled to exercise whatever rights he wishes over his own land. In effect such easements as existed prior to unification become mere quasi-easements. Such unification will only occur if a single owner acquires the freehold title to both the dominant and servient land. If the dominant owner acquires a leasehold interest in the servient land any easements will merely be suspended until the lease terminates or is assigned.[257] Where unification has occurred a subsequent re-division of the land will not revive the pre-existing easements, although any quasi-easements exercised by the unitary owner may be recreated by the rule in *Wheeldon v Burrows*.[258]

---

[252] [1971] 2 Q.B. 528 at 553; The courts will not readily infer an intention to abandon, see *CDC2020 Plc v Ferreira* [2005] 2 P. & C.R. DG 15, applying *Gotobed v Pridmore* (1971) 115 S.J. 78; Landels [2005] Conv. 481.
[253] (1993) 66 P. & C.R. 246.
[254] [2007] P. & C.R. 27.
[255] [1924] 1 Ch. 254.
[256] (1824) 3 B. & C. 332.
[257] *Thomas v Thomas* (1835) 2 Cr.M. & R. 34; *Simper v Foley* (1862) 2 Johns & H. 555.
[258] (1879) 12 Ch.D. 31.

3. Easement Rendered Obsolete

In *Huckvale v Aegean Hotels Ltd*[259] the Court of Appeal accepted the possibility that an **15–073** easement might be extinguished by frustration if it were rendered obsolete by changes in circumstances. Slade L.J. stated:

> "I would ... be prepared to accept in principle that ... circumstances might have changed so drastically since the date of the original grant of an easement (for example by supervening illegality) that it would offend common sense and reality for the court to hold that an easement still subsisted. Nevertheless, I think the court could properly so hold only in a very clear case ... [I]n the absence of evidence or proof of abandonment, the court should be slow to hold that an easement has been extinguished by frustration, unless the evidence shows clearly that because of a change in circumstances since the date of the original grant there is no practical possibility of its ever again benefiting the dominant tenement in the manner contemplated by that grant."[260]

In the event, however, it was held that a right of way was not rendered completely obsolete. Although it was presently of very limited practical use there was no certainty that it might not benefit the dominant land again in the future, especially if the ownership of the servient tenement changed. In *Jones v Cleanthi*[261] the Court of Appeal held that an easement in a lease had not been extinguished when the landlord, under a statutory obligation, erected a wall which blocked the easement. The statutory obligation might not always exist.

4. Variation of Easements

There is no right at common law to vary an easement without the agreement of both the dominant and servient owners. In *Greenwich Healthcare NHS Trust v London and Quadrant Housing Trust*[262] the plaintiff wished to develop a site as a hospital. This involved the realignment of a private right of way. The dominant owners entitled to the easement had been informed of the proposals and had raised no objection, but neither had they given any positive consent. Lightman J. held that, in the absence of any express or implied power in the grant of the easement, the servient owner had no right to realign the easement without the approval of the dominant owner. This was the case even though the new route was an improvement on the old, both for reasons of capacity and of safety. However, he was able to find a way of permitting the development to go ahead. In view of the ameliorating aspect of the changes, the absence of any objection from the dominant owners, and the importance of the hospital development, he was prepared to grant a declaration that no injunction would be granted in respect of the easement if the development went ahead. Any liability of the plaintiff would therefore sound only in damages. He did not find it necessary to decide whether the realignment constituted an actionable **15–074**

[259] (1989) 58 P. & C.R. 163.
[260] (1989) 58 P. & C.R. 163 at 173–174.
[261] [2007] 3 All E.R. 841.
[262] [1998] 3 All E.R. 437.

interference with the easement, although he doubted whether there would be any liability in damages in such a case as this. He said that the dominant owner would be entitled to use the new route,[263] and that, unless the loss of the property right to the easement over the original route could be considered a loss, "there is something to be said for the approach that the test [as to whether there has been an actionable interference] should be whether the dominant owner 'has really lost anything' by the alteration".[264]

PROFITS À PRENDRE

1. Nature of Profits

(a) *A Right to Appropriate from Land*

15–075   As has been noted above, a profit à prendre entitles a person not merely to exercise some limited right of user over the servient land it burdens, but to sever and appropriate some part of the natural produce from that land. For example, the holder of the profit might be entitled to graze his cattle on the servient land or enjoy the exclusive right to kill game.

(b) *No Requirement of a Dominant Tenement*

15–076   Whereas an easement will exist only if there is a dominant tenement, a profit à prendre can be granted over the servient land to a person even if he does not own any dominant tenement. The right to profit is enjoyed by him personally, not qua owner of some specific land. Profits are therefore said to be capable of existing in gross.[265]

(c) *Types of Profit*

15–077   A profit à prendre is described as "several" where it entitles the holder to an exclusive right to appropriate the subject of the profit from the servient land. A profit is described as "in common" where the entitlement to appropriate from the servient land is enjoyed by a number of people together, which group may include the servient owner himself.

(d) *Examples of Profits*

15–078   There are a number of well-recognised profits. The common of pasture entitles the commoners to graze their cattle on the servient common land. Where held in gross there was no limit

---

[263] Citing *Selby v Nettlefold* (1873) L.R. 9 Ch. App. 111.
[264] [1998] 3 All E.R. 437 at 443.
[265] *Lord Chesterfield v Harris* [1908] 2 Ch. 397 at 421.

to the number of cattle which could be grazed under such a common, but at common law a common of pasture appurtenant to land was restricted to the right to graze as many cattle as the dominant tenement could support through the winter,[266] a limitation removed by the Commons Registration Act 1965. The common of turbary entitles the commoners to cut such turf or peat as they need for fuel for heating and cooking. It must be appurtenant to a house.[267] The profit of piscary entitles the holders to take fish from inland waters of the servient land, but if appurtenant to land is limited to a right to take as many fish as are needed for the family of the owner of the dominant tenement,[268] and not to take fish for sale. A right to fish can be enjoyed as a several profit, thus excluding the owner of the land from fishing himself. The profit of estovers entitles the dominant owner to take wood, for use as fuel or for making or repairing furniture, fencing and equipment. It does not extend to the right to take wood for sale.

(e) Interpretation of Profits

The scope and extent of a profit is a question of construction of the terms of the grant.[269] In *Mitchell v Potter* a conveyance provided for the claimants' abstraction of water from an artificial watercourse "to draw . . . . such an amount of water as may be reasonably required for domestic and farm purposes".[270] The defendants, who also drew from the supply, argued that this should be interpreted as meaning that the water should be shared, otherwise, "they [could not] know what the residue of the water [was] at any particular time, and if they abstract water they may inevitably run the risk of facing a claim for an infringement of the claimant's right".[271] Jonathan Parker L.J. held that despite these practical difficulties, the question was one of pure construction.

15–079

> "In my judgment, that provision gives the claimant a clear right, as against the defendants (but subject always, of course, to the sufficiency of the supply of water to the reservoir from the spring), to abstract as much water from the reservoir as is reasonably required for his domestic and farm purposes."[272]

2. Acquisition of Profits

Profits may generally be acquired in the same ways as easements. These have been examined in detail above, and attention will be focused on areas of difference.

15–080

---

[266] *Robertson v Hartropp* (1889) 43 Ch.D. 484.
[267] *Att-Gen v Reynolds* [1911] 2 K.B. 888; *Warrick v Queen's College, Oxford* (1871) 6 Ch. App 716.
[268] *Lord Chesterfield v Harris* [1908] 2 Ch. 397.
[269] *Beauchamp v Frome Rural DC* [1938] 1 All ER 595; *Mitchell v Potter* [2005] EWCA Civ 88. Concerning grants of wates rights but none the less providing a useful indicator of the interpretation of profits.
[270] [2005] EWCA Civ 88, Westlaw document 2005 WL 62222. para.12.
[271] ibid, para.17.
[272] ibid, para.24.

(a) *Express Grant or Reservation*

15–081   A profit may be expressly granted or reserved by the owner of the servient land. However a profit will only be created at law if the appropriate formalities are observed. The profit must be granted by deed[273] and, since the creation of a profit is a disposition requiring registration under s.27(1)(d) of the Land Registration Act 2002, it must be completed by registration. Usually this will take the form of the entry of a notice on the register of the title of the land to which the profit relates, but in the case of a profit in gross (i.e. to a person rather than for the benefit of dominant land) for a term of more than seven years the profit must also be registered as an independent title on the Land Register.[274]

(b) *Implied Grant*

15–082   Section 62 of the Law of Property Act 1925 applies equally to profits as easements.[275] However, the rule in *Wheeldon v Burrows* will not apply because profits are not enjoyed continuously and apparently.

(c) *Prescription*

15–083   A profit may be acquired by prescription. However the Prescription Act 1832 adopts longer period for profits before its provisions apply. Thus 30 years' use will be sufficient to establish a profit by prescription if there was no permission, but where oral permission was granted 60 years is required. If there is written consent, prescription is excluded. The Prescription Act has no application to profits in gross. However, the doctrine of a lost modern grant applies to profits after 20 years, so that this will be sufficient if it cannot be proved that no such grant was made.

(d) *Registration of Profits in Common*

15–084   The Commons Registration Act 1965 required the registration of common land in England and Wales with county councils, and of its owners and those claiming to enjoy common rights over it. If such land was not registered before August 1970 it would be incapable of being registered thereafter, and any unregistered rights of common over such land were extinguished at that date. No new rights of common are capable of arising over such land after that date, but new commons may be created over other land.

---

[273] *Wood v Leadbitter* (1845) 13 M. & W. 838; *Mason v Clarke* [1954] 1 Q.B. 460.
[274] Land Registration Act 2002 Sch.2 para.6.
[275] *White v Williams* [1922] 1 K.B. 727.

3. Extinguishment of Profits

As in the case of easements, a profit will be extinguished if the holder of the profit acquires **15–085** the ownership of the servient land, or if he grants a release. Non-user of the profit will not itself extinguish the right, but alteration of the dominant land so that the profit can no longer benefit it will cause extinguishment, for example if agricultural land is developed. A profit could also be wholly or partially extinguished by means of approvement or inclosure.[276] A profit over common land acquired prior to August 1970 will have been extinguished if not registered under the Commons Registration Act 1965.

PASSING OF THE BENEFIT AND BURDEN OF EASEMENTS AND PROFITS

Easements and profits are not simply personal rights but proprietary interests in land. As such **15–086** the benefit of an easement or profit is capable of passing to a successor in title to the ownership of the dominant land, and a successor in title to the ownership of the servient land may acquire the land subject to the burden of the easement or profit.

1. Passing the Benefit of Easements and Profits

The benefit of any easements or profits is deemed to be included in a conveyance of the **15–087** dominant land, unless expressly excluded, by s.62 of the Law of Property Act 1925. A transferee of a dominant tenement will thus almost always enjoy the benefit of any easements or profits.

2. Passing of the Burden of Easements and Profits

The passing of the burden of easements and profits is an issue of priorities, in other words the **15–088** question will be whether a successor in title to the dominant land acquires it subject to the burden of the pre-existing easement or profit. Where title to the land is already registered, issues of priority will be determined by the provisions of the Land Registration Act 2002 regarding the effect of registered dispositions. Where the land is unregistered issues of priority will be determined by the provisions regarding the effect of first registration, since the only transactions which could enable the transferee of the dominant land to take free from a pre-existing easement or profit would require the title to be registered.

(a) *Priority of Easements and Profits Affecting Registered Land*

Where title to the land is already registered, issues of priority are determined by the Land **15–089** Registration Act 2002. The relevant rules vary according to the way in which the easement was created and the date at which it came into being.

---

[276] See Cheshire and Burn, *Modern Law of Real Property* (Butterworths, 15th edn), pp.572–575.

(i) Legal Easements and Profits Created Before October 13, 2003

15–090   Legal easements and profits created before the Land Registration Act 2002 came into force are overriding interests. As such they will be binding on any subsequent transferee of the servient tenement. The position of legal easements and profits created before the October 13, 2003 is a result of transitional arrangements introduced to bridge the gap between the different priority rules under the regime of the Land Registration Act 1925 and the new regime. Under the old regime all legal easements and profits, irrespective of the manner of their creation, were accorded overriding status by s.70(1)(a) of the Land Registration Act 1925. The overriding status of such pre-existing legal easements and profits is preserved by Sch.12 para.9 of the Land Registration Act 2002.

(ii) Legal Easements and Profits Created by Express Grant or Reservation after October 13, 2003[277]

15–091   As was seen above, the express grant or reservation of an easement or profit is now a registrable disposition,[278] and as such must be completed by registration, otherwise the grant or reservation will not operate at law. Since the creation of such easements and profits is completed by means of registration, they thereby enjoy priority as against all subsequent interests, and their priority is not affected by any subsequent disposition affecting the land. A transferee of the servient tenement will acquire the land subject to the burden of any such legal easements.

(iii) Legal Easements and Profits Created by Implication or Prescription after October 13, 2003 but before October 13, 2006

15–092   Different rules inevitably apply where legal easements or profits come into existence other than by express grant or reservation, since it is unrealistic to demand the registration of easements arising by implication, including by the operation of s.62 of the Law of Property Act 1925, or by prescription. Legal easements and profits created other than by express grant or reservation are accorded the status of overriding interests by Sch.3 para.3 of the Land Registration Act 2002. Special transitional arrangements exclude the operation of the exception in para.3 for a period of three years from the coming into force of Sch.3, so until the expiry of this period of grace the position for legal easements and profits is in practice identical to that which operated under the Land Registration Act 1925.

(iv) Legal Easements and Profits Created by Implication or Prescription after October 13, 2006

15–093   After three years the exception in Sch.3 para.3(1) will come into effect, so that legal easements and profits arising by implication or prescription will not automatically gain overriding status. Schedule 3 para.3(1) introduces an exception to the effect that, unless an

---

[277] Battersby [2005] Conv. 195; Kenny [2003] Conv. 304.
[278] s.27(2)(d) Land Registration Act 2002.

easement or profit has been exercised by the person entitled during the year before a disposition of the servient tenement take place,[279] it will only enjoy overriding status if it would have been obvious on a reasonably careful inspection of the land,[280] or if the person to whom the disposition is made had actual knowledge of its existence.[281]

(v) Equitable Easements and Profits

Under the regime introduced by the Land Registration Act 2002 equitable easements are excluded from enjoying overriding status. This reverses the position under the Land Registration Act 1925, where it was held that equitable interests were overriding interests within the scope of s.70(1)(a).[282] Equitable interests will therefore only enjoy priority if they are protected on the register by means of a notice.[283]

15–094

(b) *Priority of Easements and Profits Affecting Unregistered Land*

Where an easement or profit has been created over unregistered land, issues of priority will be determined by the rules regarding the effect of first registration, since any transfer of the land will necessitate the registration of title. These rules were examined in detail in Chapter 4 above. On first registration the land registrar is required to examine the title to the estate concerned, and to enter a notice in the register of any interest which affects the estate.[284] He will thus enter a notice in respect of any equitable easements which have been protected as a Class D(iii) land charge. Under Sch.1 para.3 to the Land Registration Act 2002 legal easements and profits are unregistered interests which override first registration, so that such interest will bind the proprietor on first registration.

15–095

REFORM OF THE LAW RELATING TO EASEMENTS

1. Background to Reform

In its 2008 Consultation Paper "Easements, Covenants and Profits à Prendre",[285] the Law Commission undertook an extensive review of the law of easements, covenants and profits à prendre and makes far reaching proposals for reform. It considered that reform should be consistent with the principles of land registration, given that the majority of titles are now registered:

15–096

---

[279] Sch.3 para.3(2). This exception to the exception is intended to ensure the protection of "invisible" easements which remain in use, such as rights of drainage.
[280] Land Registration Act 2002 Sch.3 para.3(1)(b).
[281] Land Registration Act 2002 Sch.3 para.3(1)(a).
[282] *Celsteel v Alton House Holdings Ltd* [1985] 1 W.L.R. 204; In *Sommer v Sweet* [2005] EWCA Civ 227; 2005 WL 513419 (Westlaw document) an easement arising under proprietary estoppel was an overriding interest under the Land Registration Act 1925; [2005] Conv. 545.
[283] Land Registration Act 2002 s.29.
[284] Land Registration Rules 2003 r.35.
[285] Law Com. No.186 (2008).

"[W]e consider that any recommendations we ultimately make must be consistent with the land registration system. There are two key aspects to the registration system that should be emphasised. First, that title is created by registration and not simply recorded by it. Second, that the register should contain as complete and as accurate a picture as possible of the nature and extent of rights relating to a particular piece of land. The need for additional enquiries beyond the register should be kept to a minimum."[286]

2. Proposals for Reform

(a) *Characteristics of Easements*

15–097 In relation to determining whether a right possesses the characteristics of an easement, the view of the Law Commission is that some reform and clarification is necessary.[287] First, in relation to the rule that the right claimed must not amount to possession of the land,[288] it was considered that the *London & Blenheim* test, that a right would not be an easement if "it would leave the servient owner without any reasonable use of his land",[289] is problematic. It is difficult to determine when it might be said that the servient owner is left with "reasonable use" and the test means that there is considerable uncertainty in relation to car parking easements. Currently it is unlikely that a right to park in a defined space, rather than in a larger area, is capable of being an easement.[290] The Law Commission considered the alternative test proposed by the House of Lords in *Moncrieff v Jamieson*,[291] to be inappropriate. Thus, returning to "first principles", it proposed an alternative: An easement is a limited right only and is entirely inconsistent with the grant of a more extensive right such as a lease:

"[T]he best approach is to consider the scope and extent of the right that is created, and to ask whether it purports to confer a right with the essential characteristics of an easement. The question should be 'What can the dominant owner do?', rather than 'What can the servient owner not do?' The right must therefore be clearly defined . . . and it must be limited in its scope".[292]

This would return the law to the position after *Copeland v Greenhalf*.[293] The test would allow a right to park in a defined space, as the use would be limited in scope to parking and would not involve any wider claim to possession, e.g. a lease.[294] Further in relation to the characteristics of an easement the Law Commission proposes "that where the benefit and burden of an easement

---

[286] Law Com. No.186 (2008), para.2.16.
[287] Law Com. No.186 (2008), para.2.16.
[288] See para.15–019 above.
[289] *London & Blenheim Ltd v Ladbroke Parks Ltd* [1992] 1 W.L.R. 1278.
[290] Law Com. No.186 (2008), paras 3.42–3.44.
[291] [2007] UKHL 42; [2007] 1 W.L.R 2620 [that the relevant enquiry is the extent to which the servient land owner retains possession and control over the land.] The test was difficult to apply in practice: para.3.47. Discussed above at para.15–019
[292] Law Com. No.186 (2008), para.3.49, footnotes omitted.
[293] Law Com. No.186 (2008), para.3.49.
[294] Law Com. No.186 (2008), para.3.52.

is registered, there should be no requirement for the owners to be different persons, provided that the dominant and servient estates in land are registered with separate title numbers".[295]

(b) *Creation of Easements*

(i) Implied Grant or Reservation

The Law Commission makes proposals for the reform of the law relating to express creation **15–098** of easements,[296] but we will deal here mainly with the proposals that concern the implication of easements. The existing rules are thought to be complex and uncertain:

> "The various methods of creation have developed in a piecemeal, uncoordinated fashion. This has led to complexity and to unnecessary and confusing overlap. To be confident whether an implied easement exists, and to understand the nature and extent of such an easement, requires specialist knowledge . . . In these circumstances, conflict may easily develop between landowners".[297]

In relation to the land registration ethic that the land register should accurately reflect all estates and interests in land, the current law on creation of easements is open to some criticism.

> "[I]t is relatively simple to create a legal easement informally, and . . . there is a significant risk that a purchaser of land burdened by the easement may be bound by it although it does not appear on the register of title."[298]

The Law Commission considers that s.62 of the Law of Property Act 1925, as a method of implying a grant of an easement, "suffers from a number of serious defects".[299] "The principal problem is that it transforms precarious interests, such as licences, into property rights".[300] Indeed, implied easements are overriding interests and can thus bind a registered proprietor even though the right has not been registered. Furthermore, people do not appreciate the effects of the section and consequently, it is a "trap for the unwary".[301] Accordingly, the Law Commission proposes that s.62 should "no longer operate to transform precarious benefits . . . into legal easements on a conveyance of the dominant estate".[302]

It was also considered unjustifiable that the law makes it harder to imply a reservation than a grant[303] and proposes that this should no longer be the case.[304]

---

[295] Law Com. No.186 (2008), para.3.66.
[296] Law Com. No.186 (2008), paras 4.24–4.35.
[297] Law Com. No.186 (2008), para.4.99.
[298] Law Com. No.186 (2008), para.4.6.
[299] Law Com. No.186 (2008), para.4.73.
[300] Law Com. No.186 (2008), para.4.73.
[301] Law Com. No.186 (2008), para.4.74.
[302] Law Com. No.186 (2008), para.4.104.
[303] See *Wheeldon v Burrows*, (1879)12 Ch D 31, para.15–030 above.
[304] Law Com. No.186 (2008), para.4.53.

The Law Commission suggests two alternative reforms on which it invites consultation[305]: (1) that the court should look at whether the parties intended an easement in the circumstances; This may be problematic given that it might be difficult to provide evidence of intentions where the land has gone through many successions of ownership. Also, the parties may not have directed their minds to the question, as was the case in *Wong v Beaumont Property Trust*[306]: It was thought that presumptions of intention based on what average people would intend on a transfer, would go some way to solving this problem.[307] (2) an easement should be implied "based on what is necessary for the use of the land in question".[308] The appropriate question was then how the law should define "necessary". The Law Commission proposed "a de minimis rule" that

> "would allow for only the absolute minimum of rights to be implied into a transaction. The absolute minimum would be an easement that permits use of the land and the buildings on the land and would generally be limited to rights of access, support and drainage."[309]

(ii) Acquisition of an Easement by Prescription

15–099 The Law Commission identified the need for a complete overhaul of the law of prescription:

> "There is no discernible need for three concurrent systems of prescriptive acquisition . . . The co-existence of three systems leads inevitably to complicated proceedings as claimants argue their case in the alternative to maximise their chances of success. As a result, it is sometimes difficult to discern from the decided cases which ground formed the basis of a successful claim. We are compelled to question whether such an unsatisfactory legal framework should have any part to play in the twenty-first century."[310]

The fact that the current law is based on a fiction of grant is considered to be unsatisfactory,[311] and under this method of acquisition it is "more difficult to determine the precise nature and extent of a right".[312] For these reasons the Law Commission recommends the prospective abolition of the current law of prescription.[313] However, because acquisition by long use still has a useful role, a replacement statutory scheme of prescription was proposed.[314] The scheme would apply to registered land and, in some respects, resembles the way rights are acquired by adverse possession under Sch.6 of the Land Registration Act 2002. Acquisition of an easement

---

[305] It also invited consultation on whether the existing law should be codified with necessary reform: There would only be three rules: necessity, the rule in *Wheeldon v Burrows*, and "intended user" (which would resemble common intention but only give effect to minimum rights): para.4.143.

[306] Law Com. No.186 (2008), para.4.110.

[307] Law Com. No.186 (2008), paras 4.113–4.117.

[308] Which could be rebutted by a contrary intention.

[309] Law Com. No.186 (2008), para.4.137. Thus, right to park, rights to light etc could not be implied under this rule: para.4.137.

[310] Law Com. No.186 (2008), para.4.168.

[311] Law Com. No.186 (2008), para.4.171.

[312] Law Com. No.186 (2008), para.4.170.

[313] Law Com. No.186 (2008), para.4.174.

[314] Law Com. No.186 (2008), para.4.183.

by statutory prescription would be based solely on long use, and not on the fiction of grant. There would have to be a "qualifying use", which means that the requirements of "not by force, or by stealth, or by permission" would apply,[315] and the right must have the characteristics of an easement.[316] The use must continue for the "prescriptive period", which is proposed to be 20 years,[317] and there should be a single prescription time period, replacing the current unsatisfactory structure under the Prescription Act 1832.[318] The right would only be acquired by registration as a notice on the burdened land.[319] However, it is suggested that a purchaser would be bound by the "inchoate right to have an easement entered on the register". In effect this would be equivalent to an overriding interest.[320] A similar scheme would apply in unregistered land, but without the registration requirement. "The easement would be a legal easement, and it would therefore be binding on successors in title to the servient land".[321]

(c) *Other Reform*

The Law Commission seeks to reform the scope of the Lands Tribunal's jurisdiction under section 84 of the Law of Property Act 1925, to discharge and modify restrictive covenants, extending it to include easements and profits.[322] Currently easements and profits cannot be discharged or modified under this provision "in the event of change of circumstances".[323] **15–100**

3. Profits à Prendre

The Law Commission proposes that "profits should only be created by express grant or reservation and by statute". "Profits should be capable of extinguishment: (1) by express release; (2) by termination of the estate to which the profit is attached; (3) by statute; and (4) by abandonment", the latter would no longer apply to registered land.[324] **15–101**

PARTY WALLS: A SPECIAL STATUTORY REGIME

One area of recent development is the enactment of a general scheme for regulating the rights of neighbouring landowners where there is a party wall on the border of their land. Although rights in relation to such walls, for example to repair, can be conferred by easements, the **15–102**

---

[315] Law Com. No.186 (2008), paras 4.195–4.196, 4.205, considered in paras 15–042-15–044 above.
[316] Law Com. No.186 (2008), para.4.233.
[317] Law Com. No.186 (2008), para.4.221.
[318] Law Com. No.186 (2008), para.4.211, under which there are two time periods.
[319] Use must be "prior to the issue arising": para.4.212 (i.e. "to within 12 months of application being made to the registrar": para.4.216).
[320] Law Com. No.186 (2008), para.4.236.
[321] Law Com. No.186 (2008), para.4.254.
[322] Law Com. No.186 (2008), Summary para.1.34. For a discussion of s.84 see Chapter 16.
[323] Law Com. No.186 (2008), para.1.11(5)).
[324] Law Com. No.186 (2008), para.6.30.

Party Wall, etc., Act 1996 provides a mechanism enabling work to be done to party walls and structures, and a means of settling disputes rapidly without the need to go to court. The system introduced by the Act is not novel, but is based on an earlier scheme operating in London.[325] Section 1 provides a mechanism for an owner who wishes to build a party wall or party fence wall on the boundary of the adjoining land. He must serve a notice on the adjoining owner a month before commencing work and describing the intended wall.[326] If consent is given he may build the wall half each on the land of the two owners and sharing the costs in proportion to their respective use of the wall, but in the absence of consent he may only build the wall placed wholly on his own land and at his own expense.[327] Section 2 provides for the repair of existing party walls and entitles an owner to a number of rights such as underpinning or thickening the wall and demolishing and rebuilding a wall which is not of sufficient specification for any building work he intends to carry out. Before exercising such rights the owner must serve a notice on the adjoining owner two months before the work is due to start.[328] The adjoining owner then has the option to serve a counter-notice requiring the building of such things as chimney flues and copings into the wall, or deeper foundations. The building owner is under a duty to compensate the adjoining owner for any loss or damage caused by work performed under the Act[329] and a building owner and his servants are entitled to enter any land during working hours to execute work pursuant to the Act.[330] Where there is a dispute, s.10 provides that the parties shall either agree on the appointment of a surveyor, or shall each appoint a surveyor, who will then appoint a third, to resolve the dispute. Where an award has been made, the parties can appeal against it to the county court.[331]

---

[325] Under the London Building Acts (Amendment) Act 1939.
[326] Party Wall, etc. Act 1996 s.1(2).
[327] Party Wall, etc. Act 1996 s.1(3).
[328] Party Wall, etc. Act 1996 s.3.
[329] Party Wall, etc. Act 1996 s.3.
[330] Party Wall, etc. Act 1996 s.3.
[331] Party Wall, etc. Act 1996 s.10(17).

Chapter 16

COVENANTS AFFECTING FREEHOLD LAND

INTRODUCTION

1. The Nature of Covenants

A covenant is simply a promise made by deed which is treated as having contractual force. **16–001**
The person who executes the covenant, termed the covenantor, makes a promise, which
promise is made for the benefit of the covenantee. The covenant is enforceable at common
law even though no consideration was provided by the covenantee. Where a covenant has
been granted the covenantee enjoys the benefit of the covenant, whereas the covenantor is
subject to the burden of the covenant. If the covenantor fails to keep his promise the covenantee will be able to recover damages for any loss he has suffered as a result of the breach. The
promise made by the covenantor may take any form. If the covenant is granted in the context
of land the covenantor may agree to do something on his land for the benefit of the covenantee, for example to build a wall along the boundary of his land. Since the obligation created
by this covenant requires the covenantor to take action it is described as a positive covenant.
Conversely the covenantor may make a promise not do some specified thing, for example that
he will not play football in his garden. Since the obligation requires the covenantor to refrain
from acting the covenant is said to be negative or restrictive.

2. The Enforceability of Covenants within the Law of Contract

(a) *Enforcement Between the Original Parties to the Covenant*

A covenant is obviously enforceable between the original parties, because they enjoy privity **16–002**
of contract. The covenantee can seek damages from the covenantor for breach, and if equitable

remedies are also available he may be able to obtain a prohibitory injunction to prevent a breach, or a mandatory injunction to restrain a continuing breach.

(b) *Enforcement by Third Parties Intended to Enjoy the Benefit of the Covenant*

16–003   The rigorous doctrine of privity of contract historically prevented a third party from enforcing a covenant or contract, even though he or she was intended to benefit from it. However the doctrine of privity of contract was radically amended by the Contracts (Rights of Third Parties) Act 1999, which entitles third parties to enforce contracts in their own right if they were intended to confer a benefit on them. The new principles only apply to contracts entered after May 11, 2000.

(c) *Assignment of the Benefit of the Covenant*

16–004   The doctrine of privity of contract did not, however, prevent a party from the contract assigning the benefit of the contract to a third party, who would thus be entitled to enforce it as against the promisor. In the context of covenants this means that the covenantee is entitled to transfer the benefit of the covenant to a third party who will be able to enforce the covenant against the covenantor. This possibility arises because the benefit of a contract is regarded as a species of property, termed a chose in action. The means by which such a transfer of the benefit of a covenant occurs is assignment, and the requirements for a legal assignment are found in s.136 of the Law of Property Act 1925.

(d) *Transfer of the Burden of a Covenant*

16–005   Although, as has been seen, the benefit of a covenant may be transferred by assignment, as a matter of contract law it was impossible for the burden of a covenant to be transferred. A contract is only enforceable against the original promisor. The doctrine of privity of contract therefore prevents the covenantor transferring his obligation to a third party such that the covenantee is entitled to enforce the contract directly against the third party.

3. Covenants Affecting Land

16–006   Where covenants are entered into by the owners of land the problems of enforceability are especially acute. For example, if Bill and Ted are neighbouring landowners and Ted enters into a covenant with Bill that he will build a boundary wall and not use his garden for playing football, clearly Bill will be able to enforce these covenants against Ted if he breaches them, either by failing to build the wall, or by playing football. However problems of enforceability arise if Bill sells his land to Wayne, and Ted his land to Garth. As a matter of contract

518

law, Bill could have expressly assigned the benefit of his covenants to Wayne, but there is no means by which the burden of the covenant could have been passed by Ted to Garth. If Garth was in breach of the covenants Wayne would perhaps be entitled to seek remedies against Ted, but not against Garth. A similar problem has already been encountered in relation to the covenants between a landlord and a tenant. Such leasehold covenants are enforceable between the original landlord and tenant, who enjoy privity of contract, but the covenants, whether positive or negative in nature, are also capable of being enforced between successors in title to the original landlord and tenant because of the doctrine of privity of estate developed in *Spencer's Case*,[1] more recently placed on a statutory footing in the Landlord and Tenant (Covenants) Act 1995. However there is no parallel doctrine operating between the successors in title to freehold owners who have granted covenants.

Despite the absence of any comprehensive mechanism for the transfer of the benefit and burden of covenants between freeholders, the law has developed so as to enable some measure of enforceability of covenants affecting freehold land between successors in title to the original covenantor and covenantee. If a covenant was made to benefit the land owned by the covenantee, and not with the original covenantee in a personal capacity, then at common law the benefit of that covenant will pass with the land so that successors in title will be able to enforce it against the original covenantor. Although there is no possibility at common law that the burden of the covenant will run with the land and bind successors in title to the original covenantor, equity has intervened to transform the contractual right generated by a negative covenant into a species of proprietary right capable of binding the land owned by the original covenantor. The burden of a negative covenant, but not of a positive covenant, is capable of running with the land so as to potentially bind a successor in title to the original covenantor in equity, and it will be enforceable by any successor in title to the original covenantee who in equity enjoys the benefit of the covenant. Such a right is described as a restrictive covenant.

PRINCIPLES OF ENFORCEABILITY OF COVENANTS AFFECTING LAND

The legal principles regulating the enforceability of freehold covenants are extremely complicated because of the distinction between contractual and proprietary rights, and the historic distinction between equity and the common law. In practice a regime ensuring the partial enforceability of covenants has been achieved by an unsatisfactory amalgam of principles drawn from equity and the common law which lacks overall coherence. The principles which determine the enforceability of covenants affecting freehold land can be summarised as follows.

16–007

1. The Enforceability of a Covenant

A covenant will only be able to be enforced, whether at common law or in equity, by a person who is entitled to the benefit of the covenant, against a person who is subject to the burden of a covenant.

16–008

---

[1] [1583] 5 Co.Rep. 16a.

2.   The Enforceability of a Covenant Between the Original Parties

16–009   A covenant will clearly be enforceable between the original parties thereto, since the original covenantee is entitled to the benefit of the covenant, and the original covenantor is subject to the burden. A third party may also be entitled to enforce a covenant against the original covenantor if it is governed by the Contracts (Rights of Third Parties) Act 1999 and it was intended to be for his benefit.

3.   The Transmissibility of the Benefit of a Covenant

16–010   The benefit of a covenant is capable of passing to another person, either at common law or in equity. At common law the benefit may pass to a successor in title to the original covenantee by assignment, either express or implied. In equity the benefit of a covenant may pass to a successor in title to the original covenantee by annexation, express assignment or through a scheme of development. Again, the Contracts (Rights of Third Parties) Act 1999 may have the effect in appropriate cases of extending the right to sue to a successor of the covenantee where the covenant was intended to benefit such a successor in title.

4.   The Transmissibility of the Burden of a Covenant

16–011   The burden of a covenant is incapable of transmission at common law because of the doctrine of privity. Except in one or two very narrow circumstances a covenant will only be able to be enforced at common law against the original covenantor who is subject to the burden thereof, and it cannot be enforced against a successor in title. In contrast in equity the burden of a covenant which is restrictive in nature is capable of passing with land. A restrictive covenant may therefore be enforced in equity against a successor in title to the original covenantor by the original covenantee, or by a successor in title to the original covenantee where the benefit of the covenant also passed with the land. In the light of these principles a positive covenant will only be able to be enforced against the original covenantor, either by the original covenantee or by a successor in title to the original covenantee who has obtained the benefit of the covenant.

5.   The Mutual Exclusivity of the Common Law and Equitable Rules

16–012   The principles developed by the common law and equity to determine the transmissibility of the benefit and burden of a covenant are mutually exclusive. A covenant can only be enforced by a person who enjoys the benefit of the covenant at common law against a person who is similarly subject to the burden of the covenant at common law, or by a person who enjoys the benefit of the covenant in equity against a person who is subject to the burden of the covenant in equity. The operation of the rules cannot be mixed. A covenant cannot be enforced by a person who enjoys only the benefit of the covenant in equity against a person who is subject only to the burden at common law, nor by a person who enjoys only the benefit of the covenant at common law against a person who is subject only to the burden in equity.

6. Determining Whether a Covenant is Enforceable

In the light of these principles a covenant affecting freehold land will only be enforceable between any two given persons where one is entitled to the benefit of the covenant at common law and the other is subject to the burden at common law, or alternatively where one is entitled to the benefit in equity and the other is subject to the burden in equity. The remainder of this chapter will examine and illustrate the detailed requirement of these principles.   **16–013**

ENFORCEMENT BETWEEN THE ORIGINAL PARTIES

1. Enforcement by the Parties of the Original Covenant

As has been noted, where the owners of freehold land have entered into covenants they are enforceable by the parties thereto on the basis of their privity of contract. For example, if Ted covenants with Bill that he will build a boundary wall; not play football in his garden; and do Bill's laundry weekly, Bill will be entitled to enforce all these covenants against him.   **16–014**

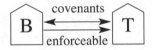

All such covenants are enforceable between the original parties to the covenant irrespective of whether they were positive or negative, personal or relating to the land.

2. Who are the Parties to the Original Covenant?

(a) *Persons Named as Parties in the Covenant*

A covenant will be enforceable by all the persons who are expressly named as covenantees in the covenant, even though they were not themselves party to it. For example, if Wayne owned other freehold land neighbouring Bill's land, and Ted covenanted "with Bill and with Wayne" that he would not use his land for industrial purposes this would entitle Wayne to enforce the covenant as an original covenantee.   **16–015**

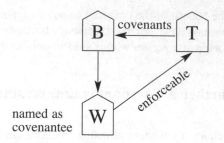

named as
covenantee

This is in contrast to the situation where a covenant is entered between two persons for the benefit of a third who is not expressly named as a covenantee. In such circumstances the third party cannot enforce the covenant because he is not a covenantee and is not therefore privy to it. For example, if Ted covenanted with Bill to build a boundary wall for all his land, and Wayne owns land neighbouring Ted's which would inevitably be benefited by the performance of the covenant, Wayne will be incapable of enforcing it against Ted.

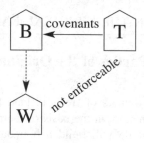

(b) *Persons Party to the Covenant by Statute: s.56(1) of the Law of Property Act 1925*

(i) Operation of s.56(1)

16–016 Section 56(1) of the Law of Property Act 1925 provides that:

> "A person may take an immediate or other interest in land or other property, or the benefit of any condition, right of entry, covenant or agreement over or respecting land or other property, although he may not be named as a party to the conveyance or other instrument."

Despite some judicial comments by Lord Denning M.R. construing this section as effecting a complete abrogation of the doctrine of privity of contract,[2] it merely enables a person to be regarded as a party to a covenant even though he is not specifically named as a covenantee if there is a generic description of the covenantees. Section 56(1) applies to all covenants, whether or not related to land, but it has an important role to play in the context of covenants

---

[2] See: *Smiths and Snipes Hall Farm Ltd v River Douglas Catchment Board* [1949] 2 K.B. 500 at 514; *Beswick v Beswick* [1966] Ch. 588 at 556.

between freehold owners in identifying the original covenantees of such a covenant. For example, if Ted covenanted with "Bill and the owners of all the other land adjoining my land" Wayne would be regarded an original party to the covenant and would be entitled to enforce the covenant against Ted even though he was not named in the covenant.

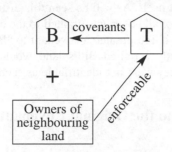

Section 56(1) operated in *Re Ecclesiastical Commissioners for England's Conveyance*.[3] In 1887 a freehold owner entered into a restrictive covenant with the Ecclesiastical Commissioners and "their successors and also as a separate covenant with their assigns owners for the time being of the land adjoining or adjacent to" a house the Commissioners were conveying to him. Luxmore J. held that by s.56(1) those persons who owned land adjacent or adjoining the land conveyed, which had also previously been owned by the Commissioners, were original covenantees of the covenant even though they were not parties to it.[4] However, s.56(1) will not operate where there is no clear statement in the covenant that it is intended to be made with a person or generic group. In *White v Bijou Mansions Ltd*[5] the purchaser of a piece of land entered into restrictive covenants in 1890 with the vendor and with "their heirs and assigns". Four years previously the vendor had sold the neighbouring land to a purchaser named Fellows. One question was whether Fellows was a party to the covenant granted in 1890. Simonds J. held that s.56 did not operate in his favour because there was no indication in the covenant that the grant was purported to be made with Fellows, but only with the vendors and those subsequently acquiring the land from the vendors.[6] Although Fellows would benefit from the covenants being observed this was not the same as his being a party to them.

(ii)   Limitation to the Operation of s.56(1)

Section 56 can only operate in favour of a person who could have been a party to the covenant when it was granted.[7] For example, if Ted granted a covenant to Bill and "the owners for the time being of the land adjacent or adjoining my land" s.56(1) would only operate to establish that the owners of such land at the date of the covenant were original covenantees. Thus, if

16–017

[3] [1936] Ch. 430.
[4] In consequence the benefit of the covenants made with them was capable of passing to their successors in title.
[5] [1937] Ch. 610; [1938] Ch. 351, CA.
[6] His successor in title could not therefore enforce the covenant because he had not been entitled to the benefit when it was granted.
[7] See *Kelsey v Dodd* (1881) 52 L.J. Ch. 34; *Stromdale and Ball Ltd v Burden* [1952] Ch. 223; *Lyus v Prowsa Developments Ltd* [1982] 1 W.L.R. 1044 at 1049, per Dillon L.J.

Wayne did not own any land adjoining Ted's land at the date of the covenant, but a year later purchased such land, he would not be able to claim that he was an original covenantee under s.56. He would be able to enforce the covenant against Ted if he had acquired the land with the benefit of the covenant, since the previous owner would have been an original covenantee, but not under the covenant itself. As will be seen this distinction is important because it is not the case that the benefit of all covenants granted to the owner of land will run with the freehold ownership. Similarly, if Ted granted a covenant to "Bill and his successors in title" those persons who subsequently acquired Bill's land would not be regarded as original parties to the covenant since they were not identifiable as such at the date of the covenant.

3. Remedies Available to the Original Covenantee

(a) *Compensation and Specific Remedies*

16–018   It has been seen how a covenant is enforceable between the original covenantor and all the original covenantees. In the event of a breach of covenant, or a threatened breach, the covenantee may be entitled either to damages for breach of covenant or an injunction.

(b) *Remedies where an Original Covenantee has Parted with his Land*

16–019   The mere fact that an original covenantee no longer owns the land to which a covenant relates does not mean that he automatically ceases to be able to enforce the covenant against the original covenantor. Unless the covenant specifically provides that he is only entitled to enforce it so long as he remains the owner of his land, as a matter of contract law the obligations created by the covenant are still owed to him and he can enforce them. For example, if Ted enters into covenants in relation to his land with Bill, and Bill then sells his land to Wayne, Bill will remain entitled to enforce the covenants against Ted.

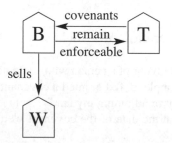

However such a liability is of little practical relevance since the covenantee will no longer be entitled to an injunction because he has no legal interest to protect and any damages would be purely nominal because he suffers no loss through the breach.[8]

[8] *Formby v Barker* [1903] 2 Ch. 539; *London County Council v Allen* [1914] 3 K.B. 642.

4. Continuing Liability of the Covenantor when he has Parted with his Land

The mere fact that the original covenantor has transferred his land does not automatically **16–020** mean that he is relieved from any continuing liability under the covenant he granted. Unless the covenant expressly provides that his liability is to cease when he no longer owns the land s.79(1) of the Law of Property Act 1925 has the effect that he remains liable for breaches committed by his successors in title. For example, if Ted covenanted with Bill that he would not use his land for industrial purposes, and he subsequently sold his land to Garth, Ted would remain liable to Bill for any breach committed by Garth.

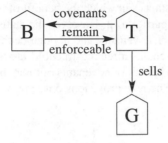

An original covenantor may protect himself to some extent from liability for breaches committed by his successors in title by ensuring that he obtains an indemnity when the land is transferred. As will be seen it is also possible that a restrictive covenant may be directly enforceable against a successor in title of the original covenantee.

Enforcement Against the Original Covenantor by Third Parties

Historically the doctrine of privity of contract has prevented third parties from enforcing con- **16–021** tracts. This doctrine has been modified by the Contracts (Rights of Third Parties) Act 1999, which provides for the enforcement of contracts by third parties in certain specified circumstances. Section 1(1) provides that a third party who is not a party to a contract may "in his own right enforce a term of the contract" if the contract expressly provides that he may,[9] or if the contract purports to confer a benefit on him[10] and "on a proper construction of the contract" it does not appear that the parties did not intend the term to be enforceable by the third party.[11] Section 1(3) provides that:

---

[9] Contracts (Rights of Third Parties) Act 1999 s.1(1)(a).
[10] Contracts (Rights of Third Parties) Act 1999 s.1(1)(b).
[11] Contracts (Rights of Third Parties) Act 1999 s.1(2).

"The third party must be expressly identified in the contract by name, as a member of a class or as answering a particular description but need not be in existence when the contract is entered into."

The statutory right of third parties to enforce contracts is thus significantly wider than the scope of s.56 of the Law of Property Act 1925, which as seen above is only capable of rendering persons in existence at the date of a covenant parties to the covenant. Under the new provisions a covenant granted by a covenantor for the benefit of a covenantee and his successors in title would seem to be enforceable by all his successors in title. Similarly if Ted covenanted with Bill and "the owners of the land adjacent or adjoining my land", and Wayne subsequently purchased neighbouring land, Wayne would be able to enforce the covenant against Ted. The statutory entitlement of third parties to enforce contracts in their own right thus greatly extends the circumstances in which the benefit of a covenant may be enforced by persons who were not original parties to it. However the statute has no implications for the transmission of the burden of such covenants, and in practice this is a far more significant barrier to the enforceability of covenants affecting freehold land. The legislation will certainly simplify the transmission of the benefit of covenants but may have little greater impact in the context of freehold covenants. The new provisions only apply in respect of contracts entered into after May 11, 2000.[12]

ENFORCEMENT AT LAW BY THE COVENANTEE'S SUCCESSORS

1. Situations where Successors in Title may Claim the Benefit of a Covenant

16–022 Where a covenant has been granted by the owner of freehold land in favour of a covenantee who also owns land, and the covenantee subsequently transfers his land to a third party, the question arises whether the successor in title to the original covenantee is able to enforce the covenant against the original covenantor. For example, if Ted covenants with Bill that he will build a boundary wall around his land; not play football in his garden; and do Bill's laundry weekly, and Bill sells his land to Wayne, will Wayne be able to enforce these covenants against Ted?

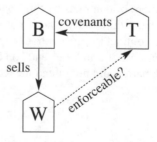

---

[12] Contracts (Rights of Third Parties) Act 1999 s.10(2).

Given that the liability of an original covenantor is not terminated if he transfers his land, the same possibility arises even if Ted has also transferred his land to Garth.

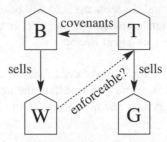

In this latter situation, the covenantee's successors may have claims against the original covenantor for breach of the covenant even though he has parted with the land. Whether the covenantor's successor in title is also liable for the breach is an entirely separate question which does not affect the liability of the original covenantor unless his undertaking was intended to operate only during his ownership of the land.

2. Does a Successor in Title to the Original Covenantee Enjoy the Benefit of the Covenant at Law?

(a) Transmission of the Benefit of a Covenant at Common Law

The benefit of a covenant can be expressly assigned by the convenantee to a third party, for example a successor in title. However, at common law it has long been held that the benefit of a covenant is capable of passing to a successor in title to the land of the original covenantee without the need for an express assignment. This was established in *The Prior's Case*[13] in the fourteenth century. The principles were identified and applied by the Court of Appeal in *Smith and Snipes Hall Farm Ltd v River Douglas Catchment Board*,[14] where the defendants had entered into a covenant in 1938 with owners of land which was subject to flooding, including a Mrs Smith who owned land known as the Low Meadows, that they would carry out works to ease the problem. Mrs Smith transferred the Low Meadows to the plaintiffs in 1940. The Court of Appeal held that as the benefit of the covenant had passed to the plaintiffs as successors in title to the original covenantee, they were entitled to enforce it against the defendant original covenantors who were in breach.

16–023

(b) Requirements for the Transmission of the Benefit of a Covenant at Common Law

The benefit of a covenant will only run with the land to a successor in title to the original covenantee if a number of conditions are met.

16–024

---

[13] (1368) Y.B. 42 Edw. 3 pl. 14 fol. 3A.
[14] [1949] 2 K.B. 500.

(i)   The Covenant Touches and Concerns the Land

16–025   Only a covenant which touches and concerns the land will be capable of passing with the land to a successor in title of the original covenantee. As Tucker L.J. stated in *Smith and Snipes Hall Farm Ltd v River Douglas Catchment Board*:

> "It is first necessary to ascertain from the deed that the covenant is one which 'touches or concerns' the land, that is, it must either affect the land as regards mode of occupation, or it must be such as per se, and not merely from collateral circumstances, affects the value of the land."[15]

This requirement of "touching and concerning" has already been encountered as a limitation in the context of leasehold covenants. It is intended to distinguish between covenants which genuinely relate to the land itself, so that it is appropriate that they should be binding on subsequent owners, and obligations which are purely personal to the original covenantor and covenantee and which it would be inappropriate to regard as passing with the land. In *P & A Swift Investments v Combined English Stores Group* Lord Oliver formulated a working test for whether in any given case a covenant touches and concerns the land:

> "(1) the covenant benefits only the [freehold owner] for the time being, and if separated from the [freehold ownership] ceases to be of benefit to the covenantee; (2) the covenant affects the nature, quality mode of user or value of the land of the [freehold owner]; (3) the covenant is not expressed to be personal (that is to say neither given only to a specific [freehold owner] nor in respect of the obligations of a specific [other owner]; (4) the fact that a covenant is to pay a sum of money will not prevent it from touching and concerning the land so long as the three forgoing conditions are satisfied and the covenant is connected with something to be done on, or in relation to the land."[16]

Applying this test, he held that the benefit of a covenant to stand as a surety of a tenant's leasehold obligations entered into with the landlord who owned the freehold reversion was a covenant which touched and concerned the land so that it was enforceable against the original covenantee by a successor in title to the freehold reversion. If a covenant touches and concerns land the benefit may pass irrespective of whether the obligation it imposes on the covenantor is positive or negative. Thus if Wayne were the successor in title to Bill, he would be able to enforce both Ted's covenant to build a boundary wall and his covenant not to play football in his garden, provided that the other requirements for the passing of the benefit were satisfied, but he would not be able to enforce the covenant to do the laundry because this does not touch and concern the land.

---

[15] [1949] 2 K.B. 500 at 506. Derived from *Congleton Corp v Pattison* (1808) 10 East 130, adopted by Farwell J. in *Rogers v Hosegood* [1900] 2 Ch. 388, and approved by Lord Oliver in *P & A Swift Investments v Combined English Stores Group* [1989] A.C. 632.
[16] [1989] A.C. 632 at 642.

(ii) The Original Covenantee must have had a Legal Estate in the Land Benefited

The benefit of a covenant which touches and concerns the land will only be capable of passing at common law if the original covenantee enjoyed a legal estate in the land benefited by the covenant.[17]

16–026

(iii) The Successor in Title has Acquired a Legal Estate in the Land

The benefit of a covenant will only pass at common law to a person who acquires a legal estate in the land. In some cases it was held that the benefit of a covenant would only pass to a person who acquired an identical legal estate to that enjoyed by the original covenantee.[18] However, in *Smith and Snipes Hall Farm Ltd v River Douglas Catchment Board*[19] the Court of Appeal held that s.78 of the Law of Property Act 1925 had the effect that the benefit of a covenant could pass to a person acquiring any legal estate in the land and not merely to a person acquiring an identical estate to that of the original covenantee. Therefore the benefit of a covenant was capable of passing to a person who had taken a legal lease from the freeholder who was the original covenantee.

16–027

(iv) The Benefit of the Covenant was Intended to Run with the Land

The mere fact that a covenant touches and concerns land will not alone suffice to establish that the benefit passes to a successor in title of the original covenantee. In *Smith and Snipes Hall Farm Ltd v River Douglas Catchment Board* Tucker L.J. stated that:

16–028

> "it must then be shown that it was the intention of the parties that the benefit thereof should run with the land."[20]

In the circumstances he found that the requirement was satisfied because the deed itself "shows that its object was to improve the drainage of land liable to flooding and prevent future flooding" and that there was an "intention that the benefit of the obligation to maintain shall attach thereto into whosoever hands the land shall come". However, for covenants entered into after 1925 the difficulties of establishing that a covenant was intended to run with the land have been greatly diminished by the decision of the Court of Appeal in *Federated Homes v Mill Lodge Properties Ltd*.[21] One central question raised in the case was as to the effect of s.78(1) of the Law of Property Act 1925, which provides that:

> "A covenant relating to any land of the covenantee shall be deemed to be made with the covenantee and his successors in title and the persons deriving title under him or them,

---

[17] *Webb v Russell* (1793) 3 T.R. 393.
[18] *Westhoughton UDC v Wigan Coal and Iron Co Ltd* [1919] 1 Ch. 159.
[19] [1949] 2 K.B. 500.
[20] [1949] 2 K.B. 500 at 506.
[21] [1980] 1 W.L.R. 594.

and shall have effect as if such successors and other persons were expressed. For the purposes of this subsection in connexion with covenants restrictive of the user of land 'successors in title' shall be deemed to include the owners and occupiers for the time being of the covenantee intended to be benefited."

Brightman L.J. considered whether this section merely reduced the length of legal documents or whether it effected a statutory annexation of the benefit of covenants to land. He concluded that:

"... if the condition precedent of s.78 is satisfied–that is to say, there exists a covenant which touches and concerns the land of the covenantee–that covenant runs with the land for the benefit of his successors in title, persons deriving title under him and other owners and occupiers."[22]

Thus the requirement that the benefit of a covenant must have been intended to run with the land will be satisfied by statutory annexation unless the deed expressly provides that the benefit is not intended to run with the land.

(v)   The Successor in Title must have Acquired the Whole Land of the Original Covenantee?

16–029   There is some suggestion that the benefit of a covenant will not pass at law to a successor in title to the original covenantee who acquires only part of his land. In *Re Union of London and Smith's Bank Ltd's Conveyance* Romer L.J. stated:

"at law the benefit of a covenant could not have been assigned in pieces. It would have to be assigned as a whole or not at all."[23]

It is unclear whether this limitation has been abrogated following *Federated Homes v Mill Lodge Properties Ltd*[24] where Brightman L.J. held that in the absence of a contrary intention the benefit of a covenant should be regarded as annexed to the whole of the land to which it relates, so that the benefit will pass to a person who acquires part of that land. The case concerned a restrictive covenant and it may be that the limitation still applies where the issue in equity is whether the benefit of a covenant has passed at law. However, there is no theoretical reason why the extent of annexation should differ between common law and equity.

(c)   *Enforcement of Covenants Executed after May 11, 2000*

16–030   As has been noted above, the traditional doctrine of privity of contract has been amended in respect of contracts entered into after May 11, 2000. If a covenant has been granted after this

---

[22] [1980] 1 W.L.R. 594 at 605.
[23] [1933] Ch. 611 at 630.
[24] [1980] 1 W.L.R. 594. See also *Smith and Snipes Hall Farm Ltd v River Douglas Catchment Board* [1949] 2 K.B. 500.

date, and the covenant is expressed to be for the benefit of the successors in title to the original covenantee, then the covenant will be enforceable by such successors in title. They are third parties "expressly identified in the contract . . . as a member of the class or as answering a particular description".[25] As such they are entitled to enforce the contract in their own right.[26]

3. Use of the Equitable Rules by a Successor in Title of the Covenantee

(a) *Circumstances in which a Covenantee's Successor will have to Rely on the Equitable Rules*

Although it has been seen that at common law the benefit of a covenant is capable of passing **16–031** to successors in title to the covenantee, there are some circumstances where a covenant has been granted and the common law rules will not apply to transmit the benefit of the covenant. In such cases the covenant may still be enforceable against the original covenantor in equity if the benefit of the covenant has passed by any of the recognised equitable mechanisms. A successor in title to the original convenantee will only need to rely on the equitable rules in the following circumstances:

(i) Original Covenantor only Enjoyed an Equitable Interest in Land

Where a covenant was granted by a covenantor who enjoyed a merely equitable interest in the **16–032** land the benefit of the covenant is incapable of passing with the land of the original covenantee at common law, and only a successor in title who can show that he was entitled to the benefit of the covenant in equity will be capable of enforcing the covenant against the original covenantee.

(ii) Original Covenantee only Enjoyed an Equitable Interest in Land

A similar consequence will follow if the original covenantee enjoyed a merely equitable inter- **16–033** est in land. A successor in title will only be able to enforce the covenant against the original covenantor if the benefit has passed in equity.[27]

(iii) An Ineffective Express Assignment

If the successor in title to the original covenantee claims to be entitled to the benefit of the **16–034** covenant by way of an express assignment, he will have to rely on equity if the assignment does not comply with s.136 of the Law of Property Act 1925.

---

[25] Contracts (Rights of Third Parties) Act 1999 s.1(3).
[26] Contracts (Rights of Third Parties) Act 1999 s.1(1).
[27] *Fairclough v Marshall* (1878) 4 Ex.D. 37; *Rogers v Hosegood* [1900] 2 Ch. 388.

(iv) Where the Original Covenantee Conveyed only Part of his Land

16–035 If it remains the case that at common law the benefit of a covenant only passes to a successor in title who acquires the whole of the land benefited, a successor in title to only part of the land of the original covenantee will have to rely on the equitable rules for the passing of benefit. In equity the benefit of a covenant is capable of passing to a successor in title to only part of the dominant tenement, who will then be able to enforce it against the original covenantee.

(b) *Equitable Mechanisms for Passing the Benefit of a Covenant*

16–036 The benefit of a covenant may pass in equity to a successor in title of the original covenantee by annexation, assignment or under a scheme of development. These mechanisms are examined in detail below in the context of restrictive covenants, but they are equally applicable where a successor in title seeks to enforce covenants, whether positive or negative, against the original covenantor and he cannot claim to be entitled to the benefit of the covenant at law.

Enforcement at Law Against Covenantor's Successors

1. Covenants cannot be Enforced at Law Against the Covenantor's Successors

16–037 In the preceding section it has been seen how the benefit of a covenant can pass with land so that a successor in title to the original covenantee is able to enforce it against the original covenantor. Although it might be thought appropriate that a covenant which touches and concerns the land should also be capable of being enforced against a successor in title to the original covenantor this is impossible at common law because of the rule that the burden of a covenant is incapable of passing with the land. This absolute inability of the burden of a covenant to pass at common law was recognised by the Court of Appeal in *Austerberry v Corporation of Oldham*.[28] The plaintiff and defendant were the successors in title to the original covenantee and covenantor of a covenant which contained an obligation to keep a road in good repair. The court held that the benefit of the covenant had not passed to the plaintiff because it did not touch and concern the land, thus rendering it unenforceable by him. However, Lindley L.J. also made clear that the burden had not passed to the defendant:

> "But it strikes me, I confess, that there is a still more formidable objection as regards the burden. Does the burden of this covenant run with the land so as to bind the defendants?

---

[28] (1885) 29 Ch.D. 750.

. . . I am not prepared to say that any covenant which imposes a burden upon land does run with the land, unless the covenant does, upon its true construction, amount to either a grant of an easement, or a rent- charge, or some other estate or interest in the land . . . I am not aware of any other case which either shews, or appears to shew, that a burden such as this can be annexed to land by a mere covenant, such as we have got here; and in the absence of authority it appears to me that we shall be perfectly warranted in saying that the burden of this covenant does not run with the land."[29]

The inability of the burden of covenants to be annexed to land and pass at common law was re-affirmed by the House of Lords in the more recent case of *Rhone v Stephens*,[30] where the issue was whether a covenant to maintain the condition of a roof was capable of binding a successor in title to the original covenantor. Lord Templeman explained why the House was unwilling to remove the limitation:

"In these circumstances your lordships were invited to overrule the decision of the Court of Appeal in the Austerberry case. To do so would destroy the distinction between law and equity . . . it is plain from the articles, reports and papers to which we were referred that judicial legislation to overrule the Austerberry case would create a number of difficulties, anomalies and uncertainties and affect the rights and liabilities of people who have for over 100 years bought and sold land in the knowledge, imparted at an elementary stage to every student of the law of real property, that positive covenants, affecting freehold land are not directly enforceable except against the original covenantor."[31]

As was noted above in the context of the passing of the benefit of a covenant, s.78 of the Law of Property Act 1925 has been construed so that the benefit of a covenant which touches and concerns land is annexed to the land in the absence of a contrary indication. Section 79(1) is a parallel provision in relation to the burden of covenants and provides:

"A covenant relating to any land of a covenantor or capable of being bound by him, shall, unless a contrary intention is expressed, be deemed to be made by the covenantor on behalf of himself, his successors in title and the persons deriving title under him or them, and subject as aforesaid, shall have effect as if such successors and other persons were expressed."

The House of Lords was unwilling to construe this section in a similar manner and hold that **16–038** it affected a statutory annexation of the burden of covenant to the land of the covenantor. Lord Templeman referred to the cases holding that s.78 effected a statutory annexation of the benefit of covenants[32] and concluded:

---

[29] (1885) 29 Ch.D. 750 at 781–783.
[30] [1994] 2 A.C. 310.
[31] [1994] 2 A.C. 310 at 321.
[32] *Smith and Snipes Hall Farm Ltd v River Douglas Catchment Board* [1949] 2 K.B. 500; *Williams v Unit Construction Co Ltd* (1955) 19 Conv. (N.S.) 262; *Federated Homes v Mill Lodge Properties Ltd* [1980] 1 W.L.R. 594 at 605–606.

"Without casting any doubt on those long standing decisions I do not consider that it follows that s.79 of the Act of 1925 had the corresponding effect of making the burden of positive covenants run with the land."[33]

Therefore, if Ted covenants with Bill that he will build a boundary wall around his land; not play football in his garden; and do Bill's laundry weekly, and Ted sells his land to Garth, Bill will be unable to enforce any of the covenants against Garth at law because the burden is incapable of passing with the land.

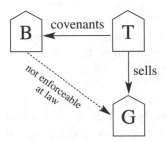

It should be remembered that the mere fact that the covenants cannot be enforced against Garth does not mean that Bill is without remedies at all. Ted remains liable to him as the original covenantor and will be held accountable even for breaches committed by Garth. Obviously the same limitations will apply if there is a successor in title to the original covenantee who enjoys the benefit of the covenants. If Ted has transferred his land to Garth, and Bill has transferred his land to Wayne, Wayne will enjoy the benefit of the covenants if the appropriate criteria are satisfied. However, as the burden of a covenant is incapable of passing with the land at law Wayne will be unable to enforce any covenants against Garth at law, but he will be able to seek remedies against the original covenantor, Ted.

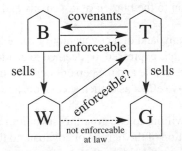

2. When a Covenant may be Enforceable Against a Covenantor's Successor in Title

16–039   Despite the general rule that the burden of covenants are incapable of passing at law there are some circumstances in which, either directly or indirectly, enforceability may be achieved.

[33] [1994] 2 A.C. 310 at 322. See also: *Jones v Price* [1965] 2 Q.B. 618; *Sefton v Tophams Ltd* [1967] 1 A.C. 50.

(a) *Enforceability of Restrictive Covenants in Equity*

The absolute inability of the burden of a covenant to pass with land is a limitation arising under the common law. However equity has intervened so that the burden of a covenant which is negative, or restrictive, in nature is capable of binding a successor in title to the original covenantor. The principles governing the enforceability of restrictive covenants in equity are examined in detail below. The availability of such equitable enforceability means that the other methods by which covenants can be rendered enforceable against a successor in title to the original covenantor are of most importance in the context of positive covenants where there is no possibility at law or in equity of the burden passing with the land.

16–040

(b) *Enforceability of Positive Covenants on the Basis of "Mutual Benefit and Burden"*

It has been suggested that where a covenant confers both benefits and burden on the covenantor a successor in title cannot take advantage of the benefit conferred without also being subject to the burden imposed. In *Halsall v Brizell*[34] the purchasers of building plots covenanted that they would contribute to the cost of the repairs and maintenance of the sewers and roads "for the common use convenience and advantage of the owners for the time being" of the plots. One subsequent owner refused to pay because he objected to the way in which his contribution had been calculated. He argued that he could not be compelled to contribute. Upjohn J. held that although the covenant was prima facie unenforceable against a successor in title to one of the original covenantors because the burden of a positive covenant was incapable of passing with the land, the successors in title could not take advantage of the right of way conferred in the same covenant without also being subject to the burden:

16–041

> "But it is conceded that it is ancient law that a man cannot take benefit under a deed without subscribing to the obligations thereunder. If authority is required for that proposition, I need only refer to one sentence during the argument in *Elliston v Reacher*[35] where Lord Cozens-Hardy M.R. observed: 'It is laid down in Co. Litt 230b that a man who takes the benefit of a deed is bound by a condition contained in it, though he does not execute it.' . . . Therefore, it seems to me, that the defendants here cannot, if they desire to use this house, as they do, take advantage of the trusts concerning the user of the roads contained in the deed and the other benefits created by it without undertaking the obligations thereunder. Upon that principle it seems to me that they are bound by this deed, if they desire to take its benefits."[36]

---

[34] [1957] Ch. 169.
[35] [1908] 2 Ch. 665 at 669.
[36] See also *Hopgood v Brown* [1955] 1 W.L.R. 213; *Ives Investments Ltd v High* [1967] 2 Q.B. 379; *Montague v Long* (1972) 24 P. & C.R. 240.

However, despite the identification of a general doctrine of benefit and burden by Megarry V.C. in *Tito v Wadell (No.2)*[37] the exact scope of the operation of the principle is in doubt. The cases from which it is drawn are concerned with enforceability between the original parties to a covenant and not to successors in title. In *Rhone v Stephens*[38] Lord Templeman accepted that the decision in *Halsall v Brizell* had been correct, but considered that the doctrine had no application where a successor in title had no real choice whether to decide to forgo the benefits conferred by the covenant which also imposed obligations upon him:

"... it does not follow that any condition can be rendered enforceable by attaching it to a right nor does it follow that every burden imposed by a conveyance may be enforced by depriving the convenantor's successor in title of every benefit which he enjoyed thereunder. The conditions must be relevant to the exercise of the right. In Halsall v Brizell there were reciprocal benefits and burdens enjoyed by the users of the roads and sewers. In the present case [the conveyance] imposes reciprocal benefits and burdens of support but clause 3 which imposed an obligation to repair the roof is an independent provision. In Halsall v Brizell the defendant could, at least in theory, choose between enjoying the right and paying his proportion of the cost or alternatively giving up the right and saving his money. In the present case the owners ... could not in theory or in practice be deprived of the benefit of the mutual rights of support if they failed to repair the roof."[39]

(c) *Indirect Enforceability of Positive Covenants by Means of a Right of Re-entry*

16–042 Indirect enforceability of positive covenants may be achieved if the covenantee subjects the land to a right of re-entry in the event of breach. Since the right of re-entry is a legal interest in the land it is capable of binding successors in title.[40] However such a mechanism may not secure absolute enforceability since the court has the jurisdiction to relieve the estate owner from forfeiture in the event of breach.

(d) *Indirect Enforceability by Means of an Estate Rentcharge*

16–043 Although in general the Rentcharges Act 1977 prevents the creation of new rent charges, s.1(4)(a) provides that it is possible to create a new "estate rentcharge", which means a rentcharge created for the purpose of "making covenants to be performed by the owner of the land affected by the rentcharge enforceable by the rent owner for the time being of the land". A right of re-entry is then annexed to the rentcharge, with the consequence that the estate can be forfeited in the event of breach of the covenant.

---

[37] [1977] Ch. 106.
[38] [1994] 2 A.C. 310.
[39] [1994] 2 A.C. 310 at 322–323.
[40] See *Shiloh Spinners v Harding* [1973] A.C. 691.

(e) *Statutory Enforceability Following Enlargement of a Leasehold Estate into Freehold Ownership*

It has already been noted that in the case of leasehold interests the burden of positive covenants   **16–044**
is capable of passing with the land by means of the doctrine of privity of estate. Some
statutory provisions allowing the conversion of long leases into freehold ownership have the
effect that any covenants of the lease are binding on the land as if it had not been converted.[41]

ENFORCEMENT OF RESTRICTIVE COVENANTS IN EQUITY

1. The Enforceability of Restrictive Covenants in Equity

(a) *Development of Restrictive Covenants in Equity*

Whereas the common law provided no general means by which the burden of a covenant was   **16–045**
capable of passing with land, equity developed a doctrine that the burden of negative covenants
was capable of passing so as to burden the land in the hands of a successor in title to the original
covenantor. This doctrine originated in *Tulk v Moxhay*[42] where it was held that the successor in
title to a piece of land in Leicester Square who had covenanted to keep it free from building
development was bound to observe the covenant because he had acquired the land with notice of
its existence. The judgments in *Tulk v Moxhay* made no distinction between positive and negative covenants, and the rationale for enforcement seems simply to be founded on the fact of
notice. However, subsequent cases fine-tuned both the scope of the doctrine and the justification
for it.[43] The doctrine which was the culmination of this judicial development was explained by
Lord Jessel M.R. in *London and South Western Railway Co v Gomm*:

> "The doctrine of [*Tulk v Moxhay*] . . . appears to me to be either an extension in equity of
> the doctrine of *Spencer's Case* to another line of cases, or else an extension in equity of the
> doctrine of negative easements; . . . The covenant in *Tulk v Moxhay* was affirmative in its
> terms, but was held by the court to imply a negative. Where there is a negative covenant
> expressed or implied . . . the court intervenes on one or other of the above grounds. This is
> an equitable doctrine, establishing an exception to the rules of common law which did not
> treat such a covenant as running with the land, and it does not matter whether it proceeds
> on an analogy to a covenant running with the land or an analogy to an easement."[44]

[41] Law of Property Act 1925 s.153; Leasehold Reform Act 1967 s.8(3).
[42] (1848) 2 Ph. 774.
[43] See *Morland v Cook* (1868) L.R. 6 Eq. 252; *Cooke v Chilcott* (1876) 3 Ch.D. 694; *Haywood v Brunswick Permanent Benefit Building Society* (1881) 8 Q.B.D. 403; *London County Council v Allen* [1914] 3 K.B. 642; (1982) 98 L.Q.R. 279 (Gardner).
[44] (1882) 20 Ch.D. 562.

In equity it is therefore possible for the burden of a negative covenant to pass with the land. Thus if Ted covenants with Bill that he will build a boundary wall around his land; not play football in his garden; and do Bill's laundry weekly, and Ted sells his land to Garth, Bill may be able to enforce the negative covenant prohibiting the playing of football against Garth in equity, provided that the relevant criteria are satisfied.

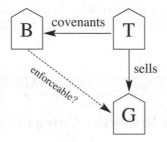

Similarly a negative covenant may be enforced by a successor in title to the original covenantee against a successor in title to the original covenantor. If Ted has transferred his land to Garth, and Bill has transferred his land to Wayne, Wayne may enjoy the benefit of the covenants which touch and concern the land. If so, he may be able to enforce the negative covenant against Garth in equity.

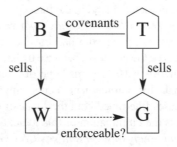

A restrictive covenant is capable not only of binding a successor in title to the freehold of the land owned by the original covenantor, but also anyone acquiring a lesser interest therein, for example a tenant under a lease[45] or a licensee.[46]

(b) *Rationale for the Enforcement of Restrictive Covenants in Equity*

16–046 Prior to the widespread intervention of the state to control the development of land by planning regulations, restrictive covenants served an important function as a means by which private owners and developers of land could effectively ensure that land was not utilised in a manner they considered inappropriate or disadvantageous to themselves. For example, a vendor who sold part of his land for development might wish to ensure that only a single

---

[45] *Wilson v Hart* (1866) L.R. 1 Ch. App. 463; *Nicoll v Fenning* (1881) 19 Ch.D. 258.
[46] *Mander v Falcke* [1891] 2 Ch. 554.

dwelling-house was build on the land sold, with the prime objective of protecting the value and amenity of the land that he retained. Similarly, the developer of an area of residential housing might wish to ensure that none of the properties could be used for other than residential purposes, thus increasing the value and saleability of the properties built. The rationale for allowing the burden of such covenants to pass in equity, since they could not at common law, was that it would be unjust for a person to acquire land knowing that it was subject to such a limitation to proceed to ignore it. For example the purchaser of a house subject to a restriction that it was not to be used for business purposes might have acquired it at a far lower price than would have been payable in the absence of such a limitation. It would be unconscionable for him to take advantage of the benefit of the reduced price yet to deny the detriment of the restriction. As Lord Cottenham L.C. stated in *Tulk v Moxhay*:

> "It is said that, the covenant being one which does not run with the land, this Court cannot enforce it; but the question is, not whether the covenant runs with the land, but whether a party shall be permitted to use the land in a manner inconsistent with the contract entered into by his vendor, and with notice of which he purchased. Of course the price would be affected by the covenant, and nothing could be more inequitable than that the original purchaser should be able to sell the property the next day for a greater price, in consideration of the assignee being allowed to escape from the liability which he had himself undertaken."[47]

(c) *Interpretation of the Meaning of a Restrictive Covenant*

The nature of the restriction imposed on the use of land by a covenant must be determined by construction of the terms of the covenant. In *Crest Nicholson Residential (South) Ltd v McAllister*[48] a covenant was granted when a company sold off plots of land on an estate not to use the premises "for any purpose other than those of or in connection with a private dwelling house". Some thirty years later a subsequent purchaser of the land sought to build new houses on the plot. The central question was whether this covenant prevented the erection of more than one single dwelling house on the plot, or whether it meant that the plot could not be used other than for residential purposes. Neuberger J. held that as a matter of construction the covenant should be taken to mean that only a single dwelling house could be built on the plot. He explained:

16–047

> "as a matter of ordinary language, the indefinite article 'a' tends to carry with it the concept of a singularity as opposed to plurality. Restriction to use as a 'private dwelling house' appears to me, at least in the absence of contextual or factual contra-indications, to mean restriction to a single dwelling house."[49]

---

[47] (1848) 2 Ph. 774 at 777.
[48] [2002] EWHC 2443, Ch; [2003] 1 All E.R. 46.
[49] [2003] 1 All ER 46 [15]; On appeal [2004] 1 W.L.R. 2409, Chadwick L.J. held that the covenant had not been annexed to the land, and it was thus unnecessary to decide the meaning of the restriction: para.53. However, he stated that he saw no reason to disagree with the judge.

(d) *Requirements for the Enforceability of a Restrictive Covenant in Equity*

(i) A Dominant Owner Entitled to the Benefit of the Covenant

16–048 A restrictive covenant will only be enforceable in equity by a person who can show that he is entitled to the benefit thereof. Clearly the original covenantee will be entitled to the benefit, but a successor in title will only be so entitled if the benefit passed to him when he acquired the land. The means by which the benefit of a covenant may pass in equity are slightly wider than at law. Despite some suggestions that a restrictive covenant is enforceable irrespective of whether the owner of the dominant land has obtained the benefit of the covenant at law[50] or in equity, the better view is that it can only be enforced against a successor in title to the original covenantor who has taken the servient land subject to the burden by a person who enjoys the benefit according to the equitable rules.[51]

(ii) A Servient Owner Subject to the Burden of the Covenant

16–049 A restrictive covenant can only be enforced against someone who owns the land affected subject to the burden of the covenant. In the case of successors in title to the original covenantor not only must the burden have been capable of passing with the land in equity, but the successor in title must have taken the land subject to the restrictive covenant as an equitable interest in the land according to the appropriate priority rules. These differ depending on whether the land is registered or unregistered. If the successor in title acquires the land in circumstances in which he takes free from the restrictive covenant it will be unenforceable against him.

2. Was the Servient Owner Subject to the Burden of the Restrictive Covenant in Equity?

(a) *Covenant must be Negative*

(i) Reassertion of the Limitation

16–050 Only the burden of a covenant which is negative in nature is capable of passing with land in equity. As has been seen this means that there is no possibility of the passing of the burden of positive covenants. This restriction was applied in *Rhone v Stephens*, where Lord Templeman stated:

> "Equity can . . . prevent or punish the breach of a negative covenant which restricts the user of land or the exercise of other rights in connection with land. Restrictive covenants

---

[50] *Rogers v Hosegood* [1900] 2 Ch. 388.
[51] *Re Union of London and Smith's Bank Ltd's Conveyance* [1933] Ch. 610 at 630.

deprive an owner of a right which he could otherwise exercise. Equity cannot compel an owner to comply with a positive covenant entered into by his predecessors in title without flatly contradicting the common law rule that a person cannot be made liable upon a contract unless he was a party to it. Enforcement of a positive covenant lies in contract; a positive covenant compels an owner to exercise his rights. Enforcement of a negative covenant lies in property; a negative covenant deprives the owner of a right over property."[52]

Therefore a covenant entered into in 1960 when a house was divided into two, whereby the owner who retained part covenanted to maintain the roof in a wind and watertight condition, was unenforceable by a successor in title to the original purchaser of the part of the house which was benefited by the covenant.

(ii)   A Question of Substance

Whether a particular obligation imposed by a covenant is positive or negative is a matter of substance rather than of form. For example, an obligation not to allow a roof to fall into disrepair is as much a positive covenant as that in *Rhone v Stephens* despite the fact that it is phrased in a negative manner. In *Haywood v Brunswick Permanent Benefit Building Society*[53] Cotton L.J. indicated that a covenant to repair was positive because it could only be enforced "by making the owner put his hand into his pocket". Thus a simple test for determining if a covenant is negative or positive is whether fulfilment of the obligation would necessitate expenditure by the owner.

16–051

(b)   *Covenant must Accommodate the Dominant Land*

Since the equitable doctrine of restrictive covenants converts what is essentially a contractual right into a property right in the nature of a negative easement, analogies can be drawn with the requirements of easements as rights in land.[54] When an equitable restrictive covenant is created, the land of the original covenantee becomes a dominant tenement and the land of the original covenantor a servient tenement. The restrictive covenant is the inverse of an easement: whereas an easement confers a right on the dominant owner to exercise some form of limited user over the servient land, a restrictive covenant entitles the dominant owner to insist that the servient owner restrains from exercising some otherwise legitimate user of his land. Although all covenants may be enforceable between the original parties in contract, only such covenants as can be said to accommodate the dominant tenement become proprietary interests capable of binding successors in title. A negative covenant can be said to be a restrictive covenant in equity which accommodates the dominant tenement if the following criteria are fulfilled:

16–052

---

[52] [1994] 2 A.C. 310.
[53] (1881) 9 Ch.D. 403 at 409.
[54] See Ch.15.

(i)   The Original Covenantee must have Owned Land to be Benefited at the Time the Covenant was Granted

16–053   A restrictive covenant will only accommodate a dominant tenement if the original covenantee was the owner of land to be benefited at the date when the covenant was granted.[55] Clearly this will be impossible if he owned no land at that date. For example, in *London County Council v Allen*[56] it was held that a covenant entered into by the owner of land that he would not build on a plot across the end of a proposed street was unenforceable against a successor in title by the Council, who were the covenantees, as they did not own any land at the time that the covenant was granted. Buckley L.J. stated that the doctrine of *Tulk v Moxhay* required the ownership of land by the covenantee as a pre-condition of enforceability of a restrictive covenant in equity against a successor in title to the covenantor:

> "The doctrine is that a covenant not running with the land, but being a negative covenant entered into by an owner of land with an adjoining owner, binds the land in equity and is enforceable against a derivative owner taking with notice. The doctrine ceases to be applicable when the person seeking to enforce the covenant against the derivative owner has no land to be protected by the negative covenant. The fact of notice is in that case irrelevant."[57]

Although a covenant granted in gross is incapable of creating a restrictive covenant, it is not a pre-requisite in equity that the covenantee must have owned the freehold of the dominant land. A restrictive covenant can be enforced in favour of the holder of the freehold reversion of land[58] or a mortgagee.[59] Once the original covenantee has parted with land he can no longer enforce a restrictive covenant in equity against the servient owner, although he may continue to enjoy purely contractual remedies. Statute has intervened so that many bodies, such as local authorities, are entitled to enforce restrictive covenants even though they do not own land benefited.

(ii)   The Dominant Tenement Enjoyed Sufficient Physical Proximity with the Servient Tenement

16–054   Just as an easement will only accommodate the dominant land if there is sufficient physical proximity with the servient tenement to justify finding that the land itself is benefited, a restrictive covenant will only be created if here is sufficient proximity between the dominant and servient land. In *London County Council v Allen* Buckley L.J. spoke of adjoining land, but contiguity is not strictly necessary. In *Kelly v Barrett*[60] Lord Pollock M.R. indicated that land at Clapham would be too remote to carry a right to enforce a covenant restrictive of the use of land at Hampstead.

---

[55] *Application of Fox* (1981) 2 B.P.R. 9310.
[56] [1914] 3 K.B. 642.
[57] [1914] 3 K.B. 642 at 654–655.
[58] *Hall v Ewin* (1988) 37 Ch.D. 74.
[59] *Regent Oil Co Ltd v J A Gregory (Hatch End) Ltd* [1966] Ch. 402.
[60] [1924] 2 Ch. 379.

(iii) The Original Parties to the Covenant must have Intended the Burden to Run with the Land

A negative covenant will not generate a restrictive covenant in equity unless it can be shown that the original parties intended the burden of the covenant to run with the land. This intention may be made clear in the deed, but this is not essential as s.79(1) of the Law of Property Act 1925 has the effect that the burden of a negative covenant will be taken as intended to run with the land unless the parties indicated a contrary intention[61] in the deed. Section 79(1) is expressly limited in scope of application to covenants "relating to land" which is the direct equivalent of the familiar concept of covenants which touch and concern the land.

16–055

(c) *Servient Tenement must have been Acquired Subject to the Burden of the Covenant*

The mere fact that a covenant is a restrictive covenant capable of passing with the land in equity does not mean that a person acquiring the servient land, or an interest in the servient land, will necessarily take his interest subject to it. This will depend upon the rules of priority regulating the land in question and whether they are entitled to take free from the burden of the restrictive covenant.

16–056

(i) Servient Tenement is Registered Land

Where title to the servient land is registered, issues of priority are determined by the provisions of the Land Registration Act 2002. Unless it has been protected by the entry of a notice on the register of title of the estate to which it relates, a restrictive covenant will lose priority if a registrable disposition of the estate is made for valuable consideration.[62] A person who purchases the land for valuable consideration will therefore acquire it free from any unprotected restrictive covenants.

16–057

(ii) Servient Tenement is Unregistered Land

Where the servient tenement is unregistered issues of priority will be determined by the rules applicable to unregistered land. However, since any transfer of ownership will have to be registered, in practice the priority rules will fall under the rules applicable to first registration under the Land Registration Act 2002. On first registration the registered proprietor will take the land subject to any interests which are the subject of an entry in the register. Since the registrar is required to enter a notice in the register of the burden of any interest which appears from his examination of the title to affect the registered estate,[63] it follows that he will enter

16–058

---

[61] See *Re Royal Victoria Pavilion, Ramsgate* [1961] Ch. 581, where Pennycuick J. held that the parties had demonstrated a counter-intention.
[62] Land Registration Act 2002 ss.29(1) and 29(2)(a)(i).
[63] Land Registration Rules 2003 r.35(1).

a notice in respect of any restrictive covenant created after January 1, 1926 which was properly protected on the land charges register as a Class D(ii) land charge.[64] An unprotected covenant created after January 1, 1926 will only be entered on the register if the registered proprietor did not acquire the land for money or money's worth.[65] In the case of restrictive covenants created before January 1, 1926 questions of priority are determined by the normal unregistered land rules including the doctrine of notice.[66] Such a covenant would therefore be entered on the register on first registration unless the registered proprietor was a bona fide purchaser for value without notice.

3. Was the Dominant Owner Entitled to the Benefit of the Restrictive Covenant?

(a) *Benefit Enjoyed by the Original Covenantee*

16–059 In order for a restrictive covenant to be enforceable the dominant land must be owned by someone entitled to the benefit of the covenant. Clearly the original covenantee will be entitled to the benefit of the covenant and will therefore be able to enforce a restrictive covenant against a successor in title to the original covenantor who has acquired the servient land subject to the burden of the covenant. More complex questions arise where the dominant land has also been transferred, so that the person with an interest in enforcing the restrictive covenant is a successor in title to the original covenantee.

(b) *Benefit of the Covenant Annexed to the Dominant Tenement*

16–060 When the benefit of a covenant is annexed to the land it is in effect attached to the dominant tenement so that it passes with the land to any successors in title without the need for an express assignment. Equitable annexation parallels the equivalent common law rules in *Smith and Snipes Hall Farm Ltd v River Douglas Catchment Board*.[67] Since annexation of the benefit of a covenant to the covenantee's land occurs when the covenant is made, there can be no such annexation if at that date the covenantee was not the owner of land capable of being benefited by the covenant. Similarly annexation can only occur of a covenant which is for the benefit of the land, so that only a covenant which satisfies the familiar requirement of touching and concerning the land is capable of being annexed to it. Ultimately annexation will only occur if the parties to the original covenant intended the benefit to be annexed to the land. Historically this intention could either be expressed in the covenant itself or implied. More recently s.78 of the Law of Property Act 1925 has been construed

---

[64] Land Charges Act 1972 s.2(5)(ii).
[65] Since in such circumstances the transferee would acquire the land subject to the unprotected land charge: Land Charges Act 1972 s.4(6).
[66] See Ch.4.
[67] [1949] 2 K.B. 500.

so that annexation is effected by statute in the absence of a counter-intention by the parties. This means that in the vast majority of cases it will be relatively easy to establish annexation in equity.

(i)   Express Annexation

It is ultimately a question of construction[68] whether a deed expressly annexes the benefit of a covenant to the covenantee's land. An intention to annex will be found if the land to be benefited is identified in the covenant, and it is stated to be for the "benefit of the land" or for the owners of the land in their capacity as such. In *Rogers v Hosegood*[69] a covenant was granted to covenantees, who enjoyed an interest in the land benefited as mortgagees, that no more than one house would be built on the land. The deed stated that the covenant was to "enure to the benefit of the [mortgagees] their heirs, and assigns and others claiming under them to all or any of their lands adjoining or near to the premises". The Court of Appeal upheld the decision of Farwell J. that this evidenced an intention that the benefit of the covenant was annexed to the land of the covenantee. In contrast, it seems that the mere fact that a covenant is made with the covenantee and his "heirs, executors, administrators and assigns" will be insufficient to effect annexation if no mention is made of the land to be benefited.[70]

16–061

(ii)   Implied Annexation

Marten v Flight Refuelling Ltd[71] is authority that an intention to annex can be implied from the circumstances surrounding the grant of a covenant even though there is no such intention in the deed itself. The case concerned a covenant granted by the purchaser of part of an estate that the land would be used solely for agricultural purposes, and which was expressed to be made with the covenantee and "its successors in title". Although there was no express statement that the covenant was intended to benefit the land Wilberforce J. held that "an intention to benefit may be found from surrounding or attending circumstances".[72] He considered the fact that the land had formed part of a larger estate which had been used exclusively for agricultural purposes, and that the purchaser had been a tenant of the farm, as had his father before him, and concluded that the covenant was taken to benefit the land of the vendors who owned the remainder of the estate. There has been a large measure of academic criticism of the decision, which has cast doubt on whether it truly establishes the possibility of an implied annexation because the plaintiffs were the original covenantees.[73] In *Sainsbury Plc v Enfield LBC*[74] Morrit J. rejected the proposition that an intention to benefit land could be inferred

16–062

---

[68] See *Chambers v Randall* [1923] 1 Ch. 149 at 155.
[69] [1900] 2 Ch. 388.
[70] *Renals v Cowlishaw* (1878) 9 Ch.D. 125; *Reid v Bickerstaff* [1909] 2 Ch. 305; *Ives v Brown* [1919] 2 Ch. 314; *Sainsbury Plc v Enfield LBC* [1989] 1 W.L.R. 591.
[71] [1962] Ch. 115.
[72] [1962] Ch. 115 at 132.
[73] (1968) 84 L.Q.R. 22 (Baker); (1972) 36 Conv. 20 (Ryder). See however (1972B) C.L.J. 151 (Wade) in support.
[74] [1989] 1 W.L.R. 590.

from the surrounding circumstances of a conveyance alone, but accepted that such circumstances might be relevant to construing the effect of a conveyance:

> "the intention must be manifested in the conveyance in which the covenant was contained when construed in the light of the surrounding circumstances, including any necessary implication in the conveyance from those surrounding circumstances."[75]

(iii) Statutory Annexation by s.78(1) of the Law of Property Act 1925

16–063   As has been noted above in the context of the passing of the benefit of covenants at law, the position with regard to covenants entered after 1925[76] is now much simplified as a result of the interpretation of s.78(1) of the Law of Property Act 1925 adopted by the Court of Appeal in *Federated Homes v Mill Lodge Properties Ltd*.[77] Section 78(1) provides that:

> "A covenant relating to any land of the covenantee shall be deemed to be made with the covenantee and his successors in title and the persons deriving title under him or them, and shall have effect as if such successors and other persons were expressed.
>
>   For the purposes of this subsection in connexion with covenants restrictive of the user of land 'successors in title' shall be deemed to include the owners and occupiers for the time being of the land of the covenantee intended to be benefited."

Federated Homes v Mill Lodge Properties Ltd concerned four equal-sized areas of land, the red, green, pink and blue land, originally owned by a single developer. The blue land was sold to the defendants who entered into a covenant that they would not build more than 300 houses on it. The plaintiffs subsequently purchased the green land, and there was an express assignment of the benefit of the covenant, and later acquired the red land but without any express assignment. On discovering that the defendants were proposing to build an additional 32 houses on the blue land the plaintiffs sought to enforce the covenant against them and restrain the proposed breach. The Court of Appeal held that the benefit of the covenant had passed with the green land by means of a chain of assignments, but the central question was whether the benefit had passed with the red land. Mills Q.C., sitting as a deputy High Court judge, held that it had not been annexed because there was no express annexation in the conveyance granting the covenant, and no such intention could be implied from the circumstances. However the Court of Appeal held that the language of the conveyance was sufficient to amount to an express annexation, but that in any event the benefit of the covenant had been annexed to the land by operation of s.78 of the Law of Property Act 1925. Brightman L.J. explained that s.78 was not merely intended to facilitate a short-cut in the drafting of conveyances, but that it has the effect that any covenant relating to land must be read as if made with the covenantor and his successors in title, and the

---

[75] [1989] 1 W.L.R. 590 at 595.

[76] s.78(1) has no application to covenants entered before January 1, 1926 and its predecessor (Conveyancing Act 1881, s.58) contains different language which has been held not to effect automatic annexation: *J Sainsbury Plc v Enfield LBC* [1989] 1 W.L.R. 590.

[77] [1980] 1 W.L.R. 594.

persons deriving title under it or them, including the owners and occupiers for the time being of the covenantee's land, and that therefore such a covenant must be regarded as annexed to the land.[78] In effect, s.78 implies into the language of the covenant words which would inevitably amount to an express annexation. Brightman L.J. stated that:

> "If, as the language of s.78 implies, a covenant relating to land which is restrictive of the user thereof is enforceable at the suit of (1) a successor in title of the covenantee, (2) a person deriving title under the covenantee or under his successors in title, and (3) the owner or occupier of the land intended to be benefited by the covenant, it must, in my view, follow that the covenant runs with the land, because ex hypothesi every successor in title to the land, every derivative proprietor of the land and every other owner and occupier has a right by statute to the covenant. In other words, if the condition precedent of s.78 is satisfied—that is to say, there exists a covenant which touches and concerns the land of the covenantee—that covenant runs with the land for the benefit of his successors in title, persons deriving title under him or them and other owners or occupiers."[79]

As Brightman L.J. noted, the operation of s.78 is limited to such covenants as are "relating to land", a requirement identical to the traditional and familiar concept of touching and concerning. A further limitation to the operation of s.78 is that its effect may be excluded by express counter-intention. This was recognised in *Roake v Chadha*.[80] The case concerned a covenant executed in 1934 that no more than one house would be built on a plot of land, and which stated that "this covenant shall not enure for the benefit of any owner or subsequent purchaser of any part of the . . . estate unless the benefit of this covenant shall be expressly assigned". Judge Paul Baker Q.C. held that even where s.78 operates so that a covenant is deemed to be made with the successors in title of the covenantee, "one still has to construe the covenant as a whole to see whether the benefit of the covenant is annexed". He held that although annexation could be readily inferred in such cases as *Federated Homes v Mill Lodge Properties Ltd* where there was no qualification to the covenant, the fact that the covenant in question expressly stated that it was not to be binding on successors in title meant that as a whole its true effect could not be to annex the covenant to the land. In *Crest Nicholson Ltd v McAllister*[81] a purchaser entered into a covenant with the vendor protecting land of the vendor that had yet to be sold off. Chadwick L.J. held that this showed that the benefit of that covenant was not intended to be annexed to that land as it was only intended to protect the vendor whilst the land had yet to be sold.[82] Where a covenant does touch and concern, and there is no counter-intention, the effect of s.78 as interpreted in Federated Homes is very wide-ranging and renders many of the formerly important mechanisms for passing the benefit of covenants at law and in equity much less relevant in practice. Its impact in the context of restrictive covenants is even more wide ranging because of the inclusion of mere occupiers within its scope, so that a restrictive covenant may be enforced by a licensee of the dominant tenement.

---

[78] For criticism see (1981) 97 L.Q.R. 32; (1982) 98 L.Q.R. 202 (Newson); (1982) 2 L.S. 53 (Hurst); [1985] Conv. 177 (Todd).
[79] [1980] 1 W.L.R. 594 at 605.
[80] [1984] 1 W.L.R. 40.
[81] [2004] EWCA Civ 410; [2004] 1 W.L.R. 2409.
[82] [2004] 1 W.L.R. 2409, para.50; see also *Sugarman v Porter* [2006] EWHC 331; [2006] 2 P & CR 14; paras 18–25.

(iv) Ineffective Annexation to the Dominant Tenement

16–064   It seems that a purported annexation of the benefit of a covenant will be ineffective if the dominant tenement is so large that the covenant could not possibly be of benefit to the majority of the land. This problem occurred in *Re Ballard's Conveyance*,[83] where a covenant was entered by the purchaser of the servient tenement not to erect buildings other than dwelling-houses in favour of the "Childwick Estate of Sir John Blundell Maple", which comprised some 1,700 acres. Clauson J. held that although the covenant touched and concerned "some comparatively small portion of the land to which it has been sought to annex it" it failed to touch and concern the larger part of the dominant tenement. He concluded that there was no authority justifying him severing the covenant and treating it as annexed only to "such part of the land as is touched and concerned with it" and that therefore "I must hold that the attempted annexation has failed and that the covenant has not been effectively annexed to the land and does not run with it".[84] However in more recent cases the size of the dominant tenement does not seem to have presented an insuperable barrier to annexation, and it is a matter of evidence in each case whether it can be established that the covenant benefited the whole of the dominant land. In *Earl of Leicester v Wells-Next-the-Sea UDC*[85] Plowman J. held that a covenant affecting a servient tenement of 19 acres was annexed to a dominant tenement of 32,000 acres on the basis of evidence by the managing agent that the covenant afforded great benefit and protection to the estate as a whole, as well as to particular parts adjacent to the servient land.[86] Perhaps more significantly, the servient owners had not attempted to counter this evidence.

(v) Problems of Annexation where the Dominant Land is Subsequently Divided

16–065   One particular problem which has arisen in the context of annexation is whether the benefit of a covenant passes to a successor in title who acquires only part of the dominant land to which the benefit was annexed. For example, if Ted covenanted with Bill and Bill sold and conveyed half of his land to Wayne, would Wayne enjoy the benefit of the covenant so that he could enforce it against Ted? As has been noted above there is some authority at common law that the benefit of a covenant can only pass with the whole of the land benefited and not with a mere part.[87] Historically it seems that if the benefit of a covenant was annexed only to the whole of the dominant tenement it would not pass in equity to a person who acquired only part thereof.[88] In contrast, in *Marquess of Zetland v Driver*[89] the Court of Appeal held that a covenant expressly annexed to any part or parts of the dominant land would be enforceable by subsequent purchaser of a part of the dominant land. However, the Court of Appeal in *Federated Homes v*

---

[83] [1937] Ch. 473.
[84] [1937] Ch. 473 at 482.
[85] [1973] Ch. 110.
[86] See also *Marten v Flight Refuelling Ltd* [1962] Ch. 115; *Wrotham Park Estate Co Ltd v Parkside Homes Ltd* [1974] 1 W.L.R. 798.
[87] *Re Union of London and Smith's Bank Ltd's Conveyance* [1933] Ch. 611.
[88] See *Re Ballard's Conveyance* [1937] Ch. 473.
[89] [1939] Ch. 1.

Mill Lodge Properties Ltd[90] made clear that it is not necessary for the covenant to expressly stipulate that the benefit is to be annexed to each and every part. Brightman L.J. stated:

> "I find the idea of the annexation of a covenant to the whole of the land but not to a part of it a difficult conception fully to grasp. I can understand that a covenantee may expressly or by necessary implication retain the benefit of a covenant wholly under his own control, so that the benefit will not pass unless the covenantee chooses to assign; but I would have thought that, if the benefit of a covenant is, on a proper construction of a document, annexed to the land, prima facie it is annexed to every part thereof, unless the contrary clearly appears."[91]

This suggests that in the absence of a clear contrary intention in the covenant that it is only intended to be annexed to the dominant land as a whole, a successor in title to part of the dominant tenement will be entitled to the benefit of the covenant.[92]

(c) *Benefit of the Covenant Expressly Assigned to the Owner of the Dominant Tenement*

(i) Continuing Relevance of Assignment

The introduction of statutory annexation in *Federated Homes v Mill Lodge Properties Ltd*[93] **16–066** has rendered assignment far less important as a means of passing the benefit of a covenant to successors in title of the original covenantee.[94] If, for whatever reason, the benefit of a covenant has not been annexed to the dominant land[95] it can still pass to a successor in title if there is an express assignment. An assignment differs from annexation in that it occurs when the dominant land is transferred by a person who enjoys the benefit of the land, whereas annexation is effected the moment that the covenant is granted.

(ii) Requirements of a Valid Express Assignment

For an effective assignment of the benefit of a covenant at common law the requirements of **16–067** s.136 of the Law of Property Act 1925 must be satisfied. In equity three requirements were identified by Romer L.J. in *Re Union of London and Smith's Bank Ltd's Conveyance*.[96] First,

---

[90] [1980] 1 W.L.R. 594.
[91] [1980] 1 W.L.R. 594 at 606.
[92] This presumption was applied in *Small v Oliver & Saunders (Developments) Ltd* [2006] EWHC 1293; Westlaw document 2006 WL 1635029 Ch; [2007] Conv. 70–77, a case which concerned a pre-1925 Act covenant and held that in the absence of express contrary wording, the benefit of a covenant, once annexed, enured to the benefit of each and every part of the land: paras 29–30. It is an example of the approach outside the statutory context: [2007] Conv. 70 at 71.
[93] [1980] 1 W.L.R. 594.
[94] (1980) 43 M.L.R. 445 (Hayton).
[95] For example, if the original covenant provides that the benefit can only be passed by express assignment: *Marquess of Zetland v Driver* [1937] Ch. 651.
[96] [1933] Ch. 611.

the covenant which is assigned must be capable of benefiting the dominant land. Secondly, the dominant land must have been "ascertainable" or "certain". Thirdly, the assignment must have occurred contemporaneously with the transfer of the dominant land, so that it formed part of the transaction transferring the dominant land. These requirements of effective equitable assignment were applied by Upjohn J. in *Newton-Abbot Co-operative Society Ltd v Williamson and Treadgold Ltd*[97] Bessie Mardon was the owner of property known as Devonia, from which she carried on a business as an ironmonger. She sold land opposite to purchasers who covenanted that they would not use it for any business in competition with her ironmongers. The covenant simply referred to Mrs Mardon "of Devonia", and did not describe the land to which it related. Bessie died and Devonia devolved under her will to her son, but her executors never expressly assigned the benefit of the covenant to him. He subsequently leased Devonia to the plaintiffs, with an express assignment of the benefit of the covenant. Upjohn J. held that in these circumstances the benefit of the covenant had passed to the plaintiffs by assignment. He held that the son enjoyed the benefit of the covenant because when his mother died her executors held it on trust for him, and his entitlement was not defeated by the absence of an express assignment. He then held that the covenant had been for the benefit of the land and not for Mrs Mardon personally. Finally, he held that it did not matter that the land benefited was not defined in the deed granting the covenant, as it could be ascertained with reasonable certainty from the attendant circumstances in which the covenant was granted.

(iii) Effect of Assignment

16–068   Where the benefit of a covenant is expressly assigned in equity the assignee is entitled to enforce the covenant against the covenantor, or his successors in title if it is restrictive, as long as he owns the dominant land. However, it has been argued that an express assignment does more than merely transfer the benefit of the covenant to the assignee personally. It has been claimed that a subsequent assignment by the original covenantee has the effect of annexing the benefit of the covenant to the land. Thus the assignment operates as a "delayed annexation" of the benefit of the covenant to the land, so that the benefit will pass to successors in title of the assignee without the need for further express assignments.[98] However, in *Re Pinewood Estate, Farnborough*,[99] Wynn-Parry J. held that in the absence of annexation or a building scheme a continuous chain of assignments was necessary to pass the benefit of a covenant to the present owner of the dominant land. In *Stillwell v Blackman*[100] Ungoed-Thomas J. indicated that: "there is no reason either in contract or in the relevant principles of equity why an express assignment of the benefit of a covenant with the passing of land should automatically operate exclusively as an annexation of the covenant to the land". The "delayed annexation" theory was also rejected by the first instance judge in *Federated Homes v Mill Lodge Properties Ltd* and is inconsistent with the reasoning of the Court of Appeal.

---

[97] [1952] Ch. 286.
[98] See *Renals v Cowlishaw* (1878) 9 Ch.D. 125; *Rogers v Hosegood* [1900] 2 Ch. 388 at 408; *Reid v Bickerstaff* [1909] 2 Ch. 305; [1938] 6 C.L.J. 339 (Bailey); [1957] C.L.J. 146 (Wade); [1962] J.P.L. 234 (Bowles); (1968) 84 L.Q.R. 22 (Baker); [1972B] C.L.J. 157 (Wade); (1971) 87 L.Q.R. 539 (Hayton).
[99] [1958] Ch. 280.
[100] [1968] Ch. 508 at 526.

(iv) Statutory Assignment by s.62(1) of the Law of Property Act 1925

In the context of leases it has been seen how s.62 of the Law of Property Act 1925 passes the **16–069** benefit of the tenant's covenants to an assignee of the freehold reversion. There has been some suggestion that this section could also operate so as to pass the benefit of freehold covenants to a transferee of the dominant land, as the section provides that:

> "A conveyance of land shall be deemed to include and shall by virtue of this Act operate to convey, with the land, all . . . rights and advantages whatsoever . . . appertaining or reputed to appertain to the land, or to any part thereof, or at the time of the conveyance . . . enjoyed with . . . the land or any part thereof."

However such an interpretation has been rejected on the grounds that the benefit of a covenant cannot be said to "appertain" to land unless it is annexed to it.[101] This was explained by Browne-Wilkinson V.C. in *Kumar v Dunning*:

> "The main intention of s.62 was to provide a form of statutory shorthand rendering it unnecessary to include such words expressly in every conveyance. It is a matter of debate whether, in the context of the section, the words 'rights . . . appertaining to the land' include rights arising under covenant as opposed to strict property rights. However, I will assume, without deciding, that rights under covenant are within the words of the section. Even on that assumption it still has to be shown that the right 'appertains to the land'. In my judgment, a right under a covenant cannot appertain to the land unless the benefit is in some way annexed to the land. If the benefit of a covenant passes under s.62 even if not annexed to the land, the whole modern law of restrictive covenants would have been established on an erroneous basis . . . It is established that, in the absence of annexation to the land or the existence of a building scheme, the benefit of a restrictive covenant cannot pass except by way of express assignment. The law so established is inconsistent with the view that a covenant, the benefit of which is not annexed to the land, can pass under the general words in s.62."[102]

In *Sugarman v Porter*,[103] Peter Smith J. thought the *Kumar* decision "equally applicable to an attempt to pass the benefits of a covenant by section 63 of the Law of Property Act 1925".[104] Section 63 ensures that a conveyance is effective to pass all the interest that the vendor has in the property. The covenant in this case was expressed to protect only that land that the vendor retained. This meant that the covenant was no longer annexed when the retained land had been sold off by the vendor. Thus, once the land had been sold off there could be no proprietary interest capable of passing under the sections.[105]

---

[101] *Roake v Chada* [1984] 1 W.L.R. 40. Judge Paul Baker Q.C. also suggested that s.62 may only operate in relation to legal rights, and that it excludes the benefit of a restrictive covenant which is equitable.
[102] [1989] Q.B. 193 at 198.
[103] [2006] EWHC 331; [2006]2 P & CR 14.
[104] [2006] EWHC 331; [2006]2 P & CR 14, para.35.
[105] [2006] EWHC 331; [2006]2 P & CR 14, para.38.

(d) Scheme of Development Establishing a "Local Law"

(i) The Need for a Separate Regime for Schemes of Development

16–070   One common situation where restrictive covenants are imposed is when the owner of land wishes to develop it and sell it as a number of separate plots, with each of the purchasers agreeing to restrict their user of their land. The objective of the scheme is straightforward, namely that the land of all of the successors in title to the developers should be subject to the restrictions, and that each owners of an individual plot should be able to enforce the restrictions against all the other owners. For example, if Bill wishes to develop his land by building three houses on separate plots, each of which is sold in turn to Ted, Wayne and Garth in successive months, he may wish to ensure that there is a restrictive covenant affecting all the houses that they be used for residential purposes only.

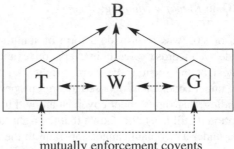

mutually enforcement covents

The rules governing annexation and assignment of the benefit of restrictive covenants are incapable of achieving the objectives of reciprocity and mutual enforceability between the three house owners. If Ted purchased the first house in July, and entered into the restrictive covenant with Bill, the benefit of the covenant would be annexed to the two plots remaining in Bill's ownership.

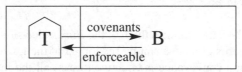

When Wayne purchased the second house from Bill in August he would take the land with the benefit of the covenant entered into by Ted, and would be able to enforce it against him if he were in breach. However, the benefit of the restrictive covenant which he himself granted to Bill would not be annexed to the land owned by Ted, meaning that Ted would not be able to enforce it against him if he was in breach.

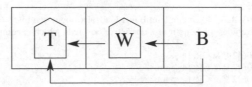

Similarly, when Garth purchased the third house in September, he would take the land with the benefit of the covenants entered into by Ted and Wayne and would be able to enforce them in the event of breach. However, there would be no land to which the benefit of the covenant he entered into could be annexed, since the covenantor, Bill, would not have retained any.

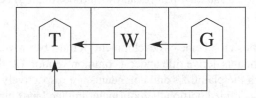

Therefore in this simple scenario the end result would be that:

(1) Garth could enforce the restrictive covenant burdening the land of Wayne.

(2) Wayne and Garth could both enforce the restrictive covenant burdening the land of Ted.

(3) Ted could not enforce the restrictive covenant burdening the land of Wayne.

(4) Neither Ted nor Wayne could enforce the restrictive covenant burdening the land of Garth.

The specifically equitable rules relating to a scheme of development enable such difficulties to be overcome and facilitate the imposition of reciprocal and mutually enforceable restrictive covenants on all the land included within the scheme.

(ii) Operation of a Scheme of Development

Where it is found that land is subject to a building scheme the consequence is that restrictive **16–071** covenants are enforceable amongst all the purchasers of plots of land subject to the development even though they would not otherwise gain the benefit of the covenants by the traditional rules regulating assignment and annexation. As Lord Browne-Wilkinson observed in *Emile Elias & Co Ltd v Pine Groves Ltd*[106] the effect of a scheme of development is to create "a local law[107] to which all owners are subject and of which all owners take the benefit".[108] Thus, if in equity it was held that Bill's land was subject to a scheme of development the restrictive covenants entered with Bill by Ted, Wayne and Garth respectively and sequentially would be enforceable between themselves inter se, and potentially by their successors in title.

---

[106] [1993] 1 W.L.R. 305.
[107] See also *Reid v Bickerstaff* [1909] 2 Ch. 305 at 319, per Cozens-Hardy M.R.
[108] A contractual analogy is *Clarke v Dunraven* [1897] A.C. 59, where it was held that competitors entering a yacht race entered into mutually enforceable obligations to adhere to the rules even though their arrangement could not be analysed using the conventional rules of offer and acceptance. See also *Law v National Greyhound Racing Club Ltd* [1983] 1 W.L.R. 1302.

(iii) Traditional Requirements of a Scheme of Development

16–072 Although nineteenth-century equity cases enforced restrictive covenants entered into under a scheme of development on the basis of broad concepts such as "community of interest",[109] in *Elliston v Reacher*[110] Parker J. adopted four criteria, subsequently approved by the Court of Appeal,[111] which had to be satisfied before land would be found to be subject to a scheme of development:

> "In order to [establish a scheme of development] it must be proved (1) that both the plain-tiffs and the defendants derive title under a common vendor; (2) that previously to selling the lands to which the plaintiff's and defendants are respectively entitled the vendor laid out his estate, or a defined portion thereof (including the lands purchased by the plaintiffs and defendants respectively), for sale in lots subject to restrictions intended to be imposed on all the lots, and which, though varying in details as to particular lots, are consistent and consistent only with some general scheme of development; (3) that these restrictions were intended by the common vendor to be and were for the benefit of all the lots intended to be sold, whether or not they were also intended to be for the benefit of other land retained by the vendor; and (4) that both the plaintiffs and the defendants, or their predecessors in title, purchased their lots from the common vendor on the footing that the restrictions subject to which the purchases were made were to enure for the benefit of the other lots included in the general scheme whether or not they were also to enure for the benefit of other lands retained by the vendors."

Applying these criteria it was held that land which was laid out into plots by a building society was subject to a scheme of development, so that restrictive covenants entered into by the purchasers of some plots that they would not use the land for a hotel or public house were enforceable against their successors in title by the successors in title of others who had purchased plots from the society and therefore enjoyed the benefit of the covenants. However the criteria appear to have presented such a barrier to establishing a scheme of development that there were only two reported cases between 1908 and 1961 where such a scheme was held to exist. In *Reid v Bickerstaff*[112] the Court of Appeal seemed to add the additional requirement that the area subject to the scheme must be well defined. Cozens-Hardy M.R. stated:

> "What are some of the essentials of a building scheme? In my opinion there must be a defined area within which the scheme is operative. Reciprocity is the foundation of the idea of a scheme. A purchaser of one parcel cannot be subject to an implied obligation to purchasers of an undefined and unknown area. He must know both the extent of his burden and the extent of his benefit."[113]

---

[109] See *Renals v Cowlishaw* (1878) 9 Ch.D. 125; *Nottingham Patent Brick and Tile Co v Butler* (1885) 15 Q.B.D. 261; *Collins v Castle* (1887) 36 Ch.D. 243; *Spicer v Martin* (1888) 14 App. Cas. 12.
[110] [1908] 2 Ch. 365 at 384.
[111] [1908] 2 Ch. 665.
[112] [1909] 2 Ch. 305.
[113] [1909] 2 Ch. 305 at 319.

(iv) Relaxation of the Traditional Requirements

Despite their long standing, a number of cases in the 1960s and 1970s backed away from a strict application of the requirements identified in Elliston v Reacher as essential for the existence of a scheme of development, and instead concentrated on the question whether there was a common intention to subject land to reciprocal covenants. In *Baxter v Four Oaks Properties Ltd*[114] Cross J. held that the court was not precluded from finding a scheme of development as a matter of law merely because the common vendor did not lay out the land in plots before the first land was sold. Instead he considered that what was required was ". . . a clearly proved intention that the purchasers were to have rights inter se".[115] In *Re Dolphin's Conveyance*[116] Stamp J. held that it was not essential that all the land subject to the scheme of development must have been sold by a common vendor. He considered that the requirements stated in *Elliston v Reacher* evidenced a common intention that the parties should be subject to mutually enforceable reciprocal covenants but that this was not the exclusive means by which such an intention could be established. He concluded that there was a building scheme because the necessary common intention was evident in the conveyances of the land from the vendors to the purchasers. Although in *Emile Elias & Co Ltd v Pine Groves Ltd*[117] the Privy Council referred to *Elliston v Reacher* as indicating "the requirements which have to be satisfied in order to establish such a building scheme", Lord Browne-Wilkinson expressly noted that there "have been certain developments in the law since that date" but that these did not bear on the case in issue. The case does not, therefore, re-assert the *Elliston v Reacher* criteria and the more liberal regime continues.[118]

16–073

(v) No Building Scheme Unless a Common Intention can be Established

The essential criterion for the establishment of a scheme of development is a common intention that the purchasers would be subject to mutual reciprocal restrictions enforceable inter se. If no such intention can be identified there will be no "local law". In *Lund v Taylor*[119] the Court of Appeal held that there was no scheme of development where there was no evidence that the purchasers of plots were told that the common vendor intended to exact similar covenants from the purchasers of other plots, nor was any such intention evidenced by the conveyances themselves. More significantly, in *Emile Elias & Co Ltd v Pine Groves Ltd*[120] the Privy Council held that a common intention could not be established if there was a lack of uniformity of the covenants required from the purchasers of different plots. The case concerned land which was formerly part of a golf club in Trinidad sold in five parcels to four purchasers, each of whom entered into restrictive covenants. All the covenants contained a restriction on erecting more than one dwelling-house, but the covenants of lots 2 and 3 also restricted the use of

16–074

---

[114] [1965] 1 Ch. 816.
[115] [1965] 1 Ch. 816 at 828.
[116] [1970] Ch. 654.
[117] [1993] 1 W.L.R. 305.
[118] Also *Small v Oliver & Saunders (Developments) Ltd* [2006] EWHC 1293, Ch; Westlaw document 2006 WL 1635029 [2007] Conv. 70–77.
[119] (1976) 31 P. & C.R. 167.
[120] [1993] 1 W.L.R. 305.

any building erected as a private dwelling-house. Lord Browne-Wilkinson explained that this meant that there was insufficient reciprocity to find the necessary common intention:

> "It is one of the badges of an enforceable building scheme . . . that they accept a common code of covenants. It is most improbable that a purchaser will have any intention to accept the burden of covenants affecting the land which he acquires being enforceable by other owners of the land in the scheme area unless he himself is to enjoy reciprocal rights over the lands of other such owners; the crucial element of reciprocity would be missing. That does not mean that all lots within the scheme must be subject to identical covenants. For example, in a scheme of mixed residential and commercial development, the covenants will obviously vary according to the use intended to be made of each category of lot. But if, as in the present case, they are all of a similar nature and all intended for high class development consisting of one dwelling house on a substantial plot, a disparity in the covenants imposed is a powerful indication that there was no intention to create reciprocally enforceable rights."[121]

(vi) No Building Scheme Unless there is a Defined Scheme Area Known to all the Original Purchasers

16–075 The second main requirement for the existence of a building scheme in the modern law is that there is a defined area of land subject to the common intention to impose mutually enforceable reciprocal covenants. As has been noted, this requirement was identified by the Court of Appeal in *Reid v Bickerstaff*.[122] In *Lund v Taylor*[123] it was claimed that a scheme of development enabled the enforcement of covenants not to erect blocks of flats on land between purchasers from a common vendor. Although the common vendor had drawn up an architect's plan for the development of part of the land the Court of Appeal held that there was insufficient evidence to establish a scheme of development. Stamp L.J. explained that the individual purchasers had not been made aware that a defined area of land was intended to be subject to reciprocal covenants:

> "In the instant case there is no evidence that the Estate Plan was brought to the attention of any of the purchasers . . . There is no evidence that any proposing purchaser of a plot was told that the vendor was proposing to exact similar covenants, or indeed any covenants, from the purchasers of other plots . . . Because there was no extrinsic evidence, nor anything in his own conveyance to show a purchaser that there was a scheme relating to a defined area, or that [the vendors] intended that stipulations should be imposed in respect of each part of that area [the plaintiff] could not on the authority of *Reid v Bickerstaff* be subject to an implied obligation to the other purchasers. On this ground alone the action must . . . fail."[124]

---

[121] [1993] 1 W.L.R. 305 at 311.
[122] [1909] 2 Ch. 305.
[123] (1976) 31 P. & C.R. 167.
[124] (1976) 31 P. & C.R. 167 at 174–176.

Similarly, in *Emile Elias & Co Ltd v Pine Groves Ltd*[125] the Privy Council held that there was no defined area subject to a scheme of development. Lord Browne-Wilkinson stated that the rationale for the requirement was that "to create a valid building scheme, the purchasers of all the land within the area of the scheme must also know what that area is". The general plan of the land sold by the golf club in five plots, which was attached to all the conveyances, did not show plot five. Lord Browne-Wilkinson explained that this had the consequence that the requirement of a defined area was not met:

> "If therefore lot 5 falls to be treated as part of the designated scheme area, it has not been proved that in 1938 the purchasers of lots 1, 2 and 3 were aware of that fact. [Counsel] suggested that it would be inferred from the fact that all the purchasers were associated with the golf club and . . . were aware of lot 5 . . . Their Lordships feel unable to attach to any such inference sufficient probative force to reach an affirmative conclusion that all the purchasers of the lots in 1938 knew that lot 5 was included. If lot 5 was to be part of a scheme area giving rise to mutually enforceable obligations between all the lots, it would surely have been shown on the plan annexed to each of the conveyances. In the view of the Board, if there was any intention to create mutually enforceable rights in a scheme area, lot 5 must have been part of that area. It was sold at the same time as lots 1–4 and was subjected to the same covenants as affected lot 4 and lot 1. It is entirely incredible that there was any intention to create rights which would be mutually enforceable between the owners of lots 1, 2, 3 and 4 but not enforceable by and against the owner of lot 5. Accordingly, lot 5 being part of any scheme that could be established and it not having been shown that the purchasers of lots 1–3 were aware of that fact, the requirement of a defined scheme area known to the original purchasers cannot be satisfied."[126]

(vii) Sub-schemes within a Wider Scheme of Development

Complex questions of enforceability arise where land subject to a scheme of development is   **16–076**
further subdivided, so that within the overall scheme there are areas subject to sub-schemes which might impose different covenants. The main issues are whether the covenants of the sub-scheme are mutually enforceable between the purchasers of the land comprising the sub-scheme, and whether the covenants of the head scheme are similarly enforceable by the purchasers of the land in the sub-scheme inter se. These questions were raised in *Brunner v Greenslade*.[127] Clearly the covenants entered by the purchasers of land subject to the sub-scheme will be enforceable inter se on the basis of the local law that the sub-scheme creates amongst them. Megarry J. rejected the view, derived from the decision of Romer J. in *Knight v Simmonds*,[128] that the covenants of a head scheme could never bind the purchasers of land subject to a sub-scheme inter se. Instead he considered that the covenants of the head

---

[125] [1993] 1 W.L.R. 305.
[126] [1993] 1 W.L.R. 305 at 310–311; In *Small v Oliver & Saunders (Developments) Ltd* [2006] EWHC 1293 the claimant was unable to establish a building scheme because he could not show that the original purchasers knew of the scheme and its reciprocity: Westlaw document 2006 WL 1635029, paras 45 and 46.
[127] [1971] Ch. 993.
[128] [1896] 1 Ch. 653.

scheme would be enforceable between them unless they had made clear an intention that the new covenants should replace the old. This would clearly be the case if the purchasers of the sub-lots had mutually covenanted that all should be released inter se from the head scheme and subjected to the sub-scheme, but this was not essential to demonstrating the necessary intention.

4. Enforcement of Restrictive Covenants

(a) *An Injunction or Damages in Lieu*

16–077   Where the equitable rules regulating the passing of the benefit and burden of restrictive covenants are satisfied, so that the servient land is subject to the burden of the covenant and the owner of the dominant land is entitled to the benefit thereof, remedies will be available to the dominant owner in the event of breach. If a breach has not yet occurred but the servient owner is proposing to act in breach the court may grant a prohibitory injunction to restrain the breach. Where the breach has already occurred the court may grant a mandatory injunction ordering the servient owner to remove whatever is causing it. This will be especially so if the servient owner has gone ahead and breached the covenant having been warned that his activities would constitute a breach. In *Wakeham v Wood*[129] the owner of servient land subject to a covenant not to erect any buildings which would obscure the sea view of the dominant land was ordered to pull down a building he had erected in flagrant disregard of the dominant owner's rights despite the fact that he had been warned by the dominant owner and his solicitor. However the court is naturally reluctant to order the wasteful destruction of buildings which have been completed, and in cases where the breach is less flagrant they are more likely to award the dominant owner damages in lieu of an injunction. For example, in *Wrotham Park Estates v Parkside Homes*[130] the servient owners built housing on land in breach of a restrictive covenant requiring them to obtain the prior approval of the dominant owner to the plans of the development. Although the dominant owners had protested at the breach and the servient owners had continued building, Brightman J. refused a mandatory injunction. He stated:

> "The erection of the houses, whether one likes it or not, is a fait accompli and the houses are now the homes of people. I accept that this particular fait accompli is reversible and could be undone. But I cannot close my eyes to the fact that the houses now exist. It would, in my opinion, be an unpardonable waste of much needed houses to direct that they now be pulled down and I have never had a moment's doubt during the hearing of this case that such an order ought to be refused."[131]

He accordingly awarded the dominant owners the equivalent of 5 per cent of the servient owners expected profits from the development in lieu of an injunction.

[129] (1982) 43 P. & C.R. 40.
[130] [1974] 1 W.L.R. 798.
[131] [1974] 1 W.L.R. 798 at 811.

(b) *Refusal of any Remedy*

Since equitable remedies are discretionary it is open for the court to refuse to award any **16–078** remedy for breach of covenant if it so chooses. In *Chatsworth Estates Co v Fewell*[132] Farwell J. anticipated the possibility that a court would not enforce a covenant restricting the use of land to residential purposes if the entire character of the neighbourhood had been changed by the dominant owner licensing non-residential use so that "there is no longer any value left in the covenants at all". However, he concluded that in the circumstances of the case the character of the neighbourhood had not been so changed by the dominant owner licensing some of the land to be used for schools, some of the houses to be converted into flats and allowing three boarding houses and a hotel to start business. Acquiescence in a breach of covenant may also disentitle a dominant owner from any remedy. This was recognised by the Court of Appeal in *Shaw v Applegate*[133] where the dominant owner took no action for three years while the servient owner used his land as an amusement arcade in breach of covenant. Buckley L.J. stated that the appropriate test was whether "the situation has become such that it would be unconscionable for the [servient owner], or the person having the right sought to be enforced, to continue to seek to enforce it". Again it was held that in the circumstances of the case the dominant owner had not acquiesced in the breach because the parties had been confused in their minds as to whether what was being done was in law a breach of the covenant. However, the failure to act meant that the appropriate remedy was not an injunction but damages in lieu.

5. Extinction of Restrictive Covenants

Since a restrictive covenant operates as a form of negative easement affecting land, just as an **16–079** easement would be extinguished by the unification of title to the dominant and servient tenements in a single owner, a restrictive covenant will also be extinguished if there is no longer any distinction of ownership between the dominant and servient land.[134] However, where the title to distinct plots in a scheme of development are unified the covenants are not extinguished but merely suspended. They will therefore revive if the land is subsequently re-divided. In *Texaco Antilles Ltd v Kernochan* Lord Cross, giving the advice of the Privy Council, stated:

> "It is no doubt true that if the restrictions in question exist simply for the mutual benefit of two adjoining properties and both those properties are bought by one man the restrictions will automatically come to an end and will not revive on a subsequent severance unless the common owner then recreates them. But their Lordships cannot see that it follows from this that if a number of people agree that the area covered by all their properties shall be subject to a 'local law' the provisions of which shall be enforceable by any owner for the time being of any part against any other owner and the whole area has

---

[132] [1931] 1 Ch. 224.
[133] [1977] 1 W.L.R. 970.
[134] *Re Tiltwood, Sussex* [1978] Ch. 269; *Re Victoria Recreation Ground, Portslade's Application* (1979) 41 P. & C.R. 119; [1973] A.C. 609 at 626.

never at any time come into common ownership an action by one owner of a part against another owner of a part must fail if it can be shown that both parts were either at the inception of the scheme or at any time subsequently in common ownership."[135]

The covenants will therefore revive on subsequent re-division of the land unless the parties have indicated a clear intention to the contrary.

6. Modification or Discharge of Restrictive Covenants

(a) *Discharge in Accordance with the Terms of the Covenant*

16–080 The terms of a restrictive covenant may provide that it is to be discharged in specified circumstances, or alternatively the terms of the covenant may be construed so as to lead to the conclusion that it must have been the intention of the parties for it to be discharged in certain circumstances. In *Crest Nicholson Residential (South) Ltd v McAllister* at first instance[136] a covenant was granted to a company which was selling off plots of land from an estate that the purchasers would not erect a dwelling house or other building on the plot unless the plans and drawings had been previously submitted to the company and approved in writing. The company was subsequently dissolved. The question was whether the covenant had thereby become absolute, thus preventing any development of the land at all because the company no longer existed to give the necessary consent, or whether it had been discharged by the dissolution of the company. Neuberger J. held that, as a matter of construction, the covenant had been discharged. Given that the covenants anticipated that the land could be developed in the future, he concluded that it was far more likely that the parties had intended that the covenant would be discharged when the company was dissolved than that it would become absolute, thus preventing all development.[137]

(b) *Modification or Discharge by the Land Tribunal*

16–081 Where land has been subjected to restrictive covenants in the past it is not necessarily the case that those covenants will be appropriate for the present. Section 84(1) of the Law of Property Act 1925 empowers the Land Tribunal "wholly or partially to discharge or modify any . . . restriction" affecting an interest in freehold land on the application of "any person interested" in the land.

---

[135] [1973] A.C. 609 at 626.
[136] [2002] EWHC 2443 (Ch.).
[137] On appeal [2004] 1 W.L.R. 2409, Chadwick L.J. held that the covenant had not been annexed to the land, and thus concluded that it was unnecessary to decide whether the restriction was now spent: para.53. However, he stated that he saw no reason to disagree with the judge's conclusions. At first instance annexation had been conceded so the judge had not had to consider the point.

(c) Grounds Justifying Exercise of the Power to Modify or Discharge

Section 84 sets out a variety of grounds entitling the Land Tribunal to modify or discharge a covenant:

16–082

(i) Obsolescence[138]

Section 84(1)(a) provides that a restrictive covenant may be modified or discharged if the restriction has become obsolete because of "changes in the character of the property or the neighbourhood or other circumstances".

16–083

(ii) Impediment to Reasonable User[139]

Section 84(1)(aa) provides for modification or discharge if the continued existence of the covenant "would impede some reasonable user of the land for public or private purposes". In order to exercise its jurisdiction on these grounds the Land Tribunal must be satisfied that the restriction impeding the reasonable user "does not secure to persons entitled to the benefit of it any practical benefits of substantial value or advantage to them", or that it "is contrary to public policy", and that "money will be an adequate compensation for the loss or disadvantage (if any)" which the dominant owner would suffer by a modification or variation.[140] The jurisdiction to modify a restrictive covenant on these grounds was examined by the Court of Appeal in *Re University of Westminster*.[141] It was held that a restriction on the use of buildings as "a School of Management Studies, a College of Architecture and Advanced Building Technology, a Hall of Residence for students, an office for a District Surveyor and for Housing purposes" could be modified on the grounds that the continued existence of the restriction would impede some reasonable user. The covenant was therefore modified to permit use for general educational purposes. In *Duffield v Gandy*[142] a covenant that restricted the building of a dwelling was of substantial benefit to the covenantee, the owner of the neighbouring land, by protecting her privacy when she used her garden, and thus the grounds for discharge under s.84(1)(aa) had not been satisfied.

16–084

(iii) Holders of Benefit have Agreed to Discharge or Modification[143]

The Land Tribunal may exercise its power by s.84(1)(b) if those entitled to the benefit of the covenant are of age and legally competent and they have "agreed, either expressly or by implication, by their acts or omissions" to a modification or discharge.

16–085

---

[138] See *Keith v Texaco Ltd* (1977) 34 P. & C.R. 249; *Re Cox's Application* (1985) 51 P. & C.R. 335; *Re Quaffers Ltd's Application* (1988) 56 P. & C.R. 142.
[139] See *Re Bass Ltd's Application* (1973) 26 P. & C.R. 156; *Gilbert v Spoor* [1983] Ch. 27; *Stannard v Issa* [1987] A.C. 175.
[140] Law of Property Act 1925 s.84(1A).
[141] [1998] 3 All E.R. 1014.
[142] [2008] EWCA Civ 379; Westlaw document 2008 WL 1737256.
[143] See *Re Fettishaw's Application (No.2)* (1973) 27 P. & C.R. 156; *Re Memvale's Securities Ltd's Application* (1975) 233 E.G. 689.

(iv) No Injury to the Holders of the Benefit[144]

16–086 Under s.84(1)(c) the Land Tribunal may modify or discharge a covenant if "the proposed discharge or modification will not injure the persons entitled to the benefit of the restriction".

(v) Imposition of Additional Limitations

16–087 When an application is sought for the modification or discharge of a restriction the Land Tribunal may add such additional limitations to the user of the land "as appear to the Lands Tribunal to be reasonable in view of the relaxation of the existing provisions".[145] Although such additional restrictions can only be imposed with the consent of the applicant, the Tribunal can "refuse to modify a restriction without some addition".

(d) *Compensation where Covenant Modified or Discharged*

16–088 Where the court modifies or discharges a covenant under s.84(1) the Land Tribunal may order the payment of compensation to the person entitled to the benefit thereof to compensate for "any loss or disadvantage suffered by that person in consequence of the discharge of modification"[146] or "to make up for any effect which the restriction had, at the time when it was imposed, in reducing the consideration then received for the land affected by it".[147] In *Winter v Traditional & Contemporary Contracts Ltd*[148] Carnwath L.J. held that the measure of compensation "is based on the impact of the development on the objectors, not on the loss of the opportunity to extract a share of the development value".[149]

REFORM OF THE LAW RELATING TO COVENANTS AFFECTING FREEHOLD LAND

1. Complexity of the Present Law

16–089 As has no doubt been appreciated, the law relating to the enforceability of covenants affecting freehold land is extremely complex. The whole area illustrates the difficulties which arise at the interface between the law of property and the law of contractual obligations, and the difference between personal and proprietary rights. There is an uncomfortable overlap

---

[144] See *Re Forestmere Properties Ltd's Application* (1980) 41 P. & C.R. 390; *Re Livingstones' Application* (1982) 47 P. & C.R. 462.
[145] Law of Property Act 1925 s.84(1B).
[146] Law of Property Act 1925 s.84(1)(i).
[147] Law of Property Act 1925 s.84(1)(ii).
[148] [2007] EWCA Civ 1088; Westlaw document 2007 WL 3236342.
[149] [2007] EWCA Civ 1088; Westlaw document 2007 WL 3236342, para.28.

between the law of property and the law of contract, with the covenant remaining enforceable "despite changes in ownership of the land".[150] This is further complicated by distinctions developed by the historic separation between equity and the common law. This causes a fundamental distinction between positive and restrictive covenants, and whilst a number of concepts are common to both for determining whether the benefit of a covenant passes with the land, namely assignment and annexation, they are applied with subtle variations. This present complexity has led to a number of reviews of the law in this area with the objective of reform and simplification.[151] In 1984 the Law Commission proposed a complete overhaul of the law in its report *Transfer of Land: The Law of Positive and Restrictive Covenants*.[152] These recommendations have not been translated into legislation. Most recently, the Law Commission has proposed extensive reform to the law of easements, covenants and profits à prendre in its Consultation Paper *Easements, Covenants and Profits à Prendre*.[153]

2. Recommendations of the Law Commission

(a) *Defects of the Present Law*

In its 2008 Consultation Paper, *Easements, Covenants and Profits à Prendre*,[154] the Law Commission identified a number of defects in the present law. First, it is inappropriate that the burden of positive covenants can never run with the land, and the present means for avoiding this limitation[155] are inadequate, "complex and insufficiently comprehensive".[156] As the Law Commission pointed out in 1984, this inability would prevent the creation of freehold flat schemes because the obligation of a lower flat to be kept in good repair for the benefit of an upper flat could not be made to pass with the title.[157] Secondly, the rules for running the burden of restrictive covenants under *Tulk v Moxhay* are unnecessarily technical and complex[158]; the rules for running the benefit in equity are yet more complicated.[159] Third, contractual liability still persists even after the parties have transferred the land.[160] Furthermore, it is important to bring substantive land law into line with the reforms to the law of registration of title introduced by the Land Registration Act 2002.[161]

16–090

---

[150] Law Commission "Easements, Covenants and Profits à Prendre": Law Com. No.186 (2008), para.1.12(6), Summary.
[151] Wilberforce Committee on Positive Covenants, Cmnd. 2719 (1965); Law Com. No.11, *Transfer of Land: Report on Restrictive Covenants* (1967); Law Commission Working Paper No.36, *Transfer of Land: Appurtenant Rights* (1971).
[152] Law Com. No.127 (1984).
[153] Law Com. No.186 (2008).
[154] Law Com. No.196 (2008), Summary.
[155] For example, a chain of indemnity covenants, rights of entry.
[156] Law Com. No.186 (2008) para.1.12(1), Summary.
[157] Law Com. No.127 (1984), para.4.4.
[158] Law Com. No.186 (2008), paras 7.36–7.37.
[159] Law Com. No.186 (2008), paras 7.36–7.37.
[160] Law Com. No.186 (2008), para.1.21, Summary; This is similar to the Law Commission's observation in 1984, para.4.9.
[161] Law Com. No.186 (2008), para 1.5, Summary.

(b) *Proposed Reform: The Creation of the "Land Obligation"*[162]

16–091 The Law Commission proposes to remedy the defects in the present law not by small piece-meal changes but by the introduction of a wholly new interest in land, the "Land Obligation". It would be "a new category of property interest" that could be attached to land so as to bind successors in title.[163] It "would cease to be enforceable by the original parties once they had parted with their respective interests in the land".[164] A Land Obligation would be capable of imposing positive obligations such as repair and maintenance.[165] To qualify as a Land Obligation a right should benefit the land and not be purely personal.[166] It should be expressly created. The Law Commission proposes that it should only be capable of creation in relation to registered land.[167] It would have to be entered on both the benefited and the burdened titles.[168] A Land Obligation would be capable of existing as a legal interest in land,[169] although the Law Commission contemplated that there could also be an "equitable Land Obligation".[170]

The proposed regime would allow developers to create a scheme of reciprocally enforceable Land Obligations when plots of a developed estate were sold off. For a Land Obligation to exist it would not be necessary for the dominant and servient land to be in separate ownership and possession, the requirement under the current law of covenants. This requirement for separate ownership and possession prevents developers, where the land is in the developer's common ownership, from imposing obligations on the various plots of land.[171] As seen above, the current law provides that covenants can be enforced if a "scheme of development" can be established, but the criteria are strict.[172] Thus the Law Commission proposes the removal of the requirement of separate ownership and possession and imposes only the condition that the dominant and servient land should have separate title numbers.[173] This would allow developers to create a scheme of common obligations enforceable against successors in title

---

[162] The expression "Land Obligation" originally emerged in the context of proposals contained in the 1967 Report, Wilberforce Committee on Positive Covenants, Cmnd. 2719 (1965); Law Com. No.11, *Transfer of Land: Report on Restrictive Covenants* (1967), which also proposed a new interest in land, proceeding on an analogy with easements: Law Com. No.186 (2008), para.7.5. In 1984 the Law Commission proposed a scheme of land obligations: *Transfer of Land: The Law of Positive and Restrictive Covenants*: Law Com. No.127 (1984). The 2008 Report examines the 1984 Report and builds on certain aspects of it, whilst rejecting others (such as the need for two types of land obligation: "neighbour obligations" and "development obligations").

[163] Law Com. No.186 (2008), Summary, para.1.15.

[164] Law Com. No.186 (2008), para.8.66.

[165] Law Com. No.186 (2008), Summary, para.1.29.

[166] The Law Commission considers that the appropriate test to apply to determine whether or not a Land Obligation is of benefit to the land is that laid down in the existing law of covenants, *P & A Swift Investments v Combined English Stores Group Plc* [1989] AC 632 para 16-025 above: Law Com. No.186 (2008), paras 8.78–8.80.

[167] Law Com. No.186 (2008), Summary, para.1.30. And thus "the first interest in land that would be capable of having effect only if title is registered": Law Com. No.186 (2008), para.8.32. The Law Commission concluded that the scheme would be unsuitable for unregistered land: para.8.34.

[168] Law Com. No.186 (2008), Summary, para.1.29.

[169] "The creation of a Land Obligation capable of comprising a legal interest would have to be completed by registration of the interest in the register for the benefited land and a notice of the interest entered in the register for the burdened land. A Land Obligation would not operate at law until these registration requirements were met". Law Com. No.186 (2008), para.8.13.

[170] Again by analogy with easements, equitable easements can exist: para.8.54.

[171] Law Com. No.186 (2008), para.8.82.

[172] Law Com. No.186 (2008), para.8.83.

[173] Law Com. No.186 (2008), para.8.85.

by applying "for the allocation of separate title numbers to each lot" and registering Land Obligations against each one.[174]

(c) The Relationship of the New Land Obligation Scheme to the Commonhold Regime

The commonhold structure provides a system of enforcing positive (and restrictive) obligations, for example, a complex system of obligations that relate to repair and maintenance of common parts. However, the Law Commission felt that there was still a need to reform the general law of covenants.[175] **16–092**

(d) Phasing Out of Restrictive Covenants

Following the introduction of the Land Obligation, it is suggested that it should no longer be possible, in relation to a registered title, to create new covenants.[176] However, if the proposed system of Land Obligations were to be introduced, one problem would be that existing restrictive covenants would not automatically become Land Obligations.[177] It is considered that there should be some scheme for the phasing out of existing covenants to prevent there being a complex dual regime.[178] It proposes various alternatives, including the extinguishment of a covenant after a certain number of years, giving owner the option of a Land Obligation to "mirror the nature of the restriction in the original covenant".[179] **16–093**

(e) Reform of Section 84 of the Law of Property Act 1925

The Law Commission seeks to reform the law in relation to the scope of the courts' jurisdiction under s.84 of the Law of Property Act 1925 to discharge and modify restrictive covenants. It proposes that it should be extended to include the new Land Obligation, and also easements and profits.[180] It also proposes that the grounds for discharge and modification should be made more transparent, in accordance with the existing practice of the Lands Tribunal.[181] **16–094**

---

[174] Law Com. No.186 (2008), para.8.85.
[175] Law Com. No.186 (2008), para.7.66.
[176] Law Com. No.186 (2008), para.13.2.
[177] Law Com. No.186 (2008), para.13.5.
[178] Law Com. No.186 (2008), para.13.5.
[179] Law Com. No.186 (2008), para.13.22 (this was similar to what was suggested in the 1991 report: Law Com. No.201, *Transfer of Land: Obsolete Restrictive Covenants* (1991)): Law Com. No.186 (2008), para.13.23.
[180] Law Com. No.186 (2008), Summary, para.1.34.
[181] Law Com. No.186 (2008), Summary, para.1.35.

Chapter 17

MORTGAGES

THE NATURE OF MORTGAGES AND SECURITY

---

1. Introduction

Most people buying a house are not in the fortunate position of having enough cash to pay for the house outright. They therefore need to borrow in order to pay for it. In comparison with their earnings, the borrowings which house buyers need to make are often relatively large. A young couple acquiring their first home may have only a small deposit and may therefore have to borrow three or four times their joint income in order to finance the purchase of even a relatively modest property. Any lender advancing this much money will want to take precautions against the possibility that the loan is not repaid. Suppose, for instance, that the borrowers die before they have repaid the loan, or some other misfortune occurs, such as one or both of them losing their job. There are various ways in which a lender can obtain protection against such events. When a lender takes protection in this way, it is said to be taking security for the loan. Of course, there are also commercial situations where a lender will want to take security. A bank lending money to a company will want protection against the possibility of the company becoming insolvent and being unable to meet all its financial obligations. It will not always be content to join a queue for payment with all the other creditors.

17–001

2. The Nature of Security

A lender is said to have security for a loan where some arrangement has been made under which the lender has some rights over and above the right to sue the borrower for the money if the loan is not repaid.[1] There are two main ways in which a lender can obtain security. The

17–002

---

[1] See Sheridan, *Rights in Security* (1974), p.1.

first is by entering into an agreement under which, if the borrower does not repay the loan, someone else is liable to do so. This is described as personal security.[2] The second is by making an agreement under which, if the loan is not repaid, the lender has limited rights against some property, for instance, by being able to sell the property in order to use the proceeds of sale to pay off the loan. This latter kind of arrangement (which includes mortgages) is described as real security, since some thing (or res, to use the Latin expression) is providing the security or safeguard to the lender. Within each of these two types of security, there are a number of variants. Although this book is primarily concerned with mortgages, it is worth briefly examining other forms of security because this helps to explain the context. Moreover, it is not uncommon for more than one form of security to be used in a single transaction. The diagram on page 000 sets out in schematic form the different types of personal and real security. In addition to the forms of security which are considered here, there are also other arrangements which can be used to protect suppliers of goods. These include conditional sales, hire-purchase, finance leases and retention of title arrangements. Descriptions of these arrangements can be found in most standard textbooks on commercial law, and are not considered further in this book.

3. Personal Security

17–003 Personal security consists of the lender's right to sue someone else if the borrower fails to repay. There are several ways in which the lender can acquire such rights. The person who undertakes to give security to the lender by agreeing to this liability is known as a surety.

(a) *Guarantee*[3]

17–004 A guarantee represents a long-stop against a failure on the part of the borrower to honour his obligation to repay. In the context of security arrangements, the term guarantee is normally confined to situations where the lender can only call upon the surety if the borrower is in default. The extent of the surety's liability rests upon the proper interpretation of the contract under which such liability was assumed.[4] For instance, where a loan is repayable in instalments, the surety might have undertaken to guarantee payment of each instalment on the date on which it falls due.[5] Alternatively, where the loan provides that on the borrower's default in paying any instalment, the whole loan is repayable, the surety's contract might oblige him

---

[2] *Islamic Press Agency Inc v Al-Wazir* [2001] EWCA Civ 1276 per Robert Walker L.J. at [18]: "I would agree that the most usual meaning of 'surety' (as applied to a person) or 'guarantor' is someone who undertakes personal liability for another person's obligation. However the expression 'surety' can be used, without solecism, to describe a person who provides some of his property as security for another person's obligation".

[3] As well as being used to describe a form of personal security, the word guarantee is used in other contexts, such as to describe a specific undertaking in a sales contract as to the quality or performance of goods.

[4] Lord Reid in *Moschi v Lep Air Services Ltd* [1972] 2 All E.R. 393 at 398, HL at 398: "Parties are free to make any agreement they like".

[5] See *Moschi v Lep Air Services Ltd* [1973] A.C. 331.

Forms of Security

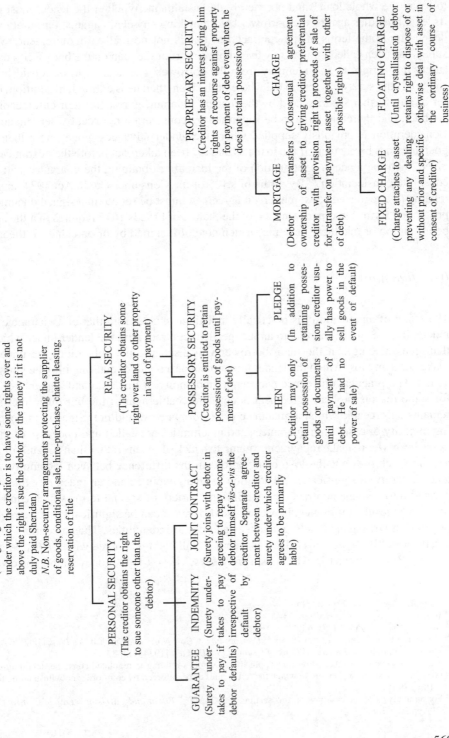

SECURITY

(The giving of security is the making of an arrangement under which the creditor is to have some rights over and above the right in sue the debtor for the money if it is not duly paid Sheridan)
N.B. Non-security arrangements protecting the supplier of goods, conditional sale, hire-purchase, chattel leasing, reservation of title

PERSONAL SECURITY

(The creditor obtains the right to sue someone other than the debtor)

GUARANTEE
(Surety undertakes to pay if debtor defaults)

INDEMNITY
(Surety undertakes to pay irrespective of default by debtor)

JOINT CONTRACT
(Surety joins with debtor in agreeing to repay become a debtor himself *vis-a-vis* the creditor Separate agreement between creditor and surety under which creditor agrees to be primarily liable)

REAL SECURITY

(The creditor obtains some right over land or other property in and of payment)

POSSESSORY SECURITY

(Creditor is entitled to retain possession of goods until payment of debt)

HEN

(Creditor may only retain possession of goods or documents until payment of debt. He had no power of sale)

PLEDGE

(In addition to retaining possession, creditor usually has power to sell goods in the event of default)

PROPRIETARY SECURITY

(Creditor has an interest giving him rights of recourse against property for payment of debt even where he does not retain possession)

MORTGAGE

(Debtor transfers ownership of asset to creditor with provision for retransfer on payment of debt)

CHARGE

(Consensual agreement giving creditor preferential right to proceeds of sale of asset together with other possible rights)

FIXED CHARGE

(Charge attaches to asset preventing any dealing without prior and specific consent of creditor)

FLOATING CHARGE

(Until crystallisation debtor retains right to dispose of or otherwise deal with asset in the ordinary course of business) to repay the whole loan,[6] and not merely the instalment. Whether the lender must pursue all its legal remedies against the borrower before making any claim against the surety will again depend upon the terms of the contract, but this is not normally a requirement.[7] Where the surety has been called upon to pay the whole or part of the loan on the borrower's default, the surety has a right to an indemnity from the borrower[8] (i.e. a right to be repaid by the borrower). If the surety has repaid the whole of the loan, then he is entitled, in addition, to a transfer of any further security held by the lender.[9] Guarantees rest for their enforceability upon contract, and therefore have to be supported by consideration, except where made by deed. Consideration is obviously supplied where the lender advances money on a loan after the guarantee has been given. If the loan has already been taken out before the guarantee has been given, then the lender's continuation of the loan after obtaining the guarantee will normally constitute consideration.[10] By virtue of s.105 of the Consumer Credit Act 1974, any security relating to a regulated consumer credit agreement must be set out in a signed document in the prescribed form.[11] In other cases, s.4 of the Statute of Frauds 1677 requires that the agreement be in writing or that there be some written note of it signed by or on behalf of the surety.[12]

(b) *Indemnity*

17–005 The effect of an indemnity is practically indistinguishable from that of a guarantee. With an indemnity, the surety enters into an independent contract with the lender under which, rather than guaranteeing that the main borrower will discharge his obligations, he undertakes to make good any loss which the lender might incur as a result of entering into the lending transaction. The practical difference between an indemnity of this kind and a guarantee is that if for some reason the loan agreement is not enforceable against the borrower, the indemnity remains enforceable whilst a guarantee of performance would not. Since in the overwhelming majority of cases both guarantees and indemnities are called upon because of the default of the borrower to make repayments owing to a lack of means rather than because of any legal reason which prevents the loan being enforced, the difference between indemnity and guarantee is rarely of significance. In addition, both a guarantee and an indemnity may be incorporated into a single contract, and the infinite variety of special terms which can be agreed further fudges the difference. However, the difference can be significant, for the requirement of proof in writing applies to guarantees and not to indemnities. Thus a contract in which a surety says, "If the borrower does not repay, I will" is a guarantee which must be proved in writing. But a contract in which the surety says, "If you lend money to the borrower, I will

---

[6] As in *Re Hawkins* [1972] Ch. 714.

[7] *Wright v Simpson* (1802) 6 Ves.Jr. 714.

[8] *Anson v Anson* [1953] 1 Q.B. 636.

[9] Mercantile Law Amendment Act 1856 s.5; *Duncan, Fox & Co v North and South Wales Bank* (1880) 6 App. Cas. 1.

[10] For an exception, see *Provincial Bank of Ireland Ltd v Donnell* [1934] N.I. 33.

[11] The Act also contains other provisions applicable to sureties relating to regulated consumer credit agreements. It is possible for a surety agreement to which the Act applies to be enforced by court order notwithstanding the absence of writing (s.105(7)).

[12] For an analysis of the case law on this section, see *Cheshire, Fifoot and Furmston's Law of Contract* (12th edn, 1991), pp.203–208.

see that you are paid", is an indemnity and does not require written proof.[13] The principles under which a surety who has honoured a guarantee is entitled to recover the sums which he has paid from the main borrower apply equally to a surety who honours an indemnity, subject to any special agreement in the contract.

(c) *Joint Liability*

In some instances a loan may be made to two persons contracting as joint borrowers, even though it is intended that only one of them will use the money.[14] From the lender's point of view, the person providing the security is not a surety in a strict sense. The lender has exactly the same rights against the "surety" as against the main borrower. Both parties can therefore be treated as principal borrowers by the lender. Subject to any special term in the contract, the lender can therefore pursue its full remedies against any one of the borrowers. The lender can, for instance, call upon either to repay the loan in full. The lender does not have to pursue all its rights and remedies against the main borrower before seeking payment from the "surety". The lender would be within its legal rights in demanding payment from the "surety" without even asking the main borrower for payment. It would then be for the main borrower and surety to sort the matter out between themselves in accordance with whatever personal arrangement they may have had. There are some special rules which apply to joint borrowing arrangements in which only one of the "borrowers" obtains the benefits of the loan and is therefore acting, in effect, as a surety. First, there will almost certainly be a contract between the borrowers under which the main borrower is liable to indemnify the surety if the latter is called upon to pay the lender. If no contract has been made expressly between the parties, then a contract to this effect is likely to be implied on the principle that a request to meet a person's debts or liabilities implies an undertaking to provide reimbursement.[15] There is no automatic right to an indemnity where the suretyship was undertaken without the request of the main borrower,[16] although there may be circumstances in which the court will consider it just and reasonable that the surety should be indemnified for meeting the payment of the loan despite the absence of any express or implied agreement.[17] The argument in favour of conferring a right of indemnity on the surety even in the absence of an express agreement or of an agreement implied on the basis of request is that the surety has enriched the main borrower at the surety's expense. However, if the enrichment was not solicited, and in some cases, perhaps not even desired, the alternative principle which comes into play is that a benefit voluntarily conferred is not recoverable.[18] There is no satisfactory explanation of how, in the grey area where these two principles meet, a decision can be made as to which is to apply. In *Owen v Tate*[19] Scarman L.J. said that "a broad approach is needed . . . and that broad approach requires the court to look at all the circumstances of the case . . . [T]he fundamental question

17–006

---

[13] *Birkmyr v Darnell* (1704) 1 Salk. 27.

[14] See for instance *CIBC Mortgage Plc v Pitt* [1993] 4 All E.R. 433.

[15] *Re a Debtor* [1937] 1 All E.R. 1; *Toussaint v Martinnant* (1787) 2 Term. 100.

[16] *Owen v Tate* [1976] Q.B. 402.

[17] *Brook's Wharf and Bull Wharf Ltd v Goodman Brothers* [1937] 1 K.B. 534.

[18] See *Re National Motor Mail-Coach Co Ltd, Clinton's Claim* [1908] 2 Ch. 515 at 520.

[19] [1975] 2 All E.R. 129 at 133–134.

is . . . whether in the circumstances it was 'just and reasonable' that a right of reimbursement should arise."

A second special rule applies to joint borrowers where only one of the borrowers benefits from the loan. This applies where the lender knows that only one of the borrowers is obtaining the benefit of the loan (as where the payments are made directly by the lender to only one of the borrowers), and where the borrowers are in a relationship in which there is a manifest danger that one can exercise undue influence over the other. In these circumstances, the lender is under a specific duty to take adequate steps to ensure that the borrower acting as surety has been properly informed of the nature of the transaction and of its possible consequences, and has been given an opportunity to obtain independent advice.[20]

(d) *Loans for House Purchase*

17–007 Personal security is often sought when a person takes out a loan to buy a house. For instance, where a couple are buying a house and the income of one of them alone is considered by the lender to be insufficient to meet the monthly repayments, the lender may insist on the loan being made to the couple jointly. This means, as has been seen above, that if the repayments are not made, the lender will be able to sue either or both of the couple for the amount outstanding. Another way in which security is sought is through a mortgage indemnity policy. Banks lending for house purchase will normally require a mortgage over the property bought. As we will see later, this means that if the loan is not repaid, the bank can ultimately sell the house in order to discharge the loan. But where the loan is for a high proportion of the value of the house—such as where 95 per cent of the purchase price is raised on mortgage—there is a danger that if property prices fall, or unpaid loan interest accumulates, the value of the house will no longer be sufficient to pay off the loan. This is often described as negative equity—the borrower owes more than the house is worth. The danger for the lender is that if a borrower with negative equity defaults—that is, fails to repay the loan—the lender is not adequately protected merely by being able to sell the house. Banks and building societies will often therefore insist that a mortgage indemnity insurance policy is taken out to provide an indemnity to the lender in the event that the loan is not repaid in accordance with its terms and on a sale of the house, too little is received to discharge the whole of the loan. The way in which these insurance policies are drawn means that a payment is not automatically triggered if the house value falls below the amount of the mortgage, even if the borrower chooses to sell. It is only if the lender sells under the mortgage and experiences a shortfall that the insurance company is obliged to provide the indemnity payment. Even then, the insurance company can bring a personal action against the borrower to recover the sums it has paid out. Since the indemnity is provided as security for the principal obligation of the borrower to repay the loan, the insurance company, as surety, is entitled to stand in the shoes of the lender to enforce that main obligation of the borrower.

---

[20] *Barclays Bank v O'Brien* [1993] 4 All E.R. 417, HL. See the discussion of undue influence below.

4. Real Security

With real security the lender has some rights in relation to property in aid of payment of the loan. Real securities divide into those where the lender has a right to retain possession of goods until payment and those (historically more recently developed) where even though the borrower is allowed to keep the property, the lender has rights which can be enforced against the property. These different ways of providing security can be categorised as possessory and proprietary. In the context of land law, we are principally concerned with proprietary security, but possessory security is worth a brief mention. **17–008**

(a) *Lien*

Liens, or rights of retention, as they might more graphically be described, arise mainly in contexts other than loan. They entitle a person who is owed money (the creditor) to refuse to hand back property to the person who owns it (the debtor), until the debt has been paid. There are a number of examples of situations where such a right can arise. For example, a car repairer who has been requested to carry out car repairs can refuse to return the vehicle to its owner until the owner has paid for the repairs.[21] Except where authorised by the court or by statute, the creditor has no right to sell the goods. Similarly, a solicitor who has carried out work for a client but who has not been paid can retain any documents he holds belonging to his client until he has received payment for his professional services.[22] **17–009**

(b) *Pledge*

A pledge (often and synonymously called a pawn) is a deposit of goods as security for meeting an obligation, usually a loan. The borrower gives goods to the lender which are then kept by the lender until the loan has been repaid. Generally under the terms of the contract, the lender is entitled to sell the goods if the loan has not been repaid within a set period of time.[23] Even where there is no express power of sale, a power to sell is implied at common law once the period for redeeming the loan has expired.[24] Most pledging transactions are now governed by the Consumer Credit Act 1974, although transactions between companies and large loans to individuals (over £15,000) are excluded by the Act. **17–010**

---

[21] *Chase v Westmore* (1816) 5 M. & S. 180 (a case involving the grinding of wheat, where earlier cases were reviewed). *Albemarle Supply Co Ltd v Hind & Co* [1928] 1 K.B. 307 is a case involving taxicabs.
[22] *Re Hawkes* [1898] 2 Ch. 1; *Hughes v Hughes* [1958] P. 224.
[23] See for instance *Franklin v Neate* (1844) 13 M. & W. 481.
[24] *Pothonier v Dawson* (1816) Holt N. P. 383.

(c) *Welsh*[25] *Mortgages*

17–011   It is not possible to make a pledge of land,[26] and it is possible that in England and Wales an attempt to pledge land would be treated as a mortgage.[27] However, some jurisdictions, including Ireland, recognise the possibility of creating what is known as a Welsh mortgage, which is in effect a form of pledge of land.[28] With this form of security, the borrower agrees that the lender may take possession of land belonging to the borrower until the loan is repaid. Instead of the borrower paying interest to the lender, the lender is entitled to retain the income or profits from the land. Unless the bargain is considered to be extortionate, or some statutory authority permits the courts to intervene,[29] the lender is able to keep the whole of the income and profits from the land, even if this exceeds what would be a reasonable return on the capital invested.[30] Similarly, if the income from the land turns out to be disappointingly poor, the lender has no right to claim more, for the right to the income from the land replaces the right to receive interest.[31] In some cases a Welsh mortgage will continue for as long as the loan remains outstanding.[32] In other cases, where the contract so provides, the lender retains the income from the land not only in lieu of interest, but also as a means of repaying the capital on the loan. It has been held that if the lender has an express power of sale, the mortgage will take effect as a conventional modern mortgage.[33]

5.   Proprietary Security

17–012   Proprietary security differs from possessory security in that the lender retains a security interest in property even though the borrower is allowed to have possession of it. Proprietary security, indeed, developed expressly for the reason that in many cases the borrower will need to have the use of the assets over which the security rights are given in order to generate the income which is needed to repay the loan. Imagine, for instance, the difficulties that would arise if the only way in which an individual borrowing money from a bank to buy a house could use the house as security was by allowing the bank to have the use of it—perhaps as a home for the bank manager! What the bank really wants is not the use of the house, but some means of being able to resort to the house if the borrower fails to repay the loan. In the meantime, the bank is quite happy for the borrower to live in it. Proprietary securities allow this.

---

[25] It is not clear why the expression "Welsh" is used since there is no evidence that this form of transaction originated in Wales. A Welsh mortgage is no more Welsh than a Dutch uncle is Dutch.

[26] Sheridan, *Rights in Security* (1974), p.145.

[27] See below.

[28] Welsh mortgages are given statutory recognition in Ireland by the Statute of Limitations Act 1957 (RI) s.34. They are also recognised in certain states of the United States of America: see for instance *Humble Oil & Refining Co v Atwood* 150 Tex 617 (1951).

[29] For example, in *Gore v Spotten* (1858) 7 I.Ch.R. 508 it was held that the usury laws then in force meant that any surplus rents from the land in excess of the statutory rate of interest had to be applied to repaying capital.

[30] *Yates v Hambly* (1741) 2 Atk. 360.

[31] See *Cassidy v Cassidy* (1889) 24 L.R. Ir. 577.

[32] *Conway v Shrimpton* (1710) 5 Bro. P.C. 187; compare *Hartpole v Walsh* (1740) 5 Bro. P.C. 267.

[33] *Re Cronin* [1914] I.R. 23.

(a) *Mortgage*

Historically, the first kind of proprietary security to be created was the mortgage, using that term in its original, narrow meaning. In return for making the loan, the lender would expect the borrower to transfer ownership of the property being used as security to the lender. Under the terms of the loan and transfer, the lender would undertake to transfer ownership back to the borrower if and when the loan was repaid or redeemed. This meant that, if the loan was not repaid, the lender would retain ownership of the property, keeping it for its own benefit or selling it. There were variants on this kind of mortgage. Although outright transfer with a right of redemption (i.e. a right to a re-transfer on repayment of the loan) was the only means by which a mortgage could be created over goods or shares or insurance policies, an alternative for land was for the borrower to grant a long lease to the lender with a provision in the lease that it would come to an end immediately the loan was repaid. This form of mortgage of land is still possible, although a mortgage by a transfer of full ownership in land is no longer permitted in England. **17–013**

(b) *Charge*

Although a mortgage gives the lender ownership of the property mortgaged, this is not really what the lender wants. The lender is simply looking for security. Equity recognised this, and therefore permitted the creation of what are known as charges. That is, the property which is being used to provide security is subject to the imposition of the remedies that the lender wants: it is charged to secure the repayment of the loan. Apart from this, the borrower's ownership of the property is not affected. The kind of charge which will most often be encountered by individuals is a fixed charge. This arises where a specific asset is subject to a charge. The borrower is unable to release the property from the charge without either repaying the loan or obtaining the prior specific consent of the lender. A fixed charge could be used by the buyer of a house to provide security for a building society loan as an alternative to creating a mortgage. Floating charges are normally only encountered where money has been lent to a trading company. A large part of a trading company's assets may be tied up in its stock-in-trade. It needs to buy goods to use in its manufacturing process, and once it has made its products it will want to sell them. It could create a fixed charge over all of its newly manufactured products, but it would then need the consent of the lender every time it wished to make a sale. The whole process would be far too cumbersome. Instead, the company enters into an agreement with the lender that all of the goods which belong to the company can be used as security for the loan, but that until some specified and identifiable event occurs, such as the company ceasing to trade in the ordinary course of business, the company has full liberty to use its stock-in-trade by selling manufactured goods and replacing them with new raw materials. Should the defined event occur, then the charge "crystallises" and fixes itself upon whatever property the company then holds. The lender is adequately protected whilst the company continues to trade normally because it is replenishing its stock of goods as rapidly as it is disposing of them. **17–014**

(c) Modern Mortgages and Charges

17–015 A charge over land is just as effective in protecting a lender as a mortgage, and, indeed, for practical purposes is indistinguishable. It would make sense for mortgages of land to be abolished, with charges being the only recognised form of proprietary security over land. The legislature has not yet chosen to adopt this simplification. Instead, charges over land are described in the legislation by reference to mortgages. This makes the rules on the creation of mortgages unnecessarily complex and obscure.

(d) Islamic Mortgages

17–016 Under the tenets of Islam, usury is not permitted. This is frequently interpreted as meaning that this prevents the lending of money at interest. This creates a problem for devout Muslims seeking to purchase their own home. Unless they have been able to save enough to pay for a purchase outright, they need assistance in finding the funds to finance their acquisition. Banks depend for their existence upon lending money at interest: they make their profits by borrowing money at a lower rate of interest than the rate at which they lend it. Some Muslim house buyers have had to compromise their religious principles by taking a mortgage,[34] and there is some theological support for the view that this is justified on the basis of necessity. However, a relatively recent development in the UK is the Islamic mortgage. This is a transaction which achieves the same outcome as the purchase of a house on mortgage, but which takes a different form. The house buyer selects the house which it is desired to purchase. However, instead of the house being bought by the purchaser, it is bought by the bank which is financing the purchase. The bank then rents the house to the "purchaser" at a rent and for a period which have been calculated as covering the full cost of the purchase together with a reasonable rate of return on monies invested to the bank. Once the final instalment of rent has been paid, the bank conveys the house to the house buyer. The transaction is therefore one which does not involve the payment of interest, but which still enables the bank to make a profit.[35] This method of financing is not, strictly speaking, a mortgage at all. It is an alternative method of financing a purchase. Nevertheless, the expression "Islamic mortgage" or "Muslim mortgage" has become a convenient label. It should be remembered that, since such transactions are not mortgages, they are not governed by the same rules as conventional mortgages.

Islamic mortgages, financed by institutional lenders rather than by individuals, are relatively recent developments, and the legal system has not yet developed to deal with some of the problems which they raise. One of the problems, that of a dual liability to pay stamp duty (which was charged both on the acquisition by the bank and on the transfer to the purchaser) has now been removed,[36] but other problems have not yet been dealt with by caselaw or

---

[34] For a business example, see *Islamic Press Agency Inc v Al-Wazir* [2001] EWCA Civ 1276.
[35] The transaction is in essence the equivalent for land of a hire-purchase transaction of consumer goods.
[36] Finance Act 2003 s.72.

legislation. For instance, where the house buyer has financial problems before making all the agreed payments under the lease, does the buyer have any greater protection than that of an ordinary tenant, perhaps because after recovering possession of the property the bank sells it at a profit?

THE CREATION OF MORTGAGES AND CHARGES

1. Obsolete Ways of Creating a Mortgage

In the past it was possible to create a mortgage by means of an outright transfer of the whole of the borrower's[37] interest in land with a provision for redemption (the return of the land discharged from the obligation) upon repayment of the loan. However, after the property reforms of 1925 it was no longer possible to create a mortgage in this way. Under the provisions of the Law of Property Act 1925 a legal mortgage or charge could be created in one of two ways,[38] either by the grant of a lease with a provision for cesser on redemption or by means of a charge by way of legal mortgage.

17–017

Where a mortgage was created by the grant of a lease with a provision for cesser on redemption, the borrower granted a lease for an extremely long period (such as 3,000 years) to the lender. The lease contained a provision that it would automatically come to an end once the loan was redeemed. If the borrower did not own the fee simple, any sub-lease granted to support a mortgage must have been for a period shorter than the borrower's own leasehold interest. In order to create a legal mortgage, the arrangement must have been made by deed. Because the borrower retained a legal estate in the land by means of the freehold reversion (or where the borrower was a leaseholder, by means of a short reversion on the borrower's own lease), it was possible for a further legal mortgage to be created through the grant of a further lease (or sub-lease), slightly longer (perhaps only by a day or two[39]) than the lease granted to the first lender. Where the owner of land attempted to grant a mortgage by way of a transfer of the whole of his freehold or leasehold estate, the Law of Property Act 1925 automatically converted the arrangement into a mortgage by way of a lease for 3,000 years in the former, and by way of a lease for 10 days less than the borrower's own lease in the latter.[40]

In deciding whether a mortgage has been created, equity looks to the intent rather than to the form. What on the face appears as a sale of land with an option to repurchase could, therefore, be held to be a mortgage if the reality of the arrangement was that the land was being used as security for a loan.[41]

---

[37] For convenience, it is assumed that in every case where a mortgage is granted, it is the borrower's land which is used as security. This will usually be the case, although it is possible for a mortgage to be granted by someone other than the borrower, for instance where a parent mortgages his or her land to support a loan made to a son or daughter.

[38] Law of Property Act 1925 ss.85(1), 86(1).

[39] For example, see the provision in Law of Property Act 1925 s.85(2)(b).

[40] Law of Property Act 1925 ss.85(2), 86(2).

[41] *Grangeside Properties Ltd v Collingwood Securities Ltd* [1964] 1 W.L.R. 139.

In the light of the virtual obsolescence of the practice of creating a mortgage by the grant of a lease with a provision for cesser on redemption, the Law Commission recommended that it should no longer be possible to create a mortgage of registered land in this way.[42] This recommendation has been implemented by s.23(1)(a) of the Land Registration Act 2002, which provides that that the owner of a registered estate has:

"power to make a disposition of any kind permitted by the general law in relation to an interest of that description, other than a mortgage by demise or sub-demise."

2. Charge by Way of Legal Mortgage of Registered Land

17–018 A charge by way of legal mortgage will only be created of registered land if the requisite formalities are observed.

(a) *Requirement of a Deed*

17–019 As with the creation of any other legal right in land, charges by way of legal mortgage must be created by deed. They must also state that they are intended to take effect as a charge by way of legal mortgage.[43] There is no other requirement as to form or content. Once created in this way, a charge by way of legal mortgage operates to confer on the mortgagee (the lender) "the same protection, powers and remedies" as if the mortgage had been created by way of lease. A charge by way of legal mortgage can therefore for convenience be called a mortgage even though a pedant could argue that a charge is not strictly speaking a mortgage, since it does not involve the conveyance of title to the land, but merely the creation of rights of security. It has been held that a mortgage by way of charge can be created before the mortgagor has acquired the legal estate in the property concerned. The mortgagor will be estopped from denying the validity of the mortgage so created, and that estoppel will be fed without the need for a new grant once the mortgagor acquires the relevant legal estate.[44]

(b) *Requirement of Registration*

17–020 The creation of a charge by way of legal mortgage of registered land must be completed by registration. This follows from s.27(2)(f) of the Land Registration Act 2002, which provides that "the grant of a legal charge" is a disposition of a registered estate required to be completed by registration. Failure to complete a legal charge by registration will have the effect that it "does not operate at law",[45] so that it will take effect only in equity.

[42] Law Com. No.245, *Land Registration for the Twenty-First Century* (1998), paras 9.4–9.5.
[43] Law of Property Act 1925 ss.85(2), 86(2).
[44] *First National Bank Plc v Thompson* [1996] 1 All E.R. 140.
[45] Land Registration Act 2002 s.27(1).

3. Mortgages of Unregistered Land

Where land is unregistered the grant of a first legal mortgage will trigger the requirement of compulsory registration of title.[46] If the estate owner does not apply to be registered as the proprietor of the estate within a two-month period of the date of the grant of the mortgage the grant "has effect as a contract made for valuable consideration to grant or create the legal estate concerned".[47] In other words, on the grant of a legal mortgage of unregistered land the title will either be registered and the mortgage will quickly become a registered charge, or in the absence of registration the mortgage will only take effect in equity. **17–021**

4. Creation of Equitable Mortgages

As has been seen above, an equitable mortgage will be created where the grant of a charge by way of legal mortgage of registered land has not been completed by registration, or where the title to unregistered land has not been registered following the grant of a legal mortgage. There are, however, other situations in which an equitable mortgage may arise. **17–022**

(a) *Mortgage of an Equitable Interest in Land*

A legal mortgage can only be granted by a person with a legal interest in the land. If the borrower has only an equitable interest in land, then any attempt to create a legal mortgage or charge can create only an equivalent equitable mortgage. The same result follows if one of two co-owners enters into a mortgage having forged the signature of the other co-owner.[48] In this case the mortgage is valid only to the extent that the fraudulent co-owner can make it, namely over that co-owner's own equitable interest. The other co-owner's beneficial interest will be unaffected by the mortgage. **17–023**

(b) *A Specifically Enforceable Contract for the Grant of a Mortgage*

Whereas a legal mortgage must be created by deed, equity recognises any specifically enforceable agreement to provide security as sufficient to create a mortgage or charge.[49] It was formerly the case that the mere deposit of the title deeds to a property in return for a loan, and with the intention of providing security, was sufficient to create an equitable mortgage.[50] That no longer applies. Since 1989[51] any contract for the grant of an interest in land must be **17–024**

---

[46] Land Registration Act 2002 s.4(1)(g).
[47] Land Registration Act 2002 s.7(2)(b).
[48] See *Thames Guarantee Ltd v Campbell* [1985] Q.B. 210.
[49] *Matthews v Goodday* (1861) 31 L.J. Ch. 282.
[50] *Russel v Russel* (1783) 1 Bro. C.C. 269.
[51] After September 26, 1989.

made in writing, contain all the relevant terms, and be signed by both parties.[52] In *Bank of Kuwait v Sahib*[53] it was held that the basis of an equitable mortgage by deposit is that there is an enforceable contract to create a mortgage. It follows, therefore, that such mortgages now require the formality of being made in writing.[54]

5. Charge Arising by Way of Subrogation

17–025 Where property is acquired by means of mortgage, almost invariably the purchase money will have to be advanced by the mortgagee to the mortgagor prior to the execution of the mortgage in order to enable the purchase to be completed.[55] Difficulties arise if the money advanced is then misapplied by the prospective mortgagor, or more usually by his solicitor who holds the funds on trust for the mortgagee in a client account. If the money is used to discharge a subsisting mortgage the lender may be entitled to claim an equivalent charge of the land by way of subrogation. This situation occurred in *Boscawen v Bajwa*.[56] Mr Bajwa had exchanged contracts to purchase a property for £165,000, and had obtained a mortgage advance from the Abbey National Building Society of £140,000. The property was already subject to a mortgage, of which the Halifax was the mortgagee. The money advanced was wrongly applied in the partial discharge of this prior mortgage without obtaining the completion of the purchase and the execution of a new mortgage in favour of the Abbey National. The Court of Appeal held that the Abbey National was entitled to a charge of the land by way of subrogation to the extent to which the money it had advanced could be traced into the discharge of the pre-existing charge.

THE RIGHTS OF THE MORTGAGOR

1. The Equity of Redemption

17–026 The fact that the lender under a mortgage or charge has either a lease in the land concerned for three millennia,[57] or is said to have the same protection, powers and remedies as if that had been the case, rather obscures the reality of the position. The reality is that the borrower is the owner.

---

[52] Law of Property (Miscellaneous Provisions) Act 1989 s.2.

[53] [1996] 3 All E.R. 215, CA.

[54] Where there has been an agreement for an interest and the claimant has relied on it to his detriment and it is unconscionable for the promisor to go back on the agreement so that a constructive trust arises, then no formality is required as s.2(5) exempts constructive trusts from this requirement. An equitable charge was created this way in *Kinane v Mackie-Conteh* [2005] EWCA Civ 45; [2005] 2 P. & C.R. D.G. 3, Court of Appeal; [2005] Conv. 501; [2005] Conv. 247.

[55] See, for example, *Abbey National Building Society v Cann* [1991] A.C. 56.

[56] [1995] 4 All E.R. 769.

[57] This is a period longer than the period since the birth of Christ; it is three times as long as the origins of the modern English law of the ownership of land. It is therefore long enough to be virtually indistinguishable from a right to the land for ever.

580

The lease (or deemed lease[58]) enjoyed by the lender confers only rights of security and not the rights which would be enjoyed by a tenant under an ordinary beneficial lease from a landowner. The borrower remains living in the property upon which the loan was secured.[59] If the property is sold, and there is an increase in value, it is the borrower who benefits. If there is any fall in value, it is the borrower who incurs the loss. This is because the borrower is entitled to the whole value of the property, subject only to repayment of the loan. All is not, therefore, what it seems. This is not the only way in which the appearance is at odds with the reality. If the property is sold under a forced sale by the lender (for instance if the borrower fails to repay the loan, or breaks some other condition of the mortgage), the lender, who has at most a long lease over the property, is able to sell the whole fee simple in the property.[60] The whole state of affairs has been described in a famous phrase as "one long suppressio veri and suggestio falsi".[61] It does no credit to the law that it has been allowed to continue without reform. It is equity which ensures that, despite the semblance of the situation, the borrower remains an effectual owner of the property. The borrower has thus been described as having an "equity" in the property, or, more fully, an "equity of redemption". This phrase describes the full bundle of the borrower's rights in the property, subject to the obligations imposed by the mortgage. This equity of redemption is capable of being bought and sold,[62] made subject to a further mortgage, given away by will, or acquired by the Crown as property without an owner.[63]

2. The Right to Redeem

One of the rights making up the equity of redemption, but by no means the only one, is the borrower's equitable right to redeem. That is the borrower's right to repay the loan and have the mortgage discharged from the property, even in cases where there has not been strict compliance with any time limits imposed by the mortgage deed or agreement. Redemption is the process by which, following the discharge of the loan or other obligation secured against property, the property is freed from the mortgage. The process is simple. In the case of unregistered land all that is required is that a receipt is endorsed on the mortgage deed, or is annexed to it.[64] In the case of registered land, application in the prescribed form must be made to the Land Registry.

    It is in the nature of a mortgage that there must always be a right to redeem, and this will normally be an express term of the agreement. A right to redeem on the basis of an express term is described as the legal right to redeem. At common law, any such express right had to

17–027

---

[58] In *Grand Junction Co Ltd v Bates* [1954] 2 Q.B. 160 at 169 Upjohn J. said that a chargee of a lease by way of legal mortgage is entitled to say "I am to be put in the same position as if I had a charge by way of sub-demise".

[59] The right of the landlord to continue living in the property which he has let to a tenant would normally be inconsistent with the tenant having exclusive possession—an essential requirement of a valid lease.

[60] Or whatever other estate the borrower holds subject to the mortgage.

[61] "One long suppression of the truth and suggestion of untruth": Maitland, *Equity* (1936), p.182.

[62] Although the usual practice in England is to repay the loan out of the proceeds of sale in order to discharge the mortgage, it is common practice in some other countries (for instance in North America) to sell a property subject to the mortgage.

[63] *Re Sir Thomas Spencer Wells* [1933] Ch. 29.

[64] Law of Property Act 1925 s.115(1); Building Societies Act 1986 Sch.4 para.2.

be exercised strictly in accordance with its terms. If a mortgage provided for repayment on a certain day, say, after six months, the borrower would be expected at common law to repay on that day, not earlier,[65] not later. Any delay in repayment would result in a forfeiture of the right to redeem.

Equity considered this rule too harsh, and moderated it by permitting borrowers to repay at any stage upon reasonable notice to the lender,[66] even if the date fixed in the contract had gone past. This right was known as the equitable right to redeem. The only way in which a borrower could lose the equitable right to redeem was if, in court proceedings, the right was "foreclosed" on the application of the lender. Even then, it was possible for a foreclosure to be reopened on the application of a borrower willing to make good any financial loss to the lender. Because of equity's intervention, the date fixed for repayment in the mortgage became of little significance, and the practice grew up of providing in the mortgage agreement for repayment after three or six months even if the loan was actually intended to last much longer. This was yet another respect in which form and substance did not correspond. Some modern mortgages continue to adopt this artificiality, but there is a growing and welcome practice to describe the obligation to repay in more accurate terms.

3. Possession

17–028

The purpose of a mortgage is normally to provide security for a loan. In most cases that loan is taken out to finance the purchase of a property in which the purchaser intends to live. The way in which a mortgage is created, however, may confer the right to possession on the lender (the mortgagee) rather than on the borrower. Where a mortgage is created by way of a demise with a proviso for cesser on redemption, the lease confers on the mortgagee an automatic right to possession. A statutory charge by way of legal mortgage is treated as conferring the same powers and remedies on the chargee as a mortgage by demise "including the right to take proceedings to obtain possession from the occupiers".[67] The wording suggests that the right to possession may require a court order.[68] Since possession will almost invariably be sought by way of court order,[69] or by consent,[70] there is, though, no practical difference between a mortgage by demise and a mortgage by legal charge except for the rare possibility of a mortgagee seeking to take possession peaceably without a court order. Harman J. in *Four Maids Ltd v Dudley Marshall Properties Ltd*[71] used colourful language to describe the position on possession:

---

[65] *Brown v Cole* (1845) 14 Sim. 427; *Burrough v Cranston* (1840) I. Eq. R. 203.

[66] By convention, this period of notice is six months (see *Cromwell Property Investment Co Ltd v Western & Toovey* [1934] Ch. 322), which is said to provide the lender with adequate time to find other ways of using or investing the money to be repaid.

[67] Law of Property Act 1925 s.87(1).

[68] A court order is required where an equitable mortgagee wishes to take possession: *Ladup Ltd v Williams & Glyn's Bank Plc* [1985] 1 W.L.R. 851; *Re O'Neill* [1967] N.I. 129.

[69] For residential property, this may be required as a consequence of the statutory jurisdiction to provide relief to mortgagors in certain circumstances under Administration of Justice Act 1970 s.36 (see below).

[70] For instance where a borrower in default under a mortgage posts the keys to the property through the building society's office door.

[71] [1957] Ch. 317 at 320.

"The right of the mortgagee to possession in the absence of some contract has nothing to do with default on the part of the mortgagor. The mortgagee may go into possession before the ink is dry on the mortgage unless there is something in the contract, express or by implication, whereby he has contracted himself out of that right. He has the right because he has a legal term of years in the property or its statutory equivalent."

In *Ropaigealach v Barclays Bank Plc*[72] Clarke L.J. considered it was correct that, in the absence of a provision to the contrary in the mortgage, a mortgagee has a right of immediate possession, but observed:

"I suspect that many mortgagors would be astonished to discover that a bank which had lent them money to buy a property for them to live in could take possession of it the next day."[73]

In practice, mortgagees will not normally take possession of the property except where there has been default by the mortgagor, and then they will do so only as a precursor to exercising their right to sell.[74] This is because this was the intention at the time of the mortgage. In addition, a mortgagee taking possession is under an obligation to take reasonable care of the physical state of the property[75] and is under a strict duty to account for any notional benefit which could be derived from possession. For instance in *White v City of London Brewery Co*,[76] the defendant mortgagees (a brewing company) took possession of a public house which the plaintiff had mortgaged to them. They leased it to a tenant with a provision tying him to obtaining all his beer from the defendants. The Court of Appeal held that the defendants were liable to account, not merely for the rent which they had received, but rather for the higher rent they could have obtained if the public house had been let as a free house.

17–029

The mortgagee's right to possession is therefore another instance of the way in which mortgages are not always what they seem. Many mortgages now reflect reality by conferring a right of possession on the mortgagor, either by means of an attornment clause (i.e. a lease-back),[77] or more usually, by providing that the mortgagee will not seek possession unless the mortgagor is in default.[78] The courts will not lightly imply a term deferring the mortgagee's right to possession where there is no express term to this effect,[79] although they are more likely to do so in the case of an instalment mortgage than in other cases.[80] The courts may, however, defer an order for possession of residential property in certain circumstances.

It has been questioned whether the immediate right of a mortgagee to possession of the land is compatible with the European Convention on Human Rights,[81] which provides in art.8:

---

[72] [1999] 4 All E.R. 235.

[73] [1999] 4 All E.R. 235 at 253.

[74] For a rare exception, where the mortgagee wished to take possession in order to preserve the value of the property, see *Western Bank Ltd v Schindler* [1977] Ch. 1.

[75] *Palk v Mortgage Services Funding Plc* [1993] Ch. 330 at 338, per Nicholls V.C.

[76] (1889) 42 Ch.D. 237.

[77] *Peckham Mutual Building Society v Registe* (1980) 42 P. & C.R. 186.

[78] *Birmingham Citizens Permanent Building Society v Caunt* [1962] Ch. 883.

[79] *Western Bank Ltd v Schindler* [1977] Ch. 1.

[80] *Esso Petroleum v Alstonbridge Properties Ltd* 1975] 1 W.L.R. 1474.

[81] Rome, November 4, 1950; TS 71 (1953); Cmd. 8969.

"1. Everyone has the right to respect for his private and family life, his home and his correspondence.
2. There shall be no interference by a public authority with the exercise of this right except such as is in accordance with the law and is necessary for the protection of the rights and freedoms of others."

The possible effects of this provision were considered by Schiemann L.J. in *Albany Home Loans v Massey*.[82] He noted that although the Article was not at that date enacted in domestic law, it provided a "clue" as to whether it would be appropriate to make an order requiring one mortgagor to leave the property whilst another joint mortgagor remains entitled to possession and is in possession.[83] Whilst the Convention has since been incorporated into domestic law by the Human Rights Act 1998, it is less than clear whether art.8 should properly have had any bearing on the issue raised in *Albany Home Loans v Massey*, as there had been no interference by a public authority. However the case suggests that the provisions of the Convention may influence the decisions of the courts even where the facts are strictly outside its scope.[84]

4. Grant of Leases

17–030 A mortgagor in possession has a statutory power to grant leases of land, normally not exceeding 50 years, binding on the mortgagee.[85] It is standard practice in mortgages for this power to be excluded. It is only in the most exceptional circumstances[86] that a lease entered into after the creation of a mortgage will be binding on the mortgagee where the statutory power has been excluded. Such a lease will be binding on the mortgagor, but not on the mortgagee.[87] In *Barclays Bank Plc v Zaroovabli*,[88] however, a bank taking a charge by way of legal mortgage over registered land had failed to register the charge as was required to complete it. The charge contained a prohibition on the creation of leases by the mortgagor. Despite this, the mortgagor granted a lease for six months to a tenant which developed, on expiry, into a statutory tenancy under the Rent Act 1977. The Court of Appeal held that this lease was binding on the bank as an overriding interest, notwithstanding the later registration of the legal charge. The delay in registering the charge meant that it initially took effect only in equity, whilst the lease, when granted, took effect as a legal interest since it was not required to be registered to have full force and effect.[89] Under the priority rules affecting registered land, the lease, being equivalent to a registered disposition of a legal estate for valuable consideration, took priority over a mortgage operating only as a minor equitable interest unprotected by any entry on the register.[90]

---

[82] [1997] 2 All E.R. 609.
[83] [1997] 2 All E.R. 609 at 612–613.[84] See: Dr Jean Howell, "Land and Human Rights" [1999] Conv. 287 at 308–309.
[85] Law of Property Act 1925 s.99.
[86] As in *Quennell v Maltby* [1979] 1 W.L.R. 318 where a mortgage was used as a device to avoid the Rent Acts. See [1979] C.L.J. 257 (R.A. Pearce).
[87] *Britannia Building Society v Earl* [1990] 1 W.L.R. 422; *Dudley and District Benefit Building Society v Emerson* [1949] 2 All E.R. 252.
[88] [1997] 2 All E.R. 19.
[89] Land Registration Act 1925 s.19.
[90] See Land Registration Act 1925 s.20. The position would be unchanged under the Land Registration Act 2002.

5. The Right to Seek an Order for Sale Against the Wishes of the Mortgagee

Whilst in most cases it will be the mortgagee who seeks an order for the sale of the property contrary to the wishes of the mortgagor, usually when the mortgage payments are in default, in some exceptional circumstances the mortgagor make seek to obtain an order from the court for the sale of the property contrary to the wishes of the mortgagee. Such exceptional circumstances arose in *Barrett v Halifax Building Society*.[91] The plaintiffs had purchased a house with the help of a joint mortgage and had found themselves experiencing negative equity and owing arrears of some £324,000. They had negotiated a sale of the property for £252,000. The mortgagee objected to the sale on the grounds that it was not in accordance with its usual policy not to permit borrowers with negative equity to conduct sales themselves without making proposals for repayment of any existing shortfall. The mortgagors sought an order for sale under s.91(2) of the Law of Property Act 1925, and it was not disputed that this section conferred upon the court a discretion to order a sale at the instance of a mortgagor against the wishes of the mortgagee if required by the justice of the case. A valuer gave evidence for the mortgagors that in the prevailing conditions of the market a higher price was likely to be obtained for property where it was sold by a mortgagor in possession than by a mortgagee which had obtained possession, in which case the forced nature of the sale would be apparent to prospective purchasers. Evans-Lombe J. held that the established policy of the mortgagee was not a relevant circumstance to be taken into account in the exercise of his discretion and ordered sale. There was no discernible advantage to the building society in refusing to allow the sale to complete, whereas there was an obvious advantage to the mortgagors to complete at what was accepted to be the best price that was likely to be obtainable.[92]

17–031

SETTING ASIDE A MORTGAGE FOR UNDUE INFLUENCE OR MISREPRESENTATION

On some occasions the presence of a mitigating factor will entitle a mortgagor to have a mortgage set aside, or to have some of its provisions modified or declared void. A mortgage can thus be set aside it if has been obtained through undue influence or misrepresentation. In recent years there has been an avalanche of cases where mortgagors (mainly but not exclusive wives) have sought to aside mortgages granted to guarantee someone else debts (usually but not exclusively their husband's debts), on the grounds that they acted under the undue influence of the person whose debts they were securing. In such cases the mortgagor is seeking to set aside a mortgage not because the mortgagor exercised undue influence, but because some third party exercised undue influence to persuade the mortgagor to enter into the mortgage. It is therefore necessary to examine both the principles of undue influence, and the principles by which the court will hold that a transaction may be set aside because one of the parties was acting under the undue influence of a third party.

17–032

[91] (1996) 28 H.L.R. 634.
[92] (1996) 28 H.L.R. 634 at 640.

1. The General Principles of Undue Influence

17–033   Equity has long exercised a jurisdiction to set aside transactions that have been obtained through the abuse of a relationship of trust and confidence. Where such an abuse has occurred equity will grant rescission of the transaction. The jurisdiction is not confined to setting aside mortgages.

(a)   *What is Undue Influence?*

17–034   The principles of undue influence emerged in equity so as to ensure that "the influence of one person over another is not abused".[93] The essence of undue influence is that, where there is a relationship of trust and confidence between two individuals, one may have enjoyed such influence, or ascendancy, over the other, as to be able to persuade that other to enter into a transaction. If the intention to enter a transaction was produced by such unacceptable means equity will act to set the transaction aside. In *Royal Bank of Scotland Plc v Etridge (No.2)* the House of Lords extensively examined the relevant principles. Lord Nicholls, who delivered a judgment which "commands the unqualified support of all members of the House"[94] stated that it was a matter of fact whether a transaction had been brought about by the exercise of undue influence, and that the person claiming undue influence bears the burden of proving that a wrong has been committed:

> "The burden of proving an allegation of undue influence rests upon the person who claims to have been wronged. This is the general rule. The evidence required to discharge the burden of proof depends on the nature of the alleged undue influence, the personality of the parties, their relationship, the extent to which the transaction cannot readily be accounted for by the ordinary motives of ordinary persons in that relationship, and all the circumstances of the case."[95]

In some circumstances the nature of the relationship between the parties will give rise to a presumption that undue influence was exercised, which will cause the burden of proof to pass to the defendant to demonstrate that the transaction was freely entered. There are therefore two categories of undue influence, actual undue influence and presumed undue influence, although the difference between these categories is essentially one of the allocation of the burden of proof.

(b)   *Actual Undue Influence*

17–035   A transaction will be set aside if a claimant is able to affirmatively prove[96] that he entered a transaction as a result of actual undue influence exerted against him. It was formerly the case

---

[93] *Royal Bank of Scotland Plc v Etridge (No.2)* [2001] UKHL 44; [2002] 2 A.C. 273 at [6], per Lord Nicholls.
[94] [2002] 2 A.C. 273 at [3], per Lord Bingham.
[95] [2002] 2 A.C. 273 at [13].
[96] *Royal Bank of Scotland v Etridge (No.2)* [1998] 4 All E.R. 705. at 711.

that a transaction would only be set aside on the grounds of actual undue influence if it could be shown that the transaction was "manifestly disadvantageous" to the person who was subject to the influence.[97] However in the context of actual undue influence this additional requirement was rejected by the House of Lords in *CIBC Mortgages Plc v Pitt*[98] although the fact that an arrangement is inexplicably disadvantageous will provide evidence that undue influence has been exercised.

(c) *Presumed Undue Influence*

A transaction will also be set aside if the facts are such as to give rise to a presumption that the it was entered through undue influence, and the presumption is not rebutted by counter evidence to show that undue influence was not exercised. The most important question is therefore as to the circumstances which will give rise to a presumption of undue influence. In *Royal Bank of Scotland Plc v Etridge (No.2)* the House of Lords held that a presumption of undue influence would arise through a combination of two factors: the existence of a relationship of trust and confidence between the parties to a transaction and the fact that the transaction was so advantageous to the party who enjoyed the trust and confidence as to require explanation.[99] Lord Nicholls explained how a presumption of undue influence would arise, and how it would shift the burden of proof from the complainant to the defendant:

> "Proof that the complainant placed trust and confidence in the other party in relation to the management of the complainant's affairs, coupled with a transaction which calls for explanation, will normally be sufficient, failing satisfactory evidence to the contrary, to discharge the burden of proof. On proof of these two matters the stage is set for the court to infer that, in the absence of a satisfactory explanation, the transaction can only have been procured by undue influence. In other words, proof of these two facts is prima facie evidence that the defendant abused the influence he acquired in the parties' relationship. He preferred his own interests. He did not behave fairly to the other. So the evidential burden then shifts to him. It is for him to produce evidence to counter the inference which otherwise should be drawn."

There are thus two elements to the presumption of undue influence. First it is necessary to establish that there was a relationship of trust and confidence between the parties, and second to show that the nature of the transaction calls for an explanation.

(i) A Relationship of Trust and Confidence Between the Parties

As Lord Nicholls further explained, some relationships give rise to an irrebuttable presumption that one party had enjoyed influence over another, so that there was no need to prove whether

17–036

17–037

---

[97] *Bank of Credit and Commerce International SA v Aboody* [1990] 1 Q.B. 923.
[98] [1993] 4 All E.R. 433.
[99] See for example [2001] UKHL 44; [2002] 2 A.C. 273 at [158], per Lord Scott.

there had been trust and confidence between the parties. Such relationships include[100] parent and child,[101] guardian and ward, trustee and beneficiary, spiritual adviser and disciple,[102] doctor and patient,[103] and solicitor and client,[104] relationships which equity characterises as being "fiduciary". However in the case of other relationships, such as that between banker and client,[105] there is no such irrebuttable presumption. It is also well established that the relationship of husband and wife is not one which gives rise to such an irrebuttable presumption of trust and confidence,[106] and this will similarly be the case between co-habiting couples,[107] whether heterosexual or homosexual, lovers[108] and close family relations.[109] Thus a wife will only be able to set aside a transaction of the grounds that she entered into it under the undue influence of her husband if she proves that there was such a relationship of trust and confidence that her husband had acquired influence, or ascendancy, over her.

(ii) The Nature of the Transaction Calls for Explanation

17–038   Where the element of trust and confidence between the parties is established, whether by irrebuttable presumption by or proof, the presumption of undue influence will only arise if it can also be shown that the "transaction is not readily explicable by the relationship".[110] In the past this requirement has been termed the need to establish that the transaction caused "manifest disadvantage" to the complainant. However Lord Nicholls preferred to discard this term, on the grounds that it was causing difficulties where wives entered transactions to guarantee their husband's business debts.[111] Although the grant of such a mortgage would plainly be disadvantageous to a wife in the sense that she would be undertaking a serious financial obligation for which she received nothing in return, in many cases it may also be for her benefit, for example if the mortgage is granted to secure the husband's business debts and his business is the source of the family income.[112] He therefore preferred to adhere to earlier formulations of the test. In *Allcard v Skinner* Lindley L.J. stated that a presumption of undue influence would only arise if the transaction cannot "reasonably be accounted for on the ground of friendship, relationship, charity, or other ordinary motives on which men act".[113] In *National Westminster Bank v Morgan* Lord Scarman said that a transaction would only be presumed to be the result of undue influence if:

---

[100] [2002] 2 A.C. 273 at [18].

[101] *Lancashire Loans Ltd v Black* [1934] 1 K.B. 380.

[102] *Allcard v Skinner* (1887) 36 Ch.D. 145; *Tufton v Sperni* [1952] 2 T.L.R. 516.

[103] *Dent v Bennett* (1839) 4 My. & Cr. 269.

[104] *Wright v Carter* [1903] 1 Ch. 27.

[105] *Lloyds Bank v Bundy* [1975] Q.B. 326.[106] [2002] 2 A.C. 273 at [19]. See also *Yerkey v Jones* (1939) 63 C.L.R. 649 at 675.

[107] *Barclays Bank v O'Brien* [1994] 1 A.C. 180.

[108] *Massey v Midland Bank Plc* [1995] 1 All E.R. 929.

[109] *Cheese v Thomas* [1994] 1 W.L.R. 129.

[110] [2002] 2 A.C. 273 at [21].

[111] He also rejected the opinion of Nourse L.J. in *Barclays Bank v Coleman* [2000] 1 All E.R. 385, who had suggested that the requirement of "manifest disadvantage" had been an original creation of the House of Lords in *National Westminster Bank Plc v Morgan*, which he respectfully considered to be wrong.

[112] [2001] UKHL 44; [2002] 2 A.C. 273 at [27].

[113] 36 Ch. D. 145 at 185.

"it constituted an advantage taken of the person subjected to the influence which, failing proof to the contrary, was explicable only on the basis that undue influence had been exercised to procure it."[114]

Lord Nicholls explained how these more broadly formulated tests would apply in the situation where a wife had acted to guarantee her husband's debts:

"I do not think that, in the ordinary course, a guarantee of the character I have mentioned is to be regarded as a transaction which, failing proof to the contrary, is explicable only on the basis that it has been procured by the exercise of undue influence by the husband. Wives frequently enter into such transactions. There are good and sufficient reasons why they are willing to do so, despite the risks involved for them and their families. They may be enthusiastic. They may not. They may be less optimistic than their husbands about the prospects of their husband's businesses. They may be anxious, perhaps exceedingly so. But this is a far cry from saying that such transactions as a class are to be regarded as prima facie evidence of the exercise of undue influence by husbands."[115]

He acknowledged that, whilst the fact that a wife had guaranteed her husband's debts did not automatically raise a presumption of undue influence, there would be cases where the circumstances were such that her signature of a guarantee or a charge of her share in matrimonial home does call for explanation. Lord Scott also explained that this second requirement simply raises a presumption of undue influence as a matter of evidence because the transaction cannot be explained by ordinary motives: **17–039**

"As to manifest disadvantage the expression is no more than shorthand for the proposition that the nature of the transaction and ingredients of the impugned transaction are essential factors in deciding whether the evidential presumption has arisen and in determining the strength of that presumption. It is not a divining-rod by means of which the presence of undue influence in the procuring of a transaction can be identified. It is merely a description of a transaction which cannot be explained by reference to the ordinary motives by which people are accustomed to act."[116]

Outside of the context of marriage, a presumption of undue influence may be raised where a person has agreed to act as a surety of the debts of another and the surety gained no personal advantage from so acting.[117] Thus in *Credit Lyonnais Bank Nederland v Burch*[118] the Court of Appeal held that an abuse of a relationship of confidence was to be presumed from the mere fact that a junior employee had executed an "extravagantly improvident" unlimited guarantee of all of her employer's debts, and that there was no further need to demonstrate any

---

[114] [1985] A.C. 686 at 704.
[115] [2001] UKHL 44; [2002] 2 A.C. 273 at [30].
[116] [2002] 2 A.C. 273 at [220].
[117] *Barclays Bank v O'Brien* [1994] 1 A.C. 180; *CIBC Mortgages Plc v Pitt* [1994] 1 A.C. 200; *Massey v Midland Bank Plc* [1995] 1 All E.R. 929; *Banco Exterior International v Thomas* [1997] 1 All E.R. 46; *Dunbar Bank Plc v Nadeem* [1997] 2 All E.R. 253.
[118] [1997] 1 All E.R. 144.

sexual or emotional tie. In *Abbey National Bank Plc v Stringer*,[119] a mother and son were joint owners of a property, the son being on the title nominally and merely because it enabled the mother to obtain a mortgage. They jointly executed a further charge in order to raise money for the son's business. The Court of Appeal held that a presumption of undue influence had been raised. The son had influence over his mother in relation to financial affairs, so that there was a relationship of trust and confidence; she had signed the document when he asked her to do so but she could not read English and he had not explained the document to her. The transaction called for explanation, as it went beyond a "mother's generosity"[120]:

> "The transaction involved putting her home at risk . . . in relation to a new business of which she knew nothing and from which she would obtain no benefit . . . she had no idea that by signing it she was putting her property up as security."[121]

In the somewhat unusual case of *Goodchild v Bradbury*,[122] a vulnerable elderly gentleman transferred land adjacent to his property to his great-nephew as a wedding gift. The nephew then sold it on to a developer, who was involved in the initial transfer. The Court of Appeal held that the relationship between great-nephew and uncle was one of trust and confidence and that the transaction was one that called for explanation. Whilst the uncle new that he wanted to give his nephew land as a wedding present, and this itself is an ordinary motive of mankind, it was unlikely he fully appreciated the effect of the gift. The land had valuable development potential which, if realised, could substantially devalue the uncle's adjacent property. Thus, it was not a transaction that anyone would enter into without considerable thought and information and could not be explained on ordinary motives of generosity. The nephew failed to discharge the onus of showing that the uncle knew what he was doing. The Court of Appeal set aside the transaction as against the developer who had notice of all the relevant circumstances. By contrast, in *Turkey v Awadh*[123] a transaction with a couple's father that he would pay the mortgage on their home in consideration of a transfer of the house to him, was explicable on ordinary motives. Even though his daughter relied on him in financial matters, it was necessary to look at the transaction in its context, including "what it was trying to achieve for the parties".[124] Chadwick L.J. confirmed the view of the 1st instance judge that the transaction did not call for explanation because the couple had got themselves into financial difficulty and this offered them "cash in hand" and alleviated their problems, and the transaction "had important family elements in it [and] thus the likelihood [was] that nothing in real terms would change as far as use of the property was concerned". Also "completion . . . was going to be delayed for years".[125]

---

[119] [2006] EWCA Civ 338; [2006] 2 P. & C.R. D.G. 15.

[120] [2006] 2 P. & C.R. D.G. 15.

[121] [2006] 2 P. & C.R. D.G. 15, per Lloyd L.J., editing supplied. In *Randall v Randall* [2004] EWHC 2258; [2005] 1 P. & C.R. D.G. 4, a presumption of undue influence arose between an aunt and her nephew when it was clear that she reposed trust and confidence in him in relation to finances and her gift of a transfer of land to that nephew could not be explained on the basis of usual motives.

[122] [2006] EWCA Civ 1868; see Westlaw document 2006 WL 3610002.

[123] [2005] EWCA Civ 382; [2005] 2 P & CR29.

[124] [2005] 2 P & CR29, para.32, per Buxton L.J.

[125] [2005] 2 P & CR29, per Chadwick L.J. at para.41; quoting the 1st instance judge.

(iii) Rebutting a Presumption of Undue Influence

The mere fact that a complainant entered into a transaction in circumstances which give rise **17–040** to a presumption of undue influence does not mean that the transaction will necessarily be set aside. The alleged wrongdoer will be entitled to adduce evidence to demonstrate that the transaction was freely entered into by the complainant, such that it should not be impugned. A presumption will be rebutted by evidence that the party who enjoyed a relationship of trust and confidence did not in fact exert undue influence. In *Royal Bank of Scotland v Etridge (No.2)*,[126] for example, a house had been purchased in the name of Mrs Etridge in 1987 using money provided by her husband. She subsequently granted the bank a mortgage of £100,000 to secure the overdraft facility of her husband's company. A year later the house was sold and a more expensive property was purchased, which was also subject to a mortgage of £100,000. The House of Lords held that on the facts, the husband had not exercised undue influence over the wife. Lord Scott explained:

> "There was evidence of the relationship between Mr and Mrs Etridge. Their relationship was, as one would expect of a married couple living together with the family income being provided by the husband's business activities and with financial decisions affecting the family being taken by the husband, a relationship of trust and confidence by her in him. But there was no evidence of abuse by Mr Etridge of that relationship, or of any bullying of Mrs Etridge to persuade her to support his decisions."[127]

A presumption of undue influence may also be rebutted by showing that the complainant received independent advice before entering the transaction. However, as Lord Nicholls explained in *Royal Bank of Scotland Plc v Etridge (No.2)*, even this may not be sufficient to rebut the presumption:

> "Proof that the complainant received advice from a third party before entering into the impugned transaction is one of the matters a court takes into account when weighing all the evidence. The weight, or importance, to be attached to such advice depends on all the circumstances. In the normal course, advice from a solicitor or other outside adviser can be expected to bring home to a complainant a proper understanding of what he or she is about to do. But a person may understand fully the implications of a proposed transaction, for instance, a substantial gift, and yet still be acting under the undue influence of another. Proof of outside advice does not, or itself, necessarily show that the subsequent completion of the transaction was free from the exercise of undue influence. Whether it will be proper to infer that outside advice had an emancipating effect, so that the transaction was not brought about by the exercise of undue influence, is a question of fact to be decided having regard to all the evidence in the case."[128]

---

[126] [2001] UKHL 44; [2002] 2 A.C. 273.
[127] [2002] 2 A.C. 273 at [221].
[128] [2001] U.K.H.L. 44; [2002] 2 A.C. 273 at [20].

2. Undue Influence Exercised by the Mortgagee Against the Mortgagor

17–041 The first situation in which a mortgage may be set aside on the grounds of undue influence is if the mortgagee has directly exercised undue influence over the mortgagor. Thus if a mortgage lender exercised actual undue influence, or took advantage of a special relationship of trust and confidence with the borrower, then the lender would not be permitted to take advantage of the breach of the position of trust and confidence by enforcing the mortgage and evicting the borrower. The lender might exercise undue influence either personally, or through an agent. Thus a lender who employed a salesman to market mortgages would be treated as having used undue influence if the salesman preyed upon the fears of an elderly householder to persuade her to take out a mortgage to invest in the purchase of an annuity[129] without ensuring that she fully understood the nature of the transaction and the risks involved in it. Where actual undue influence is exercised, it is no defence for the lender to show that in every other respect the terms of the transaction were completely fair and reasonable. There have been very few reported cases where a lender has exercised direct undue influence against a mortgagee, and the vast majority of recent cases have concerned transactions where the mortgagor was acting under undue influence exercised by a third party. However *Lloyds Bank v Bundy*[130] is an example of a case where direct undue influence was exercised. The defendant was an elderly farmer who had come to rely implicitly upon advice provided by the plaintiffs in respect of his financial affairs. His son, who also banked with the plaintiffs, owned a plant hire business which was in financial difficulties. On the advice of the bank the father charged his house, which was his sole asset, to guarantee the overdraft of his son's company. This charge was no benefit to the father and the bank had failed to suggest that he should seek independent advice before entering into the transaction. In these circumstances the Court of Appeal held that the charge, which exceeded the value of the house, should be set aside on the grounds of undue influence.

3. Undue Influence Exercised by a Third Party Against the Mortgagor

17–042 As has been noted above, most cases do not involve the direct exercise of undue influence by the lender. Instead, many recent cases have involved a situation where a mortgagor is prevailed upon to take out the mortgage by some other person who was close to them, typically a member of their family. For example in *Barclays Bank v O'Brien*,[131] which is the leading case, a wife granted the bank a joint mortgage together with her husband of their matrimonial home to secure his business debts. One question was whether the wife was entitled to set the mortgage aside on

---

[129] Using a mortgage in this way is a means of converting the capital value of a house into an income. The capital sum released by the mortgage is used to buy an annuity (a pension) of a guaranteed amount. The amount of the annuity will normally be more than the amount of interest charges incurred by the mortgage. However the borrower takes the risk that rises in mortgage interest rates may absorb a large part of the annuity income, and might even exceed it.
[130] [1975] Q.B. 326.
[131] [1994] 1 A.C. 180; [1993] 4 All E.R. 417. For commentary see: [1994] Conv 140, 421; [1994] C.L.J. 21; (1994) 110 L.Q.R. 167; (1994) 57 M.L.R. 467; [1994] R.L.R. 3; (1995) 15 L.S. 35; (1995) 15 O.J.L.S. 119.

the grounds that she had only granted it because she was subject to the undue influence of her husband. In this scenario it is clear that the bank did not itself exercise undue influence, and the question arose whether the mortgage could be impugned because of the undue influence exercised against the mortgagee by a third party. Where the undue influence was exercised by a third party against a mortgagor, the mortgagor will only be able to set aside the transaction against the mortgagee if the mortgagee was affected by the undue influence. This will only be the case if the third party had acted as the agent of the morgtagee, or if the mortgagee had notice of the undue influence exercised by the third party over the mortgagor.

(a) *Was the Third Party Acting as Agent of the Mortgagee?*

A mortgagor will be able to set aside a mortgage against a mortgagee if he or she entered the transaction whilst acting under the undue influence of a third party, and that third party was acting as an agent of the mortgagee. In such circumstances the mortgagee is obviously affected by the undue influence of the third party, since in effect the mortgagee would have exercised direct undue influence against the mortgagor. However it is clear that such a third party will only very rarely be treated as the mortgagee's agent if otherwise unconnected with the mortgagee. Suppose, for instance, that a husband, wanting to borrow money for his own purposes, goes to a bank which agrees to make the loan only if he gives the bank a mortgage over the family home owned jointly with his wife. Suppose also that the bank gives him the mortgage deed and asks him to take it home for his wife to sign. In doing so, is the husband acting as the bank's agent so that, if he improperly persuades his wife to sign, the bank will be treated as having exercised undue influence in procuring the loan? Prior to *Barclays Bank v O'Brien*[132] some cases suggested that this would, indeed, be the case. However the House of Lords considered that this was wrong, and that it would be a very rare occurrence for a husband to be treated as the lender's agent. An alternative basis was thus developed to determine whether a mortgage should be set aside on the grounds that the mortgagor had acted under the undue influence of some third party.

17–043

(b) *Did the Mortgagee have Notice of the Undue Influence Exercised by the Third Party?*

In the absence of an agency relationship between the mortgagee and the third party who exercised undue influence over the mortgagor, a mortgagee will only be affected by the undue influence of a third party if it had notice that the mortgagor had entered the transaction whilst acting under the undue influence of the third party. The application of the doctrine of notice to determine whether the mortgage should be set aside in such cases was adopted by the House of Lords in the leading case of *Barclays Bank v O'Brien*.[133] Although this case

17–044

---

[132] [1994] 1 A.C. 180.

[133] [1994] 1 A.C. 180. It should be noted that the in *Garcia v National Australia Bank Ltd* (1998) 72 A.L.J.R. 1243 the Australian High Court has declined to follow the generalised approach of the House of Lords. Following the earlier decision in *Yerkey v Jones* (1939) 63 C.L.R. 649 it was held that wives were protected by a "special equity", such that a bank will not be protected unless and until a wife who has agreed to act as a surety without benefit to herself has been fully informed of the effect of what she has done.

concerned misrepresentation, the same principles apply in the case of undue influence. Lord Browne-Wilkinson, who gave the leading judgment, explained how the doctrine of notice should operate in such circumstances:

> "The doctrine of notice lies at the heart of equity. Given that there are two innocent parties, each enjoying rights, the earlier right prevails against the later right if the acquirer of the later right knows of the earlier right (actual notice) or would have discovered it had he taken proper steps (constructive notice). In particular, if the party asserting that he takes free of the earlier rights of another knows of certain facts which put him on inquiry as to the possible existence of the rights of that other and he fails to make such inquiry or take such other steps as are reasonable to verify whether such earlier right does or does not exist, he will have constructive notice of the earlier right and take subject to it. Therefore where a wife has agreed to stand surety for her husband's debts as a result of undue influence or misrepresentation, the creditor will take subject to the wife's equity to set aside the transaction if the circumstances are such as to put the creditor on inquiry as to the circumstances in which she agreed to stand surety."[134]

Thus a mortgage will be able to be set aside if the mortgagee had actual, imputed[135] or constructive notice that the mortgagee was acting under the undue influence or a third party. In most cases the reality will be that the mortgagor is claiming that the mortgagee had constructive notice of the undue influence exercised by a third party. There are therefore two crucial questions which must be addressed. First, when will a mortgagee be put on inquiry that the mortgagor might have been acting under undue influence? Second, what must the mortgagee do to avoid being affixed with constructive notice of the undue influence?

(i)   When is a Mortgagee put on Inquiry that the Mortgagor might have been Acting under Undue Influence?

17–045   In *Barclays Bank v O'Brien* Lord Browne–Wilkinson stated the circumstances in which a bank would be put on inquiry that a mortgage had been entered through the undue influence of a third party:

> ". . . in my judgement a creditor is put on inquiry when a wife offers to stand surety for her husband's debts by the combination of two factors: (a) the transaction is on its face not to the financial advantage of the wife: and (b) there is a substantial risk in transactions of that kind that, in procuring the wife to act as surety, the husband has committed a legal or equitable wrong that entitles the wife to set aside the transaction."[136]

In *Royal Bank of Scotland Plc v Etridge (No.2)*[137] the Court of Appeal took the view this should be interpreted to mean that a bank would only be put on inquiry if it was aware that the

---

[134] [1993] 4 All E.R. 417 at 429.
[135] *Royal Bank of Scotland v Etridge (No.2)* [1998] 4 All E.R. 705.
[136] [1994] 1 A.C. 180 at 196.
[137] [1998] All E.R. 705 at 719.

parties are cohabiting, or that the particular surety places implicit trust and confidence in the debtor in relation to her financial affairs. However the House of Lords in the Etridge case rejected this interpretation in favour of a more straightforward approach. Lord Nicholls stated:

> "In my view this passage, read in context, is to be taken to mean, quite simply, that a bank is put on inquiry whenever a wife offers to stand surety for her husband's debts."[138]

The same principle will operate where a husband offers to stand surety for his wife's debts, and in the case of unmarried couples, whether heterosexual or homosexual, if the bank is aware of the relationship between the parties.[139] However a bank will not automatically be put on inquiry if the mortgage money is being advanced to the husband and wife jointly, unless the bank is aware that the loan is being made for the husband's purposes as distinct from their joint purposes.

The operation of these principles can be illustrated from a number of cases. In *Barclays Bank v O'Brien* a bank was put on notice where a wife had executed a joint mortgage of her matrimonial home to secure the overdraft facility of a manufacturing company of which her husband was a shareholder. The bank was similarly put on notice in *Massey v Midland Bank Plc*[140] where a woman acted as the guarantor for the debts of her lover of 14 years' standing, even though she did not live with him because her parents objected to the relationship, and in *Credit Lyonnais Bank Nederland v Burch*[141] the bank was put on notice where a junior employee executed an "extravagantly improvident" unlimited guarantee of all her employer's debts. In contrast in *CIBC Mortgages Plc v Pitt*[142] the House of Lords held that the bank was held not to have been put on inquiry. A wife executed a joint mortgage with her husband of their matrimonial home. She had acted under the actual undue influence of her husband, who had pressured her to agree to the mortgage in order for him to be able to invest in the stock market. The mortgage application form, which the husband and wife had signed, stated that the purpose of the loan was to enable them to pay off the existing mortgage and to purchase a holiday home. The bank was not put on inquiry because "there was nothing to indicate to the [Bank] that this was anything other than a normal advance to a husband and wife for their joint benefit".

(ii) What must the Mortgagee do to Avoid Being Affixed with Constructive Notice of the Undue Influence?

The mere fact that a mortgagee is put on inquiry that a mortgagor might be transacting subject to undue influence does not inevitably mean that the mortgage will be set aside. A mortgagee will avoid being affixed with constructive notice if it takes reasonable steps to ensure that the mortgagor was not acting under the undue influence of a third party. It should be noted that in this context the concept of constructive notice is being applied in a novel and unconventional way. As Lord Nicholls explained in *Royal Bank of Scotland Plc v Etridge (No.2)*:

17–046

---

[138] [2001] UKHL 44; [2002] 2 A.C. 273 at [44].
[139] *Barclays Bank v O'Brien* [1994] 1 A.C. 180 at 198; *Royal Bank of Scotland Plc v Etridge (No.2)* [2001] UKHL 44; [2002] 2 A.C. 273 at [47]; *Massey v Midland Bank Plc* [1995] 1 All E.R. 929.
[140] [1995] 1 All E.R. 929.
[141] [1997] 1 All E.R. 144.
[142] [1993] 4 All E.R. 433.

"There is a further respect in which O'Brien departed from conventional concepts. Traditionally, a person is deemed to have notice (that is, he has "constructive notice") of a prior right when he does not actually know of it but would have learned of it had he made the requisite inquiries A purchaser will be treated as having constructive notice of all that a reasonable prudent purchaser would have discovered. In the present type of case, the steps that a bank is required to take, lest it have constructive notice that the wife's concurrence was procured improvidently by her husband, do not consist of making inquiries. Rather, O'Brien envisages that the steps taken by the bank will reduce, or even eliminate, the risk of the wife entering into the transaction under any misapprehension or as a result of undue influence by the husband. The steps are not concerned to discover whether the wife has been wronged by her husband in this way. The steps are concerned to minimise the risk that such a wrong may be committed."[143]

Following the decision of the House of Lords in *Barclays Bank v O'Brien* many subsequent cases have sought to identify the steps a mortgagor would have to take in order to avoid constructive notice of undue influence. In *Royal Bank of Scotland Plc v Etridge (No.2)* Lord Nicholls stated what would be required:

"For the future, a bank satisfies these requirements if it insists that the wife attend a private meeting with a representative of the bank at which she is told of the extent of her liability as surety, warned of the risk she is running and urged to take independent legal advice. In exceptional cases the bank, to be safe, has to insist that the wife is separately advised."[144]

In practice most banks do not hold a private meeting to bring home to a wife who is acting as a surety for her husbands debts the risk she is running. They prefer to require the surety to seek independent legal advice, and only to proceed with the transaction on the receipt of written confirmation from a solicitor that he has explained the nature and effect of the transaction to the surety.

(c) Did the Mortgagor Receive Independent Legal Advice?

17–047 As has been seen, a mortgagee will be not be affixed with constructive notice that the mortgagor had entered the transaction under the undue influence of a third party if it ensured that the mortgagee had received independent legal advice. Much litigation has concerned the nature of the legal advice that will entitle a mortgagor to avoid constructive notice of undue influence, and the principles were thoroughly examined by the House of Lords in *Royal Bank of Scotland Plc v Etridge (No.2)*. A number of key principles were identified, which are designed to prevent such advice being delivered in a perfunctory way. Provided that these steps have been observed, a mortgagee bank will be able to rely on the confirmation of a solicitor that he has advised the mortgagor appropriately to avoid being affixed with constructive notice.

---

[143] [2001] UKHL 44; [2002] 2 A.C. 273 at [41].
[144] [2002] 2 A.C. 273 at [50].

(i) The Solicitor Need not Act for the Mortgagor Alone

The House of Lords held that a solicitor is able to provide independent legal advice to a **17–048** prospective mortgagee even if he is also acting on behalf of the third party whose debts are being guaranteed (usually the mortgagor's husband) or the mortgagee bank. Lord Nicholls explained that in such circumstances the solicitor would have a duty to act for the wife alone in giving advice, and that he must cease to advise her if at any stage he "becomes concerned that there is a real risk that other interests or duties may inhibit his advice".[145]

(ii) The Mortgagee must Ask the Mortgagor to Nominate a Solicitor Who is to Act as her Advisor[146]

The mortgagee bank must take steps to check directly with the mortgagor the name of the solic- **17–049** itor she wishes to act as her advisor. The bank must explain to the mortgagor why it will require written confirmation from a solicitor that he has fully explained the nature of the documents and the practical implications of the transaction to her. The mortgagor should then be asked to nominate a solicitor whom she is willing to instruct to advise her separately from her husband. She should be told that, if she wishes, the solicitor may be the same solicitor as is acting for her husband, although she should also be asked whether she would prefer a different solicitor.

(iii) The Mortgagee must Supply the Solicitor with All the Financial Information Required to Provide Advice[147]

Since the mortgagee bank is likely to have a better picture of the financial affairs of the **17–050** person whose debts are being guaranteed, the mortgagee must supply the solicitor who is advising the mortgagor with all the financial information needed for this purpose. Although the information required will depend upon the facts of each case, it will ordinarily include information on the purpose for which the proposed security has been requested, the current amount of the third party's indebtedness, the amount of his current overdraft facility, and the amount and terms of any new facility. A bank will need to obtain the consent of its customer to provide this information to the solicitor advising the mortgagor, but the transaction will not be able to proceed if this consent is not forthcoming.

(iv) The Mortgagee must Inform the Solicitor of any Suspicions that the Mortgagor has been Misled or Subjected to Pressure[148]

If the mortgagee bank believes or suspects that the mortgagor has been misled as to the nature of **17–051** the transaction, or is not entering it out of her own free will, it must inform the solicitor who is providing the mortgagor with independent advice of the facts giving rise to its belief or suspicion.

---

[145] [2002] 2 A.C. 273 at [74].
[146] [2002] 2 A.C. 273 at [79].
[147] [2002] 2 A.C. 273 at [79].
[148] [2002] 2 A.C. 273 at [79].

(v) The Solicitor must Explain the Nature and Risks of the Transaction to the Mortgagor

17–052 A solicitor advising a mortgagor does not need to satisfy himself that his client was free from improper influence.[149] Instead the solicitor is required to explain to the mortgagor the documents that he or she will have to sign to grant the mortgage, and advise of the risks that he or she is taking upon him or herself by so doing. Lord Nicholls identified the core advice that a solicitor should give to a mortgagor before confirming to the mortgagee that the mortgagor had been properly advised:

> "(1) He will need to explain the nature of the documents and the practical consequences they will have for the wife if she signs them. She could lose her home if the husband's business does not prosper. Her home may be her only substantial asset, as well as the family's home. She could be made bankrupt. (2) He will need to point out the seriousness of the risks involved. The wife should be told the purpose of the proposed new facility, the amount and principal terms of the new facility, and that the bank might increase the amount of the facility, or change its terms, or grant a new facility, without reference to her. She should be told the amount of the liability under her guarantee. The solicitor should discuss the wife's financial means, including her understanding of the value of the property being charged. The solicitor should discuss whether the wife or her husband has any other assets out of which repayment could be made if the husband's business should fail. These matters are relevant to the seriousness of the risks involved. (3) The solicitor will need to state clearly that the wife has a choice. The decision is hers and hers alone. Explanation of the choice facing the wife will call for some discussion of the present financial position, including the amount of the husband's indebtedness, and the amount of his current overdraft facility. (4) The solicitor should check whether the wife wishes to proceed. She should be asked whether she is content that the solicitor should write to the bank confirming that he has explained to her the nature of the documents and the practical implications they may have for her, or whether, for instance, she would prefer him to negotiate with the bank on the terms of the transaction. Matters for negotiation could include the sequence in which various securities will be called upon or a specific or lower limit to her liabilities. The solicitor should not give any confirmation to the bank without the wife's authority."[150]

The solicitor should obtain all the information he requires from the bank and give this advice in suitable non-technical language at a face-to-face meeting with the mortgagor in the absence of the person whose debts are being guaranteed.

4. The Effect of Undue Influence on a Mortgage

17–053 Where a mortgage provided by way of surety has been obtained by undue influence of which the mortgagee had actual or constructive notice, the mortgage will be set aside in its entirety

---

[149] The Court of Appeal had suggested that this was necessary in *Royal Bank of Scotland v Etridge (No.2)* [1998] 4 All E.R. 705 at 715, but this was rejected by the House of Lords. See [2001] UKHL 44; [2002] 2 A.C. 273 at [58]–[59].
[150] [2001] UKHL 44; [2002] 2 A.C. 273 at [65].

as against the surety, even where no undue influence was exercised over the surety as respects part of the mortgage. In *TSB Bank Plc v Camfield*[151] a wife had been misled into agreeing to a mortgage of the family home to secure all her husband's debts by being told that it extended only to debts up to £15,000. The Court of Appeal held that unlike the curate's egg, which was good in parts, no part of the mortgage was enforceable against the wife. However the position will be different if the mortgagor had obtained a personal benefit from the transaction which is sought to be set aside. In such circumstances it has been held that the mortgagor must make restitution of the personal benefit obtained as a pre-condition of the recission of the transaction. If such restitution cannot take place because circumstances have changed, the equitable remedy of recission of the transaction will be unavailable. In *Dunbar Bank Plc v Nadeem*[152] a husband and wife raised a loan, secured by way of a mortgage, in part to buy a long leasehold interest in their matrimonial home, and in part to pay off his business debts. The wife obtained a personal benefit because she obtained a joint beneficial interest in their matrimonial home for the first time. At first instance it was held that the mortgage could only be set aside on the grounds of undue influence if the wife refunded to the bank the proportion of the mortgage which represented the cost of financing the purchase of her half share in the beneficial interest in the property.[153] The Court of Appeal reversed this decision, finding that the transaction had not been manifestly disadvantageous, and thus that there was no presumption of undue influence. It further held that the condition imposed had been inappropriate. The majority[154] held that rather than repaying to the bank the part of the loan attributable to the acquisition of her beneficial interest she should have been required to restore her beneficial interest in the matrimonial home to her husband, as he was the true source of it. By restoring her beneficial interest to her husband the wife's personal liability would be extinguished and the bank would enjoy a legal charge over the whole of the beneficial interest. However since the property had been subject to a further subsequent charge, Morritt L.J. explained that it had become impossible for the wife to restore to her husband the unencumbered interest she had received from him thus excluding the availability of the remedy of recission.

5. An Alternative Basis for Undue Influence Cases

The result of the line of cases beginning with *Barclays Bank v O'Brien*[155] is that there are certain situations in which a bank is affected with constructive notice of undue influence being exercised against a surety unless it has taken steps to ensure that the surety was fully aware of the nature and effect of the transaction and freely consented to it. It has already been explained that the concept of constructive notice is being used in a highly idiosyncratic way, quite unlike the use of the concept in other contexts. The concept is not being used to identify when a bank must make enquiries to verify whether there is a burden which might affect it (as is the case with constructive notice in its classical guise), but it is being used to justify

17–054

---

[151] [1995] 1 All E.R. 951.
[152] [1998] 3 All E.R. 876.
[153] [1997] 2 All E.R. 253.
[154] Morritt and Potter L.JJ.
[155] [1993] 4 All E.R. 417.

imposing upon the bank a duty to ensure that the surety has obtained independent advice. In reality what is happening is that in most cases where a person acts as a surety in a personal rather than in a business capacity, the bank is placed under a positive duty to ensure that the surety has freely entered into the transaction. It would have been more straightforward and transparent for the courts to find that this was the case, rather than to use a distorted application of the doctrine of notice. To have held that there was a positive duty on a bank to ensure that a surety acted freely in all cases where there was no obvious benefit to the surety, would, however, have required the courts to depart from an established line of authority that banks owe no duties to their sureties, and the House of Lords in *Barclays Bank v O'Brien*[156] declined to do this. Instead, given the expansion of the situations in which a bank will be fixed with constructive notice, the same result has been reached by a different route.

6. Setting Aside a Mortgage Obtained by Misrepresentation

17–055 Whilst the above discussion has focused on the equitable jurisdiction to rescind a mortgage on the grounds of undue influence, it is also possible for a mortgage to be set aside if it has been obtained by misrepresentation. This will commonly occur if the mortgagor is given misleading information concerning the extent of liability secured by the mortgage. Thus in *Barclays Bank v O'Brien*[157] Mrs O'Brien granted a mortgage of her matrimonial home to guarantee the overdraft of a company of which her husband was a shareholder, which her husband had misrepresented to her was limited to £60,000 and would only last three weeks. In fact it was granted for £135,000, reducing to £120,000 after three weeks. A similar misrepresentation as to the extent of liability occurred in *TSB Bank Plc v Camfield*.[158] A mortgage will clearly be set aside if such a misrepresentation was made to the mortgagor by the mortgagee or its agent. The mortgage will also be set aside if the misrepresentation was made to the mortgagor by a third party and the mortgagee had actual or constructive notice of the misrepresentation. Thus in *Barclays Bank v O'Brien*[159] the House of Lords held that the bank was put on inquiry because of the manifest disadvantage of the transaction to the wife, and that it had failed to ensure that she received the independent advice which would have counteracted the misrepresentation.

UNCONSCIONABLE BARGAINS AND COLLATERAL ADVANTAGES

1. Equity's Jurisdiction

17–056 Equity's protection of mortgagors goes beyond merely extending the right to redeem. Doctrines of equity of general application have also found special expression in relation to mortgages. One is the right to set aside unconscionable bargains. Where a contract which no

---

[156] [1993] 4 All E.R. 417.
[157] [1993] 4 All E.R. 417.
[158] [1995] 1 All E.R. 951.
[159] [1993] 4 All E.R. 417.

properly informed legal adviser could support has been obtained from someone of weak mind, equity will not permit the bargain to stand. For instance, where a tenant and her husband prevailed upon their feeble-minded landlady (who was suffering from Parkinson's disease) to grant them a lease on terms which they knew they could not extract from her agent or anyone else, the Privy Council had no hesitation in confirming that the trial judge was right in setting the lease aside.[160] Similarly in relation to mortgages. In *Credit Lyonnais Bank Nederland v Burch*,[161] the Court of Appeal was of the view that a mortgage granted by a junior employee of her employer's debts, unlimited in time and in amount, so "shocked the conscience of the court"[162] that if it had been challenged on that basis, it would almost certainly have been held to have been an unconscionable bargain. The mortgage transaction was so extreme that "an independent solicitor would certainly have advised her as strongly as he could that she should in no circumstances enter into the mortgage".[163]

In order to show that a transaction is so harsh and oppressive that it should be set aside as unconscionable, it must be shown that "one of the parties to it has imposed the objectional terms in a morally reprehensible manner, that is, in a way which affects his conscience".[164] This may be evident from the very improvidence of the transaction in question.[165] It is not enough that a transaction is seriously disadvantageous or commercially misguided, since "the law in general leaves every man at liberty to make such bargains as he pleases, and to dispose of his own property as he chooses".[166] A good example of this is *Multiservice Bookbinding Ltd v Marden*.[167] A bookbinder, seeking to raise money for the purpose of his business, agreed to make repayments which were linked to movements in the rate of exchange between the Swiss franc and the pound sterling. He also agreed to pay interest at 2 per cent above the Minimum Lending Rate. He was accordingly agreeing to what would now be called a "double whammy", because United Kingdom interest rates were running at very high levels, and the pound was depreciating rapidly against the Swiss franc.[168] Over the 10-year fixed period of the loan, repayments of capital and interest amounted to nearly four times the amount borrowed. Despite this extremely high cost to the loan, Browne-Wilkinson J. refused to set the bargain aside. The parties to the loan agreement were not in unequal bargaining positions, there was no evidence of sharp practice, and the borrower had received independent advice. The property which he had bought with the loan had also increased in value threefold. The bargain which he had made was hard–even unreasonable–but it was not unconscionable.

By way of contrast, in *Cityland and Property Holdings Ltd v Dabrah*,[169] the tenant of residential property agreed to buy the freehold from his landlord. The majority of the purchase price was to be supplied by means of payments to the landlord secured by a mortgage against

---

[160] *Boustany v Pigott* (1993) Lawtel document No.C1605332.

[161] [1997] 1 All E.R. 144.

[162] [1997] 1 All E.R. 144 at 152.

[163] [1997] 1 All E.R. 144 at 158, per Swinton Thomas L.J.

[164] *Multiservice Bookbinding Ltd v Marden* [1979] Ch. 84 at 110, per Browne-Wilkinson J.

[165] *Alec Lobb (Garages) Ltd v Total Oil GB Ltd* [1983] 1 All E.R. 944 at 961, per Millett J.

[166] *Brusewitz v Brown* (1922) 42 N.Z.L.R. 1106 at 1110, per Sir John Salmond.

[167] [1979] Ch. 84. See [1978] C.L.J. 211 (A.J. Oakley); (1979) 42 M.L.R. 338 (W.D. Bishop and B.V. Hindley).

[168] High interest levels in the UK reflected the weak position of the pound. If the loan had been taken out in Swiss francs (exchange controls permitting), the borrower would have paid much lower interest rates. The lender was in effect having his cake and eating it.

[169] [1968] Ch. 166. See also *Kevans v Joyce* [1896] 1 I.R. 442 and *Wells v Joyce* [1905] 2 I.R. 134.

the property. These payments totalled substantially more than the portion of the purchase price which they replaced, and all of the payments were due immediately on default by the buyer, without any discount for early payment. The buyer did default relatively soon after granting the mortgage. If the whole of the amount secured was then repayable, it would have amounted to a notional interest rate of 57 per cent per annum. Goff J. held that this premium was so unreasonably high that it was unfair and unconscionable. The notional interest payable should be reduced to an amount which was fair and reasonable having regard to the risks involved.

2. Court Regulation of an "Unfair Relationship Between Creditor and Debtor"

17–057 The Consumer Credit Act 1974 gave the courts a statutory jurisdiction to reopen extortionate credit bargains.[170] A credit bargain was considered extortionate if it required the debtor "to make payments" which were "grossly exorbitant, or otherwise grossly contravene[d] ordinary principles of fair dealing".[171] Factors which the court was, under this provision, expected to take into account included the degree of risk which the creditor (lender) is taking, and the age, experience, business capacity, state of health, and financial circumstances of the debtor (borrower).[172] In *A Ketley Ltd v Scott*,[173] Foster J. held that an interest rate of 48 per cent was not excessive for a temporary bridging loan given to enable the defendants to take advantage of an opportunity to buy the flat in which they lived for a substantial discount. In other cases, apparently high interest rates have been upheld because the loan has been made as a matter of last resort to a borrower who has a poor record of repayments (and therefore represents a high risk). Conversely, in *North London Securities v Meadows*,[174] it was held that an increase of loan amount from c.£5,000 to over £140,000, due to compound interest on arrears, contravened s.138.[175] By contrast, in *I Group Mortgages Ltd v Levitt*,[176] the defendant mortgagor was unsuccessful in pleading that the mortgagees had contravened ordinary principles of fair dealing by not complying with regulatory guidelines and verifying his employment. Lingard J. held that in the event, the defendant had falsified his income so it did not lie in his mouth to complain.[177] The defence was struck out as having no reasonable prospect of success. Lingard J. stated that the breach of regulatory guidelines did not fall within s.138.

---

[170] There was no financial limit to this jurisdiction in relation to mortgages, but the Act did not apply to loans by building societies or local authorities.
[171] Consumer Credit Act 1974 s.138(1).
[172] Consumer Credit Act 1974 s.138.
[173] [1980] C.C.L.R. 37.
[174] (2005) 1 P. & C.R. D.G. 16.
[175] Brown, "The Consumer Credit Act 2006; Real Additional Mortgagor Protection" [2007] Conv. 316–339.
[176] (2004, unreported, Westlaw summary); 2004 WL 1640401.
[177] He did not come to equity with "clean hands".

The Consumer Credit Act 2006 repeals the jurisdiction to set aside an extortionate credit bargain under s.138.[178] The 2006 Act replaces it with s.140A(1) and introduces the "unfair relationship between creditor and debtor"[179]:

> "(1) The court may make an order . . . in connection with a credit agreement if it determines that the relationship between the creditor and the debtor arising out of the agreement . . . is unfair to the debtor because of . . . any of the terms of the agreement; the way in which the creditor has exercised or enforced any of his rights under the agreement; any other thing done (or not done) by, or on behalf of, the creditor."

The court, in deciding whether to make an order, "shall have regard to all matters it thinks relevant (including matters relating to the creditor and matters relating to the debtor)".[180] The court has a wide jurisdiction in relation to the agreement. The creditor may be required to repay money paid under the agreement, fulfill conditions specified by the court, alter terms, "reduce or discharge any sum payable" under the agreement, or "set aside any duty imposed on the debtor" by the agreement.[181] This test appears to be less restrictive than s.138,[182] but it remains to be seen how it is interpreted by the courts.

3. Collateral Advantages

Perhaps as a development at a time when usury laws restricted the rates of interest payable,[183] equity developed a set of rules prohibiting certain advantages which were seen as "collateral" to the mortgage; that is, as not being a part and parcel of the mortgage itself. The rules were associated with the theory that upon redemption of a mortgage, the mortgagor should receive a return of his property, free from all charges and claims against it.

17–058

(a) *There must be a Right to Redeem*

The first principle equity applied was that the nature of a mortgage required that the mortgagor had a real right to redeem his property free from the mortgage.[184] The right to redeem could not be illusory. So, although there was (and remains) in itself no objection to a mortgage which restricts the freedom of the mortgagor to redeem for a fixed period,[185] the

17–059

---

[178] Consumer Credit Act 2006 Sch.4 para.1.

[179] The Consumer Credit Act 2006 inserts s.140A into the Consumer Credit Act 1974 and came into force on April 6, 2007.

[180] Quoted in Brown, "The Consumer Credit Act 2006; Real Additional Mortgagor Protection" [2007] Conv. 316–339.

[181] There are certain exempt agreements: s.140A(5), s.140B(1), and there are savings and transitional provisions: Consumer Credit Act 2006 Sch.3.

[182] Brown [2007] Conv. 316–339.

[183] See *Jennings v Ward* (1705) 2 Vern. 520 at 521: "A man shall not have interest for his money, and a collateral advantage besides for the loan of it, or clog the equity of redemption with any by-agreement".

[184] *Cheah v Equiticorp Finance Group Ltd* [1992] 1 A.C. 472.

[185] As in *Multiservice Bookbinding Ltd v Marden* [1979] Ch. 84 where the mortgage was not to be repaid for 10 years.

mortgage must be capable of redemption while the asset subject to the mortgage still has some genuine residual value. This is neatly illustrated by two contrasting cases. In *Fairclough v Swan Brewery Co Ltd*,[186] a publican's 172-year lease was mortgaged on terms that it could not be redeemed until six weeks before the lease expired. The Privy Council held that this contractual fetter on redemption was invalid since it made the mortgage for all practical purposes irredeemable. There would have been almost no residual value. By contrast, in *Knightsbridge Estates Trust Ltd v Byrne*,[187] a commercial mortgage at competitive rates, made between two experienced parties negotiating at arm's length, provided that the loan could not be redeemed or called in for a period of 40 years. The property was freehold, and would still have had a significant residual value at the end of the mortgage period. The borrower wished to repay the loan only because interest rates had fallen before the contractual redemption date, and the loan could be replaced at lower cost. In the view of the Court of Appeal, there was no reason to set the mortgage aside. It could not be seen "as anything but a proper business transaction". In factual contrast in *Dutton v Davis*,[188] Dutton was the owner of a farm which was subject to heavy financial liabilities. He sold the farm to Davis for £250,000, who granted Dutton a lease and an option to buy back the farm. He contended that this was in reality a mortgage and that he had the right to redeem on payment of £250,000. The Court of Appeal held that it was a straightforward sale transaction.[189]

(b) *Redemption must be Free from "Clogs and Fetters"*

17–060   Since redemption is the right to the return of the property subject to the mortgage once the obligation secured by the mortgage has been discharged,[190] equity initially took the view that, upon redemption, all obligations contained in the mortgage transaction must immediately be discharged. For instance, in *Bradley v Carritt*[191] the owner of shares in a tea company mortgaged them to a broker and agreed that, even if the mortgage was repaid, he would continue to use the broker for selling the company's tea or pay him the commission that he would have earned had he been so employed. The House of Lords held that this was a fetter on the equity of redemption—an obligation continuing after the discharge of the mortgage—and was unenforceable. Similarly, in *Noakes and Co Ltd v Rice*,[192] the owner of a public house mortgaged it to a brewery. He covenanted to buy all his beer from the brewery, not only during the mortgage, but also after the mortgage was redeemed. This was held to be invalid as a restriction

---

[186] [1912] A.C. 565.
[187] [1939] Ch. 441.
[188] (2006) 2 P. & C.R. D.G. 19.
[189] It should be noted that after the Law of Property Act 1925, mortgages cannot be created by conveyance of the freehold but the Court of Appeal thought that "there is sometimes difficulty in distinguishing between an outright sale with the right to repurchase on the one hand, and an assignment by way of security subject to a right of redemption on the other". Per Lloyd L.J. (2006) 2 P. & C.R. D.G. 19.
[190] In *Santley v Wilde* [1899] 2 Ch. 474, the mortgage of a theatre provided for the mortgagee to receive a share of profits as well as the repayment of the loan with interest. The Court of Appeal held that the mortgage secured the performance of the obligation to share profits as well as the obligation to repay the loan, and accordingly the mortgage was not redeemed merely by the repayment of the loan with interest. The provision for a share of profits was justified by the high level of risk involved in making a loan against a theatrical business.
[191] [1903] A.C. 253.
[192] [1902] A.C. 24.

on the right to get back the security free from the terms of the mortgage. In both cases, had the tie agreement continued only for the duration of the mortgage, it would almost certainly have been valid,[193] unless the terms were harsh and unconscionable or in restraint of trade.[194]

(c) *Options to Purchase*

Even where a "perfectly fair bargain" has been made between two businessmen, "each of whom was quite sensible of what they were doing" and "without any trace or suspicion of oppression, surprise or circumvention", the bargain will not be upheld if it confers, as part of a mortgage, an option on the mortgagee to purchase the property mortgaged. This was the reluctant conclusion of the House of Lords in *Samuel v Jarrah Timber and Wood Paving Corporation Ltd*.[195] The House of Lords treated the rule as absolute. In Lord Lindley's words:

17–061

> "The doctrine once a mortgage, always a mortgage, means that no contract between a mortgagor and a mortgagee made at the time of the mortgage and as part of the mortgage transaction, or, in other words, as one of the terms of the loan, can be valid if it prevents the mortgagor from getting back his property on paying off what is due on his security. Any bargain which has that effect is invalid, and is inconsistent with the transaction being a mortgage."[196]

In that case, a mortgage of debenture stock in a company gave the mortgagee the option to purchase the stock at a fair valuation within 12 months of the date of the loan secured by the mortgage. It was held that the mortgagee was not entitled to enforce that option against the wishes of the mortgagor.

(d) *Independent Contractual Stipulations*

The courts' objection to collateral advantages does not extend to provisions which form no part of the mortgage itself, but which are part of an independent and distinct contract. For instance, in *Reeve v Lisle*,[197] decided by the House of Lords immediately before the *Jarrah Timber* case, the mortgagor had granted the mortgagee an option to purchase the property mortgaged in an agreement signed 10 or 11 days after the mortgage was made. This option was held to be enforceable since "the agreement to buy the equity of redemption was no part of the original mortgage transaction, but was entered into subsequently, and was an entirely separate transaction to which no objection could be taken".[198] A similar view was taken in *Kreglinger v New Patagonia Meat and Cold Storage Co Ltd*.[199] A firm of woolbrokers agreed

17–062

---

[193] [1902] A.C. 24.
[194] *Biggs v Hoddinott* [1898] 2 Ch. 307.
[195] [1904] A.C. 323.
[196] [1902] A.C. 323 at 339.
[197] [1902] A.C. 461.
[198] Per Lord Lindley in *Samuel v Jarrah Timber and Wood Paving Corp Ltd* [1902] A.C. 323.
[199] [1914] A.C. 25.

to lend £10,000 to the respondents, who packed meat. The loan was secured by a charge on the respondents' assets. The woolbrokers agreed that, although they would not call in the loan for five years, it could be repaid at any time by the respondents. The respondents, in return, agreed to give a right of first refusal on all its sheepskins to the woolbrokers, and to pay a commission on any sold to a third party, for the full period of five years, even if the loan had already been repaid. Even though this right of pre-emption was included in the same document as the mortgage, the House of Lords upheld it. Lord Haldane said that: "The question is in my opinion not whether the two contracts were made at the same moment and evidenced by the same instrument, but whether they were in substance a single and undivided contract or two distinct contracts". The right of pre-emption was a preliminary and separable condition of the loan, freely and knowingly entered into. In *Re Petrol Filling Station, Vauxhall Bridge Road, London*,[200] Ungoed-Thomas J. applied Lord Haldane's principle in holding that a solus agreement[201] made between a garage proprietor and a petrol company was enforceable after the redemption of an associated loan, even if the loan had already been repaid.

These decisions make good commercial sense. In both *Kreglinger* and *Vauxhall Bridge*, the main purpose of the mortgagee was not to make loans. The solus agreement in each case was the commercial advantage which the mortgagee sought, and there was evidence in both cases that the loan was a "sweetener" to entice the mortgagor to enter into the agreement. To deprive agreements of this kind of their validity would inhibit perfectly reasonable business arrangements between businessmen who understand fully what they are doing.

THE POSITION OF THE MORTGAGEE

1. The Right to Payment

17–063 A mortgage provides security for the performance of an obligation, normally to repay a loan. The expectation of most mortgagees is that the mortgage will be needed only as a last resort. If the loan is not repaid, the mortgagee may bring an action for repayment on the loan contract. Even where the mortgage is enforced, this right of action normally survives. For instance, in *Palk v Mortgage Services Funding Plc*,[202] where a mortgagee was seeking to take possession of the mortgagor's house, the mortgagor was still liable to make any payments due under the loan contract. Similarly, if the mortgagee enforces a mortgage through sale, and because there is negative equity, the proceeds of sale fail to meet the amount of the loan with interest and costs, the mortgagor remains liable in contract to pay the outstanding balance. The mortgagor faced with negative equity cannot therefore escape his problem by posting the keys to the property through the lender's door and walking away. In *Bristol & West Plc v Bartlett*[203] the Court of Appeal held that the relevant limitation period for the recovery of any

---

[200] (1969) 20 P. & C.R. 1.
[201] i.e. an agreement to purchase supplies exclusively from a sole supplier.
[202] [1993] Ch. 330.
[203] [2002] 4 All E.R. 544

principal sum outstanding after a mortgage had been discharged by the sale of the land was 12 years,[204] but that the relevant period for unpaid interest was six years.[205]

Even where a mortgage indemnity policy has been taken out at the mortgagor's expense to cover the possibility of a sale by the mortgagee at less than the amount of the loan, the mortgagor remains liable in contract. Except where the policy expressly provides an indemnity to the mortgagor, the insurance company making good the deficiency to the mortgagee is subrogated to the mortgagee's contractual right and may therefore take over the mortgagee's cause of action.[206]

2. The Right to Possession

It has already been seen that, although in most cases the mortgagee has the right to possession, the mortgagee will not normally exercise that right where the borrower is not in default, and there may even be an express or implied term of the mortgage that the borrower is entitled to retain possession until in default. Because the liability of a mortgagee to account while in possession is strict, it will be rare for possession to be sought except where the mortgagee intends to sell. In *Palk v Mortgage Services Funding Plc*,[207] however, the circumstances in which a mortgagee sought possession were rather unusual. A property which had been mortgaged for a very substantial sum fell in value below the amount of the mortgage during a property recession. The mortgagors were also in arrears on their mortgage payments, and arrears were building up at an alarming rate. The mortgagees sought possession with the intention of retaining the property until the market improved. In the meantime, repayment arrears were still building up. The Court of Appeal held that it had the power, at the request of the mortgagor, to order a sale[208] even if the sale would not fully discharge the debt.

The powers of a mortgagee are qualified by the general requirement that they must be "exercised in good faith for the purpose of obtaining repayment".[209] This qualification applies to the exercise of the mortgagee's right to take possession of the mortgaged land. As Lord Denning M.R. stated in *Quennell v Maltby*:

> "A mortgagee will be restrained from getting possession except where it is sought bona fide and reasonably for the purpose of enforcing the security and then only subject to such conditions as the court thinks fit to impose."[210]

17–064

---

[204] Limitation Act 1980 s.20(1); This was confirmed by the House of Lords in *West Bromwich Building Society v Wilkinson* [2005] 1 W.L.R. 2303. In this case recovery of a shortfall on a mortgage debt was statute barred because the cause of action arose when demand for payment was made, more than 12 years previously.
[205] Limitation Act 1980 s.20(5).
[206] *Woolwich Building Society v Brown*, *Independent*, January 22, 1996.
[207] [1993] Ch. 330.
[208] Under Law of Property Act 1925 s.91.
[209] *Downsview Nominees Ltd v First City Corp Ltd* [1993] A.C. 295 at 312, per Lord Templeman; In *Meretz Investments NV v ACP* [2007] Ch. 197, Lewison J held that the mortgagee in this case acted partly from improper motives but partly from the proper motive to realise his security. Thus, there was no breach of duty; see [2006] Conv. 278. The case went to appeal but not on this point. Dixon [2006] Conv. 278.
[210] [1979] 1 All E.R. 568 at 571.

(a) Jurisdiction to Postpone a Possession Order

17–065 In the case of mortgages of residential property, the Administration of Justice Act 1970 places statutory restrictions on the ability of the mortgagee to recover possession. These statutory provisions operate in addition to the court's inherent jurisdiction to grant temporary relief by staying proceedings to enable a mortgagor to assemble the funds needed to redeem the mortgage. That inherent jurisdiction is extremely limited. In *Birmingham Citizens' Permanent Building Society v Caunt*[211] it was held that the court could merely adjourn proceedings for a short time in order to "afford the mortgagor a limited opportunity to find means to pay off the mortgagee or otherwise satisfy him if there was a reasonable prospect of either of those events occurring".[212] An adjournment of more than 28 days would not normally be possible, nor could new repayment terms be forced on an unwilling mortgagee.

The Court of Appeal has held in *Cheltenham and Gloucester Plc v Booker*[213] that, although the circumstances in which the conditions are met will be rare, the inherent jurisdiction enables it to permit mortgagors to remain in possession pending a sale by the mortgagee if the mortgagors are willing to co-operate in the sale, their presence will not depress the price, and they will give up possession on completion. In *Quennell v Maltby*,[214] where an action for possession was brought by a mortgagee as a device to oust a tenant protected by the Rent Acts, Lord Denning said: "A mortgagee will be restrained from getting possession except when it is sought bona fide and reasonably for the purpose of enforcing the security and then only subject to such conditions as the court thinks fit to impose". Whilst the case illustrates that there is a jurisdiction to decline an order for possession in appropriate circumstances, the jurisdiction is probably less broad than Lord Denning asserts.

(b) Statutory Relief

(i) The Statutory Jurisdiction

17–066 Under s.36 of the Administration of Justice Act 1970 the court may adjourn possession proceedings relating to a "dwelling-house" for such period as the court considers reasonable "if it appears to the court that in the event of its exercising the power the mortgagor is likely to be able within a reasonable period to pay any sums due under the mortgage or to remedy a default consisting of a breach of any other obligation arising under or by virtue of the mortgage". There was a problem with the drafting of this provision. In *Halifax Building Society v Clarke*[215] a mortgagor had defaulted in making periodical payments under an instalment mortgage. Under a common standard provision in a mortgage repayable by instalments, the whole sum borrowed was immediately repayable if the mortgagor was late in making any single repayment. It was held that the phrase "any sums due" meant the whole of the capital debt

---

[211] [1962] Ch. 883 noted (1962) 78 L.Q.R. 171 (REM).
[212] [1962] Ch. 883 at 891 per Russell L.J.
[213] *The Times*, November 20, 1996.
[214] [1979] 1 W.L.R. 318, noted [1979] C.L.J. 257.
[215] Unreported, 1973.

and not just the outstanding arrears. The court considered that there was no prospect of this sum being found by the mortgagor "within a reasonable period". To cover this defect, amending legislation has in effect reversed the decision in *Halifax Building Society v Clarke* by defining "any sums due under the mortgage" as those sums which "the mortgagor would have expected to pay if there had been no . . . provision for earlier payment" in the event of a breach.[216] Subsequent decisions have made it clear that the Act applies both to repayment mortgages and also to mortgages where the capital sum is payable in a single instalment, for instance through a separate endowment policy,[217] and even in cases where the mortgagee is seeking possession prior to any default on the part of the mortgagor.[218] There may still, though, be some situations to which the Acts do not apply, for instance where a mortgage is used to support a bank overdraft which is repayable only on demand by the bank,[219] or where a warrant for possession has already been issued.[220]

Although a mortgagee will normally seek to obtain possession of the mortgaged land by means of a court order, *Ropaigealach v Barclays Bank Plc*[221] suggests that in some circumstances the mortgagee may be able to retake possession without the intervention of the court. The plaintiffs were in default of their mortgage payments and the mortgagee demanded payment of some £64,000. The property was empty at the time as it was undergoing repair or refurbishment. The mortgagees therefore took peaceful possession and sold the house at auction with vacant possession. The plaintiffs claimed that s.36 had the effect that a mortgagee could only obtain possession by means of an order of the court, and that the bank had therefore lacked the right to take possession and sell the property. The Court of Appeal unanimously, albeit with some reluctance, held that the section did not have this effect, and that Parliament had not intended to amend the common law right of a mortgagee to retake possession such that it could only be exercised with the assistance of the court. Thus the jurisdiction to grant relief from the mortgagee's right to possession under s.36 only arises where possession is sought by a court action. As Clarke L.J. stated:

17–067

> "I have reluctantly reached the conclusion that where a section gives the court powers 'where the mortgagee . . . brings an action in which he claims possession of the mortgaged property' it is not permissible to hold that the effect of the section is to give the court such powers whether or not the mortgagee brings such an action."[222]

It should be noted that a mortgagee will only be entitled to take possession of the land without an order of the court if there is no one present on the premises, otherwise a criminal offence will be committed.[223] The Law Commission has recommended that the common law right to take possession without court proceedings should be removed,[224] but it is clear that this reform will have to be implemented by legislation.

---

[216] Administration of Justice Act 1973 s.8.
[217] *Bank of Scotland v Grimes* [1985] Q.B. 1179, noted [1985] Conv. 407.
[218] *Western Bank Ltd v Schindler* [1977] Ch. 1.
[219] *Habib Bank Ltd v Taylor* [1982] 3 All E.R. 561.
[220] *Cheltenham and Gloucester Building Society v Obi* (1996) 28 H.L.R. 22.
[221] [1999] 4 All E.R. 235 at 253.
[222] [1999] 4 All E.R. 235 at 255.
[223] Criminal Law Act 1977 s.6.
[224] Law Com. No.204, *Transfer of Land—Land Mortgagees* (1991), para.6.16.

(ii) A Reasonable Period

17–068 The courts initially exercised the jurisdiction under s.36 of the Administration of Justice Act 1970 on the basis that the "reasonable period" over which the Act permitted the court to reschedule payments was a short period of no more than, say, one or two years.[225] In *Cheltenham & Gloucester Building Society v Norgan*,[226] however, following dicta in some earlier cases,[227] the Court of Appeal held that the whole of the remaining period of a mortgage could be taken into account in deciding what amounted to a reasonable period. Waite L.J. said:

> "The court should take as its starting point the full term of the mortgage and pose at the outset the question: would it be possible for the mortgagor to maintain payment off of the arrears by instalments over that period."[228]

According to Evans L.J., the factors to be taken into account in establishing a reasonable period include the ability of the mortgagor to make payments now and in the future, the likely duration of any temporary financial difficulty, the reason for the arrears, the period remaining of the original mortgage, and the adequacy of the security to support the loan and arrears over the repayment period.[229] The court must be satisfied that, over the period which it schedules for repayment, the mortgagor will be able to pay off the arrears and any other sums which fall due for payment under the mortgage.[230] In *Halifax Plc v Okin*[231] the Court of Appeal agreed with the judge's decision not to suspend a possession order against a mortgagor who, even though she demonstrated she had a job due to start, her past record of repayment justified the conclusion that she could not afford the mortgage. She only made one payment on a plan to pay current instalments plus an additional amount for arrears, which had been agreed under a previous postponement. The fact that the mortgagor has a cross-claim against the mortgagee is a factor which may be taken into account in deciding whether to postpone a possession order for a reasonable period, but it is not in itself sufficient to justify refusing an order for possession, even where it amounts to more than the sum owing by way of mortgage.[232]

(iii) Postponement to Enable Sale

17–069 The reason for mortgagees seeking possession of the mortgaged property is normally to facilitate a sale with vacant possession. The mortgagor may, however, feel that a sale conducted

---

[225] *Royal Trust Co of Canada v Markham* [1975] 1 W.L.R. 1416; *National Westminster Bank Plc v Skelton* (note) [1993] 1 W.L.R. 72.

[226] [1996] 1 All E.R. 449.

[227] *First Middlesburgh Trading and Mortgage Co Ltd v Cunningham* (1974) 28 P. & C.R. 69 and *Western Bank Ltd v Schindler* [1977] Ch. 1.

[228] [1996] 1 All E.R. 449 at 458.

[229] See also *First Middlesbrough Trading and Mortgage Co Ltd v Cunningham* (1974) 28 P. & C.R. 69.

[230] *First National Bank Plc v Syed* [1991] 2 All E.R. 250; *Town and Country Building Society v Julien* (1991) 24 H.L.R. 312.

[231] [2007] EWCA Civ 567; Westlaw summary.

[232] *Mobil Oil Co Ltd v Rawlinson* (1981) 43 P. & C.R. 221, noted [1982] Conv. 453; *National Westminster Bank Plc v Skelton* [1993] 1 W.L.R. 72; *Ashley Guarantee Plc v Zacaria* [1993] 1 W.L.R. 62, noted [1993] Conv. 459.

by an owner-occupier with the owner still in occupation is likely to realise a higher price than a forced sale under the mortgage of a repossessed property. In *Target Homes Ltd v Clothier*[233] there was evidence from an estate agent that the property could be sold by the owner for a price sufficient to repay the loan with arrears (no repayments had been made for over 15 months) and that an offer to purchase had already been received. Although considering that the estate agent's evidence might need to be slightly discounted, the Court of Appeal nevertheless granted a postponement of the possession order for three months to enable the mortgagor to negotiate a sale. As with the deferral of an order for possession to enable repayment by instalments, there must be a real prospect that a deferral to enable a sale to be made will not leave the lender inadequately secured and that the sale will discharge the loan.[234] As Phillips L.J. said in *Cheltenham and Gloucester Plc v Krausz*:

> "It is . . . quite clear that s.36 does not empower the court to suspend possession in order to permit the mortgagor to sell the mortgaged premises where the proceeds of sale will not suffice to discharge the mortgage debt, unless of course other funds will be available to the mortgagor to make up the shortfall."[235]

Provided that these conditions are met, the suspension of an order for possession is not necessarily confined to a period no longer than three months. In *National and Provincial Building Society v Lloyd*,[236] the mortgagor sought a delay in an order for possession in order to subdivide the mortgaged property and sell it off in lots. The Court of Appeal held that, although the "reasonable period" for which proceedings could be deferred could be for six or nine months, or even a year,[237] the mortgagor's aspirations to sell the property for enough to cover the loan and arrears owed more to hope than to reality. It therefore declined to defer the order. The court also declined on the facts to postpone a possession order in *Bristol and West Building Society v Ellis*,[238] although the court was in principle prepared to contemplate deferring an order for possession for three to five years.

(c) *Protection of Spouses*

A mortgagee seeking possession of land must serve notice on any spouse who has registered his or her rights of occupation under the Matrimonial Homes Act 1983. The spouse of the mortgagor is also entitled to any relief which is available under the statutory jurisdiction to defer an order for possession under s.36 of the Administration of Justice Act 1970. There is, however, no obligation on the mortgagee to inform the spouse of any arrears under the mortgage.[239] **17–070**

In the case of joint mortgagors, any proceedings must be brought against all the co-owners. Each will then have an opportunity to invoke the protection of s.36. Where one of two joint

---

[233] [1994] 1 All E.R. 439
[234] *Bristol and West Building Society v Ellis* (1996) E.G.C.S. 74; *The Times*, May 2, 1996.
[235] [1997] 1 All E.R. 21 at 29.
[236] [1996] 1 All E.R. 630.
[237] See also *Cheltenham and Gloucester Building Society v Johnson* (1996) 28 H.L.R. 885.
[238] *The Times*, May 2, 1996.
[239] *Hastings and Thanet Building Society v Goddard* [1970] 1 W.L.R. 1544.

mortgagors has a defence to the possession proceedings, for instance on the basis that their agreement to the mortgage was obtained through undue influence, it is possible for possession to be ordered against the mortgagor who has no such defence. Since a mortgagee is unlikely to stand to gain any benefit from an order against one co-owner alone, "it is not in general right to make an order requiring him to leave within the period during which the other mortgagee is in possession and entitled to be in possession. This must particularly be the case when the two mortgagors share the home as husband and wife".[240] The proper practice in most such cases would be to adjourn the proceedings with liberty to restore if the other mortgagor leaves the property or an order for possession is made against him or her.

3. Right to Sell

(a) Nature of the Power of Sale

17–071 The right to sell is the most potent of the mortgagee's rights, for it is normally the ultimate means of enforcing the security and repaying the debt which it secures. It is for this reason that prudent lenders ensure that the amount which they advance on loan does not amount to too high a proportion of the value of the property over which security is taken.

There is a right to sell with the authority of a court order in the case of all mortgages, whether legal or equitable. A power of sale without recourse to court can be conferred by the mortgage instrument (which will need to be by deed to confer on the mortgagee the power to grant a legal estate). In addition, for mortgages made by deed (which inevitably includes all legal mortgages), there is a statutory power of sale conferred by s.101 of the Law of Property Act 1925. This power of sale arises "when the mortgage money becomes due", but does not become exercisable until certain other conditions have been met. The purpose of this distinction between the power of sale arising and becoming exercisable is to protect purchasers from the mortgagee. The date on which the mortgage money becomes due can be verified from the mortgage deed. The conditions to be satisfied before the power becomes exercisable require an investigation of the mortgage account or actions of the mortgagor. These inquiries might be difficult or inconvenient for a purchaser, but will inevitably be known to the mortgagee. A mortgagee who sells before the relevant conditions have been satisfied will be liable to the mortgagor in damages.[241]

A purchaser is not required to make inquiries to see whether the power of sale has become exercisable.[242] However, if the purchaser has actual knowledge of an irregularity, he will be affected by it.[243]

---

[240] *Albany Home Loans Ltd v Massey* [1997] 2 All E.R. 609 at 613, per Schiemann L.J.
[241] Law of Property Act 1925 s.104(2).
[242] *Property and Bloodstock Ltd v Emerton* [1968] Ch. 94 at 114, per Danckwerts L.J.
[243] Law of Property Act 1925 s.104(2). See also *Bailey v Barnes* [1894] 1 Ch. 25 at 30 and *Lord Waring v London and Manchester Assurance Co Ltd* [1935] Ch. 310 at 318.

(b) *When the Statutory Power of Sale Arises*

The statutory power arises (i.e. the mortgagee first becomes enabled to sell the property the **17–072**
subject of the mortgage) when any special restrictions contained in the mortgage deed have
been satisfied and the mortgage money has become due under the mortgage. This latter condition is satisfied where the legal or contractual date for redemption has passed or where any
instalment of capital is due under a repayment mortgage.[244] In the case of a term mortgage
where the capital is not repayable until the end of the mortgage term, it is not sufficient that
a payment of interest has fallen due,[245] but most such mortgages, if properly drafted, will
contain an express provision under which the power of sale can be invoked.

(c) *When the Statutory Power of Sale Becomes Exercisable*

The statutory power of sale becomes exercisable when one of three alternative conditions has **17–073**
been satisfied. There must either have been three months' default after service of a notice
requiring payment of the capital moneys due under the mortgage, or some interest due under
the mortgage is in arrears and unpaid for two months after becoming due, or there has been
a breach of some other provision in the mortgage.[246]

(d) *Effect of Sale*

A sale by the mortgagee under the statutory power is effective to convey the whole of the mort- **17–074**
gagor's estate to the purchaser, be it the whole freehold or leasehold interest, rather than merely
the actual or notional leasehold interest demised to the mortgagee. The title which the purchaser receives is subject to any paramount claims, such as rights in land and mortgages having priority to the mortgagee, but it is otherwise free from any subsequent mortgages, or rights
of the mortgagor and those claiming under him. So, for instance, where the mortgagor, after
the date of the mortgage, has contracted to sell the land, the rights of the purchaser against the
land under this contract are overreached by any sale by the mortgagee.[247] The person contracting with the mortgagor will retain contractual rights against the mortgagor, but since the mortgagor will invariably be in default, those rights may be of comparatively little value.

In most cases the mortgagee will seek to obtain possession of the land prior to sale in order
to be able to offer vacant possession to potential purchasers. However in *Ropaigealach v
Barclays Bank*[248] Clarke L.J. suggested that in some cases a mortgagee might choose not to
take proceedings for possession but simply sell the property under his power of sale, leaving

---

[244] *Payne v Cardiff RDC* [1932] 1 K.B. 241 at 251 and 253.
[245] *Twentieth Century Banking Corp Ltd v Wilkinson* [1977] Ch. 99.
[246] Law of Property Act 1925 s.103.
[247] *Duke v Robson* [1973] 1 W.L.R. 267. See also *Lyus v Prowsa Developments Ltd* [1982] 1 W.L.R. 1044. In
relation to registered land see Land Registration Act 1925 s.34(4).
[248] [1999] 4 All E.R. 235.

the purchaser to take possession by evicting the mortgagor. Such a procedure might offer advantages to the mortgagee since it would be able to avoid exposure to the protection afforded the mortgagor by s.36 of the Administration of Justice Act 1970. Whilst he considered that it would be "curious that mortgagors should only have protection in the case where the mortgagee chooses to take legal proceedings"[249] he also held that it "cannot be readily inferred that Parliament intended to give protection to mortgagors in such a case".[250]

(e) *Conduct of the Sale*

17–075   The duties of a mortgagee where land is sold were summarised by Nourse L.J. in *AIB Finance Ltd v Debtors*:

> "first, that a mortgagee, although he may exercise his power of sale at any time and for his own choice, owes the mortgagor a duty to take reasonable care to obtain a proper price for the mortgaged property at that time; secondly, that the duty is not tortious in nature but one recognised by equity as arising out of the particular relationship of mortgagee and mortgagor."[251]

The mortgagee is selling in his own interest and is therefore not to be treated in the same way as a trustee exercising a power of sale under a trust instrument.[252] However, although the mortgagee "has rights of his own which he is entitled to exercise adversely to the mortgagor",[253] he "is not entitled to conduct himself in a way which unfairly prejudices the mortgagor",[254] The mortgagee owes a duty to the mortgagor in exercising the power of sale which is capable of being categorised as a duty to take reasonable care.[255] In the case of a sale of land mortgaged to a building society, the society is under a duty "to take reasonable care to ensure that the price at which the land is sold is the best price that can reasonably be obtained".[256] Even though the duty on the mortgagee can be expressed in terms of an obligation to take reasonable care, and it has been argued that it should be treated as a duty of care in negligence,[257] that view has not been approved by the Court of Appeal which, in *Parker-Tweedale v Dunbar Bank Plc*,[258] held that a mortgagee exercising a power of sale owed no duty to persons other than the mortgagor, such as the beneficiary under a trust of which the mortgagor was trustee. Nourse L.J. said that "it is both unnecessary and confusing for the duties owed by a mortgagee to the mortgagor and the surety, if there is one, to be expressed in terms of the tort of negligence". He pointed out

---

[249] [1999] 4 All E.R. 235 at 253.
[250] [1999] 4 All E.R. 235 at 252.
[251] [1998] 2 All E.R. 929 at 937.
[252] *Cuckmere Brick Co Ltd v Mutual Finance Ltd* [1971] Ch. 949; *Corbett v Halifax Plc* [2003] 4 All E.R. 180.
[253] *Farrar v Farrars Ltd* (1888) 40 Ch.D. 395 at 311, per Lindley L.J.
[254] *Palk v Mortgage Services Plc* [1993] 2 W.L.R. 415 at 420.
[255] *Standard Chartered Bank Ltd v Walker* [1982] 1 W.L.R. 1410.
[256] Building Societies Act 1986 Sch.4 para.1. *Reliance Permanent Building Society v Harwood-Stamper* [1944] Ch. 362.
[257] See *Standard Chartered Bank Ltd v Walker* [1982] 1 W.L.R. 1410; *American Express International Banking Corporation v Hurley* [1985] 3 All E.R. 564.
[258] [1991] Ch. 26.

that the origins of the mortgagee's duty preceded the development of the modern tort of negligence. More recently in *AIB Finance Ltd v Debtors*[259] the Court of Appeal reiterated that the duty of a mortgagee is equitable rather than tortious in nature.[260]

Even though the duty on the mortgagee is not a duty in the tort of negligence, it goes well beyond a duty simply to act in good faith.[261] There are many respects in which the mortgagee owes a duty to act with reasonable prudence or to take proper account of the interests of the mortgagor, and this duty is one which is unlikely to be avoided even by a widely drafted exclusion clause.[262] For instance, it has been said that the mortgagee is under no duty to exercise any of his rights or powers under a mortgage, nor is he obliged to sell, and far less to incur any expenditure in improving the mortgaged property.[263] The mortgagee can choose when to sell,[264] and is not obliged to wait for an improvement in the market.[265] Neither will the mortgagee be liable for postponing a sale, even if in consequence the security, which was sufficient to cover the debt at the time of default, subsequently declines in value.[266] However, the mortgagee "cannot sell hastily at a knock-down price sufficient to pay off his debt"[267] and he will be liable to the mortgagor if a property is sold without being left on the market for a reasonable time.[268] In *Skipton Building Society v Stott*[269] the Court of Appeal held that a mortgagee had breached its duty to obtain the current market value of the mortgaged property when it was sold to an adjoining landowner without being offered on the open market.[270] Since the market value was greater than the mortgagor's indebtedness the mortgagor was not liable for any shortfall consequent upon the sale. In *Bishop v Blake*,[271] Sir Francis Ferris held that a mortgagee was liable to account for failing to take care to achieve proper market price for an inn.[272] There was no effective attempt to market the inn and sale was made to existing tenants at an undervalue. An advertisement was "inserted at the last minute, it failed to include elementary contact details and the contract . . . was entered into before even the most alert reader of that publication had a realistic opportunity to respond".[273] If the sale is by way of auction, the sale must be properly advertised, and potential purchasers must have a reasonable opportunity to view the property and to bid for it, at least in a case where the sale was to a company associated with the mortgagees.[274] The mortgagee must also ensure that in marketing the property, the attention of purchasers is drawn to any material information which might help to improve the price. For instance, in *Cuckmere Brick Co Ltd v Mutual Finance Ltd*,[275] the mortgagee was held in breach of duty for failing to mention a planning permission which would almost certainly have increased the selling price.

17–076

---

[259] [1998] 2 All E.R. 929 at 937.
[260] See also *Yorkshire Bank Plc v Hall* [1999] 1 All E.R. 879 at 893, per Robert Walker L.J.
[261] *Kennedy v de Trafford* [1897] A.C. 180.
[262] See *Bishop v Benham* [1988] 1 W.L.R. 742.
[263] *Lloyds Bank Plc v Bryant* (1996) Lawtel document No.C0003846 (Lightman J.).
[264] *Meftah v Lloyds TSB Bank Plc* [2001] 2 All E.R. (Comm) 74.
[265] *Cuckmere Brick Co Ltd v Mutual Finance Ltd* [1971] Ch. 949.
[266] *China and South Sea Bank Ltd v Tan Soon Gin* [1990] 1 A.C. 536.
[267] *Palk v Mortgage Services Funding Plc* [1993] 2 W.L.R. 415 at 420.
[268] *Predeth v Castle Phillips Finance Co Ltd* [1986] 2 E.G.L.R. 144.
[269] [2000] All E.R. 779.
[270] Compare *Freeguard v Royal Bank of Scotland Plc* Westlaw 2002 WL 498865; [2006] Conv. 207.
[271] [2006] EWHC 831; Westlaw document 2006 WL 1078954.
[272] ibid, para.109.
[273] ibid, para.107; Dixon [2006] Conv. 278.
[274] *Tse Kwong Lam v Wong Chit Sen* [1983] 1 W.L.R. 1349.
[275] [1971] Ch. 949.

Additional difficulties occur where the mortgaged land consists of business rather than residential premises. In such cases the mortgagee is under no duty to take any steps to preserve the business unless and until he takes possession of it. In *AIB Finance Ltd v Debtors*[276] the mortgaged property consisted of a shop which the mortgagors ran as a post office, newsagent and off-licence. The mortgagees repossessed the property in December 1995 and it was sold in April 1996. The mortgagors claimed that the mortgagees had been negligent in failing to ensure that the business was preserved as a going concern pending realisation of the security. The Court of Appeal held that the mortgagees owed no such duty to the mortgagors prior to taking possession, and that at the date at which possession was obtained the mortgagors had already withdrawn the goodwill of the business by revoking their post office appointment, selling the newspaper round to another local newsagent and ceasing to trade at the shop. However the case does suggest that if a business is a going concern at the date possession is obtained the mortgagee will be subject to a duty to preserve it until sale. The prospect of such a duty, which might prove to be onerous, may well operate as an incentive to the mortgagee to delay seeking possession until the business has collapsed completely, although this carries the counter risk that it might not be able to recover as much of its loan.

(f) Sale to the Mortgagee

17–077   Where the mortgagee is selling the mortgaged property under the statutory power of sale, the mortgagee itself may not purchase the property, although the property may be sold to an associated company.[277] The burden of proof is on the mortgagee to "show that the sale was in good faith and that he took reasonable precautions to obtain the best price reasonably available at the time."[278]

However, where the sale is made by order of the court, it is possible for the mortgagee to be a purchaser.[279]

(g) Application of Proceeds of Sale

17–078   The mortgagee, following a sale, holds the proceeds of sale upon trust to apply them in the way set out in s.105 of the Law of Property Act 1925. This requires that mortgages having priority to that of the mortgagee should first be paid off and that any balance should be applied successively in paying for the costs of sale, repaying the mortgagee, repaying any subsequent mortgagee, and finally, paying the remaining balance, if any, to the mortgagor. The mortgagee is not entitled to keep the whole proceeds of the sale if they exceed the amount of the loan, even where the mortgage was obtained by fraud.[280] As has already been described, if the proceeds of sale are insufficient to repay the mortgage, the mortgagor remains contractually liable for the balance.

---

[276] [1998] 2 All E.R. 929 at 937.
[277] *Tse Kwong Lam v Wong Chit Sen* [1983] 1 W.L.R. 1349.
[278] *Mortgage Express v Mardner* [2004] EWCA Civ 1859; Westlaw document 2004 WL 2866116, para 9 per Pill LJ.
[279] *Palk v Mortgage Services Funding Plc* [1993] 2 W.L.R. 415.
[280] *Halifax Building Society v Thomas* [1995] 4 All E.R. 673.

(h) *Setting Aside a Sale*

Whilst the sale of the land by the mortgagee is not liable to be set side simply because it took **17–079** place at an undervalue, a sale may be set aside if the power of sale was improperly exercised. The sale will only be able to set aside against the purchaser of the land if he had actual knowledge of the impropriety.[281] The principles on which a sale may be set aside were considered by the Court of Appeal in *Corbett v Halifax Plc*.[282] The rather unusual facts involved the purchase of the mortgage property by an employee of the mortgagee. The claimant's house was mortgaged to the Halifax Building Society, which had a rule prohibiting members of staff from purchasing repossessed properties. The property was subsequently repossessed and purchased by the uncle of the employee who had countersigned the original mortgage offer. The sale took place at an undervalue, and the uncle immediately transferred the property to the employee. The Court of Appeal held that sale should not be set aside. Whilst the employee had deceived his employers there had not been any impropriety or bad faith between the mortgagor and the mortgagee regarding the sale. The employee had not been directly involved in the sale, was unaware of the undervalue, and the price was similar to other offers that the mortgagor had received for the property. Pumfrey J. explained that, in these circumstances, the mortgagors had no right to impugn the sale because they would not have had the right to set the sale aside against any other purchaser at an undervalue who did not know of the undervalue and was not involved in the exercise of the power of sale:

> "What makes this case unusual is that the lack of good faith has nothing to do with the [mortgagors], but has only to do with the Halifax, whose internal rules were dishonestly broken by [the employee]. The lack of good faith is thus immaterial to the [mortgagors'] interests, and did not affect those interests".[283]

4. Appointment of Receiver

A mortgagee may appoint a receiver of mortgaged property either by order of the court or, in **17–080** the case of mortgages made by deed, by virtue of s.109 of the Law of Property Act 1925. The statutory power arises and becomes exercisable upon the same events as apply to the power of sale arising and becoming exercisable.[284]

A receiver intercepts the rents and profits of land before they reach the mortgagor. The receiver then uses this income to pay off any outgoings on the land, then to meet liabilities under any prior mortgages, then to meet his own costs, and, finally, to pay off any interest or capital due under the mortgage of the mortgagee who appointed him.[285]

The nature of the functions of receivers mean that they are most likely to be appointed for commercial rather than residential property. They confer broadly the same benefits on a

---

[281] Law of Property Act 1925 s.104(2).
[282] [2002] EWCA Civ 1849; [2003] 4 All E.R. 180.
[283] at [38].
[284] Law of Property Act 1925 s.101.
[285] Law of Property Act 1925 s.109.

mortgagee as if the mortgagee had taken possession of the land with the advantage that a receiver is treated as the agent of the mortgagor rather than of the mortgagee. This means that the liability of the mortgagee to account is less strict than if he took possession.[286]

Where the mortgaged land comprises business premises the mortgagee is not under a duty to appoint a receiver to preserve the business prior to obtaining possession of the land.[287] However, where the mortgagee does decide to appoint a receiver, Scott V.C. held in *Medforth v Blake*[288] that the receiver owes a duty to the mortgagor to manage the property with due diligence, subject to a primary duty to try and bring about a situation in which interest on the secured debt can be paid and the debt itself repaid. The liability of the receiver is not confined to a duty of good faith. The duty does not mean that the receiver is obliged to carry on a business on the mortgaged premises previously carried on by the mortgagor, but that if he does carry on a business on the mortgaged premises he must take reasonable steps to try to do so profitably.[289] Thus it was held that a receiver who had managed a mortgaged pig-farming business might have breached his duty to act with due diligence by failing to obtain freely available discounts on the cost of feed, which was the main expense of the business, thus reducing its profitability.

5. Foreclosure

17–081   Foreclosure is the process by which, formerly, the mortgagor's equity of redemption was extinguished by court order. By foreclosing or terminating the mortgagor's right to redeem, the estate vested in the mortgagee became absolute. Since with modern mortgages the mortgagee has either only a notional or actual term of years by demise or sub-demise rather than a full estate, the court order has the effect of transferring title to the mortgagee.[290] The procedure is fraught with technicality, and no longer serves any real purpose. The Law Commission has recommended that the remedy should be abolished. Foreclosure, alone of all the remedies available to the mortgagee, has the effect of extinguishing the mortgagor's contractual obligation to repay the loan which the mortgage secured. It is, perhaps for this reason that the mortgagee in *Palk v Mortgage Services Funding Plc*[291] chose not to seek foreclosure. Foreclosure will be unattractive to the mortgagee in most cases where there is negative equity, since the mortgagee cannot pursue the mortgagor for the deficiency. Where the mortgaged property is worth more than the loan secured, foreclosure will be unattractive to the mortgagor, since the mortgagee would receive the surplus on a sale. The mortgagor is able to apply for an order for sale in a foreclosure action,[292] and a court would be unlikely to refuse it where the property is worth more than the loan.

---

[286] s.109; *White v Metcalf* [1903] 2 Ch. 567; *American Express International Banking Corp v Hurley* [1985] 3 All E.R. 564.
[287] *AIB Finance Ltd v Debtors* [1998] 2 All E.R. 929 at 938, per Nourse L.J.
[288] [1999] 3 All E.R. 97.
[289] [1999] 3 All E.R. 97 at 111.
[290] Law of Property Act 1925 ss.88 and 89; Land Registration Act 1925 s.34.
[291] [1993] 2 W.L.R. 415.
[292] Law of Property Act 1925 s.91.

If a mortgage is discharged using the money of a third party the original mortgagee will no longer enjoy any rights against the land concerned or the mortgagor. However the third party may be entitled to a remedy by way of subrogation. This means that the third party will enjoy a charge over the land identical to that enjoyed by the original mortgagee. Subrogation thus provides a mechanism by which an apparently discharged mortgage is preserved, albeit in favour of a different mortgagee. A remedy by way of subrogation was granted in *Boscawen v Bajwa*.[293] A house owned by Mr Bajwa was subject to a mortgage in favour of the Halifax Building Society. The mortgage was subsequently discharged using money which had been advanced to the solicitor of a prospective purchaser of the property by the Abbey National Building Society. This money had been wrongly applied since it was held by the solicitor on trust pending completion of the sale. Due to the absence of appropriate formalities there was no valid contract for the purchase of the house and the sale was never completed. The Court of Appeal held that in these circumstances the Abbey National was entitled to be subrogated to the Halifax's charge over the house. Millett L.J. stressed that the Abbey National had not intended to discharge the Halifax's charge and that it would have been "unconscionable for Mr Bajwa to assert that it had been discharged for his benefit".[294]

PRIORITY OF MORTGAGES

Complex issues of priority arise in connection with mortgages of land. It is possible for the owner of land to create more than one mortgage over it, and it is not uncommon for impecunious owners to do just that. If the value of the land is insufficient to pay off all the sums borrowed, the question may therefore arise to the priority of these mortgages between themselves. In other words, if the land is sold, which mortgage must be paid off first? In addition, there may be issues as to the extent to which a mortgagee is bound by interests created before the mortgage was made, and in some cases there may be an issue as to whether a mortgagee is bound by interests created subsequent to the mortgage. These issues are largely determined in accordance with priority rules of general application, but there are some special rules which apply exclusively to mortgages.

17–082

1. Priority of Mortgages in Registered Land

(a) *Priority of Registered Charges*

(i) Priority Between Registered Charges

Mortgages of registered land do not take effect as legal charges unless and until they have been registered.[295] Section 48(1) of the Land Registration Act 2002 provides that registered

17–083

[293] [1995] 4 All E.R. 769.
[294] [1995] 4 All E.R. 769 at 784.
[295] Land Registration Act 2002 s.27.

charges of the same registered estate are to take priority in accordance with the date order in which they were registered, not the order in which they were granted.[296] A registered legal charge will therefore automatically take priority over any subsequently created registered or unregistered charge.[297]

(ii) Priority Over Pre-existing Interests in the Land

17–084   A registered legal charge may also gain priority over any pre-existing interests in the land. Under the provisions of the Law of Property Act 1925 the grant of a legal mortgage has potentially overreaching effect.[298] Provided that the statutory criteria for the operation of overreaching are satisfied, namely that any capital moneys are paid over to at least two trustees, the grant of a legal mortgage will overreach any beneficial interests arising under a trust of the land. Overreaching has been held to operate irrespective of the fact that the beneficiary was in actual occupation of the land,[299] and irrespective of the fact that the grant of the charge did not give rise to any capital moneys.[300] The operation of overreaching has been considered in detail in Chapter 3. By s.29 of the Land Registration Act 2002 a legal charge will gain priority over any pre-existing interest in the land which did not enjoy protected priority at the time that the charge was registered,[301] either because it was protected by way of a notice in the register,[302] or because it was an overriding interest within Sch.3.[303] A beneficiary of a trust of land, whose interest has not been overreached and who was in actual occupation at the date of the registration of the charge, will therefore enjoy priority over the legal charge because his or her interest is an overriding interest, as was the case in *Williams & Glyn's Bank v Boland*.[304]

(b) *Priority of Equitable Mortgages*

17–085   As has been seen, a purported legal charge of registered land which has not been registered takes effect only as an equitable interest.[305] An equitable mortgage can be protected by way of a notice on the register. If protected it will enjoy protected priority against any subsequent interest created in the land.[306]

---

[296] Land Registration Act 2002 s.29.

[297] The priority of an earlier charge may be postponed through proprietary estoppel. In *Scottish and Newcastle Plc v Lancashire Mortgage Corp Ltd* [2007] EWCA Civ 684 Westlaw document 2007 WL 1729947, the owner of a club executed two charges on the property. The first chargee acquiesced in the second chargee's expectation that he would have priority when he made an advance of money, and benefited from the money advanced by the second chargee. The first chargee, even though he had registered his charge first, was estopped from denying that the second charge had priority. For proprietary estoppel see Ch.19.

[298] Law of Property Act 1925 s.2(1) and s.205(1)(ii).

[299] *City of London Building Society v Flegg* [1988] A.C. 54.

[300] *State Bank of India v Sood.* [1997] Ch. 279.

[301] Land Registration Act 2002 s.29(1).

[302] Land Registration Act 2002 s.29(20(a)(i).

[303] Land Registration Act 2002 s.29(20(a)(ii).

[304] [1981] A.C. 487.

[305] Land Registration Act 2002 s.27

[306] Land Registration Act 2002 s.29(2)(i).

2. Priority of Mortgages in Unregistered Land

(a) *Priority of Mortgages of Unregistered Land on First Registration*

Where the title to land is unregistered, and an event occurs which requires that that title be **17–086** registered,[307] then the priority of any existing mortgages will be determined by the rules regarding the effect of first registration.[308] On first registration the registrar is required to "enter a notice in the register of the burden of an interest which appears from his examination of the title to affect the registered estate".[309] It follows that the mortgage will gain priority, and thereby affect the estate of the registered proprietor, if it was properly protected according to the relevant rules for unregistered land at the date of registration. The rules determining the priority of mortgages affecting registered land vary depending upon whether the mortgage was protected by the deposit of title deeds or not.

(i) Mortgage Protected by the Deposit of Title Deeds

A first legal mortgagee of unregistered land has the right to possession of the title deeds relating to the land.[310] This confers important protection on the mortgagee, since anyone claiming a major interest in the land subsequent to the mortgage, for instance by way of purchase or subsequent mortgage, would normally wish to inspect the deeds. A first legal mortgagee protected by deposit of title deeds by this means has priority over all interests in the land created subsequent to the mortgage, except where this is authorised by the mortgage deed (as in a mortgage which contemplates the grant of leases by the mortgagor) or where the mortgagee has specifically authorised or adopted the transaction concerned. This is on the principle that legal rights bind the world. The only major exception to the principle that the legal rights of the first mortgagee are unassailable is where the mortgagee has deprived himself of his protection against a subsequent purchaser through fraud, misrepresentation or gross negligence, for instance by failing to take possession of all the title deeds[311] or by allowing or inducing the claimant to believe that there is no existing mortgage.[312] As was noted above, today the grant of a legal charge of unregistered land gives rise to the requirement of registration of title.

Where a first mortgage of unregistered land takes effect in equity only, the mortgagee will still have effective protection against most subsequent claims by virtue of retaining the title deeds to the property since subsequent purchasers will be put on notice of the earlier charge,[313] although this priority can be lost through the negligence or fraud of the first

17–087

---

[307] Land Registration Act 2002 s.4(1)
[308] Land Registration Act 2002 s.11 and s.12.
[309] Land Registration Rules 2003 r.35(1).
[310] Law of Property Act, 1925 s.85.
[311] *Walker v Linom* [1907] 2 Ch. 104.
[312] *Perry Herrick v Attwood* (1857) 2 De G. & J. 21.
[313] Since it was held in *United Bank of Kuwait Plc v Sahib* [1996] 3 All E.R. 215 that an equitable mortgage operates on the basis of a specifically enforceable contract to create a legal mortgage, it could be argued that equitable mortgages of a legal estate require registration as a Class C(iv) estate contract under Land Charges Act 1974. This, however, would deprive of substance the provision for registering equitable mortgages as Class C(iii) general equitable charges and cannot have been intended by the draftsman. See (1962) 26 Conv. 445 (Rowley).

mortgagee.[314] In addition, the case law suggests that it will be rare for a subsequent legal mortgagee to be bound by an earlier equitable mortgage unless the subsequent mortgagee's failure to ascertain the existence of the earlier charge can be said to arise from gross negligence.[315]

(ii) Priority of Mortgages not Protected by the Deposit of Title Deeds

17–088   Where a mortgage, whether legal or equitable, is not protected by a deposit of title deeds, it will be registrable as a Class C(i) or (iii) land charge respectively under the Land Charges Act 1972.[316] A failure to register will render the mortgage void as against a subsequent purchaser of a legal or equitable interest in the land for valuable consideration.[317] It follows that a mortgage which has not been protected in this way will lose priority on first registration of the estate to which it relates.

(b) *Priority Between Mortgages Affecting Unregistered Land*

17–089   It is not the case that every grant of a mortgage of unregistered land will trigger the requirement to register title. Only the creation of "a protected first legal mortgage of a qualifying estate" gives rise to the requirement to register,[318] and it therefore follows that the grant of a subsequent legal mortgage, or an equitable mortgage, will not require first registration. Priority between such interests will therefore have to be determined by the ordinary rules applying to unregistered land. Obviously all subsequent mortgages will yield priority to a first legal mortgage protected by the deposit of title deeds, on the principle that legal rights bind the world. However, a subsequent mortgage will gain priority over an earlier mortgage which was not a first legal mortgage protected by the deposit of title deeds, if that earlier mortgage was not protected as land charge. This follows from s.4(5) of the Land Charges Act 1972, which provides that the unprotected interest will be "void as against a purchaser of . . . any interest in such land, unless the land charge is registered in the appropriate register".[319]

---

[314] *Taylor v Russell* [1892] A.C. 244.

[315] *Oliver v Hinton* [1899] 2 Ch. 264; *Agra Bank Ltd v Barry* (1874) L.R. 7 H.L. 135 at 150 et seq.

[316] s.2(4).

[317] See Land Charges Act 1972 s.4(5) and the definition of a purchaser in s.17. There is an apparent conflict with Law of Property Act 1925 s.97, which suggests that priorities are determined by the date of registration. This would have the consequence of converting a mortgage which is void in relation to a subsequent right in accordance with the Land Charges Act into a mortgage which is inferior to it.

[318] Land Registration Act 2002 s.4(1)(g).

[319] It should be noted that there is a legislative conflict in such cases, since s.97 of the Law of Property Act 1925 appears to have the effect that the priority of mortgages affecting a legal estate in land should be determined by the date of their registration and not creation. This admits of the possibility that a pre-existing mortgage might be registered as a land charge after a subsequent mortgage has been granted, but before it has been registered. However as a matter of principle the creation of the later mortgage should have the effect of rendering the unregistered mortgage void, such that it will not revive when it is registered.

3. Postponement of Pre-existing Interests in the Land to the Rights of the Mortgagee

The rules that determine issues of priority between mortgages and other interests in registered and unregistered land have been examined. However the courts have held that, even where an application of these rules would mean that a pre-exiting interest in land would enjoy priority over a mortgage, the mortgage will take priority if the owner of the interest has expressly or impliedly postponed the interest to the mortgage.

17–090

(a) *Express Postponement*

Since the decision in *Williams & Glyn's Bank v Boland*[320] held that the rights of people sharing occupation are binding as overriding interests on a mortgagee, it has been common practice for mortgagees to require a waiver of any prior rights from any person who is, or is proposing to, share occupation of the property with the mortgagor. The consequence of such a consent is to postpone the interests of those of the mortgagee. A binding consent cannot be obtained from minors, but it has been held that their rights do not automatically bind the mortgagee.[321] In *Woolwich Building Society v Dickman*,[322] the Court of Appeal held that a form signed by Rent Act protected tenants consenting to the grant of a mortgage and postponing their rights to the mortgagee would have been effective to give the mortgagee priority except for the policy objective of the Rent Acts to confer protection on tenants, which overrode any consent given to the mortgagee.

17–091

(b) *Implied Postponement*

Even where the mortgagee has not received express consent from a person with a prior interest to the creation of a mortgage, a consent by that person to the mortgage can in some circumstances be implied. This was first established in *Bristol and West Building Society v Henning*.[323] An unmarried couple bought a house together intending that it should be half owned by each of them, but raising the purchase and the mortgage in the name of Mr Henning alone. Most of the purchase price was supplied by the mortgage, without which the purchase would not have been possible. Mrs Henning was aware of this. This was enough to give the building society priority. As Browne-Wilkinson L.J. said:

17–092

> "Mrs Henning knew of and supported the proposal to raise the purchase price of the villa on mortgage. In those circumstances, it is in my judgment impossible to impute to them any common intention other than that she authorised Mr Henning to raise the money by

[320] [1980] 2 All E.R. 408.
[321] *Hypo-Mortgage Services Ltd v Robinson* [1997] 2 F.L.R. 71.
[322] [1996] 3 All E.R. 254.
[323] [1985] 2 All E.R. 606.

mortgage to the society. In more technical terms, it was the common intention that Mr Henning as trustee should have power to grant the mortgage to the society. Such power to mortgage must have extended to granting to the society a mortgage having priority to any beneficial interests in the property."[324]

This decision has been followed and applied in *Paddington Building Society v Mendelsohn*[325] and *Abbey National Building Society v Cann*.[326] In the latter case, Mrs Cann lived in a house which had been bought in the name of her son. The purchase price had been met, in part, by a loan from the Abbey National Building Society secured by mortgage, and in part by the proceeds from the sale of the house in which Mrs Cann was previously living, and in which it was accepted that she had a beneficial interest. Mrs Cann had known that her son would be obtaining a mortgage to purchase the new property, but she expected that the mortgage would cover only a small proportion of the cost of acquisition. In fact her son pocketed much of he proceeds of their previous house, and unbeknown to her took out a much larger loan than she had been expecting. Although it was not necessary to reach a decision on the point, the House of Lords considered that, even though Mrs Cann believed that the mortgage would cover only a small proportion of the cost of acquisition, her rights were postponed to the full extent of the very much larger loan which her son negotiated. In *Equity and Law Home Loans Ltd v Prestridge*,[327] the Court of Appeal held that a person claiming an equitable interest in the property on a contribution basis whose claim was postponed to a first mortgagee was also postponed to a subsequent mortgagee to whom the property had been remortgaged, although her interest was postponed to the extent only of the amount of the original loan.

It is not yet clear from the decisions on the implied postponement of the rights of an equitable claimant whether they are based upon implied or imputed consent, agency, or estoppel.[328] In effect, where an interest in a property vested in a single legal proprietor is held on constructive trust as a result of common intention or proprietary estoppel, the rights of the beneficiary relate merely to the mortgagor's equity of redemption.[329] In any event, as has already been seen, where a mortgage is created contemporaneously with a purchase, a person claiming an equitable interest cannot claim that the mortgagee is bound by their interest on the basis of actual occupation, or presumably, under the equitable doctrine of notice in the case of unregistered land. Furthermore, even if a mortgage is not binding on one equitable owner of the property, for instance because one co-owner has procured a mortgage by fraud,[330] the mortgage will still be binding on the person who granted it to the extent of his or her putative beneficial interest. This will be sufficient to enable the mortgagee to proceed by way of an application for sale of the property under the Trusts of Land and Appointment of Trustees Act 1996 ss.13 and 14 and to use the mortgagor's portion of the proceeds of sale towards the discharge of the loan.[331]

---

[324] [1985] 2 All E.R. 606 at 609.
[325] (1985) 50 P. & C.R. 244.
[326] [1991] A.C. 56.
[327] [1992] 1 W.L.R. 137.
[328] *Skipton Building Society v Clayton* (1993) 66 P. & C.R. 223.
[329] See *Abbey National Building Society v Cann* [1991] A.C. 56 at 102.
[330] As in *First National Securites Ltd v Hegarty* [1985] Q.B. 850.
[331] See The trustee of the property of *Martin Kit Sheung Ng v Ng* (1996) Lawtel Document No.C0005225 (Lightman J.).

4. Special Priority Rules

Notwithstanding the general rules governing the priority of mortgages, it is possible for two **17–093** mortgagees to agree between themselves that their charges will rank in some other way, and such an agreement will be effective as between the parties to the arrangement.[332] However it should be noted that special priority rules operate in two situations.

(a) *Tacking*

"Tacking" occurs where a mortgagee adds a further advance to an existing mortgage. Where **17–094** land is subject to multiple mortgages tacking may enable the mortgagee of an earlier mortgage to gain priority over other later charges. The principle under which a mortgagee may gain priority by tacking vary depending upon whether the land is registered or unregistered.

(i) Tacking in Registered Land

The rules regarding the effect of tacking are now found in s.49 of the Land Registration Act **17–095** 2002. These allow for tacking to gain priority over subsequent charges in four circumstances. Section 49(1) allows the proprietor of a registered charge to gain priority where he makes further advances and he had not received notice from the subsequent chargee of the creation of the subsequent charge. Section 49(3) allows the proprietor to gain priority over the subsequent charge if the further advance was made in pursuance of an obligation to make further advances and, at the time of the creation of the subsequent charge, the obligation was entered in the register. Section 49(4) allows the proprietor to gain priority if the parties to the charge had agreed a maximum amount for which the charge is security and, at the time of the creation of the subsequent charge, the agreement was entered in the register. Finally s.49(6) allow the proprietor to gain priority if tacking occurs with the permission of the subsequent chargee.

(ii) Tacking in Unregistered Land

Tacking in unregistered land is also governed by statute. Section 94 of the Law of Property **17–096** Act 1925 provides that a mortgagee has a right to make further advances to rank in priority to subsequent mortgages:

> "(a) if an arrangement has been made to that effect with the subsequent mortgagees; or
> (b) if he had no notice of such subsequent mortgages at the time when the further advance was made by him[333]; or

---

[332] *Cheah Theam Swee v Equiticorp Finance Group Ltd* [1992] 1 A.C. 472.
[333] A mortgagee is not deemed to have notice of a mortgage for the purpose of this section merely because it was registered as a land charge: Law of Property Act 1925 s.94(2).

(c) whether or not he had such notice as aforesaid, where the mortgage imposes an obligation on him to make such further advances."

(b) *Mortgages of Interests Under Trusts*

17–097 Special rules also govern the priority of mortgages of beneficial interests under a trust of land (i.e. mortgages granted by the beneficiaries rather than by the trustees). Instead of priority being based on the ordinary land law rules, priority depends upon the order in which the trustees have been informed of the mortgage concerned. This is known as the rule in *Dearle v Hall*[334] which was extended to cover trusts of land by s.137 of the the Law of Property Act 1925. The rule that mortgages rank according to the date that notice is received by the trustees is modified where a subsequent mortgagee has actual or constructive notice of an earlier mortgage. Even if he notifies the trustees first, he will not gain priority.[335]

---

[334] (1828) 3 Russ. 1.
[335] *Re Holmes* (1885) 29 Ch.D. 786.

Chapter 18

ESTATE CONTRACTS

INTRODUCTION TO ESTATE CONTRACTS

In English law the boundary between contractual obligations and property rights is not strictly   **18–001**
drawn. It has been seen a number of times through this book that the grant of a specifically
enforceable contract for an interest in land gives rise to an equitable interest in the land by
operation of the equitable maxim that "equity treats as done that which ought to be done". For
example, a contract for the grant of a legal lease of land gives rise to an equitable lease,[1] and
a contract for the grant of a legal easement gives rise to an equitable easement.[2] A valid contract for the grant of a legal estate in land is itself regarded as a property right, termed an
estate contract. The grantee of an estate contract therefore enjoys a right in the land which is
capable of gaining priority over the subsequent rights of third parties. An estate contract is
only capable of existing as an equitable interest in the land,[3] and if it is to enjoy priority it
must be protected in the appropriate manner. For the purposes of the protection of land
charges in unregistered land, an estate contract is defined as:

> "... a contract by an estate owner or by a person entitled at the date of the contract to
> have a legal estate conveyed to him to convey or create a legal estate, including a con-
> tract conferring either expressly or by statutory implication a valid option to purchase, a
> right of pre-emption or any other like right."[4]

FORMALITIES FOR THE CREATION OF ESTATE CONTRACTS

An estate contract will only be created if the requisite formalities are observed.   **18–002**

---

[1] See *Walsh v Lonsdale* (1882) Ch.D. 9.
[2] See para.15–055.
[3] Law of Property Act 1925 s.1(3).
[4] Land Charges Act 1972 s.2(4)(iv).

1. Estate Contracts must be Made in Writing

18–003 Since an estate contract is a "contract for the sale or other disposition of an interest in land,"[5] if it was granted after September 26, 1989 it must comply with the requirements of s.2 of the Law of Property (Miscellaneous Provisions) Act 1989. It must therefore be "made in writing" and incorporate "all the terms which the parties have expressly agreed", either in one document, or where the contract is entered by means of exchange, in each document.[6] The terms of the contract may be incorporated into the relevant document either by being set out in it, or by reference to some other document.[7] The document incorporating the terms must be "signed by or on behalf of each party to the contract".[8]

2. Electronic Conveyancing and Estate Contracts in Registered Land

18–004 The Land Registration Act 2002 makes provision for the introduction of electronic conveyancing. Although these provisions have yet to be brought into force, they will have a very significant effect on the creation of estate contracts. Section 93(2) provides that:

> "A disposition to which this section applies, or a contract to make such a disposition, only has effect if it is made by means of a document in electronic form and if, when the document purports to take effect—
>
> (a) it is electronically communicated to the registrar
> (b) the relevant registration requirements are met."

The section will mean that contracts for the purchase of the freehold of registered land, a lease which is required to be registered, or the express grant of an easement, will have to be effected electronically and completed by registration.

CONTRACTS TO PURCHASE AN INTEREST IN LAND

1. A Contract for the Purchase of Land Gives Rise to a Trust of the Land

18–005 A contract for the purchase of land, whether freehold or leasehold land, is an estate contract. Since the contract is specifically enforceable it will create an immediate trust of the land in favour of the purchaser, so that from the moment that the contract is entered the vendor will

---

[5] Law of Property (Miscellaneous Provisions) Act 1989 s.2(1).
[6] Law of Property (Miscellaneous Provisions) Act 1989 s.2(2).
[7] Law of Property (Miscellaneous Provisions) Act 1989 s.2(2).
[8] Law of Property (Miscellaneous Provisions) Act 1989 s.2(3).

hold the land on constructive for the benefit of the purchaser. As Lord Jessel M.R. stated in *Lysaght v Edwards*:

> "the moment you have a valid contract for sale the vendor becomes in equity a trustee for the purchaser of the estate sold."[9]

2. The Priority of the Trust Depends Upon the Protection of the Priority of the Estate Contract

Where an estate contract for the sale of land has given rise to a constructive trust, the question has arisen as to whether issues of priority will be resolved in relation to the constructive trust, in which case the relevant rules for the priority of trust interests will be applied, or the estate contract from which it arises, in which case the relevant rules for the priority of estate contracts will be applied. This issue arose in *Lloyds Bank v Carrick*.[10] Mrs Carrick entered into a contract to purchase a maisonette, title to which was unregistered. She then moved into possession of the property, and paid the full purchase price, but the title was never conveyed to her by the vendor, who was her brother-in-law. The vendor subsequently mortgaged the property. There was no question that Mrs Carrick enjoyed a valid contract to purchase the house, and that since this contract was specifically enforceable, that it gave rise to a constructive trust in her favour. The question was whether this constructive trust was binding on the mortgagee, which was alleged to have had constructive notice thereof, even though the contract from which it arose had not been properly protected as a Class C(iv) land charge. The Court of Appeal held that the failure to protect the priority of the estate contract prevented the constructive trust from gaining priority over the interest of the mortgagee. Morritt L.J. explained:

18–006

> "One consequence of the contract becoming enforceable was that it was specifically enforceable at the suit of Mrs Carrick. Accordingly Mr Carrick became a trustee of the maisonette for Mrs Carrick... Counsel for Mrs Carrick accepted that such interest came or started from the contract but, he contended, it matured into an interest separate and distinct from the contract as soon as the purchase price was paid in full. For my part I am unable to accept this analysis... The source and origin of the trust was the contract... Section 4(6) of the 1972 Act avoids that contract as against the bank. The result, in my judgment, must be that Mrs Carrick is unable to establish the bare trust as against the bank for it has no existence except as the equitable consequence of the contract."[11]

It follows that the priority of a constructive trust arising from a specifically enforceable contract for the sale of land will fall to be determined by the appropriate rules governing the priority of the estate contract from which it proceeds, rather than from the rules governing the priority of trust interests in land. The constructive trust will only enjoy priority if the estate contract itself enjoys priority. The relevant rules for the priority of estate contracts will be explained below.

---

[9] [1876] 2 Ch. D. 499.
[10] [1996] 4 All E.R. 630.
[11] [1996] 4 All E.R. 630 at 637–638.

OPTIONS TO PURCHASE LAND

1. What is an Option?

18–007 An option to purchase land is a contract which confers upon the grantee the right to demand that the grantor convey an agreed estate in his land to him. The effect of an option was explained by Street J. in the Australia case of *Mackay v Wilson*, which was cited with approval by the Court of Appeal in *Pritchard v Briggs*:[12]

> "Speaking generally, the giving of an option to purchase land prima facie implies that the giver of the option is to be taken as making a continuing offer to sell the land, which may at any moment be converted into a contract by the optionee notifying his acceptance of that offer. The agreement to give the option imposes a positive obligation on the prospective vendor to keep the offer open during the agreed period so that it remains available for acceptance by the optionee at any moment within that period. It has more than a mere contractual operation and confers upon the optionee an equitable interest in the land."[13]

The practical nature of an option can best be illustrated by the leading cases. In *Midland Bank Trust Co v Green*[14] the owner of a farm in Lincolnshire granted his son a 10-year option to purchase a farm at a price of £75 per acre in consideration for the payment of £1. This option would entitle the son to compel his father to convey the land to him at any time during a 10-year period at the agreed price. Over the period in question the land increased very greatly in value, so that an exercise of the option would have meant that the son would be entitled to purchase the farm at a price which was very significantly below its true the market value. In *Spiro v Glencrown Properties Ltd*[15] the plaintiff granted the defendant an option to purchase a property in Finchley for £745,000, the option being exercisable by notice in writing by 5pm on the day that it was granted.

2. The Uses of Options

18–008 Options can be used for a variety of reasons. In *Midland Bank Trust Co v Green*[16] the option was intended to allow the son to acquire the ownership of the farm he was working on favourable terms. In a commercial context, an option may be granted to a tenant to allow the tenant to renew the lease, or to purchase the freehold, leaving the decision until it is possible to judge whether the commercial conditions are favourable. Options may also be used where a developer is seeking to create a "land bank" so that the current owner can continue to use the property, but the developer can "call the property in" when the developer is ready to build. A property developer may also use options where the developer needs to assemble a portfolio of

---

[12] [1980] Ch. 338.
[13] (1947) 47 S.R. (N.S.W.) 315 at 325; *Sainsbury's Supermarkets Ltd v Olympia Homes Ltd* [2005] EWHC 1235; [2006] 1 P & CR 17, para.56.
[14] [1981] A.C. 513.
[15] [1991] 1 All E.R. 600.
[16] [1981] A.C. 513.

property for development purposes—for instance by buying three adjoining premises in order to demolish and rebuild a larger building. The developer may be reluctant to go to the cost of acquiring one property until he is sure that he can acquire the others. The use of an option allows the developer, at lower cost than making a purchase, to gain the right to acquire a property which he can exercise if he succeeds in his negotiations with the other property owners.[17]

3. The Conceptual Nature of an Option

The exact nature of an option has been a matter of some debate. In some cases an option has been compared to an irrevocable offer, which does not become a contract for the sale of land until it has been accepted by the notice which exercises the option.[18] In other cases it has been regarded as a form of conditional contract to sell.[19] In *Spiro v Glencrown Properties Ltd* Hoffman J. held that, although both these analogies might be useful, neither was strictly accurate:

18–009

> "An option is not strictly speaking either an offer or a conditional contract. It does not have all the incidents of the standard form of either of these concepts. To that extent it is a relationship sui generic. But there are ways in which it resembles each of them. Each analogy is in the proper context a valid way of characterising the situation created by the option."[20]

The analogy with an irrevocable offer is thus a "useful way of describing the position of the purchaser between the grant and the exercise of the option", but it has much less explanatory power in relation to the position of the vendor because the offer which the vendor has made in the option is so different from that of an offer in the usual sense that the metaphor is of "little assistance".[21] In contrast a conditional contract provides a much better analogy for explaining the vendor's position, since the vendor is only required to sell when the grantee fulfils the requisite condition of exercising the option. Having considered the various analogies Hoffman J. stated the underlying principles of an option to purchase:

> "The granting of the option imposes no obligation upon the purchaser and an obligation upon the vendor which is contingent upon the exercise of the option. When the option is exercised vendor and purchaser come under obligations to perform as if they had concluded an ordinary contract of sale."[22]

Where an option has been granted the grantor is taken to be under an obligation not to do anything which would prevent his ability to execute the agreed conveyance. This has the effect that if the grantee chooses to exercise the option he is regarded as enjoying an equitable interest in the land from the moment that the option was validly granted.[23]

---

[17] For an example of this kind of development see *Ashburn Anstalt v Arnold* [1989] Ch. 1.

[18] *Helby v Matthews* [1895] A.C. 471; *J Sainsbury Plc v O'Connor (Inspector of Taxes)* [1990] S.T.C. 516.

[19] *Kennewell v Dye* [1949] Ch. 517; *Griffith v Pelton* [1957] 3 All E.R. 75; *Laybutt v Amoco Australia Pty Ltd* (1974) 4 A.L.R. 482.

[20] [1991] 1 All E.R. 600 at 605–606.

[21] [1991] 1 All E.R. 600 at 604.

[22] [1991] 1 All E.R. 600 at 604.

[23] See: *London and South Western Railways Co v Gomm* (1882) 20 Ch. D. 256; *First National Securities Ltd v Chiltern DC* [1975] 1 W.L.R. 1075; *London & Blenheim Estates Ltd v Ladbroke Retail Parks Ltd* [1992] 1 W.L.R. 1278.

4. Formalities for the Grant of an Option

18–010   Since an option is a contract for the "sale or disposition" of an interest in land it must, as was explained above, comply with the formality requirements of s.2 of the Law of Property (Miscellaneous Provisions) Act 1989. However there is no need for the option to be exercised in a manner which complies with these requirements. This was the central question in *Spiro v Glencrown Properties Ltd*.[24] Although the option itself had been granted in a form which met the requirement of s.2 the option was exercised in accordance with its terms by the grantee giving written notice to the grantor. The written notice did not comply with s.2 because it was signed only by the purchaser and not by the vendor. Following the exercise of the option the grantee failed to complete the purchase. In an action for breach of contract it was argued that it was the exercise of the option which created a contract for sale, and that no such contract had been created because the exercise had failed to comply with the requirements of s.2. Hoffman J. however took a purposive approach to the interpretation of s.2 and concluded that the exercise of the option did not have to comply with its requirements:

> "... it seems to me plain enough that s.2 was intended to apply to the agreement which created the option and not to the notice by which it was exercised. Section 2, which replaced s.40 of the Law of Property Act 1925, was intended to prevent disputes over whether the parties had entered into a binding agreement or over what terms they had agreed. But only the grant of the option depends upon consent. The exercise of the option is a unilateral act. It would destroy the very purpose of the option if the purchaser had to obtain the vendor's counter signature to the notice by which it was exercised. The only way in which the concept of an option to buy land could survive section 2 would be if the purchaser ensured that the vendor not only signed the agreement by which the option was granted but also at the same time provided him with a counter-signed form to use if he decided to exercise it. There seems to be no conceivable reason why the legislature should have required this additional formality."[25]

RIGHTS OF PRE-EMPTION

1. What is a Right of Pre-emption?

18–011   In contrast to an option, which entitles the grantee to demand that the grantor convey the land to him, a right of pre-emption merely entitles the grantor to a right of first refusal if the grantor decided to sell the land. The grantee of a right of pre-emption cannot in any way demand that the estate subject to the right should be conveyed to him, and the initiative remains exclusively with the grantor. The nature of a right of pre-emption can again be illustrated from two leading cases. In *Pritchard v Briggs*[26] the owners of a hotel sold and conveyed it to a purchaser, but retained

[24] [1991] 1 All E.R. 600.
[25] [1991] 1 All E.R. 600 at 602–603.
[26] [1980] Ch. 338.

some lands for their own use. The conveyance contained a covenant that the vendors would not sell any part of the retained land without first giving the purchaser the option to purchase the retained land for £3,000. In *Bircham & Co (No.2) Ltd v Worrell Holdings Ltd*[27] a lease granted a tenant a right of pre-emption in respect of the tenants reversionary interest, which would give the tenant the first option to purchase the lease. The key feature of a right of pre-emption is thus that the grantor cannot call for a conveyance of the land. In *Manchester Ship Canal Co v Manchester Racecourse Co* Oliver J. analysed the position of the grantor of a right or pre-emption:

> ". . . the disposition of the land remains a decision which is his and his alone. No doubt if he evinces a desire to sell, and thus creates the conditions in which he has undertaken to make an offer, that undertaking can be enforced inter partes, but the decision whether to create such conditions remains his and cannot be demanded or influenced by the [grantee]."[28]

2. When Might Rights of Pre-emption be Used?

A right of pre-emption might be used, as it was in *Pritchard v Briggs*[29] where the owner of property is contemplating sale but wishes to remain in control of whether or not a sale should take place. Unlike an option, in which the owner of land can be compelled to sell if the option is exercised, a right of pre-emption is triggered only if and when the owner chooses to sell. The right of pre-emption then limits the range of purchasers to whom the property can be offered, and might also have an effect upon the price. A tenant acquiring the freehold of a property under right-to-buy legislation or under favourable terms from a benevolent landlord might be required to enter into a pre-emption contract to prevent an immediate resale on the open market at the full market value. **18–012**

3. Formalities for the Grant of a Right of Pre-emption

A contract granting a right of pre-emption is similarly a contract for the "sale or disposition" of an interest in land and must, as was explained above, comply with the formality requirements of s.2 of the Law of Property (Miscellaneous Provisions) Act 1989. **18–013**

4. Does a Right of Pre-emption Create an Immediate Interest in Land?

It has been seen that an option to purchase creates an immediate equitable interest in land concerned. The position in relation to a right of pre-emption is more complex, and it appears that a distinction must now be drawn between registered and unregistered land. **18–014**

[27] (2001) 82 P. & C.R. 427.
[28] [1901] 2 Ch. 37.
[29] [1980] Ch. 338.

(a) *Rights of Pre-emption Created Before October 13, 2003*

18–015 It seems that in unregistered land a right of pre-emption does not give rise to an interest in the land until the moment that the grantor decides to sell the land. Prior to that moment, the grant of a right of pre-emption only confers a personal contractual right on the grantee. This was so held by the Court of Appeal in *Pritchard v Briggs*.[30] As was noted above, in this case the grantor sold a hotel and granted the purchaser a right of pre-emption over land that had been retained. The right of pre-emption was granted in 1944, and was duly protected as a Class C(iv) land charge. However in 1959 the retained land was leased by the grantor, and the lease granted the tenant an option to purchase the land, which was also registered as a Class C(iv) land charge. The freehold of the retained land was eventually sold to the hotel owners, but after the sale the tenant claimed to be entitled to exercise his option to purchase. The question was therefore one of priorities, namely whether the right of pre-emption enjoyed priority over the option, or the option over the right of pre-emption. Both rights had been protected as land charges, but the right of pre-emption had been registered first. The Court of Appeal held that, despite the fact of prior registration, the option took priority over the right of pre-emption, because the right of pre-emption did not exist as an interest in the land until the owners of the land decided to sell. Goff L.J. explained that a right of pre-emption should not be regarded as giving rise to an immediate interest in the land because it did not fetter the owner's freedom to alienate his land:

> ". . . a right of pre-emption gives no present right, even contingent, to call for a conveyance of the legal estate. So far as the parties are concerned, whatever economic or other pressures may come to affect the grantor, he is still absolutely free to sell or not. The grantee cannot require him to do so, or demand that an offer be made to him. Moreover, even if the grantor decides to sell and makes an offer it seems to me that so long as he does not sell to anyone else he can withdraw that offer at any time before acceptance."[31]

Although this decision is controversial,[32] and has caused some problems in practice,[33] it has been followed and approved in subsequent cases.[34] However some recent cases have indicated dissatisfaction with the decision. In *Bircham & Co (No.2) Ltd v Worrell Holdings Ltd*[35] the Court of Appeal held that a right of pre-emption would created an immediate interest in interest from the moment that the grantor offered to sell the land to the grantee if the offer is made on terms that it will remain open for a specified time, since such an offer has the effect of converting the right of pre-emption into an option to purchase. In *Dear v Reeves*[36] the Court of

---

[30] [1980] Ch. 338.
[31] [1980] Ch. 338 at 389.
[32] Megarry and Wade, *The Law of Real Property* (6th edn, 2000) describes the decision as "technically questionable", para.12–062.
[33] See Law Com. No.271, *Land Registration for the Twenty-First Century* (2001), para.5.26.
[34] *Kling v Keston Properties Ltd* (1985) 49 P. & C.R. 212; *London & Blenheim Estates Ltd v Ladbroke Retail Parks Ltd* [1994] 1 W.L.R. 31.
[35] (2001) 82 P. & C.R. 427.
[36] [2001] EWCA Civ. 277; [2002] Ch. 1.

Appeal held that a right of pre-emption constituted "property" for the purposes of s.436 of the Insolvency Act 1986 when the grantee was bankrupt. Mummery L.J. held that such a right had the "distinguishing feature of a property right," namely that it was transferable.[37] He distinguished *Pritchard v Briggs* on the grounds that:

> "It is a decision on the construction of the Land Charges Act 1925, which has a different statutory objective and the provisions referring to an 'interest' are more narrowly drafted than those in the 1986 Act."[38]

Although the Court of Appeal did not hold that *Pritchard v Briggs* was wrongly decided, Mummery L.J. acknowledged the force of the criticisms which had been made against it, and accepted that the reasoning in the judgments "may require reconsideration". However notwithstanding theses criticisms, in the absence of a clear decision to the contract the decision of the Court of Appeal in *Pritchard v Briggs* must stand as good law.

Prior to the Land Registration Act 2002 rights of pre-emption were treated identically in registered and unregistered land. It follows that rights of pre-emption which were created in respect of registered land before October 13, 2003 are not regarded as creating an immediate interest in the land.[39]

(b) *Rights of Pre-emption in Registered Land Created After October 13, 2003*

The position in relation to rights or pre-emption in registered land is now much simpler. Section 115(1) of the Land Registration Act 2002 provides that: **18–016**

> "A right of pre-emption in relation to registered land has effect from the time of creation as an interest capable of binding successors in title (subject to the rules about the effect of dispositions on priority)."

This provision only relates to rights of pre-emption granted after the legislation come into force, i.e. to rights of pre-emption created on or after October 13, 2003.

CONTRACTS CREATING AN AGENCY WITH THE OWNER OF LAND

It appears to be unlikely that a contract creating an agency arrangement with the owner of land is an estate contract which creates an interest in the land. Several cases have addressed the question whether such a contract is capable of being registered as a Class C(iv) land charge in unregistered land. In *Turley v Mackay*[40] Uthwatt J. had held that an agency agreement was a land charge within the scope of Class C(iv), and therefore capable of protection by appropriate **18–017**

---

[37] [2002] Ch. 1 at [40].
[38] [2002] Ch. 1 at [43].
[39] Land Registration Act 2002 s.115(2).
[40] [1944] Ch. 37.

registration. However in *Thomas v Rose*[41] Megarry J. held that such a contract did not give rise to an interest in land. The plaintiff entered into a contract with Rose under which Rose was appointed sole agent to clear and grade his land in preparation for use as a building site. In this agreement Rose reserved the right to accept or refuse an offer for sale of the land. Rose registered the agreement as a land charge. The plaintiff was subsequently granted an order that the agreement was not capable of registration as a land charge. Megarry J. explained why this was the case:

> "But does the contract contain any obligation on the plaintiff's part to 'create or convey' any legal estate in favour of anyone? I cannot see that it does. It gives the agent, Mr Rose, the power . . . to 'accept . . . any offer for the sale of all or any part of the area'. Let the agent do this, and there will spring into being a contract with the purchaser by the landowner, made through his agent; and doubtless that contract would be registrable. But that contract is not this contract: a contract providing for the making of a further contract to create or convey a legal estate is not itself a contract to convey or create a legal estate. I do not see how Class C(iv) can be read as embracing contracts at one remove. In my judgement, on the wording of the statute the only contracts that fall within Class C(iv) are those which themselves bind the estate owner (or other person entitled) to convey or create a legal estate. It is not enough for the contract merely to provide machinery whereby such an obligation may be created by some other transaction: the very contract itself must impose the obligation."[42]

Although the case concerned unregistered land and the interpretation of the relevant provisions of the Land Charges Act 1972 there is no reason why the position is not the same in registered land.

THE PRIORITY OF ESTATE CONTRACTS

18–018   The rules governing the priority of interests in registered and unregistered land were set out in Chapters 4 and 5 above. Only a brief summary of these rules as they apply to estate contracts will be given here.

1.   Priority of Estate Contracts in Registered Land

(a)   *Priority Between Estate Contracts*

18–019   The basic rule in registered land is that interests affecting a registered estate enjoy priority in accordance with the order of their creation, irrespective of whether they were registered or not.[43] It follows that as between themselves estate contracts will rank in priority by order of their creation. As was noted above, rights of pre-emption created after October 13, 2003 are

---

[41] [1968] 1 W.L.R. 1797.
[42] [1968] 1 W.L.R. 1797 at 1804–1805.
[43] Land Registration Act 2002 s.28.

now declared to be proprietary interests in the land, so that the decision in *Pritchard v Briggs*[44] whereby a right of pre-emption may lose priority to a subsequently granted option to purchase, will not apply in registered land.

(b) *Priority Against a Subsequent Registered Disposition*

However an estate contract will lose priority to a subsequent registered disposition of a registered estate for valuable consideration unless it enjoys protected priority.[45] There are two ways that an estate contract may enjoy protected priority. First an estate contract will enjoy protected priority if it is the subject of a notice in the register.[46] The grantee of an estate contract should thus take steps to protect his interest. Second it will enjoy protected priority if it ranks as an overriding interest because it falls within the paragraphs of Sch.3. An estate contract is likely to rank as an overriding interest if the grantee was in actual occupation of the land at the time that the disposition occurred, and that occupation would have been obvious on a reasonably careful inspection of the land, or the person to whom the disposition was made had actual knowledge of its existence.[47] Thus the estate contract of a tenant whose lease contains an option to purchase the freehold reversion, or a right of pre-emption as was the case in *Bircham & Co (No.2) Ltd v Worrell Holdings Ltd*,[48] will probably enjoy protected priority because he is in actual occupation of the land.

18–020

The operation of the relevant rules can be illustrated by reference to the facts of *Midland Bank Trust Co v Green*,[49] which involved unregistered land. As was noted above, a son had been granted a 10-year option to purchase a farm, of which he was the tenant, by his father. His estate contract was not protected by registration. His father subsequently sold the farm at a massive undervalue to his wife. If title to the land been registered it is clear that the option to purchase would have enjoyed priority and that the son would have been able to exercise it against his mother. His estate contract would have been an overriding interest because he was clearly in actual occupation of the land, and this would have been obvious from a reasonably careful inspection. Even if his occupation would not have been so obvious, his mother had actual knowledge of his estate contract, so that it would still have ranked as an overriding interest.

2. Priority of Estate Contracts in Unregistered Land

(a) *Priority Between Estate Contracts*

As was seen above in the context of the discussion of the decision of the Court of Appeal in *Pritchard v Briggs*[50] priority between estate contracts does not necessarily flow from the

18–021

---

[44] [1980] Ch. 338.
[45] Land Registration Act 2002 s.29.
[46] Land Registration Act 2002 s.29(2)(a)(i).
[47] Land Registration Act 2002 Sch.3 para.2.
[48] (2001) 82 P. & C.R. 427.
[49] [1981] A.C. 513.
[50] [1980] Ch. 338.

order of their creation or registration as land charges. A right of pre-emption is not regarded as creating an interest in land until the grantor decides to sell the land, so that an option which was granted subsequently to a right of pre-emption may gain priority over it.

(b) *Priority on First Registration of the Land*

18–022 In unregistered land an unprotected estate contract is only capable of losing priority to the interest of a purchaser of a legal estate for money or money's worth. This follows from s.4(6) of the Land Charges Act 1972, which provides that:

> "An estate contract . . . entered into on or after January 1, 1926 shall be void as against a purchaser for money or moneys worth of a legal estate in the land charged with it, unless the land charge is registered in the appropriate register before the completion of the purchase."

The operation of this section can be seen in *Midland Bank Trust Company v Green*,[51] where a father, who had granted an option to purchase a farm to his son which had not been protected as a land charge, sold and conveyed the land to his wife at a considerable undervalue. The House of Lords held that the son's option was thereby rendered void by the purchase, even though the mother knew of its existence.

Since the only situation in which such a purchase of a legal estate will not lead to the requirement to register title to the land is the grant of a legal lease for seven years or less,[52] in most cases the issue of priority will be resolved by the rules concerning the effect of first registration. The first registered proprietor will acquire the land subject only to interests which are the subject of an entry in the register, and overriding interests within Sch.1 to the Land Registration Act 2002.[53] Protection is only afforded to interests within these categories "affecting the estate at the time of registration". It would therefore appear that the grantee of an estate contract which has not been protected as a Class C(iv) land charge will lose priority on first registration, even if he was in actual occupation of the land. This follows from the fact that the estate contract will be rendered void by operation of s.4(6) of the Land Charges Act 1972 as against a purchaser of a legal estate before that purchaser is registered as the proprietor, so that the grantee no longer has any interest in the land which is capable of forming the subject matter of an overriding interest.

---

[51] [1981] A.C. 513.
[52] Land Registration Act 2002 s.4(1)(c).
[53] Land Registration Act 2002 ss.11(4) and 12(4).

Chapter 19

ESTOPPEL EQUITIES[1]

INTRODUCTION TO PROPRIETARY ESTOPPEL

1. A Means of Creating Proprietary Interests in Land

At a number of points in earlier chapters reference has been made to the doctrine of proprietary estoppel. It has been noted that this doctrine operates as a means by which a person may acquire an interest in land, whether the freehold ownership, a lease, an easement or a licence. The essence of proprietary estoppel is that the court may award an interest in land as a remedy against a landowner who has conducted himself in such a way that it would be unjust and unconscionable for him to assert his strict and unqualified right as owner to deny the claimant any entitlement because it had not been appropriately created. As Scott L.J. observed in *Layton v Martin*:

19–001

> "The proprietary estoppel line of cases are concerned with the question whether an owner of property can, by insisting on his strict legal rights therein, defeat an expectation of an interest in that property, it being an expectation which he has raised by his conduct and which has been relied on by the claimant."[2]

Proprietary estoppel provides, along with the principles of resulting and constructive trusts, a means by which interests in land may be obtained informally. The role and operation of proprietary estoppel was summarised by Stephen Moriarty:

> "The role of proprietary estoppel seems self-evident: it provides for the informal creation of interests in land whenever a person has acted detrimentally in reliance upon an oral

---

[1] See: Pearce and Stevens, *The Law of Trusts and Equitable Obligations* (4th edn, 2006), Ch. 10.
[2] [1986] 2 F.L.R. 227, 238.

assurance that he has such an interest. Oral grants of interests by themselves, therefore are insufficient; but act in reliance upon some such assurance, and proprietary estoppel will validate what the law of property says has no effect."[3]

The power of proprietary estoppel to create interests informally is well illustrated by the case of *Yaxley v Gotts*.[4] The plaintiff was a builder who wanted to acquire the freehold of a property in order to refurbish it and let it as flats. It was purchased by the defendant on the basis of an oral agreement that the plaintiff would be entitled to the ground floor flats in return for working on the flats on the upper floors and for acting as the landlord's managing agent for the whole property. This oral agreement was carried into effect. However such an oral agreement would ordinarily be incapable of giving rise to any interest in the land, since it would be rendered void for lack of formality by s.2 of the Law of Property (Miscellaneous Provisions) Act 1989. Nevertheless the Court of Appeal held that the plaintiff was entitled to ownership of the ground floor for 99 years rent free by way of the doctrine of proprietary estoppel to satisfy the equity which had arisen because he had acted to his detriment in reliance upon the oral agreement.[5]

Although the principle of proprietary estoppel is well established, its exact scope remains uncertain. The Law Commission made the following comment about the doctrine of proprietary estoppel in its discussion paper *Sharing Homes*: "It has wide application, but its boundaries are uncertain and its effects are not entirely clear".[6]

2. Elements of a Claim by Proprietary Estoppel

19–002   Acquisition of an interest in land by way of proprietary estoppel involves two essential stages:

(a) *Establishing an "Equity"*

19–003   The claimant must demonstrate that in the circumstances an estoppel has arisen which requires a remedy. More recent cases have identified three elements as necessary to the establishment of a proprietary estoppel, namely: (1) a representation or assurance; (2) reliance by the claimant on the representation or assurance; (3) change of position or detriment. When these three elements are present the claimant is said to enjoy an estoppel "equity" which requires a remedy. As recent cases have emphasised, the equity generated by estoppel requires satisfaction because it would be unconscionable to allow the representation or assurance to be repudiated[7] by allowing the other party to disregard the claimant's rights.[8]

---

[3] (1984) 100 L.Q.R. 376 at 381.
[4] [2000] 1 All E.R. 711.
[5] See also *Kinane v Mackie-Conteh* [2005] EWCA Civ 45; [2005] 2 P. & C.R. D.G. 3; *Yeoman's Row Management Ltd v Cobbe* [2006] 1 W.L.R. 2964, where an estoppel arose by virtue of detrimental reliance on an "in principle" agreement that fell outside the scope of s.2.
[6] Law Com. No.278, (2002).
[7] *Gillett v Holt* [2000] 2 All E.R. 289 at 308, per Robert Walker L.J.
[8] *Yaxley v Gotts* [2000] 1 All E.R. 711 at 724, per Robert Walker L.J.

(b) *Satisfying the "Equity"*

Once an equity has been established by a claimant it is for the court to award an appropriate **19–004** remedy in satisfaction of it. Until such time as the equity is satisfied it remains inchoate.

3. **Distinguishing the Principle of Proprietary Estoppel from the Doctrine of Constructive Trusts**

Although proprietary estoppel shares a functionally similar role in land law to that of **19–005** constructive trusts, namely to create interests in land informally, the two concepts are not synonymous. Whilst in many cases there will be a substantial overlap between them, such that it may be possible for a plaintiff to make out a claim on either ground,[9] three significant differences between their operation in practice may be observed:

(a) *"Representation" rather than "Common Intention"*

It has been seen that a constructive trust will only be established where it can be shown that **19–006** the parties shared a "common intention" that the ownership of the land should be shared, and the constructive trust arises to fulfil that intention. Although the requirement of a common intention can be criticised as the theoretical basis for the imposition of constructive trusts on the grounds of artificiality, the central question in practice is often whether such a common intention can be established. It has been seen that in *Lloyds Bank Plc v Rosset*[10] the House of Lords adopted a very narrow view of the circumstances in which such an intention could be inferred from the parties' conduct alone. In contrast proprietary estoppel operates on the basis of a "representation" or an "assurance" by the owner of land that the claimant is entitled to some interest in it. This operates as a lower threshold than "common intention" which means that it will sometimes be possible to establish an estoppel equity when a "common intention" cannot be established. As will be seen, a wider range of factual information about the nature of the parties' conduct and their relationship will be taken into account by the court in determining whether there was a representation sufficient to establish an equity.

(b) *A Range of Remedies rather than a Share of the Equitable Ownership*

Where the requirements for a constructive trust are established the only possible consequence **19–007** is that the claimant will be recognised as enjoying a share of the equitable ownership of the land subject to the trust. There is no flexibility for the court to award any alternative remedy, the land will become subject to a trust of land, and the relationship of the parties will be regulated

---

[9] See, for example, *Yaxley v Gotts* [2000] 1 All E.R. 711.
[10] [1991] 1 A.C. 107.

and determined by the rules of concurrent ownership.[11] However in the case of proprietary estoppel there is no such certainty as to the nature of the remedy that will be awarded to a successful claimant. Instead, the nature of the right awarded to satisfy the estoppel equity is a matter for the discretion of the court. As far as possible the court will attempt to fulfil the reasonable expectation of the claimant, by awarding the right it was represented that he would enjoy. A wide range of interests in land have been awarded on the basis of an estoppel, and the remedial flexibility is particularly evident where the court has refused to award an interest in land at all but has simply ordered that the claimant receive financial compensation.

(c) *Interest in Land Acquired when Awarded by the Court rather than at the Date of the Events Establishing the Cause of Action*

19–008　A third significant difference is that, where an interest in land is awarded by the court to satisfy an estoppel equity, that interest crystallises only once it is confirmed by judgment, not from the earlier date when the equity was itself raised by detrimental reliance on the relevant representation. This contrasts with a constructive trust, where the court (in theory) merely recognises the existence of the trust, which arises from the moment that the beneficiary acted to his or her detriment on the basis of the common intention that he or she was to enjoy a share of the ownership of the land. In essence the interest awarded as a response to satisfy an estoppel equity had no existence prior to the judgment awarding it and can properly be regarded as a remedy, whereas the constructive trust generates an equitable entitlement as soon as the appropriate triggers have occurred without the intervention of the court, so that it is not truly remedial but institutional in nature. The main significance of this difference is the extent to which the respective rights generated in the land are capable of binding third party interests arising in the intervening period between the events justifying the claim and the judgment of the court. In the case of a constructive trust, since the claimant's beneficial interest in the land arises from the moment that the common intention was acted upon, third parties subsequently gaining an interest in the land will potentially take their interests subject to the pre-existing equitable ownership generated by the constructive trust. Thus if a man who is the sole legal owner of a house, in which his partner enjoys a half share by way of a constructive trust, subsequently mortgages the land to a bank, the bank may take its mortgage subject to the partner's beneficial interest, dependent on the applicable rules of priority. Interests awarded by the court in satisfaction of an estoppel equity are incapable of taking priority over intervening third party interests in and of themselves. The court may even take account of the existence of such intervening third party interests in determining the appropriate remedy for the estoppel. However, although the interest awarded may not be capable of binding a third party who has become entitled to intervening rights in the land, it is an important question whether the estoppel "equity" calling for a remedy is itself a proprietary interest in land capable of binding a third

[11] It should be noted, however, that constructive trusts based upon a freely accepted obligation (rather than on common intention) have also been used to make contracts enforceable beyond the conventional limits of privity of contract, for instance to make a contractual licence enforceable against a successor in title (see *Binions v Evans* [1972] Ch. 359 and *Ashburn Anstalt v Arnold* [1989] Ch. 1). See also *Lyus v Prowsa Developments* [1982] 1 W.L.R. 1044 where a constructive trust based upon a freely accepted obligation was also imposed.

party even while it has not yet been crystallised into a traditional proprietary right by judgment of the court. For example, if a cohabitee can establish that she is entitled to an estoppel equity, but the land has been sold to a third party, will the third party take the land subject to her right to be awarded a remedy in satisfaction of the estoppel?

ESTABLISHING AN EQUITY BY PROPRIETARY ESTOPPEL

1. Historical Evolution

The doctrine of proprietary estoppel as a means of acquisition of interests in land has a long historical pedigree. In a number of cases in the nineteenth century it was held that a person's conduct could entitle a claimant to an interest in land despite the absence of the necessary formalities for the creation of such an interest.[12] Although some cases, such as *Ramsden v Dyson*,[13] suggested a broad approach to determining when such an interest should be acquired, the development of a generalised principle was stultified by *Willmott v Barber*[14] where Fry J. held that the legal owner could only be prevented from asserting his title if he had acquiesced in a mistake made by the claimant as to his rights in the land, since the foundation of the doctrine was the prevention of fraud. He laid down what have become known as the "five probanda" as pre-requisites of a successful claim:

> "A man is not to be deprived of his legal rights unless he has acted in such a way as would make it fraudulent for him to set up those rights. What, then, are the elements or requisites necessary to constitute fraud of that description? In the first place the plaintiff must have made some mistake as to his legal rights. Secondly, the plaintiff must have expended some money or must have done some act (not necessarily upon the defendant's land) on the faith of his mistaken belief. Thirdly, the defendants, the possessor of the legal right, must know of the existence of his own right which is inconsistent with the right claimed by the plaintiff. If he does not know of it he is in the same position as the plaintiff, and the doctrine of acquiescence is founded upon conduct with a knowledge of your legal rights. Fourthly, the defendant, the possessor of the legal right, must know of the plaintiff's mistaken belief of his rights. If he does not, there is nothing which calls upon him to assert his own rights. Lastly, the defendant, the possessor of the legal right, must have encouraged the plaintiff in his expenditure of money or in the other acts which he has done, either directly or by abstaining from asserting his legal right. Where all these elements exist, there is fraud of such a nature as will entitle the court to restrain the possessor of the legal title from exercising it, but, in my judgment, nothing short of this will do."[15]

19–009

---

[12] *Dillwyn v Llewellyn* (1862) 4 De G. F. & J. 517; *Ramsden v Dyson* (1866) L.R. 1 H.L. 129.
[13] (1866) L.R. 1 H.L. 129.
[14] (1880) 15 Ch.D. 96.
[15] (1880) 15 Ch.D. 96 at 105–106.

Although these probanda have been applied in subsequent cases,[16] including *Matharu v Matharu*[17] where Roch L.J. held that they had been satisfied on the facts, many other cases suggest that a less rigid approach should be taken to the question whether an equity has been established.[18] In *Ramsden v Dyson*[19] itself Lord Kingsdown articulated a much more generalised jurisdiction for establishing an equity rooted in the concept of expectations induced by the landowner rather than mistake by the claimant:

> "If a man, under a verbal agreement with a landlord for a certain interest in land, or what amounts to the same thing, under an expectation, created or encouraged by the landlord, that he shall have a certain interest, takes possession of such land, with the consent of the landlord, and upon faith of such promise or expectation, with the knowledge of the landlord and without objection by him, he lays out money upon the land, a court of equity will compel the landlord to give effect to such promise or expectation."

In the leading modern authority, *Taylor Fashions Ltd v Liverpool Victoria Trustees Co Ltd*,[20] Oliver J. re-stated the requirements for a successful estoppel claim so that it is not universally necessary to meet all five of the Willmott v Barber probanda. Instead he considered that the doctrine was founded upon a broad principle of unconscionability:

> ". . . the recent cases indicate, in my judgment, that the application of the Ramsden v Dyson principle—whether you call it proprietary estoppel, estoppel by acquiescence or estoppel by encouragement is really immaterial—requires a very much broader approach which is directed rather at ascertaining whether, in particular individual circumstances, it would be unconscionable for a party to be permitted to deny that which, knowingly or unknowingly, he has allowed or encouraged another to assume to his detriment, than to inquiring whether the circumstances can be fitted within the confines of some preconceived formula serving as a universal yardstick for every form of unconscionable behaviour."

This broader approach was been approved by the Court of Appeal in *Habib Bank Ltd v Habib Bank A.G. Zurich*[21] and was applied by the *Privy Council in Lim Teng Huan v Ang Swee Chuan*[22] where Lord Browne-Wilkinson stated:

> "The decision in *Taylor Fashions Ltd v Liverpool Victoria Trustees Co Ltd* showed that, in order to found a proprietary estoppel, it is not essential that the representor should have

---

[16] See *Crabb v Arun DC* [1976] Ch. 179; *Swallow Securities v Isenberg* [1985] 1 E.G.L.R. 132; *Coombes v Smith* [1986] 1 W.L.R. 808. In *Kammins Ballroom Co v Zenith Instruments (Torquay) Ltd* [1971] A.C. 850 and *E & L Berg Homes Ltd v Grey* (1979) 253 E.G. 473 claims of proprietary estoppel failed where the probanda were not satisifed.

[17] [1994] 2 F.L.R. 597; [1995] Conv. 61 (Welstead).

[18] See *Appleby v Cowley*, *The Times*, April 14, 1982; *Amalgamated Investment & Property Co Ltd v Texas Commerce International Bank* [1982] Q.B. 84; *Re Basham (deceased)* [1986] 1 W.L.R. 1498.

[19] (1866) L.R. 1 H.L. 129 at 170.

[20] [1982] Q.B. 133.

[21] [1981] 1 W.L.R. 1265.

[22] [1992] 1 W.L.R. 113.

been guilty of unconscionable conduct in permitting the representee to assume that he could act as he did: it is enough if, in all the circumstances, it is unconscionable for the representor to go back on the assumption which he permitted the representee to make."

This wider conception of proprietary estoppel based on principles of unconscionability has recently been accepted by the Court of Appeal in *Yaxley v Gotts*[23] and *Gillett v Holt*.[24]

2. The Modern Requirements

Following the re-statement of principle in *Taylor Fashions Ltd v Liverpool Victoria Friendly* **19–010** *Society* there are three interrelated elements that must be met to establish an estoppel equity. First, the claimant must show that there was an assurance by the landowner which gave rise to an expectation that he or she was entitled to some interest in the land. Secondly, he or she must have relied on that assurance. Thirdly, he or she must have acted to his or her detriment as a consequence of such assurance. The interrelatedness of these three requirements was reiterated by Robert Walker L.J. in *Gillett v Holt*:

"... it is important to note at the outset that the doctrine of proprietary estoppel cannot be treated as subdivided into three or four watertight compartments. In the course of oral argument in this court it repeatedly became apparent that because the quality of the relevant assurances may influence the issue of reliance, that reliance and detriment are often intertwined, and that whether there is a distinct need for a 'mutual understanding' may depend on how the other elements are formulated and understood. Moreover the fundamental principle that equity is concerned to prevent unconscionable conduct permeates all the elements of the doctrine. In the end the court must look at the matter in he round."[25]

Each of these requirements will be examined in turn.

3. An Assurance

(a) *Importance of an Assurance*

The foundation of an estoppel claim is the fact that the claimant acted on the basis that he was **19–011** entitled, or was going to become entitled,[26] to an interest in the land concerned. It is obviously not sufficient to justify a remedy if he was acting under a unilateral mistake that he was so

---

[23] [2000] 1 All E.R. 711.
[24] [2000] 2 All E.R. 289.
[25] [2000] 2 All E.R. 289 at 301.
[26] *Re Basham deceased* [1986] 1 W.L.R. 1498.

entitled, and therefore the element of assurance is the connecting factor between the expectations of the claimant and the activities of the owner of the land which call for a remedy. As Edward Nugee Q.C. stated in *Re Basham (deceased)*,[27] the essence of proprietary estoppel is that:

> "where one person, A, has acted to his detriment on the faith of a belief, which was known to and encouraged by another person, B, that he either has or is going to be given a right in or over B's property, B cannot insist on his strict legal rights if to do so would be inconsistent with A's belief."

(b) Form of Assurance

(i) Active Assurance

19–012 An active assurance or representation occurs when the owner of land by words or conduct leads the claimant to expect that he will enjoy some entitlement in the land. For example, in *Pascoe v Turner*[28] the defendant had moved in with the plaintiff first as his housekeeper and then as his lover. They moved to a new house which he purchased, but he subsequently began an affair with another woman and moved out. After he had left she remained in the house and he told her that she should not worry as the house was hers and everything in it. The Court of Appeal held that in these circumstances he had made a representation which was sufficient to establish a proprietary estoppel. In *Inwards v Baker*[29] a son was intending to purchase some land on which to build a bungalow as his home. His father persuaded him to build the bungalow on land that he owned so that it would be bigger. The Court of Appeal held that this gave rise to an expectation of the son that he would be allowed to remain in the bungalow for his lifetime which entitled him to a remedy by way of estoppel. In *Griffiths v Williams*[30] the Court of Appeal similarly held that there was a sufficient representation where a mother had assured her daughter, who was living with her and caring for her, that she would be entitled to live in the house for the whole of her life. In *Re Basham (deceased)*[31] the plaintiff was the step-daughter of the owner of a cottage who had died intestate. Prior to his death she and her husband had helped him to run his business and looked after him and the cottage, and on a number of occasions he had made clear that she was to expect to have the house when he died. When a new room was added he had told her that it was "putting money on the property for you" and when there was a boundary dispute with the neighbours he told her to sort it out herself as she was going to be entitled to the property. Edward Nugee Q.C. held that these representations encouraged the plaintiff's belief that she was going to receive the cottage and were sufficient to give rise to an estoppel equity preventing it passing to others on his intestacy. In *Gillett v Holt*[32] the Court of Appeal held that the defendant had assured the plaintiff on seven occasions that he would leave his farm

[27] [1986] 1 W.L.R. 1498 at 1503.
[28] [1979] 1 W.L.R. 431.
[29] [1965] 2 Q.B. 29.
[30] (1977) 248 E.G. 947.
[31] [1986] 1 W.L.R. 498.
[32] [2000] 2 All E.R. 289.

business to him when he died. Robert Walker L.J. stressed that it was not necessary for there to have been a "definite agreement" between the parties, provided that there was "a sufficient link between the promises relied on and the conduct which constitutes the detriment".[33] In *Yaxley v Gotts*[34] the Court of Appeal held that an estoppel equity could be established by an oral agreement for the grant of an interest in land, even where such an agreement could not give rise to an enforceable contract because it would be rendered void for lack of formalities by s.2 of the Law of Property (Miscellaneous Provisions) Act 1989. The role of estoppel in the context of an agreement for an interest in land has been considered by the Court of Appeal on two further recent occasions. In *Kinane v Mackie-Conteh*,[35] the parties had agreed that Kinane would provide a £50,000 loan and would have an interest by way of security on Mackie-Conteh's house. The agreement was not compliant with s.2(1). The Court of Appeal held that an estoppel equity could be established by the agreement "where the circumstances giving rise to proprietary estoppel also gave rise to a constructive trust".[36] The overriding factor was the unconscionability of allowing the promisor to go back on the agreement. In this case unconscionability was established because Kinane had been encouraged in his belief that he would obtain security and had relied on it to his detriment.[37] Where an estoppel does not also give rise to a constructive trust, it is unclear whether the arrangement will be invalidated by virtue of s.2(1).[38] In *Yeoman's Row Management Ltd v Cobbe*,[39] a landowner was estopped from going back on an agreement "in principle" for a joint venture with a developer when she deliberately misled him into thinking that she would enter into a contract in order that he continued to work on a planning application that enhanced the value of her land. The agreement was unconcluded and thus did not fall under s.2. Nevertheless, Mummery L.J. held that

> "proprietary estoppel could be established even where the parties anticipated that a legally binding contract would not come into existence until after planning permission had been obtained, further terms discussed and agreed and formal written contracts exchanged."[40]

Estoppel was established by unconscionability not the agreement.[41] He further considered that estoppel would not be ruled out even if an agreement was made "subject to contract": "if

---

[33] [2000] 2 All E.R. 289 at 306.

[34] [2000] 1 All E.R. 711.

[35] [2005] EWCA Civ 45; (2005) 2 P. & C.R. D.G. 3.

[36] per Arden L.J. (2005) 2 P. & C.R. D.G. 3, at D10. Section 2(5) exempts resulting and constructive trusts from s.2(1) of the Act.

[37] (2005) 2 P. & C.R. D.G. 3.

[38] Neuberger L.J. adopted a restrictive approach, doubting the observations made to opposite effect in *Yaxley v Gotts*: (2005) 2 P. & C.R. D.G. 3 at D11, Arden L.J. disagreed on this point: [2005] P. & C.R. D.G. 3 at D11. See also B. McFarlane [2005] Conv 501; M. Dixon [2005] Conv 247; There are suggestions that Mummery L.J. adopts the broad approach in *Yeoman's Row Management Ltd v Cobbe* [2006] 1 W.L.R. 2964, paras 66–67: "It is . . clear from the Law Commission Report . . . that the continued availability of proprietary estoppel was contemplated . . . Its availability does not infringe the public policy underlying section 2(1) of the 1989 Act by either directly or indirectly enforcing the . . . agreement so as to frustrate the purpose of section 2". However, in *Cobbe* the agreement was unconcluded, so did not fall within s.2.

[39] [2006] 1 W.L.R. 2964.

[40] [2006] 1 W.L.R. 2964 at para.56; Also confirming the principle that an equity could arise where there was no binding contract: *Beddow v Cayzer* [2007] EWCA Civ 644, 2007 WL 1729849, where, on the facts, no equity arose; see also *Kilcarne Holdings Ltd v Targetfollow (Birmingham) Ltd* [2006] 1 P. & C.R. D.G. 20, Court of Appeal (no constructive trust in this case).

[41] [2006] 1 W.L.R. 2964 at para.67.

the claimant established that the defendant had subsequently made a representation and had encouraged on the part of the claimant a belief or expectation that he would not withdraw from the 'subject to contract' agreement or rely on the 'subject to contract' qualification".[42]

(ii) Passive Assurance

19–013 A passive assurance occurs when the owner of land stands by and does nothing to disavow the claimant of a mistaken expectation that he was or would become entitled to an interest in the land.[43] The possibility of a passive representation was raised by Lord Wensleydale in *Ramsden v Dyson*, where he stated:

> "[If a stranger] builds on my land, supposing it to his own, and I, knowing it to be mine, do not interfere, but leave him to go on, equity considers it to be dishonest in me to remain passive and afterwards to interfere and take the profit."[44]

Although subsequent cases have made clear that it is not strictly essential to establishing an equity by proprietary estoppel that the owner knew of the claimant's mistaken belief, and also of his own legal rights to intervene,[45] these are relevant factors and it will be easier to establish an equity by passive assurance where they are present. For example, in *Scottish and Newcastle Plc v Lancashire Mortgage Corp Ltd*,[46] a first chargee stood by knowing that a chargee second in time expected to have priority. The first chargee was estopped from asserting priority when the second chargee relied on the expectation to his detriment.

(c) *Irrevocability of the Assurance*

19–014 The question has arisen in recent cases whether an assurance must have been irrevocable in order to generate an estoppel equity. A number of cases have concerned unfulfilled assurances allegedly made by the owner of land that he would leave property to the claimant by will. Whilst a claimant may have acted to his detriment on the basis of such an assurance it is also axiomatic that a testator is entitled to change his will at any time before death, and that the claimant would have been aware of this possibility. In *Taylor v Dickens*[47] an elderly lady said that she would leave her estate to her gardener, but then changed her mind without telling him after he had stopped charging her for his help with gardening and odd jobs. Judge Weeks Q.C. held that this assurance could not give rise to an estoppel equity because the elderly lady had not created or encouraged a belief that she would not exercise her right to change her will.

---

[42] [2006] 1 W.L.R. 2964, para.57 citing *Att-Gen of Hong Kong v Humphreys Estate* [1987] 1 A.C. 114; see also B. McFarlane [2005] Conv. 501; M. Dixon [2005] Conv. 247.

[43] *Willmott v Barber* (1880) 15 Ch.D. 96 concerned a problem of mistake, and Fry J.'s five probanda can most readily be justified and understood in this context.

[44] (1866) L.R. 1 H.L. 129 at 168.

[45] See *Shaw v Applegate* [1977] 1 W.L.R. 970; *Taylor Fashions Ltd v Liverpool Victoria Friendly Society* [1982] Q.B. 133. Compare *Armstrong v Sheppard & Short Ltd* [1959] 2 Q.B. 384.

[46] [2007] EWCA Civ 684; Westlaw 2007 WL 1729947.

[47] [1998] 3 F.C.R. 455.

648

This decision has been criticised by academics.[48] In *Gillett v Holt*[49] the Court of Appeal considered that these criticisms were well founded. The defendant had assured the plaintiff, who had worked for him for more than 40 years, on multiple occasions that he would leave him his farm business when he died. Robert Walker L.J. held that the inherent revocability of testamentary disposition was irrelevant in the light of the assurance given by the defendant to the plaintiff that "all this will be yours". In the circumstances the assurance was "more than a mere statement of present (revocable) intention" and was "tantamount to a promise".[50] Thus it seems that an estoppel equity will arise wherever an assurance was given which was intended to be relied upon, and which was then in fact relied upon, even if it was not expressly made irrevocable. As Robert Walker L.J. concluded, "it is the other party's detrimental reliance on the promise which makes it irrevocable".[51] The idea of when a promise of inheritance can bind a testator was the key feature of the Court of Appeal's decision in *Uglow v Uglow*.[52] The testator had encouraged the claimant to leave his family partnership in farming and set up partnership with him, by assuring him that he would leave the farm to the claimant in his will. The claimant had done so and made considerable life choices on the basis of the assurance. However, it was held that the assurance was implicitly conditional on the success of a farming partnership, which in the event did not succeed. The testator and the claimant then agreed that the claimant should have a lease of part of the farm. When the testator died the claimant argued that he was entitled to the farm on the basis of the earlier promise of inheritance. The Court of Appeal considered that the assurance should be viewed in the context of subsequent unforeseen events that might make it "conscionable" to go back on the promise, e.g. if the partnership failed and the testator wanted to change his mind about the inheritance.[53] Viewing the situation "in the round", as required by *Gillett v Holt*, it was held that

> "If there was a relevant unforeseen change of circumstances, the probable reaction of the just bystander (and it is by reference to his conscience that these matters should be judged) would be that the assurance of the Testator could be rescinded by him and replaced by a different arrangement, as long as it satisfied the equity that had arisen in favour of [the claimant] before the change of circumstances."[54]

(d) *Person Making the Assurance*

Although in most cases the assurance will have been made by the owner of the land in which an interest is claimed, an estoppel equity will also arise if the representation was made by the owner's employee or agent.[55] However a tenant cannot make assurances which will generate an equity against the freehold owner.[56]

19–015

---

[48] [1998] Conv. 220 (Thomson); [1998] R.L.R. (Swadling).
[49] [2000] 2 All E.R. 289.
[50] [2000] 2 All E.R. 289 at 304.
[51] [2000] 2 All E.R. 289 at 305.
[52] [2004] EWCA Civ 987; Westlaw document 2004 WL 1476789.
[53] ibid, para.29.
[54] ibid, para.30, which it was held to do.
[55] *Ivory v Palmer* [1975] I.C.R. 340.
[56] *Ward v Kirkland* [1967] Ch. 194; *Swallow Securities Ltd v Isenberg* (1985) 274 E.G. 1028.

(e) Object of the Assurance

19–016 An assurance will only give rise to an estoppel equity if it generated an expectation in relation to specific assets. In *Layton v Martin* Scott J. held that there was no estoppel equity where a man had given a woman who moved in with him a general assurance that he would provide for her financially. He stated that the assurance must arise:

> ". . . .in connection with some asset in respect of which it has been represented, or is alleged to have been represented that the claimant is to have some interest. . . . The present case does not raise that question. A representation that 'financial security' would be provided by the deceased to the plaintiff, and on which I will assume she acted, is not a representation that she is to have some equitable or legal interest in any particular asset or assets."[57]

However, in *Re Basham (deceased)*[58] it was held that assurance that the plaintiff would become entitled to the whole of the representor's estate on death was sufficient to give rise to an equity and that the assurance did not need to relate to a specific item of property provided that the property concerned has been sufficiently clearly identified. By analogy with the doctrine of mutual wills, Edward Nugee Q.C. stated:

> "If the belief that B will leave the whole of his estate to A is established by sufficiently cogent evidence . . . I see no reason in principle or in authority why the doctrine of proprietary estoppel should not apply so as to raise an equity against B in favour of A extending to the whole of B's estate."

4. Reliance on the Assurance

19–017 The element of reliance is closely connected with the third requirement that the claimant must have acted to their detriment on the basis of the assurance. Reliance is the element which connects any detriment with the assurance so that the claimant can be said to have so acted because of the inducement. In *Att-Gen of Hong Kong v Humphrey's Estate (Queen's Gardens) Ltd*[59] the Privy Council stated that claimants of proprietary estoppel must "show" that they had relied on the belief or expectation encouraged by the landowner.[60] In most cases the element of reliance will be obvious, and in *Greasley v Cooke*[61] Lord Denning M.R. considered that it should be presumed once a representation has been established.[62] In *Lim*

---

[57] [1986] 2 F.L.R. 227 at 238–239; In *James v Thomas* [2007] EWCA Civ 1212, the Court of Appeal held that assurances by the defendant that his cohabitee would be "provided for" when he died and that improvements to the property that the claimant was working on would "benefit" them, were not specific enough; Westlaw document WL 3389566.
[58] [1986] 1 W.L.R. 1498.
[59] [1987] A.C. 114.
[60] The assurance does not have to be the only influencing factor: *Evans v HSBC Trust Co (UK) Ltd* [2005] W.T.L.R. 1289.
[61] [1980] 1 W.L.R. 1306.
[62] For an example of the presumption of reliance in operation: *Evans v HSBC Trust Co (UK) Ltd* [2005] W.T.L.R. 1289.

Teng Huan v Ang Swee Chuan[63] the Privy Council held that reliance could be established by an inevitable inference from the facts of a case. For example, in *Van Laethem v Brooker*[64] the claimant showed reliance on the defendant's encouragement that she would have an interest in a large house and grounds bought as a development project, by raising a mortgage on her home and eventually selling it in order to contribute to the purchases and the substantial renovations. She had no other income and had compromised her home and financial security, which showed that she had relied on the belief. The element of reliance will generally only be in question in extreme situations and to eliminate those cases where the claimant cannot be shown to have changed their conduct in any way as a result of the assurance. One such case where it was held that there was no reliance is *Coombes v Smith*.[65] Mrs Coombes and Mr Smith became lovers while they were still married to different partners. Mr Smith purchased a house in which they intended to co-habit, and he said such things to Mrs Combes as "It'll be nice when we're living together—we'll spend the rest of our lives together." It was a new house and she decorated it. Just before she moved into the house Mrs Combes became pregnant. Initially she moved in alone and Mr Smith promised that he would join her after spending Christmas with his children, but in the event he never moved in. After three years Mrs Coombes and their daughter moved to a new house purchased by Mr Smith, which she again redecorated. He then began living with another woman. He undertook to permit them to remain in the house until the child was 17, but she claimed that she was entitled to have the house conveyed to her on the grounds of proprietary estoppel. Jonathan Parker Q.C. held that none of the elements of a proprietary estoppel claim were established, since Mrs Coombes had not been acting under a mistaken belief as to her legal rights and her conduct did not constitute a detriment. He also held that her acts of alleged detriment, including leaving her husband and having a child, were not causally connected with any representation so that the element of reliance was absent:

"The first act relied on by the plaintiff is allowing herself to become pregnant by the defendant. In my judgment, it would be wholly unreal, to put it mildly, to find on the evidence adduced before me that the plaintiff allowed herself to become pregnant by the defendant in reliance on some mistaken belief as to her legal rights. She allowed herself to become pregnant because she wished to live with the defendant and to bear his child . . . The second act relied on as detriment was the plaintiff's leaving her husband and moving [into the defendant's house] . . . The reality is that the plaintiff decided to [move to his house] because she preferred to have a relationship with, and a child by, the defendant rather than continuing to live with her husband. It seems to me to have been as simple as that. There is no evidence that she left her husband in reliance on the defendant's assurance that he would provide for her if and when their relationship came to an end: the idea of detriment or prejudice is only introduced ex post facto."

It is questionable whether this blanket rejection of reliance merely because the claimant also acted from personal feelings is correct, and the facts are not altogether dissimilar to those of

[63] [1992] 1 W.L.R. 113.
[64] [2005] EWHC 1478, 2005 WL 1767595 (Westlaw document), para.233.
[65] [1986] 1 W.L.R. 808.

651

Pascoe v Turner[66] where it was held that the claimant was entitled to an estoppel equity and to a conveyance of the house she occupied. Jonathan Parker Q.C. distinguished the case on the grounds that in *Pascoe v Turner* there had been a much clearer express representation that Mrs Turner was to regard the house as belonging to her, but this alone would not have been sufficient to establish the equity in the absence of reliance. The acts of Mrs Turner, such as moving into the co-habited house, could also have been explained on the basis of her affection for Mr Pascoe rather than any expectation of gaining an interest in the land, but this did not prevent a finding that she was entitled to an equity. In reality the judgment in *Coombes v Smith* seems to draw too categorical a distinction between motives of love and affection and the desire to acquire a proprietary interest. People act with mixed motives, and in many cases where a claim by proprietary estoppel has succeeded it could be said that the claimant was motivated by emotional attachment to a relationship.[67] The rejection of Mrs Coombes' claim may have been influenced by the fact that Mr Smith had already agreed that she and their daughter could remain in occupation until the child had grown up, a concession which made it somewhat easier to dismiss her claim for ownership. It is surely questionable whether the court would have refused her claim entirely if no such concession had been made so that she would not have enjoyed any right to occupy the house. Despite these criticisms of the decision the principle stands that in the absence of reliance there will be no estoppel equity. In *Stillwell v Simpson*[68] it was held that a claimant who had carried out repairs on a house of which he was the tenant had not relied on an assurance of the landlady that he would have the property, or a first option to purchase it, on her death because he had carried the work out for his own benefit, knowing that she was not able to pay for it to be done.

5. Detriment or Change of Position by the Claimant

(a) *Detrimental Reliance Generates the Estoppel*

19–018 The mere fact that an assurance was given does not, of itself, entitle a person to an interest in land, in just the same way that a mere promise to make a gift does not entitle the prospective donee to compel the donor to make it. A person is perfectly entitled to go back on his word. However if the person to whom the assurance was given has acted in some way in reliance upon it, then the representor will be estopped from denying the expectation he had generated. It is the element of detrimental reliance which renders it unconscionable[69] for the landowner to assert his strict rights against the representee. This is illustrated by the recent case of *Yeoman's Row Management Ltd v Cobbe*,[70] in which a land owner and a developer negotiated an "in principle" agreement for a joint venture to develop a block of houses in Knightsbridge.

---

[66] [1979] 1 W.L.R. 431.
[67] See for example *Greasley v Cooke* [1980] 1 W.L.R. 1306.
[68] (1983) 133 N.L.J. 894.
[69] See *Grundt v Great Boulder Gold Mines* (1937) 59 C.L.R. 641; *Yaxley v Gotts* [2000] 1 All E.R. 711; *Gillett v Holt* [2000] 2 All E.R. 289.
[70] [2006] 1 W.L.R. 2964.

The developer expended considerable time and effort in obtaining planning permission in return for which the owner had assured him she would sell him the houses and share the profits. The owner was estopped from going back on the agreement. It was held that she had taken "unconscionable advantage" of the developer by deliberately failing to tell him she had changed her mind so that he would continue to work on the planning application and thus make the land more valuable.[71] The Court of Appeal said that the focus of the doctrine of estoppel was unconscionability and not on matters such as the terms of the agreement or whether the developer had completely performed his part.[72] Although the language of "detriment" is common in the cases, more recent decisions have expressed the need for a "change of position"[73] by the representee. The latter expression is the better of the two, since the fulfilment of the expectation will normally eliminate any detriment, and in some cases the interest acquired is of greater value than the cost of the claimant's acts.[74] In *Lloyds Bank v Rosset* Lord Bridge stated that in order to generate a constructive trust or proprietary estoppel the claimant must:

"show that he or she acted to his or her detriment or significantly altered his or her position in reliance on the [representation[75]]."[76]

The requirement of detriment was recently re-examined by the Court of Appeal in *Gillett v Holt*, where Robert Walker L.J. stated:

"The overwhelming weight of authority shows that detriment is required. But the authorities also show that it is not a narrow or technical concept. The detriment need not consist of the expenditure of money or other quantifiable financial detriment, so long as it is something substantial. The requirement must be approached as part of a broad inquiry as to whether repudiation of an assurance is or is not unconscionable in all the circumstances . . . The issue of detriment must be judged at the moment when the person who has given the assurance seeks to go back on it. Whether the detriment is sufficiently substantial is to be tested by whether it would be unjust or inequitable to allow the assurance to be disregarded—that is, again, the essential test of unconscionability. The detriment must be pleaded and proved."[77]

(b) What will Constitute Detriment or "Significant Change of Position"?

There is no complete catalogue of behaviour or conduct which will be regarded as constituting sufficient detriment or change of position to establish an estoppel equity. In *Watts v*

19–019

---

[71] [2006] 1 W.L.R. 2964, para.61 per Mummery L.J.

[72] [2006] 1 W.L.R. 2964, paras 46 and 51, per Mummery L.J.

[73] See *ER Ives Investment Ltd v High* [1967] 2 Q.B. 379; *Re Basham (deceased)* [1986] 1 W.L.R. 1498.

[74] As was the case in *Yeoman's Row Management Ltd v Cobbe* [2006] 1 W.L.R. 2964.

[75] Lord Bridge actually used the term "agreement" which was appropriate in the prime context of the case, which concerned the creation of constructive trusts.

[76] [1991] 1 A.C. 107 at 132.

[77] [2000] 2 All E.R. 289 at 308.

Storey[78] the Court of Appeal said that "the categories of detriment were not closed". However certain types of conduct are well recognised as sufficient.

(i) The Claimant Improves Land Belonging to the Person Who Gave the Assurance

19–020 Expenditure by the claimant to improve the land of the representor will constitute sufficient detriment to establish an estoppel equity, provided that the expenditure was incurred in reliance upon the assurance given.[79] In *Inwards v Baker*[80] the son improved his father's land by building a bungalow on it in reliance on the assurance that he had received that he would be able to live there as long as he wished. In *Pascoe v Turner*[81] the claimant was held to have acted to her detriment when she spent money improving, repairing and redecorating the house of her former lover in reliance on his representation that she was entitled to an interest in it. Cumming-Bruce L.J. stated:

> ". . . the [claimant], having been told that the house was hers, set about improving it within and without. Outside she did not do much . . . Inside she did a great deal more. She installed gas in the kitchen with a cooker, improved the plumbing in the kitchen and put in a new sink. She got new gas fires, putting a gas fire in the lounge. She redecorated four rooms . . . We would describe the work done in and about the house as substantial in the sense that that adjective is used in the context of estoppel."[82]

In *Yaxley v Gotts*[83] the plaintiff acted to his detriment by refurbishing the house owned by the defendant, and in *Gillett v Holt*[84] the plaintiff had partly acted to his detriment by improving a farmhouse belonging to the defendant which had been barely habitable when first acquired.

(ii) The Claimant Improves his Own Land

19–021 There will also be sufficient detriment if the claimant incurs expenditure improving or changing his own land in reliance on a representation of an entitlement to the representor's land. For example, in *Rochdale Canal Co v King*[85] the claimant built a mill on his land after applying to the canal company to draw water from their canal for his steam engines and they acquiesced in his laying of pipes for that purpose. It was held that they were not entitled to an injunction restraining him from drawing water.

---

[78] [1984] 134 N.L.J. 631.
[79] *Voyce v Voyce* (1991) 62 P. & C.R. 290.
[80] [1965] 2 Q.B. 29.
[81] [1979] 1 W.L.R. 431.
[82] [1979] 1 W.L.R. 431, 435–436.
[83] [2000] 1 All E.R. 711.
[84] [2000] 2 All E.R. 289.
[85] (1853) 16 Beav. 630.

(iii)   The Claimant Purchases New Land

A claimant will have acted to his detriment if he purchases new land on the basis of an assur- **19–022**
ance. In *Salvation Army Trustees Co Ltd v West Yorkshire CC*[86] the Salvation Army purchased
a new site and built a replacement hall when the Council represented that it would be requiring
their present site for a road-widening scheme. They were later informed that the scheme would
not be adopted for some years. Although there had never been a binding contract for the sale of
the site, Woolf J. held that the Salvation Army were entitled to an equity and that the doctrine
of proprietary estoppel was "capable of extending to the disposal of an interest in land where
that disposal is closely linked by an arrangement that also involves the acquiring of an interest
in land".

(iv)   The Claimant Suffers Financial Disadvantage

A claimant will also be able to establish an estoppel equity if he acted in reliance upon an **19–023**
assurance such that he suffered a personal financial detriment unconnected with the land
itself. In *Gillett v Holt*[87] the plaintiff worked for the defendant for some 40 years on the basis
of an assurance that the defendant would leave him his farm business on his death. Mr Gillett
claimed that he had suffered detriment in respect of the opportunity cost of continuing in
Mr Holt's employment and not seeking or accepting offers of employment elsewhere, or
going into business on his own, through failing to take substantial steps to secure his future
wealth by larger pension contributions, and by stepping off the property ladder in order to
live in a farmhouse owned by Mr Holt. The evidence also suggested that his remuneration
during the period of his employment amounted to only about 80 per cent of the average for
those occupying similar positions, and that his above-average level of responsibility would
have justified him receiving earnings and benefits some 5 to 10 per cent above that average.
Mr Holt enjoyed such dominance as patron over the lives of Mr and Mrs Gillett that they were
expected to subordinate their wishes to his. He therefore decided that he would like to pay for
their eldest son to go to his old school, but he did not extend the offer to their younger son.
As parents, they felt that if one boy was to go to boarding school then both should go, which
meant that they had to send their younger son to a lesser school, paying the fees by utilising
some maturing short-term endowment policies and increasing their overdrafts. Whilst
Carnwath J. held that Mr Gillett had not acted to his detriment, the Court of Appeal held that
if he had stood back and looked at the matter in the round he would have recognised that
Mr Gillett's case on detriment "was an unusually compelling one".[88] Robert Walker L.J. suggested that in the light of all the evidence he "would find it startling if the law did not give a
remedy in such circumstances".[89]

---

[86] (1981) 41 P. & C.R. 179.
[87] [2000] 2 All E.R. 289.
[88] [2000] 2 All E.R. 289 at 309.
[89] [2000] 2 All E.R. 289 at 311.

(v) The Claimant Suffers Non-financial Personal Disadvantage

19–024   It has been a matter of some debate whether a claimant who acts to his or her personal disadvantage or changes his conduct, without any financial detriment, in reliance on an assurance will be entitled to a claim by proprietary estoppel. A narrow approach was taken by Jonathan Parker Q.C. in *Coombes v Smith*,[90] the facts of which have been discussed in detail above, where he held that the claimant's conduct in leaving her husband, having and caring for a child and redecorating the representor's house were insufficient to establish an estoppel equity. He held that becoming pregnant and giving birth was not capable of constituting detriment in the context of proprietary estoppel, and that looking after the child after it was born and redecorating the property could not give rise to "any question of prejudice or detriment". He also rejected the suggestion that her failure to take any other steps to provide for herself and her future security by looking for a job was a detriment. However, this narrow view is somewhat anomalous in the light of other cases which have taken a much more positive approach to the assessment of non-financial conduct as sufficient detriment. In *Re Basham (deceased)* Edward Nugee Q.C. stated that:

> "It is in my judgment established that the expenditure of A's money on B's property is not the only kind of detriment that gives rise to proprietary estoppel."[91]

He therefore held that the step-daughter who had cared for her step-father on the basis of his representation that she would be entitled to the cottage he owned on his death was entitled to an estoppel equity:

> ". . . the [claimant] did a very great deal for the deceased, and it is clear that she did not receive any commensurate reward for this during her lifetime. There is some evidence, though not very much, of occasions when the [claimant] or her husband acted or refrained from acting in a way in which they might have done but for their expectation of inheriting the deceased's property: I refer to the occasions when the husband refrained from selling his building land, and refrained from taking a job in Lincolnshire which would have made it impossible for the [claimant] to continue caring for her mother and the deceased, and the occasions when the [claimant] instructed solicitors at her own expense in connection with the boundary dispute between the deceased and [his neighbour], and the expenditure of time and money on the house and garden and on carpeting the house, when the deceased had ample means of his own to pay for such matters. It may be that none of these incidents, taken by itself, would be very significant, but the cumulative effect of them supports the view that the [claimant] and her husband subordinated their own interests to the wishes of the deceased."

19–025   Although there was clearly some element of financial detriment on the claimant's part a large number of these "cumulative" acts were non-financial and it was held that they went "well beyond what was called for by natural love and affection". In a number of other cases conduct which was not essentially financial in nature has been held to be sufficient detriment. For

[90] [1986] 1 W.L.R. 808.
[91] [1986] 1 W.L.R. 1498 at 1509.

example, in *Jones (AE) v Jones (FW)*[92] a son who had moved to a house purchased by his father so that he could live nearby was held to have acted to his detriment so as to be entitled to a claim by way of proprietary estoppel, and in *Greasley v Cooke*[93] the Court of Appeal held a servant who looked after the members of a family and lived with one of the owner's sons had acted to her detriment, reversing the judgment at first instance where it had been held that her activities were not capable of generating an estoppel equity. However the most important indication of the relevance of non-financial detriment was given by Browne-Wilkinson L.J. in *Grant v Edwards*.[94] Although the case concerned the question whether a common intention constructive trust had arisen, he considered that useful guidance on the question of detriment could be gained from "the principles underlying the law of proprietary estoppel":

> "In many cases of the present sort, it is impossible to say whether or not the claimant would have done the acts relied on as detriment even if she thought she had no interest in the house. Setting up house together, having a baby, making payments to the general housekeeping expenses (not strictly necessary to enable the mortgage to be paid) may all be referable to the mutual love and affection of the parties and not specifically referable to the claimant's belief that she has an interest in the house. As at present advised, once it has been shown that there was a common intention that the claimant should have an interest in the house, an act done by her to her detriment relating to the joint lives of the parties is, in my judgment, sufficient detriment to qualify."[95]

The same conclusion should also be true for proprietary estoppel, so that any conduct detrimental to a claimant, irrespective of whether it was financial or non-financial, should be capable of generating an estoppel if the requisite elements of an assurance and reliance are present. The central difference between the requirements of constructive trusts and proprietary estoppel concerns the circumstances which can generate the implication of a common intention. Whereas *Lloyds Bank v Rosset*[96] makes clear that non-financial detriment is incapable of supporting an implication of common intention in the absence of express intention, it is capable of generating an estoppel equity.

Two more recent Court of Appeal cases confirm that a claimant who has suffered a non-financial disadvantage may be regarded as having acted to his detriment. In *Campbell v Griffin*[97] a man who had initially lived with a couple as a lodger came to be regarded as a son and took care of them, undertaking cleaning, gardening, shopping and cooking. In *Jennings v Rice*[98] a part-time gardener working for an elderly widow took care of her, ran errands and did work in the house. Following a burglary of her house he spent almost every night on the sofa of her sitting room, despite the fact that he had his own house, to provide her with security.

---

[92] [1977] 1 W.L.R. 438.
[93] [1980] 1 W.L.R. 1306.
[94] [1986] Ch. 638.
[95] [1986] Ch. 638 at 657.
[96] [1991] 1 A.C. 107.
[97] [2001] EWCA Civ 990.
[98] [2002] EWCA Civ 159.

(vi) Offsetting Benefits Derived by the Claimant Against any Detriment Suffered

19–026 There is some indication that the courts are willing to weigh any benefit gained by a claimant who has acted in reliance on an assurance against any detriment that he has incurred, and that if there is an overall advantage that he will be unable to maintain a claim by way of proprietary estoppel. In *Watts v Story*[99] the Court of Appeal held that a grandson who had given up his protected tenancy in Leeds to move into his grandmother's home in Nottinghamshire when she moved to the Isle of Wight, and consequently gave up any prospects of employment in Leeds, had on balance suffered no detriment:

> ". . . when the benefits derived by him from his rent-free occupation . . . are set against any detriments suffered by him as a result of making the move from his Rent Act protected flat in Leeds, he has not on balance suffered any detriment in financial or material terms."[100]

SATISFYING THE ESTOPPEL EQUITY

1. Award of an Appropriate Remedy by the Court

19–027 A claimant who has demonstrated the requisite elements of an assurance, reliance and detriment is entitled to an estoppel equity. This is not a remedy in itself, but a right to prevent the person who gave the assurance from asserting his strict legal rights in his land to defeat the expectation he induced. It is then for the court to determine the appropriate interest which should be awarded to the claimant in satisfaction of his inchoate equity. As the Privy Council observed in *Plimmer v City of Wellington Corp*:

> "The court must look at the circumstances in each case to decide in what way the equity can be satisfied."[101]

2. A Variety of Interests Awarded in Satisfaction

19–028 The cases demonstrate that the courts have utilised a wide variety of interests as the appropriate means of satisfying an estoppel equity. These have included interests in land, occupational rights and even monetary compensation.

---

[99] (1984) 134 N.L.J. 631.
[100] See also *Appleby v Cowley*, *The Times*, April 14, 1982.
[101] (1884) 9 App. Cas. 699, 714.

(a) *Conveyance of the Freehold Ownership*

In some cases the courts have ordered the owner of land to transfer the legal fee simple estate in his land to the claimant in satisfaction of the estoppel equity. The claimant thus becomes the absolute owner of the land. Such a transfer of the freehold ownership was ordered in *Dillwyn v Llewelyn*[102] and *Pascoe v Turner*.[103] In *Gillett v Holt*[104] the court held that the estoppel equity should be satisfied in part by the conveyance to the claimant of the freehold of the farmhouse in which he and his family had been living. In some cases the court has ordered the transfer of a conditional or determinable fee simple, specifying the conditions on which the estate will come to an end.[105]

19–029

(b) *Grant of a Lease*

In some circumstances the court has ordered the owner of land to grant the claimant a leasehold estate in his land to satisfy the estoppel equity, as for example in *Siew Soon Wah v Yong Tong Hong*.[106] In *Grant v Williams*[107] a daughter who had lived for most of her life in her mother's house and had cared for her and incurred expenditure improving the property on the basis of a representation that she would be entitled to live in it for the rest of her life was held to be entitled to an interest by way of proprietary estoppel when her mother died and left the house to her granddaughter. The Court of Appeal granted her a long lease at a nominal rent of £30 per annum determinable on her death in satisfaction of her estoppel equity. Whilst this solution was proposed by the parties themselves the court may also have the power to direct such a solution if considered appropriate. As was noted at the beginning of the chapter, in *Yaxley v Gotts*[108] the Court of Appeal held that a claimant should be entitled by way of proprietary estoppel to a 99-year lease, rent-free, of the ground floor of a house he had refurbished on the basis of an oral agreement to this effect with the owner.

19–030

(c) *Transfer of a Share of the Equitable Ownership*

Where land is held on trust by tenants in common the court has ordered the co-owner to transfer his undivided share in the land to the claimant in satisfaction of the estoppel equity, as in *Lim Teng Huan v Ang Swee Chuan*[109] where one joint tenant of land in Brunei built on land when he mistakenly thought he had contracted to purchase the interest of the other joint tenant, who did nothing to disavow him of his belief and was therefore estopped from denying his title.

19–031

---

[102] (1862) 4 De G. F. & J. 517
[103] [1979] 1 W.L.R. 431. See also *Thomas v Thomas* [1956] N.Z.L.R. 785; *Cameron v Murdoch* [1983] W.A.R. 321; *Re Basham (deceased)* [1986] 1 W.L.R. 1498; *Voyce v Voyce* (1991) 62 P. & C.R. 290.
[104] [2000] 2 All E.R. 289.
[105] *Williams v Staite* [1979] Ch. 291.
[106] [1973] A.C. 836.
[107] (1977) 248 E.G. 947.
[108] [2000] 1 All E.R. 711.
[109] [1992] 1 W.L.R. 113.

(d) Grant of a Right of Occupancy

19–032   In many cases the court has determined that the appropriate remedy was that the claimant should enjoy a licence to occupy the owner's land, often for life. For example, in *Greasley v Cooke*[110] the claimant was held entitled to live in the house rent free for as long as she wished, and in *Inwards v Baker*[111] the son was similarly entitled to remain in the bungalow on his father's land as long as he wanted. In such cases the reality of the right is that it amounts to a virtual "life interest" in the land. However, the courts were historically reluctant to award a life interests as an appropriate remedy because this would lead to the creation of a strict settlement under the Settled Land Act 1925. In such an eventuality the claimant would become the tenant for life, which would vest the legal title in him and confer on him all the powers conferred by that statute on a tenant for life, including the power to sell the land. In *Grant v Williams*[112] Goff L.J. was keen to point out that the grant of a long lease determinable on death "could not in any event give [the claimant] the statutory powers under the Settled Land Act". It may be that with the replacement of the strict settlement by the trust of land in the regime introduced by the Trusts of Land and Appointment of Trustees Act 1996, where the powers of management are retained by the trustees unless they delegate them to the life tenant, the courts will feel more able to use the life interest as a means of satisfying an estoppel equity, and that the occupational licence, which confers no interest in the land and is vulnerable to third parties subsequently acquiring ownership of the land, will fall from favour.

(e) Award of Financial Compensation

19–033   In a number of cases the claimant has been awarded no interest in the land and no occupational right but merely financial compensation for any expenditure incurred by way of detriment in reliance on the representation. For example in *Dodsworth v Dodsworth*[113] the claimants, who were the owner's brother and sister-in-law, were given to believe that they could live with her in her bungalow for as long as they wished on their return from Australia. They subsequently spent some £700 on improvements to the property. Following a breakdown of the relationship between the parties the court held that their estoppel interest should not be satisfied by the award of a right to live in the bungalow rent free for life, but that they should be repaid the amount they had expended, and they were awarded a lien over the bungalow to the value of the improvements made.[114] In *Gillett v Holt*[115] the claimant was awarded a sum of £100,000 as compensation for his exclusion from the rest of the defendant's farming business in addition to the freehold of the farmhouse. In *Campbell v Griffin*[116] a single man started living with a couple as their lodger, but came to be treated as their son. He

---

[110] [1980] 1 W.L.R. 1306.
[111] [1965] 2 Q.B. 29.
[112] (1977) 248 E.G. 947.
[113] (1973) 228 E.G. 1115.
[114] See also *Unity Joint Stock Mutual Banking Association v King* (1858) 25 Beav. 72; *Taylor v Taylor* [1956] N.Z.L.R. 99.
[115] [2000] 2 All E.R. 289.
[116] [2001] EWCA Civ. 990.

assumed the role of carer, cleaning the house, maintaining the garden, helping with shopping and preparing meals. He received assurances that he had a home for life, and indeed the husband added a codicil to his will granting him a life interest in the property. In the event the husband predeceased his wife, and his will was of no effect because the house was owned as joint tenants so that survivorship operated, and the wife was unable to make a will in his favour because she was suffering from dementia. There was no doubt that in these circumstances the claimant was entitled to an equity. However the Court of Appeal held that, rather than satisfying the equity by granting him a life interest in the property he should receive a sum of £35,000. In the similar case of *Jennings v Rice*[117] the Court of Appeal held that a gardener who had acted to his detriment by looking after an elderly lady in reliance upon her assurance that she would "see to it" that he would be all right in her will should receive £200,000 from her estate. A financial remedy was again appropriate in *Powell v Benney* where the judge awarded £20,000 to a couple who acted to their detriment in reliance on the promise of an elderly gentleman to leave two properties to them in his will.[118] The couple appealed on the basis that they should be entitled to the properties. Sir Peter Gibson in the Court of Appeal held that "[I]t would offend common sense to leave out of account a benefit received in connection with a detriment when considering the detriment for the purpose of proprietary estoppel".[119] The couple had been allowed the use of the properties.

(f) *Award of an Easement*

Where appropriate the court has awarded an easement, generally a right of way, in satisfaction of the equity raised where there was an assurance that such a right would be enjoyed.[120] **19–034**

(g) *Award of a Share of the Equitable Ownership by Way of a Constructive Trust*

Although there is no case where the court has awarded a claimant a share of the equitable ownership of the land by way of a constructive trust in satisfaction of an estoppel equity there are some indications that such an interest may be capable of being so awarded. In *Hussey v Palmer* Lord Denning M.R. raised the possibility of such an award: **19–035**

> "To this I would add *Inwards v Baker*,[121] where a son built a bungalow on his father's land in the expectation that he would be allowed to stay there as his home, although there was no promise to that effect. After the father's death, his trustees sought to turn the son out. It was held that he had an equitable interest which was good against the trustees. In those cases it was emphasised that the court must look at the circumstances of each case

[117] [2002] EWCA Civ. 159.
[118] (2008) 1 P. & C.R. DG12.
[119] (2008) 1 P. & C.R. DG12.
[120] *ER Ives Investment Ltd v High* [1967] 2 Q.B. 379; *Crabb v Arun DC* [1976] Ch. 179; *Sommer v Sweet* [2005] EWCA Civ 227.
[121] [1965] 2 Q.B. 29.

to decide in what way the equity can be satisfied. In some by an equitable lien, in others by a constructive trust."[122]

This dictum has received judicial approval in New South Wales[123] and in *Re Basham (deceased)*[124] Edward Nugee Q.C. took the view that a constructive trust was also a potential remedy for proprietary estoppel. However if such a trust were to be awarded in satisfaction of an estoppel equity it would be very different from the common intention constructive trust delimited by the House of Lords in *Lloyds Bank v Rosset*,[125] which is institutional and arises when the relevant requirements of a common intention and detriment are fulfilled. The court merely recognises the trust the parties have created by their conduct. A constructive trust awarded in satisfaction of an estoppel equity would be remedial as it would only arise when awarded by the court and would not necessarily gain priority over intervening third party interests. The conceptual distinctions between constructive trusts and proprietary estoppel are well illustrated in *Preston and Henderson v St Helens MBC*.[126] A house was purchased in the name of Mr Preston with the help of a mortgage, and after Mrs Henderson moved in with him she paid the mortgage instalments and other expenses of the property. It was held that at this time she had gained a half share of the equitable ownership by way of a common intention constructive trust. He then left and represented that as far as he was concerned the house was hers. The Land Tribunal held that on the basis of this representation she had become entitled to the other half of the equitable ownership by way of proprietary estoppel.

(h) *Composite Remedies*

19–036   In some cases the courts have awarded composite remedies in satisfaction of the estoppel equity. For example, in *Re Sharpe (A Bankrupt)*[127] it was held that an aunt who had moved in with her nephew and his family and provided £12,000 of the purchase price by way of a loan was entitled to live in the house until the loan was repaid. This amounts to a composite of an occupational right and financial compensation.

(i) *No Remedy Required*

19–037   In some cases the courts have concluded that the equity raised in favour of a claimant did not require the award of any remedy in satisfaction. For example, in *Appleby v Cowley*[128] the defendant had allowed a barristers' chamber to occupy a building under a licence, paying a rent of £1,500. The barristers incurred expenditure of £7,700 on repairs and renovations. They

---

[122] [1972] 3 All E.R. 744 at 747–748.
[123] Pearce v Pearce [1977] 1 N.S.W.L.R. 170.
[124] [1986] 1 W.L.R. 1498 at 1503–1504.
[125] [1991] 1 A.C. 107.
[126] (1989) 58 P. & C.R. 500.
[127] [1980] 1 W.L.R. 219.
[128] *The Times*, April 14, 1982.

claimed a right to occupy the premises indefinitely, subject to indemnifying the owner for any expenditure incurred in relation to the building. Megarry V.C. held that although there were circumstances where it would have been unconscionable for the owner to take the benefit of the remedial work, for example if he had evicted them soon after the works had been done, on the facts there was no requirement for a remedy:

> "When the work was being done the rental value of the premises for which some £1,500 a year had been paid for some 10 years was about £4,300 . . . In those circumstances I think [the representor] may echo the phrase of Lord Hardwicke L.C. in *Attorney-General v Balliol College Oxford*[129] . . . and say that the plaintiffs have had 'sufficient satisfaction' for their expenditure."

He declined to debate the "nice academic point" whether the rationale for the refusal of the remedy was that no proprietary estoppel had been established, or whether an equity had been established but no remedy should be granted, but the many clear statements that the court has a discretion to determine how to satisfy an estoppel equity appropriately suggest that this must include the right to refuse any remedy. *Clarke v Swaby*,[130] the Privy Council took account of many years rent free accommodation. Lord Walker considered that the court has a wide discretion as to remedy, including no remedy where the equity is satisfied.[131]

3. Determining the Appropriate Satisfaction of the Estoppel Equity

It has been seen that a wide range of remedies are available to the court to satisfy an estoppel equity. However it has proved more difficult to explain how the court should determine the appropriate remedy. In the past two rival explanations have been advocated. First it has been suggested that the court possesses a broad remedial discretion to do what it just and fair to satisfy the equity. Second it has been suggested that the court should seek, as far as is possible, to award a remedy which will fulfil the expectation of the claimant. More recently the Court of Appeal seems to have adopted a composite approach, which is a synthesis of key elements of both of these alternatives.

19–038

(a) *Court Enjoys a Broad Discretion*

Some cases seem to suggest that the court possesses an unfettered discretion to decide how the estoppel equity should be satisfied. This discretion was evident in *Plimmer v City of Wellington*[132] where it was said that the "court must . . . in each case decide in what way the equity can be satisfied". In *Crabb v Arun DC*[133] Lord Denning M.R. suggested that "equity is

19–039

[129] (1744) 9 Mod. 407 at 412.
[130] (2007) 2 P. & C.R. 2.
[131] (2007) 2 P. & C.R. 2.
[132] (1884) 9 App. Cas. 699 at 714.
[133] [1976] Ch. 179.

displayed at its most flexible" in the context of determining how an established equity should be satisfied. In *Greasley v Cooke* he went on to say that:

> "The equity having thus been raised . . . it is for the courts of equity to decide in what way the equity should be satisfied."[134]

Goff L.J. also stressed the discretion of the court in *Griffiths v Williams*,[135] where he answered the question "what is the relief appropriate to satisfy the equity?" in this way:

> "The . . . question is one upon which the court has to exercise a discretion. If it finds that there is an equity, then it must determine the nature of it, and then, guided by that nature and exercising discretion in all the circumstances, it has to determine what is the fair order to make between the parties for the protection of the claimant."

However despite these judicial sentiments, and a degree of academic support,[136] it seems inappropriate that the award of a remedy should be a matter purely for the court's discretion without any principles to guide the determination of what would be appropriate. Proprietary estoppel does not yet serve as a broad remedy in the manner of the remedial constructive trust or Lord Denning's rejected "new model" constructive trust. The pure discretion theory of proprietary estoppel remedies is open to the objection of uncertainty and unpredictability. It is also inconceivable that an expectation raised of one kind of interest in land should entitle the court to award a greater interest by way of satisfaction of the estoppel equity. If the nature of the assurance was that the claimant should be entitled to occupy the owner's land this should not entitle the court to order the transfer of the freehold ownership as this would be in excess of the expectation that had been induced.

(b) *Court Constrained to Fulfil the Representee's Expectations as far as Possible*

19–040 An alternative view is that the court does not possess a broad discretion to award whatever remedy it wishes in satisfaction of the estoppel equity, but that it should select the remedy best able to fulfil the reasonable expectations of the claimant at the date that judgment is awarded in his favour. A more circumspect approach to the exercise of the court's discretion to satisfy an estoppel equity was recently supported by the Court of Appeal in *Gillett v Holt*. Robert Walker L.J. indicated how the court should go about deciding the most appropriate form for the relief to take:

> "The court approaches this task in a cautious way, in order to achieve what Scarman L.J., in *Crabb v Arun DC*,[137] called 'the minimum equity to do justice to the plaintiff'."[138]

---

[134] [1980] 1 W.L.R. 1306 at 1312.
[135] (1977) 248 E.G. 947.
[136] [1986] Conv. 406 (Thompson); (1986) 49 M.L.R. 741 (Dewar).
[137] [1976] Ch. 179 at 198.
[138] [2001] Ch. 210 at 235.

The "reasonable expectations" model explains the disparity between such cases as *Dillwyn v Llewelyn*[139] and *Pascoe v Turner*[140] where a conveyance of the freehold ownership was ordered, and *Inwards v Baker*[141] and *Williams v Staite*[142] where a mere right of occupancy was awarded. In the former cases the expectation raised by the assurance of the owner was that the land would belong to the claimant, whereas there was no such representation in the latter cases. In *Inwards v Baker*[143] the father had encouraged the son to build the bungalow on his land because it would be bigger, and although there was a clear implication that he could remain on the land as long as he wanted there was nothing from which he could reasonably expect ownership of the land. In *Williams v Staite* the assurance was merely that the claimant could "live here as long as you want". Those cases where monetary compensation was payable are explicable not on the grounds that such compensation was the expectation of the claimants, but that the breakdown of the relationship between the parties had rendered fulfilment of an expectations of shared occupancy impossible. Monetary compensation is a default remedy. For example in *Dodsworth v Dodsworth*[144] the assurance was one of occupancy for as long as the claimants wished but this would not have been possible when the parties had fallen out. As Russell L.J. observed, to grant a right of occupancy in such circumstances would merely lead to the owner having to "continue sharing her home for the rest of her life with the [claimants] with whom she was, or thought she was, at loggerheads". In *Burrows and Burrows v Sharpe*[145] an equity was established where the plaintiff and her family had moved in with her grandmother. Dillon L.J. stated that the usual approach to satisfaction of the equity was to fulfil the claimant's expectations:

> "It was often appropriate to satisfy the equity by granting the claimant the interest he was intended to have."

Having emphasised the court's discretion he considered that it should be exercised "in the light of the circumstances at the date of the hearing, taking into account, if appropriate, the conduct of the parties at that date". The relationship of the parties had broken down and the Court of Appeal rejected the solution of the first instance judge who had ordered that the plaintiff be entitled to continue to live in the house as unworkable and awarded financial compensation instead. Dillon L.J. accepted that in such circumstances the court may have to satisfy the equity in a "wholly different form from what had been intended when the parties were on good terms". The fulfilment of expectations analysis has also gained academic support. Moriarty concludes that:

> "Normally . . . a remedy will be chosen which gives the party precisely what he has been led to expect, but occasionally, where joint rights to land have been represented, he may get money instead."[146]

---

[139] (1862) 4 De G. F. & J. 517.
[140] [1979] 1 W.L.R. 431.
[141] [1965] 2 Q.B. 29.
[142] [1979] Ch. 291.
[143] [1965] 2 QB 29.
[144] [1973] 288 EG 1115.
[145] [1991] Fam Law. 67.
[146] (1984) L.Q.R. 376 at 412.

This analysis can be criticised on the grounds that often the parties' reasonable expectations cannot be easily identified because the assurance given, especially if passive, is ambiguous. For example, it is somewhat unrealistic to characterise the expectation in *Inwards v Baker*[147] as extending only to a right of occupation, since as Lord Westbury L.C. indicated in *Dillwyn v Llewelyn*, a case in which a son who built a very substantial mansion on his father's land was held to be entitled to a grant of the freehold:

> "No one builds a house for his own life only, and it is absurd to suppose that it was intended by either party that the house at the death of the son, should become the property of the father."[148]

In *Yeoman's Row Management Ltd v Cobbe*,[149] a case where an estoppel equity arose in the context of an agreement for a joint venture to develop land, whereby the appellant would sell her land to the respondent developer and they would share the profits of the development the Court of Appeal acknowledged that it was difficult to assess expectation in situations involving speculation and profit. However, to award financial compensation to reimburse the respondent for the considerable amount of work he did on an application for planning permission pursuant to the agreement,

> "would not reflect the balance of the risks and rewards to him of pursuing the planning application . . . and it would leave the [appellant] disproportionately advantaged by the grant of planning permission."[150]

Mummery L.J. concluded that the "least unsatisfactory" remedy was to award a lien for 50 per cent of the increase in value of the property.[151] Dyson L.J. agreed and considered that the appellant's conduct was relevant to the issue of remedy.[152] The respondent was denied his expectations of profit under the joint venture "by [the appellant] unconscionably taking advantage of him".[153] Here the appellant had encouraged the developer to work on the planning application, knowing it would increase the value of her land, yet all the while intending to go back on their joint venture arrangement.

(c)   *Proportionality Between the Remedy and the Detriment*

19–041   In the most recent cases the Court of Appeal has not adopted either of the approaches outlined above, but has favoured a composite approach which requires the court to ensure that the

---

[147] [1965] 2 Q.B. 29.

[148] (1862) 4 De G. F. & J. 517 at 522.

[149] [2006] 1 W.L.R. 2964.

[150] [2006] 1 W.L.R. 2964, para.39.

[151] [2006] 1 W.L.R. 2964, para.95. Even though this "would place [the respondent] in a more secure position than he might have been in if he had obtained the promised contract and gone ahead with the development with all its unknown risks on trusts and returns", per Mummery L.J., para.95.

[152] [2006] 1 W.L.R. 2964, para.126.

[153] The first instance judge's wording, [2006] 1 W.L.R. 2964, para.132.

remedy awarded to satisfy the estoppel equity is proportionate to the detriment suffered by the claimant.[154] In *Jennings v Rice*[155] the claimant was a part-time gardener who had taken care of an elderly widow on the basis of an assurance that she would "see him right", and that one day her house would be his. When she died her house was valued at £435,000, and he claimed that he was entitled to it by way of proprietary estoppel. There was no doubt that the claimant was entitled to an estoppel equity, but the question was how this equity should be satisfied. Robert Walker L.J. rejected the idea that the court possessed an unfettered discretion to choose the appropriate remedy:

> "It cannot be doubted that in this as in every other area of law, the court must take a principled approach, and cannot exercise a completely unfettered discretion according to the individual judge's notion of what is fair in any particular case."

However he also rejected the view that the court should simply act to fulfil the claimant's expectations, especially where the assurance and reliance did not relate to any specific property, so that it was more uncertain and did not have a consensual character falling not far short of an enforceable contract. Instead he stated that the underlying principle was as follows:

> ". . . once the elements of proprietary estoppel are established an equity arises. The value of that equity will depend upon all the circumstances including the expectation and the detriment. The task of the court is to do justice. The most essential requirement is that there must be proportionality between the expectation and the detriment."[156]

This principle means that where the claimant's expectations are uncertain, extravagant, or wholly out of proportion to the detriment suffered, the court should satisfy the equity in "another (and generally more limited) way".[157] Thus although the claimant's expectations are relevant to the selection of the appropriate remedy, they are not determinative. Robert Walker L.J. indicated that there were a number of factors which the court should take into account in exercising its wide judicial discretion to satisfy the equity, including: the misconduct of the claimant; particularly oppressive conduct on the part of the defendant[158]; the court's recognition that it cannot compel people who have fallen out to live peaceably together; alterations in the benefactor's assets and circumstances, the likely effects of taxation; and the other claims (legal or beneficial) on the benefactor or his or her estate.[159] Rather than awarding the claimant the freehold ownership of the widow's house, the court satisfied the claimant's equity by awarding him a sum of £200,000 from her estate. In exercising its discretion so as to satisfy the estoppel equity in a more limited way than the expectation generated, the court emphasised that the claimant had been unaware of the extent of her wealth, that the value of

---

[154] The principle of proportionality was applied in *Yeoman's Row Management Ltd. v Cobbe* [2006] 1 W.L.R. 2964.
[155] [2002] EWCA Civ 159.
[156] [2002] EWCA Civ 159 at [36].
[157] [2002] EWCA Civ 159 at [50].
[158] For example in *Pascoe v Turner* [1979] 1 W.L.R. 431, in granting the claimant the freehold of the house rather than a mere licence for life, the court took account of the owner's ruthlessness in trying to evict the claimant from the house by any possible means.
[159] [2002] EWCA Civ. 159 at [52].

her estate was out of all proportion to what he might reasonably have charged for the services he had provided, and that the house would have been unsuitable for him to reside in alone.

The operation of this composite approach can also be seen in *Campbell v Griffin*.[160] As was noted above, in this case a man who had begun by lodging with a couple acted to his detriment by taking care of them, and relied on their assurances that he would have a home for life in their house. Robert Walker L.J. held that his estoppel equity should not be satisfied by the award of a life-interest in the house, although this would have fulfilled his expectation, because this would have been "disproportionate" to the detriment he had suffered, and did not take account of the effect on other persons with claims on their estate. Instead the court awarded him the sum of £35,000.

PRIORITY AND ESTOPPEL EQUITIES

1. Priority of Interests in Land Awarded to Satisfy an Estoppel Equity

19–042   When a claim by way of proprietary estoppel has come to court, an equity is established and a remedy granted in satisfaction of it, any subsequent issues of priority will be determined by the ordinary rules applicable to the type of interest awarded.[161] For example, if the landowner is ordered to grant the claimant a lease any issues of priority concerning the claimant's lease will be resolved by the appropriate rules for leases. If the owner subsequently transfers or mortgages the freehold reversion, the transferee or mortgagee will potentially take subject to it. Greater difficulties arise where there is an award of an occupational licence to satisfy the equity[162] since it is now clear that a licence is incapable of existing as an interest in land even if it is irrevocable. In principle a licence generated by proprietary estoppel should only be capable of binding a third party who acquires a subsequent interest in the land if it was acquired subject to a constructive trust of the licence, for example if he had expressly agreed to take the land subject to the estoppel licence and paid a lower price for the land in recognition of such concession.[163] This issue is discussed more fully in Chapter 20. Obviously where satisfaction of the equity takes the form of an order to pay compensation to the representee no question of subsequent priorities will arise unless the order is also secured by an equitable lien on the land of the representor.

2. An Estoppel Equity is an Interest in Land

19–043   Prior to the Land Registration Act 2002, it was unclear whether an estoppel equity was a proprietary interest in lánd and therefore capable of binding third parties who acquired a subsequent interest in the land. An inchoate estoppel equity, which has not yet been satisfied by the award

---

[160] [2001] EWCA Civ. 990.
[161] See Battersby, "Informal Transaction in Land, Estoppel and Registration" (1998) 58 M.L.R. 637.
[162] See [1991] Conv. 36 (Battersby); (1994) 14 L.S. 147 (Baughen).
[163] See *Asburn Anstalt v Arnold* [1989] Ch. 1.

of a remedy, did not fall within the catalogue of rights and interests historically recognised as proprietary. Some academics therefore argued that the estoppel equity was incapable of binding third parties,[164] a conclusion supported by a number of authorities,[165] including *Pennine Raceway v Kirklees Council*[166] where Eveleigh L.J. expressly stated that an estoppel interest was not "an interest in land in a strict conveyancing sense". However other authorities suggested that an estoppel equity was a proprietary interest which should be capable of binding third parties,[167] and the transmissibility of an estoppel equity was accepted in Australia.[168] In England the balance of academic opinion favoured regarding an inchoate equity as a property right,[169] and in practice the Land Registry already allowed such equities to be registered as minor interests.

The matter has now been put beyond doubt by s.116(a) of the Land Registration Act 2002, which provides:

> "It is hereby declared for the avoidance of doubt that, in relation to registered land, each of the following
>
> (a) an equity by estoppel, and
> (b) a mere equity,
>
> has effect from the time the equity arises as an interest capable of binding successors in title (subject to the rules about the effect of dispositions on priority)."

3. Can an Estoppel Equity be Overreached?

The question whether an inchoate equity can be overreached has not arisen for decision. However, since under s.2(1) of the Law of Property Act 1925 overreaching operates in respect of "any equitable interest or power affecting" an estate in land, and an estoppel equity is not exempted from the scope of overreaching by s.2(3), it would appear that an estoppel equity is capable of being overreached.[170] Given the significant overlap between the principles of proprietary estoppel and resulting and constructive trusts it would be anomalous if a purchaser who paid over his purchase money to two trustees of land gained automatic priority over a resulting or constructive trust interest, but not over an estoppel equity. A number of authorities support the idea that estoppel equities should be capable of being overreached.[171] In *Birmingham*

19–044

---

[164] See [1983] Conv. 99 (Bailey); [1990] Conv. 370 (Hayton); (1990) 106 L.Q.R. 87 (Hayton).
[165] *Jones (AE) v Jones (FW)* [1977] 1 W.L.R. 438; *Fryer v Brook* [1984] L.S.Gaz.R. 2856; *United Bank of Kuwait Plc v Sahib* [1997] Ch. 107 at 142. See also *Canadian Imperial Bank of Commerce v Bello* [1992] 64 P. & C.R. 48 at 52, where Dillon L.J. held that an estoppel equity was insufficient of an interest in land to form the subject matter of an overriding interest under s.70(1)(g) of the Land Registration Act 1925.
[166] [1983] 1 Q.B. 382. See also *Plimmer v Wellington Corp* (1884) 9 App.Cas. 699.
[167] *ER Ives Investment Ltd v High* [1967] 2 Q.B. 379; *Re Sharpe (A Bankrupt)* [1980] 1 W.L.R. 219; *Voyce v Voyce* (1991) 62 P. & C.R. 290; *Lloyds Bank Plc v Carrick* [1996] 4 All E.R. 630 at 642.
[168] *Hamilton v Geraghty* (1901) 1 S.R. (N.S.W.) (Eq.) 81; *Cammeron v Murdoch* [1983] W.A.R. 321; affirmed (1986) 63 A.L.R. 575.
[169] [1991] Conv. 36 (Battersby); (1994) 14 L.S. 147 (Baughen); (1995) 58 M.L.R. 637 (Battersby).
[170] See further J. Stevens., "Is Justice a Priority in Prioirties?", Ch.8 in Meisel and Cook (eds), *Property and Protection*, Hart (2000).
[171] See: *Birmingham Midshires Mortgage Services Ltd v Sabherwal* (1999) 80 P & C.R. 256; *Lloyd v Dugdale* [2001] EWCA Civ. 1754; (2002) 2 P. & C.R. at [55].

Midshires Mortgage Services Ltd v Sabherwal[172] the suggestion was that whether a particular inchoate equity is overreachable should depend upon the nature of the underlying expectation which it protects. For example, if the inchoate equity would have given rise to an easement, or another right incapable of being overreached, the claimant would not lose the right through overreaching. Likewise, an estoppel equity which arose in circumstances where a beneficial interest under a trust was appropriate, then the claimant should be no better off than he would be with any other overreachable trust interest. Thus, the equity in these circumstances is over-reachable. The Court of Appeal seems recently to have gone further than this. In *Sommer v Sweet*,[173] it was held that an easement arising under estoppel bound a successor in title as an overriding interest under the Land Registration Act 1925. It had been argued that the con-veyance to the successor in title overreached the equity. The Vice-Chancellor dismissed the argument on the basis first that "the equity arising from a proprietary estoppel" was not an " 'equitable interest or power' affecting the estate transferred" in the contemplation of s.2 of the Law of Property Act 1925. It fell outside both the overreaching provisions and the provisions for the registration of land charges.[174] Second, the Vice-Chancellor was reluctant to hold that the estoppel equity could be overreached because it would create a conflict between s.2 of the Law of Property Act 1925 and the land registration provisions to the effect that a registered propri-etor takes subject to overriding interests.[175] Although these reasons are expressed in a general way, so that it would be possible to conclude from them that an estoppel equity is never capa-ble of being overreached, there is reason to suspect otherwise. The Vice-Chancellor observed that the decision in *Birmingham Midshires Mortgage Services Ltd*[176] was "to like effect", where as in this case the suggestion was that whether or not an estoppel equity is capable of being over-reached depended the nature of the underlying expectations. Here the expectation was an easement, which is not overreachable.

4. The Priority of Estoppel Equities in Registered Land

19–045   Where land is registered the priority of an estoppel equity will be determined by the provi-sions of the Land Registration Act 2002. These were discussed in detail in Chapter 7, so only a brief outline will be given here. The estoppel equity obviously will not gain priority over pre-exisiting interests in the land because it is not a registered disposition.[177] By virtue of s.29(1) a registered disposition of the land for valuable consideration, for example a transfer of the freehold title, the grant of a legal lease for more than seven years or a legal charge, will gain priority over a pre-existing estoppel equity unless the priority of the estoppel equity was protected at the time that registration of the disposition occurred. An estoppel equity will enjoy protected priority if it was the subject of a notice in the register[178] or if it was an

---

[172] (1999) 80 P & C.R. 256.

[173] [2005] EWCA Civ 227; 2005 W.L. 513419.

[174] 2005 WL 513419, para.26, relying on *ER Ives Investments v High* [1967] 2 Q.B. 379 and *Shiloh Spinners v Harding* [1973] A.C. 691.

[175] [2005] EWCA Civ 227; 2005 W.L. 513419, para.27.

[176] (1999) 80 P. & C.R. 256.

[177] Land Registration Act 2002 s.27 and s.28(1).

[178] Land Registration Act 2002 s.29(2)(a)(i).

overriding interest under Sch.3 to the Act.[179] Thus an estoppel equity will only enjoy priority over a subsequent registered disposition if it had been protected on the register by means of a notice, or more significantly if the owner of the equity was in actual occupation of the land at the time of the disposition, and either such occupation would have been obvious on a reasonably careful inspection of the land, or the disponee had actual knowledge of the equity.[180]

5. The Priority of Estoppel Equities in Unregistered Land

It is arguable that the proprietary status of an estoppel equity affecting unregistered land remains uncertain, since s.116(a) of the Land Registration Act 2002 only concerns the status of an equity by estoppel "in relation to registered land". Some cases suggest that an interest arising by estoppel is capable of binding a successor in title, for example in *ER Ives Investment Ltd v High*[181] the Court of Appeal held that an estoppel interest was binding on a purchaser of land who had actual notice of the easement claimed. These authorities would seem to suggest that issues of priority in relation to an estoppel equity in unregistered land will be resolved by application of the doctrine of notice as they are incapable of protection as land charges. In *Re Sharpe (A Bankrupt)*[182] Browne-Wilkinson J. seemed to suggest that a third party purchaser would acquire land free from an inchoate equity of which he had only constructive notice.[183] This, however, is contrary to principle and it is not unreasonable to expect a potential purchaser to make inquiries of the rights of any persons occupying the land and to ascertain whether they claim any entitlements therein.[184]

19–046

Since most transactions which might gain priority over an estoppel equity in unregistered land will give rise to the requirement of registration,[185] in practice issues of priority will be resolved by the rules regarding the effect of first registration. On first registration the registered proprietor of the estate will take his title subject to any overriding interests within the paragraphs of Sch.1 to the Act.[186] Provided that an estoppel equity in unregistered land is accorded the status of a proprietary right, it will rank as an overriding interest if the owner was in actual occupation of the land.[187] There is no additional requirement that the occupation must have been obvious on a reasonably careful inspection of the land.

[179] Land Registration Act 2002 s.29(2)(a)(ii).
[180] Land Registration Act 2002 Sch.3 para.2.
[181] [1967] 2 Q.B. 379.
[182] [1980] 1 W.L.R. 219.
[183] Compare *Bristol & West Building Society v Henning* [1985] 1 W.L.R. 778 where Browne-Wilkinson L.J. seemed to indicate that constructive notice would be sufficient.
[184] Compare *Kingsnorth Finance Co Ltd v Tizard* [1986] 1 W.L.R. 783.
[185] See Land Registration Act 2002 s.4.
[186] Land Registration Act 2002 s.1(4) and s.12(4).
[187] Land Registration Act 2002 Sch.1 para.2.

Chapter 20

LICENCES AND OCCUPATIONAL RIGHTS

INTRODUCTION TO LICENCES

1. The Essence of Licences

A licence is simply a permission which entitles a person to be physically present on land **20–001**
owned by someone else. Without a licence such presence would be actionable as a trespass.
As Vaughan C.J. stated in *Thomas v Sorrell*:

> "A dispensation or licence properly passeth no interest, nor alters or transfers property
> in anything, but only makes an action lawful, which without it had been unlawful."[1]

Licences are capable of authorising a very wide variety of degrees of presence on land, from
the right enjoyed by a milkman to deliver milk to the front door, to a right to occupy land
which is not a lease because there is no entitlement to exclusive possession.[2]

2. Distinguishing Between Types of Licence

Licences may take a number of forms, which are differentiated by the manner of their cre- **20–002**
ation. An express licence is one which was granted expressly by the owner of the land to
which it relates, who is termed the licensor. However in many circumstances a licence will
be taken to have arisen by implication without any express grant by the licensor. A licence is
described as a bare licence where the licensee provides no consideration in return for his entitlement to be present on the land. In contrast a licence granted in return for consideration is

---

[1] (1673) Vaughan 330 at 351.
[2] *Street v Mountford* [1895] A.C. 809.

termed a contractual licence, since it is granted by the licensor in fulfilment of a contractual obligation to do so. A licence may also arise by way of proprietary estoppel if an owner of land had given an assurance to a person that he will be able to use or occupy land and he has acted to his detriment in reliance upon that assurance. One of the most important issues regarding licences is the extent to which they are revocable, in other words when the licensor is entitled to withdraw permission to be present on land from the licensee. The extent to which a licence is revocable will vary depending how it came to be conferred. The licensee will become a trespasser if he remains on the land after the licence is revoked.

3. Licences as Purely Personal Interests

20–003 One of the key distinctions between a lease and a licence is that a licence is a purely personal interest enjoyed by the licensee, which is incapable of binding anyone other than the licensor. Thus if the licensor transfers the land over which the licence is enjoyed it will not be binding on the transferee who will acquire the land free from it. The licensee will be confined to remedies against the licensor if the licence was contractual. This traditional position has been reasserted by the courts in recent years despite the attempts of Lord Denning to elevate contractual licences to the status of proprietary rights in land by judicial pronouncement. In *Street v Mountford* Lord Templeman stated that:

> "A licence in connection with land while entitling the licensee to use the land for the purposes authorised by the licence does not create an estate in the land."[3]

However, it seems that a licence may still be capable of binding a transferee of the land in the very limited circumstances in which the court is willing to impose a constructive trust in favour of the licensee.

4. Distinguishing Between Leases and Licences

20–004 The conceptual differences between leases and licences were examined in detail in Chapter 9. In summary it was seen that an agreement conferring a right of occupancy is only capable of being a lease if it confers exclusive possession of the land. A right of occupancy that confers a lesser right of occupation will thus have to take effect as a licence. Following *Street v Mountford* it must be determined objectively whether any agreement confers a right to exclusive possession, and the subjective intentions of the parties as to whether they have granted a lease or a licence are not determinative. Because a lease is a proprietary interest in land, it might be thought that it can be granted only by a person who has the right to create such an interest. At common law, however, even a trespasser was capable of executing a grant to transfer such estate as he had in land and this grant would be effective to give an estate to the purchaser which would be completed if and when the grantor subsequently acquired the power to

---

[3] [1895] A.C. 809.

complete it.[4] In the meantime, the purchaser acquired a title which was enforceable against the grantor, and against strangers, but which was not enforceable against the true owner or anyone deriving title from him or her. The same principle was capable of applying to leases,[5] as has recently been affirmed by the decision of the House of Lords in *Bruton v London Quadrant Housing Trust*.[6] The defendant was a charitable housing association which had been granted a licence by a local authority to use a block of flats to provide short term accommodation for the homeless. The plaintiff occupied a flat in the block under a weekly agreement described as a licence and granted by the housing association. The House of Lords held that the essential nature of the agreement was in fact a lease, not a licence. It was irrelevant to the characterisation of the agreement with the claimant that the housing association was merely a licensee of the property itself, and therefore unable to grant any tenancy binding upon the local authority, even if the tenant knew of the limitation on the housing association's authority. The House of Lords held that vis-à-vis the association he was a tenant because the agreement conferred upon him the right to exclusive possession of the flat. Lord Hoffman held that an agreement did not have to create a proprietary interest in land in order to constitute a lease:

> "The decision of this House in *Street v Mountford* is authority for the proposition that a 'lease' or 'tenancy' is a contractually binding agreement, not referable to any other relationship between the parties, by which one person gives another the right to exclusive occupation of land for a fixed or renewable period or periods of time, usually in return for a periodic payment in money. An agreement having these characteristics creates a relationship of landlord and tenant to which the common law or statute may then attach various incidents. The fact that the parties use language more appropriate to a different kind of agreement, such as a licence, is irrelevant if upon its true construction it has the identifying characteristics of a lease. The meaning of the agreement, for example, as to the extent of possession which it grants, depend upon the intention of the parties, objectively ascertained by reference to the language and relevant background."[7]

Since the agreement was construed as a lease the parties were landlord and tenant. The House of Lords therefore held that the housing association was under the statutory obligation to keep the premises in repair imposed by s.11 of the Landlord and Tenant Act 1985. This decision has been heavily criticised. It seems that it was a policy motivated attempt to extend existing statutory protection regarding the condition of rented property to more vulnerable persons who are commonly provided with less secure short term accommodation. Whilst this might be a laudable objective the relevant legislation is specifically restricted to tenancies. The effect of the decision is to create a right, which is treated as a tenancy only as against the grantor, but which cannot confer a proprietary interest that is capable of binding third party successors in title who acquire the land from the owner. It is submitted that the right recognised in *Bruton v London Quadrant Housing Trust* would have been better regarded as a

---

[4] *Church of England Building Society v Piskor* [1954] Ch. 553 (overruled on the point that there is a momentary period of time between the grantor acquiring the estate and the interest he has created coming into full effect); *Rajapakse v Fernando* [1920] A.C. 892 at 897.
[5] *Cuthbertson v Irving* (1859) 4 H. & N. 742; *Mackley v Nutting* [1949] 2 K.B. 55.
[6] [1999] 3 All E.R. 481.
[7] [1999] 3 All E.R. 481 at 486.

contractual licence on the basis that the occupier should not be able to claim the advantages of a lease where he knows that the grantor has no power to grant a lease, and where the grantor does not purport to create a lease. This should be a sufficient special circumstance to displace the normal rule that a grant of exclusive possession creates a tenancy.

5. Rights Conferred by a Licence

20–005   The rights of a licensee will usually be determined by the specific terms of the licence enjoyed. Unless and until the licence is revoked the licensee will enjoy the right to be present on the land of the licensor to the extent conferred by the licence. Provided that the licensee's occupation of the land is within the scope of the licence the licensor will not be able to maintain an action for trespass against him. A licensee will also be able to enforce his right to occupy the land against third parties who are infringing his right to occupy the land. In *Dutton v Manchester Airport Plc*[8] the Court of Appeal held by a majority that a licensee was entitled to maintain an action for possession against trespassers who were occupying the land in respect of which they enjoyed a licence even though they had never possessed it themselves. The respondent company was building a second runway at Manchester Airport, and in order to accomplish this it needed to fell trees in a neighbouring wood, which was owned by the National Trust. The National Trust had granted the company a licence to do so, but protestors, who set up encampments, including tree houses, ropewalks and a tunnel, occupied the wood. Laws L.J., with whom Kennedy L.J. concurred, explained that the company was entitled to obtain an order for possession against the trespassers even thought its right was only contractual in nature and it had never possessed the land:

> ". . . the true principle is that a licensee not in occupation may claim possession against a trespasser if that is a necessary remedy to vindicate and give effect to such rights of occupation as by contract with his licensor he enjoys. This is the same principle as allows a licensee who is in de facto possession to evict a trespasser. There is no respectable distinction, in law or logic, between the two situations. An estate owner may seek an order whether he is in possession or not. So, in my judgment, may a licensee, if all other things are equal. I see no significance as a matter of principle in any distinction drawn between a plaintiff whose right to occupy the land in question arises from title and one whose right arises only from contract. In every case the question must be, what is the reach of the right, and whether it is shown that the defendant's act violates its enjoyment."[9]

A licensor is thus able to maintain an action in trespass against a third party irrespective of whether he was in possession of the land or not, and he is not dependent upon the licensor taking action to protect his rights. However a licensee cannot maintain an action against a person who enjoys a claim to possession of the land equal or superior to his own, whether by contract or estate.

---

[8] [1999] 2 All E.R. 675.
[9] [1999] 2 All E.R. 675 at 689.

BARE LICENCES

1. Creation of a Bare Licence

(a) *Express Grant*

A bare licence may be granted expressly by the owner of land. For example, when a person invites his friends round to watch the cup final, or allows a child living next door into his garden to recover a lost ball, a bare licence is granted entitling the guests or child to enter the land for the stated purpose.

20–006

(b) *Implied Licence*

A bare licence may also be implied even when there is no express grant. In *Robson v Hallett*[10] the Court of Appeal held that owners of houses impliedly license members of the public to approach their front door. Diplock L.J. stated the scope of this implied licence:

20–007

> "When a householder lives in a dwelling-house to which there is a garden in front and does not lock the gate of the garden, it gives an implied licence to any member of the public who has lawful reason for doing so to proceed from the gate to the front door or back door, and to inquire whether he may be admitted and to conduct his lawful business."

For this reason a police officer was not trespassing when he went to knock the door of a house to make inquiries. Similarly an election canvasser, double-glazing salesman or Jehovah's Witness would be entitled to enter premises. In *Holden v White*[11] the Court of Appeal held that a milkman delivering to a house enjoyed an implied licence to use a path which led to it, and in *Lambert v Roberts*[12] Donaldson L.J. considered that an implied licence is extended to all citizens who reasonably think they have legitimate business on the premises. However the implication of a licence can be rebutted. In *Robson v Hallett*[13] Diplock L.J. indicated that there would have been no implied licence if there had been a notice on the front gate stating "No admittance to police officers". In *Cole v Police Constable 443A*[14] it was held that members of the public have no implied licence to enter any church they wish to attend worship, but only their own parish church. Similarly the implied licence to customers to enter business premises would not extend to investigative journalists.

[10] [1967] 2 Q.B. 939.
[11] [1982] 1 Q.B. 679.
[12] [1981] 2 All E.R. 15 at 19.
[13] [1967] 2 Q.B. 939.
[14] [1937] 1 K.B. 316.

2.   Revocation of a Bare Licence

20–008   Where a person has entered land on the basis of a bare licence the licensor can withdraw the permission at any time, thus rendering the ex-licensee a trespasser if he continues his presence on the land. However the ex-licensee is entitled to a reasonable time to leave the land.[15] In *Robson v Hallett*[16] a licence was revoked when the owner of the house told a police sergeant, who had entered at the request of his son, to leave. Diplock L.J. stated:

> "He withdrew it, and, upon its being withdrawn, the sergeant had a reasonable time to leave the premises by the most appropriate route for doing so, namely, out of the front door, down the steps and out of the gate, and, provided that he did so with reasonable expedition, he would not be a trespasser while he was doing so."

The occupier committed an assault by using force to eject the sergeant before the sergeant had been given sufficient time to leave. What will constitute a reasonable time will depend on the nature of the land and the purpose of the licence, so that in the case of a residential licence in a family context a much longer period would apply.[17] Somewhat surprisingly, in *Gilham v Breidenbach*[18] the court held that the expression "fuck off" was to be regarded as no more than a term of abuse, rather than the withdrawal of an implied licence to enter property.

3.   User in Excess of the Licence Granted

20–009   A licensee is only entitled to use land to the extent permitted by the licence and any excessive use will constitute a trespass. For example, permission to recover a ball from a garden would not extend to playing football there. As Scrutton L.J. said in *The Carlgarth*:

> "When you invite a person into your house to use the staircase, you do not invite him to slide down the banisters."[19]

4.   Effect on Third Party Transferees of the Land

20–010   A bare licence is a purely personal interest which arises between the licensor and the licensee. It is incapable of binding a third party who acquires from the licensor title to the land to which it relates.

---

[15] *Babar v Anis* [2005] EWHC 1384; [2005] 3 F.C.R. 216.
[16] [1967] 2 Q.B. 939.
[17] See *E & L Berg Homes Ltd v Grey* (1980) 253 E.G. 473.
[18] [1982] R.T.R. 328n.
[19] [1927] P. 93 at 110.

LICENCES COUPLED WITH AN INTEREST

1. Nature of a Licence Coupled with an Interest

When the owner of land grants a person an interest or right which will only be able to be **20–011**
enjoyed by him if he enters onto his land, the grant of the right or interest will be taken to
confer a licence on the grantee such as is necessary for him to enjoy that right. For example,
in *James Jones & Sons Ltd v Earl of Tankerville*[20] a landowner had contracted to sell timber
growing on his land to a third party. Parker J. held that:

> "a contract for the sale of specific timber growing on the vendor's property, on the terms
> that such timber is cut and carried away by the purchaser certainly confers on the
> purchaser a licence to enter and cut the timber sold".

Similarly a right to take game from land will carry with it a licence to enter the land for that purpose.[21] Such licences are therefore often created by the grant of a profit à prendre,[22] and in
Hounslow LBC v Twickenham Garden Development Ltd[23] Megarry J. said "a licence to go on
land to sever and remove trees or hay, or to remove timber or hay that have already been severed,
are accepted examples of a licence coupled with an interest".[24] Such a licence will only arise if
the interest to which it is coupled is properly created. Some cases have held that a licence will
arise even where the interest granted is not a proprietary right in land. In *Vaughan v Hampson*[25]
a solicitor acting under a proxy from a creditor attended a general meeting of creditors convened
by the debtor at his solicitor's office. The solicitor refused to leave the premises when asked. The
Court of Exchequer held that the subsequent physical ejection of the solicitor was an assault
because he enjoyed a right to be present on the grounds that he enjoyed a right coupled with a
licence. In *Hurst v Picture Theatres Ltd*[26] the Court of Appeal held that a customer who had purchased a ticket for a seat at a theatre enjoyed a licence coupled with a grant and that his ejection
on the mistaken grounds that he had not paid was an assault. Buckley L.J. explained:

> "What is the grant in this case? The plaintiff in the present action paid his money to enjoy
> the sight of a particular spectacle. He was anxious to go into a picture theatre to see a
> series of views of pictures during, I suppose, an hour or a couple of hours. That which
> was granted to him was the right to enjoy looking at a spectacle, to attend a performance
> from its beginning to its end. That which was called the licence, the right to go upon the
> premises, was only something granted to him for the purpose of enabling him to have that
> which had been granted him, namely the right to see. He could not see the performance
> unless he went into the building. His right to go into the building was something given to

---

[20] [1909] 2 Ch. 440.
[21] *Frogley v Earl of Lovelace* (1859) John. 333.
[22] See above Ch. 15.
[23] [1971] Ch. 233.
[24] See also: *Wood v Manley* (1839) 11 Ad. & El. 34.
[25] (1875) 33 L.T. 15.
[26] [1915] 1 K.B. 1.

him in order to enable him to have the benefit of that which had been granted to him, namely the right to hear the opera, or see the theatrical performance, or see the moving pictures as was the case here. So that here there was a licence coupled with a grant."[27]

However in neither of these cases can it be said that the grantee enjoyed any proprietary right in the land over which he was held to have enjoyed a licence. In *Hounslow LBC v Twickenham Garden Development Ltd*[28] Megarry J. held that if such non-proprietary rights were to give rise to licences then a contractor could enjoy a licence to continue building works:

"If for this purpose 'interest' is not confined to an interest in land or in chattels on the land, what does it extend to? If a right to attend a creditor's meeting or to see a cinema performance suffices to constitute an interest, can it be said that the right and duty to do works on land fall short of being an interest? I cannot see why it should. Yet, if this be so, it is not easy to see any fair stopping place in what amounts to an interests short of any legitimate reason for being on the land."[29]

For this reason he went on hold that *Vaughan v Hampson*[30] was a "curiosity" and to conclude that a licence coupled with an interest could only arise if the interest was proprietary in nature, enjoyed either in the land itself or in chattels found on the land:

"First, as regards a licence coupled with an interest . . . I feel great doubt whether the word 'interest' means anything more than an interest in property, though it matters not whether that property is real or personal, or legal or equitable . . . I should hesitate very long before holding that a licence was coupled with an interest unless that interest was an interest in property, and that I doubt very much whether in this case the contractor's licence is coupled with an interest."[31]

2. Creation of a Licence Coupled with an Interest

20–012 Since the existence of the licence is derived from the interest to which it is coupled the licence will be created by the effective creation of the interest. In the case of a profit à prendre this will generally require a grant by deed or acquisition by prescription, but a contract for the grant of a profit creating an equitable right will also give rise to a licence.

3. Revocability of a Licence Coupled with an Interest

20–013 The nature of the interests that give rise to a licence has engendered such discussion because such licences cannot be revoked as long as the interest to which they are coupled endures.

[27] [1915] 1 K.B. 1 at 7.
[28] [1971] Ch. 233.
[29] [1971] Ch. 233 at 244.
[30] (1875) 33 L.T. 15.
[31] [1971] Ch. 233 at 254.

This was recognised in *Hounslow LBC v Twickenham Garden Development Ltd*,[32] where Megarry J. suggested that the fact that contractual licences had become capable of being irrevocable in their own right meant that there was no longer "need to torture the word 'interest' into embracing miscellaneous collections of rights".

4. Effect of a Licence Coupled with an Interest on Third Party Transferees of the Land

A licence coupled with a interest will be binding on a third party transferee of the land to which   **20–014** it relates if he acquires the land subject to the proprietary interest from which it is derived. For example, if the licensee is entitled to a profit a prendre the licence will be binding on a transferee of the servient tenement if he acquired the land subject to the burden of the profit.

CONTRACTUAL LICENCES

1. Nature of a Contractual Licence

As the name indicates, a contractual licence is a licence granted either expressly or impliedly in   **20–015** return for valuable consideration. For example, the purchase of a ticket to attend an event, whether a race meeting[33] or a cinema performance[34] will generate a contractual licence to enter the premises where the event is held. In *Ashby v Tolhurst*[35] purchase of a one-shilling ticket to use a car park at Southend was held to confer a contractual licence to park. Contractual licences are also capable of providing the basis for longer-term rights of occupation. University students with rooms in halls of residence, lodgers, hotel guests and residents of old peoples homes all have contractual licences since, as has been seen,[36] they do not enjoy the exclusive possession essential to the existence of a lease. It has been seen how in *AG Securities v Vaughan*[37] four persons occupying a flat under separate agreements for a six-month term, granted at separate times, in return for the payment of a monthly rent, were contractual licensees of the owners.

2. Creation of a Contractual Licence

A contractual licence will only come into existence if the licensee enters into a valid contract   **20–016** with the licensor. The precise terms of the licence will depend upon the terms of the contract.

---

[32] [1971] Ch. 233 at 254.
[33] *Wood v Leadbitter* (1845) 13 M. & W. 838.
[34] *Hurst v Picture Theatres* Ltd [1915] 1 K.B. 1; *Clore v Theatrical Properties Ltd and Westby & Co Ltd* [1936] 3 All E.R. 483.
[35] [1937] 2 K.B. 242.
[36] See above, Ch.9.
[37] [1990] 1 A.C. 417.

For example, a contractual licence to attend a theatrical performance will terminate when the performance is over. A contractual licence for residential occupation may be held to contain implied terms that the licensor will ensure that the licensee enjoys quiet possession,[38] and that the premises are fit for the purposes envisaged when the licence was granted.[39] As a licence is not an interest in land the contract need not be made in writing in compliance with s.2 of the Law of Property (Miscellaneous Provisions) Act 1989.

3. Revocability of a Contractual Licence

(a) *Problem of Revocability*

20–017   One central question which has arisen in the context of contractual licences is whether they can be revoked at will by the licensor. There is no doubt that where such a revocation would amount to a breach of contract the licensee is entitled to a remedy of damages to compensate him for any loss suffered as a result of the breach. However, if the court were to grant specific performance of the contract granting the licence this would have the effect of enabling the licensee to assert his contractual rights, rendering the licence irrevocable in practice. For example, if a customer purchases a ticket to watch a film at a multiplex cinema, can the management simply demand that he leave the premises, even though the film has not finished and he has not in any way broken the terms of his licence by wrong behaviour, or is the customer entitled to remain viewing? If the management uses force to remove him against his will this may amount to an assault if he enjoyed a continued right to remain on the premises, but not if he had become a trespasser.

(b) *Revocable at Common Law*

20–018   At common law a contractual licence is revocable at any time by the licensor, and the licensee's only remedy is to recover damages for breach of contract. In *Wood v Leadbitter*[40] the plaintiff had purchased a four-day ticket for a race meeting at Doncaster. He refused to leave when requested and was removed by force. He claimed that this amounted to an assault on the grounds that he enjoyed an irrevocable licence for the duration of the races. Alderson B. held that as the plaintiff did not enjoy a licence coupled with a grant it remained revocable, and that, although he might have a remedy for breach of contract against the owners of the racecourse because there had been no good reason for terminating the contract, their actions were not an assault because the revocation had rendered him a trespasser. This approach was also applied in *Thompson v Park*[41] where the owners of two prep schools agreed that they should be amalgamated for the duration of the war, and that the defendant and his pupils could enter and use the plaintiff's premises. After a year the plaintiff demanded that the defendant

---

[38] *Smith v Nottinghamshire C C*, *The Times*, November 13, 1981.
[39] *Wettern Electrical Ltd v Welsh Development Agency* [1983] Q.B. 796.
[40] (1845) 13 M. & W. 838. See also *Kerrison v Smith* [1897] 2 Q.B. 455.
[41] [1944] K.B. 408.

and his boys leave the premises, but the defendant forcibly re-entered after the Christmas holidays. The Court of Appeal held that the defendant had committed a trespass because the licence had been effectively revoked.

(c) *Potentially Irrevocable in Equity*

(i) An Injunction to Prevent Revocation

Whereas at common law a contractual licence remains revocable by the licensor at any time, **20–019** the courts have developed the jurisdiction of equity, and in particular the availability of an injunction to restrain a breach of contract, to render a contractual licence irrevocable. The House of Lords confirmed this possibility in *Millennium Productions Ltd v Winter Garden Theatre (London) Ltd*.[42] The defendants had granted the plaintiffs a licence to use their theatre for six months, with options to renew, for the production of plays, concerts or ballets. The options to renew were exercised and after several years' occupation the defendants purported to revoke the licence despite the fact that the plaintiffs were not in breach of its terms. The Court of Appeal had held that the licence was irrevocable because the contract granted the defendants no express power to revoke it. Lord Greene M.R. in the House of Lords explained the basis on which a contractual licence might be found to be irrevocable:

> "The [defendants] have purported to determine the licence. If I have correctly construed the contract their doing so was a breach of contract. It may well be that, in the old days, that would only have given rise to a right to sue in damages. The licence would have stood revoked, but after the expiration of what was the appropriate period of grace the licensees would have been trespassers and could have been expelled and their right would have been to sue for damages for breach of contract . . . But the matter requires to be considered further, because the power of equity to grant an injunction to restrain a breach of contract is, of course, a power exercisable in any court. The general rule is that before equity will grant such an injunction, there must be, on the construction of the contract, a negative clause express or implied. In the present case it seems to me that the grant of an option which, if I am right, is an irrevocable option, must imply a negative undertaking by the licensor not to revoke it. That being so, in my opinion such a contract could be enforced in equity by an injunction."[43]

In the event the House of Lords held that the contract could not be construed so as to find a term that it was irrevocable, but it accepted the principle that equity would enforce a licence where there was a contractual term that it should be irrevocable. Where the licensee has not yet entered into possession of the premises the same effect can be achieved by the award of the equitable remedy of specific performance. In *Verrall v Great Yarmouth BC*[44] the defendant council had agreed to allow the National Front to use a hall for its annual conference. After a change of political control the council repudiated the contract. The Court of

---

[42] [1946] 1 All E.R. 678.
[43] [1946] 1 All E.R. 678 at 684.
[44] [1981] Q.B. 202.

Appeal held that the principle in *Millennium Productions Ltd v Winter Garden Theatre (London) Ltd* was applicable, and ordered specific performance of the contract.

(ii)   Is there a Contractual Term that the Licence should be Irrevocable?

20–020   The central question is therefore whether a contractual licence contains a term, either express or implied, that it is not to be revoked by the licensor. Such terms are relatively easy to find where a ticket is sold for the viewing of a particular event. As Viscount Simon commented in *Millennium Productions Ltd v Winter Garden Theatre Ltd*:

> "the implication of the arrangement . . . plainly is that the ticket entitles the purchaser to enter, and if he behaves himself, to remain on the premises until the end of the event which he has paid his money to see."[45]

For this reason he held that the decision in *Wood v Leadbitter*[46] was explicable only on the grounds of the strict rules of pleading existing at the time that it was decided, and that following the fusion of law and equity it should no longer be regarded as good authority. In contrast the decision in *Hurst v Picture Theatres Ltd*[47] was approved. Although it can be criticised in as far as it suggests that the licence concerned was coupled with an interest, the Court of Appeal noted as an alternative basis for the decision that there was an irrevocable contractual licence. Buckley L.J. stated:

> "If there be a licence with an agreement not to revoke the licence, that, if given for value, is an enforceable right. If the facts here are . . . that the licence was a licence to enter the building and see the spectacle from its commencement until its termination, then there was included in that contract a contract not to revoke the licence until the play had run to its termination."

Hurst involved a licence for a short period which was reasonably clearly delineated: the duration of the performance or screening of the film. It can readily be understood how a term can be implied that the licence is irrevocable during that period. The courts have similarly been willing to imply a term into a licence of indefinite duration that it can be revoked on reasonable notice. As was pointed out in *Prudential Assurance Co Ltd v London Residuary Body*,[48] it is hard to contemplate parties entering into a hiring arrangement which can last "until the crack of doom" unless both parties agree to its termination. By way of example, in *Millennium Productions Ltd v Winter Garden Theatre Ltd*[49] the owners of a performance venue entered into a contract to allow the plaintiffs to use it for their productions. No time limit was specified for the agreement. The House of Lords held that although it was clear that the parties did not intend that the licensor should be able to make an immediate out of hand revocation, it was not intended that it

---

[45] [1948] A.C. 173.
[46] (1845) 13 M. & W. 838.
[47] [1915] 1 K.B. 1.
[48] [1992] 2 A.C. 386 (this was in the context of a lease, but the same principles apply).
[49] [1948] A.C. 173.

should be perpetual. Lord McDermott concluded that there was an implied term allowing the licensor to terminate the licence after a year by a reasonable period of notice. However it is not impossible to find that a contract for a longer-term occupation contains an implied term that it is irrevocable if the duration of the agreement has been specified. In *Hounslow LBC v Twickenham Garden Developments Ltd*[50] one question was whether builders who had entered into a contract with a council were entitled to remain in possession of the site. Megarry J. held that they were entitled to a contractual licence which contained an implied term not to revoke:

> "Now in this case the contract is one for the execution of specified works on the site during a specified period which is still running. The contract confers on each party specified rights on specified events to determine the employment of the contractor under the contract. In those circumstances, I think that there must be at least an implied negative obligation of the borough not to revoke any licence (otherwise than in accordance with the contract) while the period is still running."[51]

Although irrevocable contractual licences have usually been found in commercial contexts, they have sometimes been found to have been granted in family circumstances. In *Tanner v Tanner*[52] a milkman who was unhappy with his marriage got a girl pregnant. She took his name and became known as Mrs Tanner. After the birth of twin daughters they decided to purchase a house to provide a home. It was purchased in his name and she left her rent-controlled flat to move in with the children. He never lived there and after three years he demanded that she leave so that the house could be sold. The Court of Appeal held that she enjoyed a contractual licence to occupy the house which was irrevocable. Lord Denning M.R. explained: **20–021**

> "It is said that they were only licensees—bare licensees—under a licence revocable at will: and that the plaintiff was entitled in law to turn her and the twins out on a moments notice. I cannot believe that this is the law . . . She herself said in evidence: 'the house was supposed to be ours until the children left school.' It seems to me that enables an inference to be drawn, namely, that in all the circumstances it is to be implied that she had a licence—a contractual licence—to have accommodation in the house for herself and the children as long as they were of school age and the accommodation was reasonably required. There was, it is true, no express contract to that effect, but the circumstances are such that the court should imply a contract to that effect . . . if therefore the defendant had sought an injunction restraining the plaintiff from determining the licence, it should have been granted. The order for possession ought not to have been made."[53]

Although the decision supports the general rule that a contractual licence subject to an implied term restricting revocability will be enforced by equity, it is questionable whether the court should imply a contractual licence in such circumstances. It is highly artificial, as there is no intention for the parties to enter into a contractual relationship, and the implication is merely

---

[50] [1971] Ch. 233.
[51] [1971] Ch. 233 at 247.
[52] [1975] 1 W.L.R. 1347.
[53] [1975] 1 W.L.R. 1347 at 1350. See also *Hardwick v Johnson* [1978] 1 W.L.R. 683; *Chandler v Kerley* [1978] 1 W.L.R. 693.

an ex post facto rationalisation of the desire to find a remedy to do justice between the parties where an informal undertaking has not been kept.[54] Proprietary estoppel provides the appropriate basis for establishing an entitlement to occupation in such cases, not an implied contract.[55]

4. Effect of Contractual Licences on Third Party Transferees of the Land

(a) *Contractual Licences Historically Incapable of Binding Transferees of the Land*

20–022 The traditional common law position is that since a licence, whether contractual or not, is a purely personal interest between the licensor and the licensee, it is incapable of affecting third parties who acquire the land, or an interest in it, from the licensor. This approach was applied by the House of Lords in *King v David Allen & Sons (Billposting) Ltd*.[56] The plaintiff had been granted a contractual licence by the defendant to put up posters and advertisements on the flank wall of a cinema which a company intended to build on his land. The defendant subsequently leased his land to the company, which entered into possession and built the cinema, but then refused to allow the plaintiffs to post their bills on the wall. Buckmaster L.C. explained why the licence was unenforceable against the company, thus leaving the plaintiff with merely a remedy against the defendant for breach of contract:

> "The matter then is left in this way. There is a contract between the [plaintiffs] and the [defendant] which creates nothing but a personal obligation . . . It is difficult to see how it can be reasonably urged that anything beyond personal rights was ever contemplated by the parties. Those rights have undoubtedly been taken away by the action on the part of the company, who have been enabled to prevent the [plaintiffs] from exercising their rights owing to the lease granted by the [defendant], and he is accordingly liable in damages."

In *Clore v Theatrical Properties Ltd*[57] the Court of Appeal similarly held that the grant of a contractual licence to enjoy front of house rights of a theatre was a purely personal right and therefore only binding between the parties who enjoyed privity of contract.

(b) *Irrevocable Contractual Licences Elevated to Proprietary Status*

(i) Precedents for the Elevation of Contractual Rights to Proprietary Rights

20–023 Although contractual licences were traditionally regarded as personal rights only, there are precedents of other essentially contractual rights being elevated to the status of proprietary

[54] *Horrocks v Forray* [1976] 1 W.L.R. 230.
[55] *Coombes v Smith* [1986] 1 W.L.R. 808.
[56] [1916] 2 A.C. 54.
[57] [1936] 3 All E.R. 483.

interests. For example in *Tulk v Moxhay*[58] the doctrine was developed that the burden of a restrictive covenant was an interest in land capable of passing to bind a successor in title to the original convenantor. In a series of decisions Lord Denning M.R. attempted to elevate the status of a contractual licence to a proprietary right capable of binding third party transferees of the land.

(ii) Contractual Licences Capable of Binding a Person Claiming Title Through the Licensor

In *Errington v Errington and Woods*[59] Denning L.J. stated that the recognition by the House of Lords that a contractual licence could be irrevocable in equity should be developed a stage further so that such a licence would be capable of binding a transferee of the land:

20–024

> "Law and equity have been fused for nearly 80 years, and since 1948 it has been clear that, as a result of the fusion, a licensor will not be permitted to eject a licensee in breach of a contract to allow him to remain: see *Winter Garden Theatre London v Millennium Productions Ltd*[60] per Lord Greene, and in the House of Lords per Lord Simon; nor in breach of a promise on which the licensee has acted, even though he gave no value for it: see Foster v Robinson[61] where Sir Raymond Evershed M.R. said that as a result of the oral agreement to let the man stay, he was entitled as licensee to occupy the premises without any payment of rent for the rest of his days. This infusion of equity means that contractual licences now have a force and validity of their own and cannot be revoked in breach of contract. Neither the licensor nor anyone who claims through him can disregard the contract except a purchaser for value without notice."[62]

The case concerned a house which had been purchased by a father, with the help of a mortgage, to provide a home for his son. He had promised his son and daughter-in-law that if they continued to pay the mortgage instalments he would transfer the house to them when the mortgage was discharged. On his death the father left all his property to his widow. The son left his wife, who continued to live in the house, and returned to live with his mother. The mother sought possession of the house, which the Court of Appeal refused on the grounds that her daughter-in-law was entitled to occupy as a contractual licensee for as long as she paid the mortgage instalments. It therefore seems that a contractual licence was held enforceable against a successor in title to the original licensor, and for this reason the decision was the subject of academic[63] and judicial[64] criticism.

---

[58] (1848) 2 Ph. 774.
[59] [1952] 1 K.B. 290.
[60] [1946] 1 All E.R. 678; [1948] A.C. 173.
[61] [1951] 1 K.B. 149.
[62] [1951] 1 K.B. 149.
[63] (1952) 68 L.Q.R. 337 (Wade); (1953) 69 L.Q.R. 466 (Hargreaves); cf. (1953) 16 M.L.R. 1.
[64] *National Provincial Bank Ltd v Hastings Car Mart Ltd* [1964] Ch. 665, per Russell L.J.; *National Provincial Bank Ltd v Ainsworth* [1965] A.C. 1175; *Re Solomon* [1967] Ch. 573, per Goff J.

(iii) Contractual Licences as Equitable Interests in Land

20–025   In *Binions v Evans*[65] Lord Denning M.R. followed his earlier decision as authority for the proposition that a contractual licence gives rise to an equitable interest in land. The defendant's husband had been employed by the Tredegar Estate and lived rent-free in a cottage which it owned. On his death she was allowed to remain in the cottage and they entered an agreement that she was to reside in the cottage "as tenant at will . . . rent free for the remainder of her life", in return for which she agreed to keep the cottage in good repair and to manage the garden. The cottage was subsequently sold by the estate to the plaintiffs, who purchased the land at a reduced price because of a term in the contract of sale by which they agreed to take the land subject to the widow's interest. The plaintiffs then gave the defendant notice to quit the cottage. The Court of Appeal held that she was entitled to remain in occupation of the cottage, but for a variety of reasons. Megaw and Stephenson L.JJ. held that she was entitled to a life interest taking effect under the Settled Land Act 1925. Neither felt it necessary to consider whether a contractual licence was a proprietary right capable of binding third party successors to the licensor's title. Lord Denning M.R. however held that her right was in the nature of a contractual licence, and that it bound the plaintiffs because they had acquired the cottage, title to which was unregistered, with notice of its existence. He stated:

> "What is the status of such a licence as this? There are a number of cases in the books in which a similar right has been given. They show that a right to occupy for life, arising by contract, gives to the occupier an equitable interest in the land; just as it does when it arises under a settlement . . . The courts of equity will not allow the landlord to turn the occupier out in breach of contract; see *Foster v Robinson*[66]; nor will they allow a purchaser to turn her out if he bought with knowledge of her right—*Errington v Errington and Woods*.[67]"[68]

He also considered that, in the event that the contractual licence did not give rise to an immediate equitable proprietary interest, a constructive trust of her right to occupy would be imposed on the plaintiff purchasers because they had agreed to take the land expressly subject to her interest and it would be inequitable to turn her out. Subsequent cases followed the judgment of Lord Denning M.R. and held that occupational rights under an irrevocable contractual licence were capable of binding successors in title, as for example in *Re Sharpe (A Bankrupt)*[69] where Browne-Wilkinson J. held that a contractual licence enjoyed by an aunt to occupy a house owned by her nephew was binding on his trustee in bankruptcy.[70]

---

[65] [1972] Ch. 359.

[66] [1951] 1 K.B. 149.

[67] [1952] 1 K.B. 290.

[68] [1972] Ch. 359 at 367. Lord Denning uses an argument per saltum: having stated one proposition, he jumps to another which does not logically follow from the first. Because a landowner entering into a contract makes a promise, it does not inevitably follow that a successor in title of the landowner will be bound by that promise.

[69] [1980] 1 W.L.R. 219.

[70] See also *DHN Food Distributors Ltd v Tower Hamlets LBC* [1976] 1 W.L.R. 852.

(c) *Irrevocable Contractual Licences are Purely Personal Rights: A Re-assertion of the Traditional Orthodoxy*

The law relating to the status of contractual licences was examined in detail in *Ashburn Anstalt v Arnold*.[71] After a thorough review of the history of the law in this area the Court of Appeal categorically rejected the proposition that a contractual licence was in and of itself a proprietary interest in land capable of binding successors in title to the licensor. The court reviewed all the authorities prior to *Errington v Errington and Woods*,[72] and in particular the House of Lords decisions in *Edwards v Barrington*[73] and *King v David Allen*,[74] and concluded that:

20–026

> "Down to this point we do not think that there is any serious doubt as to the law. A mere contractual licence to occupy land is not binding on a purchaser of he land even though he has notice of the licence."[75]

The court then reviewed the authorities where it had been suggested that a contractual licence was in and of itself capable of existing as a proprietary interest, and considered that they were inconsistent with those earlier House of Lords authorities:

> "It must, we think, be very doubtful whether this court's decision in *Errington v Erington and Woods*[76] is consistent with its earlier decisions in *Daly v Edwards*[77]; *Frank Warr & Co. v London County Council*[78] and *Clore v Theatrical Properties Ltd.*[79] That decision cannot be said to be in conflict with any later decision of the House of Lords, because the House expressly left the effect of a contractual licence open in the *Hastings Car Mart* case. But there must be very real doubts whether *Errington* can be reconciled with the earlier decisions of the House of Lords in *Edwards v Barrington*[80] and *King v David Allen and Sons (Billposting) Ltd.*[81] It would seem that we must follow those cases or choose between the two lines of authority. It is not, however, necessary to consider those alternative courses in detail, since in our judgment the House of Lords cases, whether or not as a matter of strict precedent they conclude this question, state the correct principle which we should follow ... Before the *Errington* case the law appears to have been clear and well understood. It rested on an important and intelligible distinction between contractual obligations which gave rise to no estate or interest in the land and proprietary rights which, by definition, did. The far-reaching statement of principle in *Errington* was not

[71] [1989] Ch. 1. See: [1988] C.L.J. 353 (Oakley); [1988] Conv. 201 (Thompson); (1988) 104 L.Q.R. 175 (Sparkes); (1988) 51 M.L.R. 226 (Hill).
[72] [1952] 1 K.B. 290.
[73] (1901) 85 L.T. 650.
[74] 1916] 2 A.C. 54.
[75] [1989] Ch. 1 at 15.
[76] [1952] 1 K.B. 290.
[77] 83 L.T. 548.
[78] [1904] 1 K.B. 713.
[79] [1936] 3 All E.R. 483.
[80] (1901) 85 L.T. 650.
[81] [1916] 2 A.C. 54.

supported by authority, not necessary for the decision of the case and per incuriam in the sense that it was made without reference to authorities which, if they would not have compelled, would surely have persuaded the court to adopt a different ratio."[82]

(d) *Present Status of Contractual Licences*

(i) Contractual Licences are Incapable of Existing as Proprietary Rights in and of themselves

20–027   Despite the force and detailed reasoning of the Court of Appeal in *Ashburn Anstalt v Arnold*[83] and the clear renunciation of the *Errington* doctrine that an irrevocable contractual licence is a property right capable of binding third parties, the decision does not finally settle the matter. Since the Court of Appeal held that the defendant was entitled to a lease rather than a contractual licence, the comments relating to such licences were strictly obiter to the decision and do not form part of the ratio of the case. The Court of Appeal also accepted the possibility that the law might develop in the future. However, subsequent cases have treated it as repudiating the claimed proprietary status of contractual licences,[84] for example in *Camden LBC v Shortlife Community Housing*[85] Millet J. stated that the Court of Appeal had "finally repudiated the heretical view that a contractual licence creates an interest in land capable of binding third parties".

(ii) A Contractual Licence Given Effect Against a Third Party by Means of an Independent Constructive Trust

20–028   Although *Ashburn Anstalt v Arnold* effectively means that contractual licences are not to be regarded as proprietary interests in land it does not follow that there are no circumstances in which a successor in title to a licensor will acquire his interest subject to a pre-existing contractual licence. The Court of Appeal accepted that if the circumstances of acquisition entitled the court to impose a constructive trust on the successor in title to the licensor then a contractual licence would be binding on him, not in and of itself, but as a consequence of the constructive trust.[86] As has already been noted, this was a second ground for Lord Denning M.R.'s conclusion in *Binions v Evans*[87] that the contractual licence of the widow should be binding on the purchaser of the estate. The Court of Appeal considered the submission that there was general rule that "when a person sells land 'subject to' a contractual licence the court will impose a constructive trust upon the purchaser to give effect to the licence" but rejected it as too wide:

---

[82] [1989] Ch. 1 at 21–22.
[83] [1989] Ch. 1.
[84] *Canadian Imperial Bank of Commerce v Bello* (1992) 64 P. & C.R. 48.
[85] (1992) 90 L.G.R. 358 at 373.
[86] See *Lyus v Prowsa Developments* [1982] 1 W.L.R. 1044.
[87] [1972] Ch. 359.

"The court will not impose a constructive trust unless it is satisfied that the conscience of the estate owner is affected. The mere fact that that land is expressed to be conveyed 'subject to' a contract does not necessarily imply that the grantee is to be under an obligation, not otherwise existing, to give effect to the provisions of the contract. The fact that the conveyance is expressed to be subject to the contract may often . . . be at least as consistent with an intention merely to protect the grantor against claims by the grantee as an intention to impose an obligation on the grantee. The words 'subject to' will, of course, impose notice. But notice is not enough to impose on somebody an obligation to give effect to a contract into which he did not enter."[88]

The court considered the facts as if there had been a contractual licence and held that they would not have imposed a constructive trust. The major factor seems to have been the absence of any reduction in the price paid by the plaintiffs for the title to the land in consequence of their agreement to take it expressly "subject to" the defendant's rights. In contrast, the Court of Appeal held that Lord Denning M.R. had rightly found a constructive trust in *Binions v Evans*,[89] because it was established as a fact that the plaintiffs had purchased the cottage from the estate at a reduced price to reflect the fact that it was sold subject to the widow's occupancy. It therefore seems possible to conclude that a person who acquires land at a reduced value to reflect the fact that they have expressly agreed to take it subject to a pre-existing irrevocable contractual licence will not be permitted to assert that the licence is not binding because it is incapable of existing as a proprietary interest in land. Rather he will be subject to a constructive trust requiring him to give effect to his agreement to continue to allow the licensee to enjoy his entitlement.

ESTOPPEL LICENCES

1. Nature of an Estoppel Licence

It has been seen how a licence can confer a right to occupy land. An estoppel licence is a licence which arises in favour of the licensor by means of the doctrine of proprietary estoppel. The distinction between estoppel licences and the three varieties of licence which have been examined so far therefore lies in the manner by which they are brought into existence.   **20–029**

2. Creation of Estoppel Licences

(a) *Remedies Granted Under the General Doctrine of Proprietary Estoppel*

Estoppel licences are one of a number of potential remedies which may be awarded by a court to a person who is able to show that he or she is entitled to an interest by way of proprietary   **20–030**

---

[88] [1989] Ch. 1 at 25–26.
[89] [1972] Ch. 359.

estoppel. The principles of proprietary estoppel are founded in older equity cases[90] but have been brought to increasing prominence since the middle of this century. The general doctrine of proprietary estoppel was examined in detail in the previous chapter as a discrete area, and only a brief summary of its requirements will be given here.

(b) *Requirements of Proprietary Estoppel: Establishing an "Equity"*

20–031   A person seeking to claim an interest in land by way of proprietary estoppel will have to establish that they have an "equity" which calls to be remedied. This simply means that in the circumstances they are entitled to some variety of interest in land as against the owner. An "equity" will be raised whenever it would be unconscionable[91] for the owner to land to deny an interest, and this will be so when three elements are established:

(i)   An Assurance

20–032   The owner of land must have given an assurance to the person claiming an "equity" by way of proprietary estoppel that he or she would be entitled to some interest in relation to his land. This representation can be made actively or passively by failing to prevent the claimant acting when it was obvious that he was doing so with the expectation of enjoying some interest in the land.

(ii)   Reliance

20–033   The claimant will only be able to assert an "equity" if he can demonstrate that he acted in reliance on the assurance. Thus changed conduct for reasons of love or affection may not necessarily be regarded as a consequence of the assurance.[92]

(iii)   Detriment

20–034   An equity will only arise in favour of a claimant who has acted to his or her detriment in reliance upon the assurance. It is this element of detriment which renders it unconscionable for the owner to rely on his strict legal rights and to deny the claimant any entitlement to the land. In more recent cases it has been said that there is detriment whenever a claimant has changed her position in reliance on a representation.[93]

---

[90] *Ramsden v Dyson* (1866) L.R. 1 H.L. 129; *Willmott v Barber* (1880) 15 Ch.D. 96.
[91] See *Taylors Fashions Ltd v Liverpool Victoria Trustees Co Ltd* [1982] Q.B. 133; *Lim Teng Huan v Ang Swee Chuan* [1992] 1 W.L.R. 113.
[92] See *Coombes v Smith* [1986] 1 W.L.R. 808.
[93] *Grant v Edwards* [1986] Ch. 638; *Re Basham (deceased)* [1986] 1 W.L.R. 1498.

(c) Remedies Arising by Proprietary Estoppel: Satisfying the Equity

When a claimant has established that he is entitled to an "equity" by way of proprietary **20–035** estoppel this does not of itself answer the question as to the type of interest that arises in his favour. It is for the court to determine the appropriate remedy and to award the claimant what it determines, in its discretion, is the appropriate interest to "satisfy" the equity which has been raised. There is some dispute as to whether the court has a wide discretion to award whatever remedy it wishes, or whether the prime object of the court is to try to fulfil the expectations of the parties. A wide range of interests have been awarded by way of proprietary estoppel, including a transfer of the freehold ownership of the land,[94] a leasehold interest[95] and an easement.[96] In some cases a purely financial remedy has been awarded, usually because a breakdown of relationships has made it impossible for the parties to share occupation of the land in question.[97] However one common remedy has been the award of an occupational licence of the land and this is the interest with which this section is concerned.

(d) Award of an Occupational Licence as a Remedy for Proprietary Estoppel

In a number of cases it has been held that the appropriate interest to satisfy the equity raised is the **20–036** award of a licence entitling the claimant to occupy the land subject to the estoppel. In *Plimmer v Mayor of Wellington*,[98] one of the oldest cases on what today would be recognised as proprietary estoppel, the claimant was held to have become entitled to an irrevocable licence to occupy a jetty and wharf when the landowner had encouraged him to make improvements to it. In *Inwards v Baker*[99] the Court of Appeal held that a son who had been encouraged to build a bungalow on land owned by his father was entitled to an irrevocable licence to occupy the land for as long as he wanted. Similarly in *Greasley v Cooke*[100] a maid who had cohabited with the son of the owner of a house and looked after members of his family after encouragement that she was to regard the property as her home for the rest of her life was held to be entitled to remain there as long as she wished. In *Re Sharp (A Bankrupt)*[101] Browne-Wilkinson J. held that an aunt who had lent money to her nephew in return for an assurance that she would be able to live with him and his wife for life was entitled to an irrevocable licence to occupy until the loan had been repaid.

3. Revocability of an Estoppel Licence

Whether an estoppel licence is revocable by the licensor will depend upon the precise terms **20–037** of the licence awarded by the court. As has been noted in the examples cited above, the courts

[94] *Pascoe v Turner* [1979] 1 W.L.R. 431.
[95] *Griffiths v Williams* (1977) 248 E.G. 947.
[96] *Crabb v Arun DC* [1976] Ch. 179.
[97] *Dodsworth v Dodsworth* (1973) 228 E.G. 1115.
[98] (1884) 9 App. Cas. 699.
[99] [1965] 2 Q.B. 29.
[100] [1980] 1 W.L.R. 1306.
[101] [1980] 1 W.L.R. 219.

have awarded irrevocable licences where this was clearly the expectation of the licensee. As such, the licensor will be unable to terminate the licence and the licensee would be entitled to equitable remedies to enforce his interest.

4. Effect of Estoppel Licences on Third Party Transferees of the Land

(a) *Differentiating Between the Equity and the Remedy*

20–038   Despite the development of the proprietary estoppel as a means of acquiring a right to occupy land as a licensee there is little authority as to the question whether an estoppel licence is capable of binding a successor in title to the licensor obliged to observe it. This problem is complicated by the theoretical question whether an interest by way of proprietary estoppel arises at the date of the events giving rise to the "equity" or at the time when the court awards the remedy to "satisfy" the equity. The better view seems to be that before the court grants a particular right in satisfaction the equity raised by the estoppel is an inchoate interest. Different considerations may apply to the question whether an inchoate equity yet to be satisfied is capable of binding a transferee of the land to which it relates, and whether a remedy granted in satisfaction of such an equity is capable of affecting successors in title.

(b) *Can an Inchoate Equity Bind a Successor in Title?*

20–039   Prior to the Land Registration Act 2002 it was uncertain whether an inchoate estoppel equity was a proprietary interest in land, and therefore capable of binding a third party. However s.116 now provides that, for the avoidance of doubt, in relation to registered land "an equity by estoppel" has effect from the time that it arises as an interest capable of binding successors in title. It thus follows that an estoppel equity in registered land is capable of gaining priority over subsequent interests. An estoppel equity will only gain priority over a subsequent registered disposition for valuable consideration if it is protected by entry of a notice on the register, or if it ranks as an overriding interest because the owner is in actual occupation of the land.[102] The position is less clear in unregistered land, but a number of authorities suggest that an inchoate equity is capable of binding third parties, so that the claimant can obtain a remedy in satisfaction against a successor in title.[103] If this is correct then issues of priority will be determined by the operation of the traditional doctrine of notice, because an estoppel equity is not a registrable land charge.

---

[102] Land Registration Act 2002 s.29 and Sch.3 para.2.
[103] *ER Ives Investment Ltd v High* [1967] 2 Q.B. 379 at 395; *Re Sharp* [1980] 1 W.L.R. 219 at 225; *Sen v Headley* [1991] Ch. 425, 440; *Voyce v Voyce* (1991) 62 P. & C.R. 290 at 294; *Milton v Proctor* (1989) N.S.W. Conv.R. 55.

(c) *Can an Estoppel Licence Awarded in Satisfaction of an Equity Bind a Successor in Title to the Licensor?*

If a claimant has been awarded an irrevocable licence to occupy by the court as a remedy in **20–040** satisfaction of his equity it is unclear whether the licence is capable of binding a third party who acquires the land from the estopped licensor. Some authorities seem to take the view that the estoppel licence is capable of binding a third party successor in title to the land. In *Re Sharp (A Bankrupt)*[104] Browne-Wilkinson J. felt compelled to find that an estoppel licence was binding on the trustee in bankruptcy of the licensor, and potentially upon a purchaser of the legal title from the trustee, because of the authorities at that date holding that a irrevocable contractual licence was a property right binding a third party acquiring the title with notice. However following the decision of the Court of Appeal in *Ashburn Anstalt v Arnold*[105] an irrevocable licence is not of capable of binding a successor in title to the land in the absence of a constructive trust. The court doubted whether there were any grounds for finding a constructive trust against the trustee or purchaser in *Re Sharpe*.[106] As a matter of theory it seems that any right which is awarded in satisfaction of an estoppel equity must, from that point onwards, be treated according to its nature.[107] For example, if the court awards an easement or a lease in satisfaction of an estoppel equity the question whether a successor in title to the land affected will be subject to the easement or lease must be answered by application of the appropriate priorities rules relating to easements and leases respectively. Since present authorities maintain that an irrevocable licence is only able to bind a successor in title who takes the land subject to a constructive trust, a licence generated by estoppel should only be capable of binding a successor in title to the licensor if the stringent requirement for a constructive trust are met. There is no reason why a licence arising by estoppel should be treated any more favourably than a contractual licence which is expressly granted in return for consideration provided by the licensee.[108]

(d) *Inappropriateness of the Estoppel Licence as a Means of Satisfying Expectations of Residential Occupation*

The problems occasioned by the non-proprietary status of licences and the fact that they will **20–041** not bind successors in title to the licensor may simply mean that they are an inappropriate means of satisfying the equity raised by estoppel when the clear expectation of the claimant is that he or she is to be entitled to live rent free in the property for the rest of their life. The courts should perhaps avoid the use of licences altogether in such instances and award appropriate proprietary rights to achieve the same result. For example, in *Griffiths v Williams*[109] Goff J. held that the estoppel equity of a woman who had lived most of her life in her mother's

---

[104] [1980], WLR 219.
[105] [1989] Ch. 1.
[106] [1989] Ch. 1 at 25.
[107] [1991] Conv. 36 (Battersby).
[108] See also (1994) 14 L.S. 147 (Baughen).
[109] (1977) 248 E.G. 947.

house caring for her and improving the property because she expected to be entitled to live there for the rest of her life could be satisfied against the granddaughter to whom the mother had left the house on her death by the grant of a lease determinable upon death, with no power to assign, at a nominal rent. In many of the cases where an estoppel licence was found the appropriate remedy would probably have been a life interest for the claimant, which would have perfectly satisfied their expectations. However, there was a marked reluctance to grant such an entitlement in satisfaction since it would have the effect of subjecting the land in question to a strict settlement under the Settled Land Act 1925. This would have the unacceptable consequence that the life tenant would be entitled to the legal title to the land and the concomitant powers of management and disposition, which would far exceed the scope of any expectations. However, with the abolition of the strict settlement and the introduction of the new unitary trust of land by the Trusts of Land and Appointment of Trustees Act 1996,[110] where the legal title can be retained by the trustees along with all the powers of disposition, it may be that a life interest under such a trust of land is a much more appropriate means of satisfying the estoppel equity where the expectation is of residency for life. As proprietary interests in their own right, leases or life interests awarded in satisfaction of an estoppel equity would certainly be capable of binding a transferee of the land.

Another alternative, which would also avoid the difficulties associated with residential licences, would be for the court to award the claimant a purely financial remedy in satisfaction of the estoppel equity. In the previous chapter it was seen that in *Campbell v Griffin*[111] and *Jennings v Rice*[112] the Court of Appeal granted claimants who had been promised a home for life financial compensation, because it was felt that the award of the ownership of the property, or of a right to reside for life, would be disproportionate to the detriment suffered.

Occupational Rights in the Family Home

1. Introduction to Occupational Rights in the Family Home

20–042   In many cases today where a couple is cohabiting in residential property both partners will be entitled to occupy the premises, either as co-owners of the legal title or as the beneficiaries of a trust of land. This reflects the modern reality that most women, whether married or cohabiting, make some form of financial contribution to the acquisition of their family home, or are more able to insist that it should be owned jointly. However where a partner has no proprietary interest in the family home the question arises as to whether she (or, less usually, he) has any rights of occupation. Such rights will prove particularly important when the relationship breaks down, since the owner may seek to claim possession against the non-owning partner. The law has developed so that occupational rights arise in favour of spouse and civil partners, by common law and by statute, but not in favour of unmarried cohabitees.

---

[110] See Ch.14.
[111] [2001] EWCA Civ 990.
[112] [2002] EWCA Civ 159.

2. Non-statutory Occupation Rights in the Family Home

(a) *Common Law Right of the Spouse to Occupy the Matrimonial Home*

In *National Provincial Bank v Hastings Car Mart Ltd* the House of Lords recognised that at **20–043** common law a wife was entitled to occupy her matrimonial home, and that this right was not a form of licence but arose by virtue of her status as a wife. Lord Upjohn stated:

> "I think a great deal of the trouble that has arisen in this branch of the law is by reason of attaching to the wife the label of 'licensee'. But a wife does not remain lawfully in the matrimonial home by leave or licence of her husband as the owner of the property. She remains there because as a result of the status of marriage it is her right and duty so to do and if her husband fails in his duty to remain there that cannot affect her right to do so. She is not a trespasser, she is not a licensee of her husband, she is lawfully there as a wife, the situation is one sui generis."[113]

Although most of the cases concern the right of wives to occupy, the principle also extends to husbands, but it does not apply to those who are unmarried.

The common law spousal right of occupation is a personal interest enforceable only against the other spouse. As Lord Denning M.R. stated in *Gurasz v Gurasz*:

> "This right is a personal right which belongs to her as a wife. It is not a proprietary right. It is not available against third persons. It is only available against the husband."[114]

The common law right of occupation is therefore incapable (at common law) of binding a transferee of the land, although the effect of the new provision in the Land Registration Act 2002 that "mere equities" are capable of binding successors in title[115] has yet to be tested. The reasons why the House of Lords considered that the matrimonial right of occupation should not bind successors in title, even with notice, remain valid. It remains to be seen how the issues raised by the House of Lords in *National Provincial Bank Ltd v Ainsworth*[116] can be dealt with if the right does indeed bind successors in title. In practice, the impact of the new provision will be much mitigated by the need for the ordinary rules of priority for registered dispositions to be applied, and given the substantial probability that a spouse may have a proprietary interest in the matrimonial home by way of constructive trust, it is already standard practice for banks to obtain a waiver from a non-owning spouse in occupation.[117]

---

[113] [1965] A.C. 1175 at 1232. See also *Hall v King* (1988) 55 P. & C.R. 307 at 309, per Donaldson M.R.

[114] [1970] P. 11 at 16.

[115] Land Registration Act 2002 s.116: "It is hereby declared for the avoidance of doubt that, in relation to registered land . . . (b) a mere equity . . . has effect from the time the equity arises as an interest capable of binding successors in title . . .".

[116] [1965] A.C. 1175.

[117] In addition, under the Family Law Act 1996 s.31(10)(b), a spouse's matrimonial home rights are not capable of being an overriding interest even if the spouse is in actual occupation.

Although at common law a spouse's right of occupation is incapable of binding a transferee of the land the court will act to prevent a transfer occurring which would interfere with the right. In *Lee v Lee*[118] the Court of Appeal held that a county court judge had the jurisdiction to order a husband who had left his wife not to take any steps by way of sale or assignment of any interest in the matrimonial home, thus preventing him from disposing of it to the prejudice of his wife's right to occupy.

(b) An Equitable Proprietary Right to Occupy?

20–044 Given the very limited nature of the common law occupation right of spouses, and in particular its inability to affect transferees of the matrimonial home, the courts developed a species of occupational right in favour of a wife who had been left by her husband known as the "deserted wife's equity".[119] This "equity" was given a proprietary status so that it could potentially bind third party transferees of the matrimonial home. In unregistered land it would bind any purchaser with notice of the equity, and in registered land it would rank as an overriding interest under s.70(1)(g) of the Land Registration Act 1925. In *National Provincial Bank Ltd v Hastings Car Mart Ltd*[120] a husband who had left his wife subsequently transferred the title of their matrimonial home to his company, which then mortgaged the property to the bank. The Court of Appeal held that the bank took their interest subject to the wife's "equity" since she was in actual occupation of the land and it was therefore an overriding interest. However, on appeal to the House of Lords under the name *National Provincial Bank Ltd v Ainsworth*[121] the decision of the Court of Appeal was reversed and it was held that a deserted spouse has no proprietary right to occupation of the matrimonial home capable of binding a third party acquiring an interest in the land. Lord Upjohn stated:

> "The right of the wife to remain in occupation even as against her deserting husband is incapable of precise definition, it depends so much on all the circumstances of the case, on the exercise of purely discretionary remedies, and the right to remain may change overnight by the act or behaviour of either spouse. So as a matter of broad principle I am of opinion that the rights of the husband and wife must be regarded as purely personal inter se and that these rights as a matter of law do not affect third parties . . . I myself cannot see how it is possible for a 'mere equity' to bind a purchaser unless such an equity is ancillary to or dependant upon an equitable estate or interest in land . . . a 'mere equity' naked and alone is, in my opinion, incapable of binding successors in title even with notice; it is personal to the parties."[122]

This rejection of the "deserted wife's equity" ultimately ended any possibility of the judicial development of a right of occupation capable of binding transferees of land, and led to the introduction of a statutory right.

---

[118] [1952] 2 Q.B. 489.
[119] See *Bendall v McWhirter* [1952] 2 Q.B. 466; *Ferris v Weaven* [1952] 2 All E.R. 233; *Westminster Bank v Lee* [1956] Ch. 7.
[120] [1964] Ch. 667.
[121] [1965] A.C. 1175.
[122] [1965] A.C. 1175 at 1233–1238.

3. Statutory Rights of Occupation in the Family Home

(a) *Introduction of a Statutory Right*

In order to provide some protection for the rights of spouses with no share of the ownership of their matrimonial home the Matrimonial Homes Act 1967 introduced a statutory right of occupation. This legislation was first consolidated in the Matrimonial Homes Act 1983 and more recently in Pt IV of the Family Law Act 1996, as amended by the Civil Partnership Act 2004 to include civil partners.[123] **20–045**

(b) *Entitlement to "Home Rights"*

The Family Law Act 1996 introduced a new terminology for the right of occupation of the home, namely "matrimonial home rights".[124] A home right will arise if the following conditions are met: **20–046**

(i) Spouses or Civil Partners Entitled to Home Rights

The provisions of the Family Law Act 1996 conferring home rights operate only in favour of spouses or civil partners and have no application to unmarried cohabitees who may share occupation of what is in effect a quasi-matrimonial home. Sections 30(8) and 31(8) make clear that such rights can only persist for so long as the marriage or civil partnership is subsisting, and that they are automatically terminated by the termination of the marriage or civil partnership.[125] **20–047**

(ii) Spouses or Civil Partners Only Entitled to Home Rights if they have no Legal Ownership Rights in the Land

Section 30 provides that only a spouse or civil partner with no ownership rights is entitled to home rights— **20–048**

"(1) This section applies if—

    (a) one spouse or civil partner is entitled to occupy a dwelling-house by virtue of—

        (i) a beneficial estate or interest or contract; or
        (ii) any enactment giving that spouse or civil partner the right to remain in occupation;

and

    (b) the other spouse or civil partner is not so entitled."

---

[123] Sch.9. See Chapter 11.
[124] Amended to "home rights" by the Civil Partnership Act 2004.
[125] Except in so far as the court has not made an order under s.33(5) that the home rights are not brought to an end by the termination of the marriage or civil partnership.

However this is qualified by s.30(9) which provides that a person with a purely equitable interest in a house or its proceeds of sale is not to be treated as entitled to occupy by virtue of that interest, solely for the purpose of determining whether they enjoy statutory home rights. This provision is especially important in the context of unregistered land since it means that a person who enjoys an equitable interest can protect their home rights by registration as a land charge, whereas their beneficial entitlement would be subject to the doctrine of notice and cannot be protected.

(iii) Entitlement Conferred by Statutory Home Rights

20–049   Section 30(2) determines the extent of the home rights created by the statute:

> "Subject to the provisions of this Part, the spouse or civil partner not so entitled has the following rights ('home rights')—
>
> (a) if in occupation, a right not to be evicted or excluded from the dwelling-house or any part of it by the other spouse or civil partner except with the leave of the court given by an order under s.33;
> (b) if not in occupation, a right with the leave of the court so given to enter into and occupy the dwelling-house."

(c)   *Status of Home Rights*

20–050   Home rights conferred by statute remain purely personal rights enjoyed by one spouse or civil partner against another. However, by s.31(2) the home rights are given the status of a charge on the estate or interest of the owning spouse or civil partner. Section 31 provides:

> "(1) Subsections (2) and (3) apply if, at any time during a marriage or civil partnership, one spouse or civil partner is entitled to occupy a dwelling-house by virtue of a beneficial estate or interest.
> (2) The other's home rights are a charge on the estate or interest.
> (3) The charge created by subsection (2) has the same priority as if it were an equitable interest created at whichever is the latest of the following dates:
>
> (a) the date on which the spouse or civil partner so entitled acquires the estate or interest;
> (b) the date of the marriage or formation of the civil partnership; and
> (c) 1st January 1968 (the commencement date of the Matrimonial Homes Act 1967)."

Thus home rights are deemed to enjoy the equivalent proprietary status of equitable interests in the land. What judicial development was unable to achieve through the deserted wife's equity has therefore been accomplished by legislation, namely that a personal right of occupation is capable of binding successors in title to the land.

(d) *Effect of Home Rights on Third Party Transferees of the Land*

Although a home right is capable of enjoying priority over the rights of a transferee of the land, or an interest in it, whether such a right is binding will depend upon the type of land concerned.

20–051

(i) Home Rights in Registered Land

Where title to the dwelling-house in which a person enjoys a home right is registered, s.31(10) of the Family Law Act 1996 provides that the charge thereby affecting the land can be protected by registering a notice on the register. A home right can be protected by the entry of a notice without the production of the proprietor's land certificate.[126] Section 31(10)(b) provides that a home right is not an overriding interest even though the person is in actual occupation. This means that they will not be binding as against a purchaser of an interest in the land if they have not been appropriately protected.

20–052

(ii) Home Rights in Unregistered Land

In unregistered land home rights rank as Class F land charges. If they are properly protected they will be binding against any third party acquiring the land or any interest in the land.[127] Failure to register an appropriate land charge will mean that a purchaser will take his interest free from it, since s.4(8) of the Land Charges Act 1972 provides that:

20–053

> "A land charge of Class F shall be void as against a purchaser of the land charged with it, or of any interest in such land, unless the land charge is registered in the appropriate register before the completion of the purchase."

(e) *Occupation Orders where a Spouse or Civil Partner is Entitled to Home Rights*

Under s.33 of the Family Law Act 1996 the court possesses a wide jurisdiction to make an occupation order in favour of a person who "has home rights in relation to a dwelling-house".[128] Section 33(3) provides that such an order may:

20–054

> "(a) enforce the applicant's entitlement to remain in occupation as against the other person ('the respondent');
> (b) require the respondent to permit the applicant to enter and remain in the dwelling-house or part of the dwelling-house;

[126] See Land Registration Act 2002 s.34(2)(b); Matrimonial Homes and Property Act 1981 s.4(1).
[127] *Hastings and Thanet Building Society v Goddard* [1970] 1 W.L.R. 1544; *Perez-Adamson v Perez-Rivas* [1987] Fam. 89.
[128] Family Law Act 1996 s.33(1)(a)(ii), as amended by the Civil Partnership Act 2004.

    (c) regulate the occupation of the dwelling-house by either or both parties;

    (d) [inapplicable to home rights];

    (e) if the respondent has home rights in relation to the dwelling-house and the applicant is the other spouse or civil partner, restrict or terminate those rights;

    (f) require the respondent to leave the dwelling-house or part of the dwelling-house; or

    (g) exclude the respondent from a defined area in which the dwelling-house is included."

Section 33(6) requires the court to take into account all the circumstances when deciding whether to grant an order, but especially:

> "(a) the housing needs and housing resources of each of the parties and of any relevant child;
>
> (b) the financial resources of each of the parties;
>
> (c) the likely effect of any order, or of any decision by the court not to exercise its powers under subsection (3), on the health, safety, or well-being of the parties and of any relevant child;
>
> (d) the conduct of the parties in relation to each other and otherwise."

In some cases the courts have been willing to exercise their jurisdiction so as to deprive a person otherwise entitled to a home right from asserting their entitlement to occupation against a successor in title. In *Kaur v Gill*[129] a wife had enjoyed an occupational right in her matrimonial home which she protected by means of a notice on the Land Register prior to the completion of a sale by her husband to a third party. The Court of Appeal upheld the refusal of an order under the predecessor of s.33(3) of the Family Law Act 1996[130] that she should be entitled to occupy, because the purchaser was a blind man who had acquired the house because it was more convenient for him. He was only bound by notice because his solicitor had conducted an inadequate telephone search of the land register. The court held that it was perfectly legitimate to take into account the circumstances of the purchaser as well as the spouse. Dillon L.J. stated:

> "I have no doubt that the fact that a purchaser has constructive, or actual, notice of a wife's claim to rights of occupation and buys a property subject to that claim is, of itself, a highly material factor for the court to consider. Moreover, if the evidence was that the purchaser was buying by way of collusion with a husband to evict a wife, any other circumstances of merit on the purchaser's side might carry little weight in the balance. But I cannot see that the court is, without regard to merits, bound to refuse to consider the circumstances of the purchaser, or other third party deriving title under the husband subject to a wife's claim, at all."[131]

---

[129] [1988] 2 F.L.R. 328.
[130] Matrimonial Homes Act 1983 s.1(3).
[131] [1988] 2 F.L.R. 328 at 333.

INDEX